Essentials of Psychology

FIFTH EDITION

SPENCER A. RATHUS

ST. JOHN'S UNIVERSITY

Essentials of Psychology

FIFTH EDITION

HARCOURT BRACE COLLEGE PUBLISHERS

Fort Worth   Philadelphia   San Diego   New York   Orlando   Austin   San Antonio
Toronto   Montreal   London   Sydney   Tokyo

PUBLISHER	Christopher P. Klein
EXECUTIVE EDITOR	Earl McPeek
DEVELOPMENTAL EDITOR	Amy Hester
PROJECT EDITOR	Jeff Beckham
PRODUCTION MANAGER	Cynthia Young
ART DIRECTOR	Peggy Young
PHOTO AND PERMISSIONS EDITOR	Cheri Throop
PHOTO RESEARCHER	Sue C. Howard

Cover Image: © Robert Brenner/Photo Edit

ISBN: 0-15-503731-5

Library of Congress Catalog Card Number: 95-82359

Address for Editorial Correspondence: Harcourt Brace College Publishers, 301 Commerce Street, Suite 3700, Fort Worth, TX 76102.

Address for Orders: Harcourt Brace & Company, 6277 Sea Harbor Drive, Orlando, FL 32887-6777. 1-800-782-4479, or 1-800-433-0001 (in Florida).

(Copyright Acknowledgments begin on page C1, which constitutes a continuation of this copyright page.)

Harcourt Brace College Publishers may provide complimentary instructional aids and supplements or supplement packages to those adopters qualified under our adoption policy. Please contact your sales representative for more information. If as an adopter or potential user you receive supplements you do not need, please return them to your sales representative or send them to: Attn: Returns Department, Troy Warehouse, 465 South Lincoln Drive, Troy, MO 63379

Printed in the United States of America

7 8 9 0 1 2 3 4 5   032   9 8 7 6 5 4 3 2

PREFACE

Voltaire, the French man of letters, apologized to a friend for writing a long letter. He had not the time, he lamented, to write a brief one.

Similarly, writing *Essentials of Psychology* has posed a special challenge for me. The inclusion of various topics and studies in an "essentials" textbook implies that the topics and studies that go unmentioned were *not* essential—that they were, perhaps, superfluous. Yet no two psychologists would completely agree on all that is essential. It was thus necessary to make difficult decisions as to what to include and what to exclude. In the process, I learned to share Voltaire's lament that the creation of a brief work is especially arduous and time-consuming.

Having made the difficult decisions as to what to cover, the book was designed to be a complete teaching and learning tool. It contains motivational features and a thorough, built-in study guide that aims to put the student on an equal footing with the subject matter.

I also challenged the homely piece of folklore that maintains "If it ain't broke, don't fix it."

What's New In This Edition

The fifth edition of Essentials contains major advances over earlier editions. The fifth edition of *Essentials of Psychology* includes two new chapters, full integration of the sociocultural perspective, full integration of gender, "Reflections" sections, and increased emphasis on critical thinking. Even the very "language" of psychology has been modified to be consistent with psychology's emphasis on the dignity of the individual.

NEW CHAPTERS

The new chapters cover "Thinking and Language" and "Intelligence."

Chapter 8: Thinking and Language In keeping with *Essentials of Psychology's* enhanced emphasis on critical thinking, there is now full chapter coverage of the interrelated topics of thinking and language. Increased coverage of problem solving, creativity, reasoning, judgment and decision making heighten the rigor of the book. However, the increased coverage of these difficult concepts is accompanied by the traditional user-friendly approach. Relevant examples and humor motivate students and help them grasp new concepts.

Chapter 9: Intelligence Full-chapter coverage of intelligence permits us to give this key topic the attention it deserves. The fifth edition includes new coverage of artificial intelligence, the effects of musical training on intellectual performance, and the determinants of intelligence among *older adults* as well as among children. The fifth edition includes expanded coverage of Gardner's theory of multiple intelligences, Sternberg's triarchic theory of intelligence, and socioeconomic and ethnic differences in intelligence. The presentation of genetic and environmental factors in intellectual performance is balanced. Yet it is pointed out that a strong belief in the predominance of genetic factors can undermine parental and educational efforts to enhance children's intellectual development.

FULL INTEGRATION OF THE SOCIOCULTURAL PERSPECTIVE

Our population is becoming an ever richer mix of cultural traditions. The sociocultural perspective brings those various traditions within the province of psychology. It enables us to consider how best to apply psychology's research findings to people from different backgrounds. In keeping with psychology's oldest tradition, it also helps us focus more precisely on our understanding of the individual.

The sociocultural perspective is integrated throughout the book because it is relevant to all areas of psychology. Consider the following examples: Chapter 1 introduces a major section on "The Sociocultural Perspective." Chapter 2 includes a major section on "Samples and Populations: Representing Human Diversity." Chapter 8 discusses "Bilingualism" and has a new feature, "Across the Great Divide? White People Versus African Americans on the O. J. Simpson Verdict." Chapter 10 includes a section on "Sex: A Sociocultural Perspective." Chapter 12 has a major new section on "The Sociocultural Perspective" in personality. Chapter 14 includes a new feature on "Women and Psychotherapy" and expanded coverage of "Psychotherapy in the New Multicultural United States." Chapter 15 has a major new section on "Sociocultural Factors in Health and Illness: Nations Within the Nation" and a new feature on "Health and Socioeconomic Status: The Rich Get Richer and the Poor Get . . . Sicker."

FULL INTEGRATION OF GENDER

People differ not only in cultural tradition but also in gender. Focus on gender, as focus on sociocultural issues, at once helps us appreciate differences among individuals and to see through to the common core that composes the human being. Issues of gender bear on the subject matter in diverse areas of psychology and are thus integrated throughout *Essentials of Psychology*.

Following are examples of new issues in gender that are raised in various chapters: Chapter 11 discusses gender issues in level of moral judgment, formation of adolescent identity, and patterns of adult development. Chapter 12 has a new "World of Diversity" feature on "Gender Differences in Personality." Chapter 15 discusses gender differences in such issues as incidence of physical disorders and utilization of health care.

"REFLECTIONS" SECTIONS

New "Reflections" sections serve a dual function: They (1) help students learn the subject matter, and (2) stimulate critical thinking.

Psychologists and educators have shown that students learn effectively when they *reflect* on what they are learning. Reflecting on a subject means *relating* it to things they already know. (Things students already know include their own life experiences and other academic subjects.) Relating the material to things known makes it meaningful and easier to remember. Relating also makes it more likely that students will be able to *use* the new information in their own lives.

A "Reflections" section appears at the end of every major section. These sections ask students to pause before proceeding so that they may relate what they have read to their life experiences and academic knowledge.

A NEW LOOK AT THE LANGUAGE OF PSYCHOLOGY

Essentials of Psychology has always been sensitive to issues of gender and ethnicity in language. Consider gender. We do not refer to a person of unspecified gender as "he." We say, rather, "she or he" or "they." However, the new edition of the *Publication Manual of the American Psychological Association* also finds that traditional use of terms such as *subjects, receiving treatments, schizophrenics,* and *the elderly* denies individuals their dignity and the active nature of their participation in research.

Essentials of Psychology, therefore, speaks of *individuals, people,* and *participants*—not of *subjects.* Your textbook speaks of individuals as active in research—as *partaking* in research, or as *obtaining* treatments, not as *receiving* treatments. Your textbook speaks of *people with schizophrenia* or of *people diagnosed with schizophrenia,* not of *schizophrenics.* Your textbook speaks of *older people,* not of *the elderly.* In the fifth edition of *Essentials of Psychology,* the person always comes first. It is the person that defines the individual. The modifier, whether it refers to age, psychological disorders, or other matters, is secondary. This is not verbal gameplaying. People are people and deserved to be treated with dignity regardless of age, psychological disorder, or participation in research. Our descriptors expand or limit the nature of other human beings, and psychology teaches us that people deserve our very careful consideration.

Every line of *Essentials of Psychology* reflects sensitivity to the dignity of the individual.

CD-ROM MULTIMEDIA INTERFACES

Psychology: The Core on CD-ROM is a multimedia product that can be packaged with this textbook or purchased separately by students. It contains a variety of interactive multimedia features including "minilectures" on core concepts in psychology. The availability of minilectures relating to the text material is indicated by a CD-ROM icon in the margin of the textbook.

The Traditional and the Familiar

Although there are key improvements to the fifth edition, much in your textbook is traditional and familiar. The text continues to recount psychology's rich tradition, the philosophical and methodological roots that can be traced beyond the sages of the ancient Greeks. A century ago, William James wrote "I wished, by treating Psychology like a natural science, to help her become one." Psychology, as we advance into the new millennium, is very much that science of which he spoke. Your textbook explores psychology's tradition as an empirical science. It explores the research methods innovated in 19th century Germany and brought to the shores of the New World in the 20th century. It also covers the essential subjects of psychology.

The writing style of *Essentials of Psychology* continues to communicate the excitement of psychology. The text was deliberately written to be user friendly—to meet the needs of students. It uses personal anecdotes and humor to motivate students and help them understand the subject matter. The goal of the style is lofty: to engage and motivate students without descending into frivolity and condescension. The personal approach is exemplified in the way that the text walks students through the Milgram studies on obedience to authority in Chapter 2. Students vicariously experience Milgram's methods, and as a result, motivation, comprehension, and retention are enhanced.

You will also find many of the signature Rathus features and learning aids that have contributed to the success of earlier editions:

"WORLD OF DIVERSITY" FEATURES

"World of Diversity" features help students perceive why people of different cultures and genders behave and think in different ways, and how the science of psychology is enriched by addressing those differences.

"World of Diversity" features include:

- The Diversity of Contributors to the Development of Psychology (Chapter 1)
- *New to this edition:* A Sex Survey That Addresses Sociocultural Factors (Chapter 2)
- *New to this edition:* The Signs of the Times Are Changing to Reflect New Sensibilities among the Deaf (Chapter 4)
- Ethnicity and Substance Abuse among Adolescents (Chapter 5)
- *New to this edition:* Sociocultural Factors in Alcohol Abuse (Chapter 5)
- *New to this edition:* Sociocultural Factors in Learning, *or,* Donald Duck Meets a Samurai (Chapter 6)
- *New to this edition:* Across the Great Divide? White People Versus African Americans on the O. J. Simpson Verdict (Chapter 8)
- Bilingualism (Chapter 8)
- Socioeconomic and Ethnic Differences in Intelligence (Chapter 9)
- *New to this edition:* Ethnicity and Sexual Orientation: A Matter of Belonging (Chapter 10)
- *New to this edition:* Gender and Ethnicity in Adolescent Identity Formation (Chapter 11)
- Gender Differences in Personality (Chapter 12)
- Women and Psychotherapy (Chapter 14)
- Psychotherapy in the New Multicultural United States (Chapter 14)
- *New to this edition:* Health and Socioeconomic Status: The Rich Get Richer and the Poor Get . . . Sicker (Chapter 15)
- *New to this edition:* Gender Polarization and Its Costs (Chapter 16)

PROVEN PEDAGOGY

The textbook maintains the following pedagogical features that have proven useful and effective in aiding student learning:

- *Learning Objectives.* Each chapter begins with a list of learning objectives. The learning objectives serve as advance organizers that suggest the structure of the chapter and provide concrete goals for learning.

- *Pretests Composed of "Truth-or-Fiction?" Items.* Truth-or-Fiction items are not just a true-false test. They are designed to stimulate students to delve into the subject matter by challenging folk lore and common sense (which is often "common *non*sense").

- *Truth-or-Fiction Revisited.* These inserts are found in the text where discussions of the pretest topics take place. In this way, students are intermittently prompted to reflect on their answers to the pretests. Their motivation to continue to compare their preconceptions with scientific knowledge is maintained and enhanced.

- *Running Glossary.* Research shows that most students do not make use of a glossary at the end of a book. Key terms appear in **boldface** in the text and are defined in the running glossary, which is placed in the margin of the textbook. The running glossary provides ready access to the meanings of key terms so that students can maintain their concentration on the flow of material in the chapter.

BUILT-IN STUDY GUIDE

SPENCER A. RATHUS, ST. JOHN'S UNIVERSITY/SANDRA SUDWEEKS, GOLDEN WEST COLLEGE

We are particularly proud of *Essentials of Psychology's* built-in Study Guide as a vehicle for promoting student learning. The Study Guide contains the following elements:

- *Exercises with Answer Keys.* One or more exercises are found at the beginning of each Study Guide section. Exercises vary according to the nature of the material presented in the textbook chapter. For example, Chapter 1 features a fill-in-the-blank exercise on prominent people in psychology. Exercises in Chapter 4 feature graphics showing the eye and the ear where the student is asked to identify the parts. An answer key appears at the end of each exercise.

- *English as a Second Language—Bridging the Gap.* Not all introductory psychology students grew up speaking English in the home. Some students, in fact, have only recently emigrated to the United States. Some have spoken English for only a few years (or a few months!) before entering college. Prepared by Sandra Sudweeks, an ESL instructor with an MA in Intercultural Communication, the ESL sections highlight and explain idioms in the English language, cultural references to life in the United States, and phrases and expressions whose meanings are not obvious to speakers of foreign languages. Students from eleven different language backgrounds (Asian, African, Middle Eastern, and East European) read each chapter of the textbook manuscript and identified those terms and expressions they had difficulty understanding. Sandy has provided the general meaning and the meaning in the context in which it is used for each term or phrase identified as difficult by ESL students. The terms and phrases are listed alphabetically, as most students are familiar with this method of locating words, and each includes in parentheses the page number on which it is located. Many American-born, native English-speaking students are also not familiar with some American terms, phrases, and cultural references. Consequently, students may want to review this section before they start reading the chapter.

- *Chapter Review with Answer Key.* Chapter review sections are carefully programmed to prompt students' memories of the key points covered in each chapter. They foster active learning. Students fill in missing information as they read the chapter reviews. (Unique "prompts" (letters from missing words) help students complete the items. Answer keys follow the review sections.

- *Posttest with Answer Key.* Most psychologists use multiple-choice questions in their assessment of student knowledge. For this reason, each chapter concludes with a 20-item multiple-choice test that allows students to check their knowledge following the chapter review. These tests give students a way to measure their mastery and to predict their performance on their instructor's quizzes and tests. Answer keys follow the posttests.

The Ancillaries

The needs of contemporary instructors and students demand a full and broad array of ancillary materials that facilitate teaching and learning. *Essentials of Psychology* is accompanied by a complete, convenient, and carefully conceived package.

FOR THE STUDENT

Thinking and Writing About Psychology, Second Edition

SPENCER A. RATHUS, ST. JOHN'S UNIVERSITY

Shrinkwrapped with the textbook at no additional cost, *Thinking and Writing About Psychology* is designed to promote two aspects of contemporary college education: critical thinking and writing across the curriculum. To this end, the ancillary contains a discussion of what critical thinking is, a comprehensive guide to writing about psychology using the APA's latest recommendations, and dozens of writing exercises. Writing exercises may be assigned as a way of encouraging the development of thinking and writing skills, as a way of providing an opportunity for class participation, and perhaps, as a way of earning part of the grade for the course.

Thinking and Writing About Psychology can also be purchased separately.

ISBN: 0-15-504141-X

The following supplementary materials are available for purchase by students. Please contact your local college bookstore for prices and ordering information.

Psychology: The Core on CD-ROM

JOHN MITTERER, BROCK UNIVERSITY

Psychology: The Core on CD-ROM is an innovative learning tool that provides students with an interactive, multimedia introduction to psychology. More than 100 "minilectures" cover key concepts with animation, video, still images, and audio. Interactive exercises, such as experiments and demonstrations, help studetns understand how these concepts relate to "real life." Hyperlinked access to Spencer Rathus' *Psychology in the New Millennium,* sixth edition textbook gives students additional resources to search, bookmark, and read for complete understanding of the multiple perspectives and connections within psychology. In addition, the CD-ROM allows students to test their understanding of the principles of psychology via a series of multiple-choice test questions (four quizzes with 20 questions each per chapter).

Macintosh® ISBN: 0-15-503942-3
Windows™ ISBN: 0-15-503941-5

Interactive Software

- *Personal Discovery.* This unique, interactive software package allows students to explore their propensities in such areas as self-efficacy, risk taking, and coping skills.

  IBM® 3.5" ISBN: 0-15-501703-9
  Macintosh® ISBN: 0-15-501705-5

- *Supershrink I: Victor and SuperShrink II: Jennifer (IBM).* In these interactive programs, users adopt the role of counselor at a helpline clinic and interview clients, Victor and Jennifer. These programs offer extremely valuable experience to introductory students learning concepts in psychotherapy, personality, and assessment.

  IBM®
  Victor, 5.25" ISBN: 0-15-584761-9
  Jennifer, 5.25" ISBN: 0-15-584763-5
  Jennifer, 3.5" ISBN: 0-15-584764-3

FOR THE INSTRUCTOR

Harcourt Brace College Publishers may provide complimentary instructional aids and supplements or supplement packages to those adopters qualified under our adoption policy. Please contact your sales representative for more information. If, as an adopter or potential user, you receive textbooks or supplements you do not need, please return them to your sales representative or send them to:

> Attn: Returns Department
> Troy Warehouse
> 465 South Lincoln Drive
> Troy, MO 63379

Instructor's Manual with Video Instructor's Guide

RON MULSON, HUDSON VALLEY COMMUNITY COLLEGE/ALICIA GOLDNER, LONG BEACH CITY COLLEGE/MARLENE ADELMAN, NORWALK COMMUNITY-TECHNICAL COLLEGE

Ron Mulson has thoroughly revised the Instructor's Manual to include more fully-developed teaching strategies. These strategies include expanded lecture outlines, thumbnail historical insights on major researchers, brief overviews of the major studies that contributed to the chapter topics, student activities that help demonstrate concepts discussed in the textbook, and small group case studies. At the end of each chapter is a videodisc coordination section, prepared by Alicia Goldner, that lists and describes the frames from Harcourt Brace's *Dynamic Concepts in Psychology II* videodisc that relate to the topics of the chapter.

A *Video Instructor's Guide* has been combined with the manual to provide instructors with a complete resource teaching package. The guide references the Harcourt Brace Multimedia Library, with more specific teaching suggestions for using the segments from the *Discovering Psychology* Teaching Modules provided exclusively by Harcourt Brace. The guide is abundant with activities and discussions, and has been customized by Marlene Adelman to correspond with material covered in *Essentials of Psychology*.

ISBN: 0-15-503733-1

Test Bank

HARRY TIEMANN, MESA STATE UNIVERSITY/MARA MERLINO, UNIVERSITY OF NEVADA—RENO

The Test Bank has been revised and expanded to maintain 100 to 185 multiple-choice items for each chapter (total of over 2,000 items). New test items have been written for each chapter to correspond with the new topics added in the textbook. Test items appear in the order of presentation in the textbook, are keyed to learning objectives, and are coded in terms of correct answer, question type, and textbook page reference.

ISBN: 0-15-503732-3

EXAMaster+™ Computerized Test Banks: IBM, MAC, and WINDOWS versions

Offers easy-to-use options for test creation:

- *EasyTest* creates a test from a single screen in just a few easy steps. Instructors choose parameters, then select questions from the data base or let *EasyTest* randomly select them.

- *FullTest* offers a range of options that includes selecting, editing, adding, or linking questions or graphics; random selection of questions from a wide range of criteria; creating criteria; blocking questions; and printing up to 99 different versions of the same test and answer sheet.

- **On-Line Testing** allows instructors to create a test in *EXAMaster+™*, save it to the OLT subdirectory or diskette, and administer the test on-line. The results of the test can then be imported to *ESAGrade*.
- **ESAGrade** can be used to set up new classes, to record grades from tests or assignments utilizing scantron, and to analyze grades and produce class and individual statistics. *ESAGrade* comes packaged with *EXAMaster+™*.

IBM® 3.5" ISBN: 0-15-503734-X
Macintosh® ISBN: 0-15-503737-4
MS Windows™ ISBN: 0-15-503738-2

- **RequesTest** is a service for instructors without access to a computer. A software specialist will compile questions according to the instructor's criteria and mail or fax the test master within 48 hours!
- **The Software Support Hotline** is available to answer questions Monday through Friday, 9 a.m. to 4 p.m. Central Time.

(1-800 telephone numbers for these services are provided in the Preface to the printed Test Bank.)

The Whole Psychology Catalog: Instructional Resources to Enhance Student Learning

MICHAEL REINER, KENNESAW STATE COLLEGE

Instructors can easily supplement course work and assignments with this recently updated manual (copyright 1997). It has perforated pages containing experiential exercises, questionnaires, and visual aids. Each activity is classified by one of eight learning goals central to the teaching of psychology. Also included in the new version is an informative section on using the Internet.

ISBN: 0-15-504153-3

Introductory Psychology Overhead Transparencies

This set of over 130 full-color acetates covers the full range of topics typical to an introductory psychology course.

ISBN: 0-15-501456-0

The Harcourt Brace Multimedia Library

The *Harcourt Brace Multimedia Library* provides additional media for instructors for classroom use. The Library includes videos from Films for the Humanities and Sciences and Pyramid Films, as well as series such as *The Brain* Teaching Modules, *The Mind* Video Modules, *Discovering Psychology* Telecourse, *Childhood, Seasons of Life,* and *Time to Grow.* The Library also includes the following Harcourt Brace exclusives: *Discovering Psychology* Teaching Modules, *Fires of the Mind, Prisoners of the Brain, Contemporary Issues in Social Psychology,* and *VideoCases in Abnormal Psychology.*

The following videodiscs are available exclusively from the Harcourt Brace Multimedia Library: *Dynamic Concepts in Psychology I* and *Dynamic Concepts in Psychology II, Discovering Psychology* Teaching Modules, *Prisoners of the Brain,* and *Fires of the Mind* from The Infinite Voyage series, and *Development Today.*

Acknowledgments

The discipline of psychology owes its progress and its scientific standing to experts who conduct research in many different areas. Similar, the textbook *Essentials of Psychology* and its ancillaries owe a great deal of their substance and form to my colleagues who provided expert suggestions and insights at various stages of their development. My sincere thanks to the following individuals who contributed to the development of the fifth edition:

Debra Collins, Brevard Community College—Titusville

Eugenio J. Galindro, El Paso Community College

James Hart, Edison State Community College

Myles E. Johnson, Normandale Community College

Mike Knight, University of Central Oklahoma

Samuel B. Schnitzer, Indiana State University

My sincere thanks also to the reviewers of earlier editions: John Benson, Texarkana College; Ervin L. Betts, Norwalk Community College; Richard L. Cahoon, Cape Cod Community College; Albert Cohoe, Ohio Northern University; Philip W. Compton, Ohio Northern University; Bridget Coughlin, Hocking Technical Institute; James R. Council, North Dakota State University; R. Scott Ditsel, Tiffin University; George J. Downing, Gloucester County College; Barbara Engler, Union County College; Mary Farkas, Lansing Community College; Barry Fish, Eastern Michigan University; Ajaipal S. Gill, Anne Arundel Community College; Brian Gladue, North Dakota State University; John N. Goodwin, School of the Ozarks; Charles S. Grunder, University of Maine; Barbara Gryzlo, Illinois Technical College; John R. Haig, Philadelphia College of Textiles and Science; Tom Hailen, Northwestern College; George Hampton, University of Houston; James E. Hart, Edison State Community College; Kathryn Jennings, College of the Redwoods; Grace Leonard, University of Maine—Augusta; Kenneth LeSure, Cuyahoga Community College—Metro Campus; Peter C. Murrell, Milwaukee Area Technical College; Carroll S. Perrino, Morgan State University; Richard L. Port, University of Pittsburgh; Valda Robinson, Hillsborough Community College; John Roehr, Hudson Valley Community College; Laurie M. Rotando, Westchester Community College; David L. Salmond, Vincennes University; Keith Schirmer, Kellogg Community College; Linda Schwandt, Western Wisconsin Technical Institute; Joe M. Tinnin, Richland College; Carol Vitiello, Kirkwood Community College; Ann Weber, University of North Carolina; Kenneth N. Wildman, Ohio Northern University; Michael Witmer, Skagit Valley College; Cecelia K. Yoder, Oklahoma City Community College; David Zehr, Plymouth State College.

It is a continuing privilege to work with the fine publishing professionals at Harcourt Brace College Publishers. Ted Buchholz, Chris Klein, and Earl McPeek provided me with editorial support. I value Ted for his knowledge and courage and, most of all, his friendship. Amy Hester, the developmental editor, organized the commentaries of reviewers and made invaluable suggestions for developing the fifth edition. The project editor, Jeff Beckham, managed the myriad day to day activities that transformed my manuscript into a bound book. Peggy Young designed the elegant layout of the fifth edition. Sandy Lord and Sue Howard researched and obtained the vibrant photos used throughout the book and on the cover, and Kristin Bishop requested and secured the literary permissions. Senior marketing manager Susan Kindel marketed this revision to Harcourt Brace's sales force and instructors across the country.

SPENCER A. RATHUS
SHORT HILLS, NEW JERSEY
srathus@aol.com

TO THE STUDENT

How to Use This Textbook

This is your book. I wrote it with you in mind. I included a number of features to help you learn about psychology, and about yourself. This section, "To the Student" shows you how to take full advantage of those features to truly make this book your own.

Make the investment. Spend a few minutes. By doing so, you will find ways in which you can better understand the subject matter and retain it longer. You may also find ways to keep psychology an integral part of your life. Let me also confess that I envy you. I experienced the excitement of learning about psychology for the first time years ago. That excitement is now yours. Go to it!

SPENCER A. RATHUS
Short Hills, New Jersey
srathus@aol.com
74673.2251@CompuServe.com

Each chapter opens with pretest **"Truth-or-Fiction?"** items. Many students enter the course assuming that they already know a great deal about psychology—after all, by the time they enter college, they have observed people for many years. But, how much do you know? Complete these items before reading the chapter to test your knowledge.

Learning Objectives serve as advance organizers that highlight the structure of the chapter and provide concrete goals for learning.

CD-ROM icons refer to appropriate "minilectures" in *Psychology: The Core on CD-ROM* to add an interactive multimedia dimension to psychology. This may be purchased separately or packaged with this textbook at your professor's request.

"Truth-or-Fiction Revisited" inserts answer the Truth-or-Fiction? questions to which you responded before beginning the chapter. Compare the answers with your own. Did research findings support your expectations? Why or why not?

---

anxiety, mood disorders, and insomnia. The drug LSD (see Chapter 5) decreases the action of serotonin and may also influence the utilization of dopamine. With LSD, "two no's make a yes." By inhibiting an inhibitor, brain activity increases, in this case frequently leading to hallucinations.

ENDORPHINS. The word *endorphin* is the contraction of *endogenous morphine*. *Endogenous* means "developing from within." **Endorphins**, then, are similar to the narcotic morphine in their functions and effects and are produced by our own bodies. They occur naturally in the brain and in the bloodstream.

Endorphins are inhibitory neurotransmitters. They lock into receptor sites for chemicals that transmit pain messages to the brain. Once the endorphin "key" is in the "lock," pain-causing chemicals cannot transmit their (frequently unwelcome) messages. There are a number of endorphins. Beta-endorphin, for example, is many times more powerful than morphine, molecule for molecule (Snyder, 1977).

Truth or Fiction Revisited. It is true that our bodies produce natural painkillers that are more powerful than morphine. These chemicals are called *endorphins* and, ounce for ounce, they are more powerful than the narcotic morphine. Endorphins may also increase our sense of self-competence and may be connected with the "runner's high" reported by many long-distance runners.

There you have it—a fabulous forest of neurons in which billions upon billions of vesicles are pouring neurotransmitters into synaptic clefts at any given time: when you are involved in strenuous activity, now as you are reading this page, even as you are passively watching television. This microscopic picture is repeated several hundred times every second. The combined activity of all these neurotransmitters determines which messages will be transmitted and which will not. Your experience of sensations, your thoughts, and your psychological sense of control over your body are very different from the electrochemical processes we have described. Yet somehow, these many electrochemical events are responsible for your psychological sense of yourself and of the world (Greenfield, 1995).

Endorphins • (en-DOOR-fins). Neurotransmitters that are composed of amino acids and that are functionally similar to morphine.

Reflections

- How does the text use the term *message* in referring to transmission from one neuron to another? How are messages "passed along" from one neuron to another?
- Had you heard that the brain works, or operates, by means of electricity? What electrochemical processes actually account for transmission of messages in the nervous system?
- Since psychology is the study of behavior and mental processes, why are psychologists interested in biological matters such as the nervous system, the endocrine system, and heredity?

THE NERVOUS SYSTEM

As a child, I did not think it a good thing to have a "nervous" system. After all, if your system were not so nervous, you might be less likely to jump at strange noises.

Later I learned that a nervous system is not a system that is nervous. It is a system of nerves involved in thought processes, heartbeat,

visual–motor coordination, and so on. I also learned that the human nervous system is more complex than that of any other animal and that our brains are larger than those of any other animal. Now this last piece of business is not quite true. A human brain weighs about 3 pounds, but elephant and whale brains may be four times as heavy. Still, our brains compose a greater part of our body weight than do those of elephants or whales. Our brains weigh about 1/60th of our body weight. Elephant brains weigh about 1/1,000th of their total weight, and whale brains are a mere 1/10,000th of their weight. So, if we wish, we can still find figures to make us proud.

Truth or Fiction Revisited. It is not true that the human brain is larger than that of any other animal. Elephants and whales have larger brains. Our brains are more convoluted, however.

The brain is only one part of the nervous system. A **nerve** is a bundle of axons and dendrites. The cell bodies of these neurons are not considered to be part of the nerve. The cell bodies are gathered into clumps called **nuclei** in the brain and spinal cord and **ganglia** elsewhere.

The nervous system consists of the brain, the spinal cord, and the nerves linking them to receptors in the sensory organs and effectors in the muscles and glands. As shown in Figure 3.4, the brain and spinal cord make up what we refer to as the **central nervous system.** The sensory (afferent) neurons, which receive and transmit messages to the brain and spinal cord, and the motor (efferent) neurons, which transmit messages from the brain or spinal cord to the muscles and glands, make up the peripheral nervous system. There is no deep, complex reason for labeling the two major divisions of the nervous system in this way. It is just geography. The **peripheral nervous system** extends more into the edges, or periphery, of the body.

Let us now examine the nature and functions of the central and peripheral nervous systems.

FIGURE 3.4
The Divisions of the Nervous System. The nervous system contains two main divisions: the central nervous system and the peripheral nervous system. The central nervous system consists of the brain and spinal cord. The peripheral nervous system contains the somatic and autonomic systems. In turn, the autonomic nervous system is composed of sympathetic and parasympathetic divisions.

MINILECTURE: ORGANIZATION OF THE NERVOUS SYSTEM

Nerve • A bundle of axons and dendrites from many neurons.
Nuclei • (NEW-klee-eye). Plural of *nucleus*. A group of neural cell bodies found in the brain or spinal cord.
Ganglia • (GANG-lee-uh). Plural of *ganglion*. A group of neural cell bodies found elsewhere in the body (other than the brain or spinal cord).
Central nervous system • The brain and spinal cord.
Peripheral nervous system • (pair-IF-uh-ral). The part of the nervous system consisting of the somatic nervous system and the autonomic nervous system.

When you reach the end of each major section, a set of **"Reflections"** helps you learn the subject matter and stimulates critical thinking. Respond to each question in your own thoughts and words. Draw upon your own experience as well as what you have read in the book. Notice that one or more items may appear in blue type. The blue type means that the question also appears in your workbook, *Thinking and Writing About Psychology.*

The **Running Glossary** lets you learn and review key terms at your own pace, without flipping back and forth between the page you are reading and an end-of-book glossary. It includes a pronunciation guide for difficult terms and word origins.

subject of memory. And, in Chapters 8 and 9, we shall see how learning is intertwined with thinking, language, and a concept that many people think of as
learning ability: intelligence.

WORLD OF DIVERSITY

SOCIOCULTURAL FACTORS IN LEARNING, OR, DONALD DUCK MEETS A SAMURAI

The psychology of learning addresses the core of personality. Even though
what people learn is very different, it is assumed that people from different
cultures learn in the same ways. People may have very different attitudes, but
conditioning probably plays a role in the acquisition of attitudes. For example,
classic laboratory experiments have shown that attitudes toward ethnic groups
can be influenced by associating them with positive words (such as *gift* or
happy) or negative words (such as *ugly* and *failure*); (Lohr & Staats, 1973).
Parents usually positively reinforce their children for saying and doing things
that are consistent with their own attitudes. Children in the United States may
be shown approval for waving our flag, while children in hostile nations
may be smiled upon for burning our flag.

Children also acquire many attitudes, including prejudices, by means of observational learning. Children tend to imitate their parents, and parents reinforce their children for doing so (Duckitt, 1992). Prejudices can thus be
transmitted from generation to generation via learning.

People from diverse cultures share drives such as hunger and thirst, but the
foods and drinks they prefer to satisfy those drives are based on learning
within a given sociocultural setting. African and Swedish Americans may both
like chicken, but African Americans in the South may prefer their chicken prepared in a different way than Swedish Americans from Minnesota do. Once
upon a time we may have written that Mexican Americans prefer enchiladas
and burritos, that Japanese Americans prefer sushi, that Italian Americans
prefer pasta. Today, however, "ethnic foods" have become so popular that
most Americans have some familiarity with them and eat them from time to
time. There are also many acquired individual preferences within the same
ethnic group. Many White Americans like eating raw oysters, for example.
Other White Americans are revolted by them.

Our learning experiences also affect our cognition, including the nature of
the very images that swim within our consciousness. Consider, for example, a
painting by Japanese American artist Roger Shimomura (Figure 6.11). Shimomura is bicultural and blends popular Western imagery with the imagery found
in traditional Japanese prints. At first glance, the painting suggests an amusing
clash of American and Japanese popular cultures. American cartoon characters like Donald Duck, Pinocchio, Dick Tracy, and a combination Batman–
Superman vie for space on the canvas with Japanese Samurai warriors and
a contemporary Japanese. The battle of imagery from East and West may reflect the tensions within the artist regarding his ancestral roots and his chosen
country.

FIGURE 6.11
Roger Shimomura. *Untitled* (1984). Acrylic on canvas. 60" x 72". Courtesy of
Steinbaum Krauss Gallery, New York.

"World of Diversity" features and full integration of the sociocultural perspective enable you to consider how to apply psychology's research findings to people from different backgrounds.

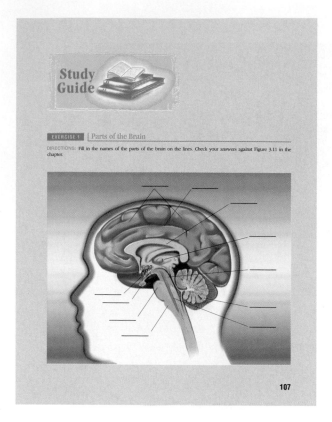

◄ The built-in **Study Guide** offers you a convenient vehicle for assessment and review of what you've learned. The Study Guide is set off from the text with blue paper and includes **exercises with answer keys, English as a Second Language sections, chapter reviews with answer keys, and posttests with answer keys.**

Study Guide

EXERCISE 1 | Parts of the Brain

DIRECTIONS: Fill in the names of the parts of the brain on the lines. Check your answers against Figure 3.11 in the chapter.

107

---

108   **CHAPTER 3** *Study Guide*

EXERCISE 2 | Major Glands of the Endocrine System

DIRECTIONS: Fill in the names of the glands of the endocrine system. List the important hormones secreted by each gland and explain their functions. Check your answers against Figure 3.17 in the chapter.

ESL | English as a Second Language — Bridging the Gap

academic competence (97)—educational abilities
aesthetic (96)—artistic ability to appreciate beauty
affliction (74)—illness or other problem that limits function
and so on (98)—continue with similar examples; et cetera (etc.)
apathy (101)—lack of interest; indifference to something
array (94)—variety of things
blind-alley entrance (90)—an entrance in a maze that stops and does not lead anywhere
block the action (79)—stop the action
bodybuilding contests (97)—contests of body muscle and strength
breathe a sigh of relief (103)—make a sound to indicate that an unpleasant situation has ended or been corrected
bred (102)—past tense of "breed," to produce offspring
buffeted about (74)—tossed back and forth roughly
butterfly pattern (83)—formed roughly in the shape of a butterfly
capable of "local government" (85)—capable of responding to something without requiring assistance from the whole system; in this case, the spinal cord can respond to something without the entire nervous system's involvement
central to (83)—very important to
clump (81)—group of something closely linked together
conception (101)—new beginning; start of development
convoluted (81)—complicated; tangled
convolutions (89)—irregular or folded-over surfaces
created anew (76)—created again and again
crossed fingers (82)—superstition that says that crossing the middle finger over the index finger (finger next to the thumb) provides good luck
crowning glory (89)—most beautiful and magnificent part

---

110   **CHAPTER 3** *Study Guide*

slightest provocation (85)—very sensitive; responding to small irritations
sparked the development (85)—caused the development
specifically tailored harbor (78)—a site, or place, that chemically fits only a specific neurotransmitter
spending of body energy from stored reserves (90)—the body is using energy from what has been saved (reserved)
stopped talking to one another (91)—stopped connecting and interacting with each other
subtle shifts (86)—small, hard-to-see changes
swear in court (71)—insist; be completely positive; speaking in a court of law under oath
syntax (95)—the way words are put together to form phrases and sentences
system of checks and balances (88)—one part of the system acts to restrain another part of the system; refers to the system of the U.S. government, which balances the powers of the three branches (parts) of the government (executive, legislative, and judicial)
tastes good/good taste (102)—in the phrase *tastes good,* taste is a verb—a person likes the flavor of the food;

in the phrase *good taste,* taste is a noun—a person has knowledge of good clothes, food, art, or manners
there you have it (80)—now you understand it
thicket of trees (73)—group of trees close together
trunklike (74)—like the trunk of a tree
twisting ladder (103)—steps that turn as they go up
unlocking the mysteries (73)—discovering what has not been understood previously
vastly (79)—enormously
vice versa (95)—and the opposite
way to prepare frog's legs (76)—frog's legs are considered by the French to be a special meal
winking out (72)—disappearing
withdrawn them (74)—taken them away; removed them
without a trace (72)—nothing remains to indicate that the creatures (people or animals) were here
work our way forward (86)—move in a forward direction; in this case, studying the brain as we move to new areas

FILL-INS | Chapter Review

SECTION 1: NEURONS: INTO THE FABULOUS FOREST

The (1) n_____ system contains billions of neurons. Neurons transmit messages to other neurons by means of chemical substances called (2) _____mitters. Neurons have a cell body, or (3) s_____; (4) d_____, which receive transmissions; and (5) a_____, which extend trunklike from the cell body. Chemicals called neurotransmitters travel across (6) s_____ to transmit messages to other neurons.

Many neurons have a fatty myelin (7) s_____. These sheaths are missing at the nodes of (8) R_____. Neural impulses travel more rapidly along myelinated (9) a_____, where they can jump from (10) n_____ to node.

Sensory or (11) _____ent neurons transmit sensory messages to the central nervous system. Motor or (12) _____ent neurons conduct messages from the central nervous system that stimulate glands or cause muscles to contract.

Neural transmission is an (13) e_____ process. An electric charge is conducted along an axon through a process that allows (14) s_____ ions into the cell and then pumps them out. The neuron has a (15) r_____ potential of −70 millivolts in relation to the body fluid outside the cell membrane and an (16) a_____ potential of +110 millivolts. The conduction of the neural impulse along the length of the neuron is what is meant by (17) _____ing.

Neurons (18) f_____ according to an all-or-none principle. Neurons may fire (19) _____s of times per second. Firing is first followed by an (20) a_____ refractory period, during which neurons do not fire in response

This one is for my daughter
Allyn, who insisted on having a
book dedicated to her alone.

CONTENTS IN BRIEF

CONTENTS

CHAPTER 3
Biology   71

CHAPTER 7
Memory   261

CHAPTER 8
Thinking and Language   313

CHAPTER 11
Development 453

CHAPTER 12
Personality   503

CHAPTER 15
Health   647

Contents

Essentials of Psychology

FIFTH EDITION

What Is Psychology?

PRETEST *Truth or Fiction?*

_____ Psychologists attempt to control behavior.

_____ A book on psychology, whose contents are similar to those of the book you are now holding, was written by Aristotle more than 2,000 years ago.

_____ The ancient Greek philosopher Socrates suggested a research method that is still used in psychology.

_____ Some psychologists look upon our strategies for solving problems as "mental programs" operated by our very "personal computers"—our brains.

_____ Women were not permitted to attend college in the United States until 1833.

_____ Men receive the majority of doctoral degrees in psychology.

"**W**HAT a piece of work is man," wrote William Shakespeare. He was writing about you: "How noble in reason! How infinite in faculty! In form and moving how express and admirable! In action how like an angel! In apprehension how like a god! The beauty of the world! The paragon of animals!"

You probably had no trouble recognizing yourself in this portrait—"noble in reason," "admirable," godlike in understanding, head and shoulders above other animals. That's you to a *tee*, isn't it? Consider some of the noble and admirable features of human behavior:

- The human abilities to think and solve problems have allowed us to build cathedrals and computers and to scan the interior of the body without surgery. Yet what is thinking? How do we solve problems?

- The human ability to create has led to great works of literature and glorious operas. Yet what is creativity?

- Human generosity and charity have encouraged us to care for older people, people who are ill, and people who are less advantaged than we are—even to sacrifice ourselves for those we love. Why do we care for others? What motivates us to care for our children and protect our families?

Human behavior varies greatly, however. Some of it is not noble or admirable. Some of it is downright puzzling. Consider these:

- Although people can be generous, most adults on crowded city streets will not stop to help a person lying on the sidewalk. Why?

- Most people who overeat or smoke cigarettes know that they are jeopardizing their health. Yet they continue in their hazardous ways. Why?

- A person claims to have raped, killed, or mutilated a victim because of insanity. An "irresistible" impulse overcame the person, or "another personality" took control. What is insanity? What is an irresistible impulse? How can we know if someone is insane? Should people who are found to be insane be judged guilty or not guilty of their crimes?

Human behavior has always fascinated people. Sometimes we are even surprised at ourselves. We have thoughts or impulses that seem to be out of character, or we can't recall something on the "tip of the tongue." Most people try to satisfy their curiosities about behavior, if at all, in their spare time. Perhaps they ask a friend for an opinion or make some casual observations. Psychologists, like other people, are also intrigued by the mysteries of behavior, but they make the scientific study of behavior their life's work.

Psychology is the scientific study of behavior and mental processes. Topics of interest to psychologists have included the nervous system, sensation and perception, learning and memory, intelligence, language, thought, growth and development, personality, stress and health, **psychological disorders,** ways of treating psychological disorders, sexual behavior, and the behavior of people in social settings such as groups and organizations.

Psychology (sigh-KOLL-oh-gee) • The science of behavior and mental processes.
Psychological disorders • Patterns of behavior or mental processes that are connected with emotional distress or significant impairment in functioning.
Theory • A formulation of relationships underlying observed events.

PSYCHOLOGY AS A SCIENCE

Psychology, like other sciences, seeks to describe, explain, predict, and control the events it studies. Psychology thus seeks to describe, explain, predict, and control behavior and mental processes.

"What a piece of work is man," wrote William Shakespeare. "How noble in reason! How infinite in faculty! In form and moving how express and admirable! In action how like an angel! In apprehension how like a god!" Psychologists also are fascinated by people's behavior and mental processes.

When possible, descriptive terms and concepts are interwoven into **theories.** Theories are formulations of apparent relationships among observed events. Psychological theories are based on assumptions about behavior and mental processes, contain statements about the principles and laws that may govern them, and allow us to derive explanations and predictions. Psychological theories may combine statements about behavior (such as eating or aggression), mental processes (such as attitudes and mental images), and anatomical structures or biological processes. For instance, many of our responses to drugs such as alcohol and marijuana can be measured as behavior, and they are presumed to reflect the biochemical actions of these drugs and our (mental) expectations about them.

Psychologists also test their theories with carefully designed methods of research such as the survey and the experiment. A satisfactory psychological theory allows us to make predictions. For instance, a satisfactory theory of hunger will allow us to predict when people will or will not eat. Yet in psychology, many theories have been found to be incapable of explaining or predicting observations. As a result, they have been discarded or revised. For example, the theory that hunger results from stomach contractions may be partially correct for normal-weight individuals, but it is inadequate as an explanation for feelings of hunger among the overweight. In Chapter 11 we shall see that stomach contractions are only one of many factors, or **variables,** involved in hunger. Contemporary theories also focus on biological variables (such as the body's muscle-to-fat ratio) and situational variables (such as the presence of other people who are eating and the time of day).

The notion of controlling behavior and mental processes is controversial. Some people erroneously think that psychologists seek ways to make people do their bidding—like puppets on strings. This is not so. Psychologists are committed to a belief in the dignity of human beings, and human dignity demands that people be free to make their own decisions and choose their own behavior. Psychologists are learning more all the time about the influences on human behavior, but they apply this knowledge only upon request and to help people meet their own needs.

Truth or Fiction Revisited. *It is true that psychologists attempt to control behavior.* However, they help clients control their own behavior to achieve their own needs.

Reflections

The research shows that if students are going to remember something, they have to think about it. They need to put it in their own heads in their own words, not just sit back passively and absorb it.

WILBERT McKEACHIE, 1994, p. 39

Variable • A condition that is measured or controlled in a scientific study. A variable can vary in a measurable manner.

Psychologists and educators have shown that you learn more effectively when you *reflect* on what you are learning. Reflecting on a subject means *relating* it to things you already know (Willoughby and others, 1994). Trying to relate the material to things you already know about makes it meaningful and easier to remember (DeAngelis, 1994a; Woloshyn and others, 1994). Relating the material to things you already know also makes it more likely that you will be able to use the new information in your own life (Kintsch, 1994).

Things you already know include your own life experiences and other academic subjects. As you read through this book, you will notice that I tell you many things about my family (including many things my family would rather keep to themselves). My reasons for doing so are to arouse your interest (attention also promotes learning) and to hand you some of my life experiences to which you can relate the subject matter. The "Reflections" sections that you will find at the end of every major section further stimulate you to relate the subject matter to your life experiences and academic knowledge. They ask you to pause before going on to the following section and to consider some questions.

For example, now that you have read the section on "Psychology as a Science," reflect on the following questions:

- **Agree or disagree with the following statement and support your answer: "Psychology is the scientific study of behavior and mental processes." How would you have defined *psychology* before you began this course or opened your book?**
- What is a theory? Do you have theories as to why people act and think as they do? What are your theories? What is the evidence for them?

- **Agree or disagree with the following statement and support your answer: "It is possible to understand people from a scientific perspective."**

The remainder of this chapter provides an overview of psychology and psychologists.

WHAT PSYCHOLOGISTS DO

Psychologists share a keen interest in behavior, but in other ways, they may differ markedly. Some psychologists engage primarily in basic research, or **pure research.** Pure research has no immediate application to personal or social problems and thus has been characterized as research for its own sake. Other psychologists engage in **applied research,** which is designed to find solutions to specific personal or social problems. Although pure research is spurred by curiosity and the desire to know and understand, today's pure research frequently enhances tomorrow's way of life. For example, pure research into learning and motivation with lower animals early in the century has found widespread applications in today's school systems. Pure research into the workings of the nervous system has enhanced knowledge of disorders such as epilepsy, Parkinson's disease, and Alzheimer's disease.

Many psychologists do not engage in research at all. Instead, they apply psychological knowledge to help people change their behavior so that they can meet their own goals more effectively. Numerous psychologists engage primarily in teaching. They disseminate psychological knowledge in classrooms, seminars, and workshops.

Many psychologists are involved in all of these activities: research, **consultation,** and teaching. For example, professors of psychology usually conduct pure or applied research and consult with individuals or industrial clients as well as teach. Full time researchers may be called on to consult with industrial clients and to organize seminars or workshops to help clients develop skills. Practitioners, such as clinical and industrial psychologists, may also engage in research—which is usually applied—and teach in the classroom or workshop. Unfortunately for psychologists who teach, conduct research, and also carry on a practice, research into expanding the week to 250 hours does not look promising.

Let us now explore some of the specialties of psychologists. Although psychologists tend to wear more than one hat, most of them carry out their functions in the following fields.

Pure research • Research conducted without concern for immediate applications.
Applied research • Research conducted in an effort to find solutions to particular problems.
Consultation • The provision of professional advice or services.
Psychotherapy (sigh-coe-THER-uh-pea) • The systematic application of psychological knowledge to the treatment of problem behavior.
Behavior therapy • Application of principles of learning to the direct modification of problem behavior.

Clinical and Counseling Psychologists

Clinical psychologists help people with psychological problems adjust to the demands of life. Clients' problems may range from anxiety and depression to sexual dysfunctions to loss of goals. Clinical psychologists evaluate problems through structured interviews and psychological tests. They help their clients resolve their problems and change maladaptive behavior through **psychotherapy** and **behavior therapy.** Clinical psychologists may work in institutions for mentally ill or mentally retarded people, in outpatient clinics, in college and university clinics, or in private practices. Clinical psychologists are the largest subgroup of psychologists (see Figure 1.1). Most people therefore

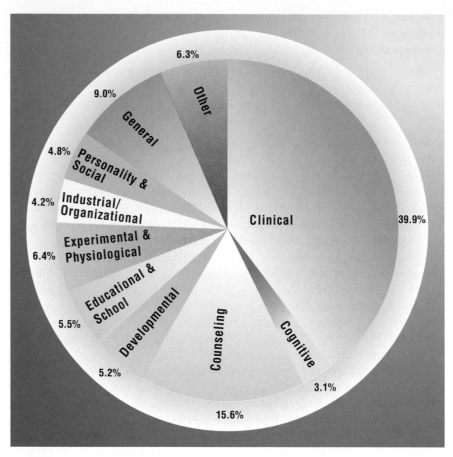

FIGURE 1.1

Recipients of Doctorates in the Various Subfields of Psychology. In 1992, nearly 40% of the doctorates in psychology were awarded in clinical psychology. The next most popular subfield was counseling psychology. From *Summary Report Doctorate Recipients from United States Universities* (Table WO4846), Office of Demographic, Employment, and Educational Research, 1994, Washington, DC: American Psychological Association. Copyright 1994 by the American Psychological Association. Reprinted with permission.

think of clinical psychologists when they hear the term *psychologist*. Many clinical psychologists divide their time among clinical practice, teaching, and research.

Clinical psychologists are not to be confused with psychiatrists. A psychiatrist is a medical doctor who specializes in the study and treatment of psychological disorders.

Counseling psychologists, like clinical psychologists, use interviews and tests to define their clients' problems. Clients of counseling psychologists have adjustment problems but not serious psychological disorders. Clients may encounter difficulty in making academic or vocational decisions or difficulty in making friends in college. They may experience marital or family conflicts or have physical handicaps. Counseling psychologists use counseling to help clients clarify their goals and find ways of surmounting obstacles. Counseling psychologists are often employed in college and university counseling and testing centers. As suggested by Figure 1.1, more than half of psychologists are clinical or counseling psychologists.

School and Educational Psychologists

School psychologists are employed by school systems to help those who encounter problems that interfere with learning. Such problems include social and family problems, emotional problems, and specific learning disorders. School psychologists define students' problems through interviews with teachers, parents, and students; psychological tests such as intelligence and achievement tests; and classroom observation. They consult with teachers, school officials, parents, and other professionals to help students overcome obstacles to learning. They help make decisions about placement of students in special education and remediation programs.

Educational psychologists, like school psychologists, optimize classroom conditions to facilitate learning. They usually focus, however, on improvement of course planning and instructional methods for a school system rather than on individual children. Educational psychologists are concerned about theoretical issues relating to learning, measurement, and child development. Their research interests include the ways in which psychological factors such as motivation and intelligence, sociocultural factors such as poverty and acculturation, and teacher behavior affect learning. Some educational psychologists prepare standardized tests such as the Scholastic Assessment Tests.

Developmental Psychologists

Developmental psychologists study the changes—physical, emotional, cognitive, and social that occur throughout the life span. They attempt to sort out the relative influences of heredity (nature) and the environment (nurture) on development. Developmental psychologists conduct research on issues such as the effects of maternal use of drugs on an embryo, the outcomes of various patterns of child rearing, children's concepts of space and time, adolescent conflicts, and adjustment among older people.

Stereotype • A fixed, conventional idea about a group.

Personality, Social, and Environmental Psychologists

Personality psychologists attempt to define human traits; to determine influences on human thought processes, feelings, and behavior; and to explain psychological disorders. They are particularly concerned with human issues such as anxiety, aggression, and gender roles.

Social psychologists are primarily concerned with the nature and causes of individuals' thoughts, feelings, and behavior in social situations. Personality psychologists look within the person for explanations of behavior. Social psychologists focus on social or external influences. Behavior is influenced from within and without.

Social psychologists have historically focused on topics such as attitude formation and attitude change, interpersonal attraction and liking, **stereotypes,** obedience to authority, and conformity to group norms. Social psychologists, like personality psychologists, study gender roles and aggression.

Environmental psychologists focus on the ways in which behavior influences, and is influenced by, the physical environment. Environmental psychologists are concerned with the ways in which buildings and cities serve, or fail to serve, human needs. They investigate the effects of extremes of temperature, noise, and air pollution.

Environmental Psychology. Environmental psychologists focus on the ways in which we affect and are affected by the physical environment. Among the concerns of environmental psychologists are the effects of crowding and "stimulus overload" on city dwellers.

Experimental Psychologists

Psychologists in all specialties may conduct experimental research. However, those called experimental psychologists conduct research into fundamental processes relevant to more applied specialties. They study the functions of the nervous system, sensation and perception, learning and memory, thought, motivation, and emotion. Experimental psychologists who focus on the relationships between biological changes and psychological events are called physiological or biological psychologists.

Experimental psychologists are more likely than other psychologists to engage in basic or pure research. Their findings are often applied by other specialists in practice. Pure research in motivation, for example, has helped clinical and counseling psychologists devise strategies for helping people control weight. Pure research in learning and memory has helped school and educational psychologists enhance learning conditions in the schools.

Psychologists in Industry

Industrial psychologists focus on the relationships between people and work. Organizational psychologists study the behavior of people in organizations such as business firms. However, many psychologists are trained in both areas. Industrial and organizational psychologists are employed by business firms to improve working conditions, enhance productivity, and—if they have counseling skills—work with employees who encounter problems on the job.

They assist in the processes of hiring, training, and promotion. They devise psychological tests to ascertain whether job applicants have the abilities, interests, and traits that predict successful performance of various jobs. They conduct research concerning job motivation, job satisfaction, the psychological and physical well-being of employees, and ways of making technical systems such as automobile dashboards and computer keyboards more user-friendly.

Consumer psychologists study the behavior of shoppers in an effort to predict and influence their behavior. They advise store managers about how to lay out the aisles of a supermarket to boost impulse buying and how to arrange window displays to attract customers. They devise strategies for enhancing the persuasiveness of newspaper ads and television commercials.

Psychologists are continually finding new areas in which to apply their knowledge and skills.

Reflections

- Which fields of psychology are most in keeping with your own interests?
- Which fields are most consistent with what you imagined psychologists did before you read this section? Which fields are most different? Why?
- What characteristics or interests are shared by all psychologists? What kinds of characteristics or interests set different kinds of psychologists apart?
- If a friend had a problem, would it be adequate to advise "Why don't you see a psychologist?" Why or why not?

WHERE PSYCHOLOGY COMES FROM: A BRIEF HISTORY

Psychology is as old as history and as modern as today. Knowledge of the history of psychology allows us to appreciate psychology's theoretical conflicts, its place among the sciences, the evolution of its methods, and its social and political roles (McGovern and others, 1991).

Although research findings and theoretical developments seem to change the face of psychology every few years, the outline for this textbook could have been written by the Greek philosopher Aristotle (ca. 384–322 B.C.). One of Aristotle's works is called *Peri Psyches,* which translates as "About the Psyche." *Peri Psyches,* like this book, begins with a history of psychological thought and historical perspectives on the nature of the mind and behavior. Given his scientific approach, Aristotle made the case that human behavior, like the movements of the stars and the seas, was subject to rules and laws. Then Aristotle delved into his subject matter topic by topic: personality, sensation and perception, thought, intelligence, needs and motives, feelings and emotion, and memory. This book reorganizes these topics, but each is here.

MINILECTURE: "A BRIEF HISTORY OF PSYCHOLOGY"

Truth or Fiction Revisited. *It is true that a book on psychology, whose contents are similar to those of the book you are now holding, was written by Aristotle more than 2,000 years ago.* The name of that book is *Peri Psyches.*

Aristotle also declared that people are basically motivated to seek pleasure and avoid pain, a view that has been employed in modern psychodynamic and learning theories.

There are other contributors from ancient Greece. Democritus (ca. 460–370 B.C.), for instance, pointed out that our behavior is influenced by external stimulation. He was one of the first to raise the issue of whether there is such a thing as free will or choice.

Plato (ca. 427–347 B.C.), the disciple of Socrates (ca. 470–399 B.C.), recorded Socrates' advice "Know thyself." It has remained a motto of psychological thought ever since. Socrates claimed that we could not attain reliable self-knowledge through our senses because the senses do not exactly mirror reality. Today, we still differentiate between the stimuli that impact upon our sensory receptors and our frequently distorted perceptions and memories. Because the senses provide imperfect knowledge, Socrates suggested that we should study ourselves through rational thought and **introspection.**

Truth or Fiction Revisited. *It is true that the ancient Greek philosopher Socrates suggested a research method that is still used in psychology.* The method is termed *introspection.*

Had we room enough and time, we could trace psychology's roots to thinkers more distant than the ancient Greeks. We could trace its development through the great thinkers of the Renaissance. We could point to 19th-century influences such as theories about evolution, the movements of the atoms, transmission of neural messages in the brain, and the association of thoughts and memories. We could also describe the development of statistics. (Psychologists use statistics to help judge the results of their research.)

As it is, we must move to the development of psychology as a laboratory science during the second half of the 19th century. Some historians set the marker date at 1860. It was then that Gustav Theodor Fechner (1801–1887) published his landmark book *Elements of Psychophysics.* It showed how physical events (such as lights and sounds) were related to psychological sensation and perception. Fechner also showed how we could scientifically measure the effect of these events. Most historians set the debut of modern psychology as a laboratory science in 1879. That is when Wilhelm Wundt (1832–1920) established the first psychological laboratory in Leipzig, Germany.

Introspection • An objective approach to describing one's mental content.

Structuralism • The school of psychology that argues that the mind consists of three basic elements—sensations, feelings, and images—that combine to form experience.

Objective • Of known or perceived objects rather than existing only in the mind; real.

Subjective • Of the mind; personal; determined by thoughts and feelings rather than by external objects.

Functionalism • The school of psychology that emphasizes the uses or functions of the mind rather than the elements of experience.

Habit • A response to a stimulus that becomes automatic with repetition.

Behaviorism • The school of psychology that defines psychology as the study of observable behavior and studies relationships between stimuli and responses.

Structuralism

Wilhelm Wundt, like Aristotle, claimed that the mind was a natural event. It could be studied scientifically, just like light, heat, and the flow of blood. Wundt used introspection to try to discover the basic elements of experience. When presented with various sights and sounds, he and his colleagues looked inward to describe their sensations and feelings.

Wundt and his students founded the school of psychology known as **structuralism.** Structuralism attempted to define the makeup of conscious experience. It broke experience down into **objective** sensations such as sight or taste, and **subjective** feelings such as emotional responses, will, and mental images (for example, memories or dreams). Structuralists believed that the mind functioned by creatively combining the elements of experience.

One of Wundt's American students was G. Stanley Hall (1844–1924). Hall's main interests included the psychological developments of childhood, adolescence, and old age. Hall is usually credited with creating the field of child psychology. He also founded the American Psychological Association.

Wilhelm Wundt

Functionalism

I wished, by treating Psychology like a natural science, to help her become one.
WILLIAM JAMES

Toward the end of the 19th century, William James (1842–1910), brother of the novelist Henry James, adopted a broader view of psychology. He focused on the relationships between experience and behavior. James argued that the stream of consciousness is fluid and continuous. Introspection convinced him that experience cannot be broken down into units, as the structuralists maintained.

James founded the school of **functionalism.** It dealt with behavior as well as consciousness. Functionalism addressed the ways in which experience permits us to adapt our behavior to our environments. It used laboratory observation to supplement introspection. The structuralists tended to ask, "What are the parts of psychological processes?" The functionalists tended to ask, "What are the purposes (functions) of behavior and mental processes? What difference do they make?"

Functionalists proposed that adaptive behavior patterns are learned and maintained. Maladaptive behavior patterns tend to drop out, or to be discontinued. Adaptive actions tend to be repeated and become **habits.** James wrote that "habit is the enormous flywheel of society." Habit maintains civilization from day to day.

The formation of habits is seen in acts such as lifting forks to our mouths and turning doorknobs. At first, these acts require full attention. If you are in doubt, stand by with paper towels and watch a baby's first efforts at self-feeding. Through repetition, the acts that make up self-feeding become automatic, or habitual. The multiple acts involved in learning to drive a car also become routine through repetition. We can then perform them without much attention. We become free to focus on our clever conversation and the cultured sounds issuing from the radio. The idea of learning by repetition is also basic to the behavioral tradition.

William James

Behaviorism

Think of placing a hungry rat in a maze. It meanders down a pathway that comes to an end. It can then turn left or right. If you consistently reward the rat with food for turning right at this choice-point, it will learn to turn right when it arrives there, at least when it is hungry. But what does the rat *think* when it is learning to turn right? "Hmm, last time I was in this situation and turned to the right, I was given some food. Think I'll try that again"?

Does it seem absurd to try to place yourself in the "mind" of a rat? So it seemed to John Broadus Watson (1878–1958), the founder of American **behaviorism.** But Watson was asked to consider just such a question. It was a requirement for his doctoral degree, which he received from the University of Chicago in 1903. Functionalism was abroad in the land and dominant at the University of Chicago. Functionalists were concerned with the stream of consciousness as well as observable behavior. Watson bridled at the introspective struggles of the functionalists to study consciousness, especially the consciousness of lower animals. He asserted that if psychology was to be a natural science, like physics or chemistry, it must limit itself to observable, measurable events. It must limit itself to behavior. Observable behavior includes activities such as pressing a lever; turning left or right; eating and mating; even involuntary body functions such as heart rate, dilation of the pupils of the eyes, blood pressure, and emission of brain waves. These behaviors are *public.* They can be measured by simple observation or laboratory instruments. Psychology must not concern itself with "elements of consciousness." Such "elements" are accessible only to the organism perceiving them. (Behaviorists define psychology as the scientific study of *behavior,* not of *behavior and mental processes.*)

John B. Watson

Reinforcement • A stimulus that follows a response and increases the frequency of the response.

Gestalt psychology (gesh-TALT) • The school of psychology that emphasizes the tendency to organize perceptions into wholes and to integrate separate stimuli into meaningful patterns.

FIGURE 1.2

A Couple of Examples of the Power of Reinforcement. In the photo on the left, we see how our feathered gift to city life has earned its keep in many behavioral experiments on the effects of reinforcement. Here, the pigeon pecks the blue button because pecking this button has been followed (reinforced) by the dropping of a food pellet into the cage. In the photo on the right, "Air Raccoon" shoots a basket. Behaviorists teach animals complex behaviors such as shooting baskets by first reinforcing approximations to the goal (or target behavior). As time progresses, closer approximations are demanded before reinforcement is given.

Harvard University psychologist B. F. Skinner (1904–1990) introduced the concept of **reinforcement** to behaviorism. Organisms, Skinner maintained, learn to behave in certain ways because they are reinforced for doing so. He demonstrated that laboratory animals will carry out various simple and complex behaviors because of reinforcement. They will peck buttons (Figure 1.2), turn in circles, climb ladders, and push toys across the floor. Many psychologists adopted the view that, in principle, one could explain intricate human behavior as the summation of instances of learning through reinforcement.

Max Wertheimer

Gestalt Psychology

In the 1920s, another school of psychology—**Gestalt psychology**—was quite prominent in Germany. In the 1930s, the three founders of the school—Max Wertheimer (1880–1943), Kurt Koffka (1886–1941), and Wolfgang Köhler (1887–1967)—left Europe to escape the Nazi threat. They carried on their work in the United States.

Wertheimer and his colleagues focused on perception and on how perception influences thinking and problem solving. In contrast to the behaviorists, Gestalt psychologists argued that one cannot hope to understand human nature by focusing only on behavior. In contrast to the structuralists, they claimed that one cannot explain human perceptions, emotions, or thought processes in terms of basic units. Perceptions were *more* than the sums of their parts. Gestalt psychologists saw our perceptions as wholes that give meaning to parts.

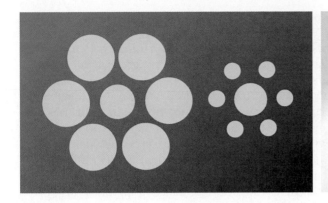

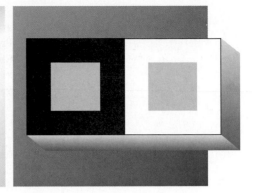

A. Are the circles in the center of the configurations the same size? Why not take a ruler and measure their diameters?

B. Is the second symbol in each line the letter B or the number 13?

C. Which one of the gray squares is brighter?

FIGURE 1.3

The Importance of Context. Gestalt psychologists have shown that our perceptions depend not only on our sensory impressions but also on the context of our impressions. They argue that human perception cannot be explained in terms of basic units because we tend to interpret our perceptions of things as wholes, in terms of the contexts in which they occur. You will interpret a man running toward you very differently depending on whether you are on a deserted street at night or at a track in the morning.

Gestalt psychologists illustrated how we tend to perceive separate pieces of information as integrated wholes, including the contexts in which they occur. Consider Figure 1.3. The dots in the centers of the configurations at the left are the same size. Yet we may perceive them as being of different sizes because of the contexts in which they appear. The inner squares in the center figure are equally bright. They may *look* different because of their contrasting backgrounds. The second symbol in each line at the right is identical. Yet in the top row we may perceive it as a B, and in the bottom row, as the number 13. The symbol has not changed, only the context in which it appears. In *The Prince and the Pauper,* Mark Twain dressed a peasant boy as a prince, and the kingdom bowed to him. Do clothes sometimes make the man or woman?

Gestalt psychologists believed that learning could be active and purposeful, not merely responsive and mechanical as in Pavlov's experiments with dogs. Wolfgang Köhler and the others demonstrated that much learning is accomplished by **insight,** not by mechanical repetition (see Chapter 9).

Insight • In Gestalt psychology, the sudden reorganization of perceptions, allowing the sudden solution of a problem.

Psychoanalysis (sigh-coe-an-AL-uh-sis) • The school of psychology that emphasizes the importance of unconscious motives and conflicts as determinants of human behavior.

Sigmund Freud

Psychoanalysis

Psychoanalysis is the school of psychology founded by a Viennese physician who fled to England in the 1930s to escape the Nazi tyranny—Sigmund Freud (1856–1939). Freud's theory, more than the others, has invaded the popular culture. You may already be familiar with it. For example, an unstable person goes on a killing spree on at least one TV crime show each season. At the show's conclusion, a psychiatrist typically explains that the killer was "unconsciously" doing away with his own mother or father. Or perhaps a friend has tried to "interpret" a slip of the tongue you made or has asked you what you thought might be the symbolic meaning of a dream.

The notions that people are driven by hidden impulses and that verbal slips and dreams represent unconscious wishes largely reflect the influence of Freud. Academic psychologists conducted their research mainly in the laboratory. Freud, however, gained his understanding of people through clinical interviews. He was astounded at how little insight people seemed to have into their motives. Some people justified, or rationalized, the most abominable behavior with absurd explanations. Others seized the opportunity to blame themselves for nearly every misfortune that had befallen the human species.

Freud came to believe that unconscious processes, especially primitive sexual and aggressive impulses, were more influential than conscious thought in determining human behavior. Freud thought that most of the mind was unconscious. It consisted of a seething cauldron of conflicting impulses, urges, and wishes. People were motivated to gratify these impulses, ugly as some of them were. But at the same time, people were motivated to judge themselves as being decent. Thus, they would often delude themselves about their real motives. Because of the assumed motion of underlying forces in personality, Freud's theory is referred to as **psychodynamic.**

Freud devised a method of psychotherapy called psychoanalysis. Psychoanalysis aims to help people gain insight into deep-seated conflicts and find socially acceptable ways of expressing wishes and gratifying needs. Psychoanalytic therapy is a process that can extend for years. We describe psychoanalysis at length (but not for years) in Chapter 13.

Now let's turn to the "top 10"—psychology's golden oldies. Table 1.1 ranks the top 10 ("most important") historic figures in psychology according to historians of psychology and chairpersons of psychology departments (Kern and others, 1991). The historians and chairpersons concur on 7 of their top 10.

Today we no longer find psychologists who describe themselves as structuralists or functionalists. Although the school of Gestalt psychology gave birth to current research approaches in perception and problem solving, few would

Psychodynamic (sigh-coe-die-NAM-ick) • Referring to Freud's theory, which proposes that the motion of underlying forces of personality determines our thoughts, feelings, and behavior. (From the Greek *dynamis,* meaning "power.")

TABLE 1.1

HISTORIANS' AND CHAIRPERSONS' RANKINGS OF THE IMPORTANCE OF FIGURES IN THE HISTORY OF PSYCHOLOGY

HISTORIANS			CHAIRPERSONS		
RANK	FIGURE	AREA OF CONTRIBUTION	RANK	FIGURE	AREA OF CONTRIBUTION
1.	Wilhelm Wundt	Structuralism	1.	B. F. Skinner	Operant Conditioning
2.	William James	Functionalism	2.	Sigmund Freud	Psychoanalysis
3.	Sigmund Freud	Psychoanalysis	3.	William James	Functionalism
4.	John B. Watson	Behaviorism	4.	Jean Piaget	Cognitive Development
5.	Ivan Pavlov	Conditioning	5.	G. Stanley Hall	Development
6.	Hermann Ebbinghaus	Memory	6.	Wilhelm Wundt	Structuralism
7.	Jean Piaget	Cognitive Development	7.	Carl Rogers	Self Theory, A Person-Centered Therapy
8.	B. F. Skinner	Operant Conditioning	8.	John B. Watson	Behaviorism
9.	Alfred Binet	Assessment of Intelligence	9.	Ivan Pavlov	Conditioning
10.	Gustav Theodor Fechner	Psychophysics	10.	Edward L. Thorndike	Learning—Law of Effect

[1] Rankings based on data from "Historians' and chairpersons' judgments of eminence among psychologists," by J. H. Kern, R. Davis, and S. F. Davis, 1991, *American Psychologist, 46,* pp. 789–792. Reprinted with permission.

consider themselves Gestalt psychologists. The numbers of orthodox behaviorists and psychoanalysts have also been declining. Many contemporary psychologists in the behaviorist tradition look on themselves as social-cognitive[1] theorists. Many psychoanalysts consider themselves neoanalysts rather than traditional Freudians. Still, the historical traditions of psychology find expression in many contemporary fields and schools of psychology.

Reflections

- Which school of psychology is most consistent with your own interests or your own views of people? Why?
- Why do behaviorists object to schools of psychology that use introspection to learn about people? Do you agree with the behaviorist point of view? Why or why not?
- Had you heard of Sigmund Freud before you began this course? What had you heard? Were your impressions accurate? Why or why not?
- **Psychology's "top 10," as selected both by historians of psychology and chairpersons of psychology departments, consists completely of White males. Why do you think this is so?**

HOW TODAY'S PSYCHOLOGISTS VIEW BEHAVIOR

First a new theory is attacked as absurd; then it is admitted to be true, but obvious and insignificant; finally it is seen to be so important that its adversaries claim that they themselves discovered it.

WILLIAM JAMES

The history of psychological thought has taken many turns, and contemporary psychologists also differ in their approaches. Today, there are six broad, influential perspectives in psychology: the biological, cognitive, humanistic–existential, psychodynamic, learning, and sociocultural perspectives. Each perspective emphasizes different topics of investigation. Each approaches its topics in its own ways.

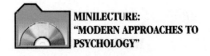

MINILECTURE: "MODERN APPROACHES TO PSYCHOLOGY"

The Biological Perspective

Psychologists assume that our thoughts, fantasies, dreams, and mental images are made possible by the nervous system, especially the brain. Biologically oriented psychologists seek the links between events in the brain—such as the activity of brain cells—and mental processes. Through biological psychology, we have discovered parts of the brain that are highly active when we listen to music, solve math problems, or have certain psychological disorders. We have learned how chemicals in the brain are essential to the storage of information—that is, the formation of memories.

Biological psychologists are also concerned about the influences of hormones and genes. For example, psychologists are interested in genetic influences on intelligence, psychological disorders, criminal behavior, even addiction to alcohol and narcotics.

---

[1] Formerly termed *social-learning theorists*.

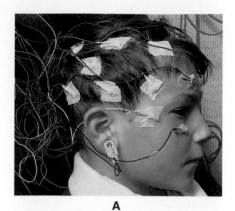

A

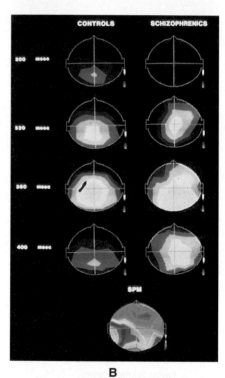

B

The Biological Perspective. Psychologists with a biological perspective investigate the connections between biological processes, overt behavior, and mental processes. They may use methods such as Brain Electrical Activity Mapping, in which electrodes measure the electrical activity of parts of the brain (photo A). The left-hand column of photo B shows the average level of electrical activity of the brains of 10 normal people at four time intervals. The right-hand column shows the average activity of 10 people diagnosed with schizophrenia. The more intense the activity, the brighter the color (white is most intense). The bottom diagram summarizes similarities and differences between the two groups.

The Cognitive Perspective

Cognitive psychologists venture into the realm of mental processes to understand human nature (Sperry, 1993). They investigate the ways in which we perceive and mentally represent the world, how we solve problems, how we dream and daydream. Cognitive psychologists, in short, study those things we refer to as the *mind.*

Today, the cognitive perspective has many faces. One is the cognitive-developmental theory of the Swiss biologist Jean Piaget (1896–1980). Another is information processing, which is related to concepts in computer science. Many cognitive psychologists focus on the processes by which information is encoded (input), stored (in long-term memory), retrieved (placed in working memory), and manipulated to solve problems (output). Our strategies for solving problems are sometimes referred to as our "mental programs" or "software." In this computer metaphor, our brains are translated into the "hardware" that runs our mental programs. Our brains, that is, become *very* personal computers.

Truth or Fiction Revisited. *It is true that some psychologists look upon our strategies for solving problems as "mental programs" operated by our very "personal computers"— our brains.* These psychologists are cognitive psychologists. They investigate the ways in which we process information.

The Humanistic–Existential Perspective

The humanistic–existential perspective is related to Gestalt psychology and is cognitive in flavor. **Humanism** stresses the human capacity for self-fulfillment and the central roles of human consciousness, self-awareness, and the capacity to make choices. Consciousness is seen as the force that unifies our personalities. **Existentialism** views people as free to choose and responsible for choosing ethical conduct.

Humanistic psychology considers subjective or personal experience to be the most important event in psychology. Humanists believe that self-awareness, experience, and choice permit us to "invent ourselves." That is, we can fashion our growth and our ways of relating to the world as we progress through life. Humanistic–existential psychology reached the peak of its popularity in the 1970s. At that time, encounter groups, Gestalt therapy, meditation, and a number of other methods were in vogue. They have been stamped collectively as the Human Potential Movement.

Critics, including those in the behaviorist tradition, argue that experiences are subjective events that are poorly suited to objective observation and measurement. Humanistic–existential psychologists such as Carl Rogers (1985) argue, however, that subjective human experience remains vital to the understanding of human nature.

The Psychodynamic Perspective

In the 1940s and 1950s, Freud's theory dominated the practice of psychotherapy. It was also widely influential in scientific psychology and the arts. Most psychotherapists were psychodynamically oriented, and many renowned artists and writers sought ways to liberate the expression of their unconscious ideas.

Today, Freud's influence continues to be felt, but it no longer dominates psychology. Psychologists who follow Freud today are likely to consider themselves to be **neoanalysts.** Neoanalysts such as Karen Horney, Erich Fromm, and Erik Erikson focus less on the roles of unconscious sexual and aggressive impulses in human behavior. They focus more on deliberate choice and self-direction.

The Learning Perspective

Many psychologists study the effects of experience on behavior. Learning, to them, is the essential factor in describing, explaining, predicting, and controlling behavior. The term *learning* has different meanings to psychologists of different persuasions, however. Some students of learning find roles for consciousness and insight. Others do not. This distinction is found among those who adhere to the behavioral and social-cognitive perspectives.

THE BEHAVIORAL PERSPECTIVE.   For John B. Watson, behaviorism was an approach to life as well as a broad guideline for psychological research. Watson despaired of measuring consciousness and mental processes in the laboratory. He also applied behavioral analysis to virtually all situations in his daily life. He viewed people as doing things because of their learning histories, situational influences, and rewards, not because of conscious choice.

Learning, for Watson and his followers, is exemplified by experiments in conditioning. The results of conditioning are explained in terms of external laboratory procedures, not in terms of changes within the organism. Behaviorists do not attempt to find out what an organism has come to "know" through learning. Cognitive psychologists, in contrast, view conditioning as a process that alters the organism's mental representation of the environment. Conditioning may encourage, but does not compel, changes in behavior (Rescorla, 1988).

THE SOCIAL-COGNITIVE PERSPECTIVE.   Since the early 1960s, **social-cognitive theorists** have gained influence in the areas of personality, psychological disorders, and methods of therapy. Theorists such as Albert Bandura, Julian Rotter, and Walter Mischel see themselves as being within the behaviorist tradition because of their focus on learning. Yet they also return to their functionalist roots by theorizing a key role for cognition. Behaviorists emphasize the importance of environmental influences and focus on acquiring habits through repetition and reinforcement. Social-cognitive theorists, in contrast, suggest that people can modify or create their environments. People also learn intentionally by observing others. Through observational learning, we acquire a storehouse of responses to life's situations. Social-cognitive theorists are also humanistic. They believe that our expectations and values help determine whether we *choose* to do what we have learned how to do.

Cognitive • Having to do with mental processes such as sensation and perception, memory, intelligence, language, thought, and problem solving.

Humanism • The philosophy and school of psychology that asserts that people are conscious, self-aware, and capable of free choice, self-fulfillment, and ethical behavior.

Existentialism (egg-ziss-TEN-shall-izm) • The view that people are completely free and responsible for their own behavior.

Neoanalysts (knee oh AN al lists) • Contemporary followers of Freud who focus less on the roles of unconscious impulses and more on conscious choice and self-direction.

Social-cognitive theory • A school of psychology in the behaviorist tradition that includes cognitive factors in the explanation and prediction of behavior. Formerly termed *social-learning theory.*

The Sociocultural Perspective

The profession of psychology focuses mainly on the individual and is committed to the dignity of the individual. We cannot understand individuals without an awareness of the richness of human diversity, however (Betancourt & López, 1993; Goodchilds, 1991). Inclusion of human diversity makes psychology a stronger science and better serves the public interest (Denmark, 1994; Reid, 1994). People differ from one another in many ways.

The **sociocultural perspective** fosters the consideration of matters of ethnicity, gender, culture, and socioeconomic status in psychology (Allen, 1993; Lewis-Fernández & Kleinman, 1994). For example, what is often seen as healthful, self-assertive, outspoken behavior by most U.S. women may be interpreted as brazen behavior within Hispanic American or Asian American communities (López & Hernandez, 1986).

One kind of diversity involves people's **ethnic groups.** Ethnic groups unite them according to cultural heritage, race, language, and common history.[2] The experiences of various ethnic groups in the United States highlight the impact of social, political, and economic factors on human behavior and development (Murray, 1995; Whitten, 1993).

The probing of human diversity enables students to appreciate the cultural heritages and historical problems of various ethnic groups. This textbook considers many psychological issues related to ethnicity, including:

- The representation of ethnic minority groups in psychological research studies
- Alcohol and substance abuse among adolescents from various ethnic minority groups
- Bilingualism
- Ethnic differences in intelligence test scores—their implications and possible origins
- The prevalence of suicide among members of different ethnic minority groups
- Ethnic differences in vulnerability to various physical problems and disorders, ranging from obesity to hypertension and cancer
- Ethnic differences in the utilization of health care for physical and psychological problems
- Multicultural issues in the practice of psychotherapy
- Prejudice

People also differ in **gender.** Gender is the state of being male or being female. Gender is not simply a matter of anatomic sex. Gender involves a complex web of cultural expectations and social roles that affect people's self-concepts and hopes and dreams, as well as their behavior. How can sciences such as psychology and medicine hope to understand the particular viewpoints, qualities, and problems of women if most research is conducted with men and by men (Hyde, 1993; Reid, 1993, 1994)?

Just as there have been prejudices against members of ethnic minority groups, so too have there been prejudices against women. Even much of the scientific research into gender roles and gender differences assumes that male behavior represents the norm (Ader & Johnson, 1994; Matlin, 1993; Walsh, 1993). The careers of women have been traditionally channeled into domestic chores, regardless of their wishes as individuals. Not until modern times were women considered suitable for higher education. (Women are still considered unsuited to education in many parts of the world!) Women have attended college in the United States only since 1833, when Oberlin opened its doors to women. Today, however, more than half (54.5%) of U.S. postsecondary students are women.

Sociocultural perspective • The view that focuses on the roles of ethnicity, gender, culture, and socioeconomic status in behavior and mental processes.
Ethnic group • A group characterized by common features such as cultural heritage, history, race, and language.
Gender • The state of being female or being male.

---

[2] I use the term *ethnicity* to include the concept of race. Some authors limit ethnicity to refer to cultural heritage, language, and common history. The root of the word, the Greek *ethnos*, was first used to refer to the people of a nation or a tribe (Betancourt & López, 1993).

PERSPECTIVE	SUBJECT MATTER	KEY ASSUMPTIONS
Biological	Nervous system, endocrine system, genetic factors	Behavior and mental processes can be explained in terms of biological processes
Cognitive	Mental imagery, information processing, thinking, language	People mentally represent the world and consciously attempt to understand it
Humanistic–existential	Subjective experience	People make free and conscious choices based on their unique experiences and frames of reference
Psychodynamic	Unconscious processes, early childhood experiences	Defensive processes prevent people from being aware of their underlying motives; people may be influenced for a lifetime by unconscious early childhood conflicts
Learning	Environmental influences on behavior; habitual behavior; observational learning	People are very similar at birth but unique histories of experience and reinforcement guide unique patterns of development of behavior and skills
Sociocultural	Effects of ethnicity, gender, culture, and socioeconomic status on behavior and mental processes	Individual differences are created by sociocultural factors as well as biological and psychological processes

FIGURE 1.4
Contemporary Perspectives at a Glance.

Truth or Fiction Revisited. It is true that women were not permitted to attend college in the United States until 1833. In that year, Oberlin began to accept women students.

Contemporary women are also making inroads into traditionally male preserves such as medicine, law, and engineering. Women now make up about 40% of U.S. medical students, for example (Angier, 1995). Women make up about 40% of Harvard Law School's students and about 40% of new associates in the 250 largest U.S. legal firms. Because women have only recently increased their numbers in these professions, their numbers are lower among doctors and lawyers in practice today. Women now make up nearly 15% of engineering graduates. Although this figure is relatively low, history provides some perspective. Only 20 years ago, women accounted for only about 4% of engineering graduates (Morrison & Von Glinow, 1990).

Contemporary psychologists continue to view behavior and mental processes from various perspectives see (Figure 1.4). The influences of the cognitive and biological perspectives appear to be on the ascent (Boneau, 1992). Yet there is little or no falloff in interest in the behavioral and psychodynamic perspectives, as measured by the number of journal articles that address these views (Friman and others, 1993).

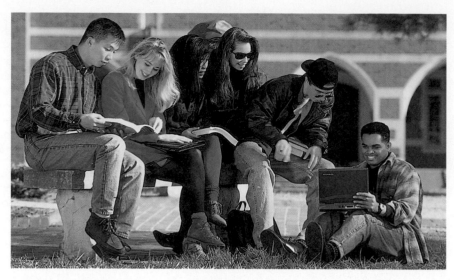

Human Diversity. How can psychologists comprehend the aspirations and problems of individuals from an ethnic group without understanding the history and cultural heritage of that group? The study of human diversity helps us to understand and appreciate the true scope of human behavior and mental processes. It is also enriching for its own sake.

Reflections

- Which psychological perspectives seem to support the view that people are free to choose their own destinies? Which do not? Does it seem to you that people are free? Why or why not?
- In what ways do some psychologists see our mental processes as computerlike? Does the comparison of human mental processes to computer information processing seem reasonable to you? Why or why not?
- Does it seem possible to you to "believe in" more than one perspective? Why or why not?
- Why is human diversity a key issue in the science of psychology? In what ways does knowledge of human diversity contribute to our understanding of behavior and mental processes?

WORLD OF DIVERSITY

THE DIVERSITY OF CONTRIBUTORS TO THE DEVELOPMENT OF PSYCHOLOGY

Have another look at psychology's "golden oldies," as listed in Table 1.1 on page 14. Did you notice something they have in common? They are all White males. Critics assert that such lists create the erroneous impression that women and people of color have not contributed to psychology (Russo, 1990a; Guthrie, 1990).

Consider some of the women. Christine Ladd-Franklin was born in 1847. In that era in American history, women were expected to remain in the home. They were excluded from careers in science (Furumoto, 1992). She nevertheless pursued a career in psychology, taught at Johns Hopkins and Columbia Universities, and formulated a theory of color vision. Mary Whiton Calkins (born in 1863), a student of William James, pioneered research in memory. She introduced the method of paired associates and discovered the primacy and recency effects (see Chapters 6 and 16; Madigan & O'Hara, 1992). She was also the first female president of the American Psychological Association in 1905. Margaret Floy Washburn (born in 1871) was the first woman to receive a PhD in psychology. Washburn also wrote *The Animal Mind,* a work that presaged behaviorism.

Then there are psychologists of different ethnic backgrounds. Back in 1901, African American Gilbert Haven Jones received his PhD in psychology in Germany. J. Henry Alston engaged in research in the perception of heat and cold. He was the first African American psychologist to be published in a key psychology journal (the year was 1920). A more contemporary African American psychologist, Kenneth B. Clark, studied ethnicity and influenced a key Supreme Court decision on desegregation (Kern and others, 1991).

Hispanic American and Asian American psychologists have also made their mark. Jorge Sanchez, for example, was among the first to show how intelligence tests are culturally biased against Mexican American children. Asian American psychologist Stanley Sue (see Chapter 9) has engaged in research in racial differences in intelligence and academic achievement and related them to discrimination and other factors.

True—psychology was once the province of White males. Today, however, more than half (59%) of the PhDs in psychology are awarded to women (see Figure 1.5; ODEER, 1994). African Americans and Hispanic Americans each

Kenneth B. Clark

Margaret Floy Washburn

FIGURE 1.5

Growth in the Percentage of Women Who Received Doctorates in the Various Subfields of Psychology, 1980 Versus 1992. This growth of the percentage of women in psychology has been dramatic. In 1980, about two doctorate recipients in five were women, as compared to nearly three in five in 1992. From *Summary Report Doctorate Recipients from United States Universities* (Table WO4846), Office of Demographic, Employment, and Educational Research, 1994, Washington, DC: American Psychological Association. Copyright 1994 by the American Psychological Association. Reprinted with permission.

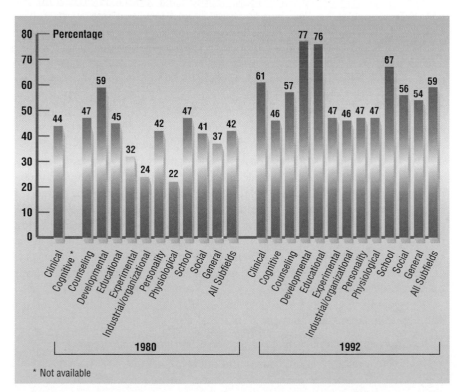

* Not available

receive 3 to 4% of the PhDs awarded in psychology, however (ODEER, 1994). This percentage is far below their representation in the general population. In a recent year, only one-tenth of 1 percent of the 65,000 members of the American Psychological Association were Native Americans (DeAngelis, 1993a). Even so, fewer than two psychology PhDs in five are now received by White males. Psychology, like the world in which it is housed, is showing diversification.

Truth or Fiction Revisited. *It is not true that men receive the majority of doctoral degrees in psychology.* Women actually receive the majority of PhDs in psychology today.

Put it another way: Psychology is for everyone.

CRITICAL THINKING AND PSYCHOLOGY

A great many people think they are thinking when they are merely rearranging their prejudices.

WILLIAM JAMES

Higher education is a broadening experience. Not only does it expose students to intellectual disciplines and human diversity. It also encourages students to learn to think critically. By thinking critically, people can challenge widely accepted but erroneous beliefs. These include their own most cherished beliefs. **Critical thinking** helps make us into active, astute judges of other people and their points of view. No longer are we passive recipients of the latest intellectual fads and tyrannies.

Critical thinking fosters skepticism. Thus we no longer so readily take certain "truths" for granted. People largely assume that authority figures like doctors and government leaders usually provide us with the facts and are best equipped to make the decisions that affect our lives (Kimble, 1994). But when doctors disagree as to whether surgery is necessary, how can they all be correct? When political leaders fling accusations and insults at one another, how can we know whom to trust? If we are to be conscientious, productive citizens of the nation and of the world, we need to learn to seek pertinent information to make our own decisions. We need to rely on our analytical abilities to judge the accuracy of this information. This textbook will help you learn to seek and analyze information that lies within the province of psychology. The critical thinking skills you acquire will also apply to other courses and all of your adult undertakings.

Critical thinking helps students evaluate other people's claims and arguments. It encourages students to reconsider and, when necessary, dispute widely held beliefs (Mayer & Goodchild, 1990). Critical thinking has many meanings. On one level, critical thinking means taking nothing for granted. It means not believing things just because they are in print or because they were uttered by authority figures or celebrities. On another level, critical thinking refers to analyzing and probing the questions, statements, and arguments of others. It means examining the definitions of terms, examining the premises or assumptions behind arguments, and scrutinizing the logic with which arguments are developed.

A psychology task force (McGovern, 1989) defined the goals of critical thinking as fostering the following thinking skills:

• Development of skepticism about explanations and conclusions

• The ability to inquire about causes and effects

Critical Thinking. Critical thinking means taking nothing for granted and analyzing other people's arguments. It means examining the definitions of terms, the premises of arguments, and the logic of arguments. Critical thinking provides the keys not only to a college education, but also to a lifetime of self-education.

- Refinement of curiosity about behavior
- Knowledge of research methods
- The ability to critically analyze arguments

Your college education is intended to do more than provide you with a data bank of useful knowledge. It is also meant to supply intellectual tools that allow you to analyze information independently. With these tools, you can continue to educate yourself for the rest of your life.

Principles of Critical Thinking

Many of the "Truth or Fiction?" items presented in this textbook are intended to encourage you to apply principles of critical thinking to the subject matter of psychology. Some of them reflect "truisms," or beliefs, that are often taken for granted within our culture. Consider a sampling of "Truth or Fiction?" items from several chapters:

- Alcohol causes aggression.
- Onions and apples have the same taste.
- We tend to act out our forbidden fantasies in our dreams.
- We must make mistakes in order to learn.
- Some people have photographic memories.
- Head Start programs have raised children's IQs.
- We value things more when we have to work for them.
- Misery loves company.
- You can never be too rich or too thin.
- People who threaten suicide are only seeking attention.
- Beauty is in the eye of the beholder.

Critical thinking • An approach to thinking characterized by skepticism and thoughtful analysis of statements and arguments—for example, probing arguments' premises and the definitions of terms.

We won't give you the answers to the items—not yet. But we will provide hints and use them to illustrate some principles of critical thinking:

1. *Be skeptical.* Politicians and advertisers strive to convince you of their points of view. Even research reported in the media or in textbooks may take a certain slant. Accept nothing as true until you have personally examined the evidence.

2. *Examine definitions of terms.* Some statements are true when a term is defined in one way but not another. Consider the statement "Head Start programs have raised children's IQs." The correctness of the statement depends on the definition of "IQ." (In Chapter 9, you will see that the term *IQ* has a specific meaning. *IQ* is not synonymous with *intelligence*.) In interpreting research, pay attention to how concepts are defined.

3. *Examine the assumptions or premises of arguments.* Consider the controversial abortion issue. The science of psychology cannot demonstrate the validity of either the pro-choice or pro-life positions (Kendler, 1993). However, critical thinking allows us to examine the assumptions that underlie assertions such as "Abortion is murder." *Murder* is a legal term that my dictionary defines as "the unlawful and malicious or premeditated killing of one human being by another." If one accepts this definition of murder as one's premise, then abortion may be murder if a fetus is considered a "human being." The question as to whether an embryo or fetus is a human being sparks considerable controversy, of course.

Also consider the view that one cannot learn about human beings by engaging in research with animals. One premise in the statement seems to be that human beings are not animals. We are, of course—thoroughly delightful animals, I might add. (Would you rather be a plant?)

4. *Be cautious in drawing conclusions from evidence.* Studies for many years had shown that most clients who receive psychotherapy improve. It was therefore generally assumed that psychotherapy worked. Some 40 years ago, however, a psychologist named Hans Eysenck pointed out that most troubled people who did *not* receive psychotherapy also improved! The question thus becomes whether people receiving psychotherapy are *more* likely to improve than those who do not.

   Correlational evidence is also inferior to experimental evidence as a way of determining cause and effect. Consider the statement "Alcohol causes aggression" in the following principle.

5. *Consider alternative interpretations of research evidence.* Does alcohol cause aggression? Is the assertion that it does so truth or fiction? Evidence certainly shows a clear *connection,* or "correlation," between alcohol and aggression. That is, many people who commit violent crimes have been drinking. Does the evidence show that this connection is *causal,* however? Tune into Chapter 2's discussion of the differences between the correlational and experimental methods to find out. You will see that rival explanations can be employed to explain correlational evidence.

6. *Do not oversimplify.* As noted in the book's discussions of language, intelligence, and development, most behavior patterns involve complex interactions of genetic and environmental influences. Also consider the complex issue as to whether psychotherapy helps people with psychological problems. In Chapter 14 you will see that it is more worthwhile to ask, What *type* of psychotherapy, practiced by *whom,* is most helpful for *what kind of problem?*

7. *Do not overgeneralize.* Consider the statement "Misery loves company." In Chapter 10 you will see that the statement is accurate under certain circumstances. Again, consider the view that one cannot learn about human beings by engaging in research with animals. Is the truth of the matter an all-or-nothing issue? Are there certain kinds of information we can obtain about people from research with animals?

8. *Apply critical thinking to all areas of life.* A skeptical attitude and a demand for evidence are not simply academic exercises that serve in college courses. They are of value in all areas of life. Be skeptical when you are bombarded by TV commercials, when political causes try to sweep you up, when you see the latest cover stories about Elvis and UFOs in the tabloids at the supermarket. How many times have you heard the claim "Studies have shown that . . ."? Perhaps such claims sound convincing, but ask yourself: Who ran the studies? Were the researchers neutral scientists or biased toward obtaining certain results?

Recognizing Fallacies in Arguments

Another aspect of critical thinking is learning to recognize the fallacies in other people's claims and arguments. Consider the following examples:

1. Arguments directed to the person *(argumentum ad hominem):* Psychological theories and research enterprises have met with historic upheavals. The

views of Sigmund Freud, for example, the founder of psychodynamic theory, were assaulted almost as soon as they were publicized both by members of his inner circle, such as Carl Jung, and by psychologists of other schools, such as behaviorists. Freud has been alternately referred to as an ingenious, compassionate scientist and as an elitist faker who spun his theories out of the fabric of the fantasy lives of bored, wealthy women. Both extremes are *ad hominem* arguments. Freud's personality and motives are of historic interest, but neither of them addresses the accuracy of his views.

2. Appeals to force *(argumentum ad baculum):* Galileo invented the telescope in the 17th century. He discovered that the Earth revolved around the sun, not vice versa. The Church had taught that the Earth was at the center of the universe, however. Galileo was condemned for heresy and warned that he would be burned to death if he did not confess the error of his ways. Galileo apparently agreed with Shakespeare's words in *King Henry IV, Part I* that "The better part of valour is discretion." He disclaimed his views. The facts, however, are what they are.

3. Appeals to authority *(argumentum ad verecundiam):* You have heard arguments to this effect many times: "Well, my mother/teacher/minister says this is true, and I think that he/she knows more about it than you do." Appeals to authority can be persuasive or infuriating, depending on whether or not you agree with them. It matters not *who* makes an assertion, however. It matters not even if that person is a psychological luminary like Sigmund Freud, William James, or John B. Watson. An argument is true or false on its own merits. Consider the evidence, not the person making the argument.

4. Appeals to popularity *(argumentum ad populum):* The appeal to popularity is cousin to the appeal to authority. The argument that one should do something because "everyone's doing it" gets some people involved in activities they later regret. The people making the pitches in TV commercials are usually popular—either because they are good looking or because they are celebrities. Evaluate the evidence. Ignore the appeal of the pitchmaker.

Acquiring an education means more than memorizing databases and learning how to solve problems in courses such as chemistry and calculus. It also means acquiring the tools to think critically. Once you do, you can continue to educate yourself for a lifetime.

Reflections

- As you reflect on your life to date, can you say that you have been a critical thinker? Why or why not? If not, are you going to do something about it? What?
- Have you been personally exposed to *ad hominem* arguments or to appeals to authority, force, or popularity? Did you recognize these arguments for what they were at the time? Are you satisfied with your response to them? Why or why not?
- Why is learning to think critically an essential part of higher education? How might critical thinking protect the individual from dictators, advertisers, and other tyrants of the mind?

We have concluded this chapter by urging students to examine the evidence before accepting the truth or falseness of other people's claims and arguments. In the following chapter, we explain how psychologists conduct research to gather evidence for their points of view.

Study Guide

The names of people who are important to psychology are in the first column. Schools of psychology and other identifying information are in the second column. Place the letter of the item that is best associated with the person in the blank space to the left of the person's name. Answers are given below.

___ 1. Aristotle

___ 2. Plato

___ 3. Wolfgang Köhler

___ 4. Gustav Theodor Fechner

___ 5. Erik Erikson

___ 6. Abraham Maslow

___ 7. B. F. Skinner

___ 8. Mary Whiton Calkins

___ 9. Carl Rogers

___ 10. Socrates

___ 11. John B. Watson

___ 12. Wilhelm Wundt

___ 13. Jean Piaget

___ 14. Ivan Pavlov

___ 15. Max Wertheimer

___ 16. G. Stanley Hall

___ 17. Kurt Koffka

___ 18. Sigmund Freud

___ 19. Karen Horney

___ 20. Kenneth B. Clark

___ 21. William James

___ 22. Christine Ladd-Franklin

A. Humanistic perspective

B. Behaviorism

C. Gestalt psychology

D. Studied ethnicity and influenced a Supreme Court decision on desegregation

E. Psychodynamic perspective

F. Author, *Elements of Psychophysics*

G. Structuralism

H. Founder of American Psychological Association

I. Introspection

J. Formulated a theory of color vision

K. Functionalism

L. Cognitive perspective

M. Author, *Peri Psyches*

N. Said "Know thyself"

O. Introduced the method of paired associates and discovered the primacy and recency effects

ANSWER KEY TO EXERCISE 1

1. M	5. E	9. A	13. L	17. C	21. K
2. I, N	6. A	10. I, N	14. B	18. E	22. J
3. C	7. B	11. B	15. C	19. E	
4. F	8. O	12. G, I	16. H	20. D	

EXERCISE 2 | Prominent Figures in the History of Psychology

This exercise is based on Table 1.1. It provides you with the opportunity to recall people whom psychological historians' and department chairpersons' rank as having made notable contributions to psychology. Write the missing name in the blank space and check your answers against the key that follows the exercise.

HISTORIANS

RANK	FIGURE	AREA OF CONTRIBUTION
1.	Wilhelm (1) W___	Structuralism
2.	William (3) J___	Functionalism
3.	(5) S___ Freud	Psychoanalysis
4.	John B. (7) W___	Behaviorism
5.	Ivan (9) P___	Conditioning
6.	Hermann (11) E___	Memory
7.	(13) J___ Piaget	Cognitive Development
8.	B. F. (15) S___	Operant Conditioning
9.	Alfred (17) B___	Assessment of Intelligence
10.	Gustav Theodor (19) F___	Psychophysics

CHAIRPERSONS

RANK	FIGURE	AREA OF CONTRIBUTION
1.	B. F. (2) S___	Operant Conditioning
2.	Sigmund (4) F___	Psychoanalysis
3.	(6) W___ James	Functionalism
4.	Jean (8) P___	Cognitive Development
5.	G. Stanley (10) H___	Development
6.	(12) W___ Wundt	Structuralism
7.	Carl (14) R___	Self Theory, A Person-Centered Therapy
8.	(16) J___ B. Watson	Behaviorism
9.	(18) I___ Pavlov	Conditioning
10.	Edward L. (20) T___	Learning—Law of Effect

ANSWER KEY TO EXERCISE 2

1. Wundt	5. Sigmund	9. Pavlov	13. Jean	17. Binet
2. Skinner	6. William	10. Hall	14. Rogers	18. Ivan
3. James	7. Watson	11. Ebbinghaus	15. Skinner	19. Fechner
4. Freud	8. Piaget	12. Wilhelm	16. John	20. Thorndike

ESL | English as a Second Language—Bridging the Gap

abominable (14)—hateful; terrible
abroad in the land (8)—known all over the country
absurd (11)—crazy, foolish
acculturation (7)—adjustment to a new culture
admirable (2)—worthy of being admired by others
adolescent conflicts (7)—problems teenagers have
adversaries (15)—opponents; people who disagree
all at once (10)—together; in one moment
asserted (11)—stated with confidence
assertions (23)—statements
astounded (14)—amazed; surprised

attain (10)—accomplish
best suited (8)—most appropriate to
biased (24)—leaning to one side or the other; prejudiced
bridled at (11)—became angry
broader view (7)—greater range of ideas
clothes . . . make the man or woman (9)—success depends upon the clothes a person wears
comes to an end (8)—stops
condemned (25)—criticized for or convicted of something
conscientious (22)—careful and responsible

contemporary (4)—modern

controversial (4)—arguable; not agreed upon

convincing (24)—persuasive

credited (10)—recognized as resposible for something

debut (10)—first appearance

differ markedly (2)—be extremely different

disciple (10)—student

discipline (9)—area of study

disorders (5)—illnesses or problems in functioning

distorted perceptions (10)—inaccurate ways of seeing or hearing

diversity (20)—difference

do their bidding (4)—do what they want

doomed to extinction (8)—definitely will not continue to live as a species

downright puzzling (2)—very confusing

dysfunction (5)—inability to perform properly

elitist (25)—one who believes only the privileged should be in charge

embryo (7)—early stages of development before birth

enterprises (24)—planned activities or projects

epilepsy (5)—a brain disorder that causes seizures

epithets (22)—insults

evolution (9)—development

exemplified (17)—illustrated; explained

facilitate (7)—assist; encourage

faker (25)—pretender; trickster

fascinated (2)—caused great interest

fashion our growth (13)—to determine what we will become

fittest (8)—best in every way

flywheel (8)—wheel that drives a machine

fosters (22)—develops

founded a school (7)—started an organized body of study or thought

free will (7)—people can decide what they will do or be

get in touch (14)—know what they feel

go on a killing spree (10)—kill many people in a short time

has taken many turns (11)—has gone in many different directions; there have been many changes in ideas

heresy (25)—going against current thought or authority figures

hypertension (18)—high blood pressure

impact upon (10)—influence

implement (4)—use

in flavor (14)—in the basic ideas

inadequate (4)—not enough

infuriating (25)—makes one angry

ingenious (25)—very clever

integrated whole (13)—something whose parts are all connected

intellectual fads and tyrannies (22)—current thoughts or strong beliefs that are used to influence others

intricate (12)—complicated detail

introspection (10)—looking inward, or thinking about oneself

irresistible impulse (2)—a desire to do something that is impossible to stop

keen (5)—strong

major figure (14)—important person

maladaptive behavior (5)—behavior that is not an effective response to situations; incorrect behavior

malicious (23)—nasty; harmful

Mark Twain (16)—a famous American writer and humorist who lived in the 1800s

maze (11)—puzzle; paths that are confusing

merits (25)—good qualities

mottos (10)—sayings

noble in reason (2)—one who is able to think well

not . . . mirror reality (7)—not the same as reality

nurture (7)—how one is cared for as a young person

obesity (18)—problem with overweight

on the tip of the tongue (2)—can almost remember something but not quite

orthodox (15)—traditional

out of character (4)—an action or thought that is not what we expected from the person

overcame (2)—took over

oversimplify (24)—made too simple; not considering everything

pertinent (22)—appropriate; related to

poverty (7)—lack of money or other resources

probing (18)—making a deep examination

province (22)—area

psychodynamic (9)—psychological processes

psychological disorder (2)—problem with the emotional or thought processes

rationalized (14)—thought of excuses for something

realize their potential (14)—become the best, most creative, and productive person possible

realm (15)—area

refinement (23)—development

remediation (7)—correction of problems

repetition (11)—doing something over and over

scrutinizing (22)—careful examination

seething cauldron (11)—angry; like a boiling pot

self-fulfillment (16)—self-development

skepticism (22)—tendency not to believe something until it's proven

spheres (18)—areas

spurred onward (5)—encouraged to continue

stand trial (7)—judged innocent or guilty in a court of law

statistics (10)—an area of study that uses numbers to indicate how often something happens

stereotypes (7)—ideas about people from different groups

stimuli (10)—things that influence

stream of consciousness (8)—flow of conscious thoughts

substances (15)—material

surprised at ourselves (2)—we discover that we think in ways that we do not expect and are surprised

that's you to a tee (2)—that is an exact description of you

theoretical perspectives (1)—points of view based on systems of thought

to a large extent (14)—in most ways

traits (8)—behaviors; characteristics

trial and error (10)—try different methods until one succeeds

tribe (18)—small group of people who live together; often used for isolated, nonmodern groups

underlying forces (14)—unseen influences

unifies (16)—connects

upheavals (24)—disturbances; problems

uppers (2)—pills (drugs) that cause a person to feel good, elated, excited

uttered by (22)—said by

verbal slips (4)—words spoken that the person didn't mean to say

vital (16)—necessary; essential

vulnerability (18)—easily influenced by

wear more than one hat (4)—do more than one job

web (18)—connections

widespread (5)—common over a large area

you can never be too rich or too thin (23)—the belief that being very wealthy or very thin is to be admired

---

FILL-INS | Chapter Review

SECTION 1: PSYCHOLOGY AS A SCIENCE

Psychology is defined as the study of (1) b_____ and mental processes. Psychology seeks to describe, explain, (2) p_____, and (3) c_____ behavior. But psychologists do not attempt to (4) c_____ the behavior of other people against their wills. Instead, they help clients (5) m_____ their own behavior for their own benefit.

Behavior is explained through psychological (6) t_____, which are sets of statements that involve assumptions about behavior. Explanations and (7) p_____ are derived from theories. Theories are revised, as needed, to accommodate new (8) ob_____. If necessary, theories are discarded.

SECTION 2: WHAT PSYCHOLOGISTS DO

Some psychologists engage in basic, or (9) p_____, research, which has no immediate applications. Other psychologists engage in (10) a_____ research, which seeks solutions to specific problems. In addition to research, many psychologists are found in (11) _____ching.

(12) _____al psychologists comprise the largest subgroup of psychologists. Clinical psychologists help people who are behaving (13) _____ally adjust to the demands of life. Clinical psychologists help clients resolve problems through (14) _____rapy and (15) b_____ therapy. (16) C_____ psychologists work with individuals who have adjustment problems but do not show seriously abnormal behavior.

School psychologists assist students with problems that interfere with (17) _____ing. School psychologists help make decisions about placement of students in (18) sp_____ education and (19) rem_____ programs. (20) Ed_____ psychologists are more concerned with theoretical issues concerning human learning.

(21) D_____ psychologists study the changes that occur throughout the life span. They attempt to sort out the relative influences of heredity and the (22) en_____ on growth. Personality psychologists seek to define human (23) _____its. They study influences on our thought processes, feelings, and (24) b_____ (25) S_____

psychologists study the nature and causes of our thoughts, feelings, and behavior in social situations. Environmental psychologists study the ways in which behavior influences and is influenced by the (26) p_____ environment.

(27) E_____ psychologists conduct research into basic psychological processes, such as sensation and perception, learning and memory, and motivation and emotion. Experimental psychologists who seek to understand the relationships between biological changes and psychological events are called (28) b_____ psychologists.

Industrial psychologists focus on the relationships between people and (29) w_____. (30) _____nal psychologists study the behavior of people in organizations. Consumer psychologists attempt to predict and influence the behavior of (31) c_____.

SECTION 3: WHERE PSYCHOLOGY COMES FROM: A BRIEF HISTORY

The Greek philosopher (32) A_____ was among the first to argue that human behavior is subject to rules and laws. Socrates proclaimed "Know thyself" and suggested the use of (33) _____tion to gain self-knowledge.

Wilhelm (34) W_____ established the first psychological laboratory in 1879. Wundt also founded the school of (35) _____alism and used introspection to study the objective and subjective elements of experience.

William James founded the school of (36) _____alism. Functionalism dealt with observable behavior, as well as conscious experience, and focused on the importance of (37) h_____, which James referred to as "the enormous flywheel of society."

John B. Watson founded the school of (38) b_____. Behaviorists argue that psychology must limit itself to (39) ob_____ behavior and forgo excursions into subjective consciousness. Watson pointed to Pavlov's experiments in (40) _____ning as a model for psychological research. Behaviorism focused on learning by conditioning, and B. F. Skinner introduced the concept of (41) _____ment as an explanation of how learning occurs.

Gestalt psychology focused on (42) p_____. Gestalt psychologists saw our perceptions as (43) wh_____ that give meaning to parts. They argued that learning can be active and (44) _____ful, not merely responsive and (45) _____ical, as in Pavlov's experiments.

Sigmund Freud founded the school of (46) p_____. According to psychodynamic theory, people are driven by hidden impulses and distort reality in order to protect themselves from (47) a_____.

SECTION 4: HOW TODAY'S PSYCHOLOGISTS VIEW BEHAVIOR

The six major perspectives in contemporary psychology include the biological, (48) co_____, (49) hu_____–existential, psychodynamic, learning, and sociocultural perspectives. Biologically oriented psychologists study the links between behavior and biological events, such as the firing of cells in the (50) b_____ and the release of hormones.

Cognitive psychologists study the ways in which we perceive and mentally (51) r_____ the world. Piaget's study of the (52) c_____ development of children has inspired many developmental and educational psychologists. Cognitive psychologists also study (53) in_____ processing—the processes by which information is perceived, stored, and (54) re_____.

Humanistic–existential psychologists stress the importance of human (55) ex_____. They also assert that people have the freedom to make responsible (56) ch_____.

Contemporary psychoanalysts are likely to consider themselves (57) ____analysts. They generally follow Freud's views but focus less on the roles of (58) un_____ sexual and aggressive impulses and see people as more capable of making conscious choices.

Watson and his followers are referred to as (59) _____ists. Social-cognitive theorists are in the behaviorist tradition because of their strong focus on the role of (60) _____ing in human behavior. Social-cognitive theorists also find roles for (61) ob_____ learning, expectations, and values in explaining human behavior.

The sociocultural perspective fosters the consideration of matters of (62) _____ity, gender, culture, and (63) socio_____ status in psychology. The profession of psychology is committed to the dignity of the (64) _____dual, but we cannot understand individuals without an awareness of the richness of human (65) _____sity. People's (66) _____nic groups are defined by features such as their common cultural heritage, race, language, and history. People also differ according to their (67) _____er—that is, the state of being male or being female.

Psychology's "golden oldies," as listed in Table 1.1, are all White (68: Females or Males?). Christine (69) Ladd-F_____ formulated a theory of color vision. Mary Whiton (70) C_____ introduced the method of paired associates and discovered the primacy and recency effects. Margaret Floy (71) W_____ wrote *The Animal Mind*. African American psychologist J. Henry (72) A_____ engaged in research in the perception of heat and cold. Kenneth B. (73) C_____ influenced a key Supreme Court decision on desegregation. Jorge (74) S_____ was among the first to show how intelligence tests are culturally biased.

SECTION 5: CRITICAL THINKING AND PSYCHOLOGY

Critical thinking is intended to foster an attitude of (75) skep_____. Critical thinking refers to thoughtfully (76) _____yzing and probing the questions, statements, and arguments of others. It means examining the (77) def_____s of terms, examining the (78) pre_____s, or assumptions, behind arguments, and scrutinizing the logic with which arguments are developed. Critical thinking within the science of psychology also refers to the ability to inquire about causes and (79) _____cts and to knowledge of (80) re_____ methods. Critical thinkers are also cautious in drawing conclusions from (81) _____ence. Critical thinkers do not (82) over_____ or (83) over_____.

Critical thinkers also learn to recognize the logical (84) fal_____s in other people's claims and arguments. Critical thinkers, for example, recognize the fallacies in arguments directed to the person *(argumentum ad (85) _____inem)*, arguments employing force *(argumentum ad baculum)*, appeals to authority *(argumentum ad (86) _____diam)*, and appeals to popularity *(argumentum ad (87) _____lum)*.

ANSWER KEY TO CHAPTER REVIEW

1. Behavior	8. Observations	15. Behavior	22. Environment	29. Work
2. Predict	9. Pure	16. Counseling	23. Traits	30. Organizational
3. Control	10. Applied	17. Learning	24. Behaviors	31. Consumers
4. Control	11. Teaching	18. Special	25. Social	32. Aristotle
5. Modify	12. Clinical	19. Remediation	26. Physical	33. Introspection
6. Theories	13. Abnormally	20. Educational	27. Experimental	34. Wundt
7. Predictions	14. Psychotherapy	21. Developmental	28. Biological	35. Structuralism

36. Functionalism
37. Habit
38. Behaviorism
39. Observable
40. Conditioning
41. Reinforcement
42. Perception
43. Wholes
44. Purposeful
45. Mechanical
46. Psychoanalysis
47. Anxiety

48. Cognitive
49. Humanistic
50. Brain
51. Represent
52. Cognitive
53. Information
54. Retrieved
55. Experience
56. Choices
57. Neoanalysts (or ego analysts)
58. Unconscious

59. Behaviorists
60. Learning
61. Observational
62. Ethnicity
63. Socioeconomic
64. Individual
65. Diversity
66. Ethnic
67. Gender
68. Males
69. Franklin
70. Calkins

71. Washburn
72. Alston
73. Clark
74. Sanchez
75. Skepticism
76. Analyzing
77. Definitions
78. Premises
79. Effects
80. Research
81. Evidence

82. Oversimplify (or overgeneralize)
83. Overgeneralize (or oversimplify)
84. Fallacies
85. *Hominem*
86. *Verecundiam*
87. *Populum*

POSTTEST | **Multiple Choice**

---

1. If you wanted to run a study in which you learned about another person's _____, you would have to rely on that person's self-report.
   a. heart rate
   b. mental images
   c. emission of a brain wave
   d. muscular responses

2. Applied research is best described as research undertaken
   a. with human beings.
   b. with lower animals.
   c. to find solutions to specific problems.
   d. for its own sake.

3. If you knew someone who was having an adjustment problem, you would be best advised to refer that person to a(n) _____ psychologist.
   a. educational
   b. developmental
   c. personality
   d. counseling

4. If you were to read an article comparing the values of breast-feeding and bottle-feeding, it would probably report research that had been carried out by _____ psychologists.
   a. clinical
   b. personality
   c. developmental
   d. school

5. _____ psychologists are most directly concerned with the investigation of issues related to gender roles, processes such as repression, and the development of traits.
   a. Personality
   b. Clinical
   c. Organizational
   d. School

6. Industrial/organizational psychologists are most likely to be consulted to
   a. assist in the processes of hiring and promotion.
   b. help workers make educational decisions.
   c. treat workers showing abnormal behavior.
   d. investigate the political and social attitudes of workers.

7. The first author of a book about psychology was
   a. Democritus.
   b. Darwin.
   c. Sophocles.
   d. Aristotle.

8. Which of the following schools of psychology originated in Germany?
   a. functionalism
   b. structuralism
   c. behaviorism
   d. psychoanalysis

9. Who argued that the mind, like light or sound, is a natural event?
   a. Carl Rogers
   b. Sigmund Freud
   c. B. F. Skinner
   d. Wilhelm Wundt

10. The school of psychology that focused most directly on perceptual processes is
    a. psychoanalysis.
    b. behaviorism.
    c. humanistic psychology.
    d. Gestalt psychology.

11. Who founded the American Psychological Association?
    a. William James
    b. Edward Bradford Titchener
    c. G. Stanley Hall
    d. Mary Whiton Calkins

12. _____ is a neoanalyst.
   a. Christine Ladd-Franklin
   b. Erik Erikson
   c. Albert Bandura
   d. Carl Rogers

13. Social-cognitive theorists differ from behaviorists in that social-cognitive theorists focus on the role of _____ in behavior.
   a. unconscious processes
   b. cognition
   c. reinforcement
   d. learning

14. Who wrote *The Animal Mind?*
   a. Margaret Floy Washburn
   b. Elizabeth Loftus
   c. Christine Ladd-Franklin
   d. Mary Whiton Calkins

15. Who introduced the methods of paired associates?
   a. Margaret Floy Washburn
   b. Elizabeth Loftus
   c. Christine Ladd-Franklin
   d. Mary Whiton Calkins

16. Who engaged in research on the perception of heat and cold?
   a. B. F. Skinner
   b. J. Henry Alston
   c. Jorge Sanchez
   d. Kenneth B. Clark

17. Who influenced a key Supreme Court decision on desegregation?
   a. B. F. Skinner
   b. J. Henry Alston
   c. Jorge Sanchez
   d. Kenneth B. Clark

18. Who was among the first to show how intelligence tests are culturally biased?
   a. B. F. Skinner
   b. J. Henry Alston
   c. Jorge Sanchez
   d. Kenneth B. Clark

19. A key value of critical thinking is that it
   a. provides a database of knowledge.
   b. makes individuals argumentative.
   c. provides people with skills to educate themselves for a lifetime.
   d. teaches people how to criticize works of art, literature, and music.

20. A student says, "I know this is true because my psychology professor says that it is true." This argument is an example of the *argumentum ad*
   a. *hominem.*
   b. *baculum.*
   c. *verecundiam.*
   d. *populum.*

ANSWER KEY TO POSTTEST

1. B	3. D	5. A	7. D	9. D	11. C	13. B	15. D	17. D	19. C
2. C	4. C	6. A	8. B	10. D	12. B	14. A	16. B	18. C	20. C

LEARNING OBJECTIVES

When you have finished studying Chapter 2, you should be able to:

THE SCIENTIFIC METHOD: PUTTING IDEAS TO THE TEST

1. Describe the features of the scientific method.

SAMPLES AND POPULATIONS: REPRESENTING HUMAN DIVERSITY

2. Explain how psychologists use samples to represent human diversity.

METHODS OF OBSERVATION: THE BETTER TO SEE YOU WITH

3. Discuss the strengths and weaknesses of various methods of observation.

THE CORRELATIONAL METHOD: SEEING WHAT GOES UP AND WHAT COMES DOWN

4. Explain the *correlational method.*
5. Discuss the limitations of the correlational method.

THE EXPERIMENTAL METHOD: TRYING THINGS OUT

6. Define *experimental method.*
7. Discuss the use of independent and dependent variables in the experimental method.
8. Discuss the use of experimental and control groups in the experimental method.
9. Discuss the use of blinds and double blinds in the experimental method.

ETHICAL ISSUES

10. Discuss ethical issues in conducting research and practice with people.
11. Discuss ethical issues concerning research with animals.

Research Methods

PRETEST *Truth or Fiction?*

_____ You could survey 20 million voters and still not predict accurately the outcome of a presidential election.

_____ Only a small minority of people would be willing to deliver agonizing electric shocks to an innocent party.

_____ Only people use tools.

_____ In many experiments, neither the participants in the experiment nor the researchers who are running the experiment know which participants are taking the real treatment and which participants are taking a placebo ("sugar pill").

_____ Psychologists would not be able to carry out certain kinds of research without deceiving participants as to the purposes and methods of the studies.

PSYCHOLOGY is the science of behavior and mental processes. Consider some questions of interest to psychologists: Do only people use tools? Does alcohol cause aggression? Why do some people hardly ever think of food, while others are obsessed with it? Why do some unhappy people attempt suicide, whereas others seek alternate ways of coping with their problems? Does having people of different ethnic backgrounds collaborate in their work decrease or increase feelings of prejudice?

Many of us have expressed opinions on questions such as these. Different psychological theories also suggest a number of possible answers. Psychology is an **empirical** science, however. Within an empirical science, assumptions about the behavior of cosmic rays, chemical compounds, cells, or people must be supported by evidence. Arguments, opinions of authorities, even time-honored theories are not scientific evidence. Scientists make it their business—literally and figuratively—to be skeptical.

Psychologists use research to study behavior and mental processes. To undertake our study of research methods, let us recount some famous research undertaken at Yale University more than 30 years ago.

THE MILGRAM STUDIES: SHOCKING STUFF AT YALE

People are capable of boundless generosity and of hideous atrocities. Throughout history, people have sacrificed themselves for the welfare of their families, friends, and nations. Throughout history, people have maimed and destroyed other people to vent their rage or to please their superiors.

Let us follow up on the negative. Soldiers have killed civilians and raped women in occupied areas to obey the orders of their superiors or to win the approval of their comrades. Millions of Native Americans, Armenians, and Jews have been slaughtered by people who were obeying the orders of their officers.

Obeying the orders of officers . . . How susceptible are people—how susceptible are you and I—to the demands of authority figures such as military officers? Is there something unusual or abnormal about people who follow orders and inflict pain and suffering on their fellow human beings? Are they very much unlike you and me? Or *are* they you and me?

Psychologist Stanley Milgram also wondered if normal people would submit to authority figures who made immoral demands. To find out, he ran a series of classic experiments at Yale University. They have become known as the Milgram studies on obedience.

In an early phase of his work, Milgram (1963) placed ads in New Haven newspapers. He was seeking participants[1] for studies on learning and memory. He enlisted 40 people ranging in age from 20 to 50—teachers, engineers, laborers, salespeople, people who had not completed elementary school, people with graduate degrees.

Let's suppose that you've answered the ad. You show up at the university for a reasonable fee ($4.50, which in the early '60s might easily fill your gas tank), for the sake of science, and for your own curiosity. You may be

Empirical • Emphasizing or based on observation and experiment.

---

[1] Also termed *subjects*. The *Publication Manual of the American Psychological Association* (1994) prefers usage of *participants* because it is more personal and acknowledges that individuals in research studies take an active role in the studies.

FIGURE 2.1

The "Aggression Machine." In the Milgram studies on obedience to authority, pressing levers on the "aggression machine" was the operational definition of aggression.

impressed. After all, Yale is a venerable institution that dominates the city. You are no less impressed by the elegant labs. You meet a distinguished behavioral scientist dressed in a white laboratory coat and another newspaper recruit like you. The scientist explains that the purpose of the experiment is to study the *effects of punishment on learning*. The experiment would require a "teacher" and a "learner." By chance, you are appointed the teacher and the other recruit the learner.

You, the scientist, and the learner enter a laboratory room. There is a threatening-looking chair with dangling straps. The scientist straps the learner in. The learner expresses some concern, but this is, after all, for the sake of science. And this is Yale University, is it not? What could happen to a person at Yale?

You follow the scientist to an adjacent room from which you are to do your "teaching." This teaching promises to have an impact. You are to punish the learner's errors by pressing levers marked from 15 to 450 volts on a fearsome-looking console (see Figure 2.1). Labels describe 28 of the 30 levers as running the gamut from "Slight Shock" to "Danger: Severe Shock." The last two levers are simply labeled "XXX." Just in case you've no idea what electric shock feels like, the scientist gives you a sample 45-volt shock. It stings. You pity the person who might receive more.

Your learner is expected to learn word pairs. Pairs of words are to be read from a list. After hearing the list once, the learner is to produce the word that pairs with the stimulus word by pressing a switch that signifies the choice from a list of four alternatives. The switch lights one of four panels in your room. If it is the correct panel, you proceed to the next stimulus word. If not, you are to deliver an electric shock. With each error, you are to increase the voltage of the shock (Figure 2.2).

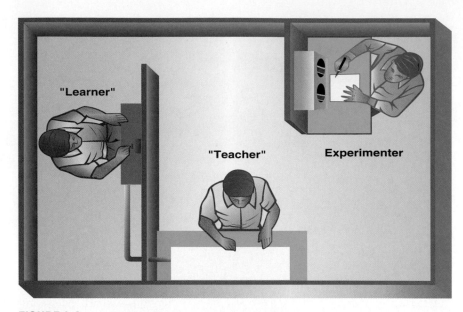

FIGURE 2.2

The Experimental Setup in the Milgram Studies. When the "learner" makes an error, the experimenter prods the "teacher" to deliver a painful electric shock.

You probably have some misgivings. Electrodes had been strapped to the learner's wrists. The scientist has applied electrode paste "to avoid blisters and burns." You also are told that the shocks will cause "no permanent tissue damage," although they might be extremely painful. Still, the learner is going along. And, after all, this is Yale.

The learner answers some items correctly and then makes some errors. With mild concern you press the levers up through 45 volts. You've tolerated that much yourself. Then a few more mistakes are made. You press the 60-volt lever, then 75. The learner makes another mistake. You pause and look at the scientist, who is reassuring: "Although the shocks may be painful, there is no permanent tissue damage, so please go on." Further errors are made, and quickly you are up to a shock of 300 volts. But now the learner is pounding on the other side of the wall! Your chest tightens and you begin to perspire. Damn science and the $4.50! you think. You hesitate and the scientist says, "The experiment requires that you continue." After the delivery of the next word, the learner makes no answer at all. What are you to do? "Wait for 5 to 10 seconds," the scientist instructs, "and then treat no answer as a wrong answer." But after the next shock, the pounding on the wall resumes! Now your heart is racing. You just know that you are causing extreme pain and discomfort. Is it possible that no lasting damage is being done? Is the experiment that important, after all? What to do? You hesitate again. The scientist says, "It is absolutely essential that you continue." His voice is very convincing. "You have no other choice," he says, "you *must* go on." You can barely think straight. For some strange reason, you feel laughter rising in your throat. Your finger shakes above the lever. What are you to do?

Milgram (1963, 1974) found out what most people in his sample would do. Of the 40 men in this phase of his research, only 5 refused to go beyond the 300-volt level. (This was the level at which the learner first pounded the wall.) Nine other "teachers" defied the scientist within the 300-volt range. But 65% of the participants complied with the scientist throughout the series. They believed that they were delivering 450-volt, XXX-rated shocks.

Were these newspaper recruits simply unfeeling? Not at all. Milgram was impressed by their signs of stress. They trembled. They stuttered. They bit their lips. They groaned. They sweated. They dug their fingernails into their flesh. Some had fits of laughter, though laughter was inappropriate. One salesperson's laughter was so convulsive that he had to drop out.

We shall return to the Milgram studies later in the chapter. They are a rich mine. Not only do they teach us about human nature. They are also useful for our discussions of research issues such as replication, the experimental method, and ethics.

Reflections

- How would you have felt if you had been a "teacher" in the Milgram study? What would you have done? Would you have delivered a shock, or would you have refused? Are you sure?
- What would you do if you heard that such an experiment was being conducted at your own college or university? Why?

Now let us consider the underpinnings of psychological research, as found in the scientific method.

THE SCIENTIFIC METHOD: PUTTING IDEAS TO THE TEST

The **scientific method** is an organized way of using experience and testing ideas to increase knowledge. Psychologists do not necessarily place a list of steps of the scientific method on the counter and follow them like a cookbook. However, there are principles that generally guide scientists' research endeavors.

Psychologists usually begin by *formulating a research question*. Research questions have many sources. Our daily experiences, psychological **theory,** even folklore all help to generate questions for research. Consider questions that may arise from daily experience. Experience with day-care centers may motivate us to conduct research into whether day care affects development of social skills or parent-child bonds of attachment.

Consider questions that might arise from psychological theory (see Figure 2.3). Social-cognitive principles of observational learning may prompt research into the effects of TV violence. Sigmund Freud's psychoanalytic theory may prompt research into whether the verbal expression of feelings of anger helps relieve feelings of depression.

Research questions may also arise from common knowledge. Consider folklore such as "Misery loves company," "Opposites attract," and "Beauty is in the eye of the beholder." (We consider these statements in Chapters 10 and 16.) Psychologists may ask, *does* misery love company? *Do* opposites attract? *Is* beauty in the eye of the beholder?

A research question may be studied in its question format. It may also be reworded into a **hypothesis** (see Figure 2.3). A hypothesis is a specific statement that is tested through research. One hypothesis about day care might be that preschoolers placed in day care will acquire greater social skills with peers than preschoolers cared for in the home. A hypothesis about TV violence might be that elementary school children who watch more violent TV shows behave more aggressively toward their peers. A hypothesis that addresses

Scientific method • A method for obtaining scientific evidence in which research questions or hypotheses are formulated and tested.

Theory • A formulation of the relationships and principles that underlie observed events. Theories allow us to explain and predict behavior.

Hypothesis • In psychology, a specific statement about behavior or mental processes that is tested through research.

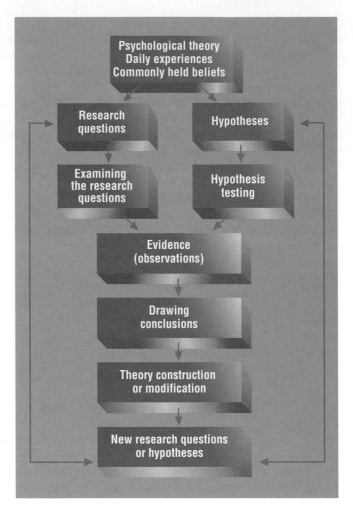

FIGURE 2.3

The Scientific Method. The scientific method is a systematic way of organizing and expanding scientific knowledge. Daily experiences, cultural beliefs, and scientific observations all foster the development of scientific theory. Theory explains observations and leads to hypotheses about events—in the case of psychology, behavior and mental processes. Our observations of hypothesized events can confirm the theory, lead to the refinement of the theory, or disconfirm the theory and possibly suggest the formulation of a new theory.

Operational definition • A definition of a variable in terms of the methods used to create or measure that variable.

Freudian theory might be that the verbal expression of feelings of anger will decrease feelings of depression.

As a science, psychology is accountable to carefully examined human experience. Therefore, psychologists next examine the research question or *test the hypothesis* through controlled methods such as naturalistic or laboratory observation and the experiment. For example, we could introduce children who are in day care and who are not to a new child and observe how each group fares with the new acquaintance.

To undertake research we must provide **operational definitions** for the variables under study. Concerning the effects of TV violence, we could have parents help us tally which TV shows their children watch and rate the shows for violent content. We could also define aggression as teacher reports on how aggressively the children act toward their peers. Then we could determine whether more-aggressive children also watch more violence on television.

Testing the hypothesis that the verbal expression of feelings of anger decreases feelings of depression might be more complex. Would the people they study include people undergoing psychoanalysis or, say, introductory psychology students? What would be the operational definition of feelings of depression? Self-ratings of depression? Scores on psychological tests? Reports of depressive behavior by spouses? Psychologists may use several definitions to study targeted behavior patterns and mental processes.

Psychologists draw conclusions about their research questions or the accuracy of their hypotheses on the basis of their research findings. When their observations do not bear out their hypotheses, they may modify the theories from which the hypotheses were derived (see Figure 2.3). Research findings often suggest refinements to psychological theories and, consequently, new avenues of research.

In our research on day care, we would probably find that children in day care show somewhat greater social skills than children cared for in the home (Clarke-Stewart, 1991; Field, 1991). We would probably also find that more-aggressive children spend more time watching TV violence (see Chapter 6). Research into the effectiveness of psychoanalytic forms of therapy is usually based on case studies.

As psychologists draw conclusions from research evidence, they try not to confuse connections between the findings with cause and effect. Yes, more-aggressive children spend more time watching TV violence. But does TV violence *cause* aggressive behavior? Perhaps there is a **selection factor** at work. Perhaps more-aggressive children are more likely than less-aggressive children to tune into violent TV programs.

To better understand the selection factor, consider a study on the relationship between exercise and health. Should we compare a group of people who exercise regularly to a group who do not? If we did, we might find that the exercisers were healthier than the couch potatoes. Could we conclude that exercise is a causal factor in good health? Perhaps not. The selection factor—the fact that one group chose to exercise and the other did not—could also suggest that healthy people are more apt to choose to exercise.[2]

As critical thinkers, psychologists attempt to avoid oversimplifying or overgeneralizing their results. The effects of day care are complex, for example. Although children in day care usually exhibit better social skills than children who are not, they are also somewhat more aggressive. If we conducted our research into the benefits of expressing feelings of anger with clients in psychoanalysis, do you think that we would be justified in generalizing the results to the population at large? If we conducted that research with introductory psychology students, could we extend or generalize the results to people in therapy for depression? Why or why not?

Some psychologists include publication of research reports in professional journals as part of the scientific method. Scientists are obligated to provide enough details of their work that other scientists will be able to repeat or **replicate** it. Psychologists may attempt to replicate a study in all its details in order to corroborate the findings. This is especially so when the findings are significant for people's health or general welfare. Sometimes psychologists replicate research methods with different kinds of participants to answer

Selection factor • A source of bias that may occur in research findings when participants are allowed to determine for themselves whether or not they will partake of a certain treatment in a scientific study. Do you think, for example, that there are problems in studying the effects of a diet or of smoking cigarettes when we allow study participants to choose whether or not they will try the diet or smoke cigarettes? Why or why not?

Replicate • Repeat, reproduce, copy. What are some reasons that psychologists replicate the research conducted by other psychologists?

---

[2] I am not suggesting that exercise does not make a contribution to health. I am merely pointing out that research that compares people who have chosen to exercise with people who have not is subject to a source of bias termed the *selection factor*. That is, the groups of exercisers and nonexercisers are not comparable, because the exercisers have chosen to exercise whereas the nonexercisers have elected not to exercise.

questions such as these: Can findings with women be generalized to men? Can findings with non-Hispanic White Americans be generalized to ethnic minority groups? Can findings with people who have sought psychotherapy be generalized to people at large?

Publication of data and researchers' interpretations of data also permits the scientific community to evaluate them.

Reflections

- Have you ever heard anyone say that "Misery loves company," "Opposites attract," or that "Beauty is in the eye of the beholder"? What was the nature of their evidence? Was it scientific? Why or why not?
- If we can demonstrate that people who exercise are healthier than people who do not, have we shown that exercise is a causal factor in good health? Why or why not?

Let us now consider the research methods used by psychologists: methods of sampling, methods of observation, the use of correlation, and the queen of the empirical approach—the experiment.

SAMPLES AND POPULATIONS: REPRESENTING HUMAN DIVERSITY

Generalize • To extend from the particular to the general; to apply observations based on a sample to a population.

Sample • Part of a population.

Population • A complete group of organisms or events.

Consider a piece of history that never quite happened: The Republican candidate Alf Landon defeated the incumbent president, Franklin D. Roosevelt, in 1936. Or at least Landon did so in a poll conducted by a popular magazine of the day, the *Literary Digest.* In the actual election, however, Roosevelt routed Landon in a landslide of 11 million votes. How, then, could the *Digest* predict a Landon victory? How was so great a discrepancy possible?

The *Digest,* you see, had surveyed voters by phone. Today, telephone sampling is a widely practiced and reasonably legitimate technique. But the *Digest* poll was taken during the Great Depression. At that time, people who had telephones were much wealthier than those who did not. People at higher income levels are also more likely to vote Republican. It should come as no surprise, then, that the overwhelming majority of those sampled said they would vote for Landon.

The principle involved here is that samples must accurately *represent* the population they are intended to reflect. Only representative samples allow us to **generalize** from research samples to populations.

Truth or Fiction Revisited. *It is true that you could survey 20 million voters and still not predict accurately the outcome of a presidential election.* Sample size alone does not guarantee that a sample will accurately represent the population from which it was drawn. In the conservative enterprise of science, we can extend, or generalize, our findings from samples only to the populations that they represent.

In surveys such as that conducted by the *Literary Digest,* and in other research methods, the individuals who are studied are referred to as a **sample.** A sample is a segment of a **population.** Psychologists and other scientists need to ensure that the people they observe *represent* their target population, such as all U.S. voters, and not subgroups such as southern California Yuppies or White members of the middle class.

A Population? Psychologists and other scientists attempt to select their research samples so that they will represent target populations. What population is suggested by the people in this photograph? How might you go about sampling them? How do people who agree to participate in research differ from those who refuse?

Problems in Generalizing from Psychological Research

All generalizations are dangerous, even this one.
ALEXANDRE DUMAS

Many factors must be considered in interpreting the accuracy of the results of scientific research. One is the nature of the research sample.

Milgram's initial research on obedience was limited to a sample of New Haven men. Could he generalize his findings to other men or to women?

Would college students, for example, who are heralded for independent thinking, show more defiance? A replication of Milgram's study with a sample of Yale men yielded similar results. What about women, who are supposedly less aggressive than men? In subsequent research, women, too, shocked the learners. All this took place in a nation that values independence and the free will of the individual.

Truth or Fiction Revisited. *It is not true that only a small minority of people would be willing to deliver agonizing electric shocks to an innocent party.* Research evidence has shown that when people are under strong social pressure, many people, even the majority, will deliver such shocks. What does this research finding say to you about "human nature"?

Later in the chapter we consider research in which the participants were drawn from a population of college men who were social drinkers. That is, they tended to drink at social gatherings but not when alone. Whom do college men represent, other than themselves? To whom can we extend, or generalize, the results?

College men tend to fall within a certain age range (about 18 to 22). They are more intelligent than the general population. We cannot be certain that the findings extend to older men of average intelligence. Social drinkers may also differ biologically and psychologically from alcoholics, who have difficulty controlling their drinking.

There is a historic bias in favor of conducting research with men (Ader & Johnson, 1994; McCarthy, 1993; Yoder & Kahn, 1993). Inadequate resources have been devoted to conducting health-related research with women (Strickland, 1991). More research with women is needed in areas such as AIDS, the effects of violence on women, and the impact of work on women's lives. It

What Are the Effects of Alcohol? Psychologists have undertaken research to determine alcohol's effects on behavior. Questions have been raised about the soundness of research in which subjects *know* they have drunk alcohol. Why?

appears that from 21% to 34% of U.S. women will be physically assaulted—slapped, beaten, choked, or attacked with a weapon—by a partner with whom they share an intimate relationship (Browne, 1993). From 14% to 25% of women have been raped (Koss, 1993). Many psychologists believe that the epidemic of violence against women will come to an end only when people in the United States confront and change the cultural traditions and institutions that give rise to violence (Goodman and others, 1993). Concerning women in the workplace, note that women are more likely than men to put in a "double shift." Women, that is, tend to put in a full day of work along with an equally long shift of shopping, mopping, and otherwise caring for their families (Chitayat, 1993; Keita, 1993).

There is a quip in psychology that experiments tend to be run with "rats, sophomores, and soldiers." Why? In part because members of these groups have been readily available. In part, perhaps, because men have historically been accorded favored treatment over women.

Research samples have also tended to underrepresent minority ethnic groups in the population. Personality tests completed by non-Hispanic White Americans and by African Americans may need to be interpreted in diverse ways if accurate conclusions are to be drawn (Nevid and others, 1997). The well-known Kinsey studies on sexual behavior (Kinsey and others, 1948, 1953) did not adequately represent African Americans, poor people, the elderly, and diverse other groups.

One way to achieve a representative sample is by means of **random sampling.** In a random sample, each member of a population has an equal chance of being selected to participate. Researchers can also use a **stratified sample,** which is drawn so that identified subgroups in the population are represented proportionately in the sample. For instance, 12% of the American population is African American. A stratified sample would thus be 12% African American. As a practical matter, a large, randomly selected sample will show reasonably accurate stratification. A random sample of 1,500 people will represent the general U.S. population reasonably well. A haphazardly drawn sample of 20 million, however, might not.

Large-scale magazine surveys of sexual behavior have asked readers to fill out and return questionnaires. Although many thousands of readers completed the questionnaires and sent them in, did they represent the general U.S. population? Probably not. These studies and similar ones may have been influenced by **volunteer bias.** People who volunteer to participate in research studies differ systematically from people who do not. In the case of research into sexual behavior, volunteers may represent subgroups of the population—or of readers of the magazines in question—who are willing to disclose intimate information (Rathus and others, 1997). Volunteers may also be more interested in research than other people. They may have more spare time. How might such differences slant or bias the research outcomes?

Random sample • A sample that is drawn so that each member of a population has an equal chance of being selected to participate.

Stratified sample • A sample that is drawn so that identified subgroups in the population are represented proportionately in the sample. How can stratified sampling be carried out to ensure that a sample represents the ethnic diversity we find in the population at large?

Volunteer bias • A source of bias or error in research that reflects the belief that people who offer to participate in research studies differ systematically from people who do not.

Reflections

- Were you surprised to find out that women in the Milgram studies obeyed orders and shocked "learners" just as men in the study did? Why or why not?
- Why do you think that there has been a historic bias toward conducting research with men?
- If scientists conducted research with a "random sample" of students from your own school, would their sample represent the general U.S. population? Why or why not?

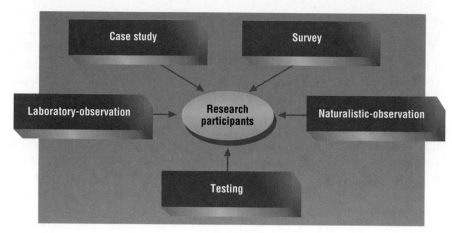

FIGURE 2.4
Methods of Observation in Psychology.

METHODS OF OBSERVATION: THE BETTER TO SEE YOU WITH

Many people consider themselves experts in psychology on the basis of their life experiences. How many times have grandparents, for example, told us what they have seen in their lives and what it means about human nature?

We see much indeed during our lifetimes. Our personal observations tend to be fleeting and uncontrolled, however. We sift through experience for the minutiae that interest us. We often ignore the obvious because it does not fit our preexisting ideas (or "schemes") of the ways that things ought to be.

Scientists, however, have devised more controlled ways of observing others. Let us consider the case-study, survey, testing, naturalistic-observation, and laboratory-observation methods (see Figure 2.4).

The Case-Study Method

We begin with the case-study method because our own informal ideas about human nature tend to be based on **case studies.** But most of us gather our information haphazardly. Often, we see what we want to see. Unscientific accounts of people's behavior are referred to as *anecdotes*. Psychologists attempt to gather information about individuals more carefully.

Sigmund Freud developed psychodynamic theory largely on the basis of case studies. Freud studied people who sought his help in depth. He looked for contributors to their personalities and problems. He followed some people for years, meeting with them several times a week.

However, there are gaps and inaccuracies in autobiographical memory (Brewin and others, 1993). People may also distort their pasts to present (or recall) a rosy picture. Researchers also have certain expectations. They may subtly encourage people to fill in gaps in ways that are consistent with their theoretical perspectives. Bandura (1986) notes, for example, that psychoanalysts have been criticized for guiding people who seek their help into viewing their own lives from the psychodynamic perspective. No wonder, then, that many people provide "evidence" that is consistent with psychodynamic theory.

Case study • A carefully drawn biography that may be obtained through interviews, questionnaires, and psychological tests.

Of course, interviewers who hold *any* theoretical viewpoint run the risk of prodding people into saying what they want to hear.

Case studies are often used to investigate rare occurrences. Consider the cases of "Eve" and "Genie." "Eve" (in real life, Chris Sizemore) was an example of a person with dissociative identity disorder (see Chapter 13). "Eve White" was a mousy, well-intentioned woman who had two other "personalities" living inside her. One was "Eve Black," a promiscuous personality who now and then emerged to take control of her behavior.

"Genie's" father locked her in a small room at the age of 20 months. He kept her there until she was discovered at the age of 13½ (Rymer, 1993). Her social contacts were limited to her nearly blind mother, who entered the room only to feed her, and to beatings by her father. No one spoke to her. After her rescue, Genie's language development followed the normal sequence outlined in Chapter 8, suggesting the universality of this sequence. Genie did not reach normal proficiency in her use of language, however. Perhaps there is a "sensitive period" for learning language in early childhood.

The Survey Method

Remember the good old days? One had to wait until the wee hours of the morning to learn the results of elections. Throughout the evening and early morning hours, suspense would build as ballots from distant neighborhoods and states were tallied. Nowadays, one is barely settled with an after-dinner cup of coffee on election night when the news-show computer cheerfully announces (computers do not, of course, have emotions or make "cheerful" announcements, but they do seem rather smug at times) that it has examined the ballots of a "scientifically selected sample." It then predicts the next president of the United States. All this may occur with less than 1% of the vote tallied. Preelection polls also do their share of eroding wonderment and doubt. In fact, some supporters of projected winners must be encouraged to actually vote so that predictions will be borne out.

Just as computers and pollsters predict election results and report national opinion on the basis of scientifically selected samples, psychologists conduct **surveys** to learn about behavior that cannot be observed or studied experimentally. Psychologists survey via questionnaires and interviews. By distributing questionnaires and analyzing answers with a computer, psychologists can survey many thousands of people at a time.

We mentioned the "Kinsey studies." Alfred Kinsey and his colleagues published two surveys of sexual behavior, based on interviews, that shocked the nation. These were *Sexual Behavior in the Human Male* (1948) and *Sexual Behavior in the Human Female* (1953). Kinsey reported that masturbation was virtually universal in his sample of men at a time when masturbation was still widely thought to impair health. He also reported that about one woman in three still single at age 25 had engaged in premarital intercourse. In addition to compiling self-reports of behavior, surveys are also used to learn about people's mental processes, including their opinions, attitudes, and values.

Interviews and questionnaires are not foolproof, of course. People may inaccurately recall their behavior. They may purposefully misrepresent it. Some people try to ingratiate themselves with their interviewers by answering in what they perceive to be the socially desirable direction. The Kinsey studies all relied on male interviewers, for example. It has been speculated that female interviewees might have been more open and honest with female interviewers. Similar problems may occur when interviewers and those surveyed are from

Survey • A method of scientific investigation in which a large sample of people answer questions about their attitudes or behavior.

different ethnic or socioeconomic backgrounds. A few people falsify attitudes and exaggerate problems to draw attention to themselves. Others just to try to foul up the results.

WORLD OF DIVERSITY

A SEX SURVEY THAT ADDRESSES SOCIOCULTURAL FACTORS

Is it possible for scientists to describe the sex lives of people in the United States? There are many difficulties in gathering data, such as the refusal of many individuals to participate in research. Moreover, we must specify *which* people we are talking about. Are we talking, for example, about the behavior of women or men, younger people or older people, White people or African Americans?

The National Health and Social Life Survey (NHSLS) sample included 3,432 people (Laumann and others, 1994). Of this number, 3,159 were English-speaking adults living in households (not dormitories, prisons, and so forth), aged 18 to 59. The other 273 were purposefully obtained by oversampling African American and Hispanic American households. More information could thus be obtained about these ethnic groups. While the sample probably represents the overall U.S. population quite well (or those aged 18–59), there may be too few Asian Americans, Native Americans, and Jews to offer much information about these groups.

The NHSLS research team identified samples of households in various locales—addresses, not names. They sent a letter to each household describing the purpose and methods of the study. An interviewer visited each household 1 week later. The people targeted were assured that the purposes of the study were important and that their identities would be kept confidential. Incentives of up to $100 were offered for cooperating. In this way, the researchers obtained a high completion rate of close to 80%.

The NHSLS considered the sociocultural factors of gender, age, level of education, religion, and race/ethnicity (Laumann and others, 1994). Consider the issue of the numbers of sex partners people have, as shown in Table 2.1.

Males, according to the survey, report having higher numbers of sex partners than females do. For example, 1 male in 3 (33%) reports having 11 or more sex partners since the age of 18. This compares with fewer than 1 woman in 10 (9%). On the other hand, most people in the United States appear to limit their numbers of sex partners to a handful or fewer.

Note that the numbers of sex partners appears to rise with age into the 40s. Why? As people gain in years, have they had more opportunity to accumulate life experiences, including sexual experiences? But then the numbers of partners fall off among people in their 50s. People in this age group entered adulthood prior to the sexual revolution. They were thus exposed to more conservative sexual attitudes.

Level of education is also connected with sexual behavior. Generally speaking, it would appear that education is something of a liberating influence. People with some college, or who have completed college, are likely to have more sex partners than those who attended only grade school or high school. If education is a liberating influence on sexuality, conservative religious experience appears to be a restraining factor. People who report having no religion

TABLE 2.1

**NUMBER OF SEX PARTNERS SINCE AGE 18
AS FOUND IN THE NHSLS† STUDY**

SOCIOCULTURAL FACTORS	NUMBER OF SEX PARTNERS (%)					
	0	1	2–4	5–10	11–20	21+
Gender						
Male	3	20	21	23	16	17
Female	3	32	36	20	6	3
Age						
18–24	8	32	34	15	8	3
25–29	2	25	31	22	10	9
30–34	3	21	29	25	11	10
35–39	2	19	30	25	14	11
40–44	1	22	28	24	14	12
45–49	2	26	24	25	10	14
50–54	2	34	28	18	9	9
55–59	1	40	28	15	8	7
Education						
Less than high school	4	27	36	19	9	6
High school graduate	3	30	29	20	10	7
Some college	2	24	29	23	12	9
College graduate	2	24	26	24	11	13
Advanced degree	4	25	26	23	10	13
Religion						
None	3	16	29	20	16	16
Liberal, moderate Protestant	2	23	31	23	12	8
Conservative Protestant	3	30	30	20	10	7
Catholic	4	27	29	23	8	9
Race/Ethnicity						
White (non-Hispanic)	3	26	29	22	11	9
African American	2	18	34	24	11	11
Hispanic American	3	35	27	17	8	9
Asian American*	6	46	25	14	6	3
Native American*	5	28	35	23	5	5

Source: Adapted from The Social Organization of Sexuality: Sexual Practices in the United States (Table 5.1C, p. 179), by E. O. Laumann, J. H. Gagnon, R. T. Michael, and S. Michaels, 1994, Chicago: University of Chicago Press.
† National Health and Social Life Survey, conducted by a research team centered at the University of Chicago.
* These sample sizes are quite small.

and liberal Protestants (for example, Methodists, Lutherans, Presbyterians, Episcopalians, and United Churches of Christ) report higher numbers of sex partners than Catholics and conservative Protestants (for example, Baptists, Pentecostals, Churches of Christ, and Assemblies of God).

Ethnicity is also connected with sexual behavior. The research findings in Table 2.1 suggest that White (non-Hispanic) Americans and African Americans have the highest numbers of sex partners. Hispanic Americans are mostly Catholic. Perhaps Catholicism provides a restraint on sexual behavior. Asian Americans would appear to be the most sexually restrained ethnic group. However, as noted in the footnote to the table, the sample sizes of Asian Americans and Native Americans are relatively small.

The Testing Method

Psychologists use psychological tests to measure traits among a population. There is a wide range of psychological tests. They measure traits ranging from intelligence and achievement to anxiety, depression, the need for social dominance, musical aptitude, and vocational interests.

Important decisions are made on the basis of psychological tests. They must thus be *reliable* and *valid*. The **reliability** of a measure is its consistency. A measure of height would not be reliable if a person appeared to be taller or shorter every time a measurement was taken. A reliable measure of personality or intelligence, like a good tape measure, yields similar results on different occasions.

There are different ways of showing a test's reliability. One of the most commonly used is **test–retest reliability.** It is shown by comparing scores of tests taken on different occasions. However, people taking intelligence and **aptitude** tests often improve their scores from one occasion to the next because of familiarity with the test items and the testing procedure. The measurement of test–retest reliability is sometimes confused by this improvement from test to test.

The **validity** of a test is the degree to which it measures what it is supposed to measure. To determine whether a test is valid, we see whether it predicts an outside standard, or external criterion. A proper standard, or criterion, for determining the validity of a test of musical aptitude is the ability to learn to play a musical instrument. Tests of musical aptitude, therefore, should predict ability to learn to play an instrument. Most psychologists assume that intelligence is one of the factors responsible for academic prowess. Thus, intelligence test scores should predict school grades. They do so moderately well (Sattler, 1988). Intelligence test scores received after the age of 7 also predict adult occupational status reasonably well (McCall, 1977).

Psychological test results, like surveys, can be distorted by respondents who answer in a socially desirable direction or exaggerate problems. For these reasons, some psychological tests have built-in **validity scales.** Validity scales are sensitive to misrepresentations. They alert the psychologist when test results may be deceptive.

Reliability • Consistency.

Test–retest reliability • A method for determining the reliability of a test by comparing (correlating) test takers' scores from separate occasions.

Aptitude • An ability or talent to succeed in an area in which one has not yet been trained.

Validity • The degree to which a test measures what it is supposed to measure.

Validity scales • Groups of test items that suggest whether the test results are valid (measure what they are supposed to measure).

Naturalistic observation • A scientific method in which organisms are observed in their natural environments.

Unobtrusive • Not interfering.

The Naturalistic-Observation Method

You use **naturalistic observation** every day of your life. That is, you observe people in their natural habitats.

So do psychologists. The next time you opt for a fast-food burger lunch, look around. Pick out slender people and overweight people and observe whether they eat their burgers and fries differently. Do the overweight eat more rapidly? Chew less frequently? Leave less food on their plates? This is the type of research psychologists use to study differences in eating habits between normal-weight and overweight people.

In naturalistic observation, scientists observe behavior in the field, or "where it happens." They try to avoid interfering with the behaviors they are observing by using **unobtrusive** measures. Jane Goodall has observed the behavior of chimpanzees in the field to learn about their social behavior, sexual behavior, and use of tools (see Figure 2.5). Her observations have shown us that we were incorrect to think that only people use tools. Moreover, kissing, as a greeting, is used by chimpanzees as well as people.

FIGURE 2.5

The Naturalistic-Observation Method. Jane Goodall has used the naturalistic-observation method with chimpanzees, quietly observing them for many years in their natural environments. In using this method, scientists try to avoid interfering with the animals or people they observe. This sometimes means allowing an animal to be mistreated by other animals or to die from a curable illness. We learn from Goodall that tools are used by primates other than human beings. The chimp in the left-hand photo is using a stick as a tool to poke around in a termite hill for food. Goodall's observations have also taught us that not only humans use kissing as a social greeting (see right-hand photo). Male chimps have even been observed greeting females by kissing their hands. Very European?

Truth or Fiction Revisited. *It is not true that only people use tools.* The naturalistic-observation method has taught us that other animals also use tools. Apes are an example. (Did you also know that otters use rocks to open the shells of mollusks?)

Laboratory • A place in which theories, techniques, and methods are tested and demonstrated.

The Laboratory-Observation Method

Psychologists also place lower animals and people into controlled laboratory environments where they can be readily observed. The effects of specific conditions can also be discerned. Figure 1.2 on page 12 shows one such environment. It is constructed so that pigeons receive reinforcers for pecking buttons.

With people, the **laboratory** takes many forms. Do not confine your imagination to rows of Bunsen burners and the smell of sulfur or to rats and pigeons in wire cages being reinforced with food pellets from heaven.

Figure 2.2 (see p. 38), for example, diagrams the laboratory setup in the Milgram studies at Yale University. Human participants (the "teacher" in the diagram) were urged to deliver electric shock to other people (so-called learners) to signal them that they had made errors on a learning task. This study was inspired by the atrocities committed by apparently typical German citizens during World War II. Its purpose was to determine how easy it would be to induce normal people to hurt others. In studies on sensation and perception, human participants may be placed in dark or quiet rooms to learn how bright or loud a stimulus must be before it can be detected.

Reflections

- What methods of observation do your family and friends use when they make assertions about human behavior? How do their methods overlap with those presented in this section? How scientific are they?

THE CORRELATIONAL METHOD: SEEING WHAT GOES UP AND WHAT COMES DOWN

Are people with higher intelligence more likely to do well in school? Do people with a stronger need for achievement climb higher up the corporate ladder? What is the relationship between stress and health?

Correlation follows observation. Psychologists use the **correlational method** to learn whether observed behavior or a measured trait is related to, or correlated with, another. Consider the variables of intelligence and academic performance. The variables of intelligence and academic performance are assigned numbers such as intelligence test scores and academic averages. Then the numbers are mathematically related and expressed as a **correlation coefficient.** A *correlation coefficient* is a number that varies between +1.00 and

Correlational method • A scientific method that studies the relationships between variables.

Correlation coefficient • A number between +1.00 to −1.00 that expresses the strength and direction (positive or negative) of the relationship between two variables.

Positive correlation • A relationship between variables in which one variable increases as the other also increases.

Negative correlation • A relationship between two variables in which one variable increases as the other decreases.

Intelligence and Achievement. Correlations between intelligence test scores and academic achievement—as measured by school grades and assessment tests—tend to be positive and strong. Does the correlational method allow us to say that intelligence *causes* or *is responsible for* academic achievements? Why, or why not?

TABLE 2.2

INTERPRETATIONS OF SOME CORRELATION COEFFICIENTS

CORRELATION COEFFICIENT	INTERPRETATION
+1.00	Perfect positive correlation, as between temperature in Fahrenheit and centigrade
+0.90	High positive correlation; adequate for test reliability
+0.60 to +0.70	Moderate positive correlation; usually considered adequate for test validity
+0.30	Weak positive correlation; unacceptable for test reliability or validity
0.00	No correlation between variables (no association indicated)
−0.30	Weak negative correlation
−0.60 to −0.70	Moderate negative correlation
−0.90	High negative correlation
−1.00	A perfect negative correlation

−1.00. Psychologists use the correlation coefficient to determine the reliability and validity of psychological tests.

Studies report **positive correlations** between intelligence and achievement. For a test to be considered reliable, correlations between a group's test results on separate occasions should be positive and high—about +0.90 (see Table 2.2). People's scores on intelligence tests are also positively correlated with their grades. Generally speaking, the higher people score on intelligence tests, the better their academic performance is likely to be. The scores attained on intelligence tests tend to be positively correlated (about +0.60 to +0.70) with academic achievement (see Figure 2.6). As noted in Table 2.2, a correlation of about +0.60 to +0.70 is adequate for purposes of test validity. However, such a correlation does not approach a perfect positive relationship. This finding suggests that factors *other* than performance on intelligence tests contribute to academic and occupational success. Motivation to do well and personal adjustment are two of them (Anastasi, 1983; Collier, 1994; Scarr, 1981).

What of the need for achievement and getting ahead? The need for achievement can be assessed by rating stories told by study participants for the presence of this need (see Chapter 10). Getting ahead can be assessed in many ways. Salary and the prestige of one's occupation or level within the corporation are two of them.

There is a **negative correlation** between stress and health. As the stress on us increases, the functioning of our immune systems decreases (see Chapter 15). Under high levels of stress, many people show poorer health.

Correlational research may suggest but does not show cause and effect. For instance, it may seem logical to assume that high intelligence makes it possible for children to profit from education. Research has also shown, however, that education contributes to higher scores on intelligence tests. Preschoolers placed in Head Start programs attain higher scores on intelligence tests than agemates who did not have this experience. The relationship between intelligence and academic performance may not be as simple as you thought. What of the link between stress and health? Does stress impair health? Or is it possible that people in poorer health encounter more stress? (See Figure 2.7.)

**MINILECTURE:
CORRELATIONS**

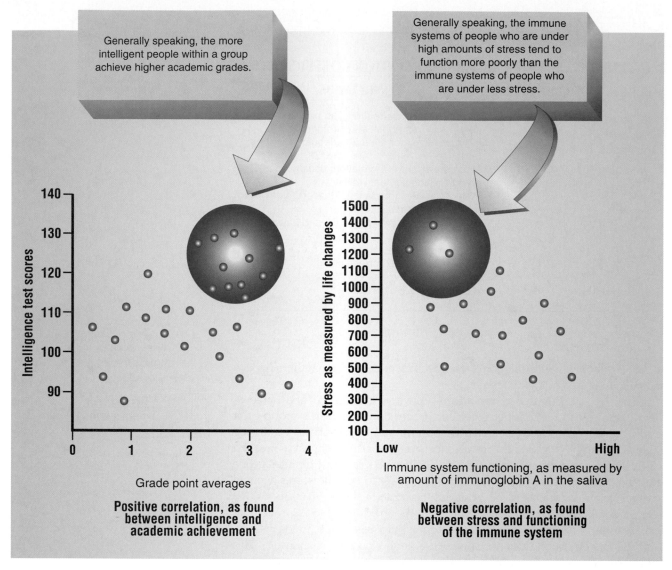

FIGURE 2.6

Positive and Negative Correlations. When there is a positive correlation between variables, as there is between intelligence and achievement, one tends to increase as the other increases. By and large, the higher people score on intelligence tests, the better their academic performance is likely to be, as in the diagram to the left. (Each dot is located to represent an individual's intelligence test score and grade point average.) Similarly, there is a positive correlation between exercise and health, as we shall see in Chapter 15. On the other hand, there is a negative correlation between stress and health. As the amount of stress we experience increases, the functioning of our immune systems tends to decrease. Correlational research may suggest but does not demonstrate cause and effect.

Reflections

- What kinds of correlations (positive? negative? strong? weak?) do you believe are found among behavior patterns such as the following: Churchgoing and crime? Language ability and musical ability? Level of education and incidence of teenage pregnancy? Grades in school and juvenile delinquency? Why?

- It happens that couples who live together before getting married are *more* likely to get divorced once they are married than couples who did not. Does

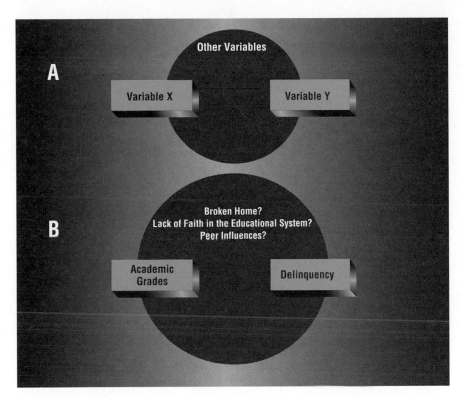

FIGURE 2.7

Correlational Relationships, Cause, and Effect. Correlational relationships may suggest but cannot demonstrate cause and effect. In part A, there is a correlation between variables *X* and *Y*. Does this mean that variable *X* causes variable *Y*, or that variable *Y* causes variable *X*? Not necessarily. Other factors, other variables, could affect both *X* and *Y*. Consider the examples of academic grades (variable *X*) and juvenile delinquency (variable *Y*) in part B. There is a negative correlation between the two. Does this mean that poor grades contribute to delinquency? Perhaps. Does it mean that delinquency contributes to poor grades? Again: perhaps. But there could also be other variables—such as a broken home, lack of faith in the educational system, or peer influences—that contribute both to poor grades and delinquency. Then again, poor grades could make youth more susceptible to negative peer influences, leading to delinquent behavior. What other possibilities are there?

Experiment • A scientific method that seeks to confirm cause-and-effect relationships by introducing independent variables and observing their effects on dependent variables.

this research finding show that living together before getting married *causes* marital instability? Why or why not? Can you think of other reasons that couples who live together before getting married may be more likely to get divorced once they are married than couples who do not?

THE EXPERIMENTAL METHOD: TRYING THINGS OUT

The people who signed up for the Milgram studies participated in an elaborate **experiment.** The participants in an experiment obtain a treatment. Milgram's participants partook of a most intricate treatment—one that involved a well-equipped research laboratory at Yale University or nearby. It also involved deception. Milgram had foreseen participants' objections to the procedure. He

MINILECTURE: THE EXPERIMENTAL METHOD

had therefore conceived standardized statements that his assistants would use when participants balked: "Although the shocks may be painful, there is no permanent tissue damage, so please go on." "The experiment requires that you continue." "It is absolutely essential that you continue." "You have no other choice. You *must* go on." These statements, the bogus "aggression machine," the use of the "learner" (who was actually a confederate of the experimenter)—all these things were part of the experimental treatment.

Most psychologists agree that the preferred method for answering questions concerning cause and effect is the experiment. In an experiment, a group of participants obtains a **treatment,** such as a dose of alcohol, a change in room temperature, perhaps an injection of a drug. The participants are observed carefully to determine whether the treatment makes a difference in their behavior. Does alcohol affect participants' ability to take tests, for example? Environmental psychologists have varied room temperatures and the levels of background noise to see whether these treatments change participants' behavior.

Experiments allow psychologists to control directly the experiences of animals and people and to draw conclusions about cause and effect. A psychologist may theorize that alcohol leads to aggression because it reduces fear of consequences or energizes the activity levels of drinkers. She or he may then hypothesize that the treatment of a specified dosage of alcohol will increase aggression. Let us follow the example of the effects of alcohol on aggression to further our understanding of the experimental method.

Independent and Dependent Variables

Consider an experiment to determine whether alcohol causes aggression. Experimental participants would be given alcohol, and its effects would be measured. In this case, alcohol is an **independent variable.** The presence of an *independent variable* is manipulated by the experimenters so that its effects may be observed. The independent variable of alcohol may be administered at different levels, or doses. It may range from none or very little to enough to cause intoxication, or drunkenness.

The measured results, or outcomes, in an experiment are called **dependent variables.** The presence of dependent variables presumably depends on the independent variables. In an experiment to determine whether alcohol influences aggression, aggressive behavior would be a dependent variable. Other dependent variables of interest in an experiment on the effects of alcohol might include sexual arousal, visual-motor coordination, and numerical computations.

In an experiment on the relationships between temperature and aggression, temperature would be an independent variable. Aggressive behavior would be a dependent variable. We could use temperature settings ranging from below freezing to blistering hot and study the effects of each. We could also use a second independent variable such as social provocation. That is, we could insult some study participants but not others. This method would allow us to study the interaction between temperature and social provocation as they affect aggression.

Experiments can be complex, with several independent and dependent variables. Psychologists often use complex experimental designs and sophisticated statistical techniques to determine the effect of each independent variable.

Treatment • In experiments, a condition received by participants so that its effects may be observed.

Independent variable • A condition in a scientific study that is manipulated so that its effects may be observed.

Dependent variable • A measure of an assumed effect of an independent variable.

Experimental and Control Groups

Ideal experiments use experimental and control groups. Experimental participants partake in the treatment. Members of control groups do not. Every effort is made to ensure that all other conditions are held constant for both groups. This method enhances researchers' abilities to draw conclusions about cause and effect. Controls heighten researchers' confidence that experimental outcomes are caused by the treatments and not by chance factors or chance fluctuations in behavior.

Return to an experiment concerning the effects of alcohol on aggression. Members of the experimental group would ingest alcohol. Members of the control group would not. In a complex experiment, different experimental groups might ingest different doses of alcohol and be exposed to different types of social provocations.

Blinds and Double Blinds

One experiment on the effects of alcohol on aggression (Boyatzis, 1974) reported that men at parties where beer and liquor were served acted more aggressively than men at parties where only soft drinks were served. But we must be cautious in interpreting these findings. Men in the experimental group *knew* that they had drunk alcohol. Men in the control group *knew* that they had not. Aggression that appeared to result from alcohol might not have reflected drinking per se. Instead, it might have reflected the individuals' expectations about the effects of alcohol. People tend to act in stereotypical ways when they believe that they have been drinking alcohol. For instance, men tend to become less anxious in social situations, more aggressive, and more sexually aroused.

A **placebo,** or "sugar pill," often results in the behavior that people expect. Physicians now and then give sugar pills to demanding, but healthy, people. Many people who receive placebos report that they feel better. When people in psychological experiments are given placebos—such as tonic water—but think that they have drunk alcohol, we can conclude that changes in behavior stem from their beliefs about alcohol, not the alcohol itself.

Well-designed experiments control for the effects of expectations by creating conditions under which participants are unaware of, or **blind** to, the treatment. Yet researchers may also have expectations. They may, in effect, be "rooting for" a certain treatment. For instance, tobacco company executives may wish to show that cigarette smoking is harmless. It is thus useful if the people measuring the experimental outcomes are also unaware of who has partaken in the treatment. Studies in which both participants and experimenters are unaware of who has obtained the treatment are called **double-blind studies.**

Double-blind studies are required by the Food and Drug Administration before it will allow the marketing of new drugs (Carroll and others, 1994). The drug and the placebo look and taste alike. Experimenters assign the drug or placebo at random to participants. Neither the participants nor the people who measure their progress know who is taking what. After the final measurements are made, an impartial panel judges whether the effects of the drug differed from those of the placebo.

Truth or Fiction Revisited. *It is true that in many experiments, neither the participants nor the researchers know which participants are taking the*

Placebo • A bogus treatment that has the appearance of being genuine.

Blind • In experimental terminology, unaware of whether or not one has received a treatment.

Double-blind study • A study in which neither the participants nor the persons measuring results know who has received the treatment.

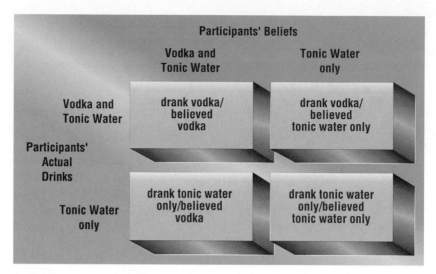

FIGURE 2.8

The Experimental Conditions in the Lang Study. The taste of vodka cannot be discerned when vodka is mixed with tonic water. For this reason, it was possible for participants to be kept "blind" as to whether or not they had drunk alcohol. Blind studies allow psychologists to control for the effects of expectations.

real treatment and which participants are taking a placebo ("sugar pill"). Such experiments are referred to as *double-blind studies*. They control for the effects of participants' and researchers' expectations. If you were running such an experiment, how would you keep track of which individuals had taken which treatments?

In one double-blind study on the effects of alcohol, Alan Lang and his colleagues (1975) pretested a highball of vodka and tonic water to determine that it could not be discriminated by taste from tonic water alone. They recruited college men who described themselves as social drinkers to participate in the study. Some men drank vodka and tonic water. Others drank tonic water only. Of the individuals who drank vodka, half were misled into believing that they had drunk tonic water only (Figure 2.8). Of those drinking tonic water only, half were misled into believing that their drink contained vodka. Thus, half the participants were blind to their treatment. Experimenters who measured aggressive responses were also blind concerning which participants had drunk vodka.

The research team found that men who believed that they had drunk vodka responded more aggressively to a provocation than men who believed that they had drunk tonic water only. The actual content of the drink was immaterial. That is, men who had actually drunk alcohol acted no more aggressively than men who had drunk tonic water only. The results of the Lang study differ dramatically from those reported by Boyatzis. Why? The Boyatzis study did not control for the effects of expectations about alcohol.

In the Lang study on alcohol and aggression, alcohol was operationally defined as a certain dose of vodka. Other types of drinks and other dosages of vodka might have had different effects. Research evidence does show that drunkenness is connected with verbal and physical aggression (Bushman & Cooper, 1990; Lau and others, 1995). In the Lang study, aggression was operationally defined in the same way as it was in the Milgram studies on obedience: selection of a certain amount of electric shock and administration of it to another participant in an experiment. College men might behave differently when they drink in other situations. How might they act when they are insulted by a supporter of an opposing football team or are threatened outside a bar?

Reflections

- **Does alcohol cause aggression? Has this chapter changed the way in which you would approach this question?**
- Can you devise a method whereby researchers can use placebos and double blinds to investigate the effects of a new drug on the urge to smoke cigarettes? Can you think of various ways in which the researchers can measure the "urge" to smoke?

ETHICAL ISSUES

It is in our discussion of ethics that we raise the most serious questions about the Milgram studies. The participants experienced severe psychological anguish. The Milgram studies on obedience made key contributions to our understanding of the limits of human nature. In fact, it is difficult for professional psychologists to imagine a history of psychology bereft of the knowledge provided by such studies. But were the Milgram studies **ethical?**

Psychologists adhere to a number of ethical standards that are intended to promote the dignity of the individual, foster human welfare, and maintain scientific integrity (McGovern and others, 1991). They also ensure that psychologists do not use research methods or treatments that are harmful to study participants or clients (American Psychological Association, 1992a).

Research with People

Lang and his colleagues (1975) gave small doses of alcohol to college students who were social drinkers. Other researchers, however, have paid alcoholics—people who have difficulties limiting their alcohol consumption—to drink in the laboratory so that they could study their reactions and those of family members (e.g., Jacob and others, 1991). Practices such as these raise more complex ethical questions (Beutler & Kendall, 1991; Stricker, 1991). For example, paying the alcoholics to drink in the laboratory, and providing the alcohol, could be construed as encouraging self-destructive behavior (Koocher, 1991).

Recall the signs of stress shown by the participants in the Milgram studies on obedience. They trembled, stuttered, groaned, sweated, bit their lips, and dug their fingernails into their flesh. In fact, if Milgram had attempted to run his experiments in the 1990s rather than the 1960s, he might have been denied permission to do so by a university ethics review committee. In virtually all institutional settings, including colleges, hospitals, and research foundations, **ethics review committees** help researchers consider the potential harm of their proposed studies. When such committees find that proposed research might be unacceptably harmful to participants, they may advise the researcher to modify the research design. They may withhold approval until the proposal has been made acceptable. Ethics review committees also weigh the potential benefits of research against the potential harm.

Today, to help avoid harming study participants, individuals must also provide **informed consent** before they participate in research programs. Having

Ethical • Moral; referring to one's system of deriving standards for determining what is moral.

Ethics review committee • A group found in an institutional setting that helps researchers consider the potential harm of their methods and reviews proposed studies according to ethical guidelines.

Informed consent • The term used by psychologists to indicate that a person has agreed to participate in research after receiving information about the purposes of the study and the nature of the treatments.

a general overview of the research and the opportunity to choose not to participate apparently gives individuals a sense of control and decreases the stress of participating (Dill and others, 1982). Is there a way in which participants in the Milgram studies could have provided informed consent? What do you think?

Psychologists treat the records of research participants and clients as **confidential.** This is because psychologists respect people's privacy and also because people are more likely to express their true thoughts and feelings when researchers or therapists keep their disclosures confidential (Blanck and others, 1992). Sometimes conflicts of interest arise, however, as when a client threatens a third party and the psychologist feels an obligation to warn the third party (Nevid and others, 1997).

Ethical standards tend to limit the types of research that psychologists may conduct. For example, how can we determine whether early separation from one's mother impairs social development? One research direction is to observe the development of children who have been separated from their mothers from an early age. It is difficult to draw conclusions from such research, however. The same factors that led to the separation—such as family tragedy or irresponsible parents—instead of the separation itself, may have led to the outcomes. Scientifically, it would be more sound to run experiments in which children are purposefully separated from their mothers at an early age and compared with children who are not. Psychologists would not seriously consider such research because of ethical standards. However, experiments in which infants are purposefully separated from mothers have been run with lower animals.

Confidential • Secret; not to be disclosed.
Debrief • To elicit information about a just-completed procedure.

THE USE OF DECEPTION.   Many psychological experiments cannot be run without deceiving their human participants. However, the use of deception raises ethical issues. Let us revisit the Milgram studies on obedience. The learners in the experiment were actually confederates of the experimenter. They had not answered the newspaper ads but were in on the truth from the start. "Teachers" were the only real study participants. They were led to believe that they were chosen at random for the teacher role. However, the choosing was rigged so that newspaper recruits would always become teachers.

Many psychologists have debated the ethics of deceiving participants in the Milgram studies (Fisher & Fyrberg, 1994). According to the American Psychological Association's (1992a) *Ethical Principles of Psychologists and Code of Conduct,* psychologists may use deception only when they believe that the benefits of the research outweigh its potential harm, when they believe that the individuals might have been willing to participate if they had understood the benefits of the research, and when participants receive an explanation afterward. Regardless of the propriety of Milgram's research, we must acknowledge that it has highlighted some hard truths about human nature.

Return to the Lang (Lang and others, 1975) study on alcohol and aggression. In this study, the researchers misinformed participants about the beverage they were drinking. They also misled individuals into believing that they were giving other participants electric shock when they, like the participants in the Milgram studies, were actually only pressing switches on a dead control board. (Pressing these switches was the operational definition of aggression in the study.) In the Lang study, students who believed they had drunk vodka were "more aggressive." That is, they selected higher levels of shock than students who believed they had not. The actual content of the beverages was immaterial.

The Lang study, like the Milgram studies, could not have been run without deception. Foiling participants' expectations was crucial to the experiment. One can debate whether the potential benefits of the research outweigh the possible harm of deception.

Yet some psychologists oppose using deception—period. Diana Baumrind (1985) argues, for example, that deception-based research can harm not only research participants but also the reputation of the profession of psychology. In a study that supports Baumrind's views, one group of students participated in experiments in which they were deceived. Afterward, they regarded psychologists as being less trustworthy than did students who were not deceived (Smith & Richardson, 1983). Baumrind argues that deception might eventually cause the public to lose trust in psychologists and other professionals.

In any event, many studies continue to employ deception (Adair and others, 1985). Psychological ethics require that research participants who are deceived be **debriefed** afterward. Debriefing helps to eliminate misconceptions and anxieties about the research and to leave participants with their dignity intact (Blanck and others, 1992). After the Lang study was completed, for example, the participants were informed of the deceptions and of the rationale for them. Participants who had actually drunk alcohol were given coffee and assessed so that the researchers could be sure they were not leaving the laboratory while intoxicated.

Truth or Fiction Revisited. *It is true that psychologists would not be able to carry out certain kinds of research without deceiving participants as to the purposes and methods of the studies.* Deception may be required to prevent participants from purposefully distorting the outcomes of the research. Psychological ethics require that psychologists weigh the potential value of research findings against the possible harm that may be done by deceiving participants.

Psychologists use deception in research only when the research could not be run without it and when they believe that the benefits will outweigh the harm.

Research with Animals

Psychologists and other scientists frequently turn to animals to conduct research that cannot be carried out with humans (Segal, 1993). For example, experiments on the effects of early separation from the mother have been done with monkeys and other animals. Such research has helped psychologists investigate the formation of parent–child bonds of attachment (see Chapter 11).

Experiments with infant monkeys highlight some of the dilemmas faced by psychologists and other scientists who contemplate potentially harmful research. Psychologists and biologists who study the workings of the brain destroy sections of the brains of laboratory animals to learn how they influence behavior. For instance, a lesion in one part of a brain structure will cause a rat to overeat (see Chapter 10). A lesion elsewhere will cause the rat to go on a crash diet. Psychologists generalize to people from experiments such as these in the hope that we may find solutions to persistent human problems such as eating disorders. Proponents of the use of animals in research argue that major advances in medicine and psychology could not have taken place without them (Fowler, 1992; Martinez, 1992; Pardes and others, 1991).

Psychologists must still face the ethical dilemma of harming animals. As with humans, psychologists follow the principle that animals should be harmed only when there is no alternative and they believe that the benefits of the research will justify the harm (American Psychological Association, 1992a).

The Ethics of Animal Research. Now and then, psychologists and other scientists harm animals to answer research questions that may yield important benefits for people. Justifying such harm poses a major ethical dilemma.

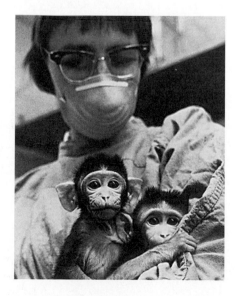

Reflections

- The Milgram studies were conducted prior to the advent of ethics review committees. (In fact, studies like Milgram's contributed to the social pressure to establish such committees.) If you were on an ethics review committee evaluating Milgram's proposed research, would you approve of his methods? Why or why not?
- **Agree or disagree with the following statement and support your answer: "Research with lower animals cannot really tell us anything about people."**
- **Is it ethical to deceive human study participants as to the nature of psychological research? Why or why not?**

Study Guide

EXERCISE	True or False?

DIRECTIONS: Circle the T or F for each of the following, to indicate whether the item is true or false. Check your answers in the key given below. It is more important at this time for you to understand why each item is true or false than to get them all right.

T   F   1. In the scientific method, participants are randomly selected and assigned to experimental groups or control groups.

T   F   2. A hypothesis is a formulation of the relationships and principles that underlie observed events that allows us to explain and predict behavior.

T   F   3. A hypothesis is a specific statement about behavior or mental processes that is tested through research.

T   F   4. Education is something of a liberating influence on sexual behavior.

T   F   5. In the Lang study on the effects of alcohol on aggression, aggression was operationally defined as selection of a level of shock to deliver to another person.

T   F   6. The most important factor about a sample is that it is very large.

T   F   7. If a sample is not randomly selected, the results of the study are inaccurate.

T   F   8. A random sample is selected by picking out telephone numbers in a directory by chance.

T   F   9. People who volunteer to participate in research studies differ from people who refuse to participate.

T   F   10. There is a positive correlation between intelligence and academic achievement.

T   F   11. There is a negative correlation between two variables. We can conclude that increasing one variable causes the other to decrease.

T   F   12. Researchers attempt to use unobtrusive measures in the naturalistic-observation method so that they do not influence the behavior they are observing.

T   F   13. Experimental blinds aim at controlling for the effects of expectations.

T   F   14. Case studies differ from surveys in the numbers of individuals studied.

T   F   15. It is unethical for a psychologist to breach confidentiality with a client, even when the client states that she or he is going to kill a third party.

ANSWER KEY TO TRUE–FALSE EXERCISE

1. F. This statement describes an experiment. The scientific method is a way of obtaining scientific evidence in which research questions or hypotheses are formulated and tested.
2. F. The statement defines a theory, not a hypothesis.
3. T.
4. T. People with more education report having more sex partners than people with less education.
5. T. The operational definition of a variable is defined in terms of the methods used to create or measure that variable.
6. F. The most important factor about a sample is that it represent the targeted population.
7. F. The results of the study may be accurate enough for the sample in the study. The results may not be able to be generalized to a target population, however.

8. F. A random sample is defined as a sample that is drawn so that each member of a population has an equal chance of being selected to participate. Telephone numbers may be used in random sampling but are not essential to the definition of random sampling.

9. T. Sure they do. They may be more willing to help other people, more interested in research, or simply have more time. In the case of sex surveys, they may also be more willing to disclose intimate information. Factors such as these may introduce volunteer bias into the results of a study.

10. T. That is, people who are more intelligent also tend to obtain better grades in school. Such a correlation does not delve into matters of cause and effect, however.

11. F. We can assume that as one variable increases, the other is *likely* to decrease. Correlation does not demonstrate cause and effect, however.

12. T.

13. T. Double-blind studies, which are the standard for demonstrating the effectiveness of new drugs, attempt to control for the expectations of both study participants and researchers.

14. T. Case studies usually address an individual or a small group, whereas surveys may address thousands of people. Ways of acquiring information may be similar, however, including interviews and questionnaires.

15. F. As pointed out in the text, such situations create ethical dilemmas, but many psychologists—and many states—require that a psychologist warn the threatened party of the danger.

ESL | Bridging the Gap

agemates (53)—people of similar ages

alluded to (47)—referred to

are held constant (57)—remain the same

assessed (53)—measured, judged

at random (57)—not in a preset or planned manner

atrocities (52)—cruel and inhuman behaviors

attained (53)—gained

ballots (41)—votes

bear out (41)—prove

bias (41)—preference for or against something; prejudice

blistering hot (56)—extremely hot

blisters (38)—skin swellings filled with fluid caused by a burn, an irritation, or a disease

borne out (47)—proved

built into (50)—already in

cause and effect (53)—something happens and as a result something else happens

chance factors . . . fluctuations (57)—occurrences that are not predictable or expected

chance fluctuations (57)—unexpected changes

chimpanzees (50)—animals like large monkeys considered to show some behaviors similar to human beings

climb higher up the corporate ladder (52)—advance to a higher position in a business organization

confederate (56)—partner who knows everything

consequences (56)—outcomes

consumption (59)—amount of food or drink taken

control groups (57)—people are selected who are similar to people being studied in an experiment, and their natural behavior is compared with that of the experimental people to judge if the experiment is actually making a difference

convulsive (39)—causing uncontrolled shaking, such as with laughter or pain

correlational method (35)—research technique of comparing the increase or decrease in two or more things to decide if they influence each other

crash diet (61)—when a person eats much less than usual for a short period of time to lose weight

critical thinkers (41)—people who try to analyze, or take apart, something to understand it

dangling straps (37)—strips of fabric or leather used to tie something that are are hanging loose

debated (60)—argued back and forth

deceptive (50)—misleading; causing someone to come to wrong conclusions

defied (38)—resisted or opposed

differ systematically (40)—be different in a predictable way

discerned (51)—identified; determined

distort (46)—change to be different from what is real

drawing conclusions (41)—making conclusions; reaching conclusions; arriving at conclusions; coming to conclusions

ethics (39)—beliefs about right and wrong behavior; standards

face the ethical dilemma (61)—consider carefully the right and wrong behaviors in a difficult situation

foiling (61)—preventing; obstructing

foolproof (47)—impossible to make a mistake

foul up the results (48)—cause the results to be invalid

further our understanding (56)—help us to understand more

historic bias (44)—long-standing preference for or against something

immune system (53)—body's defense system against disease

impair (53)—damage

impartial panel (57)—group of people who are not bi- ased or prejudiced

inflict pain (36)—cause pain

inspired by (52)—encouraged, or caused, by

insulted (59)—offended

integrity (59)—honesty

juvenile delinquency (54)—youthful wrongdoing or law- breaking

maimed (36)—injured; disabled; crippled

marital instability (54)—marriages that have serious diffi- culties

masturbation (47)—sexually stimulating oneself

misinformed or misled (60)—told incorrect information

misrepresentations (50)—things that are distorted or false

outcomes (56)—results

peers (39)—people who are equal to each other

potential (59)—possible

preexisting ideas (46)—ideas that we had before

preschoolers (53)—children less than 5 years old in spe- cial programs to learn something before starting kindergarten

rage (36)—strong anger

randomly (45)—done by chance; without a plan

recruit (37)—beginner who has been asked to join

reliable and valid (50)—dependable and accurate

rooting for (57)—hoping for; encouraging and wanting

running experiments (37)—doing experiments

running the gamut (37)—covering a variety or range of something

samples were drawn (37)—samples were taken from

self-destructive behavior (59)—behavior that hurts oneself

sexual arousal (57)—sexually stimulating

sexually restrained (49)—control or limit sexual behavior

slender (50)—thin

slight or severe shock (37)—weak or strong electrical charge that causes minor or major pain

social mover (56)—one who is influential with others in social life

social provocation (56)—doing something to offend someone

sophisticated (56)—advanced; complicated

sound as a dollar (47)—dependable

speculated (47)—considered; wondered if

statistical techniques (56)—research methods that judge the amount or frequency of something being measured

stratification (45)—organize into groups that are then ranked from high to low

sugar pill (57)—pills that look real but don't contain medicine

susceptible (36)—easily influenced by something; sensi- tive to it

tally (40)—count

target population (42)—people whom the experimenters wish to study

termed (41)—called

tissue damage (56)—injury to the body

tonic water (57)—nonalcoholic carbonated water

trustworthy (61)—honest and reliable

underpinnings (39)—structure supporting something, or beliefs behind something

urge (59)—desire

venerable (37)—highly respected for a long time

visual–motor coordination (56)—eye and body move- ment coordination

wee hours (47)—very early in the morning; before dawn

workings of the brain (61)—how the brain operates

Yuppies (42)—a term from the first letters of "Young Up- wardly mobile People," which refers to people aged about 25 to 45 who are concerned primarily with money and careers

---

FILL-INS | **Chapter Review**

SECTION 1: THE SCIENTIFIC METHOD: PUTTING IDEAS TO THE TEST

The (1) _____fic method is an organized way of going about expanding and refining knowledge. Psychologists usu- ally begin by formulating a (2) r_____ question. A research question may be studied in its question format, or it may be reworded into a (3) _____sis, which is a specific statement about behavior or mental processes that is tested through research. Psychologists next examine the research question or (4) t_____ the hypothesis through carefully controlled methods such as naturalistic or laboratory observation and the experiment. Psychologists draw (5) _____sions, about their research questions or the accuracy of their hypotheses on the basis of their research (6) ob_____s or findings. Research findings often suggest refinements to psychological (7) _____ries, and, con- sequently, new avenues of research.

SECTION 2: SAMPLES AND POPULATIONS: REPRESENTING HUMAN DIVERSITY

Samples must accurately (8) rep_____ the populations they are intended to reflect. Otherwise, we cannot (9) _____lize from research samples to populations.

Women's groups and health professionals argue that there is a historic bias in favor of conducting research with (10: men or women?). Research samples have also tended to (11: Overrepresent or Underrepresent?) minority ethnic groups in the population. The Kinsey studies on sexual behavior did not adequately represent (12) Af_____ Americans, poor people, the elderly, and diverse other groups.

In a (13) r_____ sample, each member of a population has an equal chance of being selected to participate. Researchers can also use a (14) _____fied sample, which is drawn so that identified subgroups in the population are represented proportionately in the sample. A large, randomly selected sample (15: Will or Will Not?) show reasonably accurate stratification.

The concept behind (16) _____teer bias is that people who offer to participate in research studies differ systematically from people who do not.

SECTION 3: METHODS OF OBSERVATION: THE BETTER TO SEE YOU WITH

Sigmund (17) _____d developed psychodynamic theory largely on the basis of case studies. Problems with the case study include gaps in (18) m_____ and purposeful distortion of the past. Interviewers may also have certain expectations and subtly guide people to fill in gaps in ways that are (19: Consistent or Inconsistent?) with their theoretical perspectives.

Psychologists conduct surveys to learn about behavior and mental processes that cannot be observed in the natural setting or studied (20) ex_____ally. Psychologists making surveys may employ questionnaires and interviews or examine public (21) re_____s.

In responding to surveys, people may inaccurately recall their behavior or purposefully (22) mis_____ it. Some people try to ingratiate themselves with their interviewers by answering in what they perceive to be the (23) _____ly desirable direction. Other people may falsify attitudes and exaggerate problems to draw (24) at_____ to themselves or try to foul up the results.

Psychologists use psychological tests to measure (25) t_____s and characteristics among a population. Psychological test results, like the results of surveys, can be distorted by respondents who answer in a socially (26) _____able direction or attempt to exaggerate problems. For these reasons, some psychological tests have (27) v_____ scales built into them.

The (28) _____istic-observation method observes individuals in their natural habitats. Psychologists and other scientists try to avoid interfering with the behaviors they are observing by using (29) _____sive measures. Jane (30) G_____ has extensively observed the behavior of chimpanzees in their natural environment.

Psychologists place lower animals and people into controlled laboratory environments where they can be readily observed and where the effects of specific (31) con_____s can be discerned.

SECTION 4: THE CORRELATIONAL METHOD: SEEING WHAT GOES UP AND WHAT COMES DOWN

Psychologists use the correlational method to investigate whether one observed behavior or measured trait is related to, or (32) _____lated with, another. A number called the correlation (33) co_____ indicates the direction and the magnitude of a correlation between variables. A correlation coefficient can vary between +1.00 and (34) _____.

When variables are (35) _____ly correlated, one increases as the other increases. When variables are (36) _____ly correlated, one increases as the other decreases. Numerous studies report (37) _____tive correlations between intelligence and achievement. Correlational research may suggest but does not show cause and (38) _____t.

SECTION 5: THE EXPERIMENTAL METHOD: TRYING THINGS OUT

An (39) _____ment is considered the best research method for answering questions concerning cause and effect. In an experiment, a group of participants receives a (40) _____ment, such as a dose of alcohol. The participants are then observed carefully to determine whether the treatment makes a difference in behavior. Experiments allow psychologists to (41) con_____ the experiences of participants to determine the effects of a treatment.

The presence of an (42) _____dent variable is manipulated by the experimenters so that its effects may be determined. The measured results, or outcomes, in an experiment are called (43) _____dent variables. The presence of (44) _____dent variables presumably depends on the (45) _____dent variables.

Ideal experiments use experimental and (46) con_____ groups. Individuals in (47) _____tal groups receive the treatment, whereas individuals in (48) _____ol groups do not. Every effort is made to ensure that all other (49) _____tions are held constant for experimental and control groups. In this way, researchers can have confidence that the experimental outcomes reflect the (50) _____ments and not chance factors or chance fluctuations in behavior.

A (51) p_____, or "sugar pill," often results in the behavior that people expect. When people in psychological experiments are given placebos but think that they have received the real (52) tr_____, we can conclude that changes in behavior and mental processes stem from their (53) _____fs about the treatment and not from the treatment itself.

Well-designed experiments control for the effects of expectations by creating conditions under which participants are unaware of, or (54) b_____ to, the treatment they have received. Yet researchers may also have expectations. Studies in which both study participants and experimenters are unaware of who has received the treatment are called (55) d_____-_____ studies.

SECTION 6: ETHICAL ISSUES

Psychologists adhere to a number of (56) _____cal standards that are intended to promote the dignity of the individual, foster human welfare, and maintain scientific integrity. They also assure that psychologists (57: Do or Do Not) undertake research methods or treatments that are harmful to study participants or clients.

In order to help avoid harm, human participants must provide (58) i_____ consent. Psychologists treat the records of study participants and clients as (59) _____tial because they respect people's privacy and because people are more likely to express their true thoughts and feelings when researchers or therapists keep their disclosures confidential.

Many experiments, like the Lang study on the effects of alcohol, cannot be run without (60) de_____ing people.

Psychological ethics require that study participants who are deceived be (61) _____fed afterward to help eliminate misconceptions and anxieties about the research and to leave them with their dignity intact.

Psychologists and other scientists frequently turn to (62) _____mals to conduct harmful or potentially harmful research that cannot be carried out with humans. Psychologists still face the (63) eth_____ dilemma of subjecting animals to harm. As with people, psychologists follow the principle that animals should be subjected to (64) h_____ only when there is no alternative and they believe that the benefits of the research will justify the harm.

ANSWER KEY TO CHAPTER REVIEW

1. Scientific	14. Stratified	27. Validity	40. Treatment	53. Beliefs
2. Research	15. Will	28. Naturalistic	41. Control	54. Blind
3. Hypothesis	16. Volunteer	29. Unobtrusive	42. Independent	55. Double-blind
4. Test	17. Freud	30. Goodall	43. Dependent	56. Ethical
5. Conclusions	18. Memory	31. Conditions	44. Dependent	57. Do not
6. Observations	19. Consistent	32. Correlated	45. Independent	58. Informed
7. Theories	20. Experimentally	33. Coefficient	46. Control	59. Confidential
8. Represent	21. Records	34. −1.00	47. Experimental	60. Deceiving
9. Generalize	22. Misrepresent (or misstate)	35. Positively	48. Control	61. Debriefed
10. Men	23. Socially	36. Negatively	49. Conditions	62. Animals
11. Underrepresent	24. Attention	37. Positive	50. Treatments	63. Ethical
12. African	25. Traits	38. Effect	51. Placebo	64. Harm
13. Random	26. Desirable	39. Experiment	52. Treatment	

POSTTEST | **Multiple Choice**

1. Unobtrusively observing diners at a fast-food restaurant in order to determine how frequently they take bites is an example of the
   a. experimental method.
   b. case-study method.
   c. survey method.
   d. naturalistic-observation method.

2. If you were to run an experiment on the effects of temperature on aggressive behavior, aggressive behavior would be the
   a. hypothesis.
   b. dependent variable.
   c. treatment.
   d. correlation coefficient.

3. In the Lang experiment on alcohol and aggression, the condition that led to the most aggressive behavior was
   a. drinking tonic water only.
   b. drinking vodka and tonic water.
   c. belief that one had drunk tonic water only.
   d. belief that one had drunk vodka and tonic water.

4. The Lang study on alcohol and aggression could not have been carried out without the _____ of study participants.

   a. informed consent
   b. confidentiality
   c. deception
   d. debriefing

5. Kinsey used _____ in his research on sexual behavior.
   a. laboratory observations of sexual behavior
   b. reports of former lovers of the people studied
   c. interview data
   d. psychological test data

6. A _____ sample is one in which every member of a population has an equal chance of being selected.
   a. biased
   b. chance
   c. random
   d. stratified

7. The development of psychodynamic theory relied largely on the
   a. case-study method.
   b. naturalistic-observation method.
   c. survey method.
   d. psychological testing method.

8. Of the following, the ethnic group that reported having the fewest sex partners in the National Health and Social Life Survey was
   a. White Americans.
   b. African Americans.
   c. Hispanic Americans.
   d. Asian Americans.

9. Psychologists generally agree that the best research method for determining cause and effect is the
   a. naturalistic-observation method.
   b. case-study method.
   c. correlational method.
   d. experimental method.

10. According to the text,
   a. there is a positive correlation between intelligence and academic achievement.
   b. there is a negative correlation between intelligence and academic achievement.
   c. intelligence provides the basis for academic achievement.
   d. there is no relationship between intelligence and academic achievement.

11. Which of the following is/are the source(s) of research questions?
   a. psychological theory
   b. daily experiences
   c. folklore
   d. all of the above

12. A specific statement about behavior or mental processes that is tested through research is termed a
   a. research question.
   b. hypothesis.
   c. theory.
   d. scientific principle.

13. Psychologists have observed that more-aggressive children spend more time watching TV violence than less-aggressive children. What can we conclude from this observation?
   a. TV violence causes aggression.
   b. Aggressive behavior causes the watching of violent TV shows.
   c. There is a correlation between aggression and watching TV violence.
   d. None of the above conclusions is possible.

14. According to the text, the Kinsey studies failed to in-

clude adequate numbers of _____ in the research samples.
   a. African Americans
   b. White Americans
   c. women
   d. men

15. The concept behind _____ is that people who offer to participate in research studies differ systematically from people who do not
   a. the selection factor
   b. blinds and double blinds
   c. the use of placebos
   d. volunteer bias

16. The case of _____ provides a valuable case study in the processes of language development.
   a. Genie
   b. Eve
   c. Lang
   d. Jane

17. Validity scales are most likely to be employed in the
   a. naturalistic-observation method.
   b. correlational method.
   c. testing method.
   d. experimental method.

18. Which of the following is apparently an effect of providing informed consent in psychological research?
   a. a sense of control
   b. volunteer bias
   c. selection factor
   d. violation of ethical principles

19. Diana Baumrind argues that deception-based research
   a. is necessary only with people.
   b. makes experiments less stressful.
   c. can harm the reputation of the profession of psychology.
   d. is ethical only when the benefits of the research outweigh the potential harm.

20. The most important factor in selecting a sample is that it should
   a. be large.
   b. be drawn at random.
   c. represent the targeted population.
   d. consist of people who are volunteers.

ANSWER KEY TO POSTTEST

1. D	4. C	7. A	10. A	13. C	16. A	19. C
2. B	5. C	8. D	11. D	14. A	17. C	20. C
3. D	6. C	9. D	12. B	15. D	18. A	

LEARNING OBJECTIVES

When you have finished studying Chapter 3, you should be able to:

NEURONS: INTO THE FABULOUS FOREST

1. Describe the parts and functions of the neuron.
2. Explain the electrochemical process by which neural impulses travel.
3. Explain the functions of synapses and neurotransmitters.

THE NERVOUS SYSTEM

4. Explain the functions of the divisions of the nervous system.
5. Explain how spinal reflexes work.
6. Explain how psychologists study the functions of the brain.

THE CEREBRAL CORTEX

7. Explain the functions of the lobes of the cerebral cortex.

THE ENDOCRINE SYSTEM

8. Explain the functions of various hormones.

HEREDITY: THE NATURE OF NATURE

9. Define genes and chromosomes, and describe human chromosomal structure.
10. Discuss psychologists' use of kinship studies.

Biology

PRETEST *Truth or Fiction?*

____ Some cells in your body stretch all the way down your back to your big toe.

____ Messages travel in the brain by means of electricity.

____ Our bodies produce natural painkillers that are more powerful than morphine.

____ The human brain is larger than that of any other animal.

____ Fear can give you indigestion.

____ If a surgeon were to stimulate a certain part of your brain electrically, you might swear in court that someone had stroked your leg.

____ Zookeepers who want to have baby girls or boys (crocodiles, that is) need only control the temperature at which the eggs develop.

ACCORDING to the big-bang theory, our universe began with an enormous explosion that sent countless particles hurtling into every corner of space. For billions of years, these particles have been forming immense gas clouds. Galaxies and solar systems have been condensing from the clouds, sparkling for some eons, then winking out. Human beings have only recently come into existence on an unremarkable rock circling an average star in a standard spiral galaxy.

Since the beginning of time, the universe has been in flux. Change has brought life and death and countless challenges. Some creatures have adapted successfully to these challenges and continued to evolve. Others have not met the challenges and have become extinct, falling back into the distant mists of time. Some have left fossil records. Others have disappeared without a trace.

At first, human survival on planet Earth required a greater struggle than it does today. We fought predators like the leopard. We foraged across parched lands for food. We might have warred with creatures very much like ourselves—creatures who have since become extinct. We prevailed. The human species has survived and continues to transmit its unique traits through the generations by means of genetic material whose chemical codes are only now being cracked.

Yet, what is handed down through the generations? The answer is biological, or **physiological,** structures and processes. Our biology serves as the

Pablo Picasso at Work. The great artist's nervous system was composed of neurons like those of other people. Biological psychologists delve into how our behavior and mental processes are linked to the functioning of the nervous system and other biological processes.

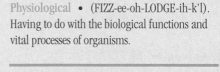

Physiological • (FIZZ-ee-oh-LODGE-ih-k'l). Having to do with the biological functions and vital processes of organisms.

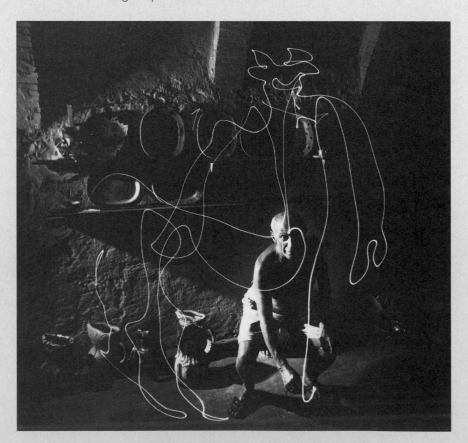

material base for our observable behaviors, emotions, and cognitions (our thoughts, images, and plans). Biology gives rise to specific behavioral tendencies in some organisms, such as the chick's instinctive fear of the shadow of the hawk (Knight, 1994). But most psychologists believe that human behavior is flexible and influenced by learning and choice as well as heredity.

Biological psychologists (or psychobiologists) work at the interfaces of psychology and biology. They study the ways in which our mental processes and observable behaviors are linked to biological structures and processes. In recent years, biological psychologists have been unlocking the mysteries of:

1. *Neurons.* Neurons are the building blocks of the nervous system. There are billions upon billions of neurons in the body—perhaps as many as there are stars in the Milky Way galaxy.

2. *The nervous system.* Neurons combine to form the structures of the nervous system. The nervous system has branches that are responsible for muscle movement, perception, automatic functions such as breathing and the secretion of hormones, and psychological phenomena such as thoughts and feelings.

3. *The cerebral cortex.* The cerebral cortex is the large, wrinkled mass inside your head that you think of as your brain. Actually, it is only one part of the brain—the part that is the most characteristically human.

4. *The endocrine system.* Through secretion of hormones, the endocrine system controls functions ranging from growth in children to production of milk in nursing women.

5. *Heredity.* Within every cell of your body there are about 100,000 genes. These chemical substances determine what type of creature you are, from the color of your hair to your body temperature to the fact that you have arms and legs rather than wings or fins.

NEURONS: INTO THE FABULOUS FOREST

Let us begin our journey in a fabulous forest of nerve cells, or **neurons,** that can be visualized as having branches, trunks, and roots—something like trees. As in other forests, many nerve cells lie alongside one another like a thicket of trees. Neurons can also lie end to end, however, with their "roots" intertwined with the "branches" of neurons that lie below. Trees receive water and nutrients from the soil. Neurons receive "messages" from a number of sources such as other neurons, pressure on the skin, and light, and they can pass these messages along.

Neurons communicate by means of chemicals called **neurotransmitters.** Neurons release neurotransmitters that are taken up by other neurons, muscles, and glands. Neurotransmitters cause chemical changes in the receiving neuron so that the message can travel along its "trunk," be translated back into neurotransmitters in its "branches," and then travel through the small spaces between neurons to be received by the "roots" of yet other neurons.

Each neuron transmits and coordinates messages in the form of neural impulses. We are born with more than 100 billion neurons (Shatz, 1992). Most of them are found in the brain. The messages transmitted by neurons somehow account for phenomena ranging from perception of an itch from a mosquito bite to the coordination of a skier's vision and muscles to the composition of a concerto to the solution of an algebraic equation.

Biological psychologists • Psychologists who study the relationships between life processes and behavior.
Neuron • (NEW-ron). A nerve cell.
Neurotransmitters • (new-row-tranz-MIT-ters). Chemical substances involved in the transmission of neural impulses from one neuron to another.

**MINILECTURE:
THE NEURON**

The Makeup of Neurons

Neurons vary according to their functions and their location. Some in the brain are only a fraction of an inch in length. Others in the legs are several feet long. Every neuron is a single nerve cell with a cell body (or **soma**), dendrites, and an axon (see Figure 3.1). The cell body contains the nucleus of the cell. The cell body uses oxygen and nutrients to generate energy to carry out the work of the cell. Anywhere from a few to several hundred short fibers, or **dendrites,** extend rootlike from the cell body to receive incoming messages from thousands of adjoining neurons. Each neuron has one **axon** that extends trunklike from the cell body. Axons are very thin, but those that carry messages from the toes to the spinal cord extend for several feet.

Truth or Fiction Revisited. It is true that some cells in your body stretch all the way down your back to your big toe. These cells are neurons. Question: How can cells that are this long be "microscopic"?

Like tree trunks, axons too can divide and extend in different directions. Axons end in smaller branching structures called **terminals.** At the tips of the axon terminals are swellings called **knobs.** Neurons carry messages in one direction only: from the dendrites or cell body through the axon to the axon terminals. The messages are then transmitted from the axon terminals to other neurons.

MYELIN.   The axons of many neurons are wrapped tightly with white, fatty **myelin sheaths.** The fat insulates the axon from electrically charged atoms, or ions, found in the fluids that encase the nervous system. Myelin minimizes leakage of the electric current being carried along the axon, thus allowing messages to be conducted more efficiently. Myelin does not uniformly coat the surface of an axon. It is missing at points called **nodes of Ranvier,** where the axon is exposed. Because of the insulation provided by myelin, neural messages, or impulses, travel rapidly from node to node.

Myelination is part of the maturation process that leads to the abilities to crawl and walk during the first year. Babies are not physiologically "ready" to engage in visual–motor coordination and other activities until the coating process reaches certain levels. In the disease multiple sclerosis, myelin is replaced with a hard fibrous tissue that throws off the timing of nerve impulses and disrupts muscular control. Affliction of neurons that control breathing can result in suffocation.

AFFERENT AND EFFERENT NEURONS.   If someone steps on your big toe, the sensation is registered by receptors or sensory neurons near the surface of your skin. Then it is transmitted to the spinal cord and brain through **afferent neurons,** which are perhaps 2 to 3 feet long. In the brain, subsequent messages might be buffeted about by associative neurons that are only a few thousandths of an inch long. You experience the pain through this process and perhaps entertain some rather nasty thoughts about the perpetrator, who is now apologizing and begging for understanding. Long before you arrive at any logical conclusions, however, motor neurons **(efferent neurons)** send messages to your foot so that you withdraw it and begin an impressive hopping routine. Other efferent neurons stimulate glands so that your heart is now beating more rapidly, you are sweating, and the hair on the back of your arms has become erect! Being a sport, you say, "Oh, it's nothing." But considering all the neurons involved, it really is something, isn't it?

In case you think that afferent and efferent neurons will be hard to distinguish because they sound pretty much the SAME to you, remember that they

---

Soma • (SO-muh). A cell body.

Dendrites • Rootlike structures, attached to the soma of a neuron, that receive impulses from other neurons.

Axon • (AX-on). A long, thin part of a neuron that transmits impulses to other neurons from branching structures called *terminals.*

Terminals • Small structures at the tips of axons.

Knobs • Swellings at the ends of terminals. Also referred to as *bulbs* or *buttons.*

Myelin sheath • (MY-uh-lin). A fatty substance that encases and insulates axons, facilitating transmission of neural impulses.

Node of Ranvier • A noninsulated segment of a myelinated axon.

Afferent neurons • Neurons that transmit messages from sensory receptors to the spinal cord and brain. Also called *sensory neurons.*

Efferent neurons • Neurons that transmit messages from the brain or spinal cord to muscles and glands. Also called *motor neurons.*

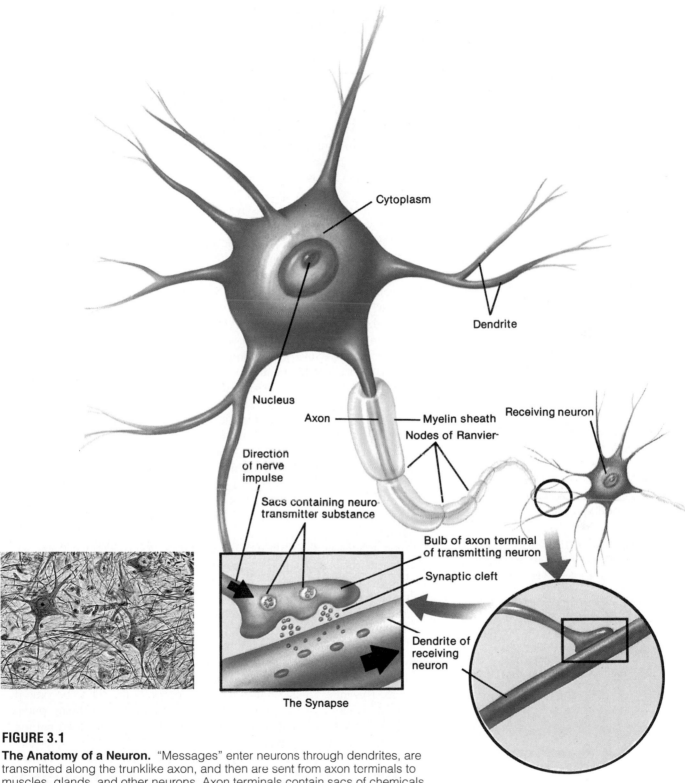

FIGURE 3.1

The Anatomy of a Neuron. "Messages" enter neurons through dendrites, are transmitted along the trunklike axon, and then are sent from axon terminals to muscles, glands, and other neurons. Axon terminals contain sacs of chemicals called neurotransmitters. Neurotransmitters are released by the transmitting neuron into the synaptic cleft, and many of them are taken up by receptor sites on the dendrites of the receiving neuron. Some neurotransmitters (called "excitatory") influence receiving neurons in the direction of firing; others (called "inhibitory") influence them in the direction of *not* firing. To date, a few dozen possible neurotransmitters have been identified.

are the "SAME." That is, *S*ensory = *A*fferent, and *M*otor = *E*fferent. But don't tell your professor I let you in on this **mnemonic** device.

The Neural Impulse: Let Us "Sing the Body Electric"[1]

In the 18th century, Italian physiologist Luigi Galvani (1737–1798) conducted a shocking experiment in a rainstorm. While his neighbors had the sense to remain indoors, Galvani and his wife were out on the porch connecting lightning rods to the heads of dissected frogs whose legs were connected by wire to a well of water. When lightning blazed above, the frogs' muscles contracted repeatedly and violently. This is not a recommended way to prepare frogs' legs. Galvani was demonstrating that the messages **(neural impulses)** that travel along neurons are electrochemical in nature.

Neural impulses travel somewhere between 2 (in nonmyelinated neurons) and 225 miles an hour (in myelinated neurons). This speed is not impressive when compared with that of an electric current in a toaster oven or a lamp, which can travel at the speed of light—over 186,000 miles per second. Distances in the body are short, however, and a message will travel from a toe to the brain in perhaps 1/50th of a second.

The process by which neural impulses travel is electrochemical. Chemical changes take place within neurons that cause an electric charge to be transmitted along their lengths. In a resting state, when a neuron is not being stimulated by its neighbors, there are relatively greater numbers of positively charged sodium ($Na+$) ions and negatively charged chloride ($Cl-$) ions in the body fluid outside the neuron than in the fluid within the neuron. Positively charged potassium ($K+$) ions are more plentiful inside, but there are many other negative ions inside that are not balanced by negative ions on the outside, lending the inside an overall negative charge in relation to the outside. The difference in electrical charge **polarizes** the neuron with a negative **resting potential** of about −70 millivolts in relation to the body fluid outside the cell membrane.

When an area on the surface of the resting neuron is adequately stimulated by other neurons, the cell membrane in the area changes its **permeability** to allow sodium ions to enter. As a consequence, the area of entry becomes positively charged, or **depolarized** with respect to the outside (Figure 3.2). The permeability of the cell membrane changes again, allowing no more sodium ions to enter.

The inside of the cell at the disturbed area has an **action potential** of 110 millivolts. This action potential, added to the −70 millivolts that characterize the resting potential, brings the membrane voltage to a positive charge of +40 millivolts. This inner change causes the next section of the cell to become permeable to sodium ions. At the same time, potassium ions are being pumped out of the area of the cell that was previously affected, which then returns to its resting potential. In this way, the neural impulse is transmitted continuously along an axon that is not myelinated. Because the impulse is created anew as it progresses, its strength does not change. Neural impulses are conducted more rapidly along myelinated axons because they jump from node to node.

Truth or Fiction Revisited. *It is true that messages travel in the brain by means of electricity.* However, this is not the whole story. Messages also

Mnemonic • (neh-MON-nick). Aiding memory, usually by linking chunks of new information to well-known schemes.

Neural impulse • (NEW-ral). The electrochemical discharge of a nerve cell, or neuron.

Polarize • To ready a neuron for firing by creating an internal negative charge in relation to the body fluid outside the cell membrane.

Resting potential • The electrical potential across the neural membrane when it is not responding to other neurons.

Permeability • The degree to which a membrane allows a substance to pass through it.

Depolarize • To reduce the resting potential of a cell membrane from about −70 millivolts toward zero.

Action potential • The electrical impulse that provides the basis for the conduction of a neural impulse along an axon of a neuron.

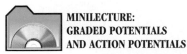

MINILECTURE: GRADED POTENTIALS AND ACTION POTENTIALS

---

[1] From "I Sing the Body Electric," a poem by Walt Whitman.

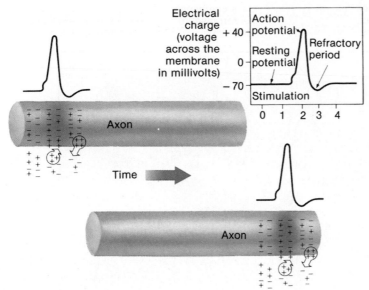

FIGURE 3.2

The Neural Impulse. When a section of a neuron is stimulated by other neurons, the cell membrane becomes permeable to sodium ions so that an action potential of about +40 millivolts is induced. This action potential is transmitted along the axon. Eventually the neuron fires (or fails to fire) according to the all-or-none principle.

travel from neurons to other neurons, muscles, or glands by means of chemical messengers termed *neurotransmitters.*

The conduction of the neural impulse along the length of a neuron is what is meant by "firing." Some neurons fire in less than 1/1,000th of a second. In firing, neurons "attempt" to transmit the message to other neurons, muscles, or glands. However, other neurons will not fire unless the incoming messages combine to reach an adequate **threshold.** A weak message may cause a temporary shift in electrical charge at some point along a neuron's cell membrane, but this charge will dissipate if the neuron is not stimulated to threshold.

A neuron may transmit several hundred such messages in a second. Each time a neuron fires, it transmits an impulse of the same strength. This fact is referred to as the **all-or-none principle.** Neurons fire more frequently when they have been stimulated by larger numbers of other neurons. Stronger stimuli cause more frequent firing.

For a thousandth of a second or so after firing, a neuron enters an **absolute refractory period.** During this period it will not fire in response to stimulation from other neurons. Then, for another few thousandths of a second, the neuron is said to be in a **relative refractory period,** during which it will fire but only in response to messages that are stronger than usual. The refractory period is a time of recovery during which sodium is prevented from passing through the neuronal membrane. When we realize that such periods of recovery might take place hundreds of times per second, it seems a rapid recovery and a short rest indeed.

The Synapse

A neuron relays its message to another neuron across a junction called a **synapse.** A synapse consists of a "branch," or axon terminal from the transmitting neuron; a dendrite ("root"), or the soma of a receiving neuron; and a

Threshold • The point at which a stimulus is just strong enough to produce a response.
All-or-none principle • The fact that a neuron fires an impulse of the same strength whenever its action potential is triggered.
Absolute refractory period • A phase following firing during which a neuron's action potential cannot be triggered.
Relative refractory period • A phase following the absolute refractory period during which a neuron will fire in response to stronger-than-usual messages.
Synapse • (SIN-apps). A junction between the axon terminals of one neuron and the dendrites or soma of another neuron.

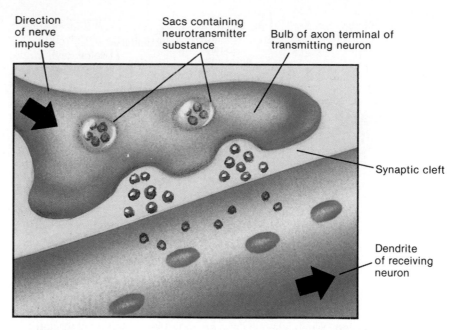

Direction
of nerve
impulse

Sacs containing
neurotransmitter
substance

Bulb of axon terminal of
transmitting neuron

Synaptic cleft

Dendrite
of receiving
neuron

FIGURE 3.3

The Synapse. Neurons relay their messages to other neurons across junctions called *synapses*. A synapse consists of an axon terminal from the transmitting neuron, the membrane of the receiving neuron, and a small gap between the two which is referred to as the *synaptic cleft*. Molecules of neurotransmitters are released into the synaptic cleft from vesicles within the axon terminal. Many molecules are taken up by receptor sites on the receiving neuron. Others are broken down or taken up again by the transmitting neuron.

Receptor site • A location on a dendrite of a receiving neuron tailored to receive a neurotransmitter.

Excitatory synapse • (EX-it-uh-TORE-ee). A synapse that influences receiving neurons in the direction of firing by increasing depolarization of their cell membranes.

fluid-filled gap between the two that is called the *synaptic cleft* (see Figure 3.3). Although the neural impulse is electrical, it does not jump the synaptic cleft like a spark. Instead, when a nerve impulse reaches a synapse, axon terminals release chemicals into the synaptic cleft like myriad ships being cast off into the sea.

Neurotransmitters

In the axon terminals are sacs, or synaptic vesicles, that contain chemicals called *neurotransmitters*. When a neural impulse reaches the axon terminal, the vesicles release varying amounts of these neurotransmitters into the synaptic cleft. From there, they influence the receiving neuron.

Dozens of neurotransmitters have been identified. Each neurotransmitter has its own chemical structure, and each can fit into a specifically tailored harbor, or **receptor site,** on the dendrite of the receiving cell. The analogy of a key fitting into a lock has been used. Once released, not all molecules of a neurotransmitter find their ways into receptor sites of other neurons. "Loose" neurotransmitters are usually either broken down or reabsorbed by the axon terminal (a process called *re-uptake*).

Some neurotransmitters act to excite other neurons—that is, to influence receiving neurons in the direction of firing. The synapses between axon terminals with excitatory neurotransmitters and receiving neurons are called **excitatory synapses.** Other neurotransmitters inhibit receiving neurons; that is, they influence them in the direction of not firing. The synapses between axon terminals with inhibitory neurotransmitters and receiving neurons are

**MINILECTURE:
NEUROTRANSMITTERS AND
THE SYNAPSE**

called **inhibitory synapses.** Neurons may be influenced by neurotransmitters that have been released by thousands of other neurons. The additive stimulation received from all these cells determines whether a particular neuron will also fire and which neurotransmitters will be released in the process.

Neurotransmitters are involved in processes ranging from muscle contraction to emotional response. Excesses or deficiencies of neurotransmitters have been linked to diseases and abnormal behavior.

ACETYLCHOLINE. **Acetylcholine** (ACh) is a neurotransmitter that controls muscle contractions. ACh is excitatory at synapses between nerves and muscles that involve voluntary movement but inhibitory at the heart and some other locations.

The effects of curare highlight the functioning of ACh. Curare is a poison that is extracted from plants by South American Indians and used in hunting. If an arrow tipped with curare pierces the skin and the poison enters the body, it prevents ACh from lodging within receptor sites in neurons, resulting in paralysis. The victim is prevented from contracting the muscles used in breathing and dies from suffocation. Botulism, a disease that stems from food poisoning, prevents the release of ACh and has the same effect as curare.

ACh is also normally prevalent in a part of the brain called the **hippocampus,** a structure involved in the formation of memories. When the ACh available to the brain decreases, memory formation is impaired.

DOPAMINE. **Dopamine** is primarily an inhibitory neurotransmitter. Dopamine is involved in voluntary movements, learning and memory, and emotional arousal. Deficiencies of dopamine are linked to Parkinson's disease, a disorder in which people progressively lose control over their muscles. They develop muscle tremors and jerky, uncoordinated movements. The drug L-dopa, a substance that the brain converts to dopamine, helps slow the progress of Parkinson's disease.

The psychological disorder schizophrenia (see Chapter 13) has also been linked to dopamine. Schizophrenic individuals may have more receptor sites for dopamine in an area of the brain that is involved in emotional responding. For this reason, they may *overutilize* the dopamine that is available in the brain, which leads to hallucinations and disturbances of thought and emotion. The phenothiazines, a group of drugs used in the treatment of schizophrenia, block the action of dopamine by locking some dopamine out of these receptor sites (Carpenter & Buchanan, 1994). Not surprisingly, phenothiazines may have Parkinson-like side effects. The side effects are usually treated by additional drugs, lowering the dose of phenothiazine, or switching to another drug.

NORADRENALINE. **Noradrenaline** is produced largely by neurons in the brain stem. Noradrenaline acts both as a neurotransmitter and a hormone. It speeds up the heartbeat and other body processes and is involved in general arousal, learning and memory, and eating. Excesses and deficiencies of noradrenaline have been linked to mood disorders (see Chapter 13).

The stimulants cocaine and amphetamines ("speed") facilitate the release of dopamine and noradrenaline and also impede their reabsorption by the releasing synaptic vesicles—that is, their re-uptake. As a result, there are excesses of these neurotransmitters in the nervous system, vastly increasing the firing of neurons and leading to a persistent state of high arousal.

SEROTONIN. Also primarily an inhibitory transmitter, **serotonin** is involved in emotional arousal and sleep. Deficiencies of serotonin have been linked to

Inhibitory synapse • A synapse that influences receiving neurons in the direction of not firing by encouraging changes in their membrane permeability in the direction of the resting potential.

Acetylcholine • (uh-SEE-till-COE-lean). A neurotransmitter that controls muscle contractions. Abbreviated *ACh*.

Hippocampus • A part of the limbic system of the brain that is involved in memory formation.

Dopamine • (DOPE-uh-mean). A neurotransmitter that is involved in Parkinson's disease and that appears to play a role in schizophrenia.

Noradrenaline • (nor-uh-DRENN-uh-lin). A neurotransmitter whose action is similar to that of the hormone adrenaline and that may play a role in depression.

Serotonin • (ser-oh-TONE-in). A neurotransmitter, deficiencies of which have been linked to affective disorders, anxiety, and insomnia.

anxiety, mood disorders, and insomnia. The drug LSD (see Chapter 5) decreases the action of serotonin and may also influence the utilization of dopamine. With LSD, "two no's make a yes." By inhibiting an inhibitor, brain activity increases, in this case frequently leading to hallucinations.

ENDORPHINS.   The word *endorphin* is the contraction of *endogenous morphine. Endogenous* means "developing from within." **Endorphins,** then, are similar to the narcotic morphine in their functions and effects and are produced by our own bodies. They occur naturally in the brain and in the bloodstream.

Endorphins are inhibitory neurotransmitters. They lock into receptor sites for chemicals that transmit pain messages to the brain. Once the endorphin "key" is in the "lock," pain-causing chemicals cannot transmit their (frequently unwelcome) messages. There are a number of endorphins. Beta-endorphin, for example, is many times more powerful than morphine, molecule for molecule (Snyder, 1977).

Truth or Fiction Revisited. *It is true that our bodies produce natural painkillers that are more powerful than morphine.* These chemicals are called *endorphins* and, ounce for ounce, they are more powerful than the narcotic morphine. Endorphins may also increase our sense of self-competence and may be connected with the "runner's high" reported by many long-distance runners.

There you have it—a fabulous forest of neurons in which billions upon billions of vesicles are pouring neurotransmitters into synaptic clefts at any given time: when you are involved in strenuous activity, now as you are reading this page, even as you are passively watching television. This microscopic picture is repeated several hundred times every second. The combined activity of all these neurotransmitters determines which messages will be transmitted and which will not. Your experience of sensations, your thoughts, and your psychological sense of control over your body are very different from the electrochemical processes we have described. Yet somehow, these many electrochemical events are responsible for your psychological sense of yourself and of the world (Greenfield, 1995).

Endorphins • (en-DOOR-fins). Neurotransmitters that are composed of amino acids and that are functionally similar to morphine.

Reflections

- How does the text use the term *message* in referring to transmission from one neuron to another? How are messages "passed along" from one neuron to another?
- Had you heard that the brain works, or operates, by means of electricity? What electrochemical processes actually account for transmission of messages in the nervous system?
- **Since psychology is the study of behavior and mental processes, why are psychologists interested in biological matters such as the nervous system, the endocrine system, and heredity?**

THE NERVOUS SYSTEM

As a child, I did not think it a good thing to have a "nervous" system. After all, if your system were not so nervous, you might be less likely to jump at strange noises.

Later I learned that a nervous system is not a system that is nervous. It is a system of nerves involved in thought processes, heartbeat, visual–motor coordination, and so on. I also learned that the human nervous system is more complex than that of any other animal and that our brains are larger than those of any other animal. Now this last piece of business is not quite true. A human brain weighs about 3 pounds, but elephant and whale brains may be four times as heavy. Still, our brains compose a greater part of our body weight than do those of elephants or whales. Our brains weigh about 1/60th of our body weight. Elephant brains weigh about 1/1,000th of their total weight, and whale brains are a mere 1/10,000th of their weight. So, if we wish, we can still find figures to make us proud.

Truth or Fiction Revisited. *It is not true that the human brain is larger than that of any other animal.* Elephants and whales have larger brains. Our brains are more convoluted, however.

The brain is only one part of the nervous system. A **nerve** is a bundle of axons and dendrites. The cell bodies of these neurons are not considered to be part of the nerve. The cell bodies are gathered into clumps called **nuclei** in the brain and spinal cord and **ganglia** elsewhere.

The nervous system consists of the brain, the spinal cord, and the nerves linking them to receptors in the sensory organs and effectors in the muscles and glands. As shown in Figure 3.4, the brain and spinal cord make up what we refer to as the **central nervous system.** The sensory (afferent) neurons, which receive and transmit messages to the brain and spinal cord, and the motor (efferent) neurons, which transmit messages from the brain or spinal cord to the muscles and glands, make up the peripheral nervous system. There is no deep, complex reason for labeling the two major divisions of the nervous system in this way. It is just geography. The **peripheral nervous system** extends more into the edges, or periphery, of the body.

Let us now examine the nature and functions of the central and peripheral nervous systems.

MINILECTURE: ORGANIZATION OF THE NERVOUS SYSTEM

Nerve • A bundle of axons and dendrites from many neurons.

Nuclei • (NEW-klee-eye). Plural of *nucleus*. A group of neural cell bodies found in the brain or spinal cord.

Ganglia • (GANG-lee-uh). Plural of *ganglion*. A group of neural cell bodies found elsewhere in the body (other than the brain or spinal cord).

Central nervous system • The brain and spinal cord.

Peripheral nervous system • (pair-IF-uh-ral). The part of the nervous system consisting of the somatic nervous system and the autonomic nervous system.

FIGURE 3.4

The Divisions of the Nervous System. The nervous system contains two main divisions: the central nervous system and the peripheral nervous system. The central nervous system consists of the brain and spinal cord. The peripheral nervous system contains the somatic and autonomic systems. In turn, the autonomic nervous system is composed of sympathetic and parasympathetic divisions.

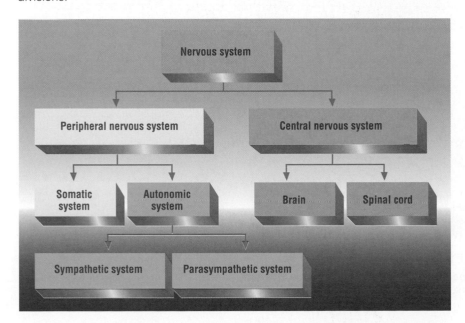

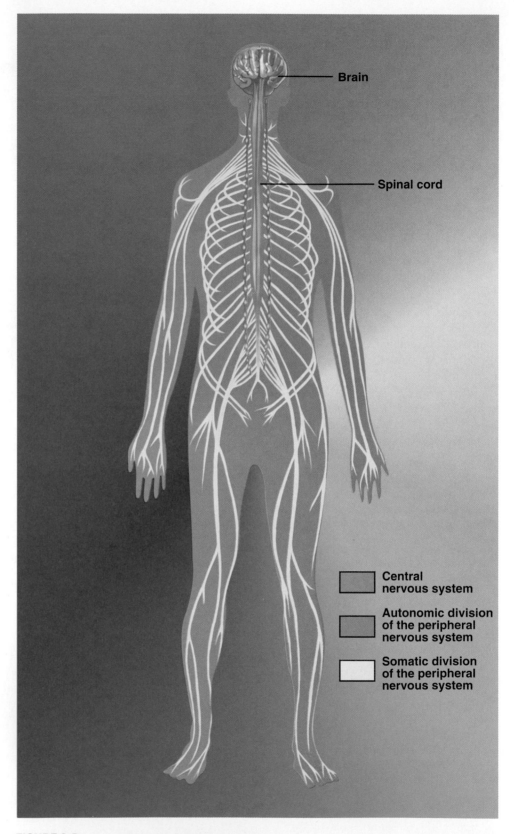

Brain

Spinal cord

Central
nervous system

Autonomic division
of the peripheral
nervous system

Somatic division
of the peripheral
nervous system

FIGURE 3.5

The Location of Parts of the Nervous System. Note that the spinal cord is protected
by a column of bones called vertebrae. The brain is protected by the skull.

The Central Nervous System

The central nervous system consists of the spinal cord and the brain.

THE SPINAL CORD. The **spinal cord** is a column of nerves about as thick as a thumb. It transmits messages from receptors to the brain and from the brain to muscles and glands throughout the body (Figure 3.5). The spinal cord is also capable of some "local government" of responses to external stimulation through **spinal reflexes.** A spinal reflex is an unlearned response to a stimulus that may involve only two neurons—a sensory (afferent) neuron and a motor (efferent) neuron (Figure 3.6). In some reflexes, a third neuron, called an **interneuron,** transmits the neural impulse from the sensory neuron through the spinal cord to the motor neuron.

The spinal cord (and the brain) consist of gray matter and white matter. The **gray matter** is composed of nonmyelinated neurons. Some of these nonmyelinated neurons are involved in spinal reflexes. Others send axons to the brain. The **white matter** is composed of bundles of longer, myelinated (and thus whitish) axons that carry messages to and from the brain. As you can see in Figure 3.6, a cross section of the spinal cord shows the gray matter, which includes cell bodies, to be distributed in a butterfly pattern.

We engage in many reflexes. We blink in response to a puff of air. We swallow when food accumulates in the mouth. A physician may tap the leg below the knee to elicit the knee-jerk reflex, a sign that the nervous system is operating adequately. Urinating and defecating are reflexes that occur in response to pressure in the bladder and the rectum. Parents spend weeks or months toilet-training infants, or teaching them to involve their brains in the process of elimination. Learning to inhibit these reflexes makes civilization possible.

Spinal cord • A column of nerves within the spine that transmits messages from sensory receptors to the brain and from the brain to muscles and glands throughout the body.

Spinal reflex • A simple, unlearned response to a stimulus that may involve only two neurons.

Interneuron • A neuron that transmits a neural impulse from a sensory neuron to a motor neuron.

Gray matter • In the spinal cord, the grayish neurons and neural segments that are involved in spinal reflexes.

White matter • In the spinal cord, axon bundles that carry messages from and to the brain.

FIGURE 3.6

The Reflex Arc. This cross section of the spinal cord shows a sensory neuron and a motor neuron, which are involved in the knee-jerk reflex. In some reflexes, interneurons link sensory and motor neurons.

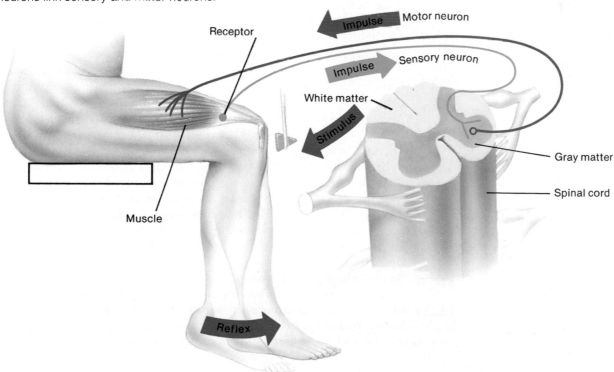

Sexual response also involves reflexes. Stimulation of the genital organs will lead to erection in the male and vaginal lubrication in the female. Both are reflexes that make sexual intercourse possible. The involuntary muscle contractions of orgasm are also reflexes. As reflexes, these processes need not involve the brain, but most often they do. Awareness of pleasurable sexual sensations in the genitals works to heighten sexual response but is not biologically required.

THE BRAIN.

> *The brain is wider than the sky,*
> *For, put them side by side,*
> *The one the other will include*
> *With ease, and you beside.*
> —Emily Dickinson

Just where is that elusive piece of business you think of as your "mind"? Thousands of years ago, it was not generally thought that the mind had a place to hang its hat within the body. It was common to assume that the body was inhabited by demons or souls that could not be explained in terms of substance. After all, if you look inside a human being, the biological structures you find do not look all that different in quality from those of many lower animals. Thus, it seemed to make sense that those qualities that made us distinctly human—such as abstract thought, poetry, science, and the composition of music—were unrelated to substances that you could see, feel, and weigh on a scale.

Ancient Egyptians attributed control of the human being to a little person, or homunculus, who dwelled within the skull and regulated our behavior. The Greek philosopher Aristotle thought that the soul set up living quarters in the heart. After all, serious injury to the heart could be said to cause the soul to take flight from the body.

MINILECTURE: METHODS IN NEUROSCIENCE RESEARCH

METHODS OF STUDYING THE BRAIN.
Today, we recognize that the mind, or consciousness, dwells essentially within the brain (Goldman-Rakic, 1995; Sperry, 1993). Our knowledge of the brain is based on a variety of accidents and research methods that are designed to allow us to discover the links between the psychological and the biological.

From injuries to the head—some of them minimal, some horrendous—we have learned that brain damage can impair consciousness and awareness. Brain damage can result in loss of vision and hearing, confusion, or loss of memory. In some cases, the loss of large portions of the brain may result in little loss of function. Ironically, the loss of sensitively located smaller portions can result in language problems, memory loss, or death.

Experiments in electrical stimulation of areas in animal and human brains (ESB) have shown that portions of the surface of the brain are associated with specific types of sensations (such as sensation of light or of a touch on the torso) or motor activities (such as movement of a leg). ESB has shown that a tiny group of structures near the center of the brain (the hypothalamus) is involved in sexual and aggressive behavior patterns. ESB has shown that a rectangular structure that rises from the back part of the brain into the forebrain (the reticular activating system) is involved in wakefulness and sleep.

Accidents have shown us how destruction of certain parts of the brain is related to behavioral changes in humans. Intentional **lesions** in the brains of laboratory animals have led to more specific knowledge. For example, lesioning one part of the limbic system causes rats and monkeys to behave gently.

Destruction of another part of the limbic system causes monkeys to rage at the slightest provocation. Destruction of yet another area of the limbic system prevents animals from forming new memories.

The **electroencephalograph** (EEG) records the electrical activity of the brain. When I was an undergraduate psychology student, I first heard that psychologists studied sleep by "connecting" people to the EEG. I had a gruesome image of people somehow being plugged in. Not so. As suggested in Figure 3.7, electrodes are simply attached to the scalp with tape or paste. Later, once the brain activity under study has been duly recorded, the electrodes are simply removed. A bit of soap and water and you're as good as new.

The EEG detects minute amounts of electrical activity—called brain waves—that pass between the electrodes. Certain brain waves are associated with feelings of relaxation and with various stages of sleep (see Chapter 5). Researchers and physicians use the EEG to locate the areas of the brain that respond to certain stimuli, such as lights or sounds, and to diagnose some kinds of abnormal behavior. The EEG also helps locate tumors.

The computer's capacity to generate images of the parts of the brain from various sources of radiation has sparked the development of imaging techniques that have been useful to researchers and physicians (Goleman, 1995; Posner & Raichle, 1994).

In one technique, **computerized axial tomography** (the CAT scan), a narrow X-ray beam is passed through the head. The amount of radiation that passes through is measured simultaneously from multiple angles (see Figure 3.8). The computer integrates these measurements into a three-dimensional view of the brain. As a result, brain damage and other abnormalities that years ago could be detected only by surgery can be displayed on a video monitor.

A second method, **positron emission tomography** (the PET scan), forms a computer-generated image of the activity of parts of the brain by tracing the

FIGURE 3.7

The Electroencephalograph. In this method of research, brain waves are detected by placing electrodes on the scalp and measuring the current that passes between them.

Lesion • (LEE-shun). An injury that results in impaired behavior or loss of a function.

Electroencephalograph • (el-eck-trow-en-SEFF-uh-lo-graf). An instrument that measures electrical activity of the brain. Abbreviated *EEG*. ("Cephalo-" derives from the Greek *kephale*, meaning "head.")

Computerized axial tomography • (AX-ee-al toe-MOG-raf-fee). Formation of a computer-generated image of the anatomical details of the brain by passing a narrow X-ray beam through the head and measuring from different angles the amount of radiation that passes through. Abbreviated *CAT scan*.

Positron emission tomography • (POZZ-i-tron). Formation of a computer-generated image of the neural activity of parts of the brain by tracing the amount of glucose used by the various parts. Abbreviated *PET scan*.

FIGURE 3.8

The Computerized Axial Tomograph (CAT) Scan. In the CAT scan, a narrow X-ray beam is passed through the head and the amount of radiation that passes through is measured simultaneously from various angles. The computer enables us to integrate these measurements into a view of the brain.

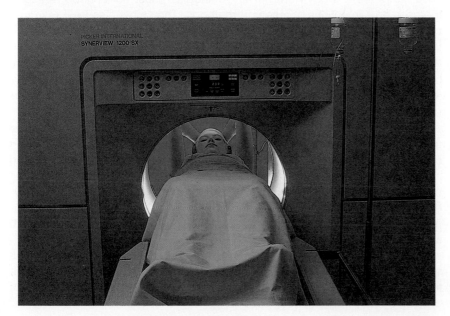

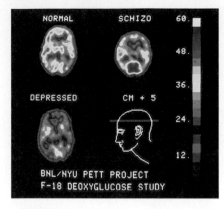

FIGURE 3.9

The Positron Emission Tomograph (PET) Scan. These PET scans of the brains of normal, schizophrenic, and depressed individuals are computer-generated images of the neural activity of parts of their brains, as formed by tracing the amount of glucose metabolized by these parts. Parts of the brain with greater neural activity metabolize more glucose. The metabolic activity ranges from low (blue) to high (red).

amount of glucose used (or metabolized) by these parts. More glucose is metabolized in the parts of the brain in which activity is greater. To trace the metabolism of glucose, a harmless amount of a radioactive compound, called a tracer, is mixed with glucose and injected into the bloodstream. When the glucose reaches the brain, the patterns of activity are revealed by measurement of the positrons—positively charged particles—that are given off by the tracer. The PET scan has been used by researchers to see which parts of the brain are most active when we are, for example, listening to music, working out a math problem, using language, or playing chess (Goldman-Rakic, 1995; "Pinpointing Chess Moves," 1994; Raichle, 1994). As shown in Figure 3.9, patterns of activity also appear to differ in the brains of normal and schizophrenic people. Researchers are exploring the meanings and potential applications of these differences.

A third imaging technique is **magnetic resonance imaging** (MRI). In MRI the person lies in a powerful magnetic field and is exposed to radio waves that cause parts of the brain to emit signals that are measured from multiple angles. The PET scan assesses brain activity in terms of metabolism of glucose. MRI relies on subtle shifts in blood flow. (More blood flows to more active parts of the brain, supplying them with oxygen.) As with the CAT scan, the signals are integrated into an anatomic image (see Figure 3.10). MRI pinpoints parts of the brain that are active when subjects engage in activities such as viewing objects of various shapes (for example, moving dots or colored stripes), pressing a lever when the name of a dangerous animal is mentioned, or reporting the first verb that comes to mind when researchers say a noun (Raichle, 1994).

Reflections

- **Agree or disagree with the following statement and support your answer: "The mind is a function of the brain."**
- Are you aware of anyone who has had her or his brain, or another part of the body, scanned by one of the techniques discussed in this section? How was the procedure described to you? Was the discussion of these methods in this section consistent with what you had heard?

The use of some research methods, such as lesioning, raise ethical issues. To properly study behavior, psychologists must not only be skilled in the uses and limitations of research methods. They must also treat research participants ethically.

FIGURE 3.10

Magnetic Resonance Imaging (MRI). This image of the brain is produced by MRI.

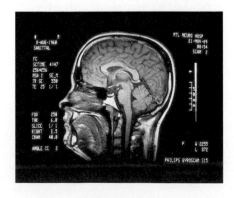

A TOUR OF THE BRAIN.   Let us look at the brain, as shown in Figure 3.11. We begin with the back of the head, where the spinal cord rises to meet the brain, and work our way forward. The lower part of the brain, or hindbrain, consists of three major structures: the medulla, the pons, and the cerebellum.

Many pathways that connect the spinal cord to higher levels of the brain pass through the **medulla.** The medulla regulates vital functions such as heart rate, blood pressure, and respiration. It also plays a role in sleep, sneezing, and coughing. The **pons** is a bulge in the hindbrain that lies forward of the medulla. *Pons* is the Latin word for "bridge," and the pons is so named because of the bundles of nerves that pass through it. The pons transmits information about body movement and is also involved in functions related to attention, sleep and alertness, and respiration.

Behind the pons lies the **cerebellum** ("little brain" in Latin). The two hemispheres of the cerebellum are involved in maintaining balance and in controlling motor (muscle) behavior. Injury to the cerebellum may lead to lack of motor coordination, stumbling, and loss of muscle tone.

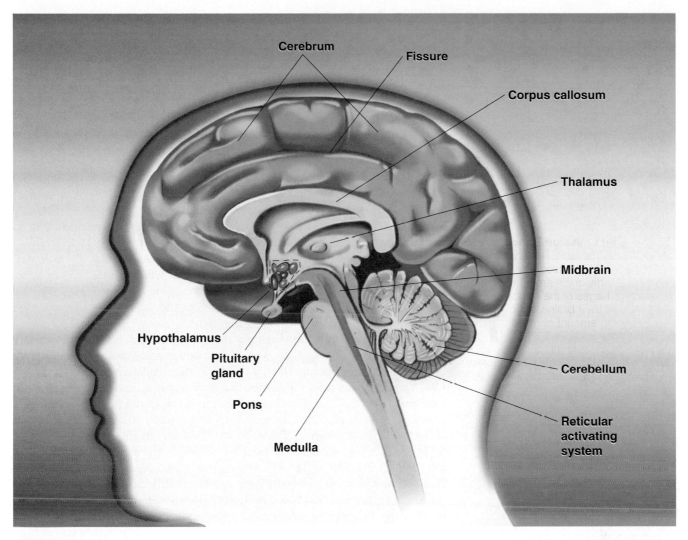

Cerebrum

Fissure

Corpus callosum

Thalamus

Midbrain

Cerebellum

Reticular activating system

Hypothalamus

Pituitary gland

Pons

Medulla

FIGURE 3.11

The Parts of the Human Brain. This view of the brain, split top to bottom, labels some of the most important structures.

The **reticular activating system** (RAS) begins in the hindbrain and ascends through the region of the midbrain into the lower part of the forebrain. The RAS is vital in the functions of attention, sleep, and arousal. Injury to the RAS may leave an animal in a coma. Stimulation of the RAS causes it to send messages to the cortex, making us more alert to sensory information. Electrical stimulation of the RAS awakens sleeping animals, and certain drugs—such as alcohol—called central-nervous-system depressants are thought to work, in part, by lowering RAS activity.

Sudden, loud noises stimulate the RAS and awaken a sleeping animal or person. But the RAS may become selective, or acquire the capacity to play a filtering role, through learning. It may allow some messages to filter through to higher brain levels and awareness while screening others out. For example, the parent who has primary responsibility for child care may be awakened by the stirring sounds of an infant. However, louder sounds of traffic or street noise are filtered out. The other parent, in contrast, may usually sleep through even loud cries. If the first parent must be away for several days, however, the

Magnetic resonance imaging • (REZZ-oh-nants). Formation of a computer-generated image of the anatomy of the brain by measuring the signals emitted when the head is placed in a strong magnetic field.

Medulla • (meh-DULL-ah). An oblong area of the hindbrain involved in regulation of heartbeat and respiration.

Pons • (ponz). A structure of the hindbrain involved in respiration, attention, and sleep and dreaming.

Cerebellum • (ser-uh-BELL-um). A part of the hindbrain involved in muscle coordination and balance.

Reticular activating system • (reh-TICK-you-lar). A part of the brain involved in attention, sleep, and arousal.

second parent's RAS may quickly acquire sensitivity to noises produced by the child. This sensitivity may rapidly fade again when the first parent returns.

Also located in the midbrain are areas involved in vision and hearing. These include the area that controls eye reflexes such as dilation of the pupils and eye movements.

Five major areas of the frontmost part of the brain, or forebrain, are the thalamus, the hypothalamus, the limbic system, the basal ganglia, and the cerebrum.

The **thalamus** is located near the center of the brain. It consists of two joined egg- or football-shaped structures. The thalamus serves as a relay station for sensory stimulation. Nerve fibers from our sensory systems enter from below. The information carried by them is then transmitted to the cerebral cortex by way of fibers that exit from above. For instance, the thalamus relays sensory input from the eyes to the visual areas of the cerebral cortex. According to neuroscientist Rodolfo Llinás, the thalamus sweeps the cerebral cortex with neural impulses every 12.5-thousandth of a second. As a result, there is synchronized firing of neurons in the cerebral cortex, which **binds** sensory information and allows us to perceive the world outside (Blakeslee, 1995a). The thalamus is also involved in controlling sleep and attention in coordination with other brain structures, including the RAS.

The **hypothalamus** lies beneath the thalamus and above the pituitary gland. It weighs only 4 grams, yet it controls the autonomic nervous system and the endocrine system. Thus, it is vital in the regulation of body temperature, the concentration of fluids, the storage of nutrients, and various aspects of motivation and emotion. Experimenters learn many of the functions of the hypothalamus by implanting electrodes in various parts of it and observing the behavioral effects when a current is switched on. In this way, it has been found that the hypothalamus is involved in hunger, thirst, sexual behavior, caring for offspring, and aggression. Among lower animals, stimulation of various areas of the hypothalamus can trigger stereotypical behaviors such as fighting, mating, or even nest building. The hypothalamus is just as important to people, but our behavior in response to messages from the hypothalamus is less stereotypical and relatively more influenced by cognitive functions such as thought, choice, and value systems.

The **limbic system** is made up of several structures, including the septum, amygdala, hippocampus, and parts of the hypothalamus (Figure 3.12). The limbic system lies along the inner edge of the cerebrum and is fully evolved in mammals only. It is involved in memory and emotion, and in the drives of hunger, sex, and aggression. People in whom operations have damaged the hippocampus can retrieve old memories but cannot permanently store new information. As a result, they may reread the same newspaper day in and day out without recalling that they have read it before. Or they may have to be perpetually reintroduced to people they have met just hours earlier (Squire, 1986). Destruction of an area within the **amygdala** leads monkeys and other mammals to show docile behavior. Destruction of the **septum** leads some mammals to respond aggressively, even with slight provocation.

The limbic system thus provides a system of "checks and balances." The amygdala and the septum appear to allow us to inhibit stereotypical behaviors that are prompted by the hypothalamus. We then have the chance to mull over situations and are less likely, when threatened, to automatically flee or attack.

The **basal ganglia** are buried beneath the cortex in front of the thalamus. The basal ganglia are involved in the control of postural movements and the

---

Thalamus • (THAL-uh-muss). An area near the center of the brain involved in the relay of sensory information to the cortex and in the functions of sleep and attention.

Bind • Integrate; piece together.

Hypothalamus • (HIGH-poe-THAL-uh-muss). A bundle of nuclei below the thalamus involved in body temperature, motivation, and emotion.

Limbic system • A group of structures involved in memory, motivation, and emotion that forms a fringe along the inner edge of the cerebrum.

Amygdala • (uh-MIG-dull-uh). A part of the limbic system that apparently facilitates stereotypical aggressive responses.

Septum • A part of the limbic system that apparently restrains stereotypical aggressive responses.

Basal ganglia • Ganglia located between the thalamus and cerebrum that are involved in motor coordination.

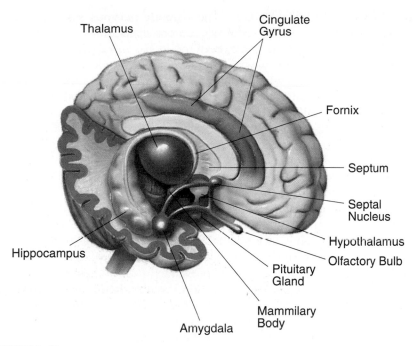

FIGURE 3.12

The Limbic System. The limbic system consists of the amygdala, hippocampus, septum and septal nuclei, fornix, cingulate gyrus, and parts of the hypothalamus.

coordination of the limbs. Most of the brain's dopamine is produced by neurons in the basal ganglia, and the degeneration of these neurons has been linked to Parkinson's disease (Rao and others, 1992). Researchers have implanted fetal neurons that produce dopamine into the brains of people with Parkinson's disease. As a result, many people regained greater control of motor functions and showed less need of L-dopa (a drug that is converted into dopamine in the body and serves as the major form of treatment of Parkinson's disease; Kolata, 1995a).

The **cerebrum** is the crowning glory of the brain. Only in human beings does the cerebrum compose such a large proportion of the brain (Figure 3.11). The surface of the cerebrum is wrinkled, or convoluted, with ridges and valleys. This surface is the **cerebral cortex.** The convolutions allow a great deal of surface area to be packed into the brain.

Valleys in the cortex are called **fissures.** A most important fissure almost divides the cerebrum in half. The hemispheres of the cerebral cortex are connected by the **corpus callosum** (Latin for "thick body" or "hard body"), a thick fiber bundle.

Cerebrum • (ser-REE-brum). The large mass of the forebrain, which consists of two hemispheres.

Cerebral cortex • (ser-REE-bral CORE-tecks). The wrinkled surface area (gray matter) of the cerebrum.

Fissures • Valleys.

Corpus callosum • (CORE-puss cal-LOSS-sum). A thick fiber bundle that connects the hemispheres of the cortex.

The Peripheral Nervous System

The peripheral nervous system consists of sensory and motor neurons that transmit messages to and from the central nervous system. Without the peripheral nervous system, our brains would be isolated from the world: They would not be able to perceive it, and they would not be able to act on it. The two main divisions of the peripheral nervous system are the somatic nervous system and the autonomic nervous system.

THE SOMATIC NERVOUS SYSTEM.   The **somatic nervous system** contains sensory (afferent) and motor (efferent) neurons. It transmits messages about sights, sounds, smells, temperature, body positions, and so on, to the central nervous system. As a result, we can experience the beauties and the horrors of the world, its physical ecstasies and agonies. Messages from the brain and spinal cord to the somatic nervous system control purposeful body movements such as raising a hand, winking, or running; breathing; and movements that we hardly attend to—movements that maintain our posture and balance.

THE AUTONOMIC NERVOUS SYSTEM.   *Autonomic* means "automatic." The **autonomic nervous system** (ANS) regulates the glands and the muscles of internal organs. Thus, the ANS controls activities such as heartbeat, respiration, digestion, and dilation of the pupils of the eyes. These activities can occur automatically, as when we are asleep. But some of them can be overridden by conscious control. You can breathe at a purposeful pace, for example. Methods like biofeedback and yoga also help people gain voluntary control of functions such as heart rate and blood pressure.

The ANS has two branches, or divisions: **sympathetic** and **parasympathetic.** These branches have largely opposing effects. Many organs and glands are stimulated by both branches of the ANS (Figure 3.13). When organs and glands are simultaneously stimulated by both divisions, their effects can average out to some degree. In general, the sympathetic division is most active during processes that involve the spending of body energy from stored reserves, such as in a fight-or-flight response to a predator or when you find out that your mortgage payment is going to be increased. The parasympathetic division is most active during processes that replenish reserves of energy, such as eating. When we are afraid, the sympathetic division of the ANS accelerates the heart rate. When we relax, it is the parasympathetic division that decelerates the heart rate. The parasympathetic division stimulates digestive processes, but the sympathetic branch inhibits digestion. Since the sympathetic division predominates when we feel fear or anxiety, fear or anxiety can cause indigestion.

Truth or Fiction Revisited.   *It is true that fear can give you indigestion.* Fear predominantly involves sympathetic activity. Digestive processes involve parasympathetic activity. Since sympathetic activity can be incompatible with parasympathetic activity, fear can be incompatible with digestion.

The ANS is of particular interest to psychologists because its activities are linked to various emotions such as anxiety and love. Some people seem to have overly reactive sympathetic nervous systems. In the absence of external threats, their bodies still respond as though they were faced with danger (see Chapter 13).

Somatic nervous system • (so-MAT-tick). The division of the peripheral nervous system that connects the central nervous system with sensory receptors, skeletal muscles, and the surface of the body.

Autonomic nervous system • (aw-toe-NOM-ick). The division of the peripheral nervous system that regulates glands and activities such as heartbeat, respiration, digestion, and dilation of the pupils. Abbreviated *ANS.*

Sympathetic • The branch of the ANS that is most active during emotional responses such as fear and anxiety that spend the body's reserves of energy.

Parasympathetic • The branch of the ANS that is most active during processes such as digestion that restore the body's reserves of energy.

Reflections

- Does it seem possible that sexual arousal and orgasm are reflexes? How do you account for the fact that you can dwell on erotic ideas and thus cause sexual reflexes to occur?

- Before taking this course, you had doubtless heard of "nerves." How do the true definitions of *neurons* and *nerves* correspond to your earlier ideas?

- Dopamine-producing neurons have been taken from the brains of aborted fetuses and implanted in the brains of people with Parkinson's disease, leading to greater control of motor functions. Do you believe that it is proper to use tissue from electively aborted fetuses in this way? Why or why not?

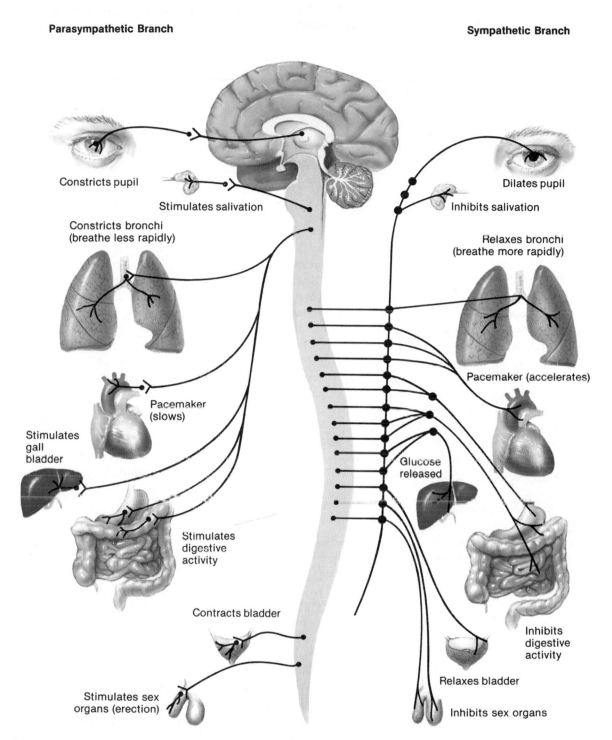

Parasympathetic Branch

Sympathetic Branch

Constricts pupil

Dilates pupil

Stimulates salivation

Inhibits salivation

Constricts bronchi
(breathe less rapidly)

Relaxes bronchi
(breathe more rapidly)

Pacemaker
(slows)

Pacemaker (accelerates)

Stimulates
gall
bladder

Glucose
released

Stimulates
digestive
activity

Inhibits
digestive
activity

Contracts bladder

Relaxes bladder

Stimulates sex
organs (erection)

Inhibits sex organs

FIGURE 3.13

**The Activities of the Two Branches of the Autonomic Nervous System
(ANS).** The parasympathetic branch of the ANS generally acts to replenish
stores of energy in the body. It is connected to organs by nerves that originate
near the top and bottom of the spinal cord. The sympathetic branch is most active during activities that expend energy. Its neurons collect in clusters or chains
of ganglia along the central portion of the spinal cord.

- Have you ever lost your appetite, been unable to eat, or thrown up because of anxiety or fear? What biological processes led fear to cause indigestion in you?

THE CEREBRAL CORTEX

Sensation and muscle activity involve many parts of the nervous system. The essential human activities of thought and language, however, involve the hemispheres of the cerebral cortex.

The Geography of the Cerebral Cortex

Each of the two hemispheres of the cerebral cortex is divided into four parts, or lobes, as shown in Figure 3.14. The **frontal lobe** lies in front of the central fissure, and the **parietal lobe** lies behind it. The **temporal lobe** lies below the side, or lateral, fissure, across from the frontal and parietal lobes. The **occipital lobe** lies behind the temporal lobe and behind and below the parietal lobe.

When light strikes the retinas of the eyes, neurons in the occipital lobe fire, and we "see." Direct artificial stimulation of the occipital lobe also produces visual sensations. You would "see" flashes of light if neurons in the occipital region of the cortex were stimulated with electricity, even if it were pitch black or your eyes were covered. The hearing or auditory area of the cortex lies in the temporal lobe along the lateral fissure. Sounds cause structures in the ear to vibrate (see Chapter 4). Messages are relayed to the auditory area of the cortex. When you hear a noise, neurons in this area are firing.

Just behind the central fissure in the parietal lobe lies an area of **somatosensory cortex,** in which the messages received from skin senses all over the body are projected. These sensations include warmth and cold, touch, pain, and movement. Neurons in different parts of the sensory cortex fire, depending on whether you wiggle your finger or raise your leg. If a brain surgeon were to stimulate the proper area of your somatosensory cortex with a small probe known as a "pencil electrode," it might seem as if someone were touching your arm or leg.

Truth or Fiction Revisited. *It is true that if a surgeon were to stimulate a certain part of your brain electrically, you might swear in court that someone had stroked your leg.* It might seem as though someone had stroked your leg.

Figure 3.14 suggests how our faces and heads are overrepresented on this cortex as compared with, say, our trunks and legs. This overrepresentation is one of the reasons that our faces and heads are more sensitive to touch than other parts of the body.

People with injuries to one hemisphere of the brain show sensory or motor deficits on the opposite side of the body. Sensory and motor nerves cross in the brain and elsewhere. The left hemisphere controls functions on, and receives inputs from, the right side of the body. The right hemisphere controls functions on, and receives inputs from, the left side of the body.

The **motor cortex** lies in the frontal lobe, just across the valley of the central fissure from the somatosensory cortex. Neurons in the motor cortex fire when we move certain parts of our body. If a surgeon were to stimulate a certain area of the right hemisphere of the motor cortex with a pencil electrode, you would raise your left leg. Raising the leg would be sensed in the somatosensory cortex, and you might have a devil of a time trying to figure out whether you had "intended" to raise that leg!

Frontal lobe • The lobe of the cerebral cortex that lies to the front of the central fissure.

Parietal lobe • (par-EYE-uh-tal). The lobe that lies just behind the central fissure.

Temporal lobe • The lobe that lies below the lateral fissure, near the temples of the head.

Occipital lobe • (ox-SIP-it-all). The lobe that lies behind and below the parietal lobe and behind the temporal lobe.

Somatosensory cortex • (so-mat-toe-SENSE-or-ree). The section of cortex in which sensory stimulation is projected. It lies just behind the central fissure in the parietal lobe.

Motor cortex • The section of cortex that lies in the frontal lobe, just across the central fissure from the sensory cortex. Neural impulses in the motor cortex are linked to muscular responses throughout the body.

MINILECTURE:
THE STRUCTURE OF
THE BRAIN

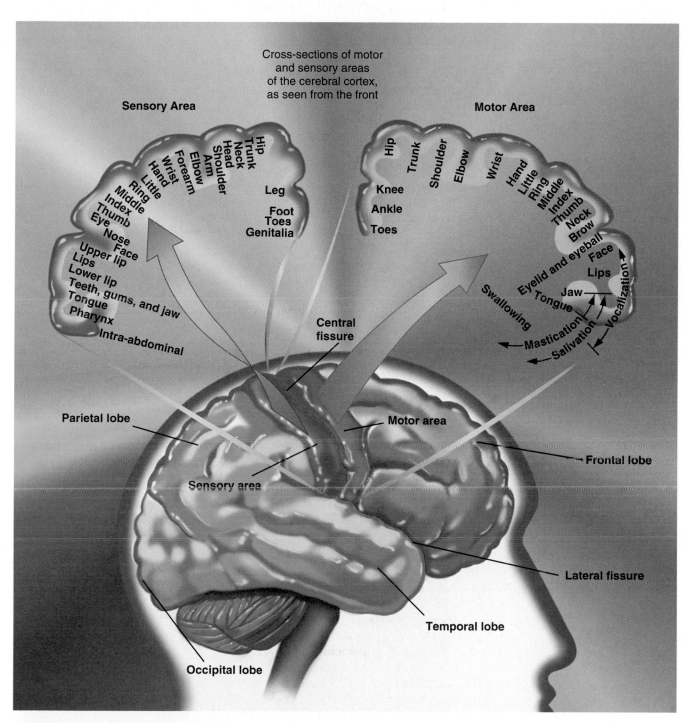

FIGURE 3.14

The Geography of the Cerebral Cortex. The cortex is divided into four lobes: frontal, parietal, temporal, and occipital. The visual area of the cortex is located in the occipital lobe. The hearing or auditory cortex lies in the temporal lobe. The sensory and motor areas face each other across the central fissure. What happens when a surgeon stimulates areas of the sensory or motor cortex during an operation?

Thought, Language, and the Cortex

Areas of the cerebral cortex that are not primarily involved in sensation or motor activity are called **association areas.** They make possible the breadth and depth of human learning, thought, memory, and language. The frontal region of the brain, near the forehead, appears to be the brain's executive center (Goldman-Rakic, 1995). This is apparently where we make plans and decisions.

Areas in the frontal lobes are involved in the memory functions required for problem solving and decision making (Goldman-Rakic, 1992; Goleman, 1995b). These areas are connected with different sensory areas and thus tap different kinds of sensory information. They retrieve visual, auditory, and other kinds of memories and manipulate them—similar to the way in which a computer retrieves information from files in storage and manipulates it in working memory (Hilts, 1995).

It is essential that we integrate sensory information. Certain neurons in the visual area of the occipital lobe fire in response to the visual presentation of vertical lines. Others fire in response to presentation of horizontal lines. Although one group of cells may respond to one aspect of the visual field and another group of cells may respond to another, association areas put it all together. As a result, we see a box or an automobile or a road map and not a confusing array of verticals and horizontals.

LANGUAGE FUNCTIONS.   In some ways, the left and right hemispheres of the brain duplicate each other's functions. In other ways, they are very different. The left hemisphere contains language functions for nearly all (97%) right-handed people (Pinker, 1994a). For two of three left-handed people (68%), the

Association areas • Areas of the cortex involved in learning, thought, memory, and language.

FIGURE 3.15

Broca's and Wernicke's Areas of the Cerebral Cortex. Areas of the dominant hemisphere most involved in speech are Broca's area and Wernicke's area. Damage to either area can produce an aphasia—that is, a disruption of the ability to understand or produce language.

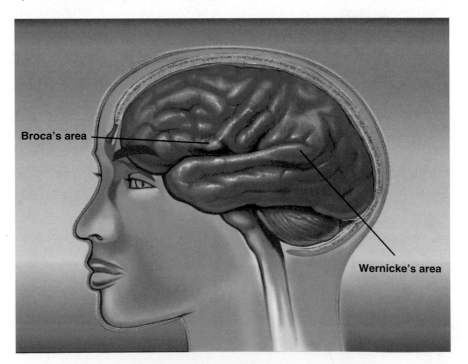

Broca's area

Wernicke's area

left hemisphere also contains language functions. The right hemisphere contains language functions for about one left-handed person in five (19%). Sensory pathways cross over in the brain. Thus, dominance of the left hemisphere is associated with dominance of the right ear, and vice versa.

Within the dominant (usually left) hemisphere of the cortex, two key language areas are Broca's area and Wernicke's area (see Figure 3.15). Damage to either area is likely to cause an **aphasia**—that is, a disruption of the ability to understand or produce language.

Wernicke's area lies in the temporal lobe near the auditory cortex. This area integrates auditory and visual information (Raichle, 1994). People with damage to Wernicke's area may show **Wernicke's aphasia,** which impairs their abilities to comprehend speech and to think of the proper words to express their own thoughts. Ironically, they usually speak freely and with proper syntax. Wernicke's area is thus essential to understanding the relationships between words and their meanings.

Broca's area is located in the frontal lobe, near the section of the motor cortex that controls the muscles of the tongue and throat and of other areas of the face that are used when speaking (Pinker, 1994a; Raichle, 1994). Broca's area and Wernicke's area are connected by nerve fibers. When Broca's area is damaged, people speak slowly and laboriously, with simple sentences. The pattern is termed **Broca's aphasia.**

Left Brain, Right Brain?

In recent years, it has become popular to speak of people as being "left-brained" or "right-brained." The notion is that the hemispheres of the brain are involved in very different kinds of intellectual and emotional functions and responses, along the lines suggested in Figure 3.16. According to this view,

FIGURE 3.16

Some of the "Specializations" of the Left and Right Hemispheres of the Cerebral Cortex. This cartoon exaggerates the "left brain–right brain" notion. The dominant (usually left) hemisphere is somewhat more involved in intellectual undertakings that require logic and problem solving. The nondominant (usually right) hemisphere is relatively more concerned with decoding visual information, aesthetic and emotional responses, and imagination. However, the functions of the hemispheres overlap.

Aphasia • (uh-FAY-she-uh). Impaired ability to comprehend or express oneself through language.

Wernicke's aphasia • (WER-nick-key). A language disorder characterized by difficulty comprehending the meaning of spoken language.

Broca's aphasia • A language disorder characterized by slow, laborious speech.

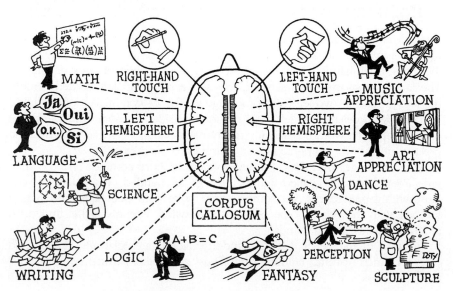

left-brained people would be primarily logical and intellectual. Right-brained people would be intuitive, creative, and emotional. Those of us fortunate enough to have our brains "in balance" would presumably have the best of it—the capacity for logic combined with emotional richness.

Like so many other popular ideas, the left-brain–right-brain notion is at best exaggerated. Research does suggest that in right-handed individuals, the left hemisphere is relatively more involved in intellectual undertakings that require logical analysis and problem solving, language, and mathematical computation (Borod, 1992; Hellige, 1990). The nondominant (usually right) hemisphere is relatively more concerned with spatial functions, aesthetic and emotional responses, imagination, understanding metaphors, and creative mathematical reasoning.

Despite these differences, however, it would be erroneous to think that the hemispheres of the brain act independently—that some people are truly left-brained and others, right-brained (Hellige, 1990). The functions of the left and right hemispheres overlap to some degree, and the hemispheres tend to respond simultaneously as we focus our attention on one thing or another. The hemispheres are aided in their "cooperation" by myelination of the corpus callosum, the bundle of nerve fibers that connects them. Myelination of the corpus callosum proceeds rapidly during early and middle childhood and is largely complete by the age of 8. By that time, we apparently have greater ability to integrate logical and emotional functioning.

We can summarize left-brain and right-brain similarities and differences as follows (Hellige, 1990):

1. The hemispheres are similar enough that each can function quite well independently but not as well as they function in normal combined usage.
2. For the great majority of people, the left hemisphere plays a special role in language. The right hemisphere seems to play a special role in emotional response.
3. Both hemispheres are involved in logic.
4. Creativity and intuition are not confined to the right hemisphere.
5. Both hemispheres are educated at the same time, even when instruction is intended to "appeal" to the right hemisphere (as in music) or the left (in a logic class).

Handedness: Is It Gauche to Be Left-Handed?

What do Michelangelo, Leonardo da Vinci, Pablo Picasso, and Steve Young all have in common? No, they are not all artists. Only one is a football player. But they are all left-handed. Yet, being a lefty is often looked on as a deficiency. The language swarms with slurs on lefties. We speak of "left-handed compliments," of having "two left feet," of strange events as "coming out of left field." The word *sinister* means "left-hand or unlucky side" in Latin. *Gauche,* moreover, is a French word that literally means "left." Compare these usages to the positive phrases "being righteous" or "being on one's right side."

Yet, 10% of us are lefties. Left-handedness is more common in boys than girls. We are usually labeled right-handed or left-handed on the basis of our handwriting preferences, yet some people write with one hand and pass a football with the other. Some people even swing a tennis racket and pitch a baseball with different hands.

Because of the belief that left-handed children are relatively clumsy and more inclined toward reading disabilities and other academic problems,

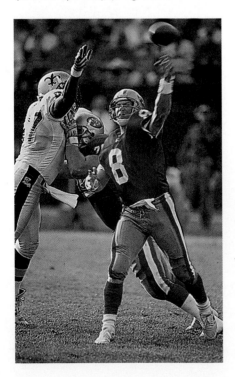

Left-Handed San Francisco 49ers Quarterback Steve Young Passes a Football. Is it gauche to be left-handed, or are lefties as competent (or incompetent) as righties?

left-handed children were once encouraged to switch to writing with their right hands. Yet, research suggests that the stereotype of left-handed children may be off base.

One study (Tan, 1985), for example, examined the relationship between preschoolers' handedness and their motor coordination. Tan found no differences in motor skills between lefties and righties. She concluded that lefties may be regarded as less well-coordinated than righties because their movements *look* so different.

What of the academic competence of lefties? There are some reports of problems, but they are sketchy. Yet, 20% of a group of several hundred mathematically gifted 12- and 13-year-olds were lefties, as compared with 10% of the general population (Benbow & Stanley, 1980, 1983).

In our discussion of the nervous system, we have described naturally occurring chemical substances that facilitate or inhibit the transmission of neural messages—neurotransmitters. Let us now turn our attention to other naturally occurring chemical substances that influence behavior—hormones. We shall see that some hormones also function as neurotransmitters.

Reflections

- As you read the words on this page, neurons in your brain are firing. Where are the neurons whose firing results in your seeing the words?
- **Agree or disagree with the following statement and support your answer: "Some people are left-brained, and other people are right-brained."**
- Would you consider yourself to be more "left-brained" or "right-brained"? Why?

THE ENDOCRINE SYSTEM

Pituitary gland • (pit-TOO-it-tar-ree). The gland that secretes growth hormone, prolactin, antidiuretic hormone, and others.

Here are some things you may have heard about hormones and behavior. Are they truth or fiction?

____ Some overweight people actually eat very little, and their excess weight is caused by "glands."

____ Injections of growth hormone have reversed some of the effects of aging in men in their 60s and 70s.

____ A woman who becomes anxious and depressed just before menstruating is suffering from "raging hormones."

____ Women who "pump iron" frequently use hormones to achieve the muscle definition that is needed to win bodybuilding contests.

____ People who receive injections of adrenaline may report that they feel as if they are about to experience some emotion, but they're not sure which one.

Let us consider each of these items. Some overweight people do eat relatively little but are "sabotaged" in their weight-loss efforts by hormonal changes that lower the rates at which they metabolize food (Brownell & Wadden, 1992). A synthetic version of growth hormone, which is normally secreted by the **pituitary gland,** has helped many older people gain muscle, shed fat, and thicken the bone in their spines (Rudman and others, 1990). Women may become somewhat more anxious or depressed at the time of menstruation, but the effects of hormones have been exaggerated. Moreover, women's response to menstruation reflects social attitudes as well as biological changes. Many top women (and men) bodybuilders do use **steroids** (hormones that are produced by the **adrenal cortex**) and growth hormone to achieve muscle mass and definition. Steroids and growth hormone promote resistance to stress and muscle growth in both genders. Finally, adrenaline, a hormone produced by the **adrenal medulla,** does generally arouse people and heighten general emotional responsiveness. The emotion to which this arousal is attributed depends in part on the person's situation (see Chapter 10).

The body contains two types of glands: glands with **ducts** and glands without ducts. A duct is a passageway that carries substances to specific locations. Saliva, sweat, tears (the name of a new rock group?), and milk all reach their destinations by means of ducts. Psychologists are interested in the substances secreted by ductless glands because of their behavioral effects (see the summary in Table 3.1). The ductless glands constitute the **endocrine system** of the body, and they secrete **hormones** (from the Greek *horman,* meaning "to stimulate" or "to excite").

Hormones are released directly into the bloodstream. As is the case with neurotransmitters,[2] hormones have specific receptor sites. Although they are poured into the bloodstream and circulate throughout the body, they act only on hormone receptors in certain locations. Some hormones released by the hypothalamus influence only the pituitary gland. Some hormones released by the pituitary influence the adrenal cortex, others influence the testes and ovaries, and so on.

THE HYPOTHALAMUS. The hypothalamus secretes a number of releasing hormones, or factors, that influence the anterior (front) lobe of the pituitary gland to secrete corresponding hormones. A dense network of blood vessels between the hypothalamus and the pituitary gland provides a direct route of influence.

THE PITUITARY GLAND. The pituitary gland lies just below the hypothalamus (see Figure 3.17). It is about the size of a pea, but it is so central to the body's functioning that it has been referred to as the "master gland."

Much hormonal action helps the body maintain steady states, as in fluid levels, blood sugar levels, and so on. Bodily mechanisms measure current levels and signal glands to release hormones when these levels deviate from optimal. The maintenance of steady states requires the feedback of bodily information to glands. This type of system is referred to as a **negative feedback** loop. That is, when enough of a hormone has been secreted, the gland is signaled to stop. With a negative feedback system in effect, even the master gland must serve a master—the hypothalamus. In turn, the hypothalamus responds to information from the body.

Prolactin largely regulates maternal behavior in lower mammals such as rats and stimulates production of milk in women. As a water-conservation measure, **antidiuretic hormone** (ADH) inhibits production of urine when fluid levels in the body are low. ADH is also connected with stereotypical paternal behavior patterns in some mammals (Insel, 1993). For example, it transforms a naive male prairie vole (a mouselike rodent) into an affectionate and protective mate and father. **Oxytocin** stimulates labor in pregnant women and is connected with maternal behavior patterns (cuddling and caring for young) in some mammals (Carter, 1993). Obstetricians may induce labor or increase the strength of uterine contractions during labor by injecting pregnant

Steroids • A family of hormones that includes testosterone, estrogen, progesterone, and corticosteroids.

Adrenal cortex • (ad-DREE-nal). The outer part of the adrenal glands located above the kidneys. It produces steroids.

Adrenal medulla • The inner part of the adrenal glands that produces adrenaline.

Duct • Passageway.

Endocrine system • (END-oh-krinn). Ductless glands that secrete hormones and release them directly into the bloodstream.

Hormone • A substance secreted by an endocrine gland that regulates various body functions.

Negative feedback • Descriptive of a system in which information that a quantity (e.g., of a hormone) has reached a set point suspends action of the agency (e.g., a gland) that gives rise to that quantity.

Prolactin • (pro-LACK-tin). A pituitary hormone that regulates production of milk and, in lower animals, maternal behavior.

Antidiuretic hormone • A pituitary hormone that conserves body fluids by increasing reabsorption of urine and is connected with paternal behavior in some mammals. Also called *vasopressin*.

Oxytocin • (OX-see-TOE-sin). A pituitary hormone that stimulates labor and lactation.

---

[2] Recall that some hormones, such as noradrenaline, also function as neurotransmitters.

TABLE 3.1
AN OVERVIEW OF SOME MAJOR GLANDS
OF THE ENDOCRINE SYSTEM

GLAND	HORMONE	MAJOR EFFECTS
Hypothalamus	Growth-hormone releasing factor	Causes pituitary gland to secrete growth hormone
	Corticotrophin-releasing hormone	Causes pituitary gland to secrete adrenocorticotrophic hormone
	Thyrotropin-releasing hormone	Causes pituitary gland to secrete thyrotropin
	Gonadotropin-releasing hormone	Causes pituitary gland to secrete follicle-stimulating hormone and luteinizing hormone
	Prolactin-releasing hormone	Causes pituitary gland to secrete prolactin
Pituitary		
Anterior Lobe	Growth hormone	Causes growth of muscles, bones, and glands
	Adrenocorticotrophic hormone (ACTH)	Regulates adrenal cortex
	Thyrotrophin	Causes thyroid gland to secrete thyroxin
	Follicle-stimulating hormone	Causes formation of sperm and egg cells
	Luteinizing hormone	Causes ovulation, maturation of sperm and egg cells
	Prolactin	Stimulates production of milk
Posterior Lobe	Antidiuretic hormone (ADH)	Inhibits production of urine
	Oxytocin	Stimulates uterine contractions during delivery and ejection of milk during nursing
Pancreas	Insulin	Enables body to metabolize sugar; regulates storage of fats
Thyroid	Thyroxin	Increases metabolic rate
Adrenal		
Cortex	Steroids (e.g., cortisol)	Increase resistance to stress; regulate carbohydrate metabolism
Medulla	Adrenaline (epinephrine)	Increases metabolic activity (heart and respiration rates, blood sugar level, etc.)
	Noradrenaline (norepinephrine)	Raises blood pressure; acts as neurotransmitter
Testes	Testosterone	Promotes growth of male sex characteristics
Ovaries	Estrogen	Regulates menstrual cycle
	Progesterone	Promotes growth of female reproductive tissues; maintains pregnancy
Uterus	(Several)	Maintain pregnancy

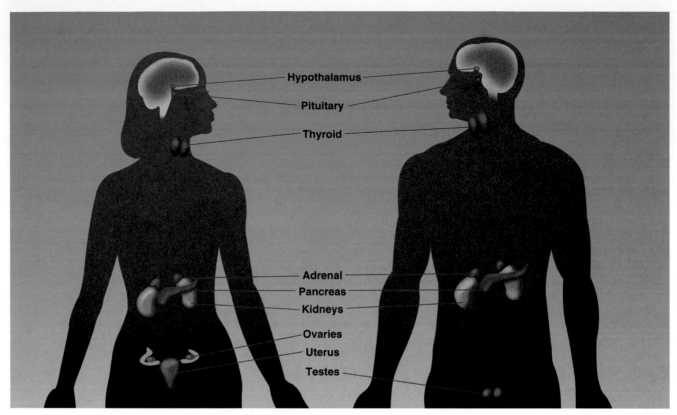

FIGURE 3.17

Major Glands of the Endocrine System. The hypothalamus is a structure of the brain. Since it secretes hormones, however, it is also an endocrine gland.

Syndrome • (SIN-drome). A cluster of symptoms characteristic of a disorder.

Corticosteroids • (CORE-tick-oh-STAIR-oids). Steroids produced by the adrenal cortex that regulate carbohydrate metabolism and increase resistance to stress by fighting inflammation and allergic reactions. Also called *cortical steroids.*

Cortisol • (CORE-tee-sol). A hormone (steroid) produced by the adrenal cortex that helps the body cope with stress by counteracting inflammation and allergic reactions.

women with oxytocin. During nursing, stimulation of nerve endings in and around the nipple sends messages to the brain that cause oxytocin to be secreted. Oxytocin then causes contractile cells in the breast to eject milk.

THE PANCREAS.   Endocrine cells within the pancreas regulate the level of sugar in the blood and the urine through *insulin* and other hormones. One form of diabetes (diabetes mellitus) is characterized by excess sugar in the blood—*hyperglycemia*—and in the urine, a life-threatening condition. Diabetes stems from inadequate secretion or utilization of insulin. People who do not secrete enough insulin of their own may need to inject this hormone daily to control diabetes.

The condition *hypoglycemia* is characterized by too little sugar in the blood. Symptoms of hypoglycemia include shakiness, dizziness, and lack of energy, a **syndrome** that is easily confused with anxiety. Many people have sought help for anxiety and learned through a series of blood tests that they are actually suffering from hypoglycemia. This disorder is generally controlled through dietary restrictions.

THE ADRENAL GLANDS.   The adrenal glands, located above the kidneys, have an outer layer, or cortex, and an inner core, or medulla. The adrenal cortex is regulated by pituitary ACTH. The cortex secretes as many as 20 different hormones known as **corticosteroids,** or cortical steroids. Cortical steroids (**cortisol** is one) increase resistance to stress; promote muscle development;

and cause the liver to release stored sugar, making energy available for emergencies.

Anabolic steroids (synthetic versions of the male sex hormone testosterone) have been used, sometimes in tandem with growth hormone, to enhance athletic prowess. Steroids stoke the muscle mass, heighten resistance to stress, and increase the body's energy supply by signaling the liver to release sugar into the bloodstream. Steroids also spur the sex drive. On a psychological level, they boost self-esteem. Steroids are generally outlawed in amateur and professional sports, although they can be prescribed by any physician. When an athlete's physician is uncooperative, steroids are readily available through illicit sources known to many team members.

The lure of steroids is understandable. Sometimes the difference between an acceptable athletic performance and a great one is rather small. Thousands of athletes try to make it in the big leagues, and the "edge" offered by steroids—even if minor—can spell the difference between a fumbling attempt and success.

If steroids help, why the fuss? Some of it is related to the ethics of competition—the notion that all athletes should "play fair." Part of it is related to the fact that steroid use is linked to liver damage and other medical problems. In addition, a number of athletes who have used growth hormone in combination with steroids, like nine-time world-champion weight lifter Larry Pacifico, have developed cardiovascular disorders such as blocked arteries. Steroids may also cause sleep disturbances and, when discontinued, depression and apathy. Moreover, the effects of long-term use remain unknown.

Adrenaline and noradrenaline are secreted by the adrenal medulla. **Adrenaline,** also known as epinephrine, is manufactured exclusively by the adrenal glands, but noradrenaline (norepinephrine) is also produced elsewhere in the body. The sympathetic branch of the autonomic nervous system causes the adrenal medulla to release a mixture of adrenaline and noradrenaline that helps arouse the body in preparation for coping with threats and stress. Adrenaline is of interest to psychologists because of its emotional, as well as physiological, effects. Adrenaline may intensify most emotions and is crucial to the experience of fear and anxiety. Noradrenaline raises the blood pressure and, in the nervous system, it acts as a neurotransmitter.

THE TESTES AND THE OVARIES. Did you know that if it were not for the secretion of the male sex hormone **testosterone** about 6 weeks after conception, we would all develop into females? Testosterone is produced by the testes and, in smaller amounts, by the ovaries and adrenal glands. A few weeks after conception, testosterone stimulates prenatal differentiation of male sex organs. (The quantities produced by the ovaries and adrenal glands are normally insufficient to foster development of male sex organs.)

During puberty, testosterone stokes the growth of muscle and bone and the development of primary and secondary sex characteristics. **Primary sex characteristics** such as the growth of the penis and the sperm-producing ability of the testes are directly involved in reproduction. **Secondary sex characteristics** such as growth of the beard and deepening of the voice differentiate males and females but are not directly involved in reproduction.

The ovaries produce **estrogen** and **progesterone.** (Estrogen is also produced in smaller amounts by the testes.) Estrogen is a generic name for several female sex hormones that foster female reproductive capacity and secondary sex characteristics such as accumulation of fat in the breasts and hips. Progesterone also has multiple functions. It stimulates growth of the female reproductive organs and maintains pregnancy.

Adrenaline • (ad-RENN-uh-lin). A hormone produced by the adrenal medulla that stimulates sympathetic ANS activity. Also called *epinephrine.*

Testosterone • (tess-TOSS-ter-own). A male sex hormone produced by the testes that promotes growth of male sexual characteristics and sperm.

Primary sex characteristics • Physical traits that distinguish males from females and are directly involved in reproduction.

Secondary sex characteristics • Physical traits that differentiate males from females but are not directly involved in reproduction.

Estrogen • (ESS-trow-jen). A generic term for several female sex hormones that promote growth of female sex characteristics and regulate the menstrual cycle.

Progesterone • (pro-JESS-ter-own). A female sex hormone that promotes growth of the sex organs and helps maintain pregnancy.

Testosterone and estrogen are connected with feelings of psychological well-being and also delay some effects of aging, such as wrinkled skin. Testosterone levels remain fairly stable. Estrogen and progesterone levels vary markedly and regulate the menstrual cycle. Following menstruation—the monthly sloughing off of the inner lining of the uterus—estrogen levels increase, leading to the development of an ovum (egg cell) and growth of the inner lining of the uterus. The ovum is released by the ovary when estrogens reach peak blood levels. Then, the inner lining of the uterus thickens in response to secretion of progesterone, gaining the capacity to support an embryo if fertilization should occur. If the ovum is not fertilized, estrogen and progesterone levels drop suddenly, triggering menstruation once more.

Reflections

- Do you know of anyone with hormonal problems? What are they? Do they result from excesses of, or deficiencies in, any of the hormones discussed in this section?

- Have you heard of athletes who were using steroids? What were the effects of the hormones?

- What hormones are involved in reproductive behavior? Has someone you know of been given any of these hormones by a physician? For what reason?

- Why do you think that psychologists are particularly interested in adrelanine and noradrenaline?

HEREDITY: THE NATURE OF NATURE

Consider some of the facts of life:

- People cannot breathe underwater (without special equipment).
- People cannot fly (again, without rather special equipment).
- Fish cannot learn to speak French or do an Irish jig even if you rear them in enriched environments and send them to finishing school (which is why we look for tuna that tastes good, not for tuna with good taste).
- Chimpanzees and gorillas can use sign language but cannot speak.

People cannot breathe underwater or fly (without oxygen tanks, airplanes, or other devices) because of their **heredity**—that is, their basic nature, as defined by the biological structures and processes they have inherited. Fish are similarly limited by the natural traits and characteristics that have been passed down from one generation to another. Because of their heredity, fish cannot speak French or do a jig. Chimpanzees and gorillas can understand many spoken words and express some concepts through nonverbal symbol systems such as American Sign Language. However, apes show no ability to speak, even though they can make sounds. They have probably failed to inherit the humanlike speech areas of the cerebral cortex. Their nature differs from ours.

Genetics are fundamental in the transmission of physical traits such as height, hair texture, and eye color. Animals can be selectively bred to enhance desired physical and psychological traits. We breed our cattle and chickens to be bigger and fatter so that they provide more food calories for less feed. We selectively breed animals to enhance psychological traits such as aggressiveness and intelligence. For example, poodles are relatively intelligent. Golden retrievers are gentle and patient with children. Border collies show a strong

---

Heredity • The transmission of traits from one generation to another through genes.

Genetics • (jen-NET-ticks). The branch of biology that studies heredity.

Behavior genetics • The study of the genetic transmission of structures and traits that give rise to behavior.

Extroversion • A trait in which a person directs his or her interest to persons and things outside the self. Sociability.

Neuroticism • A trait in which a person is given to emotional instability, anxiety, feelings of foreboding, inhibition of impulses, and avoidance behavior.

Genes • (jeans). The basic building blocks of heredity, which consist of DNA.

Chromosomes • (CROW-moe-soams). Structures consisting of genes that are found in the nuclei of the body's cells.

Sex chromosomes • The 23rd pair of chromosomes, which determine whether a child will be male or female.

herding instinct (Rosenthal, 1991). Even as puppies, Border collies will attempt to corral people who are out on a stroll.

The structures and processes we inherit at the same time make our behaviors possible and place limits on them (Kimble, 1989). The field within the science of biology that studies heredity is called **genetics. Behavior genetics** is a specialty that bridges the sciences of psychology and biology. It is concerned with the transmission of structures and traits that give rise to patterns of behavior.

Heredity also plays a role in the determination of human psychological traits (Rose, 1995). Examples include **extroversion** and **neuroticism,** shyness, social dominance, aggressiveness, leadership, effectiveness as a parent or a therapist, even an interest in arts and crafts (Carey & DiLalla, 1994; Goldsmith, 1993; Lykken and others, 1992). Genetic influences are also implicated in most psychological disorders, including anxiety and depression, schizophrenia, bipolar disorder, alcoholism, even criminal behavior (Rose, 1995). However, most behavior patterns also reflect life experiences and personal choice (Rose, 1995).

Genes and Chromosomes

Genes are the building blocks of heredity. They are the biochemical materials that regulate the development of traits. Some traits, such as blood type, are controlled by a single pair of genes. (One gene is derived from each parent.) Other traits are determined by combinations of genes. The inherited component of complex psychological traits, such as intelligence, is believed to be determined by combinations of genes (Solomon and others, 1993). We have about 100,000 genes in every cell in our bodies. Genes are segments of chromosomes.

Chromosomes each consist of more than 1,000 genes. Chromosomes are large, complex molecules of deoxyribonucleic acid, which has several chemical components. You can breathe a sigh of relief, for this acid is usually referred to simply as DNA. The tightly wound structure of DNA was first demonstrated in the 1950s by James Watson and Francis Crick (1958). DNA takes the form of a double helix, a sort of twisting ladder (see Figure 3.18). In all living things, from one-celled animals, to fish, to people, the sides of the ladder consist of alternating segments of phosphate (P) and a simple sugar (S). The "rungs" of the ladder are attached to the sugars and consist of one of two pairs of bases, either *adenine* with *thymine* (A with T) or *cytosine* with *guanine* (C with G). A single gene can contain hundreds of thousands of base pairs. The sequence of the rungs is the genetic code that will cause the unfolding organism to grow arms or wings, skin or scales.

We receive 23 chromosomes from our fathers' sperm cells and 23 chromosomes from our mothers' egg cells (ova). When a sperm cell fertilizes an ovum, the chromosomes form 23 pairs (Figure 3.19). The 23rd pair consists of **sex chromosomes,** which determine whether we are female or male. We all receive an X sex chromosome (so called because of the "X" shape) from our mothers. If we also receive an X sex chromosome from our fathers, we develop into females. If we receive a Y sex chromosome (named after the "Y" shape) from our fathers, we develop into males.

Gender is not determined by sex chromosomes throughout the animal kingdom. Reptiles such as crocodiles do not have sex chromosomes, for example. The crocodile's gender is determined by the temperature at which the egg

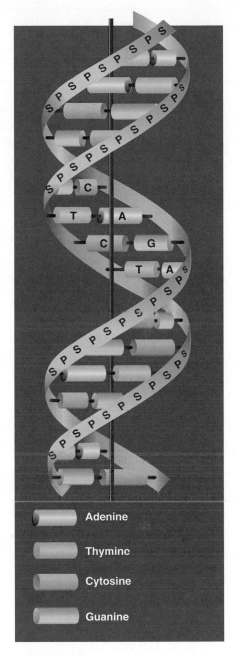

Adenine

Thymine

Cytosine

Guanine

FIGURE 3.18
The Double Helix of DNA.

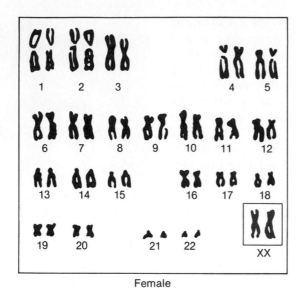

Female

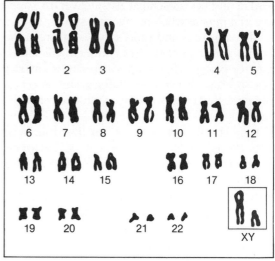

Male

FIGURE 3.19

The 23 Pairs of Human Chromosomes. People normally have 23 pairs of chromosomes. Whether one is female or male is determined by the 23rd pair of chromosomes. Females have two X sex chromosomes (left). Males have an X and a Y sex chromosome (right).

**MINILECTURE:
GENETIC
ABNORMALITIES**

develops (Crews, 1994). Some like it hot. That is, hatchlings are usually male when the eggs develop in the mid-90s Fahrenheit or above. Some like it . . . well, not cold perhaps, but certainly cooler. When crocodile eggs develop below the mid-80s Fahrenheit, the hatchlings are usually female.[3]

Truth or Fiction Revisited. *It is true that zookeepers who want to have baby girls or boys (crocodiles, that is) need only control the temperature at which the eggs develop.* The gender of baby crocodiles is determined by the temperature at which the eggs develop.

A normal human cell contains 46 chromosomes, which are organized into 23 pairs. When we do not have the normal complement of 46 chromosomes, physical and behavioral abnormalities may result. The risk of these abnormalities rises with the age of the parents (Solomon and others, 1993).

Most persons with Down syndrome have an extra, or third, chromosome on the 21st pair. The extra chromosome is usually contributed by the mother and becomes increasingly likely as women age (Solomon and others, 1993). Persons with Down syndrome show a downward-sloping fold of skin at the inner corners of the eyes, creating a superficial resemblance to Asians. Hence the old term *mongolism,* which is now recognized to be racist and no longer used. People with Down syndrome also show a characteristic round face, protruding tongue, and broad, flat nose. They are mentally retarded and may have respiratory problems and malformations of the heart. Most people with Down syndrome die by middle age.

Behavior geneticists are attempting to sort out the relative importance of **nature** (heredity) and **nurture** (environmental influences) in the origins of behavior. Psychologists are especially interested in the roles of nature and nurture in intelligence and psychological disorders.

---

[3] This does not mean that male crocodiles are hot-blooded. Reptiles are cold-blooded animals.

Behavior in general reflects the influences of both nature and nurture. Organisms inherit structures that set the stage for certain behaviors. But none of us, as we appear, is the result of heredity alone. Environmental factors such as nutrition, learning opportunities, cultural influences, exercise, and (unfortunately) accident and illness also determine whether genetically possible behaviors will be displayed. A potential Shakespeare who is reared in poverty and never taught to read or write will not create a *Hamlet*. Behavior represents the interaction of nature and nurture.

Kinship Studies

Psychologists conduct kinship studies to help determine the role of genetic factors in behavior patterns and mental processes. They locate subjects who show the behavior pattern in question and then study the distribution of the behavior among relatives. The more closely people are related, the more genes they have in common. Parents and children have a 50% overlap in their genetic endowments. So do siblings (brothers and sisters). Aunts and uncles related by blood have a 25% overlap with nieces and nephews. First cousins share 12.5% of their genetic endowment. If genes are implicated in a behavior pattern, people more closely related should be more likely to share the pattern.

TWIN STUDIES. The fertilized egg cell (ovum) that carries genetic messages from both parents is called a **zygote.** Now and then, a zygote divides into two cells that separate so that each develops into an individual with the same genetic makeup. Such people are identical twins, or **monozygotic (MZ) twins.** If the woman releases two ova in the same month, and they are both fertilized, they develop into fraternal twins, or **dizygotic (DZ) twins.** DZ twins are related in the same way as other siblings. They share 50% of their genes (Segal, 1993). MZ twins are important in the study of the relative influences of nature (heredity) and nurture (the environment) because differences between MZ twins are the result of nurture.

Physically speaking, MZ twins are more likely to look alike and be closer in height, even to have more similar blood levels of cholesterol, than DZ twins (Heller and others, 1993). Psychologically speaking, MZ twins resemble one another more strongly than DZ twins in traits such as shyness and activity levels (Emde, 1993), irritability (Goldsmith, 1993), sociability, and cognitive development (DeFries and others, 1987). MZ twins show more similarity than DZ twins in their early signs of attachment, such as smiling, cuddling, and expression of fear of strangers (Scarr & Kidd, 1983). Also, MZ twins are more likely than DZ twins to share psychological disorders such as **autism,** anxiety, substance dependence, and schizophrenia. In one study on autism, the **concordance** rate for MZ twins in one study was 96% (Ritvo and others, 1985). The concordance rate for DZ twins was only 24%.

ADOPTEE STUDIES. The interpretation of many kinship studies is confounded by the fact that relatives usually share common backgrounds as well as genes (Coon and others, 1990; Segal, 1993). This is especially true of identical twins, who are frequently dressed identically and encouraged to follow similar interests. Adoptee studies, in which children are separated from their parents at an early age (or in which identical twins are separated at an early age) and then reared apart provide special opportunities for sorting out nature and nurture. Psychologists look for the relative similarities between children and their adoptive and natural parents. When children who are reared by

Nature • In behavior genetics, heredity.

Nurture • In behavior genetics, environmental influences on behavior, such as nutrition, culture, socioeconomic status, and learning.

Zygote • (ZY-goat). A fertilized egg cell.

Monozygotic twins • (MON-oh-zy-GOT-tick). Identical, or MZ, twins. Twins who develop from a single zygote, thus carrying the same genetic instructions.

Dizygotic twins • (die-zy-GOT-tick). Fraternal, or DZ, twins. Twins who develop from separate zygotes.

Autism • A childhood disorder marked by problems such as failure to relate to others, lack of speech, and intolerance of change.

Concordance • Agreement.

adoptive parents are nonetheless more similar to their natural parents in a trait, a powerful argument is made for a genetic role in the appearance of that trait.

Reflections

- Agree or disagree with the following statement and support your answer: "Since psychological traits such as introversion, intelligence, and aggressiveness are influenced by heredity, there is no point to trying to encourage introverted people to be more sociable, to helping poor students to do better in school, or to teaching aggressive people other ways of getting what they want."
- Which family members seem to be like you physically or psychologically? Which seem to be very different? To what do you attribute the similarities and differences? Why?
- Are you aware of any individuals with genetic or chromosomal disorders?

EXERCISE 1 | **Parts of the Brain**

DIRECTIONS: Fill in the names of the parts of the brain on the lines. Check your answers against Figure 3.11 in the chapter.

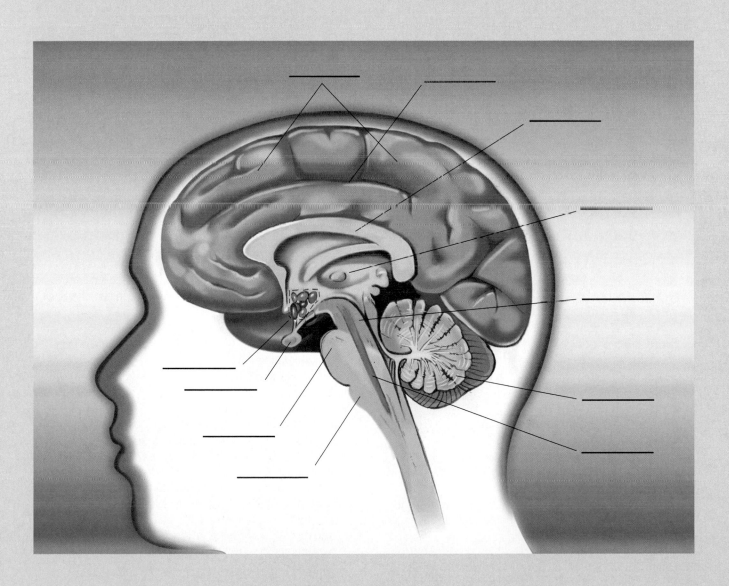

| EXERCISE 2 | Major Glands of the Endocrine System |

DIRECTIONS: Fill in the names of the glands of the endocrine system. List the important hormones secreted by each gland and explain their functions. Check your answers against Figure 3.17 in the chapter.

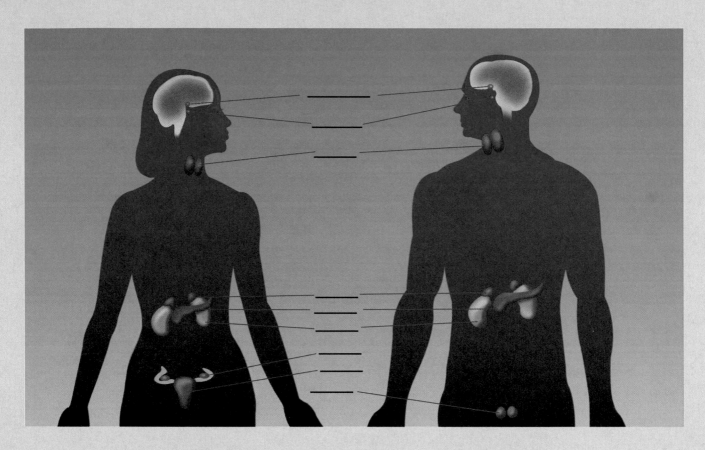

| ESL | English as a Second Language — Bridging the Gap |

academic competence (97)—educational abilities

aesthetic (96)—artistic ability to appreciate beauty

affliction (74)—illness or other problem that limits function

and so on (98)—continue with similar examples; et cetera (etc.)

apathy (101)—lack of interest; indifference to something

array (94)—variety of things

blind-alley entrance (90)—an entrance in a maze that stops and does not lead anywhere

block the action (79)—stop the action

bodybuilding contests (97)—contests of body muscle and strength

breathe a sigh of relief (103)—make a sound to indicate that an unpleasant situation has ended or been corrected

bred (102)—past tense of "breed," to produce offspring

buffeted about (74)—tossed back and forth roughly

butterfly pattern (83)—formed roughly in the shape of a butterfly

capable of "local government" (83)—capable of responding to something without requiring assistance from the whole system; in this case, the spinal cord can respond to something without the entire nervous system's involvement

central to (83)—very important to

clump (81)—group of something closely linked together

conception (101)—new beginning; start of development

convoluted (81)—complicated; tangled

convolutions (89)—irregular or folded-over surfaces

created anew (76)—created again and again

crossed fingers (82)—superstition that says that crossing the middle finger over the index finger (finger next to the thumb) provides good luck

crowning glory (89)—most beautiful and magnificent part

day in day out (88)—every day

dendrites (74)—branchlike parts of a nerve cell

devil of a time (92)—very difficult time; a lot of trouble

dissected (76)—cut open and taken apart to examine how it functions

dissipate (77)—disappear slowly; fade away

docile (88)—obedient; gentle

ecstasies (90)—great joy or happiness

egg- or football-shaped (88)—shaped like an egg or football

elusive (84)—hard to find

emotional richness (96)—emotional variety and intensity

enormous (72)—very large

entertain some rather nasty thoughts (74)—think unpleasant things

evolve (72)—develop

fabulous forest (80)—a large and beautiful group of trees

fight-or-flight response (90)—fight the predator or take flight (flee, or go away from quickly)

find a food goal (100)—find food by finding the route to it

finishing school (102)—type of school in the United States that teaches good manners and social skills

flee (88)—run away

fossil records (72)—fossils are the remains of animals and plants that died millions of years ago and became imbedded in the earth

fumbling (101)—not skillful

gruesome (85)—terrible; frightening

heighten general emotional responsiveness (98)—increase general emotional responses

highlight (79)—accentuate; emphasize

illicit (101)—forbidden; illegal

impede (79)—get in the way of; stop or delay

in a resting state (76)—when something is not moving

in flux (72)—always changing

in tandem (101)—together with

in turn (94)—the next step

integrate (94)—combine; blend; link together

intuitive (96)—able to understand things without being taught

ironically (84)—in an unexpected way

just geography (81)—refers to the physical location of something

knee-jerk reaction (83)—quick and sudden movement up of the lower leg in response to it having been hit just below the kneecap

lie end to end (73)—the end of one is next to the end of the following one, which is next to the following one, and so on

lightning rod (76)—metal wire designed to conduct lightning (redirect it) away and down into the ground where it will do less harm

maintain steady states (93)—keep the same condition or level of activity

make us proud (81)—will cause us, as human beings, to feel good about ourselves because we are better than animals

maze-bright or dull (103)—intelligent or unintelligent about figuring out a maze

maze-learning ability (103)—ability to learn how to travel a maze (puzzle of confusing paths) in order to locate the center goal or exit

mortgage payment (90)—monthly payment made to pay off a loan to a bank or mortgage company for a house that one is buying

mull over (88)—think about something for a long time to understand it

myriad (78)—a large number of something

novel approaches (81)—new and different ways

now being cracked (72)—now being understood

overutilize (79)—use too much ("too much" has a negative meaning)

Pablo Picasso (72)—a Spanish artist from the 1900s who is famous for his cubist style of modern painting

perpetrator (74)—one who causes a problem

perpetually (88)—continuously; over and over; constantly

phenomena (73)—events; happenings

piece of business (81)—item of information

pitch black (92)—completely dark; with no light

place to hang its hat (84)—having a specific location; in this case, belonging especially to the mind

play a filtering role (87)—select; leave out inappropriate or unnecessary things

potential Shakespeare (105)—person who has the ability to become a great writer; Shakespeare was a famous English writer who lived mainly in the 1500s and wrote many plays, including *Hamlet,* which is considered to be the greatest play in the English language

prowess (101)—ability; skill

pump iron (97)—exercise strenuously

put on weight (80)—increase weight; weight gain

raging hormones (97)—hormones that are flooding the body in an uncontrolled manner and causing strong emotional changes; in this case, the author is indicating this is not true

replenish (90)—replace; restore

retrieve (88)—call back

runner's high (80)—the elation, or very good feeling, experienced by people while running great distances

sabotaged (97)—tricked and prevented from accomplishing goals

screened off (80)—hidden from view

screening others out (87)—ignoring others

self-competence (80)—idea about our personal abilities

set the stage (105)—prepare for the event

sign language (102)—communication with hand and finger signals *slightest provocation* (85)—very sensitive; responding to small irritations

sparked the development (85)—caused the development

specifically tailored harbor (78)—a site, or place, that chemically fits only a specific neurotransmitter

spending of body energy from stored reserves (90)—the body is using energy from what has been saved (reserved)

stopped talking to one another (91)—stopped connecting and interacting with each other

subtle shifts (86)—small, hard-to-see changes

swear in court (71)—insist; be completely positive; speaking in a court of law under oath

syntax (95)—the way words are put together to form phrases and sentences

system of checks and balances (88)—one part of the system acts to restrain another part of the system; refers to the system of the U.S. government, which balances the powers of the three branches (parts) of the government (executive, legislative, and judicial)

tastes good/good taste (102)—in the phrase *tastes good,* taste is a verb—a person likes the flavor of the food;

in the phrase *good taste,* taste is a noun—a person has knowledge of good clothes, food, art, or manners

there you have it (80)—now you understand it

thicket of trees (73)—group of trees close together

trunklike (74)—like the trunk of a tree

twisting ladder (103)—steps that turn as they go up

unlocking the mysteries (73)—discovering what has not been understood previously

vastly (79)—enormously

vice versa (95)—and the opposite

way to prepare frog's legs (76)—frog's legs are considered by the French to be a special meal

winking out (72)—disappearing

withdrawn them (74)—taken them away; removed them

without a trace (72)—nothing remains to indicate that the creatures (people or animals) were here

work our way forward (86)—move in a forward direction; in this case, studying the brain as we move to new areas

---

FILL-INS | **Chapter Review**

SECTION 1: NEURONS: INTO THE FABULOUS FOREST

The (1) n_____ system contains billions of neurons. Neurons transmit messages to other neurons by means of chemical substances called (2) _____mitters. Neurons have a cell body, or (3) s_____; (4) d_____, which receive transmissions; and (5) a_____, which extend trunklike from the cell body. Chemicals called neurotransmitters travel across (6) s_____ to transmit messages to other neurons.

Many neurons have a fatty myelin (7) s_____. These sheaths are missing at the nodes of (8) R_____. Neural impulses travel more rapidly along myelinated (9) a_____, where they can jump from (10) n_____ to node.

Sensory or (11) _____ent neurons transmit sensory messages to the central nervous system. Motor or (12) _____ent neurons conduct messages from the central nervous system that stimulate glands or cause muscles to contract.

Neural transmission is an (13) e_____ process. An electric charge is conducted along an axon through a process that allows (14) s_____ ions into the cell and then pumps them out. The neuron has a (15) r_____ potential of −70 millivolts in relation to the body fluid outside the cell membrane and an (16) a_____ potential of +110 millivolts. The conduction of the neural impulse along the length of the neuron is what is meant by (17) _____ing.

Neurons (18) f_____ according to an all-or-none principle. Neurons may fire (19) _____s of times per second. Firing is first followed by an (20) a_____ refractory period, during which neurons do not fire in response to further stimulation. Then they undergo a (21) r_____ refractory period, during which they will fire, but only in response to stronger-than-usual messages.

A synapse consists of an axon (22) _____al from the transmitting neuron, a (23) d_____ of a receiving neuron, and a small, fluid-filled gap between them that is called the synaptic (24) c_____. (25) _____tory synapses stimulate neurons to fire. (26) _____tory neurons influence neurons in the direction of not firing.

Neurotransmitters are contained within synaptic (27) _____s. These vesicles are found in the knobs at the tips of the axon (28) _____als. Each neurotransmitter can fit into a specific (29) _____tor site on the dendrite of the receiving neuron.

(30) Ace_____ (abbreviated ACh) is the neurotransmitter that controls muscle contractions. The poison (31) c_____ acts by preventing ACh from lodging within receptor sites. ACh is normally prevalent in a brain structure essential to the formation of memories: the (32) _____pus. The neurotransmitter (33) _____ine is involved in learning and memory, and emotional arousal. Deficiencies of dopamine are linked to (34) _____son's disease. It is also theorized that schizophrenic individuals (35) over_____ dopamine because of a greater-than-normal number of receptor (36) _____s. Deficiencies of (37) _____line have been linked to depression. Amphetamines act by increasing the release of the neurotransmitters (38) d_____ and (39) n_____. Deficiencies of (40) _____nin are linked to anxiety, depression, and insomnia. The drug (41) L_____ decreases the action of serotonin, frequently leading to hallucinations. "Runner's high" may be caused by the release of chains of amino acids called (42) _____ns.

SECTION 2: THE NERVOUS SYSTEM

A nerve is composed of a bundle of (43) _____ns of neurons. The first major division of the nervous system is into the central and (44) _____al nervous systems. The brain and (45) s_____ _____ compose the central nervous system. The peripheral nervous system is divided into the (46) _____ic and (47) _____ic nervous systems. The somatic nervous system transmits sensory information about muscles, skin, and joints to the (48) c_____ nervous system. The somatic nervous system also controls (49) _____ar activity from the central nervous system. The autonomic nervous system is subdivided into sympathetic and (50) _____tic branches.

A spinal (51) r_____ is an unlearned response to a stimulus that does not involve the brain. A spinal reflex may involve as few as two neurons: a sensory or (52) _____ent neuron, and a motor or (53) _____ent neuron. A third kind of neuron, an (54) _____ron, may transmit the neural impulse from the sensory neuron through the spinal cord to the motor neuron.

In the spinal cord, (55: Gray or White?) matter consists of small, nonmyelinated neurons that are involved in reflexes. (56: Gray or White?) matter is composed of bundles of longer, myelinated axons that carry messages back and forth to and from the brain.

There are numerous ways of studying the brain. The (57) _____lograph records the electrical activity of the brain. In computerized (58) a_____ _____, a narrow X-ray beam is passed through the head; measurements of the amount of radiation that passes through permits the computer to generate a three-dimensional image of the brain.

Positron (59) e_____ _____ translates the glucose metabolized by parts of the brain into an image. In magnetic (60) r_____ imaging, radio waves cause parts of the brain to emit signals that are integrated into an image of the brain.

The hindbrain includes the (61) m_____, which is vital in heartbeat, blood pressure, and respiration. The pons transmits information concerning movement and is also involved in attention and respiration. The (62) _____lum is involved in balance and coordination.

The (63) _____ar activating system (RAS) begins in the hindbrain and continues through the midbrain into the forebrain and is vital in the functions of attention, sleep, and arousal.

Important structures of the forebrain include the thalamus, hypothalamus, limbic system, basal ganglia, and cerebrum. The (64) _____mus serves as a relay station for sensory stimulation. The (65) _____us is vital in the control of body temperature, motivation, and emotion. The (66) _____ic system is involved in memory and in the drives of hunger, sex, and aggression. The basal (67) g_____ are involved in posture and muscle coordination, and their deterioration is linked to Parkinson's disease. The surface of the cerebrum is called the (68) _____ _____tex. The cortex is (69) _____luted in shape. Valleys in the cortex are called (70) _____sures. The hemispheres of the cerebral cortex are connected by the (71) _____ _____sum.

The (72) _____ic nervous system (ANS) regulates the glands and involuntary activities such as heartbeat, digestion, and (73) d_____ of the pupils. The (74) _____tic division of the ANS dominates in activities that expend the body's resources, such as experiencing anxiety or fleeing a predator. The (75) _____tic division dominates during processes that build the body's reserves, such as eating.

SECTION 3: THE CEREBRAL CORTEX

The cerebral cortex is divided into the frontal, parietal, temporal, and (76) _____al lobes. The visual cortex is in the (77) _____al lobe, and the auditory cortex is in the (78) _____al lobe. The sensory cortex lies behind the central fissure in the (79) _____al lobe. The motor cortex lies in the (80) _____al lobe, across the (81) _____al fissure from the sensory cortex.

(82) A_____ areas of the cortex are involved in learning, thought, memory, and language. The (83) l_____ areas of the cortex lie near the intersection of the frontal, temporal, and parietal lobes in the dominant hemisphere. For the great majority of people, the (84: Left or Right?) hemisphere of the cortex contains language functions. In (85) _____'s aphasia, people speak slowly and laboriously, in simple sentences. In (86) _____'s aphasia, the ability to understand language is impaired. The (87: Left or Right?) hemisphere of the cortex seems to play a special role in understanding and producing language.

SECTION 4: THE ENDOCRINE SYSTEM

The endocrine system consists of (88) _____less glands that secrete hormones. The (89) _____mus secretes a number of hormones that regulate the functions of other glands. The pituitary gland secretes (90) _____in, which regulates maternal behavior in lower animals and stimulates production of (91) m_____ in women. ADH increases the reabsorption of (92) _____e to conserve fluid. (93) _____in stimulates labor in pregnant women.

The adrenal cortex produces (94) <u>cortico</u>___s, which promote development of muscle mass and increase resistance to stress and activity level. The adrenal medulla secretes (95) _____ine (also called epinephrine), which increases the metabolic rate and is involved in general emotional arousal.

Sex hormones secreted by the testes and (96) _____es are responsible for prenatal sexual differentiation. Female sex hormones also regulate the (97) _____al cycle. The female hormone (98) _____one helps maintain pregnancy.

SECTION 5: HEREDITY: THE NATURE OF NATURE

(99) _____s are the basic building blocks of heredity. Genes consist of (100) <u>d</u>_____ _____, which is abbreviated DNA. A large number of genes make up each (101) _____e. People normally have (102: how many?) _____ chromosomes. People receive (103: how many?) _____ chromosomes from the father and 23 from the mother.

Psychologists use kinship studies to sort out the effects of heredity and the (104) _____ment. There is reason to believe that heredity is a factor in the development of the trait when people who are (105: More or Less?) similar in kinship exhibit the trait. A fertilized egg cell is called a (106) _____e. Identical twins are formed from (107: One or Two?) zygote(s) and are termed (108) ____zygotic. Fraternal twins are formed from (109: One or Two?) zygote(s), and are termed (110) ____zygotic. It is assumed that all differences between (111: Monozygotic or Dizygotic?) twins are determined by environmental factors.

ANSWER KEY TO CHAPTER REVIEW

1. Nervous	26. Inhibitory	51. Reflex	76. Occipital
2. Neurotransmitters	27. Vesicles	52. Afferent	77. Occipital
3. Soma	28. Terminals	53. Efferent	78. Temporal
4. Dendrites	29. Receptor	54. Interneuron	79. Parietal
5. Axons	30. Acetylcholine	55. Gray	80. Frontal
6. Synapses	31. Curare	56. White	81. Central
7. Sheath	32. Hippocampus	57. Electroencephalograph	82. Association
8. Ranvier	33. Dopamine	58. Axial tomography	83. Language
9. Axons	34. Parkinson's	59. Emission tomography	84. Left
10. Node	35. Overutilize	60. Resonance	85. Broca's
11. Afferent	36. Sites	61. Medulla	86. Wernicke's
12. Efferent	37. Noradrenaline	62. Cerebellum	87. Left
13. Electrochemical	38. Dopamine (or noradrenaline)	63. Reticular	88. Ductless
14. Sodium	39. Noradrenaline (or dopamine)	64. Thalamus	89. Hypothalamus
15. Resting	40. Serotonin	65. Hypothalamus	90. Prolactin
16. Action	41. LSD	66. Limbic	91. Milk
17. Firing	42. Endorphins	67. Ganglia	92. Urine
18. Fire	43. Axons	68. Cerebral cortex	93. Oxytocin
19. Hundreds	44. Peripheral	69. Convoluted	94. Corticosteroids
20. Absolute	45. Spinal cord	70. Fissures	95. Adrenaline
21. Relative	46. Somatic (or autonomic)	71. Corpus callosum	96. Ovaries
22. Terminal	47. Autonomic (or somatic)	72. Autonomic	97. Menstrual
23. Dendrite	48. Central	73. Dilation	98. Progesterone
24. Cleft	49. Muscular	74. Sympathetic	99. Genes
25. Excitatory	50. Parasympathetic	75. Parasympathetic	100. Deoxyribonucleic acid

101. Chromosome
102. 46
103. 23
104. Environment
105. More
106. Zygote
107. One
108. Monozygotic
109. Two
110. Dizygotic
111. Monozygotic

POSTTEST | **Multiple Choice**

1. The _____ of the neuron uses oxygen to create energy to carry out the work of the cell.
   a. axon
   b. dendrite
   c. soma
   d. myelin

2. In the disease _____, myelin is replaced with a hard, fibrous tissue.
   a. cerebral palsy
   b. multiple sclerosis
   c. diabetes
   d. acromegaly

3. When a neuron is polarized, it has a resting potential of about _____ millivolts in relation to the body fluid outside the cell membrane.
   a. −70
   b. −40
   c. +40
   d. +70

4. One of the neurons in your brain receives stimulation from a few neighboring neurons and, as a result, it fires. The same receiving neuron then receives messages from larger and larger numbers of neighboring neurons. As a consequence, the receiving neuron
   a. fires more strongly.
   b. fires more frequently.
   c. shows no change in its pattern of firing.
   d. releases more inhibitory than excitatory neurotransmitters.

5. Receptor sites for neurotransmitters are found on the _____ of receiving neurons.
   a. dendrites
   b. synaptic vesicles
   c. clefts
   d. axon terminals

6. _____ is excitatory at synapses between nerves and muscles that involve voluntary movements but inhibitory at the heart and some other locations.
   a. ADH
   b. ACTH
   c. ANS
   d. ACh

7. _____ increase(s) the release of dopamine and noradrenaline, and also impede(s) their reabsorption after neurons have fired.
   a. Phenothiazines
   b. LSD
   c. Amphetamines
   d. Endorphins

8. You sit and cross your legs, and a physician taps your leg just below the knee. As a result, you kick reflexively. Which of the following is involved in your reflexive response?
   a. white matter in the spinal cord
   b. sensory cortex
   c. afferent neurons
   d. motor cortex

9. The part of the brain that gives it its wrinkled, mushroomlike appearance is
   a. the cerebellum.
   b. Broca's area.
   c. the occipital lobe.
   d. the cerebrum.

10. The left hemisphere of the cerebral cortext contains language functions for about _____% of right-handed people.
    a. 3
    b. 50
    c. 68
    d. 97

11. Messages from the brain and spinal cord to the _____ nervous system control purposeful body movements, such as raising a hand or running.
    a. autonomic
    b. somatic
    c. sympathetic
    d. parasympathetic

12. The parasympathetic division of the autonomic nervous system stimulates
    a. digestive processes.
    b. the fight-or-flight response.
    c. the heart rate.
    d. ejaculation.

13. If a person's abilities to comprehend other people's

speech and to think of the proper words to express his or her own thoughts were impaired, we should suspect damage to _____ area of the brain.
a. Levy's
b. Delgado's
c. Wernicke's
d. Gazzaniga's

14. Concerning the left brain–right brain controversy, it is most accurate to conclude that
a. the sounds of speech evoke a response in the dominant hemisphere only.
b. the sounds of speech evoke a response in the nondominant hemisphere only.
c. creativity and intuition are confined to the nondominant hemisphere.
d. the hemispheres are similar enough so that each can function quite well independently, but not as well as they function in normal combined usage.

15. Growth hormone is secreted by the
a. posterior lobe of the pituitary gland.
b. anterior lobe of the pituitary gland.
c. adrenal medulla.
d. adrenal cortex.

16. In women, prolactin
a. regulates maternal behavior.
b. causes uterine contractions.
c. stimulates production of milk.
d. maintains pregnancy.

17. Psychologists conduct kinship studies to
a. learn of the origins of physical traits such as eye color and height.
b. help determine the role of genetic factors in behavior patterns and mental processes.

c. sort out the effects of cultural beliefs and personal attitudes on behavior.
d. learn how to correct abnormalities in the endocrine system.

18. Psychologists primarily engage in adoptee studies because
a. there are no other ways to determine the effects of selective breeding in rats and other laboratory animals.
b. they are easier to conduct than physiologically based studies.
c. adopted siblings share 50% of their inheritance.
d. many kinship studies are confounded by the fact that relatives usually share common backgrounds as well as genes.

19. According to the text, which of the following hormones increases resistance to stress?
a. cortisol
b. thyroxin
c. luteinizing hormone
d. follicle stimulating hormone

20. The relationship between genetics and behavior, as expressed in the text, is that
a. genetics determines all of the behavior of rats but not of primates.
b. genetics determines all of the behavior of lower mammals, including lower primates, but not of humans.
c. genetics completely determines the level of aggressiveness but not of intelligence in mammalian species.
d. genetics makes behaviors possible and also sets limits on them.

ANSWER KEY TO POSTTEST

1. C	4. B	7. C	10. D	13. C	16. C	19. A
2. B	5. A	8. C	11. B	14. D	17. B	20. D
3. A	6. D	9. D	12. A	15. B	18. D	

Sensation and Perception

PRETEST *Truth or Fiction?*

____ People have five senses.

____ On a clear, dark night you could probably see the light from a candle burning 30 miles away.

____ If we could see lights of slightly longer wavelengths, warm-blooded animals would glow in the dark.

____ White sunlight is actually composed of all the colors of the rainbow.

____ When we mix blue light and yellow light, we attain green light.

____ A $500 machine-made violin will produce the same musical notes as a $200,000 Stradivarius.

____ Onions and apples have the same taste.

____ Many amputees experience pain in limbs that have been removed.

____ Rubbing or scratching a sore toe is often an effective way of relieving pain.

____ We have a sense that keeps us upright.

Acupuncture • The ancient Chinese practice of piercing parts of the body with needles to deaden pain and treat illness.

Sensation • The stimulation of sensory receptors and the transmission of sensory information to the central nervous system.

F IVE thousand years ago in China, give or take a day or two, an arrow was shot into the air. Where did it land? Ancient records tell us precisely where: in the hand of a fierce warrior and master of the martial arts. As the story was told to me, the warrior had grown so fierce because of a chronic toothache. Incessant pain had ruined his disposition.

One fateful day, our hero watched as invading hordes assembled on surrounding hills. His troops were trembling in the face of their great numbers, and he raised his arms to boost their morale. A slender wooden shaft lifted into the air from a nearby rise, arced, and then descended—right into the warrior's palm. His troops cringed and muttered among themselves, but our hero said nothing. Although he saw the arrow through his palm, he did not scream. He did not run. He did not even complain.

He was astounded. His toothache had vanished. His whole jaw was numb.

Meanwhile the invaders looked on—horrified. They, too, muttered among themselves. What sort of warrior could regard an arrow through his hand with such indifference? Even with a smile? If this was the caliber of the local warrior, they'd be better off traveling west and looking for a brawl in ancient Sumer or in Egypt. They sounded the retreat and withdrew.

Our warrior received a hero's welcome back in town. A physician offered to remove the arrow without a fee—a tribute to bravery. But the warrior would have none of it. The arrow had done wonders for his toothache, and he would brook no meddling. He already had discovered that if the pain threatened to return, he need only twirl the arrow and it would recede once more.

All was not well on the home front, however. Yes, his wife was thrilled to find him jovial once more, but the arrow put a crimp in romance. When he put his arm around her, she was in danger of being stabbed. Finally, she gave him an ultimatum: It was she or the arrow.

Placed in deep conflict, our warrior consulted a psychologist, who then huddled with the physician and the village elders. After much to-do, they asked the warrior to participate in an experiment. They would remove the arrow and replace it with a pin that the warrior could twirl as needed. If the pin didn't do the trick, they could always fall back on the arrow, so to speak.

To the warrior's wife's relief, the pin worked. And here, in ancient China, lay the origins of the art of **acupuncture**—the use of needles to relieve pain and treat assorted ills.

I confess that this tale is not entirely accurate. To my knowledge, there were no psychologists in ancient China. (Their loss.) Moreover, the part about the warrior's wife is fictitious. It is claimed, however, that acupuncture as a means of dealing with pain originated in ancient China when a soldier was, in fact, wounded in the hand by an arrow and discovered that a chronic toothache had disappeared. The Chinese, historians say, then set out to map the body by sticking pins here and there to learn how they influenced the perception of pain.

Control of pain is just one of the many issues that interest psychologists who study the closely related concepts of sensation and perception. **Sensation** is the stimulation of sensory receptors and the transmission of sensory information to the central nervous system (the spinal cord or brain). Sensory receptors are located in sensory organs such as the eyes and ears and, as we shall see, in the skin and elsewhere in the body. The stimulation of the senses is mechanical. It results from sources of energy like light and sound or from the presence of chemicals, as in smell and taste.

Perception is not mechanical. Perception is the process by which sensations are organized and interpreted, forming an inner representation of the world. Perception reflects learning and expectations and the ways in which we organize incoming information about the world. Perception is an active process through which we make sense of sensory stimulation. A human shape and a 12-inch ruler may stimulate paths of equal length among the sensory receptors in our eyes. Whether we interpret the human shape to be a foot-long doll or a full-grown person 15 to 20 feet away is a matter of perception.

In this chapter, you will see that your personal map of reality—your ticket of admission to a world of changing sights, sounds, and other sources of sensory input—depends largely on the so-called five senses: vision, hearing, smell, taste, and touch. We shall see, however, that touch is just one of several "skin senses," which also include pressure, warmth, cold, and pain. There are also senses that alert you to your own body position without your literally having to watch every step you take. As we explore the nature of each of these senses, we shall find that highly similar sensations may lead to quite different perceptions in different people—or within the same person in different situations.

Truth or Fiction Revisited. *It is not true that people have five senses.* People actually have many more than five senses, as we see in this chapter.

Perception • The process by which sensations are organized into an inner representation of the world.
Absolute threshold • The minimal amount of energy that can produce a sensation.
Psychophysicist • A person who studies the relationships between physical stimuli (such as light or sound) and their perception.
Method of constant stimuli • A psychophysical method for determining thresholds in which the researcher presents stimuli of various magnitudes and asks the individual to report detection.

SENSATION AND PERCEPTION: YOUR TICKET OF ADMISSION TO THE WORLD OUTSIDE

Before we begin our journey through the senses, let us consider a number of concepts that apply to all of them: absolute threshold, difference threshold, signal-detection theory, and sensory adaptation. In doing so, we shall learn why we might be able to dim the lights gradually to near darkness without people becoming aware of our mischief. We shall also learn why we might grow unaware of the most savory aromas of delightful dinners.

Sensory Thresholds. How much stimulation is necessary before you can detect a stimulus? How bright must the beacon from the lighthouse be to enable you to see it through the fog from several miles offshore?

Absolute Threshold: Is It There or Isn't It?

The weakest amount of a stimulus that can be told apart from no stimulus at all is called the **absolute threshold** for that stimulus. For example, the amount of physical energy required to activate the visual sensory system is the absolute threshold for light. Beneath this threshold, detection of light is impossible.

Psychophysicists experiment to determine the absolute thresholds of the senses by presenting stimuli of progressively greater intensity. In the **method of constant stimuli,** researchers use sets of stimuli with magnitudes close to the expected threshold. The order of the stimuli is randomized. Study participants say yes if they detect a stimulus and no if they do not. The stimuli are then repeatedly presented to the participants. An individual's absolute threshold for the stimulus is the lowest magnitude of the stimulus that he or she reports detecting 50% of the time. Weaker stimuli may be detected, but less than 50% of the time. Stronger stimuli, of course, will be detected more than 50% of the time.

TABLE 4.1

ABSOLUTE DETECTION THRESHOLDS AND OTHER CHARACTERISTICS OF HUMAN SENSORY SYSTEMS

SENSE	STIMULUS	RECEPTORS	THRESHOLD
Vision	Electromagnetic energy	Rods and cones in the retina	A candle flame viewed from a distance of about 30 miles on a clear, dark night
Hearing	Sound pressure waves	Hair cells on the basilar membrane of the inner ear	The ticking of a watch from about 20 feet away in a quiet room
Taste	Chemical substances dissolved in saliva	Taste buds on the tongue in the mouth	About 1 teaspoon of sugar dissolved in 2 gallons of water
Smell	Chemical substances in the air	Receptor cells in the upper part of the nasal cavity (the nose)	About one drop of perfume diffused throughout a small house (1 part in 500 million)
Touch	Mechanical displacement or pressure on the skin	Nerve endings located in the skin	The wing of a fly falling on a cheek from a distance of about 0.4 inch

Source: Adapted from "Contemporary Psychophysics," by E. Galanter, 1962, in R. Brown and others (Eds.), *New Directions in Psychology,* New York: Holt, Rinehart and Winston.

Psychophysical • Bridging the gap between the physical and psychological worlds.

Pitch The highness or lowness of a sound, as determined by the frequency of the sound waves.

The relationship between the intensity of a stimulus (a physical event) and its perception (a psychological event) is considered to be **psychophysical.** That is, it bridges psychological and physical events.

As you can see in Table 4.1, absolute thresholds have been determined for the senses of vision, hearing, taste, smell, and touch. Naturally, there are individual differences in absolute thresholds. Some people, that is, are more sensitive to sensory stimuli than others. The same person may also differ somewhat in sensitivity to sensory stimuli from day to day or from occasion to occasion. In the section on signal-detection theory, we shall see that sensitivity reflects psychological as well as physical and biological variables.

If the absolute thresholds for the human senses differed significantly, our daily experiences would be unrecognizable. Our ears are particularly sensitive, especially to sounds low in **pitch.** If they were any more sensitive, we might hear the collisions among molecules of air. If our eyes were sensitive to lights of slightly longer wavelengths, we would perceive infrared light waves. As a result, animals who are warm-blooded and thus give off heat—including our mates—would literally glow in the dark.

Truth or Fiction Revisited. *It is true that on a clear, dark night you could probably see the light from a candle burning 30 miles away.* This figure is in keeping with the absolute threshold for light. *It is also true that if we could see lights of slightly longer wavelengths, warm-blooded animals would glow in the dark.*

Difference Threshold:
Is It the Same or Is It Different?

How much of a difference in intensity between two lights is required before you will detect one as being brighter than the other? The minimum difference in the magnitude of two stimuli required to tell them apart is their **difference threshold**. As is the case with the absolute threshold, psychologists have agreed to the criterion of a difference in magnitudes that can be detected 50% of the time.

Psychophysicist Ernst Weber discovered through laboratory research that the difference threshold for perceiving differences in the intensity of light is about 2% (actually closer to 1/60th) of their intensity. This fraction, 1/60th, is known as **Weber's constant** for light. A closely related concept is the **just noticeable difference** (jnd), or the minimal amount by which a source of energy must be increased or decreased so that a difference in intensity will be perceived. In the case of light, people can perceive a difference in intensity 50% of the time when the brightness of a light is increased or decreased by 1/60th. Weber's constant for light holds whether we are comparing two quite bright or rather dull lights. However, it becomes inaccurate when we compare extremely bright or extremely dull lights.

As you can see in Table 4.2, Weber's research in psychophysics touched on many senses. He derived difference thresholds for different types of sensory stimulation.

A little math will show you the practical importance of jnd's. Consider weight lifting. Weber's constant for noticing differences in lifted weight is 1/53rd. (Round it off to 1/50th.) That means that one would probably have to increase the weight on a 100-pound barbell by about 2 pounds before the lifter would notice the difference. Now think of the 1-pound dumbbells used by many runners. Increasing the weight of each dumbbell by 2 pounds would be readily apparent to almost anyone because the increase would be threefold, not a small fraction. Yet the increase is still "only" 2 pounds. Return to our power lifter. When he is pressing 400 pounds, a 2-pound difference is less likely to be noticeable than when he is pressing 100 pounds. This is because our constant 2 pounds has become a difference of only 1/200th.

Difference threshold • The minimal difference in intensity required between two sources of energy so that they will be perceived as being different.

Weber's constant • The fraction of the intensity by which a source of physical energy must be increased or decreased so that a difference in intensity will be perceived.

Just noticeable difference • The minimal amount by which a source of energy must be increased or decreased so that a difference in intensity will be perceived.

TABLE 4.2
WEBER'S CONSTANTS FOR VARIOUS
SENSORY DISCRIMINATIONS

SENSE	TYPE OF DISCRIMINATION	WEBER'S CONSTANT
Vision	Brightness of a light	1/60
Hearing	Pitch (frequency) of a tone	1/333
	Loudness of a tone	1/10
Taste	Difference in saltiness	1/5
Smell	Amount of rubber smell	1/10
Touch	Pressure on the skin surface	1/7
	Deep pressure	1/77
	Difference in lifted weights	1/53

The same principle holds for the other senses: Small changes are more apt to be noticed when we begin our comparisons with small stimuli. Some dieting programs suggest that dieters reduce calorie intake by "imperceptible" amounts on a daily or weekly basis. They will eventually reach sharply reduced calorie-intake goals, but they may not feel so deprived during the reduction process.

Signal-Detection Theory: Is Being Bright Enough?

Perception is influenced by psychological factors as well as sensory stimulation (Macmillan & Creelman, 1991). **Signal-detection theory** considers the human aspects of sensation and perception.

The intensity of the signal is just one of the factors that determine whether people will perceive sensory stimuli (signals) or a difference between two signals. Another is the degree to which the signal can be distinguished from background **noise.** It is easier to hear a friend in a quiet room than in one where people are clinking silverware and glasses and engaging in competing conversations. The quality of a person's biological sensory system is still another factor. Here, we are concerned with the sharpness or acuteness of the individual's sensory system. We consider whether sensory capacity is fully developed or diminished because of illness or advanced years.

Signal-detection theory also considers psychological factors such as motivation, expectations, and learning. For example, the place in which you are reading this book may be abuzz with signals. If you are outside, perhaps there is a breeze against your face. Perhaps the shadows of passing clouds darken the scene now and then. If you are inside, perhaps there are the occasional clanks and hums of a heating system. Perhaps the odors of dinner are hanging in the air, or the voices from a TV set suggest a crowd in another room. Yet, you are focusing your attention on this page, I hope. Thus, the other signals recede

MINILECTURE: DETECTION

Signal-detection theory • The view that the perception of sensory stimuli involves the interaction of physical, biological, and psychological factors.

Noise • (1) In signal-detection theory, any unwanted signal that interferes with perception of the desired signal. (2) More generally, a combination of dissonant sounds.

Signal Detection. He sleeps while she is awakened by the baby's crying. Detection of signals, such as a baby's crying, is determined not only by the physical characteristics of the signals but also by psychological factors, such as motivation and attention.

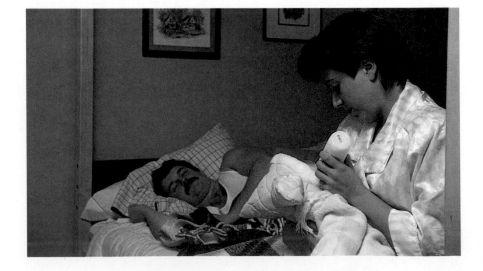

into the backdrop of your consciousness. One psychological factor in signal detection is the focusing or narrowing of attention to signals the person deems important.

Consider some examples. One parent may sleep through a baby's crying, whereas the other parent is awakened. This is not necessarily because one parent is innately more sensitive to the sounds of crying (although some men may conveniently assume that mothers are). Instead, it may be because one parent has been assigned the task of caring for the baby through the night and is thus more highly motivated to attend to the sounds. Because of training, an artist might notice the use of line or subtle colors that would go undetected by a lay person looking at the same painting. A book designer may notice subtle differences between typefaces among books; a lay person would neither be motivated nor trained to attend to these differences.

Signal-detection theory emphasizes the psychological aspects of detecting and responding to signals. The relationship between a physical stimulus and a sensory response is more than mechanical or mathematical. People's ability to detect stimuli such as meaningful blips on a radar screen depends not only on the intensity of the blips themselves but also on their training (learning), motivation (their desire to perceive meaningful blips), and psychological states such as fatigue or alertness.

MINILECTURE: DISCRIMINATION

Feature Detectors

Imagine that you are standing by the curb of a busy street and a city bus is approaching (Blakeslee, 1992c). When neurons in your sensory organs—in this case, your eyes—are stimulated by the bus, they relay information to the sensory cortex in the brain. Nobel prize winners David Hubel and Torsten Wiesel (1979) discovered that various neurons in the visual cortex fire in response to particular features of the visual input. Many cells, for example, fire in response to lines presented at various angles—vertical, horizontal, and in between. Other cells fire in response to specific colors. Because they respond to different aspects, or features, of a scene, these cells are termed **feature detectors.** In the example of the bus, visual feature detectors respond to the bus's edges, depth, contours, textures, shadows, speed, and kinds of motion (up, down, forward, and back; Blakeslee, 1992c). There are also feature detectors for other senses. Auditory feature detectors, for example, respond to the pitch, loudness, and other aspects of the sounds of the bus.

Feature detectors • Neurons in the sensory cortex that fire in response to specific features of sensory information such as lines or edges of objects.

Sensory adaptation • The processes by which organisms become more sensitive to stimuli that are low in magnitude and less sensitive to stimuli that are constant or ongoing in magnitude.

Sensitization • The type of sensory adaptation in which we become more sensitive to stimuli that are low in magnitude. Also called *positive adaptation.*

Sensory Adaptation: Where Did It Go?

There is a saying that the only constant is change. Our sensory systems are admirably suited to a changing environment. **Sensory adaptation** refers to the processes by which we become more sensitive to stimuli of low magnitude and less sensitive to stimuli of relatively constant magnitude.

Most of us are familiar with the process by which the visual sense adapts to lower intensities of light. When we first walk into a darkened movie theater, we see little but the images on the screen. As time elapses, however, we become increasingly sensitive to the faces of those around us and the inner features of the theater. The process of becoming more sensitive to stimulation is referred to as **sensitization,** or positive adaptation.

On the other hand, we become less sensitive to ongoing stimulation. Sources of light appear to grow dimmer as we adapt to them. In fact, if you

MINILECTURE: DARK ADAPTATION

could keep an image completely stable on the retinas of your eyes—which is virtually impossible to accomplish without a still image and stabilizing equipment—the image would fade within a few seconds and be very difficult to see. Similarly, at the beach we soon become less aware of the lapping of the waves. When we live in the city, we become desensitized to traffic sounds except for the occasional backfire or accident. As you may have noticed from experiences with freshly painted rooms, sensitivity to disagreeable odors fades quite rapidly. The process of becoming less sensitive to stimulation is referred to as **desensitization,** or negative adaptation.

Reflections

- How sensitive are your vision and hearing? What is the dimmest light you can see? What is the softest sound you can hear? How do psychophysicists answer such questions?
- Can you think of an example of a just noticeable difference in your life? How much weight do you have to gain or lose to notice a difference?
- **Do we sometimes fail to hear things because we don't want to hear them? How do such experiences relate to signal-detection theory?**
- Have you ever gotten used to a disagreeable odor so that you no longer noticed it? How does this experience relate to the concepts of sensory adaptation and desensitization?

Let us now examine how each of the human sensory systems perceives signals from the outer (and inner) environments.

Desensitization • The type of sensory adaptation in which we become less sensitive to constant stimuli. Also called *negative adaptation*.
Visible light • The part of the electromagnetic spectrum that stimulates the eye and produces visual sensations.

MINILECTURE: LIGHT

VISION: LETTING THE SUN SHINE IN

Our eyes are our "windows on the world." We consider information from vision to be more essential than that from hearing, smell, taste, and touch. Because vision is our dominant sense, we consider blindness our most debilitating sensory loss (Moore, 1995). An understanding of vision requires discussion of the nature of light and of the master of the sensory organs, the eye.

Light: What Is This Stuff?

In almost all cultures, light is a symbol of goodness and knowledge. We describe capable people as being "bright" or "brilliant." If we are not being complimentary, we label them as "dull." People who aren't in the know are said to be "in the dark." Just what is this stuff called light?

Visible light is the stuff that triggers visual sensations. It is just one small part of a spectrum of electromagnetic energy (see Figure 4.1) that is described in terms of wavelengths. These wavelengths vary from those of cosmic rays, which are only a few trillionths of an inch long, to some radio waves, which extend for many miles. Radar, microwaves, and X rays are also forms of electromagnetic energy.

You have probably seen rainbows or light broken down into several colors as it filtered through your windows. Sir Isaac Newton, the British scientist, discovered that sunlight could be broken down into different colors by means of a triangular solid of glass called a *prism* (Figure 4.1). When I took introductory psychology, I was taught that I could remember the colors of the spectrum, from longest to shortest wavelengths, by using the mnemonic device *Roy G.*

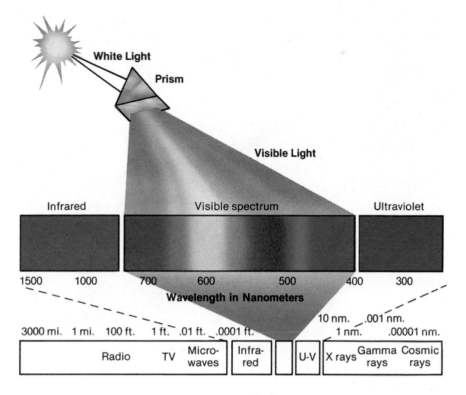

The Electromagnetic Spectrum

FIGURE 4.1

The Visible Spectrum. By passing white light, such as sunlight, through a prism, we break it down into the colors of the visible spectrum. The visible spectrum is just one part—and a narrow part indeed of the electromagnetic spectrum. The electromagnetic spectrum also includes radio waves, microwaves, X rays, cosmic rays, and many others. Different forms of electromagnetic energy have different wavelengths. They vary from a few trillionths of a meter to thousands of miles. Visible light varies in wavelength from about 400 to 700 nanometers. What is a nanometer? One *billionth* of a meter. (A meter = 39.37 inches.)

Hue • The color of light, as determined by its wavelength.

Biv (red, orange, yellow, green, blue, indigo, violet). I must have been a backward student because I found it easier to recall them in reverse order, using the meaningless acronym *vibgyor.*

Truth or Fiction Revisited. *It is true that white sunlight is actually composed of all the colors of the rainbow.*

The wavelength of visible light determines its color, or **hue.** The wavelength for red is longer than that for orange, and so on through the spectrum.

The Eye: The Better to See You With

Consider that magnificent invention called the camera, which records visual experiences. In the camera, light enters an opening and is focused onto a sensitive surface, or film. Chemicals on this surface create a lasting impression of the image that entered the camera.

The eye—our living camera—is no less remarkable. Consider its major parts (Figure 4.2). As with a film or TV camera, light enters through a narrow opening and is projected onto a sensitive surface. Light first passes through the

MINILECTURE: THE EYE

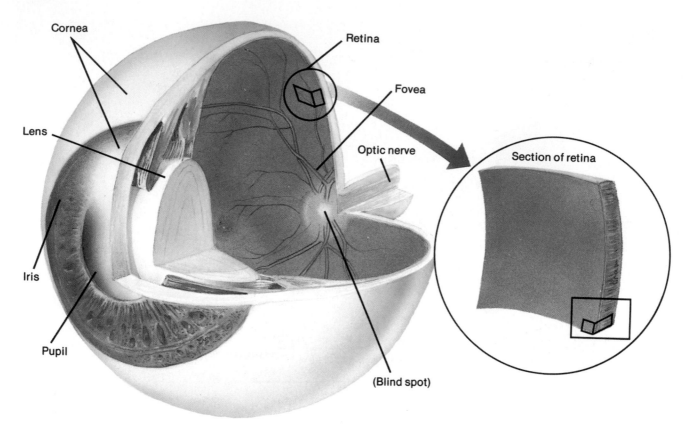

FIGURE 4.2

The Eye. In both the eye and a camera, light enters through a narrow opening and is projected onto a sensitive surface. In the eye, the photosensitive surface is called the *retina.* Information concerning the changing images on the retina is transmitted to the brain. In a camera, the photosensitive surface is usually film.

Cornea • Transparent tissue forming the outer surface of the eyeball.

Iris • A muscular membrane whose dilation regulates the amount of light that enters the eye.

Pupil • The apparently black opening in the center of the iris, through which light enters the eye.

Lens • A transparent body behind the iris that focuses an image on the retina.

Retina • The area of the inner surface of the eye that contains rods and cones.

transparent **cornea,** which covers the front of the eye's surface. The amount of light that passes through the cornea is determined by the size of the opening of the muscle called the **iris,** which is also the colored part of the eye. The opening in the iris is called the **pupil.** Pupil size adjusts automatically to the amount of light. The more intense the light, the smaller the opening. In a similar fashion, we adjust the amount of light allowed into a camera according to its brightness. Pupil size is also sensitive to emotional response: We can literally be "wide-eyed with fear."

Once light passes through the iris, it encounters the **lens.** The lens adjusts or accommodates to the image by changing its thickness. Changes in thickness permit projection of a clear image of the object onto the retina. That is, these changes focus the light according to the object's distance. If you hold a finger at arm's length, then slowly bring it toward your nose, you will feel tension in the eye as the thickness of the lens accommodates to keep the retinal image in focus. When people squint to bring an object into focus, they are adjusting the thickness of the lens. The lens in a camera does not accommodate to the distance of objects. Instead, to focus the light that is projected onto the film, the camera lens is moved farther away from or closer to the film.

The **retina** is like the film or image surface of the camera. Instead of being composed of film that is sensitive to light (photosensitive), however, the retina consists of photosensitive cells, or **photoreceptors,** called *rods* and *cones.*

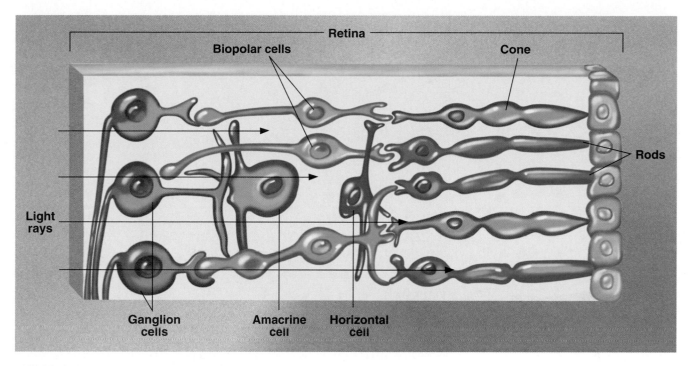

FIGURE 4.3

The Retina. After light travels through the vitreous humor of the eye, it finds its way through ganglion neurons and bipolar neurons to the photosensitive rods and cones. These photoreceptors then transmit sensory input back through the bipolar neurons to the ganglion neurons. The axons of the ganglion neurons form the optic nerve, which transmits sensory stimulation through the brain to the visual cortex of the occipital lobe. Amacrine cells and horizontal cells make connections within layers that allow photoreceptors to funnel their information into the ganglion cells.

The retina (Figure 4.3) contains several layers of cells: the rods and cones, **bipolar cells,** and **ganglion cells.** All of these cells are neurons. Light travels past the ganglion cells and bipolar cells and stimulates the rods and cones. The rods and cones then send neural messages through the bipolar cells to the ganglion cells. The axons of the million or so ganglion cells in our retinae form the **optic nerve.** The optic nerve conducts sensory input to the brain, where it is relayed to the visual area of the occipital lobe. Other neurons in the retina—amacrine cells and horizontal cells—make sideways connections at a level near the receptor cells and at another level near the ganglion cells. As a result of these lateral connections, many rods and cones funnel visual information into one bipolar cell, and many bipolar cells funnel information to one ganglion cell. Receptors outnumber ganglion cells by more than 100 to 1.

The **fovea** is the most sensitive area of the retina (see Figure 4.2). Receptors there are more densely packed. The **blind spot,** in contrast, is insensitive to visual stimulation. It is the part of the retina where the axons of the ganglion cells congregate to form the optic nerve (Figure 4.4).

RODS AND CONES. **Rods** and **cones** are the photoreceptors in the retina. About 125 million rods and 6.5 million cones are distributed across the retina (Solomon and others, 1993). The fovea is composed almost exclusively of cones. Cones then become more sparsely distributed as you work forward

Photoreceptors • Cells that respond to light.
Bipolar cells • Neurons that conduct neural impulses from rods and cones to ganglion cells.
Ganglion cells • Neurons whose axons form the optic nerve.
Optic nerve • The nerve that transmits sensory information from the eye to the brain.
Fovea • An area near the center of the retina that is dense with cones and where vision is consequently most acute.
Blind spot • The area of the retina where axons from ganglion cells meet to form the optic nerve.
Rods • Rod-shaped photoreceptors that are sensitive only to the intensity of light.
Cones • Cone-shaped photoreceptors that transmit sensations of color.

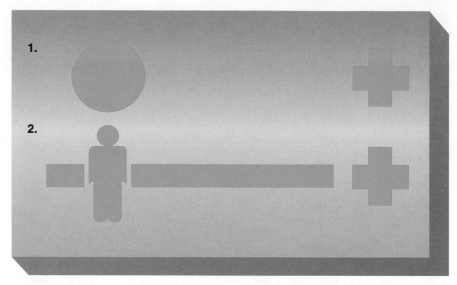

FIGURE 4.4

A "Disappearing Act." To locate the blind spots in your eyes, first look at Drawing 1. Close your right eye. Then move the book back and forth about 1 foot from your left eye while you stare at the plus sign. You will notice the circle disappear. When the circle disappears it is being projected onto the blind spot of your retina, the point at which the axons of ganglion neurons collect to form the optic nerve. Then close your left eye. Stare at the circle with your right eye and move the book back and forth. When the plus sign disappears, it is being projected onto the blind spot of your right eye. Now look at Drawing 2. You can make this figure disappear and "see" the green line continue through the spot where it was by closing your right eye and staring at the plus sign with your left. When this figure is projected onto your blind spot, your brain "fills in" the line, which is one reason that you're not usually aware that you have blind spots.

Dark adaptation • The process of adjusting to conditions of lower lighting by increasing the sensitivity of rods and cones.

MINILECTURE: DARK ADAPTATION

from the fovea toward the lens. Rods, in contrast, are nearly absent at the fovea but are distributed more densely as you approach the lens.

Rods are sensitive only to the intensity of light. They allow us to see in black and white. Cones provide color vision. In low lighting, it is possible to photograph a clearer image with black-and-white film than with color film. Similarly, rods are more sensitive to light than cones. Therefore, as the illumination grows dim, as during the evening and nighttime hours, objects appear to lose their color well before their outlines fade from view.

LIGHT ADAPTATION.   A movie theater may at first seem too dark to allow us to find seats readily. But as time goes on, we come to see the seats and other people clearly. Adjusting to lower lighting is called **dark adaptation.**

Figure 4.5 shows the amount of light needed for detection as a function of the amount of time spent in the dark. The cones and rods adapt at different rates. The cones, which permit perception of color, reach their maximum adaptation to darkness in about 10 minutes. The rods, which allow perception of light and dark only, are more sensitive and continue to adapt to darkness for up to about 45 minutes.

Adaptation to brighter lighting conditions takes place much more rapidly. When you emerge from the theater into the brilliance of the afternoon, you may at first be painfully surprised by the featureless blaze around you. The visual experience is not unlike turning the brightness of the TV set to maximum, in which case the edges of objects dissolve into light. Within a minute or so of

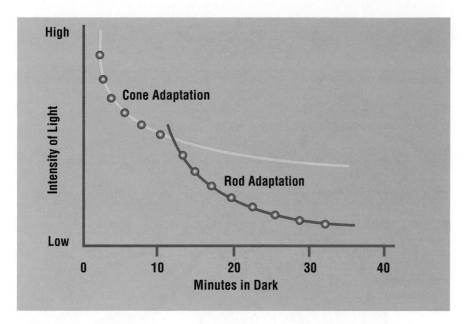

FIGURE 4.5

Dark Adaptation. This illustration shows the amount of light necessary for detection as a function of the amount of time spent in the dark. Cones and rods adapt at different rates. Cones, which permit perception of color, reach maximum dark adaptation in about 10 minutes. Rods, which permit perception of dark and light only, are more sensitive than cones. Rods continue to adapt for up to about 45 minutes.

Complementary • Descriptive of colors of the spectrum that when combined produce white or nearly white light.

entering the street, however, the brightness of the scene will have dimmed and objects will have regained their edges.

Creating an Inner World of Color: Color Vision

For most of us, the world is a place of brilliant colors—the blue-greens of the ocean, the red-oranges of the lowering sun, the deepened greens of June, the glories of rhododendron and hibiscus. Color is an emotional and aesthetic part of our everyday lives.

The wavelength of light determines its color, or hue. The brightness of a color is its degree of lightness or darkness. The brighter the color, the lighter it is.

If we bend the colors of the spectrum into a circle, we create a color wheel, as shown in Figure 4.6. Yellow is the lightest color on the color wheel. As we work our way around from yellow to violet-blue, we encounter progressively darker colors.

The colors across from one another on the color wheel are labeled **complementary.** Red-green and blue-yellow are the major complementary pairs. If we mix complementary colors together, they dissolve into gray.

"But wait!" you say. "Blue and yellow cannot be complementary because by mixing pigments of blue and yellow we create green, not gray." True enough, but we have been talking about mixing *lights,* not *pigments.* Light is the source of all color. Pigments reflect and absorb different wavelengths of light selectively. The mixture of lights is an *additive* process. The mixture of pigments is *subtractive* (see Figure 4.7).

MINILECTURE: COLOR VISION

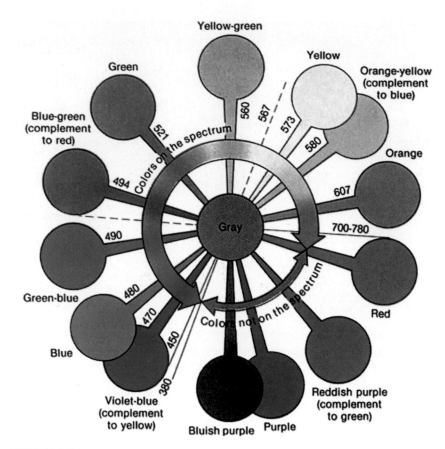

FIGURE 4.6

The Color Wheel. A color wheel can be formed by bending the colors of the spectrum into a circle and placing complementary colors across from one another. (A few colors between violet and red that are not found on the spectrum must be added to complete the circle.) When lights of complementary colors such as yellow and violet-blue are mixed, they dissolve into neutral gray. The afterimage of a color is also the color's complement.

FIGURE 4.7

Additive Color Mixtures Produced by Lights of Three Colors: Red, Green, and Violet-Blue. In the early 1800s, British scientist Thomas Young discovered that white light and all the colors of the spectrum could be produced by adding various combinations of lights of three colors and varying their intensities.

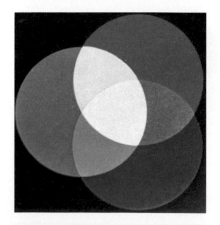

Truth or Fiction Revisited. *It is not true that we attain green light by mixing blue light and yellow light.* We attain a green pigment when we mix pigments of blue and yellow.

Pigments attain their colors by absorbing light from certain segments of the spectrum and reflecting the rest. For example, we see most plant life as green because the pigment in chlorophyll absorbs most of the red, blue, and violet wavelengths of light. The remaining green is reflected. A red pigment absorbs most of the spectrum but reflects red. White pigments reflect all colors equally. Black pigments reflect very little light.

Before reading on, why don't you try a brief experiment? Look at the strangely colored American flag in Figure 4.8 for at least half a minute. Then look at a sheet of white or gray paper. What has happened to the flag? If your color vision is working properly, and if you looked at the miscolored flag long enough, you should see a flag composed of the familiar red, white, and blue. The flag you perceive on the white sheet of paper is an **afterimage** of the first. (If you didn't look at the green, black, and yellow flag long enough the first time, you may wish to try it again. It will work any number of times.)

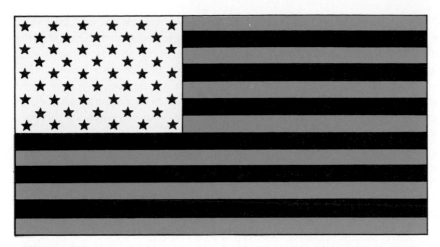

FIGURE 4.8
Three Cheers for the . . . Green, Black, and Yellow? Don't be concerned. We can readily restore Old Glory to its familiar hues. Place a sheet of white paper beneath the book, and stare at the center of the flag for 30 seconds. Then remove the book. You will see a more familiar image on the paper beneath. This is an afterimage.

In afterimages, persistent sensations of color are followed by perception of the complementary color when the first color is removed. The phenomenon of afterimages has contributed to one of the theories of color vision, as we shall soon see.

Theories of Color Vision

Adults with normal color vision can discriminate hundreds of colors across the visible spectrum. Different colors have different wavelengths. Although we can vary the physical wavelengths of light in a continuous manner from shorter to longer, many changes in color are discontinuous. Our perception of a color shifts suddenly from blue to green, even though the change in wavelength may be smaller than that between two blues. People from various cultural backgrounds divide the regions of the visible spectrum into similar groupings that correspond to the reds, yellows, greens, and blues shown in Figure 4.1.

Our ability to perceive color depends on the eye's transmission of different messages to the brain when lights of different wavelengths stimulate the cones in the retina. In this section, we shall explore and evaluate two theories of how lights of different wavelengths are perceived as being of different colors: *trichromatic theory* and *opponent-process theory.* Then we shall discuss the problems of some individuals who are blind to some or all of the colors of the visible spectrum.

TRICHROMATIC THEORY.   **Trichromatic theory** is based on an experiment that was run by British scientist Thomas Young in the early 1800s. As in Figure 4.7, Young projected three lights of different colors onto a screen so that they partly overlapped. He found that he could create any color from the visible spectrum by simply varying the intensities of the lights. When all three lights fell on the same spot, they created white light, or the appearance of no color at all. The three lights manipulated by Young were red, green, and blue-violet.

Afterimage • The lingering visual impression made by a stimulus that has been removed.
Trichromatic theory • The theory that color vision is made possible by three types of cones, some of which respond to red light, some to green, and some to blue. (From the Greek roots *treis,* meaning "three," and *chroma,* meaning "color.")

German physiologist Hermann von Helmholtz saw in Young's discovery an explanation of color vision. Von Helmholtz suggested that the eye must have three different types of photoreceptors or cones. Some must be sensitive to red light, some to green, and some to blue. We see other colors when two different types of color receptors are stimulated. The perception of yellow, for example, would result from the simultaneous stimulation of receptors for red and green. Trichromatic theory is also known as the Young–Helmholtz theory, after Thomas Young and Hermann von Helmholtz.

OPPONENT-PROCESS THEORY.   In 1870, Ewald Hering proposed the **opponent-process theory** of color vision. Opponent-process theory also holds that there are three types of color receptors, but not red, green, and blue. Hering suggested that afterimages (such as of the American flag shown in Figure 4.8) are made possible by three types of color receptors: red–green, blue–yellow, and a type that perceives differences in brightness from light to dark. A red–green cone could not transmit messages for red and green at the same time. According to Hering, staring at the green, black, and yellow flag for 30 seconds would disturb the balance of neural activity. The afterimage of red, white, and blue would represent the eye's attempt to reestablish a balance.

EVALUATION.   Both theories of color vision appear to be partially correct (Hurvich, 1981). Research supports trichromatic theory. It shows that some cones are sensitive to blue, some to green, and some to red parts of the spectrum (Solomon and others, 1993).

But studies of the bipolar and ganglion neurons suggest that messages from cones are transmitted to the brain and relayed by the thalamus to the occipital lobe in an opponent-process fashion (DeValois & Jacobs, 1984). Some opponent-process cells that transmit messages to the visual centers in the brain are excited ("turned on") by green light but inhibited ("turned off") by red light. Others can be excited by red light but are inhibited by green light. A second set of opponent-process cells responds in an opposite manner to blue and yellow. A third set responds in an opposite manner to light and dark.

A neural rebound effect apparently helps explain afterimages. That is, a green-sensitive ganglion that had been excited by green light for half a minute or so might switch briefly to inhibitory activity when the light is shut off. The effect would be to perceive red, even though no red light was being shone.

These theoretical updates allow for the afterimage effects with the green, black, and yellow flag and are also consistent with Young's experiments in mixing lights of different colors.

Color Blindness

If you can discriminate the colors of the visible spectrum, you have normal color vision and are labeled a **trichromat.** This means that you are sensitive to red–green, blue–yellow, and light–dark. People who are totally color blind are called **monochromats** and are sensitive to light–dark only. Total color blindness is quite rare. The fully color blind see the world as trichromats would on a black-and-white TV set or in a black-and-white movie.

Partial color blindness is more common than total color blindness. Partial color blindness is a gender- or sex-linked trait that strikes mostly males. The recessive genes for the disorder are found on the X sex chromosome, and thus in males they are unopposed by dominant genes on a second X sex

Opponent-process theory • The theory that color vision is made possible by three types of cones, some of which respond to red or green light, some to blue or yellow, and some only to the intensity of light.

Trichromat • A person with normal color vision.

Monochromat • A person who is sensitive to black and white only and hence color blind.

FIGURE 4.9

A Test for Color Blindness. Can you see the numbers in these plates from a test for color blindness? A person with red–green color blindness would not be able to see the 6, and a person with blue–yellow color blindness would probably not discern the 12. (Caution: These reproductions cannot be used for actual testing of color blindness.)

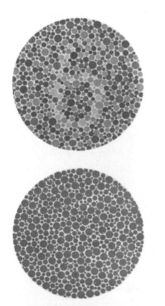

chromosome. The partially color blind are called **dichromats.** Dichromats can discriminate only two colors—red and green, or blue and yellow—and the colors that are derived from mixing these colors. Figure 4.9 shows the types of tests that are used to diagnose color blindness. Also see Figure 4.10.

A dichromat might put on one red sock and one green sock but would not mix red and blue socks. Monochromats might put on socks of any color. They would not notice a difference as long as the socks' colors did not differ in intensity, or brightness.

When we selectively breed cats and dogs, we are interested in producing coats of certain colors. But if cats and dogs bred human beings, they would be less concerned about our color because their color vision is less well developed (Rosenzweig & Leiman, 1982). Cats, for example, can distinguish fewer colors and only on large surfaces.

**MINILECTURE:
COLOR DEFICIENCY**

Dichromat • A person who is sensitive to black-white and either red–green or blue–yellow and hence partially color blind.

FIGURE 4.10

Color Blindness. The painting in the upper left-hand panel—Man Ray's *The Rope Dancer Accompanies Herself with Her Shadows*—appears as it would to a person with normal color vision. If you suffered from red–green color blindness, the picture would appear as it does in the upper right-hand panel. The lower left-hand and lower right-hand panels show how the picture would look to viewers with yellow–blue or total color blindness, respectively. (Museum of Modern Art, New York. Gift of G. David Thompson.)

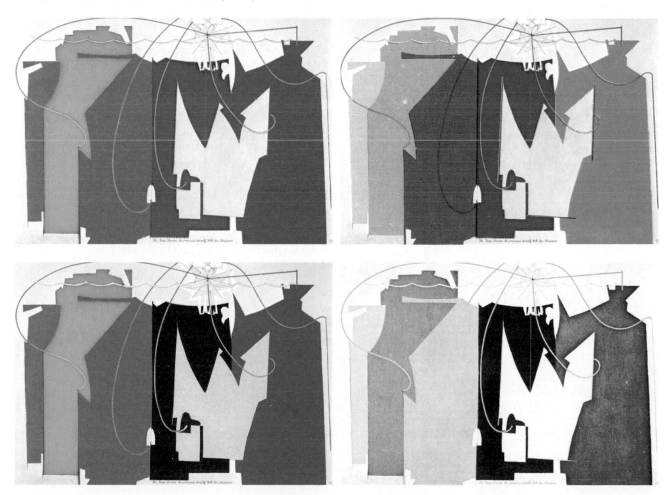

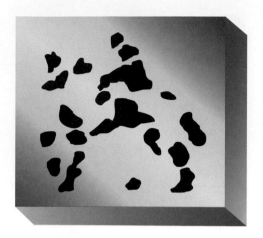

FIGURE 4.11

Closure. Meaningless splotches of ink or a horse and rider? This figure illustrates the Gestalt principle of closure.

Closure • The tendency to perceive a broken figure as being complete or whole.
Perceptual organization • The tendency to integrate perceptual elements into meaningful patterns.

**MINILECTURE:
GESTALT PRINCIPLES**

Reflections

- Have you seen a rainbow? How do you account for the colors in a rainbow?
- Hold a finger at arm's length, then bring it slowly toward your eyes, maintaining a single image as you do so. What do you feel happening as the finger approaches? Why does it happen?
- Have you had the experience of entering a dark theater and then seeing gradually more and more as you adjust? What processes account for the adjustment? Do you first see the outlines of shapes or their colors? Why?
- What does color vision add to your own life? If you are color blind or partly color blind, how have you adjusted to society's use of color? For example, how do you know when to stop and when to go at a traffic light?

VISUAL PERCEPTION

Perception is the process by which we organize or make sense of our sensory impressions. Although visual sensations are caused by electromagnetic energy, visual perception also relies on our knowledge, expectations, and motivations. Whereas sensation may be thought of as a mechanical process, perception is an active process by which we interpret the world around us.

For example, just what do you see in Figure 4.11? Do you see random splotches of ink or a rider on horseback? If you perceive a horse and rider, it is not just because of the visual sensations provided by the drawing. Each of the blobs is meaningless in and of itself, and the pattern they form is also less than clear. Despite the lack of clarity, however, you may still perceive a horse and rider. Why? The answer has something to do with your general knowledge and your desire to fit incoming bits and pieces of information into familiar patterns.

In the case of the horse and rider, your integration of disconnected shards of information into a meaningful whole also reflects what Gestalt psychologists refer to as the principle of **closure,** or the tendency to perceive a complete or whole figure even when there are gaps in the sensory input. Put another way, in perception the whole can be very much more than the mere sum of the parts. Collecting parts alone can be meaningless. It is their configuration that matters.

Perceptual Organization

Earlier in the century, Gestalt psychologists noted consistencies in our integration of bits and pieces of sensory stimulation into meaningful wholes and attempted to formulate rules that governed these processes. Max Wertheimer, in particular, discovered many such rules. As a group, these rules are referred to as the laws of **perceptual organization.** Let us examine a number of these rules, beginning with those concerning figure–ground perception. Then we consider top-down and bottom-up processing.

FIGURE–GROUND PERCEPTION.   If you look out your window, you may see people, buildings, cars, and streets, or perhaps grass, trees, birds, and clouds. All these objects tend to be perceived as figures against backgrounds. Cars against the background of the street are easier to pick out than cars piled on each other in a junkyard. Birds against the sky are more likely to be perceived than, as the saying goes, birds in the bush. Figures are closer to us than their grounds.

FIGURE 4.12

Figure and Ground. How many animals and demons can you find in this Escher print? Do we have white figures on a black background or black figures on a white background? Figure–ground perception is the tendency to perceive geometric forms against a background.

Ambiguous • Having two or more possible meanings.

When figure–ground relationships are **ambiguous,** or capable of being interpreted in various ways, our perceptions tend to be unstable, to shift back and forth. As an example, take a look at Figure 4.12—a nice leisurely look. How many people, objects, and animals can you find in this Escher print? If your eye is drawn back and forth, so that sometimes you are perceiving light figures on a dark background and then dark figures on a light background, you are experiencing figure–ground reversals. In other words, a shift is occurring in your perception of what is figure and what is ground, or backdrop. Escher was able to have some fun with us because of our tendency to try to isolate geometric patterns or figures from a background. However, in this case the "background" is as meaningful and detailed as the "figure." Therefore, our perceptions shift back and forth.

THE RUBIN VASE. In Figure 4.13 we see a Rubin vase, one of psychologists' favorite illustrations of figure–ground relationships. The figure–ground relationship in part A of the figure is ambiguous. There are no cues that suggest which area must be the figure. For this reason, our perception may shift from seeing the vase as the figure and then seeing two profiles as the figure.

There is no such problem in part B. Since it seems that a white vase has been brought forward against a colored ground, we are more likely to perceive the vase than the profiles. In part C, we are more likely to perceive the profiles than the vase because the profiles are whole, and the vase is broken against the background. Of course, we can still perceive the vase in part C, if we wish to, because experience has shown us where it is. Why not have fun

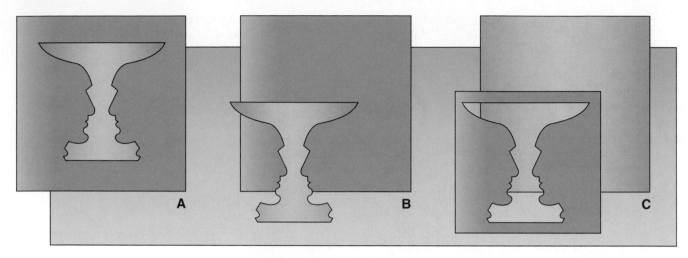

FIGURE 4.13

The Rubin Vase. A favorite drawing used by psychologists to demonstrate figure–ground perception. Part A is ambiguous, with neither the vase nor the profiles clearly the figure or the ground. In part B, the vase is the figure; in part C, the profiles are.

with some friends by covering parts B and C and asking them what they see? (They'll catch on to you quickly if they can see all three drawings at once.)

THE NECKER CUBE.   The Necker cube (Figure 4.14) provides another example of how an ambiguous drawing can lead to perceptual shifts.

Hold the figure at arm's length and stare at the center of it for 30 seconds or so. Try to allow your eye muscles to relax. (The feeling is of your eyes "glazing over.") After a while you will notice a dramatic shift in your perception of these "stacked boxes," so that what was once a front edge is now a back edge, and vice versa. Again, the dramatic perceptual shift is made possible by the fact that the outline of the drawing permits two interpretations.

SOME OTHER GESTALT RULES FOR ORGANIZATION.   In addition to the law of closure, Gestalt psychologists have noted that our perceptions are guided by rules or laws of *proximity, similarity, continuity,* and *common fate.*

Verbally describe part A of Figure 4.15 without reading further. Did you say that part A consisted of six lines or of three groups of two parallel lines? If you said three sets of lines, you were influenced by the **proximity,** or nearness, of some of the lines. There is no other reason for perceiving them in pairs or subgroups: All lines are parallel and of equal length.

Now describe part B of the figure. Did you perceive the figure as a six-by-six grid, or as three columns of *x*'s and three columns of *o*'s? According to the law of **similarity,** we perceive similar objects as belonging together. For this reason, you may have been more likely to describe part B in terms of columns than rows or a grid.

What about part C? Is it a circle with two lines stemming from it, or is it a (broken) line that goes through a circle? If you saw it as a single (broken) line, you were probably organizing your perceptions according to the rule of **continuity.** That is, we perceive a series of points or a broken line as having unity.

According to the law of **common fate,** elements seen moving together are perceived as belonging together. A group of people running in the same

FIGURE 4.14

The Necker Cube. Ambiguity in the drawing of the cubes makes perceptual shifts possible.

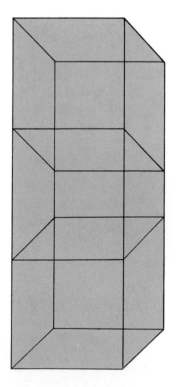

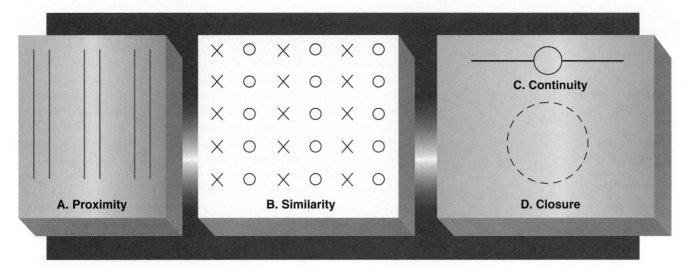

FIGURE 4.15

Some Gestalt Laws of Perceptual Organization. These drawings illustrate the Gestalt laws of proximity, similarity, continuity, and closure.

direction appear unified in purpose. Birds that flock together seem to be of a feather. (Did I get that right?)

Part D of Figure 4.15 provides another example of the law of closure. The arcs tend to be perceived as a circle (or circle with gaps) rather than as just a series of arcs.

TOP-DOWN VERSUS BOTTOM-UP PROCESSING IN PATTERN PERCEPTION. Imagine that you are trying to piece together a thousand-piece puzzle—a task that I usually avoid, despite the cajoling of my children. Now imagine that you are trying to accomplish it after someone has walked off with the box that contained the pieces—you know, the box with the picture formed by the completed puzzle.

When you have the box—when you know what the "big picture" or pattern looks like—cognitive psychologists refer to the task of assembling the pieces as **top-down processing.** The "top" of the visual system refers to the image of the pattern in the brain, and the top-down strategy for putting the puzzle together implies that you use the pattern to guide subordinate perceptual-motor tasks such as hunting for proper pieces. Without knowledge of the pattern, the assembly process is referred to as **bottom-up processing.** You begin with bits and pieces of information and become aware of the pattern formed by the assembled pieces only after you have labored for a while.

Proximity • Nearness. The perceptual tendency to group together objects that are near one another.

Similarity • The perceptual tendency to group together objects that are similar in appearance.

Continuity • The tendency to perceive a series of points or lines as having unity.

Common fate • The tendency to perceive elements that move together as belonging together.

Top-down processing • The use of contextual information or knowledge of a pattern in order to organize parts of the pattern.

Bottom-up processing • The organization of the parts of a pattern to recognize, or form an image of, the pattern they compose.

Perception of Movement

Consider the importance of the perception of movement. Moving objects—whether they are other people, animals, cars, or tons of earth plummeting down a hillside—are vital sources of sensory information. Moving objects capture the attention of even newborn infants.

To understand how we perceive movement, recall what it is like to be on a train that has begun to pull out of the station while the train on the adjacent

MINILECTURE: BIOLOGICAL MOTION

track remains stationary. If your own train does not lurch as it accelerates, you might think at first that the other train is moving. Or you might not be certain whether your train is moving forward or the other train is moving backward.

The visual perception of movement is based on change of position relative to other objects. To early scientists, whose only instrument for visual observation was the naked eye, it seemed logical that the sun circled the earth. You have to be able to imagine the movement of the earth around the sun as seen from a theoretical point in outer space—you cannot observe it directly.

How, then, do you determine which train is moving when your train is pulling out of the station (or that other train is pulling in)? One way is to look for objects you know are stable, such as station-platform columns, houses, signs, or trees. If you are stationary in relation to them, your train is not moving. Observing people walking on the station platform may not provide the answer, however, because they are also changing their position relative to stationary objects. You might also try to sense the motion of the train in your body. You know from experience how to do these things quite well, although it may be difficult to phrase explanations for them.

We have been considering the perception of real movement. Psychologists have also studied several types of apparent movement, or **illusions** of movement. These include the *autokinetic effect, stroboscopic motion,* and the *phi phenomenon.*

THE AUTOKINETIC EFFECT.
If you were to sit quietly in a dark room and stare at a point of light projected onto the far wall, after a while it might appear that the light had begun to move, even if it remained quite still. The tendency to perceive a stationary point of light as moving in a dark room is called the **autokinetic effect.**

Over the years, psychologists have run interesting experiments in which they have asked people, for example, what the light is "spelling out." The light has spelled out nothing, of course, and the words people perceive have reflected their own cognitive processes, not external sensations.

STROBOSCOPIC MOTION.
Stroboscopic motion makes motion pictures possible. In **stroboscopic motion,** the illusion of movement is provided by the presentation of a rapid progression of images of stationary objects. So-called motion pictures do not really consist of images that move. Rather, the audience is shown 16 to 22 pictures, or frames, per second, like those in Figure 4.16. Each frame differs slightly from that preceding it. Showing the frames in rapid succession then provides the illusion of movement.

At the rate of at least 16 frames per second, the "motion" in a film seems smooth and natural. With fewer than 16 or so frames per second, the movement looks jumpy and unnatural. That is why slow motion is achieved through

Illusions • Sensations that give rise to misperceptions.

Autokinetic effect • The tendency to perceive a stationary point of light in a dark room as moving.

Stroboscopic motion • A visual illusion in which the perception of motion is generated by a series of stationary images that are presented in rapid succession.

MINILECTURE: STROBOSCOPIC MOTION

FIGURE 4.16
Stroboscopic Motion. In a motion picture, viewing a series of stationary images at the rate of about 16 to 22 frames per second provides the illusion of movement. This form of apparent movement is termed *stroboscopic motion.*

filming perhaps 100 or more frames per second. When they are played back at about 22 frames per second, movement seems slowed down, yet smooth and natural.

THE PHI PHENOMENON. Have you seen news headlines spelled out in lights that rapidly wrap around a building? Have you seen an electronic scoreboard in a baseball or football stadium? When the home team scores, some scoreboards suggest the explosions of fireworks. What actually happens is that a row of lights is switched on, then off. As the first row is switched off, the second row is switched on, and so on for dozens, perhaps hundreds of rows. When the switching occurs rapidly, the **phi phenomenon** occurs: the on–off process is perceived as movement.

Like stroboscopic motion, the phi phenomenon is an example of apparent motion. Both stroboscopic motion and the phi phenomenon appear to occur because of the law of continuity. We tend to perceive a series of points as having unity, so the series of lights (points) is perceived as moving lines.

The Phi Phenomenon. The phi phenomenon is an illusion of movement that is produced by lights blinking on and off in sequence.

Depth Perception

Think of the problems you might have if you could not judge depth or distance. You might bump into other people, thinking them to be farther away than they are. An outfielder might not be able to judge whether to run toward the infield or the fence to catch a fly ball. You might give your front bumper a workout in stop-and-go traffic. Fortunately, both *monocular and binocular cues* help us perceive the depth of objects. Let us examine a number of them.

MONOCULAR CUES. Now that you have considered how difficult it would be to navigate through life without depth perception, ponder the problems of the artist who attempts to portray three-dimensional objects on a two-dimensional surface. Artists use **monocular cues,** or cues that can be perceived by one eye, to create an illusion of depth. These cues—including perspective, clearness, interposition, shadows, and texture gradient—cause certain objects to appear to be more distant from the viewer than others.

Distant objects stimulate smaller areas on the retina than nearby objects. The amount of sensory input from them is smaller, even though they may be the same size. The distances between far-off objects also appear to be smaller than equivalent distances between nearby objects. For this reason, the phenomenon known as **perspective** occurs. That is, we tend to perceive parallel lines as coming closer, or converging, as they recede from us. However, as we shall see when we discuss *size constancy,* experience teaches us that distant objects that look small will be larger when they are close. In this way, their relative size also becomes a cue to their distance from us.

The two engravings in Figure 4.17 represent impossible scenes in which the artists use principles of perspective to fool the viewer. In the engraving to the left, *Waterfall,* note that the water appears to be flowing away from the viewer in a zigzag because the stream becomes gradually narrower (that is, lines that we assume to be parallel are shown to be converging) and the stone sides of the aqueduct appear to be stepping down. However, given that the water arrives at the top of the fall, it must actually somehow be flowing upward. However, the spot from which it falls is no farther from the viewer than the collection point from which it appears to (but does not) begin its flow backward.

Again, distant objects look smaller than nearby objects of the same size. The paradoxes in the engraving to the right, *False Perspective,* are made possible by

Phi phenomenon • The perception of movement as a result of sequential presentation of visual stimuli.

Monocular cues • Stimuli suggestive of depth that can be perceived with only one eye.

Perspective • A monocular cue for depth based on the convergence (coming together) of parallel lines as they recede into the distance.

MINILECTURE: DEPTH PERCEPTION

FRONTISPIECE TO KERBY.

FIGURE 4.17

What Is Wrong with These Pictures? In *Waterfall,* to the left, how does Dutch artist M. C. Escher suggest that fallen water flows back upward, only to fall again? In *False Perspective,* to the right, how does English artist William Hogarth use monocular cues for depth perception to deceive the viewer?

Interposition • A monocular cue for depth based on the fact that a nearby object obscures a more distant object behind it.
Shadowing • A monocular cue for depth based on the fact that opaque objects block light and produce shadows.
Texture gradient • A monocular cue for depth based on the perception that closer objects appear to have rougher (more detailed) surfaces.

the fact that more-distant objects are not necessarily depicted as being smaller than nearby objects. Thus, what at first seems to be background suddenly becomes foreground, and vice versa.

The clearness of an object also suggests its distance from us. Experience shows us that we sense more details of nearby objects. For this reason, artists can suggest that certain objects are closer to the viewer by depicting them in greater detail. Note that the "distant" hill in the Hogarth engraving (Figure 4.17) is given less detail than the nearby plants at the bottom of the picture. Our perceptions are mocked when a man "on" that distant hill in the background is shown conversing with a woman leaning out a window in the middle ground.

How does artist Victor Vasarely use monocular cues to provide the illusion of a curving surface in his tapestry, *Vega-Tek* (Figure 4.18)?

We also learn that nearby objects can block our views of more-distant objects. Overlapping, or **interposition,** is the apparent placing of one object in front of another. Experience encourages us to perceive the partly covered objects as being farther away than the objects that hide parts of them from view (Figure 4.19). In the Hogarth engraving (Figure 4.17), which looks closer— the trees in the background (background?) or the moon sign hanging from the building (or is it buildings?) to the right? How does the artist use interposition to confound the viewer?

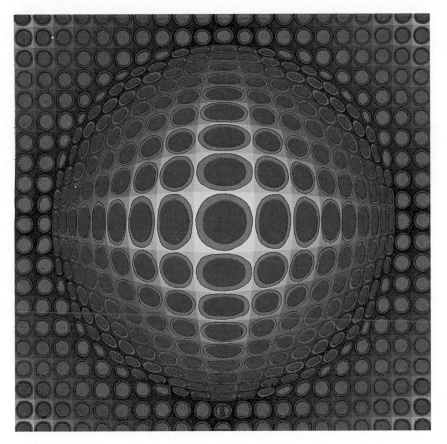

FIGURE 4.18

Creating the Illusion of Three Dimensions with Two. How does Op Artist Victor Vasarely use monocular cues for depth perception to lend this work a three-dimensional quality?

FIGURE 4.19

The Effects of Interposition. The four circles are the same size. Which circles seem closer: the complete circles or the circles with chunks bitten out of them?

FIGURE 4.20

Shadowing as a Cue in the Perception of Depth. Shadowing lends the circle on the right a sense of three-dimensionality.

Additional information about depth is provided by **shadowing** and is based on the fact that opaque objects block light and produce shadows. Shadows and highlights give us information about objects' three-dimensional shapes and about their relationships to the source of light. The left part of Figure 4.20 is perceived as a two-dimensional circle, but the right part tends to be perceived as a three-dimensional sphere because of the highlight on its surface and the shadow underneath. In the "sphere," the highlighted central area is perceived as being closest to us, with the surface then receding to the edges.

Another monocular cue is **texture gradient.** A gradient is a progressive change, and closer objects are perceived as having progressively rougher textures. In the Hogarth engraving (Figure 4.17), the building just behind the large fisherman's head has a rougher texture and thus seems to be closer than the building with the window from which the woman is leaning. Our surprise is thus heightened when the moon sign is seen as hanging from both buildings.

MOTION CUES. If you have ever driven in the country, you have probably noticed that distant objects such as mountains and stars appear to move along with you. Objects at an intermediate distance seem to be stationary, but nearby objects such as roadside markers, rocks, and trees seem to go by quite rapidly. The tendency of objects to seem to move backward or forward as a function

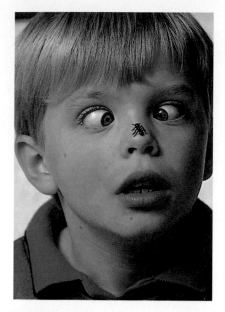

FIGURE 4.21

Retinal Disparity and Convergence as Cues for Depth. As an object nears your eyes, you begin to see two images of it because of retinal disparity. If you maintain perception of a single image, your eyes must converge on the object.

MINILECTURE: BRIGHTNESS, CONTRAST, AND CONSTANCY

of their distance is known as **motion parallax.** We learn to perceive objects that appear to move with us as being at greater distances.

Earlier we noted that nearby objects cause the lens of the eye to accommodate or bend more to bring them into focus. The sensations of tension in the eye muscles also provide a monocular cue to depth, especially when we are within about 4 feet of the objects.

BINOCULAR CUES.   **Binocular cues,** or cues that involve both eyes, also help us perceive depth. Two binocular cues are *retinal disparity* and *convergence.*

Try an experiment. Hold your index finger at arm's length. Now, gradually bring it closer until it almost touches your nose. If you keep your eyes relaxed as you do so, you will see two fingers. An image of the finger will be projected onto the retina of each eye, and each image will be slightly different because the finger will be seen at different angles. The difference between the projected images is referred to as **retinal disparity** and serves as a binocular cue for depth perception (see Figure 4.21). Note that the closer your finger comes, the farther apart the "two fingers" appear to be. Closer objects have greater retinal disparity.

If we try to maintain a single image of the approaching finger, our eyes must turn inward, or converge on it, giving us a cross-eyed look. **Convergence** is associated with feelings of tension in the eye muscles and provides another binocular cue for depth. The binocular cues of retinal disparity and convergence are strongest at near distances.

Problems in Visual Perception

PROBLEMS IN VISUAL ACUITY.   **Visual acuity** refers to sharpness of vision, as defined by the ability to discriminate visual details. People who are **nearsighted** must be unusually close to an object to discriminate its details. People who are **farsighted** have difficulty focusing on nearby objects.

You may have noticed that older people often hold newspapers or books at a distance. As you reach middle age, the lenses of the eyes become relatively brittle, making it more difficult to accommodate to, or focus on, objects. This condition is called **presbyopia,** from the Greek for "old man," although presbyopia usually begins in middle age. The lens structure of people with presbyopia differs from that of farsighted young people. Still, the effect of presbyopia is to make it difficult to perceive nearby visual stimuli. People who had normal visual acuity in their youth often require corrective lenses to read in old age. And people who were initially farsighted often have headaches linked to eyestrain.

Perceptual Constancies

The world is a constantly shifting display of visual sensations. What confusion would reign if we did not perceive a doorway to be the same doorway when seen from 6 feet as when seen from 4 feet. As we neared it, we might think that it was larger than the door we were seeking and become lost. Or consider the problems of the pet owner who recognizes his dog from the side but not from above, when the shapes differ. Fortunately, these problems tend not to occur—at least with familiar objects—because of perceptual constancies.

The image of a dog seen from 20 feet occupies about the same amount of space on your retina as an inch-long insect crawling in the palm of your hand.

Yet, you do not perceive the dog to be as small as the insect. Through your experiences you have acquired **size constancy,** or the tendency to perceive the same object as being the same size, even though the size of its image on the retina varies as a function of its distance. Experience teaches us about perspective, that the same object seen at a great distance will appear to be much smaller than when it is nearby.

SIZE CONSTANCY. Westerners may say that people or cars look like ants from airplanes, but they know that they remain people and cars even if the details of their forms are lost in the distance. We can thus say that Westerners *perceive* them to be of the same size even from great distances, and even though the images they form on the retina and in the visual cortex are extremely small.

A cross-cultural case study suggests that a person from another culture might indeed perceive people and cars to be insects from the vantage point of an airplane. It also emphasizes the role of experience in the development of size constancy. Anthropologist Colin Turnbull (1961) found that an African Pygmy, Kenge, thought that buffalo perceived across an open field were some form of insect. Turnbull had to drive Kenge down to where the animals were grazing to convince him that they were not insects. During the drive, as the buffalo gradually grew in size, Kenge muttered to himself and moved closer to Turnbull in fear. Even after Kenge saw that these animals were, indeed, familiar buffalo, he still wondered how they could grow large so quickly. Kenge, you see, lived in a thick forest and normally did not view large animals from great distances. For this reason, he had not developed size constancy for distant objects. However, Kenge had no difficulty displaying size constancy with objects placed at various distances in his home.

COLOR CONSTANCY. We also have **color constancy**—the tendency to perceive objects as retaining their color even though lighting conditions may alter their appearance. Your bright orange car may edge toward yellow-gray as the hours wend their way through twilight to nighttime. But when you finally locate it in the parking lot, you will still think of it as being orange. You expect an orange car and still judge it to be "more orange" than the (faded) blue and green cars to either side. However, it would be fiercely difficult to find it in a parking lot filled with yellow and red cars similar in size and shape.

Consider Figure 4.22. The orange squares within the blue squares are the same hue. However, the orange within the dark blue square is perceived as being purer. Why? Again, experience teaches us that the pureness of colors fades as the background grows darker. Since the orange squares are equally pure, we assume that the one in the dark background must be more saturated. We would stand ready to perceive the orange squares as being equal in purity if the square within the darker blue field actually had a bit of black mixed in with it.

BRIGHTNESS CONSTANCY. Similar to color constancy is **brightness constancy.** The same gray square is perceived as brighter when placed within a black background than when placed within a white background (see Figure 1.3 on p. 13). Again, consider the role of experience. If it were nighttime, we would expect gray to fade to near blackness. The fact that the gray within the black square stimulates the eye with equal intensity suggests that it must be very much brighter than the gray within the white square.

SHAPE CONSTANCY. We also perceive objects as maintaining their shapes, even if we perceive them from different angles so that the shape of the retinal

Motion parallax • A monocular cue for depth based on the perception that nearby objects appear to move more rapidly in relation to our own motion.

Binocular cues • Stimuli suggestive of depth that involve simultaneous perception by both eyes.

Retinal disparity • A binocular cue for depth based on the difference in the image cast by an object on the retinas of the eyes as the object moves closer or farther away.

Convergence • A binocular cue for depth based on the inward movement of the eyes as they attempt to focus on an object that is drawing nearer.

Visual acuity • Sharpness of vision.

Nearsighted • Capable of seeing nearby objects with greater acuity than distant objects.

Farsighted • Capable of seeing distant objects with greater acuity than nearby objects.

Presbyopia • A condition characterized by brittleness of the lens.

Size constancy • The tendency to perceive an object as being the same size even as the size of its retinal image changes according to the object's distance.

Color constancy • The tendency to perceive an object as being the same color even though lighting conditions change its appearance.

Brightness constancy • The tendency to perceive an object as being just as bright even though lighting conditions change its intensity.

FIGURE 4.22

Color Constancy. The orange squares within the blue squares are the same hue, yet the orange within the dark blue square is perceived as being purer. Why?

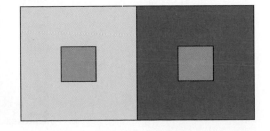

FIGURE 4.23

Shape Constancy. When closed, this door is a rectangle. When open, the retinal image is trapezoidal. But because of shape constancy, we still perceive the door as being rectangular.

FIGURE 4.24

What Is Wrong with These Drawings?

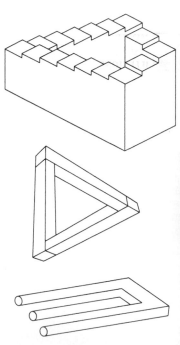

image changes dramatically. This tendency is called **shape constancy.** You perceive the top of a coffee cup or a glass to be a circle even though it is a circle only when seen from above. When seen from an angle, it is an ellipse. When seen on edge, the retinal image of the cup or glass is the same as that of a straight line. So why do you still describe the rim of the cup or glass as being a circle? Perhaps for two reasons: One is that experience has taught you that the cup will look circular when seen from above. The second is that you may have labeled the cup circular or round. Experience and labels make the world a stable place. Can you imagine the chaos that would prevail if we described objects as they stimulated our sensory organs with each changing moment, rather than according to stable conditions?

In another example, a door is a rectangle only when viewed straight on (Figure 4.23). When we move to the side or open it, the left or right edge comes closer and appears to be larger, changing the retinal image to a trapezoid. Yet we continue to think of doors as being rectangles.

The principles of perceptual organization also make it possible to create fascinating "impossible" drawings. For example, what's wrong with each of the drawings in Figure 4.24? Each has firm lines. Each has interesting shapes. In fact, if you look at any one corner of a drawing, it makes perfect sense. But take a critical view of the endless staircase in M. C. Escher's *Relativity.* What would happen if you were to walk up this staircase? Would you ever reach the top? Or what would happen if a ball rolled down and managed to turn all the corners? Would it ever reach bottom?

In each of these drawings, the artist, working in two dimensions, has used perceptual cues in such a way as to encourage us to perceive a three-dimensional figure. Any one segment of each of these drawings makes perfect sense. It's just when you put it all together that you realize that . . . well, you can't put it all together, can you? That would be impossible.

Shape constancy • The tendency to perceive an object as being the same shape although the retinal image varies in shape as it rotates.

Visual Illusions

The principles of perceptual organization make it possible for our eyes to "play tricks on us." Psychologists, like magicians, enjoy pulling a rabbit out of the hat now and then, and I am pleased to be able to demonstrate how the perceptual constancies trick the eye through so-called visual illusions.

MINILECTURE: VISUAL ILLUSIONS

The Hering-Helmholtz and Müller-Lyer illusions (Figure 4.25, part A) are named after the people who originated them. In the Hering-Helmholtz illusion, the horizontal lines are straight and parallel. However, the radiating lines cause them to appear to be bent outward near the center. The two lines in the Müller-Lyer illusion are the same length, but the line on the left, with its reversed arrowheads, looks longer.

Let us try to explain these illusions. Because of experience and lifelong use of perceptual cues, we tend to perceive the Hering-Helmholtz drawing as being three-dimensional. Because of the tendency to perceive bits of sensory information as figures against grounds, we perceive the white area in the center as being a circle in front of a series of radiating lines, all of which lies in front of a white ground. Next, because of our experience with perspective, we perceive the radiating lines as being parallel. We perceive the two horizontal lines as intersecting the "receding" lines, and we know that they would have to appear bent out at the center if they were to be equidistant at all points from the center of the circle.

Experience probably compels us to perceive the vertical lines in the Müller-Lyer illusion as being the corners of a room as seen from inside a house, at

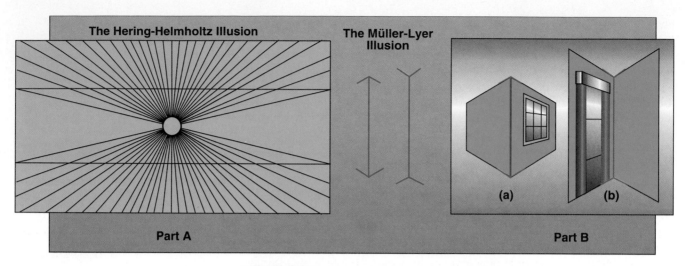

FIGURE 4.25

The Hering-Helmholtz and Müller-Lyer Illusions. In the Hering-Helmholtz illusion, are the horizontal lines straight or curved? In the Müller-Lyer illusion, are the vertical lines equal in length?

left, and outside a house, at right (see Figure 4.25, part B). In such an example, the reverse arrowheads to the left are lines where the walls meet the ceiling and the floor. We perceive such lines as extending toward us. They push the corner away from us. The arrowheads to the right are lines where exterior walls meet the roof and foundation. We perceive them as receding from us. They push the corner toward us. The vertical line to the left is thus perceived as being farther away. Since both vertical lines stimulate equal expanses across the retina, the principle of size constancy encourages us to perceive the line to the left as being longer.

Figure 4.26 is known as the Ponzo illusion. In this illusion, the two horizontal lines are the same length. However, do you perceive the top line as being longer? The rule of size constancy may also afford insight into this illusion. Perhaps the converging lines again strike us as being parallel lines receding into the distance, like the train tracks in Figure 4.26. If so, we assume from experience that the horizontal line at the top is farther down the track—farther away from us. And again, the rule of size constancy tells us that if two objects appear to be the same size and one is farther away, the farther object must be larger. So we perceive the top line as being larger.

Now that you are an expert on these visual illusions, look at Figure 4.27. First take some bets from friends about whether the three cylinders are equal in height and width. Then get a ruler. Once you have made some money, however, try to explain why the cylinders to the right look progressively larger.

FIGURE 4.26

The Ponzo Illusion. The two horizontal lines in this drawing are equal in length, but the top line is perceived as being longer. Use the principle of size constancy to explain why.

Reflections

- Why is it easier to spot your friend when she or he is walking alone than among a crowd?
- Have you ever seen two people walking next to one another and then been surprised to see them split up without saying anything to one another? How do you account for the assumption that they knew each other?
- Have you had the experience of being in a train and not knowing whether your train or a train on the next track was moving? How do you explain the confusion?

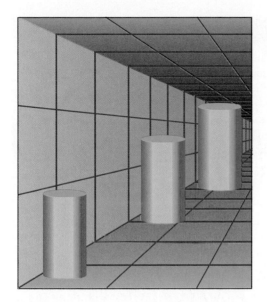

FIGURE 4.27

An Illusion Created by the Principle of Size Constancy. In this drawing, the three cylinders are the same size, yet they appear to grow larger toward the top of the picture. Use the principle of size constancy to explain why.

HEARING: TAKING IN GOOD VIBRATIONS

Consider the advertising slogan for the science fiction film *Alien:* "In space, no one can hear you scream." It's true. Space is an almost perfect vacuum, and hearing requires a medium such as air or water through which sound can travel.

Sound, or **auditory** stimulation, travels through the air in waves. Sound waves are caused by changes in air pressure that result from vibrations. These vibrations can be created by your vocal cords, guitar strings, or the clap of a book slammed down on a desk.

Pitch and Loudness

Pitch and loudness are two psychological dimensions of sound. The pitch of a sound is determined by its frequency, or the number of cycles per second. It is expressed in the unit **Hertz** (Hz). One cycle per second is one Hz. The greater the number of cycles per second (Hz), the higher the pitch of the sound. The human ear is sensitive to sound waves that vary from frequencies of 20 to 20,000 cycles per second. The pitches of women's voices are usually higher than those of men because women's vocal cords tend to be shorter and vibrate at a greater frequency. The strings of a violin are shorter than those of a viola or cello. They vibrate at greater frequencies, and we perceive them to be higher in pitch. Pitch detectors in the brain allow us to tell the difference (Blakeslee, 1995c).

The loudness of a sound is determined by the height, or **amplitude,** of sound waves. The higher the amplitude of the wave, the louder the sound. Figure 4.28 shows records of sound waves that vary in frequency and amplitude. Frequency and amplitude are independent dimensions. Sounds both high and low in pitch can be either high or low in loudness.

The loudness of a sound is usually expressed in the unit **decibel,** abbreviated *dB,* which is named after the inventor of the telephone, Alexander Graham Bell. Zero dB is equivalent to the threshold of hearing. How loud is that? It's about as loud as the ticking of a watch 20 feet away in a very quiet room (see Table 4.1).

Auditory • Having to do with hearing.

Hertz • A unit expressing the frequency of sound waves. One Hertz, or *1 Hz,* equals one cycle per second.

Amplitude • Height.

Decibel • A unit expressing the loudness of a sound. Abbreviated *dB.*

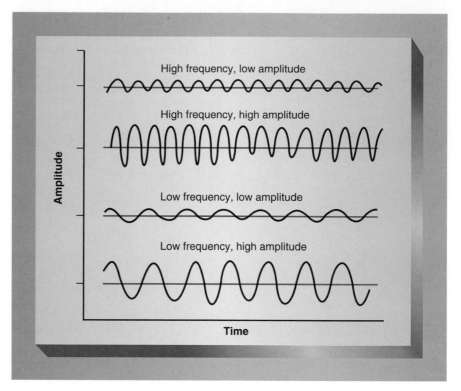

FIGURE 4.28

Sound Waves of Various Frequencies and Amplitudes. Which sounds have the highest pitch? Which are loudest?

Consonant • In harmony.

Dissonant • Incompatible, not harmonious, discordant.

Overtones • Tones of a higher frequency than those played that result from vibrations throughout a musical instrument.

Timbre • The quality or richness of a sound.

The decibel equivalents of familiar sounds are shown in Figure 4.29. Twenty dB is equivalent in loudness to a whisper at 5 feet. Thirty dB is roughly the limit of loudness at which your librarian would like to keep your college library. You may suffer hearing damage if exposed protractedly to sounds of 85 to 90 dB.

When musical sounds (also called tones) of different frequency are played together, we also perceive a third tone that results from the difference in their frequencies. If the combination of tones is pleasant, we say that they are in harmony, or **consonant** (from Latin roots meaning "together" and "sound"). Unpleasant combinations of tones are labeled **dissonant** ("the opposite of" and "sound"). The expression that something "strikes a dissonant chord" means that we find it disagreeable.

OVERTONES AND TIMBRE. In addition to producing the specified musical note, an instrument like the violin also produces a number of tones that are greater in frequency. These more highly pitched sounds are called **overtones.** Overtones result from vibrations elsewhere in the instrument and contribute to the quality or richness—the **timbre**—of a sound.

Truth or Fiction Revisited. *It is true that a $500 machine-made violin will produce the same musical notes as a $200,000 Stradivarius.* The Stradivarius has richer overtones, which lend the instrument its greater value. Professional musicians require more expensive instruments because of the richness of their overtones—their timbre.

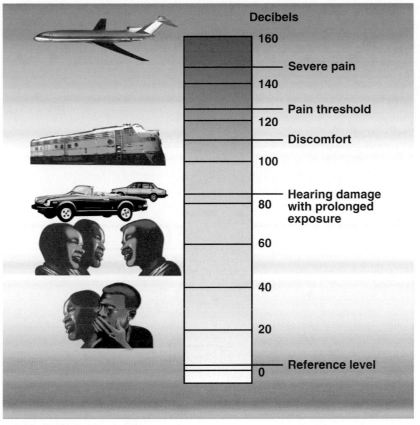

FIGURE 4.29

Decibel Ratings of Some Familiar Sounds. Zero dB is the threshold of hearing. You may suffer hearing loss if you incur prolonged exposure to sounds of 85–90 dB.

White noise • Discordant sounds of many frequencies, often producing a lulling effect.

NOISE. Noise is a combination of dissonant sounds.[1] When you place a spiral shell to your ear, you do not hear the roar of the ocean. Rather, you hear the reflected noise in your vicinity. **White noise** consists of many different frequencies of sound. Yet, the mixture can lull us to sleep if the loudness is not too great.

Now let us turn our attention to the marvelous instrument that senses all these different "vibes": the human ear.

The Ear: The Better to Hear You With

The human ear is good for lots of things—catching dust, combing your hair around, hanging jewelry from, and nibbling. It is also admirably suited for sensing sounds. The ear is shaped and structured to capture sound waves, to vibrate in sympathy with them, and to transmit all this business to centers in

---

[1] Within the broader context of signal-detection theory, *noise* has a different meaning, discussed earlier in the chapter.

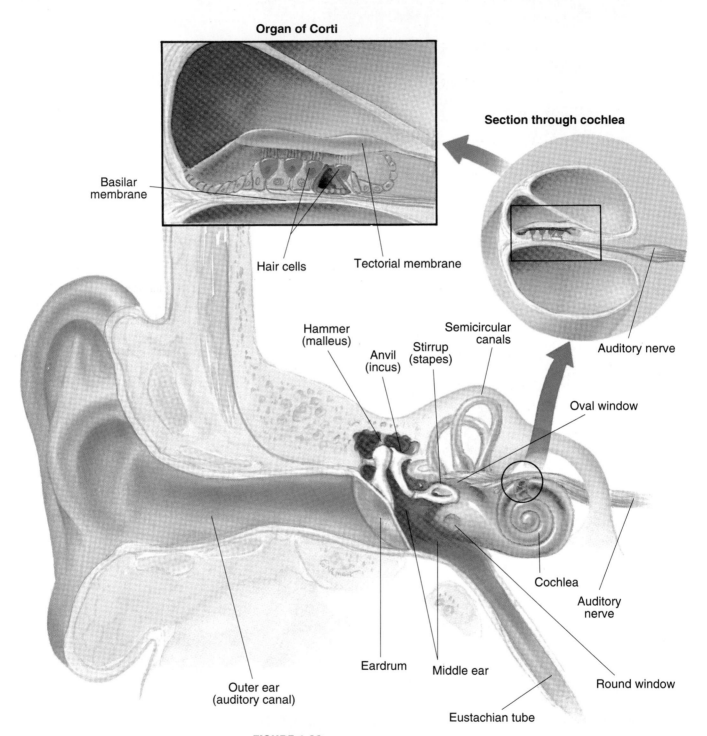

Organ of Corti

Section through cochlea

Basilar membrane

Hair cells

Tectorial membrane

Auditory nerve

Hammer (malleus)

Anvil (incus)

Stirrup (stapes)

Semicircular canals

Oval window

Cochlea

Auditory nerve

Eardrum

Middle ear

Round window

Outer ear (auditory canal)

Eustachian tube

FIGURE 4.30

The Ear. The outer ear funnels sound to the eardrum. Inside the eardrum, vibrations of the hammer, anvil, and stirrup transmit sound to the inner ear. Vibrations in the inner ear transmit the sound to the auditory nerve.

the brain. In this way, you not only hear something, you can also figure out what it is. You have an outer ear, a middle ear, and an inner ear (see Figure 4.30).

THE OUTER EAR.   The outer ear is shaped to funnel sound waves to the **eardrum,** a thin membrane that vibrates in response to sound waves and thereby transmits them to the middle and inner ears.

THE MIDDLE EAR.   The middle ear contains the eardrum and three small bones—the hammer, the anvil, and the stirrup—which also transmit sound by vibrating. These bones were given their names (actually the Latin *malleus, incus,* and *stapes* [pronounced STAY-peas], which translate as hammer, anvil, and stirrup) because of their shapes. The middle ear functions as an amplifier: It increases the magnitude of the air pressure.

The stirrup is attached to another vibrating membrane, the **oval window.** The round window shown in Figure 4.30 balances the pressure in the inner ear. It pushes out when the oval window pushes in, and it is pulled in when the oval window vibrates outward.

THE INNER EAR.   The oval window transmits vibrations into the inner ear, the bony tube called the **cochlea** (from the Greek for "snail"). The cochlea, which has the shape of a snail shell, contains two longitudinal membranes that divide it into three fluid-filled chambers. One of the membranes that lies coiled within the cochlea is called the **basilar membrane.** Vibrations in the fluids within the chambers of the inner ear press against the basilar membrane.

The **organ of Corti,** sometimes referred to as the "command post" of hearing, is attached to the basilar membrane. Thousands of hair cells (receptor cells that project like hair from the organ of Corti) "dance" in response to the vibrations of the basilar membrane (Brownell, 1992). This up-and-down movement generates neural impulses that are transmitted to the brain via the bundle of 31,000 neurons that form the **auditory nerve.** Within the brain, auditory input is projected onto the hearing areas of the temporal lobes of the cerebral cortex.

Locating Sounds

How do you balance the loudness of a stereo set? You sit between the speakers and adjust the volume until the sound seems to be equally loud in each ear. If the sound to the right is louder, the musical instruments will be perceived as being toward the right rather than straight ahead.

There is a resemblance between balancing a stereo set and locating sounds. A sound that is louder in the right ear is perceived as coming from the right. A sound from the right side also reaches the right ear first. Loudness and sequence of stimulating the ears both provide directional cues.

But it may not be easy to locate a sound that is directly in front, in back, or overhead. Such sounds are equally loud in and distant from each ear. So what do we do? Simple—usually we turn our heads slightly to determine in which ear the sound increases. If you turn your head a few degrees to the right and the loudness increases in your left ear, the sound must be in front of you. Of course we also use vision and general knowledge in locating the source of sounds. If you hear the roar of jet engines, most of the time you will make money by betting that the airplane is overhead.

Eardrum • A thin membrane that vibrates in response to sound waves, transmitting the waves to the middle and inner ears.

Oval window • A membrane that transmits vibrations from the stirrup of the middle ear to the cochlea within the inner ear.

Cochlea • The inner ear; the bony tube that contains the basilar membrane and the organ of Corti.

Basilar membrane • A membrane that lies coiled within the cochlea.

Organ of Corti • The receptor for hearing that lies on the basilar membrane in the cochlea.

Auditory nerve • The axon bundle that transmits neural impulses from the organ of Corti to the brain.

Perception of Loudness and Pitch

We know that sounds are heard because they cause vibration in parts of the ear, and information about these vibrations is transmitted to the brain. But what determines the loudness and pitch of our perceptions of these sounds?

The loudness and pitch of sounds appear to be related to the number of receptor neurons on the organ of Corti that fire and how often they fire. Psychologists generally agree that sounds are perceived as being louder when more of these sensory neurons fire. They are not so certain about the perception of pitch. Two of the theories that have been advanced to explain pitch discrimination are *place theory* and *frequency theory*.

PLACE THEORY.   According to **place theory,** the pitch of a sound is determined by the place along the basilar membrane that vibrates in response to it. In his classic research with guinea pigs and cadavers, George von Békésy (1957) found that receptors at different sites along the membrane fire in response to tones of differing frequencies. By and large, the higher the pitch of a sound, the closer the responsive neurons lie to the oval window. However, the entire membrane appears to be responsive to tones that are low in frequency.

FREQUENCY THEORY.   Place theory does not explain all the phenomena of hearing. For example, it has been found that impulses in the auditory nerve follow the pattern of the sound waves being detected. **Frequency theory** has been developed to account for such occurrences. In general, frequency theory proposes that pitch perception depends on the stimulation of neural impulses that match the frequency of the sound waves. However, frequency theory breaks down for perception of pitches higher than 1,000 Hz because neural impulses are not able to follow the forms of the sound waves at those levels.

Duplicity theory advances the view that pitch perception depends both on the place and frequency of neural response. A more comprehensive theory of pitch perception is needed to explain (1) why neurons at different sites on the basilar membrane fire in response to different pitches, (2) why impulses in the auditory nerve follow the patterns of sound waves at many frequencies, and (3) how we perceive pitches at above 1,000 Hz.

Unfortunately, not everyone perceives sound, and many of us do not perceive sounds of certain frequencies. Let us consider a number of kinds of hearing problems, or deafness.

Place theory • The theory that the pitch of a sound is determined by the section of the basilar membrane that vibrates in response to the sound.
Frequency theory • The theory that the pitch of a sound is reflected in the frequency of the neural impulses that are generated in response to the sound.
Duplicity theory • A combination of the place and frequency theories of pitch discrimination.

Deafness

An estimated 28 million Americans have impaired hearing. Two million of them are deaf (Nadol, 1993). They are thus deprived of a key source of information about the world outside. In recent years, however, society has made more of an effort to bring them into the mainstream of sensory experience. People are usually on hand to convert political and other speeches into hand signs (such as those of American Sign Language) for hearing-impaired members of the audience. Many television shows are now "closed captioned" so that they will be accessible to the hearing-impaired. Special decoders render the captions visible. Although people are more likely to encounter hearing loss as they age, educators have also grown more aware of the potential language learning problems of hearing-impaired children.

There are two major types of hearing problems or deafness: *conductive deafness* and *sensorineural deafness*.

CONDUCTIVE DEAFNESS. **Conductive deafness** occurs because of damage to the structures of the middle ear—either to the eardrum or to the three bones that conduct (and amplify) sound waves from the outer ear to the inner ear (Nadol, 1993). People with conductive hearing loss have high absolute thresholds for detection of sounds at all frequencies. This is the type of hearing impairment frequently found among older people. People with conductive deafness often profit from hearing aids, which provide the amplification that the middle ear does not.

SENSORINEURAL DEAFNESS. **Sensorineural deafness** usually stems from damage to the structures of the inner ear, most often the loss of hair cells, which will not regenerate. Sensorineural deafness can also stem from damage to the auditory nerve, for example, because of disease or because of acoustic trauma (exposure to loud sounds). In sensorineural deafness, people tend to be more sensitive to sounds of some pitches than others. In so-called Hunter's notch, hearing impairment is limited to particular frequencies—in this case, the frequencies of the sound waves generated by a gun firing. Prolonged exposure to 85 dB can cause hearing loss. People who attend high-volume rock concerts risk damaging their ears, as do workers who run pneumatic drills or drive high-volume transportation vehicles. The so-called ringing sensation that often follows exposure to loud sounds probably means that hair cells have been damaged. If you find yourself suddenly exposed to loud sounds, remember that your fingertips serve as good emergency ear protectors.

Experimental cochlear implants, or "artificial ears," contain microphones that sense sounds and electronic equipment that transmits sounds past damaged hair cells to stimulate the auditory nerve directly. Multichannel implants apply the place theory of pitch perception to enable people with hearing problems to discriminate sounds of high and low pitches. Such implants have helped many people with sensorineural deafness. However, they cannot assume the functions of damaged auditory nerves.

Conductive deafness • The forms of deafness in which there is loss of conduction of sound through the middle ear.

Sensorineural deafness • The forms of deafness that result from damage to hair cells or the auditory nerve.

Reflections

- Are you familiar with these stringed instruments: violin, viola, cello, and bass fiddle? How do their sounds differ? What accounts for their differences in sound?
- Have you ever been unsure of where a sound was coming from? How did you locate it?
- Do you know anyone who is hearing-impaired? What biological problem accounts for the impairment in hearing? How does the person cope with the impairment?

 **WORLD OF DIVERSITY**

THE SIGNS OF THE TIMES ARE CHANGING TO REFLECT NEW SENSIBILITIES AMONG THE DEAF

Deaf people used to make the sign that meant a Japanese person by twisting the little finger next to the eye (see Figure 4.31). Today many of the people who use American Sign Language have discarded this sign because it refers to the stereotypical physical feature of slanted eyes. Instead, they are adopting Japanese people's own sign for themselves: They press the thumb and index

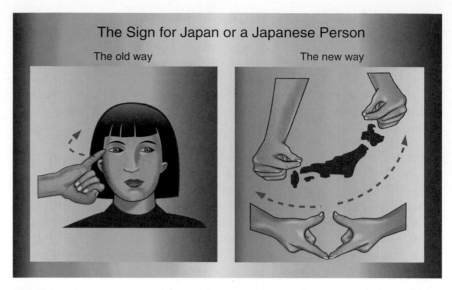

FIGURE 4.31

Old and New Signs for *Japan* or *Japanese Person* in American Sign Language. The old sign for *Japanese* is now considered offensive because it refers to the stereotypical physical feature of slanted eyes. The new sign simply outlines the island of Japan.

finger of both hands together and then pull them apart to sculpt the outline of Japan in the air (Senior, 1994).

"In American Sign Language, politically incorrect terms are often a visual representation of the ugly metaphors we have about people," notes psycholinguist Elissa Newport (1994). As with the sign for *Japanese,* the signs for *Chinese* and *Korean,* which are made by forming the letters *C* and *K* around the

FIGURE 4.32

Old and New Signs for *African Americans* in American Sign Language. The old signs for *African Americans* were considered offensive because they referred to the shape or location of the nose. The new sign outlines the African continent.

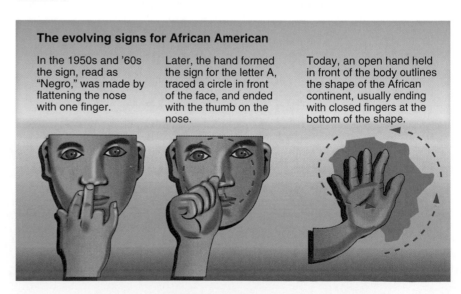

eye, are also changing. There is a new sign for *African American*. It was once indicated by flattening the nose. It was then replaced by signs for the color black—the index finger either placed by the eyebrow or wiped across the forehead. The current sign for *African American* is still centered around the nose, however, and is thus being replaced by outlining Africa in the air (see Figure 4.32).

The old sign for a gay male was an offensive swish of the wrist. Now it is more widely acceptable to simply spell out words like *homosexual, gay male,* or *lesbian* with the hands.

A sign for *stingy* shows a clenched fist in connection with stroking an imaginary beard. Stroking an imaginary beard is the sign for *Jewish,* and so the fist and beard sign has sparked discussions among deaf Jews. Still, no new sign has replaced it as of this writing.

Politically correct changes in American Sign Language have thus far caught on mainly among highly educated deaf people in urban settings. It is taking longer for them to catch on in the wider deaf community and to appear in dictionaries of sign language. Nevertheless, the clear trend is for the deaf—who in many ways have been the victims of stereotyping themselves—to learn how not to stereotype others through sign language.

SMELL

Smell and taste are the chemical senses. In the cases of vision and hearing, physical energy impacts on our sensory receptors. With smell and taste, we sample molecules of the substances being sensed.

You could say that we are underprivileged when it comes to the sense of smell. Dogs, for instance, devote about seven times as much area of the cerebral cortex to the sense of smell. Male dogs sniff to determine where the territories of other dogs leave off and to determine whether female dogs are sexually receptive. Dogs even make a living sniffing out marijuana in closed packages and suitcases.

Still, smell has an important role in human behavior. Smell makes a crucial contribution to the flavor of foods, for example (Bartoshuk & Beauchamp, 1994). If you did not have a sense of smell, an onion and an apple would taste the same to you! People's senses of smell may be lacking when we compare them to those of a dog, but we can detect the odor of one one-millionth of a milligram of vanilla in a liter of air.

An **odor** is a sample of the substance being sensed. Odors are detected by sites on receptor neurons in the **olfactory** membrane high in each nostril. Receptor neurons fire when a few molecules of the substance in gaseous form come into contact with them. Firing transmits information about odors to the brain via the **olfactory nerve.** That is how the substance is smelled.

It is unclear how many basic kinds of odors there are. In any event, olfactory receptors may respond to more than one kind of odor. Moreover, mixtures of smell sensations also help produce the broad range of odors that we can perceive (Bartoshuk & Beauchamp, 1994).

The sense of smell adapts rapidly to odors, even obnoxious ones (Solomon and others, 1993). This might be fortunate if you are using a locker room or an outhouse. It might not be so fortunate if you are being exposed to fumes from paints or second-hand smoke, since you may lose awareness of them while danger remains. One odor may also be masked by another, which is how air fresheners work.

Odor • The characteristic of a substance that makes it perceptible to the sense of smell.

Olfactory • Having to do with the sense of smell.

Olfactory nerve • The nerve that transmits information concerning odors from olfactory receptors to the brain.

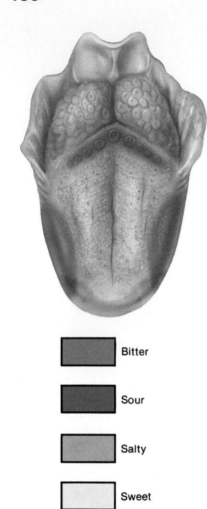

FIGURE 4.33

Location of Taste Buds. Taste buds on different areas of the tongue are sensitive to different taste qualities.

Taste cells • Receptor cells that are sensitive to taste.

Taste buds • The sensory organs for taste. They contain taste cells and are located on the tongue.

TASTE

Your cocker spaniel may jump at the chance to finish off your ice cream cone, but your Siamese cat may turn up her nose at the opportunity. Why? Dogs can perceive the taste quality of sweetness, as can pigs, but cats cannot.

There are four primary taste qualities: sweet, sour, salty, and bitter. The *flavor* of a food involves its taste but is more complex. Although apples and onions have the same taste—or the same mix of taste qualities—their flavors differ greatly. After all, you wouldn't chomp into a nice cold onion on a warm day, would you? The flavor of a food depends on its odor, texture, and temperature as well as its taste. If it were not for odor, heated tenderized shoe leather might pass for steak.

Truth or Fiction Revisited. *It is true that onions and apples have the same taste.* Their *flavors,* however, which also reflect these foods' odors and other qualities, are very different.

Taste is sensed through **taste cells**—receptor neurons that are located on **taste buds.** You have about 10,000 taste buds, most of which are located near the edges and back of your tongue. Taste buds tend to specialize a bit (see Figure 4.33). Some, for example, are more responsive to sweetness. Others react to several tastes. Receptors for sweetness lie at the tip of the tongue, and receptors for bitterness lie toward the back of the tongue. Sourness is sensed along the sides of the tongue, and saltiness overlaps the areas sensitive to sweetness and sourness (Figure 4.33). This is why people perceive a sour dish to "get them" at the sides of the tongue.

We live in different taste worlds. Some of us with a low sensitivity for the sweet taste may require twice the sugar to sweeten our food as others who are more sensitive to sweetness. Others of us who claim to enjoy very bitter foods may actually be taste-blind to them. Sensitivities to different tastes apparently have a strong genetic component.

By eating hot foods and scraping your tongue, you regularly kill off many taste cells. But you need not be alarmed at this unintended oral aggression. Taste cells are the rabbits of the sense receptors. They reproduce rapidly enough to completely renew themselves about once a week.

Older people often complain that their food has little or no "taste." However, they are more likely to experience a decline in the sense of smell (Bartoshuk & Beauchamp, 1994). Because the flavor of a food represents its tastes and odors, or aromas, older people experience loss in the *flavor* of their food. Since the flavor of food supplies some of the motivation to eat, older people are also at risk of becoming malnourished. They are often encouraged to avert malnourishment by spicing their food to enhance its flavor.

THE SKIN SENSES

The skin discriminates among many kinds of sensations—touch, pressure, warmth, cold, and pain (see Figure 4.34). We have distinct sensory receptors for pressure, temperature, and pain, but some nerve endings may receive more than one type of sensory input.

Touch and Pressure

Sensory receptors located around the roots of hair cells appear to fire in response to touching the surface of the skin. You may have noticed that if you

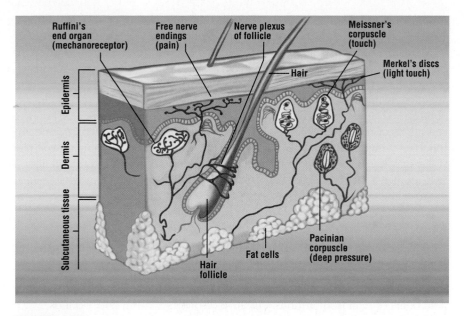

FIGURE 4.34

Skin—A Complex Organ. Your skin may be more complex than you think. It contains several layers and many kinds of sensory receptors.

are trying to "get the feel of" a fabric or the texture of a friend's hair, you must move your hand over it. Otherwise, the sensations quickly fade. If you pass your hand over the skin and then hold it still, again sensations of touching will fade. This sort of active touching involves reception of information that concerns not only touch per se but also pressure, temperature, and feedback from the muscles that are involved in movements of our hands.

Other structures beneath the skin are apparently sensitive to pressure. All in all, there are about half a million receptors for touch and pressure spaced throughout the body. Different parts of the body are more sensitive to touch and pressure than others. Psychophysicists use methods such as the **two-point threshold** to assess sensitivity to pressure. This method determines the smallest distance by which two rods touching the skin must be separated before the (blindfolded) individual will report that there are two rods, not one. As revealed by this method, our fingertips, lips, noses, and cheeks are much more sensitive than our shoulders, thighs, and calves. That is, the rods can be closer together when they touch the lips than the shoulders and still be perceived as distinct. Differential sensitivity occurs for at least two reasons: First, nerve endings are more densely packed in the fingertips and face than in other locations. Second, a greater amount of sensory cortex is devoted to the perception of sensations in the fingertips and face.

The sense of pressure, like the sense of touch, undergoes rather rapid adaptation. You may have undertaken several minutes of strategic movements to wind up with your hand on the arm or leg of your date, only to discover that adaptation to this delightful source of pressure saps the sensation.

Temperature

The receptors for temperature are neurons just beneath the skin. When skin temperature increases, receptors for warmth fire. Decreases in skin temperature cause receptors for cold to fire. Muscle changes connected with changes

Two-point threshold • The least distance by which two rods touching the skin must be separated before the individual will report that there are two rods, not one, on 50% of occasions.

in temperature may also play a role in the sensing of temperature (Schiffman, 1990).

Sensations of temperature are relative. When we are at normal body temperature, we might perceive another person's skin as being warm. When we are feverish, though, the other person's skin might seem cool to the touch. We also adapt to differences in temperature. When we walk out of an air-conditioned house into the desert sun, we at first feel intense heat. Then the sensations of heat tend to fade (although we still may be made terribly uncomfortable by high humidity). Similarly, when we first enter a swimming pool, the water may seem cool or cold because it is below body temperature. Yet after a few moments, an 80-degree-Fahrenheit pool may seem quite warm. In fact, we may chide the tentative newcomer for being overly sensitive.

FIGURE 4.35

Perception of Pain. Pain originates at the point of contact, and the pain message to the brain is initiated by the release of prostaglandins and other substances.

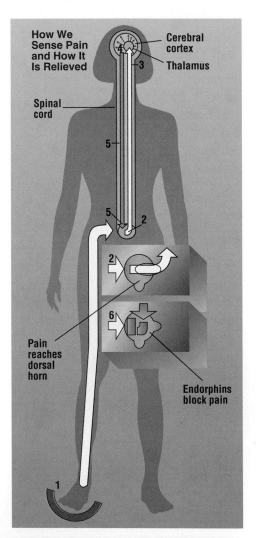

Pain: The Often Unwanted Message

Headaches, backaches, toothaches—these are only a few of the types of pain that most of us encounter from time to time. Some of us also suffer indescribable bouts of pain from arthritis, digestive disorders, cancer, and wounds.

Pain is a signal that something is wrong in the body. Pain is adaptive in the sense that it motivates us to do something about it. For some of us, however, chronic pain—pain that even lasts once injuries or illnesses have cleared up—saps our vitality and the pleasures of everyday life.

Pain originates at the point of contact, as with a stubbed toe (see Figure 4.35). The pain message to the brain is initiated by the release of various chemicals including prostaglandins. Prostaglandins facilitate transmission of the pain message to the brain and heighten circulation to the injured area, causing the redness and swelling we call inflammation. Inflammation attracts infection-fighting blood cells to the area to protect against invading bacteria. **Analgesic** drugs such as aspirin and ibuprofen (Motrin, Medipren, Advil, and so on) work by inhibiting prostaglandin production.

The pain message is relayed from the spinal cord to the thalamus and then projected to the cerebral cortex, where the location and intensity of the damage become apparent.

PHANTOM LIMB PAIN.   One of the more fascinating phenomena of psychology is found in the fact that many people experience pain in limbs that are no longer there (Blakeslee, 1995b). About two out of three combat veterans with amputated limbs report pain in missing, or "phantom," limbs (Kimble, 1992). In such cases, the pain occurs in the absence of (present) tissue damage, but the pain itself is real enough. It sometimes involves activation of nerves in the stump of the missing limb, but local anesthesia does not always eliminate the pain. Therefore, the pain must also reflect activation of the neural circuits that store memories connected with the missing limb (Melzack, 1990).

Truth or Fiction Revisited. *It is true that many amputees experience pain in limbs that have been removed.* The pain apparently reflects activation of the neural circuits that store memories connected with the limbs.

GATE THEORY.   Simple remedies like rubbing and scratching the injured toe frequently help relieve pain. Why? One possible answer lies in the gate theory of pain originated by Melzack (1980). From this perspective, only a limited amount of stimulation can be processed by the nervous system at a time. Rubbing or scratching the toe transmits sensations to the brain that, in a sense, compete for neurons. Many nerves are thus prevented from transmitting pain messages to the brain. The mechanism is analogous to shutting down a "gate" in the spinal cord. It is as if too many calls are flooding a switchboard. The flooding prevents any calls from getting through.

Truth or Fiction Revisited. *It is true that rubbing or scratching a sore toe is often an effective way of relieving pain.* Rubbing or scratching may flood the nervous system with messages so that news of the pain does not get through to the brain.

ACUPUNCTURE. Thousands of years ago, the Chinese began mapping the body to learn where pins might be placed to deaden pain elsewhere. Much of the Chinese practice of acupuncture was unknown in the West, even though Western powers occupied much of China during the 1800s. But in the 1970s, *New York Times* columnist James Reston underwent an appendectomy in China, with acupuncture as his main anesthetic. He reported no discomfort. More recently, TV journalist Bill Moyers (1993) reported on current usage of acupuncture in China. For example, one woman underwent brain surgery to remove a tumor after receiving anesthesia that consisted of a mild sedative, a small dose of narcotics, and six needles placed in her forehead, calves, and ankles. The surgery itself and the use of a guiding CAT scan were consistent with contemporary U.S. practices.

Some of the effects of acupuncture may be due to the release of endorphins. There is supportive evidence. The drug *naloxone* blocks the pain-killing effects of morphine. The analgesic effects of acupuncture are also blocked by naloxone (Kimble, 1992). Therefore, the analgesic effects of acupuncture may be linked to the morphinelike endorphins.

Analgesic • Giving rise to a state of not feeling pain though fully conscious.

Kinesthesis • The sense that informs us about the positions and motion of parts of our bodies.

KINESTHESIS

Try a brief experiment. Close your eyes. Then touch your nose with your index finger. If you weren't right on target, I'm sure you came close. But how? You didn't see your hand moving, and you (probably) didn't hear your arm swishing through the air.

You were able to bring your finger to your nose through your kinesthetic sense. **Kinesthesis** derives from the Greek words for "motion" (*kinesis*) and "perception" (*aisthesis*). When you "make a muscle" in your arm, the sensations of tightness and hardness are also provided by kinesthesis. Kinesthesis is the sense that informs you about the position and motion of parts of your body. In kinesthesis, sensory information is fed back to the brain from sensory organs in the joints, tendons, and muscles.

Imagine going for a walk without kinesthesis. You would have to watch the forward motion of each leg to be certain that you had raised it high enough to clear the curb. And if you had tried our brief experiment without the kinesthetic sense, you would have had no sensory feedback until you felt the pressure of your finger against your nose (or cheek, or eye, or forehead), and you probably would have missed dozens of times.

Are you in the mood for another experiment? Close your eyes, again. Then "make a muscle" in your right arm. Could you sense the muscle without looking at it or feeling it with your left hand? Of course you could. Kinesthesis also provides information about muscle contractions.

Kinesthesis. The acrobat receives information about the position and movement of the parts of his body through the sense of kinesthesis. Kinesthesis feeds sensory information to his brain from sensory organs in the joints, tendons, and muscles. He can sense his movements without visual self-observation.

THE VESTIBULAR SENSE: ON BEING UPRIGHT

Your **vestibular sense** tells you whether you are upright—physically, not morally. Sensory organs located in the **semicircular canals** (Figure 4.30) and elsewhere in the ears monitor your body's motion and position in relation to gravity. They tell you whether you are falling and provide cues to whether your body is changing speeds such as when you are in an accelerating airplane or automobile.

Truth or Fiction Revisited. *It is true that we have a sense that keeps us upright.* The sense—the vestibular sense—keeps us physically upright. It apparently takes more than the vestibular sense to keep us morally upright.

Vestibular sense • The sense of equilibrium that informs us about our bodies' positions relative to gravity.

Semicircular canals • Structures of the inner ear that monitor body movement and position.

Reflections

- Has food ever lost its flavor when you had a cold or an allergy attack? How do you account for the experience?
- Did a sour dish ever "get you" at the sides of the tongue? Why would it affect this area of the tongue?
- **What are the implications of knowledge of the biological aspects of sensation and perception for helping people with sensory disabilities? How might powerful computers and complex electrical circuits be used to help blind people to see, deaf people to hear?**
- **Agree or disagree with the following statement and support your answer: "The best way to cope with pain is to ignore it."**

EXERCISE 1 | **Parts of the Eye**

DIRECTIONS: Below is a drawing of the human eye. Label its parts and explain the function of each part. Check your answers against Figure 4.2.

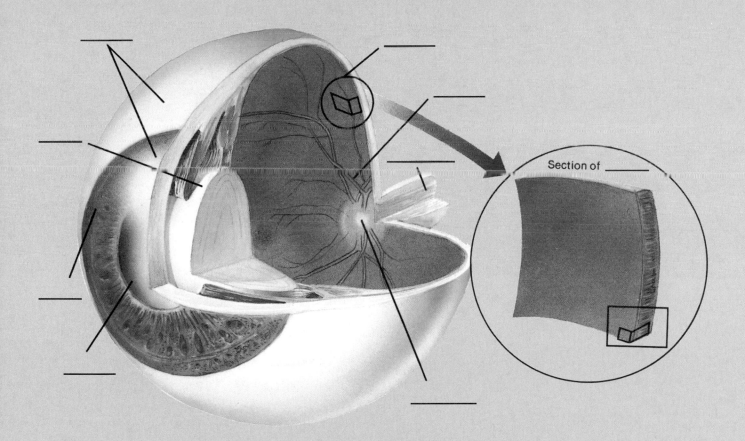

Section of _____

| Parts of the Ear

DIRECTIONS: Below is a drawing of the human ear. Label its parts and explain the function of each part. Check your answers against Figure 4.30.

Organ of _____

Section through _____

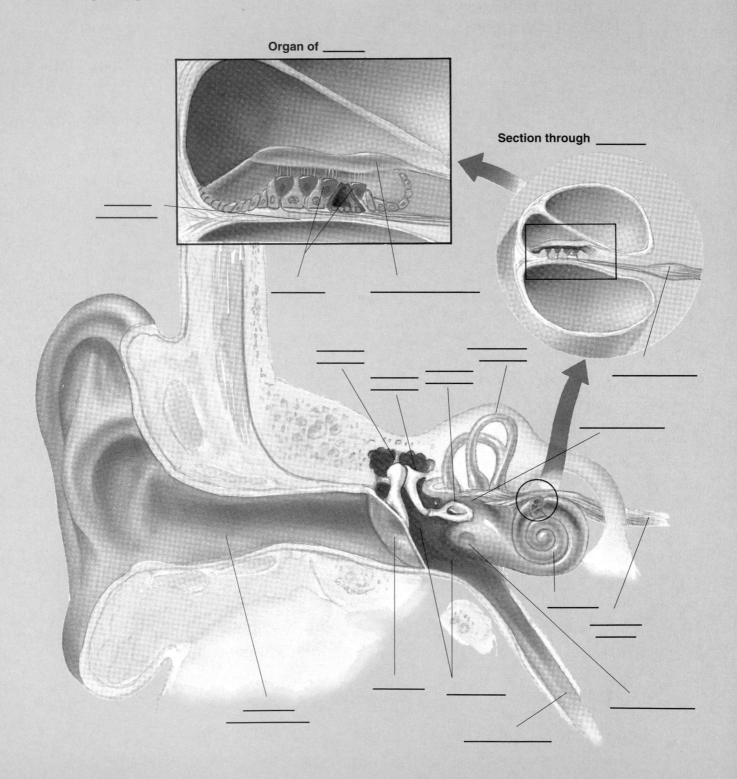

abuzz with signals (122)—having a lot of background noise

acronym (125)—a word made up of the first letters of several other words; in this case, *vibgyor* is made up of the first letter of each color

advanced years (122)—old age

advertising slogan (147)—an expression that helps to promote or sell items

afford insight (146)—give information to help in understanding something

African Pygmy (143)—race of human beings whose physical characteristics include small body size and black skin; they are nomads who generally have remained in the forests and grasslands of Africa, isolated from modern life

aggression (156)—attacking; invading

all in all (157)—when we consider all of them

appendectomy (159)—operation to remove the appendix

aqueduct (134)—a channel for directing water flow

arrowheads (145)—pieces of stone carved (cut, shaped) by American Indians to use as points on their arrows (weapons)

as the saying goes (134)—as we know the expression to be

astounded (118)—shocked; amazed

backdrop of your consciousness (123)—background of your consciousness; present, but not as noticeable as other things

background noise (122)—noise that is present but that is not the sound we are paying attention to

backward student (125)—not a good student; did not study

barbell/dumbbell (121)—mechanism for weight lifting; consists of a bar with a heavy weight on each end

birds in the bush (137)—from the expression "A bird in the hand is worth two in the bush," which means it is better to take what you can get now for certain rather than to give it up and hope you can get more later

birds that flock together seem to be of a feather (134)—A common expression that means that people who are similar like to be together

blips (123)—slight changes in measurement; refers to electronic measurements done with lines that go up or down to show changes

bridges (120)—connects; one affects the other

brittle (142)—not flexible and therefore easily broken

brook no meddling (118)—accept no interference

But wait! you say (129)—stop, I want to ask a question or make a point because I may be confused or disagree

cajoling (137)—persuading

camera buff (126)—person who enjoys photography and knows cameras

chomp (156)—take a large bite or chew hard

clanks and hums (122)—loud, abrupt noises and low, constant noises

clarity (134)—clearness

cocker spaniel (156)—type of dog

cognitive (137)—refers to conscious thought; in this case, a branch of psychology that focuses on what individuals are aware of in their mental and emotional processes

cognitive processes (138)—thought processes, which may not always reflect reality

configuration (134)—shape of a single item or pattern of a group of items

confusion would reign (142)—there would be great confusion

consider weight lifting (121)—think about lifting weights for exercise

converging (139)—coming together

cortex (143)—part of the surface of the eye

cringe (118)—react negatively to something by pulling back slightly

cross-eyed look (142)—when the eyes both look toward the nose at the same time

cycles per second (147)—a cycle is a period of time or space in which one round of events is completed; in this case, completed every second

desensitized (124)—no longer aware of, or bothered by, something

dim the lights (119)—gradually turn the lights low

ellipse (145)—an oval shape that looks like a circle held at an angle

endorphins (159)—brain hormones that have pain-killing and tranquilizing abilities

eyestrain (142)—when the eyes must work harder than usual and become tired

families intermarry (132)—colors that are related mix with other colors

featureless blaze (128)—light so bright that it is impossible to distinguish objects

fiercely difficult (143)—extremely difficult

fireworks (139)—explosives that are ignited for the noise and light they produce

foot-long doll (119)—doll that is one foot in length

from day to day/occasion to occasion (120)—from one day or event to the next

full-grown person (119)—adult who has reached his or her full size

Georges Seurat (130)—a French painter from the 1800s who is famous for his impressionist pointillist style of painting

glow in the dark (120)—shine brightly in the dark

golden opportunity (130)—wonderful opportunity

guide subordinate . . . tasks (137)—to give guidelines for minor jobs that need to be done to accomplish the whole task

hanging in the air (122)—noticeable smells in the air

home team scores (139)—the local team wins a point against the challengers

illusion (146)—a perception of something that is not accurate or is not real

imaginary (155)—not real; imagined

imperceptible (122)—amount almost too small to be measured

in contrast (130)—in looking at the differences

in other words (135)—another way to say "this is the following"

in so doing (122)—when it does this

in the mood (159)—feeling as if you want to do something

in this way (149)—this is how it occurs

incessant (118)—without stopping; always present

indescribable bouts of pain (158)—periods of pain so strong there aren't words to describe it

infrared (120)—light waves that are present but not visible to the naked eye

innately (123)—naturally; inborn

integration (134)—combination; blending things together

James Reston (159)—famous writer and an editor of the *New York Times,* a popular and influential daily newspaper

jovial (118)—cheerful and happy

jumpy (138)—not smooth

junkyard (134)—a space for disposing, or getting rid, of large pieces of trash

just a series of arcs (137)—only a number of partial circles

lapping of the waves (124)—sound of the waves on the shore

lasting impressions (125)—impression or condition that stays for a long time

layperson (123)—person who is not a professional but who is interested or experienced in the topic

lifelong (145)—all of life; to the end

literally . . . watch every step you take (119)—generally means having to be very careful about something; adding the word *literal* means that here the words mean exactly what they say—be careful about walking

lull us to sleep (149)—cause us slowly to go to sleep

lurch (138)—move with a sharp or sudden jerk

M. C. Escher (135)—modern European artist who is famous for detailed and intricate drawings that are often optical illusions

Mark Rothko; Allan d'Arcangelo (130)—modern, 20th-century American artists

meaningful whole (134)—complete concept, which has meaning

miscolored (130)—wrong colors; *mis* is a prefix that means wrong or error

mnemonic device (124)—a way of remembering something by using word association; in this case, the first letter of each name represents the first letter of each color

mocked (140)—tricked; made fun of

mutter (118)—speak in a low tone, not clearly

near darkness (119)—almost dark

neared it (142)—became closer to it

nerve endings (156)—the ends of nerves

nibbling (149)—taking very small bites

Old Glory (131)—an affectionate name for the U.S. flag

on the other hand (123)—however, there is another way to think about it

only thing that remains constant is change (123)—change always occurs and we can expect that

outfielder . . . fly ball (139)—player who is stationed in the *outfield,* any area in a baseball game that is outside of the square formed by the bases; *fly ball* is a ball that is hit high in the air toward an outfielder

paradox (139)—contradictory puzzle

partly overlapped (131)—a piece of the color was over a piece of another color

per se (157)—by itself; that and no other

perceive (132)—to sense with one of the physical senses, such as sight, hearing, touch, taste, and smell

perceptions are mocked (146)—perceptions are deceived, or tricked

play tricks on (145)—deceive; in this case, we are victims of what we think our eyes see

portray three-dimensional objects . . . two-dimensional surface (139)—to paint or draw objects that have three dimensions (length, width, and depth) on a surface that has only two dimensions (length and width)

protractedly (148)—continued for a long time

randomized (119)—the order or pattern of something is accidental, unplanned

rapidly wrap around a building (139)—move fast around a building

readily apparent (121)—very noticeable; easily seen

receding (141)—drawing back or fading out

recessive (132)—not as influential as dominant, or stronger, genes

rhododendron and hibiscus (129)—large, bright-colored flowering plants

roadside markets (139)—markets by the side of the road

roar of the ocean (149)—it is a tradition for children to be told that the noise they hear in a seashell is the sound of the ocean

round it off (121)—change it from a fraction or a decimal to the nearest whole number

scoreboard in a baseball stadium (131)—the large electric

sign where the score of the game is displayed as the game progresses

seen from above (145)—when you look down on the top of it

shards of information (134)—small pieces of information

so far (123)—from the beginning to this point

spaced throughout (157)—in different places all through the body

spectrum (129)—full range of colors

sphere (141)—round or ball shape

splotches (134)—irregular splashes or splatters

squint (126)—squeeze the eyes almost shut to improve the vision

stand ready (143)—be prepared

stemming (136)—coming, or extending out, from something

stereo set (151)—electronic device to play music from records, tapes, or compact disks; the sound comes from more than one speaker

stingy (155)—not providing much of something wanted by another, such as money, help, or favors

stop and go traffic (124)—busy street that has many stoplights and other reasons for cars to stop frequently

stroking (155)—touching in long, sweeping motions

stuff called light (124)—material they called light

stump (158)—the bottom end that is left when something has been cut short

subtle (123)—very slight; hard to notice

swish of the wrist (155)—a hand and wrist movement that is an exaggeration of a movement that some women

make; it is an offensive, prejudicial gesture used to indicate a gay male who has feminine behaviors

take some bets from friends (146)—say to friends, "If I am right, you will give something; if I am wrong, I will give something"

taste cells are the rabbits of the sense receptors (156)—rabbits have a reputation of reproducing often

tell them apart (121)—see the difference between two things

the brighter the color, the lighter it is (129)—as the color gets brighter it also gets lighter

theoretical updates (132)—recent research has changed the theory, or ideas

threefold (121)—three times

ticket of admission (119)—what is needed to gain entrance to something; refers to the ticket a person needs to be admitted to an event

trapezoid (145)—a four-sided shape with two parallel sides

true enough (129)—this is true

unexpected twists (159)—events we didn't expect; not logical

vantage point (143)—point of view; place of viewing

vibrates in response (152)—shakes in reaction to something; in this case, a thin membrane that shakes in reaction to outside sound and transmits a message to the nerves and then to the brain for interpretation

wend their way (143)—move slowly toward

when it comes to the sense of smell (155)—when we think about our sense of smell

whole platoons (148)—a great many groups

working properly (127)—operating correctly

FILL-INS | **Chapter Review**

Sensation refers to mechanical processes that involve the stimulation of (1) s_____ receptors (neurons) and the transmission of sensory information to the (2) c_____ nervous system. Perception is not mechanical. (3) P_____ is the active organization of sensations into a representation of the world. (4) P_____ reflects learning and expectations, as well as sensations.

SECTION 1: SENSATION AND PERCEPTION: YOUR TICKET OF ADMISSION TO THE WORLD OUTSIDE

The (5) a_____ threshold for a stimulus, such as light, is the lowest intensity at which it can be detected. A person's absolute threshold for light is the lowest (6) _____ty of light that he or she can see 50% of the time, according to the method of (7) _____nt stimuli. The minimum difference in intensity that can be discriminated is the (8) d_____ threshold. Difference thresholds are expressed in fractions called (9) _____'s constants.

According to (10) _____al-detection theory, several factors determine whether a person will perceive a stimulus. The detection of a signal is determined by the sensory stimuli themselves, the biological (11) s_____ system of the person, and (12) psy_____ factors, such as motivation and attention.

Sensory (13) _____tion refers to the processes by which we become more sensitive to stimuli of low magnitude and less sensitive to stimuli relatively constant in magnitude. The process of becoming more sensitive to stimulation is referred to as (14) _____tion, or positive adaptation. The process of becoming less sensitive to stimulation is referred to as (15) de_____, or (16) _____tive adaptation.

SECTION 2: VISION: LETTING THE SUN SHINE IN

(17) V_____ is our dominant sense. Visible light triggers visual (18) _____s. Visible light is one part of a spectrum of (19) _____netic energy. Electromagnetic energy is described in terms of (20) _____s. The wavelength of visible light determines its color, or (21) h_____.

The eye senses and transmits visual stimulation to the (22) _____tal lobe of the (23) ce_____ cortex. Light enters the eye through the transparent (24) c_____. The amount of light allowed in is determined by the size of the opening of the muscle called the (25) _____s. The opening in the iris is called the (26) p_____. Once past the iris, light passes through the (27) _____s, which accommodates to the image by changing its thickness. Accommodation of the lens focuses light so that a clear image is projected onto the (28) r_____. The retina is composed of (29) photo_____ called rods and (30) _____s. The rods and cones send neural messages through the (31) _____ar cells to ganglion cells. The axons of the ganglion cells constitute the (32) _____ic nerve, which conducts the sensory input to the brain.

The (33) _____a is the most sensitive part of the retina. The blind spot is the part of the retina where the axons of (34) _____n cells congregate to form the optic nerve. The fovea is populated almost exclusively by (35) _____s, which permit perception of color. Rods are spaced most densely near the (36) _____s, and they transmit sensations of light and (37) d_____ only. Rods are more (38) s_____ than cones to light. Rods continue to (39) a_____ to darkness once cones have reached peak adaptation.

White light or sunlight can be broken down into the colors of the visible (40) _____m by using a triangular glass solid called a (41) _____m. The wavelength of light determines its color, or (42) h_____. Colors across from one another on the color (43) w_____ are termed *complementary*. (44) Red–_____ and blue–yellow are the major complementary pairs. The mixture of lights is an (45) _____tive process. When we mix lights of complementary colors, they dissolve into (46) g_____. In works of art, complementary colors clash when they are placed next to one another, and there seem to be (47) _____tions where they meet. The (48) _____image of a color is its complement.

According to the (49) t_____ theory of color vision, there are three types of cones. Some cones are sensitive to red, some to blue, and some to (50) g_____ light. Opponent-process theory proposes three types of color receptors: red–green, (51) b_____, and (52) l_____. (53) O_____ theory better accounts for afterimages; however, both theories seem to have some validity.

People with normal color vision are called (54) _____mats. Color-blind people who can see only light and dark are called (55) _____mats. Dichromats are more common, and they can discriminate only two colors: red and (56) g_____, or blue and (57) y_____.

SECTION 3: VISUAL PERCEPTION

Gestalt rules of (58) _____ _____tion influence our grouping of bits of sensory stimulation into meaningful wholes. Rules of perceptual organization concern (59) f_____–ground relationships, proximity, similarity, continuity, common fate, and closure. Our perceptions seem to be unstable when figure–ground relationships are (60) _____ous. The Rubin (61) v_____ and the Necker (62) c_____ are examples of ambiguous figures.

We perceive actual movement by sensing (63) m_____ across the retina, and by sensing change of (64) p_____ of an object in relation to other objects. The (65) _____tic effect is the tendency to perceive a point of light in a darkened room as moving. (66) _____opic motion, used in films, is the perception of a rapidly presented series of still pictures as moving.

Depth perception involves monocular and (67) _____lar cues. Monocular cues include perspective, in which we tend to perceive (68) p_____ lines as converging as they recede from us; clearness—(69: Nearby or Distant)? objects are perceived as clearer; and interposition, shadowing, texture gradient, motion (70) p_____, and accommodation. According to motion parallax, distant objects appear to move more (71: Rapidly or Slowly?) than nearby objects. Binocular cues include retinal (72) d_____ and convergence of the eyes. Closer objects have (73: Greater or Lesser?) retinal disparity and require (74: Greater or Lesser?) convergence.

Through experience we develop a number of perceptual constancies. For example, we learn to assume that objects retain their size, (75) s_____, (76) b_____, and (77) c _____ despite their distance, their position, or changes in lighting conditions. In the case of size constancy, we tend to perceive an object as remaining the same size, although the size of the image on the (78) r_____ varies as a function of the object's (79) d_____ from the viewer.

Visual illusions use (80) p_____ cues as well as twists on rules for organization to deceive the eye. The effects of the Müller-Lyer and Ponzo illusions can probably be explained by using the principle of (81) s_____ constancy.

SECTION 4: HEARING: TAKING IN GOOD VIBRATIONS

(82) A_____ stimulation, or sound waves, require a medium such as air or water for transmission. Sound waves alternately (83) _____ress and expand molecules of the medium, creating (84) _____s.

The human ear can hear sounds varying in frequency from 20 to (85) _____ cycles per second. The greater the frequency of the sound (86) _____s, the higher the (87) p_____ of a sound.

The loudness of a sound is measured in (88) _____els, which are abbreviated dB. We can suffer hearing loss if exposed to protracted sounds of (89) _____ dB or more. In addition to producing specified notes, instruments may produce tones that are greater in frequency and referred to as (90) _____s. Such overtones contribute to the richness or (91) t_____ of a sound. A combination of (92) _____nt sounds is referred to as *noise*.

The ear consists of an outer, (93) m_____, and (94) i_____ ear. A thin membrane in the outer ear, called the (95) e_____, vibrates in response to sound waves and transmits them to the middle and (96) i_____ ears. The middle ear contains the three bones—the "hammer," (97) a_____, and

(98) s_____—which also vibrate and transmit sound waves to another membrane called the (99) o_____ window. The oval window then transmits sound waves to the bony tube of the inner ear called the (100) _____a. Within the cochlea are fluids that vibrate against the (101) b_____ membrane. The "command post of hearing," or organ of (102) C_____, is attached to the basilar membrane. Sound waves travel from the organ of Corti to the brain by the (103) _____ry nerve. Sounds are perceived as louder when more of the sensory neurons on the organ of (104) C_____ fire.

Two of the major theories that have been advanced to account for the perception of pitch are place theory and (105) f_____ theory. According to place theory, the pitch of a sound is determined by the segment of the (106) _____ _____ne that vibrates in response to it. According to frequency theory, the frequency with which sensory neurons fire corresponds to the (107) f_____ of the sound. So-called (108) _____ity theory advances the view that pitch perception depends both on the place and frequency of neural response.

(109) _____tive deafness occurs because of damage to the structures of the middle ear that conduct and amplify sound waves from the outer ear to the inner ear. (110) Sensori_____ deafness stems from damage to the structures of the inner ear or to the auditory nerve.

SECTION 5: SMELL

An odor is a sample of a number of (111) _____ules of the substance being smelled. Odors are detected by the (112) o_____ membrane in each nostril. The sense of smell adapts rapidly to odors, even unpleasant ones.

SECTION 6: TASTE

There are four primary taste qualities: sweet, sour, (113) s_____, and (114) b_____. Flavor involves not only the taste of food, but also its (115) o_____, texture, and temperature. The receptor neurons for taste are called (116) t_____ cells. Taste cells are located in (117) _____ _____s on the tongue. The "taste loss" found among the elderly is probably due to a decline in the sense of (118) s_____.

SECTION 7: THE SKIN SENSES

There are several skin senses, including touch, pressure, warmth, (119) c_____, and (120) p_____. The (121) _____-_____nt threshold method allows psychophysicists to assess sensitivity to pressure by determining the distance by which two rods touching the skin must be separated before a person will report that there are two rods, not one. Sensations of (122) _____ture are relative; when we are feverish, another person's skin may seem cool to the touch.

Pain originates at the point of contact and is transmitted to the brain by various chemicals, including prostaglandins. According to (123) g_____ theory, rubbing and scratching painful areas may reduce pain by sending competing messages to the brain. Naturally occurring (124) _____ins also help relieve pain.

SECTION 8: KINESTHESIS

Kinesthesis is the sensing of bodily (125) p_____ and movement. Kinesthesis relies on sensory organs in the joints, (126) t_____, and (127) _____s.

SECTION 9: THE VESTIBULAR SENSE: ON BEING UPRIGHT

The vestibular sense informs us as to whether we are in an (128) u_____ position or changing speeds. The vestibular sense is housed primarily in the (129) s_____ _____ of the ears.

ANSWER KEY TO CHAPTER REVIEW

1. Sensory	34. Ganglion	67. Binocular	100. Cochlea
2. Central	35. Cones	68. Parallel	101. Basilar
3. Perception	36. Lens	69. Nearby	102. Corti
4. Perception	37. Dark	70. Parallax	103. Auditory
5. Absolute	38. Sensitive	71. Slowly	104. Corti
6. Intensity	39. Adapt	72. Disparity	105. Frequency
7. Constant	40. Spectrum	73. Greater	106. Basilar membrane
8. Difference	41. Prism	74. Greater	107. Frequency
9. Weber's	42. Hue	75. Shape	108. Duplicity
10. Signal	43. Wheel	76. Brightness	109. Conductive
11. Sensory	44. Green	77. Color	110. Sensorineural
12. Psychological	45. Additive	78. Retina	111. Molecules
13. Adaptation	46. Gray	79. Distance	112. Olfactory
14. Sensitization	47. Vibrations	80. Perceptual	113. Salty (or bitter)
15. Desensitization	48. Afterimage	81. Size	114. Bitter (or salty)
16. Negative	49. Trichromatic	82. Auditory	115. Odor (or aroma, etc.)
17. Vision	50. Green	83. Compress	116. Taste
18. Sensations	51. Blue-yellow (or light-dark)	84. Vibrations	117. Taste buds
19. Electromagnetic	52. Light-dark (or blue-yellow)	85. 20,000	118. Smell
20. Wavelengths	53. Opponent-process	86. Waves	119. Cold (or pain)
21. Hue	54. Trichromats	87. Pitch	120. Pain (or cold)
22. Occipital	55. Monochromats	88. Decibels	121. Two-point
23. Cerebral	56. Green	89. 85–90	122. Temperature
24. Cornea	57. Yellow	90. Overtones	123. Gate
25. Iris	58. Perceptual organization	91. Timbre	124. Endorphins
26. Pupil	59. Figure	92. Dissonant	125. Position
27. Lens	60. Ambiguous	93. Middle	126. Tendons
28. Retina	61. Vase	94. Inner	127. Muscles
29. Photoreceptors	62. Cube	95. Eardrum	128. Upright
30. Cones	63. Movement	96. Inner	129. Semicircular canals
31. Bipolar	64. Position	97. Anvil (or stirrup)	
32. Optic	65. Autokinetic	98. Stirrup (or anvil)	
33. Fovea	66. Stroboscopic	99. Oval	

POSTTEST | Multiple Choice

1. Of the following, _____ have the shortest wavelengths of the spectrum of electromagnetic energy.
   a. cosmic rays
   b. X rays
   c. sound waves
   d. visible colors

2. Weber's constant for the pitch of a tone is closest to
   a. 1/7th.
   b. 1/53rd.
   c. 1/333rd.
   d. 1/20,000th.

3. You look at a lamp 10 feet away and it is clearly in focus. As you walk toward it, the lamp remains in focus. The lamp remains in focus because the _____ of your eyes are accommodating to the image of the lamp by changing their thickness.
   a. corneas
   b. irises
   c. lenses
   d. pupils

4. The cones reach their maximum adaptation to darkness in about _____ minutes.
   a. 5
   b. 10
   c. 30
   d. 45

5. Colors across from one another on the color wheel are labeled
   a. primary.
   b. afterimages.
   c. analogous.
   d. complementary.

6. _____ suggested that the eye must have three different types of cones, some sensitive to red, some to green, and some to blue.
   a. Thomas Young
   b. Sir Isaac Newton
   c. Hermann von Helmholtz
   d. Ewald Hering

7. The Rubin vase is used by psychologists to demonstrate rules of
   a. perceptual organization.
   b. perceptual constancy.
   c. depth perception.
   d. visual illusions.

8. You attend a motion picture, and it seems to you as if the people and objects being projected onto the screen are moving. Actually, your impression that the people and objects are moving is made possible by
   a. the phi phenomenon.
   b. stroboscopic motion.
   c. the autokinetic effect.
   d. motion parallax.

9. When we are driving along a dark road at night, the moon may appear to move along with us. This is an example of
   a. the autokinetic effect.
   b. perspective.
   c. motion parallax.
   d. the phi phenomenon.

10. The unit for expressing the loudness of a sound is named after
    a. Bell.
    b. Hertz.
    c. Helmholtz.
    d. Newton.

11. A combination of dissonant sounds is referred to as
    a. timbre.
    b. overtones.
    c. noise.
    d. white noise.

12. Hairlike receptor cells on the organ of Corti bend in response to vibrations of the
    a. eardrum.
    b. oval window.
    c. stirrup.
    d. basilar membrane.

13. Within the ears are found organs for
    a. vision.
    b. kinesthesis.
    c. the vestibular sense.
    d. extrasensory perception.

14. Duplicity theory advances the view that
    a. people cannot perceive pitches at above 1,000 Hz.
    b. neurons at different sites on the basilar membrane fire in response to different pitches.
    c. impulses in the auditory nerve follow the patterns of sound waves at many frequencies.
    d. pitch perception depends both on the place and frequency of neural response.

15. We have about _____ taste buds.
    a. 10
    b. 100
    c. 10,000
    d. 10,000,000

16. _____ is sensed along the sides of the tongue.
    a. Sweetness
    b. Bitterness
    c. Saltiness
    d. Sourness

17. Sensory receptors located _____ appear to fire in response to touching the surface of the skin.
    a. on the surface of the skin
    b. around the roots of hair cells
    c. at the tips of hair cells
    d. in tendons, joints, and muscles

18. According to the text, which of the following is a chemical sense?
    a. vision
    b. hearing
    c. smell
    d. kinesthesis

19. The view that pain messages may not get through to the brain when the "switchboard" that transmits pain messages becomes "flooded" is termed
    a. gate theory.
    b. opponent-process theory.
    c. volley principle.
    d. acupuncture.

20. Organs in the _____ alert you as to whether your body is changing speeds.
    a. joints
    b. tendons
    c. ears
    d. olfactory membrane

ANSWER KEY TO POSTTEST

1. A	4. B	7. A	10. A	13. C	16. D	19. A
2. C	5. D	8. B	11. C	14. D	17. B	20. C
3. C	6. C	9. C	12. D	15. C	18. C	

LEARNING OBJECTIVES

When you have finished studying Chapter 5, you should be able to:

A MINOR QUESTION: WHAT *IS* CONSCIOUSNESS?

1. Discuss the meanings of *consciousness.*

SLEEP AND DREAMS

2. Describe the stages of sleep.
3. Summarize research concerning the functions of sleep.
4. Discuss theories of dreams.

ALTERING CONSCIOUSNESS THROUGH DRUGS

5. Define *substance abuse* and *substance dependence.*
6. Describe the effects of depressants (alcohol, opiates, and so forth) on consciousness.
7. Describe the effects of stimulants (amphetamines, cocaine, and nicotine) on consciousness.
8. Describe the effects of hallucinogenics (marijuana and LSD) on consciousness.

ALTERING CONSCIOUSNESS THROUGH MEDITATION: WHEN EASTERN GODS MEET WESTERN TECHNOLOGY

9. Summarize research concerning the effects of meditation.

ALTERING CONSCIOUSNESS THROUGH BIOFEEDBACK: GETTING IN TOUCH WITH THE UNTOUCHABLE

10. Summarize research concerning the effects of biofeedback.

ALTERING CONSCIOUSNESS THROUGH HYPNOSIS: ON BEING ENTRANCED

11. Discuss the changes in consciousness that are brought about by hypnosis.
12. Discuss theories of hypnosis.

Consciousness

Truth or Fiction?

____ We act out our forbidden fantasies in our dreams.

____ Many people have insomnia because they try too hard to get to sleep at night.

____ It is dangerous to awaken a sleepwalker.

____ Alcohol "goes to women's heads" more quickly than to men's.

____ Heroin was once used as a cure for addiction to morphine.

____ Coca-Cola once "added life" through a powerful but now illegal stimulant.

____ The number of people who die from smoking-related causes is greater than the number lost to motor-vehicle accidents, abuse of alcohol and all other drugs, suicide, homicide, and AIDS combined.

____ People have managed to bring high blood pressure under control through meditation.

____ You can learn to increase or decrease your heart rate just by thinking about it.

____ People who are easily hypnotized have positive attitudes toward hypnosis.

I N 1904, William James wrote an intriguing article, "Does Consciousness Exist?" James did not think that consciousness was a proper area of study for psychologists, because no scientific method could be devised to directly observe or measure another person's consciousness.

John Watson, the "father of modern behaviorism," also insisted that only observable, measurable behavior was the proper province of psychology. In "Psychology as the Behaviorist Views It," Watson (1913) declared, "The time seems to have come when psychology must discard all references to consciousness" (p. 163). The following year, Watson was elected president of the American Psychological Association, which further cemented these ideas in the minds of many psychologists.

Consider the titles of more recent articles—"The Problem of Consciousness" (Crick & Koch, 1992) and "Trouble in Mind" (Miller, 1992). Problems in discussing consciousness have not evaporated. Psychologists have not solved all problems in defining consciousness and in measuring consciousness. Nevertheless, we devote this chapter to the exploration of the meanings and varieties of this "most profound and puzzling facet of the mind" (Crick & Koch, 1992). Many psychologists, especially cognitive psychologists, believe that we cannot capture the richness of the human experience without referring to consciousness.

A MINOR QUESTION: WHAT *IS* CONSCIOUSNESS?

Consciousness is one of those mental concepts that cannot be directly seen or touched, yet it is real enough to most people. Mental concepts such as consciousness acquire scientific status from being tied to behavior (Kimble, 1994). The concept of consciousness has several meanings. Consider a few of them.

CONSCIOUSNESS AS SENSORY AWARENESS. One meaning of consciousness is **sensory awareness** of the environment. The sense of vision permits us to be *conscious* of, or to see, the sun gleaming in the snow on the rooftops (Crick & Koch, 1992; Zeki, 1992). The sense of hearing allows us to be conscious of, or to hear, a concert.

CONSCIOUSNESS AS THE SELECTIVE ASPECT OF ATTENTION. We are not always aware of sensory stimulation, however. We can be unaware, or unconscious of, sensory stimulation when we do not pay attention to it (Greenwald, 1992). The world is abuzz with signals. Yet you are conscious of, or focusing on, the words on this page (I hope).

Focusing one's consciousness on a particular stimulus is referred to as **selective attention.** The concept of selective attention is important to psychology, and, indeed, to self-control. To pay attention in class, you must screen out the pleasant aroma of the cologne or perfume from the person in the next seat. To keep your car on the road, you must pay more attention to driving conditions than to your hunger pangs or your feelings about an argument with your family. If you are out in the woods at night, attending to rustling in the brush may be crucial to survival.

Adaptation to the environment involves learning which stimuli must be attended to and which can be safely ignored. Selective attention markedly enhances our perceptual abilities (Johnston & Dark, 1986; Moran & Desimone, 1985), to the point where we can pick out the speech of a single person across

Sensory awareness • Knowledge of the environment through perception of sensory stimulation—one definition of consciousness.

Selective attention • The focus of one's consciousness on a particular stimulus.

**MINILECTURE:
ATTENTION**

a room at a cocktail party. (This phenomenon has been suitably termed the *cocktail party effect*.)

Although we can decide where and when we shall focus our attention, some stimuli also tend to capture attention:

- Sudden changes, as when a cool breeze enters a sweltering room, or we receive a particularly high or low grade on a returned exam
- Novel stimuli, as when a dog enters the classroom, or a person has an unusual hairdo
- Intense stimuli, such as bright colors, loud noises, or sharp pain

CONSCIOUSNESS AS DIRECT INNER AWARENESS. Close your eyes. Imagine spilling a can of bright red paint across a black tabletop. Watch it spread across the black, shiny surface, then spill onto the floor. Although this image may be vivid, you did not "see" it literally. Neither your eyes nor any other sensory organs were involved. You were *conscious* of the image through **direct inner awareness.**

We are conscious of—or have direct inner awareness of—thoughts, images, emotions, and memories. Although we may not be able to measure direct inner awareness scientifically, Miller (1992) argues that "it is detectable to anyone that has it" (p. 180). These psychological processes are based on the firings of myriads of neurons—events that we do *not* experience consciously (Crick & Koch, 1992; Fischbach, 1992). Yet we are conscious of the cognitive parallels of these neural events.

Sigmund Freud, the founder of psychoanalysis, differentiated between thoughts and feelings of which we are conscious, or aware, and those that are preconscious and unconscious (see Figure 5.1). **Preconscious** material is not currently in awareness but is readily available. As you answer the following questions, you will summon up "preconscious" information: What did you eat for dinner yesterday? About what time did you wake up this morning? What's your phone number? You can make these preconscious bits of information conscious simply by directing your inner awareness, or attention, to them.

According to Freud, still other mental events are **unconscious.** They are unavailable to awareness under most circumstances. Freud believed that certain memories are painful, and certain impulses (primarily sexual and aggressive impulses) are unacceptable. Therefore, people place them out of awareness, or **repress** them, to escape feelings of anxiety, guilt, and shame.

Still, people do sometimes choose not to focus on unacceptable ideas or distractions. Consciously putting ideas or distractions out of mind is termed **suppression.** We may suppress thoughts of a date when we need to study for a test. Or, to enjoy a date, we may suppress thoughts of an unpleasant test.

Some bodily processes such as the firings of individual neurons are **nonconscious.** They cannot be experienced through sensory awareness or direct inner awareness. The growing of hair and the carrying of oxygen in the blood are nonconscious. We can see that our hair has grown, but we have no sense receptors that provide sensations related to the process. We can feel the need to breathe but do not directly experience the exchange of carbon dioxide and oxygen. We are aware that we are aware, even though we remain nonconscious of the countless biochemical events that give rise to awareness.

CONSCIOUSNESS AS PERSONAL UNITY: THE SENSE OF SELF. As we develop, we differentiate us from that which is not us. We develop a sense of being persons, individuals. There is a totality to our impressions, thoughts, and

Direct inner awareness • Knowledge of one's own thoughts, feelings, and memories without use of sensory organs—another definition of consciousness.

Preconscious • In psychodynamic theory, descriptive of material that is not in awareness but can be brought into awareness by focusing one's attention. (The Latin root *prae-* means "before.")

Unconscious • In psychodynamic theory, descriptive of ideas and feelings that are not available to awareness.

Repress • In psychodynamic theory, to eject anxiety-provoking ideas, impulses, or images from awareness, without knowing that one is doing so.

Suppression • The deliberate, or conscious, placing of certain ideas, impulses, or images out of awareness.

Nonconscious • Descriptive of bodily processes, such as the growing of hair, of which we cannot become conscious. We may "recognize" that our hair is growing but cannot directly experience the biological process.

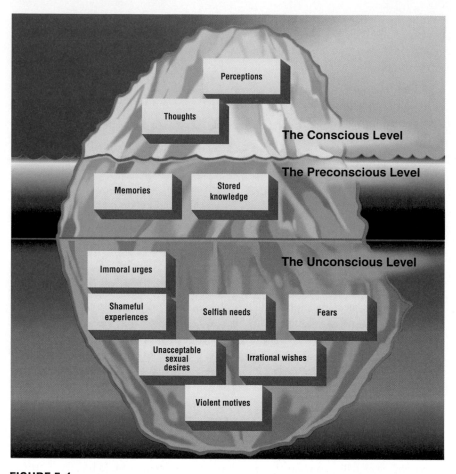

FIGURE 5.1

Levels of Consciousness, According to Sigmund Freud. According to Freud, many memories, impulses, and feelings exist below the level of conscious awareness. We could note that any film that draws an audience seems to derive its plot from items that populate the unconscious.

Self • The totality of impressions, thoughts, and feelings. The sense of self is another definition of consciousness.

Altered states of consciousness • States other than the normal waking state, including sleep, meditation, the hypnotic trance, and the distorted perceptions produced by use of some drugs.

feelings that makes up our conscious existence—our continuing sense of **self** in a changing world. In this usage of the word, consciousness *is* self.

CONSCIOUSNESS AS THE WAKING STATE.   The word *conscious* also refers to the waking state as opposed, for example, to sleep. From this perspective, sleep, meditation, the hypnotic "trance," and the distorted perceptions that can accompany use of consciousness-altering drugs are considered **altered states of consciousness.**

The remainder of the chapter explores other states of consciousness and the agents that bring them about.

Reflections

- Does consciousness exist? Do you believe that *you* have consciousness? That you are conscious, or aware, of yourself? Of the world around you? Would you bear witness to being conscious of, or experiencing, thoughts and feelings? Is the nature of your evidence scientifically compelling?

- In what ways have you used the word *consciousness*? How does your usage of the word correspond to the usages described in the chapter?

- Can we understand or study the consciousness of another person? Why or why not?

SLEEP AND DREAMS

Sleep is a fascinating topic. After all, we spend about one third of our adult lives asleep. Most of us complain when we do not sleep at least 6 hours or so. Some people sleep for an hour or two a night, however, and apparently lead otherwise normal lives (Kimble, 1992).

Our alternating periods of wakefulness and sleep provide an example of an internally generated **circadian rhythm.** People normally connect their waking and sleeping hours with the rotation of the earth. A full cycle is thus 24 hours. However, when people are removed from cues that signal day or night, a cycle tends to become extended to about 25 hours (Kimble, 1992). Why? We do not know.

Why do we sleep? Why do we dream? Why do some of us have trouble getting to sleep, and what can we do about it? In this section, we explore the stages and functions of sleep, dreams, and sleep disorders, including insomnia and sleep terrors.

The Stages of Sleep

The **electroencephalograph,** or EEG, is one of the major tools of sleep researchers. The EEG measures the electrical activity of the brain, or brain waves. Figure 5.2 shows some scrawls produced by the EEG that reflect the frequency and strength of brain waves that occur during the waking state, when we are relaxed, and when we are in one of the stages of sleep.

Brain waves, like other waves, are cyclical. During the various stages of sleep, our brains emit waves of different frequencies and amplitudes. The printouts in Figure 5.2 show what happens during a period of 15 seconds or so. Brain waves high in frequency are associated with wakefulness. The amplitude of brain waves reflects their strength. The strength or energy of brain waves is expressed in the electric unit **volts.**

Figure 5.2 shows five stages of sleep: four stages of **non-rapid-eye-movement** (NREM) sleep and one stage of **rapid-eye-movement** (REM) sleep. When we close our eyes and begin to relax before going to sleep, our brains emit many **alpha waves.** Alpha waves are low-amplitude brain waves of about 8 to 13 cycles per second. (Through biofeedback training, discussed later in the chapter, people have been taught to relax by purposefully emitting alpha waves.)

As we enter stage 1 sleep, our brain waves slow down from the alpha rhythm and enter a pattern of **theta waves.** Theta waves, which have a frequency of about 6 to 8 cycles per second, are accompanied by slow, rolling eye movements. The transition from alpha waves to theta waves may be accompanied by a **hypnagogic state,** during which we may experience brief hallucinatory, dreamlike images that resemble vivid photographs. These images may be related to creativity. Stage 1 sleep is the lightest stage of sleep. If we are awakened from stage 1 sleep, we may feel that we have not slept at all.

After 30 to 40 minutes of stage 1 sleep, we undergo a rather steep descent into sleep stages 2, 3, and 4 (see Figure 5.3). During stage 2, brain waves are medium in amplitude and have a frequency of about 4 to 7 cycles per second, but these are punctuated by more rapid **sleep spindles.**

Circadian rhythm • (sir-KADE-ee-an). Referring to cycles that are connected with the 24-hour period of the earth's rotation. (A scientific term coined from the Latin roots *circa,* meaning "about," and *diem,* meaning "day.")

Electroencephalograph • An instrument that measures electrical activity of the brain. Abbreviated *EEG.*

Volt • A unit of electrical potential.

Non-rapid-eye-movement sleep • Stages of sleep 1 through 4. Abbreviated *NREM* sleep.

Rapid-eye-movement sleep • A stage of sleep characterized by rapid eye movements, which have been linked to dreaming. Abbreviated *REM* sleep.

Alpha waves • Rapid, low-amplitude brain waves that have been linked to feelings of relaxation.

Theta waves • Slow brain waves produced during the hypnagogic state.

Hypnagogic state • The drowsy interval between waking and sleeping, characterized by brief, hallucinatory, dreamlike experiences.

Sleep spindles • Short bursts of rapid brain waves that occur during stage 2 sleep.

MINILECTURE: STAGES OF SLEEP

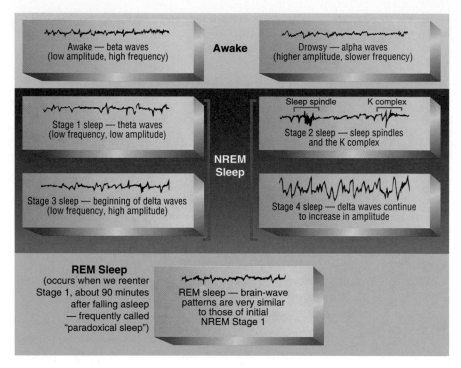

FIGURE 5.2

The Stages of Sleep. This figure illustrates typical EEG patterns for the stages of sleep. During REM sleep, EEG patterns resemble those of the lightest stage of sleep, stage 1 sleep. For this reason, REM sleep is often termed *paradoxical sleep*. As sleep progresses from stage 1 to stage 4, brain waves become slower and their amplitude increases. Dreams, including normal nightmares, are most vivid during REM sleep. More disturbing sleep terrors tend to occur during deep stage 4 sleep.

FIGURE 5.3

Sleep Cycles. This figure illustrates the alternation of REM and non-REM sleep for the typical sleeper. There are about five periods of REM sleep during an 8-hour night. Sleep is deeper earlier in the night, and REM sleep tends to become prolonged toward morning.

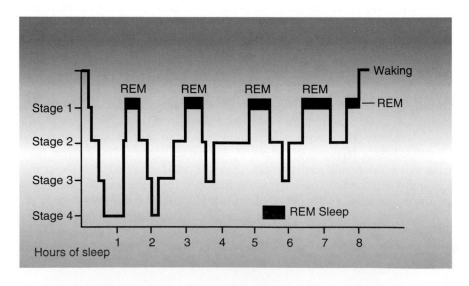

During deep-sleep stages 3 and 4, our brains produce slower **delta waves.** During stage 3, the delta waves are of about 1 to 3 cycles per second. Delta waves reach relatively great amplitude as compared with other brain waves. Stage 4 is the deepest stage of sleep, from which it is most difficult to be awakened. During stage 4 sleep, the delta waves slow to about 0.5 to 2 cycles per second, and their amplitude is greatest.

After perhaps half an hour of deep stage 4 sleep, we begin a relatively rapid journey back upward through the stages until we enter REM sleep (Figure 5.3). REM sleep derives its name from the *r*apid *e*ye *m*ovements, observable beneath our closed lids, that characterize this stage. During REM sleep, we produce relatively rapid, low-amplitude brain waves that resemble those of light stage 1 sleep. REM sleep is also called *paradoxical sleep.* This is because the EEG patterns observed during REM sleep suggest a level of arousal similar to that of the waking state (Figure 5.2). However, we are difficult to awaken during REM sleep. When we are awakened during REM sleep, as is the practice in sleep research, about 80% of the time we report that we have been dreaming. (We also dream during NREM sleep, but less frequently. We report dreaming only about 20% of the time when awakened during NREM sleep.)

We tend to undergo five trips through the stages of sleep each night (see Figure 5.3). These trips include about five periods of REM sleep. Our first journey through stage 4 sleep is usually longest. Sleep tends to become lighter as the night wears on. Our periods of REM sleep tend to become longer, and, toward morning, our last period of REM sleep may last close to half an hour.

Now that we have some idea of what sleep is like, let us examine the issue of *why* we sleep.

Functions of Sleep

Strangely enough, researchers are not at all certain as to why we sleep (Kimble, 1992). One hypothesis is that sleep helps rejuvenate a tired body. Most of us have had the experience of going without sleep for a night and feeling "wrecked" or "punch drunk" the following day. Perhaps the next evening we went to bed early to "catch up on our sleep." What will happen to you if you miss sleep for one night? For several nights?

Adler (1993b) compares people who are highly sleep-deprived with people who have been drinking heavily. Their abilities to concentrate and perform normal tasks may be seriously impaired, but they may be the last ones to recognize their limitations. Research shows that sleep deprivation mainly affects attention (Adler, 1993b). There are related psychological problems, however, including impaired memory formation, which in part may reflect lessened motivation to focus on details.

Sleep researcher Wilse Webb (1993) notes that most students can pull successful "all-nighters." That is, they can cram for a test through the night and then perform reasonably well on the test the following day. His rationale is that students will generally be highly motivated to pay attention to the details of the test. When we are sleep-deprived for several nights, aspects of psychological functioning such as attention, learning, and memory deteriorate notably. Webb (1993) also notes that many people sleep late or nap on their days off. Perhaps they are mildly deprived of sleep during the week and catch up on the weekend.

The amount of sleep we need seems to be in part genetically determined, like our heights (Webb, 1993). People also tend to need more sleep during periods of change and stress such as a change of jobs, an increase in workload,

Delta waves • Strong, slow brain waves usually emitted during stage 4 sleep.

or an episode of depression. Perhaps sleep helps us recover from the stresses of life.

In some studies, animals or people have been deprived of REM sleep. Animals and people deprived of REM sleep learn more slowly and forget what they have learned more rapidly (Adler, 1993b; Winson, 1992). Rats deprived of REM sleep for 10 days begin to eat voraciously but die of starvation (Hobson, 1992). REM sleep would appear to be essential to brain metabolism and body temperature regulation (Hobson, 1992).

In people, REM sleep may foster brain development during prenatal and infant development (McCarley, 1992). REM sleep may also help to maintain neurons in adults by "exercising" them at night (McCarley, 1992). Researchers deprive people of REM sleep by monitoring EEG records and eye movements and waking them during REM sleep. There is too much individual variation to conclude that people deprived of REM sleep learn more poorly than they otherwise would. It does seem, though, that such deprivation interferes with memory—that is, the retrieval of information that has been learned (Winson, 1992). In any event, people and lower animals deprived of REM sleep tend to show *REM-rebound*. They spend more time in REM sleep later on. They catch up.

It is during REM sleep that we tend to dream. Let us now turn our attention to dreams, a mystery about which philosophers, poets, and scientists have theorized for centuries.

Dreams: "Such Stuff as Dreams Are Made On"

Dreams • A sequence of images or thoughts that occur during sleep. Dreams may be vague and loosely plotted or vivid and intricate.

**MINILECTURE:
WHY WE DREAM**

Just what is the stuff[1] of **dreams?** What are they "made on"? Like vivid memories and daytime fantasies, dreams involve imagery in the absence of external stimulation. Some dreams are so realistic and well organized that we feel they must be real. (We simply cannot be dreaming this time!) You may have had such a dream on the night before a test. The dream would have been that you had taken the test and now it is all over. (Ah, what disappointment then prevailed when you woke up to realize that such was not the case!) Other dreams are disorganized and unformed.

Dreams are most vivid during REM sleep. Then they are most likely to have clear imagery and coherent plots, even if some of the content is fantastic. Plots are vaguer and images more fleeting during NREM sleep. You may well have a dream every time you are in REM sleep. Therefore, if you sleep for 8 hours and undergo five sleep cycles, you may have five dreams. Upon waking, you may think that time seemed to expand or contract during your dreams so that during 10 or 15 minutes, your dream content ranged over days or weeks. But dreams tend to take place in "real time": 15 minutes of events fills about 15 minutes of dreaming. Your dream theater is quite flexible: You can dream in black and white and in full color.

THEORIES OF THE CONTENT OF DREAMS.   You may recall dreams involving fantastic adventures, but most dreams are simple extensions of the activities and problems of the day (Reiser, 1992). If we are preoccupied with illness or death, sexual or aggressive urges, or moral dilemmas, we are likely to dream about them. The characters in our dreams are more likely to be friends and neighbors than spies, monsters, and princes.

---

[1] The phrase "such stuff as dreams are made on" comes from Shakespeare's *The Tempest*.

The Freudian View

"A dream is a wish your heart makes."
SONG TITLE FROM THE DISNEY FILM *CINDERELLA*

Sigmund Freud theorized that dreams reflect unconscious wishes and urges. He argued that through dreams, we can express impulses that we would censor during the day. Moreover, he said that the content of dreams is symbolic of unconscious fantasized objects such as genital organs (see Table 5.1). In Chapter 14, we shall see that a major part of Freud's method of psychoanalysis involved interpretation of his clients' dreams. Freud also believed that dreams "protect sleep" by providing imagery that would help keep disturbing, repressed thoughts out of awareness.

The view that dreams protect sleep has been challenged by the observation that disturbing events of the day tend to be followed by related disturbing dreams—not protective imagery (Reiser, 1992). Our behavior in dreams is also generally consistent with our waking behavior. Most dreams, then, are unlikely candidates for the expression (even disguised) of repressed urges. The person who leads a moral life tends to dream moral dreams.

Truth or Fiction Revisited. *It is not true that we act out our forbidden fantasies in our dreams.* Most dreams are humdrum.

The Activation-Synthesis Model According to the **activation-synthesis model,** dreams primarily reflect biological, not psychological, activity (Hobson, 1992). According to this view, an abundance of acetylcholine in the brain and a time-triggered mechanism in the pons stimulate a number of responses that lead to dreaming. One is *activation* of the reticular activating system (RAS), which arouses us but not to the point of waking. During the waking state, firing of these cells in the reticular formation is linked to movement, particularly the semiautomatic movements found in walking, running, and other

Activation-synthesis model • The view that dreams reflect activation of cognitive activity by the reticular activating system and synthesis of this activity into a pattern by the cerebral cortex.

TABLE 5.1
DREAM SYMBOLS IN PSYCHODYNAMIC THEORY

SYMBOLS FOR THE MALE GENITAL ORGANS

airplanes	fish	neckties	tools	umbrellas
bullets	hands	poles	trains	weapons
feet	hoses	snakes	trees	
fire	knives	sticks		

SYMBOLS FOR THE FEMALE GENITAL ORGANS

bottles	caves	doors	ovens	ships
boxes	chests	hats	pockets	tunnels
cases	closets	jars	pots	

SYMBOLS FOR SEXUAL INTERCOURSE

climbing a ladder	entering a room
climbing a staircase	flying in an airplane
crossing a bridge	riding a horse
driving an automobile	riding a roller coaster
riding an elevator	walking into a tunnel or down a hall

SYMBOLS FOR THE BREASTS

apples	peaches

Freud theorized that the content of dreams symbolizes urges, wishes, and objects of fantasy that we would censor in the waking state.

physical acts. During REM sleep, however, neurotransmitters generally inhibit motor (muscular) activity. Therefore, we do not thrash about as we dream (Steriade, 1992). In this way, we save ourselves (and our bed partners) some wear and tear. The eye muscles are also stimulated, and they show the rapid eye movement associated with dreaming. In addition, the RAS stimulates neural activity in the parts of the cortex involved in vision, hearing, and memory. The cortex then automatically *synthesizes,* or puts together, these sources of stimulation to yield the substances of dreams.

The activation-synthesis model explains why there is a strong tendency to dream about events of the day: The most current neural activity of the cortex would be that which represented the events or concerns of the day.

NIGHTMARES.   Have you ever dreamed that something heavy was on your chest and watching as you breathed? Or that you were trying to run from a terrible threat but couldn't gain your footing or coordinate your leg muscles?

The Scream. Norwegian artist Edvard Munch's well-known work of art contains the kind of imagery that we might find in a nightmare.

In the Middle Ages, such nightmares were thought to be the work of demons called *incubi* and *succubi* (singular: **incubus** and **succubus**). By and large, they were seen as a form of retribution. That is, they were sent to make you pay for your sins.

Nightmares, like most pleasant dreams, are generally products of REM sleep. College students keeping dream logs report an average of two nightmares a month (Wood & Bootzin, 1990). Traumatic events can spawn nightmares, as reported in a study of survivors of the San Francisco earthquake of 1989 (Wood and others, 1992). People who experience frequent nightmares are more likely than other people to also experience anxieties, depression, and other psychological problems (Berquier & Ashton, 1992). We discuss the more disturbing "sleep terrors" under the section on sleep disorders.

Sleep Disorders

There are a number of sleep disorders. Some, like insomnia, are all too familiar. Others, like narcolepsy, seem somewhat exotic. In this section, we shall discuss insomnia and the deep-sleep disorders—sleep terrors, bed-wetting, and sleepwalking.

INSOMNIA. **Insomnia** refers to three types of sleeping problems: difficulty falling asleep (sleep-onset insomnia), difficulty remaining asleep through the night, and early morning awakening (Lacks & Morin, 1992). About 15% to 20% of American adults have chronic insomnia. Thirty to 40% have occasional insomnia (Murtagh & Greenwood, 1995). Women report the disorder more frequently than men.

As a group, people who experience insomnia show greater restlessness and muscle tension than those who do not (Lacks & Morin, 1992). Those with insomnia also have greater "cognitive arousal" than those who do not. They are more likely to worry and have "racing thoughts" at bedtime (White & Nicassio, 1990). Insomnia comes and goes with many people, increasing during periods of anxiety and tension (Gillin, 1991).

Insomniacs tend to compound their sleep problems through their efforts to force themselves to get to sleep (Bootzin and others, 1991). Their concern heightens autonomic activity and muscle tension. You cannot force or will yourself to get to sleep. You can only set the stage for it by lying down and relaxing when you are tired. If you focus on sleep too closely, it will elude you. Yet, millions go to bed each night dreading the possibility of sleep-onset insomnia.

Truth or Fiction Revisited. *It is true that many people have insomnia because they try too hard to get to sleep at night.* Trying to get to sleep heightens tension and anxiety, both of which counteract the feelings of relaxation that help induce sleep.

SLEEP TERRORS. Sleep terrors, bed-wetting, and sleepwalking all occur during deep (stage 3 or 4) sleep, are more common among children, and may reflect immaturity of the nervous system.

Sleep terrors are similar to, but more severe than, nightmares. Sleep terrors usually occur during deep sleep. Nightmares take place during REM sleep. Sleep terrors occur during the first couple of sleep cycles. Nightmares more often occur later on. Experiencing a surge in the heart and respiration rates, the dreamer may suddenly sit up, talk incoherently, and move about wildly. The dreamer is never fully awake, returns to sleep, and may recall a brief image

Incubus • (1) A spirit or demon thought in medieval times to lie on sleeping people, especially on women for sexual purposes. (2) A nightmare.

Succubus • A female demon thought in medieval times to have sexual intercourse with sleeping men.

Insomnia • A term for three types of sleeping problems: (1) difficulty falling asleep, (2) difficulty remaining asleep, and (3) waking early (From the Latin *in-,* meaning "not," and *somnus,* meaning "sleep.")

Sleep terrors • Frightening dreamlike experiences that occur during the deepest stage of NREM sleep. Nightmares, in contrast, occur during REM sleep.

such as of someone pressing on the chest. In contrast to the nightmare, however, memories of the episode are not vivid. Sleep terrors are often decreased by a minor **tranquilizer** at bedtime, which reduces the amount of time spent in stage 4 sleep.

BED-WETTING.   Bed-wetting is often seen as a stigma that reflects parental harshness or the child's attempt to punish the parents, but this disorder, too, may stem from immaturity of the nervous system. In most cases, bed-wetting resolves itself before adolescence, often by age 8. Behavior-therapy methods that condition children to awaken when about to urinate have been helpful. The antidepressant drug imipramine often helps by increasing bladder capacity. Sometimes, all that is needed is reassurance that no one need be to blame for bed-wetting and that most children "outgrow" the disorder.

SLEEPWALKING.   Perhaps half of all children occasionally talk in their sleep, and as many as 15% walk in their sleep (Mindell, 1993). Sleepwalkers may roam about almost nightly while their parents fret about the accidents that could befall them. Sleepwalkers typically do not remember their excursions, although they may respond to questions while they are up and about. Contrary to myth, there is no evidence that sleepwalkers become violent or grossly disturbed if they are awakened. Mild tranquilizers and maturity typically put an end to sleepwalking.

Truth or Fiction Revisited.   It is not true that it is dangerous to awaken a sleepwalker. Sleepwalkers may be confused and startled when awakened, but they are not usually violent.

Reflections

- **How much sleep do you need? (How do you know?) How much sleep do you get? Did you ever "pull" an all-nighter? What were the effects?**
- **What things do you dream about? Agree or disagree with the following statement and support your answer: "People can gain insight into their inmost feelings and fears by interpreting their dreams."**

Drugs often play a role in the treatment of sleep disorders. But drugs are used recreationally or to "expand consciousness" as well as to treat problems. Let us now turn our attention to a number of such drugs.

ALTERING CONSCIOUSNESS THROUGH DRUGS

The world is a supermarket of **psychoactive** substances, or drugs. The United States is flooded with drugs that distort perceptions and change mood—drugs that take you up, let you down, and move you across town. Some people use drugs because their friends do or because their parents tell them not to. Some are seeking pleasure. Others are seeking inner truth.

Alcohol is the most popular drug on high school and college campuses (Johnston and others, 1993). Most college students have tried marijuana, and perhaps one in seven smokes it regularly. Many Americans take **depressants** to get to sleep at night and **stimulants** to get going in the morning. Karl Marx charged that "religion . . . is the opium of the people," but heroin is the real opium of the people. Cocaine was, until recently, the toy of the well-to-do, but price breaks have brought it into the lockers of high school students. Given

Tranquilizers   •   Drugs used to reduce anxiety and tension.

Psychoactive   •   Descriptive of drugs that have psychological effects such as stimulation or distortion of perceptions.

Depressant   •   A drug that lowers the rate of activity of the nervous system. (From the Latin *de-,* meaning "down," and *premere,* meaning "to press.")

Stimulant   •   A drug that increases activity of the nervous system.

TABLE 5.2
PERCENTAGE OF COLLEGE STUDENTS WHO REPORT
DRUG USE "DURING THE LAST 30 DAYS," 1981–1992

DRUG	1981	1982	1983	1984	1985	1986	1987	1988	1989	1990	1991	1992
Alcohol	81.9	82.8	80.3	79.1	80.3	79.7	78.4	77.0	76.2	74.5	74.7	71.4
Cigarettes	25.9	24.4	24.7	21.5	22.4	22.4	24.0	22.6	21.1	21.5	23.2	23.5
Marijuana	33.2	26.8	26.2	23.0	23.6	22.3	20.3	16.8	16.3	14.0	14.1	14.6
Cocaine	7.3	7.9	6.5	7.6	6.9	7.0	4.6	4.2	2.8	1.2	1.0	1.0
(Crack)	NA*	NA	NA	NA	NA	NA	0.4	0.5	0.2	0.1	0.3	0.1
Stimulants	12.3	9.9	7.0	5.5	4.2	3.7	2.3	1.8	1.3	1.4	1.0	1.1
Sedatives	3.4	2.5	1.1	1.0	0.7	0.6	0.6	0.6	NA	NA	NA	NA
Barbiturates	NA	NA	NA	NA	NA	NA	NA	NA	0.2	0.2	0.2	0.7
Hallucinogens	2.3	2.6	1.8	1.8	1.3	2.2	2.0	1.7	2.3	1.4	1.2	2.3
Heroin	0.0	0.0	0.0	0.0	0.0	0.0	0.1	0.1	0.1	0.0	0.1	0.0

Source: Johnston and others (1993).
* NA = Not available

laws, moral pronouncements, medical warnings, and an occasional horror story, drug use actually seems to have declined in recent years (Johnston and others, 1993). Table 5.2 shows a decade-long trend for college students, according to University of Michigan surveys. Overall, however, drugs remain a part of life in the United States.

Substance Abuse and Dependence

Where does drug use end and abuse begin? The American Psychiatric Association (1994) defines **substance abuse** as repeated use of a substance despite the fact that it is causing or compounding social, occupational, psychological, or physical problems. If you are missing school or work because you are drunk or "sleeping it off," you are abusing alcohol. The amount you drink is not as crucial as the fact that your pattern of use disrupts your life.

Dependence is more severe than abuse. Dependence has behavioral and physiological aspects (American Psychiatric Association, 1994). Behaviorally, dependence is often characterized by loss of control over the substance, as in organizing one's life around getting it and using it. Physiologically, dependence is typified by tolerance, withdrawal symptoms, or both.[2] **Tolerance** is the body's habituation to a substance so that with regular usage, higher doses are required to achieve similar effects. There are characteristic withdrawal symptoms, or an **abstinence syndrome,** when the level of usage suddenly drops off. The abstinence syndrome for alcohol includes anxiety, tremors, restlessness, weakness, rapid pulse, and high blood pressure.

When doing without a drug, people who are *psychologically* dependent show signs of anxiety (shakiness, rapid pulse, and sweating are three) that overlap abstinence syndromes. Because of these signs, they may believe that they are physiologically dependent on a drug when they are psychologically dependent. Still, symptoms of abstinence from certain drugs are unmistakably physiological. One is **delirium tremens** ("the DTs"), encountered by

Substance abuse • Persistent use of a substance even though it is causing or compounding problems in meeting the demands of life.

Tolerance • Habituation to a drug, with the result that increasingly higher doses of the drug are needed to achieve similar effects.

Abstinence syndrome • A characteristic cluster of symptoms that results from sudden decrease in an addictive drug's level of usage. (From the Latin *abstinere,* meaning "to hold back.")

Delirium tremens • A condition characterized by sweating, restlessness, disorientation, and hallucinations. The "DTs" occurs in some chronic alcohol users when there is a sudden decrease in usage. (From the Latin *de-,* meaning "from," and *lira,* meaning "line" or "furrow"—suggesting that one's behavior is off the beaten track or norm.)

[2] The lay term *addiction* is usually used to connote physiological dependence, but here, too, there may be inconsistency. After all, some people speak of being "addicted" to work or to love.

some chronic alcoholics when they suddenly lower intake. The DTs are characterized by heavy sweating, restlessness, general **disorientation,** and terrifying **hallucinations**—often of creepy, crawling animals.

Causal Factors in Substance Abuse and Dependence

There are many reasons for substance abuse and dependence. A handful include curiosity, conformity to peer pressure, parental use, rebelliousness, and escape from boredom or pressure (Botvin and others, 1990; Johnson and others, 1990; Rhodes & Jason, 1990; Sher and others, 1991). Another reason is self-handicapping: By using alcohol or another drug when we are faced with a difficult task, we can blame failure on the alcohol, not ourselves. Similarly, alcohol and other drugs have been used as excuses for behaviors such as aggression, sexual forwardness, and forgetfulness.

Psychological and biological theories also account for substance abuse in the following ways.

PSYCHOLOGICAL FACTORS.   Psychodynamic explanations of substance abuse propose that drugs help people control or express unconscious needs and impulses. Alcoholism, for example, may reflect the need to remain dependent on an overprotective mother.

Social-cognitive theorists suggest that people commonly try tranquilizing agents such as Valium and alcohol on the basis of observing others or a recommendation. Cognitive psychologists note that expectancies about the effects of a substance are powerful predictors of its use (Darkes & Goldman, 1993; Schafer & Brown, 1991). Subsequent use may be reinforced by the drug's positive effects on mood and its reduction of unpleasant sensations such as anxiety, fear, and tension. For people who are physiologically dependent, avoidance of withdrawal symptoms is also reinforcing. Carrying the substance is reinforcing, because one need not worry about having to go without it. Some people, for example, will not leave the house without taking Valium along.

Parents who use drugs may increase their children's knowledge of drugs. They also show children how to use them—for example, when they are seeking to reduce tension or to "lubricate" social interactions (Sher and others, 1991; Stacy and others, 1991).

BIOLOGICAL FACTORS.   People may have genetic predispositions toward physiological dependence on various substances, including alcohol, cocaine, and nicotine (Azar, 1995a; Haney and others, 1994; Pomerleau and others, 1993). For example, the biological children of alcoholics who are reared by adoptive parents seem more likely to develop alcohol-related problems than the natural children of the adoptive parents. An inherited tendency toward alcoholism may involve greater sensitivity to alcohol (enjoyment of it) and greater tolerance of it (Azar, 1995a; Newlin & Thomson, 1990). For example, college-age children of alcoholics exhibit better muscular control and visual–motor coordination when they drink. They feel less intoxicated when they drink low to moderate doses of alcohol and show lower hormonal response to alcohol (Pihl and others, 1990) than do children of nonalcoholics.

Let us now consider the effects of some depressants, stimulants, and hallucinogenics.

Disorientation • Loss of sense of time, place, and the identity of people.

Hallucinations • Perceptions in the absence of sensation. (From the Latin *hallucinari,* meaning "to wander mentally.")

WORLD OF DIVERSITY

ETHNICITY AND SUBSTANCE ABUSE AMONG ADOLESCENTS

Adolescent substance abuse increased through 1981 but has since been more or less in a decline (Johnston and others, 1993). Substance abuse is generally higher among African American, Hispanic American, and Native American adolescents than among White adolescents, but the extent of substance abuse also depends on where these adolescents live. The highest rates of abuse occur where economically disadvantaged minority groups live in segregated enclaves. For example, African Americans who live in the "ghetto," Hispanic Americans who dwell in the barrio, and Native Americans who live on the reservation all have high rates of use. Youth who dwell in these separate enclaves are more likely to encounter social isolation, unemployment, poverty, and deviant role models, some of which take the form of gangs (Oetting & Beauvais, 1990).

Yet, when we survey *high school seniors* only, African Americans and Hispanic Americans apparently abuse substances no more than their White counterparts do (Oetting & Beauvais, 1990). How do we account for this discrepancy? It seems that the adolescents who are at greatest risk for substance abuse also tend to drop out of school before their senior year. School-based surveys thus systematically underestimate substance abuse by some minority groups (Oetting & Beauvais, 1990).

Alcohol and tobacco appear to be taking their heaviest toll on Native Americans. Native Americans are the American ethnic group at greatest risk of incurring alcohol-related diabetes, fetal abnormalities, cirrhosis of the liver, and accident fatalities (Moncher and others, 1990). Tobacco of the smoked and smokeless varieties also places Native Americans at high risk of cardiovascular disorders and several kinds of cancer. However, these overall high rates of substance use mask the great variability in rates among Native Americans in various tribes and geographical settings (Moncher and others, 1990).

It is not enough to say that overall substance use and abuse is in a general decline in the United States. We must attend to the types of people who participate in the surveys and to ethnic diversity among participants.

Sedative • A drug that soothes or quiets restlessness or agitation. (From the Latin *sedare,* meaning "to settle.")

Alcohol

No drug has meant so much to so many as alcohol. Alcohol is our dinnertime relaxant, our bedtime **sedative,** our cocktail-party social facilitator. We celebrate holy days, applaud our accomplishments, and express joyous wishes with alcohol. The young assert their maturity with alcohol. It is used at least occasionally by 85 to 88% of the high-school population (Johnston and others, 1993). The elderly use alcohol to stimulate circulation in peripheral areas of the body. Alcohol even kills germs on surface wounds.

Alcohol is the tranquilizer you can buy without prescription. It is the relief from anxiety you can swallow in public without criticism or stigma. A man who pops a Valium tablet may look weak. A man who chugalugs a bottle of beer may be perceived as "macho."

No drug has been so abused as alcohol. Ten million to 20 million Americans are alcoholics. In contrast, 500,000 use heroin regularly and 300,000 to 500,000 abuse sedatives. Excessive drinking has been linked to lower productivity, loss of employment, and downward movement in social status (Vaillant & Milofsky, 1982). Yet, half of all Americans use alcohol, and despite widespread marijuana use, it is the drug of choice among adolescents.

EFFECTS OF ALCOHOL.   Our response to a substance reflects the physiological effects of that substance and our interpretations of those effects. Our interpretations of the drug's effects are, in turn, influenced by our expectations.

What do people expect from alcohol? Adolescent and adult Americans sampled tend to report the beliefs that alcohol reduces tension, diverts one from worrying, enhances pleasure, increases social ability, and transforms experiences for the better (Brown and others, 1985; Rohsenow, 1983). These are expectations. What *does* alcohol do?

The effects of alcohol vary with the dose and the duration of use. Low doses of alcohol may be stimulating. Higher doses of alcohol have a sedative effect (Niaura and others, 1988), which is why alcohol is classified as a depressant. Depressant drugs generally act by slowing the activity of the central nervous system. Ironically, short-term use of alcohol may lessen feelings of depression, but prolonged use may augment feelings of depression (Aneshensel & Huba, 1983). Alcohol relaxes and deadens minor aches and pains. Alcohol also intoxicates: It impairs cognitive functioning, slurs the speech, and reduces motor coordination. Alcohol is implicated in about half of U.S. automobile accidents.

Alcohol consumption is connected with a drop-off in sexual activity (Leigh, 1993). Yet some drinkers may do things they would not do if sober, such as engage in sexual activity that may lead to exposure to the AIDS virus (Cooper and others, 1994; Leigh & Stall, 1993). Why? Perhaps alcohol impairs the thought processes needed to inhibit impulses (Hull and others, 1983; Steele & Josephs, 1990). When intoxicated, people may be less able to foresee the consequences of their behavior. They may also be less likely to focus on their moral beliefs. Then too, alcohol induces feelings of elation and **euphoria** that may wash away doubts. Moreover, alcohol is associated with a liberated social role in our culture. Drinkers may place the blame on the alcohol ("It's the alcohol, not me"), even though they choose to drink.

As a food, alcohol is fattening. Yet, chronic drinkers may be malnourished. Though high in calories, alcohol does not contain nutrients such as vitamins and proteins. Moreover, alcohol can interfere with the body's absorption of vitamins, particularly thiamine, a B vitamin. Thus, chronic drinking can lead to a number of disorders such as **cirrhosis of the liver,** which has been linked to protein deficiency, and **Wernicke–Korsakoff syndrome,** which has been linked to vitamin B deficiency. In cirrhosis of the liver, connective fibers replace active liver cells, impeding circulation of the blood. Wernicke–Korsakoff syndrome is a brain dysfunction that is characterized by confusion, memory loss for recent events (that is, problems in storage of new information), and visual problems.

When alcohol is metabolized, there are increases in levels of lactic and uric acids. Lactic acid has been correlated with anxiety attacks, although there is little reason to think that alcohol causes anxiety. Uric acid can cause gout. Light to moderate drinking may increase levels of high-density lipoprotein (HDL, or "good" cholesterol) and decrease the risk of cardiovascular disorders (Fuchs and others, 1995; Gaziano and others, 1993). However, chronic heavy drinking has been linked to cardiovascular disorders and cancer. In particular, heavy

---

Euphoria   •   Feelings of well-being, elation. (From the Greek *euphoros,* meaning "healthy.")
Cirrhosis of the liver   •   A disease caused by protein deficiency in which connective fibers replace active liver cells, impeding circulation of the blood. Alcohol does not contain protein. Therefore, persons who drink excessively may be prone to this disease. (From the Greek *kirrhos,* meaning "tawny," referring to the yellow-orange color of the diseased liver.)
Wernicke–Korsakoff syndrome   •   A cluster of symptoms associated with chronic alcohol abuse and characterized by confusion, memory impairment, and filling in gaps in memory with false information (confabulation).

drinking places women at risk for breast cancer (Fuchs and others, 1995). Drinking by a pregnant woman may harm the embryo.

DRINKING YOUR TROUBLES AWAY: DRINKING AS A STRATEGY FOR COPING WITH STRESS AND FAILURE.   Adolescent involvement with alcohol has been linked repeatedly to poor school grades and other problems (Chassin and others, 1988; Mann and others, 1987; Wills, 1986). Drinking can contribute to poor grades and other problems, but people may drink to reduce academic and other stresses. Alcohol apparently disrupts ability to recognize and interpret stressful information (Sayette, 1993).

Regardless of how or why one starts drinking, regular drinking can lead to physiological dependence. People who are physiologically dependent on alcohol are motivated to drink to avoid withdrawal symptoms. Still, even when alcoholics have "dried out"—withdrawn from alcohol—many return to drinking as a way of coping with stress or as an excuse for failure.

 **WORLD OF DIVERSITY**

SOCIOCULTURAL FACTORS IN ALCOHOL ABUSE

Men are much more likely than women to become alcoholics. A cultural explanation is that tighter social constraints are usually placed on women. A biological explanation is that alcohol hits women harder. If, for example, you have the impression that alcohol "goes to women's heads" more quickly than to men's, you are probably correct. Women seem to be more affected by alcohol because they metabolize very little of it in the stomach. Thus, alcohol reaches women's bloodstreams and brains relatively intact. (Women have less of an enzyme that metabolizes alcohol in the stomach than men do [Lieber, 1990].) Women mainly metabolize alcohol in the liver. For women, reports one health professional, "drinking alcohol has the same effect as injecting it intravenously" (Lieber, 1990). Strong stuff, indeed.

Truth or Fiction Revisited. *It is true that alcohol goes to women's heads more quickly than to men's.* Women are less likely to metabolize alcohol before it affects psychological functioning. Despite their greater responsiveness to small quantities of alcohol, women who drink heavily are apparently as likely as men to become alcoholics.

Alcoholism is found at all socioeconomic levels. People low in socioeconomic status are apparently more vulnerable to the social problems connected with heavy drinking, such as incarceration and family instability. Yet, more-affluent people may be more likely to imbibe large quantities of alcohol and encounter the medical consequences of doing so, such as cirrhosis of the liver (Halldin, 1985).

Some ethnic factors are connected with alcohol abuse. Native Americans and Irish Americans have the highest rates of alcoholism in the United States (Nevid and others, 1997). Jewish Americans have relatively low rates of alcoholism, a fact for which a cultural explanation is usually offered. Jewish Americans tend to expose children to alcohol (wine) early in life, within a strong family or religious context. Wine is offered in small quantities, with consequent low blood alcohol levels. Alcohol is thus not connected with rebellion, aggression, or failure in Jewish culture.

There are also biological explanations for low levels of drinking among some ethnic groups such as Asian Americans. Asians are more likely than

White people to show a "flushing response" to alcohol, as evidenced by rapid heart rate, dizziness, and headaches (Ellickson and others, 1992). Such sensitivity to alcohol may inhibit immoderate drinking among Asian Americans as it may among women.

Opiates

Opiates are a group of depressants known as **narcotics.** Some opiates are derived from the opium poppy, from which they obtain their name. Others are similar in chemical structure but synthesized. The ancient Sumerians gave the opium poppy its name: It means "plant of joy." Opiates include morphine, heroin, codeine, Demerol, and similar drugs whose major medical application is **analgesia,** or pain relief.

Morphine was introduced at about the time of the Civil War in the United States and the Franco-Prussian War in Europe. It was used liberally to deaden pain from wounds. Physiological dependence on morphine became known as the "soldier's disease." There was little stigma attached to dependence until morphine became a restricted substance.

Heroin was so named because it made people feel "heroic" and was hailed as the "hero" that would cure physiological dependence on morphine.

Truth or Fiction Revisited. *It is true that heroin was once used as a cure for addiction to morphine.* Today, methadone is used to help addicts avert withdrawal symptoms from heroin.

Heroin is a powerful depressant that can provide a euphoric rush. Users of heroin claim that it is so pleasurable it can eradicate any thought of food or sex. Soon after its initial appearance, heroin was used to treat so many problems that it became known as G.O.M.—"God's own medicine."

Heroin is illegal. Because the penalties for possession or sale are high, it is also expensive. For this reason, many physiologically dependent people support their habits through dealing (selling heroin), prostitution, or selling stolen goods. But the chemical effects of heroin do not directly stimulate criminal or aggressive behavior. On the other hand, people who use heroin regularly may be more likely than nonusers to engage in *other* risky criminal behaviors as well.

The word seems to have gotten out that the AIDS virus can be transmitted by sharing needles to inject ("shoot up") heroin and other drugs. More and more heroin users are thus "snorting" heroin (breathing it in through the nose in powder form) rather than injecting it in liquid form (Smolowe, 1993).

Although regular users develop tolerance for heroin, high doses can cause drowsiness, stupor, altered time perception, and impaired judgment.

Methadone is a synthetic opiate. Methadone has been used to treat physiological dependence on heroin in the same way that heroin was once used to treat physiological dependence on morphine. Methadone is slower acting than heroin and does not provide the thrilling rush. Most people treated with it simply swap dependence on one drug for dependence on another. Because they are unwilling to undergo withdrawal symptoms or to contemplate a lifestyle devoid of drugs, they must be maintained on methadone indefinitely.

If methadone is injected rather than taken orally, it can provide sensations similar to those of heroin. Another drug, naloxone, prevents users from becoming high if they later take heroin. Some people are placed on naloxone after being withdrawn from heroin. However, former addicts can simply choose

"Shooting Up" Heroin. Users of heroin claim that the drug is so pleasurable that it can eradicate any thought of food or sex. Many users remain dependent on heroin because they are unwilling to undergo withdrawal symptoms or to contemplate a life devoid of drugs.

not to take naloxone. Drugs like naloxone also do not motivate former users to undertake a heroin-free lifestyle.

Narcotics can have distressing abstinence syndromes, especially when used in high doses. Such syndromes may begin with flulike symptoms and progress through tremors, cramps, chills alternating with sweating, rapid pulse, high blood pressure, insomnia, vomiting, and diarrhea. However, these syndromes are somewhat variable from person to person. Many soldiers who used heroin regularly in Vietnam are reported to have suspended usage with relatively little trouble when they returned to the United States.

Barbiturates and Methaqualone

Barbiturates such as amobarbital, phenobarbital, pentobarbital, and secobarbital are depressants with a number of medical uses including relief of anxiety and tension, deadening of pain, and treatment of epilepsy, high blood pressure, and insomnia. Barbiturates lead rapidly to physiological and psychological dependence.

Methaqualone, sold under the brand names Quaalude and Sopor, is a depressant similar in effect to barbiturates. Methaqualone also leads to physiological dependence and is quite dangerous.

Psychologists generally oppose using barbiturates and methaqualone for anxiety, tension, and insomnia. These drugs lead rapidly to dependence and do nothing to teach the individual how to alter disturbing patterns of behavior. Many physicians, too, have become concerned about barbiturates. They now prefer to prescribe minor tranquilizers such as Valium and Librium for anxiety and tension and other drugs for insomnia. However, it is now thought that minor tranquilizers may also create physiological dependence. Tranquilizers also do nothing to help people change the relationships or other factors that distress them.

Barbiturates and methaqualone are popular as street drugs because they relax the muscles and produce a mild euphoric state. High doses of barbiturates result in drowsiness, motor impairment, slurred speech, irritability, and poor judgment. A physiologically dependent person who is withdrawn abruptly from barbiturates may experience severe convulsions and die. High doses of methaqualone may cause internal bleeding, coma, and death. Because of additive effects, it is dangerous to mix alcohol and other depressants.

Amphetamines

Amphetamines are a group of stimulants that were first used by soldiers during World War II to help them remain alert through the night. Stimulants increase the activity of the nervous system and contribute to feelings of euphoria and self-confidence. Truck drivers have used amphetamines to drive through the night. Amphetamines have become perhaps more widely known through students, who have used them for all-night cram sessions, and through dieters, who use them because they reduce hunger.

Called speed, uppers, bennies (for Benzedrine), and dexies (for Dexedrine), these drugs are often used for the euphoric rush they can produce, especially in high doses. (The so-called antidepressant drugs, discussed in Chapter 14, do not produce a euphoric rush.) Some people swallow amphetamines in pill form or inject liquid methedrine, the strongest form, into their veins. They may stay awake and "high" for days on end. Such highs must come to an end.

Opiates • A group of narcotics derived from the opium poppy, or similar in chemical structure, that provide a euphoric rush and depress the nervous system.

Narcotics • Drugs used to relieve pain and induce sleep. The term is usually reserved for opiates.

Analgesia • A state of not feeling pain although fully conscious.

Morphine • An opiate introduced at about the time of the U.S. Civil War.

Heroin • An opiate. Heroin, ironically, was used as a "cure" for morphine addiction when first introduced.

Methadone • An artificial narcotic that is slower acting than, and does not provide the rush of, heroin. Methadone use allows heroin addicts to abstain from heroin without experiencing an abstinence syndrome.

Barbiturate • An addictive depressant used to relieve anxiety or induce sleep.

Methaqualone • An addictive depressant. Often called "ludes."

Amphetamines • Stimulants derived from *alpha-methyl-beta-phenyl-ethyl-amine,* a colorless liquid consisting of carbon, hydrogen, and nitrogen.

People who have been on prolonged highs sometimes "crash," or fall into a deep sleep or depression. Some people commit suicide when crashing.

A related stimulant, methylphenidate (Ritalin), is widely used to treat **attention-deficit/hyperactivity disorder** in children (Wolraich and others, 1990). Ritalin has been shown to increase the attention span, decrease aggressive and disruptive behavior, and lead to academic gains (Klorman and others, 1994; Pelham and others, 1993). Why should Ritalin, a stimulant, calm children? The prevailing view is that hyperactivity is connected with immaturity of the cerebral cortex. Ritalin may spur the cortex to exercise control over more primitive centers in the lower brain.

People can become psychologically dependent on amphetamines, especially when they are used to cope with depression. Tolerance develops rapidly, but opinion is mixed as to whether they lead to physiological dependence. High doses may cause restlessness, insomnia, loss of appetite, hallucinations, paranoid delusions, and irritability. In the amphetamine psychosis, there are hallucinations and delusions that mimic the features of paranoid schizophrenia (see Chapter 13). In addition to causing restlessness and loss of appetite with hyperactive children, Ritalin may also suppress growth and give rise to tics and cardiovascular changes. These side effects are usually reversible with "drug holidays" or dosage decreases (Whalen & Henker, 1991).

Attention-deficit/hyperactivity disorder • A disorder that begins in childhood and is characterized by a persistent pattern of lack of attention, with or without hyperactivity and impulsive behavior.

Cocaine • A powerful stimulant.

Cocaine

Do you recall the commercials claiming that Coke adds life? Given its caffeine and sugar content, "Coke"—Coca-Cola, that is—should provide quite a lift. But Coca-Cola hasn't been "the real thing" since 1906. At that time, the manufacturers discontinued the use of cocaine in its formula. Cocaine is derived from coca leaves—the plant from which the soft drink took its name.

Truth or Fiction Revisited. *It is true that Coca-Cola once "added life" through a powerful but now illegal stimulant.* That stimulant is cocaine.

Coca leaves contain **cocaine,** a stimulant that produces a state of euphoria, reduces hunger, deadens pain, and bolsters self-confidence. Cocaine's popularity with college students seems to have peaked in the mid-1980s (see Table 5.2). Today, perhaps 1% use it regularly. The great majority of high school students now believe that use of cocaine is harmful (Cohn and others, 1995). Questions remain about the prevalence of cocaine use among minority youth, high school dropouts, and young people who do not attend college, however (Oetting & Beauvais, 1990; Rhodes & Jason, 1990).

Cocaine is brewed from coca leaves as a "tea," snorted in powder form, and injected in liquid form. Repeated snorting constricts blood vessels in the nose, drying the skin and, at times, exposing cartilage and perforating the nasal septum. These problems require cosmetic surgery. The potent derivatives "crack" and "bazooka" are inexpensive because they are unrefined.

Biologically speaking, cocaine stimulates sudden rises in blood pressure, constricts the coronary arteries (which decreases the oxygen supply to the heart), and quickens the heart rate. These events can occasionally cause respiratory and cardiovascular collapse (Moliterno and others, 1994), as with the sudden deaths of a number of athletes. Overdoses can lead to restlessness and insomnia, tremors, headaches, nausea, convulsions, hallucinations, and delusions. Use of crack has been connected with strokes (Levine and others, 1990).

Cocaine—also called *snow* and *coke,* like the slang term for the soft drink—has been used as a local anesthetic since the early 1800s. It came to the attention of one Viennese neurologist in 1884, a young chap named Sigmund Freud, who used it to fight his own depression and published an early

"Snorting" Cocaine. Cocaine is a powerful stimulant whose use has become widespread because of recent price breaks. Health professionals have become concerned about cocaine's stimulation of sudden rises in blood pressure, its constriction of blood vessels, and its acceleration of the heart rate. Several athletes have died from cocaine overdoses.

supportive article, "Song of Praise." Freud's early ardor was soon tempered by awareness that cocaine was habit-forming and could cause hallucinations and delusions. Most authorities today believe that cocaine causes physiological dependence (Gold, 1993).

Although cocaine has been unavailable to the general public since the Harrison Narcotic Act of 1914, it is still commonly the anesthetic of choice for surgery on the nose and throat. Cocaine, by the way, *is* a stimulant, not a narcotic. Its classification as a narcotic was only a legality, bringing the drug under the prohibitions of the narcotics act.

Cigarettes (Nicotine)

Smoking: a "custome lothesome to the Eye, hatefull to the Nose, harmefull to the Braine, dangerous to the Lungs."

KING JAMES I, 1604

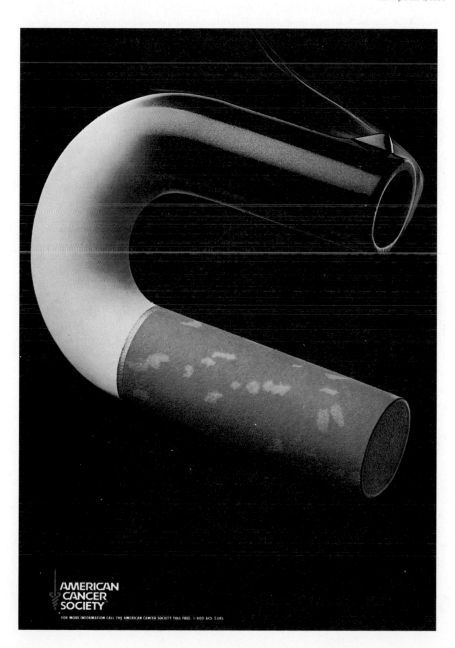

Cigarettes: Smoking Guns? The numbers of Americans who die from smoking are comparable to two jumbo jets crashing every day. If flying were that unsafe, would the government ground all flights? Would the public continue to book airline reservations?

The perils of smoking are no secret. All cigarette packs sold in the United States carry messages such as "Warning: The Surgeon General Has Determined That Cigarette Smoking Is Dangerous to Your Health." Cigarette advertising has been banned on radio and television. Nearly 420,000 Americans die from smoking-related illnesses each year (CDC, 1993b). This is the equivalent of two jumbo jets colliding in midair each day with all passengers lost. This is more than the number who die from motor-vehicle accidents, abuse of alcohol and all other drugs, suicide, homicide, and AIDS *combined* (Rosenblatt, 1994). If current worldwide trends continue, half a billion of the nearly 6 billion people alive today will eventually die from smoking (Darnton, 1994).

Truth or Fiction Revisited. *It is true that the number of people who die from smoking-related causes is greater than the number lost to motor-vehicle accidents, abuse of alcohol and all other drugs, suicide, homicide, and AIDS.*

The percentage of American adults who smoke declined from 42.2% in 1966 to 25.7% in 1991 ("Decline in smoking," 1993), but there have been recent increases among women and African Americans ("Smoke rises," 1993). As shown in Table 5.3, the incidence of smoking is connected with gender, age, ethnicity, level of education, and socioeconomic status.

Every cigarette steals about 7 minutes of a person's life (CDC, 1993b). The carbon monoxide in cigarette smoke impairs the blood's ability to carry oxygen, causing shortness of breath. The **hydrocarbons** ("tars") in cigarette smoke cause several kinds of cancer in laboratory animals. Heavy smokers are about 10 times as likely as nonsmokers to die of lung cancer (Bishop, 1993). Cigarette smoking is linked to death from heart disease, chronic lung and respiratory diseases, and other illnesses (Bartecchi and others, 1994). Women who smoke show reduced bone density, significantly increasing the risk of fracture of the hip and back (Hopper & Seeman, 1994). Pregnant women who smoke risk miscarriage, premature birth, and birth defects.

Hydrocarbons • Chemical compounds consisting of hydrogen and carbon.

TABLE 5.3
SNAPSHOT, U.S.A.: HUMAN DIVERSITY AND SMOKING

FACTOR	GROUP	PERCENT WHO SMOKE
Gender	Women	23.5
	Men	28.1
Age	18–24	22.9
	25–44	30.4
	45–64	26.9
	65–74	16.5
	75 and above	8.4
Ethnic Group	African American	29.2
	Asian American/Pacific Islander	16.0
	Hispanic American	20.2
	Native American	31.4
	Non-Hispanic White American	25.5
Level of Education	Fewer than 12 years	32.0
	12	30.0
	13–15	23.4
	16 and above	13.6
Socioeconomic Status (SES)	Below poverty level	33.3
	At poverty level or above	24.7

Source: Office of Smoking and Health, Centers for Disease Control (1993).

Passive smoking is also connected with respiratory illnesses, asthma, and other diseases (USDHHS, 1993). It accounts for more than 50,000 deaths per year (Bartecchi and others, 1994). Prolonged childhood and adolescent exposure to tobacco smoke in the household is a risk factor for lung cancer (Janerich and others, 1990). Because of the noxious effects of secondhand smoke, smoking has been banished from many public places.

Why, then, do people smoke? For many reasons—such as the desires to look sophisticated (though smokers may be more likely to be judged foolish than sophisticated these days), to have something to do with their hands, and to take in nicotine.

NICOTINE. **Nicotine** is the stimulant in cigarettes. Nicotine incites discharge of the hormone adrenaline. Adrenaline creates a burst of autonomic activity including rapid heart rate and release of sugar into the blood. As a stimulant, nicotine appears to enhance attention, improve performance on simple, repetitive tasks (Grunberg, 1993a; K. Perkins, 1993a), enhance the mood, and reduce stress (Hall and others, 1993). Nicotine does not appear to improve memory or functioning on complex cognitive tasks, such as solving math problems with many steps, however (Grunberg, 1993a; K. Perkins, 1993a). Some people smoke to control their weight (Califano, 1995). Nicotine both depresses the appetite and raises the metabolic rate (Audrain and others, 1995; Hultquist and others, 1995). People also tend to eat more when they stop smoking (Hatsukami and others, 1993; Ogden, 1994), which leads some people who have quit to return to smoking.

Cigarette smoking may be as addictive as is using heroin or cocaine (MacKenzie and others, 1994). Nicotine is the agent that creates physiological dependence on cigarettes (Kessler, 1995). Symptoms for withdrawal from nicotine include nervousness, drowsiness, energy loss, headaches, fatigue, irregular bowels, light-headedness, insomnia, dizziness, cramps, palpitations, tremors, and sweating. Since many of these symptoms mimic anxiety, it was once thought that smoking might be a habit rather than an addiction.

Passive smoking • Inhaling smoke from the tobacco products and exhalations of other people; also called *secondhand smoking*.
Nicotine • A stimulant found in tobacco smoke. (From the French name for the tobacco plant, *nicotiane*.)
Marijuana • The dried vegetable matter of the *Cannabis sativa* plant. (A Mexican-Spanish word.)
Hallucinogenic • Giving rise to hallucinations.

Marijuana

Marijuana is produced from the *Cannabis sativa* plant, which grows wild in many parts of the world. Marijuana helps some people relax and can elevate their mood. It also sometimes produces mild hallucinations, which is why marijuana is classified as a psychedelic, or **hallucinogenic,** drug.

In the 19th century, marijuana was used almost as aspirin is used today for headaches and minor aches and pains. It could be bought without prescription in any drugstore. Today, marijuana use and possession are illegal in most states. As noted by the Institute of Medicine of the National Academy of Sciences, marijuana also carries a number of health risks (Maugh, 1982). For example, marijuana impairs motor coordination and perceptual functions used in the operation of machines, such as cars and trucks. It impairs short-term memory and slows learning. Although it causes positive mood changes in many people, there are also disturbing instances of anxiety and confusion and occasional reports of psychotic reactions. Marijuana increases the heart rate up to 140–150 beats per minute and, in some people, raises blood pressure. This rise in workload poses a threat to persons with hypertension and cardiovascular disorders.

In the early 1990s, marijuana was used by about 14% of college students, down from nearly one third in 1981 (Johnston and others, 1993).

PSYCHOACTIVE EFFECTS OF MARIJUANA.   Marijuana smokers report different sensations at different levels of intoxication. The early stages of intoxication are frequently characterized by restlessness, which gives way to calmness. Fair to strong intoxication is linked to reports of heightened perceptions and increases in self-insight, creative thinking, and empathy for the feelings of others. Strong intoxication is linked to perceiving time as passing more slowly. A song, for example, might seem to last an hour rather than a few minutes. There is increased awareness of bodily sensations such as heartbeat. Smokers also report that strong intoxication heightens sexual sensations. Visual hallucinations are not uncommon.

Strong intoxication may cause smokers to experience disorientation. If the smoker's mood is euphoric, loss of identity may be interpreted as harmony with the universe. Yet, some smokers encounter negative experiences with strong intoxication. An accelerated heart rate and heightened awareness of bodily sensations leads some smokers to fear that their hearts will "run away" with them. Some smokers find disorientation threatening, and they fear failure to regain their identities. High levels of intoxication occasionally induce nausea and vomiting. Needless to say, smokers with such experiences smoke infrequently or just once.

Some people report that marijuana helps them socialize at parties. However, the friendliness characteristic of early stages of intoxication may give way to self-absorption and social withdrawal as the smoker becomes higher (Fabian & Fishkin, 1981).

People can become psychologically dependent on marijuana, as on any other drug. However, many psychologists maintain that marijuana does not cause physiological dependence. Tolerance is a sign of physiological dependence. With marijuana, however, regular usage is often associated with the need for *less,* not *more,* of the substance to achieve the same effects. Some of the substances in marijuana smoke may take a long time to be metabolized by the body. Thus, the effects of new doses may be added to those of the chemicals remaining in the body.

Marijuana's entire story has not yet been told. Some horror stories about marijuana may have been exaggerated, but one cannot assume that smoke containing 50% more carcinogenic hydrocarbon than tobacco smoke is harmless.

LSD • Lysergic acid diethylamide. A hallucinogenic drug.

Flashbacks • Distorted perceptions or hallucinations that occur days or weeks after LSD usage but mimic the LSD experience.

LSD

LSD is the abbreviation for lysergic acid diethylamide, a synthetic hallucinogenic drug. Users of "acid" claim that it "expands consciousness" and opens new worlds. Sometimes people believe they have achieved great insights while using LSD, but when it wears off they often cannot apply or recall these discoveries.

LSD and similar hallucinogenics are used by about 6% of the high school population (Johnston and others, 1991) and about 2% of the college population (see Table 5.2). As a powerful hallucinogenic, LSD produces vivid and colorful hallucinations.

FLASHBACKS.   Some LSD users have **flashbacks**—distorted perceptions or hallucinations that occur days, weeks, or longer after usage but mimic the LSD trip. Some researchers have speculated that flashbacks stem from chemical changes in the brain produced by LSD. Heaton and Victor (1976) and Matefy (1980) offer a psychological explanation for flashbacks.

An LSD "Trip"? This hallucinogenic drug can give rise to a vivid parade of colors and visual distortions. Some users claim to have arrived at great insights while "tripping," but afterward they have been typically unable to recall or apply them.

Heaton and Victor (1976) found that users who have flashbacks are more oriented toward fantasy and allowing their thoughts to wander. They are also more likely to focus on internal sensations. If they should experience sensations similar to a past trip, they may readily label them flashbacks and allow themselves to focus on them indefinitely, causing the experience to replay.

Matefy (1980) found that users who have flashbacks show greater capacity to become fully engrossed in role-playing and hypothesized that flashbacks may be nothing more than enacting the role of being on a trip. This does not necessarily mean that people who claim to have flashbacks are lying. They may be more willing to surrender personal control in response to internal sensations for the sake of altering their consciousness and having peak experiences. Users who do not have flashbacks prefer to be more in charge of their thought processes and have greater concern for meeting the demands of daily life.

Other hallucinogenic drugs include **mescaline** (derived from the peyote cactus) and **phencyclidine** (PCP). Regular use of hallucinogenics may lead to tolerance and psychological dependence. But hallucinogenics are not known to lead to physiological dependence. High doses may induce frightening hallucinations, impaired coordination, poor judgment, mood changes, and paranoid delusions.

EPILOGUE: MORE RESEARCH IS NEEDED IN USE AND ABUSE OF DRUGS

Drugs remain very much a part of U.S. society. Children and teenagers continue to become involved with drugs that impair their ability to learn at school and that are connected with reckless behavior (Cooper and others, 1994). There are also questions about the proper therapeutic use of drugs that are illicit under most circumstances. Such drugs include opiates, marijuana, and stimulants. Scientific issues often get intertwined with political and moral issues when drugs are discussed. For example, technical discussion of the benefits and dangers of marijuana is often saddled with public perceptions of marijuana that connect it with rebelliousness and sexual promiscuity. This perception originated in the "Swinging 60s."

Let us consider some key research questions about drugs—their use and abuse.

Substance Abuse in Teenagers

More research is needed into effective means of fighting substance abuse by children. Curiosity, peer pressure, parental use, rebelliousness, and the desire to escape from boredom or pressure are among the reasons children become involved with drugs. Inner-city youth are especially likely to become involved because of peer usage and the desire to escape a painful existence. Many means of fighting substance abuse have been tried with teenagers, including residential treatment centers, but their effectiveness has been shown to be modest at best (Nevid and others, 1997).

Efforts being made with younger children seem to hold somewhat more promise. For example, community psychologists are now experimenting with ways of tutoring youths to boost their self-esteem and success experiences in the schools (deGroot, 1994a, 1994b). In addition to boosting IQ scores, early childhood intervention programs also appear to decrease the likelihood of delinquent behavior, including substance abuse (Schweinhart & Weikart, 1993; Zigler and others, 1992). Perhaps these early approaches will succeed in helping children break away from poverty, a sense of lack of a future, and drug abuse.

Another positive note is that many teenagers now recognize that drugs such as crack cocaine are harmful (Johnston and others, 1993). A decade ago, teenagers were relatively more likely to attribute reports of drugs' harmfulness to horror stories concocted to scare them away from drugs. Perhaps the new

Mescaline • A hallucinogenic drug derived from the mescal (peyote) cactus. In religious ceremonies, Mexican Indians chew the button-like structures at the tops of the rounded stems of the plant.

Phencyclidine • Another hallucinogenic drug whose name is an acronym for its chemical structure. Abbreviated *PCP*.

millennium will also see more application of knowledge about the complex web of sociocultural factors that act on youths from various ethnic groups.

Treatment of Alcoholism

More research is needed into effective ways of treating alcoholism. Alcoholics Anonymous (AA) is the most widely used program to treat alcoholism. Yet the majority of those who seek help from AA appear to drop out after a handful of meetings (Miller, 1982). AA urges complete abstinence from alcohol. AA teaches that even one drink can result in relapse. Belief that one has "fallen off the wagon" can be a self-fulfilling prophecy, of course, whether one is talking about drinking, smoking, or dieting. There is also some evidence that problem drinkers who are relatively less dependent on alcohol, and who believe that they can limit their drinking, have been able to adopt the alternate strategy of controlled drinking (Rosenberg, 1993).

More research into alcoholism is needed to help determine which alcoholics need to abstain from alcohol and which can learn to exercise control in drinking. More research into the cognitive behavioral methods that hold the most promise—aversion therapy, relaxation training, covert sensitization, instruction in social skills, and self-monitoring (Elkins, 1980; Monti and others, 1993; Sanchez-Craig and others, 1984)—would also be desirable.

Therapeutic Applications of Illicit Drugs

More research is needed into the therapeutic application of various illicit drugs. For example, many people in pain who use small to moderate doses of opiates for pain relief do not experience a euphoric rush. Nor do they become psychologically dependent on them (Lang & Patt, 1994; Taub, 1993). If people who were in pain no longer need the drugs but have become physiologically dependent, they can usually quit by gradually decreasing their dosage. They encounter few, if any, side effects (Rosenthal, 1993a).

On the other hand, serious questions have been raised about using marijuana to decrease the nausea and vomiting often experienced by people with cancer who are taking chemotherapy. Supporters of marijuana argue that marijuana should be made widely available for medical purposes (Grinspoon & Bakalar, 1994). But detractors contend that carefully controlled studies on marijuana's medical benefits have not been conducted and that other drugs for nausea are available (Kolata, 1994a; Voth, 1995). The views of the medical establishment are clearly mixed (Swift, 1995).

The therapeutic usages of opiates, marijuana, and other substances need further investigation. If drugs like opiates and marijuana are to be used therapeutically, researchers need to demonstrate that they provide necessary benefits unavailable from more socially acceptable substances.

Treatment of Children with Attention-Deficit/Hyperactivity Disorder (ADHD)

More research is needed into the treatment of children with ADHD. The two major treatment methods have been stimulant medication (Ritalin) and cognitive behavior therapy. Some researchers have argued for the benefits of cognitive behavior therapy alone. Others argue for a combination of Ritalin and

Meditation • As a method for coping with stress, a systematic narrowing of attention that slows the metabolism and helps produce feelings of relaxation.

Transcendental Meditation • The simplified form of meditation brought to the United States by the Maharishi Mahesh Yogi. Abbreviated *TM*.

Mantra • A word or sound that is repeated in TM. (A Sanskrit word that has the same origin as the word *mind*.)

Meditation. People use many forms of meditation to try to expand inner awareness and experience inner harmony. The effects of meditation, like the effects of drugs, reflect both the bodily changes induced by meditation *and* the meditator's expectations.

cognitive behavior therapy (Whalen & Henker, 1991). Although some research evidence suggests that Ritalin alone is as effective as a combination of Ritalin and cognitive behavior therapy (Pelham and others, 1993), Ritalin has side effects that are a cause of concern. Its use is connected with restlessness and loss of appetite. It may also suppress growth and give rise to tics and cardiovascular changes. These side effects are usually reversible with "drug holidays" or dosage decreases (Whalen & Henker, 1991). However, it would be highly desirable to develop effective drugs that have fewer side effects or to refine cognitive behavioral techniques so that drug therapy is not necessary.

As we gather new knowledge of the nervous system and the actions of drugs, perhaps we will develop more effective therapeutic drugs and find more effective ways of helping people discontinue harmful use of drugs.

Let us now consider ways of altering consciousness that do not involve drugs.

Reflections

- **Agree or disagree with the following statement and support your answer: "People cannot be held responsible for their behavior when they have been drinking."**
- **Agree or disagree with the following statement and support your answer: "Some people just can't hold their liquor."**
- What had you heard about opiates such as heroin and morphine before reading this chapter? Is the information presented here consistent with what you had heard?
- What had you heard about marijuana? Is the information presented here consistent with what you have heard?
- **Agree or disagree with the following statement and support your answer: "Cocaine and narcotics such as heroin are the most dangerous psychoactive drugs."**

ALTERING CONSCIOUSNESS THROUGH MEDITATION: WHEN EASTERN GODS MEET WESTERN TECHNOLOGY

There are many kinds of **meditation,** but they seem to share similar psychological threads: Through rituals, exercises, and passive observation, the normal person–environment relationship is altered. Problem solving, planning, worry, awareness of the events of the day are all suspended. In this way, consciousness—that is, the normal focuses of attention—is altered, and a state of relaxation is often induced. Scientifically speaking, it is reasonable to suggest that the effects of meditation, like the effects of drugs, reflect whatever bodily changes are induced by meditation *and* one's expectations about meditation.

Transcendental Meditation, or TM, is a simplified form of Far Eastern meditation that was brought to the United States by the Maharishi Mahesh Yogi in 1959. Hundreds of thousands of Americans practice TM by repeating and concentrating on **mantras**—words or sounds that are claimed to have the capacity to help one achieve an altered state of consciousness.

TM has a number of spiritual goals such as expanding consciousness, but there are also more worldly goals such as reducing anxiety and normalizing blood pressure. In early research, Herbert Benson (1975) found no scientific evidence that TM expands consciousness, despite the claims of many practitioners. However, TM did produce what Benson labeled a **relaxation response.** During TM, the body's metabolic rate dramatically decreased. The blood pressure of people with hypertension decreased (Benson and others, 1973). In fact, people who meditated twice daily tended to show normalized blood pressure through the day. Meditators produced more frequent alpha waves—brain waves associated with feelings of relaxation but infrequent during sleep. Participants in Benson's study also showed lower heart and respiration rates. More recent research supports the usefulness of meditation in reducing anxiety (Edwards, 1991).

    Truth or Fiction Revisited. *It is true that people have managed to bring high blood pressure under control through meditation.* Meditation has been shown to normalize blood pressure.

    Other researchers agree that TM lowers a person's level of arousal, but they argue that the same relaxing effects can be achieved in other ways, such as resting quietly for the same amount of time (Holmes, 1984). Holmes found no differences between experienced meditators and novice "resters" in heart rate, respiration rate, blood pressure, and sweat in the palms of the hands (that is, galvanic skin response, or GSR). The issue here is not whether meditation helps, but whether meditation has special effects as compared with a restful break from a tension-producing routine.

    Note that formerly anxious and tense individuals who practice TM have also *chosen* to alter their stress-producing lifestyles by taking time out for themselves once or twice a day. Just taking time out for oneself may do the trick.

MINILECTURE: MEDITATION: TEACHING STORIES

ALTERING CONSCIOUSNESS THROUGH BIOFEEDBACK: GETTING IN TOUCH WITH THE UNTOUCHABLE

There is little we can take for granted in life. A few decades ago, however, psychologists were reasonably secure with the distinction between *voluntary* and *involuntary* functions. Voluntary functions, like lifting an arm or leg, were conscious. They could be directly willed. But other functions such as heart rate and blood pressure were involuntary or autonomic. They were beyond conscious control. We could no more consciously control blood pressure than, say, purposefully emit alpha waves.

    Once in a while, to be sure, we heard tales of yogis (practitioners of yoga) or other exotics who could make their hair stand literally on end or "will" their cheeks to stop bleeding after a nail had been put through. But such episodes were viewed as horror stories or stage tricks. Serious scientists went back to serious research—except for a handful of pioneering psychologists like Neal E. Miller of Rockefeller University. In classic research of the 1960s, Miller trained laboratory rats to increase or decrease their heart rates voluntarily (Miller, 1969). His procedure was simple. There is a "pleasure center" in the hypothalamus of the rat. A small burst of electricity in this center is strongly reinforcing: Rats will do whatever they can to reap this bit of shock, such as learning to press a lever.

    Miller implanted electrodes in the rats' pleasure centers. Then some rats were given electric shock whenever their heart rates happened to increase. Other rats received shock when their heart rates went lower. In other words, one group of rats was consistently "rewarded" (that is, shocked) when the rats' heart rates showed an increase. The other group was consistently rewarded for

Relaxation response • Benson's term for a group of responses that can be brought about by meditation. They involve lowered activity of the sympathetic branch of the autonomic nervous system.

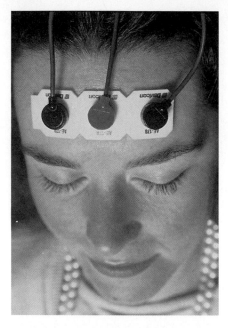

Biofeedback. Biofeedback is a system that provides, or feeds back, information about a bodily function to an organism. Through biofeedback training, people have learned to gain voluntary control over a number of functions that are normally involuntary.

Biofeedback training • The systematic feeding back to an organism information about a bodily function so that the organism can gain control of that function. Abbreviated *BFT*.

Electromyograph • An instrument that measures muscle tension. Abbreviated *EMG*. (From the Greek *mys*, meaning "mouse" and "muscle" — reflecting similarity between the movement of a mouse and the contraction of a muscle.)

a decrease. After a single 90-minute training session, rats learned to alter their heart rates by as much as 20% in the direction for which they had been rewarded.

Miller's research was an early example of **biofeedback training** (BFT). Biofeedback is simply a system that provides, or "feeds back," information about a bodily function to an organism. Miller used electrical stimulation of the brain to feed back information to rats when they had engaged in a targeted bodily response (in this case, raised or lowered their heart rates). Somehow the rats then used this information to raise or lower their heart rates voluntarily.

Similarly, people have learned to voluntarily change various bodily functions, including heart rate, that were once considered to be beyond their control.

Truth or Fiction. *It is true that you can learn to increase or decrease your heart rate just by thinking about it.* However, the "thinking about it" becomes more sophisticated through biofeedback training.

However, electrodes are not implanted in people's brains. Rather, people hear a "blip" or observe some other signal that informs them when the targeted response is being displayed.

BFT is used in many ways. In Chapter 4, we learned that BFT can be used to help people regain control over various functions when nerve pathways have been damaged. For example, a signal informs them when nervous impulses cause targeted muscles to contract, and they learn to make such control reliable by trying to cause the signal to be sounded again.

There are also many ways in which BFT helps people combat stress, tension, and anxiety. For example, people can learn to emit alpha waves (and feel somewhat more relaxed) through feedback from an EEG. A blip may increase in frequency whenever alpha waves are being emitted. The psychologist's instructions are simply to "make the blip go faster." An **electromyograph** (EMG), which monitors muscle tension, is commonly used to help people become more aware of muscle tension in the forehead and elsewhere and to learn to lower this tension. Through the use of other instruments, people have learned to lower their heart rates, their blood pressure, and the amount of sweat in the palm of the hand. All of these changes are relaxing. Biofeedback is widely used today by sports psychologists to teach athletes how to relax muscle groups that are unessential to the task at hand so that they can control anxiety and tension (Nelson, 1990).

People have also learned to elevate the temperature of a finger. Why even bother, you ask? It just so happens that limbs become subjectively warmer when more blood flows into them. Increasing the temperature of a finger—that is, altering patterns of blood flow in the body—helps some people control migraine headaches, which may be caused by dysfunctional circulatory patterns.

ALTERING CONSCIOUSNESS THROUGH HYPNOSIS: ON BEING ENTRANCED

Perhaps you have seen films in which Count Dracula hypnotized resistant victims into a stupor. Then he could get on with a bite in the neck with no further nonsense. Perhaps a fellow student labored to place a friend in a "trance" after reading a book on hypnosis. Or perhaps you have seen an audience member hypnotized in a nightclub act. If so, chances are this person acted as if he or she had returned to childhood, imagined that a snake was about to have a nip, or lay rigid between two chairs for a while.

Hypnosis, a term derived from the Greek word for sleep, has only recently become a respectable subject for psychological inquiry. Modern hypnosis seems to have begun with the ideas of Franz Mesmer in the 18th century. Mesmer asserted that the universe was connected by forms of magnetism—which may not be far from the mark. He claimed that people, too, could be drawn to one another by "animal magnetism." (No bull's-eye here.) Mesmer used bizarre props to bring people under his "spell." He did manage a respectable cure rate for minor ailments. But we skeptics are more likely to attribute his successes to the placebo effect than to animal magnetism.

Today, hypnotism retains its popularity in nightclubs, but it is also used as an anesthetic in dentistry, childbirth, even surgery. Some psychologists use hypnosis to teach clients how to reduce anxiety, manage pain, or overcome fears (Crawford & Barabasz, 1993; Edwards, 1991). Research shows that hypnosis is a useful supplement to other forms of therapy, especially in helping obese people to lose weight (Kirsch and others, 1995). Police use hypnosis to prompt the memories of witnesses.

Hypnosis. Hypnotized people become passive and tend to deploy their attention according to the instructions of the hypnotist.

Hypnotic Induction

The state of consciousness called the *hypnotic trance* is traditionally induced by asking individuals to narrow their attention to a small light, a spot on the wall, an object held by the hypnotist, or just the hypnotist's voice. There are usually suggestions that the limbs are becoming warm, heavy, and relaxed. People may also be told that they are becoming sleepy or falling asleep. Hypnosis is *not* sleep, however, as shown by differences in EEG recordings for the hypnotic trance and the stages of sleep. But the word *sleep* is understood by subjects to suggest a hypnotic trance and has a track record of success.

It is also possible to induce hypnosis through instructions that direct participants to remain active and alert (Clkurel & Gruzelier, 1990; Miller and others, 1991). So the effects of hypnosis probably cannot be attributed to relaxation.

People who are readily hypnotized are said to have *hypnotic suggestibility*. Part of hypnotic suggestibility is knowledge of what is expected during the "trance state." Generally speaking, suggestible people have positive attitudes and expectations about hypnosis and want to be hypnotized. Moreover, they focus closely on the instructions of the hypnotist (Crawford and others, 1993). Liking and trusting the hypnotist also contribute to suggestibility (Gfeller and others, 1987).

Truth or Fiction Revisited. *It is true that people who are easily hypnotized have positive attitudes toward hypnosis.* Such people look forward to the experience and cooperate with the hypnotist.

Hypnosis • A condition in which people appear to be highly suggestible and behave as though they are in a trance. (From the Greek *hypnos,* meaning "sleep.")

Changes in Consciousness Brought About by Hypnosis

Hypnotists and those who have been hypnotized report that hypnosis can bring about some or all of the following changes in consciousness. As you read them, bear in mind that changes in "consciousness" are inferred from changes in observable behavior and self-reports.

- *Passivity.* When being hypnotized, or in a trance, people await instructions and appear to suspend planning.

- *Narrowed Attention.* People may focus on the hypnotist's voice or a spot of light and avoid attending to background noise or intruding thoughts. It is claimed that individuals may not hear a loud noise behind the head if they are directed not to. (However, objective measures of hearing *do* suggest that people do not show any reduction in auditory sensitivity. Rather, they *report* greater deafness [Spanos and others, 1982].)

- *Pseudomemories and Hypermnesia.* People may be instructed to report **pseudomemories** or **hypermnesia.** In police investigations, witnesses' memories are usually heightened by instructing them to focus on selected details of a crime and then to reconstruct the entire scene. Studies suggest, however, that although people may report recalling more information when they are hypnotized, such information is often incorrect (Dwyan & Bowers, 1983; Nogrady and others, 1985; Weekes and others, 1992). But hypnotized people often report false information with conviction (Loftus, 1994; Weekes and others, 1992). Police investigators or juries may thus be misled.

- *Suggestibility.* People may respond to suggestions that an arm is becoming lighter and will rise or that the eyelids are becoming heavier and must close. They may act as though they cannot unlock hands clasped by the hypnotist or bend an arm "made rigid" by the hypnotist. Hypnotized individuals serving as witnesses are also open to the suggestions of their interviewers. They may incorporate ideas and images presented by interviewers into their memories and report them as facts (Laurence & Perry, 1983).

- *Playing Unusual Roles.* Most people expect to play sleepy, relaxed roles, but they may also be able to play roles calling for increased strength or alertness, such as riding a bicycle with less fatigue than usual. In **age regression,** people may play themselves as infants or children. Research shows that many supposed childhood memories and characteristics are played inaccurately. Nonetheless, some people show excellent recall of such details as hairstyle or speech pattern. A person may speak a language forgotten since childhood.

- *Perceptual Distortions.* Hypnotized people may act as though hypnotically induced hallucinations and delusions are real. In the "thirst hallucination," for example, people act as if they are parched, even if they have just had a drink. People may behave as though they cannot hear loud noises, smell odors (Zamansky & Bartis, 1985), or sense pain (Miller & Bowers, 1993).

- *Posthypnotic Amnesia.* Many people apparently cannot recall events that take place under hypnosis (Davidson & Bowers, 1991) or even that they were hypnotized at all, if so directed. However, they can usually recall what occurred if they are rehypnotized and instructed by the hypnotist to do so (Kihlstrom and others, 1985).

    The results of at least one experiment suggest that it may be advisable to take the phenomenon of posthypnotic amnesia with a grain of salt. People are more likely to report recalling events while "under a trance" when they are subjected to a lie detector test and led to believe that they will be found out if they are faking (Coe & Yashinski, 1985).

- *Posthypnotic Suggestion.* People may follow instructions according to prearranged cues of which they are supposedly unaware. For instance, a subject may be directed to fall again into a deep trance upon the single command "Sleep!" Smokers frequently seek the help of hypnotists to break

Pseudomemories • Hypnotically induced false memories.

Hypermnesia • Greatly enhanced or heightened memory.

Age regression • In hypnosis, taking on the role of childhood, commonly accompanied by vivid recollections of one's past.

their habits, and they are frequently given the suggestion that upon "waking," cigarette smoke will become aversive. They may also be instructed to forget that this idea originated with the hypnotist.

Theories of Hypnosis

Hypnotism is no longer explained in terms of animal magnetism, but psychodynamic theory and learning theory have offered explanations. According to Freud, the hypnotic trance represents **regression.** Hypnotized adults suspend "ego functioning," or conscious control of their behavior. They permit themselves to return to childish modes of responding that emphasize fantasy and impulse rather than fact and logic. According to learning theorist Andrew Salter, hypnosis is explained by conditioning. Words are connected with behavioral responses, and repetition of key words brings forth automatic behavior. Other theorists focus on concepts such as role-playing and dissociation.

ROLE THEORY.   Theodore Sarbin (1972) offers a **role theory** of hypnosis (Sarbin & Coe, 1972). He points out that the changes in behavior that are attributed to the hypnotic trance can be successfully imitated when people are instructed to behave *as though* they were hypnotized. For example, people can lie rigid between two chairs whether or not they are hypnotized. Also, people cannot be hypnotized unless they are familiar with the hypnotic "role"—the behavior that constitutes the trance. Sarbin is not saying that participants in hypnosis *fake* the hypnotic role. Research evidence suggests that most people who are hypnotized are not faking (Kinnunen and others, 1994). Sarbin suggests that people allow themselves to enact this role under the hypnotist's directions.

Research findings that suggestible people are motivated to enact the hypnotic role, are good role-players, and have vivid and absorbing imaginations would all seem to support role theory. The fact that the behaviors shown by hypnotized people can be mimicked by role-players means that we need not resort to the concept of the hypnotic trance—an unusual and mystifying altered state of awareness—to explain hypnotic events.

DISSOCIATION.   Runners frequently get through the pain and tedium of long-distance races by *dissociating*—by imagining themselves elsewhere, doing other things. My students inform me that they manage the pain and tedium of *other* instructors' classes in the same way. Ernest Hilgard (1977) similarly explains hypnotic phenomena through **neodissociation theory.** This is the view that we can selectively focus our attention on one thing (like hypnotic suggestions) and dissociate ourselves from the things going on around us.

In one experiment related to neodissociation theory, participants were hypnotized and instructed to submerse their arms in ice water—causing "cold pressor pain" (Miller and others, 1991). Participants were given suggestions to the effect that they were not in pain, however. Highly hypnotizable people reported dissociative experiences that allowed them to avoid the perception of pain, such as imagining that they were at the beach or imagining that their limbs were floating in air above the ice water.

Though hypnotized people may be focusing on the hypnotist's suggestions and perhaps imagining themselves to be somewhere else, they still tend to perceive their actual surroundings peripherally. In a sense, we do this all the time. We are not fully conscious, or aware, of everything going on about us.

Regression   •   Return to a form of behavior characteristic of an earlier stage of development.

Role theory   •   A theory that explains hypnotic events in terms of the person's ability to act *as though* he or she were hypnotized. Role theory differs from faking in that subjects cooperate and focus on hypnotic suggestions instead of pretending to be hypnotized.

Neodissociation theory   •   A theory that explains hypnotic events in terms of the splitting of consciousness.

Rather, at any moment we selectively focus on events such as tests, dates, or television shows that seem important or relevant. Yet while taking a test, we may be peripherally aware of the color of the wall or of the sound of rain.

Consider posthypnotic amnesia. When told to forget that they were hypnotized, people may focus on other matters. But the experience of hypnosis can be focused on afterward. Let us assume a person in a "trance" is given the posthypnotic suggestion to fall into a trance again upon hearing "sleep" but not to recall the fact that he or she was given this command. Upon "waking," the person does not focus on the posthypnotic suggestion. Hearing "Sleep!" leads to rapid refocusing of attention and return to the trance. These thoughts are all, in a sense, separated or dissociated from each other. Yet, the person's attention can focus rapidly on one, then another.

Role theory and neodissociation theory do not suggest that the phenomena of hypnosis are phony. Instead, they suggest that we do not need to explain these events through an altered state of awareness called a trance. Hypnosis may not be special at all. Rather, it is *we* who are special—through our great imaginations, our role-playing ability, and our capacity to divide our consciousness—concentrating now on one event we deem important, concentrating later on another.

Reflections

- **Agree or disagree with the following statement and support your answer: "Through meditation, people have been able to transcend the boundaries of everyday experience."**
- **Agree or disagree with the following statement and support your answer: "Research into biofeedback training has altered the traditional distinction between voluntary and involuntary body functions."**
- Had you heard of hypnosis or a hypnotic trance before taking this course? How does the information presented on hypnosis correspond to what you had heard?
- Agree or disagree with the following statement and support your answer: "You can be hypnotized only if you want to be hypnotized."

Study Guide

EXERCISE | **Types of Drugs**

DIRECTIONS: Below are the names of several types of drugs that are discussed in the text. Indicate whether each drug is a depressant (D), stimulant (S), or hallucinogenic (H) by writing the appropriate letter—D, S, or H—in the blank space to the left of the drug. The answers are given at the end of the exercise.

____ 1. Codeine
____ 2. Benzedrine
____ 3. Lysergic acid (LSD)
____ 4. Cocaine
____ 5. Demerol
____ 6. Nicotine
____ 7. Mescaline

____ 8. Methadone
____ 9. Quaalude
____ 10. Ritalin
____ 11. Phenobarbital
____ 12. Valium
____ 13. Dexedrine
____ 14. Alcohol

____ 15. Marijuana
____ 16. Morphine
____ 17. Phencyclidine (PCP)
____ 18. Heroin
____ 19. Secobarbital
____ 20. Methedrine

ANSWER KEY TO MATCHING EXERCISE

1. D	4. S	7. H	10. S	13. S	16. D	19. D
2. S	5. D	8. D	11. D	14. D	17. H	20. S
3. H	6. S	9. D	12. D	15. H	18. D	

ESL | **English as a Second Language—Bridging the Gap**

above all (201)—the important thing is

abstinence (185)—avoiding something, or staying away from

after all (177)—when you think about it

aggression (186)—hostility, or verbal or physical attacking behavior

all-night cram sessions (191)—remaining awake all night in order to study for an exam

amplitude (177)—large size

anxiety (175)—fear, worry, or nervousness about something

aroma (174)—smell; odor

arousal (179)—activity

arouse (181)—to stimulate

asserted (203)—stated

attribute (198)—identify as the cause of something

avenue to the unconscious (175)—a method of reaching the unconscious

aversive (205)—to offend; in this case, cigarette smoke will not be appealing but will be offensive

bazooka (192)—slang for a strong, cheap illegal drug; called this because it "hits" a person like a bullet from a type of gun called a bazooka

bizarre props (203)—strange or unusual things used to accomplish something

blip (202)—a short, sharp jump in a line that measures something

bolsters (192)—supports; encourages

brewed (192)—a mixture made by soaking something in a liquid

brief bursts (201)—short small explosions

bring them about (176)—cause them

came to the attention (192)—was noticed by

can take for granted in life (201)—assume, accept, and not think about or pay attention to

capture (174)—understand

catch up on our sleep (179)—get the sleep that we did not get before

chugalugs (187)—drink something quickly without stopping

Civil War (190)—(1861–1865); the American Civil War, or War Between the States, was a tragic war between the northern states and the southern states that caused much suffering

closed the gap (201)—there was not any difference

cognitive arousal (183)—level of brain activity

cologne (174)—a liquid with a light scent, not as strong as perfume

concepts (174)—ideas

concocted (198)—made up; not true

consistent (200)—agrees with

contest the view (204)—argue that

correlated (188)—associated with

cram sessions (191)—intense study periods

crucial (174)—very important

deadens pain (192)—causes a person not to feel pain

decade-long (185)—lasts for 10 years; a decade

deficiency (188)—lack of something

demons (183)—devils

despite (189)—in spite of; even though

deteriorate notably (179)—decline noticeably, significantly

detractors (200)—people who disagree with something, criticize it

deviant (187)—abnormal behavior

devised (174)—developed

dilemmas (180)—problems; difficult choices

discrepancy (187)—difference

disguised (181)—hidden or altered somehow so it is not clearly seen

distort (184)—change from what is real

dream theater (180)—the way that you dream; dream arena

droopy eyelids (204)—eyelids that are closing slowly over the eyeballs

drug of choice (188)—drug that most adolescents prefer

dwell (187)—live

elation (188)—strong sense of feeling good, happy

elude (183)—escape

enact (205)—to act something out; to do something

enclave (187)—a small area within a larger area

encounter (187)—to have or develop; to come across

engrossed in (197)—deeply involved in

episode (180)—instance

essence of (174)—basic; the basic or most important element

ethnic group (187)—group of people linked by a common culture, religion, race, or way of living

expose (189)—give the experience of something

fatalities (187)—deaths

final word on meditation is not yet in (201)—there are no conclusive research findings on meditation yet

for the sake of (198)—deprive oneself of one experience in order to have another

Franco-Prussian War (190)—(1870–1871); a war between France and Prussia (Germany) in which the Germans were the victors

from drug to drug (184)—the effects of one drug may be different from the effects of another

further cemented (174)—increased and made permanent

gain your footing (182)—remain balanced

gather some firsthand knowledge (205)—acquire some knowledge by doing it yourself

gleaming (174)—shining

grows wild (195)—grows without anyone cultivating it or planting and caring for it

habit-forming (185)—a person might acquire a habit for it; become dependent on

hair stand literally on end (201)—the hair on the head rises, which indicates there will be more success in a vertical position (this phrasing is common for expressing fear)

hallucinogenics (186)—chemicals that cause people to see imaginary sights or visions

handful (186)—a few, not all

happy-go-lucky (188)—an attitude of happiness without concern for problems that may occur later; without worry

horror stories (196)—terrible incidents

imbibe (189)—to drink or eat

impaired (179)—limited; due to a problem or injury

impulses (181)—strong, sudden wishes to do something

in effect (191)—in reality; what actually happens, although we do not plan it that way

incoherent (183)—not understandable

indeed (174)—also

inquiry (203)—investigation

insomnia (183)—difficulty with sleeping soundly

intoxicated (186)—drunk; your mind is altered by some substance

just taking this time out (200)—doing nothing else except to change activities, relax, or do nothing

Karl Marx (184)—(1818–1883); German socialist and political economist who lived in London; author of *Communist Manifesto* and *Das Kapital*

let you down (183)—make you feel calm and sometimes depressed

lie detector test (204)—mechanism that measures blood pressure and other physiological responses to determine if a person who is being questioned is telling the truth (being honest)

light-headedness (188)—a feeling that there is air in one's head

limbs (203)—arms and legs

long versus short sleepers (180)—how people who sleep many hours are different from people who sleep few hours

LSD trips (196)—journeys (fantasies and imagery) of the mind caused by LSD

macho (187)—a Spanish word that has come to be a negative slang term for a male who tries to appear extremely masculine

Marc Chagall (180)—Russian artist born in 1887 who became a famous impressionist painter in France

markedly enhances (174)—greatly increases

meant so much to so many (187)—the most important for a large number of people

mental "kick" (191)—sudden elation or good feeling

myriads (175)—too many to count

mystifying (205)—confusing; a mystery

narrow attention (192)—to focus

neural (175)—related to the brain

nightclub act (203)—entertainment in a restaurant that is known for its entertainment and not for its food

normal person–environment relationship (200)—the normal relationship of the person to the environment

not be far from the mark (203)—it may be almost accurate

novice smoker (195)—new and inexperienced smoker, or person who is beginning to smoke

once in a while (201)—it happens but not often

opens new worlds (196)—make new experience available

opinion is mixed (192)—there are different opinions

oppose (191)—to be against

outbreath (194)—a breath that you breathe out of your mouth

outdated theory (183)—a theory that does not have support now

pangs (174)—sharp feelings

peak experiences (198)—experiences of euphoria

perceptions (176)—what we see or perceive

perceptual abilities (174)—abilities to perceive, or sense, things

perils (193)—dangers

perspective (176)—point of view; way of looking at something

pioneering (201)—an innovator, someone who does something that others haven't done

poor judgment (191)—bad decision making

power isn't switched off (177)—a reference to turning off the electric current

prevailed (180)—occurred

price breaks (184)—the cost has greatly decreased

printout (177)—prints or pages that have printing on them from a computer

prolonged (188)—long-lasting

proper area (179)—a correct area; an appropriate area

proper province (174)—the correct or appropriate area for the study of psychology to have control

quickening of the heart rate (177)—the rate of the beat of the heart increases suddenly

rather steep descent (177)—extreme decline

readily available (175)—easily receive

reckless (198)—very careless; dangerous

referred to (174)—called; known as

relevant (205)—related to something important

replay of the experience (197)—unfold or repeat the experience

retribution (183)—punishment; penalty

rigid (203)—stiff and straight; held without moving

rise in workload (195)—increase in the work that the heart will have to do

scrawls (177)—scribbles; lines with no pattern that mean nothing

self-satisfied (180)—happy with oneself

semiautomatic (181)—partially automatic, almost without intention

set the stage (183)—prepare

sexual promiscuity (198)—active and immoral sexual behavior

short-term memory (195)—memory of recent events

short-term use (188)—use for a brief period of time

similar psychological threads (200)—they are connected

$64,000 question (200)—the biggest question there is

sleep it off (188)—the great length of time someone sometimes sleeps after having had a lot of alcohol

sleep-onset (177)—the point at which sleep begins

slurs the speech (188)—speech is not clear; words are not pronounced carefully

some scrawls (177)—movement of pencil or pen

speculated (196)—guessed; supposed

squelch them (190)—to eliminate them

stigma (184)—mark of social disapproval

street drugs (191)—drugs that are sold illegally on the street

summon up (175)—recall

supermarket (181)—large indoor market where customers choose from a large number of items

swear off (192)—make a positive decision not to use it or do it anymore

take . . . with a grain of salt (204)—to consider it as not very important and also not to believe it

take you up (184)—make you feel good, or euphoric

tedium (205)—boring time

tendency (182)—a preference for something; it happens often

that is (183)—this means that
thoughts . . . wander (197)—uncontrolled thoughts
thrash about (182)—move with energy
thrilling (190)—very exciting
time-triggered mechanism (199)—a mechanism that acts
  at a specific time
to be sure (201)—it is true
toy of the well-to-do (184)—plaything of the wealthy
track record (203)—has had some success in the past
trance (176)—when the mind is in a semiconscious
  state, but you are not asleep

try it out (202)—attempt it
unlikely candidates (181)—probably not good means or
  methods
vaguer (180)—not as clear
vivid (175)—strong; bright
wear and tear (182)—a little physical damage (from the
  idiom *wear out* which means "becoming unusable")
wrapped in (203)—completely involved
wrecked the following day (179)—felt very bad the
  next day

FILL-INS | **Chapter Review**

SECTION 1: A MINOR QUESTION: WHAT *IS* CONSCIOUSNESS?

In 1904, William (1) J_____ wrote an article, "Does Consciousness Exist?" John (2) W_____, the father of modern behaviorism, argued that only observable (3) b_____ should be studied by psychologists. However, (4) cog_____ psychologists believe that we cannot discuss meaningful human behavior without referring to consciousness.

    Consciousness has several meanings, including sensory awareness; the selective aspect of attention; direct (5) _____r awareness of cognitive processes; personal (6) _____y, or the sense of self; and the waking state. Sensory (7) _____ness refers to consciousness of the environment. (8) D_____ inner awareness refers to consciousness of thoughts, images, emotions, and memories.

    Sigmund Freud differentiated among ideas that are conscious; (9) _____scious, that is, available to awareness by focusing on them; and (10) _____scious, that is, unavailable to awareness under ordinary circumstances.

SECTION 2: SLEEP AND DREAMS

(11) Electro_____ (EEG) records show different stages of sleep. Different stages of sleep are characterized by different (12) b_____ waves. We have four stages of (13) non-_____-_____-_____ (NREM) sleep. Stage (14) _____ sleep is lightest, and stage (15) _____ sleep is deepest.

    The strength of brain waves is measured in the unit (16) _____s. When we close our eyes and relax before going to sleep, our brains emit (17) _____a waves. As we enter stage 1 sleep, we enter a pattern of (18) _____a waves. The transition from alpha to theta waves may be accompanied by brief hallucinatory, dream-like images referred to as the (19) _____gic state. During stage 2 sleep, sleep (20) _____les appear. We emit slow, strong (21) _____a waves during stages 3 and 4 sleep.

    After a half hour or so of stage (22) _____ sleep, we journey upward through the stages until we enter REM sleep. REM sleep is characterized by rapid (23) e_____ movements beneath closed lids, and by the emission of brain waves that resemble those of light stage (24) _____ sleep. Because EEG patterns during REM sleep resemble those of the waking state, REM sleep is also referred to as (25) _____ical sleep. During REM sleep we dream about (26) _____% of the time. We dream about (27) _____% of the time during NREM sleep.

During a typical 8-hour night, we undergo about (28: how many?) _____ trips through the different stages of sleep. Our first journey through stage 4 sleep is usually (29: Longest or Shortest?). Sleep tends to become (30: Lighter or Deeper?) as the night wears on. Periods of REM sleep tend to become (31: Longer or Shorter?) toward morning.

Sleep apparently helps restore a tired body, but we do not know exactly how sleep restores us, or how much sleep we need. People who are sleep-deprived show temporary problems in (32) _____ tion, which may reflect episodes of (33) _____ line sleep. People deprived of REM sleep show (34) REM-_____ nd during subsequent sleep periods.

Dreams are most vivid during (35: REM or NREM?) sleep. Freud theorized that dreams reflect (36) _____ scious wishes and serve the function of protecting sleep. According to the activation-synthesis model, dreams reflect activation by the (37) _____ s, and automatic integration of resultant neural activity by the (38) cerebral co _____. The content of most dreams is an extension of the events or concerns of the day.

SECTION 3: ALTERING CONSCIOUSNESS THROUGH DRUGS

Various substances or drugs alter consciousness. Substance use is considered abuse when it is continued for at least one (39) m_____ despite the fact that it is causing or compounding a social, (40) oc_____, psychological, or (41) ph_____ problem. The (42) am_____ of the substance used is not the crucial factor. Substance dependence is characterized by (43: increased or decreased?) use despite efforts to cut down and by (44) _____ cal dependence. Physiological dependence is evidenced by tolerance or by an (45) ab_____ syndrome upon withdrawal.

People usually first try drugs because of (46) _____ ity, but usage can be reinforced by anxiety reduction, feelings of euphoria, and other sensations. People are also motivated to avoid (47) _____ wal symptoms once they become physiologically dependent. Some people may have genetic predispositions to become physiologically dependent on certain substances.

Depressants acts by slowing the activity of the (48) c_____ nervous system. Alcohol is an intoxicating depressant that leads to (49) phy_____ dependence. Alcohol impairs (50) cog_____ functioning, slurs the (51) s_____, and reduces (52) m_____ coordination. Alcohol provides people with an excuse for (53) _____ re or for (54) anti_____ behavior, but alcohol has not been shown to induce antisocial behavior directly.

Opiates are (55) _____ cs derived from the opium poppy or similar in chemical structure. The opiates (56) mor_____ and (57) h_____ are depressants that reduce pain, but they are also bought on the street because of the euphoric rush they provide. Opiates can lead to (58) ph_____ dependence and distressing (59) ab_____ syndromes. The synthetic narcotic (60) _____ done has been used to treat heroin dependence.

Barbiturates are (61) _____ nts with many medical uses. These uses include treatment of (62) ep_____, of high (63) b_____ pressure, and of anxiety and insomnia. Barbiturates lead rapidly to (64) ph_____ dependence.

Stimulants act by (65: increasing or decreasing?) the activity of the nervous system. (66) _____ ines are stimulants that produce feelings of euphoria when taken in high doses. But high doses of amphetamines may also cause restlessness, insomnia, psychotic symptoms, and a "crash" upon (67) _____ al.

The stimulant (68) c_____ was used in Coca-Cola prior to 1906. Now it is an illegal drug that provides feelings of (69) _____ia and bolsters self-confidence. As with the amphetamines, overdoses can lead to (70) _____ness, (71) in_____, and psychotic reactions. There is controversy as to whether stimulants lead to (72) _____cal dependence, although it is generally agreed that any drug can lead to (73) _____cal dependence.

Cigarette smoke contains carbon (74) _____ide, hydrocarbons, and the stimulant (75) _____ine. Regular smokers adjust their smoking to maintain a consistent blood level of nicotine, suggestive of (76) _____cal dependence. Cigarette smoking has been linked to death from heart disease, cancer, and many other disorders.

Hallucinogenic substances produce (77) _____tions, or sensations and perceptions in the absence of external stimulation that become confused with reality. Marijuana is a (78) _____genic drug. Marijuana often produces heightened and distorted (79) _____tions, relaxation, feelings of (80) em_____, and reports of new insights.

LSD is a hallucinogenic drug that produces vivid (81) _____tions. So-called LSD (82) _____cks may reflect psychological rather than physiological factors. Persons prone to flashbacks are more oriented toward (83) _____sy and toward allowing their thoughts to (84) _____der. Regular use of hallucinogenics may lead to psychological (85) _____dence and to (86) tol_____. However, hallucinogenics are not known to lead to (87) _____cal dependence.

SECTION 4: ALTERING CONSCIOUSNESS THROUGH MEDITATION: WHEN EASTERN GODS MEET WESTERN TECHNOLOGY

In meditation, one focuses "passively" on an object or a (88) m_____ in order to alter the normal person–environment relationship. In this way, consciousness (that is, the normal focuses of attention) is altered and a (89) re_____ _____ is often induced. (90) Tr_____ Meditation (TM) and other forms of meditation appear to reduce high blood pressure along with producing relaxation. There is controversy as to whether meditation is more relaxing or effective in reducing (91) b_____ pressure than is simple quiet sitting or resting.

SECTION 5: ALTERING CONSCIOUSNESS THROUGH BIOFEEDBACK: GETTING IN TOUCH WITH THE UNTOUCHABLE

Biofeedback is a system that (92) _____s back information about a bodily function to an organism. Neal Miller taught rats to increase or decrease their (93) _____ _____s by giving them electric shock in their "pleasure centers" when they performed the targeted response. Through biofeedback training, people and lower animals have learned to consciously control (94) _____tary or autonomic functions. The (95) _____graph (EMG) monitors (96) m_____ tension and heightens awareness of muscle tension in the forehead and elsewhere.

SECTION 6: ALTERING CONSCIOUSNESS THROUGH HYPNOSIS: ON BEING ENTRANCED

Hypnosis in its modern form was originated by Franz (97) M_____. Mesmer explained the hypnotic "trance" through his concept of animal (98) _____ism. Hypnotism contributed to the development of the (99) _____tic theory of personality. By means of hypnosis, Charcot and Janet found that so-called (100) _____ical disorders had psychological roots. Freud suggested that hypnosis was one avenue to the (101) _____scious mind.

Today hypnotism is used in nightclub acts and thus has its sensationalistic aspects. However, psychologists responsibly use hypnosis to help clients relax, to help them (102) _____ine vivid imagery, and to help them cope with (103) p_____. Police use hypnosis to prompt the (104) m_____ of witnesses.

People who are readily hypnotized are said to have hypnotic (105) _____lity. Suggestible people have (106) _____tive attitudes toward hypnosis. They are highly (107) _____ed to become hypnotized.

Hypnosis typically brings about the following changes in consciousness: passivity, narrowed (108) _____tion, (109) _____sia (heightened memory), suggestibility, assumption of unusual roles, perceptual distortions, (110) post_____ amnesia, and posthypnotic suggestion.

According to Freud's psychoanalytic theory, the hypnotic trance represents (111) _____sion. Current theories of hypnosis do not rely on the existence of a special (112) t_____ state. According to role theory, hypnotized subjects enact the (113) r_____ of being in a hypnotic trance. In order to enact this role, they must be aware of the (114) _____iors that constitute the trance and motivated to imitate them.

ANSWER KEY TO CHAPTER REVIEW

1. James	30. Lighter	59. Abstinence	87. Physiological
2. Watson	31. Longer	60. Methadone	88. Mantra
3. Behavior	32. Attention	61. Depressants	89. Relaxation response
4. Cognitive	33. Borderline	62. Epilepsy	90. Transcendental
5. Inner	34. REM-rebound	63. Blood	91. Blood
6. Unity	35. REM	64. Physiological	92. Feeds
7. Awareness	36. Unconscious	65. Increasing	93. Heart rates
8. Direct	37. Pons	66. Amphetamines	94. Involuntary
9. Preconscious	38. Cortex	67. Withdrawal	95. Electromyograph
10. Unconscious	39. Month	68. Cocaine	96. Muscle
11. Electroencephalograph	40. Occupational	69. Euphoria	97. Mesmer
12. Brain	41. Physical	70. Restlessness	98. Magnetism
13. Non-rapid-eye-movement	42. Amount	71. Insomnia	99. Psychoanalytic (or psychodynamic)
14. 1	43. Increased	72. Physiological	100. Hysterical
15. 4	44. Physiological	73. Psychological	101. Unconscious
16. Volts	45. Abstinence	74. Monoxide	102. Imagine
17. Alpha	46. Curiosity	75. Nicotine	103. Pain
18. Theta	47. Withdrawal	76. Physiological	104. Memory
19. Hypnagogic	48. Central	77. Hallucinations	105. Suggestibility
20. Spindles	49. Physiological	78. Hallucinogenic	106. Positive
21. Delta	50. Cognitive	79. Perceptions	107. Motivated
22. 4	51. Speech	80. Empathy	108. Attention
23. Eye	52. Motor	81. Hallucinations	109. Hypermnesia
24. 1	53. Failure	82. Flashbacks	110. Posthypnotic
25. Paradoxical	54. Antisocial	83. Fantasy	111. Regression
26. 80	55. Narcotics	84. Wander	112. Trance
27. 20	56. Morphine	85. Dependence	113. Role
28. Five	57. Heroin	86. Tolerance	114. Behaviors
29. Longest	58. Physiological		

POSTTEST　| Multiple Choice

1. Sigmund Freud labeled mental events that are unavailable to awareness under most circumstances as
   a. preconscious.
   b. unconscious.
   c. repressed.
   d. dissociated.

2. According to the text, the least controversial meaning of the word *consciousness* refers to
   a. direct inner awareness.
   b. sensory awareness.
   c. the normal waking state.
   d. the sense of self.

3. Brain waves are measured by means of the
   a. electrocardiogram.
   b. electroencephalograph.
   c. electromyograph.
   d. thermistor.

4. During stage 4 sleep, the brain emits _____ waves.
   a. alpha
   b. beta
   c. delta
   d. theta

5. Sleep spindles appear during stage _____ sleep.
   a. 1
   b. 2
   c. 3
   d. 4

6. Jim usually sleeps 8 hours a night. About how many dreams is he likely to have during the night?
   a. none
   b. 1
   c. 5
   d. 25 or more

7. Freud believed that dreams "protected sleep" by
   a. causing us to emit alpha waves.
   b. inhibiting the reticular activating system.
   c. producing rapid eye movements.
   d. keeping disturbing ideas out of awareness.

8. When they drink, the college-age children of alcoholics _____ than the children of nonalcoholics.
   a. show lower tolerance
   b. develop withdrawal symptoms more rapidly
   c. show better visual–motor coordination
   d. are more likely to become physically ill

9. In terms of its action on the body, cocaine is correctly categorized as a
   a. depressant.
   b. hallucinogenic.
   c. narcotic.
   d. stimulant.

10. The most widely used drug on college campuses is
    a. cocaine.
    b. marijuana.
    c. LSD.
    d. alcohol.

11. According to the text, _____ prevents users from becoming "high" if they take heroin.
    a. Antabuse
    b. naloxone
    c. methadone
    d. imipramine

12. Which of the following is *not* part of the abstinence syndrome for alcohol?
    a. rapid pulse
    b. low blood pressure
    c. anxiety
    d. tremors

13. Methaqualone is a(n) _____ drug.
    a. depressant
    b. stimulant
    c. antidepressant
    d. hallucinogenic

14. Which of the following is least likely to cause physiological dependence?
    a. barbiturates
    b. LSD
    c. methaqualone
    d. methadone

15. TM was introduced by
    a. Maharishi Mahesh Yogi.
    b. Franz Mesmer.
    c. Herbert Benson.
    d. Neal Miller.

16. Biofeedback is defined as a system that feeds back information about _____ to an organism.
    a. autonomic functions
    b. heart rate
    c. voluntary functions
    d. a body function

17. A friend tells you that he has learned how to raise the temperature in a finger through biofeedback training. Your friend probably acquired this skill in order to
    a. relax the muscles of the forehead.
    b. control headaches.
    c. lower acid secretion in the gastrointestinal tract.
    d. emit alpha waves.

18. According to neodissociation theory,
    a. hypnotized subjects are aware of many things going on around them, even though they are focusing primarily on the hypnotist.
    b. the trance state is induced by age regression.
    c. only subjects who are highly motivated to be hypnotized can be hypnotized.
    d. one cannot enter a hypnotic trance unless one is suggestible.

19. Who first encouraged a patient to talk and express her feelings freely while she was hypnotized?
    a. Sigmund Freud
    b. Pierre Janet
    c. Josef Breuer
    d. Jean Martin Charcot

20. Arnold knows that you are taking a psychology course and asks you if you think he would be a "good subject" for hypnosis. You point out that research suggests that hypnosis is most successful with people who
    a. understand what is expected of them during the "trance state."
    b. are seeking the approval of the hypnotist.
    c. are unfamiliar with hypnosis.
    d. are below average in intelligence.

ANSWER KEY TO POSTTEST

1. B	4. C	7. D	10. D	13. A	16. D	19. C
2. A	5. B	8. C	11. B	14. B	17. B	20. A
3. B	6. C	9. D	12. B	15. A	18. A	

LEARNING OBJECTIVES

When you have finished studying Chapter 6, you should be able to:

1. Discuss controversies in defining learning.

CLASSICAL CONDITIONING

2. Explain the contribution of Ivan Pavlov to the psychology of learning.
3. Describe the types of classical conditioning.
4. Explain how contingency theory challenges the traditional explanation of classical conditioning.
5. Define *extinction, spontaneous recovery, generalization,* and *discrimination.*

OPERANT CONDITIONING

6. Explain the contributions of Edward Thorndike and B. F. Skinner to the psychology of learning.
7. Explain the process of operant conditioning.
8. Distinguish between various kinds of reinforcers, rewards, and punishments.
9. Describe various schedules of reinforcement.

COGNITIVE FACTORS IN LEARNING

10. Describe evidence that supports the view that learning can occur by insight.
11. Describe evidence that supports the existence of latent learning.
12. Discuss observational learning, including the effects of media violence.

6

Learning

PRETEST *Truth or Fiction?*

____ One nauseating meal can give rise to a food aversion that persists for years.

____ Dogs can be trained to salivate when a bell is sounded.

____ Psychologists helped a young boy overcome fear of rabbits by having him eat cookies while a rabbit was brought nearer.

____ During World War II, a psychologist devised a plan for training pigeons to guide missiles to their targets.

____ Punishment does not work.

____ Rats can be trained to climb a ramp, cross a bridge, climb a ladder, pedal a toy car, and do several other tasks — all in proper sequence.

____ Psychologists successfully fashioned a method to teach an emaciated 9-month-old infant to stop throwing up.

____ We must make mistakes if we are to learn.

WHEN I was a child in The Bronx, my friends and I would go to the movies on Saturday mornings. There would be a serial followed by a feature film, and admission was a quarter. We would also eat candy (I loved Nonpareils and Raisinets) and popcorn. One morning, my friends dared me to eat two large containers of buttered popcorn by myself. For reasons that I label "youth," I rose to the challenge. Down went an enormous container of buttered popcorn. More slowly—much more slowly—I stuffed down the second. Predictably, I felt bloated and nauseated. The taste of the butter, corn, and salt lingered in my mouth and nose, and my head spun with the repulsive sensations. It was obvious to me that I would have no more popcorn that day. However, I was surprised that I could not face buttered popcorn again for a year.

Years later, I learned that psychologists refer to my response to buttered popcorn as a **taste aversion.** Although I could not analyze my reaction in a sophisticated fashion at the time, I recognized that there was something strange about it. As I thought of it then, my "head" was telling me one thing about the popcorn while my "stomach" was telling me another. On a cognitive level, I recognized that my feelings stemmed from eating too much buttered popcorn and that smaller amounts would be safe. But something had also apparently been learned on a "gut level" that overrode my belief that I should be able to eat and enjoy reasonable amounts of buttered popcorn.

Now I know that a taste aversion is an example of classical conditioning. Classical conditioning leads organisms to anticipate events. An "overdose" of buttered popcorn had made me queasy. Afterward, the sight and odor of buttered popcorn—even the thought of it—was sufficient to make me anticipate nausea. In fact, they induced sensations of nausea in my throat and stomach. My aversion seemed silly at the time, but it is adaptive for organisms to develop taste aversions readily. Often when foods make us ill, it is because they are poisoned or unhealthful for other reasons. A taste aversion serves the adaptive function of keeping us away from them.

After I had acquired my taste aversion, I stayed away from buttered popcorn. My avoidance could be explained in terms of another kind of learning, operant conditioning, in which organisms learn to do things—and not to do other things—because of the consequences of their behavior. I stayed away from buttered popcorn to avoid anticipated nausea. But we also seek fluids when thirsty, sex when aroused, and an ambient temperature of 68 to 70 degrees Fahrenheit because we anticipate pleasant consequences. Put briefly, classical conditioning focuses on how organisms form anticipations about their environments. Operant conditioning focuses on what they do about them.

By the way, more than 30 years have now passed—how many more is my business. But I still prefer my popcorn *un*buttered.

Truth or Fiction Revisited. *It is true that one nauseating meal can give rise to a food aversion that persists for years.* In what way can the rapid development of taste aversions be said to be adaptive? Can you explain why organisms that rapidly develop taste aversions can be said to have an evolutionary advantage?

Classical and operant conditioning are two forms of learning, which is the subject of this chapter. In lower organisms, much behavior is instinctive, or inborn. Fish are born "knowing" how to swim. Salmon instinctively return to spawn in the streams of their birth after they have matured and spent years roaming the deep seas. Robins instinctively know how to sing the songs of their species and to build nests. Rats instinctively mate and rear their young. Among people, however, the variety and complexity of behavior patterns are

Taste aversion • A kind of classical conditioning in which a previously desirable or neutral food becomes repugnant because it is associated with aversive stimulation.

largely learned through experience. Experience is essential in our learning to walk and in our acquisition of the languages of our parents and communities. We learn to read, to do mathematical computations, and to symbolically rotate geometric figures. We learn to seek out the foods valued in our cultures when we are hungry. We get into the habit of starting our days with coffee, tea, or other beverages. We learn which behavior patterns are deemed socially acceptable and which are considered wrong. And, of course, our families and communities use verbal guidance, set examples, and apply rewards and punishments in an effort to teach us to stick to the straight and narrow.

Sometimes our learning experiences are direct, as was my taste aversion for buttered popcorn. But we can also learn from the experiences of others. For example, I warn my children against the perils of jumping from high places and running wild in the house. (Occasionally they heed me.) We learn about the past, about other peoples, and about how to put things together from books and visual media. And we learn as we invent ways of doing things that have never been done before.

Having noted these various ways of learning, let me admit that the very definition of **learning** stirs controversy in psychology. *Learning* may be defined in different ways.

From the behaviorist perspective, *learning* is defined as a relatively permanent change in behavior that arises from experience. Changes in behavior also arise from maturation and physical changes, but these do not reflect learning. The behaviorist definition is operational. Learning is defined in terms of the changes in behavior by which it is known. From the behaviorist perspective, buttered popcorn came to evoke nausea because it was associated with nausea. I also learned to avoid popcorn because of the consequences of consuming it—simple and not-so-sweet.

From the cognitive perspective, learning involves processes by which experience contributes to relatively permanent changes in the way organisms mentally represent the environment. Changes in representation may influence, but do not necessarily cause, changes in behavior. From this perspective, learning is *made evident* by behavioral change. However, learning is defined as an internal and not directly observable process. From the cognitive perspective, my gorging on buttered popcorn taught me to mentally represent buttered popcorn in a different way. My altered image of buttered popcorn then encouraged me to avoid it for a while. But my avoidance was not mechanical or compulsory.

Behaviorists do not concern themselves with the ways in which I mentally represent buttered popcorn. (And who can fault them?) They argue that there is no direct way of measuring my mental imagery, only my behavior. So why try to embrace imagery in a scientific theory?

Learning • (1) According to behaviorists, a relatively permanent change in behavior that results from experience. (2) According to cognitive theorists, the process by which organisms make relatively permanent changes in the way they represent the environment because of experience. These changes influence the organism's behavior but do not fully determine it.

Reflections

- Do you have a taste aversion to any kind of food? Can you recall an incident that led to the taste aversion?
- How would you have defined *learning* before beginning this chapter? Are you more in sympathy with the behavioral or cognitive perspective on learning? Why?

Let us now focus on some of the particulars of a number of kinds of learning, beginning with classical conditioning. We shall return to these theoretical matters from time to time as well.

CLASSICAL CONDITIONING

Classical conditioning involves some of the ways in which we learn to associate events. Consider: We have a distinct preference for having instructors grade our papers with *A*s rather than *F*s. We are also (usually) more likely to stop our cars for red than green traffic lights. Why? We are not born with instinctive attitudes toward the letters *A* and *F*. Nor are we born knowing that red means stop and green means go. We learn the meanings of these symbols because they are associated with other events. *A*s are associated with instructor approval and the likelihood of getting into graduate school. Red lights are associated with avoiding accidents and traffic citations.

Ivan Pavlov Rings a Bell

Lower animals also learn relationships among events, as Russian physiologist Ivan Pavlov (1849–1936) discovered in research with laboratory dogs. Pavlov was attempting to identify neural receptors in the mouth that triggered a response from the salivary glands. But his efforts were hampered by the dogs' salivating at undesired times, such as when a laboratory assistant inadvertently clanged a food tray.

Because of its biological makeup, a dog will salivate if meat powder is placed on its tongue. Salivation in response to meat powder is unlearned, a **reflex.** Reflexes are elicited by a certain range of stimuli. A **stimulus** is an environmental condition that evokes a response from an organism, such as meat powder on the tongue or a traffic light's changing colors. Reflexes are simple unlearned responses to stimuli. Pavlov discovered that reflexes can also be learned, or conditioned, through association. His dogs began salivating in response to clinking food trays because this noise, in the past, had been paired repeatedly with the arrival of food. The dogs would also salivate when an assistant entered the laboratory. Why? In the past, the assistant had brought food.

When we are striving for concrete goals, we often ignore the unexpected, even when the unexpected is just as important, or more important, than the goal. So it was that Pavlov at first saw this uncalled-for canine salivation as an

Reflex • A simple unlearned response to a stimulus.

Stimulus • An environmental condition that elicits a response.

Conditioned response (CR) • In classical conditioning, a learned response to a conditioned stimulus.

Classical conditioning • (1) According to behaviorists, a form of learning in which one stimulus comes to evoke the response usually evoked by a second stimulus by being paired repeatedly with the second stimulus. (2) According to cognitive theorists, the learning of relationships among events so as to allow an organism to represent its environment. Also referred to as *respondent conditioning* or *Pavlovian conditioning.*

Ivan Pavlov. Pavlov, his assistants, and a professional salivator (the dog) at a Russian academy early in the 20th century.

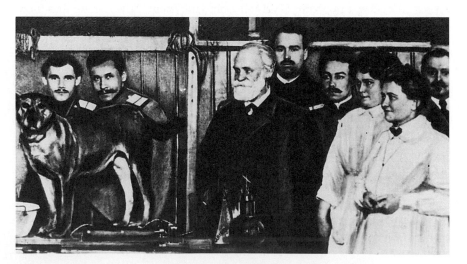

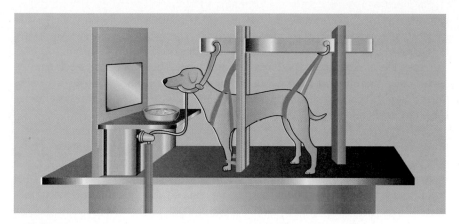

FIGURE 6.1

Pavlov's Demonstration of Conditioned Reflexes in Laboratory Dogs. From behind the two-way mirror at the left, a laboratory assistant rings a bell and then places meat powder on the dog's tongue. After several pairings, the dog salivates in response to the bell alone. A tube collects saliva and passes it to a vial. The quantity of saliva is taken as a measure of the strength of the animal's response.

annoyance, a hindrance to his research. But in 1901, he decided that his "problem" was worth looking into. He then set about to show that he could train, or condition, his dogs to salivate when he wished and in response to any stimulus he chose.

Pavlov termed these trained salivary responses *conditional reflexes.* They were *conditional* upon the repeated pairing of a previously neutral stimulus (such as the clinking of a food tray) and a stimulus (in this case, food) that predictably evoked the target response (in this case, salivation). Today, conditional reflexes are more generally referred to as **conditioned responses** (CRs). They are responses to previously neutral stimuli that are learned, or conditioned.

MINILECTURE: PAVLOV'S STUDY

Pavlov demonstrated conditioned responses by strapping a dog into a harness such as the one in Figure 6.1. When meat powder was placed on the dog's tongue, the dog salivated. Pavlov repeated the process several times, with one difference. He preceded the meat powder by half a second or so with the sounding of a bell on each occasion. After several pairings of meat powder and bell, Pavlov sounded the bell but did *not* follow the bell with the meat powder. Still the dog salivated. It had learned to salivate in response to the bell.

Truth or Fiction Revisited. *It is true that dogs can be trained to salivate when a bell is sounded.* The training is accomplished by means of the classical-conditioning method of pairing the bell with food.

Why did the dog learn to salivate in response to the bell? Behaviorists and cognitive psychologists explain the learning process in very different ways. Put on your critical-thinking cap: Would behaviorists say that after a few pairings of bell and food, a dog "knows" that the bell "means" that food is on its way? Why or why not?

Behaviorists explain the outcome of **classical conditioning** in terms of the publicly observable conditions of learning. They define classical conditioning as a simple form of learning in which one stimulus comes to evoke the response usually evoked by a second stimulus by being paired repeatedly with the second stimulus. In Pavlov's demonstration, the dog learned to salivate in

**MINILECTURE:
THE IMPORTANCE OF
TEMPORAL CONTIGUITY**

Contiguous • Next to one another.

Unconditioned stimulus (US) • A stimulus that elicits a response from an organism prior to conditioning.

Unconditioned response (UR) • An unlearned response to an unconditioned stimulus.

Orienting reflex • An unlearned response in which an organism attends to a stimulus.

Conditioned stimulus (CS) • A previously neutral stimulus that elicits a conditioned response because it has been paired repeatedly with a stimulus that already elicited that response.

Delayed conditioning • A classical-conditioning procedure in which the CS is presented before the US and left on until the response occurs.

Simultaneous conditioning • A classical-conditioning procedure in which the CS and US are presented at the same time.

Trace conditioning • A classical-conditioning procedure in which the CS is presented and then removed before the US is presented.

**MINILECTURE:
PHASES OF CLASSICAL
CONDITIONING**

response to the bell *because* the sounding of the bell had been paired with meat powder. That is, in classical conditioning, the organism forms associations between stimuli because the stimuli are **contiguous.** Behaviorists do *not* say that the dog "knew" that food was on the way. They argue that we cannot speak meaningfully about what a dog "knows." We can only outline the conditions under which targeted behaviors will reliably occur. The behaviorist focus is on the mechanical acquisition of the conditioned response.

Cognitive psychologists view classical conditioning as the learning of relationships among events. The relationships allow organisms to mentally represent their environments and make predictions (Holyoak and others, 1989; Rescorla, 1988). In Pavlov's demonstration, the dog salivated in response to the bell because the bell—from the cognitive perspective—became mentally connected with the meat powder. The cognitive focus is on the information gained by organisms. Organisms are viewed as seekers of information who generate and test rules about the relationships among events (Weiner, 1991).

Behaviorists might counter that organisms can learn to engage in conditioned responses without any evidence that they are aware of what they are learning. There are any number of classic experiments in which people learn conditioned responses that are presumably too small to perceive. In one example, people learned to engage in apparently imperceptible thumb contractions that involved only 25–30 microvolts of energy (Hefferline & Keenan, 1963). Learners, in other words, are not necessarily privy to all of their changes in behavior.

Stimuli and Responses in Classical Conditioning: US, CS, UR, and CR

In the demonstration just described, the meat powder is an unlearned or **unconditioned stimulus** (US). Salivation in response to the meat powder is an unlearned or **unconditioned response** (UR). The bell was at first a meaningless or neutral stimulus. It might have produced an **orienting reflex** in the dog because of its distinctness. But it was not yet associated with food. Then, through repeated association with the meat powder, the bell became a learned or **conditioned stimulus** (CS) for the salivation response. Salivation in response to the *bell* (or CS) is a learned or conditioned response (CR). A CR is a response similar to a UR, but the response elicited by the CS is by definition a CR, not a UR (see Figure 6.2).

Types of Classical Conditioning

Classical conditioning tends to occur most efficiently when the conditioned stimulus (CS) is presented about 0.5 second before the unconditioned stimulus (US) and is continued until the learner responds to the US. This is an example of **delayed conditioning,** in which the CS (for example, a light) can be presented anywhere from a fraction of a second to several seconds before the US (in this case, meat powder) and is left on until the response (salivation) is shown (see Figure 6.3). Conditioning can also take place via **simultaneous conditioning,** in which a CS such as a light is presented along with a US such as meat powder. In **trace conditioning,** the CS (for example, a light) is presented and then removed (or turned off) prior to presentation of the US (meat powder). Therefore, only the memory trace of the CS (light) remains to be conditioned to the US.

Conditioning occurs most effectively in delayed conditioning, perhaps because it is most adaptive. That is, in delayed conditioning, the CS signals the

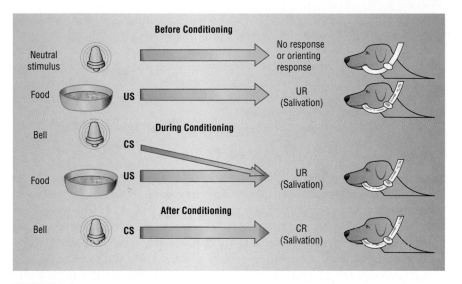

FIGURE 6.2

A Schematic Representation of Classical Conditioning. Prior to conditioning, food elicits salivation. The bell, a neutral stimulus, elicits either no response or an orienting response. During conditioning, the bell is rung just before meal powder is placed on the dog's tongue. After several repetitions, the bell, now a CS, elicits salivation, the CR.

FIGURE 6.3

Types of Classical Conditioning. In delayed conditioning (part A), the CS is presented before the US. In simultaneous conditioning (part B), the CS and US are presented together. In trace conditioning (part C), the CS is presented and then removed prior to the US. Thus only the memory trace of the CS remains when the US is presented. In backward conditioning (part D), the US is presented before the CS. Delayed conditioning is most efficient, perhaps because it allows organisms to make predictions about their environments.

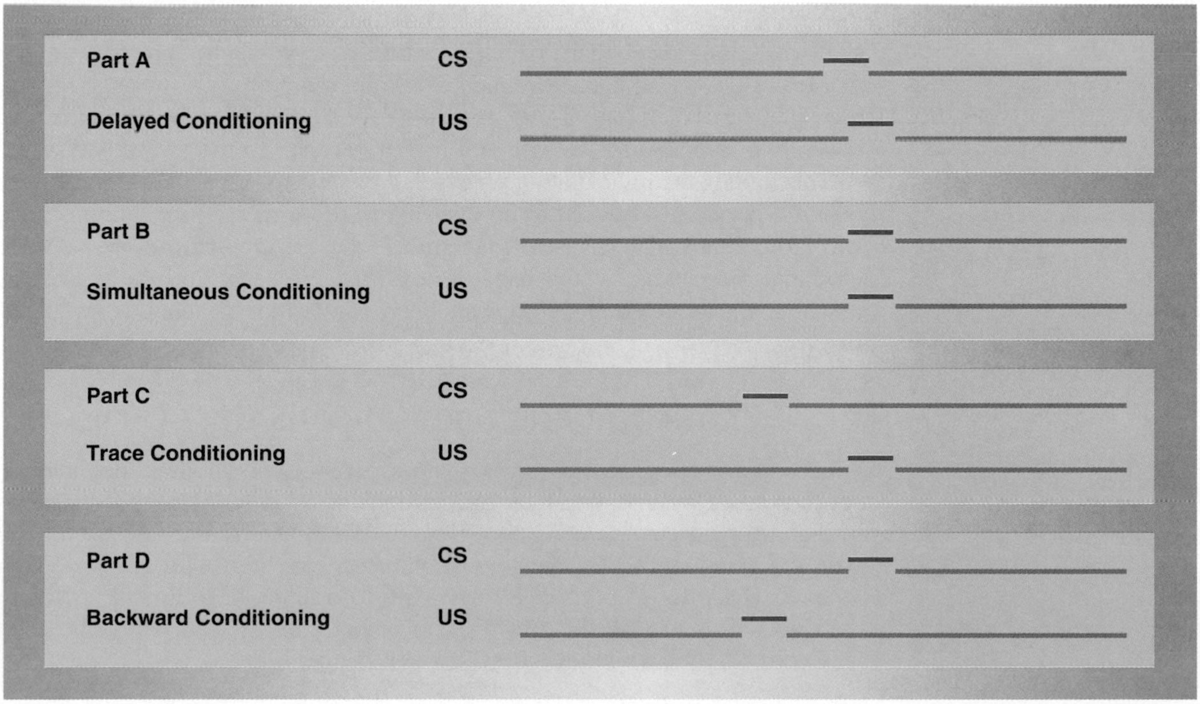

Part A	CS	
Delayed Conditioning	US	

Part B	CS	
Simultaneous Conditioning	US	

Part C	CS	
Trace Conditioning	US	

Part D	CS	
Backward Conditioning	US	

consequent appearance of the US. As a result, organisms can learn to make predictions about their environments. Predictability is adaptive because it allows organisms to prepare for future events. Learning is inefficient and may not take place at all when the US is presented before the CS (Hall, 1989), a sequence referred to as **backward conditioning.** Backward conditioning may not permit organisms to make useful predictions about their environments.

Taste Aversion

Taste aversions serve the adaptive function of motivating organisms to avoid potentially harmful foods. Although taste aversions are acquired by association, they differ from other kinds of classical conditioning in a couple of ways. First, only one association may be required. I did not have to go back for seconds at the movies to develop my aversion for buttered popcorn! Second, whereas most kinds of classical conditioning require that the US and CS be contiguous, in taste aversion the US (nausea) can occur hours after the CS (flavor of food).

Research in taste aversion challenges the behaviorist view that organisms learn to associate any stimuli that are contiguous. Not all stimuli are created equal. Instead, it seems that organisms are biologically predisposed to develop aversions that are adaptive in their environmental settings (Garcia and others, 1989). In a classic study, Garcia and Koelling (1966) conditioned two groups of rats. Each group was exposed to the same three-part CS: a taste of sweetened water, a light, and a clicker. Afterward, one group was presented a US of nausea (induced by poison or radiation), and the other group was presented a US of electric shock.

After conditioning, the rats who had been nauseated showed an aversion for sweetened water but not to the light or clicker. Although all three stimuli had been presented at the same time, *they had acquired only the taste aversion.* After conditioning, the rats who had been shocked avoided both the light and the clicker, *but they did not show a taste aversion to the sweetened water.* For each group of rats, the conditioning that took place was adaptive. In the natural scheme of things, nausea is more likely to stem from poisoned food than from lights or sounds. And so, for nauseated rats, acquiring the taste aversion was appropriate. Sharp pain, in contrast, is more likely to stem from natural events involving lights (fire, lightning) and sharp sounds (twigs snapping, things falling). Therefore, it was more appropriate for the shocked animals to develop an aversion to the light and the clicker than to the sweetened water.

This finding fits my experience as well. My nausea led to a taste aversion to buttered popcorn—but not to an aversion to the serial (which, in retrospect, was more deserving of nausea) or the movie theater. I returned every Saturday morning to see what would happen next. Yet, the serial and the theater, as much as the buttered popcorn, had been associated (contiguous) with my nausea.

Extinction and Spontaneous Recovery

Extinction and spontaneous recovery are aspects of conditioning that help organisms adapt by updating their expectations or revising their representations of the changing environment. A dog may learn to associate a new scent (CS) with the appearance of a dangerous animal. It can then take evasive action when it whiffs the scent. A child may learn to connect hearing a car pull into the driveway (CS) with the arrival of his or her parents (US). Thus, the child may come to squeal with delight (CR) when the car is heard.

Backward conditioning • A classical-conditioning procedure in which the unconditioned stimulus is presented prior to the conditioned stimulus.

Formation of a Taste Aversion?
Taste aversions may be acquired by just one association of the US and the CS. Most kinds of classical conditioning require that the US and CS be contiguous, but in a taste aversion, the US (nausea) can occur hours after the CS (flavor of food).

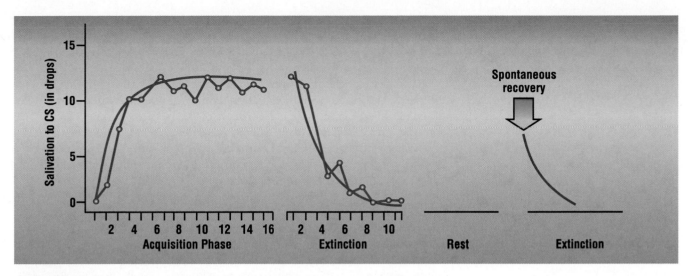

FIGURE 6.4

Learning and Extinction Curves. Actual data from Pavlov (1927) compose the jagged line, and the curved lines are idealized. In the acquisition phase, a dog salivates (shows a CR) in response to a bell (CS) after only a few trials in which the bell is paired with meat powder (the US). Afterward, the CR is extinguished in about 10 trials in which the CS is not followed by the US. After a rest period, the CR recovers spontaneously. A second series of extinction trials then leads to more rapid extinction of the CR.

But times change. The once dangerous animal may no longer be a threat. (What a puppy perceives to be a threat may lose its power to menace once the dog matures.) After moving to a new house, the child's parents may commute by means of public transportation. The sounds of a car in a nearby driveway may signal a neighbor's, not a parent's, homecoming. When conditioned stimuli (such as the scent or the sound of a car) are no longer followed by unconditioned stimuli (a dangerous animal, a parent's homecoming), they lose their ability to elicit conditioned responses. In this way, the organism adapts to a changing environment.

EXTINCTION. In classical conditioning, **extinction** is the process by which conditioned stimuli (CSs) lose the ability to elicit conditioned responses (CRs) because the CSs are no longer associated with unconditioned stimuli (USs). From the cognitive perspective, extinction teaches the organism to modify its representation of the environment because the CS no longer serves its predictive function.

In experiments in the extinction of CRs, Pavlov found that repeated presentations of the CS (or bell) without the US (meat powder) led to extinction of the CR (salivation in response to the bell). Figure 6.4 shows that a dog conditioned by Pavlov began to salivate (show a CR) in response to a bell (CS) after only a couple of pairings—referred to as **acquisition trials**—of the bell with meat powder (the US). Continued pairings of the stimuli led to increased salivation as measured in number of drops of saliva. After seven or eight trials, salivation leveled off at 11 to 12 drops.

Then, salivation to the bell (CR) was extinguished through several trials—referred to as **extinction trials**—in which the CS (bell) was presented without the meat powder (US). After about 10 extinction trials, the CR (salivation in response to the bell) was no longer shown.

Extinction • An experimental procedure in which stimuli lose their ability to evoke learned responses because the events that had followed the stimuli no longer occur. (The learned responses are said to be *extinguished.*)

Acquisition trial • In conditioning, a presentation of stimuli such that a new response is learned and strengthened.

Extinction trial • In conditioning, a performance of a learned response in the absence of its predicted consequences so that the learned response becomes inhibited.

What would happen if we were to allow a day or two to pass after we had extinguished the CR (salivation response to a bell) in a laboratory dog, and then we again presented the CS (bell)? Where would you place your money? Would the dog salivate or not?

If you bet that the dog would again show the CR (salivate in response to the bell), you were correct. Organisms tend to show **spontaneous recovery** of extinguished CRs merely as a function of the passage of time. For this reason, the term *extinction* may be a bit misleading. When a species of animal becomes extinct, all members of that species capable of reproducing have died. The species vanishes permanently. But the experimental extinction of CRs does not lead to the permanent eradication of CRs. Rather, it seems that they inhibit that response. The response does remain available for future performance.

Consider Figure 6.4 again. When spontaneous recovery of the CR does occur, the strength of the response (in this case, the number of drops of saliva) is not as great as it was at the end of the series of acquisition trials. A second set of extinction trials will also extinguish the CR more rapidly than the first series of extinction trials. Although the CR is at first weaker the second time around, pairing the CS with the US once more will build response strength rapidly.

Spontaneous recovery, like extinction, is adaptive. What would happen if the child heard no car in the driveway for several months? It could be that the next time a car entered the driveway, the child would associate the sounds with a parent's homecoming (rather than the arrival of a neighbor). This expectation could be appropriate. After all, *something* had systematically changed in the neighborhood when no car had entered the nearby driveway for so long. In the wilds, a waterhole may contain water for only a couple of months during the year. But it is useful for animals to associate the waterhole with the thirst drive from time to time so that they will return to it at the appropriate time.

As time passes and the seasons change, things sometimes follow circular paths and arrive at where they were before. Spontaneous recovery seems to provide a mechanism whereby organisms are capable of rapidly adapting to intermittently recurring situations.

Spontaneous recovery • The recurrence of an extinguished response as a function of the passage of time.

Generalization • In conditioning, the tendency for a conditioned response to be evoked by stimuli that are similar to the stimulus to which the response was conditioned.

Generalization and Discrimination

No two things are quite alike. Traffic lights are hung at slightly different heights, and shades of red and green differ a little. The barking of two dogs differs, and the sound of the same animal differs slightly from bark to bark. Adaptation requires that we respond similarly to stimuli that are equivalent in function and that we respond differently to stimuli that are not.

GENERALIZATION. Pavlov noted that responding to different stimuli as though they are functionally equivalent is adaptive for animals. Rustling sounds in the undergrowth differ, but rabbits and deer do well to flee when they perceive any of many varieties of rustling. Sirens differ, but people do well to become vigilant or to pull their cars to the side of the road when any siren is heard.

In a demonstration of **generalization,** Pavlov first conditioned a dog to salivate when a circle was presented. During each acquisition trial, the dog was shown a circle (CS), then given meat powder (US). After several trials, the dog exhibited the CR of salivating when presented with the circle alone. Pavlov demonstrated that the dog also exhibited the CR (salivation) in response to closed geometric figures such as ellipses, pentagons, and even squares. The more closely the figure resembled a circle, the greater the strength of the response (the more drops of saliva that flowed).

DISCRIMINATION.　Organisms must also learn (1) that many stimuli perceived as being similar are functionally different and (2) to respond adaptively to each. During the first couple of months of life, babies can discriminate the voices of their mothers from those of others. They will often stop crying when they hear Mother but not when they hear a stranger's voice.

Pavlov showed that a dog conditioned to salivate in response to circles could be trained *not* to salivate in response to ellipses. The type of conditioning that trains an organism to show a CR in response to a narrow range of stimuli (in this case, circular rather than elliptical geometric figures) is termed **discrimination training.** Pavlov trained the dog by presenting it with circles and ellipses but associating the meat powder (US) with circles only. After a while, the dog no longer showed the CR (salivation) in response to the ellipses. Instead, the animal showed **discrimination.** It displayed the CR in response to circles only.

Pavlov then discovered that he could make the dog behave as though it were tormented by increasing the difficulty of the discrimination task. After the dog exhibited stimulus discrimination, Pavlov showed the animal progressively rounder ellipses. Eventually, the dog could no longer discriminate them from circles. The animal then put on an infantile show. It urinated, defecated, barked profusely, and snapped at laboratory personnel.

How do we explain the dog's belligerent behavior? In a classic work written more than half a century ago, *Frustration and Aggression,* a group of behaviorally oriented psychologists suggested that frustration induces aggression (Dollard and others, 1939). Why is failure to discriminate circles from ellipses frustrating? For one thing, in such experiments, rewards—such as meat powder—are usually made contingent on correct discrimination. That is, if the dog errs, it foregoes the meat. Cognitive theorists, however, propose that organisms are motivated to construct realistic maps of the world. In building their overall images of the world, organisms—including dogs—adjust their representations to reduce discrepancies and accommodate new information (Rescorla, 1988). In the Pavlovian experiment, the dog lost the ability to meaningfully adjust its representation of the environment as the ellipses grew more circular, and so it was frustrated. Behaviorists counter that it is fruitless to speculate on what goes on in the "mind" of another organism because there is no scientific way to verify our conjectures, whether the organism is a person or a lower animal such as a dog.

Daily living requires appropriate generalization and discrimination. No two hotels are alike, but when traveling from one city to another, it is adaptive to expect to stay in some hotel. It is encouraging that green lights in Washington have the same meaning as green lights in Honolulu. But returning home in the evening requires the ability to discriminate between our homes or apartments from those of others. If we could not readily discriminate our spouses from those of others, we might land in divorce court.

Discrimination training • Teaching an organism to show a learned response in the presence of only one of a series of similar stimuli, accomplished by alternating the stimuli but following only the one stimulus with the unconditioned stimulus.

Discrimination • In conditioning, the tendency for an organism to distinguish between a conditioned stimulus and similar stimuli that do not forecast an unconditioned stimulus.

Higher-order conditioning • (1) According to behaviorists, a classical-conditioning procedure in which a previously neutral stimulus comes to elicit the response brought forth by a *conditioned* stimulus by being paired repeatedly with that conditioned stimulus. (2) According to cognitive psychologists, the learning of relationships among events, none of which evokes an unlearned response.

Higher-Order Conditioning

In **higher-order conditioning,** a previously neutral stimulus comes to serve as a CS after being paired repeatedly with a stimulus that has already become a CS. Pavlov demonstrated higher-order conditioning by first conditioning a dog to salivate (show a CR) in response to a bell (a CS). He then paired the shining of a light repeatedly with the bell. After several pairings, shining the light (the higher-order CS) came to elicit the response (salivation) that had been elicited by the bell (the first-order CS).

Consider children who learn that their parents are about to arrive when they hear a car in the driveway. It may be the case that a certain TV cartoon show starts a few minutes before the car enters the driveway. The TV show can begin to elicit the expectation that the parents are coming by being paired repeatedly with the car's entering the driveway. In another example, a boy may burn himself by touching a hot stove. After this experience, the sight of the stove may serve as a CS for eliciting a fear response. And because hearing the word *stove* may evoke a cognitive image of the stove, hearing the word alone may also elicit a fear response.

Applications of Classical Conditioning

Classical conditioning is a major avenue of learning in our daily lives. It is how stimuli come to serve as signals for other stimuli. It is why we come to expect that someone will be waiting outside when the doorbell is rung or why we expect a certain friend to appear when we hear a characteristic knock. Let us explore a number of applications of classical conditioning in the areas of child development and behavior modification.

 **MINILECTURE: BED-WETTING**

THE BELL-AND-PAD METHOD FOR BED-WETTING.   By the ages of 5 or 6, children normally awaken in response to the sensations of a full bladder. They inhibit urination, which is an automatic or reflexive response to bladder tension, and go to the bathroom. But bed wetters tend not to respond to sensations of a full bladder while asleep. And so they remain asleep and frequently wet their beds.

By means of the bell-and-pad method, children are taught to wake up in response to bladder tension. They sleep on a special sheet or pad that has been placed on the bed. When the child starts to urinate, the water content of the urine causes an electrical circuit in the pad to be closed. Closing of the circuit triggers a bell or buzzer, and the child is awakened. In terms of principles of classical conditioning, the bell is a US that wakes the child (waking up is the UR).

By means of repeated pairings, stimuli that precede the bell become associated with the bell and also gain the capacity to awaken the child. What stimuli are these? The sensations of a full bladder. In this way, bladder tension (the CS) gains the capacity to awaken the child *even though the child is asleep during the classical-conditioning procedure.*

The bell-and-pad method provides a superb example of why behaviorists prefer to explain the effects of classical conditioning in terms of the pairing of stimuli and not in terms of what the learner knows. The behaviorist may argue that we cannot assume that a sleeping child "knows" that wetting the bed will cause the bell to ring.

We can only note that by repeatedly pairing bladder tension with the bell, the child eventually *learns* to wake up in response to bladder tension alone. *Learning* is demonstrated by the change in the child's behavior. What the child *knows* about the learning process is a private matter and one on which others can only speculate.

Similar buzzer circuits have also been built into training pants as an aid to toilet training.

THE STORY OF LITTLE ALBERT: A CASE STUDY IN THE CLASSICAL CONDITION-ING OF EMOTIONAL RESPONSES. In 1920, John B. Watson and his future wife, Rosalie Rayner, published an article describing their demonstration that emotional reactions such as fears can be acquired through principles of classical conditioning. The subject of their demonstration was a lad known in the psychological literature by the name of Little Albert. Albert was a phlegmatic fellow at the age of 11 months, not given to ready displays of emotion. But he did enjoy playing with a laboratory rat. Such are the playmates to be found in psychologists' laboratories.

Using a method that some psychologists have criticized as unethical, Watson startled Little Albert by clanging steel bars behind his head when the infant played with the rat. After seven pairings, Albert showed fear of the rat even though clanging was suspended. Albert's fear was also generalized to objects similar in appearance to the rat, such as a rabbit and the fur collar on a woman's coat. Albert's conditioned fear of rats may never have become extinguished. Extinction would have required perceiving rats (the conditioned stimuli) without painful consequences (in the absence of the unconditioned stimuli). Fear, however, might have prevented Albert from facing rats. And, as we shall see in the section on operant conditioning, avoiding rats might have been *reinforced* by reduction of fear.

We must also note that other experiments in conditioning fears (e.g., by English, 1929) have not always been successful. As mentioned in our discussion of taste aversions, it may be that people are more biologically predisposed to learn fear of some objects and situations than others.

In any event, Watson and Rayner did not attempt to reverse, or undo, the effects of Little Albert's conditioning. But, as we shall see in the following sections, other psychologists have used principles of classical conditioning to do just that.

FLOODING AND SYSTEMATIC DESENSITIZATION. Two behavior-therapy methods for reducing fears are based on the classical-conditioning principle of extinction. In one called **flooding,** the client is exposed to the fear-evoking stimulus until fear responses are extinguished (Turner and others, 1994). Albert, for example, might have been placed in close contact with a rat until his fears had become fully extinguished. In extinction, the CS (in this case, the rat) is presented repeatedly in the absence of the US (the clanging of the steel bars) until the CR (fear) is no longer evoked.

Although flooding is usually effective, it is unpleasant. (When you are fearful of rats, being placed in a small room with one is not a holiday.) For this reason, behavior therapists frequently prefer to use **systematic desensitization,** in which the client is exposed gradually to fear-evoking stimuli under circumstances in which he or she remains relaxed. For example, while feeling relaxed, Little Albert might have been given the opportunity to look at photos of rats or to see live rats from a distance before they were brought closer. Systematic desensitization is described more fully in Chapter 14. Here let us note that systematic desensitization, like flooding, is highly effective. It takes longer to work than flooding, but the trade-off is that it is not as unpleasant.

COUNTERCONDITIONING. Early in the century, University of California professors Harold Jones and Mary Cover Jones (Jones, 1924) reasoned that if fears could be conditioned by painful experiences, it should be possible to *counter-condition* them by pleasant experiences. In **counterconditioning,** a pleasant stimulus is paired repeatedly with a fear-evoking object, in this way counteracting the fear response.

Flooding • A behavioral fear-reduction technique that is based on principles of classical conditioning. Fear-evoking stimuli (CSs) are presented continuously in the absence of actual harm so that fear responses (CRs) are extinguished.

Systematic desensitization • A behavioral fear-reduction technique in which a hierarchy of fear-evoking stimuli are presented while the person remains relaxed.

Counterconditioning • A fear-reduction technique in which pleasant stimuli are associated with fear-evoking stimuli so that the fear-evoking stimuli lose their aversive qualities.

Can Chocolate Chip Cookies Countercondition Fears? Yes, they taste good, but do they have the capacity to countercondition fears? At Berkeley in the 1920s, the Joneses helped a boy overcome his fear of rabbits by having him munch away as the animal was brought closer. Are contemporary behavior therapists sort of keeping up with the Joneses?

Two-year-old Peter feared rabbits intensely. The Joneses arranged for a rabbit to be gradually brought closer to Peter while he engaged in some of his favorite activities such as munching merrily away on candy and cookies. As opposed to flooding, the rabbit was not plopped in Peter's lap. Had they done so, the cookies on the plate and those already eaten might have decorated the walls. At first, they placed the rabbit in a far corner of the room while Peter munched and crunched. Peter, to be sure, cast a wary eye, but he continued to consume the treat. Gradually the animal was brought closer. Eventually, Peter ate treats and touched the rabbit at the same time. The Joneses theorized that the pleasure of eating was incompatible with fear and thus counterconditioned the fear.

Truth or Fiction Revisited. *It is true that psychologists helped a young boy overcome fear of rabbits by having him eat cookies while a rabbit was brought nearer.* It was theorized that the joy of cookies would "countercondition" fear.

Reflections

- Had you ever heard the expression "That rings a bell"? To what historic psychological events does the expression refer?
- How would you explain the process of classical conditioning? How do behaviorists explain it? Does your explanation differ from theirs? If so, how?
- How would you explain the difference between the psychological concept of *extinction* and the lay term *forgetting*?
- Do you consider Watson and Rayner's experiment with "Little Albert" to be ethical? Why or why not?
- Can you think of examples of classical conditioning in your own life?

Through classical conditioning, we learn to associate stimuli so that a simple, usually passive, response made to one is then made in response to the other. In the case of Little Albert, clanging noises were associated with a rat, so the rat came to elicit the fear response brought forth by the noise. However, classical conditioning is only one kind of learning that occurs in these situations. According to O. Hobart Mowrer's two-factor theory of learning, classical conditioning in the study with Little Albert suffices to explain the acquisition of the fear response. But then the boy's voluntary behavior changed. He avoided the rat as a way of reducing his fear. Thus, Little Albert engaged in another kind of learning—operant conditioning.

In operant conditioning, organisms learn to engage in behaviors because of their effects. The sight of a hypodermic syringe, for example, may elicit a fear response because a person once had a painful injection. The subsequent avoidance of injections is *operant behavior.* It has the effect of reducing fear. In other cases, we engage in operant behavior to attain rewards, not to avoid unpleasant outcomes.

OPERANT CONDITIONING

In **operant conditioning**—also referred to as **instrumental conditioning**—an organism learns to engage in certain behavior because of the effects of that behavior. We begin this section with the historic work of psychologist Edward L. Thorndike. Then we shall examine the more recent work of B. F. Skinner.

Edward L. Thorndike and the Law of Effect

In the 1890s, stray cats were mysteriously disappearing from the streets and alleyways of Harlem. Many of them, it turned out, were being brought to the quarters of Columbia University doctoral student Edward Thorndike. Thorndike was using them as subjects in experiments in learning by trial and error.

Thorndike placed the cats in so-called puzzle boxes. If the animals managed to pull a dangling string, a latch would be released, allowing them to jump out and reach a bowl of food.

When first placed in a puzzle box, a cat would try to squeeze through any opening and would claw and bite at the confining bars and wire. It would claw at any feature it could reach. Through such **random trial-and-error behavior,** it might take 3 to 4 minutes before the cat would chance on the response of pulling the string. Pulling the string would open the cage and allow the cat to reach the food. When placed back in the cage, it might again take several minutes for the animal to pull the string. But as these trials were repeated, it would take progressively less time for the cat to pull the string. After seven or eight trials, it might pull the string immediately when placed back in the box.

THE LAW OF EFFECT. Thorndike explained the cat's learning to pull the string in terms of his **law of effect.** According to this law, a response (such as string pulling) is "stamped in" or strengthened in a particular situation (such as being inside a puzzle box) by a reward (escaping from the box and eating). Rewards, that is, stamp in S–R (stimulus–response) connections. Punishments, in contrast, "stamp out" stimulus–response connections. Organisms would learn not to engage in punished responses. Later we shall see that the effects of punishment on learning are not so certain.

Operant conditioning • A simple form of learning in which an organism learns to engage in behavior because it is reinforced.
Instrumental conditioning • A term similar to *operant conditioning,* reflecting the fact that the learned behavior is *instrumental* in achieving certain effects.
Random trial-and-error behavior • Behavior that occurs in a novel situation prior to the reception of rewards or reinforcements.
Law of effect • Thorndike's principle that responses are "stamped in" by rewards and "stamped out" by punishments.

**MINILECTURE:
THORNDIKE AND
SKINNER**

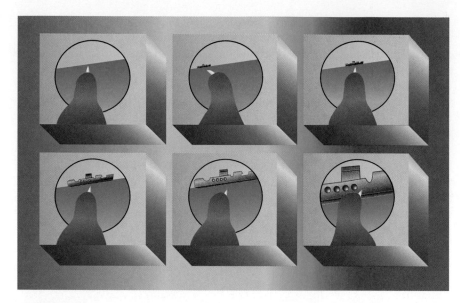

FIGURE 6.5

Project Pigeon. During World War II, B. F. Skinner suggested training pigeons to guide missiles to their targets. In an operant conditioning procedure, the pigeons would be reinforced for pecking at targets projected on a screen. Afterward, in combat, pecking at the on-screen target would keep the missile on course.

Reinforce • To follow a response with a stimulus that increases the frequency of the response.

B. F. Skinner and Reinforcement

"What did you do in the war, Daddy?" is a question familiar to many who served during America's conflicts. Some stories involve heroism, others involve the unusual. When it comes to unusual war stories, few will top that of Harvard University psychologist B. F. Skinner. For, as he relates the tale in his autobiography, *The Shaping of a Behaviorist* (1979), one of Skinner's wartime efforts was "Project Pigeon."

During World War II, Skinner proposed that pigeons be trained to guide missiles to their targets. In their training, the pigeons would be **reinforced** with food pellets for pecking at targets projected onto a screen (see Figure 6.5). Once trained, the pigeons would be placed in missiles. Pecking at similar targets displayed on a screen within the missile would correct the flight path of the missile, resulting in a "hit" and a sacrificed pigeon. However, plans for building the necessary missile—for some reason called the *Pelican* and not the *Pigeon*—were scrapped. The pigeon equipment was too bulky, and as Skinner lamented, his suggestion was not taken seriously. Apparently the Defense Department concluded that Project Pigeon was for the birds.

Truth or Fiction Revisited. *It is true that during World War II, a psychologist devised a plan for training pigeons to guide missiles to their targets.* That psychologist was B. F. Skinner, who employed principles of operant conditioning.

Project Pigeon may have been scrapped, but the principles of learning Skinner applied to the project have found wide applications in operant conditioning. In classical conditioning, an organism learns about the relationships among events. In other words, it learns to associate stimuli. As a laboratory procedure, one previously neutral stimulus (the CS) comes to elicit the response brought forth by another stimulus (the US) because they have been paired repeatedly. In operant conditioning, an organism learns to *do* something because of its effects or consequences.

This is **operant behavior,** behavior that operates on, or manipulates, the environment. In classical conditioning, involuntary responses such as salivation or eye blinks are often conditioned. In operant conditioning, *voluntary* responses such as pecking at a target, pressing a lever, or many of the athletic skills required in playing tennis are acquired, or conditioned.

In operant conditioning, organisms engage in operant behaviors, also known simply as **operants,** that result in presumably desirable consequences such as food, a hug, an A on a test, attention, or social approval. Some children learn to conform their behavior to social codes and rules to earn the attention and approval of their parents and teachers. Other children, ironically, may learn to "misbehave," since misbehavior also results in attention from other people. Children may especially learn to be "bad" when their "good" behavior is routinely ignored.

UNITS OF BEHAVIOR, "SKINNER BOXES," AND CUMULATIVE RECORDERS.

In his most influential work, *The Behavior of Organisms,* Skinner (1938) made many theoretical and technological innovations. Among them was his focus on discrete behaviors such as lever pressing as the unit, or type, of behavior to be studied (Glenn and others, 1992). Other psychologists might focus on how organisms think or "feel." Skinner focused on measurable things that they do. Many psychologists have found Skinner's kinds of behaviors inconsequential, especially when it comes to explaining and predicting human behavior. But Skinner's supporters point out that focusing on discrete behavior creates the potential for helpful behavior changes. For example, in helping people combat depression, one psychologist might focus on their "feelings." The Skinnerian would focus on cataloguing (and modifying) the types of things that people who complain of depression *do.* Directly modifying depressive behavior might also brighten clients' self-reports about their "feelings of depression," of course.

To study operant behavior efficiently, Skinner also devised an animal cage (or "operant chamber") that was dubbed the *Skinner box* by other psychologists. (Skinner himself repeatedly requested that his operant chamber *not* be called a Skinner box. History has thus far failed to honor his wishes, however.[1]) Such a box is shown in Figure 6.6. The cage is ideal for laboratory experimentation because experimental conditions (treatments) can be carefully introduced and removed, and the results on laboratory animals (defined as changes in the rate of lever pressing) can be carefully observed. The operant chamber (or Skinner box) is also energy-efficient—in terms of the energy of the experimenter. In contrast to Thorndike's puzzle box, a "correct" response does not allow the animal to escape and thus have to be recaptured and placed back in the box. According to psychologist John Garcia (1993), Skinner's "great contribution to the study of behavior was the marvelously efficient operant methodology" (p. 1158).

The rat in Figure 6.6 was deprived of food and placed in a Skinner box with a lever at one end. At first it sniffed its way around the cage and engaged in random behavior. When organisms are behaving in a random manner, responses that meet with favorable consequences tend to occur more frequently. Responses that do not meet with favorable consequences tend to be performed less frequently.

The rat's first pressing of the lever was inadvertent. However, because of this action, a food pellet dropped into the cage. The food pellet increased the

Operant behavior • Voluntary responses that are reinforced.

Operant • The same as an operant behavior.

---

[1] Of course, my using the term *Skinner box* does not exactly help Skinner's cause, either.

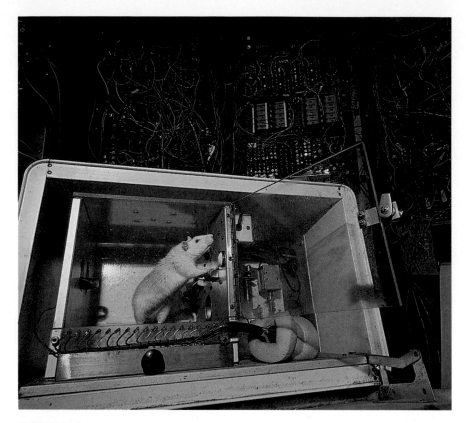

FIGURE 6.6

The Effects of Reinforcement. One of the luminaries of modern psychology, an albino laboratory rat, earns its keep in a Skinner box. The animal presses a lever because of reinforcement—in the form of food pellets—delivered through the spout of the feeder. The habit strength of this operant can be measured as the frequency of lever pressing.

FIGURE 6.7

The Cumulative Recorder. In the cumulative recorder, paper moves continuously to the left while a pen automatically records each targeted response by moving upward. When the pen reaches the top of the paper, it is automatically reset to the bottom.

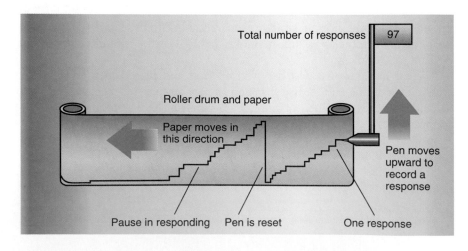

probability that the rat would press the lever again. The pellet is thus said to have served as a reinforcement for the lever pressing.

Skinner further mechanized his laboratory procedure by making use of a turning drum, or **cumulative recorder,** that had previously been used by physiologists. (See Figure 6.7.) The cumulative recorder provides a precise measure of operant behavior. The experimenter need not even be present to record correct responses. In the example used, the lever in the Skinner box is connected to the recorder so that the recording pen moves upward with each correct response. The paper moves continuously to the left at a slow but regular pace. In the sample record shown in Figure 6.7, lever pressings (which record correct responses) were at first few and far between. But after several reinforced responses, lever pressing came fast and furious. When the rat is no longer hungry, the lever pressing will drop off and then stop.

THE FIRST "CORRECT" RESPONSE.   In operant conditioning, it matters little how the first response that is reinforced comes to be made. The organism can happen on it by chance, as in random learning. The organism can also be physically guided into the response. You may command your dog to "Sit!" and then press its backside down until it is in a sitting position. Finally, you reinforce sitting with food or a pat on the head and a kind word.

Animal trainers use physical guiding or coaxing to bring about the first "correct" response. Can you imagine how long it would take to train your dog if you waited for it to sit or roll over and then seized the opportunity to command it to sit or roll over? You would both age significantly in the process.

People, of course, can be verbally guided into desired responses when they are learning tasks such as running a machine, spelling, or adding numbers. But they then need to be informed when they have made the correct response. Knowledge of results is often all the reinforcement that motivated people need to learn new skills.

Types of Reinforcers

Any stimulus that increases the probability that responses preceding it will be repeated serves as a reinforcer. Reinforcers include food pellets when an organism has been deprived of food, water when it has been deprived of liquid, the opportunity to mate, and the sound of a bell that has been previously associated with eating.

POSITIVE AND NEGATIVE REINFORCERS.   Skinner distinguished between positive and negative reinforcers. **Positive reinforcers** increase the probability that an operant will occur when they are applied. Food and approval usually serve as positive reinforcers. **Negative reinforcers** increase the probability that an operant will occur when they are *removed* (see Figure 6.8). People often learn to plan ahead so that they need not fear that things will go wrong. Fear acts as a negative reinforcer, because *removal* of fear increases the probability that the behaviors preceding it (such as planning ahead or fleeing a predator) will be repeated.

Greater reinforcers prompt more-rapid learning than do lesser reinforcers. You will probably work much harder for $1,000 than for $10. (If not, get in touch with me—I have some chores that need to be taken care of.) With sufficient reinforcement, operants become a habit. They show a high probability of recurrence in a certain situation.

IMMEDIATE VERSUS DELAYED REINFORCERS.   Immediate reinforcers are more effective than delayed reinforcers. Therefore, the short-term

Cumulative recorder   •   An instrument that records the frequency of an organism's operants (or "correct" responses) as a function of the passage of time.

Positive reinforcer   •   A reinforcer that when *presented* increases the frequency of an operant.

Negative reinforcer   •   A reinforcer that when *removed* increases the frequency of an operant.

consequences of behavior are frequently more of an incentive than the long-term consequences. Some students socialize when they should be studying because the pleasure of socializing is immediate. Studying may not pay off until the final exam or graduation. (This is why younger students do better with frequent tests.) It is difficult to quit smoking cigarettes because the reinforcement of nicotine is immediate, whereas the health hazards of smoking are more distant. Focusing on short-term reinforcement is also connected with careless sexual behavior.

PRIMARY AND SECONDARY REINFORCERS.   We can also distinguish between primary and secondary, or conditioned, reinforcers. **Primary reinforcers** are effective because of the biological makeup of the organism. Food, water, adequate warmth (positive reinforcers), and pain (a negative reinforcer) all serve as primary reinforcers. **Secondary reinforcers** acquire their value through being associated with established reinforcers. For this reason, they are also termed **conditioned reinforcers.** We may seek money because we have learned that it may be exchanged for primary reinforcers. Money, attention, social approval—all are conditioned reinforcers in our culture. We may be suspicious of, or not "understand," people who are not interested in money or the approval of others. Part of understanding others lies in being able to predict what they will find reinforcing.

Extinction and Spontaneous Recovery in Operant Conditioning

In operant conditioning, as in classical conditioning, extinction is a process in which stimuli lose the ability to evoke learned responses because the events that had followed the stimuli no longer occur. In classical conditioning, however, the "events" that normally follow and confirm the appropriateness of the

FIGURE 6.8

Positive Versus Negative Reinforcers. By definition, all reinforcers, including positive and negative reinforcers, increase the frequency of behavior. However, negative reinforcers are aversive stimuli that increase the frequency of behavior when they are *removed*. In the examples shown here, teacher approval functions as a positive reinforcer for students who study harder because of it. Teacher *disapproval* functions as a negative reinforcer when its *removal* increases the frequency of studying. Think of situations in which teacher approval might function as a negative reinforcer.

Procedure	Behavior	Consequence	Change in Behavior
Use of Positive Reinforcement	Behavior (Studying)	Positive reinforcer (Teacher approval) is *presented* when student studies	Frequency of behavior *increases* (Student studies more)
Use of Negative Reinforcement	Behavior (Studying)	Negative reinforcer (Teacher disapproval) is *removed* when student studies	Frequency of behavior *increases* (Student studies more)

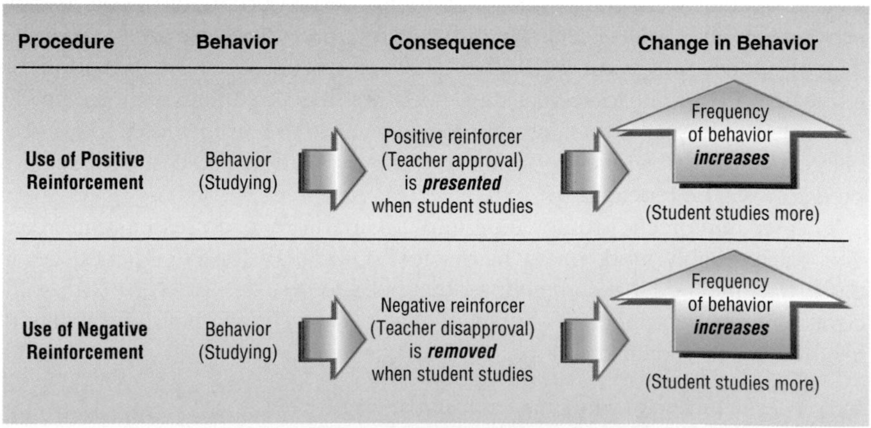

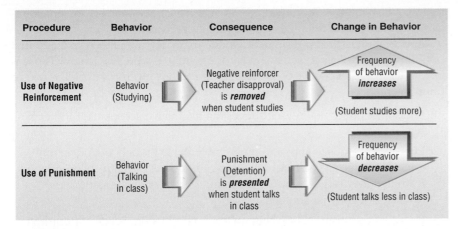

FIGURE 6.9

Negative Reinforcers Versus Punishments. Negative reinforcers and punishments both tend to be aversive stimuli. However, reinforcers *increase* the frequency of behavior. Punishments *decrease* the frequency of behavior. Negative reinforcers increase the frequency of behavior when they are removed. Punishments decrease or suppress the frequency of behavior when they are applied. Think of situations in which punishing students might have effects other than those desired by the teacher.

learned response (that is, the conditioned response) are the unconditioned stimuli. In Pavlov's experiment, the meat powder was the event that followed and confirmed the appropriateness of salivation. In operant conditioning, the ensuing events are reinforcers. Thus, in operant conditioning, the extinction of learned responses (that is, operants) results from repeated performance of operant behavior without reinforcement. After a number of trials, the operant behavior is no longer shown.

When some time is allowed to pass after the extinction process, an organism will usually perform the operant again when placed in a situation in which the operant had been reinforced previously. Spontaneous recovery of learned responses occurs in operant conditioning as well as in classical conditioning. If the operant is reinforced at this time, it quickly regains its former strength. Spontaneous recovery of extinguished operants suggests that they are inhibited or suppressed by the extinction process and not lost permanently.

Reinforcers Versus Rewards and Punishments

Rewards, like reinforcers, are stimuli that increase the frequency of behavior. But rewards are also considered to be pleasant events. Skinner preferred the concept of reinforcement to that of reward because reinforcement does not suggest trying to "get inside the head" of an organism (person or lower animal) to guess what it would find pleasant or unpleasant. A list of reinforcers is arrived at **empirically,** by observing what sorts of stimuli will increase the frequency of the behavior. However, it should be noted that some psychologists consider the term *reward* to be synonymous with positive reinforcement.

Punishments are aversive events that suppress or decrease the frequency of the behavior they follow (see Figure 6.9).[2] Punishment can rapidly suppress

Primary reinforcer • An unlearned reinforcer.

Secondary reinforcer • A stimulus that gains reinforcement value through association with established reinforcers.

Conditioned reinforcer • Another term for a secondary reinforcer.

Reward • A pleasant stimulus that increases the frequency of the behavior It follows.

Empirically • By trial or experiment rather than by logical deduction.

Punishment • An unpleasant stimulus that suppresses the behavior it follows.

---

[2] Recall that *negative reinforcers* are defined in terms of *increasing* the frequency of behavior, although the increase occurs when the negative reinforcer is *removed*. A punishment *decreases* the frequency of a behavior when it is *applied*.

undesirable behavior (Rosenfeld, 1995) and may be warranted in "emergencies" such as when a child tries to run out into the street.

Despite the fact that punishment works, many learning theorists agree that punishment often fails to achieve what the parent is trying to achieve (Rosenfeld, 1995). Consider some of the following reasons given for avoiding use of punishment:

1. Punishment does not in itself suggest an alternative acceptable form of behavior.

2. Punishment tends to suppress undesirable behavior only under circumstances in which its delivery is guaranteed. It does not take children long to learn that they can "get away with murder" with one parent, or one teacher, but not with another.

3. Punished organisms may withdraw from the situation. Severely punished children may run away, cut class, or drop out of school.

4. Punishment can create anger and hostility. Adequate punishment will almost always suppress unwanted behavior—but at what cost? A child may express accumulated feelings of hostility against other children.

5. Punishment may generalize too far. The child who is punished severely for bad table manners may stop eating altogether. Overgeneralization is more likely to occur when children do not know exactly why they are being punished and when they have not been shown alternative acceptable behaviors.

6. Punishment may be modeled as a way of solving problems or coping with stress (Strauss, 1994). We shall see that one way that children learn is by observing others. Even though children may not immediately perform the behavior they observe, they may perform it later on, even as adults, when their circumstances are similar to those of the **model.**

7. Finally, children learn responses that are punished. Whether or not children choose to perform punished responses, punishment draws their attention to them.

Truth or Fiction Revisited. *Actually, punishment does work.* Strong punishment generally suppresses the behavior it follows. The issues pertaining to punishment concern its limitations and its side effects.

It is usually preferable to focus on rewarding children for desirable behavior than on punishing them for unwanted behavior. By ignoring their misbehavior, or by using **time out** from positive reinforcement, we can consistently avoid reinforcing children for misbehavior (Budd, 1993).

To reward or positively reinforce children for desired behavior takes time and care. Simply never using punishment is not enough. First, we must pay attention to children when they are behaving well. If we take their desirable behavior for granted, and act as if we are aware of them only when they misbehave, we may be encouraging misbehavior. Second, we must be certain that children are aware of, and capable of performing, desired behavior. It is harmful and fruitless merely to punish children for unwanted behavior. We must also carefully guide them physically or verbally into making the desired responses and then reward them. We cannot teach children table manners by waiting for them to exhibit proper responses at random and then reinforcing them. If we waited by holding a half-gallon of ice cream behind our backs as a reward, we would have slippery dining room floors long before we had children with table manners.

Model • An organism that engages in a response that is then imitated by another organism.

Time out • Removal of an organism from a situation in which reinforcement is available when unwanted behavior is shown.

Discriminative Stimuli

B. F. Skinner might not have been able to get his pigeons into the drivers' seats of missiles during the war, but he had no problem training them to respond to traffic lights. Try the following experiment for yourself.

Find a pigeon. Or sit on a park bench, close your eyes, and one will find you. Place it in a Skinner box with a button on the wall. Drop a food pellet into the cage whenever the pigeon pecks the button. (Soon it will learn to peck the button whenever it has not eaten for a while.) Now place a small green light in the cage. Turn it on and off intermittently throughout the day. Reinforce button pecking with food whenever the green light is on but not when the light is off. It will not take long for this clever city pigeon to learn that it will gain as much by grooming itself or squawking and flapping around as it will by pecking the button when the light is off.

The green light will have become a **discriminative stimulus.** Discriminative stimuli act as cues. They provide information about when an operant (in this case, pecking a button) will be reinforced (in this case, by a food pellet being dropped into the cage).

Operants that are not reinforced tend to become extinguished. For the pigeon in our experiment, pecking the button *when the light is off* becomes extinguished.

A moment's reflection will suggest many ways in which discriminative stimuli influence our behavior. Would you rather ask your boss for a raise when she is smiling or when she is frowning? Wouldn't you rather answer the telephone when it is ringing? Do you think it is wise to try to get smoochy when your date is blowing smoke in your face or chugalugging a bottle of antacid tablets? One of the factors involved in gaining social skills is learning to interpret social discriminative stimuli (smiles, tones of voice, body language) accurately.

A Discriminative Stimulus. You might not think that pigeons are very discriminating, yet this gift to city life readily learns that pecking will not bring food in the presence of a discriminative stimulus such as a red light.

Schedules of Reinforcement

In operant conditioning, some responses are maintained by **continuous reinforcement.** You probably become warmer every time you put on heavy clothing. You probably become less thirsty every time you drink water. Yet, if you have ever watched people throwing money down the maws of slot machines, or "one-armed bandits," you know that behavior can also be maintained by **partial reinforcement.**

Some folklore about gambling is based on solid learning theory. You can get a person "hooked" on gambling by fixing the game to allow heavy winnings at first. Then you gradually space out the gambling behaviors that are reinforced until the gambling is maintained by infrequent winning—or even no winning at all. Partial reinforcement schedules can maintain behavior for a great deal of time, even though it goes unreinforced. Consider a critical-thinking question: Can you describe how behaviorists and cognitive psychologists might each explain the effects of a partial-reinforcement schedule on gamblers?

New operants or behaviors are acquired most rapidly through continuous reinforcement or, in some cases, through "one-trial learning" that meets with great reinforcement. So-called **pathological gamblers** often had big wins at the racetrack or casino or in the lottery in their youth. But once the operant has been acquired, it can be maintained by tapering off to a schedule of partial reinforcement.

Discriminative stimulus • In operant conditioning, a stimulus that indicates that reinforcement is available.

Continuous reinforcement • A schedule of reinforcement in which every correct response is reinforced.

Partial reinforcement • One of several reinforcement schedules in which not every correct response is reinforced.

Pathological gambler • A person who gambles habitually despite consistent losses.

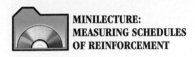

MINILECTURE: MEASURING SCHEDULES OF REINFORCEMENT

Fixed-interval schedule • A schedule in which a fixed amount of time must elapse between the previous and subsequent times that reinforcement is available.

Variable-interval schedule • A schedule in which a variable amount of time must elapse between the previous and subsequent times that reinforcement is available.

Fixed-ratio schedule • A schedule in which reinforcement is provided after a fixed number of correct responses.

Variable-ratio schedule • A schedule in which reinforcement is provided after a variable number of correct responses.

FIGURE 6.10

The "Fixed-Interval Scallop." Organisms who are reinforced on a fixed-interval schedule tend to slack off in responding after each reinforcement. The rate of response then picks up as they near the time when reinforcement will again become available. The results on the cumulative recorder look like an upward-moving series of waves, or scallops.

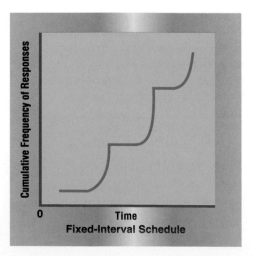

There are four basic schedules of reinforcement. They are determined by changing either the *interval* of time that must elapse between correct responses before reinforcement is made available or the *ratio* of correct responses to reinforcements. If the interval that must elapse between correct responses, before reinforcement becomes available, is zero seconds, the reinforcement schedule is continuous. A larger interval of time, such as 1 or 30 seconds, is a partial-reinforcement schedule. A one-to-one (1:1) ratio of correct responses to reinforcements is a continuous-reinforcement schedule. A higher ratio such as 2:1 or 5:1 would be a partial-reinforcement schedule.

The four basic types of schedules of reinforcement are *fixed-interval, variable-interval, fixed-ratio,* and *variable-ratio* schedules.

In a **fixed-interval schedule,** a fixed amount of time—say, 1 minute—must elapse between the previous and subsequent times that reinforcement is made available for correct responses. In a **variable-interval schedule,** varying amounts of time are allowed to elapse between making reinforcement available. In a 3-minute variable-interval schedule, the mean amount of time that would elapse between reinforcement opportunities would be 3 minutes. Each interval might vary, however, from 1 to 5 minutes.

With a fixed-interval schedule, an organism's response rate falls off after each reinforcement, then picks up as it nears the time when reinforcement will be dispensed. For example, in a 1-minute fixed-interval schedule, a rat will be reinforced with, say, a food pellet for the first operant—for example, the first pressing of a lever—that occurs after a minute has elapsed. After each reinforcement, the rat's rate of lever pressing slows down, but as the end of the 1-minute interval draws near, lever pressing increases in frequency, as suggested by Figure 6.10. It is as if the rat has learned that it must wait a while before reinforcement will be made available. The resultant record on the cumulative recorder (Figure 6.10) shows a series of characteristic upward-moving waves, or scallops, which is referred to as a *fixed-interval scallop.*

Car sales executives are employing a fixed-interval reinforcement schedule when they offer incentives for buying up the remainder of the year's line every summer and fall. In a sense, they are suppressing buying at other times, except for those consumers whose current cars are in their death throes or those who cannot exercise self-control.

In the case of the more unpredictable variable-interval schedule, the response rate is steadier but lower. If the boss calls us in for a weekly report, we will probably work hard to pull the pieces together just before the report is to be given, just as we might cram the night before a weekly quiz. But if we know that the boss might call us in for a report on the progress of a project at any time (variable-interval schedule), we are likely to keep things in a state of reasonable readiness at all times. However, our efforts are unlikely to have the intensity they would in a fixed-interval (for example, weekly) schedule. Similarly, we are less likely to cram for a series of unpredictable "pop quizzes" than for regularly scheduled quizzes. But we are likely to do at least some studying on a regular basis.

Note the effects of the reduced prices and rebates automobile companies usually offer during the period between July and September to make way for the new models. Aren't they encouraging buyers to wait for the summer and then buy in a flurry?

In a **fixed-ratio schedule,** reinforcement is provided after a fixed number of correct responses has been made. In a **variable-ratio schedule,** reinforcement is provided after a variable number of correct responses has been made. In a 10:1 variable-ratio schedule, the mean number of correct responses that would have to be made before a subsequent correct response would be reinforced is 10, but the ratio of correct responses to reinforcements might be allowed to vary from, say, 1:1 to 20:1 on a random basis.

Fixed-ratio and variable-ratio schedules maintain a high response rate. With a fixed-ratio schedule, it is as if the organism learns that it must make several responses before being reinforced. It then "gets them out of the way" as rapidly as possible. Consider the example of piecework. If a worker must sew five shirts to receive a $10 bill, he or she is on a fixed-ratio (5:1) schedule and is likely to sew at a uniformly high rate, although there might be a brief pause following each reinforcement. With a variable-ratio schedule, reinforcement can come at any time. This unpredictability also maintains a high response rate. Slot machines tend to pay off on variable-ratio schedules, and players can be seen popping coins into their maws and pulling their "arms" with barely a pause. I have seen players who do not even stop to pick up their winnings. Instead, they continue to smoothly pop in the coins, whether from their original stack or from the winnings tray.

SHAPING.   If you are teaching break dancing to people who have never danced, do not wait until they have performed a perfect moon walk before telling them they're on the right track. The foxtrot will be back in style before they have learned a thing.

We can teach complex behaviors by **shaping,** or at first reinforcing small steps toward the behavioral goals. In the beginning it may be wise to smile and say "Good" when a reluctant newcomer gathers the courage to get out on the dance floor, even if your feet get flattened by his initial clumsiness. If you are teaching someone to drive a car with a standard shift, at first generously reinforce the learner simply for shifting without stalling.

But as training proceeds, we come to expect more before dispensing reinforcement. We reinforce **successive approximations** of the goal. If you want to train a rat to climb a ladder, first reinforce it (with a food pellet) when it turns toward the ladder. Then wait until it approaches the ladder before using reinforcement. Then do not drop a food pellet into the cage until the rat touches the ladder. In this way, the rat will reach the top of the ladder more quickly than if you had waited until the target behavior had first occurred at random.

Truth or Fiction Revisited. *It is true that rats can be trained to climb a ramp, cross a bridge, climb a ladder, pedal a toy car, and do several other tasks—all in proper sequence.* The operant-conditioning procedure used to do so is called *shaping.* Do you believe that complex human behavior patterns are obtained through shaping?

Learning to drive a new standard-shift automobile to a new job also involves a complex sequence of operant behaviors. At first, we actively seek out all the discriminative stimuli or landmarks that cue us when to turn—signs, buildings, hills, and valleys. We also focus on shifting to a lower gear as we slow down so that the car won't stall. After many repetitions, though, these responses, these chains of behavior, become "habitual" and we need to pay very little attention to them.

Have you ever driven home from school or work and been suddenly unsettled as you got out of your car because you couldn't recall exactly how you had returned home? Your entire trip may seem "lost." Were you in great danger? How could you allow such a thing to happen? Actually, it may be that your responses to the demands of the route and to driving your car had become so habitual that you did not have to focus much awareness on them. You were able to think about dinner, a problem at work, or the weekend as you drove. But if something unusual such as hesitation in your engine or a

Shaping • A procedure for teaching complex behaviors that at first reinforces approximations to the target behavior.

Successive approximations • Behaviors that are progressively closer to a target behavior.

severe rainstorm had occurred on the way, you would have deployed as much attention as was needed to arrive home. Your trip was probably quite safe, after all.

Applications of Operant Conditioning

Habit is the enormous flywheel of society.
WILLIAM JAMES

Operant conditioning, like classical conditioning, is not just an exotic laboratory procedure. We use operant conditioning every day in our efforts to influence other people. Parents and peers incline children to acquire "gender-appropriate" behavior patterns through the elaborate use of rewards and punishments (see Chapter 12). Parents also tend to praise their children for sharing with others and to punish them for being too aggressive. Peers participate in the **socialization** process by playing with children who are generous and nonaggressive and, often, by avoiding those who are not (Etaugh & Rathus, 1995).

Operant conditioning may also play a role in attitude formation (see Chapter 16). Parents tend to reward their children for expressing attitudes that coincide with their own and to punish or ignore them for expressing attitudes that deviate.

Let us now consider some specific applications of operant conditioning.

BIOFEEDBACK TRAINING. Biofeedback training (BFT) is based on principles of operant conditioning. Through BFT, people and lower animals have learned to control autonomic responses to attain reinforcement. BFT has been an important innovation in the treatment of health-related problems during the past few decades.

Organisms can gain control of other autonomic functions such as blood pressure. They also can learn to improve their control over functions such as

Socialization • Guidance of people into socially desirable behavior by means of verbal messages, the systematic use of rewards and punishments, and other methods of teaching.

Taking the Pledge. Operant conditioning appears to play a role in the socialization of children. Parents and teachers tend to reward children for expressing attitudes that coincide with their own and to punish or ignore them when they express deviant attitudes.

muscle tension that are within the grasp of voluntary manipulation. When people receive BFT, reinforcement is in the form of *information*. Perhaps a "bleep" sound changes in pitch or frequency of occurrence to signal that they have modified the autonomic function in the desired direction. People, for example, can learn to emit alpha waves (and feel somewhat more relaxed) through feedback from an electroencephalograph. Through the use of other instruments, people have learned to lower muscle tension, their heart rates, even their blood pressure.

BFT is also used with accident patients who have lost neuromuscular control of parts of the body. A "bleep" informs them when they have contracted a muscle or sent an impulse down a neural pathway. By concentrating on changing the bleeps, these patients also gradually regain voluntary control over the damaged function.

TOKEN ECONOMIES.   Behavior therapists apply operant conditioning in a mental hospital to foster desired responses such as social skills and to extinguish unwanted behaviors such as social withdrawal. Several techniques such as the use of the **token economy** are outlined in Chapter 14. In token economies, psychologists give hospital residents or prison inmates tokens such as poker chips for desired behavior. The tokens reinforce desired behavior because they can be exchanged for television time, desserts, and other desired commodities.

Principles of operant conditioning have also permitted psychologists and educators to develop many beneficial innovations such as interventions with young children, behavior modification in the classroom, and programmed learning.

USING AVOIDANCE LEARNING TO SAVE A BABY'S LIFE.   Conditioning techniques have been used with children who are too young or distressed to respond to verbal forms of therapy. In one example, reported by Lang and Melamed (1969), a 9-month-old infant vomited regularly within 10 to 15 minutes after eating. Diagnostic workups found no medical basis for the problem, and medical treatments were to no avail. When the case was brought to the attention of Lang and Melamed, the infant weighed only 9 pounds and was in critical condition, being fed by a pump.

The psychologists monitored the infant for the first physical indications (local muscle tension) that vomiting was to occur. When the child tensed prior to vomiting, a tone was sounded and followed by painful but (presumably) harmless electric shock. After two 1-hour treatment sessions, the infant's muscle tensions ceased in response to the tone alone, and vomiting soon ceased altogether. At a 1-year follow-up, the infant was still not vomiting and had caught up in weight.

Truth or Fiction Revisited. *It is true that psychologists successfully fashioned a method to teach an emaciated 9-month-old infant to stop throwing up.* They derived the method from principles of conditioning. Conditioning allowed the psychologists to focus on what the child *did* and not on what the child knew or understood.

How do we explain this remarkable procedure through principles of conditioning? It appears to be an example of two-factor learning, as theorized by Mowrer (1947). The first factor was classical conditioning. Through repeated pairings, the tone (CS) came to elicit expectation of electric shock (US), so the psychologists could use the painful shock sparingly.

The second factor was operant conditioning. The electric shock and, after classical conditioning, the tone were aversive stimuli. The infant soon learned

Token economy • An environmental setting that fosters desired behavior by reinforcing it with tokens (secondary reinforcers) that can be exchanged for other reinforcers.

MINILECTURE: TREATING MALADAPTIVE VOMITING

to suppress the behaviors (muscle tensions) that were followed with aversive stimulation. By so doing, the aversive stimuli were removed. And so, the aversive stimuli served as negative reinforcers.

This learning occurred at an age long before any sort of verbal intervention could have been understood, and it apparently saved the infant's life. Similar procedures have been used to teach autistic children not to mutilate themselves.

CLASSROOM DISCIPLINE.   Remember that reinforcers are defined as stimuli that increase the frequency of behavior—not as pleasant events. Ironically, adults frequently reinforce undesirable behavior in children by attending to them, or punishing them, when they misbehave but by ignoring them when they behave in desirable ways. Similarly, teachers who raise their voices when children misbehave may be unintentionally conferring hero status on their pupils in the eyes of their peers (Wentzel, 1994). Some children may go out of their way to earn teacher disapproval, frequently to the teacher's surprise.

Teacher-preparation programs and in-service programs now usually show teachers how to use behavior modification in the classroom to reverse these response pattern. Teachers are taught to pay attention to children when they are behaving appropriately and, when possible, to ignore (avoid reinforcing) their misbehavior (Abramowitz & O'Leary, 1991). The younger the schoolchild, the more powerful teacher attention and approval seem to be.

Among older children and adolescents, peer approval is often a more powerful reinforcer than teacher approval. Peer approval may maintain misbehavior, and ignoring misbehavior may only allow peers to become more disruptive. In such cases, it may be necessary to separate troublesome children.

Teachers also frequently use time out from positive reinforcement to discourage misbehavior. In this method, children are placed in drab, restrictive environments for a specified time period, usually about 10 minutes, when they behave disruptively. When isolated, they cannot earn the attention of peers or teachers, and no reinforcing activities are present.

PROGRAMMED LEARNING.   B. F. Skinner developed an educational practice called **programmed learning** that is based on operant conditioning. Programmed learning assumes that any complex task involving conceptual learning as well as motor skills can be broken down into a number of small steps. These steps can be shaped individually and combined in sequence to form the correct behavioral chain.

Programmed learning does not punish errors. Instead, correct responses are reinforced. All children earn "100," but at their own pace. Programmed learning also assumes that it is the task of the teacher (or program) to structure the learning experience in such a way that errors will not be made.

Truth or Fiction Revisited. *It is not true that we must make mistakes if we are to learn.* The idea that we must make mistakes derives from folklore to the effect that we learn from (bad) experience. However, we also learn from good (positively reinforced) experiences and from the experiences of others.

Praise. Teacher praise reinforces desirable behavior in most children. Behavior modification in the classroom applies principles of operant conditioning.

Programmed learning • A method of learning in which complex tasks are broken down into simple steps, each of which is reinforced. Errors are not reinforced.

Reflections

- What kinds of effects have rewards and punishments had on your behavior over the years? Do you now work for rewards or to avert punishments? What kinds of rewards and punishments influence your behavior? Are the rewards and punishments that influence you less influential on other people? How so?

- What role does habit play in your life? Do you have both "good habits" and "bad habits"? What are they? How did they develop?
- Do you learn from your mistakes? Why or why not? Provide some examples.
- **Agree or disagree with the following statement and support your answer: "Complex human behavior can be explained as the summation of so many instances of conditioning."**
- **Pianists' fingers fly over the keys faster than they can read notes or even think notes. What kinds of learning are at work in learning to play the piano or in learning to perfectly execute a piece with rapid notes?**

COGNITIVE FACTORS IN LEARNING

Classical and operant conditioning were originally conceived as relatively simple forms of learning. Much of conditioning's appeal has been that it can be said to meet the behaviorist objective of explaining behavior in terms of public, observable events—in this case, laboratory conditions. Building on this theoretical base, some psychologists have suggested that the most complex human behavior involves the summation of so many instances of conditioning. However, many psychologists believe that the conditioning model is too mechanical to explain all instances of learned behavior, even in laboratory rats (Glover and others, 1990; Hayes, 1989; Weiner, 1991). They turn to cognitive factors to describe and explain additional findings in the psychology of learning.

In addition to concepts such as *association* and *reinforcement,* cognitive psychologists use concepts such as *mental structures, schemas, templates,* and *information processing.* Cognitive psychologists see people as searching for information, weighing evidence, and making decisions. Let us consider classic research that points to cognitive factors in learning, as opposed to mechanical associationism. These cognitive factors are not necessarily limited to humans, although people, of course, are the only species that can talk about them.

Contingency Theory: Contiguity or Contingency? What "Really" Happens During Classical Conditioning?

Behaviorists and cognitive psychologists interpret the events of the conditioning process in different ways. Behaviorists explain the outcomes of classical conditioning in terms of the contiguous presentation of stimuli. Cognitive psychologists explain classical conditioning in terms of the ways in which stimuli provide information that allows organisms to form and revise mental representations of their environments.

In classical-conditioning experiments with dogs, Robert Rescorla (1967) obtained some results that are difficult to explain without reference to cognitive concepts. Each phase of his work paired a tone (CS) with electric shock (US) but in different ways. With one group of animals, the shock was presented consistently after the tone. That is, the US followed on the heels of the CS as in Pavlov's studies. The dogs in this group learned to show a fear response when the tone was presented.

A second group of dogs heard an equal number of tones and received an equal number of electric shocks, but the shock never immediately followed the tone. In other words, the tone and shock were unpaired. Now, from the behavioral perspective, the dogs should not have learned to associate the tone and the shock, since one did not presage the other. Actually, the dogs learned quite a lot: They learned that they had nothing to fear when the tone was sounded! The dogs showed vigilance and fear when the laboratory was quiet—for apparently the shock could come at any time—but they were calm in the presence of the tone.

The third group of dogs also received equal numbers of tones and shocks, but these were presented at purely random intervals. Occasionally they were paired, but most often they were not. According to Rescorla, behaviorists might argue that intermittent pairing of the tones and shocks should have brought about some learning. Yet it did not. The animals showed no fear in response to the tone. Rescorla suggests that the animals in this group learned nothing because the tones provided no information about the prospect of being shocked.

Rescorla concluded that contiguity—that is, the co-appearance of two events (the US and the CS)—cannot in itself explain classical conditioning. Instead, learning occurs only when the conditioned stimulus (in this case, the tone) provides information about the unconditioned stimulus (in this case, the shock). According to so-called **contingency theory,** learning occurs because a conditioned stimulus indicates that the unconditioned stimulus is likely to ensue.

Behaviorists might counter, of course, that for the second group of dogs, the *absence* of the tone became the signal for the shock. Shock may be a powerful enough event that the fear response becomes conditioned to the laboratory environment. For the third group of dogs, the shock was as likely in the presence of the neutral stimulus as in its absence. Therefore, many behaviorists would expect no learning to occur.

Contingency theory • The view that learning occurs when stimuli provide information about the likelihood of the occurrence of other stimuli.
Latent • Hidden or concealed.

Latent Learning: When Learning Is Not Doing

I'm all grown up. I know the whole [shopping] mall.

THE AUTHOR'S DAUGHTER JORDAN AT AGE 7

Many behaviorists argue that organisms acquire only those responses, or only those operants, for which they are reinforced. E. C. Tolman, however, showed that rats also learn about their environments in the absence of reinforcement.

Tolman trained some rats to run through mazes for standard food goals. Other rats were permitted to explore the same mazes for several days without food goals or other rewards. After the unrewarded rats had been allowed to explore the mazes for 10 days, food rewards were placed in a box at the far end of the maze. The previously unrewarded explorers reached the food box as quickly as the rewarded rats after only one or two reinforced trials (Tolman & Honzik, 1950).

Tolman concluded that rats learned about mazes in which they roamed even when they were unrewarded for doing so. He distinguished between learning and performance. Rats would acquire a cognitive map of a maze, and even though they would not be motivated to follow an efficient route to the far end, they would learn rapid routes from end to end just by roaming about within the maze. Yet this learning might remain hidden, or **latent,** until they were motivated to follow the rapid routes for food goals.

Observational Learning: Monkey See, Monkey *May* Choose to Do

How many things have you learned from watching other people in real life, in films, and on television? From films and television, you may have gathered vague ideas about how to sky dive, ride surfboards, climb sheer cliffs, run a pattern to catch a touchdown pass in the Super Bowl, and dust for fingerprints, even if you have never tried these activities.

In his studies on social learning, Albert Bandura has run experiments (e.g., Bandura and others, 1963) that show we can acquire operants by observing the behavior of others. We may need some practice to refine the operants, but we can learn them by observation alone. We may also choose to allow these operants or skills to lie latent. For example, we may not imitate aggressive behavior unless we are provoked and believe that we are more likely to be rewarded than punished for it.

Observational learning may account for most human learning. It occurs when, as children, we observe parents cook, clean, or repair a broken appliance. Observational learning takes place when we watch teachers solve problems on the blackboard or hear them speak in a foreign language. Observational learning is not mechanically acquired through reinforcement. We can learn by observation without engaging in overt responses at all. It appears sufficient to pay attention to the behavior of others.

In the terminology of observational learning, a person who engages in a response to be imitated is a *model*. When observers see a model being reinforced for displaying an operant, the observers are said to be *vicariously* reinforced. Display of the operant thus becomes more likely for the observer as well as the model.

Thus, there are many different kinds of learning. We have touched on a number of them in this chapter. We have seen that psychologists disagree about what learning is, what is learned, and whether organisms are basically active or passive as they participate in the processes of learning. Nonetheless, most psychologists agree that the capacity to learn is at the heart of organisms' abilities to adapt to their environments. Some psychologists also believe that organisms, especially humans, can learn to fashion their environments in ways that enable them to meet their needs better.

Reflections

- What basic assumptions do cognitive theorists hold about human nature? How do their views correspond with your own?
- What is your own feeling as to what "really" happens during classical conditioning? How does the research evidence support or contradict your views?
- Have you ever studied an atlas, a road map, a cookbook, or a computer manual for the pleasure of doing so? In what way does the kind of learning involved in these activities reflect latent learning?
- In your own experiences, how much can you learn by observing others? What kinds of things do you have to practice for yourself in order to learn? What kinds of learnings are taking place in your classroom? As you consider these words?

It would be of little use to discuss how we learn if we were not capable of remembering what we learn from second to second, from day to day, or, in many cases, for a lifetime. In the next chapter, we turn our attention to the

Observational Learning. What is the boy learning? How?

Observational learning • The acquisition of knowledge and skills through the observation of others (who are called *models*) rather than by means of direct experience.

---

subject of memory. And, in Chapters 8 and 9, we shall see how learning is intertwined with thinking, language, and a concept that many people think of as learning ability: intelligence.

WORLD OF DIVERSITY

SOCIOCULTURAL FACTORS IN LEARNING, OR, DONALD DUCK MEETS A SAMURAI

The psychology of learning addresses the core of personality. Even though what people learn is very different, it is assumed that people from different cultures learn in the same ways. People may have very different attitudes, but conditioning probably plays a role in the acquisition of attitudes. For example, classic laboratory experiments have shown that attitudes toward ethnic groups can be influenced by associating them with positive words (such as *gift* or *happy*) or negative words (such as *ugly* and *failure*); (Lohr & Staats, 1973). Parents usually positively reinforce their children for saying and doing things that are consistent with their own attitudes. Children in the United States may be shown approval for waving our flag, while children in hostile nations may be smiled upon for burning our flag.

Children also acquire many attitudes, including prejudices, by means of observational learning. Children tend to imitate their parents, and parents reinforce their children for doing so (Duckitt, 1992). Prejudices can thus be transmitted from generation to generation via learning.

People from diverse cultures share drives such as hunger and thirst, but the foods and drinks they prefer to satisfy those drives are based on learning within a given sociocultural setting. African and Swedish Americans may both like chicken, but African Americans in the South may prefer their chicken prepared in a different way than Swedish Americans from Minnesota do. Once upon a time we may have written that Mexican Americans prefer enchiladas and burritos, that Japanese Americans prefer sushi, that Italian Americans prefer pasta. Today, however, "ethnic foods" have become so popular that most Americans have some familiarity with them and eat them from time to time. There are also many acquired individual preferences within the same ethnic group. Many White Americans like eating raw oysters, for example. Other White Americans are revolted by them.

Our learning experiences also affect our cognition, including the nature of the very images that swim within our consciousness. Consider, for example, a painting by Japanese American artist Roger Shimomura (Figure 6.11). Shimomura is bicultural and blends popular Western imagery with the imagery found in traditional Japanese prints. At first glance, the painting suggests an amusing clash of American and Japanese popular cultures. American cartoon characters like Donald Duck, Pinocchio, Dick Tracy, and a combination Batman–Superman vie for space on the canvas with Japanese Samurai warriors and a contemporary Japanese. The battle of imagery from East and West may reflect the tensions within the artist regarding his ancestral roots and his chosen country.

FIGURE 6.11
Roger Shimomura. *Untitled* (1984). Acrylic on canvas. 60" x 72". Courtesy of Steinbaum Krauss Gallery, New York.

Study Guide

Classical Versus Operant Conditioning

DIRECTIONS: Below are a number of terms that are used in discussions of conditioning. Some terms apply to classical conditioning, some to operant conditioning, and some to both. For each term place a check mark in the appropriate blank space, or spaces, to show the type(s) of learning to which it applies. The answer key is given on the next page.

CLASSICAL CONDITIONING	OPERANT CONDITIONING	TERM
_____	_____	1. Discriminative stimulus
_____	_____	2. Unconditioned stimulus
_____	_____	3. Conditioned response
_____	_____	4. Extinction
_____	_____	5. Reinforcer
_____	_____	6. Backward conditioning
_____	_____	7. Generalization
_____	_____	8. Instrumental conditioning
_____	_____	9. Bell-and-pad method
_____	_____	10. Contingency theory
_____	_____	11. Trial and error
_____	_____	12. Stimulus
_____	_____	13. Neutral stimulus
_____	_____	14. Skinner box
_____	_____	15. Operant
_____	_____	16. Spontaneous recovery
_____	_____	17. Shaping
_____	_____	18. Cumulative recorder
_____	_____	19. Conditional reflex
_____	_____	20. Variable-ratio schedule
_____	_____	21. Response
_____	_____	22. Higher-order conditioning
_____	_____	23. Successive approximations
_____	_____	24. Programmed learning
_____	_____	25. Rewards and punishments
_____	_____	26. Trace conditioning
_____	_____	27. Simultaneous conditioning

ANSWER KEY TO EXERCISE

1. O	4. C, O	7. C, O	10. C	13. C	16. C, O	19. C	22. C	25. O
2. C	5. O	8. O	11. O	14. O	17. O	20. O	23. O	26. C
3. C	6. C	9. C	12. C, O	15. O	18. O	21. C, O	24. O	27. C

ESL	# English as a Second Language—Bridging the Gap

accommodate (227)—learn

acquired (218)—to have developed or gotten something

after a while (227)—after time passes

age significantly in the process (235)—get a lot older while it happens

akin to (230)—similar to

as if on cue (224)—as if the sticks behaved from direction he gave

aspects (224)—different parts of something

at the heart of (242)—the essence of; at the base of

at what cost (238)—the other results might be worse

aversive (243)—something that causes a negative reaction

award damages (238)—to pay money to the family because the TV station was responsible for the problem

backside (235)—haunches

barely a pause (241)—almost without stopping

bed wetters . . . wet their beds (228)—children . . . urinate in their beds at night

beholder (226)—the one who looks or sees

bicultural (248)—influenced by two cultures, able to function in both

big win at the racetrack or casino or in the lottery (239)—a lot of money won from betting (wagering) on race horses, at gambling houses, and from choosing the same number that an official or licensed gambling organization has chosen

biological makeup (220)—biological composition

bit misleading (226)—difficult to understand; it appears to have one meaning but actually has another

bleep (242)—a small, short sound

body language (239)—movements of the body that communicate (without speech)

break dancing; moon walk (241)—popular and current dance steps

brim with violence (238)—have a lot of violence

broken down into (222)—separated

brought forth by (232)—created by

bulky (232)—large and hard to manage

buttered popcorn (218)—popular food sold at movie theaters, baseball games, and other entertainment events; made from corn

came fast and furious (235)—was very frequent

canned lectures (238)—lectures on videotape

cast a weary eye (230)—looked at so that he could defend himself if he had to

characteristic knock (228)—the person knocks with his or her style, or his or her personality, and we recognize that

chugalugging a bottle of antacid tablets (239)—rapidly eating, without stopping, pills that are for indigestion

clicked (224)—something had suddenly been understood

clicker (224)—any object that makes a short, sharp sound as if something is turning on and off; in this case, the clicking sound is used to train the rats to expect something to happen

clinking (220)—noise made by glass or metal objects hitting together

coaxing (234)—persuading or encouraging to do something

come to serve (228)—act as

comes to be made (235)—occurs

concrete goals (220)—specific goals; tangible goals; goals that we know we want

conferring hero status (244)—creating heroes

consequent (224)—following; subsequent

consume the treat (230)—eat the candy and cookies

controversies (217)—disagreements about an idea

cram the night before (240)—study a lot the night before a test

cut class (238)—not attend class

dangling (231)—loosely hanging down

dared me (218)—said, "We dare you"; tried to persuade me to do something that I did not want to do and that they did not want to do themselves

deemed socially acceptable (219)—thought to be the right ones by most people

desensitization (229)—to no longer be bothered by something that used to cause strong fear or dislike; in this case, it is a process in which someone is repeatedly exposed to something to help him or her become less bothered by it (discussed further in Chapter 14)

dietary staples (230)—necessary foods for health

discrete (228)—individual; separate

discrimination (227)—knowing the difference between two things

down went (218)—ate

draws their attention to (238)—causes them to pay attention to

drop out of school (238)—stop attending school

dust for fingerprints (247)—spread a chemical powder that will reveal the fingerprints (the imprint that the ends of the fingers make on surfaces); this is done in order to discover the identity of a person

elicited (220)—caused; brought forth

emit (242)—to put out

engage in (222)—do; participate in; become involved in; start to do something

ensue (246)—to follow; to come after

errs (227)—makes a mistake

extinction (229)—vanished; gone

faced with novel events (227)—confronted with "new" events, ones we have not experienced

ferret out (233)—dig out; search out, try to understand

few and far between (235)—not often

few will top that (232)—few people have a more unusual story about the war

fits (224)—corresponds to

flash of inspiration (246)—sudden inspiration

flurry (240)—a lot at the same time as opposed to a small amount at other times

focus much awareness (241)—pay much attention to

folklore (259)—tradition; old belief

follow circular paths (226)—go around in a circle

food goal (233)—to reach the goal where there was food

food pellet (233)—small, hard ball or piece of concentrated food

found wide applications (232)—been applied by many people

fox-trot (226)—a dance step that was popular before 1950; the music required slow dancing

from bark to bark (226)—each time the same dog barks, it sounds different

frustration (227)—a feeling that results when we are prevented from having or achieving something; it results in being disappointed or angry

further impair (221)—damage more

gathers the courage (241)—acquires courage

get away with murder (238)—do a negative act and not be corrected

get into the habit (219)—become accustomed to; do the same thing at the same time regularly

get out on the dance floor (241)—start dancing

get smoochy (239)—become romantic

gets inside the head of (237)—think like

good groan (248)—when a joke is heard, a person often groans (makes a long, low sound)

grooming itself (239)—cleaning itself and smoothing its feathers

hampered by (220)—hindered by; made difficult by

head spun (218)—felt sick

hindrance (221)—something that stops or slows down something else

homecoming (225)—arrival home

hooked on gambling (239)—addicted to gambling

in a couple of ways (218)—in two ways

in a flash (246)—suddenly

in the eyes of their peers (244)—the way in which the peers see

in the wilds (226)—in the forest or desert; in the natural area

incline (242)—to cause a tendency toward something

incompatible (230)—doesn't match or fit

inconsequential (233)—not important

instinctively (218)—an urge that comes from an instinct; not a conscious decision to do something

intermittent (246)—not regular; occurs now and then without a plan

just desserts (229)—reward that he deserved

land in divorce court (227)—our spouses would divorce us

latent (246)—not used

leveled off at (225)—stopped at

lies in (236)—is in

major avenue (228)—major method

matters little (235)—is not important

maws of slot machines (239)—jaws (mouths, openings) of gambling machines

may not take place at all (224)—may not occur or happen

moment's reflection will suggest (239)—if we think for a moment, we can think of many ways

munching merrily away (230)—eating without paying attention to what is occurring

nauseated (218)—feeling sick to the stomach

no avail (243)—did not correct the problem

not face (218)—not look at; not eat

not given to ready displays of emotion (229)—who did not reveal, or let people see, how he felt

not plopped in Peter's lap (230)—not suddenly dropped in Peter's lap (the position of the thighs when sitting) without gradual introduction

on a gut level (218)—on an emotional level; from strong feeling

one-armed bandits (239)—slot machines operated by pulling a lever; bandits are robbers or thieves

overgeneralization (238)—to extend too far; in this case, when a child assumes a punishment applies to more behavior than the parent intended, which causes too strong a reaction

paired repeatedly (220)—accompanied many times

pecks (239)—to pick up to hit with the beak

person dressed in unmistakable blue (245)—a police officer (it is impossible not to recognize the color of the uniform)

phlegmatic (229)—passive, indifferent; not active or lively

piecework (241)—a type of work in which a worker is paid for each piece that he or she produces, rather than paid for the amount of time it takes

plan ahead (235)—plan what to do in the future (sooner or later)

point out that (233)—emphasize

predictably (218)—could be expected to result from some action

predisposed (229)—inclined towards; a tendency towards something

presumably (222)—can be assumed or expected without knowing for sure because it's a reasonable idea

pull into the driveway (224)—drive into the driveway

purely random (221)—completely random; completely by chance

put on an infantile show (227)—acted like a baby

rebates (240)—a refund (money returned after having been delivered) of a portion (part) of a payment already made

reinforcer (217)—something that encourages existing behavior

ride a surfboard (247)—stand on a board at the edge of the ocean and move on the waves (surf)

right to free expression as guaranteed by the First Amendment (229)—the First Amendment to the Constitution provides that the goverment may not restrict the right of a person to say anything he or she wishes to say

rose to the challenge (218)—agreed

routinely ignored (233)—ignored regularly

run a pattern to catch a touchdown pass in the Super Bowl (247)—run on the field in order to make a touchdown (a score) in football in the final contest of the champions of the year

run away (238)—leave home without telling parents and not returning

rustling sounds in the undergrowth (226)—noise in the forest

sad to say (243)—unfortunately

salivary glands (220)—glands in the head that cause moisture in the mouth

scheme of things (224)—plan of events

serial (218)—adventure movies about heroes; a chapter was shown at the theater every week (serial)

Sesame Street (238)—a popular TV educational program for young children

shifting without stalling (241)—see *standard shift;* it used

to be difficult to shift gears (change the gear)—the car would often stall, or stop, before the shift had occurred completely

sky dive (247)—jump from the top of a mountain or from an airplane and "fly" with the aid of a glider or a parachute

slippery dining room floors (238)—the ice cream would melt, would become cream, and cause the floor to be slippery (a person could slide on it easily)

snapped at (227)—tried to bite

sniffed its way around (233)—walked around in the cage and sniffed (smelled) at the same time as he walked

so-called puzzle boxes (231)—the box is called this because it is a "puzzle" to the cat; the cat has to solve puzzles (problems that are like games) to get to the food

sociocultural setting (248)—the social and cultural environment that influences us

squawking (239)—making a loud, harsh sound

squeal with delight (224)—make a happy noise

standard shift (241)—in old cars, a person operated a lever by hand in order to change the ratio of the gears that connected the motor and the transmission; some newer cars also have standard shift but most are automatic shift

state of reasonable readiness (240)—a condition of always being ready

stay tuned in (238)—continue to watch TV violence

stick to the straight and narrow (219)—behave correctly; be good

strapping (221)—tying with straps (strips of cloth or leather)

stray cats (231)—cats that have no homes and live on the street

stuffed down (218)—ate with difficulty

surfboards (247)—a board that looks like a wide ski and is used for the sport of surfboarding (sliding over ocean waves)

take . . . for granted (238)—accept it but ignore it

tapering off (239)—reducing gradually

target response (221)—the response that we are looking for, or expecting

tell our spouses apart (227)—recognize our spouse (husband or wife) as being different from another spouse

thankless task (244)—a responsibility or job for which no appreciation would be given

times change (225)—the old rules and concerns do not apply now

to do just that (229)—to do *that* specifically

tormented (227)—bothered to a great degree; mistreated; abused

traffic citations (220)—tickets to indicate that a fine

(money) must be paid for violating rules for correct driving

training pants . . . toilet training (228)—underwear that is thicker than usual in order to absorb urine; it is worn by 1- to 3-year-old children while they are learning how to use the toilet

trial run (241)—an attempt to go through the maze

tune in (242)—turn on and watch TV

uncalled-for (220)—not asked for; not wanted

updating (224)—causing their expectation to change according to the current environment

vernacular (243)—to speak in an informal way, rather than using a formal style of speaking; using common, everyday speech

was for the birds (232)—was useless

went bananas (242)—became insane (crazy)

were scrapped (232)—were not continued or practiced

what, then, is there to do? (222)—so, what shall we do?

where would you place your money? (226)—what do you think? (how would you bet?); which outcome do you think would happen?

whiffs the scent (224)—smells the scent

works them up (230)—causes them to be aroused or excited and want to act

worth looking into (221)—important enough to investigate

youth (218)—young; in this case, attitudes when he was young were responsible for his doing something that he would not do now

---

FILL-INS | **Chapter Review**

From the behaviorist perspective, learning is defined as a relatively permanent change in behavior that arises from (1) _____ence. From the cognitive perspective, learning involves processes by which experience contributes to relatively permanent changes in the way organisms mentally (2) _____sent the environment.

SECTION 1: CLASSICAL CONDITIONING

Classical conditioning is defined as a simple form of learning in which an originally (3) _____al stimulus comes to bring forth, or (4) e_____, the response usually brought forth by another stimulus by being paired repeatedly with that stimulus.

When Pavlov discovered conditioning, he was attempting to identify neural receptors in the mouth that triggered a response from the (5) _____ary glands. Salivation in response to meat is unlearned, a (6) _____ex. Reflexes are elicited by (7) _____li. A stimulus may be defined as an (8) _____mental condition that evokes a response from an organism. Pavlov discovered that reflexes can also be learned, or conditioned, through (9) _____tion. Pavlov called learned reflexes (10) _____nal reflexes. Today conditional reflexes are termed (11) _____ _____ses.

In classical conditioning, a previously neutral stimulus, called the (12) _____ned stimulus (or CS) comes to elicit the response evoked by a second stimulus, called the (13) _____ned stimulus (or US) by being paired repeatedly with the second stimulus. A response to a US is called an (14) _____ned response (UR), and a response to a CS is termed a (15) _____ned response (CR).

Classical conditioning occurs efficiently when the (16) _____ned stimulus (CS) is presented about 0.5 seconds before the (17) _____ned stimulus (US). In (18) _____neous conditioning the CS is presented at the same time as the US and left on until the response occurs. In (19) _____ed conditioning the CS is presented before the US and is left on until the response is shown. In trace conditioning the CS is presented and removed (20: Prior To or After?) presentation of the US. In (21) _____ard conditioning the US is presented prior to the CS.

According to contingency theory, the (22) con_____ presentation of stimuli—that is, the co-appearance of the US and the CS—does not explain classical conditioning. Instead, learning occurs only when the CS provides (23) _____tion about the US. According to (24) con_____ theory, learning occurs because a CS indicates that the US stimulus is likely to ensue.

Taste aversions differ from other kinds of classical conditioning in a couple of ways: First, (25: Only One Association or Several Associations?) may be required. Second, the US and CS need not be presented (26) _____uously; the US (nausea) can occur hours after the CS (flavor of food). Research in taste aversion also challenges the (27) _____rist view that organisms learn to associate any stimuli that are contiguous. Instead, it seems that organisms are biologically predisposed to develop aversions that are (28) _____tive in their environmental settings.

After a US–CS association has been learned, repeated presentation of the (29) _____ned stimulus (for example, a bell) without the US (meat) will extinguish the CR (salivation). But extinguished responses may show (30) _____neous recovery as a function of time that has elapsed since the end of the extinction process.

In stimulus (31) _____ation, organisms show a CR in response to a range of stimuli similar to the CS. In stimulus (32) _____ation, organisms learn to show a CR in response to a more limited range of stimuli by pairing only the limited stimulus with the US.

In higher-order conditioning, a previously neutral stimulus comes to serve as a (33) _____ned stimulus after being paired repeatedly with a stimulus that has already been established as a CS.

Classical conditioning involves ways in which (34) _____uli come to serve as signals for other stimuli. In the (35) bell-and-p_____ method for teaching children to stop bed-wetting, a (36) b_____ is sounded when the child urinates in bed, waking the child. Urine is detected by a (37) p_____ placed beneath the sheets, and then the bell is sounded. The bell is paired repeatedly with fullness in the child's (38) bl_____. In this way, sensations of a full bladder (the conditioned stimulus) gain the capacity to wake the child just as the bell (the [39] _____ned stimulus) did.

In the case of Little (40) A_____ a young boy was taught to fear rats. In this case study, John (41) W_____ and Rosalie (42) R_____ clanged steel bars behind Albert's head as Albert played with a rat.

In the fear-reduction method of (43) _____tioning, a pleasant stimulus is paired repeatedly with a fear-evoking object, in this way counteracting the fear response.

SECTION 2: OPERANT CONDITIONING

Edward L. Thorndike used so-called (44) p_____ boxes to study learning in cats. Thorndike also originated the law of (45) _____ct, which holds that responses are "stamped in" by rewards and "stamped out" by (46) _____ments. B. F. Skinner introduced the concept of (47) _____ment. Skinner also devised a kind of cage, which has been dubbed the (48) S_____ _____, to study operant behavior in animals. Skinner's use of the (49) _____tive recorder also permitted precise measurement of operant behavior, even in the absence of the researcher.

In operant conditioning, behaviors that manipulate the environment in order to attain reinforcers are termed (50) _____ts. In operant conditioning, an organism learns to emit an operant because it is (51) _____ed.

Initial "correct" responses may be performed by random trial and (52) _____r, or by physical or verbal guiding. A reinforcement is a stimulus that increases the (53) _____cy of an operant.

Positive reinforcers increase the probability that operants will occur when they are (54: Applied or Removed?). Negative reinforcers (55: Increase or Decrease?) the probability that operants will occur when they are (56: Applied or Removed?). (57) _____ary reinforcers have their value because of the biological makeup of the organism. (58) _____ary reinforcers, such as money and approval, acquire their value through association with established reinforcers. Secondary reinforcers are also referred to as (59) _____ned reinforcers.

In operant conditioning, (60) _____tion results from repeated performance of operant behavior in the absence of reinforcement. In operant conditioning, the (61) _____nt is extinguished. (62) Sp_____ recovery of learned responses can occur as a function of the passage of time following extinction.

Rewards, like reinforcers, are (63) _____li that increase the frequency of behavior. But rewards differ from reinforcers in that rewards are considered (64) pl_____ stimuli. Punishments are defined as (65) _____sive stimuli that suppress the frequency of behavior. Skinner preferred to use the term *reinforcer* because *reinforcement* is defined in terms of its effects on observable (66) _____ior.

Many learning theorists prefer treating children's misbehavior by ignoring it or using time out from (67) _____ment rather than by using punishment. Strong punishment (68: Will or Will Not?) suppress undesired behavior. However, punishment also has some "side effects." One is that punishment (69: Does or Does Not?) teach acceptable, alternative behavior. Punishment (70) sup_____ undesired behavior only when its delivery is guaranteed. Punishment also may cause the organism to (71) w_____ from the situation, as in the child's running away from home, cutting classes, or dropping out of school. Moreover, punishment can create anger and hostility, can lead to overgeneralization, and can serve as a (72) m_____ for aggression. Finally, children (73) l_____ punished responses, whether or not they perform them.

A (74) _____ative stimulus indicates when an operant will be reinforced. A (75) co_____-reinforcement schedule leads to the most rapid acquisition of new responses, but operants are maintained most economically through (76) _____tial reinforcement. Partial reinforcement also makes responses more resistant to (77) _____tion.

There are four basic schedules of reinforcement. In a (78) f_____-_____ schedule, a specific amount of time must elapse since a previous correct response before reinforcement again becomes available. In a variable-interval schedule, the amount of (79) t_____ is allowed to vary. With a (80) f_____-interval schedule, an organism's response rate falls off after each reinforcement, then picks up as it nears the time when reinforcement will be dispensed. The resultant record on the cumulative recorder shows a series of characteristic upward-moving waves, which are referred to as fixed-interval (81) _____lops. In a (82) _____-r_____ schedule, a fixed number of correct responses must be performed before one is reinforced. In a variable-ratio schedule, the (83) n_____ of correct responses that must be performed before reinforcement becomes available is allowed to vary. Payment for piecework is an example of a (84) f_____-_____ schedule. The unpredictability of (85: Fixed or Variable?) schedules maintains a high response rate. Slot machines tend to pay off on (86) v_____-ratio schedules.

In shaping, we at first (87) r_____ small steps toward behavioral goals. We reinforce (88) _____sive approximations to the goal. Eventually we reinforce organisms for performing complex behavioral (89) _____s, with each link performed in proper sequence.

Parents and peers socialize children into acquiring (90) "gender-_____iate" behavior patterns through the elaborate use of rewards and punishments. Parents and peers also tend to (91: Reward or Punish?) their children for sharing with others and to (92: Reward or Punish?) them for being too aggressive.

Lang and Melamed used (93) _____ance learning to save the life of a baby that repeatedly threw up after eating. When the child tensed prior to vomiting, a tone was sounded and followed by painful but (presumably) harmless electric shock. We can explain this procedure through Mowrer's (94) t_____-factor learning. Through (95) _____cal conditioning, the tone (CS) came to elicit expectation of electric shock (US), so that shock could be used sparingly. But the shock and, after classical conditioning, the tone were aversive stimuli. Through (96) _____nt conditioning the infant learned to suppress the behaviors (muscle tensions) that were followed with aversive stimulation. By so doing, the aversive stimuli were removed. And so, the aversive stimuli served as (97: Positive or Negative?) reinforcers.

In using behavior (98) _____tion in the classroom, teachers usually reinforce desired behavior and attempt to (99) ex_____ undesired behavior by ignoring it. (100) _____med learning is based on the assumption that learning tasks can be broken down into a number of small steps. Correct performance of each small step is (101) _____ced.

SECTION 3: COGNITIVE FACTORS IN LEARNING

Not all learning can be explained through conditioning. Gestalt psychologist Wolfgang Köhler showed that apes can learn through sudden reorganization of (102) _____al relationships, or insight.

E. C. Tolman's work with rats suggests that they develop (103) _____ive maps of the environment. Tolman's work also suggests that operant conditioning teaches organisms where (104) rein_____ may be found, rather than mechanically increasing the frequency of (105) _____nts.

Tolman's work in (106) l_____ learning also found that organisms learn in the absence of reinforcement. Tolman also distinguished between learning and (107) _____ance, and found that organisms do not necessarily perform all the behaviors that they have learned.

Albert (108) B_____ and other social-learning theorists have shown that people can also learn by observing others. In observational learning, it is not necessary that people emit (109) _____nses of their own, nor that their behavior be (110) _____orced, in order for learning to take place. Learners may then choose to (111) p_____ the behaviors they have observed when "the time is ripe"—that is, when they believe that they will be rewarded.

ANSWER KEY TO CHAPTER REVIEW

1. Experience	6. Reflex	11. Conditioned reponses	16. Conditioned
2. Represent	7. Stimuli	12. Conditioned	17. Unconditioned
3. Neutral	8. Environmental	13. Unconditioned	18. Simultaneous
4. Elicit (or evoke)	9. Association	14. Unconditioned	19. Delayed
5. Salivary	10. Conditional	15. Conditioned	20. Prior to

21. Backward
22. Contiguous
23. Information
24. Contingency
25. Only one association
26. Contiguously
27. Behaviorist
28. Adaptive
29. Conditioned
30. Spontaneous
31. Generalization
32. Discrimination
33. Conditioned
34. Stimuli
35. Pad
36. Bell
37. Pad
38. Bladder
39. Unconditioned
40. Albert
41. Watson
42. Rayner
43. Counterconditioning

44. Puzzle
45. Effect
46. Punishments
47. Reinforcement
48. Skinner box
49. Cumulative
50. Operants
51. Reinforced
52. Error
53. Frequency
54. Applied
55. Increase
56. Removed
57. Primary
58. Secondary
59. Conditioned
60. Extinction
61. Operant
62. Spontaneous
63. Stimuli
64. Pleasant
65. Aversive
66. Behavior

67. Reinforcement
68. Will
69. Does not
70. Suppresses
71. Withdraw
72. Successive
73. Learn
74. Discriminative
75. Continuous
76. Partial
77. Extinction
78. Fixed-interval
79. Time
80. Fixed
81. Scallops
82. Fixed-ratio
83. Number
84. Fixed-ratio
85. Variable
86. Variable
87. Reinforce
88. Successive
89. Chains

90. Appropriate
91. Reward
92. Punish
93. Avoidance
94. Two
95. Classical
96. Operant
97. Negative
98. Modification
99. Extinguish
100. Programmed
101. Reinforced
102. Perceptual
103. Cognitive
104. Reinforcement
105. Operants
106. Latent
107. Performance
108. Bandura
109. Responses
110. Reinforced
111. Perform

POSTTEST | **Multiple Choice**

1. Ivan Pavlov is known for his contribution to the understanding of
   a. learning to engage in voluntary behavior.
   b. observational learning.
   c. classical conditioning.
   d. contingency theory.

2. Which school of psychologists would define learning as a change in behavior that results from experience?
   a. behaviorists
   b. cognitive psychologists
   c. Gestalt psychologists
   d. psychoanalysts

3. In Pavlov's experiments, salivation in response to meat was a
   a. CR.
   b. CS.
   c. UR.
   d. US.

4. In using the bell-and-pad method for overcoming bed-wetting, the sensations of a full bladder are the
   a. CR.
   b. CS.
   c. UR.
   d. US.

5. Extinction in classical conditioning occurs because of repeated presentation of the
   a. CR in the absence of the CS.
   b. UR in the absence of the US.
   c. CS in the absence of the US.
   d. US in the absence of the CS.

6. In higher-order conditioning, a previously neutral stimulus comes to serve as a CS after being paired with a
   a. CR.
   b. CS.
   c. UR.
   d. US.

7. Little Albert learned to fear rats as a result of
   a. the clanging of steel bars in the presence of a rat.
   b. observing a rat attack another animal.
   c. being informed that rats carry certain harmful diseases.
   d. being personally bitten by a rat.

8. Who originated the use of puzzle boxes?
   a. Ivan Pavlov
   b. John Watson
   c. B. F. Skinner
   d. Edward Thorndike

9. According to the law of effect, _____ has the effect of stamping out stimulus–response connections.
   a. forgetting
   b. negative reinforcement
   c. extinction
   d. punishment

10. Pain is an example of a
    a. primary positive reinforcer.
    b. primary negative reinforcer.
    c. secondary positive reinforcer.
    d. secondary negative reinforcer.

11. Which of the following statements about punishment is *false?*
    a. Children learn responses that are punished.
    b. Punishment increases the frequency of undesired behavior.
    c. Punished children may withdraw from the situation.
    d. Punishment may be modeled as a way of solving problems.

12. With a _____-_____ schedule, an organism's response rate falls off after each reinforcement.
    a. fixed-interval
    b. fixed-ratio
    c. variable-interval
    d. variable-ratio

13. According to the text, the best way for teachers to use behavior modification in the classroom is to
    a. pay attention to children when they are misbehaving.
    b. pay attention to children when they are behaving correctly.
    c. punish children when they are misbehaving.
    d. reward children when they are misbehaving.

14. Project Pigeon relied on principles of
    a. classical conditioning.
    b. observational learning.
    c. operant conditioning.
    d. latent learning.

15. For observational learning to take place,
    a. stimuli must be paired repeatedly.
    b. a stimulus must elicit a response.
    c. an organism must be reinforced.
    d. an organism must observe another organism.

16. The text defines a stimulus as
    a. a change in the environment.
    b. a condition that evokes a response from an organism.
    c. any change that is learned.
    d. an environmental condition that evokes a response from an organism.

17. A parent encourages a reluctant child to enter the water of a swimming pool by hugging and petting the child and murmuring "It's really nice," "You'll love it." This method is most similar to the behavior-therapy technique of
    a. extinction.
    b. systematic desensitization.
    c. counterconditioning.
    d. flooding.

18. According to contingency theory, learning occurs because
    a. a conditioned stimulus indicates that the unconditioned stimulus is likely to ensue.
    b. stimuli are contiguous.
    c. of repeated trial and error.
    d. organisms observe the outcomes of the behaviors of other organisms and act when they expect that the reinforcement contingencies will be rewarding.

19. To demonstrate that people can learn conditioned responses that are presumably too small to perceive, Hefferline and Keenan conditioned subjects to engage in apparently imperceptible
    a. eye blinks.
    b. knee jerks.
    c. galvanic skin responses.
    d. thumb contractions.

20. An important way in which the learning of taste aversions differs from other kinds of classical conditioning is that
    a. often only one pairing of the stimuli is required.
    b. learning rapidly decays.
    c. taste aversions are arbitrary, whereas other kinds of conditioning are adaptive.
    d. there is no reward for learning.

ANSWER KEY TO POSTTEST

1. C	4. B	7. A	10. B	13. B	16. D	19. D
2. A	5. C	8. D	11. B	14. C	17. C	20. A
3. C	6. B	9. D	12. A	15. D	18. A	

Memory

LEARNING OBJECTIVES

When you have finished studying Chapter 7, you should be able to:

THREE KINDS OF MEMORY
1. Describe three kinds of memory.

THREE PROCESSES OF MEMORY
2. Describe three processes of memory.

THREE STAGES OF MEMORY
3. Describe the functioning of sensory memory, short-term memory, and long-term memory.

THE LEVELS-OF-PROCESSING MODEL OF MEMORY
4. Describe the levels-of-processing model of memory.

FORGETTING
5. Explain the types of memory tasks that are used in measuring forgetting.
6. Explain the role of interference theory in forgetting.
7. Describe various kinds of amnesia.

METHODS FOR IMPROVING MEMORY
8. Describe some methods for improving memory.

THE BIOLOGY OF MEMORY
9. Describe aspects of the biology of memory.

PRETEST *Truth or Fiction?*

____ Some people have photographic memories.

____ It may be easier for you to recall the name of your first-grade teacher than of someone you just met at a party.

____ All of our experiences are permanently imprinted on the brain so that proper stimulation can cause us to remember them exactly.

____ There is no practical limit to the amount of information you can store in your memory.

____ Learning must be meaningful if we are to remember it.

____ We can remember important events that take place during the first 2 years.

____ You can use tricks to improve your memory.

____ Alzheimer's disease is a normal aspect of the aging process.

MY oldest daughter Jill was talking about how she had run into a friend from elementary school and how they had had a splendid time recalling the goofy things they had done. Her sister Allyn, age 6 at the time, was not to be outdone. "I can remember when I was born," she put in.

The family's ears perked up. Being a psychologist, I knew exactly what to say. "You can remember when you were born?" I said.

"Oh, yes," she insisted. "Mommy was there."

So far she could not be faulted. I cheered her on, and she elaborated a remarkably meticulous account of how it had been snowing in the wee hours of a bitter December morning when Mommy had to go to the hospital. You see, she said, her memory was so good that she could also summon up what it had been like *before* she was born. She wove a wonderful patchwork quilt, integrating details we had given her with her own recollections of the events surrounding the delivery of her younger sister, Jordan. All in all, she seemed quite satisfied that she had pieced together a faithful portrait of her arrival on the world stage.

Later in the chapter, we shall see that children usually cannot recall events prior to the age of 2 years, much less those of the first hours. But Allyn's tale dramatized the way in which we "remember" many of the things that have happened to us. When it comes to long-term memories, truth can take a back seat to drama and embellishment. Very often, our memories are like the bride's apparel—there's something old, something new, something borrowed, and, from time to time, something blue.

Memory is what this chapter is about. Without memory, there is no past. Without memory, experience is trivial and learning cannot abide. We shall soon contemplate what psychologists have learned about the ways in which we remember things, but first try to meet the following challenges to your memory.

FIVE CHALLENGES TO MEMORY

Before we go any further, let's test your memory. If you want to participate, find four sheets of blank paper and number them 1 through 4. Then follow the directions given below.

1. Following are 10 letters. Look at them for 15 seconds. Later in the chapter, I shall ask you if you can write them on sheet number 1. (No cheating! Don't do it now.)

   THUNSTOFAM

2. Look at these nine figures for 30 seconds. Then try to draw them in the proper sequence on sheet number 2. (Yes, right after you've finished looking at them. We'll talk about your drawings later.)

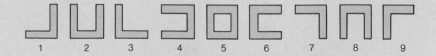

3. Okay, here's another list of letters, 17 this time. Look at the list for 60 seconds and then see whether you can reproduce it on sheet number 3. (I'm being generous this time—a full minute.)

   GMC-BSI-BMA-TTC-IAF-BI

4. Which of these pennies is an accurate reproduction of the Lincoln penny you see every day? This time there's nothing to draw on another sheet; just circle or put a checkmark by the penny you think resembles the ones you throw in the back of the drawer.

5. Examine the following drawings for 1 minute. Then copy the names of the figures on sheet number 4. When you're finished, keep reading. Soon I'll be asking you to draw those figures.

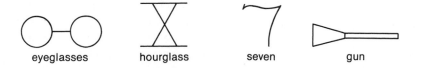

THREE KINDS OF MEMORY

Memories contain different kinds of information. Endel Tulving (1985, 1991) classifies memories according to the kind of material they hold. Return to Allyn's "recollection." Of course Allyn could not really remember her own birth. That is, she could not recall the particular event in which she had participated.

Episodic Memory

Memories of the events that happen to a person or take place in the person's presence are referred to as **episodic memory.** Your memory of what you ate for breakfast and of what your professor said in class this afternoon are examples of episodic memory.

What Allyn did recount is more accurately characterized as generalized knowledge than as visions of that important event in her young life. From listening to her parents, and from her personal experience with the events surrounding Jordan's birth, Allyn had gained extensive knowledge of what happens during childbirth. She had erroneously represented this knowledge as a precise portrayal of her birth.

Semantic Memory

Generalized knowledge is referred to as **semantic memory.** *Semantics* concerns meanings, and Allyn was reporting her understanding of the meaning of childbirth rather than an episode in her own life. You "remember" that the United States has 50 states without necessarily visiting all of them and personally adding them up. You "remember" who authored *Hamlet,* although you were not looking over Shakespeare's shoulder as he did so. These, too, are examples of semantic memory.

Your future recollection that there are three kinds of memory is more likely to be semantic than episodic. In other words, you are more likely to "know"

Episodic memory • Memories of events experienced by a person or that take place in the person's presence.

Semantic memory • General knowledge as opposed to episodic memory.

that there are three types of memory than to recall the date on which you learned about them, exactly where you were and how you were sitting, and whether or not you were also thinking about dinner at the time. We tend to use the phrase "I remember . . ." when we are referring to episodic memories, as in "I *remember* the blizzard of 1988." But we are more likely to say, "I know . . ." in reference to semantic memories, as in "I *know* about—" (or, "I heard about—") "—the blizzard of 1888." Put it another way: You may *remember* that you wrote your mother, but you *know* that Shakespeare wrote *Hamlet.*

Procedural Memory

The third type of memory is **procedural memory,** also referred to as *skill memory.* Procedural memory involves knowledge of how to do things. You have learned and "remember" how to ride a bicycle, how to swim or swing a bat, how to type (or in the case of my hunting and pecking, the approximate location of the keyboard keys), how to turn the lights on and off, and how to drive a car. Procedural memories tend to persevere even when we have not used them for many, many years. For example, it is said that we never forget how to ride a bicycle. On the other hand, procedural memories may concern skills that we cannot readily describe in words. Would you be able to explain to another person just how you manage to keep from falling when you ride a

Procedural memory • Knowledge of ways of doing things; skill memory.

Procedural Memory. Procedural memory—also referred to as skill memory—involves knowledge of how to do things. Memories of how to ride a bicycle, how to type, how to turn on and off the lights, and how to drive a car are procedural memories. Procedural memories tend to persevere even when we have not used them for many years. Here, the older developmental psychologist Jean Piaget demonstrates that we may never forget how to ride a bicycle.

bike? When you're teaching someone how to use a manual shift car, do you stick to words, or do you move your arm both to remember and to illustrate the technique?

Do you think it would help for a person to have "ESP" to remember the three types of memory? That is, E = episodic, S = semantic, and P = procedural. As we proceed, we shall see that a good deal of information about memory comes in threes. We shall also learn more about **mnemonic devices,** such as "ESP." By the way, is your use of the **acronym** *ESP* to help remember the kinds of memory an instance of episodic, semantic, or procedural memory?

Reflections

- You remember that classes have professors, and you remember your professor's name (I hope). Which of these is an episodic memory? Which is a semantic memory? Explain the difference between the two.
- **Agree or disagree with the following statement and support your answer: "You never forget how to ride a bicycle."**

Before proceeding to the next section, why don't you turn to that piece of paper on which you wrote the names of the four figures—that is, sheet number 4—and draw them from memory as exactly as you can. Then hold on to the drawings, and we'll talk about them a bit later.

Mnemonic devices • Systems for remembering in which items are related to easily recalled sets of symbols such as acronyms, phrases, or jingles.

Acronym • A word that is composed of the first letters of the elements of a phrase.

Encoding • Modifying information so that it can be placed in memory. The first stage of information processing.

Visual code • Mental representation of information as a picture.

THREE PROCESSES OF MEMORY

Psychologists and computer scientists both speak in terms of the processing of information. Think of using a computer to write a term paper. Once the system is operating, you begin to type in information. You place information into the computer's memory by typing letters on a keyboard. If you were to practice grisly surgery on your computer (which I am often tempted to do) and open up its memory, however, you wouldn't find these letters inside. This is because the computer is programmed to change the letters, the information you have typed, into a form that can be placed in its electronic memory. Similarly, when we perceive information, we must convert it into a form that can be remembered if we are to place it in memory.

Encoding

The first stage of information processing, or changing information so that we can place it in memory, is called **encoding.** Information about the world outside reaches our senses as physical and chemical stimulation. When we encode this information, we convert it into psychological formats that can be mentally represented. To do so, we commonly use visual, auditory, and semantic codes.

 **MINILECTURE: ENCODING, STORAGE, AND RETRIEVAL**

Let us illustrate the uses of coding by referring to the list of letters you first saw in the box on challenges to memory. Try to write the letters down now on sheet number 1, and then we'll talk about them. Go on, take a minute, and then come back.

Okay, now: If you had used a **visual code** to try to remember the list, you would have mentally represented it as a picture. That is, you would have maintained—or attempted to maintain—a mental image of the letters. Some artists and art historians seem to maintain marvelous visual mental representations of works of art, so that they recognize at once whether a work is authentic.

You may also have decided to read the list of letters to yourself—that is, to silently say them in sequence: "t," "h," "u," and so on. By so doing, you would have been using an **acoustic code,** or representing the stimuli as a sequence of sounds. You may also have read the list as a three-syllable word, "thun-sto-fam." This is an acoustic code, but it also involves the "meaning" of the letters, in the sense that you are interpreting the list as a word. And so this approach has elements of a semantic code.

Semantic codes represent stimuli in terms of their meaning. How can you use a semantic code to help remember the three colors blue, yellow, and gray? You may recall from Chapter 4 that blue and yellow are complementary, and when we mix lights of complementary colors we attain gray. Using this relationship among the colors to remember them lends the grouping meaning and, for this reason, is an example of a semantic code.

Our 10 letters were meaningless in and of themselves. However, they can also serve as an acronym for the familiar phrase "THe UNited STates OF AMerica," an observation that lends them meaning.

Acoustic code • Mental representation of information as a sequence of sounds.

Semantic code • Mental representation of information according to its meaning.

Storage • The maintenance of information over time. The second stage of information processing.

Maintenance rehearsal • Mental repetition of information in order to keep it in memory.

Metamemory • Self-awareness of the ways in which memory functions, allowing the person to encode, store, and retrieve information effectively.

Retrieval • The location of stored information and its return to consciousness. The third stage of information processing.

Storage

The second process of memory is **storage,** or the maintenance of information over time. If you were given the task of storing the list of letters (told to remember it), how would you attempt to place it in storage? One way would be by **maintenance rehearsal**—by mentally repeating the list, or saying it to yourself. Our awareness of the functioning of our memory, referred to by psychologists as **metamemory,** becomes more sophisticated as we develop.

You could also have condensed the amount of information you were rehearsing by reading the list as a three-syllable word; that is, you could have rehearsed three syllables rather than 10 letters. In either case, repetition would have been the key to memory. (We'll talk more about condensing, or "chunking," very soon.) However, if you had encoded the list semantically, as an acronym for "The United States of America," storage might have been instantaneous and permanent, as we shall see.

Retrieval

The third memory process is **retrieval,** or locating stored information and returning it to consciousness. With well-known information such as our names and occupations, retrieval is effortless and, for all practical purposes, immediate. But when we are trying to remember massive quantities of information, or information that is not perfectly understood, retrieval can be tedious and not always successful. To retrieve stored information in a computer, we need to know the name of the file. Similarly, retrieval of information from our memories requires knowledge of the proper cues.

If you had encoded THUNSTOFAM as a three-syllable word, your retrieval strategy would involve recollection of the word and rules of decoding. In other words, you would say the "word" *thun-sto-fam* and then decode it by spelling it out. You might err in that "thun" sounds like "thumb" and "sto" could also be spelled "stow." Using the semantic code, or recognition of the acronym for "The United States of America," could lead to flawless recollection, however.

I stuck my neck out by predicting that you would immediately and permanently store the list if you recognized it as an acronym. Here, too, there would be recollection (of the name of our country) and decoding rules. That is, to "remember" the 10 letters, you would have to envision the phrase and read off the first two letters of each word. Since using this semantic code is more complex than simply seeing the entire list (using a visual code), it may take a while to recall (actually, to reconstruct) the list of 10 letters. But by using the phrase, you are likely to remember the list of letters perpetually and flawlessly.

Now, what if you were not able to remember the list of 10 letters? What would have gone wrong? In terms of the three processes of memory, it could be that you had (1) not encoded the list in a useful way, (2) not entered the encoded information into storage, or (3) stored the information but lacked the proper cues for remembering it—such as the phrase "The United States of America" or the rule for decoding the phrase.

You may have noticed, now that we have been drawn well into the chapter, that I have discussed three kinds of memory and three processes of memory, but I have not yet *defined* memory. No apologies—we weren't ready. Now that we have explored some basic concepts, let us have a try: **Memory** is defined as the processes by which information is encoded, stored, and retrieved.

Reflections

- Consider this list of letters: THUNSTOFAM. Think of two strategies for storing the list. What are the different strategies called?
- Consider the two words *receive* and *retrieve*. How do you remember how to spell them? (That is, how do you retrieve the proper sequences of letters from your memory?)

Now let us turn our attention to two psychological models of memory—memory as stages and memory as levels of processing information.

Memory • The processes by which information is encoded, stored, and retrieved.

THREE STAGES OF MEMORY

Before the turn of the century, William James was intrigued by the fact that some memories were unreliable, "going in one ear and out the other." Others could be recalled for a lifetime:

The stream of thought flows on, but most of its elements fall into the bottomless pit of oblivion. Of some, no element survives the instant of their passage. Of others, it is confined to a few moments, hours, or days. Others, again, leave vestiges which are indestructible, and by means of which they may be recalled as long as life endures.

WILLIAM JAMES

Yes, the world is a constant display of sights and sounds and other sources of sensory stimulation, but only some of these things are remembered. James observed correctly that we remember various "elements of thought" for different lengths of time and many not at all. Atkinson and Shiffrin (1968) propose that there are three stages of information processing and that the progress of information through these stages determines whether (and how long) it will be retained (see Figure 7.1). These stages are sensory memory, short-term memory (STM), and long-term memory (LTM). Let us try to make *sense* of the *short* and the *long* of memory.

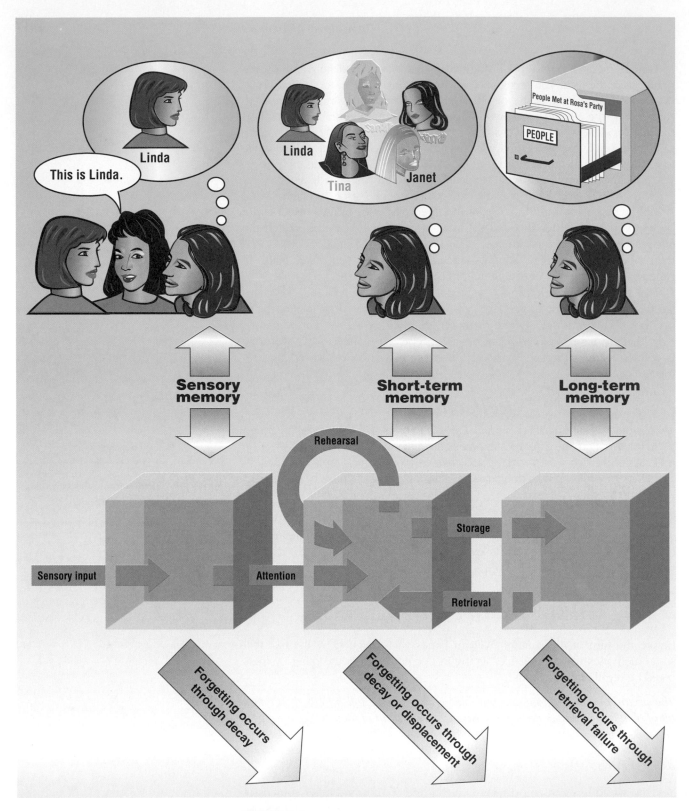

FIGURE 7.1

Three Stages of Memory. A number of psychologists hypothesize that there are three distinct stages of memory. Sensory information impacts upon the registers of sensory memory, where memory traces are held briefly before decaying. If we attend to the information, much of it is transferred to short-term memory (STM). Information in STM may decay or be displaced if it is not transferred to long-term memory (LTM). We usually use rehearsal to transfer memories to LTM. Once in LTM, memories may be retrieved through appropriate search strategies. But if information is organized poorly, or if we cannot find cues to retrieve it, it may be lost.

Sensory Memory

Consciousness . . . does not appear to itself chopped up in bits. A "river" or a "stream" are the metaphors by which it is most naturally described. In talking of it hereafter, let us call it the stream of thought, of consciousness, or of subjective life.

WILLIAM JAMES

So William James wrote of the stream of thought, or of consciousness. When we look at a visual stimulus, our impressions may seem fluid enough. Actually, they consist of a series of eye fixations referred to as **saccadic eye movement.** These movements jump from one point to another about four times each second. Yet, the visual sensations seem continuous, or streamlike, because of **sensory memory.** Sensory memory is the type or stage of memory first encountered by a stimulus. Although it holds impressions briefly, it is long enough so that series of perceptions seem to be connected.

Return to our example of the list of letters: THUNSTOFAM. If the list were flashed on a screen for a fraction of a second, the visual impression, or **memory trace,** of the stimulus would also last for only a fraction of a second afterward. Psychologists speak of the memory trace of the list as being held in a visual **sensory register**. Sensory memory, in other words, consists of registers that can briefly hold information that is entered by means of our senses.

If the letters had been flashed on a screen for, say, 1/10th of a second, your ability to remember them on the basis of sensory memory alone would be meager. Your memory would be based on a single eye fixation, and the trace of the image would vanish before a single second had passed. At the turn of the century, the social psychologist William McDougall (1904) engaged in research in which he showed study participants 1 to 12 letters arranged in rows—just long enough to allow a single eye fixation. Under these conditions, participants could typically remember only four or five letters. Thus, recollection of THUNSTOFAM, a list of 10 letters arranged into a single row, would probably depend on whether one had successfully transformed or encoded it into a form in which it could be processed by further stages of memory.

George Sperling (1960) modified McDougall's experimental method and showed that there is a difference between what people can see and what they can report. McDougall had used a *whole-report procedure,* in which participants were asked to report every letter seen in the array. Sperling used a modified *partial-report procedure,* in which participants were asked to report the contents of one of three rows of letters. In a typical procedure, Sperling flashed three rows of letters like those that follow on a screen for 50 milliseconds (1/20th of a second):

A G R E

V L S B

N K B T

Using the whole-report procedure, participants could report an average of four letters from the entire display (one out of three). But if Sperling pointed an arrow immediately after presentation at a row he wanted viewers to report, they usually reported most of the letters in the row successfully.

If Sperling presented six letters arrayed in two rows, participants could usually report either row without error. If participants were flashed three rows of 4 letters each—a total of 12—they reported correctly an average of 3 of 4 of the designated row, suggesting that about 9 letters of the 12 had been perceived.

Sperling found that the amount of time that elapsed before indicating the row to be reported was crucial. If he delayed pointing the arrow for a few fractions of a second after the display, participants were less successful in reporting the target row. If he allowed a full second to elapse, the arrow did not

MINILECTURE: SACCADIC EYE MOVEMENTS

Saccadic eye movement • The rapid jumps made by a person's eyes as they fixate on different points.

Sensory memory • The type or stage of memory first encountered by a stimulus. Sensory memory holds impressions briefly, but long enough so that series of perceptions are psychologically continuous.

Memory trace • An assumed change in the nervous system that reflects the impression made by a stimulus. Memory traces are said to be "held" in sensory registers.

Sensory register • A system of memory that holds information briefly, but long enough so that it can be processed further. There may be a sensory register for every sense.

MINILECTURE: SPERLING'S EXPERIMENTS

aid recall at all. From these data, Sperling concluded that the memory trace of visual stimuli *decays* within a second in the visual sensory register (see Figure 7.1). With a single eye fixation, participants can *see* most of a display of 12 letters clearly, as shown by their ability to immediately read off most of the letters in a designated row. Yet, as the fractions of a single second are elapsing, the memory trace of the letters is fading. By the time a second has elapsed, the trace has vanished.

ICONIC MEMORY.   Psychologists believe there is a sensory register for each one of our senses. The mental representations of visual stimuli are referred to as **icons.** The sensory register that holds icons is labeled **iconic memory.** Iconic memories are accurate, photographic memories. So those of us who can see—who mentally represent visual stimuli—have "photographic memories." However, they are very brief. What most of us normally think of as a photographic memory—the ability to retain exact mental representations of visual stimuli over long periods of time—is referred to by psychologists as *eidetic imagery*.

EIDETIC IMAGERY.   Visual stimuli, or icons, persist for remarkably long periods of time among a few individuals. About 5% of children can look at a detailed picture, turn away, and several minutes later recall the particulars of the picture with exceptional clarity—as if they were still viewing it. This extraordinary visual memory is referred to as **eidetic imagery** (Haber, 1980). Among the minority of children who have this ability, it declines with age, all but disappearing by adolescence.

Figure 7.2 provides an example of a test of eidetic imagery. Children are asked to look at the first drawing in the series for 20 to 30 seconds, after which it is removed. The children then continue to gaze at a neutral background.

Icon • A mental representation of a visual stimulus that is held briefly in sensory memory.
Iconic memory • The sensory register that briefly holds mental representations of visual stimuli.
Eidetic imagery • The maintenance of detailed visual memories over several minutes.

FIGURE 7.2

A Research Strategy for Assessing Eidetic Imagery. Children look at the first drawing for 20 to 30 seconds, after which it is removed. Next, the children look at a neutral background for several minutes. They are then shown the second drawing. When asked what they see, children with the capacity for eidetic imagery report seeing a face. The face is seen only by children who retain the first image and fuse it with the second, thus perceiving the third image.

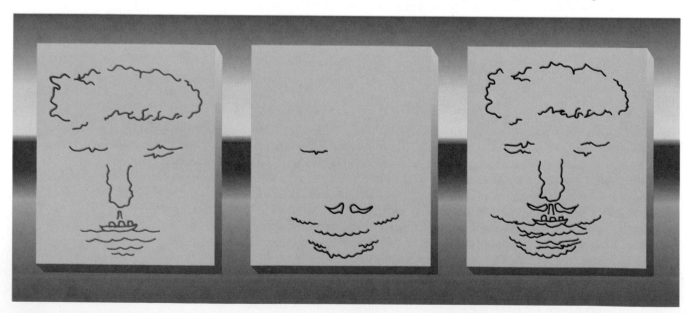

Several minutes later, the drawing in the center is placed on the backdrop. When asked what they see, many report "a face." A face would be seen only if the children had retained a clear image of the first picture and fused it with the second so that they are, in effect, perceiving the third picture in Figure 7.2 (Haber, 1980).

Eidetic imagery appears remarkably clear and detailed. It seems to be essentially a perceptual phenomenon in which coding is not a factor.

Truth or Fiction Revisited. *It is true that some people have photographic memories.* Those of us who can see have what is actually defined as *photographic*, or *iconic*, memories. However, only a few of us have *eidetic imagery*, which is closer to what lay people think of as "photographic memory." Although eidetic imagery is rare, iconic memory, as we see in the following section, universally transforms visual perceptions into smoothly unfolding impressions of the world.

ICONIC MEMORY AND SACCADIC EYE MOVEMENTS: SMOOTHING OUT THE BUMPS IN THE VISUAL RIDE.   Saccadic eye movements occur about four times every second. Iconic memory, however, holds icons for up to a second. As a consequence, the flow of visual information seems smooth and continuous. Your impression that the words you are reading flow across the page, rather than jump across in spurts, is a product of your iconic memory. Similarly, you may recall from Chapter 4 that motion pictures present 16 to 22 separate frames, or still images, each second. Iconic memory allows you to perceive the imagery as being seamless (Loftus, 1983).

ECHOIC MEMORY.   The mental representations of sounds, or auditory stimuli, are called **echoes.** The sensory register that holds echoes is referred to as **echoic memory.**

The memory traces of auditory stimuli (that is, echoes) can last for several seconds, many times longer than the traces of visual stimuli (icons). The difference in the duration of traces is probably based on biological differences between the eye and ear. This difference is one of the reasons that acoustic codes aid in the retention of information that has been presented visually—or why saying the letters or syllables of THUNSTOFAM makes the list easier to remember.

Yet echoes, like icons, will fade with the passage of time. If they are to be retained, we must pay attention to them. By selectively attending to certain stimuli, we sort them out from the background noise. For example, in studies on the development of patterns of processing information, young children have been shown photographs of rooms full of toys and then have been asked to recall as many as they can. One such study found that 2-year-old boys are more likely to attend to and remember toys such as cars, puzzles, and trains. Two-year-old girls are more likely to attend to and remember dolls, dishes, and teddy bears (Renninger & Wozniak, 1985). Even by this early age, children's patterns of attention have frequently fallen into stereotypical configurations.

Short-Term Memory

Working memory is the mental glue that links a thought through time from its beginning to its end.
                                              PATRICIA GOLDMAN-RAKIC (1995)

If you focus attention on a stimulus in the sensory register, you will tend to retain it in **short-term memory**—also referred to as **working memory**—for a minute or so after the trace of the stimulus decays (Baddeley, 1994). When

---

Echo • A mental representation of an auditory stimulus (sound) that is held briefly in sensory memory.

Echoic memory • The sensory register that briefly holds mental representations of auditory stimuli.

Short-term memory • The type or stage of memory that can hold information for up to a minute or so after the trace of the stimulus decays. Also called *working memory*.

Working memory • Same as *short-term memory*.

you are given a phone number by the information operator and then write it down or dial the number, you are retaining the number in your short-term memory. When you are told the name of someone at a party and then use that name immediately in addressing the person, you are retaining the name in short-term memory. In short-term memory, the image tends to fade significantly after 10 to 12 seconds if it is not repeated or rehearsed. It is possible to focus on maintaining a visual image in the short-term memory, but it is more common to encode visual stimuli as sounds, or auditory stimulation. Then the sounds can be rehearsed, or repeated.

As noted, most of us know that a way of retaining information in short-term memory—and possibly storing it permanently—is to rehearse it. When an information operator tells me a phone number, I usually rehearse it continuously while I am dialing it or running around frantically searching for a pencil and a scrap of paper. Most of us also know that the more times we rehearse information, the more likely we are to remember it. We have the capacity (if not the will or the time) to rehearse information and thereby keep it in short-term memory indefinitely.

ENCODING. Let us now return to the task of remembering the first list of letters in my challenge to memory. If you had coded the letters as the three-syllable word THUN-STO-FAM, you would probably have recalled them by mentally rehearsing (saying to yourself) the three-syllable "word" and then spelling it out from the sounds. A few minutes later, if someone asked whether the letters had been uppercase (THUNSTOFAM) or lowercase (thunstofam), you might not have been confident of an answer. You had used an acoustic code to help recall the list, and uppercase and lowercase letters sound alike.

Because it can be pronounced, THUNSTOFAM is not too difficult to retain in short-term memory. But what if the list of letters had been TBXLFNTSDK? This list of letters cannot be pronounced as it is. You would have had to find a complex acronym to code these letters, and within a fraction of a second—most likely an impossible task. To aid recall, you would probably have chosen to try to repeat or rehearse the letters rapidly—to read each one as many times as possible before the memory trace faded. You might have visualized each letter as you said it and tried to get back to it (that is, to run through the entire list) before it decayed.

Let us assume that you encoded the letters as sounds and then rehearsed the sounds. When asked to report the list, you might mistakenly say T-V-X-L-F-N-T-S-T-K. This would be an understandable error because the incorrect *V* and *T* sounds are similar, respectively, to the correct *B* and *D* sounds.

THE SERIAL-POSITION EFFECT. Note that you would also be likely to recall the first and last letters in the series, *T* and *K,* more accurately than the others. Why? The tendency to recall more accurately the first and last items in a series is known as the **serial-position effect.** This effect may occur because we pay more attention to the first and last stimuli in a series. They serve as the visual or auditory boundaries for the other stimuli. It may also be that the first items are likely to be rehearsed more frequently (repeated more times) than other items. The last items are likely to have been rehearsed most recently and so are most likely to be retained in short-term memory.

According to cognitive psychologists, the tendency to recall the initial items in a list is referred to as the **primacy effect.** In Chapter 16, we shall see that social psychologists also note a powerful primacy effect in our formation of impressions of other people. In other words, first impressions tend to last. The tendency to recall the last items in a list is referred to as the **recency effect.** As

---

Serial-position effect • The tendency to recall more accurately the first and last items in a series.

Primacy effect • The tendency to recall the initial items in a series of items.

Recency effect • The tendency to recall the last items in a series of items.

noted, if we are asked to recall the last items in a list soon after we have been shown the list, they may still be in short-term memory. As a result, they can be "read off." Earlier items, in contrast, may have to be retrieved from long-term memory.

CHUNKS OF INFORMATION: IS SEVEN A MAGIC NUMBER OR DID THE PHONE COMPANY GET LUCKY?   Rapidly rehearsing 10 meaningless letters is not an easy task. With TBXLFNTSDK there are 10 discrete elements, or **chunks,** of information that must be kept in short-term memory. When we encode THUNSTOFAM as three syllables, there are only three chunks to swallow at once—a memory task that is much easier on the digestion.

Psychologist George Miller noted that the average person is comfortable with digesting about seven integers at a time, the number of integers in a telephone number. In an article appearing in *Psychological Review,* he wrote:

> My problem is that I have been persecuted by an integer. For seven years this number has followed me around, has intruded in my most private data, and has assaulted me from the pages of our most public journals (1956).

In public, yet. Most people have little trouble recalling five chunks of information, as in a ZIP code. Some can remember nine, which is, for all but a few, an upper limit. So seven chunks, plus or minus one or two, is the "magic" number.

So how, you ask, do we successfully include the area codes in our recollections of telephone numbers, hence making them 10 digits long? The truth of the matter is that we usually don't. We tend to recall the area code as a single chunk of information derived from our general knowledge of where a person lives. So we are more likely to remember (or "know") the 10-digit numbers of acquaintances who reside in locales with area codes we use frequently.

Businesses pay the phone company hefty premiums so that they can attain numbers with two or three zeroes—for example, 592-2000 or 614 3300. These numbers have fewer chunks of information and hence are easier to remember. Customer recollection of business phone numbers increases sales. One financial services company uses the toll-free number CALL-IRA, which reduces the task to two chunks of information that also happen to be meaningfully related (semantically coded) to the nature of the business. Similarly, a clinic in my area that helps people quit smoking arranged for a telephone number that can be reached by dialing the letters NO SMOKE.

Return for a moment to the third challenge to memory presented on page 262. Were you able to remember the six groups of letters? Would your task have been simpler if you had grouped them differently? How about moving the dashes forward by a letter, so that they read GM-CBS-IBM-ATT-CIA-FBI? We have exactly the same list of letters, but we suddenly have six chunks of information that can be coded semantically. You may have also been able to generate the list by remembering a rule, such as "big corporations and government agencies."

If we can recall seven or perhaps nine chunks of information, how, then, do children remember the alphabet? The alphabet contains 26 discrete pieces of information. How do children learn to encode the letters of the alphabet, presented visually, as spoken sounds? The 26 letters of the alphabet cannot be pronounced like a word or phrase—despite the existence of that impossible *Sesame Street* song, "Ab k'defkey jekyl m'nop kw'r stoov w'ksizz." There is nothing about the shape of an *A* that suggests its sound. Nor does the visual stimulus *B* sound "B-ish." Children learning the alphabet and learning to

Chunk • A stimulus or group of stimuli that are perceived as a discrete piece of information.

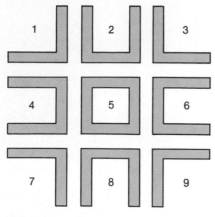

FIGURE 7.3

A Familiar Grid. The nine drawings in the second challenge to memory form this familiar tic-tac-toe grid when the numbers are placed inside them and they are arranged in numerical order, three shapes to a line. This method for recalling the shapes collapses nine chunks of information into two. One is the tic-tac-toe grid. The second is the rule for decoding the drawings from the grid.

Rote • Mechanical associative learning that is based on repetition.

Displace • In memory theory, to cause chunks of information to be lost from short-term memory by adding new items.

FIGURE 7.4

The Effect of Interference on Information in Short-Term Memory. In this experiment, college students were asked to maintain a series of three letters in their memories while they counted backward by threes from an arbitrary number. After just 3 seconds, retention was cut by half. Ability to recall the words was almost completely lost by 15 seconds.

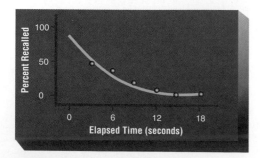

associate visually presented letters with their spoken names do so by **rote.** It is mechanical associative learning that requires time and repetition. If you think that learning the alphabet by rote is a simple child's task, now that it is behind you, try learning the Russian or Hebrew alphabet.

Now, if you had recognized THUNSTOFAM as an acronym for the first two letters of each word in the phrase "THe UNited STates OF AMerica," you also would have reduced the number of chunks of information that had to be recalled. You could have considered the phrase to be a single chunk of information, and the rule that you must use the first two letters of each word of the phrase to be another chunk.

Reconsider the second challenge to memory on page 262. You were asked to remember nine chunks of visual information. Perhaps you could have used the acoustic codes "L" and "Square" for chunks three and five, but no obvious codes are available for the seven other chunks. Now look at Figure 7.3. If you had recognized that the elements in the challenge could be arranged as the familiar tic-tac-toe grid, remembering the nine elements might have required two chunks of information. The first would have been the mental image of the grid. The second would have been the rule for decoding: Each element corresponds to the shape of a section of the grid if read like words on a page (from upper left to lower right). The number sequence 1 through 9 would not in itself present a problem, because you learned this series by rote many years ago and have rehearsed it in countless calculations since.

INTERFERENCE IN SHORT-TERM MEMORY. I mentioned that I often find myself running around looking for a pencil and a scrap of paper to write down a telephone number that has been given to me. If I keep on rehearsing the number while I'm looking, I'm okay. But I have also cursed myself repeatedly for failing to keep a pad and pencil by the telephone, and sometimes the mental dressing down interferes with my recollection of the number. (The moral of the story? Avoid self-reproach.) It has also happened that I have actually looked up a phone number for myself and been about to dial it when someone has asked me for the time or where I said we were going to dinner. Unless I say, "Now hold on a minute!" and manage to jot down the number on something, it's back to the phone book. Attending to distracting information, even briefly, prevents me from rehearsing the number, so it falls between the cracks of my short-term memory.

In an experiment with college students, Lloyd and Margaret Peterson (1959) demonstrated how prevention of rehearsal can wreak havoc with short-term memory. They asked students to remember three-letter combinations, such as HGB—normally, three easy chunks of information. They then had the students count backward from an arbitrary number, such as 181, by threes (that is, 181, 178, 175, 172, and so on). The students were told to stop counting and to report the letter sequence after the passage of the intervals of time shown in Figure 7.4. The percentage of letter combinations recalled correctly fell precipitously within seconds. After 18 seconds of interference, counting had dislodged the letter sequences in almost all of these bright young students' memories.

Psychologists say that the appearance of new information in short-term memory **displaces** the old information. Remember: Only a few bits of information at a time can be retained in short-term memory. Klatzky (1980) likens short-term memory to a shelf or workbench. Once it is full, some things fall off when new items are shoved on. Here, we have another possible explanation for the recency effect: The most recently learned bit of information is least likely to be displaced by additional information.

Displacement. Information can be lost to short-term memory by means of displacement. We may have little trouble remembering the names of the first one or two people we meet at a party. But as introductions continue, new names may displace the old, and we may forget the names of people we met only a few minutes earlier.

Displacement occurs at cocktail parties, and I'm not referring to the jostling of one's body by others in the crowd. The point is this: When you meet Jennifer or Jonathan at the party, there should be little trouble remembering the name. But then you may meet Tamara or Timothy and, still later, Stephanie or Steven. By that time you may have a hard time dredging up Jennifer or Jonathan—unless, of course, you were very, very attracted to one of them. A passionate response would set that person apart and inspire a good deal of selective attention. Recall signal-detection theory from Chapter 4: If you were enamored enough, you would probably detect the person's name (sensory signals) with a vengeance. Perhaps all the ensuing names would dissolve into background noise.

Truth or Fiction Revisited. *It is true that it may be easier for you to recall the name of your first-grade teacher than of someone you just met at a party.* Your first-grade teacher's name is stored in long-term memory. However, you may be juggling your new acquaintance's name with many others in short-term memory.

Long-Term Memory

Long-term memory is the third stage of processing of information. Think of your long-term memory as a vast storehouse of information containing names, dates, places, what Johnny did to you in second grade, and what Susan said about you when you were 12.

Some psychologists (Sigmund Freud was one) used to believe that nearly all of our perceptions and ideas were stored permanently. Of course, we might not be able to retrieve all of them, but such memories might be "lost" because of the unavailability of the proper cues, or they might be kept beneath the surface of conscious awareness by the forces of **repression.** Adherents to this view often pointed to the work of neurosurgeon Wilder Penfield (1969). Many of Penfield's patients reported the appearance of images that had something of the feel of memories, when parts of their brains were electrically stimulated.

**MINILECTURE:
THE CAPACITY OF
SHORT-TERM MEMORY**

Long-term memory • The type or stage of memory capable of relatively permanent storage.
Repression • In Freud's psychodynamic theory, the ejection of anxiety-evoking ideas from conscious awareness.

Today, most psychologists view this notion as being exaggerated. Memory researcher Elizabeth Loftus, for example, notes that the "memories" stimulated by Penfield's probes were impoverished in detail and not necessarily factual (Loftus & Loftus, 1980; Loftus, 1983).

Truth or Fiction Revisited. *It is not true that all of our experiences are permanently imprinted on the brain so that proper stimulation can cause us to remember them exactly.* Our memories are limited by such factors as the attention we pay to events (selective attention) and our inability to capture all of their details. Evidence is far from compelling that we store all of our experiences. To the contrary, we appear to be more likely to store incidents that have a greater impact on us—events more laden with personal meaning.

Now let us consider some important questions about long-term memory.

HOW ACCURATE ARE LONG-TERM MEMORIES?—MEMORY AS RECONSTRUCTIVE.

Elizabeth Loftus notes that memories are distorted by our biases and needs—by the ways in which we conceptualize our worlds. Cognitive psychologists speak of much of our knowledge of the world as being represented in terms of **schemas.**

To understand better what is meant by *schema,* consider the problems of travelers who met up with the legendary highwayman of ancient Greece, Procrustes. Procrustes had a quirk. He was interested not only in travelers' pocketbooks but also in their height. He had a concept—a schema—of just how tall people should be, and when people did not fit his schema, they were in for it. You see, Procrustes also had a very famous bed, a bed that comes down to us in history as a "Procrustean bed." He made his victims lie down in the bed, and when they were too short for it, he stretched them to make them fit. When they were too long for it, he is said to have practiced surgery on their legs. Many unfortunate passersby failed to survive.

Although the myth of Procrustes may sound absurd, it reflects a quirky truth about each of us. We all carry our cognitive Procrustean beds around with us—our unique ways of perceiving the world—and we try to make things and people fit.

Let me give you an example. Why don't you "retrieve" the fourth sheet of paper you prepared according to the instructions for the challenges to memory. The labels you wrote on the sheet will remind you of the figures. Please take a minute or two to draw them now. Then continue reading.

Now that you made your drawings, turn to Figure 7.5 on page 277. Are your drawings closer in form to those in Group 1 or those in Group 2? I wouldn't be surprised if they were more like those in Group 1. After all, they were labeled like the drawings in Group 1. The labels serve as *schemas* for the drawings—ways of organizing your knowledge of them—and these schemas may have influenced your recollections.

Consider another example of the power of schemas in processing information. Loftus and Palmer (1974) showed people a film of a car crash and then asked them to fill out questionnaires that included a question about how fast the cars were going at the time. The language of the question varied subtly, however. Some people were asked to estimate how fast the cars were going when they "hit" one another. Others were asked to estimate their speed when they "smashed" into one another. People who reconstructed the scene on the basis of the cue "hit" estimated a speed of 34 mph. People who watched the same film but reconstructed the scene on the basis of the cue "smashed" estimated a speed of 41 mph! In other words, the use of the word *hit* or *smash* caused people to organize their knowledge about the crash in different ways.

Schema • A way of mentally representing the world, such as a belief or an expectation, that can influence perception of persons, objects, and situations.

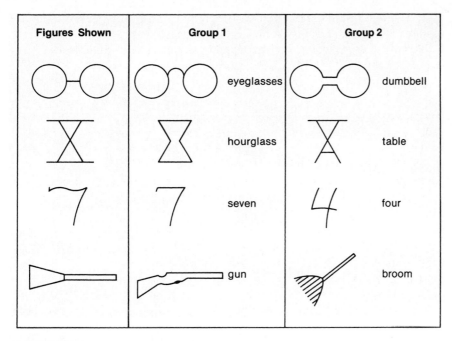

FIGURE 7.5

Memory as Reconstructive. In their classic experiment, Carmichael, Hogan, and Walter (1932) showed people the figures in the left-hand box and made remarks of the sort suggested in the other boxes. For example, the experimenter might say, "This drawing looks like eyeglasses [or a dumbbell]." When study participants later reconstructed the drawings, it was clear that they had been influenced by the experimenters' labels.

That is, the words served as diverse schemas that fostered the development of very different ways of processing information about the crash.

Participants in the same study were questioned again a week later: "Did you see any broken glass?" Since there was no broken glass shown in the film, positive replies were errors. Of those who had earlier been encouraged to process information about the accident in terms of one car "hitting" the other, 14% incorrectly answered yes. But 32% of those who had processed information about the crash in terms of one car "smashing" the other reported, incorrectly, that they had seen broken glass.

Findings such as these have important implications for eyewitness testimony.

LONG-TERM MEMORY AND EYEWITNESS TESTIMONY.   Jean Piaget, the famed investigator of children's cognitive development, distinctly remembered an attempt to kidnap him from his baby carriage along the Champs Élysées. He recalled the excited throng, the abrasions on the face of the nurse who rescued him, the police officer's white baton, and the flight of the assailant. Although graphic, Piaget's memories were false. Years later, the nurse confessed she had concocted the tale.

Nearly 80,000 U.S. trials each year rely on eyewitness testimony (Goleman, 1995a). Lawyers, judges, and other legal professionals are therefore concerned about the accuracy of our memories. As noted by psychologist Elizabeth Loftus (1993b), misidentifications of suspects "create a double horror: The wrong person is devastated by this personal tragedy, and the real criminal is still out on

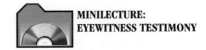

**MINILECTURE:
EYEWITNESS TESTIMONY**

How Fast Were These Cars Going When They Collided? Our schemas influence our processing of information. When shown pictures such as these, people who were asked how fast the cars were going when they *smashed* into one another offer higher estimates than people told they *hit* one another.

the streets" (p. 550). Is there reason to believe that the statements of eyewitnesses are any more factual than Piaget's?

There is cause for concern. The words chosen by an experimenter—and those chosen by a lawyer interrogating a witness—influence the reconstruction of memories (Loftus & Palmer, 1973). For example, an attorney for the plaintiff might ask the witness, "How fast was the defendant's car going when it *smashed into* the plaintiff's car?" In such a case, the car might be reported as going faster than if the question had been: "How fast was the defendant's car going when it hit the plaintiff's car?" Could the attorney for the defendant claim that use of the word *smashed* biased the witness? What of the jury who heard the word *smashed?* Would they not be biased toward assuming that the driver had been reckless?

Children tend to be more suggestible witnesses than adults, and preschoolers are more suggestible than older children (Ceci & Bruck, 1993). On the other hand, when questioned properly, even young children may be able to provide accurate and useful testimony (Ceci & Bruck, 1993).

There are cases in which the memories of eyewitnesses have been "refreshed" by hypnosis. Sad to say, hypnosis does more than amplify memories; it can also distort them (Loftus, 1994). One problem is that witnesses may accept and embellish suggestions made by the hypnotist. Another is that imagined events can seem as authentic as true events, but hypnotized people may report fantasized occurrences as compellingly as if they were real (Loftus, 1994).

There are also problems concerning the identification of criminals. For one thing, witnesses may pay more attention to the suspect's clothing than to more meaningful characteristics such as facial features, height, and weight. In one experiment, viewers of a videotaped crime incorrectly identified a man as the criminal because he wore the eyeglasses and T-shirt that had been worn by the perpetrator on the tape. The man who actually committed the crime was identified less often (Sanders, 1984).

Some other problems with eyewitness testimony:

- Identification of suspects is less accurate when suspects belong to ethnic or racial groups that differ from the witness's (Egeth, 1993).
- Identification of suspects is confused when interrogators make misleading suggestions (Lindsay & Johnson, 1989).
- Witnesses are perceived as more credible when they claim to be certain in their testimony (Wells, 1993), but there is little evidence that such claims are accurate.

As you can see, those in the legal profession are faced with a dilemma. It is recognized that our memories are distorted by our schemas—that is, the ways in which we organize experience. The ways in which we are questioned can color our recollections. And perhaps we do not pay as much attention as we should to fixed characteristics when we are trying to identify criminals. Yet research suggests that it may be possible to enhance the accuracy of eyewitness testimony. For example:

- Testimony is likely to be more accurate, and suspects are more likely to be convicted, when independent witnesses corroborate each other's testimony (Leippe, 1985; Lindsay and others, 1986).
- The accuracy of eyewitness testimony can be increased when the questioner carefully depicts the setting of the crime (Cutler and others, 1987) and asks witnesses to describe what happened rather than pump them full of suggestions (Sanders & Chiu, 1988).

Eyewitness Testimony? How trustworthy is eyewitness testimony? Memories are reconstructive rather than photographic. The wording of questioners also influences the content of the memory. Attorneys are therefore sometimes instructed not to phrase questions that "lead" the witness.

- Witnesses who first view a "blank" police lineup (one that does not have a suspect) and make no identification are more likely to make accurate identifications in subsequent lineups that contain the culprit (Wells, 1993).
- Eyewitness identification is more accurate when police present suspects in sequence rather than showing suspects all at once in the same lineup (Wells, 1993).

In sum, eyewitness testimony has its problems. Yet there may be things that can be done to improve its accuracy (Wells, 1993; Wells & Luus, 1990). And what is the alternative? If we were to prevent witnesses from testifying, how many criminals would go free (Loftus, 1993b)?

HOW MUCH INFORMATION *CAN* BE STORED IN LONG-TERM MEMORY? The human ability to store information is practically unlimited (Goldman-Rakic, 1995). New information may replace older information in short-term memory, but there is no evidence that long-term memories are lost by displacement. Long-term memories may endure for years or a lifetime. Now and then, it may seem that we have forgotten, or "lost," a long-term memory such as the names of elementary or high school classmates. Yet, it may be that we cannot find the proper cues to help us retrieve them. If long-term memories are lost, they may be lost in the same way a misplaced object is lost. It is "lost" but we sense it is still somewhere in the room. It is lost but not eradicated or destroyed.

Truth or Fiction Revisited. *It is true that there is no practical limit to the amount of information you can store in your memory.* At least no limit has been discovered to date.

Elaborative rehearsal • A method for increasing retention of new information by relating it to information that is well known.

TRANSFERRING INFORMATION FROM SHORT-TERM TO LONG-TERM MEMORY. How is information transferred from short-term to long-term memory? By and large, the more often chunks of information are rehearsed, the more likely they are to be transferred to long-term memory (Rundus, 1971). We noted that repeating information over and over to prevent it from decaying or being displaced is termed *maintenance rehearsal*. Maintenance rehearsal does not attempt to give information meaning by linking it to past learning and is not considered an effective way to place information in permanent storage (Craik & Watkins, 1973).[1]

A more effective method is to make it more meaningful—or to purposefully relate new material to information that is already well known (Woloshyn and others, 1994). To better remember the components of levers, physics students might use seesaws, wheelbarrows, and oars as examples (Scruggs & Mastropieri, 1992). The nine chunks of information in our second challenge to memory were made easier to reconstruct once they were associated with the familiar tic-tac-toe grid in Figure 7.3. Relating new material to well-known material is known as **elaborative rehearsal** (Small, 1990).

For example, have you seen this word before?

FUNTHOSTAM

Say it aloud. Do you know it? If you had used an acoustic code alone to memorize THUNSTOFAM, the list of letters you first saw on page 262, it might not have been easy to recognize FUNTHOSTAM as an incorrect spelling. Let us assume, however, that by now you have encoded THUNSTOFAM semantically as an acronym for "The United States of America." Then you would have been

---

[1] Maintenance rehearsal, however, is responsible for rote learning.

able to scan the spelling of the words in the phrase "The United States of America" to determine that FUNTHOSTAM was an incorrect spelling.

Rote repetition of a meaningless group of syllables, such as thun-sto-fam, relies on maintenance rehearsal for permanent storage. The process might be tedious (continued rehearsal) and unreliable. Elaborative rehearsal—tying THUNSTOFAM to the name of a country—might make storage instantaneous and retrieval foolproof.

Truth or Fiction Revisited. *It is not true that learning must be meaningful if we are to remember it.* Nevertheless, elaborative rehearsal, which is based on the meanings of events or subject matter, is more efficient than maintenance rehearsal, which is based on rote repetition (Simpson and others, 1994).

Language arts teachers encourage students to use new vocabulary words in sentences to help remember them. Each new usage is an instance of elaborative rehearsal. Usage helps build semantic codes that help students retrieve their meanings in the future. When I was in high school, foreign-language teachers told us that learning classical languages "exercises the mind" so that we would understand English better. Not exactly. The mind is not analogous to a muscle that responds to exercise. However, the meanings of many English words are based on foreign tongues. A person who recognizes that *retrieve* stems from roots meaning "again" (*re-*) and "find" (*trouver* in French) is less likely to forget that *retrieval* means "finding again" or "bringing back."

Think, too, of all the algebra and geometry problems we were asked to solve in high school. Each problem is an application of a procedure and, perhaps, of certain formulas and theorems. By repeatedly applying the procedures, formulas, and theorems in different contexts, we rehearse them elaboratively. As a consequence, we are more likely to remember them. Knowledge of the ways in which a formula or an equation is used helps us remember the formula. Also, by building theorem upon theorem in geometry, we relate new theorems to theorems that we already understand. As a result, we process information about them more deeply and remember them better.

Before proceeding to the next section, let me ask you to cover the preceding paragraphs. Now, which of the following words is correctly spelled: *retrieval* or *retreival?* The spellings sound alike, so an acoustic code for reconstructing the correct spelling would fail. Yet a semantic code, such as the spelling rule "*i* before *e* except after *c,*" would allow you to reconstruct the correct spelling: retr*ie*val.

FLASHBULB MEMORIES.

The attention which we lend to an experience is proportional to its vivid or interesting character; and it is a notorious fact that what interests us most vividly at the time is, other things equal, what we remember best. An impression may be so exciting emotionally as almost to leave a scar upon the cerebral tissues.

WILLIAM JAMES

Do you remember the first time you were in love? Can you remember how the streets and the trees looked somehow transformed? The vibrancy in your step? How generous you felt? How all of life's problems suddenly seemed to be solved?

We tend to remember events that occur under unusual, emotionally arousing circumstances more clearly. Those of us who are middle-aged and older tend to remember what we were doing when we heard that President John F. Kennedy had been shot in November 1963. Younger people tend to recall the events surrounding them on the day the Persian War Gulf exploded in January

Flashbulb Memories. Where were you and what were you doing when you learned that O.J. Simpson had been found not guilty by the jury of the murders of Nicole Brown Simpson and Ronald Goldman? Major happenings can illuminate everything about them, so that we clearly recall all the personal surrounding events. People who are middle-aged or older may never forget where they were or what they were doing when they heard that President Kennedy had been shot.

1991, or when they heard the verdict in the O. J. Simpson murder trial. Similarly, we may remember in detail what we were doing when we learned of a relative's death. These are all examples of "flashbulb memories," because they preserve experiences in such detail (Brown & Kulik, 1977; Thompson & Cowan, 1986).

Why does the memory become etched when the "flashbulb" goes off? One factor is the distinctness of the memory. It is easier to discriminate stimuli that stand out. Such events are salient in themselves, and the feelings that are engendered by them are also rather special. It is thus relatively easy to pick them out from the storehouse of memories. Major events such as the assassination of a president or the loss of a close relative also tend to have important effects on our lives. We are likely to dwell on them and form networks of associations. That is, we are likely to rehearse them elaboratively. Our rehearsal may include great expectations about, or deep fears for, the future. Later we will consider possible biological factors in flashbulb memories.

ORGANIZATION IN LONG-TERM MEMORY.   The storehouse of long-term memory is usually well organized. Items are not just piled on the floor or thrown into closets. We tend to gather information about rats and cats into a certain section of the storehouse, perhaps the animal or mammal section. We put information about oaks, maples, and eucalyptus into the tree section.

Categorization is a basic cognitive function. Categorizing stimuli allows us to make predictions about specific instances and to store information efficiently (Corter & Gluck, 1992).

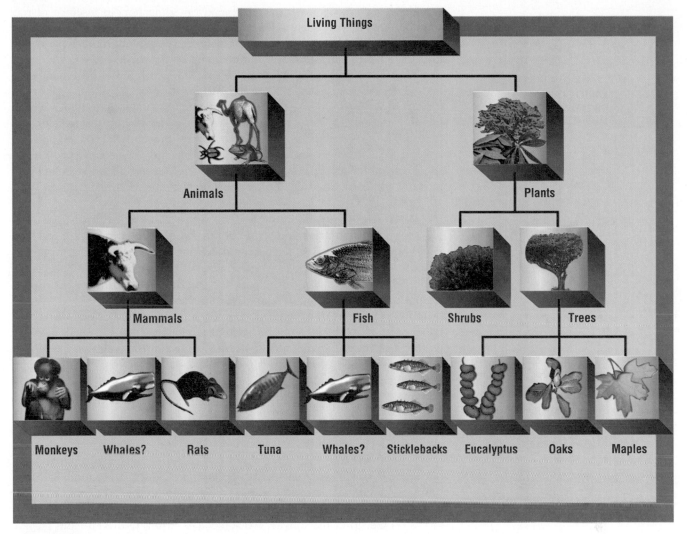

FIGURE 7.6

The Hierarchical Structure of Long-Term Memory. Where are whales filed in the hierarchical cabinets of your memory? Your classification of whales may influence your answers to these questions: Do whales breathe underwater? Are they warm-blooded? Do they nurse their young?

We tend to organize information hierarchically. A hierarchy is an arrangement of items (or chunks of information) into groups or classes according to common or distinct features. As we work our way up the hierarchy shown in Figure 7.6, we find more encompassing, or **superordinate,** classes to which the items below belong. For example, all mammals are animals, but there are many types of animals other than mammals.[2]

When items are correctly organized in long-term memory, you are more likely to recall—or know—accurate information about them (Hasselhorn, 1992; Schneider & Bjorklund, 1992). For instance, do you remember whether whales breathe underwater? If you did not know that whales are mammals (or, in Figure 7.6, **subordinate** to mammals), or if you knew nothing about

Superordinate • Descriptive of a higher (inclusive) class or category in a hierarchy.
Subordinate • Descriptive of a lower (included) class or category in a hierarchy.

---

[2] A note to biological purists: Figure 7.6 is not intended to represent phyla, classes, orders, and so on accurately. Rather, it shows how an individual's classification scheme might be organized.

**MINILECTURE:
ORGANIZATION AND
LONG-TERM MEMORY**

Tip-of-the-tongue phenomenon • The feeling that information is stored in memory although it cannot be readily retrieved. Also called the *feeling-of-knowing experience.*

Feeling-of-knowing experience • Same as *tip-of-the-tongue phenomenon.*

mammals, a correct answer might depend on some remote instance of rote learning. That is, you might be depending on chancy episodic memory rather than on reliable semantic memory. For example, you might recall some details from a Public Broadcasting System documentary on whales. If you *did* know that whales are mammals, however, you would also know—or remember—that whales do not breathe underwater. How? You would reconstruct information about whales from knowledge about mammals, the group to which whales are subordinate. Similarly, you would know, or remember, that whales, because they are mammals, are warm-blooded, nurse their young, and are a good deal more intelligent than, say, tunas and sticklebacks, which are fish. Had you incorrectly classified whales as fish, you might have searched your memory and constructed the incorrect answer that they do breathe underwater.

THE TIP-OF-THE-TONGUE PHENOMENON.   Have you ever been so close to retrieving information that it seemed to be on "the tip of your tongue"? Still, you could not quite remember it? This is a frustrating experience, similar to reeling in a fish but having it drop off the line just before it breaks the surface of the water. Psychologists term this experience the **tip-of-the-tongue (TOT) phenomenon,** or the **feeling-of-knowing experience.**

In one classic TOT experiment, Brown and McNeill (1966) defined some rather unusual words for students, such as *sampan,* which is a small riverboat used in China and Japan. Students were then asked to recall the words they had learned. Some of the students often had the right word "on the tips of their tongues" but reported words similar in meaning such as *junk, barge,* or *houseboat.* Still other students reported words that sounded similar such as *Saipan, Siam, sarong,* and *sanching.* Why?

To begin with, the words were unfamiliar, so elaborative rehearsal did not take place. The students, that is, did not have the opportunity to relate the words to other things that they knew. Brown and McNeill also suggested that our storage systems are indexed according to cues that include both the sounds and the meanings of words—according to both acoustic and semantic codes. By scanning words that are similar in sound and meaning to the word that is on the tip of the tongue, we sometimes find a useful cue and retrieve the word for which we are searching.

The feeling-of-knowing experience also seems to reflect incomplete or imperfect learning. In such cases, our answers may be "in the ballpark" if not on the mark. In some feeling-of-knowing experiments, people are often asked trivia questions. When they do not recall an answer, they are then asked to guess how likely it is that they will recognize the right answer if it is among a group of possibilities. People turn out to be very accurate in their estimations about whether they will recognize the answer. Similarly, Brown and McNeill found that the students in their TOT experiment proved to be very good at estimating the number of syllables in words they could not recall. The students often correctly guessed the initial sounds of the words and sometimes recognized words that rhymed with them.

Our sense that an answer is on the tips of our tongues thus often reflects incomplete knowledge. We may not know the exact answer, but we know something. (As a matter of fact, if we have good writing skills, we may present our incomplete knowledge so forcefully that we earn a good grade on an essay question on the topic!) At such times, the problem lies not in retrieval but in the original encoding and storage.

CONTEXT-DEPENDENT MEMORY.   The context in which we acquire information can also play a role in retrieval. I remember walking down the halls of

The Bronx apartment building where, as a child, I had lived many years earlier. I was suddenly assaulted by images of playing under the staircase, of falling against a radiator, of the shrill voice of a former neighbor calling for her child at dinnertime. Have you ever walked the halls of an old school and been assaulted by memories of faces and names that you would have guessed had been lost forever? Have you ever walked through your old neighborhood and recalled the faces of people or the aromas of cooking that were so real you salivated?

These are examples of **context-dependent memory.** Being in the proper context, that is, can dramatically enhance recall. One fascinating experiment in context-dependent memory included a number of people who were "all wet." Members of a university swimming club were asked to learn lists of words either while they were submerged or literally high and dry (Godden & Baddeley, 1975). Students who learned the list underwater showed superior recall of the list when immersed. Those who had rehearsed the list ashore, similarly, showed better retrieval on terra firma.

Other studies have found that students do better on tests when they study in the room where the test is to be given (Smith and others, 1978). When police are interviewing witnesses to crimes, they have the witnesses verbally paint the scene as vividly as possible, or they visit the crime scene with the witnesses. People who mentally place themselves back in the context in which they encoded and stored information frequently retrieve it more accurately.

STATE-DEPENDENT MEMORY. **State-dependent memory** is an extension of context-dependent memory. It sometimes happens that we retrieve information better when we are in a physiological or emotional state that is similar to the one in which we encoded and stored the information. Drugs, for example, alter our physiological response patterns. They can influence the production and uptake of neurotransmitters involved in learning and memory and can modify the general state of alertness of the body. It also happens that material that is learned "under the influence" of a drug may be most readily retrieved when the person is again under the influence of that drug (Overton, 1985).

Our moods may also serve as cues that aid in the retrieval of memories. Feeling the rush of love may trigger images of other times when we had fallen in love. The grip of anger may prompt memories of frustration and rage. Gordon Bower (1981) ran experiments in which happy or sad moods were induced in participants by hypnotic suggestion. Participants then learned lists of words. Participants who learned a list while in a happy mood showed better recall when a happy state was induced again. But participants who had learned the list when a sad mood had been induced showed superior recall when they were saddened again. Bower suggests that in day-to-day life, a happy mood influences us to focus on positive events. As a result, we will have better recall of these happy events in the future. A sad mood, unfortunately, leads us to focus on and recall the negative. Happiness may feed on happiness, but sadness under extreme circumstances can develop into a vicious cycle.

Context-dependent memory • Information that is better retrieved in the context in which it was encoded and stored, or learned.

State-dependent memory • Information that is better retrieved in the physiological or emotional state in which it was encoded and stored, or learned.

Reflections

- Agree or disagree with the following statement and support your answer: "The memory is like a muscle. The more we practice using it, the better it becomes."
- Agree or disagree with the following statement and support your answer: "People never forget their experiences—regardless of whether or not they can summon them to mind upon request."

- How is it that these "Reflections" sections may help you remember the subject matter in this course?
- **How is it that some events make such an impression on us that we never forget them, whereas many or most events are lost in the wake of time?**
- Have you ever had the experience of having something on "the tip of your tongue" but not being quite able to get at it? How does the text explain this experience?

THE LEVELS-OF-PROCESSING MODEL OF MEMORY

Not all psychologists view memory in terms of stages. Fergus Craik and Robert Lockhart (1972) suggest that we do not have a sensory memory, a short-term memory, and a long-term memory per se. Instead, our ability to remember things can also be viewed in terms of a single stage or dimension—the depth of our processing of information. This views holds that we don't form enduring memories by getting information "into" the mental structure of long-term memory. Rather, memories tend to endure when information is processed *deeply*—when it is attended to, encoded carefully, pondered, and rehearsed elaboratively or related to things we already know well.

Consider our familiar list of letters, THUNSTOFAM. In an experiment, we could ask one group of people to remember the list by repeating it aloud a few times, a letter at a time. Another group could be informed that it is an acronym for "The United States of America." If several months later each group were shown several similar lists of words and asked to select the correct list, which group do you think would be more likely to pick out THUNSTOFAM from the pack? It ought to be the group told of the acronym, because the information in that group would have been processed more deeply.

Consider why so many people have difficulty selecting the accurate drawing of the Lincoln penny. Is it perhaps because they have processed information about the appearance of a penny rather superficially? If they knew they were going to be quizzed about the features of a penny, however, wouldn't they process information about its appearance more deeply? That is, wouldn't they study the features and purposefully note whether the profile is facing left or right, what the lettering says, and where the date goes?

Consider a fascinating experiment with three groups of college students, all of whom were asked to study a picture of a living room for 1 minute (Bransford and others, 1977). Their examination entailed different approaches, however. Two groups were informed that small *x*'s were imbedded in the picture. The first of these groups was asked to find the *x*'s by scanning the picture horizontally and vertically. The second group was informed that the *x*'s could be found in the edges of the objects in the room and was asked to look for them there. The third group was asked, instead, to think about how it would use the objects pictured in the room. As a result of the divergent sets of instructions, the first two groups (the *x* hunters) processed information about the objects in the picture superficially. But the third group rehearsed the objects elaboratively—that is, the group members thought about the objects in terms of their meanings and uses. It should not be surprising that the third group remembered many times more objects than the first two groups.

Researchers more recently asked participants to indicate whether they recognized photos of faces that they had been shown under one of three conditions: being asked to recall the (1) gender or the (2) width of the nose of the person in the photo, or being asked to judge (3) whether the person is honest

(Sporer, 1991). It is likely that asking people to judge other people's honesty stimulates deeper processing of the features of the faces (Bloom & Mudd, 1991). That is, they look at more facial features, study each in more detail, and attempt to relate what they see to their ideas about human nature.

Note that the levels-of-processing model finds uses for most of the concepts employed by those who think of memory in terms of stages. For example, adherents to this model also speak of the basic memory processes (encoding, storage, and retrieval) and of different kinds of rehearsal. The essential difference is that they view memory as consisting of a single dimension that varies according to depth.

MINILECTURE: TECHNIQUES FOR MEASURING RETRIEVAL

Reflections

- **Agree or disagree with the following statement and support your answer: "The best way to remember information is to repeat it over and over again."**
- You probably do better in some subjects than others or at least find the information in some subjects easier to remember. Use the levels-of-processing model of memory to explain why the material in some subjects is easier to remember than the material in others.

We have been discussing remembering for quite some time. Since variety is supposed to be the spice of life, let's consider forgetting for a while.

Nonsense syllables • Meaningless sets of two consonants, with a vowel sandwiched in between, that are used to study memory.
Recognition • In information processing, the easiest memory task, involving identification of objects or events encountered before.

FORGETTING

What do DAL, RIK, BOF, and ZEX have in common? They are all **nonsense syllables.** Nonsense syllables are meaningless sets of two consonants with a vowel sandwiched in between. They were first used by German psychologist Hermann Ebbinghaus (1850–1909) and have since been used by many psychologists to study memory and forgetting.

Because nonsense syllables are intended to be meaningless, remembering them should depend on simple acoustic coding and maintenance rehearsal rather than on elaborative rehearsal, semantic coding, or other ways of making learning meaningful. Nonsense syllables provide a means of measuring simple memorization ability in studies of the three basic memory tasks of recognition, recall, and relearning. Studying these memory tasks has led to several conclusions about the nature of forgetting.

Memory Tasks Used in Measuring Forgetting

RECOGNITION. There are many ways of measuring **recognition.** In one study of high school graduates, Harry Bahrick and his colleagues (1975) interspersed photos of classmates with four times as many photos of strangers. Recent graduates correctly recognized persons who were former schoolmates 90% of the time. Those who had been out of school for 40 years recognized former classmates 75% of the time. A chance level of recognition would have been only 20% (one photo in five was of an actual classmate). Thus, even older graduates showed rather solid long-term recognition ability.

In many studies of recognition, psychologists ask participants to read a list of nonsense syllables. The participants then read a second list of nonsense

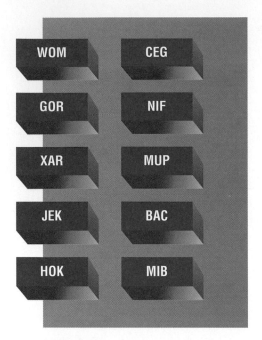

FIGURE 7.7

Paired Associates. Psychologists often use paired associates, like those shown here, to measure recall. Retrieving CEG in response to the cue WOM is made easier by an image of a WOMan smoking a "CEGarette."

Recall • Retrieval or reconstruction of learned material.

Paired associates • Nonsense syllables presented in pairs in experiments that measure recall.

Relearning • A measure of retention. Material is usually relearned more quickly than it is learned initially.

Method of savings • A measure of retention in which the difference between the number of repetitions originally required to learn a list and the number of repetitions required to relearn the list after a certain amount of time has elapsed is calculated.

syllables and indicate whether they recognize any of the syllables as having appeared on the first list. Forgetting is defined as failure to recognize a nonsense syllable that has been read before.

Recognition is the easiest type of memory task. This is why multiple-choice tests are easier than fill-in-the-blank or essay tests. We can recognize or identify photos of former classmates more easily than we can recall their names.

RECALL.   In his own studies of **recall,** another kind of memory task, Ebbinghaus would read lists of nonsense syllables aloud to the beat of a metronome and then see how many he could produce from memory. After reading through a list once, he usually would be able to recall seven nonsense syllables—the typical limit for short-term memory.

Psychologists also often use lists of pairs of nonsense syllables, called **paired associates,** to measure recall. A list of paired associates is shown in Figure 7.7. Study participants read through the lists pair by pair. Later, they are shown the first member of each pair and are asked to recall the second. Recall is more difficult than recognition. In a recognition task, one simply indicates whether an item has been seen before or which of a number of items is paired with a stimulus (as in a multiple-choice test). In a recall task, the person must retrieve a syllable with another syllable serving as a cue.

Retrieval is made easier if the two syllables can be meaningfully linked—encoded semantically—even if the "meaning" is stretched a bit. Consider the first pair of nonsense syllables in Figure 7.7. The image of a WOMan smoking a CEGarette may make CEG easier to retrieve when the person is presented with the cue WOM.

As we develop throughout childhood, our ability to recall information increases. This memory improvement is apparently linked to our growing ability to process (categorize) stimulus cues quickly (Howard & Polich, 1985). In one study, Kail and Nippold (1984) asked 8-, 12-, and 21-year-olds to name as many animals and pieces of furniture as they could during separate 7-minute intervals. The number of items recalled increased with age for both animals and furniture. For all age groups, items were retrieved according to classes. For example, in the animal category, a series of fish might be named, then a series of birds, and so on.

It is easier to recall vocabulary words from foreign languages if you can construct a meaningful link between the foreign and English words (Atkinson, 1975). The *peso,* pronounced *payso,* is a unit of Mexican money. A link can be formed by finding a part of the foreign word, such as the *pe-* (pronounced *pay*) in *peso,* and constructing a phrase such as "You pay with money." When you read or hear the word *peso* in the future, you recognize the *pe-* and retrieve the link or phrase. From the phrase, you then reconstruct the translation, "a unit of money."

RELEARNING: IS LEARNING EASIER THE SECOND TIME AROUND?   **Relearning** is a third method of measuring retention. Do you remember having to learn all of the state capitals in elementary school? What were the capitals of Wyoming and Delaware? Even when we cannot recall or recognize material that had once been learned, we can relearn it more rapidly the second time, such as Cheyenne for Wyoming and Dover for Delaware. Similarly, as we go through our 30s and 40s we may forget a good deal of our high school French or geometry. Yet, we could learn what took months or years much more rapidly the second time around.

To study the efficiency of relearning, Ebbinghaus (1885) devised the **method of savings**. First, he recorded the number of repetitions required to

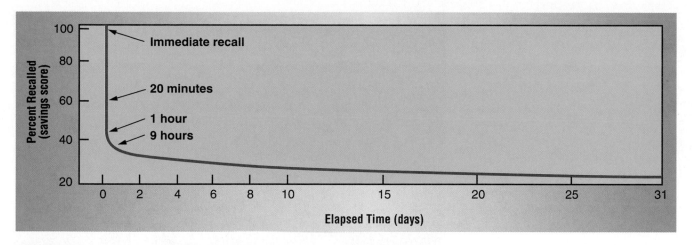

FIGURE 7.8

Ebbinghaus's Classic Curve of Forgetting. Recollection of lists of words dropped precipitously during the first hour after learning. Losses of learning then became more gradual. Retention dropped by half within the first hour. However, it took a month (31 days) for retention to be cut in half again.

learn a list of nonsense syllables or words. Then, he recorded the number of repetitions required to relearn the list after a certain amount of time had elapsed. Next, he computed the difference between the number of repetitions required to arrive at the **savings.** If a list had to be repeated 20 times before it was learned, and 20 times again after a year had passed, there were no savings. Relearning, that is, was as tedious as the initial learning. However, if the list could be learned with only 10 repetitions after a year had elapsed, half the number of repetitions required for learning had been saved. (That is, ten is half of 20.)

Figure 7.8 is Ebbinghaus's classic curve of forgetting. As you can see, there was no loss of memory as measured by savings immediately after a list had been learned. However, recollection dropped precipitously during the first hour after learning a list. Losses of learning then became more gradual. Retention dropped by half within the first hour. However, it took a month (31 days) for retention to be cut in half again. In other words, forgetting occurred most rapidly right after material was learned. We continue to forget material as time elapses but at a relatively slower rate.

Before leaving this section, I have one question for you: What are the capitals of Wyoming and Delaware?

Savings • The difference between the number of repetitions originally required to learn a list and the number of repetitions required to relearn the list after a certain amount of time has elapsed.

Interference theory • The view that we may forget stored material because other learning interferes with it.

Interference Theory

When we do not attend to, encode, and rehearse sensory input, we may forget it through decay of the trace of the image. Material in short-term memory, like material in sensory memory, can be lost through decay. It can also be lost through displacement, as may happen when we try to remember several new names at a party.

According to **interference theory,** we also forget material in short-term and long-term memory because newly learned material interferes with it. The two basic types of interference are retroactive interference (also called *retroactive inhibition*) and proactive interference (also called *proactive inhibition*).

Interference. In retroactive interference, new learning interferes with the retrieval of old learning. In proactive interference, older learning interferes with the capacity to retrieve more recently learned material. High school French vocabulary may "pop in," for example, when you are trying to retrieve Spanish words learned for a test in college.

Retroactive interference • The interference of new learning with the ability to retrieve material learned previously.

Proactive interference • The interference by old learning with the ability to retrieve material learned recently.

RETROACTIVE INTERFERENCE. In **retroactive interference,** new learning interferes with the retrieval of old learning. A medical student may memorize the names of the bones in the leg through rote repetition. Later, he or she may find that learning the names of the bones in the arm makes it more difficult to retrieve the names of the leg bones, especially if the names are similar in sound or in relative location on each limb.

PROACTIVE INTERFERENCE. In **proactive interference,** older learning interferes with the capacity to retrieve more recently learned material. High school Spanish may pop in when you are trying to retrieve college French or Italian words. All three are Romance languages, with similar roots and spellings. Old Japanese vocabulary words probably would not interfere with your ability to retrieve more-recently learned French or Italian, because Japanese roots and sounds differ considerably from those of the Romance languages.

Consider motor skills. You may learn how to drive standard shift on a car with three forward speeds and a clutch that must be let up slowly after shifting. Later, you learn to drive a car with five forward speeds and a clutch that must be released rapidly. For a while, you make a number of errors on the five-speed car because of proactive interference. (Old learning interferes with new learning.) If you return to the three-speed car after driving the five-speed car has become natural, you may stall it a few times. This is because of retroactive interference (new learning interfering with the old).

Repression

According to Sigmund Freud, we are motivated to forget painful memories and unacceptable ideas because they produce anxiety, guilt, and shame. (In terms of operant conditioning, anxiety, guilt, and shame serve as negative reinforcers. We learn to do that which is followed by their removal—in this case, to avoid thinking about certain events and ideas.) In Chapter 13, we shall see that psychoanalysts believe that repression is at the heart of disorders such as **dissociative amnesia.**

Infantile Amnesia

When he interviewed people about their early experiences, Freud discovered that they could not recall episodes that happened prior to the age of 3 and that recall was very cloudy through the age of 5. This phenomenon is referred to as **infantile amnesia.** Many of us think that we have vivid recollections of key events of infancy. Yet research that attempts to verify such memories by interviewing independent older witnesses shows that they are usually inaccurate (e.g., Sheingold & Tenney, 1982).

Infantile amnesia has nothing to do with the fact that the episodes are of the distant past. Middle-aged and elderly people have vivid memories from the ages of 6 and 10, yet the events are many decades old. But 18-year-olds show steep declines in memory when they try to recall episodes earlier than the age of 6, even though these events are fewer than 18 years away (Wetzler & Sweeney, 1986).

Freud believed that young children have aggressive impulses and perverse lusts toward their parents, and he attributed infantile amnesia to their repression (Goleman, 1993). However, the episodes lost to infantile amnesia are not weighted in the direction of such "primitive" impulses. Many such incidents are pedestrian and emotionally bland. The effects of infantile amnesia are too broad for Freud's hypothesis to hold water.

Infantile amnesia probably reflects the interaction of physiological and cognitive factors. For example, a structure of the limbic system (the **hippocampus**) that is involved in the storage of memories does not become mature until we are about 2 years old. Also, myelination of brain pathways is incomplete for the first few years, contributing to the inefficiency of information processing and memory formation. There are also cognitive reasons for infantile amnesia. One is that very young children are not particularly interested in the past (Neisser, 1993). Another is that infants, in contrast to older children, tend not to weave episodes together into meaningful stories of their own lives, or autobiographies (Hudson, 1993). Information about specific episodes thus tends to be lost. Infants also do not make reliable use of language to symbolize or classify events. Their ability to *encode* sensory input—that is, to apply the auditory and semantic codes that facilitate memory formation—is thus limited.

Truth or Fiction Revisited. *It is not true that we can remember important episodes that take place during the first 2 years of life. (Really, Allyn, believe me.) Those early childhood memories that we are so certain we can see today are probably reconstructed and mostly inaccurate. Or else they may stem from a time when we were older than we think.*

Anterograde and Retrograde Amnesia

In **anterograde amnesia,** there are memory lapses for the period following a trauma such as a blow to the head, an electric shock, or an operation. In some cases, it seems that the trauma interferes with all the processes of memory. The ability to pay attention, the encoding of sensory input, and rehearsal are all

Dissociative amnesia　•　Amnesia thought to stem from psychological conflict or trauma. (See Chapter 13.)

Infantile amnesia　•　Inability to recall events that occur prior to the age of 2 or 3. Also termed *childhood amnesia.*

Hippocampus　•　A structure in the limbic system that plays an important role in the formation of new memories.

Anterograde amnesia　•　Failure to remember events that occur after physical trauma because of the effects of the trauma.

impaired. A number of investigators have linked certain kinds of brain damage—such as that to the hippocampus—to amnesia (Corkin and others, 1985; Squire, 1994).

Consider the classic case of a man with the initials H. M. Parts of the brain are sometimes lesioned to help people with epilepsy. In H. M.'s case, a section of the hippocampus was removed (Milner, 1966). Right after the operation, the man's mental functioning appeared to be normal. As time went on, however, it became quite clear that he had severe problems in the processing of information. For example, 2 years after the operation, H. M. believed that he was 27—his age at the time of the operation. When his family relocated to a new address, H. M. could not find his new home or remember the new address. He responded with appropriate grief to the death of his uncle, yet he then began to ask about his uncle and why he did not visit. Each time he was informed of his uncle's passing, he grieved as he had when he first heard of it. All in all, it seems that H. M.'s operation prevented him from transferring information from short-term memory to long-term memory.

In **retrograde amnesia,** the source of trauma prevents people from remembering events that took place before the accident. A football player who is knocked unconscious or a person who is involved in an auto accident may be unable to recall events that occurred for several minutes prior to the trauma. The football player may not recall taking to the field. The person in the accident may not recall entering the car. It also sometimes happens that the individual cannot remember events that occurred for several years prior to the traumatic incident.

In one well-known case of retrograde amnesia, a man received a head injury in a motorcycle accident (Baddeley, 1982). When he regained consciousness, he had lost memory for all events after the age of 11. In fact, he appeared to believe that he was still 11 years old. During the next few months, he gradually recovered more knowledge of his past. He moved toward the present year by year, up until the critical motorcycle ride. But he never did recover the events just prior to the accident. The accident had apparently prevented the information that was rapidly unfolding before him from being transferred to long-term memory.

In terms of stages of memory, it may be that our perceptions and ideas need to **consolidate,** or rest undisturbed for a while, if they are to be transferred to long-term memory.

Retrograde amnesia • Failure to remember events that occur prior to physical trauma because of the effects of the trauma.

Consolidation • The fixing of information in long-term memory.

Reflections

Let's see if we can help you remember about forgetting by having you reflect on the following questions!

- Consider the memory tasks of recognition, recall, and relearning. What kinds of tasks do most of your tests rely on?
- What is an example of retroactive or proactive interference in your own life?
- What are your earliest memories? How do you know the proper dates of the experiences? How do you know how accurate your memories are? What types of experiences or processes are likely to distort these memories?

Let us now turn our attention to some of the biological events that appear to be involved in the formation of memories.

METHODS FOR IMPROVING MEMORY

A clear conscience is often the sign of a bad memory.

ANONYMOUS

We beleaguered humans have come through an Ice Age, a Stone Age, an Iron Age, and, a bit more recently, an Industrial Revolution. Now we are trying to cope with the so-called Age of Information, in which there has been an exponential explosion of information—much of it scientific. Computers have been developed to process it. We, too, process information, and there is more of it to process than ever before. Fortunately, psychologists have helped devise a number of methods for promoting the retention of information. Let us consider some of them.

Drill and Practice

Repetition (rote maintenance rehearsal) helps transfer information from short-term to long-term memory. Maintenance rehearsal may seem rather mechanical for a capable college student, but don't forget that this is how you learned the alphabet and how to count! We write spelling words over and over to remember them. Athletes and gymnasts repeat movements to facilitate their procedural memories. When you have formulas down pat, you can use your time pondering when to apply them, not trying to recall them. When the wide receiver has his moves down pat, he can focus on the defenders and not on his basic patterns.

Some students use flash cards to help them remember facts. For example, they might write "The originator of modern behaviorism is _____" on one side of the card and "John Broadus Watson" on the flip side.

In his book *Super Memory,* Douglas Herrmann (1991) recommends the following methods for helping to remember the name of someone you have just met.

1. Say the name out loud.
2. Ask your new acquaintance a question, using her or his name.
3. Use the person's name as many times as you can during your conversation. (Even seeking an opportunity to use the name will help you remember it.)
4. Write down the name, if possible, when the conversation has ended.

Relating New Information to What Is Already Known

Relating new information to what is already known is a form of elaborative rehearsal that helps us to remember it (Willoughby and others, 1994). Herrmann (1991) also suggests that you can better remember the name of a new acquaintance by thinking of a rhyme for it. Now you have done some active thinking about the name. You also have two tags for the person, not one. If you are trying to retrieve the spelling of the word *retrieve,* do so by retrieving the rule "*i* before *e* except after *c.*" There are exceptions, of course: Remember that "weird" doesn't follow the rule because it's a "weird" word.

We normally expand our knowledge base by relating new items to things already known. Children learn that a cello is like a violin, only bigger. They learn that a bass fiddle is also like a violin, but bigger yet. We remember information about whales by relating whales to other mammals. Similarly, we will better recall information about porpoises and dolphins if we think of them as small whales (and not as friendly, intelligent fish).

The media are filled with stories about people who show psychological disorders of one kind or another. To help you remember the disorders discussed in Chapter 13, think of film or TV characters who were portrayed as having the disorders. Consider how the characters' behaviors were consistent (and inconsistent) with the descriptions in the text (and those offered by your professor). You will better remember the subject matter *and* become a good critic of media portrayals of psychological problems.

Forming Unusual, Exaggerated Associations

Psychologist Charles L. Brewer uses an interesting method to teach his psychology students the fundamentals of shaping:

> In a recent class, Dr. Brewer first danced on his desk, then bleated like a sheep and finally got down on "all fours and oinked like a pig," he said. His antics were in response to a session he teaches on "successive approximation"—shaping behavior into a desired response.
>
> To get students to "shape" him, he told them he would try to figure out what they wanted him to do. If he guessed wrong, they'd "boo and hiss," while if he did what they wanted, they'd applaud him—which is why he eventually acted like a pig. "I'll do anything to get them to learn," he said. (DeAngelis, 1994a, p. 40)

It is easier to recall stimuli that stand out, that separate themselves from the crowd. We pay more attention to them, and they tend to earn more of an emotional response. Sometimes, then, we better remember information when we create unusual, exaggerated associations.

Assume that you are trying to remember the geography of the cerebral cortex, as shown in Figure 2.14. Why not think of what you look like in right profile? (Use your left profile if it is better.) Then imagine a new imaging technique in which we can see through your skull and we find four brightly colored lobes in the right hemisphere of your cerebral cortex. Not only that, but there are little people (homunculi) flapping about in the sensory and motor areas (see Figure 2.14 again). In fact, imagine that you're in a crowded line, and someone steps on your toe; thus, the homunculus in the sensory cortex has a throbbing toe. This is communicated to the association areas of the cortex, where you decide that you are rather annoyed. The language areas of the cortex think up some choice words, which are relayed to the throat and mouth of the homunculus in the motor cortex, then sent into your throat and mouth. You also send some messages through the motor cortex that tighten your muscles, in readiness to attack.

Then you see that the perpetrator of the crime is a very attractive and apologetic stranger! What part of the occipital lobe is flashing the wonderful images?

THE METHOD OF LOCI. Another example of forming unusual associations is the method of loci (pronounced LOW-sigh). With this method, you select a series of related images such as the parts of your body or the furniture in your home. Then you imagine an item from your shopping list, or another list you want to remember, as being attached to each image. Consider this meaty application: You might be better able to remember your shopping list if you imagine meatloaf in your navel or a strip of bacon draped over your nose.

By placing meatloaf or a favorite complete dinner in your navel, rather than a single item such as chopped beef, you can combine several items into one chunk of information. At the supermarket, you recall the (familiar) ingredients for meatloaf and simply recognize whether or not you need each one.

Mediation

The method of mediation also relies on forming associations: You link two items with a third that ties them together.

What if you are having difficulty remembering that John's wife's name is Tillie? You can mediate between John and Tillie as follows. Reflect that the *john* is a slang term for bathroom. Bathrooms often have ceramic *tiles*. *Tiles*, of course, sounds like *Tillie*. So it goes: John→bathroom tiles→Tillie.

I used a combination of mediation and formation of unusual associations to help me remember foreign vocabulary words in high school. For example, the Spanish verb *trabajar* means "to work," in the sense of harassing, laboring, straining. Although *-jar* is pronounced "har," I nevertheless formed a mental image of a "trial by jars" when I laid eyes on the word. I saw myself running the gauntlet with strange enemies pouring jars down upon me until I was so laden that I could barely move. "Now," I thought, "that trial by jars was really *work!*" Trabajar→trial by jars→work. And how about *mujer* (pronounced moo-hair [almost]), meaning "woman"? Women have mo' hair than I do. Woman→mo' hair→mujer. This would no longer work, because now nearly all men also have more hair than I, but the association was so outlandish that it has stuck with me.

Mnemonic Devices

Broadly speaking, the methods for jogging memory we have discussed all fall under the heading of *mnemonics*, or systems for remembering information. So-called mnemonic devices usually combine chunks of information into a format such as an acronym, jingle, or phrase. For example, recalling the phrase "Every Good Boy Does Fine" has helped many people remember the musical keys E, G, B, D, F. In Chapter 3, we saw that the acronym *SAME* serves as a mnemonic device for distinguishing between afferent and efferent neurons. And in Chapter 4, we noted that most psychology students use the acronym *Roy G Biv* to remember the colors of the rainbow, even though your "backward" author chose to use the "word" *vibgyor*.

Acronyms have found applications in many disciplines. Consider geography. The acronym *HOMES* stands for the Great Lakes: *H*uron, *O*ntario, *M*ichigan, *E*rie, and *S*uperior. In astronomy, the phrase "*M*ercury's *v*ery *e*ager *m*other *j*ust *s*erved *u*s *n*ine *p*otatoes" helps students recall the order of the planets *M*ercury, *V*enus, *E*arth, *M*ars, *J*upiter, *S*aturn, *U*ranus, *N*eptune, and *P*luto.

What about biology? You can remember that Dromedary camels have one hump while Bactrian camels have two by turning the letters *D* and *B* on their sides.

And how can you math students ever be expected to remember the reciprocal of pi (that is, 1 divided by 3.14)? Simple: Just remember the question "Can I remember the reciprocal?" and count the number of letters in each word. The reciprocal of pi, it turns out, is 0.318310. (Remember the last two digits as 10, not as one-zero.) A number of other phrases serve as mnemonic devices, as shown in Table 7.1.

TABLE 7.1
SOME MNEMONIC DEVICES

DEVICE	INFORMATION ENCODED
Washington And Jefferson Made Many A Joke. Van Buren Had To Put The Frying Pan Back. Lincoln Just Gasped, "Heaven Guard America." Cleveland Had Coats Made Ready To Wear Home. Coolidge Hurried Right To Every Kitchen Jar Nook. Ford Cut Right Brow.	U.S. Presidents: Washington, Adams, Jefferson, Madison, Monroe, Adams, Jackson Van Buren, Harrison, Tyler, Polk, Taylor, Fillmore, Pierce, Buchanan Lincoln, Johnson, Grant, Hayes, Garfield, Arthur Cleveland, Harrison, Cleveland, McKinley, Roosevelt, Taft, Wilson, Harding Coolidge, Hoover, Roosevelt, Truman, Eisenhower, Kennedy, Johnson, Nixon Ford, Carter, Reagan, Bush.
Poor Queen Victoria Eats Crow At Christmas.	The seven hills of Rome: Palatine, Quirinal, Viminal, Esquiline, Capitoline, Aventine, Caelian.
A True Conservative Can Not GOVern Virtu-ously; They Do Not Themselves Hate Avarice Altogether.	The Roman emperors: Augustus, Tiberius, Caligula, Claudius, Nero, Galba, Otho, Vitellius (the last three in the same year), Vespasian, Titus, Domitian, Nerva, Trajan, Hadrian, Antoninus Pius, Aurelius.
No Plan Like Yours To Study History Wisely	The royal houses of England: Norman, Plantagenet, Lancaster, York, Tudor, Stuart, Hanover, Windsor.
X shall stand for playmates Ten. V for Five stalwart men. I for One, D for Five. M for a Thousand soldiers true. And L for Fifty, I'll tell you.	Translation of the Roman numerals. "D for Five" means D = 500.
Mary Eats Peanut Butter.	First four hydrocarbons of the Alkane class: Methane, Ethane, Propane, and Butane, in ascending order of the number of carbon atoms in their chains.
These Ten Valuable Amino acids Have Long Preserved Life In Man.	Ten essential amino acids: Threonine, Tryptophan, Valine, Arginine, Histidine, Lysine, Phenylalanine, Leucine, Isoleucine, Methionine.
All Hairy Men Will Buy Razors.	Components of soil: Air, Humus, Mineral salts, Water, Bacteria, Rock particles.
Soak Her Toe.	Reminds one of *SohCahToa,* or: Sine = Opposite/Hypotenuse Cosine = Adjacent/Hypotenuse Tangent = Opposite/Adjacent.
Krakatoa Positively Casts Off Fumes; Generally Sulfurous Vapors.	Biological categories in descending order: Kingdom, Phylum, Class, Order, Family, Genus, Species, Variety.
On Old Olympia's Towering Tops, A Finn And a German Vault And Hop.	The twelve pairs of cranial nerves: Olfactory, Optic, Oculomotor, Trochlear, Trigeminal, Abducens, Facial, Auditory, Glossopharyngeal, Vagus, Accessory, Hypoglossal.
Never Lower Tillie's Pants; Mother Might Come Home.	The eight bones of the wrist: Navicular, Lunate, Triangular, Pisiform, Multangular greater, Multangular lesser, Capitate, Hamate.
Camels Often Sit Down Carefully. Perhaps Their Joints Creak. Persistent Early Oiling Might Pre-vent Permanent Rheumatism.	The geological time periods: Cambrian, Ordovician, Silurian, Devonian, Carboniferous, Permian, Triassic, Jurassic, Cretaceous, Paleocene, Eocene, Oligocene, Miocene, Pliocene, Pleistocene, Recent.
Lazy French Tarts Sit Naked In Anticipation.	Nerves that pass through the superior orbital fissure of the skull: Lachrymal, Frontal, Trochlear, Superior, Nasal, Inferior, Abducent.

Finally, how can you remember how to spell *mnemonics?* Easy—be willing to grant "a*MN*esty" to those who cannot.

Truth or Fiction Revisited. *It is true that you can use tricks to improve your memory.* The "tricks" all involve ways of forming associations.

Reflections

- Which methods of encoding and storing information have you used to remember the following—that the number 1 has a "wun" sound; that the visual cortex is in the occipital lobe of the brain; that B. F. Skinner was a behaviorist; a shopping list?
- What strategies could you use to learn the names of your classmates? (How did you actually come to remember the names of those classmates who are most important to you?)
- Do you have use for any of the mnemonic devices shown in Table 7.1? Which ones? What mnemonic devices have you used to help you in this and other courses?

THE BIOLOGY OF MEMORY

Psychologists generally assume that mental processes are accompanied by changes in the brain. Psychologists similarly assume that changes in the brain accompany the encoding, storage, and retrieval of information—that is, memory.

**MINILECTURE:
THE BIOLOGY OF MEMORY**

Changes at the Neural Level

Rats who are reared in richly stimulating environments develop more dendrites and synapses in the cerebral cortex than rats reared in relatively impoverished environments (Rosenzweig and others, 1972). It also has been shown that the level of visual stimulation rats receive is associated with the number of synapses they develop in the visual cortex (Turner & Greenough, 1985).

Thus, changes occur in the visual cortex as a result of visual experience. Changes are also likely to occur in the auditory cortex as a result of heard experiences. Information received through the other senses is just as likely to lead to corresponding changes in the cortical regions that represent them. The storage of experiences that are perceived by several senses involves numerous areas of the brain (Hilts, 1995). The recollection of experiences, as in the production of visual images, also apparently involves neural activity in the appropriate regions of the brain (Kosslyn, 1994).

Research with sea snails such as *Aplysia* and *Hermissenda* has offered insight into the events that take place at existing synapses when learning occurs. *Aplysia,* for example, has only about 20,000 neurons compared with humans' *billions* (Kandel & Hawkins, 1992). As a result, researchers have actually been able to study how experience is reflected at the synapses of specific neurons. When sea snails are conditioned, more of the neurotransmitter serotonin is released at certain synapses. As a consequence, transmission at these synapses becomes more efficient as trials (learning) progress (Goelet and others, 1986; Kandel & Hawkins, 1992).

Many other naturally occurring chemical substances have been shown to play roles in memory. The hormones adrenaline and noradrenaline, for example, stimulate bodily arousal and activity. They also strengthen memory when they are released following instances of learning (Cahill and others, 1994; McGaugh, 1983).

Release of the hormones adrenaline and noradrenaline may play a particular role in flashbulb memories. Because they are connected with strong emotional arousal, these hormones may etch pathways in the amygdala to record memories of highly emotional events (Goleman, 1994).

The neurotransmitter acetylcholine (ACh) is also vital in memory formation. Another hormone that can play a role in memory is antidiuretic hormone, also known as vasopressin. Vasopressin apparently stimulates social memory in male rats. Rats whose vasopressin activity has been blocked size up old acquaintances with full-body sniffs, a ritual normally reserved for strange rats (Angier, 1993). People given a synthetic form of vasopressin through nasal sprays have shown significant improvement in recall (McGaugh, 1983). Excess vasopressin, unfortunately, can have serious side effects such as constriction of the blood vessels.

Changes at the Structural Level

Consider the problems that beset H. M. following his epilepsy operation. Certain parts of the brain such as the hippocampus also appear to be involved in the formation of new memories—or the transfer of information from short-term memory to long-term memory. The hippocampus does not comprise the

FIGURE 7.9
Where Memories Are Stored.

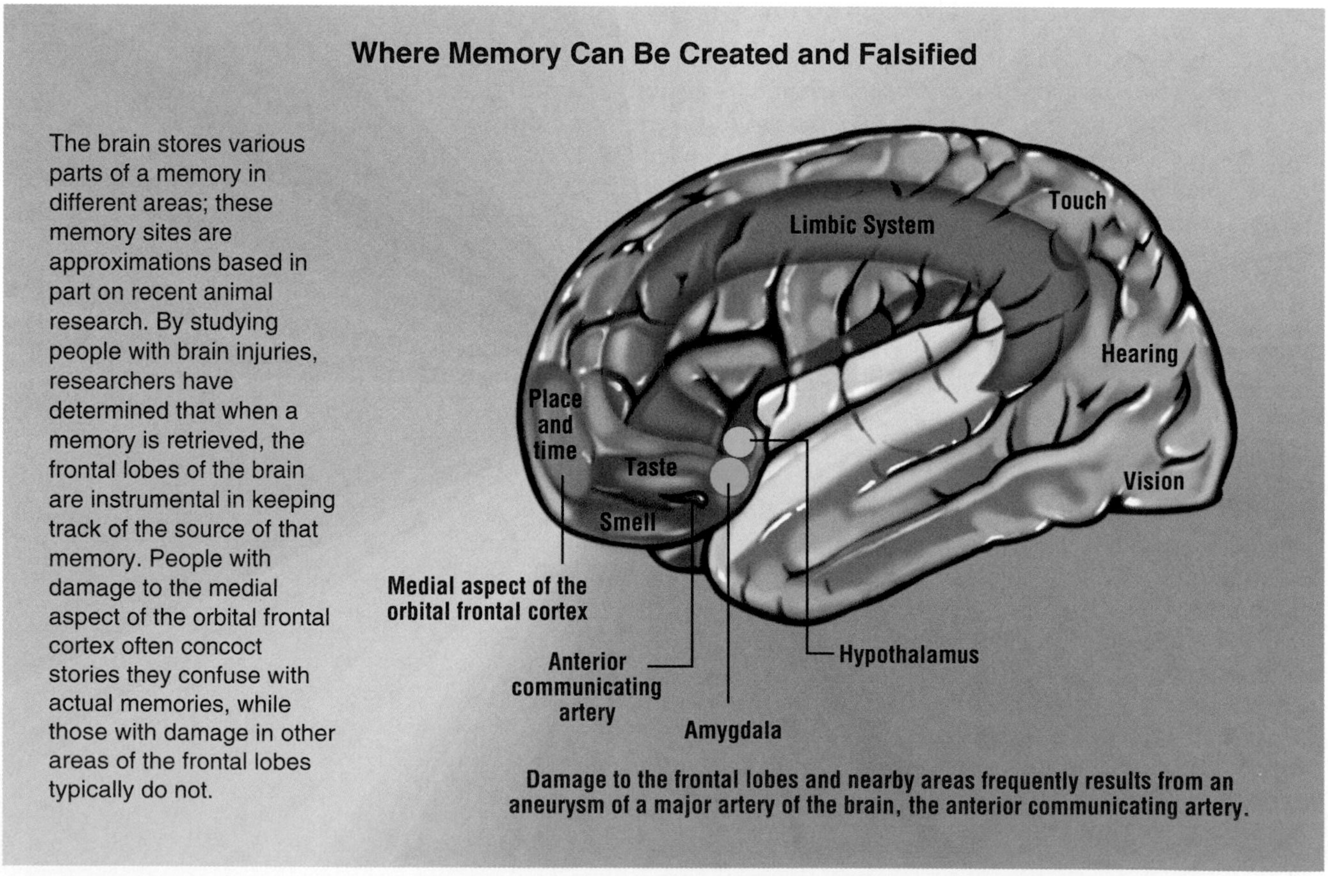

Where Memory Can Be Created and Falsified

The brain stores various parts of a memory in different areas; these memory sites are approximations based in part on recent animal research. By studying people with brain injuries, researchers have determined that when a memory is retrieved, the frontal lobes of the brain are instrumental in keeping track of the source of that memory. People with damage to the medial aspect of the orbital frontal cortex often concoct stories they confuse with actual memories, while those with damage in other areas of the frontal lobes typically do not.

Touch
Limbic System
Hearing
Place and time
Taste
Vision
Smell
Medial aspect of the orbital frontal cortex
Hypothalamus
Anterior communicating artery
Amygdala

Damage to the frontal lobes and nearby areas frequently results from an aneurysm of a major artery of the brain, the anterior communicating artery.

"storage bins" for memories themselves, because H. M.'s memories prior to the operation were not destroyed. Rather, the hippocampus is involved in relaying incoming sensory information to parts of the cortex. Therefore, it appears to be vital to the storage of new information even if old information can be retrieved without it (Murray & Mishkin, 1985; Squire, 1994).

Where are the storage bins? Figure 7.9 shows that the brain stores parts of memories in the appropriate areas of the sensory cortex (Moscovitch, 1994). Sights are stored in the visual cortex, sounds in the auditory cortex, and so on (Hilts, 1995). The limbic system is largely responsible for integrating these shards of information when we recall an event. Research with animals and people with brain injuries suggests that an area in the frontal lobe (labeled "place and time") stores information as to where and when an event occurred. People with damage to this part of the frontal lobe frequently attempt to fill in the memory gaps by making up stories as to when and where events have taken place.

The hippocampus, a part of the limbic system, is also involved in the where and when of things. The hippocampus does not become mature until we are about 2 years old. Immaturity may be connected with infantile amnesia. Adults with hippocampal damage may be able to form new procedural memories, even though they cannot form new episodic ("where and when") memories. For example, they can acquire the skill of reading words backwards even though they cannot recall individual practice sessions (Squire, 1994).

The thalamus, a structure near the center of the brain, appears to be involved in the formation of verbal memories. Part of the thalamus of an unfortunate Air Force cadet, known as N. A., was lesioned in a freak fencing accident. Following the episode, N. A. could no longer form verbal memories. However, his ability to form visual memories was unimpaired (Squire, 1994).

Alzheimer's disease • (AHLTS-high-mers). A progressive disorder characterized by loss of memory and other cognitive functions. (Named after the German physician who discovered the disease, Alois Alzheimer.)

Changes at the Neural and Structural Levels: The Case of Alzheimer's Disease

Memory functioning and memory problems are frequently characterized by changes at both the neural and structural levels. Such is the case in **Alzheimer's disease.**

Alzheimer's disease is a progressive form of mental deterioration that affects processes such as memory, language, and problem solving in as many as 4 million Americans (Angier, 1993; Growdon, 1992; Teri & Wagner, 1992). Studies in Massachusetts show that Alzheimer's affects about 10% of people over the age of 65. The risk increases dramatically with advanced age (Evans and others, 1989; Selkoe, 1992). Although Alzheimer's is connected with aging, it is a disease and not part of a normal aging process (Kolata, 1991a). Isolated memory losses (for example, forgetting where one put one's glasses) may be a normal feature of aging. Alzheimer's seriously impairs vocational and social functioning.

Truth or Fiction Revisited. *It is not true that Alzheimer's disease is a normal aspect of the aging process.*

People with Alzheimer's disease may initially find it difficult to recall recent events or basic information such as telephone numbers, area codes, ZIP codes, and the names of grandchildren. It becomes hard to manage finances and compute numbers. As the disease progresses, people require assistance to manage everyday tasks (Reisberg and others, 1986). There are large gaps in memory for recent events. People may fail to recognize familiar people or forget their names (Mendez and others, 1992). They may not recognize themselves in mirrors. Memory for remote events is also affected. They are generally unable to recall the names of their schools, parents, or birthplaces. In the most severe cases, people become helpless. They become unable to communicate or walk and require help in toileting and feeding.

Two brain abnormalities are regarded as signs of the disease: plaques (portions of degenerative brain tissue) and tangles (twisted bundles of nerve cells). The plaques are believed to destroy the adjacent brain tissue, which leads to loss of memory function and confusion. There is also a loss of synapses in the hippocampus and the frontal cortex (Tanzi, 1995). The hippocampus is vital to memory formation. Acetylcholine (ACh) is normally prevalent in the hippocampus, and people with Alzheimer's have reduced levels of ACh in their brains.

There is evidence of genetic transmission of Alzheimer's disease. More than 90% of the people who inherit a key gene from both parents contract Alzheimer's disease by the age of 75. The disease is found among 60% of those who inherit the gene from only one parent and about 20% of those who do not inherit the gene (Angier, 1993).

Because the disease is connected with reductions in ACh, chemotherapy has aimed at heightening ACh levels. For example, the drug tacrine inhibits the breakdown of ACh by decreasing the action of an enzyme that metabolizes it. As of today, however, the effects of tacrine are modest at best (Growdon, 1992). Researchers are hopeful that genetic studies of Alzheimer's disease may lead to the development of more effective medications (Roses, 1993; Tanzi, 1995).

The encoding, storage, and retrieval of information thus involves biological activity on several levels. As we learn, new synapses are developed, and changes occur at existing synapses. Various parts and structures of the brain are also involved in the formation of different kinds of memories.

Reflections

- Which biological theory of memory might have encouraged cannibalism? (Why is your psychology professor fortunate that research evidence has not confirmed this theory?)
- Assume that you could manufacture any chemical you wished and that it had no harmful side effects. What kinds of pills might you try taking during class or while reading textbooks to help you remember the subject matter?
- Do you personally know an older person who is forgetful? Forgetful in what ways? Do you know of someone with Alzheimer's disease? What behaviors characterize the disease in the individual?

Research into the biology of memory is in its infancy, but what an exciting area of research it is. What would it mean to you if you could read for an hour, pop a pill, and cause your new learnings to become consolidated in long-term memory? You would never have to reread the material; it would be at your fingertips for a lifetime. It would save a bit of study time, would it not?

A FINAL CHALLENGE TO MEMORY

Now that you've become an expert on memory, I'm going to give you a final challenge—an odd challenge but one that I bet you'll be able to meet quite well.

At the stroke of midnight on December 31, 2000, I challenge you to remember to say the following list of letters to yourself: T-H-U-N-S-T-O-F-A-M. As you join in the mass reveling of that special New Year's Eve—the one when we usher in the new millennium—repeat that list of letters silently to yourself. Oh, you may also kiss your partner, toot a horn, throw confetti into the air, and any number of other things. But also think T-H-U-N-S-T-O-F-A-M.

Why do I have such confidence in you? Why would I be willing to gamble that you'll be able to set aside other concerns for a few seconds on that New Year's Eve? There are two reasons. The first is that you'll surely be able to retrieve the letter list because of your enduring knowledge that it is an acronym for "The United States of America." The second is that this challenge is so unusual—so distinct from the other happenings in your life—that you may just store it deeply enough to jar your memory years into the future.

And if you don't meet this challenge, might you have the nagging thought that there was something you were going to do as the third millennium displaces the second? Might the challenge be—as some psychologists say—right on the tip of your tongue? And on that same New Year's Eve, my daughter Allyn—who will refuse to think T-H-U-N-S-T-O-F-A-M no matter what—will probably still be insisting that she can remember being born.

Study Guide

DIRECTIONS: In the column to the left are a number of concepts in the psychology of memory. In the column to the right are the names of individuals who have had an impact on the psychology of memory. Write the name(s) of the proper persons in the blank spaces to the left of the concepts.

___	1. Curve of forgetting	A.	Atkinson & Shiffrin
___	2. Sensory memory	B.	Brown & McNeill
___	3. Nonsense syllables	C.	Craik & Lockhart
___	4. Repression	D.	Ebbinghaus
___	5. Method of savings	E.	Freud
___	6. Levels-of-processing theory	F.	Loftus
___	7. Eyewitness testimony	G.	McDougall
___	8. Stages of memory	H.	Penfield
___	9. Neurosurgery	I.	The Petersons
___	10. Tip-of-the-tongue phenomenon	J.	Sperling
___	11. Childhood amnesia		
___	12. Interference		
___	13. Partial-report procedure		
___	14. Psychogenic amnesia		
___	15. Whole-report procedure		

ANSWER KEY TO EXERCISE

1. D	4. E	7. F	10. B	13. J
2. I, J	5. D	8. A	11. E	14. E
3. D	6. C	9. H	12. I	15. G

ESL | English as a Second Language—Bridging the Gap

a bit later (265)—a little later; a short time later

a vicious cycle (285)—occurs when one act produces a bad result, which produces another bad result, and so on (et cetera)

abide (262)—cannot remain

abrasion (277)—a scraped area where the surface is rubbed off

acronymn (266)—a word made from the first letters of words in a phrase

alter (285)—change

analogous to (281)—similar or comparable to

ashore (285)—on land; the edge of the water

assailant (277)—attacker

assaulted by images (285)—received strong mental pictures or memories

at the turn of the century (269)—when the years starting with 1800 ended and the years starting with 1900 began; each 100 years is called a *century*

at your fingertips (300)—easy to remember

attain (266)—accomplish; reach

authentic (266)—real

bank cash card (272)—a plastic credit card that allows a person to take money from a bank money machine

been drawn well into (267)—become involved in

behind you (274)—you have already done it and don't have to do it or think about it again

being seamless (271)—continuous without interruption

beleaguered (293)—to have had many problems and difficulties

biological (282)—physical

blizzard of 1988 (264)—an extremely heavy snowstorm (strong winds and a lot of snow) occurred in 1988 in the northeastern part of the United States

blow to the head (291)—a hit on the head

boo and hiss (294)—make noises that indicate the audience didn't like what he did

bride's apparel (262)—tradition that a bride should wear something old, something new, something borrowed, and something blue to guarantee future happiness

by doing so (266)—by doing this

CEGarette (288)—this is a misspelling of the word *cigarette*; however, the pronunciation is similar so the association works

chemotherapy (300)—chemical (drug) therapy for cancer treatment

cocktail parties (275)—late afternoon or evening parties where many people gather to talk and drink alcohol and eat snacks and meet new people; usually does not include dinner

color our memories (279)—have an effect on our memories

come back (265)—return to reading

conceptualize (276)—organize in our thoughts

concocted (277)—made up

condensed (266)—reduce to a smaller amount

culprit (280)—person responsible for a problem

cursed myself (274)—became angry with myself

declines with age, all but disappearing (270)—as the child gets older, the ability decreases and almost disappears

devastated (277)—damaged or destroyed

dilemma (279)—complicated difficulty

discriminate (282)—tell the difference between

distort (278)—change from accuracy

diverse (277)—different

dredging up (275)—remembering

duration (271)—length of time

dwell on (282)—continue thinking about

ears perked up (262)—listened intently and suddenly

easier on the digestion (273)—easier to undertake, or do

elaborated (262)—explained in detail

elementary school (262)—all children in the United States must start school at age 6 and attend elementary school (generally grade 1 to grade 6) and junior high school (generally grade 7 and grade 8) until age 16 years

embellishment (262)—adding extra details to make something more interesting

enamored (274)—enchanted, fascinated

ensuing (274)—following

eradicated (280)—eliminated

err in that (266)—make a mistake because

erroneously (263)—mistakenly

etched (282)—a picture or words lightly scratched into a surface

eucalyptus (282)—a type of tree that grows in warm climates

evidence is far more compelling (276)—there is no substantial proof

fallen into (271)—developed into

falls between the cracks (274)—is not retained; is lost

feed on happiness (285)—cause and also be the result of happiness

fell into (271)—could be classified, or grouped, into

first impressions tend to last (272)—what we notice or what we feel about a person the first time we meet influences how we continue to think and feel about the person

fixations (269)—when something stays focused on one object

flashed on a screen (269)—shown briefly on a screen and then removed

fostered (277)   encouraged

frantically searching (272)—looking in an urgent and upset manner

freak fencing accident (299)—an unusual and strange fencing accident; fencing is a sport involving two people fighting with swords

GM-CBS-IBM-ATT-CIA-FBI . . . (273)—GM = General Motors; CBS = Columbia Broadcasting System; IBM = International Business Machines; ATT = American Telephone and Telegraph; CIA = Central Intelligence Agency (government agency); FBI = Federal Bureau of Investigation (government agency)

go on, take a minute (265)—please, stop reading for a minute and do what I ask

going in one ear and out the other (267)—not retaining information

gone wrong? (267)—you have done wrong

got down on all fours and oinked like a pig (299)—got on his hands and knees and made noises to imitate a pig *grip of anger* (285)—the feeling of strong anger

had a quirk (276)—a particular habit that was different from other people's habits

hefty premiums (273)—a lot of extra money

high and dry (285)—to be without help when you need it (for example, when a boat is out of the water it is useless)

holds impressions briefly (269)—maintains impressions for a short time

hypnosis (278)—an artificially induced, sleeplike condition in which the person is very susceptible to suggestions from the hypnotist

impoverished (276)—didn't have much

in for it (276)—had to suffer because of it

in the ballpark (284)—close to being accurate (a reference to baseball; when a ball goes out of the ballpark it is out of bounds, or out of play)

indeed distorted by (276)—definitely altered by (emphasis)

infantile amnesia (291)—forgotten memories in children

jar your memory (301)—cause you to remember

juggling your new acquaintance's name (275)—trying to remember the new person's name

jump across in spurts (271)—cross in irregular movement

kiss your partner (301)—a custom in the United States, and perhaps other places, is to kiss the person you love at midnight on New Year's Eve

lends the grouping meaning (266)—the grouping (the way they are grouped together) then has meaning

lesioned (291)—a wound; in this case, purposely cutting away a part of the brain to help lessen a brain function problem

less than wholly reliable (276)—not completely trustworthy

let us have a try (267)—let us make an attempt

lifetime (267)—the complete life of a person

likens (274)—compares

long-term (262)—over a long period of time

manual shift (265)—a standard (hand-operated) shift to change gears in a car; it is different from an automatic shift

mass reveling (301)—large groups of people celebrating something

material they hold (263)—content they have

mental dressing down (274)—telling myself how terrible I am and that I should change

meticulous (262)—carefully accurate

might you have the nagging thought (301)—is it possible you will have a repetitive thought

much less those (262)—not even those (emphasis)

nasal sprays (298)—medicine that is sprayed (a small amount of liquid sent with force) into the nose

nature of the business (273)—type of business it is

neurosurgeon (275)—brain surgeon

no apologies (267)—I am not apologizing

no cheating! (262)—I don't want you to cheat or be unfair

not exactly (281)—this is not exactly true

not looking over Shakespeare's shoulder (263)—not standing next to Shakespeare and watching him write the play

not to be faulted (262)—no one could argue with her; she was right

not to be outdone (262)—did not want to have anyone tell better stories than she could; wanted attention

not weighted in the direction of (291)—does not support

often-cited (276)—the incident is told often

on chancy episodic memory (284)—unreliable episodic memory

on terra firma (285)—on the land; firm ground (Latin)

over time (266)—during a long period of time

participants could typically remember (289)—all of them could usually remember

persevere (264)—to continue on

persist (271)—remain

physiological response (285)—physical response

pick them out (282)—choose them

plaintiff (278)—person who brings the complaint

pop in (290)—enter the mind without trying to retrieve it

practice grisly surgery (265)—dismantle your computer, remove the mechanism; similar to conducting a surgical operation on a human

prior (262)—before

Public Broadcasting System documentary (284)—"PBS" is a TV network that has no advertising and specializes in educational programs and documentaries (nonfiction informational stories)

pushed in (290)—influenced in

put it another way (264)—say it another way; use different words

rapidly unfolding (292)—quickly occurring

read off (267)—read aloud

remarkably long periods (270)—unusually long periods; longer than expected

salient (282)—noticeable, significant

sandwiched in between (287)—put in between

self-reproach (274)—tell myself I should have done better

shoved on (274)—put on carelessly

similar to reeling in a fish but having it drop off the line just before it breaks the surface of the water (284)—like almost catching a fish but it gets free just before it comes out of the water

sort them out (271)—organize and distinguish them from each other

stall it (290)—cause the engine to stop operating because the car is in the wrong gear *stereotypical* (271)—expected because the children have learned stereotypes, or ideas in their heads, of what are appropriate toys for boys and girls

stick to words (265)—explain only in words

storage bins (299)—containers for storing things; in this case, places in the brain for storing memories

stream of thought, or of consciousness (267)—continuous thought without thinking about what is being thought

streamlike (269)—like a stream or river, a continuous flow

take a backseat (262)—become not as important as something else

tedious (266)—difficult, tiresome

tic-tac-toe grid (274)—a two-person game in which one person draws a series of intersecting lines to form squares, which each player tries to fill in with figures in a straight line while preventing the other from doing it

to date (280)—so far

toll-free (273)—no money (toll) is required to make the call

too . . . to hold water (291)—it cannot be true

too broad (291)—too wide; there are too many effects ("too" is negative here)

toot a horn, throw confetti (301)—traditional activities in the United States for celebrating the arrival of the New Year

trial by jars (295)—a series of words put together to form a memory device; the author wanted to remember an unfamiliar word that sounded like this phrase; these words aren't normally placed together, so he in

vented a story that explained them, and this mental picture helped him to remember the similar word he wanted to remember

tried to get back to it (272)—tried to do it again

trivial (262)—unimportant

truth of the matter (273)—actually

turn away (270)—stop looking at it

turn our attention to (292)—pay attention to something else

uncle's passing (292)—uncle's death

under the influence (285)—while the drug is in the body and affecting functions

upper limit (273)—the maximum

uptake (285)—taking in something

ushering in the new millennium (301)—welcome the next 1,000 years (10 centuries); the next millennium starts with the year 2000 A.D.

vast store house (275)—a very large storage area

very cloudy (291)—very unclear; not very clear

vibrancy in your step (281)—how wonderful you felt, which made you walk in an energetic, happy manner

with a vengeance (275)—emphatically; definitely; strongly

wove a wonderful patchwork quilt (262)—told a wonderful, intricate story; refers to bed covers that are made by hand and have intricate patterns

wreak havoc (274)—cause great disruption

Wyoming and Delaware (288)—Wyoming is a state in the western part of the United States, and Delaware is a state in the eastern part

ZIP code (273)—the number at the end of an address that indicates the postal region where a person lives

---

FILL-INS | **Chapter Review**

SECTION 1: THREE KINDS OF MEMORY

Memories of the events that happen to a person or take place in the person's presence are referred to as (1) _____dic memory. Generalized knowledge is referred to as (2) _____tic memory. We tend to use the phrase "I remember . . ." when we are referring to (3) _____dic memories, but we are more likely to say "I know . . ." in reference to (4) _____tic memories. (5) Pro_____ memory involves knowledge of how to do things. Procedural memory is also referred to as (6) s_____ memory.

SECTION 2: THREE PROCESSES OF MEMORY

The first stage of (7) _____ation processing, or changing information so that we can place it in memory, is called (8) _____ding. When we (9) en_____ information, we convert it into psychological formats that can be mentally represented. To do so, we commonly use (10) _____ual, (11) _____ory, and (12) _____tic codes. A visual code mentally (13) _____ sents information as a picture. An acoustic code represents information as a sequence of (14)_____ nds. Semantic codes represent stimuli in terms of their (15) _____ ing.

The second process of memory is (16) s _____, or the maintaining of information over time. One way of storing information is by (17) _____ nance rehearsal, or by mentally repeating it ("saying it to yourself").

The third memory process is (18) _____ val, or locating stored information and returning it to consciousness. Retrieval of information from memory requires knowledge of the proper (19)_____ es.

Memory is defined as the processes by which information is (20)_____ ded, stored, and (21)_____ ved.

SECTION 3: THREE STAGES OF MEMORY

The three stages of memory proposed by Atkinson and Shiffrin are (22) _____ sory memory, (23) s _____-_____ memory (STM), and (24) l _____-_____ memory (LTM). Sensory memory is the stage of memory first encountered by a (25) _____ lus. It holds impressions briefly, but long enough so that series of (26) _____ tions seem connected. The memory (27) t _____ of a stimulus lasts for only a fraction of a second. Memory traces are "held" in sensory (28) _____ ters. Sensory (29) m _____ consists of registers that can briefly hold information that is entered by means of our senses.

Sperling used the (30) p _____ -report procedure to show that there is a difference between what people can see and what they can report in the visual sensory register. Sperling concluded that the memory trace of visual stimuli (31) d _____ within a second in the visual sensory register.

The mental representations of visual stimuli are referred to as (32) _____ ns. The sensory register that holds icons is labeled (33) _____ _____ ory. Iconic memories are accurate, (34) _____ aphic memories. The ability to retain exact mental representations of visual stimuli over long amounts of time is referred to by psychologists as (35) _____ tic imagery. The mental representations of (36) _____ ory stimuli are called *echoes*. The sensory register that holds echoes is referred to as (37) _____ _____ ory. The memory (38) _____ ces of echoes can last for several seconds, many times longer than the traces of icons.

By focusing attention on a stimulus in the sensory register, you will retain it in (39) _____ -t _____ memory for a minute or so after the trace of the stimulus decays. Short-term memory is also referred to as (40) _____ ing memory. Most of us know that a way of retaining information in short-term memory—and possibly storing it permanently—is to (41) re _____ it. Rote repetition is referred to as (42) _____ ance rehearsal.

According to the (43) s _____ -position effect, we are most likely to recall the first and last items in a series. First items are likely to be rehearsed (44: More or Less?) frequently than other items. Last items are likely to have been rehearsed (45: Most or Least?) recently. The tendency to recall the initial items in a list is referred to as the (46) _____ cy effect. The tendency to recall the last items in a list is referred to as the (47) _____ cy effect.

Miller noted that the average person can maintain about (48: How Many?) chunks of information in short-term memory at a time. Children learn the alphabet by (49) r _____ —that is, by mechanical associative learning that requires time and (50) re _____. The Petersons showed that information can be displaced from short-term memory by means of (51) _____ ence. Long-term memory is the third stage of processing of (52) _____ tion.

Sigmund (53) F_____ believed that nearly all of our perceptions and ideas were stored permanently, but memories are not complete. Moreover, our memories are distorted by our (54) _____as, or ways of conceptualizing our worlds. That is, we (55) re_____ our recollections according to our schemas.

There (56: Is or Is Not?) evidence for a limit to the amount of information that can be stored in long-term memory. New information may displace older information in (57: Long or Short?) -term memory, but there is no evidence that memories in long-term memory are lost by displacement. However, we need the proper (58) c_____s to help us retrieve information in long-term memory.

Information may be transferred from short-term to long-term memory by several means, including rote repetition—also referred to as (59) _____ance rehearsal. In (60) _____tive rehearsal, new information is related to what is already known.

Psychologists have learned that we tend better to remember the events that occur under (61: Usual or Unusual?), emotionally arousing circumstances. We retain such detailed memories of events like these that they are referred to as (62) "fl_____ memories." One explanation for flashbulb memory is the (63) dis_____ of the memory. But major events, such as the assassination of a president or the loss of a close relative, also have important impacts on our lives. And so we are likely to form networks of associations to other pieces of information—that is, to rehearse them (64) _____tively.

We tend to organize information in long term memory according to a (65) _____cal structure.

The (66) t_____-of-the- (67) t_____ phenomenon—also referred to as the *feeling-of-knowing experience* seems to reflect incomplete or imperfect learning. The classic "TOT" experiment by Brown and McNeill also suggests that our storage systems are indexed according to cues that include both the sounds and the meanings of words—that is, according to both (68) _____tic and (69) _____tic codes.

(70) C_____-dependent memory refers to information that is better retrieved under the circumstances in which it was encoded and stored, or learned. State-dependent memory is an extension of (71) c_____-dependent memory and refers to the finding that we sometimes retrieve information better when we are in a (72) phys_____ or emotional state that is similar to the one in which we encoded and stored the information.

SECTION 4: THE LEVELS-OF-PROCESSING MODEL OF MEMORY

Craik and Lockhart suggest that we (73: Do or Do Not?) "have" a sensory memory, a short-term memory, and a long-term memory per se. They view our ability to remember in terms of a single stage or dimension—the degree to which we (74) pr_____ information. Put another way: According to the (75) l_____-of-processing model, memories tend to endure when information is processed deeply—when it is attended to, encoded carefully, pondered, and rehearsed elaboratively or related to things we already know well.

SECTION 5: FORGETTING

German psychologist Hermann (76) _____aus originated the use of nonsense syllables in the study of memory and forgetting. Nonsense syllables are (77: Meaningful or Meaningless?). Thus their retention is based on (78) ac_____ coding and maintenance (79) _____sal.

The three memory tasks listed in the text are (80) _____ition, (81) _____ll, and relearning. (82) Re_____ is the easiest type of memory task. In his own studies of recall, Ebbinghaus would read lists of (83) _____ _____bles aloud to the beat of a metronome and then see how many he could produce from memory. Psychologists also often use lists of pairs of nonsense syllables, called (84) _____ed _____ates, to measure recall.

People who show posthypnotic (85) _____a cannot recall previously learned word lists following hypnosis. Spanos and his colleagues hypothesize that posthypnotic amnesia occurs when hypnotized subjects interpret the suggestion not to recall information as an "invitation" to refrain from attending to (86) re_____ cues.

Ebbinghaus devised the method of (87) _____ings to study the efficiency of relearning. First he would record the number of repetitions required to learn a list of (88) n_____ syllables or words. Then he would record the number of repetitions required to (89) re_____ the list after a certain amount of time had elapsed. He would compute the difference between the numbers of (90) _____tions required to arrive at the savings. According to Ebbinghaus's classic curve of (91) _____ting, there is no loss of memory as measured by savings immediately after a list has been learned. Recollection drops (92: Gradually or Precipitously?) during the first hour after learning a list. Losses of learning then become more (93: Gradual or Precipitous?).

According to (94) _____ence theory, we forget material in short-term and long-term memory because newly learned material interferes with it. In (95) _____tive interference, new learning interferes with the retrieval of old learning. In (96) _____tive interference, older learning interferes with the capacity to retrieve more recently learned material.

According to Sigmund Freud, we repress many painful memories and unacceptable ideas because they produce (97) an_____, guilt, and shame. Psychoanalysts believe that repression is at the heart of disorders such as (98) _____tive amnesia.

Freud discovered that we usually cannot remember events that took place prior to the age of (99) _____. Freud labeled this phenomenon infantile (100) am_____ and attributed it to (101) re_____. However, the text suggests that infantile amnesia probably reflects the interaction of physiological and (102) _____tive factors. For example, the (103) hip_____, which is involved in memory formation, does not mature until about the age of 2. Moreover, infants' lack of language impairs their ability to (104) en_____ information.

In (105) _____rade amnesia there are memory lapses for the period following a traumatic event, such as a blow to the head, electric shock, or an operation. In (106) _____rade amnesia the source of trauma prevents people from remembering events that took place beforehand.

SECTION 6: METHODS FOR IMPROVING MEMORY

One way to improve memory is by rote (107) _____ance rehearsal, otherwise referred to as (108) dr_____ and practice. A method based on the concept of elaborative rehearsal is to (109) r_____ new information to that which is already known. It is also helpful to form unusual, exaggerated (110) _____tions. So-called (111) _____ic devices combine chunks of information into formats such as acronyms or phrases.

SECTION 7: THE BIOLOGY OF MEMORY

The storage of experience apparently requires that the number of avenues of communication among brain cells be increased by means of development of (112) _____ites and (113) _____pses. Research with sea snails has shown that more of the (114) _____mitter serotonin is released at certain synapses when they are conditioned. As a result, transmission at these synapses becomes (115: More or Less?) efficient as trials (learning) progress.

The hormone (116) _____line generally stimulates bodily arousal and activity. Adrenaline and (117) _____uretic hormone strengthen memory when they are released following learning.

The hippocampus is involved in relaying incoming sensory information to parts of the (118) cor_____. Therefore, it appears vital to the storage of (119: New or Old?) information, even if (120: New or Old?) information can be retrieved without it. Persons with hippocampal damage can form new (121) _____ral memories, even though they cannot form new (122) _____ic memories.

The (123) _____mus, a structure near the center of the brain, seems involved in the formation of verbal memories.

ANSWER KEY TO CHAPTER REVIEW

1. Episodic	32. Icons	63. Distinctness (or discriminability)	94. Interference
2. Semantic	33. Iconic memory	64. Elaboratively	95. Retroactive
3. Episodic	34. Photographic	65. Hierarchical	96. Proactive
4. Semantic	35. Eidetic	66. Tip	97. Anxiety
5. Procedural	36. Auditory	67. Tongue	98. Dissociative
6. Skill	37. Sensory memory	68. Acoustic	99. 3
7. Information	38. Traces	69. Semantic	100. Amnesia
8. Encoding	39. Short-term	70. Context	101. Repression
9. Encode	40. Working	71. Context	102. Cognitive
10. Visual	41. Rehearse (or repeat)	72. Physiological	103. Hippocampus
11. Auditory	42. Maintenance	73. Do not	104. Encode
12. Semantic	43. Serial	74. Process	105. Anterograde
13. Represents	44. More	75. Levels	106. Retrograde
14. Sounds	45. Most	76. Ebbinghaus	107. Maintenance
15. Meaning	46. Primacy	77. Meaningless	108. Drill
16. Storage	47. Recency	78. Acoustic	109. Relate
17. Maintenance	48. Seven	79. Rehearsal	110. Associations
18. Retrieval	49. Rote	80. Recognition	111. Mnemonic
19. Cues	50. Repetition	81. Recall	112. Dendrites
20. Encoded	51. Interference	82. Recognition	113. Synapses
21. Retrieved	52. Information	83. Nonsense syllables	114. Neurotransmitter
22. Sensory	53. Freud	84. Paired associates	115. More
23. Short-term	54. Schemas	85. Amnesia	116. Adrenaline
24. Long-term	55. Reconstruct	86. Retrieval	117. Antidiuretic
25. Stimulus	56. Is not	87. Savings	118. Cortex
26. Perceptions	57. Short	88. Nonsense	119. New
27. Trace	58. Cues	89. Relearn	120. Old
28. Registers	59. Maintenance	90. Repetitions	121. Procedural
29. Memory	60. Elaborative	91. Forgetting	122. Episodic
30. Partial	61. Unusual	92. Precipitously	123. Thalamus
31. Decays	62. Flashbulb	93. Gradual	

1. Tim remembers that Shakespeare wrote *Hamlet*. This type of memory is referred to as a(n)
   a. episodic memory.
   b. metamemory.
   c. procedural memory.
   d. semantic memory.

2. George Sperling used the _____ method in his studies of sensory memory.
   a. partial-report
   b. savings
   c. paired-associates
   d. whole-report

3. Visual impressions last for _____ in the sensory memory.
   a. up to a second
   b. about 2–5 seconds
   c. about half a minute
   d. several minutes or longer

4. Only about 5% of children show
   a. metamemory.
   b. iconic memory.
   c. photographic memory.
   d. eidetic imagery.

5. Echoic memory is defined as
   a. an acoustic code.
   b. the pathways between the thalamus and the auditory cortex.
   c. the sensory register that holds auditory stimuli.
   d. a type of procedural memory.

6. *Working memory* is another term for
   a. iconic memory.
   c. semantic memory.
   c. elaborative rehearsal.
   d. short-term memory.

7. You are given the task of remembering the written phrase "Every good boy does fine." You "say" the phrase "mentally," or "to yourself," and then you repeat it to yourself 10 times. Which of the following methods have you employed?
   a. visual encoding and elaborative rehearsal
   b. acoustic encoding and maintenance rehearsal
   c. semantic encoding and maintenance rehearsal
   d. episodic memory and procedural memory

8. You are asked to memorize this list of letters: TBJKZMGXTR. You repeat the list several times. Which letters are you most likely to recall?
   a. the sequence *JKM*
   b. the sequence *ZM*
   c. the *Z* and the *X*
   d. the first *T* and the *R*

9. A student studies for a test in the room in which the test will be administered. The student is apparently hoping that performance will be facilitated by
   a. context-dependent memory.
   b. state-dependent memory.
   c. photographic memory.
   d. iconic memory.

10. Information is least likely to be lost through decay in
    a. iconic memory.
    b. echoic memory.
    c. short-term memory.
    d. long-term memory.

11. Which of the following has been compared to a shelf or workbench so that once it is full, some things fall off when new items are shoved on?
    a. episodic memory
    b. sensory memory
    c. short-term memory
    d. long-term memory

12. Which of the following is most likely to remain firmly "embedded" in your memory over the decades?
    a. the name of your second-grade teacher
    b. a sonnet you memorized in high school
    c. how you celebrated your 11th birthday
    d. how to ride a bicycle

13. John forgets a dental appointment about which he had been extremely anxious. Freud would probably attribute his forgetting to
    a. repression.
    b. anterograde amnesia.
    c. proactive interference.
    d. decay of the memory trace.

14. Loftus and Palmer showed people a film of a car crash and then asked them to fill out questionnaires that included a question about how fast the cars were going at the time. People who reported that the car was going fastest had been asked to estimate how fast the cars were going when they _____ one another.
    a. "hit"
    b. "smashed" into
    c. "bumped" into
    d. "touched"

15. Which of the following does the text state is the most effective way of transferring information from STM into LTM?
    a. eidetic imagery
    b. maintenance rehearsal
    c. elaborative rehearsal
    d. becoming emotionally aroused

16. According to the text, the feeling-of-knowing experience seems to reflect
    a. lack of visual retrieval cues.
    b. incomplete or imperfect learning.
    c. skill memory rather than semantic memory.
    d. STM displacement by anxiety-evoking information.

17. A parent knows that you are taking a psychology course and asks how he can teach his young child the alphabet. You note that children usually learn the alphabet by
    a. mechanical associative learning.
    b. use of elaborative rehearsal.
    c. semantic coding.
    d. chunking.

18. Information in short-term memory tends to be forgotten by means of
    a. psychogenic amnesia.
    b. failure to use appropriate retrieval cues.
    c. displacement.
    d. retrograde amnesia.

19. The easiest type of memory task is
    a. recall.
    b. recognition.
    c. relearning.
    d. savings.

20. When sea snails are conditioned, more of the neurotransmitter _____ is released at certain synapses. As a result, transmission at these synapses becomes more efficient as trials (learning) progress.
    a. acetylcholine
    b. dopamine
    c. norepinephrine
    d. serotonin

ANSWER KEY TO POSTTEST

1. D	4. D	7. B	10. D	13. A	16. B	19. B
2. A	5. C	8. D	11. C	14. B	17. A	20. D
3. A	6. D	9. A	12. D	15. C	18. C	

LEARNING OBJECTIVES

When you have finished studying Chapter 8, you should be able to:

CONCEPTS AND PROTOTYPES: BUILDING BLOCKS OF THOUGHT
1. Explain how concepts and prototypes function as building blocks of thought.

PROBLEM SOLVING
2. Describe various approaches to problem solving.
3. Discuss factors that affect problem solving.

CREATIVITY
4. Discuss the relationships between problem solving, creativity, and intelligence.
5. Discuss factors that affect creativity.

REASONING
6. Describe various types of reasoning.

JUDGMENT AND DECISION MAKING
7. Discuss the role of heuristics in decision making.
8. Discuss factors that affect judgment and decision making.

LANGUAGE
9. Explain the properties of language.
10. Discuss the basics of language: phonology, morphology, syntax, and semantics.

LANGUAGE DEVELOPMENT
11. Trace the development of language.
12. Discuss theories of language development.

LANGUAGE AND THOUGHT
13. Discuss the relationships between language and thought.

Thinking and Language

PRETEST *Truth or Fiction?*

_____ It may be boring, but using the "tried and true" formula is the most efficient way to solve a problem.

_____ Only people are capable of solving problems by means of insight.

_____ The best way to solve a frustrating problem is to keep plugging away at it.

_____ Highly intelligent people are creative.

_____ We are more creative when we are paid to be creative.

_____ If *A* are *B*, and some *B* are *C*, then some *A* are *C*.

_____ If a couple has five sons, the sixth child is likely to be a daughter.

_____ An ice cream that is 97% fat free has less fat than an ice cream whose fat content makes up 10% of its calories.

_____ People change their opinions when they are shown to be wrong.

_____ The majority of people around the world speak at least two languages.

WHEN my daughter Jordan was 9 years old, she hit me with a problem about a bus driver that she had heard in school. Since I firmly believe in exposing students to the tortures I have undergone, see what you can do with her problem:

You're driving a bus that's leaving from Pennsylvania. To start off with, there were 32 people on the bus. And at the next bus stop, 11 people got off and 9 people got on. At the next bus stop, 2 people got off and 2 people got on. At the next bus stop, 12 people got on and 16 people got off. At the next bus stop, 5 people got on and 3 people got off. What color are the bus driver's eyes?

Now, I was not about to be fooled when I was listening to this problem. Although it seemed clear that I should be keeping track of how many people are on the bus, I had an inkling that a trick was involved. Therefore, I first instructed myself to remember that the bus was leaving from Pennsylvania. Being clever, I also kept track of the number of stops rather than the number of people getting on and off the bus. When I was finally hit with the question about the bus driver's eyes, I was at a loss. I protested that Jordan had said nothing about the bus driver's eyes, but she insisted that she had given me enough information to answer the question.

One of the requirements of problem solving is paying attention to relevant information (de Jong & Das-Smaal, 1995). To do that, you need some familiarity with the type of problem. I immediately classified the bus driver problem as a trick question and paid attention to apparently superfluous information. But I wasn't good enough.

The vast human ability to solve problems has allowed people to build skyscrapers, create computers, and scan the interior of the body without surgery. Some people even manage to keep track of their children and balance their checkbooks. Problem solving is one aspect of *thinking*. **Thinking** is mental activity that is involved in understanding, processing, and communicating information. Thinking entails attending to information, mentally representing it, reasoning about it, and making judgments and decisions about it. The term *thinking* generally refers to conscious, planned attempts to make sense of things (Matlin, 1994). Cognitive psychologists usually do not characterize the less deliberate cognitive activities of daydreaming or the more automatic usages of language as thinking. Yet language is entwined with much of human thought. The uniquely human capacities to conceptualize mathematical theorems and philosophical treatises rely on language. Moreover, language allows us to communicate our thoughts and record them for posterity.

In this chapter we explore the broad topics of thinking and language. We begin with concepts, which provide building blocks of thought. We wend our way toward language, which lends human thought a unique richness and beauty.

Before we proceed, I have one question for you: What color were the bus driver's eyes?

CONCEPTS AND PROTOTYPES: BUILDING BLOCKS OF THOUGHT

I began the chapter with a problem posed by my daughter Jordan. Let me proceed with a riddle from my own childhood: "What's black and white and read all over?" Since this riddle was spoken, not written, and since it involved the

---

Thinking • Mental activity that is involved in understanding, manipulating, and communicating about information. Thinking entails paying attention to information, mentally representing it, reasoning about it, and making decisions about it.

colors black and white, you would probably assume that "read" was spelled "red." Thus, in seeking an answer, you might scan your memory for an object that was red although it also somehow managed to be black and white. The answer to the riddle, "newspaper," usually met with a good groan.

The word *newspaper* is a **concept.** *Red, black,* and *white* are also concepts—color concepts. Concepts are mental categories used to classify together objects, relations, events, abstractions, or qualities that have common properties. Concepts are crucial to cognition. They represent aspects of the environment and of ourselves. In the cases of imagination and creativity, concepts can represent objects, events, activities, and ideas that never were. Much of thinking has to do with categorizing new objects and events and with manipulating the relationships among concepts.

We tend to organize concepts in hierarchies. The newspaper category includes objects such as your school paper and the *Los Angeles Times.* Newspapers, college textbooks, novels, and merchandise catalogs can be combined into higher-order categories such as *printed matter* or *printed devices that store information.* If you add CD-ROMs and floppy disks, you can create a still higher category, *objects that store information.* Now consider a question that requires categorical thinking: How are a newspaper and CD-ROM alike? Answers to such questions entail supplying the category that includes both objects. In this case, we can say that they both store information. That is, their functions are similar, even if their technology is very different. Here is another question: How are the brain and a CD-ROM alike? Yes, again, both can be said to store information. How are the brain and a CD-ROM different? To answer this question, we find a category in which only one of them belongs. For example, only the brain is a living thing. Functionally, moreover, the brain does much more than store information. The CD-ROM is an electronic device. People are not electronic devices. Could we, however, make the case that electricity is involved in human thinking? (Refer to the discussion of the neural impulse in Chapter 5.)

Prototypes are examples that best match the essential features of categories. In less technical terms, prototypes are good examples (Rosch, 1978). When new stimuli closely match people's prototypes of concepts, they are readily recognized as examples. Which animal better seems more birdlike to you? A sparrow or an ostrich? Why? Which of the following better fits the prototype of a fish? A sea horse or a shark? Both self-love and maternal love may be forms of love, but more people readily agree that maternal love is a kind of love. Maternal love apparently better fits their prototype of love (Fehr & Russell, 1991).

Many lower animals can be said to possess instinctive or inborn prototypes of various concepts. Male robins attack round reddish objects that are similar in appearance to the breasts of other male robins—even when they have been reared in isolation and have thus never seen another male robin. People, however, generally acquire prototypes on the basis of experience. Many simple prototypes such as *dog* and *red* are taught by **exemplars.** We point to a dog and say, "dog" or "This is a dog" to a child. Dogs are considered to be **positive instances** of the dog concept. **Negative instances**—that is, things that are not dogs—are then shown to the child while one says, "This is *not* a dog." Negative instances of one concept may be positive instances of another. So, in teaching a child, one may be more likely to say, "This is not a dog—it's a cat" than simply "This is not a dog."

Children may at first include horses and other four-legged animals within the dog schema or concept until the differences between dogs and horses are pointed out. (To them, the initial category could be more appropriately labeled

**MINILECTURE:
MENTAL IMAGES**

Concept • A mental category that is used to classify together objects, relations, events, abstractions, or qualities that have common properties.
Prototype • A concept of a category of objects or events that serves as a good example of the category.
Exemplar • A specific example.
Positive instance • An example of a concept.
Negative instance • An idea, event, or object that is *not* an example of a concept. Concept formation is aided by presentation of positive and negative instances.

**MINILECTURE:
THE PROTOTYPE APPROACH**

"fuzzy-wuzzies.") In language development, the overinclusion of instances in a category (reference to horses as dogs) is labeled *overextension*. Children's prototypes become refined as the result of being shown positive and negative instances and being given verbal explanations.

Abstract concepts such as *bachelor* or *square root* are typically formed through verbal explanations that involve more basic concepts (Barsalou, 1992). If one points repeatedly to *bachelors* (positive instances) and *not bachelors* (negative instances), a child may eventually learn that bachelors are males or adult males. However, it is doubtful that this show-and-tell method would ever teach them that bachelors are adult human males who are unmarried. The concept *bachelor* is best taught by explanation after the child understands the concepts of maleness and marriage.

Still more abstract concepts such as *justice, goodness, beauty,* and *love* may require complex explanations and many positive and negative instances as examples. These concepts are so abstract and instances so varied that no two people may agree on their definition. Or, if their definitions coincide, they may argue over positive versus negative instances (things that are beautiful and things that are ugly). What seems to be a beautiful work of art to me may impress you as meaningless jumbles of color. Thus the phrase "Beauty is in the eye of the beholder."

Reflections

- What strategy were you using to try to solve the bus driver problem? Were you misled or not? Why?
- When you were a child, some people were probably introduced to you as Aunt Bea or Uncle Harry. Do you remember when you first understood the concept of aunt or uncle? Can you think of ways of teaching these concepts to small children without using verbal explanation?
- Which concepts in this textbook have you found the most simple or most difficult to understand? Why?

PROBLEM SOLVING

Now I have the pleasure of sharing something personal with you. One of the pleasures I derived from my own introductory psychology course lay in showing friends the textbook and getting them involved in the problems in the section on problem solving. First, of course, I struggled with the problems myself. It's that time, now. And it's your turn. Get some scrap paper, take a breath, and have a go at the following problems. The answers will be discussed in the following pages, but don't peek. *Try* the problems first.

1. Provide the next two letters in the series for each of the following:
    a. ABABABAB??
    b. ABDEBCEF??
    c. OTTFFSSE??

2. Draw straight lines through all the points in part A of Figure 8.1, using only *four* lines. Do not lift your pencil from the paper or retrace your steps. (Answers are given in Figure 8.5.)

3. Move three matches in part B of Figure 8.1 to make four squares of the same size. You must use *all* the matches. (The answer is shown in Figure 8.5.)

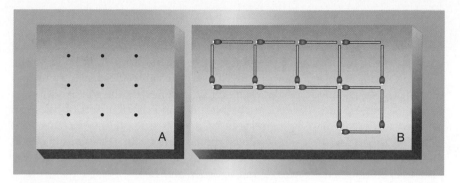

FIGURE 8.1

Two Problems. Draw straight lines through all the points in part A, using only four lines. Do not lift your pencil or retrace your steps. Move three matches in part B to make four squares equal in size. Use all the matches.

4. You have three jars—A, B, and C—which hold the amounts of water, in ounces, shown in Table 8.1. For each of the seven problems in Table 8.1, use the jars in any way you wish to arrive at the indicated amount of water. Fill or empty any jar as often as you wish. How do you obtain the desired amount of water in each problem? (The solutions are discussed on pages 323, 325 and 326.)

Approaches to Problem Solving: Getting from Here to There

What steps did you use to try to solve parts a and b of problem 1? Did you first make sure you understood the problem by rereading the instructions? Or did you dive right in as soon as you saw them on the page? Perhaps 1a and 1b came easily, but I'm sure that you studied 1c very carefully.

TABLE 8.1
WATER-JAR PROBLEMS

	THREE JARS ARE PRESENT WITH THE LISTED CAPACITY (IN OUNCES)			
PROBLEM	JAR A	JAR B	JAR C	GOAL
1	21	127	3	100
2	14	163	25	99
3	18	43	10	5
4	9	42	6	21
5	20	59	4	31
6	23	49	3	20
7	10	36	7	3

For each problem, how can you use some combination of the three jars given, and a tap, to obtain precisely the amount of water shown?

Source: Adapted from *Rigidity of Behavior* (p. 109), by A. S. Luchins and E. H. Luchins, 1959, Eugene: University of Oregon Press.

After you believed you understood what was required in each problem, you probably sought to discover the structure of the cycles in each series. Series 1a has repeated cycles of two letters: *AB, AB,* and so on. Series 1b may be seen as having four cycles of two consecutive letters: *AB, DE, BC,* and so on.

Again, did you solve 1a and 1b in a flash of insight, or did you try to find rules that govern the advance of each series? In series 1a, the rule is simply to repeat the cycle. Series 1b is more complicated, and different sets of rules can be used to describe it. One correct set of rules is that odd-numbered cycles (*1* and *3,* or *AB* and *BC*) simply repeat the last letter of the previous cycle (in this case *B*) and then advance by one letter in the alphabet. The same rule applies to even-numbered cycles (*2* and *4,* or *DE* and *EF*).

If you found rules for problems 1a and 1b, you used them to produce the next letters in the series: *AB* in series 1a, and *CD* in series 1b. Perhaps you then evaluated the effectiveness of your rules by checking your answers against the solutions in the preceding paragraphs.

Question: What alternate sets of rules could you have found to describe these two series? Would you have generated the same answers from these rules?

In this section, we explore approaches to problem solving. We begin where you may have begun with the letters series: understanding the problem. Then we discuss various strategies for attacking the problem, including the use of algorithms, heuristic devices, and analogies.

Understanding • Constructing a coherent mental representation of a problem.

UNDERSTANDING THE PROBLEM.   Let us begin our discussion of understanding problems by considering a bus driver problem that is very similar to the one my daughter Jordan gave me. This one is "official," however. That is, it appeared in the psychological literature:

> Suppose you are a bus driver. On the first stop, you pick up 6 men and 2 women. At the second stop, 2 men leave and 1 woman boards the bus. At the third stop, 1 man leaves and 2 women enter the bus. At the fourth stop, 3 men get on and 3 women get off. At the fifth stop, 2 men get off, 3 men get on, 1 woman gets off and 2 women get on. What is the bus driver's name? (Halpern, 1989, p. 392)

Both versions of the bus driver problem demonstrate that a crucial factor in understanding a problem is focusing on the key information. If we assume that it is crucial to keep track of the numbers of people getting on and off the bus, we are focusing on information that turns out to be unessential. In fact, it distracts us from focusing on the crucial information.

When we are faced with a novel problem, how can we know which information is relevant and which is irrelevant? Background knowledge in the problem area helps. If you are given a chemistry problem, it helps if you have taken some courses in chemistry. If my daughter Jordan gives you a problem, it is helpful to expect the unexpected, or to head for the hills. (In case you still haven't noticed, by the way, the critical information you need to solve both bus driver problems is indicated in the first sentence.)

Understanding a problem means constructing a coherent mental representation of the problem. The mental representation of the problem can include symbols or concepts, such as algebraic symbols or words. It can include lists, graphs, and visual images (Adeyemo, 1990; Hegarty and others, 1995). Successful understanding of a problem generally requires three features:

1. *The parts or elements of our mental representation of the problem relate to one another in a meaningful way.* If we are trying to solve a problem in

geometry, our mental triangles should have angles that total 180 degrees and not 360 degrees.

2. *The elements of our mental representation of the problem correspond to the elements of the problem in the outer world.* If we are neutralizing an acid to wind up with a salt and water, our mental representation of water should be H_2O and not OH. The elements of our mental representations must include the key elements for solving the problem, such as the information in the first sentence of the bus driver problem. We prepare ourselves to solve a problem by familiarizing ourselves with its elements and defining our goals as clearly as possible. Part of understanding algebra and geometry problems is outlining all of the givens.

3. *We have a storehouse of background knowledge that we can apply to the problem.* We have taken the necessary coursework to solve problems in algebra and chemistry. The architect has a broad understanding of building materials and styles to apply to the problem of designing a particular structure for a particular site. A broad knowledge base may allow us to classify the problem or find analogies. When given a geometry problem involving a triangle, one may think, "Does this problem seem to be similar to problems I've solved by using the quadratic equation?"

ALGORITHMS. An **algorithm** is a specific procedure for solving a type of problem. An algorithm will invariably lead to the solution—if it is used properly, that is. Mathematical formulas—such as the Pythagorean Theorem—are examples of algorithms. They will yield correct answers to problems *as long as the right formula is used*. Finding the right formula to solve a problem may require scanning one's memory for all formulas that contain variables that represent one or more of the elements in the problem. The Pythagorean Theorem concerns triangles with right angles. Therefore, it is appropriate to consider using this formula for problems concerning right angles but not for others.

Consider anagram problems, in which we try to reorganize groups of letters into words. Some anagram problems require us to use every letter from the

Algorithm • A systematic procedure for solving a problem that works invariably when it is correctly applied.

Heading for a Fight. Psychologists help people solve problems—for example, ways of averting aggression. In a particular form of therapy called problem-solving therapy, clients are encouraged to consider sample social provocations, generate multiple behavioral solutions (other than violent ones), try out the most promising, and evaluate their effectiveness.

pool of letters; others allow us to use only some of the letters. How many words can you make from the pool of letters DWARG? If you were to use the algorithm termed the **systematic random search,** you would list every possible letter combination, using from one to all five letters. You could use a dictionary or a spell-checking computer software program to see whether each result is, in fact, a word. Such a method might be plodding, but it would work.

Systematic random searches are made practical in many cases by using a computer. If you were to use a computer to solve the DWARG anagram problem, you might instruct it to engage in a systematic random search as follows: First, instruct it to list every possible letter combination, using from 1 to 5 letters. Second, instruct it to run a spell-checking program over the potential solutions. Third, instruct it to print out only the combinations that are identified as words by the spell-checking program.

Did you develop an algorithm for solving the bus driver problem? Did it involve rereading the problem slowly, checking every word to determine whether it held a clue to the solution? Have you developed an algorithm for doing well in this course? Does it involve smiling at your professor now and then and keeping your fingers crossed, or something a bit more . . . substantive?

HEURISTICS.   **Heuristics** are rules of thumb that help us simplify and solve problems. Heuristics, in contrast to algorithms, do not guarantee a correct solution to a problem. They are shortcuts. When they work, they allow for more rapid solutions (Anderson, 1991). A heuristic device for solving the anagram problem would be to look for familiar letter combinations that are found in words and then to check the remaining letters for words that include these combinations. In DWARG, for example, we can find the familiar combinations *dr* and *gr.* We may then quickly find *draw, drag,* and *grad.* The drawback to this method, however, is that we might miss some words.

Truth or Fiction Revisited. *It is not true that using the "tried and true" formula is the most efficient way to solve a problem.* Using a tried and true formula—that is, an algorithm—may be less efficient than using a heuristic device.

One type of heuristic device is the **means-end analysis.** In using this heuristic device, we assess the difference between our current situation and our goals and then do what we can to reduce this discrepancy. Let's say that you are out in your car and lost. You know that your goal is west of your current location and on the other side of the railroad tracks. A heuristic device would be to drive toward the setting sun (west) and, at the same time, to remain alert for railroad tracks. If the road comes to an end and you must turn left or right, you can scan the distance in either direction for tracks. If you don't see any, turn right or left, but then, at the next major intersection, turn toward the setting sun again. Eventually you may get there. If not, you could use that most boring of algorithms: ask people for directions until you find someone who knows the route.

When an inexperienced chess player is stuck for a move, she or he could engage in a systematic random search. That is, she could examine each piece remaining on the board and visualize every move the rules will allow each piece to make. Lengthy. She could make the process even lengthier by imagining every possible countermove to each move, several moves hence. If there are many pieces on the board, it is not difficult to imagine the combinations quickly running into the billions. Chess players—even inexperienced chess players—tend to use heuristic devices or rules of thumb, however. The ultimate goal is to win the game. Chess players focus on subgoals, for example, such as trying to capture the center of the board, protecting the king, or trying

Systematic random search   •   An algorithm for solving problems in which each possible solution is tested according to a particular set of rules.

Heuristics   •   Rules of thumb that help us simplify and solve problems.

Means-end analysis   •   A heuristic device in which we try to solve a problem by evaluating the difference between the current situation and the goal.

out a Sicilian defense. They also use means-end analysis. They consider their subgoals and imagine ways of reducing the discrepancies between their current positions and their subgoals (for example, trying to castle to protect the king). Experienced players also search their memories for games that entailed similar or identical positions.

As we see in playing chess, one strategy of achieving a sizable goal is to break it up into more manageable subgoals. The goal of writing a term paper on psychological ways of managing stress can be broken down into subgoals such as making a list of the subtopics to be included (relaxation, exercise, and so forth), taking notes on recent research on each topic, creating a first draft in each area, and so on. This approach does not mean that there is less work to do. However, it provides direction and helps outline a number of more readily attainable goals. It is thus easier to get going.

A few expert chess players are capable of reflecting on similar positions in classic chess matches. As we see in the following section, experts search for *analogies* that will help them achieve their goals.

ANALOGIES.   An *analogy* is a partial similarity among things that are different in other ways. During the cold war, some people in the United States believed in the so-called domino theory. Seeing nations as analogous to dominoes, they argued that if one nation were allowed to fall to communism, its neighbor would be likely to follow. In the late 1980s, a sort of reverse domino effect actually occurred as communism collapsed in Eastern Europe. When communism collapsed in one nation, it became likely to collapse in neighboring nations as well.

The analogy heuristic applies the solution of an earlier problem to the solution of a new one. We use the analogy heuristic frequently, whenever we try to solve a new problem by referring to a previous problem (Halpern and others, 1990). Consider the water-jar problems in Table 8.1. Problem 2 is analogous to problem 1. Therefore, the approach to solving problem 1 works with problem 2. (Later we consider what happens when the analogy heuristic fails.)

Lawyers look for analogies (called *precedents*) when they prepare cases for argument. Precedents inform them as to what types of arguments have and have not worked in the past. Psychologists and physicians consider analogies (usually in the form of case studies) when they are attempting to understand a new case and create a treatment plan. Knowing what does *not* work can be as important as knowing what works.

The chess player might think, "Karpov was in a similar [analogous] position in 1977 and was checkmated in four moves when he moved his king." (Yes, she truly might summon up such a game.) People who are good at solving math problems tend to categorize the problem properly. That is, they recognize what *type* of problem it is—and thus summon up the right formulas. Solving a problem by analogy requires locating or retrieving relevant prior problems and adapting the solution of earlier problems to the current problem (Novick & Holyoak, 1991).

Let us see whether you can use the analogy heuristic to your advantage in the following number series problem: To solve problems 1a, 1b, and 1c on page 316, you had to figure out the rules that guide the order of the letters. Survey this series of numbers and find the rule that guides their order:

8, 5, 4, 9, 1, 7, 6, 3, 2, 0

Hint: The problem is somewhat analogous to problem 1c.[1]

---

[1] The analogous element is that there is a correspondence between these numbers and the first letter in the English word that spells them out (Matlin, 1994). What would you do to the words to arrive at this order?

Factors That Affect Problem Solving

The way in which you approach a problem is central to how effective you are at solving it. Other factors also affect your effectiveness at problem solving. Three of them—your level of expertise, whether you fall prey to a mental set, and whether you develop insight into the problem—can be conceptualized as residing in you. A couple of problem characteristics also affect their solution: the extent to which the elements of the problem are fixed in function, and the way in which the problem is defined.

EXPERTISE.   To appreciate the role of expertise in problem solving, unscramble the following anagrams taken from Novick and Coté (1992). In each case, use all of the letters to form an actual English word:

DNSUO

RCWDO

IASYD

How long did it take you to unscramble each anagram? Would a person whose native language is English solve each problem (unscramble each anagram) more efficiently than a bilingual person who spoke another language in the home? Why or why not?

Experts solve problems more efficiently, more rapidly than novices do. (That is why they are called *experts*). Although it may be considered "smart" to be able to solve a particular kind of problem, experts do not necessarily exceed novices in general intelligence. Their areas of expertise may be quite limited. For example, the knowledge and skills required to determine whether a Northern Renaissance painting is a forgery are quite different from those that are used to find words that rhyme with elephant or to determine the area of a parallelogram. Generally speaking, experts at solving a certain kind of problem have a more extensive knowledge base in the area, have better memories for the elements in the problems, form mental images or representations that facilitate problem solving (Clement, 1991), relate the problem to other problems that are similar in structure, and have more efficient methods for problem solving (Hershey and others, 1990). These factors are interrelated. An art historian, for example, acquires a database that permits her or him to understand the intricacies of paintings. As a result, her or his memory for paintings—and who painted them—expands vastly. People whose native language is English are likely to have a more extensive database of English words, which should make them more efficient at unscrambling anagrams of English words. Their extensive English database should also facilitate their learning and memory of new English words.

Novick and Coté (1992) found that the solutions to the three anagram problems seemed to "pop out" in under 2 seconds among "experts." The experts apparently had more efficient methods than the novices. Experts seemed to use *parallel processing*. That is, they dealt simultaneously with two or more elements of the problems—in this case, the anagrams. In the case of DNSUO, for example, they may have played with the order of the vowels (*UO* or *OU*) at the same time they tested which consonant (*D, N,* or *S*) was likely to precede them, arriving quickly at *sou* and *sound*. Novices were more likely to engage in *serial processing*—to handle one element of the problem at a time.

MENTAL SETS.   Jordan hit me with another question: "A farmer had 17 sheep. All but 9 died. How many sheep did he have left?" Being a victim of a mental set, I assumed that this was a subtraction problem and gave the answer 8. She

**MINILECTURE:
BLOCKS OF PROBLEM
SOLVING**

gleefully informed me that she hadn't said "9 died." She had said "*all but 9* died." Therefore, the correct answer was 9. (Get it?) Put it another way: I had not *understood* the problem. My mental representation of the problem did not correspond to the actual elements of the problem. I resolved to actually pay attention when Jordan riddled me in the future.

Return to problem 1, part c, on page 316. To try to solve this problem, did you seek a pattern of letters that involved cycles and the alphabet? If so, it may be because parts a and b were solved by this approach.

The tendency to respond to a new problem with the same approach that helped solve earlier, similar-looking problems is termed a **mental set.** Mental sets usually make our work easier, but they can mislead us when the similarity between problems is illusory, as in part c of problem 1. Here is a clue: Part c is not an alphabet series. Each of the letters in the series *stands* for something. If you can discover what they stand for (that is, discover the rule), you will be able to generate the 9th and 10th letters. (The answer is in Figure 8.5 on p. 328.)

Have another look at water-jar problem 6. The formula $B-A-2C$ will solve this problem. Is that how you solved it? Note also that the problem could have been solved more efficiently by using the formula $A-C$. If the second formula did not occur to you, it may be because of the mental set you acquired from solving the first five problems.

INSIGHT: AHA!   To gain insight into the role of insight in problem solving, consider the following problem, which was posed by Janet Metcalfe:

> A stranger approached a museum curator and offered him an ancient bronze coin. The coin had an authentic appearance and was marked with the date 544 B.C. The curator had happily made acquisitions from suspicious sources before, but this time he promptly called the police and had the stranger arrested. Why? (1986, p. 624)

I'm not going to give you the answer to this problem (drat?). Instead, I'll give you a guarantee. When you arrive at the solution, it will hit you all at once. You'll think "Aha!" or "Of course!" or something a bit less polite. It will seem as though there is a sudden reorganization of the pieces of information in the problem so that the solution leaps out at you—in a flash.

Problem solving by means of insight is very important in the history of psychology (Sternberg & Davidson, 1994). Consider a classic piece of research by a German psychologist who was stranded with some laboratory subjects on a Canary Island during World War I. Gestalt psychologist Wolfgang Köhler became convinced of the reality of insight when one of his chimpanzees, Sultan, "went bananas." Sultan had learned to use a stick to rake in bananas placed outside his cage. But now Herr Köhler (pronounced *hair curler*) gave Sultan a new problem. He placed the banana beyond the reach of the stick. However, he gave Sultan two bamboo poles that could be fitted together to make a single pole long enough to retrieve the delectable reward. The setup was similar to that shown in Figure 8.2.

As if to make this historic occasion more dramatic, Sultan at first tried to reach the banana with one pole. When he could not do so, he returned to fiddling with the sticks. Köhler left the laboratory after an hour or so of frustration (his own as well as Sultan's). An assistant was assigned the thankless task of observing Sultan. But soon afterward, Sultan happened to align the two sticks as he fiddled. Then, in what seemed to be a flash of inspiration, Sultan fitted them together and pulled in the elusive banana. Köhler was summoned to the laboratory. When he arrived the sticks fell apart, as if on cue. But Sultan

Jordan. The author's daughter, Jordan, posed the problem, "A farmer had 17 sheep. All but 9 died. How many sheep were left?" What is the answer?

Mental set • The tendency to respond to a new problem with an approach that was successfully used with similar problems.

FIGURE 8.2

A Demonstration of Insight or Just Some Fiddling with Sticks? Gestalt psychologist Wolfgang Köhler ran experiments with chimpanzees to highlight the nature of problem solving by insight. This chimp must retrieve a stick outside the cage and attach it to a stick he already has before he can retrieve the distant circular object. While fiddling with two such sticks, Sultan, another chimp, seemed to suddenly recognize that the sticks could be attached. This is an example of problem solving by insight.

Insight • In Gestalt psychology, a sudden perception of relationships among elements of the "perceptual field," permitting the solution of a problem.

Cognitive map • A mental representation or picture of the elements in a learning situation, such as a maze.

**MINILECTURE:
COGNITIVE MAPS**

regathered them, fit them firmly together, and actually tested the strength of the fit before retrieving another banana.

Köhler was impressed by Sultan's rapid "perception of relationships" and used the term **insight** to describe it. He noted that such insights are not acquired gradually. Rather, they seem to occur "in a flash" when the elements of a problem had been arranged appropriately. Sultan also proved himself to be immediately capable of stringing several sticks together to retrieve various objects, not just bananas. It appeared that Sultan understood the principle of the relationship between joining sticks and reaching distant objects.

Soon after Köhler's findings were reported, psychologists in the United States demonstrated that even rats are capable of rudimentary forms of problem solving by insight. E. C. Tolman (1948) showed that rats behaved as if they had acquired **cognitive maps** of mazes. Although they would learn many paths to a food goal, they would typically choose the shortest. If the shortest path was blocked, they would quickly switch to another.

Bismarck, one of psychologist N. R. F. Maier's laboratory rats, provided further evidence of insight in laboratory rats (Maier & Schneirla, 1935). Bismarck had been trained to climb a ladder to a tabletop where food was placed. On one occasion, Maier used a mesh barrier to prevent Bismarck from reaching his goal. But, as shown in Figure 8.3, a second ladder to the table was provided. The second ladder was in clear view of the animal. At first, Bismarck sniffed and scratched and made every effort to find a path through the mesh barrier. Then Bismarck spent some time washing his face, an activity that apparently signals frustration in rats. Suddenly, Bismarck jumped into the air, turned, ran down the familiar ladder around to the new ladder, ran up the new ladder, and then claimed his just desserts. It seems that Bismarck suddenly perceived the relationships between the elements of his problem so that the solution occurred by insight. He seems to have had what Gestalt psychologists have termed an "Aha! experience."

Truth or Fiction Revisited. *It is not true that only people are capable of solving problems by means of insight.* Classic research evidence shows that lower animals, including apes and rats, are also capable of insight (a sudden reorganization of the perceptual field).

Let us return to the problems at the beginning of the section. How did you do with problem 1, part c, and problems 2 and 3? Students tend to fiddle around with them for a while, as Sultan fiddled with his sticks. The solutions, when they come, appear to arrive in a flash. Students set the stage for the flash of insight by studying the elements in the problems carefully, repeating the rules to themselves, and trying to imagine what a solution might look like. If you produced and then tried out solutions that did not meet the goals, you may have become frustrated and thought, "The heck with it! I'll come back to it later." Standing back from the problem may allow the **incubation** of insight. An incubator warms chicken eggs for a while so that they will hatch. Incubation in problem solving refers to standing back from the problem for a while as some mysterious process in us seems to continue to work on it. Later, the answer may occur to us in a flash of insight. When standing back from the problem is helpful, it may be because it provides us with some distance from unprofitable but persistent mental sets (Azar, 1995c).

Truth or Fiction Revisited. *It is not true that the best way to solve a frustrating problem is to keep plugging away at it.* It may be better to distance oneself from the problem for a while and allow it to "incubate." Eventually you may solve the problem in what seems to be a flash of insight.

Have another look at the possible role of incubation in helping us overcome mental sets. Consider the seventh water-jar problem. What if we had tried all sorts of solutions involving the three water jars, and none had worked?

Incubation • In problem solving, a hypothetical process that sometimes occurs when we stand back from a frustrating problem for a while and the solution "suddenly" appears.

FIGURE 8.3

Bismarck Uses a Cognitive Map to Claim His Just Desserts. Bismarck has learned to reach dinner by climbing ladder *A*. But now the food goal (*F*) is blocked by a wire mesh barrier (*B*). Bismarck washes his face for a while, but then, in an apparent flash of insight, runs back down ladder *A* and up new ladder *N* to reach the goal.

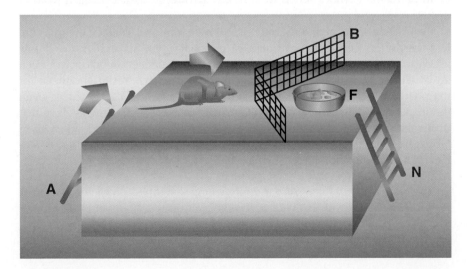

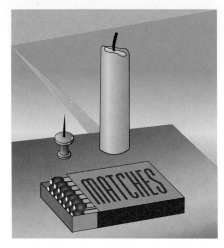

FIGURE 8.4

The Duncker Candle Problem. Can you use the objects shown on the table to attach the candle to the wall of the room so that it will burn properly?

What if we were then to stand back from this water-jar problem for a day or two? Is it not possible that with a little distance we might suddenly recall a 10, a 7, and a 3—three elements of the problem—and realize that we can arrive at the correct answer by using only two water jars? Our solution might seem too easy, and we might check Table 8.1 cautiously to make certain that the numbers are there as remembered. Perhaps our incubation period would have done nothing more than unbind us from the mental set that problem 7 *ought* to be solved by the formula *B−A−2C*.

FUNCTIONAL FIXEDNESS. **Functional fixedness** may also impair your problem-solving efforts. For example, first ask yourself what a pair of pliers is. Is it a tool for grasping, a paperweight, or a weapon? A pair of pliers could function as any of these, but your tendency to think of it as a grasping tool is fostered by your experience with it. You have probably used a pair of pliers only for grasping things. Functional fixedness is the tendency to think of an object in terms of its name or its familiar usage. Functional fixedness can be similar to a mental set in that it can make it difficult for you to use familiar objects to solve problems in novel ways.

Now that you know what functional fixedness is, let's see if you can overcome it by solving the Duncker candle problem. You enter a room that has the following objects on a table: a candle, a box of matches, and some thumbtacks (see Figure 8.4). Your task is to use the objects on the table to attach the candle to the wall of the room so that it will burn properly. (The answer is shown in Figure 8.5.)

You may know that soldiers in survival training in the desert are taught to view insects and snakes as sources of food rather than as pests or threats. But it would be understandable if you chose to show civilian functional fixedness for as long as possible if you were stuck in the desert.

THE DEFINITION OF THE PROBLEM. Problems can be well-defined or ill-defined. In a **well-defined problem,** the original state, the goal, and the rules for reaching the goal are all clearly spelled out (Medin & Ross, 1992). The water-jar problems are well-defined in that we know the size of each jar (the original state), each goal state (exactly how much water is to be obtained), and the rules (how we may use the water jars to reach the goal). Well-defined problems also have specific ways in which we can determine whether we have reached a solution. For example, we know that we have solved the anagram problem, RCWDO, when we arrive at a correctly spelled English word—*crowd.*

In an **ill-defined problem,** the original state, the goal state, or the rules are less than clear. Consider the (unlikely) possibility that an architect is simply asked to design a house. You might think that an architect would savor such an ill-defined problem because of the freedom it grants. Yet, it is difficult for the architect to know when she or he has been successful. Of course, given the inadequate definition of the problem, the architect could always claim that under the circumstances, any design is a success. In the real world, an architect would likely be given a site for a house, a budget, a requested number of bedrooms, and information about the housing styles (for example, Georgian colonial or contemporary) that a client prefers.

There are various strategies for approaching ill-defined problems (Medin & Ross, 1992). One involves dividing the problem into subproblems. The architect might begin by thinking, Let me begin by designing an ideal master bedroom. Or one could implant structure on the problem where none existed. The architect might think, Let me assume that I must design a contemporary

---

Functional fixedness • The tendency to view an object in terms of its name or familiar usage.

Well-defined problem • A problem in which the original state, the goal, and the rules for reaching the goal are clearly spelled out.

Ill-defined problem • A problem in which the original state, the goal, or the rules are less than clear.

house for a bluff that sits high above a bay. Or one could just get started and stop when she or he has arrived at a solution. The architect could simply start sketching and see what happens.

Reflections

- How did you go about solving the problems presented at the beginning of the section? Which did you get right? Which did you get wrong? Why?
- Did you develop an algorithm for solving the bus driver problem? What is it? Did you attempt to use heuristic devices? What were they?
- How can you use subgoals to develop a strategy for doing well in this course? For doing well in an athletic event?
- Are you an expert at solving math problems? Social problems? Automobile problems? Musical problems? How did you get to be an expert?
- Think of an example in which a mental set or functional fixedness interfered with your ability to solve a problem.
- Think of an example in which you were struggling and then suddenly developed insight into a problem or an academic subject.

**MINILECTURE:
WELL-FORMED VERSUS
ILL-FORMED PROBLEMS**

CREATIVITY

A creative person may be more capable of solving problems to which there are no preexisting solutions, no tried and tested formulas.

A professor of mine once remarked that there is nothing new under the sun, only novel combinations of old elements. To him, the core of **creativity** was the ability to generate novel combinations of existing elements. Many

Creativity • The ability to generate novel solutions to problems.

Creativity. This photograph shows Chinese American artist Hung Liu with her work "Burial at Little Golden Village." What is the relationship between intelligence and creativity?

psychologists concur. They view creativity as the ability to make unusual, sometimes remote, associations to the elements of a problem to generate new combinations that meet the goals (Boden, 1994). An essential aspect of a creative response is the leap from the elements of the problem to the novel solution (Amabile, 1990). A predictable solution is not particularly creative, even if it is difficult to arrive at.

According to Guilford (1967), creativity demands divergent thinking rather than convergent thinking. In **convergent thinking,** thought is limited to present facts as the problem-solver tries to narrow thinking to find the best solution. In **divergent thinking,** the problem-solver associates more fluently and freely to the various elements of the problem. The problem-solver allows "leads" to run a nearly limitless course to determine whether they will eventually combine as needed.

Successful problem solving may require both divergent and convergent thinking. At first, divergent thinking generates many possible solutions. Convergent thinking is then used to select the most probable solutions and reject the others.

Convergent thinking • A thought process that attempts to narrow in on the single best solution to a problem.

Divergent thinking • A thought process that attempts to generate multiple solutions to problems.

Creativity and Intelligence: Was Picasso Smart?

It might seem that a creative person would be highly intelligent. However, the relationship between intelligence and creativity is moderate at best. Although creative people do tend to be intelligent, intelligence is no guarantee of creativity (Sternberg, 1990). For example, a Canadian study found that a group of highly intelligent ("gifted") boys and girls aged 9 to 11 was more creative than a group of less intelligent children. However, some of the gifted children were no more creative than their less intelligent peers (Kershner & Ledger, 1985). In

FIGURE 8.5

Answers to Problems on Pages 316–317 and 326. For problem 1c, note that each of the letters is the first letter of the numbers one through eight. Therefore, the two missing letters are NT, for nine and ten. The solutions to problems 2 and 3 are shown in this illustration. Solving the Duncker candle problem requires using a thumbtack to pin the matchbox to the wall, then setting the candle on top of the box. Functional fixedness prevents many would-be problem-solvers from conceptualizing the matchbox as anything more than a device to hold the matches. Wrong answers include trying to affix the bottom of the candle to the wall with melted wax and trying to tack the candle to the wall.

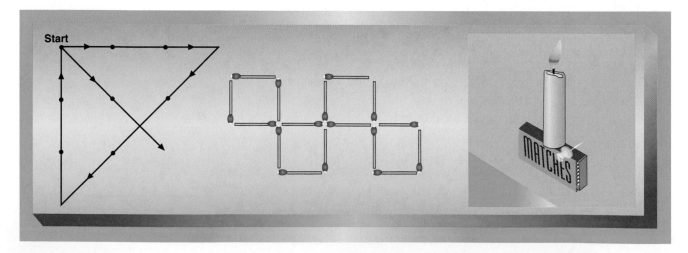

this particular study, the girls were significantly more creative than the boys, especially on verbal tasks.

Moreover, tests that measure intelligence are not useful in measuring creativity. Intelligence test questions usually require convergent thinking to narrow in on the answer. On an intelligence test, an ingenious answer that differs from the designated answer is wrong. Tests of creativity are oriented toward determining how flexible and fluent thinking can be. Here, for example, is an item from a test used by Getzels and Jackson (1962) to measure associative ability, a factor in creativity: "Write as many meanings as you can for each of the following words: (a) duck; (b) sack; (c) pitch; (d) fair." Those who write several meanings for each word, rather than only one, are rated as being potentially more creative.

Another measure of creativity might ask people to produce as many words as possible that begin with *T* and end with *N* within a minute. Still another item might give people a minute to classify a list of names in as many ways as possible. In how many different ways can you classify the following group of names?

MARTHA   PAUL   JEFFRY   SALLY   PABLO   JOAN

Truth or Fiction Revisited. *It is not necessarily true that highly intelligent people are creative.* The statement is an overgeneralization. Although highly intelligent people are more likely to be creative than people with below-average intelligence, many intelligent people are relatively unimaginative.

Factors in Creativity: Are Starving Artists More Creative?

If there is only a modest connection between creativity and intelligence, what factors do contribute to creativity? Some factors reside within the person, and some involve the social setting.

PERSONAL FACTORS. Creative people show flexibility, fluency (in generating words and ideas), and originality (Azar, 1995c). Getzels and Jackson (1962) found that creative schoolchildren tend to express, rather than inhibit, their feelings and to be playful and independent. Creative people tend to be independent and nonconformist, but independence and nonconformity do not necessarily make a person creative. Negative stereotypes of creative artists have led to exaggerations of nonconformity.

Nevertheless, creative children are often at odds with their teachers because of their independence. Faced with the chore of managing upward of 30 pupils, teachers too often label quiet and submissive children as "good" children. These studies of creativity may also explain in part why there have been many more male than female artists throughout history, even though modern research does not find boys to be more creative than girls (e.g., Kershner & Ledger, 1985). Over the years, traits like independence and nonconformity are more likely to have been discouraged in females than in males, because they are inconsistent with the passive and compliant social roles traditionally ascribed to females. Because of the women's movement, the number of women in the creative arts and sciences is growing rapidly today. In the past, the creativity of many girls may have been nipped in the bud.

SOCIAL EVALUATION. Research evidence shows that concern about evaluation by other people reduces creativity. In one experiment, college students were asked to write poems under two very different sets of expectations (Amabile, 1990). Half the students were informed that the experimenter intended only to examine their handwriting—not the aesthetic value of the poetry. The remaining students were informed that judges, who were poets, would supply them with written evaluations of their poetry's content and form. The students who expected to be evaluated according to the form and content of their work turned in significantly less creative poems.

Amabile (1990) found that the following four conditions reduce creativity:

1. Being watched while you are working
2. Being offered a reward for creativity
3. Competing for prizes
4. Having your choices or options restricted by someone else's rules

In short, when pressure prevails, creativity plummets.

Truth or Fiction Revisited. *It is not true that we are more creative when we are paid to be creative.* External pressures, including external rewards, very often dampen creativity rather than encourage it.

BRAINSTORMING.   **Brainstorming** is a group process that encourages creativity by stimulating a great number of ideas—even wild ideas—and suspending judgment until the process is completed. Note that brainstorming is not expected to work when other people evaluate one's ideas. A friendly atmosphere that supports wildly divergent ideas is assumed to be effective.

Matlin (1994) notes that psychologists have become somewhat skeptical of the brainstorming concept, however. For one thing, research evidence suggests that people who are working alone are often more creative than people who are working in groups. (Consider the cliché "A camel is a horse made by a committee.") Moreover, the ideas produced by brainstorming are frequently poorer in quality than those produced by people working alone.

Brainstorming • A group process that encourages creativity by stimulating a large number of ideas and suspending judgment until the process is completed.

Reflections

- Do you know people whom you consider to be creative? How do their traits compare with those discussed in this section?
- In your own experience, what are the connections between creativity and intelligence? Do you know people who are highly creative in art or some other area but who do not impress you as being more intelligent overall than the average person?
- Can you force creativity? You have certainly felt pressured at times to arrive at creative solutions to problems on tests. How did the pressure (for example, the amount of time left) affect you? Did it stimulate you to be more creative, or did it add to the difficulty? Why?
- Have you ever brainstormed as a group member attempting to come up with creative ideas—for example, on a class project? What was the experience like? Did the group process help or get in the way? How?

REASONING

We are not done. I have more puzzles to solve, more weighty things to consider. Ponder this preposterous proposition:

> If *A* are *B,* and some *B* are *C,* then some *A* are *C.*

Is it true or false? What say you?

I confess that upon first seeing this proposition, I believed that it was true. It seemed that we were logically progressing to higher-order categories at each step along the way (see Figure 8.6, part A). For example, if apples (*A*) are fruit (*B*), and fruit (*B*) are food (*C*), then apples (*A*) are food (*C*). But so much for categorical thinking. So much for reasoning. I was bamboozled by the "some." My example with the apples omitted the word. Consider another example of this proposition, one that uses "some": If circles (*A*) are shapes (*B*), and *some* shapes (*B*) are squares (*C*), then *some* circles (*A*) are squares (*C*). Not so! By using the qualifying term "some," we can move both up to a higher-order category (from circles to shapes) and back down to a lower-order category (from shapes to squares; see Figure 8.6, part B).

Truth or Fiction Revisited. *It is not true that if* A *are* B, *and some* B *are* C, *then some* A *are* C. We can test the truthfulness of such abstract propositions by plugging in actual objects. Critical thinkers also pay special attention to statements that have qualifying words such as *some, sometimes, always,* or *never.*

Types of Reasoning

We have been toying with an example of reasoning. **Reasoning** is the transforming of information to reach conclusions. Let us consider two kinds of reasoning: *deductive reasoning* and *inductive reasoning.*

Deductive reasoning is a form of reasoning in which the conclusion must be true if the premises are true. Consider this classic, three-sentence argument:

1. All persons are mortal.
2. Socrates is a person.
3. Therefore, Socrates is mortal.

Sentences 1 and 2 in this argument are called the **premises.** Premises provide the assumptions or basic information that allows people to draw conclusions. Sentence 3 is the conclusion. In this example, sentence 1 makes a statement about a category (persons). Sentence 2 assigns an individual (Socrates) to the category (persons). Sentence 3 concludes that what is true of the category (persons) is true for the member of the category (Socrates). The conclusion, sentence 3, is said to be *deduced* from the premises. The conclusion about Socrates is true if the premises are true.

In **inductive reasoning,** we reason from individual cases or particular facts to a general conclusion. Consider a transformation of the example of deductive reasoning:

1. Socrates is a person.
2. Socrates is mortal.
3. Therefore, persons are mortal.

The conclusion happens to be correct, but it is illogical. The fact that one person is mortal does not guarantee that all people are mortal.

Inductive reasoning, then, does not permit us to draw absolute conclusions. Yet inductive reasoning is used all the time. We conclude that a certain type of food will or will not make us ill because of our experiences on earlier occasions. ("Buttered popcorn made me nauseous. This is buttered popcorn. Therefore, this will make me nauseous.") We assume that a cheerful smile and "Hello!" will work as an icebreaker with a new acquaintance because it has worked before. Although none of these conclusions is as logical as a deductive conclusion, inductive conclusions are correct often enough so that we can get on with our daily lives with some degree of confidence.

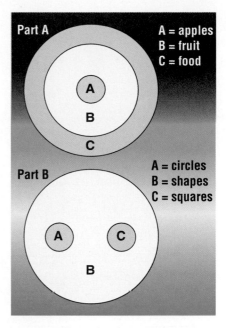

FIGURE 8.6

When Are *A* Also *C*? In part A of this figure, *A* (apples) are also *C* (food) because food represents a higher-order category that contains all apples. In part B, however, *C* (squares) is not higher order than *A* (circles). Therefore, *C* does not contain *A*. *B* (shapes), however, is higher order than both *A* and *C* and contains both.

Reasoning • The transforming of information to reach conclusions.

Deductive reasoning • A form of reasoning about arguments in which conclusions are deduced from premises. The conclusions are true if the premises are true.

Premise • A statement or assertion that serves as the basis for an argument.

Inductive reasoning • A form of reasoning in which we reason from individual cases or particular facts to a general conclusion.

Inductive reasoning is also used in psychological research. We draw samples that we believe represent certain populations. We then conduct research with those samples. We assume that the conclusions we reach with the research samples will apply to the populations. However, we cannot be absolutely certain that our samples are representative. Even if they are, there may be a few cases in the population that are so unusual that we cannot generalize to them. Nevertheless, we are correct in our conclusions often enough that the research enterprise is largely successful.

Reflections

- Do you recognize the following kind of argument?
    1. John says that too much money is spent on education.
    2. John is a (pick one: teacher, father, man, doctor, minister, congressional representative, talk show host).
    3. Therefore, too much money is spent on education.
       What sort of appeal is used in this argument? Is the argument logical? Is the conclusion correct? Think of examples of similar kinds of arguments from your own experiences.
- Provide an example of deductive reasoning and an example of inductive reasoning that is connected with your own life.

JUDGMENT AND DECISION MAKING

Decisions, decisions. Should you go for breakfast before classes begin or catch a few extra winks? Should you get married or remain single? (Should you get divorced or remain married?) Should you take a job or go on for advanced training when you complete your college program? If you opt for the job, cash will soon be jingling in your pockets. Yet, later you may wonder if you have the education to reach your potential. By furthering your education, you may have to delay independence and gratification, but you may find a more fulfilling position later on. Ah, decisions, decisions.

Other kinds of decisions are judgments about the nature of the world. We make judgments about which route to school or work will be the least crowded. We make judgments about where it is safe and convenient to live. We make judgments about political candidates and about which ice cream to buy.

You might like to think that people are so rational that they carefully weigh all the pluses and minuses when they make judgments or decisions. Or you might think that they insist upon finding and examining all the relevant information. Actually, people make most run-of-the-mill, daily decisions on the basis of limited information. They take shortcuts. They use heuristic devices— rules of thumb—in their judgments and decision making, just as they do in problem solving. Fortunately, the shortcuts tend not to land them in serious hot water—at least most of the time. In this section we consider heuristic devices and two other factors in judgments and decision making: the framing effect and overconfidence.

Heuristics in Decision Making: If It Works, Must It Be Logical?

Let us begin by asking you to imagine that you flip a coin six times. The coin has one head and one tail (take my word for it). In the following three possible outcomes, *H* stands for head and *T* stands for tail. Circle the sequence that is most likely:

H H H H H H

H H H T T T

T H H T H T

Did you select T H H T H T as the most likely sequence of events? Most people do (Matlin, 1994). Why? There are two reasons. First, people recognize that six heads in a row are unlikely. (The probability of achieving six heads is ½ x ½ x ½ x ½ x ½ x ½, or 1/64th.) Three heads and three tails are more likely than six heads (or six tails). Second, people recognize that the sequence of heads and tails ought to appear random. T H H T H T has a random look to it, whereas H H H T T T does not.

People can be said to select T H H T H T because of the **representativeness heuristic.** According to this decision-making heuristic, people make judgments about events (samples) according to the populations of events that they appear to represent (Kosonen & Winne, 1995). In this case, the sample of events is six coin tosses. The population is an infinite number of random coin tosses. But guess what, dear reader. *Each* of the sequences is equally likely (or unlikely). If the question had been whether six heads or three heads and three tails had been more likely, the correct answer would have been three and three. If the question had been whether heads and tails would be more likely to be consecutive or in random order, the correct answer would have been random order. But each of the three sequences shown is a specific sequence. What, in other words, is the probability of attaining the specific sequence T H H T H T? The probability that the first coin toss will result in a tail is ½. The probability that the second will result in a head is ½. Etc., etc. Thus, the probability of attaining the exact sequence T H H T H T is identical to that of achieving any other specific sequence: ½ x ½ x ½ x ½ x ½ x ½ = 1/64th. (Don't just sit there. Try this all out on a friend.)

Or consider this question: If a couple has five children, all of whom are boys, is their sixth child more likely to be a boy or a girl? Use of the representativeness heuristic would lead one to imagine that the couple is due for a girl. That is, five boys and one girl is closer than six boys to the assumed random distribution that accounts for roughly equal numbers of boys and girls in the world. But people with some knowledge of reproductive biology might predict that another boy is actually more likely, since five boys in a row may be too many to be a random biological event. On the other hand, if the couple's conception of a boy or girl were truly random, what would be the probability of conceiving another boy? Answer: ½.

Truth or Fiction Revisited. *It is not true that if a couple has five sons, the sixth child is likely to be a daughter.*

Another heuristic device used in decision making is the **availability heuristic.** According to this heuristic, our estimates of frequency or probability are based on how easy it is to find examples of relevant events. Let me ask you whether there are more art majors or sociology majors at your college. Unless you are familiar with the enrollment statistics, you will probably answer on the basis of the numbers of art majors and sociology majors that you personally know. Knowledge of these individuals is available to you.

Events that are more recent or more well-publicized tend to more available. Diseases such as emphysema and diabetes cause many times more death than accidents. Accidents are more likely to be reported in the media, however. Therefore, most people tend to exaggerate the number of deaths due to accidents but to underestimate the number of deaths due to emphysema and diabetes. Similarly, the media tend to focus on murder and other acts of violence,

Representativeness heuristic • A decision-making heuristic in which people make judgments about samples according to the populations they appear to represent.

Availability heuristic • A decision-making heuristic in which our estimates of frequency or probability of events are based on how easy it is to find examples.

leading people to overestimate the incidence of aggression in our society (Silver and others, 1994). I am a metropolitan New Yorker. Many people from other parts of the United States judge the Big Apple by sensationalistic news reports of violence there. Thus, as I travel around the country, I constantly run into people who seem surprised that I feel that it is safe enough to live in the area.

The **anchoring and adjustment heuristic** suggests that there can be a good deal of inertia to our judgments. In forming opinions or making estimates, we have an initial view or presumption. This is the anchor. As we receive additional information, we make adjustments. A bit begrudgingly. That is, if you grow up believing that one religion or one political party is the correct religion or political party, the belief serves as a cognitive anchor. When inconsistencies show up in your religion or political party, you may adjust your views of them, but perhaps not without some kicking and screaming.

Let us illustrate further by means of a math problem. Write each of the following multiplication problems on a separate piece of paper:

A. $8 \times 7 \times 6 \times 5 \times 4 \times 3 \times 2 \times 1$

B. $1 \times 2 \times 3 \times 4 \times 5 \times 6 \times 7 \times 8$

Show problem A to a few friends. Give them each 5 seconds to estimate the answer. Show problem B to other friends. Give them 5 seconds to estimate the answer as well.

The answers to the multiplication problems are the same since the order of the quantities being multiplied does not change the outcome. However, when Tversky and Kahneman (1982) showed these multiplication problems to high school students, the median estimate of students who were given version A was significantly higher than that of students who were given version B. Students who saw 8 in the first position offered an average estimate of 2,250. Students who saw 1 in the first position gave an average estimate of 512. That is, the estimate was larger when 8, not 1, served as the anchor. What, by the way, is the correct answer to the multiplication problems? Can you use the anchoring and adjustment heuristic to explain why both groups of students were so far off in their estimates?

Anchoring and adjustment heuristic • A decision-making heuristic in which a presumption or first estimate serves as a cognitive anchor. As we receive additional information, we make adjustments, but tend to remain in the proximity of the anchor.

The Framing Effect: Say That Again?

If you were on a low-fat diet, would you be more likely to choose an ice cream that is 97% fat free or an ice cream whose fat content makes up 10% of its calorie content? On one shopping excursion, I was impressed with an ice cream package's claims that the product was 97% fat free. Yet when I read the package closely, I noticed that a 4-ounce serving had 160 calories, 27 of which were contributed by fat. Fat, then, accounted for 27/160ths, or 16.875%, of the ice cream's calorie content. But fat only accounted for 3% of the ice cream's *weight*. The packagers of the ice cream knew all about the *framing effect*. They understood that labeling the ice cream as "97% fat free" would make it sound more healthful than "Only 17% of calories from fat."

Truth or Fiction Revisited. *It is not true that an ice cream that is 97% fat free has less fat than an ice cream whose fat content makes up 10% of its calories.* The answer depends on how the measures are taken. A brand of ice cream I bought was 97% fat free in terms of the relative weights of the ingredients, but fat contributed 16.88% of the calories. In this case, if fat had contributed 10% of the calories, the ice cream would have been more than 98% fat free in terms of weight. We tend to be impressed with the "97% fat free" claim because of the framing effect.

The **framing effect** refers to the way in which wording, or the context in which information is presented, can influence decision making. Political groups are as aware as advertisers of the role of the framing effect. For example, proponents of legalized abortion refer to themselves as "pro-choice." Opponents of abortion refer to themselves as "pro-life." Thus each group frames itself in a way that is positive ("pro" something) and refers to a value (the values of freedom and of life) with which it would be difficult to argue.

Because early detection of cancer enhances the likelihood of survival, health professionals encourage people to obtain regular screening for cancer. Their persuasive arguments can be framed to emphasize the benefits of obtaining screening or the risks of failing to do so. In an experiment run by psychologist Sara Banks and her colleagues (1995), one group of women viewed a videotape that emphasized that obtaining mammography to screen for breast cancer could save their lives. Another group of women viewed a tape that emphasized that failure to detect breast cancer early could cost them their lives. Women who were warned of the risks of failure to use mammography were more likely to obtain a mammogram in the 12 months following the treatment than were women who learned about the benefits of mammography.

Parents are also aware of the framing effect. My 3-year-old, Taylor, was invited to a play date at Abigail's house. I first asked Taylor, "Would you like to play with Abigail at her house?" The question met with a resounding no. I thought things over and reframed the question: "Would you like to play at Abigail's house and have a real fun time? She has lots of toys and games, and I'll pick you up real soon." This time Taylor's decision was yes.

Consider the following two possible survey questions to gain insight into the role of the framing effect—the effect of wording—in surveys:

1. Do you agree or disagree that women should have the same opportunities as men to seek fulfillment in the workplace?

2. Do you agree or disagree that women who have difficulty finding good day care for very young children should remain with the children in the home rather than work?

Try them out on your friends and see which earns greater agreement. Can you account for the difference?

The framing effect is also connected with the findings of Gestalt psychologists that the context in which information occurs affects its perception. In part A of Figure 1.3 on page 13, we saw that dots of the same size might be perceived as smaller or larger because of their context. Similarly, the same symbol might be interpreted as either a B or the number 13, depending on its context (see Figure 1.3, part C).

Framing effect • The influence of wording, or the context in which information is presented, on decision making.

Overconfidence: Is Your Hindsight 20–20?

Whether our decisions are correct or incorrect, most of us tend to have overconfidence in them (Gigerenzer and others, 1991; Lundeberg and others, 1994). Overconfidence applies to judgments as wide-ranging as whether one will be infected by the virus that causes AIDS (Goldman & Harlow, 1993; van der Velde and others, 1994), predicting the outcome of elections (Hawkins & Hastie, 1990), asserting that one's answers to test items are correct (Lundeberg and others, 1994), and selecting stocks. Many people refuse to alter their judgments even in the face of statistical evidence that is running against them.

WORLD OF DIVERSITY

ACROSS THE GREAT DIVIDE? WHITE AMERICANS VERSUS AFRICAN AMERICANS ON THE O. J. SIMPSON VERDICT

Through 1994 and 1995 the United States was held spellbound by the trial of sports celebrity O. J. Simpson, who had been charged with the murders of Nicole Brown Simpson and Ronald Goldman. After a parade of 126 witnesses over 133 days of testimony, a jury with a majority of African Americans acquitted Simpson.

As suggested by poll after poll, a majority of African Americans were pleased with the verdict. Most White Americans were not. Table 8.2 reports the results of a national telephone survey of 760 adults conducted for *Newsweek* magazine.

HEURISTICS IN DECISION MAKING

How do we account for the racial discrepancy? People use heuristic devices to arrive at judgments and decisions. Consider the *representativeness heuristic*. To many White observers, the Simpson case represented a more or less standard case of spouse abuse and murder. To many African American observers, the Simpson case represented a case in which the Los Angeles Police Department had proved itself to be racist.

What of the *availability heuristic?* Many White observers had skepticism available based on Simpson's financial ability to assemble a "dream team" of attorneys. Many African American observers had experiences of suffering discrimination at the hands of police available.

And what of the *anchoring and adjustment heuristic?* Most White observers began with faith in the police and the criminal justice system. Most African American observers began with lack of faith in both.

TABLE 8.2
RESULTS OF *NEWSWEEK* POLL ON ATTITUDES OF AFRICAN AMERICANS VERSUS WHITE AMERICANS TOWARD THE JURY DECISION IN THE O. J. SIMPSON MURDER CASE

	RACE	
	AFRICAN AMERICAN	WHITE
Percent agreeing with the jury's verdict of not guilty	85%	32%
Percent saying they thought the jury was fair and impartial	80%	50%

Source of data: From "Whites v. Blacks," by M. Whitaker, 1995, October 16, *Newsweek*, pp. 28–35.

Across the Great Divide. White and African American college students react to the jury verdict in the O. J. Simpson case.

FRAMING EFFECTS

Postverdict interviews of jurors also suggested the presence of framing effects. That is, some jurors who voted to acquit O. J. Simpson said that they believed he might actually have committed the murders. However, they had been asked to find him guilty or not guilty on the basis of the evidence presented. Some of this evidence had been gathered by a police officer who was revealed to be a racist. The jury had not been asked to speculate informally on Simpson's guilt or innocence.

Simpson attorney Johnnie Cochran also contributed to the framing effect. He asked the jury to use their verdict to send a message concerning racism in the Los Angeles Police Department, not just as a judgment of Simpson's guilt or innocence.

White and African American observers may agree on one thing: Their reactions to the Simpson verdict clearly reflect the use of heuristics and framing effects in judgment and decision making.

(Have you ever known someone to maintain unrealistic confidence in a candidate who was far behind in the polls?)

We also tend to view our situations with 20–20 hindsight. When we are proven wrong, we frequently find a way to show that we "knew it all along." We also at once become overconfident that we would have known the actual outcome if we had been privy to the information that became available after the event (Hawkins & Hastie, 1990). For example, if we had known that a key player would pull a hamstring muscle, we would have predicted a different outcome for the football game. If we had known that it would be blustery on Election Day, we would have predicted a smaller voter turnout and a different outcome of the election.

There are a number of reasons for overconfidence, even when our judgments are erroneous:

- We tend to be unaware of how flimsy our assumptions may be.
- We tend to focus on examples that confirm our judgments and to ignore events that do not.
- Our working memories have limited space, and we tend not to recall information that runs counter to our judgments.
- We work to bring about the events we believe in so that they sometimes come about as self-fulfilling prophecies.
- Even when people are told that they tend to be overconfident in their decisions, they usually fail to make use of this information (Gigerenzer and others, 1991). *You* are being informed, *right now*, that you may be overconfident about your decisions, even when they are based on faulty logic or inadequate information. Will *you* heed this advice, or will you continue to be overconfident and wing it day by day? (If you choose to continue to wing it, at least you'll be in good company.)

Truth or Fiction Revisited. *It is not necessarily true that people change their opinions when they are shown to be wrong.* In some cases they may, but the statement is too general to be true. Moreover, research evidence shows that people tend to attend only to information that confirms their judgments, whether or not they are correct. Also recall the anchoring and adjustment heuristic. People's opinions, erroneous or correct, serve as their cognitive anchors. Thus, even when people do change their opinions, they change them, or adjust them, as little as possible. (To be human is to anchor and adjust?)

Reflections

- Did you say that the "Truth or Fiction?" item "If a couple has five sons, the sixth child is likely to be a daughter" was truth or fiction? Why?
- Do you imagine that you could ever give up or seriously change your political or religious beliefs? Why or why not?
- Have you ever used the framing effect in trying to persuade someone to believe or do something? How?
- Do you tend to be confident in your decisions? Has your confidence—or overconfidence—ever gotten you into trouble? If so, how?
- Have you ever known people who have refused to change their minds even though they were shown to be wrong? How do you explain their reluctance to change?

Now that we have gained some insight into how people solve problems, reason, and make decisions, let us turn to the words and phrases they commonly use to think. Let us consider another aspect of cognitive science: the mechanics and development of language.

LANGUAGE

When I was in high school, I was taught that people differ from other creatures that run, swim, or fly because only we use tools and language. Then I learned that lower animals also use tools. Otters use rocks to open clam shells. Chimpanzees toss rocks as weapons and use sticks to dig out grubs for food.

In recent years, our exclusive claim to language has also been questioned, because chimps and gorillas have been taught to use **symbols** to communicate. Some communicate by making signs with their hands. Others use plastic symbols or press keys on a computer keyboard (Johnson, 1995). (See Figure 8.7.)

Language is the communication of thoughts and feelings by means of symbols that are arranged according to rules of grammar. Language makes it possible for one person to communicate knowledge to another and for one generation to communicate to another. Language creates a vehicle for recording experiences. Language allows us to don the eyes and ears of other people, to learn more than we could ever learn from direct experience. Language also provides many of the basic units of thought.

Language is one of our great strengths. Other species may be stronger, run faster, smell more keenly, even live longer, but only we have produced literature, music, mathematics, and science. Language ability has made all this possible.

Many species, including skylarks, have systems of communication. Birds warn other birds of predators. They communicate that they have taken possession of a certain tree or bush through particular chirps and shrieks. The

Symbol • Something that stands for or represents another object, event, or idea.

Language • The communication of information by means of symbols arranged according to rules of grammar.

FIGURE 8.7

An Ape Uses Signs to Communicate. Apes have been taught to express ideas by pressing keys on a computer-controlled keyboard.

MINILECTURE:
BEE LANGUAGE

Semanticity • Meaning. The quality of language in which words are used as symbols for objects, events, or ideas.

Infinite creativity • The capacity to combine words into original sentences.

Syntax • The rules in a language for placing words in proper order to form meaningful sentences.

Displacement • The quality of language that permits one to communicate information about objects and events in another time and place.

Phonology (foe-NOLL-oh-gee) • The study of the basic sounds in a language.

Phoneme (FOE-neem) • A basic sound in a language.

Morpheme (MORE-feem) • The smallest unit of meaning in a language.

MINILECTURE:
THE BASICS OF
LANGUAGE

MINILECTURE:
THE STRUCTURE OF
LANGUAGE

"dances" of bees inform other bees of the location of a food source or a predator. Vervet monkeys make sounds that signal the distance and species of predators. But these are all inborn communication patterns. Swamp sparrows reared in isolation, for example, produce songs very similar to those produced by birds reared naturally in the wild (Brody, 1991). True language is distinguished from the communication systems of lower animals by properties such as semanticity, infinite creativity, and displacement (Ratner & Gleason, 1993).

Semanticity refers to the fact that the sounds (or signs) or a language have meaning. Words serve as symbols for actions, objects, relational concepts (*over, in, more,* and so on), and other ideas. The communications systems of the birds and the bees lack semanticity. Specific sounds and—in the case of bees—specific waggles do *not* serve as symbols.

Infinite creativity refers to the capacity to combine words into original sentences. An "original" sentence is *not* one that has never been spoken before. Rather, it is a sentence that is produced by the individual instead of imitated. To produce original sentences, children must have a basic understanding of **syntax,** or the structure of grammar. Two-year-old children string signs (words) together in novel combinations.

Displacement is the capacity to communicate information about events and objects in another time or place.[2] Language makes possible the efficient transmission of complex knowledge from one person to another and from one generation to another. Displacement permits parents to warn children of their own mistakes. Displacement allows children to tell their parents what they did in school.

Basic Concepts of Language

The basic concepts of language include *phonology* (sounds[3]), *morphology* (units of meaning), *syntax* (word order), and *semantics* (the meanings of words and groups of words).

PHONOLOGY.   **Phonology** is the study of the basic sounds in a language. There are 26 letters in the English alphabet but a greater number of **phonemes.** These include the *t* and *p* in *tip,* which a psycholinguist may designate as the /t/ and /p/ phonemes. The *o* in *go* and the *o* in *gone* are different phonemes. They are spelled with the same letter, but they sound different. English speakers who learn French may be confused because /o/, as in the word *go,* has various spellings in French, including *o, au, eau,* even *eaux.*

MORPHOLOGY.   **Morphemes** are the smallest units of meaning in a language. A morpheme consists of one or more phonemes in a certain order. Some morphemes such as *dog* and *cat* function as words, but others must be used in combination. The words *dogs* and *cats* each consist of two morphemes. Adding /z/ to *dog* makes the word plural. Adding /s/ to *cat* serves the same function.

An *ed* morpheme at the end of a regular verb places it in the past tense, as with *add* and *added* and with *subtract* and *subtracted.* A *ly* morpheme at the end of an adjective often makes the word an adverb, as with *strong* and *strongly* and *weak* and *weakly.*

---

[2] The word *displacement* has a different meaning in Sigmund Freud's psychodynamic theory, as we will see in Chapter 12.

[3] American Sign Language and Signed English, which are languages used by the deaf, are exceptions.

Morphemes such as *s* and *ed* tacked on to the ends of nouns and verbs are referred to as grammatical "markers," or **inflections.** Inflections change the forms of words to indicate grammatical relationships such as *number* (singular or plural) and *tense* (for example, present or past). Languages have grammatical rules for the formation of plurals, tenses, and other inflections.

SYNTAX.

since feeling is first
who pays any attention
to the syntax of things
will never wholly kiss you . . .
                    e. e. cummings

The lines from an e. e. cummings poem are intriguing because their syntax permits various interpretations. Syntax deals with the ways words are strung together, or ordered, into phrases and sentences (Lasnik, 1990). The rules for word order are the *grammar* of a language.

In English, statements usually follow the pattern *subject, verb,* and *object of the verb.* Note this example:

The young boy (subject) → has brought (verb) → the book (object).

The sentence would be confusing if it were written "The young boy *has* the book *brought.*" But this is how the words would be ordered in German. German syntax differs. In German, a past participle ("brought") is placed at the end of the sentence, whereas the helping verb ("has") follows the subject. Although the syntax of German differs from that of English, children reared in German-speaking homes[4] acquire German syntax readily.

SEMANTICS. **Semantics** is the study of meaning. It involves the relationship between language and the objects or events language depicts. Words that sound (and are spelled) alike can have different meanings, depending on their usage. Compare these sentences:

A rock sank the boat.

Don't rock the boat.

In the first sentence, *rock* is a noun and the subject of the verb *sank.* The sentence probably means that the hull of a boat was ripped open by an underwater rock, causing the boat to sink. In the second sentence, *rock* is a verb. The second sentence is usually used as a figure of speech in which a person is being warned not to change things—not to "make waves" or "upset the apple cart."

Or compare these sentences:

The chicken is ready for dinner.

The lion is ready for dinner.

The shark is ready for dinner.

The first sentence probably means that a chicken has been cooked and is ready to be eaten. The second sentence probably means that a lion is hungry or about to devour its prey. Our interpretation of the phrase "is ready for dinner" reflects our knowledge about chickens and lions. Whether we expect a

Inflections • Grammatical markers that change the forms of words to indicate grammatical relationships such as number and tense.
Semantics • The study of the meanings of a language—the relationships between language and objects and events.

---

[4] No, homes do not really speak German or any other language. This is an example of idiomatic English. Idioms like these are readily acquired by children.

shark to be eaten or to do some eating might reflect our seafood preferences or how recently we had seen the movie *Jaws*.

Let us differentiate between the *surface structure* and the *deep structure* of sentences (Lasnik, 1990). The **surface structure** involves the superficial grammatical construction of the sentence. The surface structure of the "ready for dinner" sentences is the same. The **deep structure** of a sentence refers to its underlying meaning. The "ready for dinner" sentences clearly differ in their deep structure. "Make me a peanut butter and jelly sandwich" has an ambiguous surface structure, allowing different interpretations of its deep meaning—and the typical child's response: "Poof! You're a peanut butter and jelly sandwich!"

What of the language of apes? Linguists Steven Pinker (1994a) and Herbert Terrace (1987) conclude that apes may not really use language because they may not produce it spontaneously, and they cannot master grammar. Michael Maratsos (1983) takes a different view. He argues that this strict standard is relatively new on the scene. "Apes can probably learn to use signs to communicate meanings," Maratsos writes. "As this used to be the old boundary for language, it seems unfair [now] to raise the ante and say that [using signs to communicate meaning] is not really language" (1983, p. 771).

Reflections

- Imagine what life would be like without language. What do you believe you would have accomplished without language? What would be lacking? Why?
- Think of some English idioms or phrases that might be difficult for immigrants learning English to understand. Why?
- **Agree or disagree with the following statement and support your answer: "Only human beings can really use language."**

Now that we have explored the properties and the basics of language, let us chronicle the "child's task" of acquiring language.

LANGUAGE DEVELOPMENT

Children appear to develop language in an invariant sequence of steps. We begin with the **prelinguistic** vocalizations of crying, cooing, and babbling.

Newborn children, as parents are well aware, have an unlearned but highly effective form of verbal expression: crying and more crying. Crying is accomplished by blowing air through the vocal tract. There are no distinct, well-formed sounds.

Crying is about the only sound that babies make during the first month. During the second month, they also begin **cooing.** Babies use their tongues when they coo. For this reason, coos are more articulated than cries. Coos are often vowel-like and may resemble extended "oohs" and "ahs." Cooing appears to be linked to feelings of pleasure or positive excitement. Babies do not coo when they are hungry, tired, or in pain. Parents soon learn that different cries and coos can indicate different things: hunger, gas, or pleasure at being held or rocked.

Cries and coos are innate but can be modified by experience. When parents respond positively to cooing by talking to their babies, smiling at them, and imitating them, cooing increases. Early parent–child "conversations," in which parents respond to coos and then pause as the baby coos, may

**MINILECTURE:
THE APE LANGUAGE
DEBATE**

Surface structure • The superficial grammatical construction of a sentence.

Deep structure • The underlying meaning of a sentence.

Prelinguistic • Prior to the development of language.

Cooing • Prelinguistic, articulated, vowel-like sounds that appear to reflect feelings of positive excitement.

foster early infant awareness of turn-taking as a way of relating verbally to other people.

True language has *semanticity.* Sounds (or signs, in the case of sign language) are symbols. Cries and coos do not represent objects or events. Thus they are prelinguistic.

By about 8 months, cooing decreases markedly. By about the fifth or sixth month, children have begun to babble. **Babbling** is the first vocalizing that sounds like human speech. Children babble phonemes of several languages, including the throaty German *ch*, the clicks of certain African tribes, and rolling *r*'s. In babbling, babies frequently combine consonants and vowels, as in "ba," "ga," and, sometimes, the much valued "dada." "Dada" at first is purely coincidental (sorry, you dads), despite the family's jubilation over its appearance.

Babbling, like crying and cooing, appears to be inborn. Children from cultures whose languages sound very different all seem to babble the same sounds, including many that they could not have heard (Gleason & Ratner, 1993). As time progresses, however, their babbling takes on more of the sounds of the languages spoken in their environments.

Children seem to single out the types of phonemes used in the home within a few months. By the age of 9 or 10 months, these phonemes are repeated regularly. Foreign phonemes begin to drop out. Thus, there is an overall reduction in the variety of phonemes that infants produce.

Babbling, like crying and cooing, is a prelinguistic event. Yet infants usually understand much of what others are saying well before they utter their first words. Comprehension precedes production, and infants demonstrate comprehension with their actions and gestures.

Crying. Crying is a prelinguistic vocalization that most adults find aversive and strive to bring to an end.

Development of Vocabulary

Ah, that long-awaited first word! What a thrill! What a milestone! Sad to say, many parents miss it. They are not quite sure when their infants utter their first word, often because the first word is not pronounced clearly or because pronunciation varies from usage to usage. *Ball* may be pronounced "ba," "bee," or even "pah." The majority of early words are nouns—names for things (Nelson and others, 1993).

Vocabulary acquisition is slow at first. It may take children 3 to 4 months to achieve a 10-word vocabulary after their first word is spoken (Nelson, 1973). By about 18 months, children are producing nearly two dozen words. Many words such as *no, cookie, mama, hi,* and *eat* are quite familiar. Others, like *all-gone* and *bye-bye,* may not be found in the dictionary, but they function as words. Research evidence shows that reading to children increases their vocabulary, so parents do well to pull out the storybooks (Arnold and others, 1994; Robbins & Ehri, 1994).

Children try to talk about more objects than they have words for, and so they often extend the meaning of one word to refer to things and actions for which they do not have words. This phenomenon is termed **overextension.** At some point many children refer to horses as *doggies.* My daughter Allyn, at age 6, counted by tens as follows: sixty, seventy, eighty, ninety, *tenty.*

Babbling • The child's first vocalizations that have the sounds of speech.

Overextension • Overgeneralizing the use of words to objects and situations to which they do not apply—a normal characteristic of the speech of young children.

Development of Syntax

Although children first use one-word utterances, these utterances appear to express the meanings of sentences. Brief expressions that have the meanings of sentences are termed *telegraphic speech.* When we as adults write telegrams, we use principles of syntax to cut out all the "unnecessary" words. "Home Tuesday" might stand for "I expect to be home on Tuesday." Similarly, only the essential words are used in children's telegraphic speech—in particular, nouns, verbs, and some modifiers.

Single words that are used to express complex meanings are called **holophrases.** For example, *mama* may be used by the child to signify meanings as varied as "There goes Mama," "Come here, Mama," and "You are my Mama." Similarly, *poo-cat* can signify "There is a pussycat," "That stuffed animal looks just like my pussycat," or "I want you to give me my pussycat right now!" Most children readily teach their parents what they intend by augmenting their holophrases with gestures, intonations, and reinforcers. That is, they act delighted when parents do as requested and howl when they do not.

Toward the end of the second year, children begin to speak in telegraphic two-word sentences. In the sentence "That ball," the words *is* and *a* are implied. Two-word utterances seem to appear at about the same time in the development of all languages (Slobin, 1973). Also, the sequence of emergence of the types of two-word utterances (for example, first, agent-action; then action-object, location, and possession) is the same in languages as diverse as English, Luo (an African tongue), German, Russian, and Turkish (Slobin, 1983).

Two-word utterances, although brief, show understanding of syntax. The child will say, "Sit chair" to tell a parent to sit in a chair, not "Chair sit." (Apes do not reliably make this distinction.) The child will say, "My shoe," not "Shoe my," to show possession. "Mommy go" means Mommy is leaving. "Go Mommy" expresses the wish for Mommy to go away. For this reason, "Go Mommy" is not heard often.

Toward More Complex Language

Between the ages of 2 and 3, children's sentence structure usually expands to include the missing words in telegraphic speech. During the third year children usually add articles *(a, an, the),* conjunctions *(and, but, or),* possessive and demonstrative adjectives *(your, her, that),* pronouns *(she, him, one),* and prepositions *(in, on, over, around, under,* and *through).* Their grasp of syntax is shown in language oddities such as *your one* instead of, simply, *yours* and *his one* instead of *his.*

Usually between the ages of 2 and 3 children begin to combine phrases and clauses into complex sentences. An early example of a complex sentence is "You goed and Mommy goed, too." A more advanced example is "What will we do when we get there?"

One of the more intriguing language developments is **overregularization.** To understand children's use of overregularization, consider the formation of the past tense and of plurals in English. We add *d* or *ed* phonemes to regular verbs and *s* or *z* phonemes to regular nouns. Thus, *walk* becomes *walked* and *look* becomes *looked. Pussycat* becomes *pussycats* and *doggy* becomes *doggies.* There are also irregular verbs and nouns. For example, *see* becomes *saw, sit* becomes *sat,* and *go* becomes *went. Sheep* remains *sheep* (plural) and *child* becomes *children.*

At first, children learn a small number of these irregular verbs by imitating their parents. Two-year-olds tend to form them correctly—temporarily (Kuczaj, 1982)! Then they become aware of the syntactic rules for forming the past tense and plurals in English. As a result, they tend to make charming errors (Pinker, 1994a). Some 3- to 5-year-olds, for example, are more likely to

---

Holophrase • A single word used to express complex meanings.

Overregularization • The application of regular grammatical rules for forming inflections (e.g., past tense and plurals) to irregular verbs and nouns.

say "I seed it" than "I saw it" and more likely to say "Mommy sitted down" than "Mommy sat down." They are likely to talk about the "gooses" and "sheeps" they "seed" on the farm and about all the "childs" they ran into at the playground. This tendency to regularize the irregular is what is meant by over-regularization.

Some parents recognize that their children were at one point forming the past tense of irregular verbs correctly and that they later began to make errors. The thing to remember is that overregularization *does represent an advance in the development of syntax*. Overregularization reflects knowledge of grammar—not faulty language development. In another year or two, *mouses* will be *boringly* transformed into mice, and Mommy will no longer have *sitted* down. Parents might as well enjoy overregularization while they can.

As language develops beyond the third year, children show increasing facility with the use of pronouns (such as *it* and *she*) and with prepositions (such as *in, before,* or *on*), which represent physical or temporal relationships among objects and events. Children's first questions are telegraphic and characterized by a rising pitch (which signifies a question mark in English) at the end. "More milky?" for example, can be translated into "May I have more milk?" or "Would you like more milk?" or "Is there more milk?"—depending on the context.

It is usually during the third year that the *wh* questions appear. Consistent with the child's general cognitive development, certain *wh* questions (*what, who,* and *where*) appear earlier than others (*why, when, which,* and *how*) (Bloom and others, 1982). *Why* is usually too philosophical for the 2-year-old, and *how* is too involved. Two-year-olds are also likely to be now-oriented. Thus, *when,* too, is of less than immediate concern. By the fourth year, most children are spontaneously producing *why, when,* and *how* questions.

By the fourth year, children are asking questions, taking turns talking, and engaging in lengthy conversations. By the age of 6, their vocabularies have expanded to 10,000 words, give or take a few thousand. By 7 to 9, most children realize that words can have more than one meaning, and they are entertained by riddles and jokes that require semantic sophistication ("What's black and white and read all over?"). Between the elementary school and high school years, vocabulary continues to grow rapidly. There are also subtle advances in articulation and the capacity to use complex syntax.

Theories of Language Development

Since all normal humans talk but no house pets or house plants do, no matter how pampered, heredity must be involved in language. But since a child growing up in Japan speaks Japanese whereas the same child brought up in California would speak English, the environment is also crucial. Thus, there is no question about whether heredity or environment is involved in language, or even whether one or the other is "more important." Instead, . . . our best hope [might be] finding out *how* they interact. (Steven Pinker, 1990, p. 201)

Countless billions of children have acquired the languages spoken by their parents and passed them down, with minor changes, from generation to generation. Theories of language development are concerned with *how* they manage to do so. In language development, as in many other areas of psychology, we study the interactions between the influences of heredity (nature) and the environment (nurture). Let us see how these broad views are expressed in learning and nativist theories of language development.

LEARNING VIEWS. Learning theorists claim that language develops according to laws of learning and is similar to other kinds of learned behavior (Gleason & Ratner, 1993). They usually refer to the concepts of imitation and reinforcement. From a social-cognitive perspective, parents serve as **models.** Children learn language, at least in part, by observation and imitation. It seems likely that many vocabulary words, especially nouns and verbs (including irregular verbs), are learned by imitation.

At first children accurately repeat the irregular verb forms they observe. This repetition can probably be explained in terms of modeling, but modeling does not explain all the events of learning. Children later begin to overregularize irregular verb forms *because of* knowledge of rules of syntax, not imitation. Nor does imitative learning explain how children spontaneously utter phrases and sentences they have *not* observed. Parents, for example, are unlikely to model utterances such as "bye-bye sock" and "allgone Daddy," but children do say them.

Sometimes children steadfastly avoid imitating language forms suggested by adults, even when the adults are insistent. Note the following exchange between 2-year-old Ben and a (very frustrated!) adult:

> BEN: I like these candy. I like they.
> ADULT: You like them?
> BEN: Yes. I like they.
> ADULT: Say *them*.
> BEN: Them.
> ADULT: Say "I like *them*."
> BEN: I like them.
> ADULT: Good.
> BEN: I'm good. These candy good too.
> ADULT: Are they good?
> BEN: Yes. I like they. You like they? (Kuczaj, 1982, p. 48)

In *Verbal Behavior,* B. F. Skinner outlined his view of the role of reinforcement in language development: "A child acquires verbal behavior when relatively unpatterned vocalizations, selectively reinforced, assume forms which produce appropriate consequences in a given verbal community" (Skinner, 1957, p. 31).

Skinner allows that prelinguistic vocalizations such as cooing and babbling are inborn. But parents reinforce children for babbling that approximates real words such as *da*, which in English resembles *dog* or *daddy*. Children, in fact, do increase their babbling when it results in adults smiling at them, stroking them, and talking back to them.

As the first year progresses, children babble the sounds of their native tongues with increasing frequency. "Foreign" sounds tend to drop out. The behaviorist explains this pattern of changing frequencies in terms of reinforcement (of the sounds of the adults' language) and extinction (of foreign sounds). An alternate (nonbehavioral) explanation is that children actively attend to the sounds in their linguistic environments and are intrinsically motivated to utter them.

From Skinner's (1957, 1983) perspective, children acquire an early vocabulary through shaping. That is, parents require that children's utterances come progressively closer to actual words before they are reinforced. Skinner views multiword utterances as complex stimulus–response chains that are also taught by shaping. As children's utterances increase in length, parents foster

Models • In learning theory, persons who engage in behaviors that are imitated by others.

correct word order by uttering sentences to their children and reinforcing imitation. As with Ben, when children make grammatical errors, parents recast their utterances correctly. They then reinforce the children for repeating them.

But recall Ben's refusal to be shaped into correct syntax. If the reinforcement explanation were sufficient, parental reinforcement would facilitate children's learning of phonetics, syntax, and semantics. We do not have such evidence. For one thing, parents are more likely to reinforce their children for the accuracy, or "truth value," of their utterances than for their grammatical correctness. Parents, in other words, generally accept the syntax of their children's vocal efforts. The child who points down and says, "The grass is purple" is not likely to be reinforced, despite correct syntax. But the enthusiastic child who shows her empty plate and blurts out "I eated it all up!" is likely to be reinforced, despite overregularization of *to eat*.

Selective reinforcement of children's pronunciation, in fact, may backfire. Children whose parents reward proper pronunciation but correct poor pronunciation develop vocabulary *more slowly* than children whose parents are more tolerant of pronunciation (Nelson, 1973).

Learning theory also cannot account for the invariant sequences of language development and for children's spurts in acquisition. Even the types of two-word utterances emerge in a consistent pattern in diverse cultures. Although timing differs from child to child, the types of questions used, passive versus active sentences, and so on, all emerge in the same order.

NATIVIST VIEWS.   The nativist view of language development holds that innate or inborn factors cause children to attend to and acquire language in certain ways (Maratsos, 1983). From this perspective, children bring an inborn tendency in the form of neurological "prewiring" to language learning (Pinker, 1994a).

According to **psycholinguistic theory,** language acquisition involves the interaction of environmental influences—such as exposure to parental speech and reinforcement—and an inborn tendency to acquire language. Chomsky (1980, 1991) and some others refer to the inborn tendency as a **language acquisition device** (LAD). Evidence for an LAD is found in the universality of human language abilities and in the invariant sequences of language development.

The LAD suits the nervous system to learn grammar. On the surface, languages differ a great deal. However, the LAD serves children all over the world because languages share what Chomsky refers to as a "universal grammar"—an underlying deep structure or set of rules for turning ideas into sentences (Pinker, 1990, 1994a). Consider an analogy with computers: According to psycholinguistic theory, the universal grammar that resides in the LAD is the basic operating system of the computer. The particular language that a child learns to use is the word-processing program.

Lenneberg (1967) proposes that there is a **sensitive period** for learning language that begins at about 18 to 24 months and lasts until puberty. This period reflects neural maturation. During the sensitive period, neural development (as in the differentiation of brain structures) provides a plasticity that facilitates language learning.

Evidence for a sensitive period is found in recovery from brain injuries in some people. Injuries to the dominant hemisphere can impair or destroy the ability to speak (see Chapter 3). But prior to puberty, brain-injured children frequently recover a good deal of speaking ability.

Psycholinguistic theory • The view that language learning involves an interaction between environmental influences and an inborn tendency to acquire language. The emphasis is on the inborn tendency.

Language acquisition device • In psycholinguistic theory, neural "prewiring" that facilitates the child's learning of grammar. Abbreviated *LAD*.

Sensitive period • In linguistic theory, the period from about 18 months to puberty when the brain is thought to be particularly capable of learning language because of plasticity.

Reflections

- Have you observed an infant learning language? How did she or he communicate desires and understanding of language before she or he could speak? What was her or his first word? (Are you sure?)
- Can you recall any of your own experiences in learning the language spoken in your home? Do you recall any "cute" errors you used to make in choice of words or in pronunciation?
- **Agree or disagree with the following statement and support your answer: "People acquire knowledge on the basis of experience."**

While we as adults continue to struggle with complex concepts to explain language development, 1- and 2-year-olds go right on learning language all around us. In many cases, as we see next, those young children learn more than one.

 **WORLD OF DIVERSITY**

BILINGUALISM

It may seem strange to people in the United States, but most people throughout the world speak two or more languages (Snow, 1993). Most countries have minority populations whose languages differ from the national tongue. Nearly all Europeans are taught English and the languages of neighboring nations. Consider the Netherlands. Dutch is the native tongue, but all children are also taught French, German, and English and are expected to become fluent in each of them.

Bilingualism. Most people throughout the world speak two or more languages, and most countries have minority populations whose languages differ from the national tongue. It was once thought that children reared in bilingual homes were retarded in their cognitive and language development, but today most linguists consider bilingualism an advantage. Knowledge of more than one language certainly expands children's awareness of diverse cultures and broadens their perspectives.

TABLE 8.3
SNAPSHOT, U.S.A.: BILINGUALISM

LANGUAGE SPOKEN IN THE HOME	TOTAL NUMBER OF SPEAKERS, AGE 5 AND ABOVE		CHANGE (PERCENT)
	1990	1980	
TOTAL	31,845,000	23,060,000	38%
Spanish	17,339,000	11,549,000	50
French[1]	1,703,000	1,572,000	8
German	1,547,000	1,607,000	−4
Italian	1,309,000	1,633,000	−20
Chinese	1,249,000	632,000	98
Tagalog[2]	843,000	452,000	87
Polish	723,000	826,000	−12
Korean	626,000	276,000	127
Vietnamese	507,000	203,000	150
Portuguese	430,000	361,000	19
Japanese	428,000	342,000	25
Greek	388,000	410,000	−5
Arabic	355,000	227,000	57
Hindu, Urdu	331,000	130,000	155
Russian	242,000	175,000	39
Yiddish	213,000	320,000	−34
Thai	206,000	89,000	132
Persian	202,000	109,000	85
French Creole[3]	188,000	25,000	654
Armenian	150,000	102,000	46
Navajo[4]	149,000	123,000	21
Hungarian	148,000	180,000	−18
Hebrew	144,000	99,000	46
Dutch	143,000	146,000	−3
Mon-Khmer[5]	127,000	16,000	676

Source: U.S. Bureau of the Census (1993).
1 Spoken commonly in the home in New Hampshire, Maine, and Louisiana.
2 Main language of the Philippines.
3 Mainly spoken by Haitians.
4 Native American language.
5 Cambodian language.

Truth or Fiction Revisited. *It is true that the majority of people around the world speak at least two languages.* Bilingualism is thus the normal state of affairs, not merely an issue for immigrants to the United States.

For about 32 million people in the United States, English is a second language (Barringer, 1993b). Spanish, Russian, Chinese, or Arabic is spoken in the home and, perhaps, the neighborhood. Table 8.3 provides a snapshot of the 25 languages most commonly spoken in the home in the United States in the 1990s. Much of the 38% jump in the numbers of speakers of foreign languages is due to waves of immigration from Latin America and Asia.

Early in the century, it was widely believed that children reared in bilingual homes were retarded in their cognitive and language development. The theory was that cognitive capacity was limited. Therefore, people who stored two linguistic systems were crowding their mental abilities (Lambert, 1990). However, the U.S. Bureau of the Census reports that more than 75% of Americans who first spoke another language in the home also speak English "well" or "very well" (Barringer, 1993b). Moreover, a careful analysis of older studies in bilingualism shows that the bilingual children observed often lived in families that were low in socioeconomic status and level of education. Yet these bilingual children were compared to middle-class monolingual children. Moreover, the achievement and intelligence tests were conducted in the monolingual child's language, which was the second language of the bilingual child (Reynolds, 1991). Lack of education and testing methods rather than bilingualism per se accounted for the apparent differences in achievement and intelligence.

Today, most linguists consider it advantageous for children to be bilingual. For one thing, knowledge of more than one language expands children's awareness of different cultures and broadens their perspectives (Diaz, 1985). For example, bilingual children are more likely to understand that the symbols used in language are arbitrary. Monolingual children are more likely to erroneously think that the word *dog* is somehow intertwined with the nature of the beast. Bilingual children therefore have somewhat more cognitive flexibility. Second, learning a second language does not crowd children's available "cognitive space." Instead, learning a second language has been shown to increase children's expertise in their first (native) language. Research evidence reveals that learning French enhances knowledge of the structure of English among Canadian children whose native language is English (Lambert and others, 1991). By contrast, the worst effect of bilingualism is apparently that children occasionally forget—for a moment—which language they are using (Taylor & Taylor, 1990).

Despite the advantages of bilingualism, many immigrants have not insisted on teaching their children the languages of the lands of origin. For example, in the effort to Americanize their children, many Mexican American immigrants have not taught their children Spanish in the home (Delgado-Gaitan, 1993). As a result, many first-generation Mexican Americans do not speak Spanish.

SECOND-LANGUAGE LEARNING AND AGE

We visited Israel where the native language is Hebrew when my daughter Taylor was 19 months old. Although we stayed for a month, my wife and I barely learned to understand a word of Hebrew. A few months after we returned to the United States, however, Taylor blurted out "Sleechah!" from her seat in our shopping cart when we were trying to pass someone in an aisle of a supermarket. We realized that *sleechah* is the Hebrew for "Excuse me" and theorized that Taylor picked up the term in Israeli elevators when people were getting on and off. For a few months, when she wanted our attention, she would first try "Mommy" and "Daddy." If we were engrossed in something, however—or trying to get some sleep!—she would switch to *Eema* and *Abba,* which are the Hebrew for mother and father.

My wife and I had learned some Romance languages and German at an early age. Hebrew, however, seemed impossible to us. There were no words in common with English, and the grammar was very different. Yet here was Taylor, who knew (or pretended to know) nothing about using a potty, soaking up Hebrew like a sponge.

Painstaking research as well as anecdotal evidence reveals that people who acquire second languages at earlier ages are more likely to become fluent and sound like native speakers (Snow, 1993; Taylor & Taylor, 1990). In one study, Tahka and associates (1981) found that children who arrived in England before the age of 7 learned to speak English with no trace of a foreign accent, whether their native tongue was Armenian, Cantonese, Hindi, or French. Those who learned English at age 14 and above had pronounced accents.

Children even gain greater proficiency with American Sign Language (the language of the deaf) when they are taught it from birth (Newport & Supalla, 1993).

All in all, research evidence is consistent with Lenneberg's critical-period hypothesis. That is, young children acquire language more efficiently than older children and adults do—whether the language is their native language or another (Hurford, 1991).

Reflections

- Did you grow up speaking a language other than English in the home? If so, what special opportunities and problems were connected with the experience? Are there some family members who never learned English very well? Why did they not learn more?
- Do you believe that children who do not speak English in the home should be taught in their native languages in U.S. schools? Why or why not?

LANGUAGE AND THOUGHT

Theories of language development are of little importance to a 20-month-old who has just polished off her plate of chocolate chip cookies and exclaimed (or signed) "All gone!" In the previous section, we were concerned with how the child comes to say or sign "All gone" when she has finished her cookies. Now let us bring the chapter full circle by returning to matters of thinking: What does the child's use of "All gone" suggest about her thought processes? In other words, would the girl have *known* that there were no cookies left if she did not have a word to express this idea? (Modern theorists of language would answer yes [Larson, 1990; Miller, 1990; Pinker, 1990].) Do you always think in words? (Modern theorists of language would answer no [Larson, 1990; Miller, 1990; Pinker, 1990].) Can you think *without* using language? (Yes.) Would you be able to solve problems without using words or sentences? (That depends on the problem.)

Jean Piaget (1976) believed that language reflects knowledge of the world but that much knowledge can be acquired without language. For example, it is possible to have the concepts of roundness or redness even when we do not know or use the words *round* or *red*.

Linguistic-relativity hypothesis • The view that language structures the way in which we view the world.

The Linguistic-Relativity Hypothesis

Language may not be needed for all thought. According to the **linguistic-relativity hypothesis** proposed by Benjamin Lee Whorf (1956), however, language structures the ways in which we perceive the world. That is, the categories and relations we use to understand the world derive from our particular languages. Therefore, speakers of various languages conceptualize the world in different ways (Pinker, 1990).

According to the linguistic-relativity hypothesis, most English speakers' ability to think about snow may be rather limited when compared to that of the Inuit people. We have only a few words for snow. The Inuit people have many words, related, for example, to whether the snow is hard-packed, falling, melting, or covered by ice. When we think about snow, we have fewer words to choose from and have to search for descriptive adjectives. The Inuit people,

In an Igloo. The Inuit people of Alaska and the Canadian Northwestern Territories (shown here) have many more words for snow than most of us. They spend most of their lives in the snow, and the subtle gradations among various kinds of snow are meaningful to them.

however, can readily find a single word that describes a complex weather condition. It might then be easier for them to think about this variety of snow in relation to other aspects of their world. Similarly, the Hanunoo people of the Philippines use 92 words for rice, depending on whether the rice is husked or unhusked and on how it is prepared. And we have one word for camel; Arabs have more than 250.

In English, we have hundreds of words to describe different colors, but those who speak Shona use only three words for colors. People who speak Bassa use only two words for colors (Gleason, 1961), corresponding to light and dark. The Hopi Indians had two words for flying objects, one for birds and an all-inclusive word for anything else that may be found traveling through the air.

Does this mean that the Hopi were limited in their ability to think about bumblebees and airplanes? Are English speakers limited in their ability to think about skiing conditions? Are those who speak Shona and Bassa "color-blind" for practical purposes?

Probably not. People who use only a few words to distinguish colors seem to perceive the same color variations as people with dozens of words (Bornstein & Marks, 1982). For example, the Dani of New Guinea, like the Bassa, have just two words for colors: *mola,* which refers to yellows and reds, and *mili,* which refers to greens and blues. Still, tasks in matching and memory show that the Dani can discriminate the many colors of the spectrum when they are motivated to do so. English-speaking skiers who are concerned about different skiing conditions have developed a comprehensive special vocabulary about snow, including the terms *powder, slush, ice, hard-packed,* and *corn snow,* that might enable them to communicate and think about snow with the facility of the Inuit people. When a need to expand a language's vocabulary arises, the speakers of that language apparently have little difficulty in meeting the need.

Modern cognitive scientists generally do not accept the linguistic-relativity hypothesis (Pinker, 1990). For one thing, adults use images and abstract logical propositions as units of thought, not only words (Larson, 1990; Miller, 1990). Infants, moreover, display considerable intelligence before they have learned to speak. Another criticism is that a language's vocabulary suggests the range of concepts that the speakers of the language have traditionally found important, not their cognitive limits. For example, a person magically lifted from the 19th century and placed inside an airplane would probably not think that she or he was flying inside a bird or a large insect, even if she or he had no word for airplane.

Reflections

• How sophisticated is your thinking about electronic data processing? For example, do you know what the terms *megabyte, random access memory, CD-ROM, local bus video,* and *PCMCIA card* mean? Does your knowledge of these terms affect your ability to think about computers? Why or why not?

• Does understanding of such words as *alliteration, trochaic foot,* and *pentameter* enhance your ability to appreciate poetry? Why or why not?

We noted that infants display considerable intelligence before they can speak. Yet knowledge of the meaning of words is one of the key measures of general intelligence. Chapter 9 explores the meaning and assessment of the enigmatic concept of intelligence. We see how intelligence is intertwined with other aspects of cognition, including memory, problem solving, reasoning, decision making, and language.

Before leaving this chapter, however, I have a final problem for you:

You're driving a bus that's leaving from Pennsylvania. To start off with, there were 32 people on the bus. And at the next bus stop, 11 people got off and 9 people got on. At the next bus stop, 2 people got off and 2 people got on. At the next bus stop, 12 people got on and 16 people got off. At the next bus stop, 5 people got on and 3 people got off.

How many people are now on the bus?

Study Guide

| Matching

DIRECTIONS: Items numbered 1 through 20 represent concepts discussed in the chapter on thinking and language. Items lettered A through T represent examples of these concepts. Indicate which example matches each concept by writing the letter that represents the example in the blank space to the left of the concept.

—— 1. Algorithm

—— 2. Systematic random search

—— 3. Means-end analysis

—— 4. Mental set

—— 5. Insight

—— 6. Cognitive map

—— 7. Incubation

—— 8. Functional fixedness

—— 9. Creativity

—— 10. Divergent thinking

—— 11. Brainstorming

—— 12. Deductive reasoning

—— 13. Premise

—— 14. Inductive reasoning

—— 15. Representativeness heuristic

—— 16. Availability heuristic

—— 17. Framing effect

—— 18. Overextension

—— 19. Holophrase

—— 20. Overregularization

A. Because of sensationalistic newscasts, you assume that New York City is a terrible place to live.

B. A child says "Doggy!" but means "I want you to give me that dog right now!"

C. A child refers to a horse as a "big doggy."

D. You generate lists of all the meanings you can think of for the verbs "see" and "pull."

E. You use the formula that helped you solve one problem with problems that seem to be similar.

F. You try to figure out how to get to a certain address by picturing where you are now and attempting to reduce the discrepancy (in this case, the distance between the two locations).

G. The solution to a problem comes to you in a flash.

H. The Duncker candle problem.

I. A child says "I seed it" instead of "I saw it."

J. An attempt to solve an anagram by trying every possible letter combination.

K. You bring together a group of people to generate as many solutions as they can think of for a particular problem.

L. The statement "People are mortal" serves as this in the syllogism about Socrates.

M. Because a couple already has five daughters, you assume that their sixth child is likely to be a son.

N. You conclude that Socrates is mortal because Socrates is a person and people are mortal.

O. A politician sees that you are unwilling to consider decreasing Social Security benefits and therefore begins to argue with you about the importance of balancing the budget instead.

P. The Pythagorean Theorem.

Q. You put aside a difficult problem for a while, hoping that an effective way of approaching it will come to you later on.

R. A person assumes that a greeting that was effective with one person will be effective with another.

S. A psychological concept that involves the ability to make many associations, some of them remote, to a concept.

T. A mental image of a maze, which aids a rat in reaching a food goal.

ANSWER KEY TO EXERCISE

1. P	4. E	7. Q	10. D (or S)	13. L	16. A	19. B
2. J	5. G	8. H	11. K	14. R	17. O	20. I
3. F	6. T	9. S (or D)	12. N	15. M	18. C	

ESL | English as a Second Language—Bridging the Gap

abstract (316)   general; not specific; could be thought of differently by different people

acquired (324)—accomplished; learned

acquisition (343)—learning; accomplishment

acquisitions (323)—things that are aquired, or collected

align (323)—adjust so they line up, or fit, together

all the givens (319)—all the accepted ideas

allgone (343)—represents "all gone"; finished, there is no more

allow "leads" to run a nearly limitless course (328)—follows ideas to their limit

alternate (318)—different

ambiguous (342)—not clear

anagrams (322)—a word puzzle in which the letters are mixed up into an unrecognizable order

analogies (319)—things that are similar

analogous (321)—similar to

anchor (334)—underlying main idea

anecdotal (350)—specific instances

apes (342)—large monkeys, like chimpanzees or gorillas

apparently superfluous (314)—appears to be unnecessary

approximates (346)—resembles

arbitrary (350)—are chosen by people and don't have anything to do with the object or idea itself

articulation (345)—pronunciation

as long as (319)—if

ascribed to (329)—associated with

assumptions (331)—ideas that are understood and generally unspoken; they are used as the basis for understanding something

attend to (346)—listen to

augmenting (344)—increasing

authentic (323)—real; true

backfire (346)—have an effect that is the reverse of what was expected

bamboozled (331)—fooled; tricked

begrudgingly (334)—unwillingly; with resentment

Big Apple (334)—nickname (short or affectionate name) for New York City

blustery (336)—weather that is windy and sometimes wet or snowy

boring (320)—uninteresting; the "most boring" is the least interesting

boringly transformed (345)—will change and become uninteresting; no longer a "charming error"

brainstorming (330)—two or more people developing as many creative ideas as possible in order to have a large number from which to choose; they will then decide which are worth considering

castle (321)—a term for a move in the game of chess

categorical thinking (315)—thinking by putting things into categories

central (322)—one of the most important things

characterize the less deliberate cognitive activities (314)—call the mental activities we don't do on purpose

charming errors (344)—children's speaking mistakes that adults think are delightful or cute

chirps and shrieks (339)—different bird sounds

chronicle (342)—record

cliché (330)—familiar saying

climes (334)—climate

coherent (318)—fits together; makes sense

color-blind (352)—unable to distinguish some colors

comprehension (343)—understanding

conceptualize (314)—imagine; think about

conclusions (331)—final opinions or decisions

concur (328)—agree

confirm (336)—prove; agree with

consistent with (351)—in agreement with

contemporary (326)—current or modern; in this case, it defines a style of architecture

context (335)—things in the surrounding situation

core (327)—central or most important part

correspond to (323)—compare to; fit with

countermove (320)—a move in the opposite direction

criticism (353)—a point that disagrees with an idea

crucial (318)—extremely important

curator (323)—a person who runs a museum, library, or art gallery

delectable (323)—delicious

differentiate between (342)—look at the differences between two or more things

difficult to arrive at (328)—hard to accomplish

dive right in (317)—start right away

divergent . . . convergent (328)—moving away from . . . bringing together

don (339)—to put on

don't peek (316)—don't look

drat (323)—a slang word that is used after something happens that you don't like

drawback to (320)—the disadvantage to

e. e. cummings (341)—a modern American writer whose poems didn't follow the standard rules of English grammar

elusive (323)—hard to get or find

emerge (347)—to develop from

engage in (320)—be involved in; to do something

engrossed in (350)—deeply involved in

enhances (335)—improves; increases

entails (314)—involves; requires

enterprise (332)—project; activity

entwined (314)—wrapped around; tangled up with

erroneous (336)—wrong; in error

essential features (315)—most important characteristics

exaggeration (329)—overstatement or emphasizing too much; saying something occurs more than is true

exceed (322)—do better than; is larger than

expertise (322)—how good you are at something

facilitate (322)—make easier or better

flash of insight (318)—sudden understanding

flimsy (336)—weak; not strong

foster (342)—encourage

functionally (315)—the way it actually operates; the function, or activity, it performs

gestures (343)—movements of the arms and hands that send a message without words

gifted (328)—a person with more intelligence or other mental ability than most

go hand in hand (332)—exist together

grasping (326)—holding on to something

gratification (332)—satisfaction of your desires; pleasure

grubs (339)—small worms that are the early form of some insects

hampering mental sets (323)—ways of thinking that make it difficult for us to solve a problem

have a go (316)—try it

head for the hills (318)—run away to escape

heck with it (325)—I will not think about it anymore because I'm not interested or I think it's too difficult

heed (336)—listen to; pay attention to

hence (320)—in the future

heredity (345)—the influence of what we have inherited from our ancestors

hierarchies (314)—different levels of status; ordering things by rank of importance

hindsight (335)—how things look when we consider them after they've occurred

hypothesis (350)—an initial idea that guides research

illusory (323)—appears to be real but is not

imitated (340)—copied, or duplicated, to be exactly like another

implant (326)—insert; create; place within

in a flash (324)—suddenly

inadequate (326)—not enough

inconsistencies (334)—ideas that contradict each other

inertia (334)—resistance to change; lack of motion

inform . . . as to (321)—to tell or give an idea

ingenious (329)—very clever

inhibit (329)—to hold back; limit

inkling (314)—a little idea; a clue

instinctive (315)—natural; not learned

interpretations (341)—translations; explanations

interrelated (322)—connected

intertwined (350)—involved with; related to

intricacies (322)—fine, small, or difficult to understand parts

intriguing (344)—interesting

intrinsically motivated (346)—inborn tendency

invariably (319)—always

invariant (342)—not varying

is it not possible (326)—isn't it possible

is no guarantee of (328)—does not promise to include

jubilation (343)—excitement; celebration

jumbles (316)—things all mixed together; out of order

keep plugging away at it (325)—continue trying

lack (340)—do not have

lay in (316)—was in

let's say that (320)—let us imagine that

major intersection (320)—a place where two or more well-known streets come together

manipulating (315)—moving things around to different positions to achieve different results

matchsticks (316)—wood matches

median (334)—middle point

meeting the need (352)—doing what is necessary to accomplish what is required

mesh barrier (324)—a barrier is a block to something; a mesh barrier would be a grid made of metal or some other material that can be seen through but cannot be passed

method . . . plodding (320)—the way of doing it might be slow and a little difficult

milestone (343)—significant event

moreover (350)—in addition

much valued (331)—greatly appreciated

nauseated (331)—something that makes you feel sick to your stomach

neurological prewiring (347)—inborn, established mental pathways

nipped in the bud (329)—stopped before it can develop

nonconformist (329)—someone who doesn't do what is ordinary or expected

nothing new under the sun (327)—everything has been said and done at some time in the past

novel (326)—new

novices (322)—people who are new at doing something; not experts

now . . . it's your turn (316)—now you have the opportunity to try it

oddities (344)—strange, unusual things

opt for (332)—choose

oriented toward (316)—designed to; intended to

overconfidence (335)—too certain; sure of a particular outcome

overgeneralization (329)—a statement that is too general to be accurate; it applies to too many

overinclusion (316)—putting a variety of things that don't really match into one category or group

painstaking (350)—slow, careful, and detailed

pampered (345)—well cared for

per se (350)—by itself

persistent (325)—keeps occurring; stays and is hard to change

perspective (345)—point of view

persuasive (335)—convincing

philosophical treatises (314)—a treatise is a long written document; *philosophical* refers to attempts to understand the nature and cause of something

playground (345)—a park for children that contains play equipment

plummets (330)—declines rapidly to a very low point

polished off (351)—finished

ponder (330)—wonder about

poof (342)—a nonsense word used to express a magic command

posterity (314)—our descendants who will be born after us

practical (320)—realistic; sensible

precedents (321)—something similar to what is being looked at now that happened before

preceding (318)—things that went before

predators (339)—creatures that kill or eat other types of creatures

preposterous (330)—ridiculous

presumption (334)—assumed belief

privy to (336)—aware of

probability (333)—the probable chance of something happening a certain way

probably not (352)—it most likely is not true

problem-solvers (314)—people who solve problems

properties (314)—characteristics

proponents (335)—people who support an idea

puberty (347)—adolescence; the beginning of the period when a boy or girl starts to become a man or woman; the teenage years

raise the ante (342)—to increase expectations; make it more difficult

readily (321)—easily

reframed (335)—stated in a different way

reinforcement (348)—encouragement to continue doing something

relevant (314)—important; has something to do with the topic

reluctance (338)—not willing

retrace your steps (316)—go back and redo the task step by step

retrieving (321)—bringing back; remembering

riddle (314)—a question that asks a puzzle to be solved

rudimentary (324)—basic; undeveloped

rules of thumb (320)—practical, accepted procedures for solving problems

savor (326)—enjoy

scan (314)—to quickly search through a group of things to find a specific item

schema (315)—pattern or picture

scrap paper (316)—paper that is not needed for something else; would be thrown away if it weren't used again

seek fulfillment (335)—find happiness and satisfaction

self-fulfilling prophecies (336)—when we believe something will occur and behave as if it will, which then influences the outcome to be what we expected; if we hadn't had the expectation and behavior, it might have turned out differently

sensationalistic (334)—focusing on the exciting characteristics of something rather than the important features of it; in this case, news reports that are intended to excite people rather than inform them

sequence (333)—order in which something is arranged or occurs

signals (324)—means; indicates

simultaneously (322)—occurs at the same time

site (319)—location

sizable (321)—large; important; significant

skeptical (330)—not willing to accept or believe easily

sniffed (324)—the act of inhaling air to smell an odor

socioeconomic status (350)—social and economic level

sought (318)—tried to find (past tense of *seek,* to look for)

species (339)—classes of animals (or other creatures or plants)

spontaneously utter (345)—automatically speak without being taught

spurts (347)—sudden advances

stands for something (323)—is a symbol for something

starving (329)—doesn't have enough food and is suffering from it

steadfastly (346)—doing something consistently; with determination

stimuli (315)—ideas or objects that cause interest or a reaction

storybooks (344)—children's books that tell stories

stranded (323)—left behind without any way to leave

subgoals (320)—smaller plans that lead to achieving a larger goal

substantive (320)—important; has more meaning

suspending judgment (330)—postponing making an opinion about something until you have more information

systematic random search (320)—a step-by-step search through a variety of information that is not organized ahead of time

tacked on to (340)—added to

take a breath (316)—relax and prepare yourself

take an unpopular stand (330)—have a strong opinion about something that is different from what other people think

taking turns talking (345)—waiting until another has finished speaking before saying something; not interrupting

tap (317)—a mechanism on a pipe with a spout on the end and a handle to turn on or off the flow of a liquid in the pipe, such as water; also called a *faucet* or *spigot*

theorists (345)—scientists

thumbtacks (326)—small nails with large heads that can be pushed in with the thumb; used to pin paper or other light objects to vertical surfaces

tosses (333)—throwing something up in the air and catching it

traits (329)—characteristics

transmission (340)—the act of sending something

tried and true (320)—different alternatives or actions have been tried, and this is the one that is considered to be best and is most often used

unbind us from (326)—allow us to be free from

undergone (314)—experienced

unpatterned vocalizations (346)—sounds without a recognizable pattern of meaning

unprofitable (325)—doesn't produce good, or profitable, results

unrealistic (336)—not reasonable

unscramble (322)—take apart and put in order something that has been mixed up

versions (318)—different stories

wend our way (314)—find our path

went bananas (323)—a slang phrase that means "went crazy," or had a strong reaction from frustration, anger, or enthusiasm

wing it (336)—a slang phrase for doing something without thinking about it or practicing ahead of time

winks (332)—moments of sleep

FILL-INS | **Chapter Review**

The bus driver problem illustrates that one of the requirements of problem solving is paying attention to relevant (1) _____tion. (2) _____ing may be defined as mental activity that is involved in understanding, processing, and communicating information. Thinking entails attending to information, mentally (3) _____ting it, reasoning about it, and making judgments and (4) _____sions about it. Language allows us to (5) _____icate our thoughts and record them for posterity.

SECTION 1: CONCEPTS AND PROTOTYPES: BUILDING BLOCKS OF THOUGHT

Concepts are mental (6) _____ories used to classify together objects, relations, events, abstractions, or qualities that have common properties. Much of thinking has to do with (7) cat_____ing new objects and events and with (8) man_____ting the relationships among concepts.

We tend to organize concepts in (9) hi_____. Examples that best match the essential features of categories are termed (10) _____types. Prototypes are good (11) _____ples of concepts. Many simple prototypes such as *dog* and *red* are taught by (12) _____plars. Dogs are (13) _____tive instances of the dog concept. Cats are (14) _____tive instances of the dog concept. In language development, the overinclusion of instances in a category (reference to horses as dogs) is labeled (15) over_____.

SECTION 2: PROBLEM SOLVING

Problem solving begins with attempting to (16) _____and the problem. Understanding a problem requires focusing on the key (17) inf_____. Understanding a problem means constructing a coherent (18) m_____ (19) rep_____ of the problem. Successful understanding of a problem generally requires three features. First, the parts or elements of our (20) _____tal representation of the problem relate to one another in a meaningful way. Second, the elements of our mental representation of the problem should (21) cor_____ to the elements of the problem in the outer world. Third, we need a storehouse of background (22) _____edge that we can apply to the problem.

An (23) _____thm is a specific procedure for solving a type of problem. In solving anagram problems, the algorithm termed the (24) sys_____ random search involves listing every possible letter combination, using from one to all letters.

(25) H_____ics are rules of thumb that help us simplify and solve problems. Heuristics are shortcuts that allow for more rapid (26) _____tions. In the type of heuristic device called the (27) means-_____ analysis, we assess the difference between our current situation and our goals and then do what we can to reduce this discrepancy.

An (28) _____gy is a partial similarity among things that are different in other ways. The analogy (29) he_____ applies the solution of an earlier problem to the solution of a new one.

(30) E_____s solve problems more efficiently and rapidly than novices do. Experts at solving a certain kind of problem have a more extensive (31) kn_____ base in the area, have better memories for the elements in the problems, form mental images or (32) rep_____tions that facilitate problem solving, relate the problem to other problems that are similar in structure, and have more efficient methods for problem solving.

A (33) m_____ set is the tendency to respond to a new problem with the same approach that helped solve earlier, similar-looking problems. Some problems are solved by rapid "perception of relationships" among the elements of the problem, or (34) _____ght. Standing back from a difficult problem for a while sometimes allows the (35) _____tion of insight. When standing back from the problem is helpful, it may be because it provides us with some distance from unprofitable but persistent (36) _____tal sets.

(37) Fu_____ _____ness is the tendency to think of an object in terms of its name or its familiar usage. Functional fixedness can be similar to a (38) m_____ set in that it can make it difficult for you to use familiar objects to solve problems in novel ways.

Problems can be well-defined or (39) _____–defined. In a (40) _____–defined problem, the original state, the goal, and the rules for reaching the goal are all clearly spelled out. In an ill-defined problem, the original state, the goal state, or the rules are less than clear.

SECTION 3: CREATIVITY

A (41) _____tive person may be more capable of solving problems to which there are no preexisting solutions, no tried and tested formulas. We tend to perceive creative people as (42: Willing or Unwilling?) to take chances, unaccepting of limitations, appreciating art and music, capable of using the materials around them to make unique things, (43: Challenging or Accepting?) social norms and assumptions, willing to take an unpopular stand, and inquisitive. Many psychologists view creativity as the ability to make unusual, sometimes remote, associations to the elements of a problem to generate new (44) _____tions that meet the goals.

Creativity demands (45) _____gent thinking rather than convergent thinking. In (46) _____gent thinking, thought is limited to present facts as the problem-solver tries to narrow thinking to find the best solution. In (47) _____gent thinking, the problem-solver associates more fluently and freely to the various elements of the problem.

Creative people (48: Do or Do Not?) tend to be intelligent. Intelligence (49: Is or Is Not?) a guarantee of creativity.

Research evidence shows that concern about evaluation by other people (50: Enhances or Reduces?) creativity. Being watched while one is working (51: Enhances or Reduces?) creativity. Being offered a reward for creativity (52: Enhances or Reduces?) creativity.

(53) Br_____ing is a group process that encourages creativity by stimulating a great number of ideas—even wild ideas—and suspending judgment until the process is completed.

SECTION 4: REASONING

The text defines reasoning as the (54) _____ming of information to reach conclusions. (55) _____ive reasoning is a form of reasoning in which the conclusion must be true if the premises are true. (56) _____ses provide the assumptions or basic information that allows people to draw conclusions. In (57) _____ive reasoning, we reason from individual cases or particular facts to a general conclusion. Inductive reasoning (58: Does or Does Not?) permit us to draw absolute conclusions.

SECTION 5: JUDGMENT AND DECISION MAKING

People make most run-of-the-mill, daily decisions on the basis of (59: Complete or Limited?) information. People use rules of thumb—(60) _____tic devices—in their judgments and decision making, just as they do in problem solving.

According to the (61) rep_____ness heuristic, people make judgments about events (samples) according to the populations of events that they appear to represent. According to the (62) _____ity heuristic, our estimates of frequency or probability are based on how easy it is to find examples of relevant events.

The anchoring and (63) _____ment heuristic suggests that there can be a good deal of inertia to our judgments. In forming opinions or making estimates, we have an initial view, or presumption, that serves as the (64) a_____. As we receive additional (65) inf_____, we make adjustments.

The (66) fr_____ effect refers to the way in which wording, or the context in which information is presented, can influence decision making.

Most of us tend (67: To Have or Not To Have?) overconfidence in our decisions. One reason we tend (68: To Be or Not To Be?[5]) confident is that we tend to focus on examples that confirm our judgments and to ignore events that do not.

SECTION 6: LANGUAGE

Language is the communication of thoughts and feelings through (69) s_____. These symbols are arranged according to rules of (70) _____ar.

Language has the properties of (71) sem_____ity, infinite creativity, and (72) _____ment. Semanticity means that words serve as (73) _____ls for actions, objects, and relational concepts. Infinite creativity refers to the capacity to combine (74) _____s into original sentences. Displacement is the capacity to communicate (75) in_____ about objects or events in another time or place.

The basic components of language include phonology, (76) mor_____, (77) _____ax, and semantics. Phonology is the study of the basic (78) _____s of a language. A basic sound is labeled a (79) _____me.

Morphemes are the smallest units of (80) _____ing in a language. Morphemes consist of one or more (81) ph_____ pronounced in a particular order. Morphemes such as *s* and *ed* tacked on to the ends of nouns and verbs are examples of (82) _____cal markers, or (83) _____tions. Inflections change the forms of words to indicate grammatical relationships such as (84) n_____ (singular or plural) and (85) t_____ (e.g., present or past).

Syntax is the system of rules that determines how words are strung together to make up phrases and (86) _____ces. The rules for (87) _____rd order are the *grammar* of a language.

Semantics is the study of (88) _____ing of the relationship between language and the objects or events language depicts. The (89) s_____ structure of a sentence refers to its superficial construction—the location of words. A sentence's (90) _____p structure refers to its underlying meaning.

SECTION 7: LANGUAGE DEVELOPMENT

Children cry at birth and begin to (91) c_____ by about 2 months. (92) _____s are frequently vowel-like and may resemble repeated "oohs" and "ahs." Cooing appears associated with feelings of (93) _____sure.

(94) _____ling is the first kind of vocalization that has the sound of speech. Babbling appears at about 6 months and contains (95) _____emes found in many languages. Babbling is innate, although it can be modified by learning. Crying, cooing, and babbling are all (96) pre_____ events. They are prelinguistic because they lack (97) _____city.

Children's (98) _____ive vocabulary consists of the words that they can understand, as demonstrated, for example, by following directions. Children's (99) _____ive vocabulary consists of the words that they use in their speech. Receptive vocabulary growth (100: Lags or Outpaces?) expressive vocabulary growth.

---

[5] Sound familiar?

Children speak their first words at about the age of (101) _____. Children try to talk about more objects than they have words for, and so they often (102) over_____ the meaning of one word to refer to things and actions for which they do not have words.

Children first use (103) _____-word utterances. These utterances express the meanings found in complete sentences and are referred to as (104) _____phic speech. One-word utterances are also called (105) _____ases. Two-word telegraphic utterances appear toward the end of the (106) _____d year. Children also use (107) over___izations, as in "I seed it" and "Mommy sitted down." The "errors" made in overregularizing indicate a grasp of the rules of (108) _____ar.

Girls are slightly (109: Inferior or Superior?) to boys in their language development. Children from families of lower socioeconomic status have (110: Poorer or Richer?) vocabularies than children from middle- or upper-class families.

From a social-cognitive perspective, parents serve as (111) _____els of language usage. Children learn language, at least in part, by (112) obs_____ and (113) imi_____. Many vocabulary words, including irregular verbs, are learned by (114) imi_____. But social learning cannot account for children's (115) ___larization of regular nouns and verbs. B. F. Skinner outlined his view of the role of (116) _____ment in language development as follows: "A child acquires (117) v_____ behavior when relatively unpatterned vocalizations, selectively reinforced, assume forms which produce appropriate consequences in a given verbal community."

The (118) _____ist view of language development holds that innate factors cause children to attend to and acquire language in certain ways. According to (119) _____istic theory, language acquisition involves an interaction between environmental influences, such as exposure to parental speech and reinforcement, and an inborn tendency to acquire language. This inborn tendency has been labeled the (120) _____ _____tion device (LAD). Chomsky argues that the LAD allows children to understand a (121) "un_____ grammar," an underlying deep structure that involves rules as to how phonemes and morphemes are combined to symbolize events and yield meaning. Lenneberg proposes that there is a (122) _____tive period for learning language that begins at about 18 to 24 months and lasts until puberty. This sensitive period is based on (123) _____city of the brain.

SECTION 8: LANGUAGE AND THOUGHT

Thought is possible without (124) _____age, but language facilitates thought. According to the (125) l_____-relativity hypothesis, language structures (and limits) the way in which we perceive the world. Critics argue that a (126) _____lary may suggest the concepts deemed important by the users of a language; however, vocabulary limits do not necessarily prevent language users from making distinctions for which there are no (127) _____ds.

ANSWER KEY TO CHAPTER REVIEW

1. Information	9. Hierarchies	17. Information	25. Heuristics
2. Thinking	10. Prototypes	18. Mental	26. Solutions
3. Representing	11. Examples	19. Representation	27. Means-end
4. Decisions	12. Exemplars	20. Mental	28. Analogy
5. Communicate	13. Positive	21. Correspond	29. Heuristic
6. Categories	14. Negative	22. Knowledge	30. Experts
7. Categorizing	15. Overextension	23. Algorithm	31. Knowledge
8. Manipulating	16. Understand	24. Systematic	32. Representations

33. Mental
34. Insight
35. Incubation
36. Mental
37. Functional fixedness
38. Mental
39. Ill-defined
40. Well-defined
41. Creative
42. Willing
43. Challenging
44. Combinations
45. Divergent
46. Convergent
47. Divergent
48. Do
49. Is not
50. Reduces
51. Reduces
52. Reduces
53. Brainstorming
54. Transforming
55. Deductive
56. Premises

57. Inductive
58. Does not
59. Limited
60. Heuristic
61. Representativeness
62. Availability
63. Adjustment
64. Anchor
65. Information
66. Framing
67. To have
68. To be
69. Symbols
70. Grammar
71. Semanticity
72. Displacement
73. Symbols
74. Words
75. Information
76. Morphology
77. Syntax
78. Sounds
79. Phoneme
80. Meaning

81. Phonemes
82. Grammatical
83. Inflections
84. Number
85. Tense
86. Sentences
87. Word
88. Meaning
89. Surface
90. Deep
91. Coo
92. Coos
93. Pleasure
94. Babbling
95. Phonemes
96. Prelinguistic
97. Semanticity
98. Receptive
99. Expressive
100. Outpaces
101. 1 (12 months)
102. Overextend
103. One
104. Telegraphic

105. Holophrases
106. Second
107. Overgeneralizations
108. Grammar
109. Superior
110. Poorer
111. Models
112. Observation
113. Imitation
114. Imitation
115. Overregularization
116. Reinforcement
117. Verbal
118. Nativist
119. Psycholinguistic
120. Language acquisition
121. Universal
122. Sensitive
123. Plasticity
124. Language
125. Linguistic
126. Vocabulary
127. Words

POSTTEST | Multiple Choice

1. The bus driver problem indicates the importance of
   a. rote repetition of mental representation of the elements of a problem.
   b. prototypes.
   c. the availability heuristic.
   d. paying attention to relevant information.

2. According to the text, all of the following are examples of thinking, with the exception of
   a. mentally representing information.
   b. daydreaming.
   c. deductive reasoning.
   d. making decisions.

3. The water-jar problems indicate the role of _____ in problem solving.
   a. heuristic devices
   b. functional fixedness
   c. incubation
   d. mental sets

4. Which of the following is closest in meaning to constructing a coherent mental representation of a problem?
   a. making inferences about premises
   b. understanding a problem
   c. selecting the most efficient heuristic devices
   d. using prototypes as exemplars

5. A mathematical formula for solving a problem is an example of a(n)
   a. mental set.
   b. analogy.
   c. algorithm.
   d. heuristic device.

6. Means-end analysis is an example of a(n)
   a. mental set.
   b. analogy.
   c. algorithm.
   d. heuristic device.

7. All of the following help individuals solve problems, with the exception of
   a. insight.
   b. incubation.
   c. heuristic devices.
   d. functional fixedness.

8. Köhler's research with Sultan was an important historic event in the psychological study of
   a. problem solving by insight.
   b. creativity.
   c. the incubation effect.
   d. judgment and decision making.

9. According to Guilford, creativity involves
   a. deductive reasoning.
   b. inductive reasoning.
   c. convergent thinking.
   d. divergent thinking.

10. Which of the following enhances creativity?
    a. being offered a reward for creativity
    b. being watched while one is working
    c. competing for prizes
    d. flexibility

11. In inductive reasoning,
    a. we reason from individual cases or particular facts to a general conclusion.
    b. the conclusion must be true if the premises are true.
    c. thought is limited to present facts.
    d. the individual associates fluently and freely to the elements of the problem.

12. Consider the following two multiplication problems:
    1. $8 \times 7 \times 6 \times 5 \times 4 \times 3 \times 2 \times 1$
    2. $1 \times 2 \times 3 \times 4 \times 5 \times 6 \times 7 \times 8$
    People shown just one tend to estimate that the answer to number 1 is greater because of the
    a. representativeness heuristic.

b. anchoring and adjustment heuristic.
   c. availability heuristic.
   d. framing effect.

13. The fact that people often tend to focus on examples that confirm their judgments and ignore events that do not leads to
    a. overconfidence.
    b. the framing effect.
    c. divergent thinking.
    d. the availability heuristic.

14. The language characteristic of *semanticity* means that
    a. words can mean whatever we want them to mean.
    b. sentences have surface and deep structures.
    c. words serve as symbols.
    d. children have an intuitive grasp of meaning.

15. _____ change the forms of words to indicate grammatical relationships such as number and tense.
    a. Inflections
    b. Morphemes
    c. Phonemes
    d. Semantics

16. Which of the following is true of two-word utterances?

a. The order of appearance of types of two-word utterances is the same for such diverse languages as Russian, Luo, and Turkish.

b. The order of appearance of types of two-word utterances is the same for different European languages only.

c. The appearance of two-word utterances shows that conditioning does not play a role in language development.

d. The word order in two-word utterances tends to be haphazard.

17. A 3-year-old says, "Mommy goed away." This statement is an example of
   a. failure to understand grammar.
   b. overregularization.
   c. overextension.
   d. understanding of deep structure but not surface structure.

18. Who is credited with originating the linguistic-relativity hypothesis?

a. Chomsky
b. Whorf
c. Wechsler
d. Slobin

19. According to the text, Bismarck showed evidence of
   a. semanticity.
   b. insight.
   b. overconfidence.
   d. infinite creativity.

20. Evidence for the nativist theory of language development is found in
   a. the invariant sequences of language development.
   b. the fact that language development is made possible by cognitive analytical abilities.
   c. children's motivation to express the meanings that conceptual development makes available to them.
   d. the fact that parents reinforce children for the grammatical correctness of their utterances.

ANSWER KEY TO POSTTEST

1. D	4. B	7. D	10. D	13. A	16. A	19. B
2. B	5. C	8. B	11. A	14. C	17. B	20. A
3. D	6. D	9. D	12. B	15. A	18. B	

LEARNING OBJECTIVES

When you have finished studying Chapter 9, you should be able to:

THEORIES OF INTELLIGENCE
1. Define *intelligence.*
2. Discuss factor theories of intelligence.
3. Discuss Gardner's theory of multiple intelligences.
4. Discuss Sternberg's triarchic theory of intelligence.

ARTIFICIAL INTELLIGENCE
5. Discuss the achievements and limits of artificial intelligence.

MEASUREMENT OF INTELLIGENCE
6. Describe the development and features of intelligence tests.
7. Discuss socioeconomic and ethnic differences in intelligence.

THE TESTING CONTROVERSY: JUST WHAT DO INTELLIGENCE TESTS MEASURE?
8. Discuss the issue of whether intelligence tests contain cultural biases against ethnic minority groups and immigrants.
9. Discuss the effort to develop culture-free intelligence tests.

THE DETERMINANTS OF INTELLIGENCE: WHERE DOES INTELLIGENCE COME FROM?
10. Discuss research concerning genetic influences on intelligence.
11. Discuss research concerning environmental influences on intelligence.

Intelligence

PRETEST *Truth or Fiction?*

____ The terms *intelligence* and *IQ* can be used interchangeably.

____ Two children can answer exactly the same items on an intelligence test correctly, yet one can be above average and the other below average in IQ.

____ White Americans attain the highest scores on IQ tests.

____ Early users of IQ tests administered them in English to immigrants who did not understand the language.

____ Mental testing began in the 19th century.

____ The use of culture-free intelligence tests eliminates socioeconomic and ethnic differences in IQ.

____ Music lessons raise children's intelligence.

WHAT form of life is so adaptive that it can survive in desert temperatures of 120 degrees Fahrenheit or Arctic climes of −40 degrees Fahrenheit? What form of life can run, walk, climb, swim, live underwater for months on end, and fly to the moon and back?

I won't keep you in suspense any longer. We are that form of life. Yet, our unclad bodies do not allow us to adapt to these extremes of temperature. Brute strength does not allow us to live underwater or travel to the moon. Rather, it is our **intelligence** that permits us to adapt to these conditions and to challenge our physical limitations. The human capacity to think about abstractions like space and time sets us apart from all other species (Campbell, 1994).

The term *intelligence* is familiar enough. At an early age, we gain impressions of how intelligent we are compared to others. We associate intelligence with academic success, advancement on the job, and appropriate social behavior. Psychologists use intelligence as a **trait** that may explain, at least in part, why people do (or fail to do) things that are adaptive and inventive.

Despite our familiarity with the concept of intelligence, intelligence cannot be seen, touched, or measured physically. However, as noted by Kimble (1994), the concept of intelligence is tied to predictors, such as scores on intelligence tests, and to behavior, such as school performance. Still, the concept of intelligence is subject to various interpretations. In this chapter, we discuss different ways of looking at intelligence. We see how intelligence is measured and discuss group differences in intelligence. Finally, we examine the determinants of intelligence: heredity and the environment.

THEORIES OF INTELLIGENCE

Let us distinguish between **achievement** and intelligence. Achievement refers to knowledge and skills gained from experience. It involves specific content such as English, history, and math. The relationship between achievement and experience seems obvious: We are not surprised to find that a student who has taken Spanish, but not French, does better on a Spanish achievement test than on a French achievement test.

The meaning of *intelligence* is more difficult to pin down. Most psychologists agree that intelligence somehow provides the cognitive basis for academic achievement. Intelligence is usually perceived as underlying competence, or learning ability, whereas achievement involves acquired competencies or performance. Psychologists disagree, however, about the nature and origins of that underlying competence.

Factor Theories

Many investigators have viewed intelligence as consisting of one or more mental abilities, or **factors.** Alfred Binet, the Frenchman who developed modern intelligence-testing methods about 100 years ago, believed that intelligence consisted of several related factors. Other investigators have argued that intelligence consists of from one to hundreds of factors.

In 1904, British psychologist Charles Spearman suggested that the behaviors we consider to be intelligent have a common underlying factor. He labeled this factor **g,** for "general intelligence." *G* represented broad reasoning and problem-solving abilities. Spearman supported this view by noting that people who excel in one area can usually excel in others. But he also noted that even

---

Intelligence • A complex and controversial concept. According to David Wechsler (1975), the "capacity . . . to understand the world [and] resourcefulness to cope with its challenges."

Trait • A distinguishing characteristic that is presumed to account for consistency in behavior.

Achievement • That which is attained by one's efforts and made possible by one's abilities.

Factor • A cluster of related items such as those found on an intelligence test.

g • Spearman's symbol for general intelligence, which he believed underlay more specific abilities.

TABLE 9.1
LOUIS THURSTONE'S PRIMARY MENTAL ABILITIES

ABILITY	DESCRIPTION
Visual and spatial abilities	Visualizing forms and spatial relationships
Perceptual speed	Grasping perceptual details rapidly, perceiving similarities and differences between stimuli
Numerical ability	Computing numbers
Verbal meaning	Knowing the meanings of words
Memory	Recalling information (words, sentences, etc.)
Word fluency	Thinking of words quickly (rhyming, doing crossword puzzles, etc.)
Deductive reasoning	Deriving examples from general rules
Inductive reasoning	Deriving general rules from examples

---

the most capable people are relatively superior in some areas—whether in music or business or poetry. For this reason, he suggested that specific, or **s**, factors account for specific abilities.

To test his views, Spearman developed a statistical method called **factor analysis.** Factor analysis allows researchers to determine the relationships among large numbers of items such as those found on intelligence tests. Items that cluster together are labeled *factors*. In his research on relationships among tests of verbal, mathematical, and spatial reasoning, Spearman repeatedly found evidence supporting the existence of *s* factors. The evidence for *g* was more limited.

U.S. psychologist Louis Thurstone (1938) used factor analysis with various tests of specific abilities and also found only limited evidence for the existence of *g*. Thurstone concluded that Spearman had oversimplified the concept of intelligence. Thurstone's data suggested the presence of nine specific factors, which he labeled **primary mental abilities** (see Table 9.1). Thurstone suggested, for example, that we might have high word fluency, enabling us to rapidly develop lists of words that rhyme, yet not enabling us to be efficient at solving math problems (Thurstone & Thurstone, 1963).

This view seems to make sense. Most of us know people who are good at math but poor in English, and vice versa. Nonetheless, some link seems to connect specific mental abilities. The data still show that the person with excellent reasoning ability is likely to have a larger-than-average vocabulary and better-than-average numerical ability. Few, if any, people exceed 99% of the population in one mental ability but are exceeded by 80 or 90% of the population in others.

Over the years, psychologist J. P. Guilford (1988) expanded the numbers of factors found in intellectual functioning to as many as 180. The problem with such expansion seems to be that the more factors we generate, the more overlap we find among them (Rebok, 1987).

s • Spearman's symbol for *specific* factors, or *s* factors, which he believed accounted for individual abilities.

Factor analysis • A statistical technique that allows researchers to determine the relationships among large number of items such as test items.

Primary mental abilities • According to Thurstone, the basic abilities that make up intelligence.

Gardner's Theory of Multiple Intelligences

Howard Gardner (1983; Gardner & Hatch, 1989) proposes the existence of seven kinds of intelligence. He refers to each as "an intelligence" because they can be so different from one another (see Figure 9.1). He also

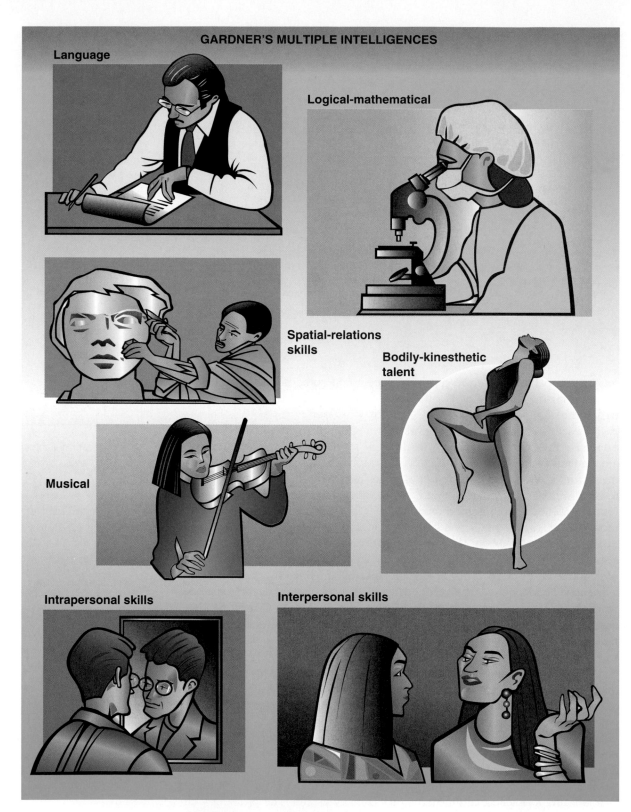

GARDNER'S MULTIPLE INTELLIGENCES

Language

Logical-mathematical

Spatial-relations skills

Bodily-kinesthetic talent

Musical

Intrapersonal skills

Interpersonal skills

FIGURE 9.1

Gardner's Theory of Multiple Intelligences. According to Gardner, there are seven intelligences, not one, and each is based in a different area of the brain. Two of these involve language ability and logic, which are familiar components of intelligence functions. But Gardner also refers to bodily talents, musical ability, spatial-relations skills, and two kinds of personal intelligence—sensitivity to one's own feelings (intrapersonal sensitivity) and sensitivity to the feelings of others (interpersonal sensitivity). According to this view, one could compose symphonies or advance mathematical theory while remaining average in, say, language skills.

believes that each kind of intelligence has its neurological base in a different area of the brain. Two such "intelligences" involve language ability and logical-mathematical ability, which are familiar enough aspects of intelligence to other theorists. However, Gardner also refers to bodily-kinesthetic talents (of the sort shown by dancers, mimes, and athletes), musical talent, spatial-relations skills, and two kinds of personal intelligence: awareness of one's own inner feelings, and sensitivity to other people's feelings and the ability to respond to them appropriately. According to Gardner, one can compose symphonies or advance mathematical theory yet be average in, say, language and personal skills. (Are not some academic "geniuses" foolish in their personal lives?)

Critics of Gardner's view grant that people do function more intelligently in some aspects of life than in others. They concur that many people have special talents, such as bodily-kinesthetic talents, whereas their overall intelligence seems average. However, they question whether such special talents are equivalent in meaning to what they see as a broader concept of intelligence (Scarr, 1985).

Sternberg's Triarchic Theory

Cognitive psychologist Robert Sternberg (1995) views intelligence in terms of information processing. He focuses on how information "flows" through us and is modified by us as we adapt to and act to change our environments.

Sternberg's analysis led him to construct a three-level, or **triarchic,** model of intelligence (see Figure 9.2). The levels are *contextual, experiential,* and *componential.* Individual differences are found at each level. The **contextual level** concerns the environmental setting. It is assumed that intelligent behavior permits people to adapt to the demands of their environments. For example, keeping a job by adapting one's behavior to the requirements of one's employer is adaptive. But if the employer is making unreasonable demands, reshaping the environment (by changing the employer's attitudes) or selecting an alternate environment (finding a more suitable job) is also adaptive.

On the **experiential level,** intelligent behavior is defined by the abilities to cope with novel situations and to process information automatically. The ability to quickly relate novel situations to familiar situations (to perceive the similarities and differences) fosters adaptation. Moreover, as a result of experience, we come to solve problems more rapidly. Intelligence and experience in reading permit the child to process familiar words more or less automatically and to decode new words efficiently. In sum, it is "intelligent" to profit from experience.

The **componential level** of intelligence consists of three processes: metacomponents, performance components, and knowledge-acquisition components. **Metacomponents** concern our awareness of our own intellectual processes. Metacomponents are involved in deciding what problem to solve, selecting appropriate strategies and formulas, monitoring the solution, and changing performance in the light of knowledge of results.

Performance components are the mental operations or skills used in solving problems or processing information. Performance components include encoding information, combining and comparing pieces of information, and generating a solution. Consider Sternberg's analogy problem:

Washington is to *one* as *Lincoln* is to (a) 5, (b) 10, (c) 15, (d) 50?

To solve the analogy, we must first correctly *encode* the elements— *Washington, one,* and *Lincoln*—by identifying them and comparing them with other information. We must first encode *Washington* and *Lincoln* as the names of

Triarchic • (try-ARK-ick). Governed by three.
Contextual level • Those aspects of intelligent behavior that permit people to adapt to their environment.
Experiential level • Those aspects of intelligence that permit people to cope with novel situations and process information automatically.
Componential level • The level of intelligence that consists of metacomponents, performance components, and knowledge-acquisition components.
Metacomponents • Components of intelligence that are based on self-awareness of our intellectual processes.
Performance components • The mental operations used in processing information.

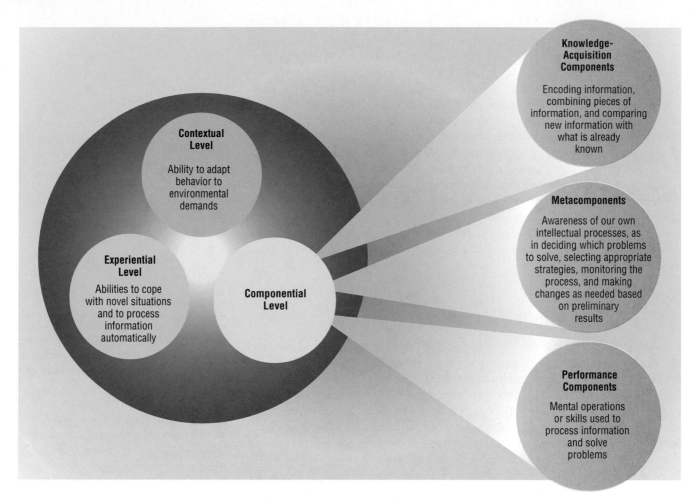

FIGURE 9.2

The Triarchic Model of Intelligence. Sternberg views intelligence as consisting of contextual, experiential, and componential levels. The componential level consists of metacomponents, performance components, and knowledge-acquisition components.

Knowledge-acquisition components • Components used in gaining knowledge, such as encoding and relating new knowledge to existing knowledge.

presidents[1] and then try to combine *Washington* and *one* in a meaningful manner. Two possibilities quickly come to mind. Washington was the first president, and his picture is on the $1 bill. We can then generate two possible solutions and try them out. First, what number president was Lincoln? Second, on what bill is Lincoln's picture found? (Do you need to consult a history book or peek into your wallet at this point?)

Knowledge-acquisition components are used in gaining new knowledge. These include encoding information (for example, Engelbert Humperdinck as the name of the contemporary singer or as the name of the 19th-century composer of the opera *Hansel and Gretel*), combining pieces of information, and comparing new information with what is already known.

Sternberg's model is complex, but it does a promising job of capturing what most investigators mean by intellectual functioning. David Wechsler, the originator of a series of widely used intelligence tests, described intelligence in terms that are simpler but, I think, consistent with Sternberg's view. Intelligence, wrote Wechsler (1975), is the "capacity of an individual to understand

---

[1] There are other possibilities. Both are the names of memorials and cities, for example.

the world [and the] resourcefulness to cope with its challenges" (p. 139). Intelligence, to Wechsler, involves accurate representation of the world (which Sternberg describes as encoding, comparing new information with old information, and so on) and effective problem solving (adapting to one's environment, profiting from experience, selecting the appropriate formulas and strategies, and so on).

Reflections

- How would you have defined *intelligence* before you began reading this chapter? How do psychologists' definitions of intelligence agree with, or differ from, your own? How would you compare your definition with those you have read about?
- From your own experiences, what seem to be the relationships between general intelligence and special talents, such as musical or artistic ability? Do you know people who are "good at everything"? Do you know people who seem extremely talented in some areas but not in others? In what areas are they talented?
- **Agree or disagree with the following statement and support your answer: "Some children are overachievers in school."**

ARTIFICIAL INTELLIGENCE

The new millennium promises to bring major developments in the realm of artificial intelligence, or *A.I.* A.I. is the replication of human intellectual functioning in computers.

The concept of A.I. has a lengthy history both in science fiction and in practice (Freedman, 1994; Gelernter, 1994). Think of HAL, the supercool computer that spoke softly but carried a big spaceship in the film *2001*. Not only was HAL capable of coordinating all the monitors and controls of a spaceship. HAL could also engage in such signature human activities as murder, lying with a straight . . . monitor, and striving to save his own . . . memory chips. The robot C3PO in *Star Wars* not only mimicked human intelligence. He also showed remarkably human anxieties and self-doubts.

So much for Hollywood. The idea that human intelligence could be copied in computer form originated in the 1950s (Chartrand, 1993). It was predicted that machines with A.I. would one day be able to understand spoken language, decipher bad handwriting, search their memories for relevant information, reason, solve problems, make decisions, write books, and explain themselves out loud. At the time these predictions were visionary. Yet, that day—"one day"—is now. Within concrete limits, today's computers are very, very good at encoding information, storing it, retrieving it, and manipulating it to solve problems and make decisions. In some ways, A.I. is even more than human. A.I. can crunch millions of numbers in a fraction of a second. A.I. can solve problems that would take people years to solve, if they could solve them at all without A.I. Given clear direction and the right formulas, computers can carry out many complex intellectual functions in a literal flash. "Who," asks Patrick Hayes (1993), a University of Illinois professor, "can keep track of 10,000 topics like a computer?"

In other ways, A.I. remains much less than human (Pinker, 1994b). Today's computers, even powerful mainframes, do not have the insights, intuitions, and creativity found in people (Gelernter, 1994). Their ability to produce original written material can be best described as lumbering. (So I will remain the

In the Eye of the (Electronic) Beholder. HAL, the computer, spoke softly but carried a big spaceship in the classic science fiction film *2001* (shown in this photo). In the 1950s, it was predicted that machines with artificial intelligence would one day be able to understand spoken language, decipher bad handwriting, search their memories for relevant information, reason, solve problems, make decisions, write books, and explain themselves out loud. That day—"one day"—is now. What forms will artificial intelligence take in the new millennium?

sole author of this book.) The sparks of brilliance we find in computational ability turn to dense wood when we ask today's computers to exercise the human functions of writing prose or composing music. (I hope my computer's not reading this.)

Despite our increasing ability to pack huge amounts of memory into tiny chips of one kind or another, the possibility of a HAL—a computer that creates original thoughts and plays upon human psychologies—still seems like science fiction, at least by the year 2001.

The ultimate goal of A.I., notes Hayes, is the creation of a computer that has a human mind. Yet, some observers suggest that this goal is unnecessary. They believe that computer science will continue to evolve by improving on the things that computers already do better than people (Carter, 1993). Freedman (1994) describes projects involving antlike robots, hybrids of computer chips and neurons, even programs that mutate and mate—allowing the survival of the fittest programs. Steven Pinker (1994b) likens these programs to "software animals that evolve in virtual worlds" (p. 13).

Whether or not scientists cease the effort to make computers think more like people, we will apparently continue to create computers that each have bits and pieces of humanlike intelligence (Gutknecht, 1992). But the whole that goes into that "piece of work" that defines the human being is likely to continue to elude us for the foreseeable future. That thought doesn't bother me a byte.

MEASUREMENT OF INTELLIGENCE

Mental age • The accumulated months of credit that a person earns on the Stanford–Binet Intelligence Scale. Abbreviated *MA*.

Although there are disagreements about the nature of intelligence, thousands of intelligence tests are administered by psychologists and educators every day. Let us explore some widely used intelligence tests.

Individual Intelligence Tests

Many of the concepts of psychology have their origins in common sense (Kimble, 1994). The commonsense notion that academic achievement depends on children's intelligence led the Frenchmen Alfred Binet and Theodore Simon to invent measures of intelligence early in this century.

**MINILECTURE:
MEASURING INTELLIGENCE**

THE STANFORD–BINET INTELLIGENCE SCALE.   The French public school system sought an instrument that could identify children who were unlikely to profit from the regular classroom so that they could receive special attention. The first version, the Binet–Simon scale, came into use in 1905. Since that time, it has undergone great revision and refinement. The current version is the Stanford–Binet Intelligence Scale (SBIS).

Despite his view that many factors are involved in intellectual functioning, Binet constructed his test to yield a single overall score so that it could be more easily used by the school system. He also assumed that intelligence increased with age. Therefore, older children should get more items right than younger children. Thus, Binet included a series of age-graded questions, as in Table 9.2. He arranged them in order of difficulty.

The Binet–Simon scale yielded a score called a **mental age,** or MA. The MA shows the intellectual level at which a child is functioning. A child with an MA of 6 is functioning, intellectually, like the average child aged 6. In taking the test, children earned "months" of credit for each correct answer. Their MA was determined by adding the years and months of credit they attained.

TABLE 9.2
ITEMS SIMILAR TO THOSE ON THE STANFORD–BINET INTELLIGENCE SCALE

LEVEL (YEARS)	ITEM
2 years	1. Children show knowledge of basic vocabulary words by identifying parts of a doll such as the mouth, ears, and hair. 2. Children show counting and spatial skills along with visual–motor coordination by building a tower of four blocks to match a model.
4 years	1. Children show word fluency and categorical thinking by filling in the missing words when they are asked questions such as "Father is a man; mother is a _____?" "Hamburgers are hot; ice cream is _____?" 2. Children show comprehension by answering correctly when they are asked questions such as "Why do people have automobiles?" "Why do people have medicine?"
9 years	1. Children can point out verbal absurdities, as in this question: "In an old cemetery, scientists unearthed a skull which they think was that of George Washington when was only 5 years of age. What is silly about that?" 2. Children show fluency with words, as shown by answering questions such as "Can you tell me a number that rhymes with snore?" "Can you tell me a color that rhymes with glue?
Adult	1. Adults show knowledge of the meanings of words and conceptual thinking by correctly explaining the differences between word pairs like "sickness and misery," "house and home," and "integrity and prestige." 2. Adults show spatial skills by answering questions such as "If a car turned to the right to head north, in what direction was it heading before it turned?"

Louis Terman adapted the Binet–Simon scale for use with children in the United States. The first version of the *Stanford*–Binet Intelligence Scale (SBIS)[2] was published in 1916. The SBIS included more items than the original test and was used with children aged 2 to 16. The SBIS also yielded an **intelligence quotient (IQ)** rather than an MA. American educators developed interest in learning the IQs of their pupils. The current version of the SBIS is used with children from the age of 2 upward and with adults.

Truth or Fiction Revisited. *It is not true that the terms* intelligence *and* IQ *can be used interchangeably.* Intelligence is a hypothetical concept on whose meanings psychologists do not agree. An *IQ* is a score on an intelligence test. What are some of the dangers in using the terms interchangeably?

The IQ reflects the relationship between a child's mental age and actual age, or chronological age (CA). Use of this ratio reflects the fact that the same MA score has different implications for children of different ages. That is, an MA of 8 is an above-average score for a 6-year-old, but an MA of 8 is below average for a 10-year-old. The German psychologist Wilhelm Stern in 1912 suggested use of the IQ to handle this problem.

Stern computed IQ by the formula IQ = (Mental Age/Chronological Age) × 100, or

$$IQ = \frac{\text{Mental Age (MA)}}{\text{Chronological Age (CA)}} \times 100$$

According to this formula, a child with an MA of 6 and a CA of 6 would have an IQ of 100. Children who can handle intellectual problems as well as older

Intelligence quotient (IQ) • (1) Originally, a ratio obtained by dividing a child's score (or mental age) on an intelligence test by his or her chronological age. (2) Generally, a score on an intelligence test.

---

[2] The test is so named because Terman carried out his work at Stanford University.

Taking the Wechsler. The Wechsler intelligence scales consist of verbal and performance subtests such as the one shown in this photograph.

children will have IQs above 100. For instance, an 8-year-old who does as well on the SBIS as the average 10-year-old will attain an IQ of 125. Children who do not answer as many items correctly as other children of their age will attain MAs lower than their CAs. Thus, their IQ scores will be below 100.

Today, IQ scores on the SBIS are derived by seeing how children's and adults' performances deviate from those of other people of the same age. People who get more items correct than average attain IQ scores above 100. People who answer fewer items correctly attain scores below 100.

Truth or Fiction Revisited. *It is true that two children can answer exactly the same items on an intelligence test correctly, yet one can be above average and the other below average in IQ.* This is because the ages of the children may differ. The more intelligent child would be the younger of the two.

THE WECHSLER SCALES. The SBIS is the "classic" individual intelligence test. However, today the Wechsler scales are more widely used (Watkins and others, 1995).

David Wechsler developed a series of scales for use with children and adults. The Wechsler scales group test questions into a number of separate subtests (such as those shown in Table 9.3). Each subtest measures a different type of intellectual task. For this reason, the test shows how well a person does on one type of task (such as defining words) as compared with another (such as using blocks to construct geometric designs). In this way, the Wechsler scales highlight children's relative strengths and weaknesses, as well as measure overall intellectual functioning.

As you can see in Table 9.3, Wechsler described some of his scales as measuring *verbal* tasks and others as assessing *performance* tasks. In general, verbal subtests require knowledge of verbal concepts, whereas performance

MINILECTURE:
THE WECHSLER SCALES:
THE WAIS

TABLE 9.3
SUBTESTS FROM THE WECHSLER
ADULT INTELLIGENCE SCALE

VERBAL SUBTESTS	PERFORMANCE SUBTESTS
1. *Information:* "What is the capital of the United States?" "Who was Shakespeare?	7. *Digit Symbol:* Learning and drawing meaningless figures that are associated with numbers.
2. *Comprehension:* "Why do we have ZIP codes?" "What does 'A stitch in time saves nine' mean?"	8. *Picture Completion:* Pointing to the missing part of a picture.
3. *Arithmetic:* "If 3 candy bars cost 25 cents, how much will 18 candy bars cost?"	9. *Block Design:* Copying pictures of geometric designs using multi-colored blocks.
4. *Similarities:* "How are good and bad alike?" "How are peanut butter and jelly alike?"	10. *Picture Arrangement:* Arranging cartoon pictures in sequence so that they tell a meaningful story.
5. *Digit Span:* Repeating a series of numbers forwards and backwards.	11. *Object Assembly:* Putting pieces of a puzzle together so that they form a meaningful object.
6. *Vocabulary:* "What does *canal* mean?"	

Items for verbal subtests 1, 2, 3, 4, and 6 are similar, but not identical, to actual test items on the WAIS.

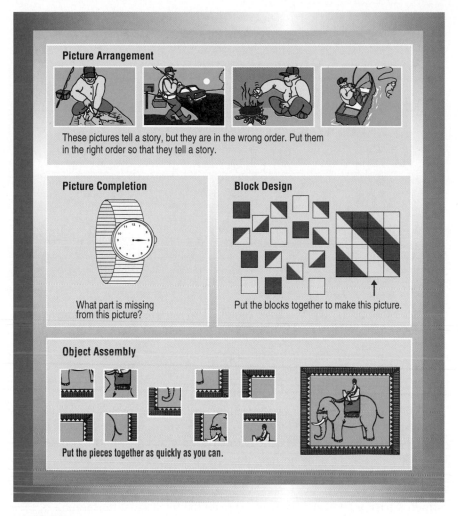

FIGURE 9.3

Performance Items of an Intelligence Test. This figure shows a number of items that resemble those in the performance subtests of the Wechsler Adult Intelligence Scale.

FIGURE 9.4

Approximate Distribution of IQ Scores. Wechsler defined the deviation IQ so that 50% of scores would fall within the broad average range of 90–110. This bell-shaped curve is referred to as a *normal curve* by psychologists. It describes the distribution of many traits, including height.

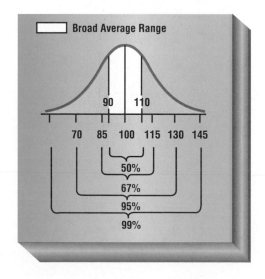

subtests require familiarity with spatial-relations concepts. (Figure 9.3 shows items similar to those found on the performance scales of the Wechsler tests.) But the two groupings are not that easily distinguished. For example, associating to the name of the object being pieced together in subtest 11—a sign of word fluency and general knowledge as well as of spatial-relations ability—helps the person construct it rapidly. In any event, Wechsler's scales permit the computation of verbal and performance IQs. It is not unusual for nontechnically oriented college students to attain higher verbal than performance IQs.

Wechsler also introduced the concept of the deviation IQ. Instead of using mental and chronological ages to compute an IQ, he based IQ scores on how a person's answers compared with (or deviated from) those attained by people in the same age group. The average test result at any age level is defined as an IQ score of 100. Wechsler then distributed IQ scores so that the middle 50% of them would fall within the "broad average range" of 90 to 110.

As you can see in Figure 9.4, most IQ scores cluster around the average. Only 4% of the population have IQ scores of above 130 or below 70. Table 9.4

TABLE 9.4
VARIATIONS IN IQ SCORES

RANGE OF SCORES	PERCENT OF POPULATION	BRIEF DESCRIPTION
130 and above	2	Very superior
120–129	7	Superior
110–119	16	Above average
100–109	25	High average
90–99	25	Low average
80–89	16	Slow learner
70–79	7	Borderline
Below 70	2	Intellectually deficient

indicates the labels that Wechsler assigned to various IQ scores and the approximate percentages of the population who attain IQ scores at those levels.

Group Tests

The SBIS and Wechsler scales are administered to one person at a time. This one-to-one ratio is considered optimal. It allows the examiner to facilitate performance (within the limits of the standardized directions) and to observe the test taker closely. Examiners are thus alerted to factors that impair performance, such as language difficulties, illness, or a noisy or poorly lit room. But large institutions with few trained examiners, such as the public schools and armed forces, have also wished to estimate the intellectual functioning of their charges. They require tests that can be administered simultaneously to large groups of people.

Group tests for children, first developed during World War I, were administered to 4 million children by 1921, a couple of years after the war had ended. At first, these tests were heralded as remarkable instruments because they eased the huge responsibilities of school administrators. However, as the years passed they came under increasing attack, because many administrators relied on them completely to track children. The administrators did not seek other sources of information about the children's abilities and achievements.

Intelligence tests provide just one source of information as to the special abilities and talents of children. Children are not to be confused with numbers, especially those in the form of IQ scores.

Reflections

- Have you ever taken an intelligence test? Was it an individual test or a group test? What was the experience like? Were you informed as to how well you did on the test? Do you believe that the test assessed you fairly or arrived at an accurate estimate of your intelligence?
- What types of items do you believe ought to be on intelligence tests? Do the tests discussed in this chapter appear to include the types of things that you consider important?

Extremes of Intelligence: Mental Retardation and Giftedness

The average IQ score in the United States is very close to 100. About 50% of U.S. children attain IQ scores in the broad average range from 90 to 110. Nearly 95% attain scores between 70 and 130. But what of the other 5%? Children who attain IQ scores below 70 are generally labeled as intellectually deficient or mentally retarded. Children who attain scores of 130 or above are usually labeled as gifted. Both labels create certain expectations. Both place burdens on children and their parents.

MENTAL RETARDATION. Mental retardation is typically assessed through a combination of children's IQ scores and behavioral observations. According to the American Association on Mental Retardation, mental retardation "refers to substantial limitations in present functioning [as] characterized by significantly sub-average intellectual functioning [including an IQ score of no more than 70 to 75], existing concurrently with related limitations in two or more of the following applicable adaptive skill areas: communication, self-care, home living, social skills, community use, self-direction, health and safety, functional academics, leisure and work" (Michaelson, 1993a). A number of scales have been developed to assess adaptive behavior. A list of 9 items from the Vineland Adaptive Behavior Scales (Sparrow and others, 1984) is shown below in Table 9.5.

Table 9.6 summarizes descriptions of a number of levels of retardation. Most of the children (about 80%) who are retarded are mildly retarded. Mildly retarded children, as the term implies, are most capable of adjusting to the demands of educational institutions and, eventually, to society at large. Mildly retarded children are also most likely to be mainstreamed in regular classrooms, as opposed to being placed in special-needs classes. Mainstreaming is intended to provide mildly retarded children with the best possible education

---

TABLE 9.5

ITEMS FROM THE VINELAND ADAPTIVE BEHAVIOR SCALES

AGE LEVEL	ITEM
1 year, 8 months	Removes front-opening coat, sweater, or shirt without assistance.
1 year, 10 months	Says at least 50 recognizable words.
3 years, 7 months	Tells popular story, fairy tale, lengthy joke, or plot of television program.
4 years, 9 months	Ties shoelaces into a bow without assistance.
5 years, 2 months	Keeps secrets or confidences for more than one day.
7 years, 7 months	Watches television or listens to radio for information about a particular area of interest.
8 years, 8 months	Uses the telephone for all kinds of calls, without assistance.
10 years, 2 months	Responds to hints or indirect cues in conversation.
12 years, 2 months	Looks after own health.

Source: Adapted from *Vineland Adaptive Behavior Scales*, by S. S. Sparrow, D. A. Ballo, and D. V. Cicchetti, 1984, Circle Pines, MN: American Guidance Service.

TABLE 9.6
LEVELS OF RETARDATION, TYPICAL RANGES OF IQ SCORES, AND TYPES OF ADAPTIVE BEHAVIORS

APPROXIMATE IQ SCORE RANGE	PRESCHOOL AGE (0–5) MATURATION AND DEVELOPMENT	SCHOOL AGE (6–21) TRAINING AND EDUCATION	ADULT (21 AND OVER) SOCIAL AND VOCATIONAL ADEQUACY
Mild (50–70)	Often not noticed as retarded by casual observer but is slower to walk, feed self, and talk than most children.	Can acquire practical skills and useful reading and arithmetic to a 3rd to 6th grade level with special education. Can be guided toward social conformity.	Can usually achieve social and vocational skills adequate to self-maintenance; may need occasional guidance and support when under unusual social or economic stress.
Moderate (35–49)	Noticeable delays in motor development, especially in speech; responds to training in various self-help activities.	Can learn simple communication, elementary health and safety habits, and simple manual skills; does not progress in functional reading or arithmetic.	Can perform simple tasks under sheltered conditions; participates in simple recreation; travels alone in familar places; usually incapable of self-maintenance.
Severe (20–34)	Marked delay in motor development; little or no communication skill; may respond to training in elementary self-help—e.g., self-feeding.	Usually walks, barring specific disability; has some understanding of speech and some response; can profit from systematic habit training.	Can conform to daily routines and repetitive activities; needs continuing direction and supervision in protective environment.
Profound (Below 20)	Gross retardation; minimal capacity for functioning in sensorimotor areas; needs nursing care.	Obvious delays in all areas of development; shows basic emotional responses; may respond to skillful training in use of legs, hands, and jaws; needs close supervision.	May walk, may need nursing care, may have primitive speech; will usually benefit from regular physical activity; incapable of self-maintenance.

and encourage socialization with children at all intellectual levels. Unfortunately, some mildly retarded children are overwhelmed by regular classrooms and are avoided by classmates.

Children with Down syndrome are most likely to fall within the moderately retarded range. As suggested in Table 9.6, moderately retarded children can learn to speak; to dress, feed, and clean themselves; and, eventually, to engage in useful work under supportive conditions, as in the sheltered workshop. However, they usually do not acquire skills in reading and arithmetic. Severely and profoundly retarded children may not acquire speech and self-help skills and remain highly dependent on others for survival throughout their lives.

CAUSES OF RETARDATION. Some of the causes of retardation are biological. Retardation, for example, can stem from chromosomal abnormalities such as Down syndrome, genetic disorders such as phenylketonuria, and brain damage. Brain damage may have many origins, including accidents during childhood and problems during pregnancy. Prenatal maternal alcohol abuse, malnutrition, or diseases can all lead to retardation.

GIFTEDNESS. Giftedness involves more than excellence in the tasks provided by standard intelligence tests. Most educators include children who have outstanding abilities, are capable of high performance in a specific academic area such as language arts or mathematics, or who show creativity or leadership, distinction in the visual or performing arts, or bodily talents as in gymnastics and dancing.

Educators suggest that it is helpful to identify gifted children early and provide them with enriched experiences so they can develop their exceptional talents. I agree. But it is also essential to provide disadvantaged children with the richest possible educational experiences. Yet, if we enrich only the gifted and the disadvantaged, we risk creating a new class of relatively deprived students—the middle 95% of the school population. I would like to see us invest enough in education to enrich every child. (I'll climb down from my soapbox now.)

Reflections

- Do you know a person who is mentally retarded? What is known of the causes of the retardation? What social and other adjustment problems seem to be connected with the person's level of intellectual functioning? What kind of educational or training experiences is the person receiving? Do these experiences seem to be appropriate? Why or why not?
- Do you know a person who is intellectually gifted? Does this person also have special talents as in math, music, or art? Does the giftedness seem to be connected with social advantages or social problems? In what ways? What kinds of educational experiences is this person receiving? Do they seem to be appropriate? Why or why not?

WORLD OF DIVERSITY

SOCIOECONOMIC AND ETHNIC DIFFERENCES IN INTELLIGENCE

Research evidence is suggestive of differences in intelligence between socioeconomic and ethnic groups (Taylor & Richards, 1991). Lower-class U.S. children attain IQ scores some 10 to 15 points lower than those of middle- and upper-class children. African American children tend to attain IQ scores some 15–20 points lower than their White agemates (Helms, 1992; Herrnstein & Murray, 1994; Storfer, 1990). Hispanic American and Native American children also score significantly below the norms of White children.

Several studies on IQ have confused the factors of social class and ethnicity because disproportionate numbers of African, Hispanic, and Native Americans are found among the lower socioeconomic classes (Patterson and others, 1990). When we limit our observations to particular ethnic groups, however, we still find an effect for social class. That is, middle-class Whites outscore lower-class Whites. Middle-class African, Hispanic, and Native Americans also all outscore lower-class members of their own ethnic groups.

Research has also discovered differences between Asians and White people. Asian Americans, for example, frequently outscore White Americans on the math portion of the Scholastic Assessment Test. Students in China (Taiwan) and Japan also outscore Americans on standardized achievement tests in math and science (Stevenson and others, 1986). British psychologist Richard Lynn (1982) has reported that Japanese (residing in Japan) attain higher IQ scores than White Britishers or U.S. citizens. The mean Japanese IQ was 111, which

Who's Smart? Asian children and Asian American children frequently outscore other American children on intelligence tests. Can we attribute the difference to genetic factors or to Asian parents' emphasis on acquiring the kinds of cognitive skills that enable children to fare well on such tests and in school? Sue and Okazaki (1990) suggest that Asian Americans place great value on education because they have been discriminated against in careers that do not require advanced education.

exceeds the top of the high average range in the United States by a point. In the United States, moreover, people of Asian Indian, Korean, Japanese, Filipino, and Chinese extraction are more likely to graduate from high school and complete four years of college than White, African, and Hispanic Americans are (Sue & Okazaki, 1990). Asian Americans are vastly overrepresented in competitive colleges and universities. They make up only 2.4% of the U.S. population but account for 12% of the undergraduates at MIT, and 24% and 33%, respectively, at the University of California campuses at Berkeley and Irvine (*Chronicle of Higher Education,* 1992).

> ***Truth or Fiction Revisited.*** *It is not true that White Americans attain the highest scores on IQ tests.* Asian Americans tend to attain higher IQ scores. What hypotheses have been generated to account for this ethnic difference in IQ scores?

Lynn (1991) argues that the greater intellectual accomplishments of Asian students are in part genetically determined. According to Sue and Okazaki (1990), however, the higher scores of Asian students may reflect different values in the home, the school, or the culture at large rather than differences in underlying competence. They argue that Asian Americans have been discriminated against in careers that do not require advanced education. Thus, they place relatively greater emphasis on the value of education. Looking to other environmental factors, Steinberg and his colleagues (1992) claim that parental encouragement and supervision in combination with peer support for academic achievement partially explain the superior performances of White and Asian Americans as compared with African and Hispanic Americans.

Reflections

MINILECTURE: GENDER COMPARISONS IN INTELLIGENCE

- Are there real social-class, racial, and ethnic differences in intelligence? (How do you interpret the meaning of the word *real?*)
- Agree or disagree with the following statement and support your answer: "Studies on IQ have confused the factors of social class and ethnicity."
- What is your own ethnic background? Are there any stereotypes as to how people from your ethnic background perform on intelligence tests? If so, what is your reaction to these stereotypes? Why?

THE TESTING CONTROVERSY: JUST WHAT DO INTELLIGENCE TESTS MEASURE?

I was almost one of the testing casualties. At 15 I earned an IQ test score of 82, three points above the track of the special education class. Based on this score, my counselor suggested that I take up bricklaying because I was "good with my hands." My low IQ, however, did not allow me to see that as desirable.

This testimony is offered by African American Robert L. Williams (1974, p. 32), who has since become a psychologist. It echoes the sentiments of many psychologists. A survey of psychologists and educational specialists by Mark Snyderman and Stanley Rothman (1987, 1990) found that most consider intelligence tests somewhat biased against African Americans and members of the lower classes. Elementary and secondary schools may also place too much emphasis on them in making educational placements.

During the 1920s, intelligence tests were misused to prevent the immigration of many Europeans and others into the United States (Kamin, 1982; Kleinmuntz, 1982). For example, test pioneer H. H. Goddard assessed 178 newly arrived immigrants at Ellis Island and claimed that "83% of the Jews, 80% of the Hungarians, 79% of the Italians, and 87% of the Russians were 'feeble-minded'" (Kleinmuntz, 1982, p. 333). Apparently it was of little concern to Goddard that these immigrants, by and large, did not understand English—the language in which the tests were administered.

Truth or Fiction Revisited. *It is true that early users of IQ tests administered them in English to immigrants who did not understand the language.*

Questions about the effects of social class on test performance, the role of tests in enhancing or inhibiting social mobility, and the like, have been asked at least since the use of mental testing in China 2,000 years ago (Matarazzo, 1990).

Truth or Fiction Revisited. *It is not true that mental testing began in the 19th century.* Records show that mental testing was used in China 2,000 years ago. Moreover, the ancient Chinese wondered about the relationship between socioeconomic status and test performance.

Twentieth-century misuse of intelligence tests has led psychologists such as Leon Kamin to complain, "Since its introduction to America the intelligence test has been used more or less consciously as an instrument of oppression against the underprivileged—the poor, the foreign born, and racial minorities" (Crawford, 1979, p. 664).

MINILECTURE: CULTURE-FAIR INTELLIGENCE TESTS

Intelligence tests measure traits that are required in modern, high-technology societies (Anastasi, 1983; Pearlman and others, 1980; Schmidt and others, 1981). The vocabulary and arithmetic subtests on the Wechsler scales, for example, clearly reflect achievements in language skills and computational ability. It is generally assumed that the broad achievements measured by these tests reflect intelligence, but they might also reflect cultural familiarity with the concepts required to answer test questions correctly. In particular, the tests seem to reflect middle-class White culture in the United States (Garcia, 1981).

Is It Possible to Develop Culture-Free Intelligence Tests?

If scoring well on intelligence tests requires a certain type of cultural experience, the tests are said to have a **cultural bias.** Children reared in African American neighborhoods could be at a disadvantage, not because of differences in intelligence but because of cultural differences (Helms, 1992) and economic deprivation. For this reason, psychologists such as Raymond B. Cattell (1949) and Florence Goodenough (1954) have tried to construct **culture-free** intelligence tests.

Cattell's Culture-Fair Intelligence Test evaluates reasoning ability through the child's ability to comprehend the rules that govern a progression of geometric designs, as shown in Figure 9.5. Goodenough's Draw-A-Person test is based on the premise that children from all cultural backgrounds have had the opportunity to observe people and note the relationships between the parts and the whole. Her instructions simply require children to draw a picture of a man or woman.

Culture-free tests have not lived up to their promise, however. Middle-class White children still outperform African American children, perhaps because they are more likely to be familiar with materials such as blocks and pencils and paper. They are more likely than disadvantaged children to have arranged blocks into various designs (practice relevant to the Cattell test) and more likely to have sketched animals, people, and inanimate objects (practice

Cultural bias • A factor that provides an advantage for test takers from certain cultural or ethnic backgrounds.

Culture-free • Describing a test in which cultural biases are absent.

FIGURE 9.5

Sample Items from Raymond Cattell's Culture-Fair Intelligence Test.
Culture-fair tests attempt to exclude items that discriminate on the basis of cultural background rather than intelligence.

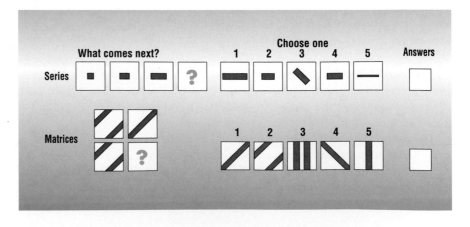

relevant to the Goodenough test). Too, culture-free tests do not predict academic success as well as other intelligence tests.

Truth or Fiction Revisited. *It is not true that the use of culture-free intelligence tests eliminates socioeconomic and ethnic differences in IQ.* Middle-class White children outperform African American children on "culture-free" tests.

Motivation to do well may also be a cultural factor. Because of socioeconomic and sociocultural differences, African American children often do not have the same motivation as White children to do well on tests (Tharp, 1991). Highly motivated children attain higher scores on intelligence tests than less-well-motivated children do (Collier, 1994). Perhaps there is no such thing as a culture-free intelligence test.

Reflections

- **Agree or disagree with the following statement and support your answer: "It is not possible to construct a truly culture-free intelligence test."**
- Consider your own ethnic group and the shared experiences of members of your ethnic group. Could you write an "intelligence test" that would provide members of your ethnic group an advantage? What types of items might you include? Would your test be a fair intelligence test, or would it be culturally biased?

THE DETERMINANTS OF INTELLIGENCE: WHERE DOES INTELLIGENCE COME FROM?

Determinants • Factors that set limits.

Because the concept of intelligence is central to what it means to be human, psychologists have intensely debated the nature of intelligence. The measurement of social-class and ethnic differences in intelligence, and the history of measurement abuse, have added social and political dimensions to the debate.

One of the more heated areas of debate concerns the **determinants** of intelligence (Azar, 1994c). That is, if different ethnic groups tend to score differently on intelligence tests, psychologists—like educators and other people involved in public life—want to know why. Yet this is one debate that is becoming supplied with important empirical findings. Here psychologists can point with pride to a rich mine of contemporary research into the roles of nature and nurture in the development of intelligence. Various ingenious approaches have been used to explore the elaborate interactions of genetic and environmental influences on intelligence.

Genetic Influences on Intelligence

Research on genetic influences on human intelligence employs strategies such as kinship studies, MZ–DZ twin studies, and adoptee studies.

KINSHIP STUDIES. Psychologists examine the IQ scores of closely and distantly related people who have been reared together or apart. If heredity is involved in human intelligence, closely related people ought to have more similar IQs than distantly related or unrelated people, even when they are reared separately.

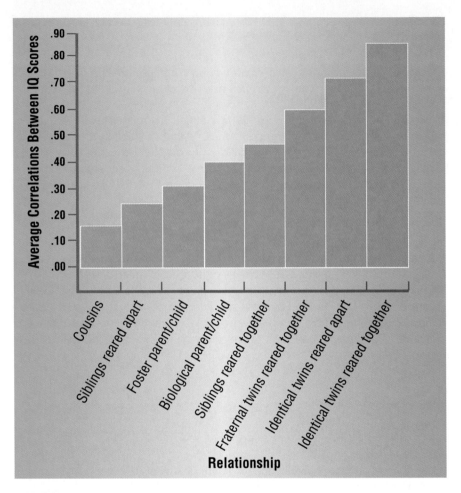

FIGURE 9.6

Findings of Studies of the Relationship Between IQ Scores and Heredity.
The data are a composite of hundreds of studies summarized in *Science* magazine (Bouchard and others, 1990). By and large, correlations are greater between pairs of people who are more closely related. Persons reared together
have more similar IQ scores than persons who were reared apart. Such findings
suggest that both genetic and environmental factors contribute to IQ scores.

Figure 9.6 is a composite of the results of more than 100 studies of IQ and
heredity in human beings, as reported by Bouchard and associates (1990). The
IQ scores of identical (MZ) twins are more alike than the scores for any other
pairs, even when the twins have been reared apart. Correlations between the
IQ scores of fraternal (DZ) twins, siblings, and parents and children are moderate. Correlations between children and their foster parents and between
cousins are weak.

TWIN STUDIES.   Large-scale twin studies are consistent with the data in Figure 9.6. Consider a study of 500 pairs of MZ and DZ twins in Louisville, Ken-
tucky (Wilson, 1983). The correlations in intelligence between MZ twins were
about the same as those for MZ twins in Figure 9.6. The correlations in intelligence between DZ twin pairs were the same as those between other siblings.
Research at the University of Minnesota with sets of twins who were reared together and others who were reunited in adulthood has obtained essentially
similar results (Bouchard and others, 1990). In the MacArthur Longitudinal

Twin Study, Robert Emde (1993) and his colleagues examined the intellectual abilities of 200 primarily White, healthy 14-month-old pairs of twins. They found that identical (MZ) twins were more similar than fraternal (DZ) twins in their spatial memory, their ability to categorize things, and their word comprehension. Emde and his colleagues concluded that genes tend to account for about 40% to 50% of the differences in cognitive skills in children (Adler, 1993a).

All in all, studies generally suggest that the **heritability** of intelligence is between 40% and 60% (Adler, 1993a; Bouchard and others, 1990; Plomin, 1989; Plomin & Rende, 1991). In other words, about half of the variations (the technical term is *variance*) in IQ scores among people can be accounted for by heredity. This is *not* the same as saying that you inherited about half of your intelligence. The implication of such a statement would be that you "got" the other half of your intelligence somewhere else. It means, rather, that about half of the difference between your IQ score and the IQ scores of other people can be explained in terms of genetic factors.

Even this view of the heritability of intelligence may be too broad to be highly accurate. Research also suggests that the heritability of verbal ability is greater than the heritability of factors such as spatial-relations ability and of memory (Thompson and others, 1991).

Note, too, that genetic pairs (such as MZ twins) reared together show higher correlations between IQ scores than similar genetic pairs (such as other MZ twins) who were reared apart. This finding holds for MZ twins, siblings, parents and children, and unrelated people. *For this reason, the same group of studies suggests that the environment plays a role in IQ scores.*

ADOPTEE STUDIES. Another strategy for exploring genetic influences on intelligence is to compare the correlations between adopted children and their biological and adoptive parents (Coon and others, 1990). When children are separated from their biological parents at early ages, one can argue that strong relationships between their IQs and those of their natural parents reflect genetic influences. Strong relationships between their IQs and those of their adoptive parents might reflect environmental influences.

Several studies with 1- and 2-year-old children in Colorado (Baker and others, 1983), Texas (Horn, 1983), and Minnesota (Scarr & Weinberg, 1983) have found a stronger relationship between the IQ scores of adopted children and those of their biological parents than with the IQ scores of their adoptive parents. The Scarr and Weinberg report concerns African American children reared by White adoptive parents. We shall return to its findings in the section on environmental influences on intelligence.

In sum, genetic factors appear to account for about half of the variation in intelligence test scores among people. Environmental factors also affect scores on intelligence tests.

MINILECTURE: THE HERITABILITY OF INTELLIGENCE

Heritability • The degree to which the variations in a trait from one person to another can be attributed to, or explained by, genetic factors.

Environmental Influences on Intelligence

Studies on environmental influences also employ a variety of research strategies. Consider the situational factors that determine IQ scores. An IQ is a score on a test. Thus in some cases, the testing situation itself can explain part of the social-class difference in IQ. In one study, the experimenters (Zigler and others, 1982) simply made children as comfortable as possible during the test. Rather than being cold and impartial, the examiner was warm and friendly. Care was also taken to see that the children understood the directions. As one result, children's test anxiety was markedly reduced. As another, the children's IQ scores were 6 points higher than those for a control group treated in a more indifferent manner, and disadvantaged children made relatively greater gains from the procedure. *By doing nothing more than make testing conditions more optimal for all children, we may narrow the IQ gap between White and African American children.*

STEREOTYPE VULNERABILITY.   **Stereotype vulnerability** also affects test scores. Psychologists Claude Steele and Joshua Aronson (1995) suggest that African American students carry an extra burden in performing scholastic tasks. They believe that they risk confirming their group's negative stereotype. This concern creates performance anxiety. Performance anxiety distracts them from the tasks at hand. Thus they perform more poorly than White students taking the same test.

In an experiment to test their view, Steele and Aronson (1995) gave two groups of African American and White Stanford undergraduates the most difficult verbal-skills test questions from the Graduate Record Exam. One group was told that the researchers were attempting to learn about the "psychological factors involved in solving verbal problems." The other group was told that the items were "a genuine test of your verbal abilities and limitations." African American students given the first message performed as well as White students. African American students given the second message—that proof of their abilities was on the line—performed significantly more poorly than the White students. Apparently the second message triggered the African American students' stereotype vulnerability. Stereotype vulnerability then led them to self-destruct.

HOME ENVIRONMENT AND STYLES OF PARENTING.   The home environment and styles of parenting also appear to have an effect on IQ (Coon and others, 1990; Olson and others, 1992; Steinberg and others, 1992b). Children of mothers who are emotionally and verbally responsive, who provide appropriate play materials, who are involved with their children, and who provide varied daily experiences during the early years attain higher IQ scores later on (Bradley and others, 1989; Gottfried and others, 1994). The extent of home organization and safety has also been linked to higher IQs at later ages and to higher achievement test scores during the first grade (Bradley and others, 1989).

Dozens of other studies support the view that the child's early environment is linked to IQ scores and academic achievement. For example, McGowan and Johnson (1984) found that good parent–child relationships and maternal encouragement of independence were both positively linked to Mexican American children's IQ scores by the age of 3. A number of studies have also found that high levels of maternal restrictiveness and punishment at 24 months are linked to *lower* IQ scores later on (Bee and others, 1982; Yeates and others, 1983).

PRESCHOOL INTERVENTION PROGRAMS.   Government-funded efforts to provide preschoolers with enriched early environments have also led to intellectual gains. Head Start programs, for example, enhance the IQ scores, achievement test scores, and academic skills of poor children (Barnett & Escobar, 1990; Hauser-Cram and others, 1991; Zigler, 1995) by exposing them to materials and activities that middle-class children take for granted. These include letters and words, numbers, books, exercises in drawing, pegs and pegboards, puzzles, toy animals, and dolls.

Stereotype vulnerability • The tendency to focus on a conventional, negative belief about one's group, such that the individual risks behaving in a way that confirms that belief.

Head Start. Preschoolers placed in Head Start programs have made dramatic increases both in readiness for elementary school and in IQ scores.

There is now good research evidence that preschool intervention programs can have major long-term effects on children. During the elementary and high school years, graduates of preschool programs are less likely to be left back or placed in classes for slow learners. They are more likely to graduate from high school, go on to college, and earn higher incomes. Early childhood intervention also decreases the likelihood of juvenile delinquency, unemployment, and being on welfare (Schweinhart & Weikart, 1993; Zigler and others, 1992). In the mid-1990s, nearly three-quarters of a million children attended Head Start programs (Kassebaum, 1994).

CAN MUSIC PROVIDE OUR CHILDREN WITH THE SWEET SOUNDS OF SUCCESS? Environmental factors that are found to enhance children's intellectual functioning may well be music to parents' ears. But it may also turn out that music is spatial reasoning to the children's ears.

Research suggests that listening to music and studying music may enhance one aspect of intellectual functioning—spatial reasoning. In October 1993, Frances Rauscher, Gordon Shaw, and Katherine Ky published an intriguing article in *Nature* on the effects of listening to Mozart. According to that study, listening to 10 minutes of Mozart's Piano Sonata K 448 on a number of occasions enhanced college students' scores on spatial reasoning tasks of the kind found on intelligence tests.

The research team of Rauscher, Shaw, Linda Levine, Ky, and Eric Wright reported the results of a follow-up study with preschoolers at the 1994 meeting of the American Psychological Association: "Music and spatial task performance: A causal relationship." They recruited 19 preschool children, ages 3 years to 4 years 9 months, and gave them 8 months of music lessons, including singing and use of a keyboard. They then found that the children's scores on an object assembly task—like that of the object assembly subtest of the Wechsler Intelligence Scale for Children—significantly exceeded those of 15 preschoolers who did not obtain the musical training.

The Sweet Sounds of Success? Research suggests that training in music advances children's spatial reasoning. Do musical activities and spatial reasoning share common neural pathways?

Truth or Fiction Revisited. *It is true that music lessons raise children's intelligence.* They contribute to the development of spatial-relations skills, which are one aspect of intellectual functioning.

How might listening to music or training in music affect spatial reasoning? The neural pathways involved in processing of music and a number of other cognitive functions—such as spatial reasoning—apparently overlap (Blakeslee, 1995c). Musical training thus develops the neural firing patterns used in spatial reasoning, which may eventually help children solve geometry problems, design skyscrapers, navigate ships, even fit suitcases into the trunk of a car (Martin, 1994).

ADOPTEE STUDIES.   The Minnesota adoption studies reported by Scarr and Weinberg suggest a genetic influence on intelligence. But the same studies (Scarr & Weinberg, 1976, 1977) also suggest a role for environmental influences. African American children who were adopted during the first year by White parents above average in income and education showed IQ scores some 15 to 25 points higher than those attained by African American children reared by their natural parents (Scarr & Weinberg, 1976). Still, the adoptees' average IQ scores, about 106, remained somewhat below those of their adoptive parents' natural children—117 (Scarr & Weinberg, 1977). Even so, the adoptive early environment closed a good deal of the IQ gap.

ENVIRONMENTAL INFLUENCES ON ADULT INTELLECTUAL FUNCTIONING. Our focus has been on the intellectual development of children. However, psychologists are also concerned about intellectual functioning among adults. They have found that older people show some decline in general intellectual ability as measured by scores on intelligence tests. The drop-off is most acute in processing speed (Schaie, 1994; Schaie & Willis, 1991). Speed is involved in timed items such as those found on the performance scales of the Wechsler Adult Intelligence Scale.

Certainly biological changes of aging are involved in the decline. For example, many older people show losses in sensory sharpness that affect their intellectual functioning. Moreover, people who retain good physical health tend to show higher levels of intellectual functioning in their later years (Schaie, 1994). It is unclear, however, whether good health is a causal factor in intelligence or whether a health-conscious lifestyle has cognitive as well as physical benefits (Gruber-Baldini, 1991).

The Seattle Longitudinal Study has been tracking intellectual changes among adults for more than 35 years as of this writing and has identified several environmental factors that affect intellectual functioning among older people (Schaie, 1993, 1994):

1. *Socioeconomic status.* People of high SES tend to maintain intellectual functioning more adequately than people low in SES. High SES is also connected with above-average income and levels of education, a history of stimulating occupational pursuits, and the maintenance of intact families.

2. *Stimulating activities.* People who maintain their levels of intellectual functioning also tend to attend cultural events, travel, participate in professional organizations, and read extensively.

3. *Marriage to a spouse with a high level of intellectual functioning.* The spouse whose level of intellectual functioning is lower at the beginning of a marriage tends to narrow the gap as time elapses. Perhaps they are continually challenged.

4. *Flexible personality.*

Yes, Head Start programs have enhanced the intellectual development of children. It also turns out that training in reasoning and visual–spatial skills improves the cognitive functioning of older people (Schaie, 1994). The benefits of such training extend to performance on the practical tasks of daily living (Willis and others, 1992).

All in all, intellectual functioning at any age appears to reflect the interaction of a complex web of genetic, physical, personal, and sociocultural factors, as suggested by Figure 9.7.

On Ethnicity and Intelligence: A Concluding Note

Many psychologists believe that heredity and environment interact to influence intelligence. Forty-five percent of Snyderman and Rothman's (1987, 1990) sample of 1,020 psychologists and educational specialists believe that African American–White differences in IQ are a "product of both genetic and environmental variation, compared to only 15% who feel the difference is entirely due to environmental variation [see Figure 9.8]. Twenty-four percent of experts do not believe there are sufficient data to support any reasonable opinion, [and 1%] indicate a belief in an entirely genetic determination" (1987, p. 141).

Diana Baumrind (1993) and Jacquelyne Jackson (1993) of the University of California Institute of Human Development argue that a strong belief in the predominance of genetic factors can undermine parental and educational efforts to enhance children's intellectual development. Jackson notes that such a view can be particularly harmful to African American children. Baumrind notes that parents are most effective when they believe their efforts will improve their children's functioning. Since parents cannot change their children's genetic codes, it is better for parents to assume that good parenting can make a difference.

Perhaps we need not be so concerned with whether we can sort out exactly "how much" of a person's IQ is due to heredity and how much is due to environmental influences. The largest number of psychologists and educators

FIGURE 9.7

The Complex Web of Factors That Appears to Affect Intellectual Functioning in Children and Adults. Intellectual functioning appears to be influenced by the interaction of genetic factors, health, personality, and a host of sociocultural factors.

FIGURE 9.8

Beliefs of Psychologists and Educational Specialists Concerning Reasons for African American/White American Differences in IQ. The largest group of psychologists and educational specialists views racial differences in IQ as reflecting the interaction of genetic and environmental factors. Source of data: Snyderman and Rothman (1987, 1990)

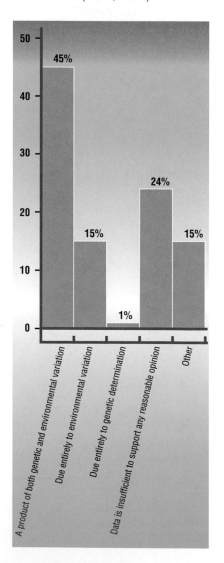

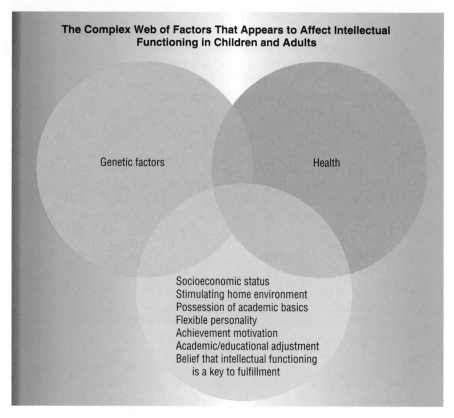

The Complex Web of Factors That Appears to Affect Intellectual Functioning in Children and Adults

Genetic factors

Health

Socioeconomic status
Stimulating home environment
Possession of academic basics
Flexible personality
Achievement motivation
Academic/educational adjustment
Belief that intellectual functioning
is a key to fulfillment

believe that IQ reflects the complex interaction of heredity, early childhood experiences, sociocultural factors and expectations, and even the atmosphere within which intelligence tests are conducted. Psychology has traditionally supported the dignity of the individual. It might be more appropriate for us to try to identify children of *all ethnic groups* whose environments place them at risk for failure and do what we can to enrich them.

As noted by Richard Rose of Indiana University,

> We inherit dispositions, not destinies. Life outcomes are consequences of lifetimes of behavior choices. . . . We actively seek opportunities to develop and display our dispositional characteristics. . . . Adult personality differences reflect, not fixed consequences of hereditary variance, but interactive processes of lifestyle selection. . . . Lives are not simple consequences of genetic [factors]. (Rose, 1995, p. 648)

Reflections

• Does your own family seem to be generally similar in overall intellectual functioning? Are there one or more family members who appear to stand out from the others because of intelligence? If so, in what ways? Where do you seem to stand in your family in terms of intellectual functioning?

• As you look back on your own childhood, can you point to any kinds of family or educational experiences that seem to have had an impact on your intellectual development? Would you say that your background, overall, was deprived or enriched? In what ways?

• **Agree or disagree with the following statement and support your answer: "The effects of Head Start programs are illusory. You can't really boost children's IQs."**

Study Guide

DIRECTIONS: Fill in the missing information in each of the following tables. Check your answers below.

TABLE 1

LOUIS THURSTONE'S (1) P_____ MENTAL ABILITIES

ABILITY	DESCRIPTION
Visual and spatial abilities	Visualizing forms and spatial relationships
(2) P_____ speed	Grasping perceptual details rapidly, perceiving similarities and differences between stimuli
Numerical ability	Computing numbers
(3) V_____ meaning	Knowing the meanings of words
Memory	Recalling information (words, sentences, etc.)
(4) W_____ fluency	Thinking of words quickly (rhyming, doing crossword puzzles, etc.)
Deductive reasoning	Deriving examples from general rules
(5) I_____ reasoning	Deriving general rules from examples

TABLE 2

SUBTESTS FROM THE WECHSLER
ADULT INTELLIGENCE SCALE

VERBAL SUBTESTS   **(6) P_____ SUBTESTS**

1. (7) I_____: "What is the capital of the United States?" "Who was Shakespeare?
2. Comprehension: "Why do we have ZIP codes?" "What does 'A stitch in time saves nine' mean?"
3. Arithmetic: "If 3 candy bars cost 25 cents, how much will 18 candy bars cost?"
4. (8) S_____: "How are good and bad alike?" "How are peanut butter and jelly alike?"
5. Digit (9) S_____: Repeating a series of numbers forwards and backwards.
6. Vocabulary: "What does *canal* mean?"

7. (10) D_____ Symbol: Learning and drawing meaningless figures that are associated with numbers.
8. (11) P_____ Completion: Pointing to the missing part of a picture.
9. (12) B_____ Design: Copying pictures of geometric designs using multicolored blocks.
10. (13) P_____ Arrangement: Arranging cartoon pictures in sequence so that they tell a meaningful story.
11. (14) O_____ Assembly: Putting pieces of a puzzle together so that they form a meaningful object.

TABLE 3

VARIATIONS IN IQ SCORES

RANGE OF SCORES	PERCENT OF POPULATION	BRIEF DESCRIPTION
130 and above	(15) _____	Very (16) s_____
120–129	(17) _____	Superior
110–119	16	Above (18) a_____
100–109	25	High average
90–99	(19) _____	(20) L_____ average
80–89	16	Slow learner
70–79	7	Borderline
Below 70	2	Intellectually deficient

ANSWER KEY TO EXERCISE

TABLE 1	TABLE 2	TABLE 3
1. Primary	6. Performance	15. 2
2. Perceptual	7. Information	16. superior
3. Verbal	8. Similarities	17. 7
4. Word	9. Span	18. average
5. Inductive	10. Digit	19. 25
	11. Picture	20. Low
	12. Block	
	13. Picture	
	14. Object	

ESL | English as a Second Language—Bridging the Gap

acute (390)—serious; most noticeable

all the givens (319)—all the accepted hypotheses

as long as (319)—if

associate (368)—connect one thing with another

barebones (345)—basics

bi (343)—bye (good-bye)

bodily-kinesthetic talents (371)—physical abilities to use the body well

bricklaying (363)—constructing buildings with brick

brute strength (368)—great strength; very strong

capturing what (372)—of explaining what

charges (378)—the people they are responsible for

climes (368)—climate

cold and impartial (387)—unfriendly and not appearing to care

colleagues (387)—people who work together who are at a similar level, or similar status, to each other

contemporary (385)—modern

correlations (387)—associations; when one thing is related to another

crunch (373)—compute or solve numerical problems

decipher (373)—interpret; figure out; understand

deficient (379)—lacking; missing something

dense wood (374)—thick wood; indicates something is not very smart

deprived (392)—lacking something; not given something

determinants (368)—things that cause something else

difficult to arrive at (368)—difficult to achieve

disproportionate (381)—out of proportation; in this case, compared with the entire population, there is a larger percentage of African, Hispanic, and Native Americans than other ethnic groups in the lower social and economic classes

don't peek (316)—don't look

downgraded (345)—made inferior

drop-off (390)—a significant drop in amount

eased (378)—made easier

enabling (369)—allowing; making it possible

encourage (379)—to give support; to help make happen

enrich (381)—to make richer or fuller

expectations (379)—occurrences we believe or hope will happen in the future

facilitate (378)—to make happen; make easier

feeble-minded (383)—retarded; did not have average intelligence

foreseeable future (374)—what can be seen of the future

go hand in hand (332)—exist together

grant (371)—agree

have a go (316)—try it

heralded (378)—praised

heredity (368)—characteristics we inherit through our genes from ancestors

heritability (387)—ability to be inherited

ingenious (385)—clever

inhibiting (383)—restricting

investigators (372)—people who seek and study information about a topic; researchers

is no guarantee of (328)—does not promise to include

juvenile delinquency (389)—teenagers who commit crimes

keep plugging away at it (325)—continue trying

later on (388)—when they are older

lay in (316)—was in

let's say that (392)—we shall imagine that

literal flash (373)—a true, short moment of time

lived up to their promise (384)—achieved what people expected

lumbering (373)—very slow; clumsy

mainframes (373)—very large, complex computers

mainstream linguistic alternative (349)—standard English

major intersection (320)—large and important area where many (at least four) streets meet or cross

matchsticks (316)—matches

mean . . . IQ (381)—average IQ

meeting the need (352)—satisfying the need to

mentally retarded (379)—intelligence or other brain function is limited

method . . . plodding (320)—the method might be slow and a little difficult

mimicked (373)—copied; imitated

moreover (391)—in addition

most boring (320)—uninteresting

much valued (331)—greatly appreciated

nothing new under the sun (327)—everything has been said and done

now it's your turn (316)—I have done it and you could not, but now you have the opportunity to do it

outperform (384)—getting better scores

outscore (381)—get higher scores

overrepresented (382)—there are more than should exist when compared with the general population

peek into your wallet (372)—look into the place where you keep your money

perceived (368)—seen as; thought to be

pin down (368)—to analyze and understand

playground (345)—a park for children that contains play equipment

poorly lit (378)—not enough light

predictor (368)—something that gives us an idea about what to expect, helps us to predict what will happen

predominance (391)—strength; most dominant factor

probably not (352)—it probably is not true

procedure (388)—process; steps to follow

prose (373)—ordinary speech or writing; not poetry

reared (386)—raised

scrap paper (316)—paper that is to be disposed of

signature human activities (373)—activities that are typical of human beings

somehow (368)—in some way, we don't know how

standard English (349)—English that is spoken with accepted grammar

stands for something (323)—is a symbol for something

supercool (373)—in this case, *cool* is slang for someone who is very relaxed, aware, and able to handle a variety of situations (it may also be a compliment for something that is liked or admired); *super* means "very"

take a breath (316)—relax and prepare yourself

take an unpopular stand (330)—have a very definite opinion about something that is different from what other people have

taken Spanish . . . taken French (368)—has studied Spanish . . . has studied French

taking turns (345)—not interrupting; one talking when the other is not

test anxiety (388)—fear of being unable to perform well on a test

test taker (378)—a person who is taking a test

the drawback to (320)—the disadvantage to

the heck with it (325)—I will dismiss it because I am not interested anymore

tried and true (320)—different alternatives or actions have been tried, and this is the one that is best and is now accepted

unclad bodies (368)—unclothed bodies; naked

unlikely to profit from (374)—probably not benefit from

visionary (373)—able to see into the future

FILL-INS | **Chapter Review**

SECTION 1: THEORIES OF INTELLIGENCE

(1) Ach_____ refers to knowledge and skills gained from experience. (2) _____ence somehow provides the cognitive basis for academic achievement. Intelligence is usually perceived as underlying competence, or (3) _____ing ability, whereas achievement involves acquired competencies or performance.

Many investigators view intelligence as consisting of one or more mental abilities, or (4) f_____s. The Frenchman Alfred (5) _____t developed modern intelligence-testing methods about 100 years ago.

Charles (6) S_____ suggested that the behaviors we consider to be intelligent have a common underlying factor. Spearman labeled this factor (7) _____, for "general intelligence." Spearman also noted that even the most capable people are relatively superior in some areas and suggested that (8) s_____, or *s*, factors account for specific abilities. To test his views, Spearman developed a statistical method called (9) f_____ _____s.

Louis Thurstone suggested the presence of nine specific factors, which he labeled (10) _____ary mental abilities. One primary mental ability, (11) w_____ fluency, enables us to rapidly develop lists of words that rhyme.

Howard Gardner proposes the existence of (12: How Many?) _____ kinds of intelligence. He believes that each kind of intelligence has its neurological base in a different area of the (13) b_____. Gardner's "intelligences" include (14) l_____ ability, logical-mathematical ability, (15) bodily-_____ talents, musical talent, (16) spacial-_____ skills, awareness of one's own inner feelings, and sensitivity to other people's feelings. Gardner's critics question whether such special talents are equivalent in meaning to what they see as a broader concept of (17) int_____.

Robert Sternberg views intelligence in terms of (18) _____tion processing. Sternberg constructed a three-level, or

(19) _____ic, model of intelligence. The levels are contextual, experiential, and (20) co_____. The contextual level permits people to adapt to the demands of their (21) _____ments. On the (22) _____tial level, intelligent behavior is defined by the abilities to cope with novel situations and to process information automatically.

The componential level of intelligence consists of three processes: (23) meta_____, performance components, and (24) knowledge-_____ components. Metacomponents concern our awareness of our own (25) _____al processes. (26) P_____ components are the mental operations or skills used in solving problems or processing information. (27) _____-acquisition components are used in gaining new knowledge.

David (28) W_____ described intelligence as the "capacity of an individual to understand the world [and the] resourcefulness to cope with its challenges."

SECTION 2: ARTIFICIAL INTELLIGENCE

Artificial intelligence is the replication of human intellectual functioning in (29) _____ters. Artificial intelligence can solve problems that would take people years to solve, if they could solve them at all. However, artificial intelligence does not have the (30) _____sights, intuitions, and (31) cre_____ found in people.

SECTION 3: MEASUREMENT OF INTELLIGENCE

Binet devised an early scale for measuring intelligence because the (32) F_____ public school system sought an instrument that could identify children who were likely to be in need of special attention. The first version was termed the (33) Binet-____ scale. The Binet–Simon scale yielded a score called a (34) m_____age, or MA.

Louis (35) T_____ adapted the Binet–Simon scale for use with children in the United States. The current version is the (36) _____–Binet Intelligence Scale (SBIS). The SBIS yields an (37) int_____ q_____ (IQ).

The IQ reflects the relationship between a child's mental age and actual age, or (38) _____cal age (CA). The IQ was first computed by the formula IQ = ([39] M_____ Age/Chronological Age) × 100.

The (40) _____ler scales group test questions into a number of separate subtests. Wechsler described some of his scales as measuring (41) v_____ tasks and others as assessing (42) _____ance tasks.

Wechsler introduced the concept of the (43) _____tion IQ. The average test result at any age level is defined as an IQ score of (44) _____. Wechsler distributed IQ scores so that the middle 50% of them fall within the "broad (45) _____age range" of 90 to 110.

Lower-class U.S. children attain IQ scores some 10 to 15 points (46: Higher or Lower?) than those of middle- and upper-class children. African American children tend to attain IQ scores some 15–20 points (47: Higher or Lower?) than their White agemates. Hispanic American and Native American children score significantly (48: Above or Below?) the norms of White children.

Asian Americans frequently obtain (49: Higher or Lower?) scores on the math portion of the Scholastic Assessment Test than White Americans. Students in China and Japan obtain (50: Higher or Lower?) scores than Americans on standardized achievement tests in math and science. According to Sue and Okazaki, the higher scores of Asian students may reflect different values in the home, the school, or the culture at large rather than differences in underlying (51) _____ ence or competence. They argue that Asian Americans place relatively greater emphasis on the value of (52) _____ tion.

SECTION 4: THE TESTING CONTROVERSY: JUST WHAT DO INTELLIGENCE TESTS MEASURE?

A survey of psychologists and educational specialists found that most (53: Do or Do Not?) consider intelligence tests somewhat biased against African Americans and members of the lower classes. During the 1920s, intelligence tests were misused to prevent the (54) im_____ion of many Europeans and others into the United States. Scores on (55) _____ ence tests may reflect cultural familiarity with the concepts required to answer test questions correctly, instead of underlying intellectual competence.

If scoring well on intelligence tests requires a certain type of cultural experience, the tests are said to have a (56) _____ al bias. Psychologists such as Raymond B. (57) C_____ and Florence (58) G_____ have tried to construct culture-free intelligence tests. Middle-class White children (59: Do or Do Not?) outperform African American children on Cattel's and Goodenough's tests.

Motivation to do well may also be a cultural factor. Highly motivated children (60: Do or Do Not?) attain higher scores on intelligence tests than less-well-motivated children do.

SECTION 5: THE DETERMINANTS OF INTELLIGENCE: WHERE DOES INTELLIGENCE COME FROM?

Psychologists examine the IQ scores of closely and distantly related people who have been reared together or (61) a_____. If heredity is involved in human intelligence, closely related people ought to have (62: More or Less?) similar IQs than distantly related or unrelated people, even when they are reared separately. The IQ scores of identical (MZ) twins are (63: More or Less?) alike than the scores for any other pairs, even when the twins have been reared apart. Correlations between children and their foster parents and between cousins are (64: Strong or Weak?).

Studies generally suggest that the (65) _____ ility of intelligence is between 40% and 60%. In other words, about half of the variations in IQ scores among people can be accounted for by (66) h_____.

Genetic pairs (such as MZ twins) reared together show (67: Higher or Lower?) correlations between IQ scores than similar genetic pairs (such as other MZ twins) who were reared apart. For this reason, the same group of studies suggests that the environment (68: Does or Does Not?) play a role in IQ scores.

Another strategy for exploring genetic influences on intelligence is to compare the correlations between adopted children and their biological and (69) _____ive parents. When children are separated from their biological parents at early ages, one can argue that strong relationships between their IQs and those of their natural parents reflect (70) _____ic influences. Strong relationships between their IQs and those of their adoptive parents are (71: More or Less?) likely to reflect environmental influences. Several studies have found a (72: Stronger or Weaker?) relationship between the IQ scores of adopted children and those of their biological parents than with the IQ scores of their adoptive parents.

The home environment and styles of parenting (73: Do or Do Not?) appear to have an effect on IQ. Children of mothers who are emotionally and verbally responsive, who provide appropriate play materials, who are involved with their children, and who provide varied daily experiences during the early years attain (74: Higher or Lower?) IQ scores later on.

The child's early environment (75: Is or Is Not?) linked to IQ scores and academic achievement. Good parent–child relationships and maternal encouragement of independence are (76: Positively or Negatively?) linked to Mexican American children's IQ scores. (77) H_____ Start programs enhance the IQ scores and academic skills of poor children by exposing them to materials and activities that middle-class children take for granted. During the elementary and high school years, graduates of preschool programs are (78: More or Less?) likely to be left back or placed in classes for slow learners.

Older people (79: Do or Do Not?) show some decline in general intellectual ability as measured by scores on intelligence tests. The drop-off is (80: Most or Least?) acute in processing speed. People of (81: High or Low?) SES tend to maintain intellectual functioning more adequately than people (82: High or Low?) in SES.

ANSWER KEY TO CHAPTER REVIEW

1. Achievement	22. Experiential	43. Deviation	64. Weak
2. Intelligence	23. Metacomponents	44. 100	65. Heritability
3. Learning	24. Knowledge-acquisition	45. Average	66. Heredity
4. Factors	25. Intellectual	46. Lower	67. Higher
5. Binet	26. Performance	47. Lower	68. Does
6. Spearman	27. Knowledge-acquisition	48. Below	69. Adoptive
7. *g*	28. Wechsler	49. Higher	70. Genetic
8. Specific	29. Computers	50. Higher	71. More
9. Factor analysis	30. Insights	51. Intelligence	72. Stronger
10. Primary	31. Creativity	52. Education	73. Do
11. Word	32. French	53. Do	74. Higher
12. Seven	33. Binet–Simon	54. Immigration	75. Is
13. Brain	34. Mental	55. Intelligence	76. Positively
14. Language	35. Terman	56. Cultural	77. Head
15. Bodily-kinesthetic	36. Stanford–Binet	57. Cattell	78. Less
16. Spatial-relations	37. Intelligence quotient	58. Goodenough	79. Do
17. Intelligence	38. Chronological	59. Do	80. Most
18. Information	39. Mental	60. Do	81. High
19. Triarchic	40. Wechsler	61. Apart	82. Low
20. Componential	41. Verbal	62. More	

POSTTEST | Multiple Choice

1. The term *intelligence* is most similar in meaning to
   a. academic achievement.
   b. musical talent.
   c. language ability.
   d. underlying competence.

2. Binet's test was developed further in the United States by
   a. Sternberg.
   b. Stern.
   c. Terman.
   d. Thurstone.

3. Whose data suggested that intelligence consists of "primary mental abilities"?
   a. Wechsler
   b. Thurstone
   c. Spearman
   d. Sternberg

4. Who suggested that awareness of one's own inner feelings is a kind of intelligence?
   a. Wechsler
   b. Binet
   c. Sternberg
   d. Gardner

5. Reshaping the environment is an example of functioning on the _____ level of intelligence.
   a. primary
   b. contextual
   c. componential
   d. experiential

6. Which of the following is not part of the componential level of intelligence?
   a. language components
   b. metacomponents
   c. performance components
   d. knowledge-acquisition components

7. Who defined intelligence as the "capacity of an individual to understand the world [and the] resourcefulness to cope with its challenges"?
   a. Sternberg
   b. Wechsler
   c. Binet
   d. Gardner

8. At the age of 2, children show counting and spatial skills along with visual–motor coordination by building a tower of four blocks to match a model. This is an example of an item similar to those found on a test created by
   a. Goodenough.
   b. Cattell.
   c. Wechsler.
   d. Binet.

9. A child has an MA of 12. From this information we can conclude that she
   a. is more intelligent than most of her peers.
   b. is less intelligent than most of her peers.
   c. has an IQ within the broad average range.
   d. is about as intelligent as the typical 12-year-old.

10. The concept of the deviation IQ was introduced by
    a. Wechsler.
    b. Stern.
    c. Gardner.
    d. Simon.

11. _____ attempted to construct a culture-free intelligence test.
    a. Gardner
    b. Simon
    c. Wechsler
    d. Goodenough

12. The symbol *g* was used by Spearman to signify
    a. general intelligence.
    b. primary mental abilities.
    c. the ability to do well on intelligence tests.
    d. IQ, but not intelligence.

13. According to Sternberg, deciding what problem to solve and selecting appropriate strategies and formulas are examples of the _____ of intellectual functioning.
    a. performance components
    b. experiential level
    c. metacomponents
    d. contextual level

14. Wechsler distributed IQ scores so that _____% of them fall within the range of 90 to 110.
    a. 2
    b. 16
    c. 32
    d. 50

15. Which of the following groups scores highest on intelligence tests?
    a. Caucasian Britishers
    b. Japanese
    c. Hispanic Americans
    d. Native Americans

16. Stern suggested that IQ be computed by the formula
    a. $(CA/MA) \times 100$.
    b. $(CA-MA) \times 100$.
    c. $(MA/CA) \times 100$.
    d. $(MA-CA) \times 100$.

17. Approximately _____% of the population obtain IQ scores suggestive of intellectual deficiency on the Wechsler scales.
    a. 2
    b. 7
    c. 16
    d. 25

18. The IQ scores of _____ show the highest correlations.
    a. identical twins reared together
    b. fraternal twins reared together
    c. identical twins reared apart
    d. fraternal twins reared apart

19. You are visiting your old high school, and a former teacher says to you, "You're taking psychology. Does it matter how children are treated while they are taking intelligence tests?" You clear your throat and say, "In a study by Zigler and his colleagues, children were made as comfortable as possible during intelligence testing. The results showed that
    a. test scores decreased for children made most comfortable."
    b. test scores were 15 points higher than those for a control group."
    c. middle-class children made relatively greater gains from this procedure."
    d. disadvantaged children made relatively greater gains from this procedure."

20. The largest group of psychologists and educational specialists voice the opinion that
    a. intelligence reflects the interaction of heredity and environmental influences.
    b. only heredity really influences intelligence.
    c. only environmental influences really affect the development of intelligence.
    d. neither heredity nor the environment has a meaningful influence on intelligence.

ANSWER KEY TO POSTTEST

1. D	4. D	7. B	10. A	13. C	16. C	19. D
2. C	5. B	8. D	11. D	14. D	17. A	20. A
3. B	6. A	9. D	12. A	15. B	18. A	

LEARNING OBJECTIVES

When you have finished studying Chapter 10, you should be able to:

COMING TO TERMS WITH MOTIVATION
1. Define *motives*, *needs*, *drives*, and *incentives*.

THEORIES OF MOTIVATION: THE WHYS OF WHY
2. Discuss various theories of motivation.

HUNGER: DO YOU GO BY "TUMMY—TIME"?
3. Discuss contributors to the hunger drive.

SEX: A SOCIOCULTURAL PERSPECTIVE
4. Explain the organizing and activating effects of sex hormones.
5. Discuss the origins of a gay male or lesbian sexual orientation.

STIMULUS MOTIVES
6. Discuss research concerning the effort to increase the stimulation one experiences.

COGNITIVE CONSISTENCY: MAKING THINGS FIT
7. Explain balance theory.
8. Explain cognitive dissonance theory.

THE THREE A'S OF MOTIVATION: ACHIEVEMENT, AFFILIATION, AND AGGRESSION
9. Discuss the need for achievement.
10. Discuss the need for affiliation.
11. Discuss various theories of aggression.

EMOTION: ADDING COLOR TO LIFE
12. Discuss lie detectors.
13. Discuss whether ways of expressing emotions are universal.
14. Explain the facial-feedback hypothesis.
15. Evaluate various theories of emotion.

Motivation and Emotion

PRETEST *Truth or Fiction?*

_____ While Christmas Eve is a time of religious devotion in most Western nations, it has become a time of sexual devotion in Japan.

_____ Getting away from it all by going on a vacation from all sensory input for a few hours is relaxing.

_____ We appreciate things more when we have to work for them.

_____ Misery loves company.

_____ Despite all the media hoopla, no scientific connection has been established between media violence and aggressive behavior.

_____ You may be able to fool a lie detector by squiggling your toes.

_____ Smiling can produce pleasant feelings.

THE Seekers were quite a group. Their brave leader, Marian Keech, dutifully recorded the messages that she believed were sent to her by the Guardians from outer space. One particular message was somewhat disturbing. It specified that the world would come to an end on December 21. A great flood was to engulf Lake City, the home of Ms. Keech and many of her faithful.

Another message brought good news, however. Ms. Keech received word that The Seekers would be spared the flood. Ms. Keech reported that she received messages through "automatic writing." The messengers would communicate through her. She would write down their words, supposedly without awareness. This bit of writing was perfectly clear: The Seekers would be saved by flying saucers at the stroke of midnight on the morning of the 21st.

In their classic observational study, Leon Festinger and his colleagues (1956) described how they managed to be present in Ms. Keech's household at the fateful hour. They pretended to belong to the faithful. Their actual purpose, however, was to observe the behavior of The Seekers during and following the prophecy's failure. The cognitive theory of motivation that Festinger was working on—**cognitive-dissonance** theory—suggested that there would be a discrepancy or conflict between two key cognitions: (1) Ms. Keech is a prophet, and (2) Ms. Keech is wrong.

How might such a conflict be resolved? One way would be for The Seekers to lose faith in Ms. Keech. But the researchers argued that according to cognitive-dissonance theory, The Seekers might be motivated to resolve the conflict by going out to spread the word and find additional converts. Otherwise the group would be painfully embarrassed.

Let us return to the momentous night. Many in the group had quit their jobs and gone on spending sprees before the end. Now they were all gathered together. They fidgeted as midnight approached, awaiting the flying saucers. Midnight came, but no saucers. Anxious glances were exchanged. Silence. Coughs. A few minutes passed by, tortuously slowly. Watches were checked, more glances exchanged. At 4:00 A.M. a bitter and frantic Ms. Keech complained that she sensed that members of the group were doubting her. At 4:45 A.M., however, she seemed suddenly relieved. Still another message was arriving, and Ms. Keech was spelling it out through automatic writing! The Seekers, it turned out, had managed to save the world through their faith. The universal powers that be had decided to let the world travel on in its sinful ways for a while longer. Why? Because of the faith of The Seekers, there was hope!

You guessed it. The faith of most of those present was renewed. They called wire services and newspapers to spread the word. All but three psychologists from the University of Minnesota. They went home, weary but enlightened, and wrote a book entitled *When Prophecy Fails,* which serves as one of the key documents of cognitive motivational theory.

Mr. Keech? He was a tolerant sort. He slept through it all.

The psychology of motivation is concerned with the *whys* of behavior. Why do we eat? Why do some of us strive to get ahead? Why do some of us ride motorcycles at breakneck speeds? Why do we try new things? Why were The Seekers in acute discomfort?

Cognitive-dissonance theory • The view that we are motivated to make our cognitions or beliefs consistent.

Motive • A hypothetical state within an organism that propels the organism toward a goal. (From the Latin *movere,* meaning "to move.")

COMING TO TERMS WITH MOTIVATION

Let us begin our journey into the *whys* of behavior with some definitions. **Motives** are hypothetical states within organisms that activate behavior and propel the organisms toward goals. Why do we say "hypothetical states"? We say so because motives are not seen and measured directly. Like many other psychological concepts, they are inferred from behavior (Kimble, 1994). Psychologists assume that behavior is largely caused by motives. *Needs, drives,* and *incentives* are closely related concepts.

Psychologists speak of physiological **needs** and psychological needs. We must meet physiological needs to survive. Examples include needs for oxygen, food, drink, pain avoidance, proper temperature, and elimination of waste products. Some physiological needs such as hunger and thirst are states of physical deprivation. When we have not eaten or drunk for a while, we develop needs for food and water. The body also has needs for oxygen, vitamins, minerals, and so on.

Examples of psychological needs are needs for achievement, power, self-esteem, social approval, and belonging. Psychological needs differ from physiological needs in two ways. First, psychological needs are not necessarily based on states of deprivation. A person with a need for achievement may have a history of success. Second, psychological needs may be acquired through experience, or learned. By contrast, physiological needs reside in the physical makeup of the organism. Because our biological makeups are similar, people share similar physiological needs. However, people are influenced by the sociocultural milieu, and needs may be expressed in divergent ways. All people need food, but some prefer a vegetarian diet whereas others prefer meat. Because learning enters into our psychological needs, people differ markedly in them (Capaldi, 1993).

Needs are said to give rise to **drives.** Depletion of food gives rise to the hunger drive, and depletion of liquids gives rise to the thirst drive. **Physiological drives** are the psychological counterparts of physiological needs. When we have gone without food and water, our bodies may *need* these substances. However, our *experience* of the drives of hunger and thirst is psychological. Drives arouse us to action. Our drive levels tend to increase with the length of time we have been deprived. We are usually more highly aroused by the hunger drive when we have not eaten for several hours than when we have not eaten for, say, 5 minutes.

Psychological needs for approval, achievement, and belonging also give rise to drives. We can be driven to get ahead in the world of business just as surely as we can be driven to eat. The drives for achievement and power consume the daily lives of many people.

An **incentive** is an object, person, or situation perceived as being capable of satisfying a need or desirable for its own sake. Money, food, a sexually attractive person, social approval, and attention can all act as incentives that motivate behavior. Needs and incentives can interact to influence the strength of drives.

Need • A state of deprivation.

Drive • A condition of arousal in an organism that is associated with a need.

Physiological drives • Unlearned drives with a biological basis, such as hunger, thirst, and avoidance of pain.

Incentive • An object, person, or situation perceived as being capable of satisfying a need.

Reflections

- Why do you think The Seekers were motivated to restore their faith in their leader?
- What are your most important biological needs? Psychological needs? How did you arrive at the list of your psychological needs?

In the following section, we explore theories of motivation. We ask the question, Just what is so motivating about motives? Researchers have spawned diverse views of the motives that propel us.

THEORIES OF MOTIVATION: THE WHYS OF WHY

Although psychologists agree that it is important to understand why people and lower animals do things, they do not agree about the whys of why—that is, the nature of motivation. Let us consider six theories of motivation: the instinct, drive-reductionist, opponent-process, humanistic, cognitive, and sociocultural theories.

Instinct Theory: "Doing What Comes Naturally"?

Animals are "prewired"—that is, born with preprogrammed tendencies—to respond to certain situations in certain ways. Birds reared in isolation from other birds build nests during the mating season even though they have never observed another bird building a nest (or, for that matter, seen a nest). Siamese fighting fish reared in isolation assume stereotypical threatening stances and attack other males when they are introduced into their tanks.

Behaviors such as these characterize particular species (species-specific) and do not rely on learning. They are called **instincts,** or **fixed-action patterns** (FAPs). Spiders spin webs. Bees "dance" to communicate the location of food to other bees. All this activity is inborn. It is genetically transmitted from generation to generation.

FAPs occur in response to stimuli that **ethologists** call **releasers.** Male members of many species are sexually aroused by **pheromones** secreted by females. Pheromones release the FAP of sexual response.

The question arises as to whether people have instincts. Around the turn of the century, psychologists William James (1890) and William McDougall (1908) argued that people have instincts that foster self-survival and social behavior.

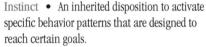

Instinct • An inherited disposition to activate specific behavior patterns that are designed to reach certain goals.

Fixed-action pattern • An instinct; abbreviated *FAP.*

Ethologist • A scientist who studies the behavior patterns that characterize different species.

Releaser • In ethology, a stimulus that elicits a FAP.

Pheromones • Chemical secretions that are detected by other members of the same species and stimulate stereotypical behaviors.

A Fixed-Action Pattern. In the presence of other males, Siamese fighting fish assume instinctive threatening stances in which they circle one another while they extend their fins and gills. If neither male retreats, there will be conflict.

James asserted that we have social instincts such as love, sympathy, and modesty. McDougall compiled 12 "basic" instincts, including hunger, sex, and self-assertion. Other psychologists have catalogued longer lists.

The psychoanalyst Sigmund Freud also used the term *instincts* to refer to physiological needs within people. Freud believed that the instincts of sex and aggression give rise to *psychic energy,* which is perceived as a feeling of tension. Tension motivates us to restore ourselves to a calmer, resting state. The behavior patterns we use to reduce the tension are largely learned.

The psychodynamic views of Sigmund Freud also coincide reasonably well with those of a group of learning theorists who presented a drive-reduction theory of learning.

Drive-Reductionism and Homeostasis: "Steady, Steady . . ."

According to **drive-reduction theory,** as framed by psychologist Clark Hull in the 1930s, **primary drives** such as hunger, thirst, and pain trigger arousal (tension) and activate behavior. We learn responses that reduce the drives. Through association, we also learn **acquired drives.** We may acquire a drive for money because money enables us to attain food, drink, and homes that protect us from predators and extremes of temperature. We might acquire drives for social approval and affiliation because other people, and their good will, help us to reduce primary drives, especially when we are infants. In all cases, tension reduction is the goal.

Primary drives like hunger are triggered when we are in a state of deprivation. Sensations of hunger motivate us to act to restore the bodily balance. The bodily tendency to maintain a steady state is called **homeostasis.** Homeostasis works much like a thermostat. When the room temperature drops below the set point, the heating system is triggered. The heat stays on until the set point is reached. Similarly, we eat until we are no longer hungry. The body's homeostatic systems involve fascinating interactions between physiological and psychological processes.

Drive-reduction theory • The view that organisms learn to engage in behaviors that have the effect of reducing drives.

Primary drives • Unlearned, or physiological, drives.

Acquired drives • Drives that are acquired through experience, or learned.

Homeostasis • (HOME-me-oh-STAY-sis). The tendency of the body to maintain a steady state.

Opponent-process theory • The view that our emotions trigger opposing emotions.

Opponent-Process Theory: From Lambs to Lions

How does the fearful soldier come to experience feelings of confidence and bravery? How do motives to retreat turn into motives to attack? How do feelings of sexual infatuation turn to disgust? How do motives to cuddle and love turn into motives to run away? Why do many people experience rebound anxiety when they go off a tranquilizer? These are complex questions that require complex answers, but part of the explanation may be found in **opponent-process theory.** According to this view, emotions tend to trigger opposing emotions. Emotional reactions are followed by their opposites, rather than by neutral feelings, when the conditions that gave rise to the first emotion change (Kimble, 1994; Solomon, 1980).

Consider this example. The "green" soldier enters combat in awe of the enemy and full of fear. She or he survives. Opposing feelings (see Figure 10.10) of anger and anticipation are triggered. Repetitions of the experience strengthen the opposing emotion. With repeated exposures to combat, then, feelings of awe and fear may diminish so that the soldier eventually comes to view combat with feelings of bravery.

Kimble (1994) connects opponent–process theory to other opponent processes that occur in people. For example, we see afterimages following visual excitation—red where there was green, yellow where there was blue. Opponent processes may be ways in which the body attempts to maintain steady states.

Humanistic Theory: "I've Got to Be Me"?

Humanistic psychologists, particularly Abraham Maslow, note that the instinct and drive-reduction theories of motivation paint people as defensive. They suggest that people behave in rather mechanical fashion to survive and reduce tension. As a humanist, Maslow asserted that behavior is also motivated by the conscious desire for personal growth. People will tolerate pain, hunger, and many other sources of tension to achieve what they perceive as personal fulfillment.

FIGURE 10.1

Maslow's Hierarchy of Needs. Maslow believed that we progress toward higher psychological needs once basic survival needs have been met. Where do you fit in this picture?

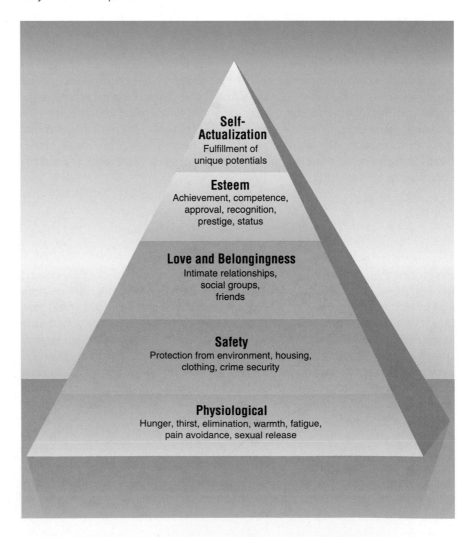

Maslow believed that we are separated from lower animals by our capacity for **self-actualization,** or self-initiated striving to become whatever we believe we are capable of being. In fact, Maslow saw self-actualization to be as essential a human need as hunger.

Maslow (1970) organized human needs into a hierarchy, from physiological needs such as hunger and thirst, through self-actualization (see Figure 10.1). He believed that in our lives, we naturally travel up through this hierarchy as long as we do not encounter insurmountable social or environmental hurdles. Maslow's hierarchy consists of the following:

1. *Physiological needs:* hunger, thirst, elimination, warmth, fatigue, pain avoidance, sexual release.

2. *Safety needs:* protection from the environment through housing and clothing; security from crime and financial hardship.

3. *Love and belongingness needs:* love and acceptance through intimate relationships, social groups, and friends. Maslow believed that in a generally well-fed society such as ours, much frustration stems from failure to meet needs at this level.

4. *Esteem needs:* achievement, competence, approval, recognition, prestige, status.

5. *Self-actualization:* fulfillment of our unique potentials. For many individuals, self-actualization involves needs for cognitive understanding (novelty, exploration, knowledge) and aesthetic needs (music, art, poetry, beauty, order).

Self-actualization • According to Maslow and other humanistic psychologists, self-initiated striving to become what one is capable of being. The motive for reaching one's full potential, for expressing one's unique capabilities.

Cognitive Theory: "I Think, Therefore I Am Consistent"?

"I think, therefore I am," said the French philosopher René Descartes. If he had been a cognitive psychologist, he might have said, "I think, therefore I am *consistent.*" Theorists such as Sandra Bem (1993) and Leon Festinger (1957) assert that people are motivated to achieve cognitive consistency. Bem argues that children try to follow the "gender schema" in their society—that is, expectations as to what behaviors are appropriate for males and females (see Chapter 12). Leon Festinger believed that people are motivated to hold harmonious beliefs and to justify their behavior. That is why we are more likely to appreciate things we must work for.

Cognitive theorists also note that people mentally represent their worlds (Rescorla, 1988). Jean Piaget and George Kelly hypothesized that people are born scientists who strive to understand the world so that they can predict and control events. Social-cognitive theorists (e.g., Bandura, 1989, 1991; Mischel, 1990, 1993; Rotter, 1990) assert that people are motivated by their expectations. On the basis of experience and reasoning, people expect that certain behaviors will lead to certain outcomes. They behave in ways that will enable them to achieve (or avert) these outcomes.

Sociocultural Theory

Sociocultural theory pervades other viewpoints. For example, primary drives may be inborn, but sociocultural experiences affect the *behavior* that satisfies them. Eating meat or fish, drinking coffee or tea, kissing lips or rubbing noses are all influenced by sociocultural factors. What stokes the sex drive is also determined by experiences within a sociocultural milieu. For example, women's breasts have become eroticized in Western culture and must usually be covered from public view. In some preliterate societies, however, the breasts are considered of interest to nursing children only, and women usually go bare-breasted. Among the Abkhasian people of Asia, men regard the female armpit as highly arousing. A woman's armpits are, therefore, a sight for her husband alone.

Self-actualization also occurs within a given sociocultural milieu. Molière was lyrical in French. Maya Angelou is poetic in English. Films of John Huston reflected the European American sense of manifest destiny in pushing back the Western frontier. Films of Spike Lee reflect the African American experience and paint the United States from a very different vantage point.

The experiences of anthropologist Margaret Mead (1935) on the South Pacific island of New Guinea showed how the sociocultural milieu influences motives such as aggressiveness and nurturance. Among the Mundugumor, a tribe of headhunters and cannibals, women and men were both warlike and aggressive. The women considered motherhood to sidetrack them from more important activities, such as butchering inhabitants of neighboring villages. In contrast, women and men of the Arapesh tribe were both gentle and nurturant of children. Then there were the Tchambuli. In that tribe the women earned a living, while the men spent most of their time nurturing the children, primping, and gossiping.

Evaluation: Which Whys Rise to the Occasion?

Instinct theory has been criticized for yielding circular explanations of behavior. If we say that mothers love and care for their children because of a maternal instinct, and then we take maternal care as evidence for such an instinct, we have come full circle. But we have explained nothing. We have only repeated ourselves. Instincts also occur within a given species. They give rise to stereotypical behaviors in all members of a class (such as adult females) within that species. There is so much variation in human behavior that it seems unlikely that much of it is instinctive. Consider William James's notion that sympathy is an instinct. Many people are cruel and cold-hearted; are we to assume that they possess less of this instinct? Such an assumption would be incompatible with the definition of an instinct.

MINILECTURE: THIRST

Drive-reduction theory appears to apply in many situations involving physiological drives such as hunger and thirst. However, we often eat when we are not hungry! Drive-reductionism also runs aground when we consider evidence that we often act to increase, rather than decrease, the tensions acting on us. Even when hungry, we may take the time to prepare a gourmet meal instead of a snack, although the snack would reduce the hunger drive as well. We drive fast cars, ride roller coasters, and sky dive for sport—all activities that heighten rather than decrease arousal. We often seek novel ways of doing things because of the stimulation they afford, shunning the tried and true. Yet, the tried and true would reduce tension more reliably. Some psychologists have theorized the existence of stimulus motives that surmount the limitations of drive-reduction theory.

Although opponent-process theory has received some empirical support, it fails to take into account many of the complexities of human behavior. The example with the soldier fails to consider cognitive issues such as belief in one's own abilities and the fatalistic belief of many soldiers that one dies when one's "time has come." Emotions involve interactions among cognitive, physiological, and behavioral factors.

Critics of Maslow argue that there is too much individual variation for the hierarchy of motivation to apply to everyone. Some people whose physiological, safety, and love needs are met show little interest in achievement and recognition. Others seek distant, self-actualizing goals while exposing themselves to great danger. Some artists, musicians, and writers devote themselves fully to their art, even at the price of poverty.

Some psychologists criticize cognitive theory for its reliance on unobservable concepts such as expectations, rather than observable behavior. Other psychologists question whether the motives to understand and manipulate the environment are inborn. Could they be acquired as we learn that understanding allows us to satisfy physiological drives such as hunger and thirst?

The sociocultural perspective explains the *whys* of behavior at the boundaries of behavior, not at the core. It focuses on external influences that affect behavior. Many psychologists prefer to consider factors within the human being that motivate and shape behavior, such as the processes by which people understand and evaluate cultural influences.

Reflections

- Do you believe that people have instincts? What kinds of instincts? What is your evidence for your belief?
- Have you ever felt powerful fear or infatuation and then had these feelings turn to anger or disgust? Can you put your finger on the factors that led to the change?
- What needs in Maslow's hierarchy are you attempting to meet by attending college?
- How have the ways in which you try to satisfy your needs been affected by sociocultural factors? Do people from other backgrounds try to satisfy the same needs, or similar needs, in different ways? How so?

Perhaps no theory explains all of psychologists' observations or satisfies all objections. Yet, there is a wealth of research on motivation. Let us first consider the drives of hunger and sex. Hunger and sex are based on physiological needs. Because physiological drives are unlearned, they are also referred to as *primary drives*.

Satiety • (SAY-she-uh-tee *or* sat-TIE-uh-tee). The state of being satisfied; fullness.

HUNGER: DO YOU GO BY "TUMMY-TIME"?

I go by tummy-time and I want my dinner.
SIR WINSTON CHURCHILL

MINILECTURE: HUNGER

We need food to survive, but food means more than survival to many of us. Food is a symbol of family togetherness and caring. We associate food with the nurturance of the parent–child relationship, with visits home during the holidays. Friends and relatives offer food when we enter their homes. Saying no may be interpreted as a personal rejection. Bacon and eggs, coffee with cream and sugar, meat and mashed potatoes—all seem to be part of sharing American values and agricultural abundance. What bodily mechanisms regulate the hunger drive? What psychological processes are at work?

In considering the bodily mechanisms that regulate hunger, let us begin with the mouth. This is an appropriate choice since we are discussing eating. Chewing and swallowing provide some sensations of **satiety.** If they did

Hunger. How do *you* feel while you wait for someone to carve the meat? Hunger is a physiological drive that motivates us to eat. What makes us feel hungry? What makes us feel satiated? Why do many of us continue to eat when we have already supplied our bodies with the needed nutrients?

Lesion • An injury that results in impaired behavior or loss of a function.

Ventromedial nucleus • A central area on the underside of the hypothalamus that appears to function as a stop-eating center.

Hyperphagic • Characterized by excessive eating.

not, we might eat for a long time after we had taken in enough food. It takes the digestive tract time to metabolize food and provide signals of satiety to the brain by way of the bloodstream.

Let us, like food, proceed to the stomach as we seek further regulatory factors in hunger. An empty stomach will lead to stomach contractions, which we call *hunger pangs*. These pangs are not as influential as had once been thought. People and animals whose stomachs have been removed still regulate food intake to maintain normal weight. This finding led to the discovery of many other hunger regulatory mechanisms including blood-sugar level, the hypothalamus, and even receptors in the liver.

When we are deprived of food, the level of sugar in the blood drops. The deficit is communicated to the hypothalamus. The drop in blood sugar apparently indicates that we have been burning energy and need to replenish it by eating.

EXPERIMENTS WITH THE HYPOTHALAMUS: THE SEARCH FOR "START EATING" AND "STOP EATING" CENTERS IN THE BRAIN.   If you were just reviving from a surgical operation, fighting your way through the fog of the anesthesia, food would probably be that last thing on your mind. But when rats are operated on and a **lesion** in the **ventromedial nucleus** (VMN) of the hypothalamus is made, they will grope toward their food supplies as soon as their eyes open. Then they eat vast quantities of Purina Rat Chow or whatever else they can find.

The VMN might function like a stop-eating center in the rat's brain. When the VMN is electrically stimulated—that is, "switched on"—a rat stops eating until the current is turned off. When the VMN is lesioned, the rat becomes **hyperphagic.** It eats until it has nearly doubled its normal weight (see Figure

10.2). Then it levels off its eating and maintains the higher weight. It is as if the set point of the stop-eating center has been raised to a higher level (Keesey, 1986).

VMN-lesioned rats are also more finicky about their food. They will eat more fats or sweet-tasting food, but they will actually eat less if their food is salty or bitter (Kimble, 1992).

The **lateral hypothalamus** might be a start-eating center in the rat's brain. If you electrically stimulate the lateral hypothalamus, the rat will start to eat. If you make a lesion in the lateral hypothalamus, the rat may stop eating altogether—that is, become **aphagic.** If you force-feed an aphagic rat for a while, however, it will begin to eat on its own and level off at a relatively low body weight. You have lowered the rat's set point. It is like turning the thermostat down from, say, 70 degrees Fahrenheit to 40 degrees Fahrenheit.

Other research suggests that receptors in the liver are also important in regulating hunger. These receptors appear to be sensitive to the blood-sugar level. In a state of food deprivation, blood sugar is low, and these receptors send rapid messages to the brain. After a meal, the blood-sugar level rises, and the receptors' rate of firing decreases (Novin and others, 1983).

Reflections

- What does food mean to you? Is food more than a way of satisfying the hunger drive? How so?
- How do you know when you are hungry? What bodily sensations do you experience?

SEX: A SOCIOCULTURAL PERSPECTIVE

Offshore from the misty coasts of Ireland lies the small island of Inis Beag. From the air it is a green jewel, warm and inviting. At ground level, things are somewhat different.

For example, the residents of Inis Beag do not believe that women experience orgasm. The woman who chances to find pleasure in sex is considered deviant. Premarital sex is all but unknown. Women engage in sexual relations to conceive children and to appease their husbands' carnal cravings. They need not worry about being called on for frequent performances, however, since the men of Inis Beag believe, erroneously, that sex saps their strength. Sex on Inis Beag is carried out in the dark—literally and figuratively—and with the nightclothes on. The man lies on top in the so-called missionary position. In accord with local concepts of masculinity, he ejaculates as fast as he can. Then he rolls over and falls asleep.

If Inis Beag does not sound like your cup of tea, you may find the atmosphere of Mangaia more congenial. Mangaia is a Polynesian pearl of an island, lifting languidly from the blue waters of the Pacific. It is on the other side of the world from Inis Beag—in more ways than one.

From an early age, Mangaian children are encouraged to get in touch with their sexuality through masturbation. Mangaian adolescents are expected to engage in sexual intercourse. They may be found on secluded beaches or beneath the listing fronds of palms, diligently practicing techniques learned from village elders.

Mangaian women are expected to reach orgasm several times before their partners do. Young men want their partners to reach orgasm and compete to see who is more effective at bringing young women to multiple orgasms.

FIGURE 10.2

A Hyperphagic Rat. This rodent winner of the basketball look-alike contest went on a binge after it received a lesion in the ventromedial nucleus (VMN) of the hypothalamus. It is as if the lesion pushed the "set point" for body weight up several notches, and the rat's weight is now about five times normal. But now it eats only enough to maintain its pleasantly plump stature, so you need not be concerned that it will eventually burst. If the lesion had been made in the lateral hypothalamus, the animal might have become the "Twiggy" of the rat world.

Lateral hypothalamus • An area at the side of the hypothalamus that appears to function as a start-eating center.

Aphagic • Characterized by undereating.

MINILECTURE:
THE SEXUAL RESPONSE
CYCLE

On the island of Inis Beag, a woman who has an orgasm is considered deviant. On Mangaia, multiple orgasms are the norm (Rathus and others, 1997). If we take a quick tour of the world of sexual diversity, we also find that:

- Nearly every society has an incest taboo, but some societies believe that a brother and sister who eat at the same table are engaging in a mildly sexual act. The practice is thus forbidden.

- What is sexually arousing varies enormously among different cultures. Women's breasts and armpits stimulate a sexual response in some cultures, but not in others.

- Kissing is a nearly universal form of petting in the United States but is unpopular in Japan and unknown among some cultures in Africa and South America. Upon seeing European visitors kissing, an African tribesman remarked, "Look at them—they eat each others' saliva and dirt."

- Sexual exclusiveness in marriage is valued highly in most parts of the United States, but among the Native American Aleut people of Alaska's Aleutian Islands, it is considered good manners for a man to offer his wife to a houseguest.

- The United States has its romantic Valentine's Day, but Japan has eroticized another day—Christmas Eve. (You read that right: Christmas Eve.) Christmas Eve may be a time of religious devotion in many Western nations, but it has become a time of sexual devotion in Japan. On Christmas Eve every single person must have a date that includes an overnight visit (Reid, 1990). During the weeks prior to Christmas, the media brim with reports on hotels for overnight stays, the correct attire, and breakfast ideas for the morning after. Where do Tokyo singles like to go before their overnighter? Tokyo Disneyland.

Truth or Fiction Revisited. *It is true that Christmas Eve has become a time of sexual devotion in Japan, even while it is a time of religious devotion in most Western nations.* There is a good deal of social pressure on single people to have a date that includes an overnight stay.

The residents of Inis Beag and Mangaia have similar anatomic features and similar sex hormones, but vastly different attitudes toward sex. Their sociocultural settings influence their patterns of sexual behavior and the pleasure they find—or do not find—in sex. Although sex is a natural function, perhaps no other natural function has been influenced so strongly by religious and moral beliefs, cultural tradition, folklore, and superstition (Rathus and others, 1997).

Let us consider the roles of sex hormones in sexual behavior. Then we turn our attention to sexual orientation.

Organizing effects • The directional effects of sex hormones—for example, along stereotypically masculine or feminine lines.

Activating effects • The arousal-producing effects of sex hormones that increase the likelihood of dominant sexual responses.

Organizing and Activating Effects of Sex Hormones

Sex hormones have many effects. They promote biological sexual differentiation, regulate the menstrual cycle, and affect sexual behavior.

Sex hormones have organizing and activating effects on behavior (Buchanan and others, 1992). They predispose lower animals toward masculine or feminine mating patterns—a directional or **organizing effect** (Crews, 1994). Hormones also affect the sex drive and promote sexual response—**activating effects.**

Sexual behavior among many lower animals is almost completely governed by hormones (Crews, 1994). The sex organs and brains of many species that are exposed to large doses of **testosterone** in utero (which occurs naturally when they share the uterus with many brothers or artificially as a result of hormone injections) become masculinized in structure (Crews, 1994). Such females are also predisposed toward masculine mating behaviors. If masculinized female rodents are given additional testosterone as adults, they attempt to mount other females about as often as males do (Goy & McEwen, 1982). Prenatal testosterone organizes the brains of these females in the masculine direction, predisposing them toward masculine behaviors in adulthood. Testosterone in adulthood then apparently activates the masculine behavior patterns.

Testosterone is also important in human behavior. As testosterone levels rise among boys during puberty, so does their interest in sex and their number of orgasms (Angier, 1994b). Although males produce 10 to 20 times the amount of androgens produced by females, androgens affect the female as well as the male sex drive. However, even though puberty brings a rise in androgens in girls as well as boys, girls do not show as dramatic a rise in sexual interest and behavior (Angier, 1994b). Peer group influences and other psychosocial factors seem to be as important as hormones for girls (Angier, 1994b).

Female mice, rats, cats, and dogs are receptive to males only during **estrus,** when female sex hormones are plentiful. During estrus, female rats respond to males by hopping, wiggling their ears, and arching their backs with their tails to one side, thus making penetration possible.

But, as noted by Kimble (1992),

> If we were to observe this same pair of rats one day [after estrus], when the female is into the first day of her new cycle, we would see a very different set of behaviors. While the male would still show signs of sexual interest, at least at first, his sniffing and attempted mounts would not be met with hopping, ear wiggling, and [back arching]. Indeed, the female is more likely to "chatter" her teeth at the male—an unmistakable sign of rodent hostility. If the male is slow to grasp her meaning, she might turn her back to him and kick at his head, mule fashion. Clearly, it is over between them. (pp. 310–311)

Women, by contrast, are sexually responsive during all phases of the menstrual cycle, even during menstruation, when hormone levels are low, and after **menopause.**

Men who are castrated or given drugs (antiandrogens) that decrease the amount of androgens in the bloodstream usually show gradual loss of sexual desire and of the capacities for erection and orgasm. Still, many castrated men remain sexually active for years. Perhaps for many people, fantasies, memories, and other cognitive stimuli are as important as hormones in sexual motivation. Women whose adrenal glands and ovaries have been removed (so that they no longer produce androgens) may gradually lose sexual interest and the capacity for sexual response. An active and enjoyable sexual history seems to ward off loss of sexual capacity, suggestive of the importance of cognitive and experiential factors in human sexual motivation. In human sexuality, biology is apparently not destiny.

Testosterone • A male hormone that promotes development of male sexual characteristics and that has activating effects on sexual arousal.

Estrus • The periodic sexual excitement of many female mammals, during which they can conceive and are receptive to the sexual advances of males.

Menopause • The cessation of menstruation.

Sexual orientation • The direction of one's erotic interests (e.g., heterosexual, gay male, lesbian, or bisexual).

Heterosexual • A person whose sexual orientation is characterized by desire for sexual activity and the formation of romantic relationships with people of the other gender.

Gay male • A male whose sexual orientation is characterized by desire for sexual activity and the formation of romantic relationships with other males.

Sexual Orientation

Sexual orientation refers to the organization or directionality of one's erotic interests. **Heterosexual** people are sexually attracted to, and interested in forming romantic relationships with, people of the other gender. **Gay males**

L'Abandon (Les Deux Amies.) This painting by Henri de Toulouse-Lautrec is of lesbian lovers.

Lesbian • A female whose sexual orientation is characterized by desire for sexual activity and the formation of romantic relationships with other females.

Bisexual • A person whose sexual orientation is characterized by desire for sexual activity and the formation of romantic relationships with both women and men.

and **lesbians** are sexually attracted to, and interested in forming romantic relationships with, people of their own gender.[1] **Bisexuals** are sexually attracted to, and interested in forming romantic relationships with, both women and men.

The concept of *sexual orientation* is not to be confused with *sexual activity*. Engaging in sexual activity with members of one's own gender does not necessarily mean that one has a gay male or lesbian sexual orientation. Sociocultural factors inform us that male–male sexual behavior may reflect limited sexual opportunities or even ritualistic cultural practices, as in the case of the New Guinean Sambian people. Adolescent boys may manually stimulate one another while fantasizing about girls. Men in prisons may similarly turn to each other as sexual outlets.

Research in the United States, Britain, France, and Denmark finds that about 3% of men surveyed identify themselves as gay (Hamer and others, 1993; Janus & Janus, 1993; Laumann and others, 1994). About 2% of the U.S. women surveyed consider themselves to have a lesbian sexual orientation (Janus & Janus, 1993; Laumann and others, 1994).

ORIGINS OF SEXUAL ORIENTATION. Psychodynamic theory ties sexual orientation to identification with male or female figures. Identification, in turn, is related to resolution of the Oedipus and Electra complexes. In men, faulty resolution of the Oedipus complex would stem from a "classic pattern" of

---

[1] In keeping with the suggestions of the American Psychological Association's (1991) Committee on Lesbian and Gay Concerns, I am using the terms *gay male* and *lesbian* instead of *homosexual* in our discussion of sexual orientation. As noted by the committee, there are several problems with the word *homosexual:* One, because it has been historically associated with concepts of deviance and mental illness, it may perpetuate negative stereotypes of gay men and lesbians. Two, the term is often used to refer to men only, thus rendering lesbians invisible. Third, the word is often ambiguous in meaning—that is, does it refer to sexual behavior or sexual orientation?

child rearing in which there is a "close binding" mother and a "detached hostile" father. Boys reared in such a home environment would identify with their mothers and not their fathers. Psychodynamic theory has been criticized, however, because many gay males have had excellent relationships with both parents. Also, the childhoods of many heterosexuals fit the "classic pattern." Because there is much variation among the families of gay men and lesbians, no single pattern applies to all cases (Isay, 1990).

From the learning perspective, early reinforcement of sexual behavior (as by orgasm achieved through interaction with members of one's own gender) can affect sexual orientation. But many gay males and lesbians are aware of their sexual orientations before they have overt sexual contacts (Bell and others, 1981).

Biological theories focus on genetic and hormonal factors. There is ample evidence of familial patterns in sexual orientation (Pillard, 1990). In one study, 22% of the brothers of 51 primarily gay men were either gay or bisexual themselves. This is about four times the percentage found in the general population (Pillard & Weinrich, 1986). A study published in *Science* reported that genes connected with sexual orientation may be found on the X sex chromosome and transmitted from mother to child (Hamer and others, 1993). Moreover, according to research by Bailey and Pillard (1991), identical (MZ) twins have a higher **concordance** rate for a gay male sexual orientation than fraternal (DZ) twins: 52% for MZ twins versus 22% for DZ twins.

Sex hormones predispose lower animals toward masculine or feminine mating patterns. Thus, it has been wondered whether gay males might be deficient in testosterone or whether lesbians might have lower-than-normal levels of estrogen and higher-than-normal levels of androgens in their bloodstreams. However, a gay male or lesbian sexual orientation has not been reliably linked to current (adult) levels of male or female sex hormones (Friedman & Downey, 1994).

But what of the effects of sex hormones on the fetus? We know that prenatal sex hormones can masculinize or feminize the brains of laboratory animals in the ways that they direct the development of brain structures.

Ellis (1990; Ellis & Ames, 1987) theorizes that sexual orientation is hormonally determined prior to birth and is affected by genetic factors, drugs (such as androgens), and maternal stress. Why maternal stress? Stress causes the release of hormones such as adrenaline and cortisol, which can interact with testosterone and affect the prenatal development of the brain. Perhaps the brains of some gay males have been prenatally feminized, and the brains of some lesbians have been masculinized (Collaer & Hines, 1995; Friedman & Downey, 1994).

The determinants of sexual orientation are mysterious and complex. Research suggests that they may involve prenatal hormone levels—which can be affected by factors such as heredity, drugs, and maternal stress—and socialization. However, the precise interaction of these influences has eluded detection.

Concordance • Agreement.

Reflections

- What sociocultural factors have affected your sexual attitudes and behavior? Are your attitudes and behavior similar to or different from those of most of your classmates? Why or why not?
- What attitudes toward gay males and lesbians were expressed in your home, in your neighborhood? Have these attitudes affected your beliefs? Has the information in this chapter changed your beliefs about gay males and lesbians?

WORLD OF DIVERSITY

ETHNICITY AND SEXUAL ORIENTATION: A MATTER OF BELONGING

Lesbians and gay men frequently suffer the slings and arrows of an outraged society. Because of societal prejudices, it is difficult for many young people to come to terms with an emerging lesbian or gay male sexual orientation (Rathus and others, 1997). You might assume that people who have been subjected to prejudice and discrimination—members of ethnic minority groups in the United States—would be more tolerant of a lesbian or gay male sexual orientation. However, according to psychologist Beverly Greene (1994) of St. John's University, such an assumption might not be warranted.

In an article that addresses the experiences of lesbians and gay men from ethnic minority groups, Greene (1994) notes that it is difficult to generalize about ethnic groups in the United States. For example, African Americans may find their cultural origins in the tribes of West Africa, but they have also been influenced by Christianity and the local subcultures of their North American towns and cities. Native Americans represent hundreds of tribal groups, languages, and cultures. By and large, however, a lesbian or gay male sexual orientation is rejected by ethnic minority groups in the United States. Lesbians and gay males are pressured to keep their sexual orientations a secret or to move to communities where they can live openly without sanction.

Within traditional Hispanic American culture, the family is the primary social unit. Men are expected to support and defend the family, and women are expected to be submissive, respectable, and deferential to men (Morales, 1992). Because women are expected to remain virgins until marriage, men sometimes engage in male–male sexual behavior without considering themselves gay (Greene, 1994). Hispanic American culture frequently denies the sexuality of women. Thus, women who label themselves lesbians are doubly condemned—because they are lesbians and because they are confronting others with their sexuality. Because lesbians are independent of men, most Hispanic American heterosexuals view Hispanic American lesbians as threats to the tradition of male dominance (Trujillo, 1991).

Asian American cultures emphasize respect for one's elders, obedience to parents, and sharp distinctions in masculine and feminine gender roles (Chan, 1992). The topic of sex is generally taboo within the family. Asian Americans, like Hispanic Americans, tend to assume that sex is unimportant to women. Women are also considered to be less important than men. Open admission of a lesbian or gay male sexual orientation is seen as a rejection of one's traditional cultural roles and a threat to the continuity of the family line (Chan, 1992; Garnets & Kimmel, 1991).

Because many African American men have had difficulty finding jobs, gender roles among African Americans have been more flexible than those found among White Americans and most other ethnic minority groups (Greene, 1994). Nevertheless, the African American community appears to strongly reject gay men and lesbians, pressuring them to remain secretive about their sexual orientations (Gomez & Smith, 1990; Poussaint, 1990). Greene (1994) hypothesizes a number of factors that influence African Americans to be hostile toward lesbians and gay men. One is strong allegiance to Christian beliefs and biblical scripture. Another is internalization of the dominant culture's stereotyping of African Americans as highly sexual beings. That is, many

African Americans may feel a need to assert their sexual "normalcy" or even a sense of sexual superiority.

Prior to the European conquest, sex may not have been discussed openly by Native Americans, but sex was generally seen as a natural part of life. Individuals who incorporated both traditional feminine and masculine styles were generally accepted and even admired. The influence of the religions of colonists led to greater rejection of lesbians and gay men and to pressure to move off the reservation to the big city (Greene, 1994). Native American lesbians and gay men, like Asian American lesbians and gay men, thus often feel doubly removed from their families.

All in all, lesbians and gay men may find more of a sense of belonging in the gay community than in their ethnic communities.

STIMULUS MOTIVES

One day when my daughter Taylor was 5 months old, I was batting her feet. (Why not?) She was sitting back in her mother's lap, and I repeatedly batted her feet up toward her middle with the palms of my hands. After a while, she began to laugh. When I stopped, she pushed a foot toward me, churned her arms back and forth, and blew bubbles as forcefully as she could. So I batted her feet again. She laughed and pushed them toward me again. This went on for a while, and it dawned on me that Taylor was doing what she could to make the stimulation last.

Physical needs give rise to drives like hunger and thirst. In such cases, organisms are motivated to *reduce* the tension or stimulation that impinges on them. But in the case of **stimulus motives,** organisms seek to *increase* stimulation, like Taylor sought to have me bat her feet. Stimulus motives include sensory stimulation, activity, exploration, and manipulation of the environment.

There are ways in which some stimulus motives provide a clear evolutionary advantage. People and lower animals who are motivated to learn about and manipulate the environment are more likely to survive. Learning about the environment increases awareness of resources and of potential dangers, and manipulation permits one to change the environment in beneficial ways. Learning and manipulation increase the chances of survival until sexual maturity and of transmitting whatever genetic codes may underlie these motives to future generations.

Stimulus motives • Motives to increase the stimulation impinging upon an organism.

Sensory deprivation • A research method for systematically decreasing the amount of stimulation that impinges upon sensory receptors.

Sensory Stimulation and Activity

When I was a teenager during the 1950s, I was unaware that some lucky students at McGill University in Montreal were being paid $20 a day (which, with inflation, would be well above $100 today) for doing absolutely nothing. Would you like such "work" for $100 a day? Don't answer too quickly. According to the results of classic research into **sensory deprivation,** you might not like it much at all.

Student volunteers were blindfolded in quiet cubicles (Bexton and others, 1954). Their arms were bandaged, and they could hear nothing but the dull, continuous hum of air conditioning. With nothing to do, many students slept for a while. After a few hours of sensory-deprived wakefulness, most felt bored and irritable. As time went on, many of them grew more uncomfortable, and some reported hallucinations, as of images of dots and geometric shapes.

Many students quit during the first day despite the financial incentive and the desire to contribute to science. Many of those who remained for a few days found it temporarily difficult to concentrate on simple problems afterward. For many, the experimental conditions did not provide a relaxing vacation. Instead, they instigated boredom and disorientation.

Truth or Fiction Revisited. *It is not true that getting away from it all by going on a vacation from all sensory input for a few hours is relaxing.* If carried out as it was at McGill University, such a "vacation" may be highly stressful.

INDIVIDUAL DIFFERENCES IN DESIRE FOR STIMULATION. Some people seek higher levels of stimulation and activity than others. John is a couch potato, content to sit by the TV set all evening. Marsha doesn't feel right unless she's out on the tennis court or jogging. Cliff isn't content unless he has ridden his motorcycle over back trails at breakneck speeds, and Janet feels exuberant when she's catching the big wave or free-fall diving from an airplane. One's preference for tennis, motorcycling, or skydiving reflects one's geographical location, social class, and learning experiences. But it just may be that the levels of arousal at which we are comfortable would be too high or too low for other people. It also may be that these levels are determined to some degree by **innate** factors.

Innate • Inborn, unlearned.

Novel stimulation • (1) An unusual source of arousal or excitement. (2) A hypothesized primary drive to experience new or different stimulation.

Copulate • To engage in sexual intercourse.

Exploration and Manipulation

Have you ever brought a dog or cat into a new home? At first, it may show general excitement. New kittens are also known to hide under a couch or bed for a few hours. But then they will begin to explore every corner of the new environment. When placed in novel environments, many animals appear to possess an innate motive to engage in exploratory behavior.

Once they are familiar with the environment, lower animals and people appear to be motivated to seek **novel stimulation.** For example, when they have not been deprived of food for a great deal of time, rats will often explore unfamiliar arms of mazes rather than head straight for the section of the maze in which they have learned to expect food. Animals who have just **copulated** and thereby reduced their sex drives will often show renewed interest in sexual behavior when presented with a novel sex partner. Monkeys will learn how to manipulate gadgets for the incentive of being able to observe novel stimulation through a window (see Figure 10.3). Children will spend hour after hour manipulating the controls of video games for the pleasure of zapping video monsters.

The question has arisen whether people and animals seek to explore and manipulate the environment *because* these activities help them reduce primary drives such as hunger and thirst or whether they engage in these activities for their own sake. Many psychologists do believe that such stimulating activities are reinforcing in and of themselves. Monkeys do seem to get a kick out of "monkeying around" with gadgets (see Figure 10.4). They learn how to manipulate hooks and eyes and other mechanical devices without any external incentives whatsoever (Harlow and others, 1950). Children engage in prolonged play with "busy boxes"—boxes filled with objects that honk, squeak, rattle, and buzz. They seem to find discovery of the cause-and-effect relationships in these gadgets pleasurable even though they are not rewarded with food, ice cream, or even hugs from parents.

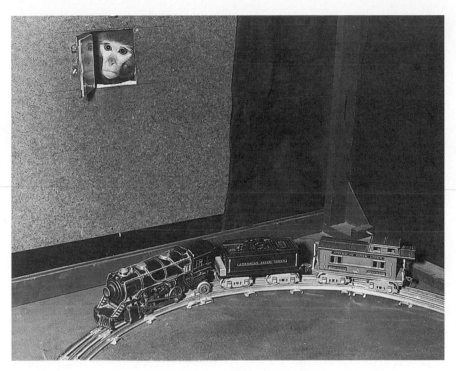

FIGURE 10.4

A Manipulation Drive? These young rhesus monkeys appear to monkey around with gadgets for the sheer pleasure of monkeying around. No external incentives or reinforcements are needed. Children similarly enjoy manipulating gadgets that honk, squeak, rattle, and buzz, even though the resultant honks and squeaks do not satisfy physiological drives such as hunger or thirst.

FIGURE 10.3

The Allure of Novel Stimulation. People and many lower animals are motivated to explore the environment and to seek novel stimulation. This monkey has learned to unlock a door for the privilege of viewing a model train.

Reflections

- Can you think of times when you were tired but "got a new wind" when you started to do something new or intriguing? Why do you think this happened?
- **Agree or disagree with the following statement and support your answer: "Some people may find a long, relaxing vacation on the beach to be highly annoying."**

COGNITIVE CONSISTENCY: MAKING THINGS FIT

Balance theory • The view that people have a need to organize their perceptions, opinions, and beliefs in a harmonious manner.

Cognitive theorists propose that organisms are motivated to create realistic mental maps of the world. Organisms therefore adjust their representations of the world, as needed, to reduce discrepancies and accommodate new information (Rescorla, 1988). In this section we consider two theories that address our efforts to create consistent mental maps: balance theory and cognitive-dissonance theory.

Balance Theory

According to **balance theory,** originated by Fritz Heider (1958), we are motivated to maintain harmony among our beliefs and attitudes. For example, when people we like share our attitudes, there is balance and all is well (see

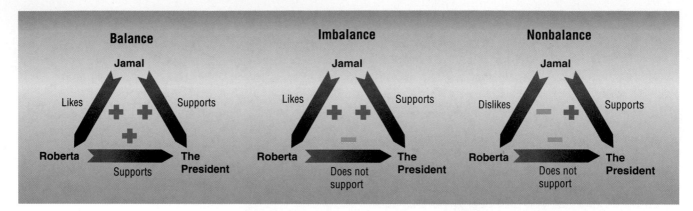

FIGURE 10.5

Balance Theory. According to Heider, we are motivated to maintain harmony among our attitudes. As in the triangle to the left, when people we like share our attitudes, there is a state of balance and all is well. However, as in the triangle in the center, when someone we care about disagrees with us, there is an uncomfortable state of imbalance. The triangle on the right shows a state of nonbalance in which we dislike someone else, so that her or his attitudes are not of much interest to us one way or the other.

Nonbalance • In balance theory, a condition in which persons whom we dislike do not agree with us.

Imbalance • In balance theory, an uncomfortable condition in which persons whom we like disagree with us.

Figure 10.5). It works the other way as well: If we support the president of the United States and she or he expresses an attitude, our own cognitions will remain in balance if we agree. For this reason, we are likely to develop favorable attitudes toward unfamiliar objects that the president seems to endorse. If we dislike other people, we might not care very much about their attitudes. They may disagree with us, but this state of **nonbalance** leaves us indifferent.

When someone we care about expresses a discrepant attitude, however, we *are* likely to be concerned. The relationship will survive if we like chocolate and our friend prefers vanilla, but what if the discrepancy concerns religion, politics, or child rearing? A state of **imbalance** now exists. What if the president, whom we like, reports favorably on an object we dislike? There is now an uncomfortable state of imbalance. What can we do to end such a state? We can try to induce others to change their attitudes. Or we can change our feelings about the other person.

Cognitive-Dissonance Theory: "If I Did It, It Must Be Important"?

Do I contradict myself?
Very well then I contradict myself,
(I am large, I contain multitudes.)
        WALT WHITMAN, *SONG OF MYSELF*

Walt Whitman may not have minded contradicting himself, but according to Leon Festinger (Festinger, 1957; Festinger & Carlsmith, 1959), the originator of cognitive-dissonance theory, most people do not like their attitudes (cognitions) to be inconsistent. Awareness that two cognitions are dissonant, or that our attitudes are incompatible with our behavior, is unpleasant and motivates us to reduce the discrepancy.

In the first and one of the classic studies on cognitive dissonance, one group of participants received $1 for telling someone else that a boring task was interesting (Festinger & Carlsmith, 1959). A second group received $20 to describe the chore positively. Both groups were paid to engage in **attitude-discrepant behavior**—that is, behavior that ran counter to their cognitions. After "selling" the job to others, the participants were asked to rate their own liking for it. Ironically, the group paid *less* rated the task as more interesting. Why?

According to learning theory, the result would be confusing. After all, shouldn't we learn to like that which is highly rewarding? But cognitive-dissonance theory would predict this "less-leads-to-more effect" for the following reason: The cognitions "I was paid very little" and "I told someone that this assignment was interesting" are dissonant. People tend to engage in **effort justification.** They tend to explain their behavior to themselves in such a way that unpleasant undertakings seem worth it. Study participants paid only $1 may have justified their lie by concluding that they may not have been lying in the first place. Similarly, we appreciate things more when they are more difficult to obtain.

Truth or Fiction Revisited. *It is true that we appreciate things more when we have to work for them.* This is an example of the principle of effort justification.

Cognitive dissonance would also be created if we were to believe that our preferred candidate was unlikely to win the American presidential election. One cognition would be that our candidate is better for the country or, at an extreme, would "save" the country from harmful forces. A second, and dissonant, cognition would be that our candidate does not have a chance to win. Research shows that in the presidential elections from 1952 to 1980, people by a four-to-one margin helped reduce such dissonance by expressing the belief that their candidate would win (Granberg & Brent, 1983). They often clung to these beliefs despite lopsided polls to the contrary.

MINILECTURE: ATTITUDE-DISCREPANT BEHAVIOR

Attitude-discrepant behavior • Behavior that is inconsistent with an attitude and may have the effect of modifying an attitude.

Effort justification • In cognitive-dissonance theory, the tendency to seek justification (acceptable reasons) for strenuous efforts.

Reflections

- Have you ever changed your opinion of someone when you learned that she or he liked something that you disliked? What happened? Why did it happen?
- Were you ever subjected to difficult hazing upon joining a sorority, fraternity, or other kind of club? Did the experience affect your feelings about being a member of the group? How? Can you connect your experience to the concept of *effort justification?*

THE THREE A'S OF MOTIVATION: ACHIEVEMENT, AFFILIATION, AND AGGRESSION

Let us consider some of the powerful motives that bind us together and tear us asunder: achievement, affiliation, and aggression. Harvard University psychologist Henry Murray hypothesized that each of these "A's" reflects a psychological need. Murray also referred to them as *social motives,* which he believed differed from primary motives such as hunger in that they were acquired through social learning. However, contemporary researchers do not rule out a role for hereditary predispositions toward these behavior patterns.

FIGURE 10.6

Tapping Fantasies in Personality Research. This picture is similar to a Thematic Apperception Test card that is frequently used to measure the need for achievement. What is happening in this picture? What is the person thinking and feeling? What is going to happen? Your answers to these questions reflect your own needs as well as the content of the picture itself.

Thematic Apperception Test • A test devised by Henry Murray to measure needs through fantasy production.

Achievement

We all know students who persist at academic tasks despite distractions. We all know adults who strive relentlessly to get ahead, to "make it," to earn vast sums of money, to invent, to accomplish the impossible. Such people are said to have strong achievement motivation.

Psychologist David McClelland (1958) helped pioneer the assessment of achievement motivation through fantasy. One method involves the **Thematic Apperception Test** (TAT), which was developed by Henry Murray. The TAT contains cards with pictures and drawings that are subject to various interpretations (see Chapter 12). Individuals are shown one or more TAT cards and asked to construct stories about the pictured theme: to indicate what led up to it, what the characters are thinking and feeling, and what is likely to happen.

One TAT card is similar to that in Figure 10.6. The meaning of the card is ambiguous—unclear. Is the boy sleeping, thinking about the violin, wishing he were out playing? Consider two stories that could be told about this card:

Story 1: "He's upset that he's got to practice the violin because he's behind in his assignments and doesn't particularly like to work. He'd much rather be out playing with the other kids, and he'll probably sneak out to do just that."

Story 2: "He's thinking, 'Someday I'll be a great violinist. I'll play at Carnegie Hall, and everybody will be proud of me.' He practices constantly."

Formal standards enable psychologists to derive achievement motivation scores from stories such as these, but you need not be acquainted with them to see that the second story suggests more achievement motivation than the first. Classic studies find that people with high achievement motivation earn higher grades than people of comparable learning ability but lower achievement motivation. They are more likely to earn high salaries and be promoted than less motivated people with similar opportunities. They perform better at math problems and unscrambling anagrams such as decoding RSTA into STAR, TARS, ARTS, or RATS.[2]

McClelland (1965) found that 83% of college graduates with high achievement motivation took positions characterized by risk, decision making, and the chance for great success, such as business management, sales, or businesses of their own making. Seventy percent of the graduates who chose nonentrepreneurial positions showed low achievement motivation. People with high achievement motivation seem to prefer challenges and are willing to take moderate risks to achieve their goals.

WHAT FLAVOR IS YOUR ACHIEVEMENT MOTIVATION?　Carol Dweck (1990) finds that achievement motivation can be driven by different forces. Do you want to do well in this course? If you do, why is that so? Are you mainly motivated by performance goals? That is, is the course grade the key to you? If it is, it may be in part because your motives concern tangible rewards such as getting into graduate school, getting a good job, reaping approval from parents or your instructor, or averting criticism. Or are you motivated mainly by learning goals? Is your central motive the enhancing of your knowledge and skills— your abilities to understand and master the subject matter? Performance goals in life are usually met through extrinsic rewards—for example, a good income and prestige. Learning goals usually lead to intrinsic rewards, such as personal self-satisfaction. Many of us strive to meet both performance and learning goals in many subjects, and in other areas of life.

Affiliation • Association or connection with a group.

DEVELOPMENT OF ACHIEVEMENT MOTIVATION.　Parents with strong achievement motivation tend to encourage their children to think and act independently from an early age. In terms of schoolwork, parents help children develop learning goals by encouraging persistence, enjoyment, and independence in schoolwork (Ginsburg & Bronstein, 1993; Gottfried and others, 1994). They expose their children to new, stimulating experiences. Parents of children who develop performance goals are more likely to reward children with toys or money for getting good grades and to respond to poor grades with anger and the removal of privileges (Ginsburg & Bronstein, 1993; Gottfried and others, 1994). Parents of children with strong achievement motivation also show warmth and praise their children profusely for their accomplishments. Children of such parents frequently set high standards for themselves, associate their achievements with self-worth, and come to attribute their achievements to their own efforts rather than to chance or to the intervention of others (Dweck, 1990; Ginsburg & Bronstein, 1993).

Affiliation: "People Who Need People"

The motive for **affiliation** prompts us to make friends, join groups, and to prefer to do things with others rather than go it alone. Affiliation motivation

---

[2] You can count on a psychologist not to miss an opportunity to toss a few rats into his or her book.

contributes to the social glue that creates families and civilizations. In this sense, it is certainly a positive trait. Yet, some people have such a strong need to affiliate that they find it painful to make their own decisions or to be in solitude. Research by Stanley Schachter suggests that a very high need to affiliate may indicate anxiety, such as when people "huddle together" in fear of some outside force.

In a classic experiment on the effects of anxiety on affiliation, Schachter (1959) manipulated study participants' anxiety levels by leading them to believe that they would receive either painful electric shocks (the high-anxiety condition) or mild electric shocks (the low-anxiety condition). Participants were then asked to wait while the shock apparatus was supposedly being set up. They could choose to wait alone or in a room with others. The majority (63%) of those who expected a painful shock chose to wait in a room with other people. Only one third (33%) of those who expected a mild shock chose to wait with others.

Truth or Fiction Revisited. *Schachter found that misery does love company—but only company of a special sort.* Highly anxious study participants were placed in two social conditions. In the first, they could choose either to wait alone or with others who would also receive painful shocks. Sixty percent of these people chose to affiliate—that is, to wait with others. In the second condition, highly anxious participants could choose to wait alone or with people they believed were not involved with the study. In this second condition, no one chose to affiliate.

Why did those in Schachter's study wish to affiliate only with people who shared their misery? Schachter explained their choice through the **theory of social comparison.** This theory holds that in an ambiguous situation—that is, a situation in which we are not certain about what we should do or how we should feel—we will affiliate with people with whom we can compare feelings and behaviors. Schachter's anxious recruits could compare their reactions with those of other "victims," but not with people who had no reason to feel anxious. Anxious participants may also have resented uninvolved people for "getting away free."

Theory of social comparison • The view that people look to others for cues about how to behave when they are in confusing or unfamiliar situations.

Aggression: Some Facts of Life and Death

Ponder some facts of life and death:

- Following the demise of the cold war and the Soviet Union, you might have expected the world to become more peaceful. Yet wars rage on almost every continent.

- In the United States, violence replaced communicable diseases as the leading cause of death among young people during the past generation. Homicide has become the second-leading cause of death, following accidents, among 15- to 24-year-olds (Lore & Schultz, 1993).

- Aggression is not limited to foreign battlefields or dark streets and alleyways. Each year, more than a million U.S. children are brought to the attention of authorities as victims of child abuse.

- The video games *Mortal Kombat* and *Night Trap* are best-sellers with U.S. children. In *Mortal Kombat,* the player can decapitate the loser. In *Night Trap,* the player attempts to prevent a gang of vampires from capturing scantily clad sorority sisters. If the player fails, the vampires drain the women's blood from their necks.

Why do people treat each other like this? Let us consider some theories of aggression.

THE BIOLOGICAL PERSPECTIVE.   Numerous biological structures and chemicals appear to be involved in aggression. One is the hypothalamus. In response to releasers, many lower animals show instinctive aggressive reactions. The hypothalamus appears to be involved in this inborn reaction pattern: Electrical stimulation of part of the hypothalamus triggers stereotypical aggressive behaviors in many lower animals. In people, however, whose brains are more complex, other brain structures apparently moderate possible instincts.

An offshoot of the biological perspective called *sociobiology* suggests that aggression is natural and even desirable for people. Sociobiology views much social behavior, including aggressive behavior, as genetically determined. Consider Darwin's theory of evolution. Darwin held that many more individuals are produced than can find food and survive into adulthood. Therefore, a struggle for survival ensues. Those individuals who possess characteristics that provide them with an advantage in the struggle for existence are more likely to survive and contribute their genes to the next generation (Dawkins, 1995; Dennett, 1995). In many species, such characteristics include aggressiveness. Because aggressive individuals are more likely to survive and reproduce, whatever genes are linked to aggressive behavior are more likely to be transmitted to subsequent generations.

The sociobiological view has been attacked on numerous grounds. One is that people's intelligence (their capacity to outwit other species), not their aggressiveness, appears to be the dominant factor in human survival. Another is that there is too much variation among people to believe that they are dominated by, or at the mercy of, aggressive impulses.

THE PSYCHODYNAMIC PERSPECTIVE.   Sigmund Freud believed that aggressive impulses were inevitable reactions to the frustrations of daily life. Children (and adults) normally desire to vent aggressive impulses on other people, including parents, because even the most attentive parents cannot gratify all of their demands immediately. Yet children, also fearing their parents' retribution and loss of love, come to repress most aggressive impulses. The Freudian perspective, in a sense, sees us as "steam engines." By holding in rather than venting "steam," we set the stage for future explosions. Pent-up aggressive impulses demand outlets. They may be expressed toward parents in roundabout ways such as destroying furniture, or they may be expressed toward strangers later in life.

According to psychodynamic theory, the best ways to prevent harmful aggression may be to encourage less harmful aggression. In the steam-engine analogy, verbal aggression (as through wit, sarcasm, or expression of negative feelings) may vent some of the aggressive steam in the unconscious. So might cheering on one's football team or attending prize fights. Psychoanalysts refer to the venting of aggressive impulses as **catharsis.** Catharsis is theorized to be a safety valve. But research findings on the usefulness of catharsis are mixed. Some studies suggest that catharsis leads to pleasant reductions in tension and a lowered likelihood of future aggression (e.g., Doob & Wood, 1972). Other studies, however, suggest that letting some steam escape actually encourages more aggression later on (e.g., Geen and others, 1975).

THE COGNITIVE PERSPECTIVE.   Cognitive psychologists assert that our behavior is influenced by our values, by the ways in which we interpret our

Catharsis   •   In psychodynamic theory, the purging of strong emotions or the relieving of tensions. (A Greek word meaning "purification.")

situations, and by choice. From the cognitive perspective, for example, people who believe that aggression is necessary and justified—as during wartime—are likely to act aggressively. People who believe that a particular war or act of aggression is unjust, or who universally oppose aggression, are less likely to behave aggressively (Feshbach, 1994).

One cognitive theory suggests that aggravating and painful events trigger unpleasant feelings (Rule and others, 1987). These feelings, in turn, prompt aggression. Aggression is *not* automatic, however. Cognitive factors intervene (Berkowitz, 1994). People *decide* whether they will strike out or not on the basis of factors such as their experiences with aggression and their interpretation of the other person's motives.

Researchers find that many aggressive people distort other people's motives. For example, they assume that other people mean them ill when they do not (Akhtar & Bradley, 1991; Crick & Dodge, 1994; Dodge and others, 1990). Similarly, some date rapists misread women as really meaning yes when they say no (e.g., Lipton and others, 1987; Malamuth and others, 1991).

Cognitively oriented psychotherapists note that we are more likely to respond aggressively to a provocation when we magnify the importance of the insult or otherwise stir up feelings of anger (e.g., Lochman, 1992; Lochman & Dodge, 1994).

THE LEARNING PERSPECTIVE: TV OR NOT TV?—THAT IS THE QUESTION. From the behavioral perspective, learning is acquired through principles of reinforcement. Organisms that are reinforced for aggressive behavior are more likely to behave aggressively in similar situations. Environmental consequences make it more likely that strong, agile organisms will be reinforced for aggressive behavior.

From the social-cognitive perspective, aggressive skills are acquired largely by observing others. Social-cognitive theorists, however, find roles for consciousness and choice. They believe that we are not likely to act aggressively unless we believe that aggression is appropriate under the circumstances.

Much of human learning occurs by observation. Observational learning extends to observing parents and peers, classroom learning, reading books, and—in one of the more controversial aspects of modern life—learning from media such as television and films (American Psychological Association, 1992b). Children are routinely exposed to murders, beatings, and sexual assaults—just by turning on the TV set (Huesmann & Miller, 1994). In fact, a child who watches 2 to 4 hours of television a day will have seen 8,000 murders and another 100,000 acts of violence—*by the time she or he has finished elementary school* (Eron, 1993). Do media portrayals of violence beget violence in the streets and in the home?

In study after study, children and adults who view violence in the media show higher levels of aggressive behavior than people who are not exposed to media violence (DeAngelis, 1993; Liebert and others, 1989). There are thus *connections* between violence in the media and real violence. Most psychologists thus agree that media violence *contributes* to aggression (Huesmann, 1993; NIMH, 1982). Consider ways in which media violence makes this contribution.

- *Observational Learning* Children learn from observing the behavior of their parents and other adults (Bandura, 1973, 1986; DeAngelis, 1993). TV violence supplies *models* of aggressive "skills." Acquisition of these skills, in turn, enhances children's aggressive *competencies*. In fact, children are more likely to imitate what their parents do than to heed what they say. If adults

FIGURE 10.7

A Classic Experiment in the Imitation of Aggressive Models. Research by Albert Bandura and his colleagues has shown that children frequently imitate the aggressive behavior that they observe. In the top row, an adult model strikes a clown doll. The lower rows show a boy and a girl imitating the aggressive behavior.

say they disapprove of aggression but smash furniture or slap each other when frustrated, children are likely to develop the notion that aggression is the way to handle frustration. Classic experiments have shown that children tend to imitate the aggressive behavior they see on television, whether the models are cartoons or real people (Bandura and others, 1963; see Figure 10.7).

- *Disinhibition* The expression of operants or skills may be inhibited by punishment or by the expectation of punishment. Conversely, media violence may disinhibit the expression of aggressive impulses that would otherwise have been controlled, especially when media characters "get away" with violence or are rewarded for it.

    Bandura's research has shown that the probability of aggression increases when the models are similar to the observers and when the models are rewarded for aggression. Viewers have been theorized to be *vicariously* reinforced when they observe another person being reinforced for engaging in operants. And perhaps observers of rewarded aggressors are more likely to come to believe that aggression may be appropriate for them as well.

- *Increased Arousal* Media violence and aggressive video games increase viewers' levels of arousal. In the vernacular, television "works them up." We are more likely to engage in dominant forms of behavior, including aggressive behavior, under high levels of arousal.

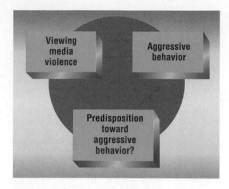

FIGURE 10.8

What Are the Connections Between Media Violence and Aggressive Behavior? Does media violence lead to aggression? Does aggressive behavior lead to a preference for viewing violence? Or does a third factor, such as a predisposition toward aggressive behavior, contribute to both? Might such a predisposition be at least in part genetic?

• *Priming of Aggressive Thoughts and Memories* Media violence has cognitive effects that parallel those of biological arousal. It primes or arouses aggressive ideas and memories (Berkowitz, 1988). Media violence also provides viewers with aggressive *scripts*—that is, ideas on how to behave in situations that seem to parallel those they have observed (Huesmann & Miller, 1994).

• *Habituation* We become used to, or habituated to, many stimuli that impinge on us repeatedly. Repeated exposure to TV violence may therefore decrease viewers' emotional response to real violence (Huesmann, 1993). If children come to perceive violence as the norm, their own attitudes toward violence may become less condemnatory and they may place less value on constraining aggressive urges (Eron, 1993; Huesmann, 1993).

Truth or Fiction Revisited. *Actually, a scientific connection has been established between TV violence and aggression in real life.* Now put on your critical-thinking cap and consider definitions: Is it necessary that we establish that media violence *causes* aggression for there to be a *connection* between the two? What are some of the relationships between media violence and aggression (see Figure 10.8)?

Although media violence encourages aggression in viewers, its greatest impact is on children who are *already* considered by teachers to be most aggressive (Josephson, 1987). There seems to be a circular relationship between viewing media violence and aggressive behavior (DeAngelis, 1993; Eron, 1982). Yes, TV violence contributes to aggressive behavior, but aggressive children are also more likely to tune in and stay tuned to it.

Aggressive children are frequently rejected by their nonaggressive peers—at least within the middle-class culture (Eron, 1982; Patterson, 1993). Aggressive children may watch more television because their peer relationships are less fulfilling and because the high incidence of TV violence tends to confirm their view that aggressive behavior is normal (Eron, 1982). Media violence also interacts with other contributors to violence. For example, parental rejection and use of physical punishment further increase the likelihood of aggression in children (Eron, 1982). Harsh home life may further confirm the TV viewer's vision of the world as a violent place and further encourage reliance on television for companionship.

What, then, should be done about media violence? One issue is whether the government will—or should—take steps to curtail violence in the media. Another is what we as parents and educators can do to mitigate the impact of media violence. Huesmann and his colleagues (1983) have shown that children who watch violent shows act less aggressively when they are informed of the following:

1. The violent behavior they observe in the media does *not* represent the behavior of most people.

2. The apparently aggressive behaviors they watch are not real. They reflect camera tricks, special effects, and stunts.

3. Most people resolve conflicts by nonviolent means.

THE SOCIOCULTURAL PERSPECTIVE. The sociocultural perspective focuses on matters of ethnicity and gender in aggression. Note the following facts:

• African American men aged 15 to 34 are about 9 times as likely as non-Hispanic White Americans to be victims of homicide (Tomes, 1993).

• Hispanic American men are about 5 times as likely as non-Hispanic White Americans to be homicide victims (Tomes, 1993).

- Each year in the United States about 30 women per 1,000 are victims of violence at the hands of their male partners (Tomes, 1993).
- Perhaps half the women in the United States have been battered—that is, subjected to severe physical, sexual, or psychological abuse (Walker, 1993).

Sociocultural theorists note that U.S. culture—like the culture of the Mundugumor—has a way of breeding violence. For example, the countries of Thailand and Jamaica discourage aggression in children and foster politeness and deference (Tharp, 1991). In the United States, by contrast, competitiveness, independence, and differentiation is widely encouraged. In Thailand and Jamaica, then, children are more likely to be "overcontrolled" and complain of sleeping problems, fears, and physical problems. In the United States, children are more likely to be "undercontrolled"—argumentative, disobedient, and belligerent (Tharp, 1991).

Reflections

- **Why do some people seem satisfied to just get by, whereas other people are driven to work and improve despite their achievements?**
- Do you feel a strong need to make friends, join groups, and do things with other people? Why or why not?
- Do you feel a greater need to be around other people when you are upset about something? If so, why?
- **Does violence on television and in films cause aggression in viewers? How much violence have you witnessed on television, in films, on the streets? Has observation of violence affected your behavior?**

EMOTION: ADDING COLOR TO LIFE

Emotions color our lives. We are green with envy, red with anger, blue with sorrow. The poets paint a thoughtful mood as a brown study. Positive emotions such as love and desire can fill our days with pleasure. Negative emotions such as fear, depression, and anger can fill us with dread and make each day a chore.

An emotion can at once be a response to a situation (in the way that fear is a response to a threat) and motivate behavior (in the way that anger can motivate us to act aggressively). An emotion can also be a goal in itself. We may behave in ways that will lead us to experience joy or feelings of love.

Emotions are states of feeling that have cognitive, physiological, and behavioral components (Carlson & Hatfield, 1992; Fischer and others, 1990; Haaland, 1992). Many strong emotions spark activity in the autonomic nervous system (LeDoux, 1986). Fear, which usually occurs in response to a threat, involves cognitions that one is in danger, predominantly **sympathetic** arousal (rapid heartbeat and breathing, sweating, muscle tension), and tendencies to avoid or escape from the situation (see Table 10.1). As a response to a social provocation, anger involves cognitions that a provocateur should be paid back, both sympathetic and **parasympathetic** arousal, and tendencies to attack. Depression usually involves cognitions of helplessness and hopelessness, predominantly parasympathetic arousal, and behavioral tendencies toward inactivity—or, sometimes, self-destruction. Joy, grief, jealousy, disgust, embarrassment, liking—all have cognitive, physiological, and behavioral components. Generally speaking, the greater the autonomic arousal, the more intense the emotion (Chwalisz and others, 1988).

Emotion • A state of feeling that has cognitive, physiological, and behavioral components.

Sympathetic • Of the sympathetic division of the autonomic nervous system.

Parasympathetic • Of the parasympathetic division of the autonomic nervous system.

TABLE 10.1
COMPONENTS OF THREE COMMON EMOTIONS

| | COMPONENTS | | |
EMOTION	COGNITIVE	PHYSIOLOGICAL	BEHAVIORAL
Fear	Belief that one is in danger	Sympathetic arousal	Avoidance tendencies
Anger	Frustration or belief that one is being mistreated	Sympathetic and parasympathetic arousal	Attack tendencies
Depression	Thoughts of helplessness, hopelessness, worthlessness	Parasympathetic arousal	Inactivity, possible self-destructive tendencies

The connection between autonomic arousal and emotions has led to the development of many kinds of "lie detectors." Such instruments detect something, but do they detect specific emotional responses that signify lies?

Arousal, Emotions, and Lie Detection

One may smile, and smile, and be a villain.
SHAKESPEARE, *HAMLET*

Lying—for better and for worse—is an integral part of life (Saxe, 1991a). Political leaders lie to get elected. Some students lie about why they have not completed assignments (Greene & Saxe, 1990). ('Fess up!) The great majority of us lie to our lovers—most often about other relationships (Shusterman & Saxe, 1990). (Is it really true that you never held anyone's hand before?) People also lie about their qualifications to obtain jobs and, of course, to deny guilt for crimes. Although we are unlikely to subject our political leaders, students, and lovers to "lie detector" tests, such tests are frequently used in hiring and police investigative work.

Facial expressions often offer clues to deceit, but some people can lie with a straight face—or a smile. The use of devices to detect lies has a long, if not laudable, history:

> The Bedouins of Arabia . . . until quite recently required conflicting witnesses to lick a hot iron; the one whose tongue was burned was thought to be lying. The Chinese, it is said, had a similar method for detecting lying: Suspects were forced to chew rice powder and spit it out; if the powder was dry, the suspect was guilty. A variation of this test was used during the Inquisition. The suspect had to swallow a "trial slice" of bread and cheese; if it stuck to the suspect's palate or throat he or she was not telling the truth. (Kleinmuntz & Szucko, 1984, pp. 766–767)

These methods may sound primitive, even bizarre, but they are broadly consistent with modern psychological knowledge. Anxiety concerning being caught in a lie is linked to arousal of the sympathetic division of the autonomic nervous system. One sign of sympathetic arousal is lack of saliva, or dryness in the mouth. The emotions of fear and guilt are also linked to sympathetic arousal and, hence, dryness in the mouth.

Modern lie detectors, or polygraphs (see Figure 10.9), monitor indicators of sympathetic arousal while a witness or suspect is being examined: heart rate, blood pressure, respiration rate, and electrodermal response (sweating). Questions have been raised about the validity of the polygraph, however.

The American Polygraph Association (1992) claims that the polygraph is 85% to 95% accurate. Critics, however, find polygraphs less accurate and sensitive to more than lies (Bashore & Rapp, 1993; Furedy, 1990; Saxe, 1991b; Steinbrook, 1992). Studies have found that factors such as tensing muscles, drugs, and previous experience with polygraph tests all significantly reduce the accuracy rate (Steinbrook, 1992). In one experiment, people were able to reduce the accuracy rate to about 50% by biting their tongues (to produce pain) or pressing their toes against the floor (to tense muscles) while being interviewed (Honts and others, 1985).

Truth or Fiction Revisited. *It is true that you may be able to fool a lie detector by squiggling your toes.* Squiggling creates patterns of autonomic arousal that may be misread by interpreters of polygraphs.

In a review of the literature, the government Office of Technology Assessment (OTA) found that there was little valid research into the use of the polygraph in preemployment screening, "dragnet" investigations (attempts to ferret out the guilty from many subjects), or determining who should be given access to classified information (U.S. Congress, 1983). OTA also looked into studies involving investigations of specific indictments. The studies' conclusions varied widely. In 28 studies judged to have adequate methodology, accurate detections of guilt ranged from 35% to 100%. Accurate judgments of innocence ranged from 12.5% to 94%.

In sum, no identifiable pattern of autonomic arousal has been connected with lying, and with lying alone (Bashore & Rapp, 1993; Saxe, 1991b; Steinbrook, 1992). Because of validity problems, results of polygraph examinations

FIGURE 10.9

What Do "Lie Detectors" Detect? The polygraph monitors heart rate, blood pressure, respiration rate, and sweat in the palms of the hands. Is the polygraph sensitive to lying only? Is it foolproof? Because of the controversy surrounding these questions, many courts no longer admit polygraph evidence.

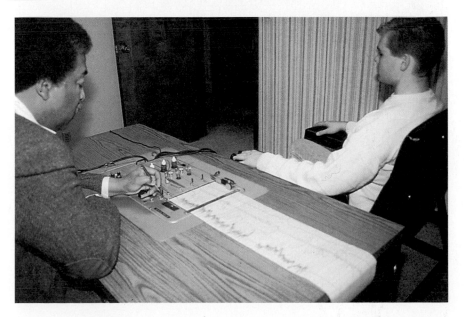

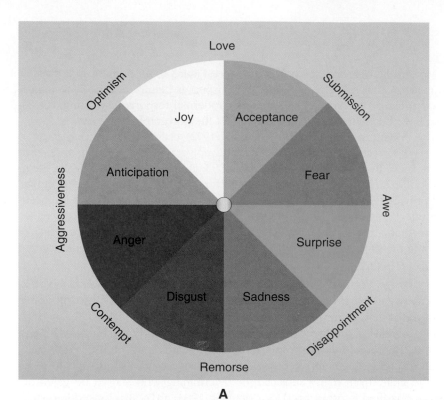

A

B

FIGURE 10.10

Plutchik's Theory of Emotions. Part A shows Plutchik's "circle of emotions." Plutchik theorizes that there are eight basic, or primary, emotions. Secondary emotions such as love are derived from combinations of primary emotions—in this case, joy and acceptance. Part B shows Plutchik's "emotion solid." The vertical axis of this toplike figure repesents degrees of emotional intensity. Intensity increases as we journey upward. Anger is more intense than the related emotion of annoyance, and rage is more intense still.

are no longer admitted as evidence in many courts. Polygraph interviews are still often conducted in criminal investigations and in job interviews, but these practices are also being questioned. Bashore and Rapp (1993) suggest that measures of electrical brain activity might be found to be more accurate than the polygraph.

How Many Emotions Are There? Where Do They Come From?

The ancient Chinese believed that there were four basic or instinctive emotions—happiness, anger, sorrow, and fear. They arose, respectively, in the heart, liver, lungs, and kidneys (Carlson & Hatfield, 1992). (No, there is no evidence for this view.) Behaviorist John B. Watson (1924) believed that there were three basic or inborn emotions: fear, rage, and love. Others, such as Paul Ekman (1980, 1992) and Robert Plutchik (1984) have argued for somewhat larger numbers of basic emotions (see Figure 10.10). The question remains unresolved (Fischer and others, 1990).

In 1932, Katherine Bridges proposed that people are born with a single basic emotion—diffuse excitement—and that other emotions become differentiated as children develop. Carroll Izard (1984, 1990, 1992) more recently argued that all emotions are present and differentiated at birth. However, they are not exhibited all at once. Instead, they emerge in response to the child's developing needs and maturational sequences. In keeping with Izard's view, researchers have found that infants appear to show a number of different emotions at ages earlier than those suggested by Bridges. In one study of the emotions shown by babies during their first 3 months, 99% of the mothers interviewed reported that their babies showed the emotion of interest. Ninety-five percent of mothers reported joy; 84%, anger; 74%, surprise; and 58%, fear (Johnson and others, 1982).

MINILECTURE: TYPES OF EMOTION

The Expression of Emotions

*There's no art
To find the mind's construction in the face.*

SHAKESPEARE, *MACBETH*

Joy and sadness are found in diverse cultures around the world, but how can we tell when other people are happy or despondent? It turns out that the expression of many emotions may be universal (Rinn, 1991). Smiling is apparently a universal sign of friendliness and approval. Baring the teeth, as noted by Charles Darwin (1872) in the last century, may be a universal sign of anger. As the originator of the theory of evolution, Darwin believed that the universal recognition of facial expressions would have survival value. For example, facial expressions could signal the approach of enemies (or friends) in the absence of language.

Most investigators (e.g., Brown, 1991; Buss, 1992; Ekman, 1992, 1994; Izard, 1992, 1994) concur that certain facial expressions suggest the same emotions in all people. Moreover, people in diverse cultures recognize the emotions manifested by the facial expressions. In classic research, Paul Ekman (1980) took photographs of people exhibiting the emotions of anger, disgust, fear, happiness, sadness, and surprise, similar to those shown in Figure 10.11. He then asked people around the world to indicate what emotions were being depicted. Those queried ranged from European college students to members of

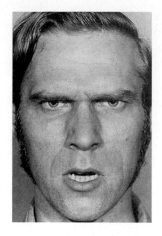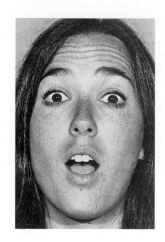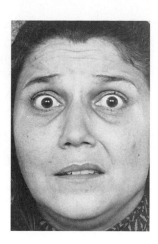

FIGURE 10.11

Photographs Used in Research by Paul Ekman. Ekman's research suggests that the expression of several basic emotions—such as happiness, anger, surprise, and fear—is universally recognized.

**MINILECTURE:
FACIAL EXPRESSION OF
EMOTION**

the Fore, a tribe that dwells in the New Guinea highlands. All groups, including the Fore, who had almost no contact with Western culture, agreed on the portrayed emotions. The Fore also displayed familiar facial expressions when asked how they would respond if they were the characters in stories that called for basic emotional responses. Ekman and his colleagues (1987) more recently obtained similar results in a study of 10 cultures in which participants were permitted to report that multiple emotions were shown by facial expressions. The participants generally agreed on which two emotions were being shown and which emotion was most intense.

Facial-feedback hypothesis • The view that stereotypical facial expressions can contribute to stereotypical emotions.

The Facial-Feedback Hypothesis

We generally recognize that facial expressions reflect emotional states. In fact, various emotional states give rise to certain patterns of electrical activity in the facial muscles and in the brain (Cacioppo and others, 1988; Ekman and others, 1990).

The **facial-feedback hypothesis** argues, however, that the causal relationship between emotions and facial expressions can also work in the opposite direction. Consider Darwin's words:

> The free expression by outward signs of an emotion intensifies it. On the other hand, the repression, as far as possible, of all outward signs softens our emotions. (Darwin, 1872, p. 22)

Can smiling give rise to feelings of good will, for example, or frowning, to anger?

Psychological research has given rise to some interesting findings concerning the facial-feedback hypothesis (Ekman, 1993b). Inducing participants in experiments to smile, for example, leads them to report more positive feelings and to rate cartoons as being more humorous. When induced to frown, they rate cartoons as being more aggressive. When participants pose expressions of pain, they rate electric shocks as being more painful.

What are the possible links between facial feedback and emotion? One link is arousal. Intense contraction of facial muscles such as those used in signifying fear heightens arousal (Zuckerman and others, 1981). Self-perception of heightened arousal then leads to heightened emotional activity. Other links may involve changes in brain temperature and the release of neurotransmitters (Zajonc, 1985). Kinesthetic feedback of the contraction of facial muscles may also induce feeling states. Ekman (1993b) has found that the so-called Duchenne smile, which is characterized by "crow's feet wrinkles around the eyes and a subtle drop in the eye cover fold so that the skin above the eye moves down slightly toward the eyeball," can induce pleasant feelings.

Truth or Fiction Revisited. *It is true that smiling can produce pleasant feelings.* Research has shown that the Duchenne smile can indeed give rise to pleasant feelings.

You may have heard the British expression "keep a stiff upper lip" as a recommendation for handling stress. It might be that a "stiff" lip suppresses emotional response—as long as the lip is relaxed rather than quivering with fear or tension. But when a lip is stiffened through strong muscle tension, facial feedback may heighten emotional response. In the following section, we see that the facial-feedback hypothesis is related to the James–Lange theory of emotion.

Theories of Emotion: *Is* Feeling First?

**MINILECTURE:
THEORIES OF EMOTION**

In Chapter 8, we asked you to consider the syntax of the following lines from an e. e. cummings poem:

> *since feeling is first*
> *who pays any attention*
> *to the syntax of things*
> *will never wholly kiss you . . .*

Now let us address the subject matter of the poem—no, not the kiss, but the question, *Does* feeling, in fact, come first?

Emotions have physiological, situational, and cognitive components, but psychologists have disagreed about how these components interact to produce feeling states and actions. Some psychologists argue that physiological arousal ("feeling" in the cummings poem) is a more basic component of emotional response than cognition and that the type of arousal we experience strongly influences our cognitive appraisal and our labeling of the emotion (e.g., Izard, 1984; Zajonc, 1984). For these psychologists, "feeling is first." Other psychologists argue that cognitive appraisal and physiological arousal are so strongly intertwined that cognitive processes may determine the emotional response (e.g., Lazarus, 1984, 1991a).

The commonsense theory of emotions is that something happens (situation) that is cognitively appraised (interpreted) by the person and the feeling state (a combination of arousal and thoughts) follows. For example, you meet someone new, appraise that person as being delightful, and feelings of attraction follow. Or you flunk a test, recognize that you're in trouble, and feel down in the dumps.

However, historic and contemporary theories of how the components of emotions interact are at variance with the commonsense view. Let us consider a number of more important theories and see if we can arrive at some useful conclusions.

THE JAMES–LANGE THEORY.   At the turn of the century, William James suggested that our emotions follow, rather than cause, our behavioral responses

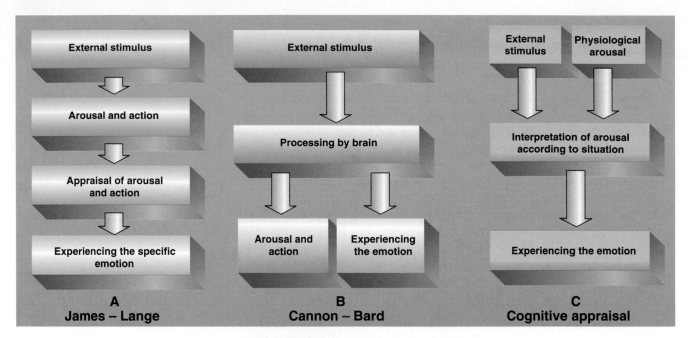

FIGURE 10.12

What Are the Major Theories of Emotion? Several theories of emotion have been advanced, each of which proposes a different role for the components of emotional response. According to the James–Lange theory (part A), events trigger specific arousal patterns and actions. Emotions result from our appraisal of our body responses. According to the Cannon–Bard theory (part B), events are first processed by the brain. Body patterns of arousal, action, and our emotional responses are then triggered simultaneously. According to the theory of cognitive appraisal (part C), events and arousal are appraised by the individual. The emotional response stems from the person's appraisal of the situation and his or her level of arousal.

to events. This view was also proposed by a contemporary of James's, the Danish physiologist Karl G. Lange. It is thus termed the James–Lange theory of emotion.

According to James and Lange (see Figure 10.12, part A), certain external stimuli instinctively trigger specific patterns of arousal and action such as fighting or fleeing. We then become angry *because* we act aggressively. We then become afraid *because* we run away. Emotions are simply the cognitive representations (or by-products) of automatic physiological and behavioral responses.

Walter Cannon (1927) criticized the James–Lange assertion that each emotion has distinct physiological correlates. Cannon argued that the physiological arousal that accompanies emotion A is not as distinct from the arousal that accompanies emotion B as the theory asserts. We can also note that the James–Lange view ascribes a very meager function to human cognition; it denies the roles of cognitive appraisal, personal values, and personal choice.

On the other hand, the James–Lange theory is consistent with the facial-feedback hypothesis. That is, smiling apparently can induce pleasant feelings, "even though we don't know if the effect is strong enough to override sadness" (Ekman, 1993b). The theory also suggests that we may be able to change our feelings by changing our behavior. Changing one's behavior to change one's feelings is one aspect of behavior therapy, which is discussed in Chapter 14.

THE CANNON–BARD THEORY. Walter Cannon was not content to criticize the James–Lange theory. He (Cannon, 1927) and Philip Bard (1934) suggested that an event would trigger bodily responses (arousal and action) and the experience of an emotion simultaneously. As shown in Figure 10.12 (part B), when an event is perceived (processed by the brain), the brain stimulates autonomic and muscular activity (arousal and action) *and* cognitive activity (experience of the emotion). According to the Cannon–Bard theory, emotions *accompany* bodily responses. Emotions are not *produced* by bodily changes, as in the James–Lange theory.

The central criticism of the Cannon–Bard theory focuses on whether bodily responses (arousal and action) and emotions are actually stimulated simultaneously. For example, pain or the perception of danger may trigger arousal before we begin to feel distress or fear. Also, many of us have had the experience of having a "narrow escape" and then becoming aroused and shaky afterward, when we have finally had time to consider the damage that might have occurred. What is needed is a theory that allows for an ongoing interaction of external events, physiological changes (such as autonomic arousal and muscular activity), and cognitive activities.

THE THEORY OF COGNITIVE APPRAISAL. Recent theoretical approaches to emotion have stressed cognitive factors. Among those psychologists who argue that thinking comes first are Gordon Bower, Richard Lazarus, Stanley Schachter, and Robert Zajonc.

Stanley Schachter (1971) asserts that emotions have generally similar patterns of bodily arousal. The essential way in which they vary is along a weak–strong dimension that is determined by one's level of arousal. The label we give to an emotion largely depends on our cognitive appraisal of our situation. Cognitive appraisal is based on many factors, including our perception of external events and the ways in which other people seem to respond to those events (see Figure 10.12, part C). Given the presence of other people, we engage in social comparison to arrive at an appropriate response.

In a classic experiment, Schachter and Singer (1962) showed that arousal can be labeled quite differently, depending on a person's situation. The investigators told study participants that their purpose was to study the effects of a vitamin on vision. Half of the participants received an injection of adrenaline, a hormone that increases autonomic arousal (see Chapter 3). A control group received an injection of an inactive solution. Those given adrenaline then received one of three "cognitive manipulations," as shown in Table 10.2. Group 1 was told nothing about possible emotional effects of the "vitamin." Group 2

TABLE 10.2

INJECTED SUBSTANCES AND COGNITIVE MANIPULATIONS IN THE SCHACHTER–SINGER STUDY

GROUP	SUBSTANCE	COGNITIVE MANIPULATION
1	Adrenaline	No information given about effects
2	Adrenaline	Misinformation given: itching, numbness, etc.
3	Adrenaline	Accurate information: physiological arousal
4	(Inactive)	None

Source: Schachter & Singer (1962).

was deliberately misinformed; group members were led to expect itching, numbness, or other irrelevant symptoms. Group 3 was informed accurately about the increased arousal they would experience.

After receiving injections and cognitive manipulations, study participants were asked to wait, in pairs, while the experimental apparatus was being set up. Participants did not know that the person with whom they were waiting was a confederate of the experimenter. The confederate's purpose was to model a response that the participant would believe resulted from the injection.

Some who took part in the experiment waited with a confederate who acted in a happy-go-lucky manner. He flew paper airplanes about the room and tossed paper balls into a wastebasket. Other participants waited with a confederate who acted angry, complaining about the experiment, tearing up a questionnaire, and departing the waiting room in a huff. As the confederates worked for their Oscars, the real participants were observed through a one-way mirror.

The people in groups 1 and 2 were likely to imitate the behavior of the confederate. Those exposed to the **euphoric** confederate acted jovial and content. Those exposed to the angry confederate imitated that person's complaining, aggressive ways. But those in groups 3 and 4 were less influenced by the confederate's behavior.

Schachter and Singer concluded that those in groups 1 and 2 were in an ambiguous situation. Members of these groups felt arousal from the adrenaline injection but had no basis for attributing it to any event or emotion. Social comparison with the confederate led them to attribute their arousal either to happiness or to anger, whichever was displayed by the confederate. Group 3 members expected arousal from the injection with no particular emotional consequences. These people did not imitate the confederate's display of happiness or anger because they were not in an ambiguous situation. Group 4 members had no physiological arousal for which they needed an attribution, except perhaps for some induced by observing the confederate. Group 4 members also failed to imitate the confederate.

Now, happiness and anger are quite different emotions. Happiness is a positive emotion, and anger, for most of us, is a negative emotion. Yet, Schachter and Singer suggest that any physiological differences between these two emotions are so slight that opposing cognitive appraisals of the same situation can lead one person to label arousal as happiness and another person to label arousal as anger. The Schachter–Singer view could not be farther removed from the James–Lange theory, which holds that each emotion has specific and readily recognized body sensations.

The truth, it happens, may lie somewhere in between.

In science, it must be possible to replicate experiments and attain identical or similar results. The Schachter and Singer study has been replicated with *different* results, however (Ekman, 1993a). For instance, a number of studies found that participants were less likely to imitate the behavior of the confederate and were likely to perceive unexplained arousal in negative terms such as nervousness, anger, even jealousy (Zimbardo and others, 1993).

EVALUATION.   What do we make of all this? Research by Paul Ekman and his colleagues (1983) suggests that the patterns of arousal connected with various emotions are apparently more specific than suggested by Schachter and Singer—although less specific than suggested by James and Lange. Similarly, recent research with the PET scan suggests that different emotions such as happiness and sadness involve different structures of the brain (Goleman,

Euphoric • Characterized by feelings of well-being, elation.

1995b). Moreover, lack of control over our emotions and lack of understanding of what is happening to us appear to be disturbing experiences (Zimbardo and others, 1993). Thus our cognitive appraisals of our situations apparently do affect our emotional responses, even if not quite in the way envisioned by Schachter.

In sum, various components of an experience—cognitive, physiological, and behavioral—contribute to our emotional responses. People are thinking beings who gather information from all three sources in determining their behavioral responses and labeling their emotional responses. The fact that none of the theories we have discussed applies to all people in all situations is comforting. Our emotions are not quite as easily understood or manipulated as some theorists have suggested.

Reflections

- Do you know people whom you consider to be highly emotional? What behavior patterns lead you to infer that they are emotional?
- **What do lie detectors detect? Have you ever tried to discern whether someone was lying to you? What types of clues did you look for? Do you think that you were successful in determining the truth?**
- Have you had any experiences that seem to support one of the theories of emotion presented in the chapter? What were they? Which theory do they seem to support?

Study Guide

| **Exercise: Matching Scientists and Concepts**

DIRECTIONS: Here are a number of statements that express various concepts or positions that concern the psychology of motivation and emotion. Below them are the names of a number of psychologists and other scientists discussed in Chapter 10. Write the number of the statement to the left of the name of the appropriate scientist. The answer key follows the exercise.

1. We are motivated to maintain harmony among our beliefs and attitudes. For example, when people we like share our attitudes, there is balance and all is well.

2. People have 12 basic instincts, including hunger, sex, and self-assertion.

3. Once people have met their lower-level needs, they naturally try to find personal fulfillment by actualizing their unique potentials.

4. When people are in an ambiguous situation, they tend to look to other people in the same situation for information as to how they ought to behave.

5. The reason that people and lower animals find rewards to be pleasant is that rewards have the effect of reducing primary or acquired drives.

6. Awareness that two cognitions are dissonant, or that our attitudes are incompatible with our behavior, is unpleasant and motivates us to reduce the discrepancy.

7. External events trigger instinctive patterns of arousal and action such as fighting or fleeing. We then become angry *because* we fight; we become afraid *because* we run away.

8. The instincts of hunger, sex, and aggression give rise to psychic energy, which is perceived as tension. This tension motivates us to find ways to restore ourselves to a calmer, resting state.

9. The free expression by outward signs of an emotion intensifies it. On the other hand, the repression, as far as possible, of all outward signs softens our emotions.

10. Social motives differ from primary motives such as hunger in that they are acquired through social learning.

___ A. Charles Darwin   ___ F. Abraham Maslow
___ B. Sigmund Freud   ___ G. William McDougall
___ C. Clark Hull   ___ H. Leon Festinger
___ D. William James   ___ I. Stanley Schachter
___ E. Fritz Heider   ___ J. Henry Murray

ANSWER KEY TO EXERCISE

| A. 9 | C. 5 | E. 1 | G. 2 | I. 4 |
| B. 8 | D. 7 | F. 3 | H. 6 | J. 10 |

acquainted with (425)—familiar with

agile (428)—active, quick

ambiguous situation (440)—a situation that was not clear

apparatus (426)—mechanical device

apparently moderate possible instincts (427)—appear to limit behaviors that possibly are caused by instinct

appease (413)—to calm, satisfy

armpit (410)—the underside area where the arm joins the body

as far as possible (436)—as much as possible

as time went on (420)—as time progressed; as the moments passed

ascribes (438)—makes responsible for

assume female mating stances (415)—become sexually receptive to the males

at the price of poverty (411)—they will be poor; they'll have careers that are satisfying but do not provide much money

at variance with (437)—not in agreement with

attributing it (440)—believing it was caused by

automatic writing (403)—unconscious writing; some people believe it is possible to receive messages from creatures in outer space and that these messages are transmitted through human beings who write what they are told to by the creature

awe (407)—strong respect and admiration

baring the teeth (435)—holding the lips up and over the teeth, revealing the teeth; an angry expression in animals

batting her feet (419)—lightly and playfully hitting her feet

beget (428)—cause

berths (426)—positions

binge eating (413)—eating very large amounts in a very short time

biology apparently is not destiny (415)—biology evidently does not determine our behavior

bounce up and down in weight (413)—gain and lose weight

by-products (438)—unintended results

castrated (415)—to remove the male reproductive glands called the *testicles*

circular explanation (410)—an explanation that goes around and around without getting to an end point

circular relationship (430)—things that influence each other

classic experiment (426)—a famous experiment

climbed (412)—rose; increased

cognitive appraisal (437)—judgment

cognitive manipulations (439)—attempts to influence thinking

cognitive, physiological, and behavioral components (431)—thought, physical, and action parts

coincide reasonably well (407)—match fairly well; are very similar

color our lives (431)—provide our lives with variety, interest, enjoyment, and feeling

come full circle (410)—started at one point (place), moved, and then ended at the same point

concur (435)—agree

condemned (418)—criticized

confederate of the experimenter (440)—an assistant of the experimenter; he or she had been told by the experimenter how to act

consistency (421)—behavior that matches expectations

conversely (429)—the reverse; on the other hand

converts (404)—new believers; they changed from one belief to another

couch potato (420)—slang term for someone who is content to sit around and not do anything that requires physical effort

could not be farther removed from (440)—is extremely different from

critical-thinking cap (430)—think in a way that will allow you to take apart an idea to examine and understand it

cuddle (407)—to hug or snuggle with something

curtail (430)—limit

decapitate (426)—cut off the head

demise (426)—end; death

deviant (413)—abnormal; peculiar

diminish (407)—decrease

directionality (415)—the direction toward which something is aimed

discrepant (422)—doesn't fit or agree with; is contradictory

dissonant (423)—contradict; are not in agreement

don't answer too quickly (419)—think about it before you answer because what you think now might not be what you would think later, or after the activity

down in the dumps (437)—depressed

eluded (417)—escaped

empirical support (410)—observed occurrences of something

enlightened (404)—educated about something; now knowing the truth

envisioned (441)—pictured or imagined

eroticize (414)—to give erotic, or sexual, overtones

experiential (415)—related to actual experience

extrinsic . . . intrinsic rewards (425)—external or internal benefits

exuberant (420)—enthusiastic, lively

far from (404)—not like this at all (strong emphasis)

fateful (417)—the special time at which an important, feared thing is expected to happen

faulty resolution (431)—not resolved, or handled, correctly or completely

fill our days . . . pleasure (431)—cause us to feel pleasure during our lives; cause each day to be pleasurable

fill us with (431)—cause us to have

finicky about their food (413)—hard to please about what they eat; very picky

flying saucers (404)—some people believe that large, flat, saucer-shaped vehicles carry creatures who fly in outer space

foster (406)—encourage

framed by (407)—explained or laid out by

gadgets (420)—mechanical objects

get away with (429)—do something wrong and not be punished

get by (431)—do the minimum necessary

getting away scot-free (426)—not having to suffer or pay a penalty

give rise to (410)—cause to develop

go it alone (425)—do things alone

gratify (427)—satisfy

grope toward (412)—move toward in an uncertain manner

happy-go-lucky (440)—happy and carefree; relaxed

harsh (430)—cruel, severe, or unkind

having a narrow escape (439)—getting out of a dangerous position

hazing (423)—to play rough practical jokes on someone; hazing rituals may be used by some groups to initiate new people who want to join the group or club

hierarchy (409)—a series of levels, or ranks; the bottom level is the least important, or easiest, to reach, and the top level is the most important, or hardest, to reach

huddle together (426)—stay closely together

hypothetical states (404)—conditions that are unseen or imagined but could be real

impinge on us (430)—influence us

in a huff (440)—angrily

in sum (433)—in the end; after all is considered

incest taboo (414)—a strong rule against sexual intercourse between closely related family members

incompatible (422)—don't agree with each other; don't fit together

indictments (433)—accusations of wrongdoing

inducing (436)—causing or influencing

infatuation (407)—a strong preoccupation or obsession for somebody or something

inferred (405)—assumed or gathered from

inhibited; disinhibited (429)—to inhibit is when something prevents or slows down the occurrence of a behavior; the opposite is to disinhibit, when something

which was stopping or slowing a behavior is removed and the behavior is no longer discouraged

instigated (420)—caused or created

insurmountable . . . hurdles (409)—barriers that are impossible to overcome

internalization (418)—accepting ideas from outside influences as one's own guiding ideas

intervene (426)—influence the situation

jovial (440)—cheerful and happy

keep a stiff upper lip (437)—to not reveal emotion and appear to be calm; it comes from the idea that when a person keeps the upper lip in an unmovable position, the person shows no emotion

key cognitions (404)—important ideas

largely learned (407)—mainly learned; primarily learned

last thing on your mind (412)—not what you would think about at that moment

leading them to believe (426)—causing them to think

lengthy, if not laudable (425)—has been occurring for a long time and can be criticized

limited-time-only, half-price sale (424)—a sale at half the original price for a very short time

lopsided (423)—leaning strongly to one side

made more demands (425)—required more performance

manifested (435)—shown

manipulate (419)—to direct or control

media hoopla (403)—a lot of attention and publicity by the news media

milieu (405)—people in the surrounding environment

misery loves company (403)—people who are feeling unhappy want to be with other people who are feeling unhappy

misread (428)—misunderstand

modesty (407)—the attitude of being reserved or humble; not drawing attention to oneself

momentous (404)—important

monkeying around with (420)—playing with

motives (428)—reasons for doing something

multiyear contracts (426)—legal agreements for more than one year

must be met (424)—must be attended to

nonentrepreneurial positions (425)—jobs that did not involve business development

offshoot (427)—a development in another direction

on the eve of (414)—the night before

operants (429)—behaviors

outer space (404)—the area outside of the world we know

outward signs (436)—external indications

outwit (427)—be more clever than others and gain an advantage

over between them (415)—they do not have a love relationship anymore

paid back (431)—punished

paint (408)—represent

parallel (430)—are comparable or similar to

parental rejection (430)—when parents strongly disapprove of or don't care for their children

pent-up (427)—held in and built up to high levels

persistence (425)—the ability to persist, or stick with, something

personal fulfillment (408)—a sense of personal accomplishment and satisfaction

petting (414)—forms of caressing that demonstrate physical affection

portrayed (436)—shown

pose (436)—imitate

predispose (414)—to encourage a tendency toward

predominantly (431)—mainly; primarily

preliterate societies (410)—societies that do not have a written language

primitive, even bizarre (432)—crude, uncivilized; even weird or strange

primping (410)—decorating and grooming oneself

prod them to extend themselves (425)—encourage them to try to exert great effort

profusely (425)—extravagant; a large amount

propel (404)—cause to move

prophecy (404)—a forecast; an expectation based on a belief that someone uses to predict the future

provocation . . . provocateur (431)—to cause something to happen . . . the one who causes the event

psych themselves up (425)—become enthusiastic and aroused

queried (435)—asked

question has arisen (420)—question has been asked

rage (426)—occurs with strong intensity

receptors (412)—locations in the body where chemicals attach

regulatory factors (412)—conditions that direct, or regulate, the occurrence or development of something

releasers (427)—events or factors that allow something to occur

reliance on (430)—to depend on

replicate (440)—duplicate

represent (409)—understand and operate from an idea

repress (427)—not show; hide from awareness

resented (426)—be annoyed by, disliked; blaming the other

roundabout ways (427)—indirect ways; not obvious

runs aground (410)—no longer makes sense; runs into trouble like a boat that runs up on the shore

see their fate as being in their own hands (425)—think of their future as something they can control

Seekers (404)—the name of a group of people who believed the world would come to an end by an invasion of creatures from outer space

shaky (439)—unsteady; trembling from being scared

shunning (410)—rejecting, ignoring

sidetrack (410)—to distract from something; take it in a different direction, like a small train track going away from the main track

signify (432)—indicate

simultaneously (439)—happens at the same time

sissies (410)—boys who are perceived as acting like girls; a negative term

slings and arrows (418)—insults and rejection

slow to grasp her meaning (415)—not understanding (reluctant to stop his advances)

social glue (426)—social structure that joins people together; glue is an adhesive

softens our emotions (436)—calms our emotions

sorority or fraternity (423)—social clubs for men or women on college and university campuses

spawned (405)—thought of; taken from a term meaning "to give birth"

squiggling your toes (403)—wiggling or moving your toes up and down

stokes (410)—fuels; causes

strive relentlessly (424)—effort without stopping

subject to various interpretations (424)—can be explained in different ways; have different meanings

submissive . . . deferential (418)—to submit, or defer, to men; to follow a man's wishes and direction

suggestive of (415)—it suggests or indicates

supposedly (426)—it was not occurring, but it was supposed to be occurring

syntax (437)—the order of words to make a phrase or sentence

tangible rewards (425)—actual, real benefits

tear us asunder (423)—pull us apart

this is indeed the case (410)—this is certainly true (strong emphasis)

took positions (425)—accepted jobs

trigger (407)—to cause or start something

truth, it turns out, may lie somewhere in between (440)—the truth, we discovered later, may not be one or the other, but may be in between the two

tummy-time (411)—*tummy* is a child's word for stomach; tummy-time would be the stomach's messages of hunger

universal powers that be (404)—a humorous reference to the possible powers outside of our awareness that regulate our world and our lives

universally (428)—generally always; widespread occurrence

unscrambling (425)—deciphering; solving the anagram puzzle

validity (433)—truth; dependability

venting (427)—releasing

vernacular (430)—common way of speaking; everyday, informal words *vicariously* (429)—having an experience by watching another do something, as if the watcher were doing the action

ward off (415)—prevent; protect against

warranted (418)—justified or reasonable

whatsoever (420)—at all (emphatic)

whereas (405)—but in comparison

wink (432)—the rapid lowering and raising of one eye-lid; it is a signal of affection, interest, or joking

work in concert (435)—operate together, at the same time

worked for their Oscars (440)—acted well; Oscars are awards for good acting in the movies

works them up (430)—gets people excited

yielding circular explanations (410)—producing explanations that are circular, or start in one place and end in the same place

zapping (420)—slang for attacking suddenly with something

FILL-INS | **Chapter Review**

SECTION 1: COMING TO TERMS WITH MOTIVATION

Motives are hypothetical states within organisms that (1) _____vate behavior and direct organisms toward (2) _____s. Physiological needs generally reflect states of physical (3) _____tion. Psychological needs (4: Are or Are Not?) necessarily based on states of deprivation and may be learned, or acquired through (5) ex_____. Needs give rise to (6) _____s, which are psychological in nature and arouse us to action. An (7) _____tive is an object, person, or situation that is perceived as being capable of satisfying a need.

SECTION 2: THEORIES OF MOTIVATION: THE WHYS OF WHY

According to the (8) in_____ theory of motivation, animals are born with preprogrammed tendencies to behave in certain ways in certain situations. Within instinct theory, stimuli called (9) _____sers elicit innate fixed-(10) a_____ patterns, or *FAPs*. William James and William (11) Mc_____ argued that people have various instincts that lead not only to survival, but also to (12) s_____ behavior.

According to Clark (13) _____'s drive-reduction theory of motivation, (14) _____ds are pleasant because they reduce drives. As a consequence, we are motivated to engage in (15) be_____ that leads to rewards. Drive-reduction theorists differentiate between (16) pr_____ (innate) drives and (17) _____red (learned) drives. The body's tendency to maintain a steady state is called (18) _____stasis.

According to (19) o_____-process theory, emotions tend to trigger opposing emotions. (20) _____istic psychologists argue that behavior can be growth-oriented. Humanists believe that people are motivated to consciously strive for personal (21) _____ment. Abraham (22) M_____ hypothesized that people have a hierarchy of needs, including an innate need for self-actualization. Maslow's hierarchy includes physiological needs, safety needs, love and (23) _____ness needs, esteem needs, and, at the top, the need for (24) self-_____ation.

Cognitive psychologists such as Sandra Bem and Leon (25) F_____ assert that people are motivated to achieve cognitive consistency. Jean (26) P_____ and George Kelly hypothesized that people are born scientists who strive to understand the world so that they can predict and control events.

(27) Socio_____ theory pervades other viewpoints. For example, primary drives may be inborn, but sociocultural experiences affect the (28) b_____ that satisfies them.

SECTION 3: HUNGER: DO YOU GO BY "TUMMY-TIME"?

Hunger is regulated by several internal mechanisms, including (29) _____ch contractions, blood-(30) s_____ level, receptors in the mouth and liver, and the responses of the hypothalamus. Chewing and swallowing provide some sensations of (31) _____ty. The (32) _____al nucleus (VMN) of the hypothalamus apparently functions as a stop-eating center. Lesions in this area lead to (33) _____gia in rats, a condition in which the animals grow to several times their normal body weight, but then level off. It is as if lesions in the VMN raise the (34) _____t point of the stop-eating center to be triggered at a much higher level. The (35) _____al hypothalamus apparently functions as a start-eating center. Lesions in the lateral hypothalamus can lead to (36) _____gia in rats.

SECTION 4: SEX: A SOCIOCULTURAL PERSPECTIVE

Sex hormones promote biological sexual (37) _____tiation, regulate the menstrual cycle, and influence sexual behavior. Sexual behavior among many lower animals is almost completely governed by (38) _____ones. Hormones predispose lower animals toward (39) _____line or feminine mating patterns (an organizing effect) and influence the sex drive and facilitate sexual (40) re_____ (activating effects).

Male rats who have been castrated at birth—and thus deprived of (41) _____erone—make no effort to mate as adults. When male rats are castrated in adulthood, injections of testosterone cause them to resume stereotypical (42) _____ine sexual behavior patterns. Men who are castrated or given antiandrogens usually show gradual loss of sexual desire and of the capacities for (43) _____tion and orgasm. Female mice, rats, cats, and dogs are receptive to males only during (44) _____us. But women are sexually responsive during all phases of the menstrual cycle and even after (45) _____pause.

A gay male or lesbian sexual (46) _____ation is an erotic response to members of one's own gender. Psychodynamic theory ties a gay male sexual orientation to a "classic pattern" of a (47) "close—_____ing" mother and a (48) "_____ed—hostile" father. From the perspective of learning theory, early reinforcement of sexual behavior can influence sexual orientation. A gay male or lesbian sexual orientation (49: Has or Has Not?) been reliably linked to current (adult) levels of male or female sex hormones. But sexual orientation may be connected with (50) _____tal exposure to sex hormones.

SECTION 5: STIMULUS MOTIVES

Stimulus motives are like physiological needs in that they are also (51) _____nate. Physiological needs motivate us to (52: Increase or Reduce?) the stimulation that impinges upon us. Stimulus motives, by contrast, motivate us to (53: Increase or Decrease?) the stimulation impinging upon us.

People and many lower animals have needs for stimulation and activity, for exploration and manipulation. Sensation-seekers engage in behavior that results in a high level of (54) _____tion.

Studies in sensory (55) _____ation show that lack of stimulation is aversive. After a few hours, subjects in these studies become bored and (56) _____table. As time goes on, some of them report visual (57) _____ations, which tend to be limited to geometric figures. After a few days, subjects find it difficult to (58) co_____ on problems.

SECTION 6: SOCIAL MOTIVES

Social motives differ from primary motives in that they are (59) _____ired through social learning experiences. Harvard University psychologist Henry (60) M_____ referred to social motives as (61) _____ical needs.

Psychologist David (62) Mc_____ pioneered the assessment of achievement motivation through fantasy. In doing so, McClelland used Murray's Thematic (63) _____tion Test.

People with high achievement motivation attain (64: Higher or Lower?) grades and earn (65: More or Less?) money than people of comparable ability with lower achievement motivation. Parents with high achievement motivation tend to encourage their children to think and act (66) _____dently.

The need for (67) _____ation prompts us to join groups and make friends. Stanley Schachter found that anxiety tends to (68: Increase or Decrease?) the need for affiliation. When anxious, we prefer to affiliate with people who (69: Share or Do Not Share?) our predicaments. Schachter explains this preference through the theory of social (70) _____ison. This theory holds that when we are in (71) _____guous situations, we seek to affiliate with people with whom we can compare feelings and behaviors.

(72) Socio_____ views much social behavior, including aggressive behavior, as genetically determined. Because aggressive individuals are more likely to (73) _____duce, whatever genes are linked to aggressive behavior are more likely to be transmitted to subsequent generations. According to (74) psycho_____ theory, the best ways to prevent harmful aggression may be to encourage less harmful aggression. From the (75) c_____ perspective, people who believe that aggression is necessary and justified—as during wartime—are likely to act aggressively. People who believe that a particular war or act of aggression is unjust, or who universally oppose aggression, are (76: More or Less?) likely to behave aggressively.

From the behavioral perspective, learning is acquired through principles of (77) _____ment. People who view violence in the media show (78: Higher or Lower?) levels of aggressive behavior than people who are not exposed to media violence. Media violence supplies (79) _____els of aggressive "skills." Repeated exposure to media violence may (80: Increase or Decrease?) viewers' emotional response to real violence. The (81) socio_____ perspective focuses on matters of ethnicity and gender in aggression.

SECTION 7: EMOTION: ADDING COLOR TO LIFE

An emotion is a state of (82) _____ing. Emotions have physiological, (83) _____al, and cognitive components. Emotions motivate behavior, but can also serve as (84) _____nses to situations and as goals in themselves. The emotion of anxiety involves predominantly (85) _____etic arousal. The emotion of depression involves predominantly (86) _____etic arousal.

Lie detectors are known technically as (87) _____aphs. Polygraphs assess sympathetic (88) _____al rather than lies per se. Polygraphs monitor four bodily functions: heart rate; blood (89) _____e; respiration rate; and (90) ____dermal response, which is an index of sweating. Supporters of the polygraph claim that it is successful in more than (91) _____% of cases. However, subjects can reduce the accuracy rate of polygraphs, as lie detectors, by thinking about disturbing events during the interview, biting their tongues, or creating (92) _____etic arousal in other ways.

The expression of many emotions appears to be (93) _____sal. (94) Sm_____ appears to be a universal sign of friendliness and approval. Psychologist Paul (95) E_____ showed subjects throughout the world photographs of people posing emotions such as anger, disgust, fear, happiness, sadness, and surprise. All groups correctly identified the emotions being portrayed.

According to the (96) f_____-f_____ hypothesis, posing intense facial expressions can heighten emotional response. Inducing (97) _____ing leads subjects to report more positive feelings. Subjects who are induced to frown rate cartoons as more (98) ag_____.

Psychologists do not agree as to the relative importance of physiological arousal and (99) co_____ appraisal in activating particular emotions. According to the James–Lange theory, emotions have specific patterns of (100) ar_____ and (101) ac_____ that are triggered by certain external events. Emotions follow, rather than cause, the overt behavioral (102) re_____s to events.

The Cannon–Bard theory proposes that processing of events by the brain gives rise simultaneously to (103) ____nomic activity (arousal), (104) _____lar activity (action), and cognitive activity (the mental experiencing of the emotion). From this view, emotions (105) ac_____ bodily responses, but are not produced by bodily changes.

According to the theory of cognitive appraisal, emotions have largely similar patterns of (106) _____al. Emotions essentially vary along a (107) _____g to weak dimension that is determined by one's level of arousal. The emotion a person will experience in response to an external stimulus reflects that person's (108) ap_____ of the stimulus—that is, the meaning of the stimulus to him or her. A classic study by (109) Sch_____ and Singer suggested that a similar pattern of arousal can be labeled quite differently, depending on a person's situation. However, the Schachter and Singer study has been replicated with different results.

Research seems to suggest that patterns of arousal are more specific than suggested by the theory of (110) _____tive appraisal, but that cognitive appraisal does play an important role in determining our responses to events.

ANSWER KEY TO CHAPTER REVIEW

1. Motivate	12. Social	23. Belongingness	34. Set
2. Goals	13. Hull	24. Self-actualization	35. Lateral
3. Deprivation	14. Rewards	25. Festinger	36. Aphagia
4. Are not	15. Behavior	26. Piaget	37. Differentiation
5. Experience	16. Primary	27. Sociocultural	38. Hormones
6. Drives	17. Acquired	28. Behavior	39. Masculine
7. Incentive	18. Homeostasis	29. Stomach	40. Response
8. Instinct	19. Opponent	30. Sugar	41. Testosterone
9. Releasers	20. Humanistic	31. Satiety	42. Masculine
10. Action	21. Fulfillment	32. Ventromedial	43. Erection
11. McDougall	22. Maslow	33. Hyperphagia	44. Estrus

45. Menopause
46. Orientation
47. Close-binding
48. Detached-hostile
49. Has not
50. Prenatal
51. Innate
52. Reduce
53. Increase
54. Stimulation
55. Deprivation
56. Irritable
57. Hallucinations
58. Concentrate
59. Acquired
60. Murray
61. Psychological
62. McClelland
63. Apperception
64. Higher
65. More
66. Independently
67. Affiliation
68. Increase
69. Share
70. Comparison
71. Ambiguous
72. Sociobiology
73. Reproduce
74. Psychodynamic (or psychoanalytic)
75. Cognitive
76. Less
77. Reinforcement
78. Higher
79. Models
80. Decrease
81. Sociocultural
82. Feeling
83. Situational
84. Responses
85. Sympathetic
86. Parasympathetic
87. Polygraphs
88. Arousal
89. Pressure
90. Electrodermal
91. 90
92. Sympathetic
93. Universal
94. Smiling
95. Ekman
96. Facial-feedback
97. Smiling
98. Aggressive
99. Cognitive
100. Arousal
101. Action
102. Responses
103. Autonomic
104. Muscular
105. Accompany
106. Arousal
107. Strong
108. Appraisal
109. Schachter
110. Cognitive

POSTTEST | Multiple Choice

1. Physiological _____ are the psychological counterparts of physiological needs.
   a. drives
   b. incentives
   c. responses
   d. behaviors

2. Inherited dispositions that activate behavior patterns designed to reach specific goals are referred to as
   a. motives.
   b. drives.
   c. instincts.
   d. releasers.

3. A reward of $1,000 for returning a wallet would serve as a(n)
   a. need.
   b. incentive.
   c. drive.
   d. social motive.

4. Drive-reduction theory has the greatest difficulty explaining
   a. seeking of sensory stimulation.
   b. the thirst drive.
   c. the hunger drive.
   d. avoidance of extremes in temperature.

5. When the ventromedial nucleus of a rat's hypothalamus is lesioned, the animal becomes
   a. hyperglycemic.
   b. hyperphagic.
   c. hypoglycemic.
   d. aphagic.

6. According to the text, _____ theory argues that people are motivated by the conscious desire for personal growth.
   a. instinct
   b. sociocultural
   c. cognitive
   d. humanistic

7. According to the text, the greatest impact of media aggression is on
   a. adults who are unaggressive.
   b. adults who are already aggressive.
   c. children who are unaggressive.
   d. children who are already aggressive.

8. All of the following except _____ are thought to contribute to the likelihood that people who view media violence will behave aggressively.
   a. inhibition
   b. increased arousal
   c. priming of aggressive thoughts and memories
   d. habituation

9. Participants in sensory-deprivation experiments are reported to have experienced all of the following *except* for
   a. boredom.
   b. irritability.
   d. hallucinations.
   d. delusions.

10. Which of the following asserts that people are motivated to achieve cognitive consistency?
    a. Clark Hull

b. Leon Festinger
c. William McDougall
d. Charles Darwin

11. The polygraph is used to detect
    a. cognitive dissonance.
    b. media violence.
    c. pangs of hunger.
    d. lies.

12. David McClelland assessed achievement motivation by using the
    a. MMPI.
    b. Rorschach inkblot test.
    c. TAT.
    d. interview.

13. Who believed that we become angry *because* we fight? That we become afraid *because* we run away from threats?
    a. Karl Lange
    b. Stanley Schachter
    c. Robert Zajonc
    d. Jerome Singer

14. Stanley Schachter explains the findings of his research into anxiety and affiliation by means of
    a. James–Lange theory.
    b. cognitive dissonance theory.
    c. the theory of social comparison.
    d. drive-reductionism.

15. According to the text, the emotion of _____ involves predominantly sympathetic arousal.
    a. depression
    b. anger
    c. acceptance
    d. fear

16. According to opponent-process theory, emotional reactions are followed by _____ when the conditions that gave rise to the first emotion change.

a. neutral feelings
b. their opposites
c. confusion
d. exaggerated forms of the initial emotion

17. It is theorized that the facial-feedback hypothesis may influence the experience of emotions in all of the following ways, with the exception of
    a. kinesthetic feedback.
    b. feedback from other people.
    c. release of neurotransmitters.
    d. modifying the person's level of arousal.

18. Which of the following noted that baring the teeth may be a universal sign of anger?
    a. Charles Darwin
    b. Robert Zajonc
    c. Stanley Schachter
    d. William James

19. A person tries to get herself out of a state of depression by engaging in behaviors that were once enjoyable. This approach to overcoming depression is most consistent with a theory proposed by
    a. William James.
    b. Walter Cannon.
    c. Henry Murray.
    d. Stanley Schachter.

20. Which of the following statements contradicts the theory of emotion proposed by Schachter and Singer?
    a. Strong arousal is associated with stronger emotions.
    b. Situations influence the experience of emotions.
    c. In ambiguous situations, we may try to determine how we should feel by observing others in the same situation.
    d. There are some reasonably distinct patterns of arousal that are not fully exchangeable.

ANSWER KEY TO POSTTEST

1. A	4. A	7. D	10. B	13. A	16. B	19. A
2. C	5. B	8. A	11. D	14. C	17. B	20. D
3. B	6. C	9. D	12. C	15. D	18. A	

Development

PRETEST *Truth or Fiction?*

_____ Fertilization takes place in the uterus.

_____ Your heart started beating when you were only one-fifth of an inch long and weighed a fraction of an ounce.

_____ The way to a baby's heart is through its stomach — that is, babies become emotionally attached to those who feed them.

_____ The highest level of moral reasoning involves relying on our own views of what is right and wrong.

_____ Girls are capable of becoming pregnant when they have their first menstrual periods.

_____ Menopause signals the end of a woman's sexual interests.

_____ Mothers suffer from the "empty-nest syndrome" when the youngest child leaves home.

_____ Most older people are dissatisfied with their lives.

_____ Older people who blame health problems on aging rather than on specific factors such as a virus are more likely to die in the near future.

O N a summerlike day in October, Ling and Patrick Chang rush out to their jobs as usual. While Ling, a buyer for a New York department store, is arranging for dresses from the Chicago manufacturer to arrive in time for the spring line, a very different drama is unfolding in her body. Hormones are causing a follicle (egg container) in one of her ovaries to rupture and release an egg cell, or ovum. Ling, like other women, possessed from birth all the egg cells she would ever have. How this ovum was selected to ripen and be released this month is unknown. But in any case, Ling will be capable of becoming pregnant for only a couple of days following ovulation.

When it is released, the ovum begins a slow journey down a 4-inch-long fallopian tube to the uterus. It is within this tube that one of Patrick's sperm cells will unite with the egg.

Truth or Fiction Revisited. *It is not true that fertilization takes place in the uterus.* Fertilization normally occurs in a fallopian tube.

Like many other couples, Ling and Patrick engaged in sexual intercourse the night before. But unlike most other couples, their timing and methodology were preplanned. Ling used a kit bought in a drugstore to predict when she would ovulate. She chemically analyzed her urine for the presence of luteinizing hormone, which surges 1 to 2 days prior to ovulation. The results suggested that Ling would be most likely to conceive today.

When Ling and Patrick made love, he ejaculated hundreds of millions of sperm, with about equal numbers of Y and X sex chromosomes. By the time of conception, only a few thousand had survived the journey to the fallopian tubes. Several bombarded the ovum, attempting to penetrate. Only one succeeded. It carried a Y sex chromosome, so the couple conceived a boy. The fertilized ovum, or **zygote,** is 1/175th of an inch across—a tiny stage for the drama yet to unfold.

Developmental psychologists would be pleased to study the development of Patrick and Ling's new son from conception throughout his lifetime. There are several reasons for this. One approach to the explanation of adult behavior lies in the discovery of early influences and developmental sequences. An answer to the question of *why* we behave in certain ways lies in outlining the development of behavior patterns over the years. There also is interest in the effects of genetics, of early interactions with parents and **siblings,** and of the school and the community on traits such as aggressiveness and intelligence.

Developmental psychologists also seek insight into the causes of developmental abnormalities. This avenue of research can contribute to children's health and psychological well-being. For instance, should pregnant women abstain from smoking and drinking? Is it safe for the **embryo** for pregnant women to take aspirin for a headache or tetracycline to ward off a bacterial invasion? Need we be concerned about placing our children in day care? What factors contribute to child abuse? Developmental psychologists are also concerned about issues in adult development. For example, what conflicts and disillusionments can we expect as we journey through our 30s, 40s, and 50s? The information acquired by developmental psychologists can help us make decisions about how we rear our children and lead our own lives.

Of course, there is another very good reason for studying development. Thousands of psychologists enjoy it.

Zygote • A fertilized ovum.
Siblings • Brothers and sisters.

CONTROVERSIES IN DEVELOPMENTAL PSYCHOLOGY

Throughout this textbook, we have seen that psychologists see things in very different ways. Diverse views give rise to controversies in developmental psychology as well.

Does Development Reflect Nature or Nurture?

There is continuing interest in sorting out what human behavior is the result of nature and of nurture. What aspects of behavior originate in a person's genes—that is, nature—and are biologically "programmed" to unfold in the child as long as minimal nutrition and social experience are provided? What aspects of behavior can be largely traced to environmental influences such as nutrition and learning—that is, nurture?

Psychologists seek to understand the influences of nature in our genetic heritage, in the functioning of the nervous system, and in the process of **maturation.** Psychologists look for the influences of nurture in our nutrition, cultural and family backgrounds, and opportunities to learn about the world, including early cognitive stimulation and formal education. The U.S. psychologist Arnold Gesell (1880–1961) leaned heavily toward natural explanations of development, arguing that all areas of development are self-regulated by the unfolding of natural plans and processes. John Watson and other behaviorists leaned heavily toward environmental explanations. (Watson, of course, was focusing primarily on adaptive behavior patterns. Gesell was focusing on many aspects of development, including physical and motor growth and development.) Today, nearly all researchers would agree, broadly speaking, that nature and nurture interact as children develop.

Embryo • (EM-bree-oh). The baby from the third through the eighth weeks following conception, during which time the major organ systems undergo rapid differentiation.

Maturation • (mat-your-RAY-shun). The orderly unfolding of traits, as regulated by the genetic code.

Stage • A distinct period of life that is qualitatively different from other stages.

Is Development Continuous or Discontinuous?

Do developmental changes occur gradually (continuously) or in major qualitative leaps (discontinuously) that dramatically alter our bodies and behavior?

Watson and other behaviorists have viewed human development as being a continuous process in which the effects of learning mount gradually, with no major sudden qualitative changes. Maturational theorists, in contrast, believe that there are a number of rapid qualitative changes that usher in new **stages** of development. Maturational theorists point out that the environment, even when enriched, profits us little until we are ready, or mature enough, to develop in a certain direction. For example, newborn babies will not imitate their parents' speech, even when parents speak clearly and deliberately. Nor does aided practice in "walking" during the first few months after birth significantly accelerate the emergence of independent walking.

Stage theorists such as Sigmund Freud (see Chapter 12) and Jean Piaget saw development as being discontinuous. Both theorists saw biological changes as providing the potential for psychological changes. Freud focused on the ways in which physical sexual developments might provide the basis for personality development. Piaget centered on the ways in which maturation of the nervous system permitted cognitive advances. Stage theorists see the sequences of development as being invariant, although they allow for individual differences in timing.

Certain aspects of physical development do appear to occur in stages. For example, from the age of 2 to the onset of **puberty,** children gradually grow larger. Then the adolescent growth spurt occurs, ushered in by hormones and characterized by rapid biological changes in structure and function (as in the development of the sex organs) as well as in size. So it would appear that a new stage of life has begun. Psychologists disagree more strongly on whether aspects of development such as cognitive development, attachment, and gender-typing occur in stages.

PHYSICAL DEVELOPMENT

Physical development includes gains in height and weight; maturation of the nervous system; and development of bones, muscles, and the sex organs. Let us first consider the physical developments that occur between conception and birth.

Prenatal Development

During the months following conception, the single cell formed by the union of sperm and egg will multiply—becoming two, then four, then eight, and so on. By the time a **fetus** is ready to be born, it will contain trillions of cells. Prenatal development is divided into three periods: the germinal stage (approximately the first 2 weeks), the embryonic stage (which lasts from 2 weeks to about 2 months after conception), and the fetal stage.

THE GERMINAL STAGE.   The zygote divides repeatedly as it proceeds on its 3- to 4-day journey to the uterus. A few days into the germinal stage, cells are separating into groups according to what they will become. What has become a ball-like mass wanders the uterus for another 3 to 4 days before beginning to implant in the uterine wall. Implantation takes another week or so. Prior to implantation, the dividing ball of cells is nourished solely by the yolk of the original egg cell, and it does not gain in mass. The period from conception to implantation is called the **germinal stage,** or the **period of the ovum.**

THE EMBRYONIC STAGE.   The embryonic stage lasts from implantation until about the eighth week of development. During this stage, the major body organ systems differentiate. Development follows two general trends—**cephalocaudal** and **proximodistal.** The growth of the head precedes the growth of the lower parts of the body. If you also think of the body as containing a central axis that coincides with the spinal cord, the growth of the organ systems close to this axis (that is, *proximal*) takes precedence over the growth of the extremities (*distal* areas). Relatively early maturation of the brain and the major organ systems allows them to participate in the nourishment and further development of the embryo.

During the third week after conception, the head and the blood vessels begin to form. During the fourth week, a primitive heart begins to beat and pump blood—in an organism that is one-fifth of an inch long. The heart will continue to beat without rest every minute of every day for perhaps 80 or 90 years.

Truth or Fiction Revisited. *It is true that your heart started beating when you were only one-fifth of an inch long and weighed a fraction of an ounce.* This occurred within a month following conception.

Puberty • (PEW-burr-tee *or* POO-burr-tee). The period of early adolescence during which hormones spur rapid physical development.

Fetus • (FEE-tuss). The baby from the third month following conception through birth, during which time there is maturation of organ systems and dramatic gains in length and weight.

Germinal stage • The first stage of prenatal development, during which the dividing mass of cells has not become implanted in the uterine wall.

Period of the ovum • Another term for the *germinal stage.*

Cephalocaudal • (SEFF-uh-lo-CAW-d'l). Proceeding from top to bottom.

Proximodistal • (PROX-ee-mo-DISS-t'l). Proceeding from near to far.

**MINILECTURE:
PRENATAL DEVELOPMENT**

An Exercise Class for Pregnant Women. Years ago, the rule of thumb was that pregnant women were not to exert themselves. Today, it is recognized that exercise is healthful for pregnant women, because it promotes cardiovascular fitness and increases muscle strength. Fitness and strength are assets during childbirth—and at other times.

Arm buds and leg buds begin to appear toward the end of the first month. Eyes, ears, nose, and mouth begin to take shape. By this time, the nervous system, including the brain, has also begun to develop.

The upper arms and legs develop first, followed by the forearms and lower legs. Next come hands and feet, followed at 6 to 8 weeks by webbed fingers and toes. By the end of the second month, the limbs are elongating and separated. The webbing is gone. The head has become rounded and the facial features distinct—all in an embryo about 1 inch long and weighing 1/30th of an ounce. During the second month, the nervous system begins to transmit messages.

By 5 to 6 weeks, the embryo is only a quarter to a half an inch long, yet nondescript sex organs have formed. By about the seventh week, the genetic code (XY or XX) begins to assert itself, causing sex organs to differentiate. If a Y sex chromosome is present, testes form and begin to produce **androgens,** which further masculinize the sex organs. Without male sex hormones, the embryo will develop female sex organs.

The embryo and fetus develop suspended within a protective **amniotic sac** in the mother's uterus. Amniotic fluid serves as a natural air bag. It allows the fetus to move or even jerk around without injury. It also helps maintain an even temperature.

The **placenta** permits the embryo (and later on, the fetus) to exchange nutrients and wastes with the mother. The placenta is unique in origin: It grows from material supplied by both mother and embryo. The fetus is connected to the placenta by the **umbilical cord.** The mother is connected to the placenta by the system of blood vessels in the uterine wall.

The circulatory systems of mother and baby do not mix. A membrane in the placenta permits only certain substances to pass through. Oxygen and nutrients are passed from the mother to the embryo. Carbon dioxide and other wastes are passed from the child to the mother, where they are removed by the mother's lungs and kidneys. Unfortunately, a number of other substances can pass through the placenta. They include some microscopic disease

Androgens • (AND-row-jennz). Male sex hormones.
Amniotic sac • (am-knee-OTT-tick). A sac within the uterus that contains the embryo or fetus.
Placenta • (pluh-SENT-uh). A membrane that permits the exchange of nutrients and waste products between the mother and her developing child but does not allow the maternal and fetal bloodstreams to mix.
Umbilical cord • (um-BILL-lick-al). A tube between the mother and her developing child through which nutrients and waste products are conducted.

organisms—such as those that cause syphilis and German measles—and some chemical agents, including drugs for acne, aspirin, narcotics, alcohol, and tranquilizers. Because these and other agents may be harmful to the embryo and fetus, pregnant women are advised to consult their physicians about the advisability of using any chemical agents, even those that are available without prescription.

THE FETAL STAGE. The fetal stage lasts from the beginning of the third month until birth. The fetus begins to turn and respond to external stimulation at about the ninth or tenth week. By the end of the third month, all the major organ systems have been formed. The fourth through sixth months are characterized by maturation of fetal organ systems and dramatic gains in size. During these months, the fetus advances from 1 *ounce* to 2 *pounds* in weight and grows three to four times in length, from about 4 to 14 inches.

In the middle of the fourth month, the mother usually detects the first fetal movements. By the end of the sixth month, the fetus moves its limbs so vigorously that the mother may complain of being kicked. The fetus opens and shuts its eyes, sucks its thumb, alternates between periods of wakefulness and sleep, and perceives light. It also turns somersaults, which can be clearly perceived by the mother. The umbilical cord is composed so that it will not break or become dangerously wrapped around the fetus, no matter how many acrobatic feats the fetus performs.

During the last 3 months, the organ systems of the fetus continue to mature. The fetus gains about 5½ pounds and doubles in length. Newborn boys average about 7½ pounds and newborn girls about 7 pounds.

Neonate • A newly born child.

Reflex • A simple unlearned response to a stimulus.

AND AFTER BIRTH . . . Within 9 months, the fetus develops from a nearly microscopic cell to a **neonate** about 20 inches in length. Weight increases by the billions. During infancy, dramatic gains continue. Babies usually double their birth weight in about 5 months and triple it by the first birthday. Their height increases by about 10 inches in the first year. Children grow another 4 to 6 inches during the second year and gain some 4 to 7 pounds.

Following the gains of infancy, children gain about 2 to 3 inches a year until they reach the adolescent growth spurt. Weight gains also remain fairly even at about 4 to 6 pounds per year.

In one of the more fascinating aspects of the development of the nervous system, newborn babies show a number of automatic behavior patterns that are essential to survival—reflexes.

Reflexes

Soon after you were born, a doctor or a nurse probably pressed her fingers against the palms of your hands. Although you would have had no "idea" as to what to do, most likely you grasped the fingers firmly—so firmly that you could actually have been lifted from your cradle by holding on! Grasping at birth is inborn, just one of the neonate's many **reflexes.** Reflexes are simple, unlearned, stereotypical responses that are elicited by specific stimuli. They do not involve higher brain functions. They occur automatically, without thinking.

Many reflexes such as the breathing reflex have survival value. The breathing rate is regulated by body levels of oxygen and carbon dioxide. We take in oxygen and give off carbon dioxide. Newborns normally take their first breath before the umbilical cord is cut. The breathing reflex continues to work for a lifetime, though we can take conscious control of breathing when we choose.

Newborn children do not "know" that it is necessary to eat to survive, so it is fortunate that they have **rooting** and sucking reflexes. Neonates will turn their heads (root) toward stimuli that prod or stroke the cheek, chin, or corners of the mouth. They will suck objects that touch their lips. Neonates reflexively withdraw from painful stimuli (the withdrawal reflex), and they draw up their legs and arch their backs in response to sudden noises, bumps, or loss of support while being held (the startle, or Moro, reflex). They reflexively grasp objects that press against the palms of their hands (the grasp, or palmar, reflex). They spread their toes when the soles of their feet are stimulated (the Babinski reflex). Babies also show sneezing, coughing, yawning, blinking, and many other reflexes. It is guaranteed that you will learn about the **sphincter** reflex if you put on your best clothes and hold an undiapered neonate on your lap for a while. Pediatricians assess the adequacy of babies' neural functioning largely by testing their reflexes.

As children develop, their muscles and neural functions mature, and they learn to coordinate sensory and motor activity. Many reflexes drop out of their storehouse of responses. Many processes, such as the elimination of wastes, come under voluntary control. Some highlights of children's motor development are chronicled in Figure 11.1.

Perceptual Development

William James (1890) wrote that the newborn baby must sense the world as "one great booming, buzzing confusion." The neonate emerges from being literally suspended in a temperature-controlled environment to being—again, in James's words—"assailed by eyes, ears, nose, skin, and entrails at once." Despite his eloquence, James may have exaggerated the disorganization of the neonate's world.

Newborn children spend about 16 hours a day sleeping and do not have much opportunity to learn about the world. Yet, they are capable of perceiving the world reasonably well soon after birth (Pick, 1991).

VISION. The **pupillary reflex** is present at birth. By the age of 3 months, infants can discriminate most, if not all, of the colors of the visible spectrum (Banks & Shannon, 1993; Teller & Lindsey, 1993). Newborns can fixate on a light. Within a couple of days, they follow, or track, a moving light with their eyes (Kellman & von Hofsten, 1992).

The lenses of the eyes of neonates do not adjust to the distance of objects. They therefore see as through a fixed-focus camera. They are nearsighted and see objects 7 to 9 inches away most clearly. By about the age of 4 months, however, infants seem able to focus about as well as adults can. Visual acuity makes dramatic gains during the first 2 months (Hainline & Abramov, 1992) and approaches adult levels by 1 year of age (Haith, 1990).

DEPTH PERCEPTION. Classic research shows that infants tend to respond to cues for depth by the time they are able to crawl (at about 6 to 8 months). Most also have the good sense to avoid crawling off ledges and table tops into open space (Campos and others, 1978). Note the setup (Figure 11.2) in the classic "visual cliff" experiment run by Walk and Gibson (1961). An 8-month-old infant crawls freely above the portion of the glass with a checkerboard pattern immediately beneath but hesitates to crawl over the portion of the glass beneath which the checkerboard has been dropped a few feet. Since the glass alone would support the infant, this is a "visual cliff," not an actual cliff.

Rooting • The turning of an infant's head toward a touch, such as by the mother's nipple.

Sphincter • (SFINK-ter). A ringlike muscle that circles a body opening such as the anus. An infant will exhibit the sphincter reflex (have a bowel movement) in response to intestinal pressure.

Pupillary reflex • (PEW-pill-air-ee). The automatic adjustment of the irises to permit more or less light to enter the eye.

MINILECTURE: DEVELOPMENT OF VISUAL ACUITY

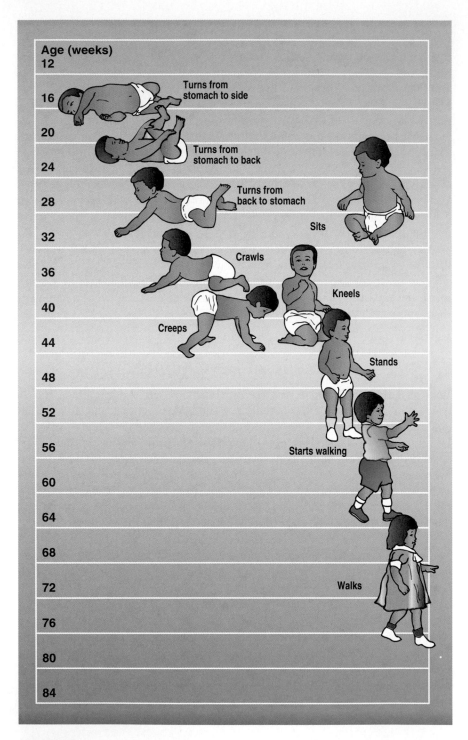

Age (weeks)
12
16 — Turns from stomach to side
20
24 — Turns from stomach to back
28 — Turns from back to stomach
— Sits
32 — Crawls
36 — Kneels
40 — Creeps
44 — Stands
48
52
56 — Starts walking
60
64
68
72 — Walks
76
80
84

FIGURE 11.1

Motor Development in Infancy. At birth, infants appear to be bundles of aimless "nervous energy." They have reflexive responses, but they also engage in random movements. Random movement is replaced by purposeful activity as they mature. Motor development proceeds in an orderly sequence. Practice prompts sensorimotor coordination, but maturation is essential. During the first 6 months, cells in the motor and sensorimotor areas of the brain mature to allow activities such as crawling and, later, walking. The times in the figure are approximate: An infant who is a bit behind may develop with no problems at all. A precocious infant will not necessarily become a rocket scientist (or gymnast).

FIGURE 11.2

The Classic Visual Cliff Experiment. This young explorer has the good sense not to crawl out onto an apparently unsupported surface, even when Mother beckons from the other side. Rats, pups, kittens, and chicks also will not try to walk across to the other side. (So don't bother asking why the chicken crossed the visual cliff.)

HEARING. Months before they are born, fetuses respond to sounds. Normal neonates reflexively turn their heads toward unusual sounds and suspend other activities. This finding, along with findings about visual tracking, suggests that infants are preprogrammed to survey their environments. Neonates are more responsive to high-pitched than low-pitched sounds. On the other hand, speaking or singing softly in a low-pitched voice soothes infants (Papousek and others, 1991). This is well-known to parents who use lullabies to get infants to sleep (Trehub and others, 1993).

Babies a few days old prefer their mothers' voices to those of other women, but they do not show similar preferences for the voices of their fathers (De-Casper & Prescott, 1984; Freeman and others, 1993). By birth, of course, fetuses have had many months of "experience" in the uterus. For at least 2 or 3 months, they have been capable of sensing sounds. Because they are predominantly exposed to sounds produced by their mothers, learning may contribute to neonatal preferences.

SMELL: THE NOSE KNOWS EARLY. The nasal preferences of babies are similar to those of adults. Newborn infants spit, stick out their tongues, and literally wrinkle their noses at the odor of rotten eggs. But they smile and show licking motions in response to chocolate, strawberry, vanilla, and honey.

The sense of smell, like the sense of hearing, may provide a vehicle for mother–infant recognition. By 15 days, nursing infants prefer their mothers' underarm odors to those of other women (Porter and others, 1992). Bottle-fed babies do not show this preference.

TASTE. Shortly after birth, infants show the ability to discriminate taste. They suck liquid solutions of sugar and milk but grimace and refuse to suck salty or bitter solutions. Sweet solutions tend to calm newborns (Blass & Smith, 1992). The tongue pressure of 1-day-old infants sucking on a nipple correlates with the amount of sugar in their liquid diet.

SKIN SENSES.   Newborn babies are sensitive to touch. Many reflexes (rooting and sucking are two) are activated by pressure against the skin. Newborns are relatively insensitive to pain, however, which may be adaptive considering the squeezing of the birth process. Sensitivity increases dramatically within a few days.

The skin senses are an extremely important avenue of learning and communication for babies. Sensations of skin against skin also appear to provide feelings of comfort and security that may contribute to the formation of affectionate bonds between infants and caregivers.

Attachment • The enduring affectional tie that binds one person to another.

Reflections

- Agree or disagree with the following statement and support your answer: "Human development is self-regulated by the unfolding of natural plans and processes."
- How can you make use of knowledge of prenatal development in your own life?
- What are your beliefs concerning *why* newborn babies have reflexes that drop out as the weeks and months proceed?
- Agree or disagree with the following statement and support your answer: "The newborn baby must sense the world as 'one great booming, buzzing confusion.'"

SOCIAL DEVELOPMENT

At the age of 2, my daughter Allyn almost succeeded at preventing publication of an earlier edition of this book. When I locked myself into my study, she positioned herself outside the door and called, "Daddy, oh Daddy." Next came, "Pencer, oh Pencer." At other times, she would bang on the door or cry outside. When I would give in (several times a day) and open the door, she would run in and say, "I want you to pick up me" and hold out her arms or climb into my lap. Then she would say, "I want to play." I would beg, "I'm in the middle of something. Just give me a second to finish it." Then, when I would look back at my monitor, she would try to turn my face to hers or turn the computer off. Or, if I were trying to jot down some notes from a journal, she would try to yank them from my hands and toss them across the room. (I have sometimes wanted to do that to the journals, too.) Although we were separate human beings, it was as though she were very much *attached* to me.

I am a psychologist. Solutions thus came easily. For example, I could write outside the home. But this solution had the drawback of distancing me from my family. Another solution was to let my daughter cry and ignore her. If I refused to reinforce crying, crying would become extinguished. There were only two problems with this solution. First, I was incapable of ignoring her crying. Second, I didn't *want* to extinguish her efforts to get to me. Feelings of attachment, you see, are a two-way street.

Mary D. Salter Ainsworth (1989), a preeminent researcher in attachment, defines **attachment** as an emotional tie that is formed between one animal or person and another specific individual. Attachment keeps organisms together and tends to endure. Attachment is essential to the very survival of the infant (Bowlby, 1988).

Allyn. When she was 2 years old, the author's daughter Allyn nearly succeeded in preventing the publication of an earlier edition of this book by pulling him away from the computer while he was at work. Because of their mutual attachment, separation was painful. According to Ainsworth, attachment is an emotional bond between one animal or person and another specific individual. Secure attachment paves the way for healthy social development.

The behaviors that define attachment include (1) attempts to maintain contact or nearness and (2) shows of anxiety when separated. Babies and children try to maintain contact with caregivers to whom they are attached. They engage in eye contact, pull and tug at them, ask to be picked up, and may even jump in front of them in such a way that they will be "run over" if they are not picked up!

Attachment is one measure of the care that infants receive. The mothers of securely attached children are more likely to be affectionate and reliable caregivers (Cox and others, 1992; Isabella, 1993). **Securely attached** children are happier, more sociable with unfamiliar adults, more cooperative with parents, and get along better with peers than do **insecurely attached** children (Belsky and others, 1991; Thompson, 1991a). Securely attached preschoolers have longer attention spans, are less impulsive, and better at solving problems (Frankel & Bates, 1990; Lederberg & Mobley, 1990). At ages 5 and 6, securely attached children are liked better by their peers and teachers, are more competent, and have fewer behavior problems than insecurely attached peers (Lyons-Ruth and others, 1993; Youngblade & Belsky, 1992).

STAGES OF ATTACHMENT. The study of attachment is greatly indebted to the individual and collaborative efforts of Mary Ainsworth and John Bowlby (1991), whose "partnership [has] endured for 40 years across time and distance" (p. 333). In a review of their research, they refer to critical cross-cultural studies such as one conducted by Ainsworth in Uganda, which led to a theory of stages of attachment.

Ainsworth tracked the attachment behaviors of Ugandan infants. She noted their efforts to maintain contact with the mother, their protests when separated, and their use of the mother as a base for exploring the environment. At first, the Ugandan infants showed **indiscriminate attachment.** That is, they preferred being held or being with someone to being alone, but they showed no preferences. Specific attachment to the mother began to develop at about 4 months of age and grew intense by about 7 months of age. Fear of strangers, if it developed at all, followed by 1 or 2 months.

From studies such as these, Mary Ainsworth identified three stages of attachment:

1. The **initial-preattachment phase,** which lasts from birth to about 3 months and is characterized by indiscriminate attachment.

2. The **attachment-in-the-making phase,** which occurs at about 3 or 4 months and is characterized by preference for familiar figures.

3. The **clear-cut-attachment phase,** which occurs at about 6 or 7 months and is characterized by intensified dependence on the primary caregiver— usually the mother.

Bowlby noted that children's attachment behaviors are also characterized by fear of strangers ("stranger anxiety"). But not all children show fear of strangers.

Theories of Attachment

Attachment, like so many other behavior patterns, seems to develop as a result of the interaction of nature and nurture.

A BEHAVIORAL VIEW OF ATTACHMENT: MOTHER AS A REINFORCER. Early in the century, behaviorists argued that attachment behaviors are learned through conditioning. Caregivers feed their infants and tend to their other physiological

Secure attachment • A type of attachment characterized by positive feelings toward attachment figures and feelings of security.
Insecure attachment • A negative type of attachment, in which children show indifference or ambivalence toward attachment figures.
Indiscriminate attachment • Showing attachment behaviors toward any person.
Initial-preattachment phase • The first phase in forming bonds of attachment, characterized by indiscriminate attachment.
Attachment-in-the-making phase • The second phase in forming bonds of attachment, characterized by preference for familiar figures.
Clear-cut-attachment phase • The third phase in forming bonds of attachment, characterized by intensified dependence on the primary caregiver.

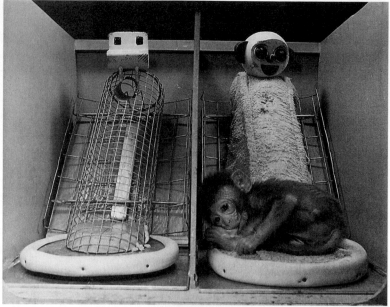

FIGURE 11.3

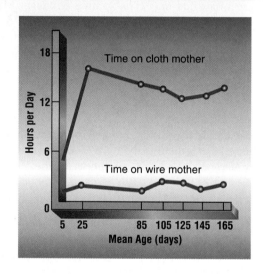

Attachment in Infant Monkeys.
Although this rhesus monkey infant is fed by the "wire mother," it spends most of its time clinging to the soft, cuddly "terry-cloth mother." It knows where to get a meal, but contact comfort is apparently a more central determinant of attachment in infant monkeys (and infant humans?) than is the feeding process.

Contact comfort • A hypothesized primary drive to seek physical comfort through contact with another.

Critical period • A period of time when a fixed-action pattern can be elicited by a releasing stimulus.

Imprinting • A process occurring during a critical period in the development of an organism, in which that organism responds to a stimulus in a manner that will afterward be difficult to modify.

needs. Thus, infants associate their caregivers with gratification and learn to approach them to meet their needs. From this perspective, a caregiver becomes a conditioned reinforcer. The feelings of gratification that are associated with meeting basic needs generalize into feelings of security when the caregiver is present.

HARLOW'S VIEW OF ATTACHMENT: MOTHER AS A SOURCE OF CONTACT COMFORT. Classic research by psychologist Harry F. Harlow casts doubt on the behaviorist view that attachment is learned mechanically. Harlow had noted that infant rhesus monkeys reared without mothers or companions became attached to pieces of cloth in their cages. They maintained contact with them and showed distress when separated from them. Harlow conducted a series of experiments to find out why (Harlow, 1959).

In one study, Harlow placed rhesus monkey infants in cages with two surrogate mothers, as shown in Figure 11.3. One "mother" was made from wire mesh from which a baby bottle was extended. The other surrogate mother was made of soft, cuddly terry cloth. Infant monkeys spent most of their time clinging to the cloth mother, even though "she" did not gratify the need for food (see Figure 11.3). Harlow concluded that monkeys—and perhaps humans—have a primary (unlearned) need for **contact comfort** that is as basic as the need for food. Gratification of the need for contact comfort, rather than food, might be why infant monkeys (and humans) cling to their mothers.

Truth or Fiction Revisited. *It is not true that the way to a baby's heart is through its stomach. That is, babies do not necessarily become emotionally attached to those who feed them.* Contact comfort may be a stronger wellspring of attachment. Let's put it another way: The path to a monkey's heart may be through its skin, not its stomach.

Harlow and Zimmerman (1959) found that a surrogate mother made of terry cloth could also serve as a comforting base from which a rhesus infant could explore the environment. Toys such as stuffed bears (see Figure 11.4) and oversized wooden insects were placed in cages with rhesus infants and their surrogate mothers. When the infants were alone or had wire surrogate mothers for companions, they cowered in fear as long as the "bear monster" or "insect monster" was present. But when the terry-cloth mothers were present, the infants clung to them for a while, then explored the intruding "monster." With human infants, too, bonds of mother–infant attachment appear to provide a secure base from which infants feel encouraged to express their curiosity motives.

IMPRINTING: AN ETHOLOGICAL VIEW OF ATTACHMENT. Ethologists note that for many animals, attachment is an inborn fixed action pattern (FAP). The FAP of attachment, like other FAPs, is theorized to occur in the presence of a species-specific releasing stimulus and during a **critical period** of life.

Some animals become attached to the first moving object they encounter. The unwritten rule seems to be "If it moves, it must be mother." It is as if the image of the moving object becomes "imprinted" on the young animal, and so the formation of an attachment in this manner is called **imprinting.**

Ethologist Konrad Lorenz (1981) became well known when pictures of his "family" of goslings were made public (see Figure 11.5). How did Lorenz acquire his following? He was present when the goslings hatched, during their

FIGURE 11.4

Security. With its terry-cloth surrogate mother nearby, this infant rhesus monkey apparently feels secure enough to explore the "bear monster" placed in its cage. But infants with only wire surrogate mothers, or with no mothers, remain cowering in a corner when the bear or other "monsters" are introduced.

FIGURE 11.5

Imprinting. Quite a following? Konrad Lorenz may not look like Mommy to you, but these goslings became attached to him because he was the first moving object they perceived and followed. This type of attachment process is referred to as *imprinting.*

critical periods, and he allowed them to follow him. The critical period for geese and some other animals is bounded, at the younger end, by the age at which they first engage in locomotion and, at the older end, by the age at which they develop fear of strangers. The goslings followed Lorenz persistently, ran to him when frightened, honked with distress at his departure, and tried to overcome barriers between them. If you substitute crying for honking, it all sounds rather human.

If imprinting occurs with children, it does not follow the mechanics that apply to waterfowl. Not all children develop fear of strangers. When they do, it occurs at about 6 to 8 months of age—*prior to* independent locomotion, or crawling, which usually occurs 1 or 2 months later. Yet, Ainsworth and Bowlby (1991) also hold an ethological view of human attachment. However, the critical period with humans would be extensive.

Reflections

- How would you characterize your own attachment to the parent figures in your life? How did your feelings of attachment affect your behavior as a child?

COGNITIVE DEVELOPMENT

The developing thought processes of children—their cognitive development—is explored in this section. Cognitive functioning develops over a number of years, and children have ideas about the world that differ considerably from those of adults. Many of these ideas are charming but illogical. Swiss psychologist Jean Piaget (1896–1980) contributed significantly to our understanding of children's cognitive development.

Jean Piaget's Cognitive-Developmental Theory

Piaget is more than a historical figure, large as he looms in the historical landscape of developmental psychology. His theory is still very much a contending presence in the free-for-all that defines current psychological theorizing.

HARRY BEILIN (1992)

In his early 20s, Jean Piaget obtained a job at the Binet Institute in Paris. His initial task was to develop a standardized version of the Binet intelligence test in French. In so doing, he questioned many children using potential items and became intrigued by their *incorrect* answers. Another investigator might have shrugged them off and forgotten them. Young Piaget realized that there were methods to his children's madness. The wrong answers reflected consistent, if illogical, cognitive processes.

Piaget (1963) hypothesized that children's cognitive processes develop in an orderly sequence of stages. Although some children may be more advanced than others at particular ages, the developmental sequence is invariant. Piaget identified four major stages of cognitive development (see Table 11.1): sensorimotor, preoperational, concrete operational, and formal operational.

Piaget regarded children as natural physicists who actively intend to learn about and manipulate their worlds. In the Piagetan view, children who squish their food and laugh enthusiastically, for example, are often acting as budding scientists. In addition to enjoying a response from parents, they are studying the texture and consistency of their food. (Parents, of course, often wish that

TABLE 11.1
PIAGET'S STAGES OF COGNITIVE DEVELOPMENT

STAGE	APPROXIMATE AGE	DESCRIPTION
Sensorimotor	Birth–2 years	Behavior suggests that child lacks language and does not use symbols or mental representations of objects in the environment. Simple responding to the environment (through reflexive schemes) draws to an end, and intenional behavior—such as making interesting sights last—begins. The child develops the object concept and acquires the basics of language.
Preoperational	2–7 years	The child begins to represent the world mentally, but thought is egocentric. The child does not focus on two aspects of a situation at once and therefore lacks conservation. The child shows animism, artificialism, and immanent justice.
Concrete operational	7–12	The child shows conservation concepts, can adopt the viewpoint of others, can classify objects in series (for example, from shortest to longest), and shows comprehension of basic relational concepts (such as one object being larger or heavier than another).
Formal operational	12 years and above	Mature, adult thought emerges. Thinking seems to be characterized by deductive logic, consideration of various possibilities before acting to solve a problem (mental trial and error), abstract thought (for example, philosophical weighing of moral principles), and the formation and testing of hypotheses.

their children would practice these experiments in the laboratory, not the dining room.)

Piaget's view differs markedly from the behaviorist view that people merely react to environmental stimuli rather than intending to interpret and act on the world. Piaget saw people as actors, not reactors. Piaget believed that people purposefully form cognitive representations of, and seek to manipulate, the world.

PIAGET'S BASIC CONCEPTS: ASSIMILATION AND ACCOMMODATION. Piaget described human thought or intelligence in terms of *assimilation* and *accommodation*. **Assimilation** is responding to a new stimulus through a reflex or existing habit. Infants, for example, usually try to place new objects in their mouths to suck, feel, or explore. Piaget would say that the child is assimilating a new toy to the sucking **scheme.** A scheme is a pattern of action or a mental structure that is involved in acquiring or organizing knowledge.

Accommodation is the creation of new ways of responding to objects or looking at the world. In accommodation, children transform existing schemes—action patterns or ways of organizing knowledge—in order to incorporate new events. Children (and adults) accommodate to objects and situations that cannot be integrated into existing schemes. The ability to accommodate to novel stimulation advances as a result of maturation and experience.

Most of the time, newborn children assimilate environmental stimulation according to reflexive schemes, although adjusting the mouth to contain the nipple is a primitive kind of accommodation. Reflexive behavior, to Piaget, is not characteristic of "true" intelligence. True intelligence involves adapting to the world through a smooth, fluid balancing of the processes of assimilation and

Assimilation • (as SIM-mc-LAY-shun). According to Piaget, the inclusion of a new event into an existing scheme.

Scheme • According to Piaget, a hypothetical mental structure that permits the classification and organization of new information.

Accommodation • (ack-KOM-me-DAY-shun). According to Piaget, the modification of schemes so that information inconsistent with existing schemes can be integrated or understood.

MINILECTURE:
OBJECT PERMANENCE

accommodation (Beilin, 1992). Let us now return to the stages of cognitive development.

THE SENSORIMOTOR STAGE.

The newborn infant is capable of assimilating novel stimulation only to existing reflexes (or ready-made schemes) such as the rooting and sucking reflexes. But by the time an infant reaches the age of 1 month, it will already show purposeful behavior by repeating behavior patterns that are pleasurable, such as sucking its hand. During the first month or so, an infant apparently does not connect stimulation perceived through different senses. Crude turning toward sources of auditory and olfactory stimulation has a ready-made look about it that cannot be considered purposeful searching. But within the first few months, the infant begins to coordinate vision with grasping so that it simultaneously looks at what it is holding or touching.

A 3- or 4-month-old infant may be fascinated by its own hands and legs. It may become absorbed in watching itself open and close its fists. The infant becomes increasingly interested in acting on the environment to make interesting results (such as the sound of a rattle) last. Behavior becomes increasingly intentional and purposeful. Between 4 and 8 months of age, the infant explores cause-and-effect relationships such as the thump that can be made by tossing an object or the way kicking can cause a hanging toy to bounce.

Prior to the age of 6 months or so, out of sight is literally out of mind. Objects are not yet mentally represented. For this reason, as you can see in Figure 11.6, a child will make no effort to search for an object that has been removed or placed behind a screen. By the ages of 8 to 12 months, however, infants realize that objects removed from sight still exist and attempt to find them. In this way, they show what is known as **object permanence.**

During the second year of life, children begin to show interest in how things are constructed. It may be for this reason that they persistently touch and finger their parents' and their own faces. Toward the end of the second year, children begin to engage in mental trial and error before they try out overt behavior. For instance, when they look for an object you have removed, they will no longer begin their search in the last place it was seen. Rather, they may follow you, assuming that you are carrying the object even though it is not visible. It is as though they are anticipating failure in searching for the object in the place where it was most recently seen.

Because the first stage of development is dominated by learning to coordinate perception of the self and of the environment with motor (muscular) activity, Piaget termed it the **sensorimotor stage.** The sensorimotor stage comes to a close at about the age of 2, with the acquisition of the basics of language.

THE PREOPERATIONAL STAGE.

When Tony gets little, I'll marry him, okay?

THE AUTHOR'S DAUGHTER TAYLOR, AT AGE 2 YEARS 10 MONTHS. (TONY WAS A WAITER AT A RESTAURANT.)

The **preoperational stage** is characterized by children's early use of words and symbols to represent objects and the relationships among them. But be warned—any resemblance between the logic of children between the ages of 2 to 7 and your own logic very often appears to be purely coincidental. Children may use the same words as adults do, but this does not mean that their views of the world are similar to adults'. A major limit on preoperational children's thinking is that it tends to be one-dimensional—to focus on one aspect of a problem or situation at a time.

One consequence of one-dimensional thinking is **egocentrism.** Preoperational children cannot understand that other people do not see things as they

Object permanence • Recognition that objects removed from sight still exist, as demonstrated in young children by continued pursuit.

Sensorimotor stage • The first of Piaget's stages of cognitive development, characterized by coordination of sensory information and motor activity, early exploration of the environment, and lack of language.

Preoperational stage • The second of Piaget's stages, characterized by illogical use of words and symbols, spotty logic, and egocentrism.

Egocentric • (ee-go-SENT-trick). According to Piaget, assuming that others view the world as one does oneself.

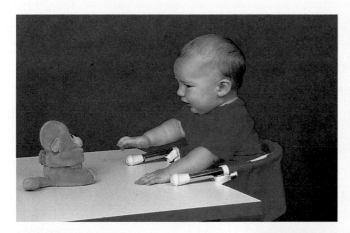
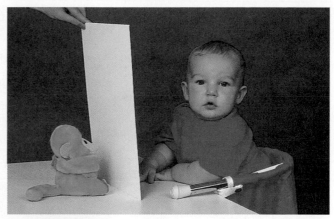

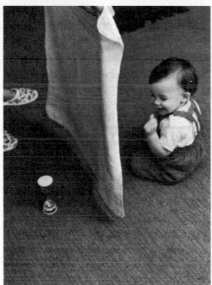

FIGURE 11.6

Object Permanence. To the infant at the top, who is in the early part of the sensorimotor stage, out of sight is truly out of mind. Once a sheet of paper is placed between the infant and the toy monkey, the infant loses all interest in the toy. From evidence of this sort, Piaget concluded that the toy is not mentally represented. The bottom series of photos shows a child in a later part of the sensorimotor stage. This child does mentally represent objects and pushes through a towel to reach an object that has been screened from sight.

Animism • The belief that inanimate objects move because of will or spirit.

Artificialism • The belief that natural objects have been created by human beings.

do. When Allyn was 2½, I asked her to tell me about a trip to the store with her mother. "You tell me," she replied. Upon questioning, it seemed that she did not understand that I could not see the world through her eyes.

To egocentric preoperational children, all the world's a stage that has been erected to meet their needs and amuse them. When asked, "Why does the sun shine?" they may say, "To keep me warm." If asked, "Why is the sky blue?" they may respond, "'Cause blue's my favorite color." Preoperational children also show **animism.** They attribute life and consciousness to physical objects like the sun and the moon (Beilin, 1992). They also show **artificialism.** They believe that environmental events like rain and thunder are human inventions (Beilin, 1992). Asked why the sky is blue, 4-year-olds may answer, "'Cause

TABLE 11.2
EXAMPLES OF PREOPERATIONAL THOUGHT

TYPE OF THOUGHT	SAMPLE QUESTIONS	TYPICAL ANSWERS
Egocentrism	Why does it get dark out?	So I can go to sleep.
	Why does the sun shine?	To keep me warm.
	Why is there snow?	For me to play in.
	Why is grass green?	Because that's my favorite color.
	What are TV sets for?	To watch my favorite shows and cartoons.
Animism (attributing life and consciousness to physical objects)	Why do trees have leaves?	To keep them warm.
	Why do stars twinkle?	Because they're happy and cheerful.
	Why does the sun move in the sky?	To follow children and hear what they say.
	Where do boats go at night?	They sleep like we do.
Artificialism (assuming that environmental events are human inventions)	What makes it rain?	Someone emptying a watering can.
	Why is the sky blue?	Somebody painted it.
	What is the wind?	A man blowing.
	What causes thunder?	A man grumbling.
	How does a baby get in Mommy's tummy?	Just make it first. (How?) You put some eyes on it, put the head on (etc.).

Conservation • According to Piaget, recognition that basic properties of substances such as weight and mass remain the same when superficial features change.

Center • According to Piaget, to focus one's attention.

Mommy painted it." Examples of egocentrism, animism, and artificialism are shown in Table 11.2.

To gain further insight into preoperational thinking, consider these problems:

1. Imagine that you pour water from a tall, thin glass into a low, wide glass. Now, does the low, wide glass contain more, less, or the same amount of water as was in the tall, thin glass? I won't keep you in suspense. If you said the same amount of water (with possible minor exceptions for spillage and evaporation), you were correct. Now that you're rolling, here is the other problem:

2. If you flatten a ball of clay into a pancake, do you wind up with more, less, or the same amount of clay? If you said the same amount of clay, you are correct once more.

To arrive at the correct answers to these questions, you must understand the law of **conservation.** This law holds that basic properties of substances such as mass, weight, and volume remain the same—or are *conserved*—when you change superficial properties such as their shape or arrangement.

Conservation requires the ability to think about, or **center** on, two aspects of a situation at once, such as height and width. Conserving the mass, weight, or volume of a substance requires recognition that a change in one dimension can compensate for a change in another. But the preoperational boy in Figure 11.7 focuses on just one dimension at a time. First, he is shown two tall, thin

FIGURE 11.7

Conservation. The boy in these photographs agreed that the amount of water in two identical containers is equal. He then watched as water from one container was poured into a tall, thin container. In the left-hand photograph, he is examining one of the original containers and the new container. When asked whether he thinks that the amounts of water in the two containers are now the same, he says no. Apparently, he is impressed by the height of the new container, and, prior to the development of conservation, he focuses on only one dimension of the situation at a time—in this case, the height of the new container.

glasses of water and agrees that they have the same amount of water. Then, while he watches, water is poured from one tall glass into a squat glass. Now, he is asked which glass has more water. After mulling over the problem, he points to the tall glass. Why? When he looks at the glasses, he is "overwhelmed" by the fact that the thinner glass is taller. The preoperational child focuses on the most apparent dimension of the situation—in this case, the greater height of the thinner glass. He does not realize that the gain in width in the squat glass compensates for the loss in height. By the way, if you ask him whether any water has been added or taken away in the pouring process, he will readily reply no. But if you then repeat the question about which glass has *more* water, he will again point to the taller glass.

If all this sounds rather illogical, that is because it is illogical—or to be precise, preoperational.

After you have tried the experiment with the water, try the following. Make two rows with five pennies each. In the first row, place the pennies about half an inch apart. In the second row, place the pennies 2 to 3 inches apart. Ask a 4- to 5-year-old child which row has more pennies. What do you think the child will say? Why?

Piaget (1962) found that the moral judgment of preoperational children is also one-dimensional. Five-year-olds are slaves to rules and authority. When you ask them why something should be done in a certain way, they may insist "Because that's the way to do it!" or "Because my Mommy says so!" Right is right and wrong is wrong. Why? "Because!"—that's why.

 **MINILECTURE: CONSERVATION**

According to most older children and adults, an act is a crime only when there is criminal intent. Accidents may be hurtful, but the perpetrators are usually seen as blameless. But in the court of the one-dimensional, preoperational child, there is **objective responsibility.** People are sentenced (and harshly!) on the basis of the amount of damage they have done, not their motive or intentions.

To demonstrate objective responsibility, Piaget would tell children stories and ask them which character was naughtier and why. John, for instance, accidentally breaks 15 cups when he opens a door. Henry breaks one cup when he sneaks into a kitchen cabinet to find forbidden jam. The preoperational child usually judges John to be naughtier. Why? He broke more cups.

THE CONCRETE-OPERATIONAL STAGE.   By about the age of 7, the typical child is entering the stage of **concrete operations.** In this stage, which lasts until about the age of 12, children show the beginnings of the capacity for adult logic. However, their logical thought, or operations, generally involves tangible objects rather than abstract ideas. Concrete operational children are capable of **decentration.** They can center simultaneously on two dimensions of a problem. This attainment has implications for moral judgments, conservation, and other intellectual undertakings.

Children now become **subjective** in their moral judgments. They center on the motives of wrongdoers as well as the amount of damage done when assigning guilt. Concrete-operational children judge Henry more harshly than John, since John's misdeed was an accident.

Concrete-operational children understand the laws of conservation. The boy in Figure 11.7, now a few years older, would say that the squat glass still has the same amount of water. If asked why, he might reply, "Because you can pour it back into the other one." An answer to this effect also suggests awareness of the concept of **reversibility**—recognition that many processes can be reversed or undone so that things can be restored to their previous condition. Centering simultaneously on the height and the width of the glasses, the boy recognizes that the loss in height compensates for the gain in width.

Concrete-operational children can conserve *number* as well as weight and mass. They recognize that there is the same number of pennies in each of the rows described earlier, even though one row may be spread out to look longer than the other.

Children in this stage are less egocentric. They are able to take on the roles of others and to view the world, and themselves, from other peoples' perspectives. They recognize that people see things in different ways because of different situations and different sets of values.

During the concrete-operational stage, children's own sets of values begin to emerge and acquire stability. Children come to understand that feelings of love between them and their parents can endure even when someone feels angry or disappointed at the moment.

THE FORMAL-OPERATIONAL STAGE.   The stage of **formal operations** is the final stage in Piaget's theory. It begins at about the time of puberty and is the stage of cognitive maturity. Not all children enter this stage at puberty, and some people never reach it.

Formal-operational children (and adults) think abstractly. They become capable of solving geometric problems about circles and squares without reference to what the circles and squares may represent in the real world. Children derive rules for behavior from general principles and can focus, or center, on

---

Objective responsibility • According to Piaget, the assignment of blame according to the amount of damage done rather than the motives of the actor.

Concrete-operational stage • Piaget's third stage, characterized by logical thought concerning tangible objects, conservation, and subjective morality.

Decentration • (DEE-sent-TRAY-shun). Simultaneous focusing on more than one dimension of a problem, so that flexible, reversible thought becomes possible.

Subjective moral judgment • According to Piaget, moral judgments that are based on the motives of the perpetrator.

Reversibility • According to Piaget, recognition that processes can be undone, that things can be made as they were.

Formal-operational stage • Piaget's fourth stage, characterized by abstract logical thought; deduction from principles.

many aspects of a situation at once in arriving at judgments and solving problems.

In a sense, it is during the stage of formal operations that people tend to emerge as theoretical scientists—even though they may see themselves as having little or no interest in science. They become capable of dealing with hypothetical situations. They realize that situations can have different outcomes, and they think ahead, experimenting with different possibilities. Children— adolescents by now—also conduct experiments to determine whether their hypotheses are correct. These experiments are not conducted in the laboratory. Rather, adolescents may try out different tones of voice, ways of carrying themselves, and ways of treating others to see what works best for them.

Children in this stage can reason deductively, or draw conclusions about specific objects or people once they have been classified accurately. Adolescents can be somewhat proud of their new logical abilities. A new sort of egocentrism can develop in which adolescents emotionally press for acceptance of their logic without recognition of the exceptions or practical problems that are often considered by adults. Consider this example: "It is wrong to hurt people. Industry A occasionally hurts people (perhaps through pollution or economic pressures). Therefore, Industry A must be severely punished or dismantled." This thinking is logical. By impatiently pressing for immediate major changes or severe penalties, however, one may not fully consider various practical problems such as thousands of resultant layoffs.

EVALUATION OF PIAGET'S COGNITIVE-DEVELOPMENTAL THEORY. A number of questions, such as the following, have been raised concerning the accuracy of Piaget's views:

1. *Was Piaget's timing accurate?* Some critics argue that Piaget's methodology led him to underestimate the abilities of children. U.S. researchers have used different methods and have found, for example, that preschoolers are less egocentric and that children are capable of conservation at earlier ages than Piaget's research suggested. On the other hand, Piaget himself admitted that the ages at which his subjects showed certain developments were a function of the methods he used (Beilin, 1992). Piaget himself was not locked into particular age norms.

2. *Is cognitive development discontinuous?* The most damaging criticism leveled at Piaget is that cognitive skills such as egocentrism and conservation appear to develop more continuously than Piaget thought—rather than in stages. Flavell and his colleagues (1993) argue that cognitive development does *not* appear to be very stagelike. Although cognitive developments appear to build on other cognitive developments, the process may be more gradual than discontinuous.

3. *Are developmental sequences invariant?* Here, Piaget's views have fared better. It seems that the sequences of development are indeed invariant, as Piaget believed. I also think it is fair to say that the sequences of development might be more essential to Piaget's theory than their timing.

In sum, Piaget's theoretical edifice has been rocked, but it has not been dashed to rubble. Research continues to wear away at his timing and at his belief that the stages of cognitive development are discontinuous, but his views on the sequences of development remain relatively inviolate.

Let us now turn our attention to Lawrence Kohlberg's theory of moral development and see how children process information that leads to judgments of right and wrong.

Lawrence Kohlberg's
Theory of Moral Development

Psychologist Lawrence Kohlberg (1981) originated a cognitive-developmental theory of children's moral reasoning. Before we describe Kohlberg's views, read the following tale he used in his research and answer the questions that follow.

> In Europe a woman was near death from a special kind of cancer. There was one drug that the doctors thought might save her. It was a form of radium that a druggist in the same town had recently discovered. The drug was expensive to make, but the druggist was charging ten times what the drug cost him to make. He paid $200 for the radium and charged $2,000 for a small dose of the drug. The sick woman's husband, Heinz, went to everyone he knew to borrow the money, but he could only get together about $1,000, which was half of what it cost. He told the druggist that his wife was dying and asked him to sell it cheaper or let him pay later. But the druggist said: "No, I discovered the drug and I'm going to make money from it." So Heinz got desperate and broke into the man's store to steal the drug for his wife. (Kohlberg, 1969)

What do you think? Should Heinz have tried to steal the drug? Was he right or wrong? As you can see from Table 11.3, the issue is more complicated than a simple yes or no. Heinz is caught up in a moral dilemma in which a legal or social rule (in this case, laws against stealing) is pitted against a strong human need (Heinz's desire to save his wife). According to Kohlberg's theory, children and adults arrive at yes or no answers for different reasons. These reasons can be classified according to the level of moral development they reflect.

As a stage theorist, Kohlberg argues that the stages of moral reasoning follow an invariant sequence. Children progress at different rates, and not all children (or adults) reach the highest stage. But children must go through stage 1 before they enter stage 2, and so on. According to Kohlberg, there are three levels of moral development and two stages within each level.

Preconventional level • According to Kohlberg, a period during which moral judgments are based largely on expectation of rewards or punishments.

Conventional level • According to Kohlberg, a period during which moral judgments largely reflect social conventions. A "law-and-order" approach to morality.

THE PRECONVENTIONAL LEVEL. The **preconventional level** applies to most children through about the age of 9. Children at this level base moral judgments on the consequences of behavior. For instance, stage 1 is oriented toward obedience and punishment. Good behavior is obedient and allows one to avoid punishment.

In stage 2, good behavior allows people to satisfy their needs and those of others. (Heinz's wife needs the drug. Therefore, stealing the drug—the only way of attaining it—is not wrong.)

THE CONVENTIONAL LEVEL. In the **conventional level** of moral reasoning, right and wrong are judged by conformity to conventional (family, church, societal) standards of right and wrong. According to the stage 3 "good-boy orientation," it is moral to meet the needs and expectations of others. Moral behavior is what is "normal"—what the majority does. (Heinz should steal the drug because that is what a "good husband" would do. It is "natural" or "normal" to try to help one's wife. Or, Heinz should *not* steal the drug because "good people do not steal.")

In stage 4, moral judgments are based on rules that maintain the social order. Showing respect for authority and doing one's duty are valued highly. (Heinz must steal the drug. It would be his responsibility if he let his wife die.

TABLE 11.3
KOHLBERG'S LEVELS AND STAGES OF MORAL DEVELOPMENT

STAGE OF DEVELOPMENT	EXAMPLES OF MORAL REASONING THAT SUPPORT HEINZ'S STEALING THE DRUG	EXAMPLES OF MORAL REASONING THAT OPPOSE HEINZ'S STEALING THE DRUG
LEVEL I: PRECONVENTIONAL		
Stage 1: Judgments guided by obedience and the prospect of punishment (The consequences of the behavior.)	It isn't wrong to take the drug. After all, Heinz tried to pay the druggist for it, and it's worth only $200, not $2,000.	It's wrong to take the drug because taking things without paying is against the law; Heinz will get caught and go to jail.
Stage 2: Naively egoistic, instrumental orientation (Things are right when they satisfy peoples needs.)	Heinz ought to take the drug because his wife really needs it. He can always pay the druggist back.	Heinz shouldn't take the drug. If he gets caught and winds up in jail, it won't do his wife any good.
LEVEL II: CONVENTIONAL		
Stage 3: "Good-boy orientation" (That which helps others and is socially approved is right.)	Stealing is a crime, so it's bad, but Heinz should take the drug to save his wife or else people would blame him for letting her die.	Stealing is a crime. Heinz shouldn't just take the drug because his family will be dishonored and they will blame him.
Stage 4: Law-and-order orientation (Doing one's duty and showing respect for authority are right.)	Heinz must take the drug to do his duty to save his wife. Eventually, he has to pay the druggist for it, however.	If everybody took the law into his or her own hands, civilization would fall apart, so Heinz shouldn't steal the drug.
LEVEL III: POSTCONVENTIONAL		
Stage 5: Contractual, legalistic orientation (It is moral to weigh pressing human needs against society's need to maintain the social order.)	This thing is complicated because society has a right to maintain law and order, but Heinz has to take the drug to save his wife.	I can see why Heinz feels he has to take the drug, but laws exist for the benefit of society as a whole and can't simply be cast aside.
Stage 6: Universal ethical principles orientation (People must act in accord with universal ethical principles and their own conscience, even if they must break the law in doing so.)	This is a case in which the law comes into conflict with the principle of the sanctity of human life. Heinz must take the drug because his wife's life is more important than the law.	If Heinz, in his own conscience, believes that stealing the drug is worse than letting his wife die, he should not take it. People have to make sacrifices to do what they believe is right.

He would pay the druggist when he could.) Many people do not mature beyond the conventional level.

Stage 3 moral judgments are found most frequently among 13-year-olds, and stage 4 judgments most often among 16-year-olds (Kohlberg, 1963).

THE POSTCONVENTIONAL LEVEL. In the **postconventional level,** moral reasoning is based on the person's own moral standards. In each instance, moral judgments are derived from personal values, not from conventional standards or authority figures. In stage 5's contractual, legalistic orientation, it is recognized that laws stem from agreed-upon procedures and that many laws have great value and should not be violated. But under exceptional circumstances, laws cannot bind the individual. (Although it is illegal for Heinz to steal the drug, in this case it is the right thing to do.)

Stage 6 thinking relies on supposed universal ethical principles such as those of human life, individual dignity, justice, and **reciprocity.** Behavior that

Postconventional level • According to Kohlberg, a period during which moral judgments are derived from moral principles and people look to themselves to set moral standards.
Reciprocity • Mutual action.

is consistent with these principles is moral. If a law is unjust or contradicts the rights of the individual, it is wrong to obey it.

Postconventional people look to their consciences as the highest moral authority. This point has created confusion. To some it suggests that it is right to break the law when it is convenient. But this interpretation is incorrect. Kohlberg means that postconventional people must do what they believe is right even if it counters social rules or laws or requires personal sacrifice.

Not all people reach the postconventional level of moral reasoning. Postconventional moral judgments were absent among the 7- to 10-year-olds in Kohlberg's (1963) sample of American children. Postconventional judgments are found more frequently during the early and middle teens. By age 16, stage 5 reasoning is shown by about 20% and stage 6 reasoning by about 5% of adolescents. However, stage 3 and 4 judgments are made more frequently at all ages, 7 through 16, studied by Kohlberg and other investigators (Colby and others, 1983; Rest, 1983).

EVALUATION OF KOHLBERG'S THEORY. Research suggests that moral reasoning does follow a developmental sequence (Snarey and others, 1985), even though most children do not reach postconventional thought. Postconventional thought, when found, first occurs during adolescence. It also seems that formal operational thinking is a precedent for postconventional reasoning, which requires the capacities to understand abstract moral principles and to empathize with the attitudes and emotional responses of other people (Flavell and others, 1993).

Consistent with Kohlberg's theory, children do not appear to skip stages as they progress (Flavell and others, 1993). When children are exposed to adult models who enact a lower stage of moral reasoning, they can be induced to follow along (Bandura & McDonald, 1963). Children exposed to examples of moral reasoning above and below their own stage generally prefer the higher stage, however (Rest, 1983). Thus the thrust of moral development is from lower to higher, even if children can be sidetracked by social influences.

However, a key issue in moral development is whether Kohlberg's theory has gender and ethnocentric biases. One of the more controversial notions in the history of child development is that males show higher levels of moral development than females. From his psychoanalytic perspective, Freud assumed that males would have stronger "superegos" than females because of the wrenching Oedipus complex and the male's consequent identification with authority figures and social codes. But Freud's views on the Oedipus complex were speculative, and his views on women reflected the ignorance and prejudice of his times.

In more recent years, however, some researchers have reported gender differences in moral development in the United States in terms of responses to Heinz's dilemma. Some studies have found that boys reason at higher levels of moral development than girls. Carol Gilligan (1982; Gilligan and others, 1989) argues that this gender difference reflects different patterns of socialization for boys and girls.

Gilligan makes her point through two examples of responses to Heinz's dilemma. Eleven-year-old Jake views the dilemma as a math problem. He sets up an equation showing that life has greater value than property. Heinz is thus obligated to steal the drug. Eleven-year-old Amy vacillates. She notes that stealing the drug and letting Heinz's wife die would both be wrong. Amy searches for alternatives, such as getting a loan, stating that it would profit Heinz's wife little if he went to jail and were no longer around to help her.

According to Gilligan, Amy is showing a pattern of reasoning that is as sophisticated as Jake's. Still, Amy would be rated as showing a lower level of moral development. Gilligan asserts that Amy, like other girls, has been socialized into focusing on the needs of others and foregoing simplistic judgments of right and wrong. As a consequence, Amy is more likely to appear to show stage 3 reasoning, which focuses in part on empathy for others. Jake, by contrast, has been socialized into making judgments based purely on logic. To him, clear-cut conclusions are to be derived from a set of premises. Amy was aware of the logical considerations that struck Jake, of course. However, she processed them as one source of information—not as the sole acceptable source. It is ironic that Amy's empathy, a trait that has "defined the 'goodness' of women," marks Amy "as deficient in moral development" (Gilligan, 1982, p. 18). Prior to his death in 1987, Kohlberg had begun efforts to correct the sexism in his scoring system.

Kohlberg's critics have suggested that postconventional reasoning, especially stage 6 reasoning, may reflect Kohlberg's personal ideals and not a natural, universal stage of development. Stage 6 reasoning is based on supposedly omnipresent ethical principles. The principles of justice, equality, integrity, and reverence for life may have a high appeal to you, but you were reared in a culture that idealizes them. They are not universal, however—witness the brutality of Adolph Hitler, Joseph Stalin, and Saddam Hussein. These principles are more reflective of Western ideals than of cognitive development. In his later years, Kohlberg virtually dropped stage 6 reasoning from his theory, in recognition of these problems.

Truth or Fiction Revisited. *It is true within our culture that the highest level of moral reasoning involves relying on our own views of what is right and wrong.* However, postconventional thought is not found in all cultures, and there is more support for stage 5 reasoning than for stage 6 reasoning.

Adolescence • The period of life bounded by puberty and the assumption of adult responsibilities.

Reflections

- **Agree or disagree with the following statement and support your answer: "Children are natural scientists who actively intend to learn about and manipulate their worlds."**
- Can you provide some examples of assimilation and accommodation in your own learning about the various areas of psychology?
- What cognitive strategies are you using to learn the material in this chapter? Are they planned or automatic?
- Agree or disagree with the following statement and support your answer: "Postconventional moral judgments represent the highest level of moral reasoning."
- How would you characterize your own level of cognitive development, in terms of both Piaget's and Kohlberg's theories of development? Support your characterizations.

ADOLESCENCE

Adolescence is a time of transition from childhood to adulthood. In our society, adolescents often feel that they are "neither fish nor fowl," as the saying goes—neither children nor adults. Although adolescents may be old enough to reproduce and are as large as their parents, they are often treated quite differently. They may not be eligible for driver's licenses until they are 16 or 17.

Adolescents. In our culture, adolescents are "neither fish nor fowl." Although they may be old enough to reproduce and may be as large as their parents, adolescents are often treated like children.

Secondary sex characteristics • Characteristics that differentiate the sexes, such as distribution of body hair and depth of voice, but that are not directly involved in reproduction.

Menarche • (men-ARK-key *or* may-NARSH). The beginning of menstruation.

They cannot attend R-rated films unless accompanied by an adult. They are prevented from working long hours. They are required to remain in school usually through age 16. They may not marry until they reach the "age of consent." Let us consider the physical, social, and personal changes of adolescence.

Physical Development

Adolescence is heralded by puberty. Puberty begins with the appearance of **secondary sex characteristics** such as body hair, deepening of the voice in males, and rounding of the breasts and hips in females. In boys pituitary hormones stoke the testes to increase the output of testosterone, causing the penis and testes to grow and bodily hair to appear. By the early teens, erections become common, and boys may ejaculate. Ejaculatory ability usually precedes the presence of mature sperm by at least a year. Ejaculation is thus not evidence of reproductive capacity.

In girls, pituitary secretions cause the ovaries to begin to secrete estrogen, which stimulates growth of breast tissue and fatty and supportive tissue in the hips and buttocks. Thus the pelvis widens, rounding the hips. Small amounts of androgens produced by the adrenal glands, along with estrogen, spur growth of pubic and underarm hair. Estrogen and androgens together stimulate the growth of female sex organs. Estrogen production becomes cyclical in puberty and regulates the menstrual cycle. First menstruation, or **menarche,** usually occurs between the ages of 11 and 14. Girls cannot become pregnant until they begin to ovulate, which may occur as much as 2 years later.

Truth or Fiction Revisited. *It is not usually true that girls are capable of becoming pregnant when they have their first menstrual periods.* Menarche can precede ovulation by a year or more.

Puberty ends when the long bones make no further gains in length so that full height is attained. But adolescence ends with psychosocial markers such as assumption of adult responsibilities. Adolescence is a psychological concept with biological aspects, but puberty is a biological concept.

The stable growth patterns in height and weight that characterize early and middle childhood come to an abrupt end with the adolescent growth spurt, which lasts for 2 to 3 years. Adolescents add some 8 to 12 inches in height. Most boys wind up taller and heavier than most girls.

In boys, the muscle mass increases notably in weight, and there are gains in shoulder width and chest circumference. Adolescents may eat enormous quantities of food to fuel their growth spurts. Adults fighting the battle of the bulge stare at them in wonder as they wolf down french fries and shakes at the fast-food counter and later go out for pizza.

Social and Personality Development

In the last century, psychologist G. Stanley Hall described adolescence as a time of *Sturm und Drang*—storm and stress. Certainly, many American teenagers abuse drugs, have unplanned pregnancies, contract sexually transmitted diseases, become involved in violence, and encounter psychological and social problems that are connected with academic failure and suicide attempts (Garland & Zigler, 1993; Gentry & Eron, 1993; Kazdin, 1993). Nearly 1 in 10 adolescent girls becomes pregnant each year. Nearly 10% of teenaged boys and 20% of teenaged girls attempt suicide. Alcohol-related incidents are the overall leading cause of death among adolescents.

Hall attributed the conflicts and distress of adolescence to biological changes. Research evidence suggests that the hormonal changes of adolescence may have some effect on the activity levels, mood swings, and aggressive tendencies of many adolescents (Buchanan and others, 1992). Overall, however, it would appear that cultural influences and social expectations may have a greater impact on adolescents than hormones do (Buchanan and others, 1992).

Yet the picture of adolescence as a state of constant rebellion against parents and society is overblown. Yes, adolescence is a time of redefinition of parent–child relationships. However, many of these changes are positive and not negative (Collins, 1990; Steinberg, 1991). Moreover, there are many individual differences.

Adolescents do strive to become more independent from their parents. This striving is manifested by some bickering, especially in early adolescence (Smetana and others, 1991). Conflicts typically center around the details of everyday family life—issues such as homework, chores, money, appearance, curfews, and dating (Galambos & Almeida, 1992; Smetana and others, 1991). Arguments are common when adolescents maintain that personal choices, such as those that concern clothes and friends, should be made by them and not their parents (Smetana and others, 1991).

The striving for independence is also characterized by withdrawal from family life, at least relative to the prior involvement. In one study, children ranging in age from 9 to 15 carried electronic pagers for a week so that they could report what they were doing and whom they were with when signaled (Larson & Richards, 1991). The amount of time spent with the family decreased dramatically as age increased. The 15-year-olds spent only half as much time with their families as the 9-year-olds. Yet this change does not mean that most adolescents spend their time on the streets. For 15-year-old boys in the study, time with the family tended to be replaced by time spent alone. For older girls, this time was divided between friends and solitude.

Adolescents, like younger children, interact with their mothers more so than their fathers. When parent–adolescent conflict arises, then, it is more likely to be with the mother. But most adolescents also see their mothers as more supportive than their fathers, as knowing them better, and as being more likely to tolerate their opinions (Collins & Russell, 1991; Noller & Callan, 1990). Teenagers are also more likely to seek and follow advice from their mothers than their fathers (Greene & Grimsley, 1991).

Adolescents and parents are often in conflict because adolescents experiment with many things that can be harmful to their health. Yet they often do not perceive such activities to be as risky as their parents do. Lawrence Cohn and his colleagues (1995) found, for example, that parents perceive drinking, smoking, failure to use seat belts, drag racing, and a number of other activities to be riskier than their teenagers did (see Table 11.4). Activities were rated according to a scale in which 1 = no harm and 5 = very great harm.

Some distancing from parents is adaptive for adolescents (Galambos, 1992). After all, they do have to form relationships outside the family. But greater independence does not necessarily mean that adolescents become emotionally detached from their parents or fall completely under the influence of their peers. Most adolescents continue to feel love, respect, and loyalty toward their parents (Montemayor & Flannery, 1991). Adolescents who feel close to their parents actually show greater self-reliance and independence than those who are distant from their parents. Adolescents who retain close ties with parents also fare better in school and have fewer adjustment problems (Davey, 1993; Papini & Roggman, 1992; Steinberg, 1991).

Despite parent–adolescent conflict over issues of control, many studies confirm that parents and adolescents share quite similar social, political, religious, and economic views (Paikoff & Collins, 1991). In sum, there are frequent parent–adolescent differences on issues of personal control. However, there is apparently no "generation gap" on broader matters.

TABLE 11.4
MEAN RATINGS OF PERCEIVED HARMFULNESS OF VARIOUS ACTIVITIES

ACTIVITY	EXPERIMENTAL INVOLVEMENT (DOING ACTIVITY ONCE OR TWICE TO SEE WHAT IT IS LIKE)		FREQUENT INVOLVEMENT	
	TEENAGER	TEENAGER'S PARENTS	TEENAGER	TEENAGER'S PARENTS
Drinking alcohol	2.6	3.5	4.4	4.8
Smoking cigarettes	3.0	3.6	4.4	4.8
Using diet pills	2.8	3.8	4.1	4.7
Not using seat belts	3.0	4.3	4.0	4.8
Getting drunk	3.2	4.2	4.4	4.8
Sniffing glue	3.6	4.6	4.6	4.9
Driving home after drinking a few beers	3.8	4.5	4.6	4.8
Drag racing	3.8	4.6	4.5	4.8
Using steroids	3.8	4.4	4.7	4.9

Ratings based on a scale of 1 to 5, in which 1 = "no harm" and 5 = "very great harm."

WORLD OF DIVERSITY

GENDER AND ETHNICITY IN ADOLESCENT IDENTITY FORMATION

Erik Erikson's views of the development of identity were intended to apply primarily to males (Archer, 1992; Patterson and others, 1992). In Erikson's theory, the stage of identity development includes embracing a philosophy of life and commitment to a career. It is in the next stage that people develop the capacity to form intimate relationships. Erikson believed that the development of interpersonal relationships was more important to women's identity than occupational and ideological issues. Revealing his theoretical indebtedness to Sigmund Freud, Erikson believed that women's identities were intimately connected with women's roles as wives and mothers. Men's identities did not depend on their roles as husbands and fathers. Erikson argued, therefore, that women tended to resolve concerns about identity and intimacy simultaneously and later than men resolved identity concerns (Patterson and others, 1992).

Yet contemporary research shows that women in the United States approach identity formation in a manner that is much more similar to, than different from, men (Archer, 1992). The realities of contemporary life in the United States call for full participation of women in the workplace. It is not surprising, then, that adolescent girls voice about equal concern with boys about their occupational plans. Girls, however, also voice concern about the interrelatedness of family concerns and occupational concerns in their daily lives (Archer, 1992). This is not surprising when we consider that despite their investment in the workplace, U.S. women still often have the primary responsibility for rearing the children and maintaining the home (Archer, 1991). (When is the last time you heard a man wonder how he will balance the demands of a career and a family?)

Identity formation is more complicated for adolescents from ethnic minority groups (Cross, 1991; Spencer & Markstrom-Adams, 1990). Unlike adolescents who are a part of the dominant culture, minority adolescents may be faced with two sets of cultural values: those of their ethnic group and those of the dominant culture (Markstrom-Adams, 1992; Phinney & Rosenthal, 1992). When these values are in conflict, the minority adolescent needs to reconcile the differences and, frequently, decide where she or he stands. Maha Alkhateeb, an Arab American Muslim adolescent, talks about why she skipped the prom: "At the time of the prom, I was sad, but just about everyone I knew had sex that night, which I think was immoral. Now, I like saying that I didn't go. I didn't go there just because it was a cool thing to do" ("Muslim Women," 1993, p. B9).

Biracial adolescents or adolescents whose parents are of different religions wrestle not only with these issues, but with issues as to what constitutes their own dominant cultural heritage (Gibbs, 1992; Johnson, 1992; Miller, 1992). Parents from different ethnic groups may decide to spend their lives together, but their values may not dwell so contentedly side by side within the minds of their children.

EGO IDENTITY VERSUS ROLE DIFFUSION.   According to psychoanalyst Erik Erikson, the major challenge of adolescence is the creation of an adult identity.

This is accomplished primarily through choosing and developing a commitment to an occupation or a role in life. But identity extends to sexual, political, and religious beliefs and commitments.

Erikson (1963) theorizes that adolescents experience a life crisis of *ego identity versus role diffusion*. If this crisis is resolved properly, adolescents develop a firm sense of who they are and what they stand for. This sense of **ego identity** can carry them through difficult times and color their achievements with meaning. If they do not resolve this life crisis properly, they may experience **role diffusion.** They then spread themselves thin, running down one blind alley after another and placing themselves at the mercy of leaders who promise to give them the sense of identity they cannot mold for themselves.

Reflections

- G. Stanley Hall wrote that adolescence is a period of *Sturm und Drang*—storm and stress. Is it? If so, why?
- Consider your own experiences as an adolescent. How did your gender or ethnic group influence the formation of your own identity? Did the process of building your identity require you to resolve any conflicts related to your gender or ethnicity?

Ego identity • Erikson's term for a firm sense of who one is and what one stands for.

Role diffusion • Erikson's term for lack of clarity in one's life roles—a function of failure to develop ego identity.

Intimacy versus isolation • Erikson's life crisis of young adulthood, which is characterized by the task of developing abiding intimate relationships.

Trying 20s • Sheehy's term for the third decade of life, when people are frequently occupied with advancement in the career world.

ADULT DEVELOPMENT

Development continues throughout a lifetime. Many theorists believe that adult concerns and involvements are patterned so that we can speak of stages of adult development. Yet others point out that there may no longer be a standard life cycle with predictable stages (Sheehy, 1995). People are living longer and are in many ways freer than ever to choose their own destinies. Let us consider the adult years according to three broad categories: young adulthood, middle adulthood, and late adulthood.

Young Adulthood

Young or early adulthood covers the two decades from ages 20 to 40. According to Erik Erikson (1963), young adulthood is the stage of **intimacy versus isolation.** Erikson saw the establishment of intimate relationships as central to young adulthood. Young adults who have evolved a firm sense of identity during adolescence are now ready to "fuse" their identities with those of other people through marriage and abiding friendships.

Erikson warns that we may not be able to commit ourselves to others until we have achieved ego identity, or established stable life roles. Achieving ego identity is the central task of adolescence. Lack of personal stability is connected with the high divorce rate in teenage marriages.

Erikson argues that people who do not reach out to develop intimate relationships risk retreating into isolation and loneliness.

Adults in their 20s tend to be fueled by ambition as they strive to establish their pathways in life. Journalist Gail Sheehy (1976) labeled the 20s the **Trying 20s**—a period during which people basically strive to advance themselves in the career world. They are concerned with establishing their pathways in life. They are generally responsible for their own support, make their own choices, and are largely free from parental influences.

MINILECTURE: PSYCHOSOCIAL DEVELOPMENT IN ADULTHOOD

Establishing Intimate Relationships. According to Erik Erikson, establishing intimate relationships is a central task of young adulthood.

During our 20s, many of us feel "buoyed by powerful illusions and belief in the power of the will [so that] we commonly insist . . . that what we have chosen to do is the one true course in life" (Sheehy, 1976, p. 33). This "one true course" usually turns out to have many swerves and bends. As we develop, what seemed to be important one year can lose some of its allure in the next. That which we hardly noticed can gain prominence.

GENDER DIFFERENCES IN DEVELOPMENTAL PATTERNS OF YOUNG ADULTHOOD. Most Western men consider separation and individuation to be key goals of personality development during young adulthood (Guisinger & Blatt, 1994). For women, however, the establishment and maintenance of social relationships are also of primary importance (Gilligan and others, 1990, 1991; Jordan and others, 1991). Women are relatively more likely to be guided by changing patterns of attachment and caring. In becoming adults, men are likely to undergo a transition from restriction to control. Women, as pointed out by Gilligan (1982), are relatively more likely to undergo a transition from being cared for to caring for others, however.

According to Levinson (1978), men enter the adult world in their early 20s. Upon entry, they are faced with the tasks of exploring adult roles (in terms of careers, intimate relationships, and so on) and of establishing stability in the chosen roles. At this time, men also often adopt a **dream**—the drive to "become" someone, to leave their mark on history—which serves as a tentative blueprint for their lives.

Although there are differences in the development of women and men, a study by Ravenna Helson and Geraldine Moane (1987) of the University of California found that between the ages of 21 and 27, college women develop in terms of individuation and autonomy. That is, they, like men, tend to assert increasing control over their own lives. College women, of course, are relatively liberated and career-oriented in comparison with their less-well-educated peers.

Dream • In this usage, Levinson's term for the overriding drive of youth to become someone important, to leave one's mark on history.

THE AGE-30 TRANSITION.   Levinson labeled the ages of 28 to 33 the **age-30 transition.** For many, this is a period of reassessment of the choices made during their early 20s. A number of researchers have noted that women frequently encounter a crisis that begins between the ages of 27 and 30 (Reinke and others, 1985). During the early 30s, many of the women studied by Helson and Moane (1987) felt exploited by others, alone, weak, limited, and as if they would "never get myself together." Concerns about nearing the end of the fertile years, opportunities closing down, and heightened responsibilities at home and work all make their contributions.

For men and women, the late 20s and early 30s are commonly characterized by self-questioning: "Where is my life going?" "Why am I doing this?" Sheehy (1976) labeled the 30s the **Catch 30s** because of such reassessment. During our 30s, we often find that the lifestyles we adopted during our 20s do not fit as comfortably as we had anticipated.

One response that people have to the disillusionments of the 30s, according to Sheehy,

> is the tearing up of the life we have spent most of our 20s putting together. It may mean striking out on a secondary road toward a new vision or converting a dream of "running for president" into a more realistic goal. The single person feels a push to find a partner. The woman who was previously content at home with children chafes to venture into the world. The childless couple reconsiders children. And almost everybody who is married . . . feels a discontent. (1976, p. 34)

SETTLING DOWN AND ROOTING.   According to Levinson, the ages of about 33 to 40 are characterized by settling down. Men during this period still strive to forge ahead in their careers, their interpersonal relationships, and their communities. During the latter half of their 30s, men are also concerned about "becoming one's own man." That is, they desire independence and autonomy in their careers and adult relationships. Promotions and pay increases are important as signs of success.

Sheehy found that young adults who had successfully ridden out the storm of reassessments of the Catch 30s begin the process of "rooting" at this time. They feel a need to put down roots, to make a financial and emotional investment in their homes. Their concerns become more focused on promotion or tenure, career advancement, and long-term mortgages.

Middle Adulthood

Middle adulthood spans the years from 40 to 60 or 65. Sheehy (1995) terms the years from 45 onward "second adulthood." Rather than viewing them as years of decline, her interviews suggest that many Americans find them to be opportunities for new direction and fulfillment.

GENERATIVITY VERSUS STAGNATION.   Erikson (1963) labels the life crisis of the middle years that of **generativity versus stagnation.** Are we striving to produce or to rear our children well, or are we marking time, treading water? Generativity by and large requires doing things that we believe are worthwhile. In so doing, we enhance and maintain our self-esteem. Generativity also involves the Eriksonian ideal of helping shape the new generation. This shaping may involve rearing our own children or generally working to make the world a better place.

Age-30 transition • Levinson's term for the ages from 28 to 33, which are characterized by reassessment of the goals and values of the 20s.

Catch 30s • Sheehy's term for the fourth decade of life, when many people undergo major reassessments of their accomplishments and goals.

Generativity versus stagnation • Erikson's term for the crisis of middle adulthood, characterized by the task of being productive and contributing to younger generations.

MIDLIFE TRANSITION.   According to Levinson, there is a **midlife transition** at about age 40 to 45 that is characterized by a shift in psychological perspective. Previously, we had thought of our ages in terms of the number of years that have elapsed since birth. Now we begin to think of our ages in terms of the number of years we have left. Men in their 30s still think of themselves as part of the Pepsi Generation, older brothers to "kids" in their 20s. At about age 40 to 45, however, some marker event—illness, a change on the job, the death of a friend or of a parent, or being beaten at tennis by one's child—leads men to realize that they are a full generation older. Suddenly there seems to be more to look back on than forward to. It dawns on men that they'll never be president or chairperson of the board. They'll never play shortstop for the Dodgers. They mourn their own youth and begin to adjust to the specter of old age and the finality of death.

MASTERY.   Sheehy (1995) is much more optimistic than Levinson. She terms the years from 45 to 65 "the Age of Mastery," because people are frequently at the height of their productive powers. Sheehy believes that the key task for people aged 45 to 55 is to decide what they will do with their "second adulthoods"—the 30 to 40 healthy years that they may have left once they reach 50. She believes that both men and women can experience great success and joy if they find their passion and pursue it wholeheartedly.

"MIDDLESCENCE".   Yet people do need to find their passion. Sheehy coins the term **middlescence** to describe a period of searching that is in some ways akin to adolescence. Both are an age of transition. Middlescence involves a search for new identity: "Turning backward, going around in circles, feeling lost in a buzz of confusion and unable to make decisions—all this is predictable and, for many people, a necessary precursor to making the passage into midlife" (Sheehy, 1995).

Women, as suggested by Sheehy and other writers (e.g., Reinke and others, 1985), may undergo a midlife transition a number of years earlier than men do. Sheehy (1976) writes that women enter midlife about 5 years earlier than men do, at about age 35 instead of 40. Once they turn 35, women are usually advised to have their fetuses tested for Down syndrome and other chromosomal disorders. At age 35, women also enter higher risk categories for side effects from birth control pills.

Yet women frequently experience a renewed sense of self in their 40s and 50s, as they emerge from "middlescence" (Apter, 1995; Sheehy, 1995). Many women in their early 40s are already emerging from some of the fears and uncertainties that are first confronting men. Helson and Moane (1987) found that women at age 43 are more likely than women in their early 30s to feel confident; to exert an influence on their communities; to feel secure and committed; to feel productive, effective, and powerful; and to extend their interests beyond their own families.

MENOPAUSE.   **Menopause,** or the cessation of menstruation, usually occurs during the late 40s or early 50s, although there are wide variations. Menopause is the final stage of a broader female experience, the climacteric, which is caused by a falling off in the secretion of the hormones estrogen and progesterone. The climacteric begins with irregular periods and ends with menopause.[1] With menopause, ovulation also draws to an end. There is some

Middlescence (Middlescence?). Gail Sheehy believes that the key task for people in middle age is to decide what they will do with their "second adulthood"—that is, the 30 to 40 healthy years that most people have left once they reach 50. She coins the term *middlescence* to suggest that this is a period of searching. Middlescence, like adolescence, involves a search for new identity.

Midlife transition • Levinson's term for the ages from 40 to 45, which are characterized by a shift in psychological perspective from viewing ourselves in terms of years lived to viewing ourselves in terms of the years we have left.
Middlescence • Sheehy's term for a stage of life, from 45 to 55, when people seek new identity and are frequently "lost in a buzz of confusion."
Menopause • (MEN-no-paws). The cessation of menstruation.

---

[1] There are other reasons for irregular periods. Women who encounter them are advised to discuss them with their doctors.

atrophy of breast tissue and a decrease in the elasticity of the skin. Women can also experience a loss of bone density that leads to osteoporosis in late adulthood.

During the climacteric, many women encounter symptoms such as hot flashes (uncomfortable sensations characterized by heat and perspiration) and loss of sleep. However, women are more likely to suffer from depression prior to menopause, when they may buckle from the combined demands of the workplace, child rearing, and home-making (Brody, 1993b). In most cases, mood changes are relatively mild. According to psychologist Karen Matthews, who has been following a sample of 451 women through menopause, some women do encounter problems. "But studies show that they are in the minority," Matthews (1994, p. 25) points out. "The vast majority have no problem at all getting through the menopausal transition."

Menopause does not signal the end of a woman's sexual interests (Brody, 1993b). Many women find the separation of sex from reproduction to be sexually liberating. Some of the physical problems that may stem from falloff in hormone production may be alleviated by hormone-replacement therapy (Belchetz, 1994). A more important issue may be the meaning of menopause to the individual. Women who equate menopause with loss of femininity are likely to encounter more distress than those who do not (Rathus and others, 1997).

Truth or Fiction Revisited. *It is not true that menopause signals the end of a woman's sexual interests.* Many women find the separation of sex from reproduction to be sexually liberating.

Empty-nest syndrome • A sense of depression and loss of purpose felt by some parents when the youngest child leaves home.

THE EMPTY-NEST SYNDROME. In earlier decades, psychologists placed great emphasis on a concept referred to as the **empty-nest syndrome** that applied to women in particular. It was assumed that women experienced a profound sense of loss when the youngest child went off to college, got married, or moved into an apartment. Research findings paint more of a mixed and optimistic picture, however. Certainly there can be problems, and these apply to both parents. Perhaps the largest of these is letting go of one's children after so many years of mutual interdependence (Bell, 1983). The stresses of letting go can be compounded when the children are ambivalent about independence.

Many mothers report increased marital satisfaction and personal changes such as greater mellowness, self-confidence, and stability after the children have left home, however (Reinke and others, 1985). Middle-aged women show increased dominance and assertiveness, an orientation toward achievement, and greater influence in the worlds of politics and work. It is as if they are cut free from traditional shackles by the knowledge that their child-bearing years are behind them.

Truth or Fiction Revisited. *It is not true that mothers generally suffer from the "empty-nest syndrome" when the youngest child leaves home.* Most mothers (and fathers) do *not* suffer when the youngest child leaves home.

Role reversals are not uncommon in family life once the children have left home (Wink & Helson, 1993). Given traditional sociocultural expectations of men and women, men are frequently more competent than their wives in the world outside the family during the early stages of marriage, and their wives are more emotionally dependent. But in the postparental period, these differences decrease or actually become reversed both because of the women's enhanced status in the world of work and because of the influence of the mother role.

Late Adulthood

You know you're getting old when you stoop to tie your shoes and wonder what else you can do while you're down there.

GEORGE BURNS

Late adulthood begins at age 65. One reason that developmental psychologists have become concerned about the later years is that with improved health care and knowledge of the importance of diet and exercise, more Americans than ever before are 65 or older. By the year 2000, nearly 35 million Americans, more than 13% of the population, will be 65 or older (Farley, 1993b). In 1900, only 1 American in 30 was over 65, as compared with 1 in 9 in 1970. By the year 2020, perhaps 1 American in 5 will be 65 or older (Figure 11.8). Another reason for the increased interest in aging is the recognition that, in a sense, *all* development involves aging. A third reason for studying the later years is to learn how we can further promote the health and psychological well-being of older people.

PHYSICAL DEVELOPMENT.   Various changes—some of them problematic—do occur during the later years. Changes in calcium metabolism lead to increased brittleness in the bones and heightened risk of breaks from accidents like falls. The skin becomes less elastic and subject to wrinkles and folds.

The senses become less acute. Older people see and hear less acutely. Because of a decline in the sense of smell, they may use more seasonings to flavor their food. Older people require more time (called **reaction time**) to respond to stimuli. Older drivers need more time to respond to traffic lights, other vehicles, and changing road conditions.

As we grow older, our immune systems also function less effectively, leaving us more vulnerable to disease.

COGNITIVE DEVELOPMENT.   Although there are some declines in reaction time, intellectual functioning, and memory among older people, they are not as large as many people tend to assume they are (Benson, 1995). However, we understand very little about why they occur. Losses of sensory acuity and of motivation to do well may contribute to lower scores. Psychologist B. F. Skinner (1983) argued that much of the falloff is due to an "aging environment" rather than an aging person. That is, the behavior of older people often goes unreinforced. Nursing home residents who are rewarded for remembering recent events show improved scores on tests of memory (Langer and others, 1979; Wolinsky, 1982).

THEORIES OF AGING.   Although it may be hard to believe that it will happen to us, everyone who has so far walked the Earth has aged—which may not be a bad fate, considering the alternative. Why do we age? Various factors, some of which are theoretical, apparently contribute to aging.

Heredity plays a role. **Longevity** runs in families. People whose parents and grandparents lived into their 80s and 90s have a better chance of reaching these years themselves.

Environmental factors also influence aging. People who exercise regularly seem to live longer. Disease, stress, obesity, and cigarette smoking can contribute to an early death. Fortunately, we can exert control over some of these factors.

Older people show better health and psychological well-being when they do exert control over their own lives (Rodin, 1986; Wolinsky, 1982). About 29%

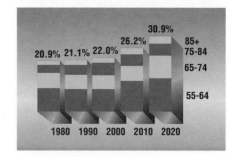

FIGURE 11.8

The Aging of America. Because of factors such as improved health care, diet, and exercise, Americans are living longer. By the year 2020, for example, about 31% of us will be at least 55 years old, as compared with about 21% today.

Reaction time   •   The amount of time required to respond to a stimulus.

Longevity   •   A long span of life.

of older people will spend at least some time in a nursing home (Kemper & Murtaugh, 1991), however, where many of them surrender much of their independence. Even in the nursing home, older people fare better when they are kept well-informed and allowed to make decisions on matters that affect them.

Disturbances in the abilities of cells to regenerate and repair themselves accompany aging. It is unclear whether these disturbances are genetically pre-programmed or are caused by external factors (such as ultraviolet light) or by an accumulation of random internal changes. More research is needed into the basic processes of aging, including the relationships between biological processes, lifestyle factors, and psychological problems such as confusional states and Alzheimer's disease (Lonergan & Krevans, 1991).

EGO INTEGRITY VERSUS DESPAIR.   According to Erikson, late adulthood is the stage of **ego integrity versus despair.** The basic challenge is to maintain the belief that life is meaningful and worthwhile in the face of the inevitability of death. Ego integrity derives from wisdom, as well as from the acceptance of one's life span as occurring at a certain point in the sweep of history and as being limited. We spend most of our lives accumulating things and relationships. Erikson argues that adjustment in the later years requires the wisdom to be able to let go.

Erikson was optimistic. He believed that we can maintain a sense of trust through life and avoid feelings of despair.

ADJUSTMENT AMONG THE ELDERLY.   Despite the changes that occur with aging, the majority of people in their 70s report being generally satisfied with their lives (Margoshes, 1995). A study of people retired for 18 to 120 months found that 75% rated retirement as mostly good (Hendrick and others, 1982a). More than 90% were generally satisfied with life. More than 75% reported their health as good or excellent.

> ***Truth or Fiction Revisited.***   *It is not true that most older people are dissatisfied with their lives.*

SUCCESSFUL AGING.   The concept of "successful aging" has sprung into the lexicons of developmental psychologists (Margoshes, 1995). The idea is not simply to put a positive spin on the inevitable. Psychologists have found that "successful agers" have a number of characteristics that can inspire all of us to lead more enjoyable and productive lives.

One component of successful aging is reshaping one's life to concentrate on what one finds to be important and meaningful. Laura Carstensen's (1995) research on people aged 70 and above reveals that successful agers form emotional goals that bring them satisfaction. For example, rather than cast about in multiple directions, they may focus on their families and friends. Successful agers may have less time left than those of us in earlier stages of adulthood, but they tend to spend it more wisely (Garfinkel, 1995).

Paul and Margret Baltes (1995) use the term "selective optimization and compensation" to describe the manner in which successful agers lead their lives. That is, successful agers no longer seek to compete in arenas best left to younger people—such as certain kinds of athletic or business activities. Rather, they focus on matters that allow them to maintain a sense of personal control. Moreover, they use available resources to make up for losses. If their memories are not quite what they once were, they make notes or other reminders. If their senses are no longer as acute, they use devices such as hearing aids or allow themselves more time to take in information. There are also ingenious individual strategies. The great pianist Arthur Rubinstein performed

---

Ego integrity versus despair • Erikson's term for the crisis of late adulthood, characterized by the task of maintaining one's sense of identity despite physical deterioration.

into his 80s, when he had lost much of his speed. In his later years, however, he would slow down before playing faster passages to enhance the impression of speed during faster passages (Margoshes, 1995).

A second component of successful aging is a positive outlook. For example, some older people attribute occasional health problems—such as aches and pains—to specific and unstable factors, such as a cold or jogging too long. Others attribute aches and pains to global and stable factors such as aging itself. Not surprisingly, those who attribute these problems to specific, unstable factors are more optimistic that they will surmount them. They thus have a more positive outlook or attitude. Of particular interest here is research conducted by William Rakowski (1995). Rakowski followed 1,400 people aged 70 and above with nonlethal health problems such as aches and pains. He found that those who blamed the problems on aging itself were significantly more likely to die in the near future than those who blamed the problems on specific, unstable factors.

Truth or Fiction Revisited. *It is true that older people who blame health problems on aging rather than on specific factors such as a virus are more likely to die in the near future.*

A third component of successful aging is challenging oneself. Many individuals look forward to late adulthood as a time when they can rest from life's challenges. However, sitting back and allowing the world to pass by is a prescription for vegetating, not living life to its fullest. Consider an experiment conducted by Curt Sandman and Francis Crinella (1995) with 175 people of an average age of 72. They randomly assigned participants either to a foster grandparent program with neurologically impaired children or to a control group and followed them for 10 years. As compared with people in the control group, the foster grandparents carried out various physical challenges, such as walking a few miles each day, and also had new social interactions. At assessment, the foster grandparent program had improved participants' overall cognitive functioning, including memory functioning, and their sleep patterns. Moreover, the foster grandparents showed superior functioning in these areas as compared with people assigned to the control group.

Doing less is no prescription for health and adjustment among older people. Focusing in on what is important, maintaining a positive attitude, and accepting new challenges is as important for older people as for any of us.

ON DEATH AND DYING.

Of all the wonders that I yet have heard,
It seems to me most strange that men should fear;
Seeing that death, a necessary end,
Will come when it will come.
                        SHAKESPEARE, *JULIUS CAESAR*

Death is the last great taboo. Psychiatrist Elisabeth Kübler-Ross commented on our denial of death in her landmark book *On Death and Dying:*

> We use euphemisms, we make the dead look as if they were asleep, we ship the children off to protect them from the anxiety and turmoil around the house if the [person] is fortunate enough to die at home, [and] we don't allow children to visit their dying parents in the hospitals. (1969, p. 8)

From her work with terminally ill patients, Kübler-Ross found some common responses to news of impending death. She identified five stages of dying through which many patients pass, and she suggests that older people who suspect that death is approaching may under go similar stages:

1. *Denial.* In the denial stage, people feel, "It can't be me. The diagnosis must be wrong."

2. *Anger.* Denial usually gives way to anger and resentment toward the young and healthy and, sometimes, toward the medical establishment—"It's unfair. Why me?"

3. *Bargaining.* Next, people may try to bargain with God to postpone death, promising, for example, to do good deeds if they are given another 6 months, another year.

4. *Depression.* With depression come feelings of loss and hopelessness—grief at the specter of leaving loved ones and life itself.

5. *Final acceptance.* Ultimately, an inner peace may come, a quiet acceptance of the inevitable. Such "peace" does not resemble contentment. It is nearly devoid of feeling.

Psychologist Edwin Shneidman (1984), who has specialized in the concerns of suicidal and dying individuals, acknowledges the presence of feelings such as those described by Kübler-Ross, but he does not perceive them to be linked in sequence. Instead, Shneidman suggests that dying people show a variety of emotional and cognitive responses that tend to be fleeting or relatively stable, to ebb and flow, and to reflect pain and bewilderment. He also points out that the kinds of responses shown by individuals reflect their personality traits and their philosophies of life.

"LYING DOWN TO PLEASANT DREAMS . . ." The American poet William Cullen Bryant is best known for his poem "Thanatopsis," which he composed at the age of 18. "Thanatopsis" expresses Erik Erikson's goal of ego integrity—optimism that we can maintain a sense of trust through life. By meeting squarely the challenges of our adult lives, perhaps we can take our leave with dignity. When our time comes to "join the innumerable caravan"—the billions who have died before us—perhaps we can depart life with integrity.

Live, wrote the poet, so that

> *. . . when thy summons comes to join*
> *The innumerable caravan that moves*
> *To that mysterious realm, where each shall take*
> *His chamber in the silent halls of death,*
> *Thou go not, like the quarry-slave at night,*
> *Scourged to his dungeon, but, sustained and soothed*
> *By an unfaltering trust, approach thy grave*
> *Like one that wraps the drapery of his couch*
> *About him, and lies down to pleasant dreams.*

Bryant, of course, wrote "Thanatopsis" at age 18, not at 85, the age at which he died. At that advanced age, his feelings—and his verse—might have differed. But literature and poetry, unlike science, need not reflect reality. They can serve to inspire and warm us.

Reflections

- Consider the middle-aged and older people in your own life. Are their behavior and personalities in any way consistent with the descriptions in this section? How or how not?

- Erik Erikson wrote that one aspect of wisdom was the ability to visualize one's role in the march of history and to accept one's own death. Do you believe that acceptance of death is a sign of wisdom? (Or that wisdom means being able to accept one's own death?) Why or why not?

Study Guide

Stages and Ages in Piaget's Theory

DIRECTIONS: List the names of each of Piaget's stages of cognitive development and the approximate ages at which they take place.

STAGE   APPROXIMATE AGES

1. _____   _____

2. _____   _____

3. _____-_____   _____

4. _____-_____   _____

ANSWER KEY TO EXERCISE 1

1. Sensorimotor stage: first 2 years
2. Preoperational stage: ages 2–6
3. Concrete-operational stage: ages 7–12
4. Formal-operational stage: adolescence and adulthood

Events That Take Place During Piaget's Stages of Development

DIRECTIONS: Following are a number of events that take place during Piaget's stages of cognitive development. In the blank space to the left of each event, write the letter (A, B, C, or D) that indicates the stage during which the event first takes place.

A = Sensorimotor

B = Preoperational

C = Concrete-operational

D = Formal-operational

____ 1. Artificialism

____ 2. Subjective moral judgments

____ 3. Abstract thinking

____ 4. Object permanence

____ 5. Children emerge as theoretical scientists

____ 6. Animism

____ 7. Conservation

____ 8. Assimilation of novel stimulation to ready-made schemes

____ 9. Objective moral judgments

____ 10. Reversibility

ANSWER KEY TO EXERCISE 2

1. B	3. D	5. D	7. C	9. B
2. C	4. A	6. B	8. A	10. C

agreed-upon (475)—procedures that everyone (society) agrees to

akin (485)—similar to

ambivalent (486)—to have conflicting feelings about something; to not be sure

arriving at (473)—deciding

as well as (488)—and it also happens

attainment (472)—accomplishment

beckoned (461)—called to the child with hand movements

bewilderment (490)—confusion; lack of understanding

biologically programmed (455)—does a plan exist in the genes that affects some of our behavior

blind alley (482)—a pointless direction; an activity that does not result in something useful

booming, buzzing (459)—sudden loud, or constant high-pitched, noises

bouyed by powerful illusions (483)—cheered up or encouraged by strong ideas we have that might not be realistic

but be warned (468)—but be aware of something

call for (481)—demand

caregivers (462)—people who care for the infants

carry them through (482)—help them through

caution us not to attach too much importance to (480)—warn us not to believe completely

center on (470)—notice particularly

center simultaneously on two dimensions (472)—focus on two parts at the same time

central task (482)—important action

chafes to venture into the world (484)—to be eager to be involved in the world outside the home

chatting animatedly (455)—talking happily

checkerboard (459)—pattern of black and white squares that alternate

closing down (484)—not available anymore

cognitive stimulation (455)—experiences and activities that encourage development of thinking abilities

color their achievements with meaning (482)—give their accomplishments meaning

come to terms with (498)—understand and accept something; the dream may not be reached

comforting base (465)—comfortable place

coming apart at the seams (456)—feels very unhappy with life; depressed and not able to figure out how to feel better

conditioned reinforcer (463)—each time a need is met by someone, we become more and more accustomed (conditioned) to thinking of that person (reinforcer) as important to us

conscience (476)—a person's standards about what is

right and wrong behavior; also called values, morals, or ethics

crude turning (468)—inexperienced and clumsy movement toward something

cut free from (486)—become less attached to

dashed to rubble (473)—destroyed

dawned on me (485)—it occurred to me; I realized

dawns on men (485)—men think; men realize

dignity (490)—honor and distinction

disturbances (488)—disruption; interference

diverse views (455)—different opinions

dominance and assertiveness (486)—a desire to control (dominate) and to be confident and self-assured (assertive)

drama was unfolding (454)—an exciting occurrence was happening

dramatic shift (455)—a big, important change

dwell so contentedly (481)—exist together comfortably

ebb and flow (490)—to not occur and to occur

edifice has been rocked (473)—structure has been questioned

egocentric (468)—being self-centered; looking at everything in terms of how it will affect the infant

eloquence (459)—ability to speak well; ability to use creative words to explain something or create a picture

emerge from (485)—to come out of

euphemisms (489)—gentler words for something that is difficult to discuss frankly

exaggerated (459)—overstated something; made it seem greater than it is

exploited (484)—taken advantage of by others

extramarital affairs (486)—emotional and sexual attachments that are not with the spouse but with someone else

facelike patterns (468)—designs that look like faces

fair to say (473)—reasonable to say

falling off (485)—decrease

fare better (488)—act and feel better

fared better (473)—have been accepted more

fate (487)—future; destiny; outcome

fetuses routinely tested (485)—unborn babies checked regularly for problems with the development

fighting the battle of the bulge (479)—trying not to gain weight

find their passion and pursue it wholeheartedly (485)—to discover what makes them happy and focus on it with all their attention

firm sense (482)—a strong feeling

flip side of the coin (480)—the other side of the issue

for their own good (463)—so they do not physically or psychologically hurt themselves *for their own support* (482)—for earning by themselves the money for rent and food

forge ahead (484)—try to succeed

free themselves from their dreams (480)—decide that their unrealistic dream will not occur

freer than ever to choose their own destinies (482)—more capable than before of deciding by themselves how they want their futures to develop

fueled by ambition (482)—motivated by the desire to succeed

generalize into (463)—when we apply something experienced in a specific situation to many situations

gratification (463)—satisfaction; getting your needs and wants met

grew intense (463)—became very strong

grinding out accounts (465)—involved in a boring job

growth spurts (479)—short, rapid periods of growth

heritage (455)—background; the genes we inherited from our ancestors

idealize (477)—to consider to be extremely important

inevitability (488)—an outcome that is unavoidable

judge . . . more harshly (472)—criticize . . . much more strongly

landmark book (489)—an important book that many people paid attention to

largely traced to (455)—mainly caused by

last chance (470)—something must be accomplished now or it will never be accomplished

layoffs (473)—loss of jobs; firing people

leaned heavily toward (455)—believed that

letting go of one's children (486)—allowing one's children to become independent

long-term mortgages (484)—a loan to buy a house that takes many years to pay back

lose some of its allure (483)—becomes less important or interesting

loss of purpose (498)—that there is no goal

made public (465)—were publicized; were put in national magazines or newspapers

major . . . leaps (455)—important periods of growth that are separate from each other

mark on history (483)—do something that future generations will remember

marker event (485)—an important event that symbolizes a change

marking time, treading water (484)—not moving forward; not progressing in a job or career; just passing time

means to do so (473)—ability to do it

meeting squarely the challenges (490)—accepting and directly handling the difficulties

mellowness (486)—calmness; serenity

methods to his children's madness (466)—good reasons for the incorrect answers

middle-level (485)—middle position (job); not at the top and not at the bottom

mold (482)—to shape

mold for themselves (482)—create for themselves

mourn (485)—to be sad that something has gone or died

naughtier (472)—more disobedient than another

nearing the end of the fertile years (484)—arriving at the end of the time when a woman can get pregnant

need we be concerned (470)—should we worry

neither fish nor fowl (477)—neither children nor adults; neither one definite group or the other; in between

nourished solely by the yolk (456)—fed only by the nutritional material in the center of the egg cell

otherwise linked (468)—connected in some other way

out of sight is literally out of mind (469)—if the baby cannot see the object or person, the baby does not think about it

overriding drive (483)—main effort

oversized (465)—bigger than normal size

paint more of a mixed and optimistic picture (486)—indicate that a situation is more different and more hopeful than previously thought

path to a monkey's heart (465)—the way to make a monkey happy

pathways in life (482)—directions in life

placed face down (462)—placed with the face looking down at the surface

placing themselves at the mercy of (482)—allowing another to make decisions for you; leaving your well-being to another

preference for familiar figures (463)—wanting to be with someone who is familiar

prom (481)—a special formal dance that is scheduled every year in high schools, generally for students who are in their last year (seniors)

prominence (483)—importance

psychological well-being (487)—mental and emotional health

pull and tug (463)—hold and pull their arms or clothes to get their attention

put aside the issue of (470)—we will not think about

put down roots (489)—to build a life, with a job and a family

reared (477)—raised or taught by family or other caregivers

remiss (476)—was not correct; was a mistake

reverence for life (477)—a belief that life is something to be respected, honored, and cared for

ridden out the storm (484)—survived the difficult years

role in life (482)—a position in life, or a way of living that is accepted by the person and society

run over (463)—stepped on

saw development as being (455)—believed that development was

self-reliance (480)—the ability to depend on yourself

sense of urgency (487)—a feeling that there is not much time left

settling down (484)—becoming involved with a job and a family

shrugged them off (466)—didn't pay attention to them

signal the end (453)—a sign that the end is near

small (474)—small difference; not a lot of difference

so far walked the Earth (487)—lived up to this time; lived before us

soft, cuddly terry cloth (464)—terry cloth is a soft, fuzzy material; like the material towels are made of

somersaults (458)—rolling over in a complete circle with the feet going over the head

soothe (461)—to calm; to comfort

specter of old age (485)—the unpleasant idea of old age

spread themselves thin (482)—do too many things

squat glass (471)—a short and wide glass

storm and stress (479)—upset and strain

strikes men that (485)—men suddenly think that

strive (479)—to make an effort to gain or achieve something

sweep of history (488)—the many years in the past and in the future

swerves and bends (483)—frequently changing direction

tangible (472)—actual physical objects that can be touched

tentative blueprint (483)—temporary plan

tenure (484)—a guarantee that many university and college teachers are given that they will always have their jobs

terminally ill (489)—people who will die from the illness

thrust of (476)—the direction of

timed items (466)—items that have a time limit

timing (454)—the time that they choose

tomboyishness (468)—when a young woman behaves like a young male

tracked their attachment (463)—watched and studied how the babies showed their attachment to their mothers

traditional shackles (486)—traditional confinements

try out (468)—attempt

trying out (468)—experimenting with

turmoil (489)—when things are in a state of confusion and upset; difficulty

unwritten rule (465)—informal and nonspecific idea that is accepted and followed by many

upon entry (483)—when we enter the adult world

usher in (455)—introduce

venture onto (484)—to go onto

was once believed (487)—people used to believe

waterfowl (466)—birds that live in the water, such as ducks

ways of carrying themselves (473)—methods of dressing, walking, talking, and acting

wear away at (473)—to question and to criticize

webbed fingers and toes (457)—not completely developed fingers and toes that still have skin attaching them to each other; they look like the webbed feet of a frog

when so placed (469)—when they were placed this way

why me? (490)—why did this happen to me and not someone else?

wind up (479)—become; when they are finished growing

wolf down (479)—quickly eat a lot in a short period like a wild animal might

would "never get myself together" (484)—would never organize myself and my life

wrapped up in the ways (458)—concerned with the ways

wrenching Oedipus complex (476)—a difficult and upsetting (wrenching) emotional separation from the parent of the opposite sex, which is considered to be necessary for an individual to develop as a healthy person; Oedipus was the tragic hero of a famous Greek myth, or teaching story

wrestle (481)—to have difficulty deciding what is the best decision

wrongdoer (472)—a person who does something wrong

yearning for independence (498)—a great desire to be independent

---

FILL-INS   **Chapter Review**

SECTION 1: CONTROVERSIES IN DEVELOPMENTAL PSYCHOLOGY

Aspects of behavior that originate in our genes and unfold in the child as long as minimal nutrition and social experience are provided are referred to as our (1) _____ure. Those aspects of behavior that can be largely traced to environmental influences such as nutrition and learning are said to reflect our (2) _____ure. Psychologist Arnold (3) G_____ endorsed natural explanations of development. Gesell argued that development is self-regulated by the unfolding of natural plans and processes, or by (4) _____ation. John Watson and other behaviorists leaned heavily toward (5) _____mental explanations. (6) W_____ focused primarily on adaptive behavior patterns, whereas (7) _____ell focused on including physical and motor growth and development.

Psychologists argue as to whether developmental changes occur gradually—that is, (8) _____ously, or in major qualitative leaps that dramatically alter the ways in which we are structured and behave—that is, (9) _____ously. Behaviorists view development as a (10) _____ous process in which the effects of learning mount gradually, with no major sudden qualitative changes. (11) _____tional theorists, by contrast, believe that there are periods of life during which development occurs so dramatically that we can speak of its occurring in (12) _____ges.

SECTION 2: PHYSICAL DEVELOPMENT

It is possible to become pregnant for a day or so following (13) _____tion. Ovulation is defined as the releasing of an (14) o_____ from an ovary. A person begins to grow and develop when a sperm cell combines with an ovum to become a (15) z_____. Sperm cells can carry X or (16) _____ sex chromosomes. If a sperm cell with (17: an X or a Y?) sex chromosome fertilizes an ovum, a boy is conceived.

Prenatal development may be divided into (18: How Many?) _____ stages or periods. These are the (19) _____nal stage (approximately the first 2 weeks), the (20) em_____ stage (which lasts from 2 weeks to about 2 months after conception), and the (21) f_____ stage. During the germinal stage, the zygote divides repeatedly as it travels through the (22) f_____ tube and then within the uterus. Then the zygote becomes implanted in the wall of the (23) u_____.

The (24) _____ic period lasts from implantation until the end of the second month. During the embryonic period, the major (25) o_____ systems of the unborn child undergo rapid development. Development follows two general trends: (26) _____caudal and (27) prox_____.

The most dramatic gains in height and weight occur during (28) _____tal development. Babies usually double their birth weight in about (29: How Many?) _____ months and triple it by the (30: Which?) _____ birthday. Following the gains of infancy, children gain about (31: How Many?) _____ to 3 inches a year and (32: How Many?) _____ to 6 pounds a year until they reach the adolescent growth spurt.

Infants are born with a number of reflexes. Reflexes are (33) _____typical responses elicited by specific stimuli. Reflexes occur automatically; they do not involve higher (34) b_____ functions. The most basic reflex for survival is (35) _____hing. In the (36) _____ing reflex, infants turn their heads toward stimuli that touch the cheek. In the (37) _____ing reflex, infants suck objects that touch the lips. In the (38) s_____, or Moro reflex, infants arch their backs and draw up their legs in response to sudden noises and bumps. In the grasp, or (39) _____r reflex, infants grasp objects pressed against the palms of the hands. In the (40) B_____ reflex, they spread their toes when the soles of the feet are stimulated. Reflexes like rooting and sucking promote survival and phase out as neural functioning (41) _____ures and many previously automatic processes come under (42) vol_____ control.

Newborn children sleep about (43: How Many?) _____ hours a day. The (44) _____ary reflex is present at birth, so the irises widen automatically to admit more light when it is dark, and vice versa. Neonates do not show visual (45) _____dation; they see as through a fixed-focus camera. Infants are generally capable of depth perception, as measured by behavior on the visual cliff, by the time they are able to (46) c_____.

Most newborns (47) _____xively turn their heads toward unusual sounds. Three-day-old babies prefer their (48) _____rs' voices to those of other women, but do not show similar preferences for the voices of their fathers. Newborns can discriminate different odors, and they breathe (49: More or Less?) rapidly and are (50: More or Less?) active when presented with powerful odors. Newborns can discriminate sweet tastes. The tongue pressure of neonates sucking on a nipple correlates with the amount of (51) s_____ in their liquid diet. Newborns are sensitive to touch, but relatively insensitive to (52) p_____, which may reflect an adaptive response to the process of birth.

SECTION 3: SOCIAL DEVELOPMENT

Ainsworth defines attachment "as an (53) _____tional tie that one person or animal forms between himself and another specific one—a tie that binds them together in (54) s_____ and endures over time." Securely attached babies cry (55: More or Less?) frequently and are (56: More or Less?) likely to show affection toward their mothers than insecurely attached babies.

Ainsworth identified three stages of attachment: the (57) _____-_____chment phase, which lasts from birth to about 3 months and is characterized by indiscriminate attachment; the (58) attachment-in-the-_____ing phase, which occurs at about 3 or 4 months and is characterized by preference for familiar figures; and the (59) c_____-cut-attachment phase, which occurs at 6 or 7 months and is characterized by greater dependence on the primary caregiver.

Behaviorists argue that children become attached to mothers through (60) _____ning, because their mothers feed them and attend to other primary needs. From this view, mothers serve as conditioned (61)_____ers.

The Harlow studies with rhesus monkeys suggest that an innate motive, referred to as (62) c_____ comfort, is more important than conditioning in the development of attachment. Harlow's infant monkeys spent more time on soft terry-cloth (63) su_____ "mothers" than on wire "mothers," even when their feeding bottles protruded from the wire mothers.

Ethologists argue that attachment occurs during a (64) c_____ period. During this critical period, young animals such as ducks and geese form (65) _____ive attachments to the first moving objects they encounter. The process of forming an attachment in this manner is called (66) _____ing. Attachment in these animals is bounded at the early end by the age at which they first engage in (67) lo_____ and, at the upper end, by the development of (68) _____r of strangers.

SECTION 4: COGNITIVE DEVELOPMENT

Jean Piaget has advanced our knowledge of children's (69) c_____ development. Piaget saw children as budding (70)_____ists, who actively strive to make sense of the perceptual world. Piaget referred to action patterns and mental structures that are involved in acquiring or organizing knowledge as (71) _____s. He defined intelligence as involving processes of (72) _____tion, or responding to events according to existing schemes, and (73) _____tion, or the changing of schemes to permit effective responses to new events.

Piaget's view of cognitive development includes (74: How Many?) _____ stages or periods. First comes the (75) _____ or, period, which occurs prior to use of symbols and language. During the sensorimotor period, the child comes to mentally represent objects and thus develops object (76) per_____. Second is the (77) _____tional period, which is characterized by egocentric thought (or inability to see the world as it is seen by others); animism; artificialism; inability to (78) _____ter on more than one aspect of a situation at a time; and (79: Objective or Subjective?) moral judgments. Third is the (80) c_____-operational period, which is characterized by conservation; less egocentrism; reversibility; and (81: Objective or Subjective?) moral judgments. The fourth period is the (82) f_____-operational period, which is characterized by capacity for abstract logic.

Various issues have been raised about Piaget's views. For example, Piaget's methodology led him to (83: Overestimate or Underestimate?) the ages at which children can carry out certain kinds of tasks. Also, cognitive skills such as egocentrism and conservation may develop (84: More or Less?) continuously than Piaget thought—not in general stages. On the positive side, it seems that the sequences of development are indeed (85: Variant or Invariant?), as Piaget believed.

Kohlberg's theory of cognitive development focuses on the development of (86) _____al reasoning. Kohlberg hypothesizes that the processes of moral reasoning develop through (87: How Many?) _____ "levels" and (88: How Many?) _____ stages within each level. In the (89) _____tional level, judgments are based on expectation of rewards or punishments. Stage 1 is oriented toward obedience and (90) _____ment. In stage 2, good behavior is equated with what will allow people to satisfy (91) _____ds. Conventional-level moral judgments reflect the need to conform to conventional standards of right or wrong. According to the stage 3 (92) " g_____-_____ orientation," it is good to meet the needs and expectations of others. In stage 4, moral judgments are based on rules that maintain the social (93) _____r. The third level in Kohlberg's theory is termed (94) _____tional, and it consists of stages 5 and 6. In stage 5's (95) co_____, legalistic orientation, it is recognized that laws stem from agreed-upon procedures and that existing laws cannot bind the individual's behavior in unusual circumstances. In stage 6's conscience, or (96) _____ed, orientation, people consider behavior that is consistent with their own ethical standards as right.

Critics suggest that postconventional reasoning, especially stage (97) _____ reasoning, may be more reflective of Kohlberg's philosophical ideals than of a natural stage of cognitive development.

SECTION 5: ADOLESCENCE

Adolescence begins at (98) p_____ and ends with assumption of adult responsibilities. Puberty begins with the appearance of (99) _____ary sex characteristics, such as the growth of bodily hair, deepening of the (100) v_____ in males, and rounding of the breasts and hips in females. Changes that lead to reproductive capacity and secondary sex characteristics are stimulated by (101) _____rone in the male and by (102) _____en and androgens in the female. Testosterone causes the penis and (103) _____es to grow and pubic hair to appear. Small amounts of (104) _____gens, along with estrogen, stimulate growth of pubic and axillary hair in the female. First menstruation is termed (105) _____che.

Gould and other researchers have found that adolescents frequently yearn for (106) _____ence from parents. Erikson considers ego (107) _____y, or the defining of a life role, the major challenge of adolescence. Adolescents who do not develop ego identity may encounter role (108) d_____.

SECTION 6: ADULT DEVELOPMENT

Adulthood can be divided into young, middle, and (109) l_____ adulthood. According to Sheehy, young adulthood is generally characterized by striving to advance in the (110) c_____ world. Erikson considers the development of (111) _____te relationships a central task of young adulthood. Erikson labels young adulthood the stage of intimacy versus (112) i_____. According to Levinson, young adults often adopt a (113) d_____, which serves as a tentative blueprint for their lives and is characterized by the drive to "become" someone, to leave their mark on history.

During the late 20s and 30s, many women encounter a crisis involving concerns about nearing the end of the (114) f_____ years, closing opportunities, and heightened responsibilities. Sheehy labels the 30s the (115) C_____ 30s, because many adults encounter disillusionment and reassess their lives at this time.

Many middle-aged people encounter feelings of entrapment and loss of purpose that are termed the (116) mi_____ _____. Erikson labels middle age the stage of (117) g_____ versus stagnation. Middle adulthood is a time when we must come to terms with the discrepancies between our (118) _____ments and the dreams of youth.

Sheehy coins the term (119) mid_____ to describe a period of searching among the middle-aged that is in some ways similar to adolescence. Both are an age of (120) _____tion. Middlescence involves a search for new (121) _____ity.

It was once thought that middle-aged women experience the (122) "e_____-_____ syndrome" (when the youngest child leaves home), but research does not support this view. However, many women at this time show increased (123) dom_____ and (124) _____iveness. It is as if the children's leaving home has freed them from (125) tr_____ expectations of how women are supposed to behave.

Late adulthood begins at age (126) _____. Psychologists have become (127: More or Less?) concerned about late adulthood in recent years. In late adulthood, changes in (128) _____m metabolism lead to increased brittleness in the bones. The senses become (129: More or Less?) acute, and so the elderly frequently season their food more heavily. The time required to respond to stimuli—that is, (130) _____ion time—increases. "Successful agers" reshape their lives to concentrate on what they find to be important and (131) _____ful.

Heredity plays a role in having a long life span, or (132) _____ity. According to the (133) _____ar aging theory, the ability to repair DNA within cells decreases as we age. Environmental factors such as exercise, proper diet, and the maintenance of (134) c_____ over one's life can all apparently delay aging to some degree.

Kübler-Ross identifies five stages of dying among the terminally ill: (135) de_____, anger, bargaining, (136) de_____, and final (137) _____ance. Research by other investigators finds that psychological reactions to approaching death are (138: More or Less?) varied than Kübler-Ross suggests.

Erikson terms late adulthood the stage of ego (139) _____ty versus despair. Ego integrity is the ability to maintain one's sense of identity in spite of progressive physical deterioration. Erikson argues that ego integrity is derived from (140) w_____, and he argues that adjustment in the later years requires the wisdom to be able to let go.

ANSWER KEY TO CHAPTER REVIEW

1. Nature	36. Rooting	71. Schemes	106. Independence
2. Nurture	37. Sucking	72. Assimilation	107. Identity
3. Gesell	38. Startle	73. Accommodation	108. Diffusion
4. Maturation	39. Palmar	74. Four	109. Late
5. Environmental	40. Babinski	75. Sensorimotor	110. Career
6. Watson	41. Matures	76. Permanence	111. Intimate
7. Gesell	42. Voluntary	77. Preoperational	112. Isolation
8. Continuously	43. 16	78. Center	113. Dream
9. Discontinuously	44. Pupillary	79. Objective	114. Fertile
10. Continuous	45. Accommodation	80. Concrete	115. Catch
11. Maturational	46. Crawl	81. Subjective	116. Midlife crisis
12. Stages	47. Reflexively	82. Formal	117. Generativity
13. Ovulation	48. Mothers'	83. Underestimate	118. Achievements
14. Ovum	49. More	84. More	119. Middlescence
15. Zygote	50. More	85. Invariant	120. Transition
16. Y	51. Sugar	86. Moral	121. Identity
17. a Y	52. Pain	87. Three	122. Empty-nest
18. Three	53. Affectional	88. Two	123. Dominance
19. Germinal	54. Space	89. Preconventional	124. Assertiveness
20. Embryonic	55. Less	90. Punishment	125. Traditional
21. Fetal	56. More	91. Needs	126. 65
22. Fallopian	57. Initial-preattachment	92. Good-boy	127. More
23. Uterus	58. Attachment-in-the-making	93. Order	128. Calcium
24. Embryonic	59. Clear-cut-attachment	94. Postconventional	129. Less
25. Organ	60. Conditioning	95. Contractual	130. Reaction
26. Cephalocaudal	61. Reinforcers	96. Principled	131. Meaningful
27. Proximodistal	62. Contact	97. 6	132. Longevity
28. Prenatal	63. Surrogate	98. Puberty	133. Cellular
29. 5	64. Critical	99. Secondary	134. Control
30. First	65. Instinctive	100. Voice	135. Denial
31. 2	66. Imprinting	101. Testosterone	136. Depression
32. 4	67. Locomotion	102. Estrogen	137. Acceptance
33. Stereotypical	68. Fear	103. Testes	138. More
34. Brain	69. Cognitive	104. Androgens	139. Integrity
35. Breathing	70. Scientists	105. Menarche	140. Wisdom

POSTTEST | Multiple Choice

1. Conception normally takes place in the
   a. uterus.
   b. fallopian tube.
   c. ovary.
   d. vagina.

2. Development tends to be continuous, according to the views of
   a. Sigmund Freud.
   b. Erik Erikson.
   c. John Watson.
   d. Jean Piaget.

3. The embryonic period lasts from _____ until about the eighth week of prenatal development.
   a. implantation
   b. conception
   c. ovulation
   d. the time the zygote reaches the uterus

4. There is a sudden noise in the nursery, and a newborn baby draws up his legs and arches his back in response. This response is an example of the _____ reflex.
   a. Babinski
   b. palmar
   c. sphincter
   d. Moro

5. Which of the following is true of perception in babies?
   a. They prefer the voices of their fathers to those of other men.
   b. They cannot hear until they are 2 to 3 weeks old.
   c. They can perceive depth within a few days after birth.
   d. They are born with the pupillary reflex.

6. All of the following are known for research in the area of attachment, with the exception of
   a. Konrad Lorenz.
   b. Mary Ainsworth.
   c. Jown Bowlby.
   d. Sandra Bem.

7. In Harlow's experiments, infant rhesus monkeys showed preference for surrogate mothers
   a. of their own species.
   b. that were made from soft material.
   c. that fed them.
   d. that were present when they wanted to explore the environment.

8. Piaget viewed children as
   a. reacting mechanically to environmental stimuli.
   b. at the mercy of instinctive impulses.
   c. budding scientists.
   d. having a hierarchy of needs.

9. According to Piaget, children first show object permanence during the
   a. sensorimotor period.
   b. preoperational period.
   c. concrete-operational period.
   d. formal-operational period.

10. According to Piaget, children first center on the motives of wrongdoers, as well as the amount of damage done, during the

    a. sensorimotor period.
    b. preoperational period.
    c. concrete-operational period.
    d. formal-operational period.

11. Which of the following stages of moral development comes earliest, according to Kohlberg?
    a. good-boy orientation
    b. contractual, legalistic orientation
    c. naively egoistic orientation
    d. obedience-and-punishment orientation

12. According to Kohlberg, stage _____ moral judgments are characterized by respect for authority and social order.
    a. 1
    b. 2
    c. 3
    d. 4

13. Carstensen's research on people aged 70 and above reveals that successful agers
    a. do not experience menopause or manopause.
    b. are fixated in the stage of middlescence.
    c. compete with younger people in all areas.
    d. form emotional goals that bring them satisfaction.

14. The period of adolescence is defined by
    a. biological changes only.
    b. psychosocial changes only.
    c. both biological and psychosocial changes.
    d. neither biological nor psychosocial changes.

15. Sheehy uses the term "middlescence" to suggest that
    a. adolescence occurs in the middle of life.
    b. middle age has become a second adolescent period.
    c. psychologists take a scientific approach to the study of middle age.
    d. there is a stage of life between childhood and adolescence.

16. Menarche is defined as
    a. the beginning of puberty in girls.
    b. the appearance of secondary sex characteristics in girls.
    c. the complete maturation of secondary sex characteristics in girls.
    d. first menstruation.

17. According to Erikson, adolescence is characterized by the crisis of
    a. ego identity versus role diffusion.
    b. intimacy versus isolation.
    c. autonomy versus doubt.
    d. ego integrity versus despair.

18. Sheehy labels the 30s the "Catch 30s" because
    a. the long bones make no further gains in length.
    b. of disillusionments and reassessments.
    c. women enter midlife at about age 35.
    d. we reach the halfway point of the typical life span.

19. Research shows that middle-aged women
    a. frequently show increased dominance and assertiveness.
    b. most often report decreased marital satisfaction.

c. cannot make the transition from motherhood to socially useful occupations.
d. come under the influence of the dream.

20. According to the cellular aging theory, the ability to repair _____ decreases as we age.
    a. the cell wall
    b. the myelin sheath
    c. DNA
    d. RNA

ANSWER KEY TO POSTTEST

1. B	4. D	7. B	10. C	13. D	16. D	19. A
2. C	5. D	8. C	11. D	14. C	17. A	20. C
3. A	6. D	9. A	12. D	15. B	18. B	

LEARNING OBJECTIVES

When you have finished studying Chapter 12, you should be able to:

"WHY ARE THEY SAD AND GLAD AND BAD?":
INTRODUCTION TO PERSONALITY
1. Define *personality*.

THE TRAIT PERSPECTIVE
2. Describe the contributions of Gordon Allport and Raymond Cattell to trait theory.
3. Describe the trait theory of Hans Eysenck.
4. Describe the Big Five trait theory.

THE PSYCHODYNAMIC PERSPECTIVE
5. Describe the psychodynamic views of Sigmund Freud.
6. Describe the psychodynamic views of Carl Jung, Alfred Adler, Karen Horney, and Erik Erikson.

THE LEARNING PERSPECTIVE
7. Describe the behaviorist approach to personality.
8. Describe the social-cognitive approach to personality.

THE HUMANISTIC–EXISTENTIAL PERSPECTIVE
9. Describe Abraham Maslow's views on personality.
10. Describe Carl Rogers's self theory.

THE SOCIOCULTURAL PERSPECTIVE
11. Discuss research concerning sociocultural issues in personality.

MEASUREMENT OF PERSONALITY
12. Describe some of the major objective and projective measures of personality.

GENDER DIFFERENCES IN PERSONALITY
13. Describe gender differences in personality.
14. Describe theoretical views of gender differences in personality.

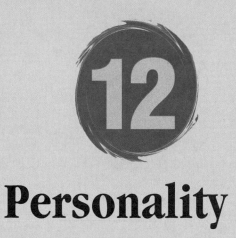

12

Personality

PRETEST *Truth or Fiction?*

_____ Obese people are jolly.

_____ According to Sigmund Freud, the human mind is like a vast submerged iceberg, only the tip of which rises above the surface into conscious awareness.

_____ According to Freud, biting one's fingernails or smoking cigarettes as an adult is a sign of conflict during very early childhood.

_____ We are more likely to persist at difficult tasks when we believe that we shall succeed.

_____ Psychologists can determine whether a person has told the truth on a personality test.

_____ There is a psychological test made up of inkblots, and one of them looks like a bat.

_____ Men behave more aggressively than women do.

*A*N unlearned carpenter of my acquaintance once said in my hearing: "There is very little difference between one [person] and another; but what little there is, is very important." This distinction seems to me to go to the heart of the matter.

WILLIAM JAMES

I was reading Dr. Seuss's *One Fish, Two Fish* to my daughter, Taylor, when she was 2 years old. The sneaky author set up a trap for fathers. A part of the book reads that "Some [fish] are sad. And some are glad. And some are very, very bad. Why are they sad and glad and bad? I do not know. Go ask your dad."

Thanks, Dr. Seuss.

For many months I had just recited this section and then moved on. On one particular day, however, Taylor's cognitive development had apparently flowered. No longer would she let me gloss this over. Why, indeed, she wanted to know, were some fish sad? Why were others glad and bad? I paused and then, being a typical American dad, I gave the answer I'm sure has been given by thousands of other fathers:

"Uh, some fish are sad and others are glad or bad because of, uh, the interaction of nature and nurture—I mean, you know, heredity and environmental factors."

To which Taylor laughed and replied "Not!"

Personality • The distinct patterns of behavior, thoughts, and feelings that characterize a person's adaptation to life.

Trait • A relatively stable aspect of personality that is inferred from behavior and assumed to give rise to consistent behavior.

"WHY ARE THEY SAD AND GLAD AND BAD?": INTRODUCTION TO PERSONALITY

I'm still not certain whether Taylor thought my words came out silly or that my psychological theorizing was simplistic or off base. But this question applied to people—that is, why people are sad or glad or bad—is the kind of question that is of interest to psychologists who investigate matters of **personality.**

Now, people do not necessarily agree on what the word *personality* means. Many lay people equate personality with liveliness, as in, "She's got a lot of personality." Others characterize a person's personality as consisting of the most striking or dominant traits. Someone may be described as having a "shy personality" or a "happy-go-lucky personality." Psychologists define personality as the reasonably stable patterns of emotions, motives, and behavior that distinguish people from one another.

Psychologists also seek to explain how personality *develops*—that is, why some (people) are sad or glad or bad. We begin this chapter with a descriptive approach to personality—the trait perspective. Then we explore the grand theories of personality: the psychodynamic, learning, humanistic–existential, and sociocultural theories. Finally, we describe methods of measuring whether people are sad, glad, bad, and lots of other things—personality tests.

THE TRAIT PERSPECTIVE

If I asked you to describe yourself, you would probably do so in terms of **traits.** Traits such as bright, sophisticated, and witty. (That is you, is it not?) We usually describe people in terms of traits.

Traits are reasonably stable elements of personality that are inferred from behavior. If you describe a friend as "shy," it may be because you have observed social anxiety or withdrawal in the friend's encounters. Traits are assumed to account for similar behavior in different situations. You probably expect your "shy" friend to be retiring in most social situations—"all across the board," as the saying goes. The concept of traits also finds a place in other approaches to personality. Sigmund Freud, for example, linked development of traits to children's experiences.

From Hippocrates to the Present Day

The history of the trait approach dates at least to Hippocrates (ca. 460–377 B.C.), the physician of the Golden Age of Greece (Maher & Maher, 1994). Hippocrates believed that traits were embedded in people's bodily fluids, or humors, and gave rise to certain types of personalities. People's personalities depended on the balance of four "basic fluids," or humors, in their bodies. Yellow bile was associated with a choleric (quick-tempered) disposition; blood, a sanguine (warm, cheerful) one; phlegm, a phlegmatic (sluggish, calm, cool) disposition; and black bile, a melancholic (gloomy, pensive) temperament. Disease was believed to reflect an imbalance in humors. Methods such as bloodletting and vomiting were recommended to restore the balance and one's health (Maher & Maher, 1994). Although Hippocrates' theoretical edifice lies in ruins, the terms *choleric, sanguine, phlegmatic,* and *melancholic* remain in use.

Early in the 20th century, William Sheldon suggested that personality traits were linked to body types (Maher & Maher, 1994). His types were derived from distinctions between layers of embryonic tissue. Sheldon's theory has not drawn much interest in recent years, in part because it perpetuated stereotypes such as the notion that obese people are jolly.

Truth or Fiction Revisited. *It is not true that obese people are jolly.* For the statement to be true, it would have to apply universally. It doesn't. Moreover, this view serves to perpetuate a stereotype.

More enduring trait theories, like that of Gordon Allport, have assumed that traits are heritable and embedded in the nervous system. They have used the mathematical technique of **factor analysis** to try to determine basic human traits.

Sir Francis Galton was among the first scientists to recognize the **lexical hypothesis.** It holds that many of the world's languages will use single words to describe fundamental human differences in personality (Goldberg, 1993). More than 50 years ago, Gordon Allport and a colleague (Allport & Oddbert, 1936) catalogued some 18,000 human traits from a search through word lists of the sort found in dictionaries. Some were physical traits such as short, black, and brunette. Others were behavioral traits such as shy and emotional. Still others were moral traits such as honest. This exhaustive list has served as the basis for personality research by many other psychologists, including Raymond Cattell.

Raymond Cattell (1965) refined the Allport catalogue. He removed unusual terms and grouped the remaining traits. Cattell also distinguished between surface traits and source traits. **Surface traits** describe characteristic ways of behaving—for example, cleanliness, stubbornness, thrift, and orderliness. Surface traits form meaningful patterns that are suggestive of underlying **source traits.** Cattell argued that psychological measurement of a person's source traits would enable us to predict his or her behavior.

Cattell's research led him to suggest the existence of 16 source traits. They can be measured by means of his Sixteen Personality Factors Scale. The "16 PF" is frequently used in psychological research that explores differences

Factor analysis • A statistical technique that identifies variables or traits that tend to belong together or, as items on a personality test, to be answered in the same direction. For example, test items assessing organization, thoroughness, and reliability would tend to be answered in the same direction to form a factor that can be labeled *conscientiousness.*

Lexical hypothesis • The view that fundamental human differences in personality traits may be studied by surveying which traits are described by many of the world's languages in single words. People, that is, from various cultures will need concise ways of describing common personality traits.

Surface traits • Cattell's term for characteristic, observable ways of behaving.

Source traits • Cattell's term for underlying traits from which surface traits are derived.

Creative Artists. Artist Faith Ringgold (right) works on a quilt with a colleague. What traits are shown by creative artists? What are their strengths, their weaknesses? How do their personalities compare, say, to those of airline pilots? How do psychologists measure traits?

FIGURE 12.1

Three Personality Profiles According to Cattell's Personality Factors. How do the traits of writers, airline pilots, and creative artists compare? Where would you place yourself within these personality dimensions?

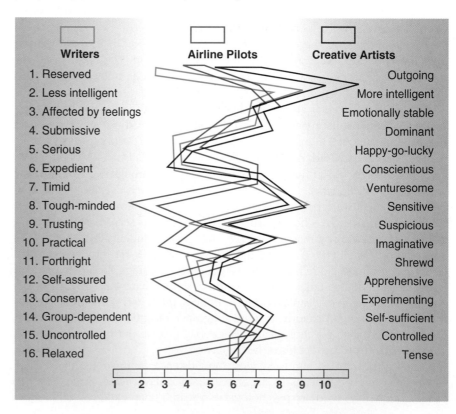

between groups of people and individuals. Figure 12.1. shows the differences, according to the 16 PF, between airline pilots, creative artists, and writers. Notice that the pilots are more stable, conscientious, tough-minded, practical, controlled, and relaxed than the other two groups. The artists and writers are more intelligent, sensitive, and imaginative.

Hans Eysenck

British psychologist Hans J. Eysenck (1960; Eysenck & Eysenck, 1985) has focused much of his research on the relationships between two important traits: **introversion–extroversion** and emotional stability **(neuroticism).** He has catalogued various personality traits according to where they are "situated" along these dimensions or factors (refer to Figure 12.2). For instance, an anxious person would be high both in introversion and in neuroticism—that is, preoccupied with his or her own thoughts and emotionally unstable.

Eysenck's scheme is reminiscent of that of Hippocrates. According to Eysenck's dimensions, the choleric type would be extroverted and unstable; the sanguine type, extroverted and stable; the phlegmatic type, introverted and stable; and the melancholic type, introverted and unstable.

FIGURE 12.2

Eysenck's Personality Dimensions and Hippocrates' Personality Types. Various personality traits shown in the outer ring fall within the two major dimensions of personality suggested by Hans Eysenck. The inner circle shows how Hippocrates' four major personality types—choleric, sanguine, phlegmatic, and melancholic—fit within Eysenck's modern dimensions.

Introversion • A source trait characterized by intense imagination and the tendency to inhibit impulses.

Extroversion • A source trait characterized by tendencies to be socially outgoing and to express feelings and impulses freely.

Neuroticism • Eysenck's term for emotional instability.

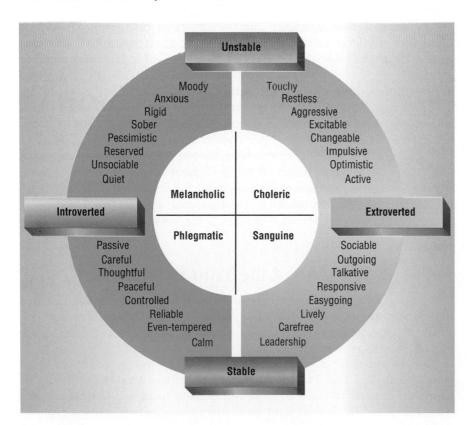

TABLE 12.1
THE BIG FIVE PERSONALITY FACTORS

FACTOR	NAME	TRAITS
I	Extroversion	Contrasts talkativeness, assertiveness, and activity with silence, passivity, and reserve
II	Agreeableness	Contrasts kindness, trust, and warmth with hostility, selfishness, and distrust
III	Conscientiousness	Contrasts organization, thoroughness, and reliability with carelessness, negligence, and unreliability
IV	Emotional stability	Includes traits such as nervousness, moodiness, temperamentality, and sensitivity to negative stimuli
V	Openness to experience	Contrasts imagination, curiosity, and creativity with shallowness and imperceptiveness

Sources: Clark and others, 1994; Goldberg, 1993.

The Big Five Factor Structure

Empirical studies (Digman, 1990; Trull, 1992) suggest that there may be five basic personality factors (Goldberg, 1993; Kimble, 1994). They include the two found by Eysenck—introversion–extroversion and emotional stability—and three suggested by Raymond Cattell—conscientiousness, agreeableness, and openness to new experience (akin to Cattell's experimenting-conservative dimension; see Table 12.1). Many personality theorists, especially Louis Thurstone, Raymond Cattell, and Donald Fiske, can be said to have had a part in the development of the Big Five. However, Tupes and Christal (1992) are usually credited because of their key studies for the U.S. Air Force (Goldberg, 1993; McCrae, 1992). The Big Five have found practical applications in areas such as personnel selection and classification (Goldberg, 1993) and psychological disorders (Clark and others, 1994; Widiger & Costa, 1994).

There continues to be disagreement on the number of basic personality factors (Block, 1995). Zuckerman (1992), for example, questions the ways in which researchers determine which personality factors are basic and which are not. Hans Eysenck is less charitable. He argues that the Big Five factor theory is unscientific, even "a grotesque product of the imagination" (Eysenck, 1993, p. 1299).

Evaluation of the Trait Perspective

Trait theories have their strengths and weaknesses. Trait theorists have focused much attention on the development of useful tests such as Cattell's Sixteen Personality Factors Scale to measure traits. Others are discussed in the section on measurement of personality.

Trait theorists have also spawned theories concerning the fit between personality and jobs. The qualities that suit us for various kinds of work can be expressed in terms of our abilities, our personality traits, and our interests. By using interviews and tests to learn about our abilities and our traits, testing and

MINILECTURE:
TRAIT THEORIES

counseling centers can make valuable suggestions about the likelihood for our success and fulfillment in various kinds of jobs.

Freud developed his theories about "oral," "anal," and other traits on the basis of clinical case studies. However, trait theorists have administered broad personality tests to thousands of people and have used sophisticated statistical techniques to identify the basic traits, or factors, that tend to describe us.

One weakness of trait theory is that it is descriptive, not explanatory. Trait theory focuses on describing traits rather than tracing their origins or investigating how they may be modified. Moreover, the "explanations" that are provided by trait theory are often criticized as being **circular explanations.** That is, they restate what is observed and do not explain what is observed. Saying that John failed to ask Marsha on a date *because* of shyness is an example of a circular explanation: We have merely restated John's (shy) behavior as a trait (shyness).

The trait concept requires that traits show stability. Although many personality traits seem to do so, behavior may vary more from situation to situation than trait theory would allow (Mischel, 1993).

Reflections

- How would you describe yourself in terms of traits? Why?
- Where would you place athletes and artists in terms of the dimensions of introversion–extroversion and emotional stability? Where would you place yourself?

THE PSYCHODYNAMIC PERSPECTIVE

There are several **psychodynamic theories** of personality, but they have things in common. Each teaches that personality is characterized by a dynamic struggle. Drives such as sex, aggression, and the need for superiority come into conflict with laws, social rules, and moral codes. The laws and social rules become internalized. We make them parts of ourselves. After doing so, the dynamic struggle becomes a clashing of opposing *inner* forces. At any moment, our behavior, thoughts, and emotions represent the outcome of these inner contests.

Each psychodynamic theory owes its origin to the thinking of Sigmund Freud.

Sigmund Freud's Theory of Psychosexual Development

He was born with a shock of dark hair—in Jewish tradition, the sign of a prophet. In 1856, in a Czechoslovakian village, an old woman told his mother that she had given birth to a great man. The child was reared with great expectations. His sister, in fact, was prohibited from playing the piano when Freud was reading or reflecting in his room.[1] In manhood, Sigmund Freud himself would be cynical about the prophecy. Old women, after all, would earn greater favors by forecasting good tidings than doom. But the forecast about Freud was not pure fantasy. Few have influenced our thinking about human nature so deeply.

Circular explanation • An explanation that merely restates its own concepts instead of offering additional information.

Psychodynamic theory • Sigmund Freud's perspective, which emphasizes the importance of unconscious motives and conflicts as forces that determine behavior.

---

[1] My wife believes that Freud's sister was running into standard 19th-century sexism. She might have been prevented from playing the piano if playing interfered with the activities of any man, not just the "local family genius."

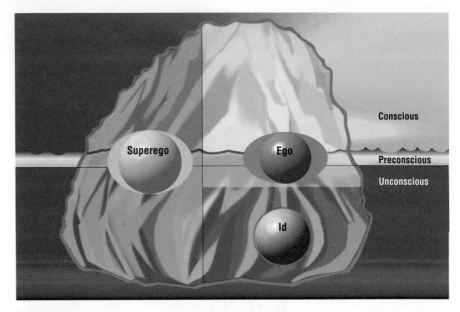

FIGURE 12.3

The Human Iceberg According to Freud. According to psychodynamic theory, only the tip of human personality rises above the surface of the mind into conscious awareness. Material in the preconscious can become conscious if we direct our attention to it, but unconscious material tends to remain shrouded in mystery.

Conscious • Self-aware.

Preconscious • Capable of being brought into awareness by the focusing of attention.

Unconscious • In psychodynamic theory, not available to awareness by simple focusing of attention.

How Much Are We Aware Of? Freud suggested that people are aware of but a few of the ideas and the impulses that dwell within their minds. The greater mass of the mind, our deepest images, thoughts, fears, and urges, remain beneath the surface of awareness.

Freud was trained as a physician. Early in his practice, he was astounded to find that some people apparently experienced loss of feeling in a hand or paralysis of the legs in the absence of any medical disorder. These odd symptoms often disappeared once people had recalled and discussed stressful events and feelings of guilt or anxiety that seemed to be related to the symptoms. For a long time, these events and feelings had been hidden beneath the surface of awareness. Even so, they had the capacity to influence people's behavior.

From this sort of clinical evidence, Freud concluded that the human mind is like an iceberg (Loftus & Klinger, 1992). Only the tip of an iceberg rises above the surface of the water, while the great mass of it darkens the deep (see Figure 12.3). Freud came to believe that people, similarly, were aware of only a small number of the ideas and impulses that dwelled within their minds. Freud argued that the greater mass of the mind—our deepest images, thoughts, fears, and urges—remained beneath the surface of conscious awareness, where little light illumined them.

Truth or Fiction Revisited. *According to Sigmund Freud, it is true that the human mind is like a vast submerged iceberg, only the tip of which rises above the surface into conscious awareness.* We will see that most personality theorists credit conscious thought with more importance than Freud did.

Freud labeled the region that poked through into the light of awareness the **conscious** part of the mind. He called the regions that lay below the surface the *preconscious* and the *unconscious*. The **preconscious** mind contains elements of experience that are presently out of awareness but that can be made conscious simply by focusing on them. The **unconscious** mind is shrouded in mystery. It contains biological instincts such as sex and aggression. Some unconscious urges cannot be experienced consciously because mental images and words could not portray them in all their color and fury. Other unconscious urges may be kept below the surface by repression.

Repression is the automatic ejection of anxiety-evoking ideas from awareness. Research evidence suggests that many people repress ugly childhood experiences (Myers & Brewin, 1994). Perhaps "something shocking happens, and the mind pushes it into some inaccessible corner of the unconscious" (Loftus, 1993a). Repression may also protect us from perceiving morally unacceptable impulses.

In the unconscious mind, primitive drives seek expression. Internalized values try to keep them in check. The resultant conflict can precipitate outbursts and psychological problems.

We cannot view the unconscious mind directly. Freud explored the unconscious through a method of mental detective work called **psychoanalysis.** In this method, people are prodded to talk about anything that "pops" into their minds while they remain comfortable and relaxed. People may gain some useful **self-insight** by pursuing some of the thoughts that pop into awareness. But they are also motivated to evade threatening subjects. Repression not only ejects unacceptable thoughts from awareness. It also prompts **resistance**—the desire to avoid thinking or talking about them. Repression and resistance can make psychoanalysis a tedious process that lasts for years, even decades.

THE STRUCTURE OF PERSONALITY.   When is a structure not a structure? When it is a mental or **psychic structure.** Sigmund Freud labeled the clashing forces of personality *psychic structures.* They could not be seen or measured directly, but their presence was suggested by behavior, expressed thoughts, and emotions. Freud hypothesized the existence of three psychic structures: the *id, ego,* and *superego.*

The **id** is present at birth. It represents physiological drives and is fully unconscious. Freud described the id as "a chaos, a cauldron of seething excitations" (1964, p. 73). The conscious mind might find it inconsistent to love and hate a person at the same time, but Freud believed that conflicting emotions could dwell side by side in the id. In the id, we could feel hatred for our mothers for failing to immediately gratify all of our needs even as we sense love for them.

The id follows what Freud termed the **pleasure principle.** It demands instant gratification of instincts without consideration of law, social custom, or the needs of others.

The **ego** begins to develop during the first year of life, largely because a child's demands for gratification cannot all be met immediately. The ego "stands for reason and good sense" (Freud, 1964, p. 76), for rational ways of coping with frustration. The ego curbs the appetites of the id and makes plans that are compatible with social convention. Thus, a person can find gratification yet avoid social disapproval. The id lets you know that you are hungry. The ego formulates the idea of microwaving some enchiladas.

The ego is guided by the **reality principle.** It takes into account what is practical along with what is urged. The ego also provides the conscious sense of self.

Although most of the ego is conscious, some of its business is carried out unconsciously. For instance, the ego also acts as a censor that screens the impulses of the id. When the ego senses that improper impulses are rising into awareness, it may use psychological defenses to deter them from surfacing. Repression is one such psychological defense, or **defense mechanism.** Various defense mechanisms are described in Table 12.2.

Repression • A defense mechanism that protects the person from anxiety by ejecting anxiety-evoking ideas and impulses from awareness.

Psychoanalysis • In this usage, Freud's method of exploring human personality.

Self-insight • Accurate awareness of one's motives and feelings.

Resistance • A blocking of thoughts whose awareness could cause anxiety.

Psychic structure • In psychodynamic theory, a hypothesized mental structure that helps explain different aspects of behavior.

Id • The psychic structure, present at birth, that represents physiological drives and is fully unconscious.

Pleasure principle • The governing principle of the id; the seeking of immediate gratification of instinctive needs.

Ego • The second psychic structure to develop, characterized by self-awareness, planning, and delay of gratification.

Reality principle • Consideration of what is practical and possible in gratifying needs; the governing principle of the ego.

Defense mechanism • In psychodynamic theory, an unconscious function of the ego that protects it from anxiety-evoking material by preventing accurate recognition of this material.

TABLE 12.2
SOME DEFENSE MECHANISMS OF THE EGO, ACCORDING TO PSYCHODYNAMIC THEORY

DEFENSE MECHANISM	DEFINITION	EXAMPLES
Repression	The ejection of anxiety-evoking ideas from awareness.	A student forgets that a difficult term paper is due. A person in therapy forgets an appointment when anxiety-evoking material is to be discussed.
Regression	The return, under stress, to a form of behavior characteristic of an earlier stage of development.	An adolescent cries when forbidden to use the family car. An adult becomes highly dependent on his parents following the breakup of his marriage.
Rationalization	The use of self-deceiving justifications for unacceptable behavior.	A student blames her cheating on her teacher's leaving the room during a test. A man explains his cheating on his income tax by saying, "Everyone does it."
Displacement	The transfer of ideas and impulses from threatening or unsuitable objects to less threatening objects.	A worker picks a fight with her spouse after being criticized sharply by her supervisor.
Projection	The thrusting of one's own unacceptable impulses onto others so that others are assumed to harbor them.	A hostile person perceives the world as being a dangerous place. A sexually frustrated person interprets innocent gestures of others as sexual advances.
Reaction formation	Assumption of behavior in opposition to one's genuine impulses in order to keep impulses repressed.	A person who is angry with a relative behaves in a "sickly sweet" manner toward that relative. A sadistic individual becomes a physician.
Denial	Refusal to accept the true nature of a threat.	Belief that one will not contract cancer or heart disease although one smokes heavily. "It can't happen to me."
Sublimation	The channeling of primitive impulses into positive, constructive efforts.	A person paints nudes for the sake of "beauty" and "art." A hostile person becomes a tennis star.

Superego • The third psychic structure, which functions as a moral guardian and sets forth high standards for behavior.

Identification • In psychodynamic theory, the unconscious assumption of the behavior of another person.

Moral principle • The governing principle of the superego, which sets moral standards and enforces adherence to them.

The **superego** develops throughout early childhood, usually incorporating the moral standards and values of parents and important members of the community through **identification.** The superego functions according to the **moral principle.** The superego holds forth shining examples of an ideal self and also acts like the conscience, an internal moral guardian. Throughout life, the superego monitors the intentions of the ego and hands out judgments of right and wrong. It floods the ego with feelings of guilt and shame when the verdict is negative.

The ego hasn't an easy time of it. It stands between id and superego, braving the arrows of each. It strives to satisfy the demands of the id and the moral sense of the superego. The id may urge, "You are sexually aroused!" But the superego may warn, "You're not married." The poor ego is caught in the middle.

From the Freudian perspective, a healthy personality has found ways to gratify most of the id's demands without seriously offending the superego. Most of the id's remaining demands are contained or repressed. If the ego is not a good problem-solver, or if the superego is too stern, the ego will have a hard time of it.

STAGES OF PSYCHOSEXUAL DEVELOPMENT. Freud stirred controversy within the medical establishment of his day by arguing that sexual impulses were pivotal factors in personality development, even among children. Freud saw children's basic ways of relating to the world, such as sucking their mothers' breasts and moving their bowels, as entailing sexual feelings.

Freud believed that a major instinct, which he termed **Eros,** aimed at preserving and perpetuating life. Eros is fueled by psychological, or psychic, energy that Freud labeled **libido.** Libidinal energy involved sexual impulses, so Freud considered it to be *psychosexual*. Libidinal energy would be expressed through sexual feelings in different parts of the body, or **erogenous zones,** as the child developed. To Freud, human development involved the transfer of libidinal energy from one zone to another. He hypothesized five periods of **psychosexual development:** oral, anal, phallic, latency, and genital.

During the first year of life, a child experiences much of its world through the mouth. If it fits, into the mouth it goes. This is the **oral stage.** Freud argued that oral activities such as sucking and biting bring the child sexual gratification as well as nourishment.

Freud believed that children would encounter conflicts during each stage of psychosexual development. During the oral stage, conflict would center around the nature and extent of oral gratification. Early **weaning** could lead to frustration. Excessive gratification, on the other hand, could lead an infant to expect that it would routinely be handed everything in life. Insufficient or excessive gratification in any stage could lead to **fixation** in that stage and to the development of traits characteristic of that stage. Oral traits include dependency, gullibility, and optimism or pessimism.

Freud theorized that adults with an **oral fixation** could experience exaggerated desires for "oral activities," such as smoking, overeating, alcohol abuse, and nail biting. Like the infant whose very survival depends on the mercy of an adult, adults with oral fixations may be disposed toward clinging, dependent interpersonal relationships.

Truth or Fiction Revisited. *According to Freud, it is true that biting one's fingernails or smoking cigarettes as an adult is a sign of conflict during very early childhood.* Freud believed that adult problems tend to have their origins in childhood conflicts that are long lost to conscious awareness.

Note that according to psychodynamic theory, people are largely at the mercy of events that occurred long before they can weigh alternatives and make decisions about how to behave. Freud's own "oral fixation," cigar smoking, seems to have advanced the cancer of the mouth and jaw that killed him in 1939.

During the **anal stage,** sexual gratification is attained through contraction and relaxation of the muscles that control elimination of waste products. Elimination, which was controlled reflexively during most of the first year of life, comes under voluntary muscular control, even if such control is not reliable at first. The anal stage is said to begin in the second year of life.

During the anal stage, children learn to delay the gratification of eliminating as soon as they feel the urge. The general issue of self-control may become a source of conflict between parent and child. **Anal fixations** may stem from this conflict and lead to two sets of anal traits. So-called **anal-retentive** traits involve excessive use of self-control. They include perfectionism, a strong need for order, and exaggerated neatness and cleanliness. **Anal-expulsive** traits, on the other hand, "let it all hang out." They include carelessness, messiness, even **sadism.**

Children enter the **phallic stage** during the third year of life. During this stage, the major erogenous zone is the phallic region (the **clitoris** in girls). Parent–child conflict is likely to develop over masturbation, which parents may treat with punishment and threats. During the phallic stage, children may

Eros • In psychodynamic theory, the basic instinct to preserve and perpetuate life.

Libido • (1) In psychodynamic theory, the energy of Eros; the sexual instinct. (2) Generally, sexual interest or drive.

Erogenous zone • An area of the body that is sensitive to sexual sensations.

Psychosexual development • In psychodynamic theory, the process by which libidinal energy is expressed through different erogenous zones during different stages of development.

Oral stage • The first stage of psychosexual development, during which gratification is hypothesized to be attained primarily through oral activities.

Weaning • Accustoming a child not to suck the mother's breast or a baby bottle.

Fixation • In psychodynamic theory, arrested development; attachment to objects of an earlier stage.

Oral fixation • Attachment to objects and behaviors characteristic of the oral stage.

Anal stage • The second stage of psychosexual development, when gratification is attained through anal activities.

Anal fixation • Attachment to objects and behaviors characteristic of the anal stage.

Anal-retentive • Descriptive of behaviors and traits that have to do with "holding in," or self-control.

Anal-expulsive • Descriptive of behaviors and traits that have to do with unregulated self-expression such as messiness.

Sadism • Attaining gratification from inflicting pain on, or humiliating, others.

Phallic stage • The third stage of psychosexual development, characterized by a shift of libido to the phallic region.

Clitoris • An external female sex organ that is highly sensitive to sexual stimulation.

develop strong sexual attachments to the parent of the other gender and begin to view the parent of the same gender as a rival for the other parent's affections. Boys may want to marry Mommy, and girls may want to marry Daddy.

Feelings of lust and jealousy are difficult for children to handle. Home life would be tense indeed if they were aware of them. Thus, these feelings remain unconscious, but their influence is felt through fantasies about marriage and hostility toward the parent of the same gender. Freud labeled this conflict in boys the **Oedipus complex,** after the legendary Greek king who unwittingly killed his father and married his mother. Similar feelings in girls give rise to the **Electra complex.** According to Greek legend, Electra was the daughter of the king Agamemnon. She longed for him after his death and sought revenge against his slayers—her mother and her mother's lover.

The Oedipus and Electra complexes become resolved by about the ages of 5 or 6. Children then repress their hostilities toward, and identify with, the parent of the same gender. Identification leads to playing the social and gender roles of the parent of the same gender and internalizing that parent's values. Sexual feelings toward the parent of the other gender are repressed for a number of years. When the feelings emerge during adolescence, they are **displaced,** or transferred, to socially appropriate members of the other gender.

By the age of 5 or 6, Freud believed that children would have been in conflict with their parents over sexual feelings for several years. The pressures of the Oedipus and Electra complexes would motivate them to repress all sexual urges. In so doing, they would enter **latency,** a period of life during which sexual feelings remain unconscious. They would use this period to focus on schoolwork and to consolidate earlier learning, most notably of appropriate gender-role behaviors. During the latency phase, it would not be uncommon for children to prefer playmates of their own gender.

Freud wrote that we enter the final stage of psychosexual development, or **genital stage,** at puberty. Adolescent males again experience sexual urges toward their mothers and adolescent females toward their fathers. However, the **incest taboo** encourages repression of these impulses and their displacement onto other adults or adolescents of the other gender. Boys still might seek girls "just like the girl that married dear old Dad." Girls still might be attracted to men who resemble their fathers.

People in the genital stage prefer, by definition, to find sexual gratification through intercourse with a member of the other gender. In Freud's view, oral or anal stimulation, masturbation, and homosexual activity would all represent **pregenital** fixations and immature forms of sexual conduct. They would not be consistent with the life instinct Eros.

Other Psychodynamic Theorists

Several personality theorists are intellectual heirs of Sigmund Freud. Their theories, like Freud's, include roles for unconscious motivation, for motivational conflict, and for defensive responses to anxiety that involve repression and cognitive distortion of reality. In other respects, theories differ considerably.

CARL JUNG.

The brain is viewed as an appendage of the genital glands.

CARL JUNG (ON FREUD'S PSYCHODYNAMIC THEORY)

Carl Jung (1875–1961) was a Swiss psychiatrist who had been a member of Freud's inner circle. He fell into disfavor with Freud when he developed his

---

Oedipus complex • A conflict of the phallic stage in which the boy wishes to possess his mother sexually and perceives his father as a rival in love.

Electra complex • A conflict of the phallic stage in which the girl longs for her father and resents her mother.

Displaced • Transferred.

Latency • A phase of psychosexual development characterized by repression of sexual impulses.

Genital stage • The mature stage of psychosexual development, characterized by preferred expression of libido through intercourse with an adult of the other gender.

Incest taboo • The cultural prohibition against marrying or having sexual relations with a close blood relative.

Pregenital • Characteristic of stages less mature than the genital stage.

own psychodynamic theory—**analytical psychology.** As suggested by the above quotation, Jung downplayed the importance of the sexual instinct. He saw it as but one of several important instincts.

Jung, like Freud, was intrigued by unconscious processes. He believed that we not only have a *personal* unconscious that contains repressed memories and impulses, but also an inherited **collective unconscious.** The collective unconscious contains primitive images, or **archetypes,** which reflect the history of our species. Examples of archetypes are the All-Powerful God, the young hero, the fertile and nurturing mother, the wise old man, the hostile brother, even fairy godmothers, wicked witches, and themes of rebirth or resurrection. Archetypes themselves remain unconscious, but Jung declared that they influence our thoughts and emotions and render us responsive to cultural themes in stories and films.

Despite his interest in the collective unconscious, Jung granted more importance to conscious motives than Freud did. Jung believed that one of the archetypes is a **Self,** a unifying force of personality that gives direction and purpose to human behavior. According to Jung, the Self aims to provide the personality with wholeness or fullness.

ALFRED ADLER. Alfred Adler (1870–1937), another follower of Freud, also believed that Freud had placed too much emphasis on sexual impulses. Adler believed that people are basically motivated by an **inferiority complex.** In some people, feelings of inferiority may be based on physical problems and the need to compensate for them. Adler believed, however, that all of us encounter some feelings of inferiority because of our small size as children, and these feelings give rise to a **drive for superiority.** For instance, the English poet Lord Byron, who had a crippled leg, became a champion swimmer. Adler as a child was crippled by rickets and suffered from pneumonia, and it may be that his theory developed in part from his own childhood striving to overcome repeated bouts of illness.

Adler, like Jung, believed that self-awareness plays a major role in the formation of personality. Adler spoke of a **creative self,** a self-aware aspect of personality that strives to overcome obstacles and develop the individual's potential. Because each person's potential is unique, Adler's views have been termed **individual psychology.**

Adler introduced the term *sibling rivalry* to describe the jealousies that are found among brothers and sisters.

KAREN HORNEY. Karen Horney (1885–1952) agreed with Freud that childhood experiences played a major role in the development of adult personality. But like many other neoanalysts, she believed that sexual and aggressive impulses took a backseat in importance to social relationships. Moreover, she disagreed with Freud that anatomical differences between the genders led girls to feel inferior to boys.

Horney, like Freud, saw parent–child relationships to be of paramount importance. Small children are completely dependent: When their parents treat them with indifference or harshness, they develop feelings of insecurity and what Horney terms **basic anxiety.** Children also resent neglectful parents, and Horney theorized that a **basic hostility** would accompany basic anxiety. Horney agreed with Freud that children would repress rather than express feelings of hostility toward their parents because of fear of reprisal and, just as important, fear of driving them away. But in contrast to Freud, she also believed that genuine and consistent love could mitigate the effects of even the most traumatic childhoods (Quinn, 1987).

Analytical psychology • Jung's psychodynamic theory, which emphasizes the collective unconscious and archetypes.

Collective unconscious • Jung's hypothesized store of vague racial memories.

Archetypes • Basic, primitive images or concepts hypothesized by Jung to reside in the collective unconscious.

Self • In analytical psychology, a conscious, unifying force to personality that provides people with direction and purpose.

Inferiority complex • Feelings of inferiority hypothesized by Adler to serve as a central motivating force.

Drive for superiority • Adler's term for the desire to compensate for feelings of inferiority.

Creative self • According to Adler, the self-aware aspect of personality that strives to achieve its full potential.

Individual psychology • Adler's psychodynamic theory, which emphasizes feelings of inferiority and the creative self.

Basic anxiety • Horney's term for lasting feelings of insecurity that stem from harsh or indifferent parental treatment.

Basic hostility • Horney's term for lasting feelings of anger that accompany basic anxiety but are directed toward nonfamily members in adulthood.

TABLE 12.3
ERIK ERIKSON'S STAGES OF PSYCHOSOCIAL DEVELOPMENT

TIME PERIOD	LIFE CRISES	THE DEVELOPMENTAL TASK
Infancy (0–1)	Trust versus mistrust	Coming to trust the mother and the environment—to associate the surroundings with feelings of inner goodness
Early childhood (2–3)	Autonomy versus shame and doubt	Developing the wish to make choices and the self-control to exercise choice
Preschool years (4–5)	Initiative versus guilt	Adding planning and "attacking" to choice; becoming active and on the move
Grammar school years (6–12)	Industry versus inferiority	Becoming eagerly absorbed in skills, tasks, and productivity; mastering the fundamentals of technology
Adolescence	Identity versus role diffusion	Connecting skills and social roles to formation of career objectives
Young adulthood	Intimacy versus isolation	Committing the self to another; engaging in sexual love
Middle adulthood	Generativity versus stagnation	Needing to be needed; guiding and encouraging the younger generation; being creative
Late adulthood	Integrity versus despair	Accepting the timing and placing of one's own life cycle; achieving wisdom and dignity

Source: Erikson, 1963, pp. 247–269.

Psychosocial development • Erikson's theory of personality and development, which emphasizes social relationships and eight stages of growth.

Ego identity • A firm sense of who one is and what one stands for.

ERIK ERIKSON. Erik Erikson (1902–1994) also believed that Freud had placed undue emphasis on sexual instincts. He asserted that social relationships are more crucial determinants of personality. To Erikson, the general climate of the mother–infant relationship is more important than the details of the feeding process or the sexual feelings that might be stirred by contact with the mother. Erikson also argued that, to a large degree, we are the conscious architects of our own personalities. His view grants more powers to the ego than Freud had allowed. Within Erikson's theory, it is possible for us to make real choices. Within Freud's theory, we may think that we are making choices, but we may only be rationalizing the compromises forced upon us by intrapsychic warfare.

Erikson, like Freud, is known for devising a comprehensive developmental theory of personality. But whereas Freud proposed stages of psycho*sexual* development, Erikson proposed stages of psycho*social* development. Rather than label a stage after an erogenous zone, Erikson labeled stages after the traits that might be developed during that stage (see Table 12.3). Each stage is named according to the possible outcomes. For example, the first stage of **psychosocial development** is named the stage of trust versus mistrust because of the two possible major outcomes. (1) A warm, loving relationship with the mother (and others) during infancy might lead to a sense of basic trust in people and the world. (2) A cold, nongratifying relationship might generate a pervasive sense of mistrust. Erikson believed that most of us would wind up with some blend of trust and mistrust—hopefully more trust than mistrust. A basic sense of mistrust could mar the formation of relationships for a lifetime unless we came to recognize and challenge it. For Erikson, the goal of adolescence is the attainment of **ego identity,** not genital sexuality.

Erikson extended Freud's five developmental stages to eight. Freud's developmental theory ends with adolescence. Erikson's includes the changing concerns of adulthood.

Evaluation of the Psychodynamic Perspective

Psychodynamic theories have had tremendous appeal. They are "rich" theories. They involve many concepts and explain many varieties of human behavior and traits.

Although concepts such as "intrapsychic conflict" and "psychic energy" strike many psychologists as unscientific today, Freud fought for the idea that human personality and behavior are subject to scientific analysis. Freud's theorizing took place at a time when many people still viewed grave psychological problems as signs of possession by the devil or evil spirits, as they had during the Middle Ages. Freud argued that psychological disorders stem from problems within the individual—not evil spirits. Freud's thinking contributed to the development of compassion for, and methods of helping, people with psychological disorders.

Psychodynamic theory has also focused the attention of scientists and helping professionals on the far-reaching effects of childhood events. The developmental theories of Freud and Erikson suggest ways in which early childhood traumas can affect us for a lifetime. Horney believed that Freud was too pessimistic about the ability of children to recover from trauma and that Freud underestimated the saving powers of love. Yet, Freud and other psychodynamic theorists are to be credited for suggesting that personality and behavior *develop*—and that it is important for us as parents to be aware of the emotional needs of our children.

Freud has helped us recognize that sexual and aggressive urges are commonplace and that there is a difference between acknowledging these urges and acting on them. As W. Bertram Wolfe put it, "Freud found sex an outcast in the outhouse, and left it in the living room an honored guest."

Freud also noted that people have defensive ways of looking at the world. The defense mechanisms he listed have become part of everyday parlance. Whether or not we attribute these cognitive distortions to unconscious ego functioning, our thinking may be distorted by our efforts to avert anxiety and guilt. If these concepts no longer strike us as being innovative, it is largely because of the influence of Sigmund Freud. Psychodynamic theorists also innovated many methods of psychotherapy, which we describe in Chapter 14.

Despite their richness, psychodynamic theories, particularly the original psychodynamic views of Sigmund Freud, have met with criticism. Some followers of Freud, such as Horney and Erikson, have argued that Freud placed too much emphasis on human sexuality and neglected the importance of social relationships. Other followers have argued that Freud placed too much emphasis on unconscious motives. They assert that people consciously seek self-enhancement and intellectual pleasures. They do not merely try to gratify the dark demands of the id.

A number of critics note that "psychic structures" such as the id, ego, and superego have no substance. They are little more than useful fictions—poetic ways to express inner conflict. It is debatable whether Freud ever attributed substance to the psychic structures. He, too, may have seen them more as poetic fictions than as "things." If so, his critics have the right to use other descriptive terms and write better "poems."

Some critics have argued that Freud's hypothetical mental processes fail as scientific concepts because they can neither be observed nor can they predict observable behavior with precision (Hale, 1995; Robinson, 1993). Scientific propositions must be capable of being proved false. But Freud's statements about mental structures are unscientific because no conceivable type of evidence can disprove them. Any behavior can be explained in terms of these hypothesized (but unobservable) "structures."

Nor have the stages of psychosexual development escaped criticism. Children begin to masturbate as early as the first year, not in the phallic stage. As parents know from discovering their children play "doctor," the latency stage is not as sexually latent as Freud believed. Much of Freud's thinking concerning the Oedipus and Electra complexes remains speculation. The evidence for some of Erikson's developmental views seems somewhat sturdier. For example, adolescents who fail to develop ego identity seem to encounter problems developing intimate relationships later on.

Freud's method of gathering evidence from the clinical session is also suspect (Robinson, 1993). Therapists may subtly influence clients to produce what they expect to find. Therapists may also fail to separate reported facts from their own interpretations. Also, Freud and many other psychodynamic theorists restricted their evidence gathering to case studies with individuals who sought therapy for adjustment problems. Their clients were also mostly White and drawn from the middle and upper classes. Persons seeking therapy are likely to have more problems than the general population.

Reflections

- **Do unconscious impulses and ideas influence our behavior? (What would Freud have said about your answer?)**
- **Agree or disagree with the following statement and support your answer: "People are basically antisocial. Their primitive impulses must be suppressed and repressed if they are to function productively within social settings."**
- If you were fixated in a stage of psychosocial development, which stage would it be? Why?

THE LEARNING PERSPECTIVE

The learning perspective has also contributed to the understanding of personality. We shall focus on two learning approaches: behaviorism and social-cognitive theory.

Behaviorism

You have freedom when you're easy in your harness.
                                                    ROBERT FROST

At Johns Hopkins University in 1924, psychologist John B. Watson announced the battle cry of the behaviorist movement:

> Give me a dozen healthy infants, well-formed, and my own specified world to bring them up in and I'll guarantee to take any one at random and train him to become any type of specialist I might suggest—doctor, lawyer, merchant-chief and, yes, even beggar-man and thief, regardless of his talents, penchants, tendencies, abilities, vocations, and the race of his ancestors. (p. 82)

Watson proclaimed that environmental influences—not thinking or choice—shape human preferences and behaviors. As a counterbalance to the psychoanalysts and structuralists of his day, Watson argued that unseen, undetectable mental structures must be rejected in favor of that which can be seen and measured. In the 1930s, Watson's hue and cry was taken up by B. F. Skinner. Skinner agreed that we should avoid trying to see within the "black box" of the organism and emphasized the effect that reinforcements have on behavior.

Watson and Skinner largely discarded the notions of personal freedom, choice, and self-direction. Most of us assume that our wants originate within us. But Skinner suggests that environmental influences such as parental approval and social custom shape us into *wanting* certain things and *not wanting* others (Delprato & Midgley, 1992).

In his novel *Walden Two,* Skinner (1948) describes a Utopian society in which people are happy and content, because they are allowed to do as they please. However, they have been trained or conditioned from early childhood to engage in **prosocial** behavior and to express prosocial attitudes. Because of their reinforcement histories, they *want* to behave in a decent, kind, and unselfish way (Dinsmoor, 1992). They see themselves as being free because society makes no effort to force them to behave as they do as adults.

Skinner elaborated on his beliefs about people and society in *Beyond Freedom and Dignity* (1972). According to Skinner, adaptation to the environment requires acceptance of behavior patterns that ensure survival. If the group is to survive, it must construct rules and laws that foster social harmony. People are then rewarded for following these rules and punished for disobeying them. None of us is really free, even though we think of ourselves as coming together freely to establish the rules and as choosing to follow them.

Some object to behaviorist notions because they sidestep consciousness and choice. Others argue that people are not so blindly ruled by pleasure and pain. People have rebelled against the so-called necessity of survival by choosing pain and hardship over pleasure, or death over life. Many people have sacrificed their own lives to save those of others. The behaviorist defense might be that the apparent choice of pain or death is forced on the altruist as inevitably as conformity to social custom is forced on others.

Prosocial • Behavior that is characterized by helping others and making a contribution to society.

Social-cognitive theory • A cognitively oriented learning theory in which observational learning and person variables such as values and expectancies play major roles in individual differences.

Person variables • Factors within the person, such as expectancies and competencies, that influence behavior.

Expectancies • Personal predictions about the outcomes of potential behaviors.

Subjective value • The desirability of an object or event.

Social-Cognitive Theory

Social-cognitive theory[2] is a contemporary view of learning that is being developed by Albert Bandura (1986, 1989, 1991) and other psychologists (e.g., Cantor, 1990; Dweck, 1990; Higgins, 1990; Mischel, 1990). Social-cognitive theory focuses on the importance of learning by observation and on the cognitive processes that underlie individual differences. Social-cognitive theorists see people as influencing the environment just as the environment influences them. Social-cognitive theorists agree with behaviorists and other empirical psychologists that discussions of human nature should be tied to observable experiences and behaviors. They assert, however, that variables within people—**person variables**—must also be considered if we are to understand them.

One goal of psychological theories is the prediction of behavior. Social-cognitive theorist Julian B. Rotter (1972) argues that we cannot predict behavior from situational variables alone. Behavior also depends on the person's **expectancies** about its outcomes and the perceived or **subjective value** of those outcomes.

---

[2] Formerly termed *social-learning theory.*

To social-cognitive theorists, people are self-aware and engage in purposeful learning. People are not simply at the mercy of the environment. Instead, they seek to learn about their environment. They alter and construct the environment to make reinforcers available.

Social-cognitive theorists also note the importance of rules and symbolic processes in learning. Children, for example, learn more effectively how to behave in specific situations when parents explain the rules involved. In inductive methods of discipline, parents use the situation to teach children about general rules and social codes that should govern their behavior. Inductive methods are more effective at fostering desirable behavior than punishment alone.

Model • In social-cognitive theory, an organism that exhibits behaviors that others imitate or acquire through observational learning.

Encode • Interpret; transform.

Self-efficacy expectations • Beliefs to the effect that one can handle a task.

OBSERVATIONAL LEARNING.   Observational learning (also termed **modeling** or cognitive learning) refers to acquiring knowledge by observing others. For operant conditioning to occur, an organism (1) must engage in a response, and (2) that response must be reinforced. But observational learning occurs even when the learner does not perform the observed behavior. Therefore, direct reinforcement is not required either. Observing others extends to reading about them or perceiving what they do and what happens to them in media such as radio, television, and film.

Our expectations stem from our observations of what happens to ourselves and other people. For example, teachers are more likely to call on males and more accepting of "calling out" in class from males than females (Sadker & Sadker, 1994). As a result, many males expect to be rewarded for calling out. Females, however, may learn that they will be reprimanded for behaving in what traditionalists might term an "unladylike" manner.

How Do Competencies Contribute to Performance? There are great individual differences in our competencies, based on genetic variation, nourishment, differences in learning opportunities, and other environmental factors. What factors contribute to this girl's performance on the balance beam?

PERSON AND SITUATIONAL VARIABLES.   Social-cognitive theorists view behavior as stemming from the interaction between person variables and situational variables. Person variables include competencies, encoding strategies, expectancies, subjective values, and self-regulatory systems and plans (Mischel, 1993, pp. 403–411; see Figure 12.4).

- *Competencies.* Competencies include knowledge of the physical world, of cultural codes of conduct, and of the behavior expected in certain situations. They include academic skills such as reading and writing, athletic skills such as swimming and tossing a football, social skills such as knowing how to ask someone out on a date, job skills, and many others.

- *Encoding Strategies.* Different people **encode** (symbolize, or represent) the same stimuli in different ways, and their encoding strategies are an important factor in their overt behavior. One person might encode a tennis game as a chance to bat the ball back and forth and have some fun. Another might encode the same game as a demand to perfect his or her serve. One person might encode a date that doesn't work out as a sign of his social incompetence. Another might encode the experience as reflecting the fact that people are not always "made for each other."

- *Expectancies.* Expectancies are predictions about what will happen. Key expectancies are **self-efficacy expectations.** These are our beliefs that we can accomplish things such as speak before a group, or do a backflip into a swimming pool, or solve math problems (Pajares & Miller, 1994). People with positive self-efficacy expectations are more likely to try difficult tasks than people who do not believe that they can master them.

Truth or Fiction Revisited. *It is true that we are more likely to persist at difficult tasks when we believe we shall succeed.* Positive self-efficacy

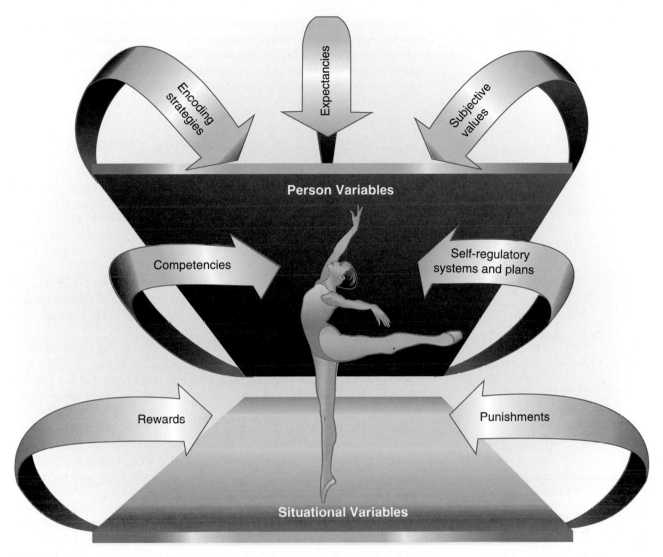

FIGURE 12.4

Person Variables and Situational Variables in Social-Cognitive Theory. According to social-cognitive theory, person variables and situational variables interact to influence behavior.

expectations apparently motivate us to persevere. Bandura (1986) suggests that one way in which psychotherapy helps people is by changing their self-efficacy expectations from "I can't" to "I can." As a result, people are motivated to try out new patterns of behavior.

- *Subjective Values.* People place different values on things. What is frightening to one person may entice another. What is somewhat desirable to one may be irresistible to another. From the social-cognitive perspective, in contrast to behaviorist perspective, we are not controlled by stimuli. Instead, stimuli have meanings for us, and these meanings are one factor in influencing behavior.

- *Self-Regulatory Systems and Plans.* Social-cognitive theory recognizes that one of the features of being human is our tendency to regulate our own behavior, even in the absence of observers and external constraints. We set goals and standards for ourselves, construct plans for achieving them, and congratulate or criticize ourselves, depending on whether or not we reach them (Bandura, 1991). Self-regulation amplifies our opportunities for influencing our environment. We can select the situations to which we expose ourselves and the arenas in which we shall contend. Based on our expectancies, we may choose to enter the academic or athletic worlds.

Evaluation of the Learning Perspective

Learning theorists have made monumental contributions to the scientific understanding of behavior, but they have also left some psychologists dissatisfied.

Psychodynamic theorists and trait theorists propose the existence of psychological structures that cannot be seen and measured directly. Learning theorists—particularly behaviorists—have dramatized the importance of referring to publicly observable variables, or behaviors, if psychology is to be accepted as a science.

Similarly, psychodynamic theorists and trait theorists focus on internal variables such as intrapsychic conflict and traits to explain and predict behavior. Learning theorists have emphasized the importance of environmental conditions, or situational variables, as determinants of behavior.

Learning theorists have elaborated on the conditions that foster learning—even automatic kinds of learning. They have shown that involuntary responses—including fear responses—may be conditioned, that we can learn to do things because of reinforcements, and that many broad behavior patterns are acquired by observing others.

Learning theorists have devised methods for helping individuals solve adjustment problems that probably would not have been derived from any other theoretical perspective. These include the behavioral, extinction-based fear-reduction methods of flooding and systematic desensitization and the operant-conditioning method of biofeedback training.

On the other hand, behaviorism is limited in its ability to explain personality. Behaviorism does not describe, explain, or even suggest the richness of inner human experience. We experience thoughts and feelings and peruse our complex inner maps of the world, and behaviorism does not deal with these phenomena. To be fair, however, the "limitations" of behaviorism are self-imposed. Personality theorists have traditionally dealt with thoughts, feelings, and behavior. Behaviorism, in its insistence on studying only that which is observable and measurable, deals with behavior alone.

Critics of social-cognitive theory cannot accuse its supporters of denying the importance of cognitive activity and feelings. But they often contend that social-cognitive theory has not derived satisfying statements about the development of traits or accounted for self-awareness. Also, social-cognitive theory—like its intellectual forebear, behaviorism—may not have always paid sufficient attention to genetic variation in explaining individual differences in behavior.

Social-cognitive theorists seem to be working on these theoretical flaws. Social-cognitive theorists, unlike behaviorists, view people as active, not as reacting mechanically to environmental pressures.

Reflections

- **Given cultural and social conditioning, is true freedom possible? To behaviorists, our telling ourselves that we have free will is determined by the environment. Is free will merely an illusion? What is the evidence for your belief?**

- Which theorists believe that people are "ruled" by pleasure and pain? Do you share this belief? Why or why not?
- **Agree or disagree with the following statement and support your answer: "Success breeds success." Do examples from your own life support this view?**

Now let us consider theories that begin with the assumption of consciousness and dwell on the importance of our cognitive functioning.

THE HUMANISTIC–EXISTENTIAL PERSPECTIVE

You are unique, and if that is not fulfilled, then something has been lost.

MARTHA GRAHAM

Humanists and existentialists dwell on conscious, personal experience and on the meaning of life. **Humanism** became a third force in American psychology in the 1950s and 1960s, in part as a reply to the predominant psychodynamic and behavioral models. Humanism also represented a reaction to the "rat race" spawned by industrialization and automation. Humanists opposed the posting of people on the gray, anonymous treadmills of industry. "Alienation" from inner sources of meaning distressed them. Against this backdrop emerged the humanistic views of Abraham Maslow and Carl Rogers.

Existentialism in part reflects the horrors of mass destruction of human life through war and genocide. The European existentialist philosophers Jean-Paul Sartre and Martin Heidegger saw human life as trivial in the grand scheme of things. But seeing human existence as meaningless can lead to withdrawal and apathy—even suicide. Psychological salvation therefore requires implanting personal meaning on things and making personal choices. Yes, there is pain in life, and yes, life sooner or later comes to an end, but people can see the world for what it is and make real, **authentic** choices.

Freud argued that defense mechanisms prevent us from seeing the world as it is. Therefore, the concept of free choice is meaningless. Behaviorists viewed freedom as an illusion determined by social forces. Social-cognitive theorists also speak of external or situational forces that influence us. To existentialists, we are really and painfully free to do as we choose with our lives.

Humanists and existentialists share a search for meaning in life and a belief that freedom and personal responsibility are the essence of being human. Let us now consider the humanistic views of Abraham Maslow and Carl Rogers.

Humanism • The view that people are capable of free choice, self-fulfillment, and ethical behavior.

Existentialism • The view that people are completely free and responsible for their own behavior.

Authentic • Genuine; consistent with one's values and beliefs.

Self-actualization • In humanistic theory, the innate tendency to strive to realize one's potential.

Abraham Maslow and the Challenge of Self-Actualization

Humanists see Freud as preoccupied with the "basement" of the human condition. Freud wrote that people are basically motivated to gratify defensive, biological drives. (Maslow's theoretical *hierarchy of needs* is discussed in Chapter 10.) Abraham Maslow argued that people also have growth-oriented needs for **self-actualization**—to become all that they can be. Because people are unique, they must follow unique paths to self-actualization. Self-actualization requires taking risks. People who adhere to the "tried and true" may find their lives degenerating into monotony and predictability.

Carl Rogers's Self Theory

Unique. According to humanistic psychologists like Carl Rogers, each of us views the world and ourselves from a unique frame of reference. What is important to one individual may hold little meaning for another.

Gestalt • In this usage, a quality of wholeness.

Frame of reference • One's unique patterning of perceptions and attitudes according to which one evaluates events.

Self-esteem • One's evaluation and valuing of oneself.

Unconditional positive regard • A persistent expression of esteem for the value of a person, but not necessarily an unqualified acceptance of all of the person's behaviors.

Conditional positive regard • Judgment of another person's value on the basis of the acceptability of that person's behaviors.

Conditions of worth • Standards by which the value of a person is judged.

Carl Rogers (1902–1987) was a minister before he became a psychologist. Like Maslow, he wrote that people shape themselves through free choice and action.

Rogers defined the *self* as an "organized, consistent, conceptual **gestalt** composed of perceptions of the characteristics of the 'I' or 'me' and the perceptions of the relationships of the 'I' or 'me' to others and to various aspects of life, together with the values attached to these perceptions" (1959, p. 200). Your self is your center of experience. It is your ongoing sense of who and what you are, your sense of how and why you react to the environment and how you choose to act on the environment. Your choices are made on the basis of your values, and your values are also parts of your self.

To Rogers, the sense of self is inborn, or innate. The self provides the experience of being human in the world. It is the guiding principle behind personality structure and behavior.

THE SELF-CONCEPT AND FRAMES OF REFERENCE. Our self-concepts comprise our impressions of ourselves and our evaluations of our adequacy. It may be helpful to think of us as rating ourselves according to various scales or dimensions such as good–bad, intelligent–unintelligent, strong–weak, and tall–short.

Rogers stated that we all have unique ways of looking at ourselves and the world, or unique **frames of reference.** It may be that we each use a different set of dimensions in defining ourselves and that we judge ourselves according to different sets of values. To one person, achievement–failure may be the most important dimension. To another person, the most important dimension may be decency–indecency. A third person may not even think in terms of decency.

SELF-ESTEEM AND POSITIVE REGARD. Rogers assumed that we all develop a need for self-regard, or **self-esteem,** as we develop and become aware of ourselves. At first, self-esteem reflects the esteem in which others hold us. Parents help children develop self-esteem when they show them **unconditional positive regard**—that is, when they accept them as having intrinsic merit regardless of their behavior at the moment. But when parents show children **conditional positive regard**—accept them only when they behave in a desired manner—children may learn to disown the thoughts, feelings, and behaviors that parents have rejected. Conditional positive regard may lead children to develop **conditions of worth,** or to think that they are worthwhile only if they behave in certain ways.

Because each of us is thought to have a unique potential, children who develop conditions of worth must be somewhat disappointed in themselves. We cannot fully live up to the wishes of others and remain true to ourselves. This does not mean that the expression of the self inevitably leads to conflict. Rogers was optimistic about human nature. He believed that we hurt others or act in antisocial ways only when we are frustrated in our efforts to develop our potential. But when parents and others are loving and tolerant of our differentness, we, too, are loving—even if some of our preferences, abilities, and values differ from those of our parents.

However, children in some families learn that it is bad to have ideas of their own, especially about sexual, political, or religious matters. When they perceive their parents' disapproval, they may come to see themselves as rebels and label their feelings as being selfish, wrong, or evil. If they wish to retain a consistent self-concept and self-esteem, they may have to deny many of their genuine feelings, or disown parts of themselves. In this way, the self-concept becomes distorted. According to Rogers, anxiety often stems from partial perception of feelings and ideas that are inconsistent with the distorted self-concept. Since anxiety is unpleasant, such individuals may deny that these feelings and ideas exist.

PSYCHOLOGICAL CONGRUENCE AND THE SELF-IDEAL. When we accept our feelings as our own, we experience psychological integrity or wholeness. There is a "fit" between our self-concept and our behavior, thoughts, and emotions, which Rogers called **congruence.**

According to Rogers, the path to self-actualization requires getting in touch with our genuine feelings, accepting them as ours, and acting on them. This is the goal of Rogers's method of psychotherapy, person-centered therapy, which we discuss in Chapter 14. Here, it is sufficient to say that person-centered therapists provide an atmosphere in which clients can cope with the anxieties of focusing on disowned parts of the self.

Rogers also believed that we have mental images of what we are capable of becoming, or **self-ideals.** We are motivated to reduce the discrepancy between our self-concepts and our self-ideals. As we undertake the process of actualizing ourselves, our self-ideals may gradually grow more complex. Our goals may become higher or change in quality. The self-ideal is something like a carrot dangling from a stick strapped to a burro's head. The burro strives to reach the carrot, as though it were a step or two away, without recognizing that its own progress also causes the carrot to advance. Striving to meet meaningful goals, the good struggle, yields happiness.

Congruence • According to Rogers, a fit between one's self-concept and one's behaviors, thoughts, and feelings.

Self-ideal • A mental image of what we believe we ought to be.

Evaluation of the Humanistic-Existential Perspective

Humanistic–existential theories usually have tremendous appeal for college students because of their focus on the importance of personal experience. We tend to treasure our conscious experiences (our "selves") and those of the people we care about. For lower organisms, to be alive is to move, to process food, to exchange oxygen and carbon dioxide, and to reproduce one's kind. But for human beings, an essential aspect of life is conscious experience—the sense of one's self as progressing through space and time. Humanistic–existential theorists grant consciousness the cardinal role it occupies in our daily lives.

Psychodynamic theories see us largely as victims of our childhoods. Learning theories, to some degree, see us as "victims of circumstances"—or, at least, as victims of situational variables. But humanistic–existential theorists envision us as being free to make choices. Psychodynamic theorists and learning theorists wonder whether our sense of freedom is merely an illusion. Humanistic–existential theorists begin with an assumption of personal freedom.

Humanistic–existential theorists have made important innovations and contributions to the practice of psychotherapy, such as person-centered therapy, the type of therapy originated by Carl Rogers (see Chapter 14).

Ironically, the primary strength of the humanistic–existential approaches—their focus on conscious experience—is also their primary weakness. Conscious experience is private and subjective. Therefore, the validity of formulating theories in terms of consciousness has been questioned. On the other hand, some psychologists (e.g., Bevan & Kessel, 1994) believe that the science of psychology can afford to loosen its methods somewhat if loosening will help it to better address the richness of human experience.

The concept of self-actualization, like trait theory, yields circular explanations for behavior. When we see someone engaged in what seems to be positive striving, we gain little insight by attributing this behavior to a self-actualizing force. We have done nothing to account for the origins of the self-actualizing force.

Humanistic–existential theories, like learning theories, have little to say about the development of traits and personality types. Humanistic–existential theorists assume that we are all unique, but they do not predict the sorts of traits, abilities, and interests we shall develop.

Reflections

- Maslow believed that self-actualization requires taking risks. Are you a self-actualizer? Why do you think that you are—or are not?
- What factors in your life have contributed to your self-esteem? Do your experiences support Rogers's views on the origins of self-esteem?

THE SOCIOCULTURAL PERSPECTIVE

Thirteen-year-old Hannah brought her lunch tray to the table in the cafeteria. Her mother Julie eyed in horror the french fries, the plate of mashed potatoes in gravy, the bag of potato chips, and the large paper cup brimming with soda. "You cannot eat that!" she said. "It's garbage!"

"Oh come on, Mom! Chill, okay?" Hannah rejoined, and she took her tray to sit with friends rather than with us.

I spend my Saturdays with my children at the Manhattan School of Music. Not only do they study voice, piano, and violin. They—and I—have widened our cultural perspective by relating to families and students from all parts of the world.

Julie and Hannah are Korean Americans. Flustered, Julie shook her head and said, "I've now been in the United States longer than I was in Korea, and I still can't get used to the way children act here." A Polish American parent, Barbara, at the table chimed in, "I never would have spoken to my parents the way Thomas speaks to me. I would have been . . . whipped or beaten."

"I try to tell Hannah she is part of the family," Julie continued. "She should think of other people. When she talks that way, it is embarrassing."

"Over here children are not part of the family," said Ken, an African American parent. "They are either part of their own crowd or they are 'individuals.'"

"Being an individual does not mean that you must be mean to your mother," Julie said. "What do you think, Spencer? You're the psychologist."

I think I made some unhelpful comments about the ketchup on the french fries having vitamin C and some slightly helpful comments about what is typical for teenagers in the United States. But I'm not sure, because I was thinking deeply about Hannah at the time. Not about her lunch, but about the formation of her personality and the influences on her behavior.

Personality in our new multicultural United States cannot be understood without reference to the sociocultural perspective. Multiple traditions characterize our nation as it evolves into a "social mosaic" (Portes & Stepick, 1993).

Back to Hannah. Perhaps there were unconscious psychodynamic influences operating on her. Her traits included exceptional intelligence and musical aptitude, which were at least partly determined by her heredity. Clearly, she was consciously striving to become a great violinist. But one could not make inroads into Hannah's personality structure without also considering the **sociocultural perspective**—the sociocultural influences acting on her.

Here was a youngster strongly affected by her school peers—she was completely at home in her blue jeans and with her luncheon choices. She was also a daughter in an immigrant group that views education as a key to success (Gibson & Ogbu, 1991; Ogbu, 1993). Her group had contributed to her personal ambition. But being a Korean American had not prevented her from becoming an outspoken American teenager. (Would she have been outspoken if she had been reared in Korea, I wondered, but this question can never be answered with certainty.) Hannah's outspokenness struck her mother as brazen and inappropriate (Lopez & Hernandez, 1986). Julie was deeply offended by behavior that rolls off my back with my own children. Julie reeled off the things that were "wrong" with Hannah from her Korean American perspective. I listed some things that were very right with Hannah and encouraged Julie to worry less.

Let us consider ways in which sociocultural factors can affect one's sense of self.

Individualism Versus Collectivism

In a sense, Julie's complaint was that Hannah saw herself too much as an individual and an artist rather than as a family member and a Korean girl. Cross-cultural research reveals that people in the United States and many northern European nations tend to be individualistic. **Individualists** tend to define themselves in terms of their personal identities and to give priority to their personal goals. When asked to complete the statement "I am," they are likely to respond in terms of their personality traits ("I am outgoing," "I am artistic") or their occupations ("I am a nurse," "I am a systems analyst") (Triandis, 1990). In contrast, many people from cultures in Africa, Asia, and Central and South America tend to be collectivistic. **Collectivists** tend to define themselves in terms of the groups to which they belong and to give priority to the goals of their group. They feel complete only in terms of their social relationships with others (Markus & Kitayama, 1991; see Figure 12.5). When asked to complete the statement "I am," they are more likely to respond in terms of their families, gender, or nation ("I am a father," "I am a Buddhist," "I am a Japanese") (Draguns, 1988; Triandis, 1990, 1994).

The seeds of individualism and collectivism are found in the cultures in which the person grows up. The capitalist system fosters individualism to some degree. It assumes that individuals are entitled to amass personal fortunes and that the process of doing so creates jobs and wealth for large numbers of people. The individualist perspective is found in the self-reliant heroes and anti-heroes in Western media—from Homer's Odysseus to Clint Eastwood's gritty cowboys and Walt Disney's Princess Jasmine (in the film *Aladdin*). The traditional writings of the East have exalted people who resisted personal temptations to do their duty and promote the welfare of the group.

There are, of course, conflicting ideals within a given culture, individual differences, and even gender differences. In the United States, for example, children are taught to share with other children as well as to be "Number 1." Children are encouraged to give to charity as well as to be independent and successful.

Sociocultural perspective • The view that focuses on the roles of ethnicity, gender, culture, and socioeconomic status in personality formation, behavior, and mental processes.
Individualist • A person who defines herself or himself in terms of personal traits and gives priority to her or his own goals.
Collectivist • A person who defines herself or himself in terms of relationships to other people and groups and gives priority to group goals.

Is This "Iron John"? Do Western theories of personality present the masculine gender role stereotype—as characterized by separation and individuation—as the highest goal of personality development? Women more so than men emphasize interpersonal relatedness as a key goal of personality development. Although their needs to be strong individuals may prevent men from getting in touch with their feelings, they may suffer from feelings of alienation and grief over lack of relatedness to other people.

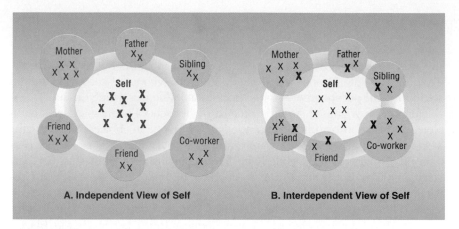

FIGURE 12.5

The Self in Relation to Others from the Individualist and Collectivist Perspectives. To an individualist, the self is separate from other people (part A). To a collectivist, the self is complete only in terms of relationships to other people (part B). (Based on Markus & Kitayama, 1991).

Acculturation • The process of adaptation in which immigrants and native groups identify with a new, dominant culture by learning about that culture and making behavioral and attitudinal changes.

Note, too, that neither individualism nor collectivism in its extreme form is desirable. Extreme greed or selfishness tears the social fabric. Extreme collectivism discourages inventiveness and creativity and denies the dignity of the individual.

Sociocultural Factors and the Self

Sociocultural factors also affect the self-concept and self-esteem of the individual. Carl Rogers noted that our self-concepts tend to reflect the ways in which other people see us. Thus, members of the dominant culture in the United States are likely to have a positive sense of self. They share in the expectations of personal achievement and respect that are typically accorded those who ascend to power. Similarly, members of ethnic groups that have been subjected to discrimination and poverty may have poorer self-concepts and lower self-esteem than members of the dominant culture (Greene, 1993, 1994; Lewis-Fernández & Kleinman, 1994).

Acculturation and Self-Esteem

Should Hindu women who emigrate to the United States surrender the sari in favor of California Casuals? Should Russian immigrants teach their children Russian in the home? Should African American children be acquainted with the music and art of African peoples? Should women from traditional Islamic societies lift the veil and enter the workplace alongside American Murphy Browns? How does **acculturation** affect the psychological well-being of immigrants and their families?

Self-esteem is connected with patterns of acculturation among immigrants to the United States. There are various patterns of acculturation. Some immigrants are completely *assimilated* by the dominant culture. They lose the language and customs of their country of origin and become like the dominant culture in the new host country. Others maintain *separation*. They retain the

Three Generations of the Wong Family. Chinese American artist Hung Liu's triptych traces the history of the Wong family, as they emigrated from China, and then over the course of two generations in the United States. Contemporary descendants of the Wongs are influenced by acculturation and intermarriage with Americans from other backgrounds.

language and customs of their country of origin and never become comfortable with the language and customs of the new host country. Still others become *bicultural*. They become fluent in the languages of their countries of origin and their new countries and integrate the customs and values of both cultures.

Research evidence suggests that people who identify with the bicultural pattern have the highest self-esteem (Phinney and others, 1992). For example, Mexican Americans who are more proficient in English are less likely to be anxious and depressed than less proficient Mexican Americans (Salgado de Snyder and others, 1990). The ability to adapt to the ways of the new society combined with a supportive cultural tradition and a sense of ethnic identity apparently helps people to adjust.

Evaluation of the Sociocultural Perspective

The sociocultural perspective thus provides valuable insights into the roles of ethnicity, gender, culture, and socioeconomic status in personality formation. When we ignore sociocultural factors, we deal only with the core of the human being—the potentials that permit adaptation to external forces. Sociocultural factors are external forces that are internalized and affect all of us. They run through us deeply, touching many aspects of our cognitions, motives, emotions, and behavior. Without reference to sociocultural factors, we may be able to understand generalities about behavior and cognitive processes. However, we will not be able to understand how individuals think, behave, and feel about themselves within a given cultural setting. The sociocultural perspective enhances our sensitivity to cultural differences and expectations and allows us to appreciate much of the richness of human behavior and mental processes.

Reflections

- When you were a child, were you given conflicting messages about the importance of competing successfully and of sharing? Do you think that the experiences in your own home were oriented more toward encouraging individualism or collectivism? How so?
- How have sociocultural factors affected your own self-concept?
- For how many generations have the families of your parents been in the United States? What acculturation problems did your forebears experience? If you do not have specific information about their experiences, what do you imagine they might have been like? Why?

Aptitude • A natural ability or talent.

MEASUREMENT OF PERSONALITY

Psychologists usually date psychological assessment to the 19th century—with the works of Francis Galton, James McKeen Cattell, Alfred Binet, and others. However, many people were selected for government service on the basis of assessment of individual differences in mental and physical abilities 2,500 years ago during the Golden Age of Greece (Matarazzo, 1990). In China some 2,000 years ago, objective tests were also used to select applicants for civil service (Bowman, 1989). These tests measured aptitudes such as verbal and mathematical abilities as well as knowledge of law and geography. All these measures took a sample of behavior to predict future behavior. Contemporary measures of personality similarly sample behavior, usually in the form of a self-report, to predict future behavior. Standardized interviews are often used. Many psychologists even have computers conduct some routine interviews (Bloom, 1992).

Measures of personality are used to make important decisions such as whether a person is suited for a certain type of work, for a particular class in school, or for a drug to reduce agitation (Saccuzzo, 1994). As part of their admissions process, graduate schools often ask professors to rate prospective students on scales that assess traits such as intelligence, emotional stability, and cooperation. Students may take tests of **aptitudes** and interests to gather insight into whether they are suited for certain occupations. It is assumed that students who share the aptitudes and interests of people who are well-adjusted in certain positions are also likely to be well-adjusted in those positions.

Objective Tests

Objective tests present respondents with a **standardized** group of test items in the form of a questionnaire. Respondents are limited to selecting among specific answers.

The Minnesota Multiphasic Personality Inventory (MMPI) contains hundreds of items presented in a true–false format. The MMPI was intended to be used by clinical and counseling psychologists to help diagnose psychological disorders (see Chapter 13). Accurate measurement of people's problems should point to appropriate treatment. The MMPI is the most widely used psychological test in clinical work (Helmes & Reddon, 1993; Watkins and others, 1995). It is also the most widely used instrument for personality measurement in psychological research.

The MMPI is usually scored for the 4 **validity scales** and 10 **clinical scales** described in Table 12.4. The validity scales suggest whether answers represent the person's thoughts, emotions, and behaviors. However, they cannot guarantee that deception will be disclosed.

Truth or Fiction Revisited. *Psychologists cannot invariably determine whether a person has told the truth on a personality test.* However, validity scales allow psychologists to make educated guesses.

The validity scales in Table 12.4 assess different **response sets,** or biases, in answering the questions. For example, some people try to present themselves as excessively moral and well-behaved individuals. Others try to look bizarre or answer haphazardly. Many personality measures have some kind of validity scale. The clinical scales of the MMPI assess the problems shown in Table 12.4, as well as stereotypical masculine or feminine interests and introversion.

The MMPI scales were constructed empirically on the basis of actual clinical data rather than on the basis of psychological theory. A test-item bank of

Objective tests • Tests whose items must be answered in a specified, limited manner and whose items have concrete answers that are considered correct.

Standardized test • Given to a large number of respondents so that data concerning the typical responses can be accumulated and analyzed.

Validity scales • Groups of test items that indicate whether a person's responses accurately reflect that individual's traits.

Clinical scales • Groups of test items that measure the presence of various abnormal behavior patterns.

Response set • A tendency to answer test items according to a bias—for instance, to make oneself seem perfect or bizarre.

TABLE 12.4
COMMONLY USED VALIDITY AND CLINICAL SCALES OF THE MMPI

SCALE	ABBREVIATION	POSSIBLE INTERPRETATIONS
VALIDITY SCALES		
Question	?	Corresponds to number of items left unanswered
Lie	L	Lies or is highly conventional
Frequency	F	Exaggerates complaints or answers items haphazardly
Correction	K	Denies problems
CLINICAL SCALES		
Hypochondriasis	Hs	Has bodily concerns and complaints
Depression	D	Is depressed, guilty; has feelings of guilt and helplessness
Hysteria	Hy	Reacts to stress by developing physical symptoms; lacks insight
Psychopathetic deviate	Pd	Is immoral, in conflict with the law; has stormy relationships
Masculinity/femininity	Mf	High scores suggest interests and behavior patterns considered stereotypical of the other gender
Paranoia	Pa	Is suspicious and resentful, highly cynical about human nature
Psychasthenia	Pt	Is anxious, worried, high-strung
Schizophrenia	Sc	Is confused, disorganized, disoriented; has bizarre ideas
Hypomania	Ma	Is energetic, restless, active, easily bored
Social introversion	Si	Is introverted, timid, shy; lacks self-confidence

several hundred items was derived from questions often asked in clinical interviews. Here are some of the items that were used:

My father was a good man.	T	F
I am very seldom troubled by headaches.	T	F
My hands and feet are usually warm enough.	T	F
I have never done anything dangerous for the thrill of it.	T	F
I work under a great deal of tension.	T	F

The items were administered to people with previously identified symptoms such as depressive or schizophrenic symptoms. Items that successfully set apart people with these symptoms were included on scales named accordingly. Figure 12.6 is the personality profile of a 27-year-old barber who consulted a psychologist because of depression and difficulty in making decisions. The barber scored abnormally high on the Hs, D, Pt, Sc, and Si scales, suggestive of concern with body functions (Hs), depression (D), persistent feelings of anxiety and tension (Pt), insomnia and fatigue, and some difficulties relating to

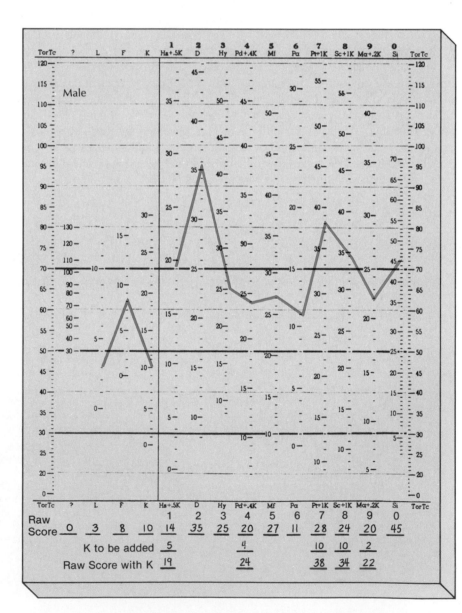

FIGURE 12.6

An MMPI Personality Profile. This profile was attained by a depressed barber. On this form, scores at the standard level of 50 are average for males, and scores above the standard score of 70 are considered abnormally high. The raw score is the number of items answered in a certain direction on a given MMPI scale. K is the correction scale. A certain percentage of the K-scale score is added onto several clinical scales to correct for denial of problems.

other people (Sc, Si). Note that the high Sc score does not in itself indicate that the barber should be diagnosed with schizophrenia.

Projective Tests

FIGURE 12.7
A Rorschach Inkblot. What does this look like? What could it be?

You may have heard that there is a personality test that asks people what a drawing or inkblot looks like and that people commonly answer "a bat." There are a number of such tests, the best known of which is the Rorschach inkblot test, named after its originator, Swiss psychiatrist Hermann Rorschach (1884–1922).

THE RORSCHACH INKBLOT TEST.   The Rorschach test is a **projective test.** In projective techniques, there are no clear, specified answers. People are presented with **ambiguous** stimuli such as inkblots or vague drawings and may be asked to report what these stimuli look like to them or to tell stories about them. Because there is no one proper response, it is assumed that people *project* their own personalities into their responses. The meanings they attribute to these stimuli are assumed to reflect their personalities as well as the drawings or blots themselves.

The facts of the matter are slightly different. Yes, there is no single "correct" response to the Rorschach inkblot shown in Figure 12.7. However, some responses are not in keeping with the features of the blot. Figure 12.7 could be a bat or a flying insect, the pointed face of an animal, the face of a jack-o'-lantern, or many other things. But responses like "an ice cream cone," "diseased lungs," or "a metal leaf in flames" are not suggested by the features of the blot and may suggest personality problems.

Truth or Fiction Revisited. *It is true that there is a psychological test made up of inkblots, and one of them looks like a bat.* This is the Rorschach inkblot test.

People are given the cards, one by one, and are asked what they look like or what they could be. People can give no, one, or several responses to each card. They can hold the card upside down or sideways. The Rorschach test is thought to provide insight into a person's intelligence, interests, cultural background, degree of introversion or extroversion, level of anxiety, reality testing, and a host of other variables.

THE THEMATIC APPERCEPTION TEST.   The Thematic Apperception Test (TAT) was developed in the 1930s by psychologist Henry Murray at Harvard University. It consists of drawings like that shown in Figure 10.6 (see p. 424). They are open to several interpretations. People are given the cards one at a time and are asked to make up stories about them.

The TAT is widely used in research into motivation and in clinical practice (Watkins and others, 1995). In an experiment described in Chapter 10, need for achievement was assessed from people's responses to a picture of a boy and a violin. The notion is that we are likely to be preoccupied with our own needs to some degree and that our needs will be projected into our responses to ambiguous situations. The TAT is also widely used to assess attitudes toward other people, especially parents, lovers, and spouses.

Projective test • A psychological test that presents ambiguous stimuli onto which the test taker projects his or her own personality in making a response.

Ambiguous • Having two or more possible meanings.

Reflections

- Did you ever take any psychological tests? For what purposes? What were your feelings about the tests at the time? Did they seem valid to you? Why or why not?

• Do you believe that psychological tests should be used as the sole means for making decisions about people's personalities or assessing psychological problems? Why or why not?

WORLD OF DIVERSITY

GENDER DIFFERENCES IN PERSONALITY

The anatomical differences between women and men are obvious and are connected with the biological role of each gender in the process of reproduction. Biologists, therefore, have a relatively easy time of it describing and interpreting the gender differences that they study.

The task of psychology is more complex and wrapped up with sociocultural and political issues (Eagly, 1995; Marecek, 1995). Differences in personality between women and men are not so obvious as biological differences.

Put it another way: To fulfill certain biological roles, women and men have to be biologically different. Throughout history, it has also been assumed that women and men must be psychologically different in order to fulfill different roles in the family and society at large.

Psychological research has brought us to question whether women are actually different in personality, however. If they are different in personality, just *how* different are they? And, of course, psychologists are vitally concerned with just how women and men get to be different in personality. In the case of anatomy, it is clear that gender differences are predominantly genetic. In the case of personality, psychological and sociocultural influences also come into play.

GENDER DIFFERENCES: VIVE LA DIFFÉRENCE OR VIVE LA SIMILARITÉ?

What psychological differences are found between women and men? It was once believed that males were more intelligent than females because of their greater knowledge of world affairs and their skill in science and industry. We

Bucking the Stereotypes. Many contemporary women and men are bucking the stereotypes and pursuing careers in fields that previously were reserved for the other gender. Women now make up 11% of the two million Americans in the armed forces, although there is continuing conflict over sending them into combat. Some men are now found in nursing.

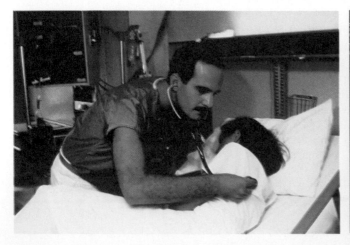

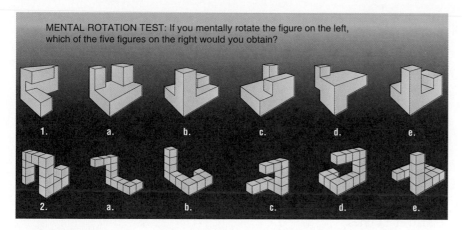

FIGURE 12.8

Rotating Figures in Space. Males as a group outperform females on spatial-relations tasks, such as rotating figures in space and picturing the results. However, females do as well as males when they receive some training in the task.

now recognize that greater male knowledge and skill reflected not differences in intelligence but the systematic exclusion of females from world affairs, science, and industry. Studies in the assessment of intelligence do not show overall differences in cognitive abilities between males and females. However, a classic review of the research literature by Maccoby and Jacklin (1974) found persistent suggestions that girls are somewhat superior to boys in verbal ability. Males, on the other hand, seem to be somewhat superior in visual–spatial abilities. Differences in mathematical ability are more complex.

Girls seem to acquire language somewhat faster than boys. Girls make more prelinguistic vocalizations and utter their first word a half month earlier. They acquire additional words more rapidly, and their pronunciation is clearer (Hyde & Linn, 1988; Nelson, 1973). High school girls excel in spelling, punctuation, reading comprehension, solving verbal analogies (such as Washington : one :: Lincoln : ?), and solving anagrams (scrambled words). Also, far more boys in the United States than girls have reading problems, ranging from reading below grade level to severe disabilities.

On the other hand, at least the males headed toward college seem to catch up in verbal skills. On the 1988 Scholastic Assessment Tests, for example, males outscored females by an average score of 435 to 422 (Carmody, 1988).

Males apparently excel in visual–spatial abilities (Voyer and others, 1995). Beginning in adolescence, boys usually outperform girls on tests of spatial ability (Maccoby & Jacklin, 1974; Halpern, 1986). These tests assess skills such as mentally rotating figures in space (see Figure 12.8) and finding figures embedded within larger designs (see Figure 12.9).

Concerning math, differences at all ages are small and narrowing (Hyde and others, 1990). Females excel in computational ability in elementary school, however, and males excel in mathematical problem solving in high school and in college (Hyde and others, 1990). Differences in problem solving are reflected on the mathematics test of the Scholastic Assessment Test (SAT). The mean score is 500, and about two thirds of the test takers receive scores between 400 and 600. Boys outperform girls on SAT math items (Byrnes & Takahira, 1993). Twice as many boys as girls attain scores over 500 (Benbow & Stanley, 1980). According to Byrnes and Takahira (1993), boys' superiority in

FIGURE 12.9

Items from an Embedded-Figures Test.

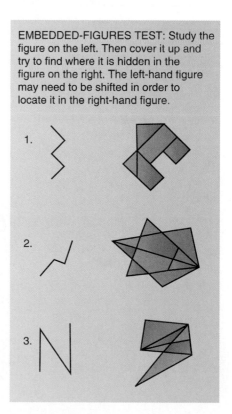

EMBEDDED-FIGURES TEST: Study the figure on the left. Then cover it up and try to find where it is hidden in the figure on the right. The left-hand figure may need to be shifted in order to locate it in the right-hand figure.

math does not reflect gender per se. Instead, boys do as well as they do because of prior knowledge of math and their strategies for approaching math problems.

In any event, psychologists note that three factors should caution us not to attach too much importance to apparent gender differences in cognition:

1. In most cases they are small (Hyde & Plant, 1995). Differences in verbal, mathematical, and spatial abilities are also getting smaller (Hyde and others, 1990; Maccoby, 1990; Voyer and others, 1995).

2. These gender differences are *group* differences. Variation in these skills is larger *within* the groups than between males and females (Maccoby, 1990). Millions of females outdistance the "average" male in math and spatial abilities. Men have produced their Shakespeares. Women have produced their Madame Curies.

3. Many differences that exist may largely reflect sociocultural expectations and environmental influences (Tobias, 1982). Spatial and math abilities are stereotyped as masculine in our culture. Female introductory psychology students given just 3 hours of training in various visual–spatial skills, such as rotating geometric figures, showed no performance deficit in these skills when compared with men (Stericker & LeVesconte, 1982).

Differences in Aggression.   In most cultures, it is the males who march off to war and who battle for glory and shaving-cream commercial contracts. Most psychological studies of aggression have found that male children and adults behave more aggressively than females (Eagly, 1987; Maccoby, 1990; Maccoby & Jacklin, 1980).

**MINILECTURE:
GENDER COMPARISONS IN
INTELLIGENCE**

Truth or Fiction Revisited. It is true that men behave more aggressively than women do—at least in most cultures. The issue is whether this gender difference is inborn or reflects sociocultural conditioning.

Individuality Versus Relatedness.   Males reared in Western culture tend to view the self as supreme and distinct from other people. Moreover, separation and individuation are conceived as the highest goal of personality development. Yet a woman's sense of self is more commonly wrapped up in her sense of relatedness—her establishment and maintenance of social relationships (Gilligan and others, 1991; Jordan and others, 1991).

Guisinger and Blatt (1994) suggest that the male tendency toward individualism might arise from the different developmental tasks faced by boys and girls. For example, when a boy recognizes that he and his mother are not of the same gender, he must set himself apart from her. This process of differentiation may lead boys to greater concern about being separate and distinct from other people. For girls, of course, such differentiation from the mother is unnecessary.

Gender stereotypes and cultural expectations also enter the picture early. True—in our society the great majority of women are in the workforce. Yet girls are still taught from an early age that they will have the primary responsibilities for homemaking and child rearing. Even in an age where women and men share child-rearing chores more so than they did in the past, the developmental research still shows that women are more likely than men to supply the emotional glue that holds the family together.

Grand theories of personality and human development have been accused of having a "phallocentric" and individualist bias (Jordan and others, 1991). This criticism applies to the views of Freud, Erikson, and Kohlberg, among others. Each view has been accused of using the yardsticks of male development as the norms. Each view neglects important aspects of personality development, such as the relatedness of the individual to other people (Guisinger & Blatt, 1994).

ON BECOMING A WOMAN OR A MAN: THE DEVELOPMENT OF GENDER DIFFERENCES

There are thus gender differences in personality. They include minor differences in cognitive functioning and differences in aggressiveness and communication styles. In this section, we consider the biological and psychological factors that appear to contribute to the development of gender differences.

Biological Influences. Biological views on gender differences tend to focus on two issues: brain organization and sex hormones.

A number of studies suggest that we can speak of "left brain" versus "right brain" functions. Language skills seem to depend more on left-brain functioning. Right-brain functioning may be more involved in spatial relations and in aesthetic and emotional responses. The brain hemispheres appear to be more specialized in males than in females. Evidence for this view derives from adults who receive brain injuries. Men with damage to the left hemisphere are more likely to show verbal deficits than women with similar damage (McGlone, 1980). Men with damage to the right hemisphere are more likely to show spatial-relations deficits than similarly injured women.

Gender differences in brain organization might, in part, explain why women exceed men in verbal skills that require some spatial organization, such as reading, spelling, and crisp articulation of speech. Men might be superior at more specialized spatial-relations tasks, however, such as interpreting road maps and visualizing objects in space.

Sex hormones are responsible for prenatal differentiation of sex organs. Prenatal sex hormones may also "masculinize" or "feminize" the brain by creating predispositions that are consistent with some gender-role stereotypes (Crews, 1994). Yet Money (1977, 1987) argues that social learning plays a stronger role in the development of **gender identity,** personality traits, and preferences. Money claims that social learning is powerful enough to counteract many prenatal predispositions.

Evidence for the possible role of hormonal influences derives from animal studies (Collaer & Hines, 1995; Crews, 1994). Male rats are generally superior to females in maze-learning ability, for example, a task that requires spatial skills. Female rats that are exposed to androgens in the uterus or soon after birth learn maze routes as rapidly as males, however (Vandenbergh, 1993).

Males are more aggressive than females, and aggression in lower animals has been connected with the male sex hormone testosterone (Collaer & Hines, 1995). As Benderly puts it, this finding has led to one scientific version of the view that "boys have no choice but to be boys" (1993, p. 10). However, cognitive psychologists, as we shall see, argue that boys (and girls) can choose whether or not to act aggressively, regardless of the levels of hormones in their bloodstreams.

Psychodynamic Theory. Sigmund Freud explained the acquisition of gender roles in terms of **identification.** Freud believed that gender identity remains flexible until the resolution of the Oedipus and Electra complexes at about the age of 5 or 6. Appropriate gender-typing requires that boys identify with their fathers and surrender the wish to possess their mothers. Girls have to identify with their mothers and surrender the wish to have a penis.

Boys and girls develop stereotypical preferences for toys and activities much earlier than might be predicted by psychodynamic theory, however.

Gender identity • One's sense of being female or male.

Identification • (1) In psychodynamic theory, unconscious incorporation of the personality of another person. (2) In social-learning theory, a broad, continuous process of imitation during which children strive to become like role models.

Even within their first year, boys are more explorative and independent. Girls are relatively more quiet, dependent, and restrained (Etaugh & Rathus, 1995). By 18 to 36 months, girls are more likely to play with soft toys and dolls and to dance. Boys of this age are more likely to play with blocks and toy cars, trucks, and airplanes.

Social-Cognitive Theory.   Social-cognitive theorists explain the acquisition of gender roles and gender differences in terms of observational learning, identification, and socialization. Children learn much of what is considered masculine or feminine by observational learning. Social-cognitive theorists view identification as a broad, continuous learning process in which children are influenced by rewards and punishments to imitate adults of the same gender—particularly the parent of the same gender. In identification, as opposed to imitation, children do not simply imitate a certain behavior pattern. They also try to become broadly like the model.

Socialization also plays a role. Parents and other adults—even other children—inform children about how they are expected to behave. They reward children for behavior they consider gender-appropriate. They punish (or fail to reinforce) children for behavior they consider inappropriate. Girls, for example, are given dolls while they still sleep in cribs. They are encouraged to rehearse caregiving behaviors in preparation for traditional feminine adult roles. Girls frequently learn to respond to social provocations by feeling anxious about the possibility of acting aggressively. Boys are generally encouraged to retaliate (Frodi and others, 1977).

From the social-cognitive perspective, males and females both tend to view aggression as a way in which people control other people. Men are more aggressive than women, however, because men tend to think of aggression as a more or less legitimate weapon in the male struggle for status and power (Campbell, 1993). Women, by contrast, usually think of aggression as the result of a *failure* of self-control.

Social-cognitive theory has helped outline the ways in which rewards, punishments, and modeling foster "gender-appropriate" behavior. Gender-schema theory suggests that we tend to assume gender-appropriate behavior patterns as a result of blending our self-concepts with sociocultural expectations.

Gender-Schema Theory: Blending the Self-Concept with Sociocultural Expectations.   You have heard the expression, "looking at the world through rose-colored glasses." According to Sandra Bem (1993), the originator of **gender-schema theory,** people look at the social world through "the lenses of gender." Bem argues that our culture polarizes females and males by organizing social life around mutually exclusive gender roles or scripts. Children, and later adults, come to internalize, or accept, the polarizing scripts without realizing it. Unless parents or unusual events encourage them to challenge the validity of gender polarization, children attempt to construct identities that are consistent with the "proper" script. Most children perceive gender polarization as normal. They reject behavior—in others and in themselves—that deviates from it. Children's self-esteem soon becomes wrapped up in the ways in which they measure up to the gender schema.

Within gender-schema theory, gender identity is sufficient to prompt "gender-appropriate" behavior. Once children understand the labels *boy* and *girl,* they have a basis for blending their self-concepts with the gender schema of their culture. No external reinforcement is required. Children who have developed a sense of being male or being female, which usually occurs by the age of 3, actively seek information about the gender schema.

Socialization • Guidance of people—and children in particular—into socially desirable behavior by means of verbal messages, the systematic use of rewards and punishments, and other methods of teaching.

Gender-schema theory • The view that gender identity and knowledge of the distribution of behavior patterns into feminine and masculine roles motivates and guides the gender-typing of the child.

Study Guide

DIRECTIONS: In the column to the right are the names of personality theorists. In the column to the left is a list of personality-theory concepts. Match the concept with the theorist by writing the letter(s) of the appropriate theorist(s) in the blank space to the left of the concept.

____ 1. Surface trait

____ 2. Self

____ 3. Big Five factors

____ 4. Id

____ 5. 16 PF Scale

____ 6. Psychosocial development

____ 7. Frame of reference

____ 8. Behaviorism

____ 9. Inferiority complex

____ 10. Basic anxiety

____ 11. Self-efficacy expectations

____ 12. Introversion

____ 13. Trust versus mistrust

____ 14. Latency

____ 15. Conditions of worth

____ 16. Electra complex

____ 17. Archetype

____ 18. Creative self

____ 19. Source trait

____ 20. Person variables

A. Alfred Adler

B. B. F. Skinner

C. Albert Bandura

D. Raymond Cattell

E. Erik Erikson

F. Hans Eysenck

G. Sigmund Freud

H. Karen Horney

I. Carl Jung

J. Carl Rogers

K. Julian Rotter

L. John B. Watson

M. Tupes and Christal

ANSWER KEY TO EXERCISE

1. D	4. G	7. J	10. H	13. E	16. G	19. D
2. A, I, J	5. D	8. B, L	11. C	14. G	17. I	20. C, K
3. M	6. E	9. A	12. F	15. J	18. A	

address traits (505)—consider characteristics

adjusting a carburetor (529)—changing the mixture of air and gasoline in the engine of a car in order to obtain better operation of the car

aesthetic (537)—artistic

after doing so (509)—after we do this

all across the board (505)—in every situation; all the time

altruist (519)—someone who cares deeply for other human beings

amass (527)—gather

anatomical (534)—physical

aptitudes (530)—abilities

as surely as (504)—is the same way as

astounded (510)—amazed; shocked

at the mercy of (513)—victims of

backflip (520)—a dive that involves doing a backward somersault in the air, ending with the diver entering the water headfirst as in a regular dive

blindly ruled by pleasure and pain (519)—allow pleasure and pain to determine their actions without thinking about it

braving the arrows (512)—risking the criticisms and attacks

brazen (527)—disrespectful

brimming (526)—full to the very top with liquid

broadest effect (522)—the widest effect; an effect on most of the issues

calling out (520)—speaking aloud without asking for permission to speak

cardinal role (525)—the most important role

carrot dangling from a stick (525)—a motivation; something good that is not close enough to reach, but we try hard to reach it

cauldron (511)—a large pot used for boiling something

charitable (508)—generous

check off (534)—show that it occurred by making a checkmark

chess (524)—a game, played on a board, that requires a great amount of skill; a player needs to plan future moves in order to capture the opponent's chess pieces

chimed in (526)—joined the conversation by adding something

clinging (513)—attaching physically and emotionally

codes of conduct (520)—rules for behavior

conformity (510)—obedience

conscious architects (516)—deliberate builder; in this case, we make our own personalities

consolidate (514)—bring together

curbs the appetites (511)—limits the desires

date (520)—an invitation to another person to go to a social function

desensitization (522)—a process of minimizing someone's fear or discomfort with something by slowly exposing him or her to it more and more often so he or she no longer has a strong reaction to it

deter (511)—stop

disown (524)—deny

driving them away (515)—causing the parents to not care any longer

dwell side by side (511)—live or exist next to each other

easy time of it (534)—things are easy

edifice (505)—structure

embedded in (505)—buried in

embryonic (505)—not completely developed; in the early stages

erogenous zone (513)—area of sexual sensitivity

exalted (527)—respected; admired; held in high esteem

facts of the matter (533)—the facts in the situation

far-reaching effects (517)—effects that will continue and may cause problems in the future

feeling at home at gatherings (527)—feel comfortable with groups of people in a social setting

fell into disfavor (514)—became disliked

fit our jobs (508)—that our jobs are appropriate to our abilities

floods the ego (512)—overwhelms the ego

for fear of (515)—because we are afraid

for the thrill of it (532)—because I only wanted the exciting sensations

forced-choice format (531)—a question-asking form that requires that people answer one way or another, without offering a neutral (neither one nor the other) choice

forced upon us by intrapsychic warfare (516)—the compromises we did not choose that result from the conflicts among the ego, superego, and id

forecasting good tidings, then doom (509)—predicting good news, then bad news

fought for the idea that (517)—tried to convince people that

fueled by (513)—caused to operate

further clouded (515)—made additionally unclear

fury (510)—strong intensity; fierceness

general climate (516)—general feeling

genocide (523)—when one group of people tries to kill all members of another group *getting in touch with* (525)—becoming aware of

given moment (509)—a specific moment

gloss over (504)—handle something in a surface, or superficial, way

golf (534)—a sport requiring hitting a small ball over a large area of ground and ultimately hitting it into a hole

grants more powers to (516)—gives more powers to

gratify (511)—satisfy

guardian (511)—caregiver

hands out judgments (512)—dispenses judgments

haphazardly (531)—without direction or purpose; not regularly

harbor feelings (512)—have feelings and continue to have them

hard time of it (512)—things are difficult

hatred (511)—strong dislike and resentment

holds forth shining examples (512)—displays excellent examples

hue and cry (519)—strong statement of ideas

importance to conscious motives (515)—fully conscious functions must be considered important

in part (515)—not completely, but enough to be considered

inkblots (533)—large areas of ink on a piece of paper

inner circle (514)—the friends and colleagues who worked closely with Freud

intellectual forebear (522)—the theories that came before it and influenced it

introversion (507)—a personality type characterized by preferring to spend time alone

jack-o'-lantern (533)—a Halloween tradition in which people carve faces in pumpkins and then make lamps by putting lighted candles inside

jolly (503)—cheerful; happy

largely discard the notions (519)—almost completely dismiss the ideas

legitimate (538)—appropriate

let it all hang out (513)—say everything you are thinking or feeling

Lord Byron (515)—one of the English Romantic poets of the 19th century

luncheon (527)—lunch

made for each other (520)—of compatible personality; personalitities that fit well together

make up stories (533)—create stories

mar the formation of (516)—obstruct or slow the development of

mental detective work (511)—a method of figuring out answers from evidence and clues

met (511)—be gratified

nourishment (513)—nutrition

obese (503)—fat

off base (504)—wrong; not focused on the right area

outbursts (511)—explosions of emotion

overly anxious to please (507)—a strong need to please others, but with anxiety that it might not work

owes its origin (509)—has its beginning

paramount importance (515)—the most important

penchants (518)—preferences; tendencies

perpetuated (505)—maintained; encouraged

placed undue emphasis (516)—had considered much too strongly the importance of something

poked through (510)—went through to

polar opposites (538)—extreme opposites; *polar* refers to the North and South Poles

pops into their minds (511)—suddenly enters their mind

price (517)—the negative emotional result

prodded to talk (511)—urged and encouraged to talk

puberty (513)—the time when a young girl's or boy's body is becoming a woman or a man; it usually starts in the early teen years

reduce the discrepancy (525)—make the differences smaller

reeled off (527)—stated a list

reminiscent (507)—it reminds us of something else

render (515)—cause to be

resurrection (515)—coming back to life

rich mind (517)—an effective method

rising into awareness (511)—becoming known

Robert Louis Stevenson (518)—a 19th-century Scottish author who wrote many stories and poems that are still popular

sanguine (507)—cheerful; optimistic; confident

serve (520)—refers to the game of tennis; the serve puts the ball in the game, and there is an advantage to the server if she can hit a powerful and accurate serve

set apart (532)—identifed

shadowy parts (524)—unpleasant, hidden aspects

shock of dark hair (509)—a lot of dark hair

short-sighted hedonism (509)—enjoying the moment without thinking about what the negative results might be

shrouded in mystery (570)—unknown

sidestep the roles of (519)—ignore the expectations

simplistic (504)—very basic; uses only the simplest concepts

sneaky (504)—tricky

sole criteria (534)—only requirements

spawned (508)—created

spouse (512)—husband or wife

spurred him on (510)—caused him to work harder and achieve

stirred controversy (512)—caused disagreement

stormy relationships (531)—unstable relationships

strike many psychologists as being (517)—are concepts that many psychologists think are

submerged (503)—hidden under water

suit us (508)—make us the right person
suspect (518)—to be questionable
tedious (511)—tiring; dull; requires a lot of effort
to a large degree (516)—to a great extent; almost completely
tossing a football properly (520)—throwing a football in the correct way in order to play football well

unearthing elements (518)—discovering elements
unladylike (520)—not behaving like a lady should behave
victims of circumstance (525)—other situations and the evironment affect us, and we cannot control that
wicked (515)—evil; extremely bad

FILL-INS | **Chapter Review**

SECTION 1: "WHY ARE THEY SAD AND GLAD AND BAD?": INTRODUCTION TO PERSONALITY

Psychologists define *personality* as the reasonably stable patterns of (1) _____ions, motives, and (2) b_____ that distinguish people from one another.

SECTION 2: THE TRAIT PERSPECTIVE

Traits are personality elements that are inferred from (3) _____or. Traits are said to endure and to account for behavioral (4) _____ency.

Allport and Oddbert catalogued 18,000 human traits from a search through word lists of the sort found in (5) _____aries. According to Raymond Cattell, (6) s_____ traits are characteristic ways of behaving that seem linked in an orderly manner. (7) S_____ traits are underlying traits from which surface traits are derived. Cattell constructed the (8) S_____ Personality Factors Scale, a test that measures source traits.

Hans J. (9) E_____ has focused on the relationships between two source traits: introversion–extroversion and emotional (10) _____ity. Eysenck notes that his scheme is reminiscent of that suggested by (11) _____ates, the Greek physician.

Recent research suggests that there may be five basic personality factors: introversion–extroversion, emotional stability, (12) con_____, agreeableness, and (13) _____ness.

SECTION 3: THE PSYCHODYNAMIC PERSPECTIVE

(14) Psycho_____ theories of personality teach that personality is characterized by a struggle between drives such as sex and aggression on the one hand, and laws, social rules, and moral codes on the other. The laws and social rules become (15) _____lized; that is, we make them parts of ourselves.

Sigmund Freud labeled the clashing forces of personality (16) _____ic structures. Psychodynamic theory assumes that we are driven largely by (17) _____scious motives. Conflict is inevitable as instincts of hunger, (18) s_____, and (19) ag_____ come up against social pressures to follow laws and social codes.

Freud hypothesized the existence of (20: How Many?) _____ psychic structures. The unconscious (21) i_____ is the psychic structure present at birth. The id represents psychological drives and operates according to the (22) pl_____ principle, seeking instant gratification.

The psychic structure called the (23) e_____ is the sense of self, or "I." The ego develops through experience and operates according to the (24) re_____ principle. So-called (25) de_____ mechanisms protect the ego from anxiety by repressing unacceptable ideas or distorting reality.

The third psychic structure is the (26) s_____. The superego is the moral sense. It develops throughout early childhood, including the standards of parents and others by means of (27) ____fication. The superego operates according to the (28) m_____ principle.

People undergo psychosexual development as psychosexual energy, or (29) l_____, is transferred from one (30) _____nous zone to another during childhood. There are (31: How Many?) _____ stages of psychosexual development. They are the oral, (32) a_____, phallic, (33) l_____, and genital stages.

(34) Fi_____ in a stage may lead to the development of traits associated with that stage. Fixation in the oral stage, for example, may lead to oral traits such as (35) dep_____ and (36) g_____ility. Anal fixation may result in extremes of (37) cl_____ness versus messiness, or of (38) per_____ism versus carelessness.

The Oedipus and Electra complexes are conflicts of the (39) _____ic stage. In these conflicts, children long to possess the parent of the (40: Same or Other?) gender and resent the parent of the (41: Same or Other?) gender. Under normal circumstances, these complexes eventually become resolved by identifying with the parent of the (42: Same or Other?) gender.

Carl Jung's psychodynamic theory is called (43) _____cal psychology. Jung believed that in addition to a personal unconscious mind, we also have a (44) _____tive unconscious, which contains primitive images or (45) _____pes that are reflections of the history of our species.

Alfred Adler's psychodynamic theory is called (46) _____ual psychology. Adler believed that people are basically motivated by an (47) _____ity complex and that this complex gives rise to a compensating drive for (48) _____ity.

Karen (49) H_____, like Freud, saw parent–child relationships as paramount in importance. When parents treat children indifferently or harshly, the children develop feelings of insecurity that Horney labeled basic (50) _____ty.

Erik Erikson's psychodynamic theory is called the theory of (51) psycho_____ development. Erikson highlights the importance of early (52) _____al relationships rather than the gratification of childhood (53) _____al impulses. Erikson extended Freud's five developmental stages to (54: How Many?) _____. Erikson's stages are characterized by certain life (55) _____ses. These are the crises of (56) _____ versus mistrust, (57) _____my versus shame and doubt, initiative versus (58) g_____, (59) _____try versus inferiority, identity versus (60) _____ diffusion, (61) _____vity versus stagnation, and integrity versus (62) de_____.

SECTION 4: THE LEARNING PERSPECTIVE

The behaviorists John B. Watson and B. F. (63) S_____ discarded notions of personal freedom and argued that environmental contingencies can shape people into wanting to do the things that the physical environment and society requires of them.

Social-cognitive theory, in contrast to behaviorism, has a strong (64) cog_____ orientation and focuses on the importance of learning by (65) _____tion. Rotter argues that behavior depends upon the person's (66) _____ancies concerning the outcome of that behavior and the perceived or (67) _____tive values of those outcomes.

Social-cognitive theorists do not consider only situational rewards and (68) _____ents important in the prediction of behavior. They also consider the roles of (69) p_____ variables. Person variables include (70) co_____cies, (71) en_____ing strategies, expectancies, subjective values, and (72) self-_____tory systems and plans. Bandura refers to beliefs that one can handle a task as (73) self-e_____ expectations. We are (74: More or Less?) likely to persist at difficult tasks when we believe that we shall succeed at them.

SECTION 5: THE HUMANISTIC–EXISTENTIAL PERSPECTIVE

Abraham Maslow argued that people have growth-oriented needs for (75) self-_____ation. Carl Rogers's theory begins with the assumption of the existence of the (76) s_____. According to Carl (77) R_____, the self is an organized and consistent way in which a person perceives his or her "I" to relate to others and the world.

The self is innate and will attempt to become actualized (develop its unique potential) when the person receives (78) _____ional positive regard. We all have needs for self-esteem and see the world through unique frames of (79) _____nce. Conditions of (80) w_____ lead to a distorted self-concept, to the disowning of parts of the self, and, often, to anxiety. When we accept our feelings as our own, there is a fit between our self-concepts and our behavior, thoughts, and emotions that Rogers calls psychological (81) _____ence.

SECTION 6: THE SOCIOCULTURAL PERSPECTIVE

The (82) _____cultural perspective considers ethnic and other sociocultural influences on personality. People in the United States and many northern European nations tend to be (83) _____istic. They tend to define themselves in terms of their personal identities and to give priority to their personal goals. (84) _____ists tend to define themselves in terms of the groups to which they belong and to give priority to the goals of their group.

Members of minority ethnic groups who have been subjected to discrimination and poverty may have (85: Higher or Lower?) self-esteem than members of the dominant culture. Immigrants who identify with the bicultural pattern of assimilation have the (86: Highest or Lowest?) self-esteem.

SECTION 7: MEASUREMENT OF PERSONALITY

In personality measurement, psychologists take a sample of (87) b_____ in order to predict future behavior.

(88) _____ive tests present test takers with a standardized set of test items in the form of questionnaires. Projective tests present (89) _____uous stimuli and permit the respondent a broad range of answers.

The (90) M_____ M_____ Personality Inventory (MMPI) is the most widely used psychological test in the clinical setting. The MMPI is an (91) _____ive personality test that uses a true–false format to assess psychological disorders. The MMPI contains (92) _____ity scales as well as clinical scales.

The foremost projective technique is the (93) R_____ inkblot test, in which test takers are asked to report what inkblots look like or could be. The (94) T_____ A_____ Test (TAT) consists of ambiguous drawings that test takers are asked to interpret.

SECTION 8: GENDER DIFFERENCES IN PERSONALITY

Research suggests that (95: Boys or Girls?) are somewhat superior in verbal ability. Males seem somewhat superior in (96) v_____–spatial abilities and (97) _____tics. Three factors should caution us not to attach too much importance to these cognitive gender differences. First, in most cases they are (98: Large or Small?). Second, these gender differences are (99) g_____ differences. Third, they may largely reflect cultural (100) _____tions.

Most psychological studies of aggression have found that (101: Males or Females?) behave more aggressively.

(102) Pre_____ sex hormones may "masculinize" or "feminize" the brain by creating predispositions that are consistent with some gender-role stereotypes.

Social-cognitive theorists explain the acquisition of gender roles and gender differences in terms such as (103) _____tional learning, identification, and (104) so_____tion. Children learn much of what is considered masculine or feminine behaviors by (105) ob_____nal learning of the relative frequencies with which men and women perform them. Social-cognitive theorists view (106) _____ation as a broad, continuous learning process in which children are influenced by rewards and punishments to imitate adults of the same gender.

(107) Gender-s_____ theory holds that children use gender as one way of organizing their perceptions of the world. Children learn to judge themselves according to the traits, or constructs, considered relevant to their (108) _____er. In so doing, their (109) self-_____s become blended with the gender schema of their culture.

ANSWER KEY TO CHAPTER REVIEW

1. Emotions	29. Libido	57. Autonomy	85. Lower
2. Behavior	30. Erogenous	58. Guilt	86. Highest
3. Behavior	31. Five	59. Industry	87. Behavior
4. Consistency	32. Anal	60. Role	88. Objective
5. Dictionaries	33. Latency	61. Generativity	89. Ambiguous
6. Surface	34. Fixation	62. Despair	90. Minnesota Multiphasic
7. Source	35. Dependence (or depression)	63. Skinner	91. Objective
8. Sixteen	36. Gullibility	64. Cognitive	92. Validity
9. Eysenck	37. Cleanliness	65. Observation	93. Rorschach
10. Stability	38. Perfectionism	66. Expectancies	94. Thematic Apperception
11. Hippocrates	39. Phallic	67. Subjective	95. Girls
12. Conscientiousness	40. Other	68. Punishments	96. Visual-spatial
13. Openness	41. Same	69. Person	97. Mathematics
14. Psychodynamic	42. Same	70. Competencies	98. Small
15. Internalized	43. Analytical	71. Encoding	99. Group
16. Psychic	44. Collective	72. Regulatory	100. Expectations
17. Unconscious	45. Archetypes	73. Self-efficacy	101. Males
18. Sex	46. Individual	74. More	102. Prenatal
19. Aggression	47. Inferiority	75. Self-actualization	103. Observational
20. Three	48. Superiority	76. Self	104. Socialization
21. Id	49. Horney	77. Rogers	105. Observational
22. Pleasure	50. Anxiety	78. Unconditional	106. Identification
23. Ego	51. Psychosocial	79. Reference	107. Schema
24. Reality	52. Social	80. Worth	108. Gender
25. Defense	53. Sexual	81. Congruence	109. Self-concepts
26. Superego	54. Eight	82. Sociocultural	
27. Identification	55. Crises	83. Individualistic	
28. Moral	56. Trust	84. Collectivists	

1. Freud labeled the clashing forces of personality
   a. repression and resistance.
   b. conscious and unconscious.
   c. defense mechanisms.
   d. psychic structures.

2. According to psychodynamic theory, the _____ follows the reality principle.
   a. id
   b. ego
   c. superego
   d. libido

3. According to psychodynamic theory, the superego usually incorporates the standards of parents through
   a. identification.
   b. repression.
   c. unconditional positive regard.
   d. classical and operant conditioning.

4. John throws his clothing and books all over the floor, leaves his hair unkempt, and rarely cleans his room. According to psychodynamic theory, John's behavior is suggestive of conflict during the _____ stage of psychosexual development.
   a. genital
   b. oral
   c. phallic
   d. anal

5. Alfred Adler believed that people are basically motivated by
   a. the collective unconscious.
   b. hostility.
   c. biological and safety needs.
   d. an inferiority complex.

6. Karen Horney agreed with Freud that
   a. a woman's place is in the home.
   b. there are eight stages of psychosocial development.
   c. parent–child relationships are very important.
   d. sexual impulses are more important than social relationships.

7. According to the text, which of the following theorists believed that a basic element of personality was the Self?
   a. John B. Watson
   b. Carl Jung
   c. Sigmund Freud
   d. Hans J. Eysenck

8. Gordon Allport looked upon traits as
   a. archetypes.
   b. basic instincts.
   c. generalized expectancies.
   d. embedded in the nervous system.

9. Raymond Cattell hypothesized the existence of two types of traits: _____ traits and source traits.
   a. surface
   b. cardinal
   c. secondary
   d. central

10. The outlooks of John B. Watson and B. F. Skinner discarded all of the following notions, with the exception of
    a. self-direction.
    b. personal freedom.
    c. learning.
    d. choice.

11. _____ has argued for the inclusion of cognitive points of view within learning theory.
    a. Carl Rogers
    b. Albert Bandura
    c. John B. Watson
    d. B. F. Skinner

12. Which of the following is a situational variable?
    a. a self-efficacy expectation
    b. the subjective value of a reward
    c. a generalized expectancy
    d. a reward

13. According to Carl Rogers, the sense of self
    a. is an archetype.
    b. develops as a result of conditions of worth.
    c. is innate.
    d. develops once biological and safety needs have been met.

14. A mother and father tell you that their most important goal for their new child is that she develop a strong sense of self-esteem. According to self theory, parents are likely to help their children develop self-esteem when they show them
    a. conditional positive regard.
    b. conditions of worth.
    c. unconditional positive regard.
    d. psychological congruence.

15. Which theorist has focused on the relationships between introversion–extroversion and neuroticism?
    a. Carl Jung
    b. Hans J. Eysenck
    c. Raymond Cattell
    d. Karen Horney

16. The view that children adopt gender roles by blending their self-concepts with the distribution of gender roles in society is most consistent with
    a. psychodynamic theory.
    b. self theory.
    c. social-cognitive theory.
    d. gender-schema theory.

17. Research into gender differences suggests that
    a. boys are more aggressive than girls.
    b. boys have greater verbal skills than girls.
    c. girls have greater math skills than boys.
    d. girls have greater spatial-relations skills than boys.

18. Which of the following theorists would be most likely to agree that people are capable of recognizing and understanding their own feelings?
    a. B. F. Skinner
    b. John Watson
    c. Abraham Maslow
    d. Sigmund Freud

19. Objective personality tests
    a. show test takers ambiguous figures.
    b. are easier to answer than projective tests.
    c. limit respondents to a specific range of answers.
    d. are less valid than projective personality tests.

20. The name Rorschach is connected with
    a. a projective testing method.
    b. the Big Five factor structure.
    c. social-cognitive theory.
    d. gender-schema theory.

ANSWER KEY TO POSTTEST

1. D	4. D	7. B	10. C	13. C	16. D	19. C
2. B	5. D	8. D	11. B	14. C	17. A	20. A
3. A	6. C	9. A	12. D	15. B	18. C	

Psychological Disorders

PRETEST *Truth or Fiction?*

_____ A man shot the president of the United States in front of millions of television witnesses, yet was found not guilty by a court of law.

_____ In the Middle Ages, innocent people were drowned to prove that they were not possessed by the Devil.

_____ Some people have more than one identity, and the identities may have different allergies and eyeglass prescriptions.

_____ It is abnormal to feel depressed.

_____ People who threaten suicide are only seeking attention.

_____ You can never be too rich or too thin.

_____ Some college women control their weight by going on cycles of binge eating followed by self-induced vomiting.

THE Ohio State campus lived in terror one long fall. Four college women were abducted, were forced to cash checks or obtain money with their instant-cash cards, then were raped. A mysterious phone call led to the arrest of a 23-year-old drifter, William, who had been dismissed from the Navy.

William was not the boy next door.

Psychologists and psychiatrists who interviewed William concluded that 10 personalities—8 male and 2 female—resided within him (Scott, 1994). His personality had been "fractured" by an abusive childhood. The personalities showed distinct facial expressions, vocal patterns, and memories. They even performed differently on personality and intelligence tests.

Arthur, the most rational personality, spoke with a British accent. Danny and Christopher were quiet adolescents. Christene was a 3-year-old girl. It was Tommy, a 16-year-old, who had enlisted in the Navy. Allen was 18 and smoked. Adelena, a 19-year-old lesbian personality, had committed the rapes. Who had made the mysterious phone call? Probably David, aged 9, an anxious child personality.

The defense claimed that William's behavior was caused by a psychological disorder: **dissociative identity disorder** (also referred to as **multiple personality disorder**). Several distinct identities or personalities dwelled within him. Some were aware of the others. Some believed that they were the sole occupants. Billy, the core identity, had learned to sleep as a child to avoid the abuse of his father. A psychiatrist asserted that Billy had also been "asleep," in a "psychological coma," during the abductions. Billy should therefore be found innocent by reason of **insanity.**

Billy was found not guilty by reason of insanity. He was committed to a psychiatric institution and released 6 years later.

In 1982, John Hinckley was also found not guilty of the assassination attempt on President Reagan's life by reason of insanity. Expert witnesses testified that he should be diagnosed with **schizophrenia.** Hinckley, too, was committed to a psychiatric institution.

Truth or Fiction Revisited. *It is true that a man shot the president of the United States in front of millions of television witnesses, yet was found not guilty by a court of law.* He was found not guilty by reason of insanity.

Dissociative identity disorder and schizophrenia are two **psychological disorders.** If William and John had lived in Salem, Massachusetts, in 1692, just 200 years after Columbus set foot in the New World, they might have been hanged or burned as witches. At that time, most people assumed that psychological disorders were caused by possession by the Devil. Nineteen people lost their lives that year in that colonial town for allegedly practicing the arts of Satan.

Throughout human history, most people have attributed unusual behavior and psychological disorders to demons. The ancient Greeks by and large believed that the gods punished humans by causing confusion and madness. An exception was Hippocrates, the Greek physician of the Golden Age of art and literature (4th century B.C.). Hippocrates made the radical suggestion that psychological disorders were caused by an abnormality of the brain. The notion that biology could affect thoughts, feelings, and behavior was to lie dormant for about 2,000 years.

During the Middle Ages in Europe, as well as during the early days of European American colonization of the rocky coast of Massachusetts, it was generally believed that psychological disorders were signs of possession by agents of the Devil. Possession could stem from retribution, or God's having the Devil possess your soul as punishment for sins. Agitation and confusion were ascribed to retribution. Possession was also believed to result from deals with the Devil, in which people traded their souls for earthly gains. Such traders were called witches. Witches were held responsible for unfortunate events ranging from a neighbor's infertility to a poor crop. At least 200,000 accused witches were killed during the next 2 centuries. Europe was no place to practice strange ways. The goings-on at Salem were trivial by comparison.

Ingenious "diagnostic" tests were used to ferret out possession. The water-float test was based on the principle that pure metals sink to the bottom during smelting. Impurities float to the surface. Suspects were thus kept in deep water. Those who sank to the bottom and drowned were judged to be pure. Suspects who managed to keep their heads above water were assumed to be "impure" and in league with the Devil. Then they were in real trouble. This ordeal is the origin of the phrase "Damned if you do and damned if you don't."

Truth or Fiction Revisited. *It is true that innocent people were drowned in the Middle Ages as a way of proving that they were not possessed by the Devil.* The method was based on a water-float test designed to determine whether metals are pure.

Few people in the United States today would argue that unusual or unacceptable behavior is caused by demons. Still, the English language continues to harbor phrases suggestive of demonology. How many times have you heard the expressions "Something got the best of me" or "The Devil made me do it"?

In this chapter, we first define what is meant by a psychological disorder. We then discuss various psychological disorders, including anxiety disorders, dissociative disorders, somatoform disorders, mood disorders, schizophrenia, personality disorders, and eating disorders.

WHAT ARE PSYCHOLOGICAL DISORDERS?

Psychology is the study of behavior and mental processes. Psychological disorders are patterns of behavior or mental processes that are connected with notable distress or disability. However, they are not predictable responses to specific events.

For example, some psychological disorders are characterized by anxiety or depression, but many of us are anxious or depressed now and then without being considered disordered. It is appropriate to be anxious before a big date or on the eve of a midterm exam. It is appropriate to be depressed if a friend is upset with you or if you have failed at a test or job.

When, then, are feelings like anxiety and depression deemed to be abnormal or signs of a psychological disorder? For one thing, anxiety and depression may suggest a disorder when they are not appropriate to our situations. It is inappropriate to be depressed when things are going well or to be distraught when entering an elevator or looking out of a fourth-story window. The magnitude of the problem may also suggest that a disorder is present. Though some anxiety is to be expected before a job interview, feeling that your heart is pounding so intensely that it might leap out of your chest—and then avoiding the interview—are not. Nor is sweating so profusely that your clothing literally becomes soaked.

Behaviors or mental processes that meet one or more of the following criteria are suggestive of psychological disorders:

1. *Unusual.* Although people with psychological disorders are in a minority, uncommon behavior or mental processes are not in themselves abnormal. Only one person holds the record for running or swimming the fastest mile.

That person is different from you and me but is not abnormal. Only a few people qualify as geniuses in mathematics, but mathematical genius is not a sign of a psychological disorder.

Rarity or statistical deviance may not be sufficient for behavior or mental processes to be labeled abnormal, but it helps. Most people do not see or hear things that are not there, and "seeing things" and "hearing things" are considered abnormal. We must also consider the situation. Although many of us feel "panicked" when we recall that a term paper or report is due, most of us do not have panic attacks "out of the blue." Unpredictable panic attacks are thus suggestive of psychological disorder.

2. *Faulty in perception or interpretation of reality.* It is considered normal to talk to God through prayer, but people who claim that God talks back to them may be committed to a psychiatric institution. Our society considers it normal to be inspired by religious beliefs, but abnormal to believe that God is literally speaking to you. "Hearing voices" and "seeing things" are considered **hallucinations.** Similarly, **ideas of persecution** such as believing that the Mafia or the FBI are "out to get you" are considered signs of disorder. (Unless they *are* out to get you, of course.)

3. *Distressful.* Anxiety, depression, exaggerated fears, and other psychological states cause personal distress, and severe personal distress may be considered abnormal. Anxiety and depression may also be appropriate responses to one's situation, however, as in a real threat or loss. In such cases, they are not abnormal unless they persevere long after the source of distress has been removed or after most people would have adjusted.

Hallucination (hal-LOOSE-sin-nay-shun) • A perception in the absence of sensory stimulation that is confused with reality.

Ideas of persecution • Erroneous beliefs that one is being victimized or persecuted.

Hallucinations. Hallucinations are perceptions that occur in the absence of external stimulation that cannot be distinguished from real perceptions, as in "hearing voices" or "seeing things." Are the cats in this Sandy Skoglund photograph real or hallucinatory?

4. *Self-defeating.* Behavior or mental processes that cause misery rather than happiness and fulfillment may be suggestive of psychological disorders. Chronic drinking that impairs work and family life and cigarette smoking that impairs health may thus be deemed abnormal.

5. *Dangerous.* Behavior or mental processes that are hazardous to the self or others may be considered suggestive of psychological disorders. People who threaten or attempt suicide may be considered abnormal, as may people who threaten or attack others. Yet criminal behavior or aggressive behavior in athletic contests does not necessarily imply a psychological disorder.

6. *Socially unacceptable.* We must consider the cultural context of a behavior pattern in judging whether the behavior is normal. In the United States, it is deemed normal for males to be aggressive in sports and in combat. In other situations warmth and tenderness are valued. Many in the United States admire women who are self-assertive, yet Hispanic American, Asian American, and "traditional" non-Hispanic White American communities groups may find outspoken women to be brazen and insolent.

CLASSIFYING PSYCHOLOGICAL DISORDERS

Toss some people, apes, seaweed, fish, and sponges into a room—preferably a well-ventilated room. Stir slightly. What do you have? It depends on how you classify this hodgepodge.

Classify them as plants versus animals and you lump the people, chimpanzees, fish, and, yes, sponges together. Classify them as stuff that carries on its business on land or underwater, and we throw in our lots with just the chimps. How about those that swim and those that don't? Then the chimps, the fish, and some of us are pigeonholed together.

Classification is at the heart of science (Barlow, 1991). Without labeling and ordering psychological disorders, investigators would not be able to communicate with each other, and progress would be at a standstill. The most widely used classification scheme for psychological disorders[1] is the *Diagnostic and Statistical Manual* (DSM) of the American Psychiatric Association (Maser and others, 1991). The DSM was developed to provide a uniform way of classifying psychological disorders (Widiger and others, 1991), and it has undergone several revisions.

The current edition of the DSM—the DSM-IV—employs a multiaxial, or multidimensional, system of assessment. It provides a broad range of information about an individual's functioning, not just a diagnosis. The axes are shown in Table 13.1.

Separating the diagnostic categories into two axes provides diagnostic flexibility. People may receive Axis I or Axis II diagnoses, or a combination of the two.

Axis III, general medical conditions, lists physical disorders or problems that may affect people's functioning or response to psychotherapy or drug treatment. Axis IV, psychosocial and environmental problems, includes difficulties that may affect the diagnosis, treatment, or outcome of a psychological disorder. Axis V, the global assessment of functioning, allows the clinician to rate

---

[1] The American Psychiatric Association refers to psychological disorders as *mental disorders.*

TABLE 13.1

THE MULTIAXIAL CLASSIFICATION
SYSTEM OF THE DSM-IV

AXIS	TYPE OF INFORMATION	BRIEF DESCRIPTION
I	Clinical Syndromes (a wide range of diagnostic classes, such as substance-related disorders, anxiety disorders, mood disorders, schizophrenia, somatoform disorders, and dissociative disorders)	Patterns of abnormal behavior that impair functioning and are stressful to the individual
II	Personality Disorders	Deeply ingrained, maladaptive ways of perceiving others and behavior that are stressful to the individual or those who relate to the individual
III	General Medical Conditions	Chronic and acute illnesses, injuries, allergies, and so on, that affect functioning and treatment, such as cardiovascular disorders, athletic injuries, and allergies to medication
IV	Psychosocial and Environmental Problems	Stressors that occurred during the past year that may have contributed to the development of a new mental disorder or the recurrence of a prior disorder or that may have exacerbated an existing disorder, such as divorce occurring during a depressive episode. Stressors can be marital, parental, occupational, financial, legal, developmental, physical, and so on.
V	Global Assessment of Functioning	Overall judgment of current functioning and the highest level of functioning in the past year according to psychological, social, and occupational criteria

the client's current level of functioning and highest level of functioning prior to the onset of the psychological disorder. The purpose is to help set goals as to what kinds of psychological functioning are to be restored.

The DSM-IV groups disorders on the basis of observable features or symptoms, which is logical enough. However, early editions of the DSM grouped many disorders on the basis of assumptions about their causes (Millon, 1991). Because Freud's psychodynamic theory was widely accepted at the time, one major diagnostic category contained the so-called neuroses.[2] From the psychodynamic perspective, all neuroses—no matter how differently people with various neuroses might behave—stemmed from unconscious neurotic conflict.

---

[2] The neuroses included what are today referred to as anxiety disorders, dissociative disorders, somatoform disorders, mild depression, and some other disorders, such as sleepwalking.

Each neurosis was thought to reflect a way of coping with unconscious fear that primitive impulses might break loose. As a result, sleepwalking was included as a neurosis (psychoanalysts assumed that sleepwalking contained impulses by permitting their partial expression during the night). Now that the focus is on the observable, sleepwalking is classified as a sleep disorder, not as a kind of neurosis. I mention all this because the words *neurosis* and *neurotic* are still heard today. Without some explanation, it might seem strange that they have been largely abandoned by professionals.

We must also consider the reliability and validity of the DSM categories. The reliability of a diagnosis such as dissociative identity disorder is its consistency, usually measured as the extent of agreement among professionals who make diagnoses. For example, the agreement rates among pairs of professionals for diagnoses of schizophrenia and mood disorders are about 81% and 83%, respectively (Spitzer and others, 1979). These are reasonably respectable numbers. One reason the DSM is reliable is that the diagnostic categories have been narrowed in recent years, meaning that fewer people are likely to show the lists of behaviors required for various diagnoses. There is a downside to this reliability: Some observers wonder whether the descriptions of some diagnostic categories are so narrow that many people who actually have the disorders, such as many people with schizophrenia, fail to be properly diagnosed (Andreasen, 1990).

The validity of a diagnosis is the degree to which it reflects an *actual* disorder. For example, there is question as to whether the kinds of depression listed in the DSM are really all that distinct (Keller and others, 1990) and whether "substance abuse" is really all that different from "substance dependence" (Helzer & Schuckit, 1990).

Some professionals, like psychiatrist Thomas Szasz, believe that the categories described in the DSM are really "problems in living" rather than "disorders." They are not disorders, at least, in the sense that high blood pressure, cancer, and the flu are disorders. Szasz argues that labeling people with problems in living as being "sick" degrades them and encourages them to evade their personal and social responsibilities. Since sick people are encouraged to obey doctors' orders, Szasz (1984) also contends that labeling people as "sick" accords too much power to health professionals. Instead, troubled people need to be encouraged to take greater responsibility for solving their own problems.

In sum, questions remain about classification. These include questions about the reliability and validity of the diagnostic categories in the DSM and broader philosophical questions. Yet, in considering abnormal behavior, I shall refer to the DSM. This is a convenience, however, and not an endorsement.

Reflections

- Do any family members or friends have psychological disorders? Do their behaviors or mental processes correspond to the six criteria discussed in the chapter? How are the disorders being treated?
- **Agree or disagree with the following statement and support your answer: "Normalcy and abnormality must be understood within a particular cultural context."**
- **Agree or disagree with the following statement and support your answer: "People should not feel anxious or depressed."**

Let us now consider the more prominent psychological disorders.

ANXIETY DISORDERS

Anxiety is characterized by subjective and physical features (Beck and others, 1988). Subjective features include fear of the worst happening, fear of losing control, nervousness, and inability to relax. Physical features reflect arousal of the sympathetic branch of the autonomic nervous system. They entail trembling, sweating, a pounding or racing heart, elevated blood pressure (a flushed face), and faintness. Anxiety is an appropriate response to a threat. Anxiety can be abnormal, however, when its extent is out of proportion to the threat or when it "comes out of the blue"—that is, when events do not seem to warrant it.

Types of Anxiety Disorders

The anxiety disorders include phobic, panic, generalized anxiety, obsessive–compulsive, post-traumatic stress, and acute stress disorders.

PHOBIAS.   There are several types of phobias, including specific phobias, social phobia, and agoraphobia. **Specific phobias** are excessive, irrational fears of specific objects or situations. **Social phobias** are persistent fears of scrutiny by others or of doing something that will be humiliating or embarrassing. Stage fright and speech anxiety are common social phobias.

Some people with social phobia cannot sign their names in public, as in the case of Brett:

> Brett had a signature phobia. She was literally terrified of signing her name in public. She had structured her life to avoid situations requiring a signature. She paid cash rather than by credit card. She filed documents by mail rather than in person. She even registered her car in her husband's name so that he would be responsible for signing the motor vehicle forms. Like many people with phobias, Brett was clever at restructuring her life so that she could avoid exposing herself to these fearful situations. She had even kept her phobia from her husband for 15 years.
>
> Brett's phobia was maintained by an underlying fear of social embarrassment. She feared ridicule for an illegible or sloppy signature, or that authority figures like bank officers or motor vehicle officials would think that her signature was phony or a forgery. Brett knew that she could prove her identity by other means than her signature and also recognized that no one really cared whether or not her signature was legible. Brett had created a vicious cycle of anxiety: She felt she must prevent her hands from shaking so that she could write legibly. But her anxiety was so strong that she began to shake whenever her signature was required. The more she tried to fend off the anxiety, the stronger it became. Her anxiety confirmed her belief that her signature would be ridiculed. (Adapted from Nevid and others, 1997)

One specific phobia is fear of elevators. Some people will not enter elevators despite the hardships they incur (such as walking six flights of steps) as a result. Yes, the cable *could* break. The ventilation *could* fail. One *could* be stuck waiting in midair for repairs. These problems are uncommon, however, and it does not make sense for most of us to repeatedly walk flights of stairs to elude them. Similarly, some people with specific phobias for hypodermic needles will not receive injections, even when they are the advised remedy for profound illness. Injections can be painful, but most people with phobias

Specific phobia • Persistent fear of a specific object or situation.
Social phobia • An irrational, excessive fear of public scrutiny.

for needles would gladly accept an excruciating pinch if it would help them fight illness. Other specific phobias include **claustrophobia** (fear of tight or enclosed places), **acrophobia** (fear of heights), and fear of mice, snakes, and other creepy-crawlies.

Phobias can seriously disrupt one's life. A person may know that a phobia is irrational yet still experience acute anxiety and avoid the phobic article or circumstance.

Fears of animals and imaginary creatures are common among children. **Agoraphobia** is among the most widespread phobias among adults. Agoraphobia is derived from the Greek meaning "fear of the marketplace," or of being out in open, busy areas. Persons with agoraphobia fear being in places from which it might be difficult to escape or in which help might be unavailable if they become disquieted. In practice, people who receive this label are often loath to venture out of their homes, especially when they are alone. They find it trying or infeasible to hold jobs or to sustain an ordinary social life.

PANIC DISORDER.

My heart would start pounding so hard I was sure I was having a heart attack. I used to go to the emergency room. Sometimes I felt dizzy, like I was going to pass out. I was sure I was about to die.
                                                                    KIM WEINER

Panic disorder is an abrupt attack of acute anxiety that is not triggered by a specific object or situation. People with panic disorder experience strong physical sensations such as shortness of breath, heavy sweating, quaking, and pounding of the heart (Goleman, 1992). As was the case with Kim Weiner (1992), they are particularly aware of cardiac sensations (Ehlers & Breuer, 1992), and it is not unusual for them to think that they are having a heart attack. People may also experience choking sensations; nausea; numbness or tingling; flushes or chills; chest pain; and fear of dying, going crazy, or losing control. Panic attacks may last from a minute or two to an hour or more. Afterwards, people usually feel spent.

Perhaps half of us panic now and then (Wilson and others, 1991). The diagnosis of panic disorder is reserved for people who undergo series of attacks or live in dread of attacks, however. Fewer than 10% of us meet this standard (Wilson and others, 1992).

Because panic attacks seem to descend from nowhere, some people who have had them generally remain in the home for fear of having an attack in public. In such cases, they are diagnosed as having panic disorder with agoraphobia.

GENERALIZED ANXIETY DISORDER.

The central feature of **generalized anxiety disorder** is persistent anxiety. As with panic disorder, the anxiety cannot be attributed to a phobic object, situation, or activity. Rather, it seems to be free floating. Features may include motor tension (shakiness, inability to relax, furrowed brow, fidgeting); autonomic overarousal (sweating, dry mouth, racing heart, light-headedness, frequent urinating, diarrhea); feelings of dread and foreboding; and excessive vigilance, as shown by distractibility, insomnia, and irritability.

OBSESSIVE-COMPULSIVE DISORDER.

Obsessions are recurrent thoughts or images that seem irrational and beyond control. Obsessions are accompanied by anxiety (Foa, 1990). They are so compelling and recurrent that they disrupt daily life. They may include doubts about whether one has locked the doors and shut the windows; impulses such as the wish to strangle one's spouse;

Claustrophobia (claws-troe-FOE-bee-uh) • Fear of tight, small places.

Acrophobia (ack-row-FOE-bee-uh) • Fear of high places.

Agoraphobia (ag-or-uh-FOE-bee-uh) • Fear of open, crowded places.

Panic disorder • The recurrent experiencing of attacks of extreme anxiety in the absence of external stimuli that usually elicit anxiety.

Generalized anxiety disorder • Feelings of dread and foreboding and sympathetic arousal of at least 6 months' duration.

Obsession • A recurring thought or image that seems beyond control.

Compulsion • An apparently irresistible urge to repeat an act or engage in ritualistic behavior such as hand-washing.

Obsessive–Compulsive Disorder. The "woman" in this photograph, *Red Library #2,* by Laurie Simmons, is apparently transfixed by the absence of perfection. It seems that one picture is missing. People with obsessive–compulsive disorder engage in repetitious behaviors as a way of managing troubling thoughts.

and images such as one mother's repeated fantasy that her children had been run over by traffic on the way home from school. In another case, a 16-year-old boy found "numbers in my head" whenever he was about to study or take a test. A woman became obsessed with the idea that she had contaminated her hands with Sani-Flush and that the chemicals were spreading to everything she touched.

Compulsions are thoughts or behaviors that tend to reduce the anxiety connected with obsessions (Foa, 1990). They are seemingly irresistible urges to engage in acts, often repeatedly, such as elaborate washing after using the bathroom. The impulse is recurrent and forceful, interfering with daily life. The woman who felt contaminated by Sani-Flush engaged in intricate hand-washing rituals to reduce the anxiety connected with the obsession. She spent 3 to 4 hours daily at the sink and complained, "My hands look like lobster claws."

POST-TRAUMATIC STRESS DISORDER. Fire, stabbings, shootings, suicides, medical emergencies, accidents, bombs, and hazardous material explosions—these are just some of the traumatic experiences firefighters confront on a fairly regular basis. Because of such experiences, one study found that the prevalence of **post-traumatic stress disorder** (PTSD) among firefighters was 16.5%. This rate was 1% higher than the rate among Vietnam veterans and compared with a rate of 1% to 3% among the general population (DeAngelis, 1995a).

PTSD is known by intense and persistent feelings of anxiety and helplessness that are caused by a traumatic experience such as a physical threat or assault of oneself or one's family, destruction of one's community, or witnessing a death. PTSD may occur many months after the event. PTSD has troubled many combat veterans and people who have seen their homes and communities inundated by floods, swept away by tornadoes, or subjected to toxic hazards (Baum & Fleming, 1993). A study of victims of Hurricane Andrew, which assailed South Florida, found that one man in four and about one woman in three (36%) had developed post-traumatic stress disorder (Ironson, 1993). A national study of more than 4,000 women found that PTSD had occurred among about one woman in four who had been victimized by crime (Resnick and others, 1993; see Figure 13.1).

The event that precipitates PTSD is incessantly reexperienced as intrusive memories, recurrent dreams, and flashbacks—the sudden feeling that the event is reoccurring. When combat veterans with PTSD imagine the events of

A Traumatic Experience from the Vietnam War. Physical threats and other traumatic experiences can lead to post-traumatic stress disorder (PTSD). PTSD is characterized by intrusive memories of the experience, recurrent dreams about it, and the sudden feeling that it is, in fact, recurring (as in flashbacks).

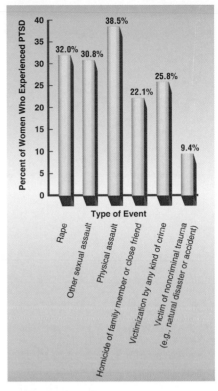

FIGURE 13.1

Incidence of Post-Traumatic Stress Disorder Among Female Victims of Crime and Among Other Women. According to Resnick and her colleagues (1993), about 1 woman in 4 (25.8%) who was victimized by crime could be diagnosed with PTSD at some point following the crime. By contrast, fewer than 1 woman in 10 (9.4%) who was not victimized by crime experienced PTSD.

Post-traumatic stress disorder • A disorder that follows a psychologically distressing event outside the range of normal human experience and that is characterized by features such as intense fear, avoidance of stimuli associated with the event, and reliving of the event. Abbreviated *PTSD*.

the battlefield, they show a great deal of muscle tension and other physiological signs of anxiety (Orr and others, 1993; Pitman and others, 1990).

The person with PTSD typically attempts to avoid thoughts and activities connected to the traumatic event. He or she may also display sleep problems, irritable outbursts, difficulty concentrating, extreme vigilance, and an intensified "startle" response.

ACUTE STRESS DISORDER.   **Acute stress disorder,** like PTSD, is characterized by feelings of anxiety and helplessness that are caused by a traumatic event. However, PTSD can occur 6 months or more after the traumatic event and tends to persist. Acute stress disorder occurs within a month of the event and lasts from 2 days to 4 weeks. Women who have been raped, for example, experience immediate high levels of distress that tend to peak in severity about 3 weeks after the assault (Davidson & Foa, 1991; Rothbaum and others, 1992).

Theoretical Views

According to the psychodynamic perspective, phobias symbolize conflicts of childhood origin. Psychodynamic theory explains generalized anxiety as persistent difficulty in maintaining repression of primitive impulses. Psychoanalysts view obsessions as the leakage of unconscious impulses and compulsions as acts that allow people to keep such impulses partly repressed.

Some learning theorists consider phobias to be conditioned fears that were acquired in early childhood. Therefore, their origins are beyond memory. Avoidance of feared stimuli is reinforced by reduction of anxiety. In the case of women who have been raped, evidence suggests that exposure to the situation (for example, the neighborhood, one's workplace) in which the attack occurred, in the absence of further attack, can extinguish some of the post-traumatic distress (Wirtz & Harrell, 1987).

Susan Mineka (1991) suggests that people (and nonhuman primates) are genetically predisposed to fear stimuli that may have once posed a threat to their ancestors. Evolutionary forces would have favored the survival of individuals who were predisposed toward acquiring fears of large animals, spiders, snakes, heights, entrapment, sharp objects, and strangers. In laboratory experiments, people view photographs of various objects and then receive electric shock (Hugdahl & Ohman, 1977; Ohman and others, 1976). Participants more readily acquire fear reactions to some stimuli (for example, spiders and snakes) than others (for example, flowers and houses), as measured by sweat in the palm of the hand. These experiments, however, do not show that the participants are genetically predisposed to develop fear responses to stimuli such as snakes and spiders. The participants were reared in a society in which many people react negatively to these creepy-crawlies. Thus their learning experiences, and not genetic factors, may have predisposed them to fear these stimuli.

Similarly, social-cognitive theorists note a role for observational learning in fear acquisition (Bandura and others, 1969). If parents squirm, grimace, and shudder at mice, blood, or dirt on the kitchen floor, children might encode these stimuli as being awful and imitate their behavior. Learning theorists suggest that generalized anxiety is often nothing more than fear that has been associated with situations so broad that they are not readily identified, such as social relationships or personal achievement. Cognitive theorists suggest that anxiety can be maintained by thinking that one is in a terrible situation and is helpless to change it. Mineka (1991) argues that people with anxiety disorders

Acute stress disorder • A disorder, like PTSD, that is characterized by feelings of anxiety and helplessness and caused by a traumatic event. Unlike PTSD, acute stress disorder occurs within a month of the event and lasts from 2 days to 4 weeks. (A category first included in DSM-IV.)

are cognitively biased toward paying more attention to threatening objects or situations. Psychoanalysts and learning theorists broadly agree that compulsive behavior reduces anxiety.

Cognitive theorists note that our appraisals of the magnitude of the threats in events help determine whether events are traumatic and lead to PTSD (Creamer and others, 1992). People with panic attacks tend to misinterpret bodily cues and to view them as threats (Meichenbaum, 1993). Obsessions and compulsions may serve to divert people's attention from more intimidating issues such as "What am I to do with my life?" When anxieties are acquired at a young age, we may later interpret them as enduring traits and label ourselves as "people who fear _____" (you fill it in). We then live up to the labels. We also entertain thoughts that heighten and perpetuate anxiety such as "I've got to get out of here," or "My heart is going to leap out of my chest." Such ideas intensify physical signs of anxiety, disrupt planning, magnify the aversiveness of stimuli, motivate avoidance, and decrease self-efficacy expectations about ability to manage the situation. Belief that we shall not be able to handle a threat heightens anxiety. Belief that we are in control lessens anxiety (Bandura and others, 1985).

Biological factors play a role in anxiety disorders. Genetic factors are implicated in most psychological disorders, including anxiety disorders (Carey & DiLalla, 1994). For one thing, anxiety disorders tend to run in families (Michels & Marzuk, 1993b; Turner and others, 1987). Twin studies also find the **concordance** rate for anxiety disorders to be higher among pairs of identical than fraternal twins (Torgersen, 1983). Adoptee studies similarly show that the biological parent places the child at risk for anxiety and related traits (Pedersen and others, 1988).

Perhaps a predisposition toward anxiety—in the form of a highly reactive autonomic nervous system—can be inherited. What might make a nervous system "highly reactive"? In the case of panic disorder, faulty regulation of serotonin and norepinephrine may be involved (Clum and others, 1993). In other anxiety disorders, one possibility is that receptor sites in the brain are not sensitive enough to **gamma-aminobutyric acid (GABA),** an inhibitory neuro transmitter that may help quell anxiety reactions. The **benzodiazepines,** a class of drugs that reduce anxiety, are thought to work by increasing the sensitivity of receptor sites to GABA. However, it is unlikely that excesses or deficiencies in the levels of a single neurotransmitter can explain any psychological disorder (Michels & Marzuk, 1993a).

Many cases of anxiety disorders may reflect the interaction of biological and psychological factors. In panic disorder, biological imbalances may initially trigger attacks, but subsequent fear of attacks—and of the bodily cues that signal the onset of attacks—may heighten people's discomfort and give them the idea that there is nothing they can do about them (McNally, 1990; Meichenbaum, 1993). Feelings of helplessness increase fear. People with panic disorder can thus be helped by psychological methods that provide ways of reducing physical discomfort—including regular breathing—and that show them that there are, after all, things they can do to cope with attacks (Clum and others, 1993; Klosko and others, 1990). The origins of many patterns of abnormal behavior seem quite complex, involving the interaction of biological and psychological factors.

Concordance (con-CORD-ants) • Agreement.

Gamma-aminobutyric acid (GABA) (a-me-no-byoo-TIE-rick) • An inhibitory neurotransmitter that is implicated in anxiety reactions.

Benzodiazepines (ben-zoe-die-AZZ-uh-peans) • A class of drugs that reduce anxiety; minor tranquilizers.

Reflections

• Have you ever felt anxious? Did your anxiety strike you as being normal under the circumstances? Why or why not?

- Do you know anyone with a phobia? What kind of phobia? Does the phobia seriously interfere with his or her life? How so?
- Do you ever find yourself "in a panic"? Under what circumstances? What is the difference between "being in a panic" and having a panic disorder?
- Do you know any people who are obsessive–compulsive? What behavior leads you to apply this label?
- Do you tend to pay a great deal of attention to potential threats or to put them out of your mind? How does your response to threats affect your feelings about them?

DISSOCIATIVE DISORDERS

In the **dissociative disorders,** there is a separation of mental processes such as thoughts, emotions, identity, memory, or consciousness—the processes that make the person feel whole (Spiegel & Cardeña, 1991).

Types of Dissociative Disorders

Dissociative disorders (diss-SO-she-uh-tivv) • Disorders in which there are sudden, temporary changes in consciousness or self-identity.

Dissociative amnesia (am-KNEE-she-uh) • A dissociative disorder marked by loss of memory or self-identity; skills and general knowledge are usually retained. Previously termed *psychogenic amnesia*.

Malingering • Pretending to be ill in order to escape duty or work.

Dissociative fugue (FYOOG) • A dissociative disorder in which one experiences amnesia and then flees to a new location. Previously termed *psychogenic fugue*.

The DSM lists several dissociative disorders, including dissociative amnesia, dissociative fugue, dissociative identity disorder, and depersonalization.

DISSOCIATIVE AMNESIA. In **dissociative amnesia,** there is sudden inability to recall important personal information. Memory loss cannot be attributed to organic problems such as a blow to the head or alcoholic intoxication. It is thus a psychological dissociative disorder, and not an organic disorder. In the most common example, the person cannot recall events for a number of hours after a stressful incident, as in warfare or in the case of the uninjured survivor of an accident. In generalized amnesia, people forget their entire lives. Amnesia may last for hours or years. Termination of amnesia is also sudden.

People sometimes claim that they cannot recall engaging in socially unacceptable behavior, promising to do something, and so on. Claiming to have a psychological problem such as amnesia in order to escape responsibility is known as **malingering.** Current research methods do not guarantee that we can distinguish malingerers from people with dissociative disorders.

DISSOCIATIVE FUGUE. In **dissociative fugue,** the person shows loss of memory for the past and travels abruptly from his or her home or place of work. Either the person does not think about the past, or the person reports a past filled with sham memories that are not known to be erroneous. Following recovery, the events that occurred during the fugue are not recalled.

DISSOCIATIVE IDENTITY DISORDER. Dissociative identity disorder (formerly termed *multiple personality disorder*) is the name given to William's disorder, as described at the beginning of the chapter. In this disorder, two or more identities or personalities, each with distinct traits and memories, "occupy" the same person, with or without awareness of the others. Different identities might even have different eyeglass prescriptions (Braun, 1988).

Braun reports cases in which assorted identities showed different allergic responses. In one person with dissociative identity disorder, an identity named Timmy was not sensitive to orange juice. But when other identities who alternated control over him drank orange juice, they would break out with hives. Hives would also erupt after Timmy drank orange juice if another identity

Dissociative Identity Disorder. In the film *The Three Faces of Eve,* Joanne Woodward played three personalities in the same woman: the shy, inhibited Eve White (lying on couch); the flirtatious and promiscuous Eve Black (in dark dress); and a third personality (Jane) who could accept her sexual and aggressive impulses and still maintain her sense of identity.

emerged while the juice was being digested. If Timmy reappeared when the allergic reaction was present, the itching of the hives would cease and the blisters would start to subside. In other cases reported by Braun, different identities in one person might show various responses to the same medicine. Or one identity might exhibit color blindness while others had intact color vision.

Truth or Fiction Revisited. It is true that some people have more than one identity, and the identities may have different allergies and eyeglass prescriptions. Nevertheless, many individuals may feign dissociative identity disorder in an effort to evade responsibility for unacceptable behavior.

A few celebrated cases have been portrayed in the popular media. In one that became the subject of the film *The Three Faces of Eve,* a timid housewife named Eve White harbored two other identities. Eve Black was a sexually aggressive, antisocial personality. Jane was an emerging identity who was able to accept the existence of her primitive impulses, yet show socially appropriate behavior. Finally, the three faces merged into one—Jane. Ironically, Jane (Chris Sizemore, in real life) reportedly split into 22 identities later on. Another well-publicized case is that of Sybil, a woman with 16 identities who was played by Sally Field in a film of the same name.

DEPERSONALIZATION DISORDER. **Depersonalization disorder** is characterized by persistent or recurrent feelings that one is detached from one's own body, as if one is observing one's thought processes from the outside. One may also feel as though he or she is functioning on automatic pilot, or as if in a dream.

The case of Richie illustrates a transient (passing) episode of depersonalization:

"We went to Orlando with the children after school let out. I had also been driving myself hard, and it was time to let go. We spent three days 'doing' Disneyworld, and it got to the point where we were all wearing shirts with mice and ducks on them and singing Disney songs like 'Yo ho, yo ho, a pirate's life for me.' On the third day I began to feel unreal and ill at ease while we were watching these middle-American Ivory-soap teenagers singing and dancing in front of Cinderella's Castle. The day was finally cooling down, but I broke into a sweat. I became shaky

Depersonalization disorder • A dissociative disorder in which one experiences persistent or recurrent feelings that one is not real or is detached from one's own experiences or body.

Feelings of Depersonalization. Episodes of depersonalization are typified by a sense of detachment from oneself. It may seem that one is outside of one's own body or walking in a dream.

and dizzy and sat down on the cement next to the 4-year-old's stroller without giving [my wife] an explanation. There were strollers and kids and [adults'] legs all around me, and for some strange reason I became fixated on the pieces of popcorn strewn on the ground. All of a sudden it was like the people around me were all silly mechanical creatures, like the dolls in the 'It's a Small World' [exhibit] or the animals on the 'Jungle Cruise.' Things sort of seemed to slow down, the way they do when you've smoked marijuana, and there was this invisible wall of cotton between me and everyone else.

"Then the concert was over and my wife was like 'What's the matter?' and did I want to stay for the Electrical Parade and the fireworks or was I sick? Now I was beginning to wonder if I was going crazy and I said I was sick, that my wife would have to take me by the hand and drive us back to the [motel]. Somehow we got back to the monorail and turned in the strollers. I waited in the herd [of people] at the station like a dead person, my eyes glazed over, looking out over kids with Mickey Mouse ears and Mickey Mouse balloons. The mechanical voice on the monorail almost did me in and I got really shaky.

"I refused to go back to the Magic Kingdom. I went with the family to Sea World, and on another day I dropped [my wife] and the kids off at the Magic Kingdom and picked them up that night. My wife thought I was goldbricking or something, and we had a helluva fight about it, but we had a life to get back to and my sanity had to come first." (Nevid and others, 1997)

Theoretical Views

According to psychodynamic theory, people with dissociative disorders use massive repression to avert recognition of improper impulses (Vaillant, 1994). In dissociative amnesia and fugue, the person forgets a profoundly disturbing event or impulse. In dissociative identity disorder, the person expresses unacceptable impulses through alternate identities. In depersonalization, the person stands outside—removed from the turmoil within.

According to learning theorists, people with dissociative disorders have learned *not to think* about disturbing acts or impulses to avoid feelings of guilt and shame. Technically speaking, *not thinking about these matters* is reinforced[3] by *removal* of the aversive stimuli of guilt and shame.

Social-cognitive theory suggests that many people come to role-play dissociative identity disorder through observational learning. This is not quite the same thing as faking, because people can "forget to tell themselves" that they have assumed a role. Reinforcers are made available by role-playing individuals with dissociative identity disorder: Drawing attention to oneself and escaping responsibility for unacceptable behavior are two (Spanos and others, 1985; Thigpen & Cleckley, 1984). Although role-playing is not the same as faking, many psychologists are suspicious that people in individual cases claim to have dissociative identity disorder as a way of evading responsibility for unacceptable behavior (McMinn & Wade, 1995).

Perhaps all of us are capable of dividing our awareness so that we become unaware, at least temporarily, of events that we usually focus more attention on. The dissociative disorders raise fascinating questions about the nature of human self-identity and memory (Kihlstrom and others, 1994). Perhaps it is no marvel that attention can be divided. Perhaps the marvel is that human consciousness normally integrates experience into a meaningful whole.

Reflections

- Have you ever known people to claim that they had "amnesia" for some episode or event? Do you think that the term was used correctly? Why or why not?
- Have you ever felt removed from the world—as though the things around you could not be really happening? Do these feelings seem connected with depersonalization? Why or why not?
- Have you seen a film or a TV show in which a character was supposed to have dissociative identity disorder (perhaps it was called "multiple personality")? What kind of behavior did the character display? Does the behavior seem consistent with the description of the disorder in the text? In the film or TV show, what were the supposed origins of the disorder?

Somatoform disorders (so-MAT-oh-form) •
Disorders in which people complain of physical (somatic) problems even though no physical abnormality can be found.

SOMATOFORM DISORDERS

In **somatoform disorders,** people show or complain of physical problems such as paralysis, pain, or the persistent belief that they have a serious disease, yet no evidence of a physical abnormality can be found.

Types of Somatoform Disorders

In this section, we discuss two somatoform disorders: conversion disorder and hypochondriasis.

---

[3] This is an example of negative reinforcement. The frequency of behavior—in this case, the frequency of diverting one's attention from a certain topic—is increased by *removal* of a stimulus—in this case, by removal of feelings of, say, guilt or shame.

CONVERSION DISORDER. **Conversion disorder** is characterized by a major change in, or loss of, physical functioning, although there are no medical findings to explain the loss of functioning. The behaviors are not intentionally produced. That is, the person is not faking.

If you lost the ability to see at night, or if your legs became paralyzed, you would understandably show concern. But some people with conversion disorder show indifference to their symptoms, a remarkable feature referred to as **la belle indifférence.** Conversion disorder is so named because it appears to "convert" a source of stress into a physical difficulty.

During World War II, a number of bomber pilots developed night blindness. They could not carry out their nighttime missions, although no damage to the optic nerves was found. In rare cases, women with large families have been reported to become paralyzed in the legs, again with no medical findings.

HYPOCHONDRIASIS. Persons with **hypochondriasis** insist that they have profound physical illness, even though no medical evidence can be found. They become preoccupied with minor physical sensations and maintain their belief despite medical reassurance. They may run from doctor to doctor, seeking the one who will find the causes of the sensations. Fear may disrupt work or home life.

Conversion disorder • A disorder in which anxiety or unconscious conflicts are "converted" into physical symptoms that often have the effect of helping the person cope with anxiety or conflict.

La belle indifférence (lah bell an-DEEF-fay-rants) • A French term descriptive of the lack of concern sometimes shown by people with conversion disorders.

Hypochondriasis (high-poe-con-DRY-uh-sis) • Persistent belief that one has a medical disorder despite lack of medical findings.

Theoretical Views

Consistent with psychodynamic theory, early versions of the DSM labeled what are now referred to as *somatoform disorders* to be "hysterical neuroses." "Hysterical" derives from the word *hystera,* the Greek term for the uterus or womb. Like many other Greeks, Hippocrates believed that hysteria was a sort of female trouble that was caused by a wandering uterus. It was erroneously thought that the uterus could roam the body—that it was not anchored in place! As the uterus meandered, it could cause pains and odd sensations almost anywhere. The Greeks also believed that pregnancy anchored the uterus and ended hysterical complaints. What did Greek physicians thus prescribe to bring monthly aches and pains to an end? Good guess.

Even in the earlier years of the 20th century, it was suggested that strange sensations and medically unfounded complaints were largely the province of women. Moreover, considering the problem to be a neurosis suggested that it stemmed from unconscious childhood conflicts. The psychodynamic view of conversion disorders is that the symptoms protect the individual from feelings of guilt or shame or from another source of stress. Conversion disorders, like dissociative disorders, often seem to serve a purpose. The "blindness" of the pilots may have afforded them respite from stressful missions or may have allowed them to evade the guilt from bombing civilian populations.

Reflections

- What kinds of problems do you think are involved in trying to determine whether someone has a medical problem or a conversion disorder?
- Have you heard the term *hypochondriac* used sarcastically or as an insult? How so?

MOOD DISORDERS

Mood disorders are characterized by disturbance in expressed emotions. The disruption generally involves depression or elation. Most instances of depression are normal, or "run-of-the-mill." If you have failed an important test, if a business investment has been lost, or if your closest friend becomes ill, it is understandable and fitting for you to be depressed about it. It would be odd, in fact, if you were *not* affected by adversity.

Truth or Fiction Revisited. *It is not abnormal to feel depressed.* It is normal—indeed, it is psychologically appropriate—for one to feel depressed when one's situation is depressing. As with anxiety disorders, feelings of depression are considered abnormal when they are magnified beyond one's circumstances or when there is no apparent reason for them.

Types of Mood Disorders

In this section, we discuss two mood disorders: major depression and bipolar disorder.

MAJOR DEPRESSION. Depression is the "common cold" of psychological problems, perhaps affecting upward of 10% of us at any given time (Alloy and others, 1990). People with run-of-the-mill depression may feel sad, blue, or "down in the dumps." They may complain of lack of energy, loss of self-esteem, difficulty concentrating, loss of interest in other people and usually enjoyable activities, pessimism, crying, and thoughts of suicide.

These feelings tend to be more intense among people with **major depression.** People with major depression may also show poor appetite and serious weight loss, agitation or **psychomotor retardation,** inability to concentrate and make decisions, complaints of "not caring" anymore, and suicide attempts.

Persons with major depression may also show faulty perception of reality—so-called psychotic behaviors. Psychotic behaviors include delusions of unworthiness, guilt for imagined wrongdoings, even ideas that one is rotting from disease. There may also be hallucinations such as of the Devil administering just punishment or of strange bodily sensations.

BIPOLAR DISORDER. In **bipolar disorder,** formerly known as manic-depression, there are mood swings from elation to depression. These cycles seem to be unrelated to external events. In the elated, or **manic** phase, people may show excessive excitement or silliness, carrying jokes too far. They may show poor judgment, sometimes destroying property, and be argumentative. Roommates may avoid them, finding them abrasive. Manic people often speak rapidly ("pressured speech") and jump from topic to topic, showing **rapid flight of ideas.** It is hard to get a word in edgewise. They may make extremely large contributions to charity or give away expensive possessions. They may not be able to sit still or to sleep restfully.

Depression is the other side of the coin. People with bipolar depression often sleep more than usual and are lethargic. People with major (or unipolar) depression are more likely to have insomnia and agitation. People with bipolar depression also exhibit social withdrawal and irritability.

Some people with bipolar disorder attempt suicide on the way down from the elated phase. They will do almost anything to escape the depths of depression that lie ahead.

Major depression • A severe depressive disorder in which the person may show loss of appetite and psychomotor behaviors, and impaired reality testing.

Psychomotor retardation • Slowness in motor activity and (apparently) in thought.

Bipolar disorder • A disorder in which the mood alternates between two extreme poles (elation and depression). Also referred to as *manic-depression.*

Manic • Elated, showing excessive excitement.

Rapid flight of ideas • Rapid speech and topic changes, characteristic of manic behavior.

Theoretical Views

Depression is an appropriate reaction to losses and unpleasant events. Problems such as marital discord, physical discomfort, incompetence, and failure or pressure at work all contribute to feelings of depression. We tend to be more depressed by things we bring upon ourselves, such as academic problems, financial problems, unwanted pregnancy, conflict with the law, arguments, and fights (Hammen & Mayol, 1982; Simons and others, 1993). Many people recover from depression less readily than others, however. People who remain depressed have lower self-esteem (Andrews & Brown, 1993), are less likely to be able to solve social problems (Marx and others, 1992; Nezu & Ronan, 1985), and have less social support (Asarnow and others, 1987; Pagel & Becker, 1987).

Women are more likely than men to be diagnosed with depression (Nolen-Hoeksema & Girgus, 1994; Russo, 1990b). Fluctuating hormone levels may play a role (Pool, 1994), but Belle (1990) points out that sociocultural factors are also important. Women—especially single mothers—have lower socioeconomic status than men in our society, and depression and other psychological disorders are more common among poor people (Hobfoll and others, 1995). Even capable, hard-working women are likely to become depressed when they see how society limits their opportunities (Rothbart & Ahadi, 1994). Employed mothers are also frequently depressed by the difficulty of finding adequate child care (Ross, 1993).

PSYCHODYNAMIC VIEWS.   Psychoanalysts suggest various explanations for depression. In one, people at risk for depression are overly concerned about hurting others' feelings or losing their approval. As a result, they hold in rather than express feelings of anger. Anger becomes turned inward and is experienced as misery and self-hatred. From the psychodynamic perspective, bipolar disorder may be seen as alternating dominance of the personality by the superego and the ego. In the depressive phase of the disorder, the superego dominates, flooding the individual with exaggerated ideas of wrongdoing and associated feelings of guilt and worthlessness. After a while, the ego defends itself by rebounding and asserting supremacy, accounting for the elation and self-confidence that in part characterize the manic phase. Later, in response to the excessive display of ego, feelings of guilt return, again plunging the person into depression.

LEARNING VIEWS.   Many people with depressive disorders have an external locus of control. That is, they do not believe that they can control events to achieve desired outcomes (Weisz and others, 1993). Some people with depressive disorders lack skills, such as social skills, that might lead to rewards (Gotlib, 1984).

Research has also found links between depression and **learned helplessness.** In classic research, Seligman taught dogs that they were helpless to escape an electric shock by preventing them from leaving a cage in which they received repeated shock. Later a barrier to a safe compartment was removed, allowing the animals a way out. When they were shocked again, however, the dogs made no effort to escape. They had apparently learned that they were helpless. Seligman's dogs were also, in a sense, reinforced for doing nothing. That is, the shock *eventually* stopped when the dogs were showing helpless behavior—inactivity and withdrawal. "Reinforcement" might have increased the likelihood of repeating their "successful behavior"—that is, doing nothing—in a similar situation. This helpless behavior resembles that of people who are depressed.

COGNITIVE FACTORS.   The concept of learned helplessness bridges learning and cognitive approaches in that it is an attitude, a general expectation. Other cognitive factors also contribute to depression. For example, perfectionists set themselves up for depression through irrational self-demands. They are likely

---

Learned helplessness • A model for the acquisition of depressive behavior, based on findings that organisms in aversive situations learn to show inactivity when their operants go unreinforced.

to fall short of their (unrealistic) expectations and, as a result, to feel depressed (Blatt and others, 1995; Hewitt & Flett, 1993; Persons and others, 1993).

People with depression pay more attention to negative information (Mineka, 1991). They tend to be self-critical (Zuroff & Mongrain, 1987) and pessimistic (Alloy & Ahrens, 1987; Pyszczynski and others, 1987). People, moreover, who respond to feelings of depression by focusing on their symptoms and the possible causes and effects of their symptoms tend to prolong depressive episodes (Nolen-Hoeksema, 1991). Susan Nolen-Hoeksema and her colleagues (1993) found that women are more likely than men to focus on their symptoms and thereby prolong feelings of depression. Men seem somewhat more likely to try to fight off negative feelings by distracting themselves (Parrot & Sabini, 1990). She points out that men are more likely to distract themselves by turning to alcohol, however, thus exposing themselves and their families to additional problems (Nolen-Hoeksema, 1991).

Seligman and his colleagues (1979) note that when things go wrong, we may think of the causes of failure as *internal* or *external, stable* or *unstable, global* or *specific*. Let us explain these various **attributional styles** through the example of having a date that does not work out. An internal attribution involves self-blame, as in "I really loused it up." An external attribution places the blame elsewhere (as in "Some couples just don't take to each other," or, "She was the wrong sign for me"). A stable attribution ("It's my personality")

Why Did He Miss That Tackle? This football player is compounding his feelings of depression by attributing his shortcomings on the field to factors that he cannot change. For example, he tells himself that he missed the tackle because of stupidity and lack of athletic ability. He ignores the facts that his coaching was poor and that his teammates failed to come to his support.

Attributional style (at-rib-BYOO-shun-al) • One's tendency to attribute one's behavior to internal or external factors, stable or unstable factors, and so on.

suggests a problem that cannot be changed. An unstable attribution ("It was the head cold") suggests a temporary condition. A global attribution of failure ("I have no idea what to do when I'm with people") suggests that the problem is quite large. A specific attribution ("I have problems making small talk at the very outset of a relationship") chops the problem down to a manageable size.

Research shows that people who are depressed are more likely than other people to attribute the causes of their failures to internal, stable, and global factors—factors that they are relatively helpless to change (Gotlib and others, 1993; Metalsky and others, 1993; Simons and others, 1995). Such attributions can give rise to feelings of hopelessness.

BIOLOGICAL FACTORS. Researchers are also searching for biological factors in mood disorders. Depression, for example, is often associated with the trait of **neuroticism,** which is heritable (Clark and others, 1994). Anxiety is also connected with neuroticism, and mood and anxiety disorders are frequently found in the same person (Clark and others, 1994).

Mood swings also tend to run in families (Rose, 1995; Wachtel, 1994). There is a higher concordance rate for bipolar disorder among identical than fraternal twins (Goodwin & Jamison, 1990; Klein and others, 1985).

Other researchers focus on the actions of the neurotransmitters serotonin and noradrenaline (Cooper and others, 1991; Michels & Marzuk, 1993b). Deficiencies in serotonin may create a general disposition toward mood disorders. Serotonin deficiency *combined with* noradrenaline deficiency may be linked with depression. People with severe depression often respond to antidepressant drugs that heighten the action of noradrenaline and serotonin. The metal lithium, moreover, which is the major chemical treatment for bipolar disorder, apparently flattens out manic-depressive cycles by moderating levels of noradrenaline.

Many cases of depression may reflect the interaction of biological factors (such as neurotransmitters) and psychological factors (such as learned helplessness). For example, Seligman (1975) and Weiss (1982) found that dogs who learn that they are helpless to escape electric shocks also have less noradrenaline available to the brain. Helplessness is thus linked to low noradrenaline levels. The relationship might be a vicious cycle: A depressing situation may decrease the action of noradrenaline, and this chemical change may aggravate depression.

Relationships between mood disorders and biological factors are complex and under intense study. Even if people are biologically predisposed toward depression, self-efficacy expectations and attitudes—particularly attitudes about whether one can change things for the better—may also play a role.

Neuroticism • A personality trait characterized largely by persistent anxiety.

Suicide

Consider some facts about suicide:

- Three times as many women as men attempt suicide, but about four times as many men succeed (see Figure 13.2; Rich and others, 1988; CDC, 1985a).

- Men prefer to use guns or to hang themselves, but women prefer to use sleeping pills. Males, that is, tend to use quicker and more-lethal means. A study of 204 San Diego County suicides found that males were more likely to use guns (60% of the males versus 28% of the females; Rich and others, 1988). Females more often used drugs or poisons (44% of the females versus 11% of the males).

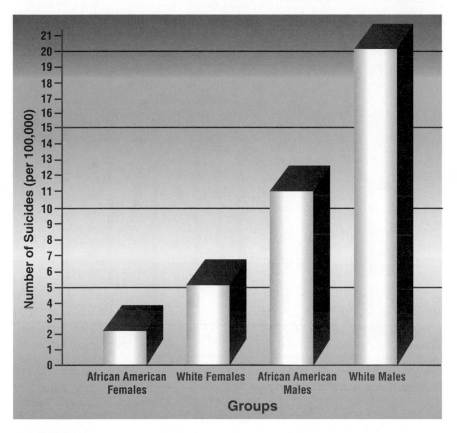

FIGURE 13.2

Suicide Rates According to Gender and Ethnicity. Men are more likely than women to commit suicide. Women, however, make more suicide attempts. How can we account for this discrepancy? White people are also more likely to commit suicide than African Americans. (Source of figure: U.S. Bureau of the Census, 1989.)

- Although African Americans are more likely than White Americans to live in poverty and experience discrimination, the suicide rate is about twice as high among White Americans (Figure 13.2).

- One in four Native American teenagers has attempted suicide—a rate that is four times higher than that of other U.S. teenagers (Resnick and others, 1992). Among Zuni adolescents of New Mexico, the rate of completed suicides is more than twice the national rate (Howard-Pitney and others, 1992).

- Teenage suicides loom large in the media spotlight, but older people are actually much more likely to commit suicide (McIntosh and others, 1995; Richman, 1993; see Figure 13.3). The suicide rate among older people is nearly twice the national rate.

All in all, about 30,000 people each year take their lives in the United States (Michels & Marzuk, 1993a). We discuss suicide within the context of mood disorders because most suicides are linked to feelings of depression and hopelessness (Beck and others, 1990; Lewinsohn and others, 1994a, 1994b). Additional factors connected with suicide include anxiety, panic attacks, lack of pleasure, alcohol abuse, problems concentrating, and insomnia (Sommers-Flanagan & Sommers-Flanagan, 1995). Among Native American Zuni adolescents in New Mexico, drug abuse, problems in school, and problems in

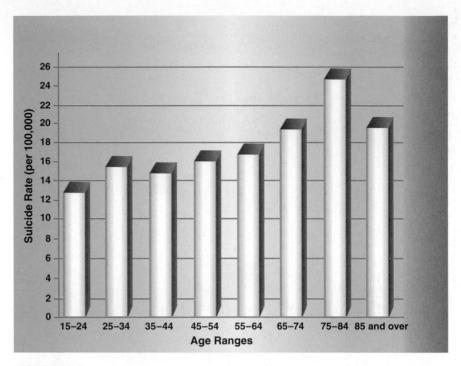

FIGURE 13.3

Suicide Rates According to Age. Older people (aged 65 and above) are more likely to commit suicide than the young and the middle-aged, yet suicide is the second leading cause of death among college students. (Source of figure: U.S. Bureau of the Census, 1989.)

communicating with other people are also connected with suicide (Howard-Pitney and others, 1992). Exposure to other people who are committing suicide can increase the risk that an adolescent will attempt suicide (CDC, 1995). People who attempt suicide are usually trying to end extreme psychological anguish (Shneidman, 1985).

Suicide attempts are more frequent following stressful events, especially events that entail loss of social support—as in the loss of a spouse, friend, or relative. People under stress who consider suicide have been found to be less capable of solving problems—particularly interpersonal problems—than non-suicidal people (Rotheram-Borus and others, 1990; Sadowski & Kelley, 1993; Schotte and others, 1990). Suicidal people are thus less likely to find productive ways of changing the stressful situation.

Suicide, like so many other psychological problems, tends to run in families. Nearly one in four people who attempt suicide reports that a family member has committed suicide (Sorensen & Rutter, 1991). Psychological disorders among family members may also make a contribution (Sorensen & Rutter, 1991; Wilson, 1991). The causal connections are unclear, however. Do suicide attempters inherit disorders that can lead to suicide? Does the family environment subject several family members to feelings of hopelessness? Does the suicide of a family member give one the idea of committing suicide or create the impression that one is somehow fated to commit suicide? Perhaps these possibilities and others—such as poor problem-solving ability—form a complex web of contributory factors.

MYTHS ABOUT SUICIDE.   Some believe that people who threaten suicide are only seeking attention. The serious just "do it." Actually, most people who commit suicide give clear clues concerning their intentions (Nevid and others, 1997).

Truth or Fiction Revisited. *It is not true that people who threaten suicide are only seeking attention.* The statement is too general to be accurate. Although there are some pretenders, many people who threaten suicide attempt to take their lives. Some believe that those who fail at suicide attempts are only seeking attention. But many people who commit suicide have made prior attempts (Lewinsohn and others, 1994a). Contrary to myth, discussion of suicide with a person who is depressed does not prompt suicide (CDC, 1995). Extracting a promise that the person will not commit suicide before calling or visiting a helping professional seems to prevent some suicides.

Some believe that only "insane" people (meaning people who are out of touch with reality) would take their own lives. However, suicidal thinking is not necessarily a sign of psychosis, neurosis, or personality disorder. Instead, the contemplation of suicide reflects a narrowing of the range of options that people think are available to them (Rotheram-Borus and others, 1990; Schotte and others, 1990).

Reflections

- Do you think that you would find it easy or difficult to admit to having feelings of depression? Why?
- How would you distinguish between "normal" depression or "normal" enthusiasm and a mood disorder?
- Do you ever feel depressed? What kinds of experiences lead you to feel depressed? When you fall short of your goals, do you tend to be merciless in your self-criticism or to blame other people or "circumstances"? Do your views of your shortcomings tend to worsen or to ease your feelings of depression?
- Did you ever feel that there was nothing you could do to improve your situation or to solve a personal problem? How did the feeling that you could do nothing affect your mood? Why?
- Is any of the information on suicide, or on people who attempt suicide, a surprise to you? If so, in what way?
- **Agree or disagree with the following statement and support your answer: "You have to be insane to want to take your own life."**

SCHIZOPHRENIA

Joyce was 19. Her husband Ron brought her into the emergency room because she had slit her wrists. When she was interviewed, her attention wandered. She seemed distracted by things in the air, or something she might be hearing. It was as if she had an invisible earphone.

She explained that she had cut her wrists because the "hellsmen" had told her to. Then she seemed frightened. Later she said that the hellsmen had warned her not to reveal their existence. She had been afraid that they would punish her for talking about them.

Ron told the emergency room physician that Joyce did not want to be near other people and had convinced him to rent a bungalow in the country. There she would make fantastic drawings of goblins and monsters during the day. Now and then she would become agitated and act as if invisible things were giving her instructions.

"I'm bad," Joyce would mutter. "I'm bad." She would begin to jumble her words. Ron would then try to convince her to go to the hospital, but she would refuse. Then the wrist cutting would begin. Ron thought he

MINILECTURE: DEFINING SCHIZOPHRENIA

had made the cottage safe by removing knives and blades. But Joyce would always find something.

Then Joyce would be brought to the hospital, have stitches put in, be kept under observation for a while, and medicated. She would explain that she cut herself because the hellsmen had told her that she was bad and must die. After a few days she would deny hearing the hellsmen, and she would insist on leaving the hospital.

Ron would take her home. The pattern continued.

When the emergency room staff examined Joyce's wrists and heard that she believed she had been following the orders of "hellsmen," they suspected that she could be diagnosed with schizophrenia. Schizophrenia touches every aspect of people's lives. Schizophrenia is characterized by disturbances in (1) thought and language, (2) perception and attention, (3) motor activity, and (4) mood, and by (5) withdrawal and absorption in daydreams or fantasy.

Schizophrenia has been referred to as the worst disorder affecting human beings (Carpenter & Buchanan, 1994). It affects nearly 1% of the population worldwide. Its onset is relatively early in life, and its adverse effects tend to endure. It has been estimated that one third to one half of the homeless people in the United States have schizophrenia (Bachrach, 1992).

Schizophrenia is known primarily by disturbances in thought, which are inferred from verbal and other behavior. Persons with schizophrenia may show *loosening of associations*. Unless we are daydreaming or deliberately allowing our thoughts to "wander," our thinking is normally tightly knit. We start at a certain point, and the things that come to mind (the associations) tend to be logically and coherently connected. But people with schizophrenia often think in an illogical, disorganized manner. Their speech may be jumbled, combining parts of words or making rhymes in a meaningless fashion. People with schizophrenia may also jump from topic to topic, conveying little useful information. They usually have no insight that their thoughts and behavior are abnormal.

Many people with schizophrenia have **delusions**—for example, delusions of grandeur, persecution, or reference. In the case of delusions of grandeur, a person may believe, for example, that he is Jesus or a person on a special mission, or he may have grand, illogical plans for saving the world. Delusions tend to be unshakable, despite disconfirming evidence. Persons with delusions of persecution may believe that they are sought by the Mafia, CIA, FBI, or some other group or agency. A woman with delusions of reference expressed the belief that national news broadcasts contained coded information about her. A man with such delusions complained that neighbors had "bugged" his walls with "radios." Other people with schizophrenia may have delusions to the effect that they have committed unpardonable sins, that they are rotting away from a hideous disease, or that they or the world do not really exist.

The perceptions of people with schizophrenia often include hallucinations—imagery in the absence of external stimulation that the person cannot distinguish from reality. In Shakespeare's play, after the killing of King Duncan, feelings of guilt apparently cause Macbeth to hallucinate a knife:

> *Is this a dagger which I see before me,*
> *The handle toward my hand? Come, let me clutch thee:*
> *I have thee not, and yet I see thee still.*
> *Art thou not, fatal vision, sensible*
> *To feeling as to sight? or art thou but*
> *A dagger of the mind, a false creation,*
> *Proceeding from the heat-oppressed brain?*

Delusions • False, persistent beliefs that are unsubstantiated by sensory or objective evidence.

Stupor (STEW-pour) • A condition in which the senses and thought are dulled.

Paranoid schizophrenia • A type of schizophrenia characterized primarily by delusions—commonly of persecution—and by vivid hallucinations.

Disorganized schizophrenia • The type of schizophrenia that is characterized by disorganized delusions and vivid hallucinations.

Catatonic schizophrenia • The type of schizophrenia that is characterized by striking impairment in motor activity.

Waxy flexibility • A feature of catatonic schizophrenia in which persons maintain postures into which they are placed.

Macbeth is a fictional character, of course. Joyce, however, a true case study, apparently believed that she heard "hellsmen." Other hallucinators may see colors or even obscene words spelled out in midair. Auditory hallucinations are most common.

Motor activity may become wild and excited or may slow to a **stupor.** There may be strange gestures and peculiar facial expressions. Emotional response may be flat or blunted, or inappropriate—as in giggling at bad news. Research evidence suggests that many people with schizophrenia experience emotional responses but that their expression is inhibited (Kring and others, 1993). People with schizophrenia tend to withdraw from social contacts and become wrapped up in their own thoughts and fantasies.

Types of Schizophrenia

There are three major types of schizophrenia: paranoid, disorganized, and catatonic.

PARANOID TYPE.   People with **paranoid schizophrenia** have systematized delusions and, frequently, related auditory hallucinations. They usually show delusions of grandeur and persecution, but they may also show delusions of jealousy, in which they believe that a spouse or lover has been unfaithful. They may show agitation, confusion, and fear, and may experience vivid hallucinations that are consistent with their delusions. The person with paranoid schizophrenia often constructs a complex or systematized delusion involving themes of wrongdoing or persecution.

The disorganized and catatonic subtypes are relatively rare (Andreasen, 1990).

DISORGANIZED TYPE.   People with **disorganized schizophrenia** show incoherence, loosening of associations, disorganized behavior, disorganized delusions, fragmentary delusions or hallucinations, and flat or highly inappropriate emotional responses. Extreme social impairment is common among people with disorganized schizophrenia. They may also show silliness and giddiness of mood, giggling, and nonsensical speech. They may neglect their appearance and hygiene and lose control of their bladder and their bowels. Emilio showed some of these behaviors:

> A 40-year-old man who looks more like 30 is brought to the hospital by his mother, who reports that she is afraid of him. It is his twelfth hospitalization. He is dressed in a tattered overcoat, baseball cap, and bedroom slippers, and sports several medals around his neck. His affect ranges from anger (hurling obscenities at his mother) to giggling. He speaks with a childlike quality and walks with exaggerated hip movements and seems to measure each step very carefully. Since stopping his medication about a month ago, . . . he has been hearing voices and looking and acting more bizarrely. He tells the interviewer he has been "eating wires" and lighting fires. His speech is generally incoherent and frequently falls into rhyme. (Adapted from Spitzer and others, 1989, pp. 137–138)

CATATONIC TYPE.   People with **catatonic schizophrenia** show striking impairment in motor activity. Impairment is characterized by slowing of activity into a stupor that may change suddenly into an agitated phase. Catatonic individuals may hold unusual, even difficult postures for hours, even as their limbs grow swollen or stiff. A striking feature is **waxy flexibility,** in which they

Paranoid Schizophrenia. Paranoid schizophrenics hold systematized delusions, often involving ideas that they are being persecuted or are on a special mission. Although they cannot be argued out of their delusions, their cognitive functioning is relatively intact compared to that of disorganized and catatonic schizophrenics.

maintain positions into which they have been manipulated by others. Catatonic individuals may also show **mutism,** but afterward they usually report that they heard what others were saying at the time.

People who show grossly psychotic characteristics such as hallucinations, delusions, incoherence, or disorganized behavior, but do not fit the definitions of these three types of schizophrenia, are considered to be of an undifferentiated type.

Theoretical Views

Psychologists have investigated various factors that may contribute to schizophrenia.

PSYCHODYNAMIC VIEWS.   According to the psychodynamic perspective, schizophrenia is the overwhelming of the ego by sexual or aggressive impulses from the id. The impulses threaten the ego and cause intense intrapsychic conflict. Under this threat, the person regresses to an early phase of the oral stage in which the infant has not yet learned that it and the world are separate. Fantasies become confused with reality, giving birth to hallucinations and delusions. Primitive impulses may carry more weight than social norms.

Critics point out that schizophrenic behavior is not the same as infantile behavior. Moreover, psychoanalysts have not been able to predict a schizophrenic outcome on the basis of theoretically predisposing childhoods.

LEARNING VIEWS.   Learning theorists explain schizophrenia through conditioning and observational learning. From this perspective, people show schizophrenic behavior when it is more likely than normal behavior to be reinforced. This may occur when the person is reared in a socially unrewarding or punitive situation; inner fantasies then become more reinforcing than social realities.

People in the psychiatric hospital may learn what is "expected" of them by observing other hospitalized individuals. Hospital staff may reinforce schizophrenic behavior by paying more attention to people who behave bizarrely. This view is consistent with folklore that the child who disrupts the class earns more attention from the teacher than the "good" child.

Critics note that many of us are reared in socially punitive settings but are apparently immune to extinction of socially appropriate behavior. Others develop schizophrenic behavior without the opportunity to observe other people with schizophrenia.

SOCIOCULTURAL VIEWS.   Many investigators have considered whether and how social and cultural factors such as poverty, discrimination, and overcrowding contribute to schizophrenia—especially among people who are genetically vulnerable to schizophrenia. Some sociocultural theorists suggest that adequate "treatment" of schizophrenia requires changing society to eradicate social ills, rather than changing the person whose behavior is deviant. Such theorists point out that schizophrenia is most common among the lowest socioeconomic classes (e.g., Kety, 1980). A classic study in New Haven, Connecticut, showed that the rate of schizophrenia was twice as high in the lowest socioeconomic class as in the next class on the socioeconomic ladder (Hollingshead & Redlich, 1958). More recent research revealed that schizophrenia is five times more common at the lowest rung of the socioeconomic ladder than at the highest (Keith and others, 1991).

Mutism (MU-tizm) • Refusal to talk.

Critics of this view suggest that low socioeconomic status may be a *conse-quence* and not an *antecedent* of schizophrenia. People with schizophrenia may drift downward in social status because they lack the social skills and cognitive abilities to function at higher levels. Thus, they may wind up in more impoverished areas in disproportionately high numbers.

Evidence for the hypothesis that people with schizophrenia drift downward in socioeconomic status is mixed (Nevid and others, 1997). Many people with schizophrenia do drift downward occupationally in comparison with their fathers' occupations. Many are also reared in families in which the fathers come from the lowest socioeconomic class, however. Because the stresses of poverty may play a role in the development of schizophrenia, many researchers are interested in the possible interactions of psychosocial stressors and biological factors (Carpenter & Buchanan, 1994).

BIOLOGICAL RISK FACTORS.　　Research has suggested that there are three biological risk factors for schizophrenia: heredity, complications during pregnancy and birth, and birth during the winter (Carpenter & Buchanan, 1994).

Schizophrenia, like many other psychological disorders, runs in families (Grove and others, 1991). People with schizophrenia constitute about 1% of the population, but children with one parent diagnosed with schizophrenia have about a 10% chance of being diagnosed with schizophrenia themselves. Children with two such parents have about a 35–40% chance of doing so (Gottesman, 1991; Straube & Oades, 1992). Twin studies also find about a 40–50% concordance rate for the diagnosis among pairs of identical (MZ) twins, whose genetic codes are the same, as compared with about a 10% rate among pairs of fraternal (DZ) twins (Gottesman, 1991; Straube & Oades, 1992). Sharing genes with people with schizophrenia apparently places one at risk.

However, these kinship studies did not generally control for environmental influences. Adoptee studies do, and they find that the biological parent typically places the child at greater risk than the adoptive parent—even though the child has been reared by the adoptive parent (Gottesman, 1991; Carpenter & Buchanan, 1994).

Evidence for a genetic role in schizophrenia seems strong. However, heredity cannot be the sole factor. If it were, we might expect a 100% concordance rate for schizophrenia between pairs of identical twins, as opposed to the 40–50% rate found in research (Carpenter & Buchanan, 1994). It also turns out that many people with schizophrenia have undergone complications during pregnancy and birth. For example, the mothers of many people who are diagnosed with schizophrenia had influenza during the sixth or seventh month of pregnancy (C. E. Barr and others, 1990; Sham and others, 1992; Torrey and others, 1992). Maternal starvation has also been implicated (Susser & Lin, 1992). Individuals diagnosed with schizophrenia are also somewhat more likely to be born during the winter than would be predicted by chance (Carpenter & Buchanan, 1994). Considered together, these three biological risk factors suggest that schizophrenia involves atypical development of the central nervous system (Bracha and others, 1992; Carpenter & Buchanan, 1994). As we see next, problems in the nervous system may involve neurotransmitters as well as the development of brain structures.

MINILECTURE: CAUSES OF SCHIZOPHRENIA

THE DOPAMINE THEORY OF SCHIZOPHRENIA.　　Over the years, much research has also been conducted into the chemistry of schizophrenia. Numerous chemical substances have been thought to play a role in schizophrenic disorders. Much current theory and research focus on the neurotransmitter dopamine (Carpenter & Buchanan, 1994). According to the dopamine theory of schizophrenia, people with schizophrenia *use* more dopamine than other people, although they do not necessarily produce more of it. Why? They may have more dopamine receptors in the brain than other people, or their dopamine receptors may be hyperactive (Davis and others, 1991). Postmortem studies of the brains of people with schizophrenia have yielded evidence consistent with both possibilities.

Many researchers agree that dopamine plays a role in schizophrenia but argue that other neurotransmitters are also involved (Maas and others, 1993; van Kammen and others, 1990). Supportive evidence is found in the fact that drugs that act on dopamine alone are not always effective in the treatment of schizophrenia (Carpenter & Buchanan, 1994).

Because so many psychological and biological factors have been implicated in schizophrenia, most investigators today favor a *multifactorial* model of schizophrenia. According to this model, genetic factors create a predisposition toward schizophrenia. A genetic vulnerability to the disorder then interacts with other factors such as viral infections, complications during pregnancy and birth, stress, and the quality of parenting to produce schizophrenic behavior (Michels & Marzuk, 1993a; Gottesman, 1991).

Reflections

- Have you ever heard the expression "split personality"? Does the expression seem to apply more to dissociative identity disorder or schizophrenia? Why?
- Had you heard of hallucinations or delusions before reading this section? Did your impressions of the meanings of these words match the descriptions in the text? What were the differences?
- Can you imagine what it might be like to be schizophrenic? Can you imagine why it might be frightening not to be able to distinguish between reality and hallucinations?

PERSONALITY DISORDERS

Personality disorders • Enduring patterns of maladaptive behavior that are sources of distress to the individual or others.

Paranoid personality disorder • A disorder characterized by persistent suspiciousness, but not involving the disorganization of paranoid schizophrenia.

Schizotypal personality disorder • A disorder characterized by oddities of thought and behavior, but not involving bizarre psychotic behaviors.

Personality disorders, like personality traits, are characterized by enduring patterns of behavior. Personality disorders, however, are inflexible and maladaptive. They impair personal or social functioning and are a source of distress to the individual or to other people (Widiger & Costa, 1994).

Types of Personality Disorders

There are a number of personality disorders, including the paranoid, schizotypal, schizoid, antisocial, and avoidant personality disorders. The defining trait of the **paranoid personality disorder** is the tendency to interpret other people's behavior as being deliberately threatening or demeaning. Although persons with the disorder do not show grossly disorganized thinking, they are mistrustful of others, and their social relationships suffer for it. They may be suspicious of coworkers and supervisors, but they can generally hold on to jobs.

Schizotypal personality disorder is characterized by pervasive peculiarities in thought, perception, and behavior such as excessive fantasy and suspiciousness, feelings of being unreal, or odd usage of words. The bizarre behaviors that characterize schizophrenia are absent, so this disorder is schizo-*typal*, not schizophrenic. Because of their oddities, persons with the disorder are often maladjusted on the job.

TABLE 13.2

**CHARACTERISTICS OF PEOPLE DIAGNOSED WITH
ANTISOCIAL PERSONALITY DISORDER**

Persistent violation of the rights of others	Persistent lying
Irresponsibility	Sexual promiscuity
Lack of loyalty or of formation of enduring relationships	Substance abuse
	Impulsivity
Failure to maintain good job performance over the years	Glibness; superficial charm
	Exaggerated sense of self-worth
Failure to develop or adhere to a life plan	Inability to tolerate boredom
History of truancy	At least 18 years of age
History of delinquency	Juvenile delinquency
History of running away	

Sources: Hare and others, 1991; Harris and others, 1994; White and others, 1994.

The **schizoid personality** is defined by indifference to social relationships and flatness in emotional responsiveness. People with schizoid personality are loners. They do not develop warm, tender feelings for others. They have few friends and rarely get married. Some people with schizoid personality do very well on the job, as long as continuous social interaction is not required. Hallucinations and delusions are absent.

Persons with **antisocial personality disorder** persistently violate the rights of others and are in conflict with the law (see Table 13.2). They often show a superficial charm and are at least average in intelligence. Striking features are their lack of guilt or anxiety about their misdeeds and their failures to learn from punishment and form meaningful bonds with other people (Widiger, 1990). Though they are often heavily punished by parents and rejected by peers for their misconduct, they carry on their impulsive, careless styles of life (Patterson, 1993; White and others, 1994). Many people with antisocial personality disorder are also alcoholic (Sher & Trull, 1994). Women are more likely than men to have anxiety and depressive disorders. Men are more likely to have antisocial personality disorder (Russo, 1990b).

People with **avoidant personality disorder** are generally unwilling to enter relationships without assurance of acceptance because of fear of rejection and criticism. As a result, they may have few close relationships outside their immediate families. Unlike people with schizoid personality, however, people with avoidant personality have interest in, and feelings of warmth toward, other people.

Theoretical Views

Many of the theoretical accounts of personality disorders derive from the psychodynamic model. Traditional Freudian theory focuses on Oedipal problems as the foundation for many psychological disorders, including personality disorders. Faulty resolution of the Oedipus complex might lead to antisocial personality disorder since the moral conscience, or superego, is believed to depend on proper resolution of the Oedipus complex. Research concurs with psychodynamic theory that lack of guilt, as found among people with antisocial personality disorder, is more likely to develop among children who receive parental rejection and punishment rather than warmth and affection (Baumeister and others, 1994; Zahn-Waxler & Kochanska, 1990). Psychodynamic theory

Schizoid personality disorder • A disorder characterized by social withdrawal.

Antisocial personality disorder • The diagnosis given a person who is in frequent conflict with society, yet who is undeterred by punishment and experiences little or no guilt and anxiety.

Avoidant personality disorder • A personality disorder in which the person is generally unwilling to enter relationships without assurance of acceptance because of fears of rejection and criticism.

proposed that men were more likely to experience feelings of guilt than women because men were subjected to the throes of the Oedipus complex. However, empirical research shows that women are more likely than men to feel guilty about moral transgressions (Baumeister and others, 1994; Tangney, 1990). Men, by contrast, are more likely to fear being caught.

Learning theorists suggest that childhood experiences can contribute to maladaptive ways of relating to others (personality disorders) in adulthood. Cognitive psychologists find that antisocial adolescents encode social information in ways that bolster their misdeeds. For example, they tend to interpret other people's behavior as threatening, even when it is not (Crick & Dodge, 1994; Dodge and others, 1990; Lochman, 1992). Cognitive therapists have encouraged some antisocial adolescents to view social provocations as problems to be solved rather than as threats to their "manhood," with some favorable initial results (Lochman, 1992).

From a trait-theory perspective, Widiger and Costa (1994) note that many personality disorders seem to be extreme variations of normal personality traits. Referring to the Big Five model of personality, they note that people with schizoid personalities tend to be highly introverted. People with avoidant personalities tend to be both introverted and emotionally unstable (neurotic).

Genetic factors may be involved in some personality disorders (Nigg & Goldsmith, 1994). For example, antisocial personality disorder tends to run in families. Adoptee studies reveal higher incidences of antisocial behavior among the biological than the adoptive relatives of persons with the disorder (DiLalla & Gottesman, 1991). There is also evidence that genetic influences are moderate at best and that the family environment contributes to antisocial behavior (Carey, 1992).

If there are genetic factors in antisocial personality disorder, they may influence the individual's characteristic level of arousal of the nervous system. Consider that antisocial personality disorder is characterized by deficiency in self-control (Sher & Trull, 1994). People with the disorder are unlikely to show guilt for their misdeeds or to be deterred by punishment. Low levels of guilt and anxiety may reflect lower-than-normal levels of arousal, which, in turn, may have a partial genetic basis (Lykken, 1982). Experiments show that people with antisocial personality disorder do not learn as rapidly as others equal in intelligence when the payoff is avoidance of impending electric shock. But when their levels of arousal are increased by injections of adrenaline, they learn to avoid punishment as rapidly as others (Schachter & Latané, 1964; Chesno & Kilmann, 1975). Patrick and his colleagues (1993) found that people with antisocial personality disorder did not show a startle response to unpleasant slides that included mutilated people and snakes. This finding provides additional evidence that antisocial personality disorder is connected with a deficit in the biological systems that regulate fear.

A lower-than-normal level of arousal would not ensure the development of an antisocial personality. Perhaps a person must also be reared under conditions that do not foster the self-concept of a law-abiding citizen. Punishment for deviant behavior would then be unlikely to induce feelings of guilt and shame. The individual might well be "undeterred" by punishment.

Reflections

- Agree or disagree with the following statement and support your answer: "Criminals have antisocial personality disorder."
- Do you know some people whom you consider to have "bad personalities"? How does the term "bad personality" differ from the diagnosis of personality disorder?

EATING DISORDERS

Most of us deprive ourselves or consume vast quantities of food now and then. The **eating disorders** listed in the DSM are characterized by persistent, gross disturbances in eating patterns, however. They include anorexia nervosa and bulimia nervosa.

Types of Eating Disorders

ANOREXIA NERVOSA. There is a saying that you can never be too rich or too thin. Excess money may be pleasant enough, but as in the case of Karen, one can certainly be too thin.

> Karen was the 22-year-old daughter of a renowned English professor. She had begun her college career full of promise at the age of 17. But two years ago, after "social problems" occurred, she had returned to live at home and taken progressively lighter course loads at a local college. Karen had never been overweight, but about a year ago her mother noticed that she seemed to be gradually "turning into a skeleton."
>
> Karen spent hours every day shopping at the supermarket, butcher, and bakeries; and in conjuring up gourmet treats for her parents and younger siblings. Arguments over her lifestyle and eating habits had divided the family into two camps. The camp led by her father called for patience. That headed by her mother demanded confrontation. Her mother feared that Karen's father would "protect her right into her grave" and wanted Karen placed in residential treatment "for her own good." The parents finally compromised on an outpatient evaluation.
>
> At an even 5 feet, Karen looked like a prepubescent 11-year-old. Her nose and cheekbones protruded crisply, like those of an elegant young fashion model. Her lips were full, but the redness of the lipstick was unnatural, as if too much paint had been dabbed on a corpse for the funeral. Karen weighed only 78 pounds, but she had dressed in a stylish silk blouse, scarf, and baggy pants so that not one inch of her body was revealed. More striking than her mouth was the redness of her rouged cheeks. It was unclear whether she had used too much makeup or whether minimal makeup had caused the stark contrast between the parts of her face that were covered and those that were not.
>
> Karen vehemently denied that she had a problem. Her figure was "just about where I want it to be" and she engaged in aerobic exercise daily. A deal was struck in which outpatient treatment would be tried as long as Karen lost no more weight and showed steady gains back to at least 90 pounds. Treatment included a day hospital with group therapy and two meals a day. But word came back that Karen was artfully toying with her food—cutting it up, sort of licking it, and moving it about her plate—rather than eating it. After three weeks Karen had lost another pound. At that point her parents were able to persuade her to enter a residential treatment program where her eating could be carefully monitored. (Nevid and others, 1997)

Karen was diagnosed with **anorexia nervosa,** a life-threatening disorder characterized by refusal to maintain a healthful body weight, intense fear of being overweight, a distorted body image, and, in females, lack of menstruation (amenorrhea.) Anorexic persons usually weigh less than 85% of their expected body weight.

Eating disorders • Psychological disorders that are characterized by distortion of the body image and gross disturbances in eating patterns. **Anorexia nervosa** • A life-threatening eating disorder characterized by refusal to maintain a healthful body weight, intense fear of being overweight, a distorted body image, and, in females, lack of menstruation (amenorrhea).

By and large, eating disorders affect women during adolescence and young adulthood. Nearly 1 in 200 school-aged girls has trouble gaining or maintaining weight, and the incidences of anorexia nervosa and bulimia nervosa have increased markedly in recent years (Strober, 1986). Anorexic women greatly outnumber anorexic men, as noted in the following section.

Anorexic women may drop 25% or more of their body weight in a year. Severe weight loss triggers amenorrhea. Their general health declines.

Truth or Fiction Revisited. *The statement that "You can never be too rich or too thin" is false.* I won't pass judgment on whether or not you can be too rich. You can clearly be too thin, however. About 4% of anorexic women die from weight-loss-related problems such as weakness or imbalances in body chemistry (Herzog and others, 1988).

The typical anorexic or bulimic person is a young White female of higher socioeconomic status, although anorexia is also becoming more prevalent among other ethnic groups and older age groups (Mitchell & Eckert, 1987). Women with eating disorders vastly outnumber men with them.

Theorists account for the gender gap in different ways. Because anorexia is connected with amenorrhea, some psychodynamic theorists suggest that anorexia represents an effort by the girl to remain prepubescent. Anorexia allows the girl to avoid growing up, separating from the family, and assuming adult responsibilities. Because of the loss of fatty deposits, their breasts and hips flatten. In their fantasies, perhaps, anorexic women remain children, sexually undifferentiated.

Cognitive-behavioral approaches suggest that weight loss acquires its powerful reinforcement value because of a combination of feelings of personal perfectibility and the cultural idealization of the slender female (Vitousek & Manke, 1994). Brenner (1992) notes that female models, who tend to represent the female ideal, are 9% taller and 16% slimmer than the average woman. Sixteen percent! For most women, that is at least 16 pounds!

Consider the sociocultural aspects of the eating disorders: As the cultural ideal grows slimmer, women with average or heavier-than-average figures come under more pressure to control their weight (Bordo, 1993; Wolf, 1991). Agras and Kirkley (1986) documented the interest in losing weight by counting the numbers of diet articles printed in three women's magazines since the year 1900. The magazines reviewed were *Ladies' Home Journal, Good Housekeeping,* and *Harper's Bazaar.* Diet articles were absent until the 1930s. During the 1930s and 1940s, only about one article appeared in every 10 issues. During the 1950s and 1960s, the number of diet articles jumped to about one in every other issue. During the 1980s, however, the number mushroomed to about 1.3 articles per issue. In recent years, that is, there has been an average of *more than one* diet article per issue!

In the typical pattern, girls notice some weight gain after menarche and decide that it must come off. However, dieting—and, often, exercise—continue at a fever pitch. They persist after girls reach average body weights, even after family members and others have told them that they are losing too much. Anorexic girls almost always adamantly deny that they are wasting away. They may point to their fierce exercise regimens as proof. Their body images are distorted (Williamson and others, 1993). Penner and his colleagues (1991) studied women who averaged 31% below their ideal body weights, according to Metropolitan Life Insurance Company charts. The women ironically overestimated the size of parts of their bodies to be 31% larger than they actually were! Others perceive anorexic women as "skin and bones." The women themselves frequently sit before the mirror and see themselves as they were.

Many people with anorexia become obsessed with food and are constantly around it. They may engross themselves in cookbooks, take on the family shopping chores, and prepare elaborate dinners for others.

BULIMIA NERVOSA. The case of Nicole provides a vivid account of a young woman diagnosed with **bulimia nervosa:**

Nicole awakens in her cold dark room and already wishes it was time to go back to bed. She dreads the thought of going through this day, which will be like so many others in her recent past. She asks herself the question every morning, "Will I be able to make it through the day without being totally obsessed by thoughts of food, or will I blow it again and

Bulimia nervosa • An eating disorder characterized by recurrent cycles of binge eating followed by dramatic measures to purge the food.

On a Binge. Bulimia nervosa is defined as recurrent cycles of binge eating and the taking of dramatic measures, such as self-induced vomiting, to purge the food. Why do you think that so many more women than men are diagnosed with anorexia nervosa and bulimia nervosa?

spend the day [binge eating]"? She tells herself that today she will begin a new life, today she will start to live like a normal human being. However, she is not at all convinced that the choice is hers. (Boskind-White & White, 1983, p. 29)

It turns out that this day Nicole begins by eating eggs and toast. Then she binges on cookies; doughnuts; bagels smothered with butter, cream cheese, and jelly; granola; candy bars; and bowls of cereal and milk—all within 45 minutes. When she cannot take in any more food, she turns her attention to purging what she has eaten. She goes to the bathroom, ties back her hair, turns on the shower to mask any noise she will make, drinks a glass of water, and makes herself vomit. Afterward she vows, "Starting tomorrow, I'm going to change." But she knows that tomorrow it will probably be the same story.

Truth or Fiction Revisited. *It is true that some college women control their weight by going on cycles of binge eating followed by self-induced vomiting.* Many other women do so as well. People who behave in this way are said to have bulimia nervosa. Bulimia nervosa is defined as recurrent cycles of binge eating followed by dramatic measures to purge the food. Binge eating frequently follows food deprivation, as through severe dieting (Polivy and others, 1994). A binge involves eating much larger-than-normal quantities of food and a sense of loss of control over eating (Wilson & Walsh, 1991). Purging includes self-induced vomiting, fasting or strict dieting, use of laxatives, and vigorous exercise. As with anorexia, there is overconcern about body shape and weight (Gleaves and others, 1993). Like anorexia, bulimia affects many more women than men.

Theoretical Views

Numerous explanations of anorexia nervosa and bulimia nervosa have been advanced. Some psychoanalysts suggest that anorexia represents an unconscious effort by the girl to cope with sexual fears, particularly the prospect of pregnancy. Some psychoanalytically oriented theorists suggest that adolescents may use refusal to eat as a weapon against their parents. One study compared mothers of adolescents with eating disorders with mothers of adolescents without such problems. Mothers of adolescents with eating disorders were relatively more likely to be unhappy with their families' functioning, to have problems with eating and dieting themselves, to think that their daughters should lose weight, and to consider their daughters unattractive (Pike & Rodin, 1991). The researchers speculate that some adolescents develop eating disorders as ways of coping with feelings of loneliness and alienation they experience in the home. Could binge eating, as suggested by Humphrey (1986), symbolize the effort to gain nurturance and comfort not offered by the mother? Could purging be a symbolic ridding oneself of negative feelings toward the family?

Other psychologists view anorexia as an excessive fear of gaining weight that derives from cultural idealization of the slender female. This ideal may contribute to distortion of the body image.

Over the years, anorexia nervosa and bulimia nervosa have generally been attributed to psychological origins, but research has also implicated biological factors such as neurotransmitters. When noradrenaline acts on one part of the hypothalamus, it stimulates animals to eat (Kaplan & Woodside, 1987; Mitchell & Eckert, 1987). Serotonin, in contrast, appears to induce feelings of satiation and suppress the appetite (Halmi and others, 1986; Kaplan & Woodside, 1987).

A biological condition that would increase the effect of serotonin could thus have a negative impact on the desire to eat, as in anorexia. A biological condition that decreased the effect of serotonin, which normally suppresses the appetite, could result in periodic binge eating, as in bulimia.

Reflections

- Are you happy with your body shape? Do you feel pressure to be thinner than you are? Why or why not?
- Consider your sociocultural background. Are women from this background traditionally expected to be well-rounded or slender? What attitudes are connected with weight and body shape within your traditions?

Although the causes of many psychological disorders remain in dispute, a number of therapy methods have been devised to deal with them. Those methods are the focus of Chapter 14.

Study Guide

| **Matching Symptoms and Psychological Disorders**

DIRECTIONS: In the first column are symptoms of psychological disorders. The second column lists disorders. Write the letter of the type of disorder in the appropriate blank space. More than one type of disorder may apply. Answers are given below.

____ 1. Waxy flexibility

____ 2. Flashbacks

____ 3. Binge eating

____ 4. Nervousness

____ 5. Weight loss

____ 6. Free-floating anxiety

____ 7. Loss of a sense of one's personal identity

____ 8. Pressured speech

____ 9. Vivid, abundant hallucinations

____ 10. Delusions of persecution

____ 11. Delusions of unworthiness

____ 12. Self-induced vomiting

____ 13. Sudden anxiety attacks in the absence of threatening stimuli

____ 14. Lack of guilt over misdeeds

____ 15. Elation

____ 16. Hallucinations

____ 17. Lack of energy

____ 18. Suspiciousness

____ 19. La belle indifférence

____ 20. Compulsive behavior

____ 21. Social withdrawal

____ 22. Fear of public scrutiny

____ 23. Physical complaints

____ 24. Loose associations

____ 25. Giddiness

A. Phobic disorder

B. Panic disorder

C. Generalized anxiety disorder

D. Obsessive–compulsive disorder

E. Post-traumatic stress disorder

F. Dissociative amnesia

G. Dissociative identity disorder

H. Depersonalization disorder

I. Conversion disorder

J. Hypochondriasis

K. Anorexia nervosa

L. Bulimia nervosa

M. Major depression

N. Bipolar disorder

O. Disorganized schizophrenia

P. Catatonic schizophrenia

Q. Paranoid schizophrenia

R. Paranoid personality

S. Schizoid personality

T. Antisocial personality

ANSWER KEY TO EXERCISE

1. P	6. C	11. M	16. O, P, Q	21. M, S
2. E	7. F, H	12. L	17. M	22. A
3. L	8. N	13. B	18. Q, R	23. J
4. A, B, C, etc.	9. O	14. T	19. I	24. O, P, Q
5. K, M	10. Q	15. N	20. D, W	25. O

<table><tr><td>ESL</td><td>English as a Second Language — Bridging the Gap</td></tr></table>

---

accords (555)—gives

afforded them respite (566)—gave them relief

around it (583)—where food is being sold, prepared, or eaten

ascribed to (550)—credited to

automatic teller machine cards (550)—plastic cards that can be put into bank machines to get money from a person's account without going into the bank

avert (564)—avoid; turn away from

Band-Aid (555)—a superficial treatment that does not cure; Band-Aid is the brand name of a small adhesive strip bandage

blue (567)—a little depressed

bolster (580)—support; encourage

boy next door (550)—an expression that refers to a nice, friendly young man who would never do anything wrong

brazen (553)—not modest

break out with hives (562)—have an allergic reaction consisting of red areas on the skin

bridges (568)—connects

broken through (563)—to have traveled through

bugged his walls with radios (574)—installed machines in his walls that could listen to and record what he was saying

by reason of (550)—because of

call it quits (562)—allow you to be free

can never be too rich or too thin (581)—an expression that reflects a value held by some women in the United States who believe that being extremely wealthy and extremely thin is important

can't get a word in edgewise (567)—unable to join in a conversation because there is no time when the other person isn't talking

carrying jokes too far (567)—allowing a joke to hurt someone

causal connections (572)—connections between the cause and effect

certain ends (574)—specific results

chops the problem down to a manageable size (570)—focuses in on the main points of a problem to make it seem like one that can be dealt with

come to (565)—begin

comes out of the blue (552)—occurs without warning

complex web (572)—a complicated tangle

compulsions (560)—a strong urge to do something

conjuring up (581)—dreaming up; imagining; creating

conveying (574)—communicating; sending

coworkers (578)—people who work together in the same company

creepy-crawlies (557)—bugs

cycles of binge eating (549)—periods of rapid and excessive eating; considered to be a psychological disorder

deemed (553)—called; considered to be

deeply ingrained (554)—deeply rooted in the person

degrades (555)—says something negative; dishonors

demonology (551)—the belief that people can be possessed by demons

descend from nowhere (557)—occur without warning

deterred by (580)—prevented; stopped

deviant (551)—not normal

did me in (564)—overwhelmed me; was more than I could handle

distraught (551)—to be very upset

does not work out (569)—is not successful

down in the dumps (567)—depressed

downside (555)—negative side

drifter (550)—someone who doesn't live or work permanently in any one spot but travels from place to place

earphone (573)—small receiver in the ear

elation (566)—extreme happiness; joy

elude (556)—escape; avoid

empirical research (580)—observing actual occurrences of something

entail (556)—involve

erroneously (566)—in error; incorrectly

exacerbated (559)—made worse

excruciating pinch (557)—extremely painful hurt, like a sharp squeeze

faking (565)—pretending; trying to trick another

fall short (568)—to not reach

falls under the control of (562)—controlled by

feel whole (562)—feel like one complete person

feign (562)—pretend; imitate

ferret out (551)—discover

fever pitch (582)—intensely and continually

fidgeting (557)—to behave or move around nervously; to be restless; to handle something in a preoccupied way

fitting (567)—natural and appropriate

flashbacks (559)—sudden memories that are so realistic it feels as if we are there again

fluctuating (568)—changing; increasing or decreasing

forgery (556)—a copy of the real thing

free-floating (557)—without attachment

furrowed brow (557)—when someone squeezes the eyebrows together and makes a wrinkle between the eyebrows; often indicates worry or difficulty of some kind

goings-on (551)—occurrences

goldbricking (564)—being lazy

grossly disorganized (578)—extremely out of order

harbor (551)—contain

helluva (569)—slang for "one hell of a," which is an adjective for very big or strong; can be used as a negative or a positive

hives (562)—skin rash often resulting from allergic reactions

hold on to jobs (578)—maintain their employment

impairs (553)—limits; damages

in full sway (552)—the accepted idea

in league with (551)—acting in a way that the Devil wanted

infantile (576)—like an infant

inhibitory (561)—stops or slows down something

insolent (553)—discourteous

intrusive (559)—annoying or troublesome; something that invades

jumbled (574)—confused

jump from topic to topic (567)—move from one topic to another topic that is not relevant

kinship studies (577)—studying people who are related to each other

leakage of (560)—slow withdrawing of

lie dormant (550)—not be considered

live up to (561)—meet the expectations

loath to venture out of (557)—afraid to go out of

loners (579)—people who prefer to be alone most of the time

loused it up (569)—caused the bad experience

lump . . . together (553)—place them in the same category even though they may not belong together

Mafia (552)—a national organized crime group that began in Italy

magnified beyond (567)—greater than is expected

magnitude (551)—large size

making small talk (570)—talking about things that are not personal; general discussion topics that are typical when first meeting someone

maladaptive (554)—not well adjusted in dealing with other people; sees others and relationships with others in ways that cause difficulty

massive (564)—extremely big

meandered (566)—wandered about with purpose or direction

meaningful whole (565)—a complete identity with meaning

menarche (580)—the start of menstruation

midair (556)—between elevator stops

misdeeds (580)—wrongdoing

multidimensional (553)—many dimensions, or things to look at, in a system or issue being considered

nonsensical speech (575)—speech that has no meaning

on the way down (567)—as they move into depression

onset (574)—beginning; start of something

other side of the coin (567)—the other part of the same disorder

out of proportion to (556)—a reaction that is larger than the situation calls for

out of the blue (552)—unexpectedly; without warning

out of touch with reality (573)—disconnected from the immediate circumstances, situation, or environment

out to get you (552)—looking for you in order to kill you

overly concerned (568)—too concerned (negative)

payoff (580)—positive result

pervasive (578)—widespread and lasting

phony (556)—fake; not real

pigeonholed (553)—classified in a small category

point to . . . evidence (582)—indicated . . . evidence as proof

predisposing childhood (576)—experiences in childhood that might cause a person to have a tendency toward some problem

predisposition (561)—tendency toward something

promising avenue of research (562)—direction of research that might be important

psychiatric institution (552)—hospital where people with psychiatric disorders can be treated

psychotherapy (553)—treatment of psychological problems

quell (561)—reduce or stop

racing heart (556)—a heart that feels as though it is beating more quickly than usual

recurrent (559)—happens again and again

reliability and validity (555)—dependability (will the concepts apply to many people or only some) and accuracy (is it really what we think it is)

retribution (550)—a punishment or penalty one must pay for wrongdoing

rocky coast of Massachusetts (550)—refers to the town of Salem, Massachusetts, where the witch trials were held

rotting away from disease (574)—slowly dying from a disease

run from doctor to doctor (566)—continuously search for a doctor by visiting one and then another

run-of-the-mill (566)—common

Salem, Massachusetts . . . burned as a witch (550)—Arthur Miller, an American playwright of this century, wrote a play called *The Crucible* about a famous place and time in U.S. history when people were judged and killed for being witches

Sani-Flush (558)—the brand name for a chemical mixture that is used to clean toilets

self-assertive (552)—outspoken and self-assured

self-concept (580)—our ideas about who we are

serve a purpose (566)—to accomplish something; to have a reason for occurring

sexual promiscuity (579)—frequent and random sexual activity with people with whom a person does not have a strong emotional relationship

sham (562)—artificial; false

slit her wrists (573)—cut the wrists where it is difficult to stop the bleeding; it is a way to kill oneself

social norms (576)—"rules" about correct behaviors that are expected by others

something all too real (552)—an actual or real illness

spent (557)—extremely tired; exhausted

squirm (560)—wiggle or twist around

stage fright (556)—fear of speaking in front of or of performing in front of a group of people

stands outside (565)—feels as though he or she is outside of his or her personality

stem from (550)—develop from

stitches (574)—using a special thread and needle to sew up a skin wound

strike you (561)—impress you

striking feature (579)—most noticeable characteristic

taking a person's mind off (562)—redirecting; causing the person not to think about something

terminated the . . . behavior . . . and the patient (562)—both the behavior and the patient were ended

The Three Faces of Eve (563)—a 1950s movie about a woman with multiple personalities

throes (580)—struggles; difficulties

thus removed from the real world (565)—removed from the real world this way

tightly knit (574)—connected by associations

tingling (557)—a prickling, stinging feeling

transgressions (580)—intrusions; violations; moral transgressions would be doing something that goes against our ideas of good behavior

traumatic (559)—very upsetting

turned inward (568)—focuses in on the person himself or herself

wandering uterus (566)—a uterus that moves inside the body

wasting away (582)—becoming so thin that they look like they are going to die

weapon against (584)—as a way of expressing anger at

were at work (573)—were operating

were in for it (551)—could expect the worst situation to happen to you

wrapped up in (575)—focused only on

wrong sign (570)—refers to astrological signs, which some believe can predict personality traits of people according to the placement of the stars and planets when they were born; the belief is that people's signs can tell whether they would be good or bad partners; a wrong sign would mean that person is not a good match for another

---

FILL-INS | **Chapter Review**

SECTION 1: WHAT ARE PSYCHOLOGICAL DISORDERS?

The text lists (1: how many?) _____ criteria for determining whether behavior is abnormal. Behavior tends to be labeled abnormal when it is unusual or (2) _____cally deviant, when it is socially (3) un_____ble, when it involves faulty (4) _____tion of reality, when it is dangerous, when it is (5) self-_____ing, or when it is personally distressing.

SECTION 2: CLASSIFYING PSYCHOLOGICAL DISORDERS

The DSM-IV employs a (6) <u>multi</u>_____, or multidimensional, system of assessment. The DSM-IV groups disorders on the basis of observable features or (7) _____<u>toms</u>. The DSM is reliable in part because diagnostic categories have been (8: Widened or Narrowed?) in recent years. The (9) _____<u>ity</u> of a diagnosis is the degree to which it reflects an actual disorder.

SECTION 3: ANXIETY DISORDERS

The anxiety disorders include irrational fears, or (10) _____ias; panic disorder, which is characterized by sudden attacks in which people typically fear that they may be losing (11) <u>con</u>_____ or going crazy; free-floating, or (12) _____<u>ized</u>, anxiety; (13) obsessive–<u>c</u>_____ disorder, in which people are troubled by intrusive thoughts or impulses to repeat some activity; and (14) <u>post-</u>_____ stress disorder (PTSD).

(15) _____<u>phobia</u> is fear of being out in open, busy areas. Stage fright and speech anxiety are examples of (16) _____<u>al</u> phobias, in which people have excessive fear of public scrutiny. Panic disorder differs from other anxiety disorders in part because there is a stronger bodily component to the anxiety, including heavy (17) <u>sw</u>_____ing and pounding of the (18) <u>h</u>_____. An (19) _____<u>ion</u> is a recurring thought or image that seems irrational and beyond control. A (20) _____<u>ion</u> is a seemingly irresistible urge to engage in an act, often repeatedly. Post-traumatic (21) <u>s</u>_____ disorder (PTSD) involves intense and persistent feelings of anxiety and helplessness that are caused by a traumatic experience. The precipitating event is reexperienced in the form of intrusive memories, recurrent dreams, and (22) _____<u>cks</u>, or feeling that the event is recurring.

Psychodynamic theory explains generalized anxiety as persistent difficulty in maintaining (23) _____<u>ion</u> of primitive impulses. According to psychodynamic theory, phobias symbolize (24) _____<u>cious</u> conflicts. From the behaviorist perspective, phobias are (25) _____<u>ned</u> fears. Susan (26) <u>M</u>_____ suggests that people are genetically predisposed to fear stimuli that may have once posed a threat to their ancestors. Given the apparent independence of panic attacks from (27: Internal or External?) events, researchers are investigating possible organic causes for panic disorder. Psychoanalysts and learning theorists agree that compulsive behavior may be maintained because it reduces (28) _____<u>ty</u>.

Anxiety disorders (29: Do or Do Not?) tend to run in families. Some people may have a biological predisposition to anxiety in that their receptors to (30) gamma-_____<u>ric</u> acid (GABA) may not be sensitive enough. GABA is a (31) _____<u>mitter</u> that may help quell anxiety reactions.

SECTION 4: DISSOCIATIVE DISORDERS

Dissociative disorders are characterized by a sudden temporary change in (32) <u>co</u>_____<u>ness</u> or self-identity. The dissociative disorders include (33) dissociative <u>a</u>_____ (motivated forgetting); fugue (forgetting plus fleeing and adopting a new identity); dissociative (34) <u>i</u>_____ disorder, in which a person behaves as if distinct personalities occupy the body; and (35) _____<u>zation</u> disorder, in which people feel as if they are not themselves.

According to psychodynamic theory, dissociative disorders involve massive use of (36) _____<u>sion</u>. According to learning theory, dissociative disorders are conditions in which people learn not to (37) <u>t</u>_____ about disturbing acts or impulses in order to avoid feelings of guilt and shame. Cognitive theorists explain dissociative disorders in terms of where we focus our (38) _____ion at a given time.

SECTION 5: SOMATOFORM DISORDERS

In (39) so_____ disorders, people show or complain of physical problems, such as paralysis, pain, or the persistent belief that they have a serious disease. Evidence of a medical problem (40: Can or Cannot?) be found.

The somatoform disorders include (41) con_____ disorder and (42) hypo_____is. In a conversion disorder, there is a major change in or loss of (43) p_____ functioning with no organic basis. Some victims of conversion disorder show a remarkable lack of concern over their loss of function, a symptom known as la (44) b_____ indifférence. The (45) _____ic view of conversion disorders is that the symptoms produced by the victim protect the victim from guilt or another source of stress.

SECTION 6: MOOD DISORDERS

Mood disorders are characterized by disturbance in expressed (46) _____ions. Mood disorders include major (47) _____sion and (48) bi_____ disorder.

Depression is characterized by sadness, lack of (49) _____gy, loss of self-esteem, difficulty in concentrating, loss of (50) in_____ in other people and activities that were enjoyable, (51: Optimism or Pessimism?), crying, and, sometimes, by thoughts of suicide. (52) M_____-depression can reach psychotic proportions, with grossly impaired reality testing.

(53) B_____ disorder was formerly known as manic-depression. In bipolar disorder there are mood swings from (54) _____ion to depression and back. Manic people may show pressured speech, have grand, delusional schemes, and jump from topic to topic, a symptom called rapid (55) f_____ of ideas.

Depression is a(n) (56: Normal or Abnormal?) reaction to a loss or to exposure to unpleasant events. Recent research emphasizes the possible roles of learned helplessness, (57) _____tional styles, and the roles of (58) _____mitters in prolonged depression.

According to psychodynamic theory, prolonged depression may reflect feelings of (59) a_____ that are turned inward rather than expressed. Learning theorists have noted similarities between depressed people and animals who are not (60) _____ced for instrumental behavior. People and animals both show (61) in_____ty and loss of interest when they have repeatedly failed to receive reinforcement.

Martin (62) Se_____ and his colleagues have explored links between depression and learned helplessness. Depressed people are more likely than nondepressed people to make (63: Internal or External?), (64: Stable or Unstable?), and (65: Specific or Global?) attributions for failures.

Research suggests that deficiencies in the neurotransmitter (66) _____in may create a general predisposition toward mood disorders. A concurrent deficiency of the neurotransmitter (67: Adrenaline or Noradrenaline?) may then contribute to depression. Concurrent (68: Excesses or Deficiencies?) of noradrenaline may contribute to manic behavior.

Suicide is more common among (69: College Students or Nonstudents?). Three times as many (70: Men as Women? or Women as Men?) attempt suicide. Suicide is most often linked to feelings of (71) de_____ and hopelessness. People who threaten suicide are (72: More or Less?) likely to carry out the threat than people who do not.

SECTION 7: SCHIZOPHRENIA

Schizophrenic disorders are characterized by disturbances in (73) th_____ and language (as found, for example, in the loosening of associations and in delusions); in (74) per_____ and attention (as found, for example, in hallucinations); in (75) m_____ activity (as found, for example, in a stupor); in mood (as found, for example, in flat emotional responses); and by withdrawal and autism.

Major types of schizophrenia include (76) dis_____ schizophrenia, catatonic schizophrenia, and paranoid schizophrenia. Disorganized schizophrenia is characterized by disorganized (77) del_____s and vivid, abundant (78) _____nations. Catatonic schizophrenia is characterized by impaired motor activity, as in a catatonic (79) _____or, and by (80) w_____ flexibility. Paranoid schizophrenia is characterized by paranoid (81) _____ions.

According to psychodynamic theory, schizophrenic behavior occurs when impulses of the (82: Id, Ego, or Superego?) overwhelm the (83: Id, Ego, or Superego?). Schizophrenia (84: Does or Does Not?) tend to run in families. Children with two schizophrenic parents have about a (85) _____% chance of becoming schizophrenic. Current theory and research concerning an organic basis for schizophrenia focus on the neurotransmitter (86) _____ine. According to the dopamine theory of schizophrenia, schizophrenics may (87) u_____ more dopamine than normal people do.

SECTION 8: PERSONALITY DISORDERS

Personality disorders, like personality traits, are characterized by enduring patterns of (88) be_____. Personality disorders are inflexible, (89) mal_____ive behavior patterns that impair personal or social functioning and are a source of (90) dis_____ to the individual or to others.

The defining trait of the (91) _____oid personality is suspiciousness. Persons with (92) sch_____ personality disorders show oddities of thought, perception, and behavior. However, schizotypal personalities do not show bizarre (93) _____tic behavior. Social (94) _____al is the major characteristic of the schizoid personality. Persons with (95) _____oid personality disorder prefer to be by themselves and do not develop warm, tender feelings for others.

Persons with (96) _____ial personality disorders persistently violate the rights of others. They show little or no (97) g_____ or shame over their misdeeds and are largely undeterred by (98) _____ment.

Various factors seem to contribute to antisocial behavior. One is parental (99) re_____ion during childhood. Second is inconsistent (100) _____line. Third is an organic factor. Research suggests that persons with antisocial personalities have (101: Higher or Lower?)-than-normal levels of arousal, which might explain why they are undeterred by most forms of punishment. Cognitive psychologists find that antisocial adolescents tend to interpret other people's behavior as (102) _____ning, even when it is not.

SECTION 9: EATING DISORDERS

The eating disorders include (103) an_____ nervosa and bulimia (104) n_____. Anorexia is characterized by refusal to maintain a healthful body weight, intense fear of being overweight, a distorted (105) b_____ image, and, in females, (106) amen_____. Anorexia is more likely to afflict young (107: Men or Women?). Bulimia nervosa is defined as recurrent cycles of (108) b_____ eating and the taking of dramatic measures to (109) p_____ the food, such as self-induced vomiting. Both disorders tend to begin in (110) _____ence.

Psychoanalysts suggest that anorexia may represent an unconscious effort by the girl to remain (111) pre_____. As noted by Polivy and Herman, cultural (112) _____zation of the slender female has become so ingrained that "normal" eating for American women today is characterized by dieting.

ANSWER KEY TO CHAPTER REVIEW

1. Six
2. Statistically
3. Unacceptable
4. Perception (or interpretation)
5. Self-defeating
6. Multiaxial
7. Symptoms
8. Narrowed
9. Validity
10. Phobias
11. Control
12. Generalized
13. Obsessive–compulsive
14. Post-traumatic
15. Agoraphobia
16. Social
17. Sweating
18. Heart
19. Obsession
20. Compulsion
21. Stress
22. Flashbacks
23. Repression
24. Unconscious
25. Conditioned
26. Mineka
27. External
28. Anxiety

29. Do
30. Aminobutyric
31. Neurotransmitter
32. Consciousness
33. Amnesia
34. Identity
35. Depersonalization
36. Repression
37. Think
38. Attention
39. Somatoform
40. Cannot
41. Conversion
42. Hypochondriasis
43. Physical
44. Belle
45. Psychodynamic
46. Emotions
47. Depression
48. Bipolar
49. Energy
50. Interest
51. Pessimism
52. Major
53. Bipolar
54. Elation
55. Flight
56. Normal

57. Attributional
58. Neurotransmitters
59. Anger
60. Reinforced
61. Inactivity
62. Seligman
63. Internal
64. Stable
65. Global
66. Serotonin
67. Noradrenaline
68. Excesses
69. College students
70. Women as men
71. Depression
72. More
73. Thought
74. Perception
75. Motor
76. Disorganized
77. Delusions
78. Hallucinations
79. Stupor
80. Waxy
81. Delusions
82. Id
83. Ego
84. Does

85. 35
86. Dopamine
87. Utilize
88. Behavior
89. Maladaptive
90. Distress
91. Paranoid
92. Schizotypal
93. Psychotic
94. Withdrawal
95. Schizoid
96. Antisocial
97. Guilt
98. Punishment
99. Rejection
100. Discipline
101. Lower
102. Threatening
103. Anorexia
104. Nervosa
105. Body
106. Amenorrhea
107. Women
108. Binge
109. Purge
110. Adolescence
111. Prepubescent
112. Idealization

POSTTEST | Multiple Choice

1. Throughout human history, most people have attributed unusual behavior and psychological disorders to
   a. poverty.
   b. unconscious urges.
   c. demons.
   d. observational learning.

2. The most widely used system of classification of psychological disorders in the United States is written by the
   a. American Psychiatric Association.
   b. American Psychological Association.
   c. American Medical Association.
   d. World Health Organization.

3. According to the chapter, the most widespread phobia among adults is
   a. speech anxiety.
   b. claustrophobia.
   c. agoraphobia.
   d. fear of injections.

4. Dan has a problem in which he encounters heavy sweating and a pounding heart—both for no apparent reason. Dan would probably be diagnosed as having a(n)
   a. phobic disorder.
   b. panic disorder.
   c. generalized anxiety disorder.
   d. obsessive–compulsive disorder.

5. A difference between a phobic disorder and a fear is that the phobic response
   a. is out of proportion to the actual danger.
   b. involves cognitive as well as behavioral reactions.
   c. is characterized by rapid heart rate.
   d. encourages avoidance of the feared object or situation.

6. By definition, all dissociative disorders involve
   a. massive repression of unacceptable impulses.
   b. a sudden, temporary change in consciousness or identity.
   c. the presence of at least two conflicting personalities.
   d. malingering.

7. In which of the following does the individual feel unreal and separated from his or her body?
   a. depersonalization disorder
   b. schizotypal personality disorder
   c. dissociative identity disorder
   d. schizoid personality disorder

8. Mary believes that she is suffering from a serious stomach or intestinal disease, because she has difficulty keeping food down and has unusual sensations in these regions of the body. However, repeated visits to physicians have not uncovered evidence of any medical disorder. Mary is most likely to be diagnosed as suffering from
   a. conversion disorder.
   b. malingering.
   c. anorexia nervosa.
   d. hypochondriasis.

9. Mood disorders are primarily characterized by disturbance in
   a. thought processes.
   b. biological processes.
   c. expressed emotions.
   d. motor responses.

10. The symptom that differentiates bipolar disorder from other disorders is
    a. suicide attempts.
    b. severe bouts of depression.
    c. delusional thinking.
    d. rapid flight of ideas.

11. Deficiencies of _____ are most likely to be connected with both types of mood disorders discussed in the chapter.
    a. adrenaline
    b. noradrenaline
    c. serotonin
    d. dopamine

12. Schizophrenic disorders are known primarily by disturbances in
    a. motor responses.
    b. thought.
    c. expressed emotions.
    d. physical functioning.

13. A person with _____ is most likely to show confused, jumbled thinking.
    a. schizotypal personality disorder
    b. paranoid schizophrenia
    c. paranoid personality disorder
    d. schizoid personality disorder

14. Evidence seems clearest that people with schizophrenia
    a. produce more dopamine than other people do.
    b. have a greater number of dopamine receptors in the brain than other people do.
    c. are more sensitive to dopamine than other people are.
    d. utilize more dopamine than other people do.

15. The defining trait of the paranoid personality disorder is
    a. social withdrawal.
    b. oddities of thought.
    c. suspiciousness.
    d. self-absorption.

16. According to Susan Nolen-Hoeksema, people who respond to feelings of depression by focusing on their symptoms and the possible causes and effects of their symptoms tend to
    a. develop insight into the origins of their problems.
    b. prolong depressive episodes.
    c. increase the amount of noradrenaline available to the brain.
    d. utilize lower-than-normal levels of dopamine.

17. According to the chapter, evidence suggests that there is a role for genetic factors in each of the following disorders, *with the exception of*
    a. anxiety disorders.
    b. schizophrenia.
    c. bipolar disorder.
    d. dissociative fugue.

18. Which of the following statements about suicide is true?

14

Therapy

PRETEST *Truth or Fiction?*

_____ People in Merry Old England used to visit the local insane asylum for a fun night out on the town.

_____ Some psychotherapists interpret clients' dreams.

_____ To be of help, psychotherapy must continue for months, perhaps years.

_____ Well-adjusted women wish to remain in the home and rear children.

_____ Other psychotherapists encourage their clients to take the lead in the therapy session.

_____ Lying around in your reclining chair and fantasizing can be an effective way of confronting your fears.

_____ Smoking cigarettes can be an effective treatment for helping people to . . . stop smoking cigarettes.

_____ You might be able to gain control over bad habits merely by keeping a record of where and when you practice them.

_____ Still other psychotherapists tell their clients precisely what to do.

_____ The originator of a surgical technique intended to reduce violence learned that it was not always successful . . . when one of his patients shot him.

J ASMINE, a 19-year-old college sophomore, has been crying almost without letup for several days. She feels that her life is falling apart. Her college aspirations lie in shambles. She has brought shame upon her family. Thoughts of suicide have crossed her mind. She can barely drag herself out of bed in the morning. She is avoiding friends. She can pinpoint some sources of stress in life: a couple of less-than-shining grades, an argument with a boyfriend, friction with roommates. Still, her misery seemed to descend on her from nowhere.

Jasmine is depressed—so depressed that family and friends have finally prevailed upon her to seek professional help. Had she broken her leg, her treatment from a qualified professional would have followed a fairly standard course. Yet treatment of psychological problems and disorders like depression may be approached from very different perspectives. Depending on whom Jasmine sees, she may be

- Lying on a couch talking about anything that pops into awareness and exploring the hidden meanings of a recurrent dream
- Sitting face to face with a gentle, accepting therapist who places the major burden for what happens in therapy on Jasmine's shoulders
- Listening to a frank, straightforward therapist assert that her problems stem from self-defeating attitudes and perfectionistic beliefs
- Taking pills
- Participating in some combination of the above

These methods, though different, all represent methods of therapy. To make sense of what is happening to Jasmine, we first define *psychotherapy*. We consider the history of therapy and examine several of the major current psychotherapies including psychodynamic, humanistic–existential, cognitive, behavior, and group therapies. After exploring these approaches to psychotherapy, we shall turn our attention to biological therapies including drug therapy, electroconvulsive shock therapy, and psychosurgery.

Psychotherapy • A systematic interaction between a therapist and a client that brings psychological principles to bear on influencing the client's thoughts, feelings, or behavior in order to help that client overcome abnormal behavior or adjust to problems in living.

WHAT IS THERAPY? IN SEARCH OF THAT "SWEET OBLIVIOUS ANTIDOTE"[1]

The form of therapy practiced by a psychologist or another helping professional is related to her or his assumptions about personality and psychological disorders. Treatment is not, or ought not to be, a matter of chance.

Although there are many different kinds of psychotherapy, they have a number of things in common. **Psychotherapy** is a systematic interaction between a therapist and a client that brings psychological principles to bear on influencing the client's thoughts, feelings, or behavior in order to help the client overcome psychological disorders, adjust to problems in living, or develop as an individual.

Quite a mouthful? True. But note the essentials:

1. *Systematic Interaction.* Psychotherapy is a systematic interaction between a client and a therapist. The client's needs and goals and the therapist's theoretical point of view interact to determine how the therapist and client relate to one another.

---

[1] The phrase is from Shakespeare's *Macbeth,* as seen in the following pages.

2. *Psychological Principles.* Psychotherapy brings psychological principles to bear on the client's problems or goals. Psychotherapy is based on psychological theory and research in areas such as personality, learning, motivation, and emotion. Psychotherapy is not based on, say, religious or biological principles, although there is no reason why psychotherapy cannot be compatible with both.

3. *Thoughts, Feelings, and Behavior.* Psychotherapy influences clients' thoughts, feelings, and behavior. Psychotherapy can be aimed at any or all of these aspects of human psychology.

4. *Psychological Disorders, Adjustment Problems, and Personal Growth.* Psychotherapy is used with at least three types of clients. First, there are people who have psychological disorders. Other people seek help in adjusting to problems such as social shyness, weight problems, loss of a spouse, or career confusion. Still other people use psychotherapy because they want to learn more about themselves and reach their full potential as individuals, creative artists, parents, and members of social groups.

**MINILECTURE:
APPROACHES TO
PSYCHOTHERAPY**

History of Therapies

Ancient and medieval "treatments" of psychological disorders often reflected the demonological model. As such, they tended to involve cruel practices such as exorcism and death by hanging or burning, as was practiced some 300 years ago. In Europe and the United States, some people who could not meet the demands of everyday life were also thrown into prisons (Grob, 1994). Others begged in city streets, stole produce and food animals from farms, or entered marginal societal niches occupied by prostitutes and petty thieves. A few might have found their ways to monasteries or other retreats that offered a kind word and some support. Generally speaking, they all had one thing in common: They died early.

**MINILECTURE:
THE HISTORY OF
THERAPY**

ASYLUMS. **Asylums** originated in European monasteries. They were the first institutions meant primarily for persons with psychological disorders. Their function was human warehousing, not treatment. Asylums mushroomed in population until the daily stresses created by noise, overcrowding, and unsanitary conditions undoubtedly heightened the problems they were meant to ameliorate. Inmates were frequently chained and beaten. Some were chained for decades.

The word *bedlam* is derived from the name of the London asylum St. Mary's of Bethlehem, which opened its gates in 1547. Here, the unfortunate were chained between the inner and outer walls, whipped, and allowed to lie in their own waste. And here, the ladies and gentlemen of the British upper class might go for a stroll on a lazy afternoon to take in the sights. The admission for such amusement? One penny.

Truth or Fiction Revisited. *It is true that people in Merry Old England used to visit the local insane asylum for a fun night out on the town.* St. Mary's of Bethlehem was the best known asylum.

Humanitarian reform movements began in the 18th century. In Paris, Philippe Pinel unchained the residents at the asylum known as La Bicêtre. The populace was amazed that most of them, rather than run amok, profited from kindness and greater freedom. Many could eventually function in society once more. Reform movements were later led by the Quaker William Tuke in England and by Dorothea Dix in America.

Asylum • (uh-SIGH-lum). An institution for the care of the mentally ill.

St. Mary's of Bethlehem. This famous London institution is the source of the term *bedlam*.

MENTAL HOSPITALS. Mental hospitals gradually replaced asylums in the United States. In the mid-1950s, more than a million people resided in state, county, Veterans Administration, or private facilities. Treatment, not warehousing, is the function of the mental hospital. Still, because of high hospital populations and understaffing, many individuals have received little attention. Even today, with somewhat improved conditions, one psychiatrist may be responsible for the welfare of several hundred residents on a weekend.

THE COMMUNITY MENTAL HEALTH MOVEMENT. Since the 1960s, efforts have been made to maintain people with psychological disorders in the community. The Community Mental-Health Centers Act of 1963 provided funds for creating hundreds of community mental health centers, in which people would be

---

TABLE 14.1

FUNCTIONS OF A COMMUNITY MENTAL HEALTH CENTER

Outpatient treatment
Short-term hospitalization
Partial hospitalization (e.g., individual sleeps in the hospital and works outside
   during the day)
Crisis intervention
Community consultation and education about abnormal behavior

The Community Mental-Health Centers Act provided funds for community agencies that attempt to intervene in psychological disorders as early as possible and to maintain people in the community.

charged according to their ability to pay, in order to accomplish this goal. These centers attempt to maintain new patients as outpatients, to serve hospital residents who have been released into the community, and to provide other services listed in Table 14.1. Today, the majority of the people with chronic psychological disorders live in the community, not the hospital.

Critics note that many people who had resided in hospitals for decades were suddenly discharged to "home" communities that seemed foreign and frightening. Many people do not obtain adequate follow-up care in the community following discharge. Many join the ranks of the nation's homeless (Carling, 1990; Levine & Rog, 1990). Some people try to return to the protected world of the hospital and become trapped in a "revolving door" between the hospital and the community.

Reflections

- Have people you know said they have gone for "therapy"? What kind of therapy? What are your attitudes toward people who seek professional help for psychological or adjustment problems? Why?
- Had you heard of insane asylums or mental hospitals? What pictures were conjured up in your mind? How did your impressions match the information in this chapter?
- Is there a community mental health center or home for homeless people in your neighborhood? How would your family or your neighbors feel about having these agencies in your neighborhood? Why?

Let us consider the different kinds of therapies available today.

PSYCHODYNAMIC THERAPIES: TO "RAZE OUT THE WRITTEN TROUBLES OF THE BRAIN"

Psychodynamic therapies are based on the thinking of Sigmund Freud, the founder of psychodynamic theory. Broadly speaking, they are based on the view that our problems largely reflect early childhood experiences and internal conflicts. According to Freud, this internal conflict involves the shifting of psychic, or libidinal, energy among the three psychic structures—the id, ego, and superego. The sway of psychic energy determines our behavior. When primitive urges threaten to break through from the id or when the superego floods us with excessive guilt, it prompts the establishment of defenses and creates distress. Freud's psychodynamic therapy method—psychoanalysis—aims to modify the flow of energy among these structures, largely to bulwark the ego against the torrents of energy loosed by the id and the superego. With impulses and feelings of guilt and shame placed under greater control, clients are emotionally freed to develop more adaptive behavior patterns.

Not all psychodynamically oriented therapists view internal conflict in terms of unconscious forces. In this section, we first outline Freud's psychoanalytic methods for shoring up the ego—"traditional" psychoanalysis. We then examine more modern psychoanalytic approaches, whose concepts of conflict and methods differ from those of Freud.

Traditional Psychoanalysis: "Where Id Was, There Shall Ego Be"

Canst thou not minister to a mind diseas'd,
Pluck out from the memory a rooted sorrow,
Raze out the written troubles of the brain,
And with some sweet oblivious antidote
Cleanse the stuff'd bosom of that perilous stuff
Which weighs upon the heart?

SHAKESPEARE, *MACBETH*

In this passage, Macbeth asks a physician to minister to Lady Macbeth after she has gone mad. In the play, her madness is in part caused by current events—namely, her guilt for participating in murders designed to seat her husband on the throne of Scotland. There are also hints of more deeply rooted and mysterious problems, however, such as conflicts about infertility.

If Lady Macbeth's physician had been a traditional psychoanalyst, he might have asked her to lie on a couch in a slightly darkened room. He would have sat just behind her and encouraged her to talk about anything that came to mind, no matter how trivial, no matter how personal. To avoid interfering with her self-exploration, he might have said little or nothing for session after session. That would have been par for the course. A traditional **psychoanalysis,** you see, can extend for months, or years.

Psychoanalysis is the clinical method devised by Freud for plucking "from the memory a rooted sorrow," for razing "out the written troubles of the brain." Psychoanalysis is the method used by Freud and his followers to "cleanse . . . that perilous stuff which weighs upon the heart"—to provide insight into the

Psychoanalysis • Freud's method of psychotherapy.

Traditional Psychoanalysis. In traditional psychoanalysis, the analyst sits in a chair by the head of a couch while a client free-associates. The cardinal rule of free association is that no thought is to be censored.

conflicts presumed to lie at the roots of a person's problems. Insight involves a number of things: knowledge of the experiences that lead to conflicts and maladaptive behavior; identification and labeling of feelings and conflicts that lie below conscious awareness; and objective evaluation of one's beliefs and ideas, feelings, and overt behavior.

Psychoanalysis also seeks to allow the client to express emotions and impulses that are theorized to have been dammed up by the forces of repression. Freud was fond of saying, "Where id was, there shall ego be." In part, he meant that psychoanalysis could shed light on the inner workings of the mind. Freud did not believe that we ought to, or need to, become conscious of all of our conflicts and primitive impulses, however. Instead, he sought to replace impulsive and defensive behavior with coping behavior. He believed that impulsive behavior reflects the urges of the id. Defensive behavior such as timidly avoiding confrontations represents the ego's compromising efforts to protect the client from these impulses and the possibility of retaliation. Coping behavior would allow the client to partially express these impulses, but in socially acceptable ways. In so doing, the client would find gratification but avoid social and self-condemnation.

In this way, a man with a phobia for knives might discover he had been repressing the urge to harm someone who had taken advantage of him. He might also find ways to confront his antagonist verbally. A woman with a conversion disorder—for example, paralysis of the legs—could see that her disability allows her to avoid unwanted pregnancy without guilt. She might also realize her resentment at being pressed into a stereotypical feminine gender role and decide to expand her options.

Freud also believed that psychoanalysis allows the client to spill forth the psychic energy that was repressed by conflicts and guilt. He called this spilling forth **abreaction,** or **catharsis.** Abreaction would provide feelings of relief by alleviating some of the forces assaulting the ego.

FREE ASSOCIATION. Early in his career as a therapist, Freud found that hypnosis allowed his clients to focus on repressed conflicts and talk about them. The relaxed "trance state" provided by hypnosis seemed to allow clients to break through to topics of which they were otherwise unaware. Freud also found that many clients denied the accuracy of this material once they were out of the trance, however. Other clients found these revelations to be premature and painful. Freud thus turned to **free association,** a more gradual method of breaking down the walls of defense that block insight into unconscious processes.

In free association, the client is made comfortable, as by lying on a couch, and is asked to talk about any topic that comes to mind. No thought is to be censored—that is the cardinal rule. Psychoanalysts ask their clients to wander "freely" from topic to topic, but they do not believe that the process *within* the client is fully free. Repressed impulses press for release. A client may begin to free associate with meaningless topics, but pertinent repressed material may eventually surface.

The ego persists in trying to repress unacceptable impulses and threatening conflicts. As a result, clients might show **resistance** to recalling and discussing threatening ideas. Clients might claim "My mind is blank" when they are about to entertain such thoughts. They might accuse the analyst of being demanding or inconsiderate. They might "forget" their appointment when threatening material is due to be uncovered.

The therapist observes the dynamic struggle between the compulsion to utter and resistance. Through discreet remarks, the analyst subtly tips the balance

Abreaction • (AB-ree-ACK-shun). In psychoanalysis, expression of previously repressed feelings and impulses to allow the psychic energy associated with them to spill forth.

Catharsis • (cuh-THAR-sis). Another term for *abreaction.*

Free association • In psychoanalysis, the uncensored uttering of all thoughts that come to mind.

Resistance • The tendency to block the free expression of impulses and primitive ideas—a reflection of the defense mechanism of repression.

in favor of uttering. A gradual process of self-discovery and self-insight ensues. Now and then, the analyst offers an **interpretation** of an utterance, showing how it suggests resistance or deep-seated feelings and conflicts.

DREAM ANALYSIS.

Sometimes a cigar is just a cigar.
SIGMUND FREUD, ON DREAM ANALYSIS

Freud often had clients jot down their dreams upon waking so that they could be discussed in therapy. Freud considered dreams the "royal road to the unconscious." He believed that dreams were determined by unconscious processes as well as by the events of the day. Unconscious impulses tend to be expressed in dreams as a form of **wish fulfillment.**

But unacceptable sexual and aggressive impulses are likely to be displaced onto objects and situations that reflect the client's era and culture. These objects become symbols of the unconscious wishes. For example, long, narrow dream objects might be **phallic symbols,** but whether the symbol takes the form of a spear, rifle, stick shift, or spacecraft partially reflects one's cultural background.

In psychodynamic theory, the perceived content of the dream is called its shown or **manifest content.** Its presumed hidden or symbolic content is referred to as its **latent content.** A man might dream that he is flying. Flying is the manifest content of the dream. Freud usually interpreted flying as being symbolic of erection, so issues concerning sexual potency might make up the latent content of such a dream.

Truth or Fiction Revisited. *It is true that some psychotherapists interpret clients' dreams.* Psychoanalysis is a case in point. Despite his interest in possible dream symbols, even Freud allowed that "Sometimes a cigar is just a cigar."

Psychoanalysis saw its heyday in the 1950s (Hale, 1995). Since then, its influence and adherents have declined. One reason is that intellectuals and the public fell too quickly and too deeply in love with psychoanalysis (Robinson, 1993). Thus there is a rebound. Other forces that contributed to the decline of psychoanalysis include the rise of the women's movement, which, as we see later in the chapter, has found psychoanalysis to be degrading to women.

Modern Psychodynamic Approaches

Some psychoanalysts adhere faithfully to Freud's protracted techniques. They continue to practice traditional psychoanalysis. In recent years, however, briefer, less intense forms of psychodynamic therapy have been devised (Hale, 1995; Strupp, 1992). These methods are "psychoanalytically oriented." They make treatment available to clients who do not have the time or money for protracted therapy (Strupp, 1992). Also, frankly, many of these therapists believe that protracted therapy is not needed or justifiable in terms of the ratio of cost to benefits.

Truth or Fiction Revisited. *It is not true that psychotherapy must continue for months, perhaps years, to be of help.* There are many effective brief forms of psychotherapy.

Although some modern psychodynamic therapies continue to focus on revealing unconscious material and on breaking through psychological defenses or resistance, there are a number of differences from traditional psychoanalysis. One is that client and therapist usually sit face to face, as opposed to

---

Interpretation • An explanation of a client's utterance according to psychoanalytic theory.

Wish fulfillment • A primitive method used by the id to attempt to gratify basic instincts.

Phallic symbol • A sign that represents the penis.

Manifest content • In psychodynamic theory, the reported content of dreams.

Latent content • In psychodynamic theory, the symbolized or underlying content of dreams.

the client's reclining on a couch. The therapist is usually more directive than the traditional psychoanalyst. Modern therapists often suggest productive behavior instead of focusing solely on self-insight. Finally, there is usually more focus on the ego as the "executive" of personality. Accordingly, there is less emphasis on the role of the id. For this reason, many modern psychodynamic therapists are considered **ego analysts.**

Many of Freud's followers, the "second generation" of psychoanalysts—from Jung and Adler to Horney and Erikson—believed that Freud had placed too much emphasis on sexual and aggressive impulses and underestimated the importance of the ego. Freud, for example, aimed to establish conditions under which clients could spill forth psychic energy and eventually shore up the position of the ego. Erikson, in contrast, spoke to clients directly about their values and concerns and encouraged them to consciously fashion desired traits and behavior patterns. Freud saw clients as victims of the past and doubted their ability to overcome childhood trauma. Karen Horney, on the other hand, deemed clients capable of overcoming early abuse and deprivation through self-understanding and adult relationships (Quinn, 1987). Even Freud's daughter, the psychoanalyst Anna Freud (1895–1982), was more concerned with the ego than with unconscious forces and conflicts.

Today, there are many psychodynamic therapies. Many approaches show the influence of Sigmund Freud. As a group they continue to use terms such as *conflict* and *ego*. They differ in the prominence they ascribe to unconscious forces and in their perception of the role of the ego.

Reflections

- Did you have a picture of psychoanalysis in your mind before reading this section? What was it like? Did it differ from the information presented in this chapter?
- Does it make you or other people you know feel good to talk with someone about your problems? Are there some thoughts or experiences you are unwilling to talk about or share with others? How do you think a psychoanalyst would respond if you brought them up? Why?

Ego analyst • A psychodynamically oriented therapist who focuses on the conscious, coping behavior of the ego instead of the hypothesized, unconscious functioning of the id.

WORLD OF DIVERSITY

WOMEN AND PSYCHOTHERAPY

Why discuss women and psychotherapy? Don't psychotherapy and the theories on which therapy is based apply to both genders? They do. But the most prominent form of therapy in the 20th century—psychoanalysis—set forth a view of women that has reinforced male dominance and the view that a woman's place is in the home (Robinson, 1993).

Traditional psychoanalysis professes that it is normal for little girls to experience penis envy. However, proper resolution of the Oedipus complex results in women's (unconsciously) replacing the desire for a penis of their own with the desire to bear children. Well-adjusted women, according to the theory, accept the authority of their husbands and wish to remain in the home and rear children. This degrading view of women has been attacked as groundless not only by critics of psychoanalysis, but also by modern-day ego analysts such as Karen Horney (Robinson, 1993).

Truth or Fiction Revisited. *It is not true that well-adjusted women wish to remain in the home and rear children.* This traditional psychodynamic view has not found empirical support and has been fiercely attacked by critics.

Social critics have attacked traditional psychodynamic theory as one more cultural ideology that subjugates women (Lerman & Porter, 1990; Greene, 1993; Robinson, 1993). For example, women who act assertively have often been perceived by traditional psychoanalysts as manifesting unresolved penis envy. Assertive men were viewed as appropriately masculinized. A more enlightened approach to therapy emerged as a response not only to psychoanalysis but also to male dominance of the mental health professions.

Psychoanalysts have a tendency to interpret clients' expressions of anger and indignation as *transference*—that is, as signs of maladjustment and reactions to historic events and figures in their lives. However, women have had ample cause to be angry toward, and suspicious of, male therapists. Anger is, after all, an appropriate response to prejudice and discrimination. Only 40 to 50 years ago most therapists considered women who chose to work as maladjusted.

Most contemporary therapists are guided by the goal of raising awareness of the harmful effects of discrimination against, and harassment of, women on the job, of placement of men in positions of dominance over women, and of treatment of women as sex objects.

The Case of Women and Depression. Sociocultural theorists note that social inequality, rather than individual psychopathology, creates and maintains many of the problems presented in psychotherapy. This is particularly so when

HUMANISTIC–EXISTENTIAL THERAPIES: TOWARD AUTHENTIC LIVING

Psychodynamic therapies focus on internal conflicts and unconscious processes. Humanistic–existential therapies focus on the quality of clients' subjective, conscious experience. Psychodynamic therapies tend to focus on the past, and particularly on early childhood experiences. Humanistic–existential therapies usually focus on what clients are experiencing today—on "the here and now."

These differences are frequently ones of *emphasis,* however. The past has a way of influencing current thoughts, feelings, and behavior. Carl Rogers, the originator of person-centered therapy, believed that childhood experiences gave rise to the conditions of worth that troubled his clients here and now. Rogers and Fritz Perls, the originator of Gestalt therapy, recognized that early incorporation of other people's values often leads clients to "disown" parts of their own personalities.

Person-Centered Therapy: Removing Roadblocks to Self-Actualization

Person-centered therapy was originated by Carl Rogers (1951). Rogers believed that we are free to make choices and control our destinies, despite the burdens of the past.

clients are members of oppressed groups, such as women (Brown, 1992). For example, women are more likely than men to be depressed (Coryell and others, 1992; Weissman and others, 1991). A major survey of five U.S. communities showed that major depression affected 7% of the women surveyed during their lifetimes, as compared with 2.6% of the men (Weissman and others, 1991).

Some therapists, like many uneducated lay people, assume that biological gender differences largely explain why women are more likely to get depressed. How often do we hear degrading remarks such as "It must be that time of the month" when women express feelings of anger or irritation? Hormonal changes during the menstrual cycle and childbirth may contribute to depression in women (McGrath and others, 1990). However, a panel convened by the American Psychological Association attributed most of the difference to the greater stresses placed on women (McGrath and others, 1990). Women are more likely to encounter socioeconomic and sociocultural stressors such as physical and sexual abuse, poverty, single parenthood, and sexism. Women are also more likely than men to support others who are undergoing stress. In supporting others, they heap additional caregiving burdens on themselves (Shumaker & Hill, 1991). One panel member, Bonnie Strickland, expressed surprise that still more women are not clinically depressed, given that they are treated as second-class citizens.

A part of "therapy" for women, then, is to modify the overwhelming demands that are made of women in contemporary society (Comas-Diaz, 1994). The pain may lie in the individual, but the cause often lies in society.

Person-centered therapy • Carl Rogers's method of psychotherapy, which emphasizes the creation of a warm, therapeutic atmosphere that frees clients to engage in self-exploration and self-expression.

Rogers also believed that we have natural tendencies toward health, growth, and fulfillment. Given this view, Rogers wrote that psychological problems arise from roadblocks placed in the path of our own self-actualization. Because others show us selective approval when we are young, we learn to disown the disapproved parts of ourselves. We don masks and facades to earn

Person-Centered Therapy. By showing the qualities of unconditional positive regard, empathic understanding, genuineness, and congruence, person-centered therapists create an atmosphere in which clients can explore their feelings.

social approval. We may learn to be seen but not heard—not even heard, or examined fully, by ourselves. As a result, we might experience stress and discomfort and the feeling that we—or the world—are not real.

Person-centered therapy aims to provide insight into the parts of us that we have disowned so that we can feel whole and head toward authentic living. It stresses the importance of a warm, therapeutic atmosphere that encourages client self-exploration and self-expression. Therapist acceptance of the client is thought to foster client self-acceptance and self-esteem. Self-acceptance frees the client to make choices that develop his or her unique potential.

Person-centered therapy is nondirective. The client takes the lead, listing and exploring problems. The therapist reflects or paraphrases expressed feelings and ideas, helping the client get in touch with deeper feelings and follow the strongest leads in the quest for self-insight.

Truth or Fiction Revisited. *It is true that some psychotherapists encourage their clients to take the lead in the therapy session.* Person-centered therapists provide an example.

Person-centered therapy is practiced widely in college and university counseling centers, not just to help students experiencing, say, anxieties or depression but also to help them make decisions. Many college students have not yet made career choices or wonder whether they should become involved with particular people or in sexual activity. Person-centered therapists provide an encouraging atmosphere in which clients can verbally explore choices and make decisions. Person-centered therapists do not tell clients what to do. Instead, they help clients arrive at their own decisions.

The effective person-centered therapist also shows four qualities: unconditional positive regard, empathic understanding, genuineness, and congruence. **Unconditional positive regard** is respect for clients as important human beings with unique values and goals. Clients are provided with a sense of security that encourages them to follow their own feelings. Psychoanalysts might hesitate to encourage clients to freely express their impulses because of the fear that primitive forces might be unleashed. Person-centered therapists believe that people are basically *pro*social, however. If people follow their own feelings, rather than act defensively, they should not be abusive or *anti*social.

Empathic understanding is shown by accurately reflecting the client's experiences and feelings. Therapists try to view the world through their clients' **frames of reference** by setting aside their own values and listening closely.

Psychoanalysts are trained to be opaque. Person-centered therapists are trained to show **genuineness.** Person-centered therapists are open about their feelings. It would be harmful to clients if their therapists could not truly accept and like them, even though their values might differ from those of the therapists. Rogers admitted that he sometimes had negative feelings about clients, usually boredom. He usually expressed these feelings rather than hold them in (Bennett, 1985). Person-centered therapists must also be able to tolerate differentness, because they believe that every client is different in important ways.

Person-centered therapists also try to show **congruence,** or a fit between their thoughts, feelings, and behavior. Person-centered therapists serve as models of integrity to their clients.

Transactional Analysis: I'm OK—You're OK—We're All OK

Transactional analysis (TA) is also rooted in the psychodynamic tradition. According to Thomas Harris, author of *I'm OK—You're OK* (1967), many of us

---

Unconditional positive regard • Acceptance of the value of another person, although not necessarily acceptance of everything the person does.

Empathic understanding • (em-PATH-ick). Ability to perceive a client's feelings from the client's frame of reference. A quality of the good person-centered therapist.

Frame of reference • One's unique patterning of perceptions and attitudes, according to which one evaluates events.

Genuineness • Recognition and open expression of the therapist's own feelings.

Congruence • (con-GREW-ants). A fit between one's self-concept and behaviors, thoughts, and emotions.

Transactional analysis • A form of psychotherapy that deals with how people interact and how their interactions reinforce attitudes, expectations, and "life positions." Abbreviated *TA*.

have inferiority complexes of the sort described by the psychoanalyst Alfred Adler. Even though we have become adults, we might continue to see ourselves as dependent children. We might think other people are OK but not see ourselves as being OK.

Within TA, *I'm not OK—You're OK* is one of four basic "life positions," or ways of perceiving relationships with others. A major goal of TA is to help people adopt the life position *I'm OK—You're OK,* in which they accept others and themselves. Unfortunately, people tend to adopt "games," or styles of relating to others, that are designed to confirm one of the unhealthy life positions: I'm OK—You're not OK, I'm not OK—You're OK, or I'm not OK—You're not OK.

Psychiatrist Eric Berne (1976), the originator of TA, described our personalities as containing three "ego states": **Parent, Child,** and **Adult.** The "parent" is a moralistic ego state. The "child" is an irresponsible and emotional ego state. The "adult" is a rational ego state. It is easy to confuse the child ego state with the id, the adult ego state with the ego, and the parent ego state with the superego. But note that these are three hypothesized ego states, or ways of coping. The id is unconscious and so is some of the functioning of the superego. In TA, however, we can be fully conscious of the child and parent ego states.

Many interpersonal troubles occur because people tend to relate to each other as parents, children, or adults. A social exchange between two people is called a **transaction**. A transaction is said to fit, or be **complementary,** when a social exchange follows the same lines. In one type of complementary transaction, people relate as adults. A transaction can also be complementary, even if it is upsetting, when two people relate as parent and child (Parent: "You shouldn't have done that"; Child: "I'm sorry; I promise it won't happen again"). Communication breaks down when the social exchange between the parties does not follow complementary lines (as in Figure 14.1).

NATALIE (adult to adult): Did you have a good time tonight?
HAL (child to parent): Why do you wanna know?

Or:

BILL (adult to adult): Nan, did you see the checkbook?
NAN (parent to child): A place for everything and everything in its place!

TA is often carried out with couples who complain of communication problems. It encourages people to relate to each other as adults.

Gestalt Therapy: Getting It Together

Gestalt therapy was originated by Fritz Perls (1893–1970). Gestalt therapy, like person-centered therapy, aims to help individuals integrate conflicting parts of the personality. Perls used the term *Gestalt* to signify his interest in providing the conflicting parts of the personality an integrated form or shape. He aimed to have his clients become aware of inner conflict, accept the reality of conflict rather than deny it or keep it repressed, and make productive choices despite misgivings and fear.

Although Perls's ideas about conflicting personality elements owe much to psychodynamic theory, his form of therapy, unlike psychoanalysis, focuses on the here and now. In Gestalt therapy, clients undergo exercises to heighten awareness of current feelings and behavior rather than explore the past. Perls also believed, along with Carl Rogers, that people are free to make choices

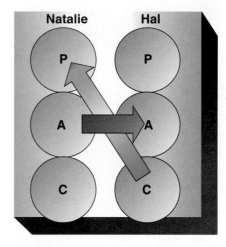

FIGURE 14.1

A Crossed Transaction. Transactions are social exchanges. "Crossed" transactions hamper communication. In this crossed transaction, Natalie asks Hal, "Did you have a good time tonight?" Hal replies, "Why do you wanna know?" Thus communication is broken off.

Parent • In TA, a moralistic ego state.
Child • In TA, an irresponsible, emotional ego state.
Adult • In TA, a rational, adaptive ego state.
Transaction • In TA, an exchange between two people.
Complementary • In TA, descriptive of a transaction in which the ego states of two people interact harmoniously.
Gestalt therapy • Fritz Perls's form of psychotherapy, which attempts to integrate conflicting parts of the personality through directive methods designed to help clients perceive their whole selves.

and to direct their personal growth. Unlike person-centered therapy, however, Gestalt therapy is highly directive. The therapist leads the client through planned experiences.

One Gestalt technique that increases awareness of internal conflict is the **dialogue.** Clients undertake verbal confrontations between opposing wishes and ideas. An example of these clashing personality elements is "top dog" and "underdog." One's top dog might conservatively suggest, "Don't take chances. Stick with what you have or you might lose it all." One's frustrated underdog might then rise up and assert, "You never try anything. How will you ever get out of this rut if you don't take on new challenges?" Heightened awareness of the elements of conflict can clear the path toward resolution, perhaps through compromise.

Body language also provides insight into conflicting feelings. Clients might be instructed to attend to the ways in which they furrow their eyebrows and tense their facial muscles when they express ideas that they think they support. In this way, they often find that their body language asserts feelings that they have been denying.

To increase clients' understanding of opposing points of view, Gestalt therapists might encourage them to argue in favor of ideas opposed to their own. They might also have clients role-play people who are important to them to become more in touch with their points of view.

Psychodynamic theory views dreams as the "royal road to the unconscious." Perls saw the stuff of dreams as disowned parts of the personality. Perls would often ask clients to role-play the elements in their dreams to get in touch with these parts. In *Gestalt Therapy Verbatim,* Perls—known to clients and friends alike as Fritz—describes a session in which a client, Jim, is reporting a dream:

> JIM: I just have the typical recurring dream which I think a lot of people might have if they have a background problem, and it isn't of anything I think I can act out. It's the distant wheel—I'm not sure what type it is—it's coming towards me and ever-increasing in size. And then finally, it's just above me and it's no height that I can determine, it's so high. And that's—
>
> FRITZ: If you were this wheel, . . . what would you do with Jim?
>
> JIM: I am just about to roll over Jim. (Perls, 1971, p. 127)

Perls encourages Jim to undertake a dialogue with the wheel. Jim comes to see that the wheel represents fears about taking decisive action. Through this insight, the "wheel" becomes more manageable in size, and Jim is able to use some of the "energy" that he might otherwise have spent in worrying to begin taking charge of his life.

Dialogue • A Gestalt therapy technique in which clients verbalize confrontations between conflicting parts of their personality.

Reflections

- How would you feel if you went for help and your therapist followed your lead rather than offered concrete advice? Why?
- Have you experienced unconditional positive regard or conditional positive regard in your home life? How do you think your experiences have shaped your self-esteem?
- Do you believe that you are "OK"? Why or why not?
- Do you feel that parts of your personality pull you in different directions? If so, how?

Let us now turn our attention to another group of therapies that are concerned with subjective experience and the here and now—cognitive therapies. Humanistic–existential therapists tend to focus on clients' personalities. However, cognitive therapists tend to focus on mental processes such as thoughts, strategies for interpreting experience, plans, problem-solving techniques, and attitudes—especially self-defeating attitudes.

COGNITIVE THERAPIES: "THINKING MAKES IT SO"

There is nothing either good or bad, but thinking makes it so.
SHAKESPEARE, *HAMLET*

In this line from *Hamlet,* Shakespeare did not mean to suggest that injuries and misfortunes are painless or easy to manage. Rather, he meant that our cognitive appraisals of unfortunate circumstances can heighten our discomfort and impair our coping ability. In so doing, Shakespeare was providing a kind of motto for cognitive therapists.

Although there are many cognitively oriented therapists and more than one type of **cognitive therapy,** cognitive therapists would generally agree with Carl Rogers that people are free to make choices and develop in accord with their concepts of what they are capable of being. Cognitive therapists would also agree with Fritz Perls that it is appropriate for clients to focus on the here and now. Cognitive therapists, like Perls, are also reasonably directive in their approaches.

Cognitive therapists focus on the beliefs, attitudes, and automatic types of thinking that create and compound their clients' problems (Beck, 1993; Ellis, 1993). Cognitive therapists, like psychodynamic and humanistic–existential therapists, are interested in fostering client self-insight. However, they aim to heighten clients' insight into *current cognitions* as well as those of the past (Jones & Pulos, 1993). Cognitive therapists also aim to directly *change* maladaptive cognitions to reduce negative feelings, provide a more realistic view of the world, and help clients solve problems.

Let us look at the approaches of the cognitive therapists Albert Ellis and Aaron Beck.

Cognitive therapy • A form of therapy that focuses on how clients' cognitions (expectations, attitudes, beliefs, etc.) lead to distress and may be modified to relieve distress and promote adaptive behavior.

Rational-emotive therapy • Albert Ellis's form of cognitive psychotherapy, which focuses on how irrational expectations create anxiety and disappointment and which encourages clients to challenge and correct these expectations.

Rational-Emotive Therapy: Overcoming "Musts" and "Shoulds"

Albert Ellis (1977, 1993), the founder of **rational-emotive therapy,** points out that our beliefs about events, as well as the events themselves, shape our responses to them. Moreover, many of us harbor a number of irrational beliefs that can give rise to problems or magnify their impact. Two of the most important ones are the belief that you must have the love and approval of people who are important to you and the belief that you must prove yourself to be thoroughly competent, adequate, and achieving. (Others are elaborated in Chapter 15.)

Ellis's methods are active and directive. He does not sit back like the traditional psychoanalyst and occasionally offer an interpretation. Instead, he urges clients to seek out their irrational beliefs, which can be hard to pinpoint. He then shows clients how their beliefs lead to misery and challenges them to change their beliefs. According to Ellis, we need less misery and less blaming but more action.

Cognitive Therapy: Correcting Cognitive Errors

Psychiatrist Aaron Beck (1991, 1993) also focuses on clients' cognitive distortions. He questions them in a manner that encourages them to see the irrationality of their own ways of thinking—how, for example, their minimizing of their accomplishments and their pessimistic assumptions that the worst will happen heighten feelings of depression. Beck, like Ellis, notes that our cognitive distortions can be fleeting and automatic, difficult to detect. His therapy methods help clients pin them down and challenge them.

Beck notes in particular the pervasive influence of four basic types of cognitive errors that contribute to clients' miseries:

1. Clients may *selectively perceive* the world as a harmful place and ignore evidence to the contrary.

2. Clients may *overgeneralize* on the basis of a few examples. For example, they may perceive themselves as worthless because they were laid off at work or as grossly unattractive because they were refused a request for a date.

3. Clients may *magnify,* or blow out of proportion, the importance of negative events. As noted in the discussion of Ellis's views, clients may catastrophize flunking a test by assuming they will flunk out of college or catastrophize losing a job by believing that they will never work again and that serious harm will befall their families.

4. Clients may engage in *absolutist thinking,* or looking at the world in black and white rather than in shades of gray. In doing so, a rejection on a date takes on the meaning of a lifetime of loneliness; a discomforting illness takes on life-threatening proportions.

The concept of pinpointing and modifying errors may become clearer from reading an excerpt from a case in which a 53-year-old engineer obtained cognitive therapy for severe depression. The engineer had left his job and become inactive. As reported by Beck and his colleagues, the first treatment goal was to foster physical activity—even things like raking leaves and preparing dinner—because activity is incompatible with depression. Then:

> [The engineer's] cognitive distortions were identified by comparing his assessment of each activity with that of his wife. Alternative ways of interpreting his experiences were then considered.
>
> In comparing his wife's résumé of his past experiences, he became aware that he had (1) undervalued his past by failing to mention many previous accomplishments, (2) regarded himself as far more responsible for his "failures" than she did, and (3) concluded that he was worthless since he had not succeeded in attaining certain goals in the past. When the two accounts were contrasted, he could discern many of his cognitive distortions. In subsequent sessions, his wife continued to serve as an "objectifier."
>
> In midtherapy, [he] compiled a list of new attitudes that he had acquired since initiating therapy. These included:
>
> 1. "I am starting at a lower level of functioning at my job, but it will improve if I persist."
> 2. "I know that once I get going in the morning, everything will run all right for the rest of the day."
> 3. "I can't achieve everything at once."
> 4. "I have my periods of ups and downs, but in the long run I feel better."

5. "My expectations from my job and life should be scaled down to a realistic level."
6. "Giving in to avoidance [e.g., staying away from work and social interactions] never helps and only leads to further avoidance."

He was instructed to re-read this list daily for several weeks even though he already knew the content. (Rush and others, 1975)

Rereading the list of productive attitudes is a variation of the cognitive technique of having clients rehearse or repeat rational ideas so that they come to replace cognitive distortions and irrational beliefs. The engineer gradually became less depressed in therapy and returned to work and an active social life. Along the way, he learned to combat inappropriate self-blame for problems, perfectionistic expectations, magnifications of failures, and overgeneralizations from failures.

Becoming aware of cognitive errors and modifying catastrophizing thoughts help us cope with stress. Internal, stable, and global attributions of failure lead to depression and feelings of helplessness. Cognitive therapists also alert clients to cognitive errors such as these so that the clients can change their attitudes and pave the way for more effective behavior.

Many theorists consider cognitive therapy to be a collection of techniques that belong within the province of behavior therapy, which is discussed in the following section. Some members of this group prefer the name "cognitive *behavior* therapy." Others argue that the term *behavior therapy* is broad enough to include cognitive techniques. Many cognitive therapists and behavior therapists differ in focus, however. Behavior therapists deal with client cognitions to change behavior. Cognitive therapists also see the value of tying treatment outcomes to behavior, but they assert that cognitive change is itself a key goal.

Behavior therapy • Systematic application of the principles of learning to the direct modification of a client's problem behaviors.

Reflections

- Do you believe that you must have the love and approval of people who are important to you? (How do you think you can know if you do?) If so, does this belief ever give rise to feelings of frustration, anxiety, or depression in you?
- Do you believe that you must prove yourself to be thoroughly competent, adequate, and achieving? (How do you think you can know if you do?) If so, does this belief ever give rise to feelings of frustration, anxiety, or depression in you?
- Do you ever engage in any of Beck's cognitive errors? For example, do you magnify the importance of negative events? (Here we go again: How do you think you can know if you do?) If so, does this belief ever give rise to feelings of frustration, anxiety, or depression in you?

BEHAVIOR THERAPY: ADJUSTMENT IS WHAT YOU DO

Behavior therapy—also called *behavior modification*—is the direct promotion of desired behavioral change by means of systematic application of principles of learning. Many behavior therapists incorporate cognitive processes in their theoretical outlook and cognitive procedures in their methodology (Meichenbaum, 1993). For example, techniques such as systematic desensitization, covert sensitization, and covert reinforcement ask clients to focus on visual imagery. Behavioral methods for treating bulimia nervosa focus on clients' irrational attitudes toward their weight and body shape as well as foster healthful eating habits (Wilson & Fairburn, 1993).

Behavior therapists rely heavily on principles of conditioning and observational learning. They help clients discontinue self-defeating behavior patterns such as overeating, smoking, and phobic avoidance of harmless stimuli. They also help clients acquire adaptive behavior patterns such as the social skills required to start social relationships and to say no to insistent salespeople.

Behavior therapists may help clients gain "insight" into maladaptive behavior in the sense of fostering awareness of the circumstances in which it occurs. They do not foster insight in the psychoanalytic sense of unearthing the childhood origins of problems and the symbolic meanings of maladaptive behavior. Behavior therapists, like other therapists, may also build warm, therapeutic relationships with clients, but they see the efficacy of behavior therapy as deriving from specific, learning-based procedures (Wolpe, 1990). Behavior therapists insist that their methods be established by experimentation (Wolpe, 1990) and that therapeutic outcomes be assessed in terms of observable, measurable behavior.

Let us consider some behavior-therapy techniques.

Fear-Reduction Methods

Behavior therapists use many methods for reducing fears, including flooding (see Chapter 6), systematic desensitization, and modeling.

SYSTEMATIC DESENSITIZATION.

> Adam has a phobia for receiving injections. His behavior therapist treats him as he reclines in a comfortable padded chair. In a state of deep muscle relaxation, Adam observes slides projected on a screen. A slide of a nurse holding a needle has just been shown three times, 30 seconds at a time. Each time Adam has shown no anxiety. So now a slightly more discomforting slide is shown: one of the nurse aiming the needle toward someone's bare arm. After 15 seconds, our armchair adventurer notices twinges of discomfort and raises a finger as a signal (speaking might disturb his relaxation). The projector operator turns off the light, and Adam spends 2 minutes imagining his "safe scene"—lying on a beach beneath the tropical sun. Then the slide is shown again. This time Adam views it for 30 seconds before feeling anxiety.

Adam is undergoing **systematic desensitization,** a method for reducing phobic responses originated by psychiatrist Joseph Wolpe (1990). Systematic desensitization is a gradual process. Clients learn to handle increasingly disturbing stimuli while anxiety to each one is being counterconditioned. About 10 to 20 stimuli are arranged in a sequence, or **hierarchy,** according to their capacity to elicit anxiety. In imagination or by being shown photos, the client travels gradually up through this hierarchy, approaching the target behavior. In Adam's case, the target behavior was the ability to obtain an injection without undue anxiety.

Wolpe developed systematic desensitization on the assumption that maladaptive anxiety responses, like other behaviors, are learned or conditioned. He reasoned that they can be unlearned by counterconditioning or by extinction. In counterconditioning, a response that is incompatible with anxiety is made to appear under conditions that usually elicit anxiety. Muscle relaxation is incompatible with anxiety. For this reason, Adam's therapist is teaching Adam to experience relaxation in the presence of (usually) anxiety-evoking slides of needles. (Muscle relaxation is usually achieved by means of

Systematic desensitization • Wolpe's method for reducing fears by associating a hierarchy of images of fear-evoking stimuli with deep muscle relaxation.

Hierarchy • An arrangement of stimuli according to the amount of fear they evoke.

Overcoming Fear of Flying. This woman has undergone group systematic desensitization in order to overcome her fear of flying. For several sessions, she engaged in tasks such as viewing pictures of airplanes and imagining herself in one. Now in the final stages of her program, she actually flies in an airplane with the support of group members and her therapist.

FIGURE 14.2

Modeling. Modeling is a behavior-therapy technique that is based on principles of observational learning. In these photos, people with a fear of snakes observe, then imitate, models who are unafraid. Parents often try to convince children that something tastes good by eating it before them and saying "Mmm!"

progressive relaxation, which we describe in Chapter 15 as a method for lowering the arousal that attends anxiety reactions.)

Remaining in the presence of phobic imagery, rather than running from it, is also likely to enhance our self-efficacy expectations (Galassi, 1988). Self-efficacy expectations are negatively correlated with levels of adrenaline in the bloodstream (Bandura and others, 1985). Raising clients' self-efficacy expectations may thus help lower their adrenaline levels, counteract feelings of nervousness, and lessen the physical signs of anxiety.

Truth or Fiction Revisited. *It is true that lying around in your reclining chair and fantasizing can be an effective way of confronting your fears.* This description is consistent with the method of systematic desensitization.

MODELING. **Modeling** relies on observational learning. In this method, clients observe, then imitate, people who approach and cope with the objects or situations the clients fear. Bandura and his colleagues (1969) found that modeling worked as well as systematic desensitization—and more rapidly—in reducing fear of snakes (see Figure 14.2). Modeling also is likely to increase self-efficacy expectations in coping with feared stimuli.

**MINILECTURE:
TREATING MALADAPTIVE
VOMITING**

Modeling • A behavior-therapy technique in which a client observes and imitates a person who approaches and copes with feared objects or situations.

Aversive Conditioning. In aversive conditioning, unwanted behaviors take on a noxious quality as a result of pairing them repeatedly with aversive stimuli. Overexposure is making cigarette smoke aversive to the smoker in this photograph.

Aversive conditioning • A behavior-therapy technique in which undesired responses are inhibited by pairing repugnant or offensive stimuli with them.

Rapid smoking • An aversive-conditioning technique for quitting smoking in which the would-be quitter inhales frequently, thus rendering once-desirable cigarette smoke aversive.

Aversive Conditioning

Aversive conditioning is one of the more controversial procedures in behavior therapy. In aversive conditioning, painful or aversive stimuli are paired with unwanted impulses, such as desire for a cigarette or desire to engage in antisocial behavior, to make the goal less appealing. For example, to help people control alcohol intake, tastes of different alcoholic beverages can be paired with drug-induced nausea and vomiting or with electric shock.

Aversive conditioning has been used with problems as divergent as cigarette smoking (Lichtenstein & Glasgow, 1992), sexual abuse (Rice and others, 1991), and retarded children's self-injurious behavior. **Rapid smoking** is an aversive-conditioning method designed to help smokers quit. In this method, the would-be quitter inhales every 6 seconds. In another aversive-conditioning method for quitting smoking, the hose of an everyday hair dryer is hooked up to a chamber with several lit cigarettes. Smoke is blown into the quitter's face as he or she also smokes a cigarette. In a third, branching pipes are used so that the smoker draws in smoke from two or more cigarettes simultaneously. In all of these methods, overexposure renders once-desirable cigarette smoke aversive. The quitter becomes motivated to avoid, rather than seek, cigarettes and stops smoking on a preplanned date. Many reports have shown a quit rate of 60% or higher at 6-month follow-ups. Yet interest in these methods for quitting smoking has waned because of side effects such as raising the blood pressure and decreasing the blood's capacity to carry oxygen.

Truth or Fiction Revisited. *It is true that smoking cigarettes can be an effective treatment for helping people to stop smoking cigarettes.* The trick is to inhale enough smoke so that it is aversive rather than enjoyable.

In one study of aversive conditioning in the treatment of alcoholism, 63% of the 685 people treated remained abstinent for 1 year afterward, and about a third remained abstinent for at least 3 years (Wiens & Menustik, 1983). It may seem ironic that punitive aversive stimulation is sometimes used to stop children from punishing themselves, but people sometimes hurt themselves to obtain sympathy and attention from others. If self-injury leads to more pain than anticipated and no sympathy, it might be discontinued.

Operant Conditioning Procedures

We usually prefer to relate to people who smile at us rather than ignore us and to take courses in which we do well rather than fail. We tend to repeat behavior that is reinforced. Behavior that is not reinforced tends to become extinguished. Behavior therapists have used these principles of operant conditioning with people with psychotic disorders as well as those with milder problems.

The staff at one mental hospital was at a loss about how to encourage withdrawn people diagnosed with schizophrenia to eat regularly. Ayllon and Haughton (1962) observed that staff members were exacerbating the problem by coaxing people with schizophrenia into the dining room, even feeding them. Increased staff attention apparently reinforced their lack of cooperation. Some rules were changed. Individuals who did not arrive at the dining hall within 30 minutes after serving were locked out. Staff could not interact with diners at mealtime. With uncooperative behavior no longer reinforced, the hospital residents quickly changed their eating habits.

THE TOKEN ECONOMY.   Many psychiatric wards and hospitals now use **token economies** in which tokens such as poker chips must be used by residents to purchase TV viewing time, extra visits to the canteen, or private rooms. The tokens are reinforcements for productive activities such as making beds, brushing teeth, and socializing. Token economies have not eliminated all problems of people diagnosed with schizophrenia. However, they have enhanced these individuals' activity and cooperation. Tokens have also been used successfully in programs designed to modify the behavior of children with conduct disorders. For example, Schneider and Byrne (1987) gave children tokens for helpful behaviors such as volunteering and removed tokens for behaviors such as arguing and inattention.

SUCCESSIVE APPROXIMATIONS.   The operant conditioning method of **successive approximations** is often used to help clients build good habits. Let us use a (not uncommon!) example: You wish to study 3 hours an evening but can maintain concentration for only half an hour. Rather than attempting to increase study time all at once, you could do so gradually by, say, 5 minutes an evening. After every hour or so of studying, you could reinforce yourself with 5 minutes of people-watching in a busy section of the library.

SOCIAL-SKILLS TRAINING.   In social-skills training, behavior therapists decrease social anxiety and build social skills through operant-conditioning procedures that employ **self-monitoring,** coaching, modeling, role-playing, **behavior rehearsal,** and **feedback.** Social-skills training has been used to help former hospital residents maintain jobs and apartments in the community.

Social-skills training is effective in groups. Group members can role-play important people—such as parents, spouses, or potential dates—in the lives of other members. The trainee then can engage in behavior rehearsal with the role-player.

BIOFEEDBACK TRAINING.   Through **biofeedback training** (BFT), therapists help clients become more aware of, and gain control over, various bodily

---

Token economy • A controlled environment in which people are reinforced for desired behaviors with tokens (such as poker chips) that may be exchanged for privileges.

Successive approximations • In operant conditioning, a series of behaviors that gradually become more similar to a target behavior.

Self-monitoring • Keeping a record of one's own behavior to identify problems and record successes.

Behavior rehearsal • Practice.

Feedback • In assertiveness training, information about the effectiveness of a response.

Biofeedback training • The systematic feeding back to an organism information about a bodily function so that the organism can gain control of that function. Abbreviated *BFT*.

functions. Therapists attach clients to devices that measure bodily changes such as heart rate. "Bleeps" or other electronic signals are used to indicate (and thereby reinforce) bodily changes in the desired direction. (Knowledge of results is a powerful reinforcer.) The electromyograph (EMG), for example, monitors muscle tension. It has been used to augment control over muscle tension in the forehead and elsewhere, thereby alleviating anxiety and stress.

BFT also helps clients voluntarily regulate functions such as heart rate and blood pressure that were once thought to be beyond conscious control. Hypertensive clients use a blood-pressure cuff and electronic signals to gain control over their blood pressure. The electroencephalograph (EEG) monitors brain waves and can be used to teach people how to produce alpha waves, which are associated with relaxation. Some people have overcome insomnia by learning to produce brain waves associated with sleep.

Self-Control Methods

Do mysterious forces sometimes seem to be at work? Forces that delight in wreaking havoc on New Year's resolutions and other efforts to take charge of bad habits? Just when you go on a diet, that juicy pizza stares at you from the TV set. Just when you resolve to balance your budget, that sweater goes on sale. Behavior therapists have developed a number of self-control techniques to help people cope with such temptations.

FUNCTIONAL ANALYSIS OF BEHAVIOR. Behavior therapists usually begin with a **functional analysis** of the problem behavior. In this way, they help determine the stimuli that trigger problem behavior and the reinforcers that maintain it. You can use a diary to jot down each instance of a problem behavior. Note the time of day, location, your activity (including your thoughts and feelings), and reactions (yours and others'). Functional analysis serves a number of purposes. It makes you more aware of the environmental context of your behavior and can boost your motivation to change.

Truth or Fiction Revisited. *It is true that you might be able to gain control over bad habits merely by keeping a record of where and when you practice them.* The record may help motivate you, make you more aware of the problems, and suggest strategies for behavior change.

Brian used functional analysis to master his nail biting. Table 14.2 shows a few items from his notebook. He discovered that boredom and humdrum activities seemed to serve as triggers for nail biting. He began to watch out for feelings of boredom as signs to practice self-control. He also made some changes in his life so that he would feel bored less often.

Self-control strategies can be aimed at (1) the stimuli that trigger behavior, (2) the behaviors themselves, and (3) reinforcers.

STRATEGIES AIMED AT STIMULI THAT TRIGGER BEHAVIOR.

Restriction of the stimulus field. Gradually exclude the problem behavior from more environments. For example, at first make smoking off limits in the car, then in the office.

Avoidance of powerful stimuli that trigger habits. Avoid obvious sources of temptation. People who go window-shopping often wind up buying more than windows. If eating at The Pizza Glutton tempts you to forget your diet, eat at home or at The Celery Stalk instead.

Functional analysis • A systematic study of behavior in which one identifies the stimuli that trigger problem behavior and the reinforcers that maintain it.

TABLE 14.2
EXCERPTS FROM BRIAN'S DIARY OF NAIL BITING FOR APRIL 14

INCIDENT	TIME	LOCATION	ACTIVITY (THOUGHTS, FEELINGS)	REACTIONS
1	7:45 A.M.	Freeway	Driving to work, bored, not thinking	Finger bleeds, pain
2	10:30 A.M.	Office	Writing report	Self-disgust
3	2:25 P.M.	Conference	Listening to dull financial report	Embarrassment
4	6:40 P.M.	Living room	Watching evening news	Self-disgust

A functional analysis of problem behavior like nail biting increases awareness of the environmental context in which it occurs, spurs motivation to change, and, in highly motivated people, might lead to significant behavioral change.

Stimulus control. Place yourself in an environment in which desirable behavior is likely to occur. Maybe it's difficult to lift your mood directly at times, but you can place yourself in the audience of that uplifting concert or film. It might be difficult to force yourself to study, but how about rewarding yourself for spending time in the library?

STRATEGIES AIMED AT BEHAVIOR.

Response prevention. Make unwanted behavior difficult or impossible. Impulse buying is curbed when you shred your credit cards, leave your checkbook home, and carry only a couple of dollars. You can't reach for the strawberry cream cheese pie in your refrigerator if you have left it at the supermarket (that is, have not bought it).

Competing responses. Engage in behaviors that are incompatible with the bad habits. It is difficult to drink a glass of water and a fattening milk shake simultaneously. Grasping something firmly is a useful competing response for nail biting or scratching.

Chain breaking. Interfere with unwanted habitual behavior by complicating the process of engaging in it. Break the chain of reaching for a readily available cigarette and placing it in your mouth by wrapping the pack in aluminum foil and placing it on the top shelf in the closet. Rewrap the pack after taking one. Put your cigarette in the ashtray between puffs, or put your fork down between mouthfuls of dessert. Ask yourself if you really want more.

Successive approximations. Gradually approach targets through a series of relatively painless steps. Increase studying by only 5 minutes a day. Decrease smoking by pausing for a minute when the cigarette is smoked halfway, or by putting it out a minute before you would wind up eating the filter. Decrease your daily intake of food by 50 to 100 calories every couple of days, or cut out one type of fattening food every few days.

STRATEGIES AIMED AT REINFORCEMENTS.

Reinforcement of desired behavior. Why give yourself something for nothing? Make pleasant activities such as going to films, walking on the beach, or reading a new novel contingent upon meeting reasonable, daily behavioral goals. Put one dollar away toward that camera or vacation trip each day you remain within your calorie limit.

Response cost. Heighten awareness of the long-term reasons for dieting or cutting down on smoking by punishing yourself for not meeting a daily goal or for practicing a bad habit. Make out a check to your most hated cause and mail it at once if you bite your nails or inhale that cheesecake.

"Grandma's method." Remember Grandma's method for inducing children to eat their vegetables? Simple: no veggies, no dessert. In this method, desired behaviors such as studying and brushing teeth can be increased by insisting that they be done before you carry out a favored or frequently occurring activity. For example, don't watch television unless you have studied first. Don't leave the apartment until you've brushed your teeth. You can also place reminders of new attitudes you're trying to acquire on little cards and read them regularly. For example, in quitting smoking, you might write "Every day it becomes a little easier" on one card and "Your lungs will turn pink again" on another. Place these cards and others in your wallet and read them like clockwork before you leave the house.

Covert sensitization. Create imaginary horror stories about problem behavior. Psychologists have successfully reduced overeating and smoking by having clients imagine that they become acutely nauseated at the thought of fattening foods or that a cigarette is made from vomit. Some horror stories are not so "imaginary." Deliberately focusing on heart strain and diseased lungs every time you overeat or smoke, rather than ignoring these long-term consequences, might also promote self-control.

Covert reinforcement. Create rewarding imagery for desired behavior. When you have achieved a behavioral goal, fantasize about how wonderful you are. Imagine friends and family patting you on the back. Fantasize about the *Playboy* or *Playgirl* centerfold for a minute.

Truth or Fiction Revisited. *It is true that some psychotherapists tell their clients precisely what to do.* That is, they outline behavioral prescriptions for their clients. Behavior therapists, Gestalt therapists, and some cognitive therapists provide examples.

Reflections

- **Is behavior therapy behavioral? Do some methods seem more behavioral than others? Explain.**
- Can you relate the methods discussed in this section to principles of conditioning and observational learning? As an example, how about the methods of fear reduction?
- Consider some of your own life concerns. Do you think they can be dealt with by means of behavior therapy? Why or why not?

GROUP THERAPIES

When a psychotherapist has several clients with similar problems—whether anxiety, depression, adjustment to divorce, or lack of social skills—it often makes sense to treat these clients in groups rather than individual sessions. The methods and characteristics of the group reflect the needs of the members and the theoretical orientation of the leader. In group psychoanalysis, clients might interpret one another's dreams. In a person-centered group, they might

Group Therapy. Group therapy has a number of advantages over individual therapy for many clients. It's economical, provides a fund of information and experience for clients to draw upon, elicits group support and reassurance, and provides the opportunity to relate to other people. On the other hand, some clients do require individual attention.

provide an accepting atmosphere for self-exploration. Members of behavior-therapy groups might obtain joint desensitization to anxiety-evoking stimuli or practice social skills together.

Group therapy has the following advantages:

1. Group therapy is economical (Sleek, 1995). It allows the therapist to work with several clients at once. Since good therapists are usually busy, the group format allows them to see people who might otherwise have to wait.

2. As compared with one-to-one therapy, group therapy provides a greater fund of information and life experience for clients to draw upon. When a group member explains how something worked out (or didn't work out) for him or her, it might have more impact than a theoretical discussion or a secondhand story from a therapist.

3. Appropriate behavior receives group support. Clients usually appreciate approval from their therapists, but an outpouring of peer approval is quite powerful.

4. When we run into troubles, it is easy to imagine that we are different from other people or inferior. Group members frequently learn that other people have had similar problems and self-doubts. Affiliating with people who have similar problems is reassuring.

5. Group members who show improvement provide hope for other members.

6. Many individuals seek therapy because of problems relating to other people. People who seek therapy for other reasons are also frequently socially inhibited. Members of groups have the opportunity to practice social skills in a relatively nonthreatening atmosphere. In a group consisting of men and women of different ages, group members can role-play one another's employers, employees, spouses, parents, children, and friends. A 20-year-old can practice refusing unreasonable requests from a 47-year-old as a way of learning how to refuse such requests from a parent. Members can role-play asking one another out on dates, saying no (or yes) to sexual requests, and so on.

On the other hand, group therapy is not for everyone. Some clients fare better with individual treatment. Many clients prefer not to disclose their problems to a group. They may be inhibited in front of others, or they may want individual attention. Many group clients share these concerns. Therefore, it is the responsibility of the therapist to insist that group disclosures be kept confidential, to establish a supportive atmosphere, and to ensure that group members obtain the attention they need.

Many types of therapy can be conducted either individually or in groups. Encounter groups, couple therapy, and family therapy are conducted in group format only.

Encounter Groups

Encounter groups are not appropriate for treating serious psychological problems. Rather, they are intended to promote personal growth by heightening awareness of one's own needs and feelings and those of others. This goal is sought through intense confrontations, or encounters, between strangers. Like ships in the night, group members come together out of the darkness, touch one another briefly, then sink back into the shadows of one another's lives. But something is thought to be gained from the passing.

Encounter groups stress interactions between group members in the here and now. Discussion of the past may be outlawed. Interpretation is out. Expression of genuine feelings toward others is encouraged. When group members think that a person's social mask is phony, they might descend en masse to rip it off.

Professionals recognize that encounter groups can be damaging when they urge overly rapid disclosure of intimate matters or when several members attack one member in unison. Responsible leaders do not tolerate these abuses and try to keep groups moving in growth-enhancing directions.

Encounter group • A type of group that aims to foster self-awareness by focusing on how group members relate to each other in a setting that encourages open expression of feelings.

Family therapy • A form of therapy in which the family unit is treated as the client.

Couple Therapy

Couple therapy helps unmarried and married couples enhance their relationships by improving communication skills and helping them manage conflict (Markman and others, 1993). There are often power imbalances in relationships, and couple therapy helps individuals find "full membership" in the couple. Correcting power imbalances increases marital happiness and can decrease the incidence of domestic violence. Ironically, the partner with *less* power in the relationship is usually the violent partner. Violence would sometimes appear to be a way of compensating for inability to share power in other areas of the relationship (Babcock and others, 1993).

The main approach to couple therapy today appears to be cognitive-behavioral (Jacobson & Addis, 1993; Markman and others, 1993). It focuses on teaching couples specific communications skills (such as how to listen to one another and how to express feelings), ways of handling feelings like depression and anger, and ways of solving problems.

Family Therapy

In **family therapy,** one or more families constitute the group. Family therapy may be undertaken from various theoretical viewpoints. One is the "systems approach," in which the family system of interaction is studied and modified to enhance the growth of family members and of the family unit as a whole (Annunziata & Jacobson-Kram, 1995; Mikesell and others, 1995).

It is often found that family members with low self-esteem cannot tolerate different attitudes and behaviors from other family members. Faulty family communications also create problems. It is also not uncommon for the family to present an "identified patient"—that is, the family member who has *the* problem and is *causing* all the trouble. Yet family therapists usually assume that the identified patient is a scapegoat for other problems within and among family members. It is a sort of myth: Change the bad apple—or identified patient—and the barrel—or family—will be functional once more.

The family therapist—who is often a specialist in this field—attempts to teach the family to communicate more effectively and to encourage growth and the eventual autonomy, or independence, of each family member. In doing so, the family therapist will also show the family how the identified patient has been used as a focus for the problems of other members of the group.

There are many other types of groups: marathon groups, sensitivity-training groups, and psychodrama, to name just a few.

Reflections

- If you went for therapy, do you think that you would prefer being treated on a one-to-one basis or in a group? Why?
- Could a couple or a family you know of profit from couple therapy or family therapy? If so, in what way? Can you foresee problems in encouraging a couple or family to go for therapy? What might they be?

Now that we have explored some of the types of psychotherapy in use today, let us consider a question that may have occurred to you: Does psychotherapy work?

DOES PSYCHOTHERAPY WORK?

Many of us know people who swear by their therapists, but the evidence is often shaky—for example, "I was a wreck before, but now . . . ," or "I feel so much better now." Anecdotes like these are encouraging, but we do not know what would have happened to these people had they not sought help. Many people feel better about their problems as time goes on, with or without therapy. Sometimes, happily, problems seem to go away by themselves. Sometimes, people find solutions on their own. Then, too, we hear some stories about how therapy was to no avail and about people hopping fruitlessly from therapist to therapist.

Problems in Conducting Research on Psychotherapy

Before we report on research into the effectiveness of therapy, let us review some of the problems of this kind of research.

PROBLEMS IN RUNNING EXPERIMENTS ON PSYCHOTHERAPY. The ideal method for evaluating a treatment—such as a method of therapy—is the experiment. However, "Experiments [on therapeutic methods] are not easy to arrange and control, outcomes are difficult to measure—often even to define—and results are often disappointing" (Smith & Sechrest, 1991, p. 233).

Consider psychoanalysis. In well-run experiments, individuals are randomly assigned to experimental and control groups. Thus, a sound experiment on psychoanalysis might require randomly assigning people seeking therapy to psychoanalysis and to a control group or other kinds of therapy for comparison (Luborsky and others, 1993). A person may have to remain in traditional psychoanalysis for years to attain results, however. Could we create control "treatments" comparable in duration? Moreover, some people seek psychoanalysis per se rather than psychotherapy in general. Would it be ethical to assign them at random to other treatments or to a no-treatment control group? Clearly not.

In an ideal experiment, participants and researchers are blind as to the treatment the participants obtain. In the Lang (1975) experiment on the effects of alcohol (see Chapter 2), participants were blind as to whether they had ingested alcohol. The researchers could thus control for participants' expectations about alcohol's effects. In an ideal experiment on therapy, individuals would be similarly blind as to the type of therapy they are obtaining—or as to whether they are obtaining a placebo (Carroll and others, 1994). It is difficult to mask the type of therapy clients are obtaining, however (Margraf and others, 1991). Even if we could conceal it from clients, could we hide it from therapists?

PROBLEMS IN MEASURING THE OUTCOMES OF THERAPY.　Consider problems we run into when measuring the outcomes of therapy (Azar, 1994b). Behavior therapists define their goals in behavioral terms—such as a formerly phobic individual being able to obtain an injection or look out of a 20th-story window. Therefore, behavior therapists do not encounter too many problems in this area. But what of the person-centered therapist who fosters insight and self-actualization? Or of the cognitive therapist who alters the ways in which clients perceive the world or who replaces irrational beliefs with rational ones? We cannot directly measure an insight, self-actualization, or a rational belief. We must assess what clients say and do and make inferences about such variables.

There are also problems with the amount of change. A therapy method may produce statistically significant changes that are not necessarily meaningful (Christiensen, 1994). The issue is not simply whether psychologists can use sophisticated mathematic means to show that clients change. The question is whether such change makes profound differences in clients' lives.

ARE CLINICAL JUDGMENTS VALID?　Because of problems such as these, many clinicians believe that important clinical questions cannot be answered through research (Newman & Howard, 1991). For them, clinical judgment is the basis for evaluating the effectiveness of therapy. Unfortunately, therapists have a stake in believing that their clients profit from treatment. Therapists are not unbiased judges, even when they try to be.

DOES THERAPY HELP BECAUSE OF THE METHOD OR BECAUSE OF "NONSPECIFIC FACTORS"?　It is a staggering task to sort out the benefits of therapy per se from other aspects of the therapy situation. These aspects are termed *nonspecific factors* and refer to features that are found in most therapies, such as the instillation of hope and the relationship with a therapist (Crits-Christoph & Mintz, 1991). Common threads among therapists include the showing of warmth and empathy and the encouragement of exploration (Burns &

Nolen-Hoeksema, 1992; Lambert and others, 1986; Rounsaville and others, 1987). The benefits of therapy could thus stem largely from such nonspecific factors. If so, the method itself might have little more value than a "sugar pill" has in combating physical ailments.

WHAT IS THE EXPERIMENTAL TREATMENT IN PSYCHOTHERAPY OUTCOME STUDIES? We may also inquire, what exactly is the experimental "treatment" being evaluated? Various therapists may say that they are practicing psychoanalysis, but they differ as individuals and in their training. It is therefore difficult to specify just what is happening in the therapeutic session (Luborsky and others, 1993).

Analyses of Therapy Effectiveness

Despite these evaluation problems, research into the effectiveness of therapy has been highly encouraging (Barlow, 1994; Lipsey & Wilson, 1993). Since the late 1970s, this research has relied heavily on a technique termed **meta-analysis** by researcher Gene Glass. Meta-analysis combines and averages the results of individual studies. Generally speaking, the included studies address similar issues in a similar way. Moreover, the analysts judge them to have been conducted in a valid manner.

In their classic early use of meta-analysis, Mary Lee Smith and Gene Glass (1977) analyzed the results of dozens of outcome studies on types of therapies. They concluded that people who obtained psychodynamic therapy showed greater well-being, on the average, than 70% to 75% of those who did not obtain treatment. Similarly, nearly 75% of the clients obtaining person-centered therapy were better off than people without treatment. Psychodynamic and person-centered therapies appear to be most effective with well-educated, verbal, strongly motivated clients who report problems with anxiety, depression (of light to moderate proportions), and interpersonal relationships. Neither form of therapy appears to be effective with people with psychotic disorders such as major depression, bipolar disorder, and schizophrenia. Smith and Glass (1977) found that people who obtained TA were better off than about 72% of those without treatment. People who obtained Gestalt therapy showed greater well-being than about 60% of those without treatment. The effectiveness of psychoanalysis, person-centered therapy, and TA was thus reasonably comparable. Gestalt therapy fell behind.

Smith and Glass (1977) did not include cognitive therapies in their meta-analysis because many cognitive approaches were relatively new at the time of their study. Because behavior therapists also incorporate many cognitive techniques, it can be difficult to sort out which aspects—cognitive or otherwise—of behavioral treatments are most effective. However, many meta-analyses of cognitive-behavioral therapy have been conducted since the early work of Smith and Glass. Their results are strongly encouraging (Lipsey & Wilson, 1993).

A number of studies of cognitive therapy per se have also been conducted. For example, they show that rational-emotive therapy helps people with emotional problems such as anxiety and depression (Engels and others, 1993; Haaga & Davison, 1993). Modifying self-defeating beliefs of the sort outlined by Beck also frequently alleviates anxiety and depression (Robins & Hayes, 1993; Whisman and others, 1991). Cognitive therapy is effective in the treatment of major depression (Muñoz and others, 1994). Cognitive therapy has also helped people with personality disorders (Beck & Freeman, 1990). It

Meta-analysis • A method for combining and averaging the results of individual research studies.

has even helped outpatients with schizophrenia (who are also using drug therapy) to modify delusional beliefs (Chadwick & Lowe, 1990).

Behavior therapy has provided people with strategies for alleviating anxiety, depression, social-skills deficits, and problems in self-control. These strategies have proved effective for most clients in terms of quantifiable behavioral change (Lazarus, 1990). Behavior therapists have also been innovative with a number of problems such as anxiety and sexual disorders for which there had not previously been effective treatments. Overall, Smith and Glass (1977) found behavior-therapy techniques to be somewhat more effective than psychodynamic or humanistic–existential methods. About 80% of people who obtained behavior-therapy treatments such as systematic desensitization and strategies for self-control showed greater well-being than people who did not. The 80% figure compares favorably with percentages in the low to middle 70s for people who obtained psychodynamic and humanistic–existential therapies.

Many studies that directly compare treatment techniques find behavior-therapy, psychodynamic, and humanistic–existential approaches to be about equal in overall effectiveness (Berman and others, 1985; Smith and others, 1980). Psychodynamic and humanistic–existential approaches seem to foster greater self-understanding. Behavior therapy (including cognitive-behavioral therapy) shows superior results in treatment of specific problems such as headaches (Blanchard, 1992b) and anxiety disorders (Borkovec & Costello, 1993). Behavior therapy has also been effective in helping coordinate the care of institutionalized people, including people with schizophrenia and those with mental retardation (Spreat & Behar, 1994). However, there is little evidence that behavior therapy alone is effective in treating the quirks of thought found in people with severe psychotic disorders (Wolpe, 1990).

Thus, it is not enough to ask which type of therapy is most effective. We must ask which type of therapy is most effective for a particular problem (Beutler, 1991; Shoham-Salomon, 1991; Snow, 1991). What are its advantages? What are its limitations? Clients may successfully use systematic desensitization to overcome stage fright, as measured by ability to speak to a group of people. If clients also want to know *why* they have stage fright, however, behavior therapy alone will not provide the answer.

Reflections

- Agree or disagree with the following statement and support your answer: "Psychotherapy is just common sense."
- Justin swears he feels much better because of psychoanalysis. Deborah swears by her experience with Gestalt therapy. Are these endorsements acceptable as scientific evidence? Why or why not?
- Agree or disagree with the following statement and support your answer: "It has never been shown that psychotherapy does any good."
- Agree or disagree with the following statement and support your answer: "The effects of traditional psychoanalysis cannot be determined by the experimental method."
- Do you believe that you might profit from psychotherapy? Why or why not?

WORLD OF DIVERSITY

PSYCHOTHERAPY IN THE NEW MULTICULTURAL UNITED STATES

The United States they are a-changing. Most of the "prescriptions" for psychotherapy discussed in the chapter were originated by, and intended for use with, European Americans. Yet the United States has many millions of African Americans, Asian Americans, Hispanic Americans, and Native Americans who seek or would profit from the benefits of psychotherapy. However, people from ethnic minority groups are less likely than European Americans to seek therapy (Cheung & Snowden, 1990; Ho, 1985; Yamamoto, 1986). They are also more likely to quit therapy after a visit or two (Tharp, 1991). Reasons for their lower participation rate include the following:

- Lack of recognition that therapy is indicated
- Ignorance of the availability of mental health services, or inability to pay for them (DeAngelis, 1995b)
- Distrust of mental health workers, particularly White workers and (in the case of many women) male workers (Greene, 1992)
- Language barriers (American Psychological Association, 1993; Martinez, 1986)
- Reluctance to open up about personal matters to strangers—especially strangers who are not members of one's ethnic group (LaFramboise, 1994)
- Cultural inclinations toward other approaches to problem solving, such as religious approaches
- Negative experiences with mental health workers

It might seem that it would be wisest for ethnic minorities to work only with therapists who share their ethnic backgrounds, and, perhaps, for women to work with female therapists. There are two problems with this approach, however. First, there are not enough minority therapists to go around (Allison and others, 1994; Tomes, 1995). For example, only about 12% of the psychologists employed by the U.S. Indian Health Service, which serves people living on reservations, are Native Americans (DeAngelis, 1993). Second, such limitations would unfairly stereotype European American therapists as insensitive, particularly males. They would similarly unfairly characterize therapists from ethnic minority groups as sensitive. Neither stereotype is necessarily true. One cannot make assumptions about the cultural sensitivity of the therapist on the basis of ethnicity alone (Bernal & Castro, 1994; Greene, 1991).

Generally speaking, clinicians need to avoid stereotypes and be sensitive to the cultural heritages, languages, and values of people in psychotherapy (American Psychological Association, 1993; Comas-Diaz, 1994; Yetrzenka, 1995). White clinicians need to avoid stereotypes and to be sensitive to the languages, behavior patterns, and values of minority group members in making diagnoses and doing therapy (Bernal & Castro, 1994; Comas-Diaz, 1994; Greene, 1992). Many graduate programs in psychology now offer courses in working with individuals from minority groups (Mintz and others, 1995; Pope-Davis and others, 1995).

Let us consider some of the issues involved in psychotherapy with African Americans, Asian Americans, Hispanic Americans, and Native Americans.

Can White Therapists Conduct Effective Psychotherapy with Members of Minority Groups? Why are members of minority groups less likely than the White majority to seek therapy for their problems? What kinds of issues arise when majority therapists engage in therapy with members of minority groups?

African Americans and Psychotherapy. In addition to the particular psychological problems that are presented by African American clients, therapists often need to help them develop ways of coping with prejudice and discrimination. Some African Americans also show low self-esteem because of the internalization of negative stereotypes that are maintained by the dominant culture (Greene, 1992; Pinderhughes, 1989).

African Americans are frequently reluctant to seek psychological help, both because of cultural assumptions that people should manage their own problems and because of mistrust of the therapy process. African Americans tend to assume that people are supposed to be resilient to stress and manage their problems by themselves. Signs of emotional weakness such as tension, anxiety, and depression are stigmatized and may lead to the individual's being perceived—by herself or himself as well as others—as having a "nervous breakdown" (Boyd-Franklin, 1995; Childs, 1990; Greene, 1993). The cultural expectation that people should get over such feelings by themselves often discourages them from seeking psychological intervention until the problem becomes more serious.

Many African American clients are then suspicious of their therapists—especially when therapists are non-Hispanic White Americans. They may withhold a good deal of personal information because of the history of extreme racial discrimination in such areas as employment, housing, education, and access to health care (Boyd-Franklin, 1995; Greene, 1990, 1993). When African Americans are suspicious, it is often because of awareness of the potential for maltreatment and exploitation. African American clients frequently minimize their vulnerability to exploitation by being less self-disclosing, especially when the relationship with the therapist is just under way. Such mistrust should not be confused with paranoia, however (Boyd-Franklin, 1995; Greene, 1986).

Therapists need to be familiar with African American culture and alert to their own attitudes and feelings about African Americans (Greene, 1992;

Pinderhughes, 1989). Therapists—regardless of their ethnicity—are exposed to the same stereotypes of African Americans as other people are and need to examine whether they believe them. Therapists need to confront their own prejudices and strive to replace stereotypes with knowledge of their African American clients as individuals.

Then there is the issue of cultural competence (Tomes, 1995). Therapists need to be aware of the cultural characteristics of African American families (American Psychological Association, 1993). There are typically strong kinship bonds among family members that often include people who are not biologically related. A close friend of a parent, for example, may enact some parenting role and be addressed as "Aunt." African American families usually have a strong spiritual and religious orientation. Households tend to be multigenerational. Because African American women have a long history of working outside the home, gender roles may be relatively flexible. Child-rearing responsibilities may be shared by various family members (Boyd-Franklin, 1995; Collins, 1990; Greene, 1990). Grandmothers, for example, often function as parents and may even be referred to by the children as "mother."

Asian Americans and Psychotherapy. Asian Americans tend to stigmatize people with problems in mental health, so that troubled people may deny that such problems exist and refuse to seek help for them (Sue, 1991). Asian Americans, especially recent immigrants, may also not understand or believe in Western approaches to psychotherapy. For example, Western psychotherapy typically encourages people to express their feelings openly, a mode of behavior that may conflict with traditional Asian public restraint. Western insight-oriented therapies also tend to be unstructured, open-ended, and ambiguous. Many Asians prefer to obtain advice that is structured and concrete. Western therapists usually try to help clients clarify their feelings and arrive at their own decisions. Asians may prefer therapists to function as authority figures who provide direct advice (Isomura and others, 1987).

Asian Americans also tend to view mental health differently. They tend to believe that mental health requires diverting one's thoughts from painful experiences or "morbid" concerns. Many Western therapy approaches aim to help clients get in touch with negative thoughts and feelings, however (Sue, 1991).

Because of the tendency to turn away from painful thoughts, many Asians experience and express psychological complaints as physical symptoms (Zane & Sue, 1991). Rather than thinking of themselves as being anxious, they may focus on physical symptoms of anxiety such as a pounding heart and heavy sweating. Rather than thinking of themselves as depressed, they may center on their fatigue and low levels of energy.

To help Asian Americans, therapists—whether Asian American or of another ethnic group—must be sensitive to the cultural beliefs and values of Asians and use knowledge of these beliefs and values in therapy (American Psychological Association, 1993). Therapy must be consistent with clients' cultural expectations. Consider the therapeutic relationship between therapists and Japanese clients. Traditional Japanese culture endorses restraint in self-disclosure. Therapists who work with Japanese clients must thus be patient and not anticipate early self-disclosures (Henkin, 1985).

There can also be other conflicts between the goals of Western therapy and the values of a certain culture. Psychology emphasizes the dignity and importance of the individual, for example, and many Japanese are reared with cultural beliefs that the individual is subordinate to the group (Henkin, 1985).

Hispanic Americans and Psychotherapy. Hispanic American subcultures differ a great deal from one another. One cannot assume that cultural values that are found among Cuban Americans will also be found among Mexican Americans, Puerto Ricans, and Hispanic Americans from South America (Greene, 1994). Yet some values and beliefs do appear to be shared by the many Hispanic American subgroups, including adherence to a definite patriarchal (male-dominated) family structure and strong kinship ties. Many Hispanic Americans also share the following values:

> One's identity is in part determined by one's role in the family. The male, or *macho,* is the head of the family, the provider, the protector of the family honor, and the final decision maker. The woman's role (*Marianismo*) is to care for the family and the children. Obviously, these roles are changing, with women entering the work force and achieving greater educational opportunities. Cultural values of *respeto* (respect), *confianza* (trust), *dignidad* (dignity), and *personalismo* (personalism) are highly esteemed and are important factors in working with many [Hispanic Americans]. (De la Cancela & Guzman, 1991, p. 60)

Therapists need to be aware of potential conflicts between the traditional Hispanic American value of interdependency on the family and the typical non-Hispanic White American belief in independence and self-reliance (De la Cancela & Guzman, 1991). Psychotherapy appears to be more effective when therapists respect cultural differences in values rather than attempt to remold people from ethnic minority groups according to the values of the dominant culture (De la Cancela & Guzman, 1991).

Other problems that may sap the effectiveness of therapy arise from the cultural gulf that may exist between the typically middle-class, non-Hispanic White American therapist and the typically lower socioeconomic class Hispanic American client (Malgady and others, 1990; Tomes, 1995). Measures such as the following may help bridge the gaps between psychotherapists and Hispanic American clients:

1. Interacting with clients in the language requested by clients or, if this is not possible, referring clients to professionals who can do so (American Psychological Association, 1993). Enlisting bilingual/bicultural staff and establishing a therapeutic atmosphere that accepts Hispanic American cultural values (Malgady and others, 1990).

2. Using methods that are consistent with Hispanic American clients' values. One might also tailor the treatment approach to the client's level of **acculturation,** as suggested by number of generations in the United States, number of years in the United States, fluency in English, level of education, relationships with people from the dominant culture, and similar factors (American Psychological Association, 1993). More acculturated clients may be assumed to share more of the values of the dominant culture (Ruiz, 1981).

3. Innovating therapy methods that incorporate clients' cultural values. Malgady and his colleagues (1990), for example, have integrated cultural values into psychotherapy through the use of *cuento therapy* with Puerto Ricans. *Cuento therapy* is a form of storytelling that adapts Hispanic folktales, or *cuentos,* in such a way that the characters serve as models for adaptive behavior. The child characters in the stories embody culturally desirable and effective values and behavior patterns.

Acculturation • The process of becoming adapted to a new or different culture, according to such factors as the language of the culture and relationships with people from that culture.

Native Americans and Psychotherapy. Many psychological disorders among Native Americans reflect the disruption in traditional culture caused by European colonization (LaFramboise, 1994). Native Americans have also been denied full access to the dominant Western culture (LaFramboise, 1994). Loss of cultural identity and social disorganization have set the stage for problems such as alcoholism, substance abuse, and depression. These problems dispose Native American adults to a high incidence of child abuse and neglect, which, in turn, contributes to feelings of depression among adolescents. Adolescents may then try to escape their feelings through alcohol and other drugs.

Many Native American cultures classify their problems according to those that are believed to arise from outside influences ("White man's sicknesses"), such as alcoholism and drug addiction, and those that arise from lack of harmony with traditional tribal life and thought ("Indian sicknesses"; Trimble, 1991). "White man's medicine" may be sought to cope with "White man's sicknesses," but traditional healers, shamans, and medicine men and women may be asked to treat "Indian sicknesses."

Theresa LaFramboise (1994) argues that if psychologists are to help Native Americans cope with psychological disorders, they must be sensitive to their culture, customs, and values. Efforts at preventing disorders should focus on strengthening Native American cultural identity, pride, and cohesion. They should help Native Americans regain a sense of mastery over their world. When cultural and language differences create so great a gulf between Native Americans and the dominant culture, perhaps only trained Native Americans will be able to provide effective counseling, as was the case among the Native American Papago people of Arizona (Kahn, 1982).

Therapists can also use indigenous ceremonies that reflect clients' cultural or religious traditions (Edwards, 1995). Purification and cleansing rites are therapeutic for many Native Americans in the United States and elsewhere, as among the Brazilian *umbanda,* the African-Cuban *santeria,* and the Haitian *vodou* (Lefley, 1990). Such rites are commonly sought by Native Americans who believe that their problems are caused by failure to placate malevolent spirits or to perform required rituals (Lefley, 1990).

Although the names of the religions are different, members of all ethnic groups in the United States also seek the help of clergy to cleanse their spirits of unacceptable urges and ideas. Such measures provide comfort and may have powerful placebo effects, even if they fail to address directly the biological or psychological roots of problems.

Reflections

- Consider your sociocultural background. Do people from your background generally feel comfortable with the thought of going for psychotherapy? Why or why not?
- Do you think that the goals of psychoanalysis and other forms of psychotherapy are consistent with the values and customs of people from your particular background? Why or why not?
- Would you feel comfortable seeing a psychotherapist who was from another ethnic background? Why or why not? A psychotherapist of the other gender? Why or why not?

MINILECTURE: BIOLOGICAL THERAPIES

BIOLOGICAL THERAPIES: IN SEARCH OF THE MAGIC PILL

In the 1950s, Fats Domino popularized the song "My Blue Heaven." Fats was singing about the sky and happiness. Today, "blue heavens" is one of the street names for the 10-milligram dose of the antianxiety drug, Valium. Clinicians prescribe Valium and other drugs for people with various psychological disorders. In this section, we discuss drug therapy, electroconvulsive therapy, and psychosurgery, three biological, or medical, approaches to treating people with psychological disorders.

Drug Therapy

In this section, we discuss antianxiety drugs, antipsychotic drugs, antidepressants, and lithium.

ANTIANXIETY DRUGS.   Most antianxiety drugs (also called *minor tranquilizers*) belong to the chemical class *benzodiazepines*. Valium (diazepam) is a benzodiazepine. Other benzodiazepines include chlordiazepoxide (for example, Librium), oxazepam (Serax), and alprazolam (Xanax). Antianxiety drugs are usually prescribed for outpatients who complain of generalized anxiety or panic attacks, although many people also use them as sleeping pills. Valium and other antianxiety drugs depress the activity of the central nervous system (CNS). The CNS, in turn, decreases sympathetic activity, reducing the heart rate, respiration rate, and feelings of nervousness and tension.

Most people use antianxiety drugs for brief periods of time (Shader & Greenblatt, 1993). Some people come to tolerate small dosages of these drugs very quickly, however (Gillin, 1991). When tolerance occurs, dosages must be increased for the drug to remain effective. Some people become embroiled in tugs-of-war with their clinicians when the clinicians become concerned about how much they are taking. Clinicians may ask people to cut down "for their own good." People sometimes resent clinicians for getting them started with the drug and then playing moralists.

Sedation (feelings of being tired or drowsy) is the most common side effect of antianxiety drugs (Shader & Greenblatt, 1993). Problems that may be associated with withdrawal from them include **rebound anxiety.** That is, some people who have been using these drugs regularly report that their anxiety returns in exacerbated form once they discontinue them. Antianxiety drugs can induce physical dependence, as evidenced by withdrawal symptoms such as tremulousness, sweating, insomnia, and rapid heartbeat.

ANTIPSYCHOTIC DRUGS.   People diagnosed with schizophrenia are likely to take antipsychotic drugs (also called *major tranquilizers*). In most cases, antipsychotic drugs reduce agitation, delusions, and hallucinations (Gilman and others, 1990; Michels & Marzuk, 1993). Many antipsychotic drugs, including phenothiazines (for example, Thorazine) and clozapine (Clozaril) are thought to act by blocking dopamine receptors in the brain (Carpenter & Buchanan, 1994; Michels & Marzuk, 1993). Research along these lines supports the dopamine theory of schizophrenia (see Chapter 13).

ANTIDEPRESSANTS.   People with major depression often take so-called **antidepressant** drugs. Antidepressants are also sometimes helpful with people

---

Rebound anxiety • Strong anxiety that can attend the suspension of usage of a tranquilizer.
Antidepressant • (ant-eye-dee-PRESS-ant). Acting to relieve depression.

with eating disorders (Craighead & Agras, 1991) and panic disorder (Clum and others, 1993). Problems in the regulation of noradrenaline and serotonin may be involved in these other disorders as well as depression. Antidepressants are believed to work by increasing the amount of one or both of these neurotransmitters available in the brain, which can affect both depression and eating disorders. However, cognitive-behavior therapy addresses irrational attitudes concerning weight and body shape, fosters normal eating habits, and helps people resist the urges to binge and purge. Cognitive-behavior therapy is therefore apparently more effective than antidepressants with people with bulimia (Wilson & Fairburn, 1993).

There are various kinds of antidepressant drugs. Each type increases the brain concentrations of noradrenaline or serotonin (Potter and others, 1991). **Monoamine oxidase (MAO) inhibitors** block the activity of an enzyme that breaks down noradrenaline and serotonin. Nardil and Parnate are examples of MAO inhibitors. **Tricyclic antidepressants** such as Tofranil and Elavil prevent reuptake of noradrenaline and serotonin by the axon terminals of the transmitting neurons. **Serotonin-uptake inhibitors,** such as fluoxetine hydrochloride (Prozac) and sertraline (Zoloft), also block the reuptake of serotonin by presynaptic neurons (Gram, 1994). As a result, the neurotransmitters remain longer in the synaptic cleft, enhancing the probability that they will influence receiving neurons.

Antidepressants tend to alleviate the physical aspects of depression. For example, they tend to increase a person's activity level and to reduce eating and sleeping disturbances (Lyons and others, 1985). Severely depressed people often have insomnia, and it is not unusual for antidepressant drugs, which have a strong **sedative** effect, to be given at bedtime. Typically, antidepressant drugs must build up to a therapeutic level, which may take several weeks. Because overdoses of antidepressants can be lethal, some people enter the hospital during the build-up period to prevent suicide attempts.

LITHIUM. It could be said that the ancient Greeks and Romans were among the first to use the metal lithium as a psychoactive drug. They would prescribe mineral water for people with bipolar disorder. They had no inkling as to why this treatment sometimes helped, but it might have been because mineral water contains lithium. A salt of the metal lithium (lithium carbonate), in tablet form, flattens out cycles of manic behavior and depression for most people. It is not known how lithium works, although it affects functioning of the neurotransmitters dopamine, acetylcholine, serotonin, and norepinephrine (Price & Heninger, 1994).

Because lithium is more toxic than most drugs, the dose must be carefully monitored during early phases of therapy. It might be necessary for persons with bipolar disorder to use lithium indefinitely, just as a person with diabetes must continue insulin to control the illness. Lithium also has been shown to have side effects such as hand tremors, memory impairment, and excessive thirst and urination (Price & Heninger, 1994). Memory impairment is reported as the main reason that people discontinue lithium.

EVALUATION. There is little question that drug therapy has helped many people with severe psychological disorders. Antipsychotic drugs largely account for the lessened need for restraint and supervision (padded cells, straitjackets, hospitalization, and so on) used with people with schizophrenia. Antipsychotic drugs have allowed hundreds of thousands of people to lead largely normal lives in the community. Most problems related to these drugs concern their side effects.

Monoamine oxidase inhibitors • (MON-oh-ah-mean OX-see-dase) Antidepressant drugs that work by blocking the action of an enzyme that breaks down noradrenaline and serotonin. Abbreviated *MAO inhibitors*.

Tricyclic antidepressants • (try-SIGH-click). Antidepressant drugs that work by preventing the reuptake of noradrenaline and serotonin by transmitting neurons.

Serotonin-uptake inhibitors • Antidepressant drugs that work by blocking the reuptake of serotonin by presynaptic neurons.

Sedative • Relieving nervousness or agitation.

On the other hand, most comparisons of psychotherapy (in the form of cognitive therapy) and drug therapy for depression suggest that cognitive therapy is at least comparable in effectiveness to use of antidepressants (Hollon and others, 1991; Imber and others, 1990). In fact, cognitive therapy may be more effective (Antonuccio, 1995; Muñoz and others, 1994). For one thing, cognitive therapy provides coping skills that reduce the risk of recurrence of depression once treatment ends (Hollon and others, 1993). Moreover, a combination of antidepressant medication and psychotherapy is apparently no more effective than either form of treatment alone (Burns & Nolen-Hoeksema, 1992; Robinson and others, 1990; Wexler & Cicchetti, 1992).

Many psychologists and psychiatrists are comfortable with the short-term use of antianxiety drugs in helping clients manage periods of unusual anxiety or tension. Antianxiety drugs do not cure anxiety disorders, however (Shader & Greenblatt, 1993). Many people use antianxiety drugs routinely to dull the arousal that stems from anxiety-producing lifestyles or interpersonal problems. Rather than make painful decisions to confront their problems, they prefer to pop a pill. Unfortunately, some physicians also find it easier to prescribe antianxiety drugs than to help people examine and change their lives. The physician's lot is not eased by the fact that many people want pills, not talk.

Although drug therapy is helpful in some disorders that do not respond to psychotherapy alone, no chemical can show a person how to change an idea or solve an interpersonal problem. In some cases, chemicals only dull the pain of failure and postpone the day when people must seize control of their lives.

Electroconvulsive therapy • Treatment of disorders like major depression by passing an electric current (that causes a convulsion) through the head. Abbreviated *ECT*.

Electroconvulsive Therapy

Electroconvulsive therapy (ECT) was introduced by Italian psychiatrist Ugo Cerletti in 1939 for use with people with psychological disorders. Cerletti had noted that some slaughterhouses used electric shock to render animals unconscious. The shocks also produced convulsions. Cerletti erroneously believed, as did other European researchers of the period, that convulsions were incompatible with schizophrenia and other major psychological disorders.

ECT was originally used for a variety of psychological disorders. Because of the advent of antipsychotic drugs, however, the American Psychiatric Association (1990) now recommends ECT mainly for people with major depression who are not responsive to antidepressants. ECT is still sometimes obtained by people with intense manic episodes, schizophrenia, and other disorders, however (Sakheim, 1990).

People typically obtain one ECT treatment three times a week for up to 10 sessions. Electrodes are attached to the temples, or on one side of the head only (in "unilateral ECT"), and an electrical current strong enough to produce a convulsion is induced. The shock causes unconsciousness, so people do not recall it. Still, people take a sedative so they sleep during treatment. In the past, people who obtained ECT flailed about wildly during the convulsions, sometimes breaking bones. Today, they take muscle-relaxing drugs, and convulsions are barely perceptible to onlookers. ECT is not advised for people with high blood pressure or heart ailments.

ECT is controversial for many reasons. First, many professionals are distressed by the thought of passing electric shock through the head and producing convulsions, even if they are suppressed by drugs. Second are the side effects. ECT disrupts recall of recent events. Although memory functioning usually seems near normal for most people a few months after treatment, some appear to have permanent memory impairment (Coleman, 1990). Third, nobody knows *why* ECT works. For reasons such as these, ECT was outlawed in Berkeley, California, by voter referendum in 1982. This decision was later overturned in the courts, but it remains of interest because it marked the first time that a specific treatment found its way to the ballot box.

Psychosurgery

Psychosurgery is more controversial than ECT. The best-known modern technique, the **prefrontal lobotomy,** has been used with people with severe disorders. In this method, a picklike instrument is used to crudely sever the nerve pathways that link the prefrontal lobes of the brain to the thalamus. The prefrontal lobotomy was pioneered by the Portuguese neurologist Antonio Egas Moniz and was brought to the United States in the 1930s. As pointed out by Valenstein (1986), the theoretical rationale for the operation was vague and misguided. Moreover, Moniz's reports of success were exaggerated. Nevertheless, the prefrontal lobotomy was performed on more than a thousand people by 1950 in an effort to reduce violence and agitation. Anecdotal evidence of the method's unreliable outcomes is found in an ironic footnote to history: One of Dr. Moniz's "failures" shot him, leaving a bullet lodged in his spine and paralyzing his legs.

> **Truth or Fiction Revisited.** *It is true that the originator of a surgical technique intended to reduce violence learned that it was not always successful . . . when one of his patients shot him.* The technique in question is the prefrontal lobotomy.

Psychosurgery • Surgery intended to promote psychological changes or to relieve disordered behavior.

Prefrontal lobotomy • The severing or destruction of a section of the frontal lobe of the brain.

The prefrontal lobotomy also has a host of side effects including hyperactivity and distractibility, impaired learning ability, overeating, apathy and withdrawal, epileptic-type seizures, reduced creativity, and, now and then, death. Because of these side effects, and because of the advent of antipsychotic drugs, the prefrontal lobotomy has been largely discontinued in the United States.

Reflections

- **Agree or disagree with the following statement and support your answer: "Drugs cause more problems than they solve when they are used to treat people with psychological disorders."**
- Agree or disagree with the following statement and support your answer: "Biological treatments provide only a sort of Band-Aid therapy for psychological disorders. They don't get at the heart of the problems."

Study Guide

| Matching Therapy Methods and Kinds of Therapy

DIRECTIONS: In the first column are a number of therapy methods. In the second column are types of therapy. Match the method to the type of therapy by placing the letter of the type of therapy in the blank space to the left of the method. Answers are given below. (More than one answer may apply.)

THERAPY METHODS

____ 1. Dialogue

____ 2. Showing genuineness

____ 3. Lithium carbonate

____ 4. Free association

____ 5. Restriction of the stimulus field

____ 6. Dream analysis

____ 7. Prefrontal lobotomy

____ 8. Empathic understanding

____ 9. Phenothiazines

____ 10. Interpretation

____ 11. Aversive conditioning

____ 12. Token economy

____ 13. Challenging irrational beliefs

____ 14. Showing congruence

____ 15. Systematic desensitization

____ 16. Biofeedback training

KINDS OF THERAPY

A. Psychoanalysis

B. Person-centered therapy

C. Gestalt therapy

D. Cognitive therapy

E. Behavior therapy

F. Drugs

G. Psychosurgery

ANSWER KEY TO EXERCISE 1

1. C	5. E	9. F	13. D
2. B	6. A, C	10. A, C	14. B
3. F	7. G	11. E	15. E
4. A	8. B	12. E	16. E

| EXERCISE 2 | Matching Names and Kinds of Therapy |

DIRECTIONS: In the column to the left are the names of people who have made a contribution to the development of therapy methods. In the column to the right are therapy methods. Match the person to the therapy method by writing the letter that signifies the method in the blank space to the left of the name.

PERSON

____ 1. Aaron Beck

____ 2. Carl Rogers

____ 3. Fritz Perls

____ 4. Albert Ellis

____ 5. Joseph Wolpe

____ 6. Erik Erikson

____ 7. Ugo Cerletti

____ 8. Thomas Harris

____ 9. Antonio Egas Moniz

____ 10. Sigmund Freud

THERAPY METHOD

A. Psychoanalysis

B. Behavior therapy

C. Cognitive therapy

D. Family therapy

E. Gestalt therapy

F. Person-centered therapy

G. Electroconvulsive therapy

H. Psychosurgery

I. Transactional analysis

ANSWER KEY TO EXERCISE 2

| 1. C | 3. E | 5. B | 7. G | 9. H |
| 2. F | 4. C | 6. A | 8. I | 10. A |

| ESL | English as a Second Language — Bridging the Gap |

a host of (635)—a great number of

adhere faithfully (604)—stick to something without fail

aimed at (599)—relevant to

ameliorate (599)—to make better

antagonist (602)—challenger; enemy; opponent

are blind (624)—are not aware of

armchair adventurer (614)—one who satisfies the need for adventure by reading or watching a television program about it

as such (599)—because they are this

as time goes on (623)—as time passes

aspirations (598)—ambitions; dreams for the future

attend to (610)—pay attention to

authentic (608)—true; real

be fleeting (612)—quick to appear and disappear

blocked insight (603)—stopped; insight that cannot occur

blow out of proportion (612)—exaggerate

break down the defensive barrier (603)—destroy his defensive barriers

brings . . . to bear on influencing (598)—using . . . in order to influence

build . . . relationships (614)—develop relationships

bulwark the ego against (601)—to protect the ego from

by setting aside (608)—by not considering

come to tolerate (632)—become used to something; in this case, their bodies become adjusted to the medicine, and it no longer has the effect it used to

compulsion to utter (603)—irresistible desire to say something that reveals a hidden feeling

concrete advice (610)—specific suggestions

conjured up (601)—dreamed up; invented

contingent upon (620)—making a condition or requirement; in this case, that you can't do something pleasant unless you first take care of a responsibility

dammed up (603)—to have been held back, stopped up

deep-seated feelings (604)—feelings that are very deep and entrenched

delusional beliefs (626)—false or imaginary beliefs

descend en masse (622)—come forward as a group

discreet remarks (604)—careful, sensitive comments

disown (606)—reject

divergent (616)—different

don masks and facades (607)—act falsely; "to don" something means to put it on

don't take chances . . . (610)—don't risk failure

embroiled (632)—deeply involved; tangled up in something

empirical support (605)—evidence of actual occurrences

ensues (604)—follows

everyday hair dryer (616)—an ordinary hair dryer

exacerbating the problem (617)—making a problem worse

face to face (598)—the front of one person directly in front of the front of the other person

fashion desired traits (605)—create the characteristics they want

father figure (629)—a substitute for a father

Fats Domino (632)—a popular 1950s entertainer who was famous for rock and roll music

fiercely attacked (605)—strongly criticized

follow-up care (601)—care given to someone after he or she has been treated for the initial problem

for one thing (634)—one of the reasons

found its way to the ballot box (635)—became an issue that the public would vote on in local elections

frankly (604)—honestly; candidly; I shall be direct and say this, even though it may be negative

get going in the morning (612)—start to function in the morning

get out of this rut (610)—remove yourself from the boring routine

give . . . a chance (610)—not allow the relationship to develop because we are afraid of having a bad experience

given this view (607)—if we accept this opinion, then

go about it (623)—to do it; to find help

go for a stroll on a lazy afternoon (599)—walk slowly and leisurely on an afternoon in which they did not have to do anything important

gray automaton in a mechanized society (621)—a robot in an impersonal society

grist for the therapeutic mill (613)—information for the therapist to use in treatment

groundless (605)—without reason; not true

gulf (630)—a separation between two things

harbor a number of irrational beliefs (611)—hold several ideas about ourselves that are not realistic or true

hard to catch (611)—hard to notice

heighten our discomfort (611)—increase our negative feelings

human warehousing (599)—to provide only a place to stay; to provide "storage space" without any care

humdrum activities (618)—boring, ordinary activities

impair our coping ability (611)—making it harder for us to respond to situations successfully

in the long run (612)—finally; at the end

in their wake (616)—afterward

inner workings of (603)—the way it works inside

innovative (626)—creative; original; inventive

is no (599)—is not a

laid off at work (612)—lost their jobs; were told they could not work there anymore

laypeople (607)—people who are not trained specifically in something but who may have some experience

lengthy process (604)—a long process

loosed by the id (601)—released by the id

maladaptive behavior (614)—behavior that is not appropriate or well-adjusted

maladjustment (606)—poor adjustment to problems

manifesting (606)—appearing

marginal societal niche (599)—a place in society that is out of the mainstream, or outside the accepted values and attitudes of society

matter of chance (598)—not carefully planned

may eventually surface (603)—may be revealed in the future

mind is blank (603)—I have no idea; there are no thoughts in my mind

monasteries (599)—group homes for people with religious vows, such as monks

morbid (629)—unpleasant; depressing; sad

mushroomed in population (599)—increased in number

no matter how trivial . . . personal (602)—it did not matter how unimportant or personal

not based on, say, (599)—not established on, for example,

not meet demands . . . life (599)—don't support themselves and don't have money for food and shelter

not work out (621)—not be successful

on their own (623)—without help

one of many (616)—there are many that are acceptable, and this is one of them

oppressed (607)—persecuted; held down; denied rights or advantages

out on the town (597)—going places for entertainment

outlook . . . looks brighter (613)—the future appears better for this situation

overexposure renders it aversive (616)—being forced to experience something more than you would like makes it unpleasant

padded cells, straitjackets (633)—devices to limit people who are out of control; rooms with pads on the walls so a person can't get hurt; jackets that tie a person's arms down so they can't hurt themselves or someone else

par for the course (602)—what was expected

paranoia (628)—unreasonable fear or distrust

passing blurs on the street (622)—people we see on the street about whom we know nothing; because of this, we pay very little attention to them

per se (625)—by itself; identified only as these

perilous (602)—dangerous; tricky

phobia (602)—strong, irrational fear

phobic (624)—extremely fearful of something

physician's lot is not eased (634)—the doctor's work is not made easier

pin down (612)—notice and pay attention

placebo effect (631)—an effect that does not change the underlying problem but which the individual believes has created an improvement in his or her condition or situation

places major burden . . . on . . . shoulders (598)—expects Jasmine to take the major responsibility for solving her own problems

plead not guilty of encouraging (618)—say that he or she did not encourage

plucking (602)—taking; pulling

pop a pill (634)—to take a pill

pops into (598)—enters

professes (605)—states; says

proper resolution (605)—correct way to solve a problem

protracted techniques (604)—techniques that take a long time

Quakers (604)—an American religious group, also called *Society of Friends,* which originated in England in 1620; known for their work in helping others and improving the fairness of societies

quite a mouthful (598)—This is an overwhelming statement, isn't it?

ratio of cost to benefits (604)—the results received compared with what it cost to get them

raze out the written troubles of the brain (601)—to get rid of established emotional or mental problems

remold (630)—to make someone or something different from the original

resilient (628)—flexible; able to handle problems without difficulty

revolving door (601)—a situation in which they left the hospital feeling all right, became disturbed again, and then returned to the hospital, and this cycle continued

roadblocks placed in the path of (607)—barriers that prevent something

role-playing (610)—imagining a social situation and acting it out as an opportunity to practice how to handle the situation in real life

royal road (604)—the best way

run all right (612)—be all right

running amok (608)—becoming confused, disorganized, and out of control

saw its heyday (604)—was popular

scaled down (613)—reduced

scapegoat (623)—someone who is blamed for a problem that is actually caused by another or several others

seemed foreign and frightening (601)—appeared too strange and scary

seen but not heard (608)—be quiet and unobtrusive and not express our feelings; an expression referring to children—that they are to speak only when an adult speaks to them

self-efficacy (614)—our beliefs about our competency, or ability to do things or respond to situations well

sex object (606)—an impersonalized person to enjoy sexually

shape our responses to them (611)—influence how we react

shoring up the ego (601)—strengthening the ego

6-month follow-ups (616)—to check the condition of something every 6 months

somewhat flamboyant ad (614)—an advertisement that was excessive in its explanation of services

spent in worrying (610)—used in worrying to shape our responses to them

spill forth (603)—to be released and come out

squarely in the eye (621)—directly

staggering task (624)—enormous and overwhelming job

stick with what you have (610)—remain the way you are

stigmatized (628)—considered to be shameful or negative

subtly tips the balance (604)—delicately influences the outcome in a particular direction

swear by (623)—think they are very good

take in the sights (599)—to look at things that are interesting in the area

take the lead (597)—to direct the discussion and emphasis themselves

tips the balance in favor of (603)—changes the balance so that the person speaks about it

tokens (617)—something that represents something else; in this case, money

top dog (610)—a boss

torrents of energy (601)—large amounts of energy

twinges of discomfort (614)—feelings of being uncomfortable

two-way street (613)—the feelings are from the client to the therapist, and they are also from the therapist to the client

underdog (610)—a person who has nothing or who is at a disadvantage in a situation

unleashed (608)—released

uplifting experience (619)—exciting and happy experience

Voice (621)—*The Village Voice* is a popular New York City newspaper that has a large section of sometimes unusual personal and business advertisements

voter referendum (635)—when voters decide whether to bring a proposed law up for consideration in local elections

weighs upon the heart (602)—causes depression

worst will happen (612)—the worst event will happen

would-be quitters (616)—people who are trying to quit

FILL-INS | Chapter Review

Psychotherapy is a systematic interaction between a therapist and a client that brings (1) _____ical principles to bear on influencing clients' thoughts, feelings, or behavior. Psychotherapy helps clients overcome psychological (2) _____rs or adjust to problems in living.

Historic treatments of psychological disorders involved cruel practices such as the (3) ex_____ of the Middle Ages. The first institutions intended primarily for the mentally ill were called (4) _____ms. St. Mary's of (5) B_____ is the name of a well-known London asylum.

Humanitarian reform movements began in the (6) _____ century. Philippe (7) P_____ unchained the patients at the asylum called La Bicêtre. Mental (8) _____tals replaced asylums in the United States.

Psychodynamic therapies are based on the thinking of Sigmund (9) F_____. Freud's method of psychoanalysis attempts to shed light on (10) _____cious conflicts that are presumed to lie at the roots of clients' problems. Freud sought to replace impulsive and defensive behavior with (11) _____ng behavior. Freud also believed that psychoanalysis would allow clients to engage in (12) _____sis or abreaction.

The chief psychoanalytic method is (13) f_____ association. The cardinal rule of free association is that no thought is to be (14) _____ed. In this way, material that has been (15) _____sed should eventually come to the surface of awareness.

Freud considered (16) _____s to be the "royal road to the unconscious." The perceived content of a dream is termed its (17) _____t content. The presumed symbolic content of a dream is termed its hidden or (18) _____t content.

Contemporary psychodynamic approaches tend to be (19: Longer or Briefer?) and (20: More or Less?) intense than Freud's. Modern psychodynamic therapists focus more on the (21) e_____ as the "executive" of personality.

Humanistic–existential therapies focus on the quality of clients' (22) _____tive, conscious experience. Person-centered therapy was originated by (23) _____ _____s. Person-centered therapy is a (24: Directive or Nondirective?) method that provides clients with a warm, accepting atmosphere that enables them to explore and overcome roadblocks to self-actualization. The characteristics shown by the person-centered therapist include (25: Conditional or Unconditional?) positive regard, (26) em_____ understanding, (27) gen_____, and (28) _____ence.

Gestalt therapy was originated by (29) _____ _____s. Gestalt therapy provides (30: Directive or Nondirective?) methods that are designed to help clients integrate conflicting parts of the (31) _____ity.

Cognitive therapists focus on the (32) be_____s, attitudes, and (33) _____tic types of thinking that create and compound their clients' problems.

(34) Rational-e_____therapy is one type of cognitive therapy. It was originated by (35) A_____ _____. Rational-emotive therapy confronts clients with the ways in which (36) _____nal beliefs contribute to problems such as anxiety, depression, and feelings of hopelessness.

Psychiatrist Aaron Beck has focused on ways in which cognitive errors or (37) dis_____s heighten feelings of (38) de_____. Beck notes the pervasive influence of four basic types of cognitive errors that contribute to clients' miseries: selective (39) _____tion of the world as a harmful place; (40) over_____zation on the basis of a few examples; (41) mag_____tion of the significance of negative events; and (42) _____tist thinking, or looking at the world in black and white rather than in shades of gray.

SECTION 5: BEHAVIOR THERAPY: ADJUSTMENT IS WHAT YOU DO

Behavior therapy is also referred to as behavior (43) _____tion. Behavior therapy is defined as the systematic application of principles of (44) _____ing to bring about desired behavioral changes. Behavior therapists insist that their methods be established by (45) _____tation and that therapeutic outcomes be assessed in terms of (46) ob_____ble, measurable behavior.

Two behavior-therapy methods for reducing fears are systematic (47) de_____tion, in which a client is gradually exposed to more fear-arousing stimuli, and (48) p_____ modeling, in which a client observes and then imitates a model who handles fear-arousing stimuli. In systematic desensitization, clients confront a (49) h_____ of anxiety-evoking stimuli while they remain relaxed.

In the method of aversive conditioning, undesired responses are decreased in frequency by being associated with (50) _____ive stimuli. An example of aversive conditioning is (51) r_____ smoking, in which cigarette smoke is made aversive by frequent puffing.

In operant-conditioning methods, desired responses are (52) _____ced and undesired responses are (53) _____shed. In social-skills training, behavior therapists decrease social anxiety and build social skills through operant-conditioning procedures that employ (54) s_____-monitoring, coaching, modeling, (55) r_____-playing, (56) b_____rehearsal, and (57) _____back. Through (58) _____back training (BFT), therapists help clients become more aware of, and gain control over, various bodily functions. "Bleeps" or other electronic signals are used to (59) r_____ bodily changes in the desired direction. The (60) _____ograph (EMG) monitors muscle tension. The (61) _____ograph (EEG) monitors brain waves. The EEG can be used to teach people how to produce (62) _____a waves, which are associated with relaxation.

In self-control methods, clients first engage in a (63) _____nal analysis of their problem behavior. A functional analysis helps them learn what stimuli trigger and (64)_____ain the behavior. Then clients are taught how to manipulate the antecedents and (65) _____nces of their behavior and how to increase the frequency of desired responses and decrease the frequency of undesired responses.

SECTION 6: GROUP THERAPIES

The methods and characteristics of group therapy reflect the clients' needs and the (66) _____ical orientation of the group leader. There are a number of advantages to group therapy. Group therapy can be more (67) _____ical than individual therapy, allowing several clients to be seen at once. Clients may draw upon the (68) exp_____ of other group members as well as the knowledge of the therapist. Too, clients can receive (69) em_____ support from other group members.

SECTION 7: DOES PSYCHOTHERAPY WORK?

Smith and Glass found that people who receive psychoanalysis show greater well-being than (70) _____% of those who are left untreated. Psychoanalysis is most effective with clients who are (71: Well or Poorly?) educated, highly verbal, and (72: Highly or Poorly?) motivated. About (73) _____% of clients obtaining person-centered therapy were better off than people left untreated. People receiving TA were better off than about (74) _____% of people left untreated. People receiving Gestalt therapy showed greater well-being than about 60% of those who were left untreated.

Critics of psychodynamic and humanistic—existential methods assert that it has not been shown that their benefits can be attributed to the (75) th_____ methods per se. Benefits may derive from the (76) non_____ factors found in many types of therapy, such as showing warmth, (77: Encouraging or Discouraging?) exploration, and combating feelings of hopelessness.

SECTION 8: BIOLOGICAL THERAPIES: IN SEARCH OF THE MAGIC PILL

Valium is an example of (78) d_____ therapy. (79: Minor or Major?) tranquilizers are usually prescribed for outpatients who complain of anxiety or tension. (80) V_____ and other minor tranquilizers are theorized to depress the activity of the (81) c_____ nervous system, which, in turn, decreases sympathetic activity. Many patients who have regularly used minor tranquilizers encounter (82) re_____ anxiety when they discontinue.

Major tranquilizers are sometimes referred to as (83) anti_____ drugs. In most cases, major tranquilizers reduce agitation, (84) del_____s, and hallucinations. Major tranquilizers that belong to the chemical class of (85) _____iazines are thought to work by blocking the action of the neurotransmitter (86) _____ine in the brain.

(87) Anti_____ drugs have relieved many instances of major depression. Antidepressants are believed to work by increasing the amounts of the neurotransmitters (88) nor_____ine and (89) _____nin available in the brain.

Lithium helps flatten out the cycles of (90) m_____ behavior and depression found in (91) _____ar disorder. Lithium appears to moderate the level of (92) _____line available to the brain.

Electroconvulsive therapy (ECT) was introduced by Ugo (93) C_____ in 1939. ECT uses electric shock to produce (94) _____ions. Since the advent of major tranquilizers, use of ECT has been generally limited to people with (95) _____ _____sion. ECT is controversial because it impairs (96) m_____, and nobody knows why it works.

Psychosurgery was pioneered by Antonio Egas (97) M_____. The best-known technique is called the (98) pre_____ _____omy. The prefrontal lobotomy has been used with severely disturbed patients and severs the nerve pathways that link the prefrontal (99) _____s of the brain to the (100) _____mus. The prefrontal lobotomy has been largely discontinued because of the advent of major tranquilizers and because of (101) s_____ effects.

ANSWER KEY TO CHAPTER REVIEW

1. Psychological	27. Genuineness	53. Extinguished	79. Minor
2. Disorders	28. Congruence	54. Self	80. Valium
3. Exorcism	29. Fritz Perls	55. Role	81. Central
4. Asylums	30. Directive	56. Behavior	82. Rebound
5. Bethlehem	31. Personality	57. Feedback	83. Antipsychotic
6. 18th	32. Beliefs	58. Biofeedback	84. Delusions
7. Pinel	33. Automatic	59. Reinforce	85. Phenothiazines
8. Hospitals	34. Rational-emotive	60. Electromyograph	86. Dopamine
9. Freud	35. Albert Ellis	61. Electroencephalograph	87. Antidepressant
10. Unconscious	36. Irrational	62. Alpha	88. Noradrenaline
11. Coping	37. Distortions	63. Functional	89. Serotonin
12. Catharsis	38. Depression	64. Maintain	90. Manic
13. Free	39. Perception	65. Consequences	91. Bipolar
14. Censored	40. Overgeneralization	66. Theoretical	92. Noradrenaline
15. Repressed	41. Magnification	67. Economical	93. Cerletti
16. Dreams	42. Absolutist	68. Experiences	94. Convulsions
17. Manifest	43. Modification	69. Emotional	95. Major depression
18. Latent	44. Learning	70. 70–75	96. Memory
19. Briefer	45. Experimentation	71. Well	97. Moniz
20. Less	46. Observable	72. Highly	98. Prefrontal lobotomy
21. Ego	47. Desensitization	73. 75	99. Lobes
22. Subjective	48. Participant	74. 72	100. Thalamus
23. Carl Rogers	49. Hierarchy	75. Therapy	101. Side
24. Nondirective	50. Aversive	76. Nonspecific	
25. Unconditional	51. Rapid	77. Encouraging	
26. Empathic	52. Reinforced	78. Drug	

POSTTEST | Multiple Choice

1. A leader of the humanitarian reform movement in the United States was
   a. Philippe Pinel.
   b. Dorothea Dix.
   c. Sigmund Freud.
   d. William Tuke.

2. Of the following, the form of treatment that seems to be most helpful with severe depression is
   a. cognitive therapy.
   b. behavior therapy.
   c. traditional psychoanalysis.
   d. person-centered therapy.

3. Sigmund Freud remarked, "Where id was, there shall ego be." According to the text, Freud meant that
   a. all unconscious ideas should be made conscious.
   b. feelings of guilt should be removed.
   c. coping behavior should replace impulsive behavior.
   d. defense mechanisms should be destroyed.

4. A person has a dream in which she is flying. According to Sigmund Freud, the perceived subject matter of a dream—in this case, flying—is its
   a. manifest content.
   b. objective content.
   c. symbolic content.
   d. latent content.

5. Congruence may be defined as
   a. honesty in interpersonal relationships.
   b. a fit between one's behavior and feelings.
   c. ability to perceive the world from a client's frame of reference.
   d. genuine acceptance of the client as a person.

6. According to the text, which form of therapy set forth a view of women that has reinforced male dominance and the view that a woman's place is in the home?
   a. Gestalt therapy
   b. person-centered therapy

    c. psychoanalysis

    d. Transactional analysis

7. According to Albert Ellis, the central factors in our problems are
    a. genetic factors.
    b. maladaptive habits.
    c. unconscious conflicts.
    d. irrational beliefs.

8. Behavior rehearsal is most similar in meaning to
    a. practice.
    b. role-playing.
    c. modeling.
    d. countertransference.

9. According to the text, the technique of modeling is connected with
    a. person-centered therapy.
    b. traditional psychoanalysis.
    c. social-skills training.
    d. Gestalt therapy.

10. The technique called _____ is an example of aversive conditioning.
    a. "Grandma's method"
    b. restriction of the stimulus field
    c. operant conditioning
    d. rapid smoking

11. Tom cut down on his cigarette intake by simply pausing between puffs. This technique is an example of
    a. successive approximations.
    b. chainbreaking.
    c. response prevention.
    d. avoiding stimuli that trigger unwanted behavior.

12. Which of the following forms of therapy is nondirective?
    a. Gestalt therapy
    b. behavior therapy
    c. cognitive therapy
    d. person-centered therapy

13. According to the studies analyzed by Smith and Glass, the *least* effective form of therapy is
    a. Gestalt therapy.
    b. psychoanalysis.
    c. cognitive therapy.
    d. behavior therapy.

14. Valium and other minor tranquilizers are thought to depress the activity of the _____, which, in turn, decreases, sympathetic activity.
    a. central nervous system
    b. parasympathetic nervous system
    c. adrenal medulla
    d. adrenal cortex

15. Phenothiazines are thought to work by blocking the action of
    a. acetylcholine.
    b. noradrenaline.
    c. dopamine.
    d. serotonin.

16. Which of the following is widely used to treat bipolar disorder?
    a. ECT
    b. the prefrontal lobotomy
    c. lithium carbonate
    d. major tranquilizers

17. According to the text, each of the following is a problem in assessing the effectiveness of psychotherapy, except for
    a. availability of appropriate statistical techniques.
    b. difficulty in conducting experiments in psychotherapy.
    c. the role of nonsepecific factors in therapy.
    d. difficulty in defining the outcomes of therapy.

18. According to the text, the person who wrote that many people are depressed because they are pessimistic and tend to minimize their own accomplishments is a
    a. cognitive therapist.
    b. traditional psychoanalyst.
    c. behavior therapist.
    d. transactional analyst.

19. Psychosurgery was pioneered by
    a. Wolpe.
    b. Dix.
    c. Moniz.
    d. Perls.

20. The self-control technique of _____ is a strategy that is aimed at the reinforcements that maintain behavior.
    a. response prevention
    b. stimulus control
    c. successive approximations
    d. covert sensitization

ANSWER KEY TO POSTTEST

1. B	4. A	7. D	10. D	13. A	16. C	19. C
2. A	5. B	8. A	11. B	14. A	17. A	20. D
3. C	6. C	9. C	12. D	15. C	18. A	

Health

LEARNING OBJECTIVES

When you have finished studying Chapter 15, you should be able to:

HEALTH PSYCHOLOGY
1. Define *health psychology.*

STRESS: PRESSES, PUSHES, AND PULLS
2. Enumerate sources of stress.
3. Describe moderators of the impact of stress.
4. Describe the general adaptation syndrome.
5. Describe the effects of stress on the immune system.

A MULTIFACTORIAL APPROACH TO HEALTH AND ILLNESS
6. Discuss the roles of biological, psychological, and other factors in health and illness.

SOCIOCULTURAL FACTORS IN HEALTH AND ILLNESS: NATIONS WITHIN THE NATION
7. Discuss the roles of ethnicity, socioeconomic status, and gender in health and illness.

UNDERSTANDING AND COPING WITH MAJOR HEALTH PROBLEMS IN THE UNITED STATES TODAY
8. Describe the relationships between psychological factors and health problems such as headaches, heart disease, cancer, AIDS, and obesity.

PRETEST *Truth or Fiction?*

____ The more change the merrier — variety's the spice of life.

____ A sense of humor can moderate the impact of stress.

____ Single men live longer.

____ At any given moment, countless microscopic warriors within our bodies are carrying out search-and-destroy missions against foreign agents.

____ Poor people in the United States eat less than more affluent people.

____ Stress can influence the course of cancer.

____ Only gay males and substance abusers are at serious risk for contracting AIDS.

____ Because of better diets, young adults in the United States are trimmer in the 1990s than they were in the 1980s.

____ Americans overeat by enough to feed the nation of Germany.

SIRENS. Ambulances. Stretchers. The emergency room at Dallas's public Parkland Memorial Hospital is a busy place. Sirens wail endlessly as ambulances pull up to the doors and discharge people in need of prompt attention. Because of the volume of patients, beds line the halls. People who do not require immediate care cram the waiting room. Many hours may pass before they are seen. It is not unusual for people who are not considered in danger to wait for 10 to 12 hours.

All this may sound rather foreboding, but good things are happening at Parkland as well. One of them is the attention that physicians attempt to pay to people's psychological needs as well as to their physical needs. Influenced both by his own clinical experience and Native American wisdom about the healing process, for example, Dr. Ron Anderson teaches his medical students that caring about people is not just an outdated ideal that typifies backwoods practices. Rather, it is a powerful weapon against disease.

Journalist Bill Moyers describes Anderson on rounds with students:

> I listen as he stops at the bedside of an elderly woman suffering from chronic asthma. He asks the usual questions: "How did you sleep last night?" "Is the breathing getting any easier?" His next questions surprise the medical students: "Is your son still looking for work?" "Is he still drinking?" "Tell us what happened right before the asthma attack." He explains to his puzzled students. "We know that anxiety aggravates many illnesses, especially chronic conditions like asthma. So we have to find out what may be causing her episodes of stress and help her find some way of coping with it. Otherwise she will land in here again, and next time we might not be able to save her. We cannot just prescribe medication and walk away. That is medical neglect. We have to take the time to get to know her, how she lives, her values, what her social supports are. If we don't know that her son is her sole support and that he's out of work, we will be much less effective in dealing with her asthma." (Moyers, 1993, p. 2)

Health psychology • The field of psychology that studies the relationships between psychological factors (e.g., attitudes, beliefs, situational influences, and behavior patterns) and the prevention and treatment of physical illness.

Pathogen • A microscopic organism (e.g., bacterium or virus) that can cause disease.

HEALTH PSYCHOLOGY

Note some key concepts from the slice of hospital life reported by Moyers: "Anxiety aggravates many illnesses." "We have to find out what may be causing . . . stress and . . . find some way of coping with it." "We cannot just prescribe medication and walk away." "We have to take the time to get to know [people], how [they] live, [their] values, what [their] social supports are."

We could say that Anderson and Moyers collaborated on an introduction to the field of health psychology. **Health psychology** studies the relationships between psychological factors and the prevention and treatment of physical illness (Taylor, 1990). The case of the woman with asthma is a useful springboard for discussion because, in recent years, health psychologists have been exploring the ways in which

- psychological factors (e.g., stress, behavior patterns, and attitudes) can lead to or exacerbate physical illness;
- people can cope with stress;
- stress and **pathogens** can interact to influence the immune system (Kiecolt-Glaser & Glaser, 1992);
- people decide whether to seek health care;

- health-care providers can encourage people to comply with professional advice;
- psychological forms of intervention such as health education (for example, concerning nutrition, smoking, and exercise) and behavior modification can contribute to physical health (Blanchard, 1992a; Castelli, 1994; Dubbert, 1992; Lehrer and others, 1992).

Because of the links between psychological factors and physical health, 3,500 psychologists are now estimated to be on the faculties of medical schools (Matarazzo, 1993). Psychologists are found in medical schools' departments of family practice, neurology, pediatrics, psychiatry, and rehabilitation medicine (Michaelson, 1993b; Wiggins, 1994). In this chapter, we consider a number of issues in health psychology: sources of stress, factors that moderate the impact of stress, the body's response to stress, and the connections between psychology and physical disorders.

STRESS: PRESSES, PUSHES, AND PULLS

Americans will put up with anything provided it doesn't block traffic.
DAN RATHER

In physics, stress is the pressure or force exerted on a body. Tons of rock pressing on the earth, one car smashing into another, a rubber band stretching—all are types of physical stress. Psychological forces, or stresses, also "press," "push," or "pull." We may feel "crushed" by the "weight" of a big decision, "smashed" by adversity, or "stretched" to the point of "snapping."

In psychology, **stress** is the demand made on an organism to adapt, to cope, or to adjust. Some stress is healthful and necessary to keep us alert and occupied. Stress researcher Hans Selye (1980) referred to such healthful stress as **eustress.** But intense or prolonged stress can tax our adjustive capacity, dampen our moods, and harm our bodies (Berenbaum & Connelly, 1993; Cohen and others, 1993; Repetti, 1993).

Stress • The demand that is made on an organism to adapt.

Eustress • (YOU-stress). Stress that is healthful.

Daily hassles • Notable daily conditions and experiences that are threatening or harmful to a person's well-being.

Uplifts • Notable pleasant daily conditions and experiences.

Sources of Stress: Don't Hassle Me?

Let us consider various sources of stress, including daily hassles, life changes, conflict, irrational beliefs, and Type A behavior.

**MINILECTURE:
STRESS AND
STRESSORS**

DAILY HASSLES. It is the "last" straw that will break the camel's back—so goes the saying. Similarly, stresses can pile atop one another until we can no longer cope. Some of these stresses are **daily hassles,** or notable daily conditions and experiences that are threatening or harmful to a person's well-being. Others are life changes. Lazarus and his colleagues (1985) analyzed a scale that measures daily hassles and their opposites—**uplifts**—and found that hassles could be grouped as follows:

1. *Household hassles:* preparing meals, shopping, and home maintenance
2. *Health hassles:* physical illness, concern about medical treatment, and the side effects of medication
3. *Time-pressure hassles:* having too many things to do, too many responsibilities, and not enough time

4. *Inner-concern hassles:* being lonely and fearful of confrontation
5. *Environmental hassles:* crime, neighborhood deterioration, and traffic noise
6. *Financial-responsibility hassles:* concern about owing money such as mortgage payments and loan installments
7. *Work hassles:* job dissatisfaction, not liking one's work duties, and problems with coworkers
8. *Future-security hassles:* concerns about job security, taxes, property investments, stock market swings, and retirement

Hassles are linked to psychological variables such as anxiety, depression, and feelings of aloneness. For example, 83% of people in the United States will be victimized by a violent crime at some time, and victimization is connected with problems such as anxiety, physical complaints, hostility, and depression (Norris & Kaniasty, 1994).

LIFE CHANGES: "GOING THROUGH CHANGES." Too much of a good thing can make you ill. You might think that marrying Mr. or Ms. Right, finding a prestigious job, and moving to a better neighborhood all in the same year would propel you into a state of bliss. It might. But all these events, one on top of the other, may also lead to headaches, high blood pressure, and other ailments (Holmes & Rahe, 1967). As pleasant as they may be, they entail major life changes, and life changes are another source of stress.

Life changes differ from daily hassles in two ways: (1) Many life changes are positive and desirable, whereas all hassles, by definition, are negative. (2) Hassles occur regularly. Life changes are relatively more isolated.

Richard Lazarus and his colleagues (e.g., Kanner and others, 1981) constructed a list of 117 daily hassles for their research. They asked people to indicate which of these hassles they had encountered and how intense they were. Holmes and Rahe (1967) constructed a scale to measure the impact of life changes by assigning marriage an arbitrary weight of 50 "life-change units." Then they asked people to assign units to other life changes, with marriage as the baseline. Most events were rated as less stressful than marriage. Some, such as the death of a spouse (100 units) and divorce (73 units), were more stressful. Changes in work hours and residence (20 units each) were included, regardless of whether they were negative or positive. Positive life changes such as an outstanding personal achievement (28 units) and going on vacation (13 units) also made the list.

HASSLES, LIFE CHANGES, AND ILLNESS. Hassles and life changes—especially negative life changes—affect us psychologically. They are connected with anxiety and depression. But stressors such as hassles and life changes also predict physical illnesses such as heart disease and cancer, even athletic injuries (Kanner and others, 1981; Smith and others, 1990; Stewart and others, 1994). Holmes and Rahe found that people who "earned" 300 or more life-change units within a year on their scale were at greater risk for illness. Eight of ten developed medical problems as compared with only one of three people whose life-change-unit totals were below 150.

Truth or Fiction Revisited. *Although variety may be the very spice of life, psychologists have not found that "the more change the merrier."* Changes, even changes for the better, are sources of stress in that they require adjustment. Since stress is connected with physical illness, it may even be that too much of a good thing—too many positive life changes—do indeed make one ill.

Life Changes. Life changes differ from daily hassles in that they tend to be more episodic. Life changes can also be positive as well as negative. What is the relationship between life changes and illness? Is the relationship causal?

QUESTIONS ABOUT THE LINKS BETWEEN HASSLES, LIFE CHANGES, AND ILLNESS. The links between daily hassles, life changes, and illness have been supported by research. However, critical thinking reveals a number of limitations:

1. *Correlational Evidence.* The links between hassles, life changes, and illness are correlational rather than experimental. It may seem logical that the hassles and life changes caused the disorders, but these variables were not manipulated experimentally. Rival explanations of the data are therefore possible (Figure 15.1). One is that people who are predisposed toward medical or psychological problems encounter more hassles and amass more life-change units. For example, medical disorders may contribute to sexual problems, arguments with spouses or in-laws, changes in living conditions

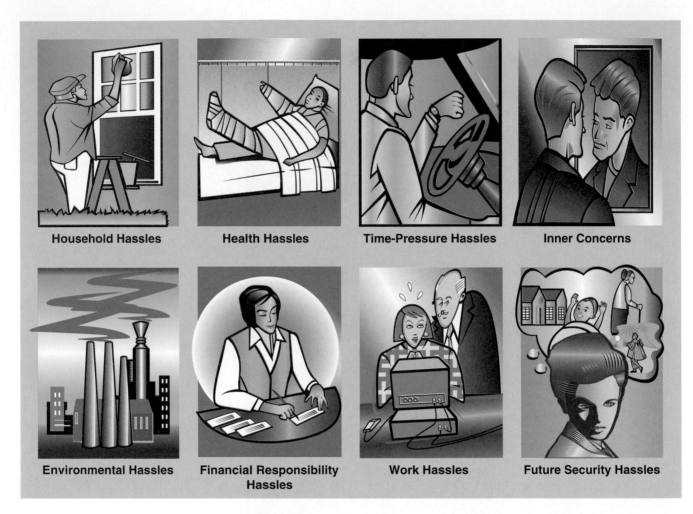

FIGURE 15.1

Daily Hassles. Daily hassles are recurring sources of aggravation. Which of the hassles shown here are regular parts of your life?

and personal habits, and changes in sleeping habits before they are diagnosed. People may also generate the life events that then lead to physical and psychological disorders (Simons and others, 1993).

2. *Positive Versus Negative Life Changes.* Other aspects of the research into the relationship between life changes and illness have also been challenged. For instance, positive life changes may be less disturbing than hassles and negative life changes, even when the number of life-change units is the same (Lefcourt and others, 1981).

3. *Personality Differences.* People with different kinds of personalities respond to life stresses in different ways (Vaillant, 1994). People who are easygoing or psychologically hardy are apparently less likely to become ill under stress.

4. *Cognitive Appraisal.* The stress of an event reflects the meaning of the event to the individual (Lazarus, 1991b; Whitehead, 1994). Pregnancy, for example, can be a positive or negative life change, depending on whether one is prepared for a child. We appraise hassles, traumatic experiences, and life changes (Creamer and others, 1992; Kiecolt-Glaser, 1993; Lazarus, 1991a). In

responding to them, we assess their danger, our values and goals, our beliefs in our coping ability, our social support, and so on. The same event is less taxing to people who have greater coping ability and support.

Despite these methodological flaws, hassles and life changes still require adjustments. It seems wise to be aware of the hassles and life changes in our lifestyles.

CONFLICT.

> *I am*
> *At war 'twixt will and will not.*
> SHAKESPEARE, *MEASURE FOR MEASURE*

Have you ever felt "damned if you did and damned if you didn't"? Regretted that you couldn't do two things, or be in two places, at the same time? This is **conflict**—being torn in two or more directions by opposing motives. Conflict is frustrating and stressful.

You may be fearful of visiting the dentist but also fear that your teeth will decay if you do not. Cream cheese pie may be delicious, but oh the calories! You may not want to contribute to the Association for the Advancement of Lost Causes, but you fear that your friends will consider you cheap or uncommitted if you do not. When conflict is stressful, and no resolution is in sight, some people withdraw from the conflict by focusing their attention on other matters or by suspending their behavior altogether. Highly conflicted people have refused to get out of bed in the morning and start the day.

When conflicting motives are powerful, people are faced with the need to make a decision. Yet decision making can also be stressful, especially when there is no clear correct choice. For this reason, people sometimes decide *not* to decide.

IRRATIONAL BELIEFS: TEN DOORWAYS TO DISTRESS.

Psychologist Albert Ellis (1977, 1993) notes that our beliefs about events, as well as the events themselves, can be stressors. Consider a case in which one is fired from a job and is anxious and depressed about it. It may seem logical that losing the job is itself responsible for the misery. However, Ellis points out how beliefs about the loss compound misery.

According to Ellis's $A \rightarrow B \rightarrow C$ approach, losing the job is an *activating event* (A). The eventual outcome, or *consequence* (C), is misery. Between the activating event (A) and the consequence (C), however, lie *beliefs* (B), such as "This job was the most important thing in my life," "What a no-good failure I am," "My family will starve," "I'll never find a job as good," "There's nothing I can do about it." Beliefs such as these compound misery, foster helplessness, and divert us from planning what to do next. The belief "There's nothing I can do about it" fosters helplessness. The belief "What a no-good failure I am" internalizes the blame and may be an exaggeration. The belief "My family will starve" may also be an exaggeration.

We can diagram the situation like this:

Activating events $\rightarrow$ Beliefs $\rightarrow$ Consequences

Anxieties about the future and depression over a loss are normal and to be expected. However, the beliefs of the person who lost the job tend to **catastrophize** the extent of the loss and to contribute to anxiety and depression. By heightening emotional reaction to the loss and fostering feelings of helplessness, these beliefs also impair coping ability. They lower people's self-efficacy expectations and divert their attention from problem solving.

Ellis proposes that many of us harbor irrational beliefs. We carry them with us. They are our personal doorways to distress. They can give rise to problems

Conflict • Being torn in different directions by opposing motives. Feelings produced by being in conflict.

Catastrophize • (kuh-TASS-trow-fize). To interpret negative events as being disastrous; to "blow out of proportion."

in themselves, and, when problems assault us from other sources, these beliefs can magnify their effect. How many of these beliefs do you harbor? Are you sure?

Irrational Belief 1: You must have sincere love and approval almost all the time from the people who are important to you.

Irrational Belief 2: You must prove yourself to be thoroughly competent, adequate, and achieving at something important.

Irrational Belief 3: Things must go the way you want them to go. Life is awful when you don't get your first choice in everything.

Irrational Belief 4: Other people must treat everyone fairly and justly. When people act unfairly or unethically, they are rotten.

Irrational Belief 5: When there is danger or fear in your world, you must be preoccupied with and upset by it.

Irrational Belief 6: People and things should turn out better than they do. It's awful and horrible when you don't find quick solutions to life's hassles.

Irrational Belief 7: Your emotional misery stems from external pressures that you have little or no ability to control. Unless these external pressures change, you must remain miserable.

Irrational Belief 8: It is easier to evade life's responsibilities and problems than to face them and undertake more rewarding forms of self-discipline.

Irrational Belief 9: Your past influenced you immensely and must therefore continue to determine your feelings and behavior today.

Irrational Belief 10: You can achieve happiness by inertia and inaction, or by just enjoying yourself from day to day.

Ellis finds it understandable that we would want the approval of others but irrational to believe that we cannot survive without it. It would be nice to be competent in everything we do, but it's unreasonable to expect it. Sure, it would be nice to serve and volley like a tennis pro, but most of us haven't the time or natural ability to perfect the game. Demanding self-perfection prevents us from going out on the courts on weekends and batting the ball back and forth for fun. Belief 5 is a prescription for perpetual emotional upheaval. Beliefs 7 and 9 lead to feelings of helplessness and demoralization. Sure, Ellis might say, childhood experiences can explain the origins of irrational beliefs, but it is our own cognitive appraisal—here and now—that causes us misery. Research supports the connections between irrational beliefs (for example, excessive dependence on social approval and perfectionism) and feelings of anxiety and depression (Hewitt & Flett, 1993; Persons and others, 1993).

TYPE A BEHAVIOR.   Some people create stress for themselves through the **Type A behavior** pattern. Type A people are highly driven, competitive, impatient, and aggressive (Thoresen & Powell, 1992). They feel rushed and under pressure and keep one eye glued firmly on the clock. They are not only prompt but often early for appointments. They eat, walk, and talk rapidly and become restless when others work slowly. They attempt to dominate group discussions. Type A people find it difficult to surrender control or to share power. They are often reluctant to delegate authority in the workplace and thus increase their own workloads. Type A people "accentuate the negative." They are merciless in their self-criticism when they fail at a task (Moser & Dyck, 1989). They even seek out negative information about themselves in order to better themselves (Cooney & Zeichner, 1985).

Type A behavior • Behavior characterized by a sense of time urgency, competitiveness, and hostility.

Type A Behavior. The Type A behavior pattern is characterized by a sense of time urgency, competitiveness, and hostility.

Type A people find it difficult to go out on the tennis court and just bat the ball back and forth. They watch their form, perfect their strokes, and demand regular self-improvement. The irrational belief that they must be perfectly competent and achieving in everything they undertake seems to be their motto.

Type B people, in contrast, relax more readily and focus more on the quality of life. They are less ambitious and less impatient, and they pace themselves. Type A people earn higher grades and more money than Type Bs of equal intelligence. Type A people also seek greater challenges than Type Bs (Ortega & Pipal, 1984).

Self-efficacy expectations • Our beliefs that we can bring about desired changes through our own efforts.

Psychological Moderators of Stress

There is no one-to-one relationship between the amount of stress we undergo and physical illness or psychological distress. Physical factors account for some of the variability in our responses: Some people inherit predispositions toward specific disorders. Psychological factors also play a role, however (Holahan & Moos, 1990). They can influence, or *moderate,* the effects of sources of stress. In this section, we discuss a number of psychological moderators of stress: self-efficacy expectations, psychological hardiness, a sense of humor, predictability, and social support.

SELF-EFFICACY EXPECTATIONS: "THE LITTLE ENGINE THAT COULD." Our **self-efficacy expectations** affect our abilities to withstand stress (Bandura, 1982, 1991). For example, when we are faced with fear-inducing objects, high self-efficacy expectations are accompanied by relatively *lower* levels of adrenaline and noradrenaline in the bloodstream (Bandura and others, 1985). Adrenaline is secreted when we are under stress, and it arouses the body by means such as accelerating the heart rate and releasing glucose from the liver. As a result, we may have "butterflies in the stomach" and feelings of nervousness. Excessive arousal can impair our ability to manage stress by upsetting us and

Psychological hardiness • A cluster of traits that buffer stress and are characterized by commitment, challenge, and control.

Self-Efficacy Expectations and Performance. Outstanding artists like this Native American hoop dancer tend to have high self-efficacy expectations. That is, they believe in themselves. High self-efficacy expectations—beliefs that we can cope—moderate the amount of stress impacting upon us.

distracting us from the tasks at hand. People with higher self-efficacy expectations thus have biological as well as psychological reasons for remaining calmer.

People who are self-confident are less prone to become depressed in response to negative life events (Holahan & Moos, 1991). Moreover, people with positive self-efficacy expectations respond more positively to treatment for depression (Hoberman and others, 1988).

People with higher self-efficacy expectations are more likely to lose weight or quit smoking and are less likely to relapse afterward (DiClemente and others, 1991). Women with higher self-efficacy expectations are more likely to persist without medication in controlling pain during childbirth (Manning & Wright, 1983).

PSYCHOLOGICAL HARDINESS. **Psychological hardiness** also helps people resist stress. The research on psychological hardiness is largely indebted to the pioneering work of Suzanne Kobasa (1979) and her colleagues, who studied business executives who resisted illness despite heavy loads of stress. In one phase of her research, Kobasa administered a battery of psychological tests to hardy and nonhardy executives and found that the hardy executives differed from the nonhardy in three important ways (Kobasa and others, 1982, pp. 169–170):

1. Hardy individuals were high in *commitment*. That is, they showed a tendency to involve themselves in, rather than experience alienation from, whatever they were doing or encountering.

2. Hardy individuals were high in *challenge*. They believed that change rather than stability was normal in life. They appraised change as an interesting incentive to personal growth, not as a threat to security.

3. Hardy individuals were also high in perceived *control* over their lives. They felt and behaved as though they were influential rather than helpless in facing the various rewards and punishments of life. Psychologically hardy people tend to have what Julian B. Rotter (1990) terms an internal **locus of control.**

According to Kobasa, hardy people are more resistant to stress because they see themselves as *choosing* to be in their stress-producing situations. They also interpret, or encode, the stress impacting upon them as making life more interesting, not as compounding the pressures to which they are subjected. Their activation of control allows them to regulate to some degree the amount of stress they will encounter at any given time (Maddi & Kobasa, 1984). Even the *illusion* of being in control of one's situation tends to enhance one's mood in the face of stress (Alloy & Clements, 1992).

Kobasa and Pucetti (1983) suggest that psychological hardiness helps individuals by buffering stressful life events. Buffering stress gives people the opportunity to draw on social supports (Ganellen & Blaney, 1984) and to use coping mechanisms such as controlling what they will be doing from day to day. Type A individuals who show psychological hardiness are more resistant to illness, including heart disease, than Type A individuals who do not (Friedman & Booth-Kewley, 1987; Krantz and others, 1988).

SENSE OF HUMOR: DOES "A MERRY HEART DOETH GOOD LIKE A MEDICINE"?

The idea that humor lightens the burdens of the day and helps us cope with stress has been with us for millennia (Lefcourt & Martin, 1986). Consider the biblical maxim "a merry heart doeth good like a medicine" (Proverbs 17:22).

Anatomy of an Illness is Norman Cousins's (1979) anecdotal report of his bout with a painful collagen illness that is similar to arthritis. Cousins found that 10 minutes of belly laughter of the sort he experienced while watching Marx brothers movies had a powerful anesthetic effect on his pain. Laughter allowed him to sleep and may also have reduced his inflammation, which is consistent with some findings that emotional responses such as happiness and anger may have beneficial effects on the immune system (Kemeny, 1993). The benefits of humor may also reflect the cognitive shifts they entail and the emotional changes that accompany them.

Research has also shown that humor can moderate the moderating effects of stress. Martin and Lefcourt (1983) administered a negative-life-events checklist and a measure of mood disturbance to college students. The mood-disturbance measure also yielded a stress score. Students self-rated their sense of humor. Behavioral assessments were made of their ability to produce humor under stress. Overall, there was a significant relationship between negative life events and stress scores: High accumulations of negative life events predicted higher levels of stress. However, students who had a greater sense of humor and who produced humor in difficult situations were less affected by negative life events than other students.

Truth or Fiction Revisited. *It is true that a sense of humor can moderate the impact of stress.* In the experiment run by Martin and Lefcourt, humor played its conjectured stress-buffering role.

Locus of control • The place (locus) to which an individual attributes control over the receiving of reinforcers—either inside or outside the self.

PREDICTABILITY.   Ability to predict a stressor apparently moderates its impact. Predictability allows us to brace ourselves for the inevitable and, in many cases, to plan ways of coping with it. People who want information about medical procedures and what they will feel cope with pain more effectively than those who do not when given that information (Ludwick-Rosenthal & Neufeld, 1993).

There is also a relationship between the desire to assume control over one's situation and the usefulness of information about impending stressors (Lazarus & Folkman, 1984). Predictability is of greater benefit to **"internals"**—that is, to people who wish to exercise control over their situations—than to **"externals"** (Affleck and others, 1987; Martelli and others, 1987).

Animal research tends to support the view that there are advantages to predictability, especially when predictability allows one to control a stressor (Weinberg & Levine, 1980). Providing laboratory rats with a signal that a stressor is approaching apparently buffers its impact.

In one study, Weiss (1972) placed three sets of rats matched according to age and weight into individual soundproof cages, as shown in Figure 15.2. The rat on the left received electric shock following a signal. It could then terminate the shock by turning the wheel. The rat in the center was shocked in tandem with the rat to the left, but it received no warning signal and could do nothing to terminate the shock. The rat to the right received no signal and no electric shock. However, it was placed in the identical apparatus, including having electrodes attached to its tail, to control for any effects of this unnatural environment.

"Internals" • People who perceive the ability to attain reinforcements as being largely within themselves.

"Externals" • People who perceive the ability to attain reinforcements as being largely outside themselves.

FIGURE 15.2

The Experimental Setup in the Weiss Study on Ulcer Formation in Rats. The rat to the left is signaled prior to receiving electric shock and can terminate the shock by turning the wheel. The rat in the center receives a shock of the same intensity and duration but is not warned of its onset and cannot terminate it. The rat to the right receives no signal and no shock.

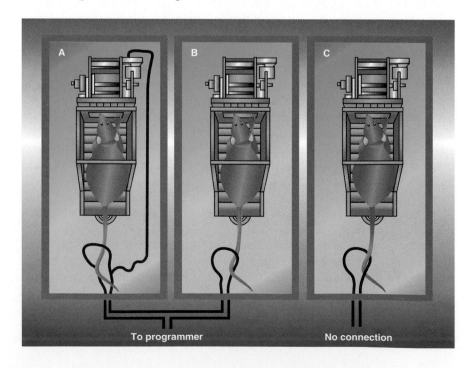

As shown in Figure 15.3, shock led to ulceration in the rats—the definition of stressful experience in this study. The rats to the right, which received no signal and no shock, showed hardly any ulceration. Rats that received shock without warning showed the greatest amount of ulceration. Rats given warning signals and allowed to terminate the shock also developed ulcers, but to a significantly lesser degree. The Weiss study suggests that inescapable stressors may be less harmful when they are predictable and when we act purposefully upon their arrival. Knowledge of them permits us to brace ourselves and plan effective responses. We may not avert stress, but we may buffer its impact.

SOCIAL SUPPORT. Social support, like psychological hardiness, seems to buffer the effects of stress (Burman & Margolin, 1992; Coyne & Downey, 1991; Holahan & Moos, 1990). Introverts, people who lack social skills, and people who live by themselves seem more prone to developing infectious diseases under stress (Cohen & Williamson, 1991).

Social supports include the following:

1. *Emotional concern.*
2. *Instrumental aid* (the material supports and services that aid adaptive behavior).
3. *Information* (guidance and advice that enhances people's ability to cope).
4. *Appraisal* (feedback from others as to how one is doing). This kind of support involves helping people interpret, or "make sense of," what has happened to them.
5. *Socializing* (simple conversation, recreation, even going shopping with another person).

Research supports the value of social support. Elderly people who have social support recover more rapidly from physical disabilities (Wilcox and others, 1994). People who have buddies who help them start exercising or quit drinking or smoking are more likely to succeed (Gruder and others, 1993; Nides and others, 1995). Social support appears to protect us, and to help us recover, from feelings of depression (Holahan and others, 1995; Lewinsohn and others, 1994b; McLeod and others, 1992). A study of men who were infected with the AIDS virus (HIV) showed that men who received more satisfying social support were less depressed and found HIV-related symptoms less stressful than men who received less satisfying social support (Hays and others, 1992). Stress is less likely to induce high blood pressure in women who have social support than in women who do not (Linden and others, 1993).

People who receive social support may even live longer, as was found in studies of Alameda County, California (Berkman & Breslow, 1983), and Tecumseh, Michigan (House and others, 1982). In the Tecumseh study, adults were followed during a 12-year period. The mortality rate was significantly lower for men who were married, who regularly attended meetings of voluntary associations, and who frequently engaged in social leisure activities.

Truth or Fiction Revisited. *It is not true that single men live longer.* Actually, married men live longer than single men.

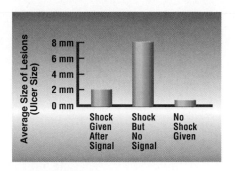

FIGURE 15.3

Effects of Predictability and Ability to Control a Stressor on Ulcer Formation in Rats. Rats that received no signals or shocks formed hardly any ulcers, as shown in part C. Rats that received shocks but could not predict or terminate them showed the most ulcer formation. Part B shows that rats that were warned of impending shocks and could terminate them showed more ulcer formation than rats that were not shocked but not nearly as much ulceration as rats that could not predict the onset of shocks.

The General Adaptation Syndrome

How is it that too much of a good thing—or that stress—can make us ill? Hans Selye (1976) suggested that the body under stress is like a clock with an alarm system that does not shut off until its energy is dangerously depleted.

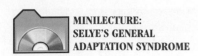
Selye observed that the body's response to different stressors shows some similarities or generalities, whether the stressor is a bacterial invasion, perceived danger, or a major life change. He labeled this response the **general adaptation syndrome** (GAS). The GAS consists of three stages: an alarm reaction, a resistance stage, and an exhaustion stage.

THE ALARM REACTION. The **alarm reaction** is triggered by perception of a stressor. This reaction mobilizes or arouses the body in preparation for defense. Early in the century, physiologist Walter Cannon termed this alarm system the **fight-or-flight reaction.** The alarm reaction involves a number of body changes that are initiated by the brain and further regulated by the endocrine system and the sympathetic division of the autonomic nervous system (ANS; Gallucci and others, 1993). Let us consider the roles of these two body systems.

Stress has a domino effect on the endocrine system (Figure 15.4). The hypothalamus secretes corticotrophin-releasing hormone (CRH). CRH causes the pituitary gland to secrete adrenocorticotrophic hormone (ACTH). ACTH then causes the adrenal cortex to secrete cortisol and other corticosteroids (steroidal hormones produced by the adrenal cortex). Corticosteroids help protect the body by combatting allergic reactions (such as difficulty breathing) and by producing inflammation. Inflammation increases circulation to parts of the body that are injured, carrying hordes of white blood cells to fend off invading pathogens.

General adaptation syndrome • Selye's term for a hypothesized three-stage response to stress. Abbreviated *GAS.*

Alarm reaction • The first stage of the GAS, which is triggered by the impact of a stressor and characterized by sympathetic activity.

Fight-or-flight reaction • An innate adaptive response to the perception of danger.

FIGURE 15.4

Stress and the Endocrine System. Stress has a domino effect on the endocrine system, leading to the release of corticosteroids and a mixture of adrenaline and noradrenaline. Corticosteroids combat allergic reactions (such as difficulty breathing) and cause inflammation. Adrenaline and noradrenaline arouse the body to cope by accelerating the heart rate and providing energy for the fight-or-flight reaction.

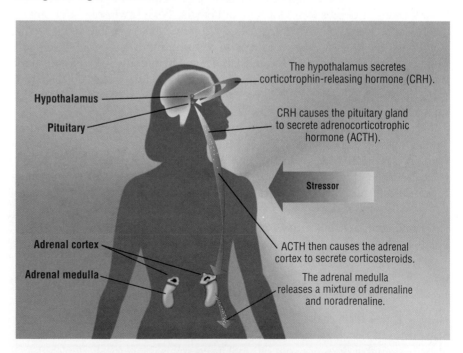

TABLE 15.1
COMPONENTS OF THE ALARM REACTION

Corticosteroids are secreted	Muscles tense
Adrenaline is secreted	Blood shifts from internal organs of the
Noradrenaline is secreted	skeletal musculature
Respiration rate increases	Digestion is inhibited
Heart rate increases	Sugar is released from the liver
Blood pressure increases	Blood coagulability increases

The alarm reaction is triggered by various types of stressors. It is defined by release of cortico-steroids and adrenaline and by activity of the sympathetic branch of the autonomic nervous system. It prepares the body to fight or flee from a source of danger.

Two other hormones that play a major role in the alarm reaction are secreted by the adrenal medulla. The sympathetic division of the ANS activates the adrenal medulla, causing a mixture of adrenaline and noradrenaline to be released. The mixture arouses the body to cope with threats and stress by accelerating the heart rate and causing muscle tissue and the liver to release glucose (sugar). In this way, energy is provided for the fight-or-flight reaction, which was inherited from a time when many stressors were life threatening. This reaction activates the body so that it is prepared to fight or flee from a predator. Adrenaline and noradrenaline also appear to etch memories of stressful events in the limbic system so that we are apt to remember them (Cahill and others, 1994; Goleman, 1994).

Many of the bodily changes that occur in the fight-or-flight reaction are outlined in Table 15.1. Historically, the reaction was triggered by a predator at the edge of a thicket or by a sudden rustling in the undergrowth. Today, it is also aroused when you chafe at the bit in stop-and-go traffic or learn that your mortgage payments are going to be increased. Once the threat is removed, the body returns to a lower state of arousal.

THE RESISTANCE STAGE.   If the alarm reaction mobilizes the body and the stressor is not removed, we enter the adaptation stage, or **resistance stage,** of the GAS. The levels of endocrine and sympathetic activity are not as high as in the alarm reaction, but they are still greater than normal. In this stage, the body attempts to restore lost energy and repair bodily damage.

THE EXHAUSTION STAGE.   If the stressor is still not adequately dealt with, we may enter the final or **exhaustion stage** of the GAS. Our individual capacities for resisting stress vary, but all of us eventually become exhausted when stress persists indefinitely. Our muscles become fatigued, and we deplete our bodies of resources required for combating stress. With exhaustion, the parasympathetic division of the ANS may predominate. As a result, our heartbeats and respiration rates slow down, and many of the body responses that had characterized sympathetic activity are reversed. It might sound as if we would profit from the respite, but remember that we are still under stress—and possibly an external threat. Continued stress in the exhaustion stage may lead to what Selye terms "diseases of adaptation"—from allergies and hives to ulcers and heart disease—and, ultimately, to death.

Resistance stage • The second stage of the GAS, characterized by prolonged sympathetic activity in an effort to restore lost energy and repair damage. Also called the *adaptation stage*.

Exhaustion stage • The third stage of the GAS, characterized by weakened resistance and possible deterioration.

Let us now consider the effects of stress on the body's immune system. Our discussion will pave the way for understanding the links between various psychological factors and physical illnesses.

Effects of Stress on the Immune System

Research shows that chronic stress suppresses the **immune system** (Coe, 1993; O'Leary, 1990). Research also demonstrates how psychological factors such as control and social support moderate the effects of stress on the immune system. Let us first review the nature and functions of the immune system. Then we shall consider the effects of stress on the immune system in more detail.

NATURE AND FUNCTIONS OF THE IMMUNE SYSTEM. Given the complexities of our bodies and the fast pace of scientific change, it is common for us to think of ourselves as being highly dependent on trained professionals such as physicians to cope with illness. Yet, we actually do most of this coping by ourselves, by means of our immune systems.

The immune system has several functions that help us combat disease. One way in which we combat physical disorders is by producing white blood cells that routinely engulf and kill pathogens such as bacteria, fungi, and viruses; worn-out body cells; even cells that have changed into cancerous cells. White blood cells are technically termed **leukocytes** (Figure 15.5). Leukocytes carry

---

Immune system • (im-YOON). The system of the body that recognizes and destroys foreign agents (antigens) that invade the body.

Leukocytes • (LOO-coe-sites). White blood cells. (Derived from the Greek words *leukos,* meaning "white," and *kytos,* literally meaning "a hollow" but used to refer to cells.)

FIGURE 15.5

Microscopic Warfare. The immune system helps us to combat disease. It produces white blood cells (leukocytes), such as the one shown here, that routinely engulf and kill pathogens such as bacteria and viruses. Leukocytes recognize pathogens by the shapes of their surfaces. The surface shapes are termed *antigens* (short for "antibody generators") because the body reacts to their presence by developing specialized proteins (the *antibodies*) that attach to the pathogens, inactivating them and marking them for destruction.

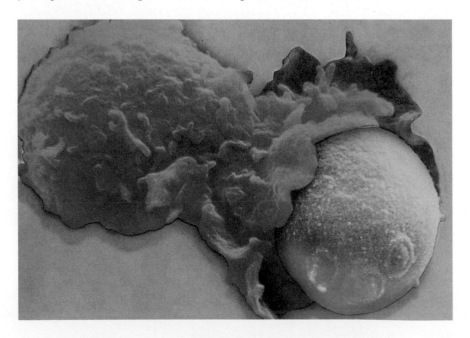

on microscopic warfare. They engage in search-and-destroy missions in which they "recognize" and then eliminate foreign agents and unhealthy cells.

Leukocytes remember foreign agents by the shapes of their surfaces to enhance the effectiveness of future combat. The surface shapes are termed **antigens** because the body reacts to their presence by developing specialized proteins, or **antibodies,** that attach to the foreign bodies, inactivating them and marking them for destruction. The immune system "remembers" how to battle antigens by maintaining antibodies to them in the bloodstream, often for years.[1]

Inflammation is another function of the immune system. When injury occurs, blood vessels in the area first contract (to stem bleeding) but then dilate. Dilation increases the flow of blood to the damaged area, causing the redness and warmth that characterize inflammation. The increased blood supply also brings in large numbers of white blood cells to combat invading microscopic life forms such as bacteria that might otherwise use the local damage as a port of entry into the body.

Truth or Fiction Revisited. *It is true that countless microscopic warriors within our bodies are carrying out search-and-destroy missions against foreign agents at any given moment.* The warriors are the white blood cells of the immune system.

STRESS AND THE IMMUNE SYSTEM.   Psychologists, biologists, and medical researchers have combined their efforts in a field of study that addresses the relationships between psychological factors, the nervous system, the endocrine system, the immune system, and disease: **psychoneuroimmunology** (Maier and others, 1994). One of the major concerns of psychoneuroimmunology is the effect of stress on the immune system.

One of the reasons that stress eventually exhausts us is that it stimulates us to produce steroids. Steroids suppress the functioning of the immune system. Suppression has negligible effects when steroids are secreted intermittently, but persistent secretion impairs the functioning of the immune system by decreasing inflammation and interfering with the formation of antibodies. As a consequence, susceptibility to various illnesses, including the common cold (Cohen and others, 1993), increases.

An experiment with laboratory rats and electric shock mirrored the method of Weiss (1972), as described earlier. In the later study, however, the dependent variable was activity of the immune system, not ulcer formation (Laudenslager and others, 1983). The rats were exposed to inevitable electric shocks, but, as in the Weiss study, one group of rats could terminate the shock. Rats who could *not* exert control over the stressor showed immune-system deficits, but the rats who could terminate the shock showed no deficiency.

One study with people focused on dental students (Jemmott and others, 1983). Students showed lower immune-system functioning, as measured by lower levels of antibodies in the saliva, during stressful school periods than immediately following vacations. Moreover, students with many friends showed less suppression of the immune system than students with few friends. Social support apparently buffered school stresses.

Other studies have found that the stress of examinations depresses immune-system response to the Epstein-Barr virus, which causes fatigue and other

Antigen • (ANT-tee-jenn or ANT-eye-jenn). A substance that stimulates the body to mount an immune-system response to it. (The contraction for *anti*body *gen*erator.)

Antibodies • Substances formed by white blood cells that recognize and destroy antigens.

Inflammation • (IN-flam-MAY-shun). Increased blood flow to an injured area of the body, resulting in redness, warmth, and an increased supply of white blood cells.

Psychoneuroimmunology • (sigh-coe-new-row-im-you-NOLL-oh-gee). The field that studies the relationships between psychological factors (e.g., attitudes and overt behavior patterns) and the functioning of the immune system.

---

[1] Vaccination is the introduction of a weakened form of an antigen (usually a bacteria or a virus) into the body to stimulate the production of antibodies. Antibodies can confer immunity for many years, in some cases for a lifetime. Smallpox has been eradicated by means of vaccination, and scientists are searching for a vaccine against the AIDS virus.

problems (Glaser and others, 1991, 1993). Moreover, students who are lonely show greater suppression of the immune system than students who have more social support. In a study of elderly people, it was found that a combination of relaxation training, which decreases sympathetic activity, and training in coping skills *improves* the functioning of the immune system (Glaser and others, 1991).

Reflections

- What kinds of life changes and daily hassles are you experiencing these days? Do you find these events stressful? How do you know?
- Hassles and life changes can predict physical illness. Does this mean that we should try to avoid making changes in our lives? Why or why not?
- What kinds of conflict, if any, are you in? What are you doing to attempt to resolve these conflicts?
- Are you a Type A person? Why do you think that you are or are not?
- Agree or disagree with the following statement and support your answer: "It is better not to know about bad things that are going to happen."
- Why do you think that married men live longer than single men do? (See Figure 15.6.) Is it because marriage is a more healthful state than singlehood, or do these findings reflect a selection factor? That is, do the same factors that lead men to get married and to stay married also lead to better health? If so, what might these factors be?

FIGURE 15.6

Why Do Married Men Live Longer Than Single Men? Does marriage lead to longevity, or does another factor contribute both to longevity and a tendency to get married? What might that other factor (or factors) be?

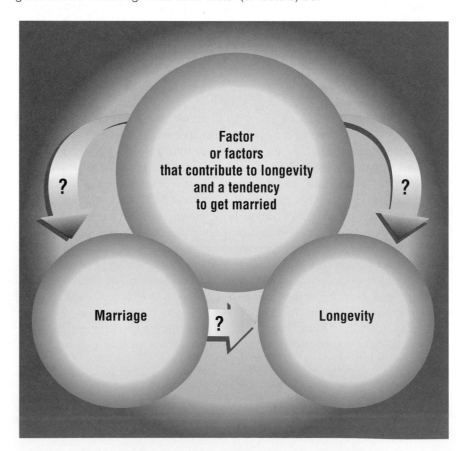

- Do you tend to get ill—for example, to "catch what's going around"—at a certain time of the year? If so, what time of year? Why do you think that you are more vulnerable to illness at this time of year?

Now that we have considered the nature of stress and the body's response to stress, let us more broadly consider the factors involved in physical illness.

A MULTIFACTORIAL APPROACH TO HEALTH AND ILLNESS

The only way to keep your health is to eat what you don't want, drink what you don't like, and do what you'd rather not.

MARK TWAIN

Why do people get sick? Why do some of us develop cancer? Why do others have heart attacks? Why do still others seem to be immune to these illnesses? Why do some of us seem to come down with everything that is going around, while others ride out the roughest winters with nary a sniffle? There is no single, simple answer to these questions. The likelihood of contracting an illness—whether a case of the flu or a kind of cancer—can reflect the interaction of many factors (Coie and others, 1993; Stokols, 1992). Biological factors such as family history of disease, pathogens, inoculations, injuries, age, and gender may strike us as the most obvious causes of disease. However, as shown in Table 15.2, psychological, social, technological, and natural environmental factors also play key roles in health and illness. For example, the Los Angeles earthquake of 1994 not only killed more than 40 people and cost billions of dollars. It also caused life changes to pile atop one another by disrupting community life. Services that had been taken for granted, such as electricity and water, were lost. Businesses and homes were destroyed, so that people had to rebuild or relocate. Such disasters reveal the thinness of the veneer of technology on which civilization depends. It is understandable that many survivors report stress-related problems such as anxiety and depression for months after the fact.

Many diseases are influenced by psychological factors, such as our attitudes and patterns of behavior (Ader, 1993; Angell, 1993; Farley, 1993a). Psychological states such as anxiety and depression can also impair the functioning of the immune system, rendering us more vulnerable to physical illness in general (Esterling and others, 1993; Herbert & Cohen, 1993; Kemeny and others, 1994; Weisse, 1992).

In the following section we focus on some of the sociocultural factors that are connected with health and illness, as reflected in human diversity. Then we turn our attention to a number of health problems including headaches, heart disease, asthma, cancer, and AIDS.

SOCIOCULTURAL FACTORS IN HEALTH AND ILLNESS: NATIONS WITHIN THE NATION

In 1990, a cigarette company began to market a new brand, Uptown, which was specifically designed to appeal to African Americans. There was such a clamor from civil rights groups and the media, however, that the ad campaign was canceled, and manufacture of the brand was discontinued ("Decline in

TABLE 15.2
FACTORS IN HEALTH AND ILLNESS: BIOLOGICAL, PSYCHOLOGICAL, SOCIAL, TECHNOLOGICAL, AND NATURAL ENVIRONMENTAL

BIOLOGICAL	PERSONALITY	BEHAVIORAL	SOCIOCULTURAL	TECHNOLOGICAL	NATURAL ENVIRONMENTAL
Family history of illness	Self-efficacy expectations	Diet (intake of calories, fats, fiber, vitamins, etc.)	Socioeconomic status	Adequacy of available health care	Natural disasters (earthquakes, floods, hurricanes, drought, extremes of temperature, tornados)
Exposure to infectious pathogens (e.g., bacteria and viruses)	Psychological hardiness	Consumption of alcohol	Availability and use of social support vs. peer rejection or isolation	Vehicular safety	Radon
Functioning of the immune system	Psychological conflict (approach–approach, avoidance–avoidance approach–avoidance)	Cigarette smoking	Family circumstances: social class, family size, conflict, disorganization	Architectural features (e.g., injury-resistant design, nontoxic construction materials, aesthetic design, air quality, noise insulation)	
Inoculations	Optimism	Level of physical activity	Social climate in the workplace, sexual harrassment		
Medication history	Attributional style (how one explains one's failures to oneself)	Sleep patterns	Prejudice and discrimination		
Congenital disabilities, perinatal complications	Health locus of control (belief that one is in charge of one's own health)	Safety practices (e.g., driving with seat belts; careful driving; practice of sexual abstinence, monogamy, or "safe sex"; attaining of comprehensive prenatal care)	Major life changes of a social nature such as death of a spouse or divorce	Aesthetics of residential, workplace, and communal architecture and landscape architecture	
Physiological conditions (e.g., hypertension, serum cholesterol level)	Introversion/ extroversion	Regular medical and dental checkups	Health-related cultural and religious beliefs and practices	Water quality	
Reactivity of the cardiovascular system (e.g., "hot reactor")	Coronary-prone (Type A) personality	Compliance with medical and dental advice	Major economic life changes such as taking out a large mortgage or losing one's job	Solid waste treatment and sanitation	
Pain and discomfort	Tendencies to express feelings of anger and frustration	Interpersonal/ social skills	Health promotion programs in the workplace or the community	Pollution	
Age	Depression/ anxiety		Health-related legislation	Radiation	
Gender	Hostility/ suspiciousness		Availability of health insurance	Global warming	
			Availability of transportation to health-care facilities	Ozone depletion	

This table incorporates elements from Coie and others (1993) and Stokols (1992).

Smoking," 1993). The cigarette brand Virginia Slims is designed and marketed to appeal to women (McCarthy, 1990). Virginia Slims is very much alive and economically successful, sad to say. In fact, whereas most population groups are now smoking less than they did a generation ago, young career women are smoking more. We thus find a greater incidence of lung cancer and other smoking-related illnesses within this group than we have in past years.

Health psychologists have noted that in the realms of health-related behaviors and the incidence of various physical disorders, we are many nations and not just one. Many factors influence whether people make an effort to prevent illness or succumb to illness. As noted in Table 15.2, they include ethnicity, gender, level of education, and socioeconomic status.

For example, African Americans between the ages of 25 and 64 have a much higher mortality rate than White Americans in the same age group. Moreover, this gap has been widening over the past few decades (Pappas and others, 1993). The death rate does not appear to be due to ethnicity per se, but rather to factors such as income (Angell, 1993) and level of education (Guralnik and others, 1993). (African Americans tend to be poorer and less well educated than White Americans.) African Americans not only have less access to health care than White Americans do. African Americans are also more likely to live in unhealthful neighborhoods, eat high-fat diets, and smoke (Pappas and others, 1993).

MINILECTURE: PERSONALITY AND HEALTH

Disproportionate numbers of deaths from AIDS also occur within ethnic minorities in the United States, predominantly among African Americans and Hispanic Americans. Only 12% of the U.S. population is African American, but African American men account for more than 30% of those with AIDS (Amaro, 1995). African American women account for more than 54% of the women with AIDS. Only 9% of the population is Hispanic American, but Hispanic Americans account for more than 17% of people with AIDS (Amaro, 1995). Hispanic American women account for 20% of the women with AIDS. Yet minority adolescents still think of AIDS as a disease of White gay males. Thus, they perceive themselves to be at little risk for contracting AIDS (St. Lawrence and others, 1995).

The incidence of sickle-cell anemia is highest among African and Hispanic Americans. The incidence of Tay-Sachs disease is greatest among Jews of East European origin. The connection between these disorders and the ethnic groups they assault is genetic.

African Americans are five to seven times more likely than European Americans to suffer from hypertension (Leary, 1991). However, African Americans are also more likely to suffer from hypertension than Black Africans are. Many health professionals thus infer that environmental factors that are found among many African Americans—such as stress, diet, and smoking—contribute to high blood pressure in people who are genetically vulnerable to it (Betancourt & López, 1993; Leary, 1991).

Anorexia and bulimia nervosa are uncommon among poor people, but obesity is most prevalent among them (see Chapter 10). The incidence of obesity is also greater among cultural groups in which many people associate obesity with happiness and health—as among some Haitian (Laguerre, 1981) and Puerto Rican groups (Harwood, 1981). The urban ghetto fosters obesity because junk food is heavily promoted, and many residents eat as a way of coping with stress (Freeman, 1991).

Truth or Fiction Revisited. *It is not true that poor people in the United States eat less than more affluent people.* Obesity is actually most prevalent among the lowest socioeconomic groups. Why? (This is not to deny the sad fact that some poor people in the United States go hungry.)

African Americans are more likely than White Americans to suffer heart attacks and to die from them (Becker and others, 1993). Early diagnosis and treatment might help decrease the racial gap (Ayanian, 1993). African Americans who suffer from heart disease are less likely than White Americans to undergo surgical procedures such as bypass surgery, even in Veterans Administration hospitals, where diagnosis and treatment are free (Whittle and others, 1993).

African Americans are also more likely than White Americans to contract most forms of cancer. Possibly because of genetic factors, the incidence of lung cancer is significantly higher among African Americans than White Americans (American Cancer Society, 1995; Blakeslee, 1994). Once they contract cancer, African Americans are more likely than White Americans to die from it (Andersen, 1992; Bal, 1992). The discouraging results for African Americans are connected with their lower socioeconomic status (Baquet and others, 1991). Consider research on women with breast cancer. Cancer is more curable when it is detected early. Yet women who do not carry health insurance coverage, or who have Medicaid (public health insurance for people of low socioeconomic status), are less likely than women who have private health insurance to detect cancer early and are more likely to die from it (Ayanian and others, 1993).

Also consider some cross-cultural differences in health. Death rates from cancer are higher in nations such as the Netherlands, Denmark, England, Canada, and—yes—the United States, where the population has a high daily fat intake (Cohen, 1987). Death rates from cancer are much lower in nations such as in Thailand, the Philippines, and Japan, where the daily fat intake is markedly lower. Don't assume that the difference is racial just because Thailand, the Philippines, and Japan are Asian nations! The diets of Japanese Americans are similar in fat content to those of other Americans—and so are their death rates from cancer.

Because of dietary differences, Japanese American men living in California and Hawaii are two to three times more likely to become obese than Japanese men who live in Japan (Curb & Marcus, 1991).

The type of fat also makes a difference. Saturated fats, found in meat and butter, heighten the risk of cancer. Monounsaturated olive oil may lower the risk of cancer. In Mediterranean countries such as Italy and Greece, where olive oil is used widely for cooking and salads, the incidence of breast cancer is much lower than in the United States (Brody, 1995b).

Then consider a few gender differences. Men are more likely than women to suffer from heart disease. Women are apparently "protected" by high levels of estrogen until menopause (Brody, 1993b). After menopause, women are dramatically more likely to incur heart disease. Hormone replacement therapy apparently continues to lower the risk of heart disease, however (Brody, 1995a).

At all ages, men are more likely than women to drink alcohol heavily. Heavy drinking is found less often among the elderly than among young and middle adults. The incidence of heavy drinking is highest in the nation's capitol—Washington, DC, and lowest in the states of Utah and West Virginia.

The gender of the physician can also make a difference. According to a study of more than 90,000 women, women whose internists or family practitioners are women are more likely to have screenings for cancer (mammograms and Pap smears) than women whose internists or family practitioners are men (Lurie and others, 1993). It is unclear from this study, however, whether women physicians are more likely than their male counterparts to encourage women to seek preventive care, or whether women who choose female physicians are also more likely to seek preventive care. Other research shows that female physicians are more likely than male physicians to conduct breast examinations properly (Hall and others, 1990).

There are health-care "overusers" and "underusers" among cultural groups. For example, Hispanic Americans visit physicians less often than African Americans and non-Hispanic White Americans do because of lack of health insurance, difficulty speaking English, misgivings about medical technology, and—for illegal aliens—fear of deportation (Ziv & Lo, 1995).

Men's life expectancies are 7 years shorter on average than women's. A survey of 1,500 physicians suggests that the difference is due, at least in part, to women's greater willingness to seek health care ("Doctors Tie Male Mentality," 1995). Men often let symptoms go until a problem that could have been prevented or readily treated becomes serious or life threatening. Some men, according to the survey, have a "bulletproof mentality."

WORLD OF DIVERSITY

HEALTH AND SOCIOECONOMIC STATUS: THE RICH GET RICHER AND THE POOR GET . . . SICKER

Socioeconomic status (SES) and health have been intimately connected throughout history (Abraham, 1993; Rogers & Ginzberg, 1993). Generally speaking, people higher in SES enjoy better health and lead longer lives (Leary, 1995). The question is *why*.

Nancy Adler and her colleagues (1994) suggest various possible explanations for the link between health and SES. One possibility is that the connection between health and SES is not causal but that SES and health may both reflect genetic factors. For example, a genetically based solid constitution might lead both to good health and social standing. Second, poor health might lead to socioeconomic "drift" (that is, loss of social standing). Third, SES might affect biological functions that, in turn, influence one's health.

How might SES influence health? SES is defined in part in terms of level of education. That is, people who attain low levels of education are also likely to be low in SES. Less-well-educated people are more likely to smoke (Winkleby and others, 1991), and smoking is connected with many physical illnesses. People lower in SES are also less likely to exercise and more likely to be obese—both of which are, again, linked to poor health outcomes (Ford and others, 1991).

Moreover, psychological stress places people at greater risk of physical illness. By altering hormonal responses and suppressing the immune response, people under stress are more likely to develop illnesses ranging from gastrointestinal disorders to heart attacks, and to succumb to infectious agents (Cohen and others, 1993). People who are lower in SES are more likely to suffer stress for two reasons. First, poor people are more likely to encounter stressors, such as daily financial hassles, crowding, and pollution. Second, poor people are less likely to have the resources to cope with stressful experiences (Adler and others, 1994).

Let us also not forget that poorer people have less access to health care (Abraham, 1993; Leary, 1995; Rogers & Ginzberg, 1993). The problem is compounded by the fact that people of low SES are less likely to be educated concerning the values of regular health checkups and of early medical intervention when symptoms arise.

Socioeconomic status • One's social and financial level, as indicated by measures such as income, level of education, and occupational status. Abbreviated *SES*.

UNDERSTANDING AND COPING WITH MAJOR HEALTH PROBLEMS IN THE UNITED STATES TODAY

Let us now consider a number of health problems including headaches, heart disease, asthma, cancer, and AIDS. In each case we consider the interplay of biological, psychological, social, technological, and environmental factors in the origins of the problem. Although these are medical problems, psychologists have contributed to their understanding and treatment. Moreover, psychologists sometimes help people adjust when there is nothing to be done (McCarthy, 1995).

Headaches

Headaches are among the most common stress-related physical ailments. Nearly 20% of people in the United States suffer from severe headaches.

MUSCLE-TENSION HEADACHE.   The single most frequent kind of headache is the muscle-tension headache. We are likely to contract muscles in the shoulders, neck, forehead, and scalp during the first two stages of the GAS. Persistent stress can lead to persistent contraction of these muscles, giving rise to muscle-tension headaches. Such headaches usually come on gradually. They are most often characterized by dull, steady pain on both sides of the head and feelings of tightness or pressure.

MIGRAINE HEADACHE.   Most other headaches, including the severe **migraine headache,** are vascular in nature—that is, stemming from changes in the blood supply to the head (Welch, 1993). There is often a warning "aura" that may be characterized by visual problems and perception of unusual odors. The attacks themselves are often attended by intensified sensitivity to light; loss of appetite, nausea, and vomiting; sensory and motor disturbances such as loss of balance; and changes in mood. The so-called common migraine headache is identified by sudden onset and throbbing on one side of the head. The so-called classic migraine is known by sensory and motor disturbances that precede the pain.

The origins of migraine headaches are not clearly understood. It is believed, however, that they can be induced by barometric pressure; pollen; specific drugs; the chemical monosodium glutamate (MSG), which is often used to enhance the flavor of food; chocolates; aged cheeses; beer, champagne, and red wines; and the hormonal changes connected with menstruation (Brody, 1992a). Type A behavior may also be an important contributor to migraine headaches. In one study, 53% of 30 migraine sufferers showed the Type A behavior pattern, as compared with 23% of 30 muscle-tension headache sufferers (Rappaport and others, 1988).

Regardless of the original source of the headache, we can unwittingly propel ourselves into a vicious cycle. Headache pain is a stressor that can lead us to increase, rather than relax, muscle tension in the neck, shoulders, scalp, and face.

TREATMENT.   Aspirin and ibuprofen frequently decrease pain, including headache pain, by inhibiting the production of the prostaglandins that help initiate transmission of pain messages to the brain. Drugs that affect the blood flow in the brain help many people with migraines (Welch, 1993). Behavioral methods can also help. Progressive relaxation focuses on decreasing muscle tension and has been shown to be highly effective in relieving muscle-tension headaches (Blanchard, 1992b; Blanchard and others, 1990a, 1991). Biofeedback training that alters the flow of blood to the head has helped many people with migraine headaches (Blanchard and others, 1990b; Gauthier and others, 1994). People who are sensitive to MSG or red wine can ask that MSG be left out of their dishes and can switch to a white wine.

Why, under stress, do some of us develop ulcers, others develop heart disease, and still others suffer no physical problems? In the following sections, we see that there may be an interaction between stress and predisposing biological and psychological differences between individuals.

Migraine headaches • (MY-grain). Throbbing headaches that are connected with changes in the supply of blood to the head.

Heart Disease

Coronary heart disease (CHD) causes nearly half the deaths in the United States (USDHHS, 1991). Consider the risk factors for CHD:

1. *Family History.* People whose families show a history of CHD are more likely to develop CHD themselves (Marenberg and others, 1994).

2. *Physiological Conditions.* Obesity, high **serum cholesterol** levels (Keil and others, 1993; Manson and others, 1990; Rossouw and others, 1990; Stampfer and others, 1991), and **hypertension** are examples.

    About one American in five has hypertension, or abnormally high blood pressure (Leary, 1991). When high blood pressure has no identifiable causes, it is referred to as *essential hypertension.* There appears to be a genetic component to essential hypertension (Caulfield and others, 1994). However, our blood pressure also rises in situations in which people are constantly on guard against threats, whether in combat, in the workplace, or in the home. When we are under great stress, we may believe that we can feel our blood pressure "pounding through the roof," but this notion is usually inaccurate. Most people cannot recognize symptoms of hypertension. It is thus important for us to have our blood pressure checked regularly.

3. *Patterns of Consumption.* Patterns include heavy drinking, smoking, overeating, and eating food high in cholesterol, like saturated fats (Castelli, 1994; Jeffery, 1991; Keil, 1993). Smoking raises the blood level of cholesterol and weakens the walls of blood vessels (Bartecchi and others, 1994).

4. *Type A Behavior.* Evidence is mixed as to whether the Type A behavior pattern—or one or more of its components, such as hostility—places people at risk for CHD. However, most studies suggest that there is at least a modest relationship between Type A behavior and CHD (Thoresen & Powell, 1992). It also seems that alleviating Type A behavior patterns may reduce the risk of *recurrent* heart attacks (Friedman & Ulmer, 1984).

5. *Hostility and Holding in Feelings of Anger* (Kneip and others, 1993; Suarez and others, 1993).

6. *Job Strain.* Overtime work, assembly-line labor, and exposure to conflicting demands all make their contributions (Jenkins, 1988). High-strain work, which makes high demands on workers but affords them little personal control, places workers at the highest risk (Karasek and others, 1982; Krantz and others, 1988). As shown in Figure 15.7, the work of waiters and waitresses may best fit this description.

7. *Chronic Fatigue and Chronic Emotional Strain.*

8. *A Physically Inactive Lifestyle* (Dubbert, 1992; Lakka and others, 1994).

BEHAVIOR MODIFICATION FOR REDUCING RISK FACTORS FOR HEART DISEASE. Once heart disease has been diagnosed, there are a number of medical treatments, including surgery and medication. However, persons who have not had CHD (as well as those who have) can profit from behavior modification that is intended to reduce the risk factors. These methods include the following:

1. *Stopping Smoking.* (See methods in Chapter 5.)

2. *Weight Control.* (See methods in Chapter 10.)

3. *Reducing Hypertension.* Relaxation training (Agras and others, 1983), meditation (Benson and others, 1973), aerobic exercise (Brownell & Wadden,

Serum cholesterol • (SEE-rum coe-LESS-ter-all). Cholesterol found in the blood.

Hypertension • (HIGH-purr-TEN-shun). High blood pressure.

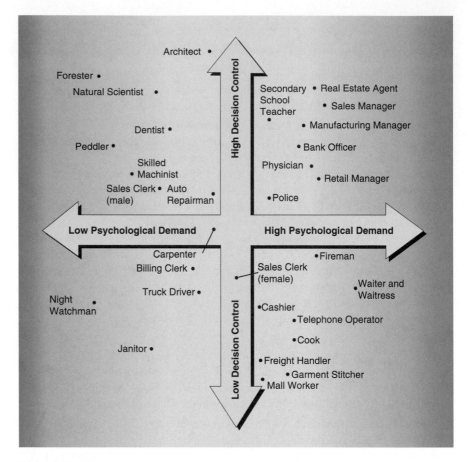

FIGURE 15.7

The Job-Strain Model. This model highlights the psychological demands made by various occupations and the amount of personal (decision) control they allow. Occupations characterized by both high demand and low decision control place workers at greatest risk for heart disease.

1992; Danforth and others, 1990), maintenance of normal weight, and cutting down on dietary salt (Langford and others, 1985) all show promise in the treatment of hypertension.

4. *Lowering Low-Density Lipoprotein (Harmful) Serum Cholesterol.* The major method involves cutting down on foods high in cholesterol and saturated fats, but exercise and medication may also help (Castelli, 1994). Interestingly, people assume that foods that are low in fat will not taste as good as high-fat foods, even when their flavor is comparable. Subjects in one laboratory experiment rated food labeled "high-fat" as tasting better than food labeled "low-fat" (Wardle & Solomons, 1994). However, they were tasting the same exact food!

5. *Modifying Type A Behavior.* Taking time out for ourselves and working on feelings of hostility modify Type A behavior and decrease the risk of heart attacks, even for people who have previously suffered them (Friedman & Ulmer, 1984; Roskies and others, 1986).

6. *Exercise.* Sustained physical activity protects people from CHD (Castelli, 1994; Curfman, 1993b). However, studies in the United States (Mittelman and others, 1993) and Germany (Willich and others, 1993) show that

strenuous physical exertion by people who are not used to exercise can trigger heart attacks. Sedentary people are therefore advised to begin exercise programs under their physicians' guidance.

We conclude this section with good news for readers of this book: *Better educated* people are more likely to modify health-impairing behavior and reap the benefits of change (Angell, 1993; Guralnik and others, 1993; Johnston and others, 1992; Pappas and others, 1993).

Asthma

Asthma is a respiratory disorder characterized by episodic constriction of the main tubes of the windpipe (the bronchi), oversecretion of mucus, and inflammation of air passageways (Israel and others, 1990). Sufferers may wheeze and intermittently find it difficult to breathe. Asthma affects about 9% of African American children and 6% of White children in the United States (DeAngelis, 1994b). Nearly 5,000 Americans die from asthma each year. African Americans and older people are the most vulnerable (Altman, 1993).

Although the causes of asthma are unknown, the lungs of people with asthma are more irritable than those who do not suffer from the disease (Altman, 1993). Attacks can be triggered by allergic reactions; cold, dry air; stress; emotional responses such as anger; laughing too hard; and exercise (McFadden & Gilbert, 1994). Although the link to stress is less than fully clear, the stress of worrying about an attack can apparently help bring one on.

There are medical treatments for asthma, including bronchodilators and inhaled steroids (Altman, 1993). A number of reports suggest that asthma sufferers may also improve their breathing by muscle relaxation training, biofeedback that helps relax facial muscles, and family therapy that reduces the interpersonal stresses that affect asthmatic children (Lehrer and others, 1992). Asthma has also been connected with respiratory infections and with maternal smoking during pregnancy (Martinez and others, 1992). Such evidence again suggests an interaction between the psychological and the physiological.

Cancer

Cancer is characterized by the development of abnormal, or mutant, cells that reproduce rapidly and rob the body of nutrients. Cancerous cells may take root anywhere: in the blood (leukemia), bones, digestive tract, lungs, and genital organs. If not controlled early, the cancerous cells may metastasize (establish colonies elsewhere in the body). We apparently develop cancer cells quite frequently, but the immune system normally surveys the body and destroys cancer cells. Evidence suggests that people whose immune systems are compromised by physical or psychological factors are more likely to develop tumors (Antoni, 1987; Greenberg, 1987).

RISK FACTORS.　As with many other disorders, people can inherit dispositions toward cancer (Eysenck, 1991). Carcinogenic genes may remove the usual brakes on cell division, allowing cells to propagate wildly. Or they may allow mutations to accumulate unchecked in other genes (Kolata, 1993b). However, many behavior patterns markedly heighten the risk for cancer, such as smoking (Bartecchi and others, 1994), drinking alcohol (especially in women), ingesting animal fats (Willett and others, 1990), and sunbathing (which because of ultraviolet light causes skin cancer). Prolonged psychological conditions such as depression or stress also heighten the risk (Antoni, 1987).

STRESS AND CANCER. Researchers have begun to uncover links between stress and cancer. For example, a study of children with cancer by Jacob and Charles (1980) revealed that a significant percentage had encountered severe life changes within a year of the diagnosis, often involving the death of a loved one or the loss of a close relationship.

Numerous studies also connect stressful life events to the onset of cancer among adults. However, this research has been criticized because it tends to be retrospective (Krantz and others, 1985). That is, people with cancer are interviewed about events preceding their diagnoses and about their psychological well-being prior to the onset of the disease. Self-reports are confounded by problems in memory and other inaccuracies. Moreover, the causal relationships in such research are clouded. For example, development of the illness might have precipitated stressful events. Stress, in other words, might have been the result of the illness rather than the cause.

Experimental research that could not be conducted with humans has been conducted with rats and other animals. In one type of study, animals are injected with cancerous cells or with viruses that cause cancer and then exposed to various conditions. In this way, it can be determined which conditions influence the likelihood that the animals' immune systems will be able to fend off the antigens. Such experiments with rodents suggest that once cancer has affected the individual, stress can influence its course. In one study, for example, rats were implanted with small numbers of cancer cells so that their own immune systems would have a chance to successfully combat them (Visintainer and others, 1982). Some of the rats were then exposed to inescapable shocks, whereas others were exposed to escapable shocks or to no shock. The rats exposed to the most stressful condition—the inescapable shock—were half as likely as the other rats to reject the cancer and two times as likely to die from it.

In a study of this kind with mice, Riley (1981) studied the effects of a cancer-causing virus that can be passed from mothers to offspring by means of nursing. This virus typically produces breast cancer in 80% of female offspring by the time they have reached 400 days of age. Riley placed one group of female offspring at risk for cancer in a stressful environment of loud noises and noxious odors. Another group was placed in a less stressful environment. At the age of 400 days, 92% of the mice who developed under stressful conditions developed breast cancer, compared with 7% of those in the control group. Moreover, the high-stress mice showed increases in levels of steroids, which depress the functioning of the body's immune system, and lower blood levels of disease-fighting antibodies. However, the "bottom line" in this experiment is of major interest: By the time another 200 days had elapsed, the low-stress mice had nearly caught up to their high-stress peers in the incidence of cancer. Stress appears to have hastened along the inevitable for many of these mice, but the ultimate outcomes were not overwhelmingly influenced by stress.

Truth or Fiction Revisited. *It is true that stress can influence the course of cancer.* Whether stress ever affects the ultimate outcome remains an open question.

PSYCHOLOGICAL FACTORS IN THE TREATMENT OF CANCER. Not only must people with cancer cope with the biological aspects of their illnesses. They are

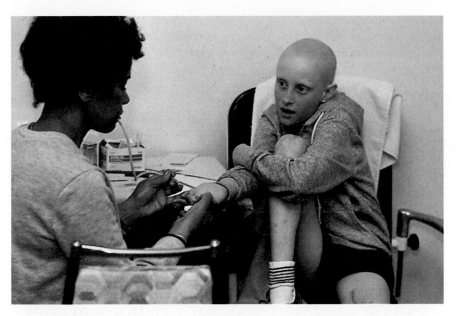

How Have Health Psychologists Helped This Young Person with Cancer?
Cancer is a medical disorder, but psychologists have contributed to the treatment of cancer patients. For example, psychologists help cancer patients remain in charge of their lives, combat feelings of hopelessness, cope with stress, and manage the side effects of chemotherapy.

also often faced with a host of psychological problems. These include feelings of anxiety and depression about treatment methods and the eventual outcome, changes in body image after the removal of a breast or testicle, feelings of vulnerability, and family problems, as in the cases of families who criticize people with cancer for feeling sorry for themselves or for not fighting hard enough (Andersen and others, 1994; Rosenthal, 1993b). Psychological stress due to cancer can impair the immune system, setting the stage for additional health problems, such as respiratory tract infections (Andersen and others, 1994).

It is understandable that people with cancer will be sad about it, but severe depression is often treatable in people with cancer (Holland, 1993). In former years, a cancer survivor who complained that his treatment left him unable to function sexually might be told that he was lucky to be alive by his physician (Holland, 1993). Today such people are more likely to be treated with sensitivity.

Many people with cancer are more concerned about their pain, or the pain they fear they will experience in the late stages of the illness, than they are about death. People with cancer may refuse narcotics like morphine for fear that they will no longer be effective later on, when they "really need it." Or they may fear that they will become addicted or tolerant. Accurate information is often helpful because specialists today say that addiction is not a problem for people with cancer and that tolerance can be dealt with by combinations of therapies (Brody, 1994). Psychological methods such as relaxation, meditation, biofeedback training, and exercise can also be of help (Lang & Patt, 1994).

There are also psychological interventions for the nausea that often accompanies chemotherapy. People undergoing chemotherapy who also use relaxation training and guided imagery techniques have significantly less nausea and vomiting than people who do not use these techniques. Moreover, their blood pressure and pulse rates are lower, and their moods are less negative than those who do not obtain the psychological help (Burish and others, 1987). Studies with preteenagers and teenagers find that playing video games also lessens the discomfort of chemotherapy (Kolko & Rickard-Figueroa, 1985; Redd and others, 1987). The children focus on battling computer-generated monsters rather than the effects of the chemicals being injected.

Yes, cancer is a medical disorder. However, health psychologists have improved the treatment of people with cancer. For example, a crisis like cancer can induce perceptions that life has spun out of control and become unpredictable. Control and predictability are factors in psychological hardiness, so perceptions of lack of control and unpredictability can lead to psychological vulnerability and heighten stress. Health psychology therefore stresses the value of encouraging people with cancer to remain in charge of their lives (Jacox and others, 1994). Yes, cancer does require medical treatment and, in too many cases, there are few options. However, people with cancer can still choose their attitudes. A 10-year follow-up of women with breast cancer found a significantly higher survival rate for women who met their diagnosis with anger and a "fighting spirit" rather than stoic acceptance (Pettingale and others, 1985). Emotional states like hostility, anxiety, even horror are all associated with increased rates of survival in breast cancer. Desire to fight the illness is apparently a vital treatment component.

Health psychologists have also found that the feelings of hopelessness and helplessness that often accompany the diagnosis of cancer may hinder recovery (Levy and others, 1985). Such feelings can depress the responsiveness of the person's immune system (Brody, 1994). Hospitalization itself is stressful because it removes people from their normal sources of social support and reduces their sense of control. If handled insensitively, hospitalization may further depress people's own ability to fight illness.

Psychologists are teaching coping skills to people with cancer to relieve psychological as well as physical distress. In one study, cognitive-behavioral coping methods were found superior to supportive group therapy and a no-treatment control condition in reducing emotional distress and helping people meet the demands of daily life (Telch & Telch, 1986). Treatment included relaxation training, stress management techniques, assertive communication training, cognitive restructuring, problem-solving techniques, management of emotions, and engaging in pleasant activities. Coping skills are beneficial in themselves and help people with cancer regain a sense of control and mastery.

Yet another psychological application is helping people undergoing chemotherapy keep up their strength by eating. The problem is that chemotherapy often causes nausea, and nausea becomes associated with foods eaten earlier in the day, causing enduring taste aversions in about 45% of the individuals obtaining treatment (Carey & Burish, 1988). So people with cancer, who are often already losing weight because of their illness, may find that taste aversions exacerbate the problems caused by lack of appetite. To combat taste aversions in people obtaining chemotherapy, Bernstein (1985) recommends feeding them atypical foods prior to chemotherapy. If taste aversions develop, they are associated with the unusual food, and their appetites for dietary staples may remain unaffected. Relaxation training also appears to increase food intake in people undergoing chemotherapy (Carey & Burish, 1987).

In sum, cancer is frightening and, in many cases, there may be little that we can do about its eventual outcome. However, we are still not helpless in the face of cancer. We can take measures like the following:

1. We can limit our exposure to the behavioral risk factors for cancer.

2. We can modify our diets by reducing intake of fats and increasing our intake of fruits and vegetables (Mevkens, 1990; Willett and others, 1990). Crucifers such as broccoli, cauliflower, and cabbage appear to be of particular value (Angier, 1994a). (Yes, Grandma was right.)

3. We can have regular medical checkups to detect cancer early. Unfortunately, people may not go for regular checkups or diagnostic procedures, such as mammograms to detect breast cancer, unless they believe that they are susceptible to the disease, believe in the benefits of mammography, and are not put off by barriers such as inconvenience or cost (Aiken and others, 1994).

4. We can regulate the amount of stress that affects us.

5. If we are struck by cancer, we can battle it energetically rather than assume the roles of passive victims.

AIDS

It really is demeaning for someone in my situation to have the 1990s' version of leprosy, to have to walk around on eggshells when we know that I am absolutely no danger to anyone. . . . You can kiss me, you can hug me, you can shake my hand, you can drink out of the same glass. I can sneeze on you, I can cough on you—you're not going to get it from me.

ARTHUR ASHE (1992), FORMER TENNIS PLAYER AND WIMBLEDON CHAMPION, WHO DIED OF AIDS IN 1993

The "1990s' version of leprosy" is acquired immunodeficiency syndrome (AIDS). AIDS is a fatal condition in which one's immune system is so weakened that it falls prey to "opportunistic" diseases. (Opportunistic diseases are those that would not stand much of a chance of developing in people whose immune systems were intact.) AIDS is caused by the human immunodeficiency virus (HIV). Although it takes an average (median) of 10 years for people who are infected with HIV to develop full-blown cases of AIDS (Altman, 1995), researchers believe that nearly all of those who are infected will eventually do so.

HIV is transmitted by heterosexual vaginal intercourse, anal intercourse, sharing contaminated hypodermic needles (as when a group of people "shoots up" a drug), transfusions of contaminated blood, and childbirth (Glasner & Kaslow, 1990). There is no evidence that public toilets, holding or hugging an infected person, or living or attending school with one transmit the virus.

HIV has an affinity for, and kills, white blood cells called *CD4 lymphocytes*[2] (or, more simply, *CD4 cells*) that are found in the immune system. CD4 cells recognize viruses and other germs and "instruct" other white blood cells—called *B lymphocytes*—to make antibodies. When CD4 cells are depleted, the body is left vulnerable to opportunistic diseases.

AIDS is characterized by fatigue, fever, unexplained weight loss, swollen lymph nodes, diarrhea, and, in many cases, impairment in learning and memory (Grant & Heaton, 1990). Opportunistic infections such as the following take hold: Kaposi's sarcoma, a cancer of the blood cells, that is seen in many gay males who contract AIDS; PCP (pneumocystis carinii pneumonia), a kind of pneumonia that is characterized by coughing and shortness of breath; and, in women, invasive cancer of the cervix.

---

[2] Also called T_4 *cells* or *helper T cells*.

People in the United States have been most likely to become infected with HIV by engaging in male–male sexual activity or injecting ("shooting up") illicit drugs (CDC, 1994). Other people who have been at particular risk include sex partners of people who inject drugs, babies born to women who inject drugs or whose sex partners inject drugs, prostitutes, men who visit prostitutes, sex partners of men who visit infected prostitutes, and people receiving blood transfusions—for example, people obtaining surgery and hemophiliacs. This last avenue of infection has become rare, however, because the medical community routinely screens blood supplies.

One psychological risk factor for being infected with HIV is that people tend to underestimate their risk of being infected (van der Velde and others, 1994). This finding is true of almost all groups, including poor inner-city residents (Hobfoll and others, 1993) and college students (Goldman & Harlow, 1993). Because AIDS has often been characterized as transmitted by anal intercourse (a practice that is not uncommon among gay males) and the sharing of contaminated needles, many heterosexual, non-drug-abusing Americans have dismissed the threat of AIDS (Kolata, 1993a). Yet male–female sexual intercourse accounts for a majority of cases worldwide (Kolata, 1993a). Although gays and drug abusers have been hit hardest by the epidemic, HIV cuts across all boundaries of gender, sexual orientation, ethnicity, and socioeconomic status.

Truth or Fiction Revisited. *It is not true that only gay males and substance abusers are at serious risk for contracting AIDS.* We all need to be aware of the risk factors and take appropriate precautions.

Infection by HIV is generally diagnosed by blood or saliva tests that show antibodies to the virus. Because it can take months after infection for antibodies to develop, repeated tests may be in order.

Unfortunately, we do not have a safe, effective vaccine for HIV. Nor is there a cure for AIDS. A number of antiviral drugs and behavioral interventions are under investigation, singly and in combination. However, none of them has cured anyone of AIDS to date (Eckholm, 1994). The only known way to effectively cope with AIDS is by *prevention* (Chesney, 1993; Kelly and others, 1993).

WHAT TO DO.

You're not just sleeping with one person, you're sleeping with everyone they ever slept with.

DR. THERESA CRENSHAW, PRESIDENT, AMERICAN ASSOCIATION OF SEX EDUCATORS, COUNSELORS AND THERAPISTS

Most college students appear to be reasonably well-informed about HIV transmission and AIDS (Wulfert & Wan, 1993). However, knowledge of AIDS and methods of HIV transmission are apparently insufficient in themselves to induce self-protective behavior (Bandura, 1990). Many college students assume that a partner is not infected with HIV. They simply hope for the best—even in the age of AIDS (Wulfert & Wan, 1993).

What can we do to prevent the transmission of HIV? A number of things.

1. *Refuse to deny the prevalence and harmful nature of AIDS.* Many people try to put AIDS and other sexually transmitted diseases (STDs) out of their minds and wing it when it comes to sex. The first and most important aspect of primary prevention is psychological: keeping AIDS in mind—refusing to play the dangerous game (at least for the moment) that it does not exist or is unlikely to strike you. Other measures involve modifying our behavior.

2. *Remain abstinent.* One way to curb the sexual transmission of HIV is sexual abstinence. Most people who remain abstinent do so while they are looking for Mr. or Ms. Right, of course. They thus eventually face the risk of engaging in sexual intercourse. Moreover, students want to know just what "abstinence" means. Does it mean avoiding sexual intercourse (yes) or any form of sexual activity with another person (not necessarily)? Kissing, hugging, and petting to orgasm (without coming into contact with semen or vaginal secretions) are generally considered safe.

3. *Engage in a monogamous relationship with someone who is not infected.* Sexual activity within a monogamous relationship with an uninfected person is safe. The questions here are how certain one can be that one's partner is indeed uninfected and monogamous.

For those who are unwilling to abstain from sexual relationships or to limit themselves to a monogamous relationship, some things can be done that make sex safer—if not perfectly safe:

4. *Be selective.* Engage in sexual activity only with well-known people who do not belong to the high-risk groups for AIDS.

5. *Inspect one's partner's genitals.* People who have been infected by HIV often have other sexually transmitted diseases. Examining one's partner's genitals for blisters, discharges, chancres, rashes, warts, lice, and unpleasant odors while engaged in foreplay may yield signs of such diseases.

6. *Wash one's own genitals before and after contact.* Washing beforehand helps protect one's partner. Washing promptly afterward with soap and water helps remove germs.

7. *Use spermicides.* Many spermicides kill HIV as well as sperm. Check with a pharmacist.

8. *Use condoms.* Latex condoms (but not condoms made from animal membrane) protect the man from vaginal (or other) body fluids and protect the woman from having infected semen enter the vagina.

9. *Contribute to research on AIDS.* If you can afford it, make a contribution to the American Foundation for AIDS Research (AMFAR) or to the Pediatric AIDS Foundation. Both organizations are based in Los Angeles.

10. *When in doubt, stop.* If one is not sure that sex is safe, one can stop and mull things over or seek expert advice.

If you think about it, this last piece is rather good general advice. When in doubt, why not stop and think, regardless of whether the doubt is about one's sex partner, one's college major, or a financial investment? In sex and in most other areas of life, hesitating when in doubt pays off in many, many ways.

Obesity

There is no sincerer love than the love of food.
GEORGE BERNARD SHAW

The two biggest sellers in any bookstore are the cookbooks and the diet books. The cookbooks tell you how to prepare the food and the diet books tell you how not to eat any of it.
ANDY ROONEY

Obesity is one of the banes of modern life. Even though young Americans are eating a lower-fat diet than they were in the 1980s, they weigh 10 pounds more on the average than they did in the 1980s ("Despite Better Diets," 1994; see Table 15.3).

TABLE 15.3
SNAPSHOT, U.S.A.: AVERAGE WEIGHT IN POUNDS OF AMERICANS AGED 25–30 IN THE 1980S VERSUS THE 1990S

	1985–1986	1992–1993	GAIN IN POUNDS
African American men	174.2	185.8	11.6
White men	171.1	181.9	10.8
African American women	158.5	166.2	7.7
White women	140.6	150.8	10.2

Based on a survey of 5,115 Americans.
Source of data: Cora E. Lewis, University of Alabama at Birmingham. Cited in "Despite Better Diets, Adults in Their 20s Are Weighing More," 1994, *The New York Times,* March 18, p. A17.

Truth or Fiction Revisited. *It is not true that young adults in the United States are trimmer than they were in the 1980s.* Young Americans now eat less fat and their cholesterol levels are 9 points lower on the average, but they weigh in, on average, at 10 pounds more. Eating more and exercising less are two of the reasons ("Despite Better Diets," 1994).

Here are some other facts about weight:

• One out of four American adults is obese—that is, weighs more than 20% above his or her recommended weight (Kuczmarski, 1992).

• Americans consume 815 billion calories of food each day, which is 200 billion calories more than they need to maintain their weight (Jenkins, 1988). The excess calories could feed a nation of 80 million people (Jenkins, 1988).

Truth or Fiction Revisited. *It is true that Americans overeat by enough to feed the nation of Germany.* They overeat by enough to feed another 80 million people!

• At any given time, 25% to 50% of the adult American population is on a diet (Bouchard, 1991).

• Within a few years, most dieters regain most of the weight they have lost (Wilson, 1993).

This nation idealizes slender heroes and heroines. For those of us who "measure more than up" to TV and film idols, food may have replaced sex as the central source of guilt. Obese people encounter more than their fair share of illnesses, including heart disease, diabetes, gout, respiratory problems, even certain kinds of cancer (Leary, 1991; Manson and others, 1990). Obesity is also connected with psychological, social, and economic problems (Fitzgibbon and others, 1993; Stunkard & Sørensen, 1993). If obesity is connected with health problems and unhappiness with the image reflected in the mirror, why do so many people overeat? Psychological research has made major contributions to our knowledge concerning why so many people are obese and what can be done about it.

HEREDITY.   Obesity runs in families. It used to be the conventional wisdom that obese parents encouraged their children to be overweight by having fattening foods in the house and setting poor examples. However, a study of Scandinavian adoptees by Stunkard and his colleagues (1990) found that children bear a closer resemblance in weight to their biological parents than to their adoptive parents. There may also be a gene that contributes to obesity because those with the gene are not signaled by the brain when they have eaten enough to sustain them (Lindpaintner, 1995). Heredity, then, plays a role in obesity (Friedman & Brownell, 1995).

FAT CELLS. The efforts of obese people to maintain a slender profile might be sabotaged by microscopic units of life within their own bodies: fat cells. No, fat cells are not overweight cells. They are adipose tissue, or cells that store fat. Hunger might be related to the amount of fat stored in these cells. As time passes after a meal, the blood-sugar level drops. Fat is then drawn from these cells to provide further nourishment. At some point, referred to as the *set point,* the hypothalamus is signaled of the fat deficiency in these cells, triggering the hunger drive.

People with more adipose tissue than others feel food-deprived earlier, even though they may be equal in weight. This might be because more signals are being sent to the brain. Obese people, and *formerly* obese people, tend to have more adipose tissue than people of normal weight. Thus, many people who have lost weight complain that they are always hungry when they try to maintain normal weight levels.

Fatty tissue also metabolizes food more slowly than muscle. For this reason, a person with a high fat-to-muscle ratio will metabolize food more slowly than a person of the same weight with a lower fat-to-muscle ratio. In other words, two people identical in weight will metabolize food at different rates, according to their bodies' distribution of muscle and fat. Obese people are therefore doubly handicapped in their efforts to lose weight—not only by their extra weight but by the fact that much of their body is composed of adipose tissue.

In a sense, the normal distribution of fat cells could be considered "sexist." The average man is 40% muscle and 15% fat, whereas the average woman is 23% muscle and 25% fat. Therefore, if a man and woman with typical distributions of muscle and fat are of the same weight, the woman—who has more fat cells—will have to eat less to maintain that weight.

DIETING AND METABOLISM. People on diets and those who have lost substantial amounts of weight burn fewer calories. That is, their metabolic rates slow down (Leibel and others, 1995; Shah & Jeffery, 1991).

Other factors, such as stress and our emotional states, also play a role in obesity (Greeno & Wing, 1994). Efforts to diet may be impeded by negative emotions like depression and anxiety (Cools and others, 1992).

METHODS OF WEIGHT CONTROL. Before discussing methods of losing weight, let us note that not everyone who is a few pounds overweight should be trying to slim down (Brownell, 1993; Brownell & Rodin, 1994). For example, women are under extreme pressure to conform to an unnaturally slender cultural ideal (Bordo, 1993; Wolf, 1991). Moreover, most attempts to lose weight do not work. On the other hand, for many obese people, shedding excess pounds lowers the risks of diabetes and heart disease (Brody, 1992d).

Research on motivation and on cognitive and behavioral methods of therapy has enhanced our knowledge of healthful ways of losing weight. Sound weight-control programs do not involve fad diets such as fasting, eliminating carbohydrates, or eating excessive amounts of grapefruit or rice. Instead, they involve changes in lifestyle that include improving nutritional knowledge, decreasing calorie intake, exercising, and modifying behavior (Brownell & Rodin, 1994; Brownell & Wadden 1992).

A Sampler of Dietary Methods. At any given time, 25% to 50% of the adult American population is on a diet. Dieting has become the "normal" pattern of eating for women in the United States. Dozens of diets vie for attention on the bookshelves on any given day. How can we know which contain truth and which contain fiction?

Nutritional knowledge helps ensure that we will not deprive ourselves of essential food elements and suggests strategies for losing weight without making us feel overly deprived. For example, eating foods that are low in saturated fats and cholesterol is not only good for the heart. Because dietary fat is converted to bodily fat more efficiently than carbohydrates are, a low-fat diet also leads to weight loss (Brownell & Wadden, 1992; Wood and others, 1991). Nutritional knowledge also leads to suggestions for taking in fewer calories. We can lessen our calorie intake by switching to lower-calorie foods—relying more on fresh, unsweetened fruits and vegetables (eating apples rather than apple pie), lean meats, fish and poultry, and skim milk and cheese. We can also cut down on—or eliminate—butter, margarine, oils, and sugar.

The same foods that help us control our weight also tend to be high in vitamins and fiber and low in fats. Such foods may thus also lower our risks of heart disease, cancer, and a number of other illnesses.

Dieting plus exercise is more effective than dieting alone (Epstein and others, 1995; Wood and others, 1991). Remember that when we restrict calories, our metabolic rates compensate by slowing down. Exercise burns calories and builds muscle tissue. Muscle metabolizes more calories than bodily fat.

Cognitive and behavioral methods have also provided many strategies for losing weight:

Establish calorie-intake goals and heighten awareness of whether you are meeting them. Get a calorie book and keep a diary of your calorie intake.

Substitute low-calorie foods for high-calorie foods. Fill your stomach with celery rather than cheesecake and enchiladas. Eat frozen yogurt rather than ice cream. Eat preplanned low-calorie snacks such as unbuttered popcorn instead of binge eating a jar of peanuts.

Take a 5-minute break between helpings. Ask yourself whether you're still hungry. (If not, stop eating!)

Avoid sources of external stimulation (temptations) to which you have succumbed in the past. Shop at the mall with the Alfalfa Sprout, not the Gushy Gloppy Shoppe. Plan your meal before entering a restaurant. (Avoid that tempting menu.) Attend to your own plate, not to the sumptuous dish at the next table. (Your salad probably looks greener to them, anyhow.) Shop from a list. Walk briskly through the supermarket, preferably after dinner when you're no longer hungry. Don't be sidetracked by pretty packages (fattening things may come in them). Keep out of the kitchen. Study, watch TV, write letters elsewhere. Prepare only enough food to remain within your calorie goals.

Exercise to burn more calories and maintain your predieting metabolic rate. Reach for your mate, not your plate (to coin a phrase). Jog rather than eat an unplanned snack. Build exercise routines by a few minutes each week.

Reward yourself for meeting calorie goals— but not with food. Imagine how great you'll look in that new swimsuit next summer. Do not go to see that great new film unless you have met your weekly calorie goal. Each time you meet your weekly calorie goal, put cash in the bank toward a vacation or new camera.

Use imagery to help yourself lose weight. Tempted by a fattening dish? Imagine that it's rotten, that you would be nauseated by it and have a sick taste in your mouth for the rest of the day. Tempted to binge? Strip before the mirror and handle a fatty area of your body. Ask yourself if you really want to make it larger or if you would prefer to exercise self-control.

Mentally walk through solutions to problem situations. Consider how you will politely refuse when cake is handed out at the office party. Rehearse your next visit to "the relatives"—the ones who tell you how painfully thin you look and try to stuff you. Imagine how you'll politely (but firmly) refuse seconds, and thirds, despite their protestations.

Above all, if you slip from your plan for a day, don't blow things out of proportion. Dieters are often tempted to binge, especially when they rigidly see themselves either as perfect successes or complete failures or when they experience powerful emotions—either positive or negative. Consider the weekly or monthly trend, not just the day. Credit yourself for the long-term trend. If you do binge, resume dieting the next day.

Losing weight—and keeping it off—is not easy, but it can be done. Making a personal commitment to losing weight and formulating a workable plan for doing so are two of the keys.

Reflections

- **Agree or disagree with the following statement and support your answer: "Good health is basically a matter of heredity or good luck. People cannot really do much to enhance their health or stave off illness."**

- Consider your sociocultural background: What health problems are more common, or less common, among people of your background than among the U.S. population at large? Why do you think that these problems are more common or less common among people of your background?
- Agree or disagree with the following statement and support your answer: "Some people can 'refuse' to become ill."
- **Agree or disagree with the following statement and support your answer: "One's behavior, and not one's group membership, places one at risk of HIV infection."**
- **Agree or disagree with the following statement and support your answer: "Dieting is the normal way of eating for American women."**
- How do you feel about your own weight and body shape? Why?
- How many dieters do you know? What methods, if any, seem to work for them?
- **Agree or disagree with the following statement and support your answer: "People who are overweight simply eat too much."**

Study Guide

| **True-False Questions**

DIRECTIONS: Consider each of the following statements. Circle the T if it is true and the F if it is false. Answers and explanations follow the exercise.

NOTE: I'm going to be impossibly tricky, so keep in mind that this is a learning exercise for you and not a real test! The items should increase your test-wiseness.

T   F   1. If we become ill and require hospitalization, we should keep in mind, like Norman Cousins, that laughter is the best medicine.

T   F   2. Daily hassles are the same as life changes.

T   F   3. Life changes are to be avoided, if we wish to remain healthy.

T   F   4. The research links between life changes and illness are correlational, not experimental.

T   F   5. Type A people become restless when they see others working slowly.

T   F   6. Psychological factors can moderate the impact of sources of stress.

T   F   7. It has been shown experimentally that high self-efficacy expectations are accompanied by low levels of adrenaline and norepinephrine in the bloodstream.

T   F   8. People in whom high self-efficacy expectations are experimentally induced complete tasks more successfully than people of comparable ability but lower self-efficacy expectations.

T   F   9. Psychologically hardy individuals show a tendency to involve themselves in, rather than experience alienation from, whatever they are doing or encountering.

T   F 10. Psychological hardiness can help people resist stress.

T   F 11. Psychologically hardy people tend to have an external locus of control.

T   F 12. In an important psychological study of the moderating effects of humor on stress by Canadian psychologists Rod Martin and Herbert Lefcourt, students with a greater sense of humor, and who produced humor in difficult situations, were less affected by negative life events than other students.

T   F 13. In the Weiss study, rats that received shock without warning showed greatest ulceration.

T   F 14. If you get married, you will live longer.

T   F 15. The GAS consists of three stages: an adaptation stage, a resistance stage, and an exhaustion stage.

T   F 16. The alarm reaction involves a number of body changes that are initiated by the brain and further regulated by the endocrine system and the sympathetic division of the autonomic nervous system.

T   F 17. The hypothalamus secretes corticotrophin-releasing hormone, which, in turn, stimulates the pituitary gland to secrete adrenocorticotrophic hormone.

T   F 18. The parasympathetic division of the ANS activates the adrenal medulla, causing a mixture of adrenaline and norepinephrine to be released.

T   F 19. In their research, psychologists use the amount of cortisol in the adrenal glands as a biological measure of stress.

T	F	20. One way in which we combat physical disorders is by producing white blood cells that routinely engulf and kill pathogens.
T	F	21. The foreign agents that are recognized and destroyed by leukocytes are called *antibodies*.
T	F	22. Steroids heighten the functioning of the immune system.
T	F	23. The single most frequent kind of headache is the migraine headache.
T	F	24. Arousal of the sympathetic division of the ANS heightens blood pressure.
T	F	25. People whose families show a history of heart disease are more likely to develop heart disease themselves.
T	F	26. According to the text, people with Type A behavior are twice as likely as people with Type B behavior to have heart attacks.
T	F	27. Asthma attacks can be triggered by stress.
T	F	28. Cancer rates have been skyrocketing.
T	F	29. Stress can cause cancer.
T	F	30. Women are more likely to seek medical help than men are.

ANSWER KEY TO EXERCISE

Answer Comment

1. F. Let us not overgeneralize from the anecdote about Norman Cousins to the point where we jeopardize our health!
2. F. The text points out that daily hassles differ from life changes in two ways. What are they?
3. F. The text points out that *high numbers* of life changes place us in higher risk groups. Even so, there is no experimental evidence that high numbers of life changes directly cause illness in people.
4. T. Again, this is why we cannot assume that life changes cause illness.
5. T. This is one "side effect" of their sense of time urgency.
6. T. Sure they can.
7. T. Here the "trick" is to carefully check out the adjectives "high" and "low."
8. T. Again, the task is to check out the relationships between the words "high," "more," and "lower."
9. T. This is what is meant by their sense of commitment.
10. T.
11. F. *Internal,* not *external.*
12. T. You need to check out the names of the researchers (accurate) as well as the relationships between "greater" and "less" (all accurate).
13. T. True in that the study was run by Weiss and the results are accurate.
14. F. Again we have correlational evidence. Therefore, while it is true that married men live longer than single men, it may be that the factors that lead to the decision to get married, and not marriage itself, make the difference. Also, findings are less clear-cut for women.
15. F. Tricky! Yes there are three stages, but the adaptation stage *is* the resistance stage; the alarm reaction has been erroneously omitted.
16. T. All parts true (a difficult question!).
17. T. Another difficult item, with all parts true. It may help to recall, from Chapter 3, that the hypothalamus secretes many releasing factors that cause the pituitary to secrete related hormones.
18. F. The sympathetic division, not the parasympathetic division, does this.
19. T. False. Cortisol is produced by the adrenal glands.
20. T. This is one of the functions of the immune system.
21. F. They are called *antigens,* not *antibodies.*
22. F. Steroids *suppress* the functioning of the immune system.
23. F. The muscle-tension headache is more common.
24. T. A simple statement of fact.
25. T. There is a genetic risk factor.
26. F. There is no statement in the text that twice as many Type A people as Type B people have heart attacks.
27. T. A simple statement of fact.
28. F. Actually, many better educated people have been modifying their behavior and placing themselves in lower risk categories for many kinds of cancer.

29. F. Although stress appears to exacerbate the course of cancer (see the previous item), there is no evidence that stress *causes* cancer.

30. T. A factual gender difference related in the text.

| ESL | **English as a Second Language—Bridging the Gap** |

abstinent (666)—to avoid doing something

accentuate (654)—emphasize

affords (671)—gives

ailments (650)—illnesses

amass more life-change units (651)—collect more points for having made changes in life

anecdotal (657)—telling the story of an individual's experience

apparatus (658)—machine; device

assembly-line labor (671)—factory work, involving people standing in front of a moving table; each person attaches a part to an item that then moves to the next worker, who adds another part until it is completed

Association for the Advancement of Lost Causes (653)—the author's joking name for a charitable organization that asks for contributions; this one doesn't really exist

at the drop of a hat (670)—at the first suggestion

atypical (676)—not common

aura (670)—feeling; atmosphere

aversions (676)—dislikes

backfire (665)—have the opposite effect of what was intended

banes (679)—problems; afflictions

baseline (650)—item against which all others are measured

bat the ball back and forth (655)—two people who hit a ball back and forth, without paying attention to the rules of the game

belly laughter (657)—strong, deep laughter

bliss (650)—extreme happiness

bottom line (674)—the most significant thing to look at in the end

brace ourselves (658)—to be prepared

bridle at (670)—become very annoyed

bring one on (673)—cause an attack

buffering (657)—providing some form of protection so something isn't so difficult or painful

buffers between themselves (658)—shields or protection between themselves

bulletproof mentality (668)—belief that they are so strong they can't be injured or ill

clamor (665)—a loud noise; many people responding negatively

coin a phrase (683)—to create a saying

come on (670)—begin

competent (654)—capable of doing things well

compound (653)—multiply; increase

confounded (674)—confused; made hard to understand

confrontation (649)—a conflict; fight

coping skills (676)—techniques for handling difficulties

correlational (651)—are associated with each other; occur at the same time but may not cause each other

credit yourself (683)—give yourself a compliment

cross-country skiing (680)—skiing is a snow sport in which a long, narrow "board" is strapped to each foot, and the person slides down a snow-covered hill or mountain; *cross-country* means that instead of sliding down a mountain, the person slides in a walking motion on level ground

damned if you did and damned if you didn't (652)—a saying that means "no matter which decision you make there will be a problem"

dampen our moods (649)—depress us a little

demoralization (654)—feeling discouraged

diagnosed (652)—recognized as a medical problem

easygoing (652)—relaxed and flexible

episodic (673)—occurs over periods of time; starts and stops and starts again

exaggeration (653)—something that is made to look bigger than it really is

face of stress (657)—confronted with, or facing, stress

fear-inducing (655)—causing fear

fend off (674)—resist

fighting spirit (676)—the will to fight against something

foodstuffs (680)—food

foreboding (648)—predicting unpleasant outcomes

foster (653)—encourage

from time to time (665)—sometimes

full-blown cases (677)—completely developed illness

give in to illness (667)—emotionally accept illness without fighting it

given . . . and fast pace of scientific change (662)—because our bodies are so complex, and because scientific changes are occurring very often

hard hit (675)—be influenced strongly by; hurt a lot

hardy or nonhardy (656)—emotionally strong or weak

hassle (649)—to bother me; give me problems or difficulties

illicit drugs (678)—illegal drugs

immensely (654)—a great deal; extremely

in-laws (651)—parents and other relatives of a spouse

inaction (654)—not doing anything; taking no action

indebted to (656)—owed to

induce (678)—persuade someone to do something

inescapable (659)—cannot be avoided

inoculations (665)—injections to prevent illnesses

jumping rope (683)—a play or exercise activity that involves swinging a rope above the head and jumping over it when it goes under the feet

keep one eye glued firmly on the clock (654)—watch the time continually and therefore not relax

last straw that breaks the camel's back (649)—a saying that means "I have been able to handle all the problems until now—it is this last problem that has finally made me unable to cope"

leisure (659)—relaxation

loan installments (650)—monthly payments required to repay a loan

longshoremen (662)—people employed to unload cargo from ships

low-interest loans (650)—loans that have low interest rates (the amount a person pays to have the loan)

marrying Mr. or Ms. Right (650)—marrying the perfect mate

menopause (668)—the time in women's lives when menstruation cycles end

merry heart doeth good like a medicine (657)—a happy person is healthy

methodological flaws (652)—problems with the research method techniques

millennia (657)—thousands of years

mirrored (663)—imitated; was the same as

motto (655)—a person's private rule or a general saying

mull things over (679)—think about something deeply to make a good decision

nary a sniffle (665)—hardly (not even) a runny nose

no one-to-one relationship (655)—no relationship between the amount of stress to the amount or kind of illness

on guard (671)—aware of protecting themselves

one on top of the other (650)—one added to the other

overtime work (671)—additional hours of work for which one is paid extra

pace themselves (655)—go at a slow, steady speed; allow periods of time between stressful occurrences

pathogens (660)—things that cause disease

pave the way for understanding (662)—help you to understand

pediatrics (649)—medical care of children

postal workers (662)—people who work for the U.S. Post Office

preoccupied with (654)—think and worry about something frequently

prestigious (650)—impressive; has a high status

propagate (673)—reproduce

propel you into a state of bliss (650)—make you extremely happy

property investments (650)—buying property to make money from using or selling it

prostitutes (679)—men and women who take money for doing a sex act with someone

psychologically hardy (652)—emotionally strong

put off by (677)—stopped by something

racial gap (667)—difference in the results between the two racial groups; in this case, research is showing that, most likely because of social problems, people from some racial groups have more health difficulties

reasonably (678)—somewhat adequate; have some knowledge

relapse (656)—to begin something again

reluctant (654)—not willing to do something

remains an open question (674)—is not known

resemblance (680)—similarity

reside with (660)—remain with; the responsibility of

retirement (650)—the period of life when a person stops his or her regular job and lives on accumulated savings and company or government social security payments

right from the start (651)—to begin an activity from the start

rob the body of nutrients (673)—take vitamins that the body needs

rodents (674)—rats and mice

self-discipline (654)—self-control

self-efficacy (653)—beliefs about our ability to be able to do things and handle problems

short bursts (657)—short intensive periods

sidetracked (683)—distracted by

singly and in combination (678)—one and combined

skyrocketing (686)—rising quickly

slim chance of a full recovery (681)—might not recover completely

so goes the saying (649)—this is the expression

sound (681)—sensible; good

stand much chance (677)—to have an opportunity

stick to (670)—stay with

stock market swings (650)—the prices of stocks traded on the stock market tend to go up and down together

stoic (676)—willing to handle difficulties quietly, with patience and no complaints

strenuous (673)—difficult
stressor (658)—the thing that causes stress
sudden cognitive shifts (659)—sudden thought changes
sumptuous (683)—magnificent; elaborate; delicious
tandem (658)—at the same time
tax our adjustive capacity (649)—put a burden on, or use up, our ability to adjust to changes
taxes (650)—everyone's obligation to pay a portion of his or her income to the government to contribute to national needs
temporary setbacks (651)—temporary reverses
Ten Doorways to Distress (653)—10 ways to be upset
threat to security (657)—something that causes insecurity
throbbing (670)—pounding or beating feeling
too much of a good thing (665)—attaining success in many areas in the same time period
tracking (662)—researching
traumatic (652)—very upsetting; causes serious problems

trimmer (647)—more slender; thinner
truly hit home (649)—are obvious
typifies backwoods practices (648)—is typical of health practices in places far away from cities and towns
ulceration (659)—creation of ulcers
uncritically endorse (650)—recommend without criticism
unwittingly propel ourselves (670)—without being aware of it, we can do something that can cause us trouble
upheaval (654)—upset; distress
urban ghetto (667)—areas in cities where poor people live
veneer (665)—surface appearance; implies that there is not much substance and it only appears to be there
wing it (678)—do it without preparation or information
withstand stress (655)—to be able to endure stress; not be hurt by stress
worn-out body cells (662)—body cells that do not function anymore

---

FILL-INS | **Chapter Review**

SECTION 1: HEALTH PSYCHOLOGY

The field of health psychology studies the relationships between (1) _____ ical factors (e.g., stress, behavior, and attitudes) and the prevention and treatment of physical illness.

SECTION 2: STRESS: PRESSES, PUSHES, AND PULLS

In psychology, (2) s_____ is the demand made on an organism to adjust. Many sources of stress reflect external factors—daily (3) _____les, life changes, pain and discomfort, frustration, and conflict. Others such as Type (4) _____ behavior are self-imposed.

(5) D_____ hassles are notable daily conditions and experiences that are threatening or harmful to a person's well-being. Life changes differ from daily hassles in that many life changes are (6) _____ive and desirable, whereas hassles are all negative. (7) L_____ changes are also more isolated than daily hassles.

Type A behavior is characterized by a sense of time (8) _____cy, competitiveness, and (9) ag_____ness. Type B people, by contrast, relax (10: Less or More?) readily and focus (11: Less or More?) on the quality of life.

Our (12) self-e_____ expectations are our perceptions of our capacities to bring about change. People with (13: Higher or Lower?) self-efficacy expectations tend to cope better with stress.

Kobasa and her colleagues have found that psychologically hardy executives differ from the nonhardy in three ways: Hardy individuals are high in (14) _____ment (they involve themselves in, rather than experience alienation from, what they are doing); hardy individuals are high in challenge; hardy individuals are (15: High or Low?) in perceived control over their lives.

Being able to predict the onset of a stressor (16: Increases or Decreases?) its impact upon us.

Social support (17: Does or Does Not?) buffer the effects of stress. Numerous studies have found a lower mortality rate for (18: Single or Married?) men.

The general adaptation syndrome (GAS) consists of (19: How Many?) _____ stages. These stages are the (20) a _____ reaction, a resistance stage, and the (21) _____tion stage. The alarm reaction (22) m____izes, or arouses, the body for defense. Cannon had earlier termed this alarm system the (23) f_____-or-f_____ reaction.

The alarm reaction involves a number of body changes that are initiated by the brain and further regulated by the (24) _____rine system and the (25) _____etic division of the autonomic nervous system. Under stress, the pituitary gland secretes (26) A_____. ACTH causes the adrenal cortex to release (27) _____sol and other steroids that help the body respond to stress by fighting (28) in_____tion and allergic reactions. Two other hormones that play a major role in the alarm reaction are secreted by the adrenal medulla: (29) ad_____ine and (30) nor_____rine.

In the (31) _____tion stage, or resistance stage, of the GAS, the body attempts to restore lost energy and repair whatever damage has been done. All of us eventually reach the (32) _____tion stage when stress persists. With exhaustion, the (33) para_____tic division of the ANS may become predominant.

The immune system produces (34) w_____ blood cells that routinely engulf and kill pathogens. White blood cells are technically termed (35) _____ytes. The immune system "remembers" foreign agents so that future combat will be more efficient. Pathogens that are recognized and destroyed by leukocytes are called (36) _____ens. Some leukocytes produce (37) _____dies, or specialized proteins that bind to their antigens and mark them for destruction.

One reason that stress eventually exhausts us is that it stimulates us to produce (38) _____oids. Steroids (39: Enhance or Suppress?) the functioning of the immune system. Dental students in one study showed (40: Higher or Lower?) immune-system functioning during stressful school periods than immediately following vacations.

SECTION 3: A MULTIFACTORIAL APPROACH TO HEALTH AND ILLNESS

The likelihood of contracting an illness reflects the (41) inter_____ of many factors. Biological factors such as family history, (42) _____gens , inoculations, injuries, and age play a role. However, psychological, social, (43) tech_____, and environmental factors also play roles. Many diseases are influenced by (44) _____cal factors, such as our attitudes and patterns of behavior. Psychological states such as anxiety and depression impair the functioning of the (45) i_____ system, rendering us more vulnerable to illness.

SECTION 4: SOCIOCULTURAL FACTORS IN HEALTH AND ILLNESS: NATIONS WITHIN THE NATION

The cigarette brand Virginia Slims is designed and marketed to appeal to (46) w_____.

African Americans between the ages of 25 and 64 have a (47: Higher or Lower?) mortality rate than White Americans in the same age group. The death rate appears to be due to factors such as income and level of (48) _____tion. African Americans have (49: Greater or Less?) access to health care than White Americans do.

The incidences of sickle-cell anemia and hypertension are highest among (50) A_____ Americans. The incidence of Tay-Sachs disease is greatest among (51) J_____ of East European origin. Anorexia and (52) b_____nervosa are uncommon among poor people. Obesity is (53: Most or Least?) prevalent among poor people.

Death rates from cancer are higher in nations where the population has a (54: High or Low?) daily fat intake.

Men's life expectancies are 7 years (55: Longer or Shorter?) than women's. The difference is due, at least in part, to women's (56: Greater or Lesser?) willingness to seek health care.

SECTION 5: UNDERSTANDING AND COPING WITH MAJOR HEALTH PROBLEMS IN THE UNITED STATES TODAY

The most common kind of headache is the (57) m_____-_____ headache. Most other headaches, including the migraine, stem from changes in the (58) b_____ supply to the head. (59) Mi_____ headaches have pre-headache phases during which there is decreased blood supply to the head, and headaches phases, during which the (60) _____ries are dilated, increasing the flow of blood.

Arousal of the (61) _____tic division of the ANS heightens the blood pressure. Hypertension predisposes victims to other (62) car_____lar disorders such as (63) art_____rosis, heart attacks, and strokes. Blood pressure (64: Decreases or Increases?) in situations in which people must be constantly on guard against threats. Blood pressure appears to be higher among (65: African Americans or White People?).

There are several risk factors for heart disease: family history; (66) phy_____gical conditions such as obesity, hypertension, and high levels of serum (67) _____erol; patterns of consumption, such as heavy drinking and smoking; Type (68) _____ behavior; and work (69) o_____ (e.g., overtime work and assembly-line labor).

Asthma is a respiratory disorder that is often the result of an (70) _____ic reaction in which the main tubes of the windpipe—the bronchi—contract, making it difficult to breathe. Asthma attacks (71: Can or Cannot?) be triggered by stress.

People (72: Can or Cannot?) inherit dispositions toward developing cancer, but many behavior patterns, such as smoking, drinking, and eating animal fats, heighten the risk for cancer. Numerous studies connect stressful life events to the onset of cancer in people, but this research has been criticized in that it is (73) ret_____tive. Experimental research with animals shows that once cancer has affected the individual, stress can (74: Accelerate or Retard?) its course.

HIV is the virus that causes the disease called (75) _____. HIV (76: Can or Cannot?) be transmitted by heterosexual vaginal intercourse. HIV has an affinity for, and kills, (77: Red or White?) blood cells, thereby weakening the immune system. AIDS patients typically die from (78) _____istic infections. In the United States, the two groups who have been hit hardest by the AIDS epidemic are (79) g_____ males and people who (80) i_____ drugs.

Obesity (81: Runs or Does Not Run?) in families. A study of Scandinavian adoptees by Stunkard found that children bear a closer resemblance in weight to their (82: Adoptive or Biological?) parents than to their (83: Adoptive or Biological?) parents.

One reason that obese people may desire to eat more than normal-weight people is that they have larger numbers of (84) f_____ cells, or adipose tissue. As time passes after eating, the (85) _____d-sugar level drops, causing fat to be drawn off from these cells in order to provide further nourishment. The resultant fat deficiency is signaled to the (86) _____amus, triggering the hunger drive. Obese people may send (87: Stronger or Weaker?) signals to the hypothalamus because of the larger number of fat cells.

Fatty tissue metabolizes food more (88: Rapidly or Slowly?) than muscle. For this reason, a person with a high fat-to-muscle ratio will metabolize food (89: Less or More?) slowly than a person of the same weight with a (90: Higher or Lower?) fat-to-muscle ratio. The average man has a (91: Higher or Lower?) fat-to-muscle ratio than the average woman.

People who are dieting and people who have lost much weight usually do not eat enough to satisfy the (92) _____t points in their hypothalamuses. As a consequence, compensating metabolic forces are set in motion; that is, (93: Fewer or More?) calories are burned.

Effective diets tend to use combinations of the following elements: improving (94) <u>nu</u>_____<u>al</u> knowledge, decreasing intake of (95) _____ries, (96) <u>exer</u>_____, and behavior (97) _____cation.

ANSWER KEY TO CHAPTER REVIEW

1. Psychological	21. Exhaustion	41. Interaction	60. Arteries	79. Opportunistic
2. Stress	22. Mobilizes	42. Pathogens	61. Sympathetic	80. Inject
3. Hassles	23. Fight-or-flight	43. Technological	62. Cardiovascular	81. Runs
4. A	24. Endocrine	44. Psychological	63. Arteriosclerosis	82. Biological
5. Daily	25. Sympathetic	45. Immune	64. Increases	83. Adoptive
6. Positive	26. ACTH	46. Women	65. African Americans	84. Fat
7. Life	27. Cortisol	47. Higher	66. Physiological	85. Blood
8. Urgency	28. Inflammation	48. Education	67. Cholesterol	86. Hypothalamus
9. Aggressiveness	29. Adrenaline	49. Less	68. A	87. Stronger
10. More	30. Norepinephrine	50. African	69. Overload	88. Slowly
11. More	31. Adaptation	51. Jews	70. Allergic	89. More
12. Efficacy	32. Exhaustion	52. Bulimia	71. Can	90. Lower
13. Higher	33. Parasympathetic	53. Most	72. Can	91. Lower
14. Commitment	34. White	54. High	73. Retrospective	92. Set
15. High	35. Leukocytes	55. Shorter	74. Accelerate	93. Fewer
16. Decreases	36. Antigens	56. Greater	75. AIDS	94. Nutritional
17. Does	37. Antibodies	57. Muscle-tension	76. Can	95. Calories
18. Married	38. Steroids	58. Blood	77. White	96. Exercise
19. Three	39. Suppress	59. Migraine	78. Opportunistic	97. Modification
20. Alarm	40. Lower	60. Arteries		

POSTTEST | **Multiple Choice**

1. Which is the most accurate statement about stress?
   a. Stress is the painful price we must pay for living.
   b. The most stressed people are usually unaware of stress.
   c. Some stress is necessary to keep us alert and occupied.
   d. All stress is harmful to the body.

2. Hassles differ from life changes in that
   a. hassles require adaptation.
   b. hassles are a source of stress.
   c. life changes occur more frequently.
   d. life changes can be positive as well as negative.

3. Type A people are characterized by
   a. need for affiliation.
   b. secretion of excessive ACTH.
   c. competitiveness and impatience.
   d. predisposition toward alcoholism.

4. As compared with Type B people, Type A people
   a. perceive time as passing more rapidly.
   b. earn less money.
   c. smoke less frequently.
   d. are better adjusted in their marriages.

5. Psychologically hardy individuals show all of the following, *with the exception of*
   a. competitiveness.
   b. commitment.
   c. control.
   d. challenge.

6. Nancy has just had a frightening experience in which she thought her car was going off the road. Which of the following is likely to be happening inside her?
   a. Her respiration rate is decreasing.
   b. Her blood pressure is decreasing.
   c. Her digestive processes are speeding up.
   d. Her blood flow is shifting away from her skeletal musculature.

7. Unrelieved stress during the _____ may lead to diseases of adaptation and death.
   a. fight-or-flight reaction
   b. exhaustion stage
   c. resistance stage
   d. alarm reaction

8. According to the text, people who inject drugs are at risk for contracting

a. AIDS.
b. heart disease.
c. cancer.
d. headaches.

9. The text mentions that hypertension predisposes people to all of the following *with the exception of*
   a. arteriosclerosis.
   b. strokes.
   c. heart attacks.
   d. ulcers.

10. A vascular headache is caused by
    a. muscle tension.
    b. change in blood supply to the head.
    c. injury.
    d. chronic stress.

11. Which of the following is *not* a risk factor for heart disease?
    a. low serum cholesterol
    b. family history of heart disease
    c. hypertension
    d. physical inactivity

12. The so-called common migraine headache is identified by
    a. muscle tension in the shoulders and back of the neck.
    b. hypertension.
    c. sudden onset and throbbing on one side of the head.
    d. sensory and motor disturbances that precede the pain.

13. Which of the following is a component of the alarm reaction?
    a. Muscles relax.
    b. Adrenaline is secreted.
    c. Blood coagulability decreases.
    d. Heart rate decreases.

14. According to the text, so-called diseases of adaptation are caused by
    a. life changes.
    b. fear that one will contract the disease.
    c. genetic factors.
    d. a combination of stress and some predisposing factor.

15. Bacteria and viruses are examples of
    a. antigens.
    b. antibodies.
    c. leukocytes.
    d. pathogens.

16. The immune system has all of the following functions, *with the exception of*
    a. producing white blood cells.
    b. producing red blood cells.
    c. causing inflammation.
    d. recognizing pathogens.

17. Which of the following suppresses the functioning of the immune system?
    a. leukocytes
    b. vaccination
    c. steroids
    d. relaxation

18. According to the text, which of the following is a reason that health psychologists study HIV infection and AIDS?
    a. They are of enormous concern to the public.
    b. The costs of the AIDS epidemic have been skyrocketing.
    c. Our behavior patterns place us at risk for being infected with HIV.
    d. Stress-management techniques can cure AIDS.

19. The first and foremost recommendation in the chapter for preventing transmission of HIV is to
    a. refuse to deny the prevalence and harmful nature of AIDS.
    b. use condoms.
    c. abstain from sexual activity.
    d. limit sexual activity to partners whom one knows very well.

20. The body of the average woman is made up of _____% fat.
    a. 5
    b. 15
    c. 25
    d. 40

ANSWER KEY TO POSTTEST

1. C	4. A	7. B	10. B	13. B	16. B	19. A
2. D	5. A	8. A	11. A	14. D	17. C	20. C
3. C	6. D	9. D	12. C	15. D	18. C	

Social Psychology

PRETEST *Truth or Fiction?*

_____ Airing a television commercial repeatedly hurts sales.

_____ First impressions have powerful effects on our social relationships.

_____ We take others to task for their misdeeds but tend to see ourselves as victims of circumstances when our conduct falls short of our ideals.

_____ Beauty is in the eye of the beholder.

_____ People are perceived as being more attractive when they are smiling.

_____ Love makes the world go round — romantic love is found in every culture in the world, that is.

_____ Nearly 40 people stood by and did nothing while a woman was being stabbed to death.

CANDY and Stretch. A new technique for controlling weight gains? No, these are the names of a couple who have just met at a camera club that doubles as a meeting place for singles.

Candy and Stretch stand above the crowd—literally. Candy, an attractive woman in her early 30s, is almost 6 feet tall. Stretch is more plain-looking, but wholesome, in his late 30s, and 6 feet 5 inches.

Stretch has been in the group for some time. Candy is a new member. Let's listen in on them as they make conversation during a coffee break.[1] As you will see, there are differences between what they say and what they are thinking:

THEY SAY	THEY THINK
Stretch: Well you're certainly a welcome addition to our group.	(Can't I ever say something clever?)
Candy: Thank you. It certainly is friendly and interesting.	(He's cute.)
Stretch: My friends call me Stretch. It's left over from my basketball days. Silly, but I'm used to it.	(It's safer than saying my name is David Stein.)
Candy: My name is Candy.	(At least my nickname is. He doesn't have to hear Hortense O'Brien.)
Stretch: What kind of camera is that?	(Why couldn't a girl named Candy be Jewish? It's only a nickname, isn't it?)
Candy: Just this old German one of my uncle's. I borrowed it from the office.	(He could be Irish. And that camera looks expensive.)
Stretch: May I? (He takes her camera, brushing her hand and then tingling with the touch.) Fine lens. You work for your uncle?	(Now I've done it. Brought up work.)
Candy: Ever since college. It's more than being just a secretary. I get into sales, too.	(So okay, what if I only went for a year. If he asks what I sell, I'll tell him anything except underwear.)
Stretch: Sales? That's funny. I'm in sales, too, but mainly as an executive. I run our department. I started using cameras on trips. Last time I was in the Bahamas. I took—	(Is there a nice way to say used cars? I'd better change the subject.) (Great legs! And the way her hips move—)
Candy: Oh! Do you go to the Bahamas, too? I love those islands.	(So I went just once, and it was for the brassiere manufacturers' convention. At least we're off the subject of jobs.)

---

[1] Source of dialogue: *Pairing*, by G. R. Bach, and R. M. Deutsch, 1970, New York: Peter H. Wyden.

Stretch:	(She's probably been around. Well, at least we're off the subject of jobs.)
I did a little underwater work there last summer. Fantastic colors. So rich in life.	(And lonelier than hell.)
Candy:	(Look at that build. He must swim like a fish. I should learn.)
I wish I'd had time when I was there. I love the water.	(Well, I do. At the beach, anyway, where I can wade in and not go too deep.)

So begins a relationship. Candy and Stretch have a drink and talk, sharing their likes and dislikes. Amazingly, they seem to agree on everything—from cars to clothing to politics. The attraction is very strong, and neither is willing to risk turning the other off by disagreeing.

Soon they feel that they have fallen in love. They still agree on everything they discuss, but they scrupulously avoid one topic: religion. Their religious differences became apparent when they exchanged last names. But that doesn't mean they have to talk about it.

They also put off introductions to their parents. The O'Briens and the Steins are narrow-minded about religion. If the truth be known, so are Candy and Stretch.

What happens in this tangled web of deception? After some deliberation, and not without misgivings, they decide to get married. Do they live happily ever after? We can't say. "Ever after" isn't here yet.

We do not have all the answers, but we have some questions. Candy and Stretch's relationship began with a powerful attraction. What is *attraction?* How do we determine who is attractive? Candy and Stretch fell in love. What is *love?* They pretended to share each other's attitudes. What are *attitudes?* Also, why were they so reluctant to disagree?

Candy and Stretch were both a bit prejudiced about religion. What is *prejudice?* Why didn't they introduce each other to their parents? Did they fear that their parents would want them to *conform* to their own standards? Would their parents try to *persuade* them to limit dating to people of their own religions? Would they *obey?*

Attraction, attitudes, prejudice, conformity, persuasion, obedience—these topics are the province of the branch of psychology called **social psychology.** Social psychologists study the nature and causes of our behavior and mental processes in social situations. The social psychological topics we discuss in this chapter include attitudes, social perception, attraction, social influence, and group behavior.

Social psychology • The field of psychology that studies the nature and causes of individual thoughts, feelings, and overt behavior in social situations.

ATTITUDES

How do you feel about abortion, Japanese cars, and the Republican party? The only connection I draw among these items is that people have *attitudes* toward them. They each tend to elicit cognitive evaluations (such as approval or disapproval), feelings (liking, disliking, or something stronger), and behavioral tendencies (as of approach or avoidance). Although I asked you how you "feel," attitudes are not just feelings or emotions (Pratkanis and others, 1989).

Most psychologists agree that thinking (judgment) is primary. Feelings and behavior follow (Breckler & Wiggins, 1989; Eagly & Chaiken, 1993; Petty & Cacioppo, 1986).

Attitudes are behavioral and cognitive tendencies that are expressed by evaluating particular people, places, or things with some degree of favor or disfavor (Eagly & Chaiken, 1993). Attitudes are learned and affect behavior (Shavitt, 1990; Snyder & DeBono, 1989). Attitudes can foster love or hate. They can give rise to helping behavior or to mass destruction. They can lead to social conflict or to conflict resolution. Attitudes can change, but they tend to remain stable unless shoved. Most people do not change their religion or political affiliation without serious reflection or coercion.

The A–B Problem: Do We Do as We Think?

Our definition of attitude implies that our behavior is consistent with our cognition—our beliefs and our feelings. When we are free to do as we wish, it often is. But, as indicated by the term **A–B problem,** the link between attitudes (A) and behaviors (B) tends to be weak to moderate (Eagly & Chaiken, 1993). For example, research reveals that attitudes toward health-related behaviors such as use of alcohol and cigarettes, and drunken driving, are not strong or consistent predictors of these behaviors (Stacy and others, 1994).

A number of factors influence the likelihood that we can predict behavior from attitudes:

1. *Specificity.* We can better predict specific behavior from specific attitudes than from global attitudes. We can better predict church attendance by knowing people's attitudes toward church attendance than by knowing whether they are Christian. A study of female juvenile delinquents found that prostitutes made weaker judgments against prostitution than other delinquents did (Bartek and others, 1993).

2. *Strength of attitudes.* Strong attitudes are more likely to determine behavior than weak attitudes (Fazio, 1990). A person who believes that the nation's destiny depends on Republicans taking control of Congress is more likely to vote than a person who leans toward Republicanism but does not believe that the outcome of elections makes much difference.

3. *Vested interest.* People are more likely to act on their attitudes when they have a vested interest in the outcome (Johnson & Eagly, 1989). People are more likely to vote for (or against) unionization of their workplace, for example, when they believe that their job security depends on the outcome.

4. *Accessibility.* People are more likely to express their attitudes when they are accessible—that is, when they are brought to mind (Fazio, 1990; Krosnick, 1989). This is why politicians attempt to "get out the vote" by means of media blitzes just prior to an election. It does politicians little good to have supporters who forget them on election day. Attitudes that have strong emotional impact are more accessible (Wu & Shaffer, 1987), which is one reason that politicians strive to get their supporters "worked up" over the issues.

Candy and Stretch avoided discussing matters on which they differed. One motive might have been to avoid heightening the *accessibility* of their clashing attitudes. By keeping them under the table, Candy and Stretch might be less likely to act on them and go their separate ways.

Attitude • An enduring mental representation of a person, place, or thing that evokes an emotional response and affected behavior.

A–B problem • The issue of how well we can predict behavior on the basis of attitudes.

Origins of Attitudes

You were not born a Republican or a Democrat. You were not born a Catholic or a Jew—although your parents may have practiced one of these religions when you came along. Political, religious, and other attitudes are learned.

CONDITIONING. Conditioning may play a role in the acquisition of attitudes. Classic experiments suggested that attitudes toward national groups can be influenced by associating them with positive words (such as *gift* or *happy*) or negative words (such as *ugly* and *failure;* Lohr & Staats, 1973). President George Bush's references to Iraq's Saddam Hussein as "another Hitler" prior to the Persian Gulf War encouraged people to associate their hatred for Hitler with Hussein. Parents often reward children for saying and doing things that are consistent with their own attitudes. Patriotism is encouraged by approving of children when they sing the national anthem or wave the flag.

OBSERVATIONAL LEARNING. Attitudes formed through direct experience may be stronger and easier to recall, but we also acquire attitudes by observing others. The approval or disapproval of peers molds adolescents to prefer short or long hair, blue jeans, or preppy sweaters. Television shows us that body odor, bad breath, and the frizzies are dreaded diseases—and, perhaps, that people who use harsh toilet paper are somehow un-American.

COGNITIVE APPRAISAL. Yet, all is not so mechanical. Now and then we also evaluate information and attitudes on the basis of evidence. We may revise **stereotypes** on the basis of new information (Weber & Crocker, 1983). We are especially likely to scrutinize our attitudes when we know that we shall have to justify them to people who may dissent (Tetlock, 1983).

Still, initial attitudes tend to serve as cognitive anchors. They help mold the ways in which we perceive the world and interpret events. Attitudes we encounter later are thus often judged in terms of how much they deviate from the initial set. Accepting larger deviations demands greater adjustments in information processing (Quattrone, 1982). For this reason, perhaps, great deviations are apt to be resisted. Yet once people begin to think deeply about issues, changes in attitudes are likely to persist (Verplanken, 1991).

Stereotype • A fixed, conventional idea about a group.

Elaboration likelihood model • The view that persuasive messages are evaluated (elaborated) on the basis of central and peripheral cues.

Changing Attitudes Through Persuasion

Let advertisers spend the same amount of money improving their product that they do on advertising and they wouldn't have to advertise it.

WILL ROGERS

Rogers's social comment sounds on the mark, but he was probably wrong. It does little good to have a wonderful product if its existence remains a secret.

Petty and Cacioppo (1986) have devised the **elaboration likelihood model** for understanding the processes by which people examine the information in persuasive messages. According to this view, there are at least two routes to persuading others to change attitudes—that is, two ways of responding to, or elaborating, persuasive messages. The first, or central route, involves thoughtful consideration of arguments and evidence (Eagly & Chaiken, 1993). The second, or peripheral route, involves associating objects with positive or negative cues. When politicians avow that "this bill is supported by Jesse Jackson (or Jesse Helms)," they are seeking predictable, knee-jerk reactions, not

MINILECTURE: FACTORS IN PERSUASIVE COMMUNUICATION

careful consideration of a bill's merits. Other cues are rewards (such as a smile or a hug), punishments (such as parental disapproval), and factors such as the trustworthiness and attractiveness of the communicator.

Advertisements, which are a form of persuasive communication, also rely on central and peripheral ones. Some ads focus on the quality of the product (central route). Others attempt to associate the product with appealing images (peripheral route). Ads for Total cereal, which highlight its nutritional benefits, provide information about the quality of the product. So, too, do the "Pepsi Challenge" taste-test ads, which claim that Pepsi tastes better than Coca-Cola. Marlboro cigarette ads that focus on the masculine, rugged image of the "Marlboro man"[2] offer no information about the product itself. Nor do Virginia Slims cigarette ads, which show attractive women smoking.

In this section, we shall examine one central factor in persuasion—the nature of the message itself—and three peripheral factors: (1) the messenger, (2) the context of the message, and (3) the audience. We shall also examine a method of persuasion used frequently by persons seeking charitable contributions: the foot-in-the-door technique.

THE PERSUASIVE MESSAGE: SAY WHAT? SAY HOW? SAY HOW OFTEN? How do we respond when TV commercials are repeated until we have memorized every dimple on the actors' faces? Research suggests that familiarity breeds content, not contempt.

You might not be crazy about *zebulons* and *afworbu*s at first, but Zajonc (1968) found that people began to react favorably toward these bogus Turkish words[3] on the basis of repeated exposure. Political candidates who become well known to the public through regular TV commercials attain more votes (Grush, 1980). People respond more favorably to abstract art, classical music, and photographs of people from various ethnic minority groups on the basis of repetition. Love for classical art and music may begin through exposure in the nursery, not the college appreciation course.

> ***Truth or Fiction Revisited.*** *It is not true that airing a TV commercial repeatedly hurts sales.* Repeated exposure frequently leads to liking and acceptance.

The more complex the stimuli, the more likely it is that frequent exposure will have favorable effects. The 100th playing of a Bach fugue may be less tiresome than the 100th performance of a pop tune.

In two-sided arguments, the communicator recounts the arguments of the opposition in order to refute them. Theologians and politicians sometimes expose their followers to the arguments of the opposition. By refuting them one by one, they impart to their followers a kind of psychological immunity to them. Two-sided product claims, in which advertisers admitted their product's weak points in addition to highlighting its strengths, are the most believable (Bridgwater, 1982).

It would be nice to think that people are too sophisticated to be persuaded by a **fear appeal.** However, women warned of the dire risks of failing to be screened for breast cancer are more likely to obtain mammograms than women who are informed of the benefits of mammography (Banks and others, 1995). Fear appeals are also more effective at persuading college students

Fear appeal • A type of persuasive communication that influences behavior on the basis of arousing fear instead of rational analysis of the issues.

---

[2] The rugged actor in the original TV commercials died from lung cancer. Cigarettes were apparently more rugged than he.

[3] *Zebulun,* it happens, is the name of Jacob's 10th son, as reported in Genesis. Driving through the Carolinas one summer, your author noted a town named Zebulon. (I'm a repository of useless information.)

to use condoms to prevent transmission of the AIDS virus (Struckman-Johnson and others, 1994). Sun tanning has been shown to increase the likelihood of skin cancer. Interestingly, however, warnings against sun tanning were shown to be more effective among a group of Wake Forest University students when they were based on risks to students' *appearance* (premature aging, wrinkling, and scarring of the skin) rather than on the risk to their health (Jones & Leary, 1994). That is, students who read essays about the sun's cosmetic effects were more likely to say they would protect themselves from the sun than were students who read essays about the sun and cancer. Generally speaking, fear appeals are most effective when they are strong, when the audience believes the dire outcomes, and when the audience believes that it can change (Eagly & Chaiken, 1993).

Audiences also tend to believe arguments that appear to run counter to the vested interests of the communicator (Eagly & Chaiken, 1993). People may pay more attention to a whaling-fleet owner's claim than to a conservationist's that whales are becoming extinct. If the president of Chrysler or General Motors said that Toyotas and Hondas were superior, you can bet that we would prick up our ears.

THE PERSUASIVE COMMUNICATOR: WHOM DO YOU TRUST? Would you buy a used car from a person convicted of larceny? Would you attend weight-control classes run by a 350-pound leader? Would you leaf through fashion magazines featuring homely models? Probably not. Research shows that persuasive communicators show expertise, trustworthiness, attractiveness, or similarity to their audiences (Mackie and others, 1990; Wilder, 1990). Because of the adoration of their fans, sports superstars such as Michael Jordan have also solidified their places as endorsers of products (Goldman, 1993). Fans may consider Jordan to be an MVP, or Most Valuable Player. To Madison Avenue, however, Jordan is an MVE, or Most Valuable Endorser (Goldman, 1993).

TV news anchors enjoy high prestige. One study (Mullen and others, 1987) found that before the 1984 presidential election, Peter Jennings of ABC News had shown significantly more favorable facial expressions when reporting on Ronald Reagan than on Walter Mondale. Tom Brokaw of NBC and Dan Rather of CBS had not shown favoritism. The researchers also found that viewers of ABC News voted for Reagan in greater proportions than viewers of NBC or CBS News. It is tempting to conclude that viewers were subtly persuaded by Jennings to vote for Reagan—and maybe this happened in a number of cases. But viewers do not simply absorb, spongelike, whatever the tube feeds them. Instead, they show **selective avoidance** and **selective exposure** (Sweeney & Gruber, 1984). They tend to switch channels when they are faced with news coverage that counters their own attitudes. They also seek communicators whose outlooks coincide with their own. Thus, it may simply be that Reaganites favored Jennings over Brokaw and Rather.

THE CONTEXT OF THE MESSAGE: "GET 'EM IN A GOOD MOOD." You are too shrewd to let someone persuade you by buttering you up, but perhaps someone you know would be influenced by a sip of wine, a bite of cheese, and a sincere compliment. Atmospheric elements like good food and pleasant music boost acceptance of persuasive messages. When we are in a good mood, we are apparently less likely to carefully evaluate the situation (Mackie & Worth, 1989; Petty and others, 1991; Schwarz and others, 1991).

It is also counterproductive to call your dates fools when they differ with you—even though their ideas are bound to be foolish if they do not concur with yours. Agreement and praise are more effective at encouraging others to

Selective avoidance • Diverting one's attention from information that is inconsistent with one's attitudes.
Selective exposure • Deliberately seeking and attending to information that is consistent with one's attitudes.

Would You Buy These Products?
Advertisers use a combination of central and peripheral cues to hawk their wares. What factors contribute to the persuasiveness of messages? To the persuasiveness of communicators? Why is Michael Jordan considered an MVE ("most valuable endorser")?

embrace your views. Appear sincere or else your compliments will look manipulative. (It seems unsporting to divulge this information.)

THE PERSUADED AUDIENCE: ARE YOU A PERSON WHO CAN'T SAY NO? Why do some people have sales resistance? Why do others enrich the lives of every door-to-door salesperson? It may be that people with high self-esteem and low social anxiety are more likely to resist social pressure (Santee & Maslach, 1982). Baumeister and Covington (1985) challenge the view that persons with low self-esteem are more open to persuasion, however. Persons with high self-esteem may also be persuaded, but they may be less willing to confess that others have influenced them. Knowledge of the areas that a communicator is addressing also tends to lessen persuadableness (Wood, 1982).

A classic study by Schwartz and Gottman (1976) reveals the cognitive nature of the social anxiety that can make it hard for some of us to refuse requests. Schwartz and Gottman found that people who comply with unreasonable requests are more apt to report thinking, "I was worried about what the other person would think of me if I refused," "It is better to help others than to be self-centered," or "The other person might be hurt or insulted if I refused." People who did not comply reported thoughts such as "It doesn't matter what the other person thinks of me," "I am perfectly free to say no," or "This request is an unreasonable one" (p. 916).

THE FOOT-IN-THE-DOOR TECHNIQUE. You might suppose that contributing money to door-to-door solicitors for charity will get you off the hook. That is, they'll take the cash and leave you alone for a while. Actually, the opposite is true. The next time they mount a campaign, they may call on generous you to go door to door! Organizations compile lists of persons they can rely on. Giving an inch apparently encourages others to go for a yard. They have gotten their "foot in the door."

Consider a classic experiment on the **foot-in-the-door technique** by Freedman and Fraser (1966). Groups of women received phone calls from a consumer group requesting that they let a six-person crew drop by their homes to catalog their household products. The job could take hours. Only 22% of one group acceded to this irksome entreaty. But 53% of another group of women assented to a visit from this wrecking crew. Why was the second group more compliant? The pliant group had been phoned a few days earlier and had agreed to answer a few questions about the soap products they used. They had been primed for the second request. The caller had gotten a "foot in the door."

Research suggests that people who accede to small requests become more amenable to larger ones because they come to see themselves as the kind of people who help in this way (Eisenberg and others, 1987). Regardless of how the foot-in-the-door technique works, if you want to say no, it may be easier to do so (and stick to your guns) the first time a request is made. Later may be too late.

In the following section, we discuss a particularly troubling kind of attitude: prejudice.

> **Foot-in-the-door technique** • A method for inducing compliance in which a small request is followed by a larger request.

Prejudice and Stereotypes

Too often we consider race as something only Blacks have, sex orientation as something only gays have, gender as something only women have. If we don't fall into any of these categories, then we don't have to worry.

HENRY LOUIS GATES, JR., CHAIR, HARVARD UNIVERSITY'S AFRICAN AMERICAN STUDIES DEPARTMENT

I imagine one of the reasons people cling to their hates so stubbornly is because they sense, once hate is gone, they will be forced to deal with pain.

JAMES BALDWIN

I am free of all prejudices. I hate everyone equally.

W. C. FIELDS

People have condemned billions of other people. Without ever meeting them. Without ever learning their names.

Prejudice is an attitude toward a group that leads people to evaluate members of that group negatively. On a cognitive level, prejudice is linked to expectations that the target group will behave poorly, say, in the workplace or by engaging in criminal behavior. On an affective level, prejudice is associated with negative feelings such as dislike or hatred. Behaviorally, prejudice is connected with avoidance, aggression, and discrimination.

DISCRIMINATION.   One form of negative behavior that results from prejudice is called **discrimination.** Many groups have suffered discrimination in the United States—women, gay males and lesbians, older people, and ethnic groups such as African Americans, Asian Americans, Hispanic Americans, Irish Americans, Jewish Americans, and Native Americans (Takaki, 1993). Discrimination takes many forms, including denial of access to jobs, housing, and the voting booth—even avoidance of eye contact (Neuberg, 1989). Many people have forgotten that African American men gained the right to vote decades before women did.

STEREOTYPES.   Are Jewish Americans shrewd and ambitious? Are African Americans superstitious and musical? Are gay men and lesbians unfit for military service? Such ideas are stereotypes—prejudices about groups that lead people to interpret their observations in a biased fashion (Herek, 1993). Table 16.1 shows common stereotypes about various sociocultural groups.

SOURCES OF PREJUDICE.   The sources of prejudice are many and varied. Let us consider some contributors:

1. *Assumptions of dissimilarity.* We are apt to like people who share our attitudes. In forming impressions of others, we are influenced by attitudinal similarity and dissimilarity (Duckitt, 1992). People of different religions and races often have different backgrounds, however, giving rise to dissimilar attitudes. Even when people of different races share important values, they may assume they do not.

2. *Social conflict.* There is a lengthy history of social and economic conflict between people of different races and religions. For example, Southern White people and African Americans have competed for jobs, giving rise to negative attitudes, even lynchings (Hepworth & West, 1988).

3. *Social learning.* Children acquire some attitudes from others, especially parents. Children tend to imitate their parents, and parents reinforce their children for doing so (Duckitt, 1992). In this way, prejudices can be transmitted from generation to generation.

4. *Information processing.* One cognitive view is that prejudices act as cognitive filters through which we perceive the social world. Prejudice is a way of processing social information. It is easier to attend to, and remember, instances of behavior that are consistent with our prejudices than it is to reconstruct our mental categories (Bodenhausen, 1988; Devine, 1989; Dovidio and others, 1986; Fiske, 1993). If you believe that Jewish Americans are stingy, it is easier to recall a Jewish American's negotiation of a price than a

Prejudice • The belief that a person or group, on the basis of assumed racial, ethnic, sexual, or other features, will possess negative characteristics or perform inadequately.

Discrimination • The denial of privileges to a person or group because of prejudice.

Stereotyping. How well is this child performing on her test? An experiment by Darley and Gross showed that our expectations concerning a child's performance on a test are linked to our awareness of that child's socioeconomic background.

TABLE 16.1
SOME STEREOTYPES OF SOCIOCULTURAL GROUPS WITHIN THE UNITED STATES

African Americans
Physically powerful and well-coordinated
Unclean
Unintelligent and superstitious
Musically talented
Excellent as lovers
Lazy
Emotional and aggressive
Flashy (gaudy clothes and big cars)

Chinese Americans
Deceitful
Inscrutable
Wise
Cruel
Polite, quiet, and deferential
Possessing strong family ties
Law-abiding

Hispanic Americans
Macho
Unwilling to learn English
Disinterested in education
Not concerned about being on welfare
Warm, expressive
Lazy
Hot-tempered and violent

Irish Americans
Sexually repressed
Heavy drinkers
Overly religious
Political and nationalistic
Outgoing, witty, and literary
Hot-tempered ("fighting Irish")

Italian Americans
Overly interested in food
Ignorant, suspicious of education
Clannish
Great singers
Great shoemakers and barbers
Hot-tempered and violent
Connected to the Mafia
Talk with their hands
Cowardly in battle

Japanese Americans
Ambitious, hardworking, and competitive
Intelligent, well-educated
Obedient, servile women
Sneaky
Poor lovers
Possessing strong family ties
Great imitators, not originators
Law-abiding

Jewish Americans
Cheap, shrewd in business
Clannish
Control banks, Wall Street, and the media
Wealthy and showy
Big-nosed
Pushy
Smothering mother

Polish Americans
Unintelligent and uneducated
Overly religious
Dirty
Racist, bigoted
Boorish, uncultured

White Anglo-Saxon Protestants ("WASPs")
Hardworking, ambitious, thrifty
Honorable
Wealthy, powerful
Insensitive, emotionally cold
Polite, well-mannered, genteel
Snobbish
Guilt-ridden do-gooders

Stereotypes are fixed, conventional ideas about groups of people and can give rise to prejudice and discrimination. Do you believe the stereotypes listed in this table? What is the evidence for your beliefs?
Sources of stereotypes: *Sociology in a changing world* (3rd ed.), by W. Kornblum, 1994, Fort Worth: Harcourt Brace College Publishers; *A different mirror: A history of multicultural America*, by R. Takaki, 1993, Boston: Little, Brown & Company.

Jewish American's charitable donation. If you believe that Californians are "airheads," it may be easier to recall TV images of surfing than of scientific conferences at Caltech and Berkeley.

5. *Social categorization.* A second cognitive perspective focuses on people's tendencies to divide the social world into "us" and "them." People usually view those who belong to their own groups—the "in-group"—more favorably than those who do not—the "out-group" (Duckitt, 1992; Linville and others, 1989; Schaller & Maas, 1989). Moreover, there is a tendency for us to assume that out-group members are more alike, or homogeneous, in their attitudes and behavior than members of our own groups (Judd & Park, 1988; Wilder, 1986). Our isolation from out-group members makes it easier to maintain our stereotypes.

6. *Victimization by prejudice.* Ironically, people who have been victims of prejudice sometimes attempt to gain a sense of pride by asserting their superiority over other socioeconomic or ethnic groups (Van Brunt, 1994).

MINILECTURE: STEREOTYPE AND PREJUDICE

Reflections

- **Agree or disagree with the following statement and support your answer: "People vote their consciences."**

- What are your political attitudes? Liberal? Conservative? Middle of the road? (Something else?) How did you develop these attitudes? (Are you sure?) Do your political attitudes represent the attitudes of many people from your socio-cultural background? Why or why not?
- Are you entertained by any radio or TV commercials? Which ones? Why? Did these commercials ever convince you to buy a product? Which product? Was the commercial accurate?
- Do you ever get involved in arguments in which you try to change other people's attitudes? Can you provide an example? Do you tend to win or lose such arguments? Why?
- What stereotypes, if any, do you hold of other ethnic groups, such as those included in Table 16.1? How did these stereotypes develop? Has taking this course affected your tendency to hold such stereotypes? If so, in what way?

Let us now turn our attention to some of the factors involved in the formation of our impressions of other people.

WORLD OF DIVERSITY

GENDER POLARIZATION AND ITS COSTS

Psychologist Sandra Lipsitz Bem (1993) writes that three beliefs about women and men have prevailed throughout the history of Western culture and polarized our views of women and men:

1. Women and men have basically different psychological and sexual natures.
2. Men are the superior, dominant gender.
3. Gender differences and male superiority are "natural."

What does "natural" mean? Throughout most of history, people viewed naturalness in terms of religion, or God's scheme of things (Bem, 1993). For the past century or so, naturalness has been seen in biological, evolutionary terms—at least by most scientists.

What are perceived as the "natural" gender roles? In what Bem (1993) refers to as our "gender-polarizing society," people tend to see the feminine gender role as warm, emotional, dependent, gentle, helpful, mild, patient, submissive, and interested in the arts. The typical masculine gender role is perceived as independent, competitive, tough, protective, logical, and competent at business, math, and science. Women are typically expected to care for the kids and cook the meals.

U.S. gender polarization is connected with the traditional distribution of men into breadwinning roles and women into homemaking roles. When the wife works, she is less likely to be perceived as stereotypically feminine—unless she works because of financial necessity and not because of choice. Despite the persistence of the stereotype that men put bread on the table, 6 of every 10 new U.S. jobs in the 1990s are being filled by women (National Institute of Occupational Safety and Health, 1990).

COSTS OF GENDER POLARIZATION

Gender polarization exacts costs in terms of education, activities, careers, psychological well-being, and interpersonal relationships.

Costs in Education. Polarization has historically worked to the disadvantage of women. In past centuries, girls were considered to be unsuited to education. Even the great Swiss-French philosopher Jean-Jacques Rousseau, who was in the forefront of an open approach to education, believed that girls were basically irrational and naturally disposed to child rearing and homemaking tasks—certainly not to commerce, science, and industry.

In the United States today, boys and girls are looked upon as being about equal in overall learning ability. Girls are expected to excel in language arts, and boys, in math and science, however. Such expectations dissuade girls from taking advanced courses in the "male domain." Boys take more math courses in high school than girls do (AAUW, 1992), and math courses open doorways to occupations in the natural sciences, engineering, and economics, among many other fields. There are several reasons why American boys are more likely than American girls to feel at home with math (AAUW, 1992):

1. Fathers are more likely than mothers to help children with math homework.

2. Advanced math courses are more likely to be taught by men.

3. Teachers often show higher expectations for boys in math courses.

4. Teachers of math courses spend more time instructing and interacting with boys than girls.

By junior high, boys view themselves as more competent in math than girls do, even when they receive identical grades (AAUW, 1992). Boys are more likely to have positive feelings about math. Girls are more liable to have math anxiety. It becomes increasingly hard to convince high school and college women to take math courses, even when they have superior ability. Even girls who excel in math and science are less likely than boys to choose careers in math and science (AAUW, 1992).

If women are to find their places in professions related to math, science, and engineering, we may need to provide more female role models in these professions. As we enter the new millennium, such models will help shatter the stereotype that these occupations are meant for men. We also need to encourage girls to take more courses in math and science. Experimental programs such as Operation Smart (for *Science, Math, and Relevant Technology*), run by Girls, Inc., show that with a little encouragement, many female middleschoolers overcome any anxieties they may have about math and science (Marriott, 1991).

Reviews of the research (AAUW, 1992; Sadker & Sadker, 1994) reveal the following:

- Teachers pay more attention to boys than to girls.

- Girls continue to lag behind boys on achievement test scores in math and science.

- Girls are reporting an increased incidence of sexual harassment by boys.

- A number of standardized tests are biased against girls, which hurts their chances of being accepted into college and receiving scholarships.

- Textbooks still tend to ignore or stereotype women.

- Girls receive virtually no information about pressing concerns such as sexual discrimination, sexual abuse and harassment, and depression.

Costs in Careers. Women are less likely than men to enter careers in math, science, and engineering. Although women are awarded more than half of the bachelor's degrees in the United States, they receive fewer than one third of the degrees in science and engineering. Moreover, women account for only

15% of the nation's scientists and engineers (Hafner, 1993). Why? It is partly because math, science, and engineering are perceived as being inconsistent with the feminine gender role. Many little girls are dissuaded from thinking about professions such as engineering and architecture because they are given dolls, not firetrucks and blocks, to play with (Marriott, 1991). Many boys are likewise deterred from entering child-care and nursing professions because others look askance at them when they reach for dolls.

Then there are the inequities in the workplace that are based on gender polarization. For example, women earn less than men for comparable work. Women are less likely than men to be promoted into responsible managerial positions (Kilborn, 1995; Rosenberg and others, 1993). Once in managerial positions, women often feel pressured to be "tougher" than men in order to seem as tough. They also feel pressured to pay more attention to their appearance than men do, because coworkers pay more attention to what they wear, how they crop their hair, and so forth. If they don't look crisp and tailored every day, others will think they are unable to exert the force to remain in command. If they dress up too much, however, they may be denounced as fashion plates rather than serious workers! Female managers who choose to be deliberate in decision making—and, consequently, to take some time—may stand accused of being "wishy-washy." What happens when female managers change their minds? They run the risk of being labeled fickle and indecisive, rather than flexible and willing to consider new information.

Women in the workplace are also often expected to engage in traditionally feminine tasks, such as making the coffee or cleaning up after the conference lunch, along with the jobs they were hired to do. Finally, women usually have the dual responsibility of being the major caregiver for the children in the home.

Costs in Psychological Well-Being and Interpersonal Relationships.   Polarization also interferes with our psychological well-being and our interpersonal relationships. Women who assume the traditional feminine gender role appear to have lower self-esteem than women who also show masculine traits (Bem, 1993). They are more likely to believe that women are to be seen and not heard. They are therefore unlikely to assert themselves by making their needs and wants known. As a consequence, they are likely to encounter frustration.

Men who accept the traditional masculine gender role are less likely to feel comfortable performing the activities involved in caring for children, such as bathing them, dressing them, and feeding them (Bem, 1993). Such men are less likely to ask for help—including medical help—when they need it ("Doctors tie male mentality," 1995). They are also less likely to be sympathetic and tender or express feelings of love in their marital relationships (Coleman & Ganong, 1985).

Social perception • A subfield of social psychology that studies the ways in which we form and modify impressions of others.

SOCIAL PERCEPTION

Why do you wear your best outfit to a job interview? Why do defense attorneys dress their clients neatly and cut their hair before they are seen by the jury? Because first impressions are important and reasonably accurate (Burnstein & Schul, 1982; Wyer, 1988).

First impressions are one of the topics in the psychology of **social perception.** In this section, we explore several factors that contribute to social perception: primacy and recency effects, attribution theory, and body language. Then, we survey the determinants of interpersonal attraction.

Primacy and Recency Effects: The Importance of First Impressions

When I was a teenager, a young man was accepted or rejected by his date's parents the first time they were introduced. If he was considerate and made small talk, her parents would allow the couple to stay out past curfew, even to watch submarine races at the beach during the early morning hours. If he was boorish or uncommunicative, he was a cad forever. Her parents would object to him, no matter how hard he worked to gain their favor later on.

First impressions can make or break us. This is the **primacy effect.** We infer traits from behavior. If we act considerately at first, we are labeled considerate. The trait of consideration is used to explain and predict our future behavior. If, after being labeled considerate, one keeps a date out past curfew, this lapse is likely to be seen as an exception to a rule—excused by circumstances or external causes. If one is first seen as inconsiderate, however, several months of considerate behavior may be perceived as a cynical effort to "make up for it."

Participants in a classic experiment on the primacy effect read different stories about "Jim" (Luchins, 1957). The stories consisted of one or two paragraphs. One-paragraph stories portrayed Jim as friendly or unfriendly. These paragraphs were also used in the two-paragraph stories but were read in opposite order. Of those reading only the "friendly" paragraph, 95% rated Jim as friendly. Of those who read just the "unfriendly" paragraph, 3% rated him as friendly. Seventy-eight percent of those who read two-paragraph stories in the "friendly–unfriendly" order labeled Jim as friendly. When they read the paragraphs in the reverse order, only 18% rated Jim as friendly.

MINILECTURE: ATTRIBUTION

Primacy effect   •   The tendency to evaluate others in terms of first impressions.

First impressions. Why is it important to make a good first impression? What are some ways of doing so?

Truth or Fiction Revisited. *It is true that first impressions have power-ful effects on our social relationships.* People apparently interpret future events in the light of first impressions. If you have made a poor first impression with someone, should you attempt to change her or his impression or just give up on the relationship?

How can we encourage people to pay more attention to more recent im-pressions? Luchins accomplished this by allowing time to elapse between pre-senting the paragraphs. In this way, fading memories allowed more recent information to take precedence. This is the **recency effect.** Luchins found a second way to counter first impressions: He simply asked people in the study to avoid snap judgments and to weigh all the evidence.

Attribution Theory: You're Free but I'm Caught in the Middle?

At the age of 3, one of my daughters believed that a friend's son was a boy be-cause he *wanted* to be a boy. Since she was 3 at the time, this error in my daughter's **attribution** for the boy's gender is understandable. Adults tend to make somewhat similar attribution errors, however. No, adults do not believe that people's preferences have much to do with their gender. However, adults do tend to exaggerate the role of choice in other aspects of their behavior.

An assumption about why people do things is called an *attribution for be-havior* (Jones, 1990). Our inference of the motives and traits of others through the observation of their behavior is called the **attribution process.** We now focus on attribution theory, or the processes by which people draw conclu-sions about the factors that influence one another's behavior.

Attribution theory is very important, because our attributions lead us to per-ceive others either as purposeful actors or as victims of circumstances.

DISPOSITIONAL AND SITUATIONAL ATTRIBUTIONS. Social psychologists de-scribe two types of attributions—dispositional attributions and situational attri-butions. **Dispositional attributions** ascribe a person's behavior to internal factors, such as personality traits and free will. **Situational attributions** at-tribute a person's actions to external factors such as social influence or social-ization.

THE FUNDAMENTAL ATTRIBUTION ERROR. People tend to attribute too much of other people's behavior to internal factors such as free will (Kimble, 1994). This bias in the attribution process is the **fundamental attribution error.** When we observe the behavior of others, we apparently focus too much on their actions and too little on the circumstances that surround their actions. We tend to be more aware of the networks of forces acting on ourselves.

One reason for the fundamental attribution error is that we tend to infer traits from behavior. When we overhear a woman screaming at her husband in a supermarket, we tend to assume that she is impulsive and boisterous. We are usually not aware of the many things that her husband might have done to in-furiate her. The fundamental attribution error is linked to another bias in the at-tribution process: the actor–observer effect.

THE ACTOR–OBSERVER EFFECT. When we see ourselves and others engag-ing in behavior that we do not like, we tend to see the others as willful actors but to perceive ourselves as victims of circumstances (Fiske & Taylor, 1984).

Recency effect • The tendency to evaluate others in terms of the most recent impression.

Attribution • A belief concerning why people behave in a certain way.

Attribution process • The process by which people draw inferences about the motives and traits of others.

Dispositional attribution • An assumption that a person's behavior is determined by inter-nal causes such as personal attitudes or goals.

Situational attribution • An assumption that a person's behavior is determined by external circumstances such as the social pressure found in a situation.

Fundamental attribution error • The ten-dency to assume that others act predominantly on the basis of their dispositions, even when there is evidence suggesting the importance of their situations.

The tendency to attribute the behavior of others to dispositional factors and our own behavior to situational influences is termed the **actor–observer effect.**

Consider an example. When parents and children argue about the children's choice of friends or dates, the parents infer traits from behavior and tend to perceive their children as stubborn, difficult, and independent. The children also infer traits from behavior. They may thus perceive their parents as bossy and controlling. Parents and children alike attribute the others' behavior to internal causes. They both make dispositional attributions about other people's behavior, that is.

How do the parents and children perceive themselves? The parents probably see themselves as being forced into combat by their children's foolishness. If they become insistent, it is in response to their children's stubbornness. The children probably see themselves as responding to peer pressures and, perhaps, to sexual urges that may have come from within but do not seem "of their own making." The parents and the children both tend to see their own behavior as being motivated by external factors. That is, they make situational attributions for their own behavior.

Truth or Fiction Revisited. It is true that we take others to task for their misdeeds but tend to see ourselves as victims of circumstances when our conduct falls short of our ideals. This bias in the attribution process is referred to as the actor–observer effect. What factors seem to account for the actor–observer effect?

The actor–observer effect extends to our perceptions of the in-group (an extension of ourselves) and the out-group. Consider conflicts between nations. Both sides may engage in brutal acts of violence. Each side usually considers the other to be calculating, inflexible, and—not infrequently—sinister. Each side also typically views its own people as victims of circumstances and its own violent actions as being vindicated or dictated by the situation. After all, we may look at the other side as being in the wrong, but can we expect the out-group to agree with us?[4]

THE SELF-SERVING BIAS. There is also a **self-serving bias** in the attribution process. We are likely to ascribe our successes to internal, dispositional factors but our failures to external, situational influences (Baumgardner and others, 1986; Van der Plight & Eiser, 1983). When we have done well on a test or impressed a date, we are likely to credit these outcomes to our intelligence and charm. But when we fail, we are likely to ascribe them to bad luck, an unfairly demanding test, or our date's bad mood.

It seems that we extend the self-serving bias to others in our perceptions of why we win or lose when we gamble. When we win bets on football games, we tend to attribute our success to the greater ability of the winning team—a dispositional factor (Gilovich, 1983). But when we lose our bets, we tend to ascribe the game's outcome to a fluke, such as an error by a referee.

An ironic twist to the self-serving bias is that we tend to see ourselves as less self-centered than others (Rempel and others, 1985).

There are exceptions to the self-serving bias. We are more likely to own up to our responsibility for our failures when we think that other people will not accept situational attributions (Reiss and others, 1981). Depressed people are

Actor–observer effect • The tendency to attribute our own behavior to situational factors but to attribute the behavior of others to dispositional factors.

Self-serving bias • The tendency to view one's successes as stemming from internal factors and one's failure as stemming from external factors.

---

[4] I am not suggesting that all nations are equally blameless (or blameworthy) for their brutality toward other nations. I am merely pointing out that there is a tendency for the people of a nation to perceive themselves as being driven to unwanted behavior. Yet, they are also likely to perceive other nations' negative behavior as willful and directed by national dispositions.

also more likely than nondepressed people to ascribe their failures to internal factors, even when dispositional attributions are not justified.

Another interesting attribution bias is a gender difference in attributions for friendly behavior. Men are more likely than women to interpret a woman's friendliness toward men as flirting (Abbey, 1987). Perhaps gender roles apparently still lead men to expect that "decent" women are passive.

FACTORS CONTRIBUTING TO THE ATTRIBUTION PROCESS: CONSENSUS, CONSISTENCY, AND DISTINCTIVENESS.   According to Kelley and Michela (1980), our attribution of behavior to internal or external causes can be influenced by three factors: consensus, consistency, and distinctiveness. When few people act in a certain way—that is, when **consensus** is low—we are likely to attribute behavior to dispositional (internal) factors. Consistency refers to the degree to which the same person acts in the same way on other occasions. Highly consistent behavior can often be attributed to dispositional factors. Distinctiveness is the extent to which the person responds differently in different situations. If the person acts similarly in different situations, distinctiveness is low. We are thus likely to attribute his or her behavior to dispositional factors.

Let us apply the criteria of consensus, consistency, and distinctiveness to a customer in a restaurant. She takes one bite of her blueberry cheesecake and calls for the waiter. She argues that her food is inedible and demands that it be replaced. The question is whether she complained as a result of internal causes (for example, because she is difficult to please) or external causes (that is, because the food really is bad). Under the following circumstances, we are likely to attribute her behavior to internal, dispositional causes: (1) No one else at the table is complaining, so consensus is low. (2) She has returned food on other occasions, so consistency is high. (3) She complains in other restaurants also, so distinctiveness is low (see Table 16.2).

Under the following circumstances, however, we are likely to attribute her behavior to external situational causes: (1) Everyone else at the table is also complaining, so consensus is high. (2) She has not returned food on other occasions, so consistency is low. (3) She usually does not complain at restaurants, so distinctiveness is high. Given these conditions, we are likely to believe that the blueberry cheesecake really is awful, and our friend is justifiably responding to the circumstances.

Consensus • General agreement.

TABLE 16.2

FACTORS LEADING TO INTERNAL OR EXTERNAL ATTRIBUTIONS OF BEHAVIOR

	INTERNAL ATTRIBUTION	**EXTERNAL ATTRIBUTION**
Consensus	*Low:* Few people behave this way.	*High:* Most people behave this way.
Consistency	*High:* The person behaves this way frequently.	*Low:* The person does not behave this way frequently.
Distinctiveness	*Low:* The person behaves this way in many situations.	*High:* The person behaves this way in few situations.

We are more likely to attribute behavior to internal, dispositional factors when it is low in consensus, high in consistency, and low in distinctiveness. In the example given in the textbook, we will be most likely to attribute a complaint about one's food to external factors if other people also complain (high consensus) and if the complainer usually does not (high distinctiveness).

Body Language

Body language is important in social perception. Nonverbal behavior can express internal states, such as feelings. It can regulate social interactions (Patterson, 1991). People even use body language to deceive other people as to how they feel (DePaulo, 1992).

At an early age, we learn that the ways people carry themselves provide cues to how they feel and are likely to behave (Saarni, 1990). You may have noticed that when people are "uptight," they may also be rigid and straight-backed. People who are relaxed are more likely, literally, to "hang loose." Factors such as eye contact, posture, and distance between people provide broadly recognized cues to their moods and feelings toward their companions. When people face us and lean toward us, we may assume that they like us or are interested in what we are saying. If we are privy to a conversation between a couple and observe that the woman is leaning toward the man, but that the man is sitting back and toying with his hair, we are likely to infer that he is not having any of what she is selling.

Touching also communicates. Women are more likely than men to touch other people when they are interacting with them (Stier & Hall, 1984). In one touching experiment, Kleinke (1977) showed that appeals for help can be more effective when the distressed person engages in physical contact with people being asked for aid. A woman obtained more dimes for phone calls when she touched the person she was asking for money on the arm. In another experiment, waitresses obtained higher tips when they touched patrons on the hand or the shoulder while making change (Crusco & Wetzel, 1984).

In these experiments, touching was noncontroversial. It was usually gentle, brief, and occurred in familiar settings. However, when touching suggests greater intimacy than is desired, it can be seen as negative. A study in a nursing home found that responses to being touched depended on factors such as the status of the staff member, the type of touch, and the part of the body that was touched (Hollinger & Buschmann, 1993). Touching was considered positive when it was appropriate to the situation and did not appear to be condescending. Touching was seen as negative when it was controlling, unnecessary, or overly intimate.

Body language can also be used to establish and maintain territorial control (Brown & Altman, 1981), as anyone who has had to step aside because a football player was walking down the hall can testify. Werner and her colleagues (1981) found that players in a game arcade used touching as a way of signaling others to keep their distance. Solo players engaged in more touching than did groups, perhaps because they were surrounded by strangers.

GAZING AND STARING: THE EYES HAVE IT. We usually feel that we can learn much from eye contact. When others "look us squarely in the eye," we may assume that they are being assertive or open with us. Avoidance of eye contact may suggest deception or depression. Gazing is interpreted as a sign of liking or friendliness (Kleinke, 1986). In one penetrating study, as a matter of fact, men and women were asked to gaze into each other's eyes for 2 minutes (Kellerman and others, 1989). Afterward, they reported passionate feelings toward one another. (Watch out!)

Gazes differ, of course, from persistent hard stares. Hard stares are interpreted as provocations or signs of anger. Adolescent males sometimes engage in staring contests as an assertion of dominance. The male who looks away first loses. In a classic series of field experiments, Phoebe Ellsworth and her colleagues (1972) subjected drivers stopped at red lights to hard stares from

FIGURE 16.1

Diagram of an Experiment in Hard Staring and Avoidance. In the Ellsworth study, the confederate of the experimenter stared at some drivers and not at others. Recipients of the stares drove across the intersection more rapidly once the light turned green. Why?

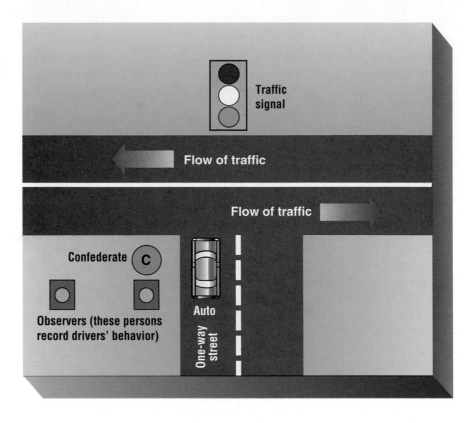

Attraction • In social psychology, an attitude of liking or disliking (negative attraction).

riders of motor scooters (see Figure 16.1). People who were stared at crossed the intersection more rapidly than people who were not when the light changed. Staring at people apparently increases their physiological arousal to uncomfortable levels.

Reflections

- Think of an instance in which you tried to make a good first impression on someone. How did you do it? Why was it important to try to make a good first impression?
- Give an example of an instance in which you, or someone you know, tried to excuse your behavior by making a situational attribution. Do you make the fundamental attribution error of attributing too much of other people's behavior to choice? Give an example.
- How do you feel when strangers touch you? Why? How do you feel when a physician or nurse touches you during an examination? Why?
- Did you ever leave a situation in which you were stared at in order to lower feelings of arousal and avert the threat of danger?

INTERPERSONAL ATTRACTION: LIKING AND LOVING

Whether we are discussing the science of physics, a pair of magnetic toy dogs, or a couple in a singles bar, **attraction** is a force that draws bodies together. In psychology, attraction is also thought of as a force that draws bodies, or people, together—an attitude of liking. Magnetic "kissing" dogs are usually constructed so that the heads attract one another, but (unlike their flesh-and-blood counterparts) a head and tail repel one another. Attraction can lead to feelings of liking and loving. We shall see that when there is a matching of the heads—that is, a meeting of the minds—people experience *positive attraction* to one another. As with the toy dogs, when we believe that another person's opinions are, well, asinine, we experience *negative attraction* and are repelled.

Physical Attractiveness: How Important Is Looking Good?

Are we all so intelligent and sophisticated that we rank physical appearance low on the roster of qualities we seek in a date—below sensitivity and warmth, for example? No. Physical appearance has been found to be a key factor in attraction and consideration of partners for dates and marriage (Hendrick & Hendrick, 1992). Physical attractiveness also influences prospective employers during job interviews (Mack & Rainey, 1990).

IS BEAUTY IN THE EYE OF THE BEHOLDER? What determines physical allure? Are our standards subjective—that is, "in the eye of the beholder?" Or is there agreement on what is appealing?

Some aspects of beauty appear to be cross-cultural. For example, a study of people in England and Japan found that both British and Japanese men considered women with large eyes, high cheekbones, and narrow jaws to be most attractive (Perret and others, 1994). In his research, Perrett created computer composites of the faces of 60 women and, as shown in part A of Figure 16.2,

FIGURE 16.2

What Features Contribute to Facial Attractiveness? Both in England and Japan, features such as large eyes, high cheekbones, and narrow jaws contribute to perceptions of the attractiveness of women. Part A shows a composite of the faces of 15 women rated as the most attractive of a group of 60. Part B is a composite in which the features of these 15 women are exaggerated—that is, developed further in the direction that separates them from the average of the entire 60.

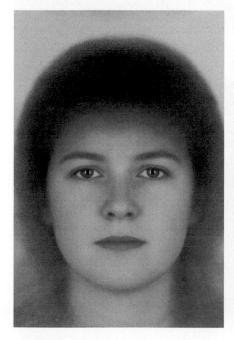
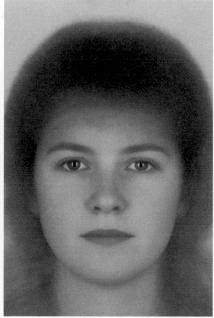

"Looking Good." Tia Carrere, Rosie Perez, Denzel Washington, and Kevin Costner are among those who set the standards for beauty in contemporary American culture. How important is physical attractiveness? What are our stereotypes of attractive people? Do we see them as being more successful? As making better spouses and parents?

of the 15 women who were rated the most attractive. He then used computer enhancement to exaggerate the differences between the composite of the 60 and the composite of the 15 most attractive, arriving at the image shown in part B of Figure 16.2. Part B, which shows higher cheekbones and a narrower jaw than part A, was rated as the most attractive image. Similar results were found for the image of a Japanese woman. Works of art suggest that the ancient Greeks and Egyptians favored similar facial features (Etcoff, 1994).

Psychologist Judith Langlois (1994) has found that the tendency to prefer attractive faces, as determined by amount of time spent looking at various faces, is found in infants by the age of 2 months. She concludes that infants' preferences are likely to be inborn.

In our society, tallness is an asset for men, but tall women are viewed less positively (Sheppard & Strathman, 1989). College woman prefer their dates to be about 6 inches taller than they are. College men tend to fancy women who are about 4½ inches shorter (Gillis & Avis, 1980).

Stretch and Candy were tall. Since we tend to connect tallness with social dominance, many women of Candy's height may be concerned that their stature will compromise their femininity. Some women fear that shorter men are disinclined to ask them out. A few walk with a hunch, trying to downplay their height. A neighbor of the author describes herself as 5 feet 13 inches tall.

Although preferences for facial features may transcend time and culture, preferences for body weight and shape may be more culturally determined (Etcoff, 1994). For example, plumpness has been valued in many cultures. Grandmothers who worry that their granddaughters are starving themselves often come from cultures in which stoutness is acceptable or desirable.[5] In current Western society, both genders find slenderness engaging (Franzoi & Herzog, 1987).

Truth or Fiction Revisited. *It is not true that beauty is in the eye of the beholder,* despite the familiarity of the adage. It appears that some aspects of physical appeal may be innate or inborn. There are also cultural standards for beauty that influence people who are reared in that culture.

Although both genders perceive overweight people as unappealing, there are fascinating gender differences in perceptions of desirable body shapes. College men generally find their current physique similar to the ideal male build and to the one that women find most appealing (Fallon & Rozin, 1985). College women, in contrast, generally see themselves as markedly heavier than the figure that is most appealing to men and heavier still than the ideal (see Figure 16.3). Both mothers and fathers of college students see themselves as heavier than their ideal weights (Rozin & Fallon, 1988). Both genders err in their estimates of the other's likes, however. Men of both generations actually prefer women to be heavier than women presume. Women of both generations fancy men who are slimmer than the men imagine.

A flat-chested look was a hallmark of the enchanting profile of the 1920s flapper era, but U.S. women today are likely to think of their bust size as too small (even though they consider themselves to be generally too heavy!). Despite the medical risks, about 120,000 U.S. women a year had breast-implant surgery for cosmetic reasons through 1991. The numbers included such public figures (pardon the pun) as Cher and Mariel Hemingway (Williams, 1992). Ironically, we tend to perceive large-busted women as less intelligent, competent, moral, and modest than women with smaller breasts (Kleinke & Staneski, 1980). Unless there is known to be a silicone implant, this is clearly a case in which people overattribute a physical feature to dispositional factors!

---

[5] The other side of the coin, as noted in Chapter 13's discussion of anorexia nervosa, is that some granddaughters *are* literally starving themselves today.

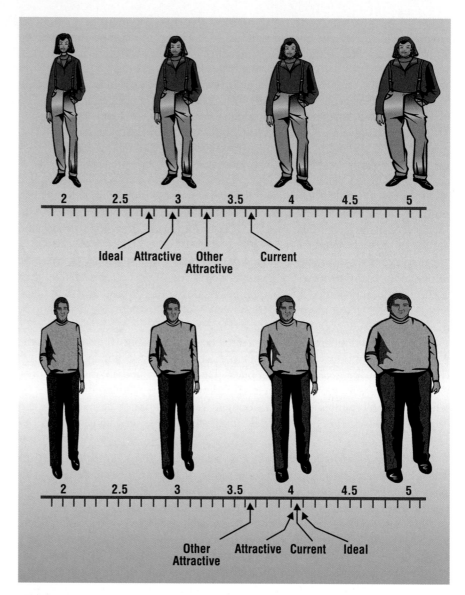

FIGURE 16.3

Can You Ever Be Too Thin? Research suggests that most college women believe that they are heavier than they ought to be. However, men actually prefer women to be a bit heavier than women assume the men would like them to be.

"PRETTY IS AS PRETTY DOES?" Men and women are both perceived as more attractive when they are smiling (Reis and others, 1990). There is thus ample reason to, as the song goes, "put on a happy face" when you are meeting people or looking for a date.

Truth or Fiction Revisited. *It is true that people are perceived as being more attractive when they are smiling.* Does this research finding provide a reason to "put on a happy face" early in the development of social relationships?

Other aspects of behavior also affect interpersonal attraction. Women shown videotapes of prospective dates prefer men who act outgoing and self-expressive (Riggio & Wolf, 1984). College men who show dominance (operationally defined as control over a social interaction with a professor) in a videotape are rated as more attractive by women (Sadalla and others, 1987). College men respond negatively to women who show self-assertion and social dominance, however (Riggio & Wolf, 1984; Sadalla and others, 1987). Despite the liberating forces of recent years, the cultural stereotype of the ideal woman still finds a place for demureness. I am *not* suggesting that self-assertive, expressive women take a back seat to make themselves appealing to traditional men. Assertive women might find nothing but conflict with such men anyhow.

"YOUR DADDY'S RICH AND YOUR MA IS GOOD LOOKIN'": GENDER DIFFERENCES IN THE IMPORTANCE OF PHYSICAL ATTRACTIVENESS.

Your Daddy's rich
And your Ma is good lookin',
So hush, little baby,
Don't you cry.

"SUMMERTIME," FROM THE OPERA *PORGY AND BESS*

College men and women report that the importance of physical attractiveness depends on the type of relationship (Nevid, 1984). In relationships that are predominantly sexual, the physical attractiveness of one's partner is the primary consideration. Psychological traits such as honesty, fidelity, warmth, and sensitivity become relatively more important in long-term relationships.

Men are relatively more swayed than women by their partners' physical characteristics, however. Women place relatively greater emphasis on personal qualities such as warmth, assertiveness, need for achievement, and wit (Hendrick & Hendrick, 1992; Sprecher and others, 1994).

These findings are replicated in studies on mate selection. Women tend to place greater emphasis than men on traits such as professional status, consideration, dependability, kindness, and fondness for children. Men place relatively greater emphasis on physical allure, cooking ability (can't they turn on the microwave oven themselves?), even thrift (Buss, 1994; Feingold, 1992a).

On the surface, gender differences in the traits that affect perceptions of attractiveness seem unbearably sexist—and, perhaps they are. Some sociobiologists believe that evolutionary forces favor the survival of men and women with these preferences because they provide reproductive advantages (Buss, 1995; Fisher, 1992). Physical features such as cleanliness, good complexion, clear eyes, good teeth and good hair, firm muscle tone, and a steady gait are universally appealing to both genders (Rathus and others, 1997). Perhaps such traits have value as markers of better reproductive potential in prospective mates. According to the "parental investment model," a woman's appeal is strongly connected with her age and health, both of which are markers of reproductive capacity. The value of men as reproducers, however, could be more intertwined with factors that contribute to a stable environment for child rearing—such as social standing and reliability (Feingold, 1992a). For such reasons, sociobiologists speculate that these qualities may have grown relatively more alluring to women over the millennia (e.g., Buss, 1994; Fisher, 1992).

Stereotypes of Attractive People: Do Good Things Come in Pretty Packages?

By and large, we rate what is beautiful as good. We expect physically attractive people to be poised, sociable, popular, intelligent, mentally healthy, fulfilled, persuasive, and successful in their jobs and marriages (Eagly and others, 1991;

Feingold, 1992b). Unattractive people are more likely to be judged as outside of the mainstream—for example, politically radical or psychologically disordered (Brigham, 1980; O'Grady, 1982; Unger and others, 1982). Unattractive college students are also more apt to rate themselves as susceptible to personal problems.

These stereotypes seem to have some basis in reality. For one thing, attractive people *do* seem less likely to develop psychological disorders. The disorders of unattractive people are also more severe (e.g., Archer & Cash, 1985; Farina and others, 1986; Burns and Farina, 1987). For another, attractiveness correlates positively with popularity, social skills, and sexual experience (Feingold, 1992b). The correlations between physical attractiveness and most measures of mental ability and personality are trivial, however (Feingold, 1992b).

One way to interpret the data on the correlates of beauty is to assume that they are all innate. In other words, we can believe that beauty and social competence go genetically hand in hand. We can believe that biology is destiny and throw up our hands in despair. Another (more adaptive!) interpretation is that we can do things to make ourselves more attractive and also more successful and fulfilled. Smiling, for example, is linked to attractiveness. So is having a decent physique or figure (which we can work on) and attending to grooming and dress. So don't give up the ship.

Attractive people are also more likely to be judged innocent of crimes in mock jury experiments and observational studies (Mazzella & Feingold, 1994). When found guilty, they are given less severe sentences (Stewart, 1980). Perhaps we assume that attractive people have less need to resort to deviant behavior to achieve their goals. Even when they have erred, perhaps they will have more opportunity for personal growth and be more likely to change their evil ways.

Attractive children learn early of the expectations of others. Even during the first year, adults tend to rate attractive babies as good, smart, likeable, even well-behaved (Stephan & Langlois, 1984). Parents, teachers, and other children expect attractive children to get good grades and be popular, well behaved, and talented.

Matching hypothesis • The view that people tend to choose persons similar to themselves in attractiveness and attitudes in the formation of interpersonal relationships.

Similarity: Do "Opposites Attract" or Do "Birds of a Feather Flock Together"?

Although we may rate highly attractive people as being most desirable, most of us are not left to blend in with the wallpaper. According to the **matching hypothesis,** we tend to ask out people who are similar to ourselves in physical attractiveness rather than the local Denzel Washington or Cindy Crawford look-alike. One motive for asking out "matches" seems to be fear of rejection by more attractive people (Bernstein and others, 1983).

The similarity we seek extends well beyond physical attractiveness. Our marital and sex partners tend to be like us in race/ethnicity, age, level of education, and religion. Consider some findings of the National Health and Social Life Survey (Michael and others, 1994, pp. 45–47):

- Nearly 94% of single White men have White women as their sex partners; 2% are partnered with Hispanic American women, 2% with Asian American women, and less than 1% with African American women.

- About 82% of African American men have African American women as their sex partners; nearly 8% are partnered with White women, and almost 5% with Hispanic American women.

The Matching Hypothesis. Do opposites attract, or do we tend to pair off with people who look and think as we do? As suggested by these photographs, similarity often runs at least skin-deep.

- About 83% of the women and men in the study chose partners within 5 years of their own age and of the same or a similar religion.
- Of nearly 2,000 women in the study, not one with a graduate college degree had a partner who had not finished high school.

SIMILARITY IN ATTITUDES: YOU'RE ENTITLED TO YOUR OWN OPINION, SO LONG AS IT AGREES WITH MINE?   Why do the great majority of us have partners from our own background? One reason is that marriages are made in the neighborhood and not in heaven (Michael and others, 1994). That is, we tend to live among people who are similar to us in background and thus to come into contact with them. Another is that we are drawn to people who are similar in their attitudes. People similar in background are more likely to be similar in their attitudes. Similarity in attitudes and tastes is a key contributor to attraction, friendships, and love relationships (Cappella & Palmer, 1990; Griffin & Sparks, 1990; Laumann and others, 1994). Not all attitudes are equal, however. Attitudes toward religion and children are more important in mate selection than characteristics like kindness and professional status (e.g., Buss & Barnes, 1986; Howard and others, 1987).

We also tend to *assume* that alluring people share our attitudes (Dawes, 1989; Marks and others, 1981). Is this wish fulfillment? When feelings of attraction are strong, as with Candy and Stretch, perhaps we want to think that the kinks in the relationship will be small or that we can iron them out. Similarly, we tend to assume that the presidential candidates we support share our political views (Brent & Granberg, 1982). We may even forget public statements that conflict with our views (Johnson & Judd, 1983). Then, once they are in office, we may be disillusioned when they swerve from our expectations.

We have seen how our feelings of attraction are influenced by physical attractiveness and similarity to other people. Let us now see what happens when feelings of attraction blossom into love.

Love: Doing What Happens . . . Culturally?

Love—the ideal for which we make great sacrifice. Love—the sentiment that launched a thousand ships in the Greek epic *The Iliad*. Through the millennia, poets have sought to capture love in words. Dante Alighieri, the poet who shed some light on the Dark Ages, wrote of "the love that moves the sun and the other stars." Poet Robert Burns wrote that his love was like "a red, red rose." Love is beautiful and elusive. Passion and romantic love are also earthy and lusty, surging with sexual desire.

We use the label "love" to describe everything from affection to sex ("making love"). During adolescence, lust is often tagged as love. We use "love" to describe lust, because sexual desire in the absence of a committed relationship may be viewed as primitive—especially by parents who fear that adolescents may become pregnant if they give in to it. "Being in love" puts the cultural stamp of approval on sexual feelings. "Love" can be discussed even at the dinner table.

THE LOVE TRIANGLE.   No, this love triangle does not refer to two men wooing the same woman. It refers to Robert Sternberg's triangular model of love. Sternberg (1988) believes that love can include combinations of three components: intimacy, passion, and decision/commitment (see Figure 16.4).

Intimacy refers to a couple's closeness, to their mutual concern and sharing of feelings and resources. Passion means romance and sexual feelings. Decision/commitment refers to deciding that one is in love and, in the long term,

FIGURE 16.4

The Triangular Model of Love. According to this model, love has three components: intimacy, passion, and decision/commitment. The ideal of consummate love consists of romantic love plus commitment.

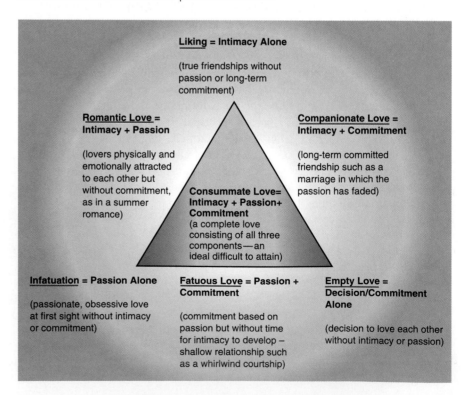

the commitment to enhance and maintain the relationship. Passion is most cru-cial in short-term relationships. Intimacy and commitment are relatively more important in enduring relationships. The ideal form of love, which combines all three, is consummate love. Consummate love, within this model, is roman-tic love plus commitment.

ROMANTIC LOVE IN CONTEMPORARY WESTERN CULTURE: A SOCIOCULTURAL APPROACH. Romantic love is characterized by passion and intimacy. Passion involves feelings of fascination, as shown by preoccupation with the loved one, sexual craving, and the desire for exclusiveness (a special relationship with the loved one). Intimacy involves caring—championing the interests of the loved one, sacrificing one's own interests, if necessary. College undergrad-uates see helping one's lover as being more central to the concept of love than seeking to meet one's own needs with one's lover (Steck and others, 1982). ("Ask not what your lover can do for you. Ask what you can do for your lover.") People who are dating, or who expect to be dating one another, are cognitively biased toward evaluating one another positively (Fiske, 1993). They tend to pay attention to information that confirms their romantic interests. In less technical terms, romantic lovers often idealize one another. They magnify each other's positive features and overlook their flaws.

To experience romantic love, in contrast to attachment or sexual arousal, one must be exposed to a culture that idealizes the concept. In Western cul-ture, romantic love blossoms within the fairy tales about Sleeping Beauty, Cin-derella, Snow White, and all their Princes Charming. It matures with romantic novels, television tales and films, and the personal tales of friends and relatives about dates and romances.

Truth or Fiction Revisited. *Romantic love is not found in every cul-ture in the world.* Romantic love is found only in cultures that idealize the concept.

Romantic Love. There are many kinds of love. Romantic love is an in-tense, positive emotion that involves sexual attraction, feelings of caring, a cultural setting that idealizes love, and the *belief* that one is "in love."

Reflections

- Agree or disagree with the following statement and support your answer: "Beauty is in the eye of the beholder."
- What do the men you know look for in a date? What do the women look for? Are the desired traits similar or dissimilar? In what ways?
- What do the men you know look for in a *mate*? What do the women look for in a mate? Are the desired traits similar or dissimilar to those sought in a date? In what ways?
- **Can love last, or is it but a passing fancy?**
- **Agree or disagree with the following statement and support your answer: "Opposites attract."**

SOCIAL INFLUENCE

Asking me why I don't feel comfortable praying in front of other people here in the United States is like asking me why I don't wear shorts in Cairo.

MAYADA EL-ZOGHBI, A 24-YEAR-OLD EGYPTIAN WOMAN WHO GREW UP IN EGYPT AND MINNESOTA[6]

Most of us would be reluctant to wear blue jeans to a funeral, to walk naked on city streets, or, for that matter, to wear clothes at a nudist colony. Other

---

[6] Citations in this section are drawn from "Muslim Women Bridging Culture Gap," 1993, *The New York Times*, November 8, p. B9.

people and groups can exert enormous pressure on us to behave according to their wishes or according to group norms. As an example, consider the experiences of some Muslim women who have immigrated to the United States:

- "People look at me and they're like, 'She wants to work here?'" complained 19-year-old Maha Alkateeb. After a frustrating job search at the mall, she pulled off her hejab, the black scarf with which many Muslim women cover their hair, and allowed her long, dark hair to cascade out.

- Wanda Khan, 37, suffered a similar setback in Charlotte, North Carolina. She was denied a teaching job because of her hejab. "I know that I am more than qualified," she said, "but a school official told me that there is a school policy against wearing hats. I told him it was a religious thing, and that I couldn't remove it, and that I would take it up with the school board."

- "Here in America, you are constantly forced to question the things we took for granted back home," explains Ferial Masry, a Saudi Arabian immigrant who runs a photography shop in Southern California. "Here, you need to really understand your values and get the children to feel close to their culture while still letting them assimilate." Ferial, like many other Arabian Americans, attempts to balance the sacred and the secular in her personal life. She studies Islamic history, takes Arabic folk dancing, but also lets her children watch the cable program *Nick at Nite*.

- Single Muslim women in the United States have additional problems. In the old country, no one (or hardly anyone) engaged in premarital sexual activity. But in the United States, the media provide a very different impression about sexual norms. Thus, single Muslim women often find secular U.S. culture to be very seductive.

- Muslim women in the United States debate the merits of wearing veils (there is nothing in the Islamic religion that requires the hejab per se, but wearing one is a traditional way for Muslim women to meet Islamic mandates for modesty). For some, the issue seems to be how to continue to embrace Islam and at the same time adopt appealing values of the dominant U.S. culture concerning independence, self-assertiveness, and advancement in the workplace.

The long and the short of it is that Muslim immigrants to the United States, like other immigrants, are being exposed to, and influenced by, the dominant culture in the United States. That culture is exerting social influence. **Social influence** is the area of social psychology that studies the ways in which people alter the thoughts, feelings, and behavior of others. We already learned how attitudes can be changed through persuasion. In this section, we describe a couple of classic experiments to show various ways in which people influence others to engage in destructive obedience and conform to social norms.

Social influence • The area of social psychology that studies the ways in which people influence the thoughts, feelings, and behavior of others.

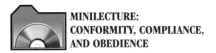

MINILECTURE: CONFORMITY, COMPLIANCE, AND OBEDIENCE

Obedience to Authority: Does Might Make Right?

Throughout history soldiers have followed orders—even when it comes to slaughtering innocent civilians. The Turkish slaughter of Armenians, the Nazi slaughter of Jews, the Serbian slaughter of Bosnian Muslims, the slaughter in Rwanda—these are historic and not so historic examples of the tragedies that can arise from following orders. We may say that we are horrified by such crimes and that we can't imagine why people engage in them. But how many of us would resist orders issued by authority figures?

THE MILGRAM STUDIES. Stanley Milgram also wondered how many of us would resist authority figures who made immoral requests. To find out, he ran a series of experiments that we reviewed in Chapter 2. People responded to newspaper ads to participate in research on "the effects of punishment on learning." The experiment required a "teacher" and a "learner." The newspaper recruit was appointed the teacher—supposedly by chance.

Figures 2.1 and 2.2 show the bogus shock apparatus that was employed in the studies and the layout of the laboratory. "Teachers" were given the task of administering shock to learners when they made errors. The shock was to increase with each consecutive error. Despite the professed purpose of the research, Milgram's sole aim was to determine how many people would deliver high levels of apparently painful electric shock to "learners."

In various phases of Milgram's research, nearly half or the majority of participants complied throughout the series, believing that they were delivering 450-volt, XXX-rated shocks. These findings held for men from the New Haven community, for Yale students, and for women as well as men.

Many people thus obey the commands of others, even when pressed to perform immoral tasks. But *why?* Why did Germans "just follow orders" and commit atrocities? Why did "teachers" obey the experimenter? We do not have all the answers, but we can offer a number of hypotheses:

1. *Socialization.* Despite the expressed American ideal of independence, we are socialized to obey authority figures such as parents and teachers from early childhood. Obedience to immoral demands may be the ugly sibling of socially desirable respect for authority figures (Blass, 1991).

2. *Lack of social comparison.* In Milgram's experimental settings, experimenters showed command of the situation, whereas "teachers" were on the experimenter's ground and very much on their own. Being on their own, they did not have the opportunity to compare their ideas and feelings with those of people in the same situation. They were thus less likely to have a clear impression of what to do.

3. *Perception of legitimate authority.* The phase of Milgram's research just described took place within the hallowed halls of Yale University. Those participating in the study there might have been overpowered by the reputation and authority of the setting. An experimenter at Yale might have appeared to be very much the legitimate authority figure—as might a government official or a high-ranking officer in the military. Yet, further research showed that the university setting contributed to compliance but was not fully responsible for it. The percentage of individuals complying with the experimenter's demands dropped from 65% to 48% when Milgram (1974) replicated the study in a dingy storefront in a nearby town. At first glance, this finding might even seem encouraging. But the main point of the Milgram studies is that most of us remain willing to engage in morally reprehensible acts at the behest of a legitimate-looking authority figure. Hitler and his henchmen were very much the legitimate authority figures in Nazi Germany. "Science" and Yale University legitimized the authority of the experimenters in the Milgram studies. The problem of acquiescence to authority figures remains.

4. *The foot-in-the-door technique.* The foot-in-the-door technique might also have contributed to the obedience of the teachers (Gilberg, 1981). Once they had begun to deliver shocks to learners, they might have found it progressively more difficult to extricate themselves. Soldiers, similarly, are first taught to obey unquestioningly in innocuous matters such as dress and drill.

By the time they are ordered to risk their lives, they have been saluting smartly and following commands for quite some time.

5. *Inaccessibility of values.* People are more likely to act in accord with their attitudes when their attitudes are readily available, or accessible. Most people believe that it is wrong to harm innocent people. But as the teachers in the Milgram experiments became more and more aroused, their attitudes might have become less accessible. As a consequence, it might have become progressively more difficult for them to behave according to them.

6. *Buffers.* Several buffers decreased the effect of the learners' pain on the teachers. Learners (confederates of the experimenter), for example, were in another room. When they were in the same room with teachers—that is, when teachers had full view of their victims—the compliance rate dropped from 65% to 40% (Miller, 1986). Moreover, when the teacher held the learner's hand on the shock plate, the compliance rate dropped to 30%. In modern warfare, opposing soldiers may be separated by great distances. They may be little more than a blip on a radar screen. It is one thing to press a button to launch a missile or to aim a piece of artillery at a distant troop or a distant ridge. It is another to hold a weapon to the victim's throat.

There are thus numerous theoretical explanations for obedience. Regardless of the exact nature of the forces that acted on the participants in the Milgram studies, Milgram's research has alerted us to a real and present danger—the tendency of many, if not most, people to obey an authority figure even when the figure's demands contradict the person's moral values. It has happened before. Unless we remain alert, it will happen again.

In the section on conformity, we describe another classic study. Imagine how you would behave if you were involved in it.

Conformity: Do Many Make Right?

We are said to **conform** when we change our behavior to adhere to social norms. **Social norms** are widely accepted expectations concerning social behavior. Explicit social norms require us to whisper in libraries and to slow down when driving past a school. One unspoken or implicit social norm is to face front in elevators. Another implicit norm is to be fashionably late for social gatherings.

The tendency to conform to social norms is often a good thing. Many norms have evolved because they favor comfort and survival. Group pressure can also promote maladaptive behavior, as when people engage in risky behavior because "everyone is doing it."

Let us look at a classic experiment on conformity run by Solomon Asch in the early 1950s. We shall then examine factors that promote conformity.

SEVEN LINE JUDGES CAN'T BE WRONG: THE ASCH STUDY. Do you believe what you see with your own eyes? Seeing is believing, is it not? Not if you were a participant in the Asch (1952) study.

You would enter a laboratory room with seven other participants in an experiment on visual discrimination. There was a man at the front of a room with some cards with lines drawn on them.

The eight of you would be seated in a series. You would be given the seventh seat, a minor fact at the time. The man would explain the task. There was a single line on the card on the left. Three lines were drawn on the card at the

---

Conform • To change one's attitudes or overt behavior to adhere to social norms.

Social norms • Explicit and implicit rules that reflect social expectations and influence the ways people behave in social situations.

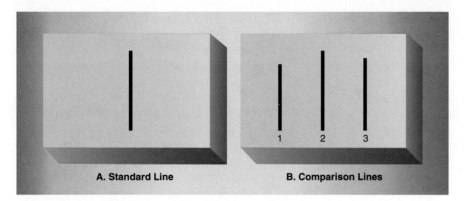

FIGURE 16.5

Cards Used in the Asch Study on Conformity. Which line on card B—1, 2, or 3—is the same length as the line on card A? Line 2, right? But would you say "2" if you were a member of a group and six people answering ahead of you all said "3"? Are you sure?

right (Figure 16.5). One line was the same length as the line on the other card. You and the other participants need only call out, one at a time, which of the three lines—1, 2, or 3—was the same length. Simple.

You would try it out. Those to your right spoke out in order: "3," "3," "3," "3," "3," "3." Now it was your turn. Line 3 was clearly the same length as the line on the first card, so you said "3." The fellow after you then chimed in: "3." That's all there was to it. Two other cards were then set up in the front of the room. This time line 2 was clearly the same length as the line on the first card. The answers: "2," "2," "2," "2," "2," "2." Your turn again: "2," you said, and perhaps your mind began to wander. Your stomach was gurgling a bit. That night you would not even mind dorm food particularly. The fellow after you said "2."

Another pair of cards was held up. Line 3 was clearly the correct answer. The six people on your right spoke in turn: "1," "1 . . ." Wait a second! ". . . 1," "1—" You forgot about dinner and studied the lines briefly. No, 1 was too short, by a good half an inch. But ". . . 1," "1," and suddenly it was your turn. Your hands had quickly become sweaty and there was a lump in your throat. You wanted to say 3, but was it right? There was really no time, and you had already paused noticeably: "1," you said, "1," the last fellow confirmed matter-of-factly.

Now your attention was riveted on the chore. Much of the time you agreed with the other seven line judges, but sometimes you did not. And for some reason beyond your understanding, they were in perfect agreement, even when they were wrong—assuming that you could trust your eyes. The experiment was becoming an uncomfortable experience, and you began to doubt your judgment.

The discomfort in the Asch study was caused by the pressure to conform. Actually, the other seven recruits were confederates of the experimenter. They prearranged a number of incorrect responses. The sole purpose of the study was to see whether you would conform to the erroneous group judgments.

How many people in Asch's study caved in? How many went along with the crowd rather than assert what they thought to be the right answer? Seventy-five percent. *Three of four agreed with the majority wrong answer at least once.*

FACTORS INFLUENCING CONFORMITY.   Several personal and situational factors prompt conformity to social norms. Personal factors include the desires to be liked by other members of the group and to be right (Insko, 1985), low self-esteem, high self-consciousness, social shyness (Santee & Maslach, 1982), and lack of familiarity with the job. Situational factors include group size and social support.

There has been a great deal of controversy about whether women conform to social norms more than men do. Old-fashioned stereotypes portray men as rugged individualists and women as civilizing influences, so it is not surprising that women have been generally perceived as more conformist. Yet, many psychologists argue that there are no major gender differences in conformity. Eagly (1987) suggests that people perceive women as being easier to "push around" because women usually have lower social status than men—in society at large and in the workforce.

Situational factors include the number of people who hold the majority opinion and the presence of at least one other person who shares the discrepant opinion. Likelihood of conformity, even to incorrect group judgments, increases rapidly as a group grows to five members, then rises more slowly to about eight members (Tanford & Penrod, 1984). At about that point, the maximum chance of conformity is reached. Yet finding just one other person who supports your minority opinion is apparently enough to encourage you to stick to your guns (Morris and others, 1977).

Reflections

- Why do you think that participants in the Milgram studies obeyed orders? How would you describe the pressures acting on them?
- It has been shown that people who value being right more than being liked by others are less likely to conform to group pressure (Insko and others, 1985). Which is more important to you?
- Can you think of some instances in which you have conformed to social pressure? (Would you wear blue jeans if everyone else wore slacks or skirts?) Have the pressures placed on you by your own sociocultural group ever come into conflict with the values and customs of the United States at large? If so, how?

Social facilitation • The process by which a person's performance is increased when other members of a group engage in similar behavior.

GROUP BEHAVIOR

To be human is to belong to groups. Groups help us satisfy the needs for affection, attention, and belonging (Robbins, 1989). They empower us to do things we could not manage by ourselves.

In this section, we look at a number of aspects of group behavior: social facilitation, group decision making, mob behavior, and the bystander effect.

Social Facilitation: Monkey See, Monkey Do Faster?

One effect of groups on individual behavior is **social facilitation,** or the effects on performance that result from the presence of others. Bicycle riders and runners tend to move more rapidly when they are members of a group. This effect is not limited to people. Dogs and cats eat more rapidly around others. Even roaches—yes, roaches—run more rapidly when other roaches are present (Zajonc, 1980).

Social Facilitation. Runners tend to move more rapidly when they are members of a group. Does the presence of others raise our levels of arousal or give rise to evaluation apprehension?

According to Robert Zajonc (1980), the presence of others influences us by increasing our levels of arousal, or motivation. When our levels of arousal are highly increased, our performance of simple, dominant responses is facilitated. Our performance of complex, recently acquired responses may be impaired, however. For this reason, a well-rehearsed speech may be delivered more masterfully before a larger audience. An offhand speech or a question-and-answer session may be hampered by a large audience.

Social facilitation may be influenced by **evaluation apprehension** as well as level of arousal (Bray & Sugarman, 1980; Sanna & Shotland, 1990). Our performance before a group is affected not only by the presence of others, but also by concern that they are evaluating us. When giving a speech, we may "lose our thread" if we are distracted by the audience and focus too much on its apparent reaction to us (Seta, 1982). If we believe that we have begun to flounder, evaluation apprehension may skyrocket. As a result, our performance may falter further.

The presence of others can also impair performance—not when we are acting *before* a group, but when we are anonymous members *of* a group (Harkins, 1987; Shepperd, 1993). Workers, for example, may "goof off" or engage in "social loafing" on humdrum jobs when they believe they will not be found out and held accountable. There is then no evaluation apprehension. There may also be **diffusion of responsibility** in groups. Each person may feel less obligation to help because others are present. Group members may also reduce their efforts if an apparently capable member makes no contribution but "rides free" on the efforts of others.

Evaluation apprehension • Concern that others are evaluating our behavior.

Diffusion of responsibility • The spreading or sharing of responsibility for a decision or behavior within a group.

Group Decision Making

In 1986 and 1987, President Ronald Reagan's popularity took a drubbing when it was alleged that he had authorized the sale of American weapons to Iran to try to gain the release of American hostages being held by pro-Iranian groups in Lebanon. This occurred at a time when the American public was very hostile toward Iran. Reagan had also sworn he would never negotiate with terrorists and had branded Iran a "terrorist nation." The decision to trade weapons for hostages apparently resulted from heated discussions in the White House during which the secretaries of state and defense took one position and the national security adviser took another position.

How do group decisions get made? Social psychologists have discovered a number of "rules," or **social decision schemes,** that govern much of group decision making (Davis and others, 1984; Kerr & MacCoun, 1985; Stasser and others, 1989). Note some examples:

1. *The majority-wins scheme.* In this commonly used scheme, the group arrives at the decision that was initially supported by the majority. This scheme appears to guide decision making most often when there is no objectively correct decision. An example would be a decision about which car models to build when their popularity has not been tested in the court of public opinion.

2. *The truth-wins scheme.* In this scheme, as more information is provided and opinions are discussed, the group comes to recognize that one approach is objectively correct. For example, a group deciding whether to use SAT scores in admitting students to college would profit from information about whether these scores actually predict college success.

3. *The two-thirds majority scheme.* This scheme is frequently adopted by juries, who tend to convict defendants when two-thirds of the jury initially favors conviction.

4. *The first-shift rule.* In this scheme, the group tends to adopt the decision that reflects the first shift in opinion expressed by any group member. If a car-manufacturing group is equally divided on whether to produce a convertible, it may opt to do so after one group member initially opposed to the idea changes her mind. If a jury is deadlocked, the members may eventually follow the lead of the first juror to switch his position.

Now let us consider whether group members are likely to make compromise decisions or to take relatively extreme viewpoints as a result of diverse initial positions.

Social decision schemes • Rules for predicting the final outcome of group decision making on the basis of the members' initial positions.

Groupthink • A process in which group members are influenced by cohesiveness and a dynamic leader to ignore external realities as they make decisions.

Groupthink

Groupthink is a problem that sometimes arises in group decision making (Janis, 1982). Group problem solving may degenerate into groupthink when a group senses an external threat. Groupthink is usually unrealistic and fueled by a dynamic group leader. The perception of external threat heightens group cohesiveness and serves as a source of stress. When under stress, group members tend not to consider all their options carefully (Keinan, 1987). Flawed decisions are therefore common.

Groupthink has been connected with fiascos such as President Kennedy's decision to support the Bay of Pigs invasion of Cuba, the Watergate affair, and NASA's decision to launch the *Challenger* space shuttle despite engineers' warnings that cold weather might endanger the launching (Aldag & Fuller, 1993). The Iran-Contra affair of the 1980s, which made Colonel Oliver North a household name, offers another example. Janis notes five characteristics of groupthink that play roles in such flawed group decisions:

1. *Feelings of invulnerability.* Each decision-making group might have believed that it was beyond the reach of critics or the law—in some cases, because

the groups consisted of powerful individuals close to the president of the United States.

2. *Group belief in its rightness.* These groups apparently believed in the rightness of what they were doing. In some cases, the groups were carrying out the president's wishes. In the case of the *Challenger* launch, NASA had a track record of nearly unblemished success.

3. *The discrediting of information opposed to the group's decision.* At the time that Oliver North's group decided to divert funds from (secret) sales of arms to Iran to the Contras, it was illegal for the U.S. government to do so. The group apparently discredited the law by (1) deciding that it was inconsistent with the best interests of the United States and (2) enlisting private citizens to divert profits from sales to the Contras so that the U.S. government was not directly involved.

4. *Pressures on group members to conform.* Groupthink pressures group members to conform (McCauley, 1989).

5. *Stereotyping of members of the out-group.* Oliver North's group reportedly stereotyped persons who would oppose them as communist "sympathizers"; "knee-jerk liberals"; and, in the case of the Congress that had made helping the Contras illegal, "slow-acting," "vacillating" (that is, voting to aid the Contras in one bill and prohibiting aid to the Contras in another), and "irresolute."

The negative outcomes of groupthink can be averted when group leaders encourage group members to remain skeptical about options and to feel free to ask probing questions and disagree with other members.

Mob Behavior and Deindividuation

Deindividuation • The process by which group members may discontinue self-evaluation and adopt group norms and attitudes.

Gustave Le Bon (1960), the French social thinker, branded mobs and crowds irrational, like a "beast with many heads." Mob actions such as race riots and lynchings sometimes seem to operate on a psychology of their own. Do mobs elicit the beast in us? How is it that mild-mannered people commit mayhem as members of a mob? In seeking an answer, let us examine a lynching and the baiting type of crowd that often seems to attend threatened suicides.

THE LYNCHING OF ARTHUR STEVENS.   In their classic volume *Social Learning and Imitation,* Neal Miller and John Dollard (1941) vividly described a Southern lynching. Arthur Stevens, an African American, was accused of murdering his lover, a White woman, when she wanted to break up with him. Stevens was arrested and confessed to the crime. The sheriff feared violence and moved Stevens to a town 200 miles distant during the night. But his location was uncovered. The next day, a mob of a hundred persons stormed the jail and returned Stevens to the scene of the crime.

Outrage spread from person to person like a plague bacillus. Laborers, professionals, women, adolescents, and law-enforcement officers alike were infected. Stevens was tortured and murdered. His corpse was dragged through the streets. The mob then went on a rampage in town, chasing and assaulting other African Americans. The riot ended only when troops were sent in to restore law and order.

DEINDIVIDUATION.   When we act as individuals, fear of consequences and self-evaluation tend to prevent antisocial behavior. But as members of a mob, we may experience **deindividuation,** a state of reduced self-awareness and lowered concern for social evaluation (Mann and others, 1982). Many factors lead to deindividuation, including anonymity, diffusion of responsibility, arousal due to noise and crowding, and a focus on emerging group norms rather than one's own values (Diener, 1980). Under these circumstances, crowd members behave more aggressively than they would as individuals.

Police know that mob actions are best averted early by dispersing the small groups that may gather into a crowd. On an individual level, perhaps we can resist deindividuation by instructing ourselves to stop and think whenever we begin to feel highly aroused as group members. If we dissociate ourselves from such groups when they are forming, we shall be more likely to remain critical and avoid behavior that we shall later regret.

THE BAITING CROWD IN CASES OF THREATENED SUICIDE. As individuals, we often feel compassion when we observe people who are so distressed that they are considering suicide. Why is it, then, that when people who are considering suicide threaten to jump from a ledge, the crowd often baits them, urging them on?

Such baiting occurred in 10 of 21 cases of threatened suicide studied by Mann (1981). Analysis of newspaper reports suggested a number of factors that might have prompted deindividuation among crowd members. They all contributed to anonymity: The crowds were large. It was dark (past 6 P.M.). The victim and the crowd were distant from one another (with the victim, for example, on a high floor). Baiting was also linked to high temperatures (the summer season) and lengthy episodes. Crowd members were thus likely to be tired and under stress.

Altruism • Unselfish concern for the welfare of others.

**MINILECTURE:
KITTY GENOVESE**

Altruism and the Bystander Effect: Some Watch While Others Die

The nation was shocked by the murder of 28-year-old Kitty Genovese in New York City. Murder was not unheard of in the Big Apple, but Kitty had screamed for help as her killer stalked her for more than half an hour and stabbed her in three separate attacks (Rosenthal, 1994). Thirty-eight neighbors heard the commotion. Twice their voices and their bedroom lights interrupted the assault. Each time the attacker returned. Still, nobody came to her aid. No one even called the police. Why? Some witnesses said matter-of-factly that they did not want to get involved. One said that he was tired. Still others said, "I don't know." As a nation, are we a callous bunch who would rather watch than help when others are in trouble?

Truth or Fiction Revisited. *It is true that nearly 40 people stood by and did nothing while a woman was being stabbed to death.* Their failure to come to her aid has been termed the *bystander effect.* What factors determine whether we help others who are in trouble?

THE HELPER: WHO HELPS? Some theorists (e.g., Guisinger & Blatt, 1994; Rushton, 1989) suggest that **altruism** is a natural aspect of human nature. Self-sacrifice sometimes helps close relatives or others who are similar to us to survive. Ironically, self-sacrifice is selfish from a genetic or sociobiological point of view. It helps us perpetuate a genetic code similar to our own. This view suggests that we are more likely to be altruistic with our relatives rather than strangers, however. The Kitty Genoveses of the world remain out of luck unless they are surrounded by kinfolk or friends.

Would You Stop to Help This Person? What factors enter into our decisions to help people in trouble or pass them by?

Most psychologists focus on the roles of a helper's mood and personality traits. By and large, we are more likely to help others when we are in a good mood (Berkowitz, 1987; Manucia and others, 1984). Perhaps good moods impart a sense of personal power (Cunningham and others, 1990). We may help others when we are miserable ourselves, however, if our own problems work to increase our empathy or sensitivity to the plight of others (Thompson and others, 1980). People with a high need for approval may help others to earn social approval. People who are empathic, who can take the perspective of others, are also likely to help (Batson and others, 1989a).

There are many reasons bystanders are reluctant to aid people in distress. First, bystanders may not fully understand what they are seeing and fail to recognize that an emergency exists. The more ambiguous the situation, that is, the less likely bystanders are to help (Shotland & Heinold, 1985). Perhaps some who heard Kitty Genovese's calls for help were not certain as to what was happening. (But remember that others admitted they did not want to get involved.) Second, bystanders who are not certain that they possess the competencies to take charge of the situation may stay on the sidelines for fear of making a social blunder and being subject to ridicule (Pantin & Carver, 1982). Or they may fear getting hurt themselves. (Perhaps some who heard Kitty Genovese thought, "If I try to intervene I may get killed or make an idiot of myself.") Bystanders who believe that others get what they deserve may rationalize not helping by thinking that a person would not be in trouble unless this outcome was just (Lerner and others, 1975). (Perhaps some who heard Kitty Genovese thought, "She probably wouldn't be under attack if she hadn't done something bad to the guy.")

A sense of personal responsibility increases the likelihood of helping. Such responsibility may stem from having made a verbal commitment to help (e.g., Moriarty, 1975) or from having been designated by others as being responsible for carrying out a helping chore (Maruyama and others, 1982). This, of course, is the central question: How can people be made to feel responsible for one another?

THE VICTIM: WHO IS HELPED?   Although gender roles have been changing, it is traditional for men to help women in our society. Women were more likely than men to receive help, especially from men, when they dropped coins in Atlanta (a southern city) than in Seattle or Columbus (northern cities; Latané & Dabbs, 1975). The researchers suggest that traditional gender roles persevere more strongly in the South.

Women are also more likely than men to be helped when their cars have broken down on the highway or they are hitchhiking (Pomazal & Clore, 1973). There may be sexual overtones to some of this "altruism." Attractive and unaccompanied women are most likely to be helped by men (Benson and others, 1976; Snyder and others, 1974).

As in the research on interpersonal attraction, similarity also seems to promote helping behavior. Poorly dressed people are more likely to succeed in requests for a dime with poorly dressed strangers. Well-dressed people are more likely to get money from well-dressed strangers (Hensley, 1981).

SITUATIONAL DETERMINANTS OF HELPING: "AM I THE ONLY ONE HERE?"   It may seem logical that a group of people would be more likely to have come to the aid of Kitty Genovese than a lone person. After all, a group could more effectively have overpowered her attacker. Research by Darley and Latané (1968) suggests that a lone person may have been more likely to try to help her, however.

In their classic experiment, male participants were performing meaningless tasks in cubicles when they heard a (convincing) recording of a person apparently having an epileptic seizure. When the men thought that four other persons were immediately available to help, only 31% made an effort to help the victim. When they thought that no one else was available, however, 85% of them tried to offer aid. As in other areas of group behavior, it seems that diffusion of responsibility inhibits helping behavior in groups or crowds. When we are in a group, we are often willing to let George (or Georgette) do it. When George isn't around, we are more willing to help others ourselves. (Perhaps some who heard Kitty Genovese thought, "Why should I get involved? Other people can hear her too.")

In most studies on the bystander effect, the bystanders are strangers (Latané & Nida, 1981). Research shows that bystanders who are acquainted with victims are more likely to respond to the social norm of helping others in need (Rutkowski and others, 1983). Aren't we also more likely to give to charity when asked directly by a coworker or supervisor in the socially exposed situation of the office as compared with a letter received in the privacy of our own homes?

We are more likely to help when we understand what is happening (for instance, if we clearly see that the woman whose car has broken down is alone), when the environment is familiar (when we are in our hometown rather than a strange city), and when we have the competencies. Registered nurses, for example, are more likely than people with no medical training to come to the aid of accident victims (Cramer and others, 1988).

Reflections

- Families, classes, religious groups, political parties, nations, circles of friends, bowling teams, sailing clubs, conversation groups, therapy groups—to how many groups do you belong? How does belonging to groups influence your behavior?

- Do you work harder or less hard than you would as an individual when you are given a group assignment? Why?
- Have you ever been a member of a committee or other group decision-making body? Did the group make the decisions democratically, or did a powerful leader emerge? Were the decisions made more or less conservative than the decisions you would probably have made on your own? Why?
- Have you ever done something as a member of a mob that you would not have done if you had been acting on your own? What? How did being a member of the mob influence you?
- Altruism and the bystander effect highlight the fact that we are members of a vast, interdependent social fabric. The next time you see a stranger who is in need of help, what will you do? Are you sure?

Study Guide

DIRECTIONS: The numbered items represent a number of concepts in social psychology. The lettered items are instances of behavior that serve as examples of these concepts. Match the example with the appropriate concept by writing the letter of the example in the blank space to the left of the concept. Answers are given below.

CONCEPT

___ 1. Prejudice

___ 2. Bystander effect

___ 3. Recency effect

___ 4. Discrimination

___ 5. Conformity

___ 6. Dispositional attribution

___ 7. Emotional appeal

___ 8. Foot-in-the-door technique

___ 9. Matching hypothesis

___ 10. Actor–observer effect

___ 11. Primacy effect

___ 12. Evaluation apprehension

___ 13. Consummate love

___ 14. Self-serving bias

___ 15. Situational attribution

___ 16. Deindividuation

___ 17. Diffusion of responsibility

___ 18. Fundamental attribution error

___ 19. The first-shift rule

___ 20. Buffer

___ 21. Inaccessibility of attitudes

___ 22. A–B problem

___ 23. Groupthink

EXAMPLES

A. A person assumes that someone who bumped into him did so on purpose.

B. A man does not ask a beautiful woman out for fear of rejection.

C. We have done well on a test and credit the outcome to our intelligence and charm.

D. A person asks a small favor to prepare someone to grant a larger favor later.

E. A new worker is late and the boss conceptualizes him as "a late person."

F. John blames his mood on the weather.

G. A person does not come to the aid of a crime victim because many people surround the victim.

H. A person feels romantic love plus commitment toward another person.

I. A mob member adopts the norms of the crowd.

J. Parents and their teenagers are arguing about the teenagers' choices of dates, and the parents therefore perceive their children to be stubborn, difficult, and independent.

K. A student wears blue jeans because "everyone" is wearing them.

L. An athlete runs faster because he is concerned that fellow racers are aware of his performance.

M. A man assumes that a woman will not be assertive in the business world.

N. The man in item M, above, chooses not to hire a woman.

O. A dentist shows photos of diseased gums to convince patients to improve their oral hygiene.

P. Fading memories allow recent information to take precedence.

Q. A group with a dynamic leader ignores the evidence and makes foolish decisions.

R. A person becomes so aroused as a member of a mob that he completely forgets his personal moral values.

S. A psychologist cannot predict a voter's behavior because the voter's political beliefs are very generalized.

T. A "teacher" in the Milgram study shocks the "learner" because the learner is out of sight, behind a wall.

U. A deadlocked jury votes to convict a defendant after one person who had previously thought the defendant not guilty changes his mind.

ANSWER KEY TO EXERCISE

1. M	5. K	9. B	13. H	17. G	21. R
2. G	6. A	10. J	14. C	18. A	22. S
3. P	7. O	11. E	15. F	19. U	23. Q
4. N	8. D	12. L	16. I	20. T

ESL | English as a Second Language—Bridging the Gap

---

acceded to (703)—agreed to

acquainted with (734)—to know or be familiar with

acquiescence (725)—to agree with another; do what he or she wants

adage (717)—old, common saying

adhere to (726)—to follow; conform to

airheads (705)—people who don't think or are not very intelligent; who are interested only in superficial things

allure (715)—attractive; tempting

altruism (732)—selflessness; putting others' needs first

ambiguous (733)—unclear

amenable to (703)—agreeable to

ample (718)—plenty; a lot

anonymity (732)—not known; no one knows the individuals

apparatus (725)—device; mechanism

assimilate (724)—becoming adjusted to a new culture; taking on some (or all) of the characteristics of the new culture

associate (699)—to connect

at the behest of (725)—at the request of someone else

Atlanta . . . Seattle or Columbus . . . the South (734)— cities and areas in the United States where it is assumed that people tend to hold more conservative political and social views than in other parts of the United States; a stereotype

atrocities (725)—horrible acts; inhuman behaviors

avow (699)—state; declare

baiting (732)—encouraging or challenging someone to do something

barged into (695)—went into, quickly and with anger

beauty is in the eye of the beholder (697)—a person is beautiful because another person believes it

been around (697)—had a very active social life; known a lot of people of the opposite sex

Big Apple (732)—a nickname (short and affectionate name) for New York City

bigoted (705)—narrow-minded; prejudiced

blend in with the wallpaper (720)—to be ignored, as if we were only part of the room's decoration

blue jeans (699)—popular, casual pants traditionally made of strong dark blue cloth

bogus (700)—phony

boisterous (710)—noisy; rowdy

boorish (705)—rude; crude

break-in (721)—use of force to enter a locked building

buffers (726)—something that protects and softens the effect of something difficult

bust size (717)—size of the breasts

buttering you up (701)—flattering you; telling you wonderful things about yourself that may or may not be true to persuade you to believe, say, or do something

cad (709)—a man who is not trustworthy with women; not a gentleman *calculating, inflexible, and . . . sinister* (711)—interested only in their own advantage; not willing to bend in their opinions; and dangerous

callous bunch (732)—an unfeeling group of people

car model (730)—car manufacturers make several new styles of cars each year

cascade (724)—to fall like water

caved in (727)—gave up; stopped participating in the experiment

central to the concept (723)—a more important part

championing (723)—supporting; defending

changes her mind (730)—expresses a different opinion from the one previously expressed

charitable donation (705)—an amount of money that a person gives to a charity (an organization that helps people in trouble)

Cher . . . Mariel Hemingway (717)—movie actresses

Chrysler, General Motors, Toyota, Honda (704)—large car manufacturers

clannish (705)—stick only to others like them

coercion (698)—persuasion; pressure; force

cognitive anchors (699)—cognitive bases

college appreciation course (700)—college music or art appreciation course

come to grips with (699)—tried to understand

come to our aid (721)—help us

commercial (695)—advertisement

commotion (732)—noise and disturbance

compromise (717)—to give something up; in this case, make her appear less feminine

confederates (727)—helpers; partners

consensus (712)—when everyone agrees on something and behaves in that way

correlates (720)—is associated with; correlate positively means when the level of one thing goes up, the other does also

cover-up (712)—concealment

crisp and tailored (708)—well-groomed and conservative in dress

crop their hair (708)—cut their hair very short, like a man's

curfew (709)—the time when someone is supposed to be home

cynical (709)—doubting; negative; insincere; in this case, making an effort to do something only to impress others and not because the person really wants to do it

daredevils (710)—reckless people

defense attorneys (708)—the lawyers responsible for defending the accused person in a court of law

deferential (705)—agreeable

deliberation (697)—thought

demureness (719)—shy and modest

denounced (708)—criticized

Denzel Washington or Cindy Crawford look-alike (720)—someone who looks like the popular movie actor or model

despite lopsided polls to the contrary (722)—even though the answers to the questions that had been distributed (polls) did not make it appear that the candidate would win

destiny (698)—future

deviate (699)—go in a different direction from

diffusion (734)—spread out; not specifically focused on one point

dingy storefront (703)—small, unpainted, unrepaired, and unoccupied store

dire risks (700)—dangerous chances

discrepant (728)—different; contradictory

disillusioned (721)—become disappointed in them; lose our good expectations

disinclined (717)—not inclined, or want, to do something

dissuade (707)—discourage someone; persuade someone not to do something

divulge (703)—reveal

don't abandon ship (720)—don't stop trying to change or improve; continue to try

dorm food (727)—food provided in college dormitories, or student residence buildings

doubles as (695)—also has the function of being

dreaded diseases (699)—feared illnesses

earthy and lusty (722)—earthy is basic, down-to-earth; lusty is strong, energetic (generally has a sexual meaning)

elicit (697)—bring out

elusive (722)—hard to define or find

empathy (733)—ability to imagine how the other feels

enhance and maintain (723)—improve and keep in good condition

enrich the lives of every door-to-door salesperson (703)—always buy something from salespeople who come to the home, and help them to live better

entitled (721)—to have the right to something

episodes (732)—events; occurrences

ever after (697)—forever

exception to a rule (709)—not our usual behavior

exert enormous pressure (724)—use strong persuasion to get others to do something; in this case, use strong social approval and disapproval to influence people's social behavior

experimenter's ground (699)—the experimenter's territory

explicit (726)—very specific

extricate (726)—get out of a situation

eyes have it (713)—a saying that means "the eyes are the most important message sender"

falling for (714)—believing

falls short of our ideals (695)—is not what we think it should be *falter* (729)—to hesitate or hold back; in this case, to begin to deteriorate

familiarity breeds content, not contempt (700)—the original expression is "familiarity breeds contempt," which means that we become bored or indifferent with what we know very well; in this case, the research indicates the opposite—that we like things we're familiar with

fancy men (717)—to like men

fashion plates (708)—people who focus too much on looking fashionable and not on more important things

favors conviction (730)—is in favor of judging someone as guilty

fearsome looking console (700)—a cabinet (a piece of furniture) that looks frightening

fiascos (730)—big mistakes

fidelity (719)—faithfulness

flapper era (717)—a time during the 1920s when women's fashion emphasized a flat-chested appearance

flashy (705)—showy; not in good taste

flaws (723)—imperfections; defects

flounder (729)—to be confused and not sure of what we should do

fluke (711)—a rare, accidental incident which is not really by how the game was played

forced into combat (711)—having to argue, disagree, and disapprove

frizzies (699)—split ends in the hair

fueled by (730)—caused and maintained by

genteel (705)—refined; mannerly

get out the vote (698)—encourage people to vote

get you off the hook (703)—you will not be asked or required to do anything else

giving an inch . . . go for a yard (703)—if you give or do a little, others will then expect you to give or do a lot more

go hand in hand (720)—coincide in the same person

go their separate ways (698)—part, not see each other anymore

goof off . . . social loafing (729)—play and not work when they should; talking and socializing instead

grisly films (719)—terrible, horrible, bloody films

ground to a halt (708)—stopped

group cohesiveness (730)—closeness of a group

gurgling a bit (727)—making hunger noises

hallowed halls (725)—long-respected, even sacred, buildings; in this case, Yale University is a very old and prestigious American university that has high status

hang loose (713)—be flexible and not worry

hard stares (713)—unrelenting stares

hard truths (697)—unfortunate facts

hejab (724)—head covering or veil that Islamic women sometimes wear

homely models (701)—unattractive models

hometown (734)—the town (small city) where a person was born and lived when he or she was a child

humdrum (729)—boring; repetitive; ordinary

hunch (717)—standing with their backs bent forward a little to appear shorter

hurts sales (695)—has a negative effect on selling the product; the product won't sell well

if the truth be known (697)—if you want to know the truth

impart (700)—give

implies (698)—suggests

inedible (712)—can't be eaten; not worth eating

inhibits (734)—limits or prevents; holds back

innocuous matters (726)—unimportant things

inscrutable (705)—mysterious

interpret (699)—to take meaning from

invulnerability (730)—the sense of being completely right; can't make an error

irksome (703)—irritating

ironed out (721)—can be solved; made smooth and without any wrinkles

ironic twist (711)—an outcome that you did not expect

ironically (717)—a sometimes humorous contradiction

irrational (707)—not logical; controlled too much by emotions

irresolute (731)—not strong and determined in your opinion or behavior

it does . . . little good (698)—politicians may have supporters, but if the supporters don't vote, their support does not help

jury (708)—a group of selected citizens who decide whether a defendant in a court of law is guilty or innocent

keeping them under the table (698)—not discussing them; by not acknowledging that they have different attitudes

kinfolk (732)—relatives

kinks in a relationship (720)—disagreements and unresolved issues

knee-jerk liberals (731)—a negative term for someone who reacts on the basis of emotion instead of considered opinion; in this case, a liberal is a person who has political positions that do not agree with traditional, or conservative, positions

knee-jerk reactions (699)—responses based on impulse, not thought

lag behind (707)—fall behind; not achieve as much

leans toward (698)—tends to think in this way

leaves us (720)—causes us to be

liberating (719)—freeing

long and short of it (724)—in the end, the main point

look-alike (720)—imitation

look askance (708)—look at with disapproval, surprise, suspicion *lose our thread* (729)—forget what we planned to say next

lust (722)—sexual desire

lynching (704)—killing someone by hanging them by the neck

Madison Avenue (710)—the advertising industry

make conversation (696)—talk to each other for the purpose of getting to know each other, not to give information or to solve problems

make or break us (709)—establish us as wonderful or establish us as unattractive and awful

make up for it (709)—to compensate for it; to create a better image

makes much difference (698)—will cause changes in what the government does (both the Democrats and the Republicans will act in the same way)

mandates (724)—rules; regulations

manipulative (703)—controlling; dominating

matter-of-factly (727)—stated simply and frankly

meaningful relationships (719)—relationships that have some level of emotional involvement and commitment

media blitzes (698)—a great number of advertisements very close together on radio, television, and in the newspapers

meeting of the minds (715)—when two people have similar opinions and ideas; when they agree

merits (724)—good points; benefits

misgivings (726)—doubts; think that maybe it wasn't a good idea

mob behavior (728)—the behavior of people when they get in a group

mold the ways (699)—create the ways

monkey see, monkey do faster (728)—"monkey see, monkey do" is an old saying that refers to the fact that when a person sees another doing something, he or she may imitate the behavior

mount a campaign (703)—begin a campaign

movie buffs (699)—fans who know a lot about movies

narrow-minded (697)—believe that their religion or point of view is the only good one

networks of forces acting on ourselves (710)—pressures that affect us

noncontroversial (713)—there is no disagreement about the meaning

not at all (723)—no, that was not true (emphatic)

not have a chance to win (710)—cannot win (emphatic)

not having any of what she is selling (713)—does not want what she has to offer; is not interested in her

nudist colony (723)—a private community where people who don't like to wear clothes can go to vacation or live

offhand speech (729)—informal, not practiced speech

on their own (699)—alone

operationally defined as (719)—the behavior being observed was

outside of the mainstream (720)—not among the accepted groups in the society; separate from most people

overtones (734)—suggestions; unspoken feelings

pardon the pun (717)—please excuse my play on words

patriotism (699)—love and devotion to your country

peripheral (699)—superficial; less valuable

perpetuate (732)—continue

Peter Jennings, Tom Brokaw, Dan Rather (701)—news commentators on three major television news programs

physique (717)—body size and shape

plague bacillus (731)—a rapidly spreading organism that causes a widespread, serious disease

plain-looking but wholesome (696)—not handsome, but looks decent and pleasant

pliant (703)—receptive; willing to do what others want

plumpness (717)—to be a little fat; chubby

polarized (706)—having opposite opinions and being unable to see the other side's point of view

political affiliation (698)—political party membership

pop tune (700)—current popular music (not traditional classical music)

preppy sweaters (699)—now-popular sweaters that traditionally were worn by people who went to preparatory ("prep") schools (private, expensive high schools) and "ivy league" colleges (private, expensive colleges in the northeastern United States)

prescription for totalitarianism (701)—a plan that indicates how to establish totalitarianism

prick up our ears (703)—listen in a very interested manner

primed for (703)—prepared for

privy to a conversation (713)—overhear a conversation between two other people; hear a conversation we are not involved in

prospective (715)—future

provocations (713)—something that challenges, or irritates, another

put on a happy face (718)—a line from an old song that means to smile and look happy

rationalize (733)—to justify; make it acceptable to think or do something

referee (711)—an official who judges the rules and plays in a contest

references (699)—mention of

refute (700)—contradict; disagree with

reprehensible acts (726)—disgraceful, bad behaviors

rides free (729)—obtain credit for what other members of the group have done

riveted on the chore (727)—focused on the job to be done

roster (715)—list

running the gamut (721)—being all degrees

sacred and the secular (724)—religious and nonreligious (daily life) activities

sake of science (712)—because you wanted to help science

SAT scores (731)—Scholastic Assessment Test scores, which influence college admission

scrupulously (697)—very careful and precise

scrutinize (699)—examine closely

seductive (724)—alluring; focuses on physical attraction

self-serving bias (711)—a tendency to have viewpoints and make decisions that favor ourselves

servile (705)—cooperative; behave like a servant

sexually repressed (705)—controlled; not sexually active

shatter (707)—break into small pieces, such as when glass breaks

shift in opinion (730)—change in opinion

shrewd (701)—clever

signing petitions (703)—requests by citizens to other citizens that they sign their names on a piece of paper to show support for an issue and petition (ask) the government to act on it

sip of wine (701)—a small drink of wine

slaughtering (724)—killing in large numbers, without apparent feeling

Sleeping Beauty, Cinderella, Snow White . . . Princes Charming (723)—female heroines and male heroes from children's storybooks

smothering mother (705)—overwhelming mother who worries about her child constantly

snap judgments (710)—decisions made without thought

sneaky (705)—tricky in a hidden way

snobbish (705)—self-important; think they're better than others

so do (700)—the ads also do that

social blunder (733)—doing something that would be socially wrong

social norm (695)—what is considered to be "correct" behavior in a society

solidified (701)—established

somehow un-American (699)—they are not respecting the American ideals in some way

spongelike (701)—like a sponge (a material that absorbs liquid)

stature (717)—height

stay on the sidelines (733)—stay on the side

steady gait (719)—firm, straight walk, which we interpret to mean someone who is self-confident and trustworthy

stick to your guns (703)—do not change your mind or weaken your decision

stoutness (717)—heavy; large size; sturdy

subject to ridicule (733)—be the recipient of ridicule

submissive (706)—obedient; willing to follow other's directions

susceptible (720)—a tendency to "get something"; be vulnerable to some influence, problem, or disease

Suzy Wongs, Charlie Chans, and Fu Manchus (704)—stereotyped Asian characters in American movies

swayed (719)—influenced

sweep it under the rug (701)—hide it

swerve from our expectations (721)—do not do what we expect

Szechuan tidbits, the nouveau Fresno film, the disco party (723)—an evening of fashionable entertainment: special Chinese food, a new and important movie, a discotheque party

tagged as (722)—labeled as

tail end of a date (723)—the last few minutes of a date

take a backseat (719)—assume a less important position

take others to task (695)—criticize others

take precedence (710)—to be more important

tangled web of deception (697)—confusing situation in which each person is deceiving the other

taste-test (700)—testing products by deciding which has the best flavor

The King and I (721)—a popular 1950s movie about a British woman who goes to Siam in the 1800s

their own making (711)—to be their responsibility

they're like (724)—West Coast teenage slang which means "they said or appeared to think"

throw up our hands in despair (720)—give up; not care about trying any more because we don't think it will make any difference

thus begins a relationship (697)—in this way the relationship begins

took a drubbing (729)—took a beating; decreased a great deal

took for granted (724)—assumed and expected as natural; didn't appreciate or pay much attention to something

toying with his hair (713)—play with his hair

transcend (717)—to cut across; go beyond

trivial (720)—not important; insignificant

trust your eyes (727)—trust what you were seeing

tube feeds them (701)—is on the television

turning the other off (697)—saying or doing something that will cause the other person not to be interested anymore

unblemished (731)—without any errors

unsporting (703)—not being courteous; not following appropriate rules of the game

uptight (713)—tense and worried

vacillating (731)— undecided; changing your position frequently

vested interest (698)—the beliefs a person holds because they benefit him or her

vividly (731)—in clear and distinct detail

voting booth (704)—the designated area of privacy where a person casts his or her vote to elect representatives or approve or disapprove laws

well-rehearsed (729)—well-practiced

went along with (727)—continued to do what everyone was expecting him or her to do

were in on (703)—knew

whaling fleet (701)—commercial boats that hunt whales

what about you? (711)—what would you do?

what to do? (710)—you thought, "What should I do?"

whereas (725)—in contrast; on the other hand

wine that was sold at its time (709)—wine that was sold when the taste was the best

wishy-washy (708)—lacking strength and ability to make clear decisions

wooing (722)—dating; seeking a romantic relationship

worked up over the issue (698)—deeply concerned and upset

works the other way (700)—it is also the reverse

wrecking crew (702)—people whose job it is to destroy a building

you're not alone (705)—you're not the only person who feels that way

---

FILL-INS | Chapter Review

SECTION 1: INTRODUCTION

Social psychology is the study of the nature and causes of our behavior and (1) m_____ processes in (2) _____al situations.

SECTION 2: ATTITUDES

Attitudes are behavioral and (3) _____tive tendencies that are expressed by evaluating particular people, places, or things with some degree of favor or (4) dis_____. When we are free to do as we wish, our behavior (5: Is or Is Not?) most often consistent with our attitudes. According to the (6) A_____ problem, the link between attitudes and behavior tends to be weak.

Attitudes may be acquired through conditioning, observational learning, and (7) cog_____ appraisal. Attitudes toward national groups can be influenced by (8) _____ing them with positive or negative words. Parents often (9) re_____ children for doing or saying things that are consistent with their own attitudes. Early attitudes tend to serve as cognitive (10) _____ors. We judge subsequent points of view in terms of how much they (11) d_____ from the first set.

Petty and Cacioppo have devised the (12) e_____ likelihood model for understanding the processes by which people examine the information in persuasive messages. According to this view, there are central and (13) _____ral routes to persuading others to change attitudes. That is, there are two ways of responding to, or (14) _____ting, persuasive messages. The (15) _____ral route views elaboration and possible attitudinal change as resulting from conscientious consideration of arguments and evidence. The (16) _____ral route involves elaboration of the objects of attitudes by associating them with positive or negative cues.

Repeated messages generally "sell" (17: Better or Worse?) than messages delivered once. (18) Two-_____d arguments, in which the communicator recounts the arguments of the opposition in order to (19) re_____ them, can be especially effective when the audience is at first uncertain about its position. People tend to show greater response to (20) e_____al appeals than to purely factual presentations, especially when emotional appeals offer concrete advice for avoiding negative consequences. Audiences also tend to believe arguments that appear to (21: Be In Agreement With or Run Counter To?) the personal interests of the communicator.

Persuasive communicators tend to show (22) ex_____, trustworthiness, attractiveness, or (23) _____ity to the audience. People show selective avoidance of and selective (24) ex_____ to communicators. People who are easily persuaded frequently show (25: High or Low?) self-esteem and (26: High or Low?) social anxiety. They also tend (27: To Be or Not To Be?) highly concerned with what the persuader might think of them if they fail to comply. According to the (28) f_____-in-the-door effect, people are more likely to accede to large requests after they have acceded to smaller requests.

Prejudice is an (29) at_____ toward a group. Denial of access to privileges is termed (30) _____nation. A (31) _____type is a fixed, conventional idea about a group that can lead us to make certain assumptions about group members we have not met.

Sources of prejudice include attitudinal (32: Similarity or Dissimilarity?). We tend to assume that members of out-groups hold attitudes that are (33: Similar or Dissimilar?) to our own. Other sources may include social and (34) ec_____ conflict, an authoritarian society in which minority group members serve as (35) _____goats, social learning from parents, and the tendency to divide the social world into two categories: "us" and "them."

SECTION 3: SOCIAL PERCEPTION

The psychology of social (36) _____tion concerns our perception of others. We often perceive others in terms of first impressions; this is an example of the (37) _____cy effect. In a classic experiment on the primacy effect, (38) L_____ had subjects read different stories about "Jim." In the (39) _____cy effect, fading memories allow more recent information to take precedence.

Our inference of the motives and traits of others through the observation of their behavior is called the (40) _____tion process. When we make dispositional attributions, we attribute people's behavior to (41: Internal or External?) factors, such as their personality traits and decisions. When we make (42) _____nal attributions, we attribute people's behavior to their circumstances or external forces.

Certain biases operate in the attribution (43) _____ss. The (44) _____tal attribution error is the tendency to attribute too much of other people's behavior to dispositional factors. According to the (45) actor–_____er effect, we tend to attribute the behavior of others to internal, (46) _____nal factors. We tend to attribute our own behavior to external, (47) _____nal factors. According to the (48) self-_____ing bias, we are more likely to ascribe our successes to internal, dispositional factors but our failures to external, (49) _____nal influence.

At an early age we learn to "read" body language. People who feel (50: Positively or Negatively?) toward one another tend to position themselves close together and to touch. Women are (51: More or Less?) likely than men to touch other people when they are interacting with them. Gazing into another's eyes can be a sign of love, but a so-called (52) h_____ stare is an aversive challenge.

SECTION 4: INTERPERSONAL ATTRACTION: LIKING AND LOVING

In social psychology, (53) _____tion has been defined as an attitude of liking (positive attraction) or disliking (54) (_____tive attraction). In our culture, (55: Obesity or Slenderness?) is found attractive in both men and women, and tallness is valued in (56: Men or Women?). Women generally see themselves as (57: Slimmer or Heavier?) than the figure that is attractive to most males. Men actually prefer women to be somewhat (58: Slimmer or Heavier?) than women expect. Women prefer men to be somewhat (59: Slimmer or Heavier?) than men expect. We tend to find the same people (60: More or Less?) attractive when they are smiling.

We are more attracted to good-looking people. We tend to assume that attractive people are (61: More or Less?) likely to be talented and (62: More or Less?) likely to engage in criminal behavior. According to the (63) _____ing hypothesis, we tend to seek dates and mates at our own level of attractiveness. The matching tendency seems to be motivated largely by fear of (64) _____tion.

We are (65: More or Less?) attracted to people who share our attitudes.

SECTION 5: SOCIAL INFLUENCE

Most people comply with the demands of authority figures, even when these demands seem immoral, as shown in the studies on obedience run by Stanley (66) M_____. The following factors appear to have contributed to obedience in the Milgram studies: participants' history of socialization, lack of (67) _____al comparison, perception of experimenters as being legitimate (68) _____ity figures, the (69) foot-in-the-d_____ technique, inaccessibility of values, and the presence of (70) _____ers that separated "teachers" from their victims.

In Asch's studies of conformity to group pressure, (71) _____% of the participants agreed with an incorrect majority judgment at least once. People experience increasing pressure to conform to group norms and opinions as groups grow to (72: How Many?) _____ people. (73: Men or Women?) are more likely to conform. The presence of at least (74: How Many?) _____ person(s) who share(s) one's minority view, and familiarity with the tasks at hand, decrease conforming behavior.

SECTION 6: GROUP BEHAVIOR

Social (75) _____tion refers to the effects on performance that result from the presence of others. According to Zajonc, the presence of others influences us by increasing our levels of (76) _____sal. We may also be concerned that the other people present are evaluating our performance—a phenomenon termed (77) _____ _____sion. However, Latané and other researchers have found that task performance may decline when we are (78) _____mous members of a group. This phenomenon is referred to as social (79) _____ing.

Social psychologists have discovered a number of rules, or (80) so_____-_____sion schemes, that seem to govern group decision making. In the (81) m_____-wins scheme, the group arrives at the decision that was initially supported by the majority. In the (82) t_____-wins scheme, the group comes to recognize that one approach is objectively correct as more information is provided and opinions are discussed. The (83) _____-_____ds majority scheme is frequently adopted by juries, who tend to convict defendants when two-thirds of the jury initially favors conviction. In the (84) f_____-shift rule, the group tends to adopt the decision that reflects the first shift in opinion expressed by any group member.

Groupthink is usually (85: Realistic or Unrealistic?) and can lead to flawed decisions. Groupthink is usually instigated by a dynamic group leader. It tends to be fueled by the perception of (86) _____nal threats to the group or to those the group wishes to protect. The perception of external threat heightens group (87) co_____ness and serves as a source of stress. When under stress, group members (88: Tend or Tend Not?) to weigh carefully all their options. The following factors contribute to groupthink: feelings of (89: Vulnerability or Invulnerability?), group belief in its rightness, discrediting of (90) _____tion opposed to the group's decision, pressures on group members to conform, and stereotyping of members of the (91) out-_____.

As members of a group, we may experience (92) _____duation, which is a state of reduced self-awareness and lowered concern for social (93) ev_____tion. Factors that lead to deindividuation include anonymity, (94) _____sion of responsibility, a high level of (95) ar_____ due to noise and crowding, and focusing of individual attention on the group process.

Helping behavior is otherwise termed (96) _____ism. We are more likely to help others when we are in a (97: Good or Bad?) mood. According to the (98) _____der effect, people are less likely to aid others in distress when they are members of crowds. A powerful case in point is the tragedy of Kitty (99) Ge_____, who was stabbed to death while neighbors did nothing to help. One reason for failure to help is that in a crowd there is diffusion of (100) re_____ity. We are more likely to help people in need when we think we are the only one available, when we have a (101: Clear or Unclear?) view of the situation, and when we (102: Are or Are Not?) afraid that we shall be committing a social blunder.

ANSWER KEY TO CHAPTER REVIEW

1. Mental	27. To be	53. Attraction	79. Loafing
2. Social	28. Foot	54. Negative	80. Social decision
3. Cognitive	29. Attitude	55. Slenderness	81. Majority
4. Disfavor	30. Discrimination	56. Men	82. Truth
5. Is	31. Stereotype	57. Heavier	83. Two-thirds
6. A–B	32. Dissimilarity	58. Heavier	84. First-shift
7. Cognitive	33. Dissimilar	59. Slimmer	85. Unrealistic
8. Associating (or pairing)	34. Economic	60. More	86. External
9. Reinforce (or reward)	35. Scapegoats	61. More	87. Cohesiveness
10. Anchors	36. Perception	62. Less	88. Tend not
11. Deviate	37. Primacy	63. Matching	89. Invulnerability
12. Elaboration	38. Luchins	64. Rejection	90. Information
13. Peripheral	39. Recency	65. More	91. Out-group
14. Elaborating	40. Attribution	66. Milgram	92. Deindividuation
15. Central	41. Internal	67. Social	93. Evaluation
16. Peripheral	42. Situational	68. Authority	94. Diffusion
17. Better	43. Process	69. Door	95. Arousal
18. Sided	44. Fundamental	70. Buffers	96. Altruism
19. Refute	45. Observer	71. 75	97. Good
20. Emotional	46. Dispositional	72. Eight	98. Bystander
21. Run counter to	47. Situational	73. Women	99. Genovese
22. Expertise	48. Serving	74. One	100. Responsibility
23. Similarity	49. Situational	75. Facilitation	101. Clear
24. Exposure	50. Positively	76. Arousal	102. Are not
25. Low	51. More	77. Evaluation apprehension	
26. High	52. Hard	78. Anonymous	

POSTTEST | *Multiple Choice*

1. Which of the following most nearly expresses the relationship between attitudes and behaviors?
   a. People always behave in ways that are consistent with their attitudes.
   b. People always change their attitudes so that they are consistent with their behavior.
   c. There is no relationship between attitudes and behaviors.
   d. People are likely to act in accord with strong, specific attitudes.

2. Which of the following is a central cue for persuading people to drink Coke or Pepsi?

   a. providing information about the taste of the drink

   b. having a rock star deliver a television commercial

   c. showing attractive, slender people drinking the soda

   d. using a person with a fine voice to sell the product

3. People tend to be easy to persuade when they
   a. have high self-esteem.
   b. focus on the needs and feelings of the persuader.
   c. have low social anxiety.
   d. focus on their own needs and feelings.

4. One teacher of religion believes that children are more likely to adhere to their own religion's beliefs when they are also taught opposing beliefs. Another teacher of religion believes that it is dangerous to teach children opposing beliefs. Research concerning persuasion shows that two-sided arguments have the advantage of
   a. offering peripheral cues for persuasion.
   b. conditioning the audience.
   c. appealing to the intellect only, not the emotions.
   d. showing the audience how to refute the opposition's arguments.

5. Physically attractive people are perceived as _____ than other people.
   a. poorer parents
   b. having less stable marriages
   c. more mentally healthy
   d. more likely to commit crimes

6. When Milgram moved the site of his research on obedience from Yale University to a storefront in a nearby city,
   a. no one complied with the demands of the authority figure.
   b. fewer people complied with the demands of the authority figure.
   c. more people complied with the demands of the authority figure.
   d. the results were about the same.

7. Which of the following sources of prejudice is reflected in the statement that "It is easier to attend to, and remember, instances of behavior that are consistent with our prejudices than it is to reconstruct our mental categories"?
   a. assumptions of dissimilarity
   b. social conflict
   c. authoritarianism
   d. information processing

8. One form of behavior that results from prejudice is called

   a. authoritarianism.
   b. deindividuation.
   c. attitude-discrepant behavior.
   d. discrimination.

9. Which of the following statements reflects a clear dispositional attribution?
   a. "Something got the best of him."
   b. "He did what he thought was right."
   c. "He did it that way because of the weather."
   d. "He could not refuse the money."

10. Attributing too much of other people's behavior to dispositional factors is called
   a. the fundamental attribution error.
   b. the actor–observer effect.
   c. internalization.
   d. evaluation apprehension.

11. Which of the following is true about standards for attractiveness in our culture?
   a. Tallness is an asset for women.
   b. Women prefer their dates to be about the same height as they are.
   c. Women prefer their men somewhat heavier than men expect.
   d. Men prefer their women somewhat heavier than women expect.

12. In their dating practices, people tend to ask out persons who are similar in attractiveness largely because of
   a. fairness.
   b. fear of rejection.
   c. balance theory.
   d. evaluation apprehension.

13. Important experiments on obedience to authority were carried out by
   a. Stanley Milgram.
   b. Solomon Asch.
   c. Abraham Luchins.
   d. John Dollard.

14. Mob behavior appears to be characterized by all of the following, with the exception of
   a. reduced self-awareness.
   b. focusing of individual attention on the group process.
   c. arousal due to noise and crowding.
   d. heightened concern for social evaluation.

15. Conformity is defined as
   a. obedience to authority.
   b. deindividuation.
   c. behavior in accordance with social norms.
   d. diffusion of responsibility.

16. When we are members of a group, we are most likely to engage in social loafing when
    a. we experience evaluation apprehension.
    b. our level of arousal increases.
    c. we are anonymous.
    d. the leader is an authority figure.

17. When juries are deadlocked, they are most likely to arrive at a verdict by means of the
    a. two-thirds rule.
    b. majority-wins scheme.
    c. first-shift rule.
    d. truth-wins scheme.

18. Luchins had subjects read different stories about "Jim" in order to study
    a. cognitive dissonance.
    b. the primacy effect.
    c. diffusion of responsibility.
    d. factors that contribute to attraction.

19. All of the following appear to lead to deindividuation, with the exception of
    a. a low level of arousal.
    b. anonymity.
    c. diffusion of responsibility.
    d. focusing of individual attention on the group process.

20. The case of Kitty Genovese illustrates
    a. cognitive-dissonance theory.
    b. group decision making.
    c. the bystander effect.
    d. the principle of social loafing.

ANSWER KEY TO POSTTEST

1. D	4. D	7. D	10. A	13. A	16. C	19. A
2. A	5. C	8. D	11. D	14. D	17. C	20. C
3. B	6. B	9. B	12. B	15. C	18. B	

APPENDIX

Statistics

IMAGINE that some visitors from outer space arrive outside Madison Square Garden in New York City. Their goal this dark and numbing winter evening is to learn all they can about the inhabitants of planet Earth. They are drawn inside the Garden by lights, shouts, and warmth. The spotlighting inside rivets their attention to a wood-floored arena where the New York Apples are hosting the California Quakes in a briskly contested basketball game.

Our visitors use their sophisticated instruments to take some measurements of the players. Some surprising statistics are sent back to the planet of their origin: It appears that (1) 100% of Earthlings are male, and (2) the height of Earthlings ranges from 6 feet 1 inch to 7 feet 2 inches.

Statistics is the name given the science concerned with obtaining and organizing numerical measurements or information. Our imagined visitors have sent home some statistics about the sex and size of human beings that are at once accurate and misleading. Although they accurately measured the basketball players, their small **sample** of Earth's **population** was quite distorted. Fortunately for us Earthlings, about half of us are female. And the **range** of heights observed by the aliens, of 6 feet 1 to 7 feet 2, is both restricted and too high. People vary in height by more than 1 foot and 1 inch. And our **average** height is not between 6 feet 1 inch and 7 feet 2 inches but a number of inches below.

Psychologists, like our imagined visitors, are vitally concerned with measuring human as well as animal characteristics and traits—not just physical characteristics like sex and height but also psychological traits like intelligence, aggressiveness, anxiety, or self-assertiveness. By observing the central tendencies (averages) and variations in measurements from person to person, psychologists can state that some person is average or above average in intelligence or that another person is less assertive than, say, 60% of the population.

But psychologists, unlike our aliens, are careful in their attempts to select a sample that accurately represents the entire population. Professional basketball players do not represent the human species. They are taller, stronger, and more agile than the rest of us, and they make more shaving-cream commercials.

In this appendix, we shall survey some of the statistical methods used by psychologists to draw conclusions about the measurements they take in research activities. First, we shall discuss *descriptive statistics* and learn what types of statements we can make about the height of basketball players and some other human traits. Then, we shall discuss the *normal curve* and learn why basketball players are abnormal—at least in terms of height. We shall explore *correlation coefficients* and provide you with some less-than-shocking news: More intelligent people attain higher grades than less intelligent people. Finally, we shall have a brief look at inferential *statistics* and see why we can be bold enough to say that the difference in height between basketball players and other people is not just a chance accident, or fluke. Basketball players are in fact statistically significantly taller than the general population.

Statistics • Numerical facts assembled in such a manner that they provide significant information about measures or scores. (From the Latin word *status,* meaning "standing" or "position.")

Sample • Part of a population.

Population • A complete group from which a sample is selected.

Range • A measure of variability; the distance between extreme measures or scores.

Average • Central tendency of a group of measures, expressed as mean, median, and mode.

Descriptive Statistics

Being told that someone is a "10" is not very descriptive unless you know something about how possible scores are distributed and how frequently one finds a 10. Fortunately—for 10s, if not for the rest of us—one is usually informed that someone is a 10 on a scale of 1 to 10 and that 10 is the positive end of the scale. If this is not sufficient, one will also be told that 10s are few and far between—rather unusual statistical events.

This business of a scale from 1 to 10 is not very scientific, to be sure, but it does suggest something about **descriptive statistics.** We can use descriptive statistics to clarify our understanding of a distribution of scores such as heights, test grades, IQs, or increases or decreases in measures of sexual arousal following the drinking of alcohol. For example, descriptive statistics can help us to determine measures of central tendency, or averages, and to determine how much variability there is in the scores. Being a 10 loses some of its charm if the average score is an 11. Being a 10 is more remarkable in a distribution whose scores range from 1 to 10 than in one that ranges from 9 to 10.

Let us now examine some of the concerns of descriptive statistics: the frequency distribution, measures of central tendency (types of averages), and measures of variability.

THE FREQUENCY DISTRIBUTION. A **frequency distribution** takes scores or items of raw data, puts them into order as from lowest to highest, and groups them according to class intervals. Table A.1 shows the rosters for a recent California Quakes–New York Apples basketball game. The members of each team are listed according to the numbers on their uniforms. Table A.2 shows a frequency distribution of the heights of the players of both teams combined, with a class interval of 1 inch.

It would also be possible to use 3-inch class intervals, as in Table A.3. In determining how large a class interval should be, a researcher attempts to collapse that data into a small enough number of classes to ensure that they will appear meaningful at a glance. But the researcher also attempts to maintain a

Descriptive statistics • The branch of statistics that is concerned with providing information about a distribution of scores.

Frequency distribution • An ordered set of data that indicates how frequently scores appear.

TABLE A.1
ROSTERS OF QUAKES VERSUS APPLES AT NEW YORK

CALIFORNIA		NEW YORK	
2 Callahan	6′−7″	3 Roosevelt	6′−1″
5 Daly	6′−11″	12 Chaffee	6′−5″
6 Chico	6′−2″	13 Baldwin	6′−9″
12 Capistrano	6′−3″	25 Delmar	6′−6″
21 Brentwood	6′−5″	27 Merrick	6′−8″
25 Van Nuys	6′−3″	28 Hewlett	6′−6″
31 Clemente	6′−9″	33 Hollis	6′−9″
32 Whittier	6′−8″	42 Bedford	6′−5″
41 Fernando	7′−2″	43 Coram	6′−2″
43 Watts	6′−9″	45 Hampton	6′−10″
53 Huntington	6′−6″	53 Ardsley	6′−10″

A glance at the rosters for a recent California Quakes–New York Apples basketball game shows you that the heights of the team members, combined, ranged from 6 feet 1 inch to 7 feet 2 inches. Are the heights of the team members representative of those of the general male population?

TABLE A.2
FREQUENCY DISTRIBUTION OF HEIGHTS OF BASKETBALL PLAYERS, WITH A ONE-INCH CLASS INTERVAL

CLASS INTERVAL	NUMBER OF PLAYERS IN CLASS
6–1 to 6–1.9	1
6–2 to 6–2.9	2
6–3 to 6–3.9	2
6–4 to 6–4.9	0
6–5 to 6–5.9	3
6–6 to 6–6.9	3
6–7 to 6–7.9	1
6–8 to 6–8.9	2
6–9 to 6–9.9	4
6–10 to 6–10.9	2
6–11 to 6–11.9	1
7–0 to 7–0.9	0
7–1 to 7–1.9	0
7–2 to 7–2.9	1

large enough number of categories to ensure that important differences are not obscured.

Table A.3 obscures the fact that no players are 6 feet 4 inches tall. If the researcher believes that this information is extremely important, a class interval of 1 inch may be maintained.

Figure A.1 shows two methods for representing the information in Table A.3 with graphs. Both in frequency **histograms** and frequency **polygons,** the class intervals are typically drawn along the horizontal line, or X-axis, and the number of scores (persons, cases, or events) in each class is drawn along the vertical line, or Y-axis. In a histogram, the number of scores in each class interval is represented by a rectangular solid so that the graph resembles a series of steps. In a polygon, the number of scores in each class interval is plotted as a point, and the points are then connected to form a many-sided geometric figure. Note that class intervals were added at both ends of the horizontal axis of the frequency polygon so that the lines could be brought down to the axis to close the geometric figure.

Histogram • A graphic representation of a frequency distribution that uses rectangular solids. (From the Greek *historia,* meaning "narrative," and *gramma,* meaning "writing" or "drawing.")

Polygon • A closed figure. (From the Greek *polys,* meaning "many," and *gōnia,* meaning "angle.")

TABLE A.3
FREQUENCY DISTRIBUTION OF HEIGHTS OF BASKETBALL PLAYERS, WITH A THREE-INCH CLASS INTERVAL

CLASS INTERVAL	NUMBER OF PLAYERS IN CLASS
6–1 to 6–3.9	5
6–4 to 6–6.9	6
6–7 to 6–9.9	7
6–10 to 7–0.9	3
7–1 to 7–3.9	1

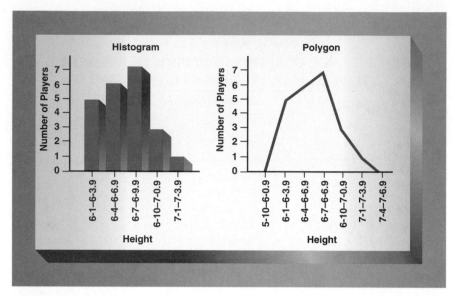

FIGURE A.1

Two Graphical Representations of the Data in Table A.3.

Mean • A type of average calculated by dividing the sum of scores by the number of scores. (From the Latin *medius,* meaning "middle.")

Median • The score beneath which 50% of the class fall. (From the Latin *medius,* meaning "middle.")

**MINILECTURE:
CENTRAL TENDENCY**

MEASURES OF CENTRAL TENDENCY.

Never try to walk across a river just because it has an average depth of four feet.
MARTIN FRIEDMAN

There are three types of measures of central tendency, or averages: *mean, median,* and *mode.* Each tells us something about the way in which the scores in a distribution may be summarized by a typical or representative number.

The **mean** is what most people think of as "the average." The mean is obtained by adding up all the scores in a distribution and then dividing this sum by the number of scores. In the case of our basketball players, it would be advisable first to convert all heights into one unit, such as inches (6'1" becomes 73", and so on). If we add all the heights in inches, then divided by the number of players, or 22, we obtain a mean height of 78.73", or 6'6.73".

The **median** is the score of the middle case in a frequency distribution. It is the score beneath which 50% of the cases fall. In a distribution with an even number of cases, such as the distribution of the heights of the 22 basketball players in Table A.2, the median is determined by finding the mean of the two middle cases. Listing these 22 cases in ascending order, we find that the 11th case is 6'6" and the 12th case is 6'7". Thus the median is (6'6" + 6'7")/2, or 6'6$\frac{1}{2}$".

In the case of the heights of the basketball players, the mean and the median are similar, and either serves as a useful indicator of the central tendency of the data. But suppose we are attempting to determine the average savings of 30 families living on a suburban block. Let us assume that 29 of the 30 families have savings between $8,000 and $12,000, adding up to $294,000. But the 30th family has savings of $1,400,000! The mean savings for a family on this block would thus be $56,467. A mean can be greatly distorted by one or two extreme scores, and for such distributions the median is a better indicator of the central tendency. The median savings on our hypothetical block would lie between $8,000 and $12,000 and so would be more representative of the central tendency of savings. Studies of the incomes of American families usually report median rather than mean incomes just to avoid the distortions that would result from treating incomes of the small numbers of multimillionaires in the same way as other incomes.

The **mode** is simply the most frequently occurring score in a distribution. The mode of the data in Table A.1 is 6′9″ because this height occurs most often. The median class interval for the data in Table A.3 is 6′6½″ to 6′9½″. In these cases, the mode is somewhat higher than the mean or median height.

In some cases, the mode is a more appropriate description of a distribution than the mean or median. Figure A.2 shows a **bimodal** distribution, or a distribution with two modes. In this hypothetical distribution of the test scores, the mode at the left indicates the most common class interval for students who did not study, and the mode at the right indicates the most frequent class interval for students who did. The mean and median test scores would probably lie within the 55–59 class interval, yet use of that interval as a measure of central tendency would not provide very meaningful information about the distribution of scores. It might suggest that the test was too hard, not that a number of students chose not to study. One would be better able to visualize the distribution of scores if it is reported as a bimodal distribution. Even in similar cases in which the modes are not exactly equal, it might be more appropriate to describe a distribution as being bimodal or even multimodal.

MEASURES OF VARIABILITY. Measures of variability of a distribution inform us about the spread of scores, or about the typical distances of scores from the average score. Measures of variability include the *range* of scores and the *standard deviation*.

The **range** of scores in a distribution is defined as the difference between the highest score and the lowest score, and it is obtained by subtracting the lowest score from the highest score. The range of heights in Table A.2 is 7′2″ minus 6′1″, or 1′1″. It is important to know the range of temperatures if we move to a new climate so that we may anticipate the weather and dress appropriately. A teacher must have some understanding of the range of abilities or skills in a class to teach effectively.

MINILECTURE: VARIABILITY

Mode • The most frequently occurring number or score in a distribution. (From the Latin *modus,* meaning "measure.")

Bimodal • Having two modes.

Range • The difference between the highest and the lowest scores in a distribution.

FIGURE A.2

A Bimodal Distribution. The hypothetical distribution represents students' scores on a test. The mode at the left represents the central tendency of students who did not study, and the mode at the right represents the mode of students who did study.

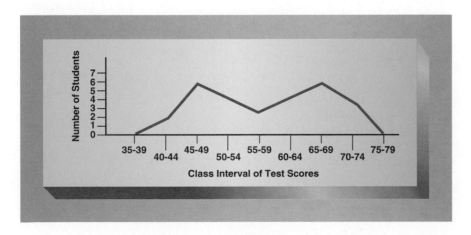

The range is an imperfect measure of variability because of the manner in which it is influenced by extreme scores. In our earlier discussion of the savings of 30 families on a suburban block, the range of savings is $1,400,000 to $8,000, or $1,392,000. This tells us little about the typical variability of savings accounts, which lie within a restricted range of $8,000 to $12,000. The **standard deviation** is a statistic that indicates how scores are distributed about a mean of a distribution.

The standard deviation considers every score in a distribution, not just the extreme scores. Thus, the standard deviation for the distribution on the right in Figure A.3 would be smaller than that of the distribution on the left. Note that each distribution has the same number of scores, the same mean, and the same range of scores. But the standard deviation for the distribution on the right is smaller than that of the distribution on the left, because the scores tend to cluster more closely about the mean.

The standard deviation (S.D.) is calculated by the formula

$$\text{S.D.} = \sqrt{\frac{\text{Sum of } d^2}{N}}$$

where d equals the deviation of each score from the mean of the distribution, and N equals the number of scores in the distribution.

Let us find the mean and standard deviation of the IQ scores listed in column 1 of Table A.4. To obtain the mean, we add all the scores, attain 1,500, and then divide by the number of scores (15) to obtain a mean of 100. We obtain the deviation score (d) for each IQ score by subtracting the score from 100. The d for an IQ of 85 equals 100 minus 85, or 15, and so on. Then we square each d and add these squares. The S.D. equals the square root of the sum of squares (1,426) divided by the number of scores (15), or 9.75.

As an additional exercise, we can show that the S.D. of the test scores on the left (in Figure A.3) is greater than that for the scores on the right by assigning the grades points according to a 4.0 system. Let A = 4, B = 3, C = 2, D = 1, and F = 0. The S.D. for each distribution of test scores is computed in

Standard deviation • A measure of the variability of a distribution, attained by the formula

$$\sqrt{\frac{\text{Sum of } d^2}{N}}$$

FIGURE A.3

Hypothetical Distributions of Student Test Scores. Each distribution has the same number of scores, the same mean, and even the same range, but the standard deviation is greater for the distribution on the left because the scores tend to be farther from the mean.

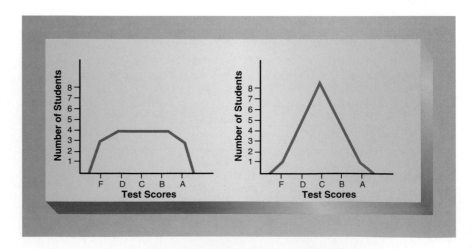

TABLE A.4

HYPOTHETICAL SCORES ATTAINED FROM AN IQ TESTING

IQ SCORE	*d* (DEVIATION SCORE)	*d*² (DEVIATION SCORE SQUARED)
85	15	225
87	13	169
89	11	121
90	10	100
93	7	49
97	3	9
97	3	9
100	0	0
101	−1	1
104	−4	16
105	−5	25
110	−10	100
112	−12	144
113	−13	169
117	−17	289

Sum of IQ scores = 1,5000
Sum of d^2 scores = 1,426

$$\text{Mean} = \frac{\text{Sum of scores}}{\text{Number of scores}}$$

$$= \frac{1,500}{15} = 100$$

Standard Deviation (S.D.)

$$= \sqrt{\frac{\text{Sum of } d^2}{\text{Number of Scores}}}$$

$$= \sqrt{\frac{1,426}{15}} = \sqrt{95.07} = 9.75$$

Normal distribution • A symmetrical distribution in which approximately 68% of cases lie within a standard deviation of the mean.
Normal curve • Graphic presentation of a normal distribution, showing a bell shape.

Table A.5. The greater S.D. for the distribution on the left indicates that the scores in that distribution are more variable, or tend to be farther from the mean.

The Normal Curve

Many human traits and characteristics such as height and intelligence seem to be distributed in a pattern known as a normal distribution. In a **normal distribution,** the mean, median, and mode all fall at the same data point or score. Scores cluster most heavily about the mean, fall off rapidly in either direction at first (as shown in Figure A.4), and then taper off more gradually.

The curve in Figure A.4 is bell shaped. This type of distribution is also called a **normal curve.** It is hypothesized to reflect the distribution of variables in which different scores are determined by chance variation. Height is thought to be largely determined by chance combinations of genetic material. A distribution of the heights of a random sample of the population approximates normal distributions for men and women, with the mean of the distribution for men a few inches higher than the mean for women.

Test developers traditionally assumed that intelligence was also randomly or normally distributed among the population. For that reason, they constructed

TABLE A.5

COMPUTATION OF STANDARD DEVIATIONS FOR TEST-SCORE DISTRIBUTIONS IN FIGURE A.3

DISTRIBUTION AT LEFT: GRADE	d	d^2	DISTRIBUTION AT RIGHT: GRADE	d	d^2
A (4)	2	4	A (4)	2	4
A (4)	2	4	B (3)	1	1
A (4)	2	4	B (3)	1	1
B (3)	1	1	B (3)	1	1
B (3)	1	1	B (3)	1	1
B (3)	1	1	C (2)	0	0
B (3)	1	1	C (2)	0	0
C (2)	0	0	C (2)	0	0
C (2)	0	0	C (2)	0	0
C (2)	0	0	C (2)	0	0
C (2)	0	0	C (2)	0	0
D (1)	−1	1	C (2)	0	0
D (1)	−1	1	C (2)	0	0
D (1)	−1	1	D (1)	−1	1
D (1)	−1	1	D (1)	−1	1
F (0)	−2	4	D (1)	−1	1
F (0)	−2	4	D (1)	−1	1
F (0)	−2	4	F (0)	−2	4

Sum of grades = 36
Mean grade =
36/18 = 2
Sum of d^2 = 32
    S.D. = $\sqrt{32/18}$
       = 1.33

Sum of grades = 36
Mean grade =
36/18 = 2
Sum of d^2 = 16
    S.D. = $\sqrt{16/18}$
       = 0.94

intelligence tests so that scores would be distributed as close to "normal" as possible. In actuality, IQ scores are also influenced by environmental factors and chromosomal abnormalities, so the resultant curves are not perfectly normal. Most IQ tests have means defined as scores of 100 points, and the Wechsler scales are constructed to have standard deviations of 15 points, as shown in Figure A.4. This means that 50% of the Wechsler scores fall between 90 and 100 (the "broad average" range), about 68% (or two of three) fall between 85 and 115, and more than 95% fall between 70 and 130—that is, within two S.D.s of the mean.

The Scholastic Assessment Test (SATs) were constructed so that the mean scores would be 500 points, and an S.D. would be 100 points. Thus, a score of 600 would equal or excel that of some 84 to 85% of the test takers. Because of the complex interaction of variables determining SAT scores, the distribution of SAT scores is not exactly normal either. The normal curve is an idealized curve.

The Correlation Coefficient

What is the relationship between intelligence and educational achievement? Between cigarette smoking and lung cancer in human beings? Between introversion and frequency of dating among college students? We cannot run

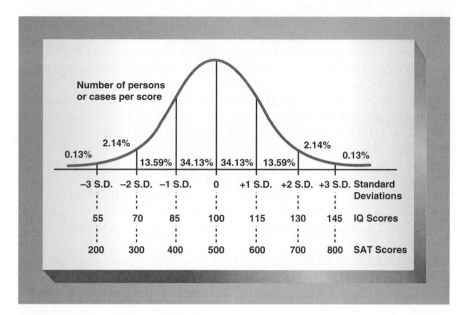

FIGURE A.4

A Bell-Shaped or Normal Curve. In a normal curve, approximately 68 percent of the cases lie within a standard deviation (S.D.) from the mean, and the mean, median, and mode all lie at the same score. IQ tests and Scholastic Assessment Tests have been constructed so that distributions of scores approximate the normal curve.

Correlation coefficient • A number between −1.00 and +1.00 that indicates the degree of relationship between two variables.

experiments to determine whether the relationships between these variables are causal, because we cannot manipulate the independent variable. For example, we cannot randomly assign a group of people to cigarette smoking and another group to nonsmoking. People must be permitted to make their own choices, and so it is possible that the same factors that lead people to choose to smoke may also lead to lung cancer. However, the **correlation coefficient** may be used to show that there is a relationship between smoking and cancer.

The correlation coefficient is a statistic that describes the relationship between two variables. It varies from +1.00 to −1.00; therefore, a correlation coefficient of +1.00 is called a perfect positive correlation, a coefficient of −1.00 is a perfect negative correlation, and a coefficient of 0.00 shows no correlation between variables. The meanings of various correlation coefficients are discussed further in Chapter 2.

Inferential Statistics

In a study reported in Chapter 9, children enrolled in a Head Start program earned a mean IQ score of 99, whereas children similar in background who were not enrolled in Head Start earned a mean IQ score of 93. Is this difference of six points in IQ significant, or does it represent chance fluctuation of scores? In a study reported in Chapter 2, people who believed they had drunk alcohol chose higher levels of electric shock to be applied to persons who had provoked them than did people who believed they had not drunk alcohol. Did the difference in level of shock chosen reflect an actual difference between the two groups, or could it have been a chance fluctuation? Inferential statistics help us make decisions about whether differences found between such groups reflect the real differences or just fluctuations.

Figure A.5 shows the distribution of heights of 1,000 men and 1,000 women selected at random. The mean height for men is greater than the mean height for women. Can we draw the conclusion, or **infer,** that this difference in heights represents the general population of men and women? Or must we avoid such an inference and summarize our results by stating only that the sample of 1,000 men in the study had a higher mean height than that of the sample of 1,000 women in the study?

If we could not draw inferences about populations from studies of samples, our research findings would be very limited indeed—limited only to the specific individuals studied. However, the branch of statistics known as **inferential statistics** uses mathematical techniques in such a way that we can draw conclusions about populations from which samples have been drawn.

STATISTICALLY SIGNIFICANT DIFFERENCES.   In determining whether differences in measures taken of research samples may be applied to the populations from which they were drawn, psychologists use mathematical techniques that indicate whether differences are statistically significant. Was the difference in IQ scores for children attending and those not attending Head Start significant? Did it represent only the children participating in the study, or can it be applied to all children represented by the sample? Is the difference between the height of men and the height of women in Figure A.5 statistically significant? Can we apply our findings to all men and women?

Psychologists use formulas involving the means and standard deviations of sample groups to determine whether group differences are statistically significant. As you can see in Figure A.6, the farther apart the group means are, the more likely it is that the difference between them is statistically significant. This makes a good deal of common sense. After all, if you were told that your

Infer • To draw a conclusion, to conclude. (From the Latin *in*, meaning "in," and *ferre*, meaning "to bear.")

Inferential statistics • The branch of statistics concerned with the confidence with which conclusions drawn about samples may be extended to the populations from which they were drawn.

FIGURE A.5

Distribution of Heights for Random Samples of Men and Women. Inferential statistics permit us to apply our findings to the populations sampled.

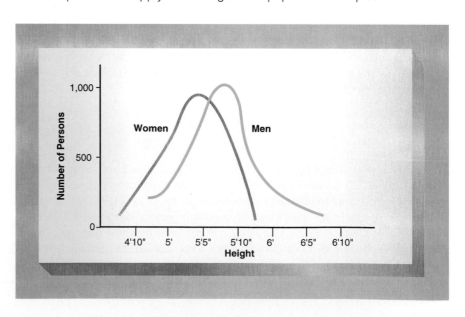

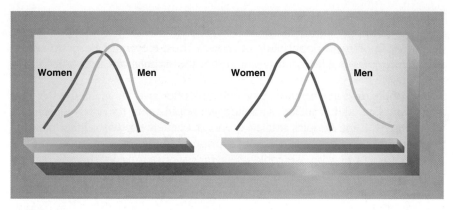

FIGURE A.6

Psychologists use group means and standard deviations to determine whether the difference between group means is statistically significant. The difference between the means of the groups on the right is greater and thus more likely to be statistically significant.

neighbor's car had gotten one-tenth of a mile more per gallon of gasoline than your car had last year, you might assume that this was a chance difference. But if the difference was farther apart, say 14 miles per gallon, you might readily believe that this difference reflected an actual difference in driving habits or efficiency of the automobiles.

As you can see in Figure A.7, the smaller the standard deviations (a measure of variability) of the two groups, the more likely it is that the difference of the means is statistically significant. As an extreme example, if all women sampled were exactly 5′5″ tall, and all men sampled were exactly 5′10″, we would be highly likely to assume that the difference of 5 inches in group means is statistically significant. But if the heights of women varied from 2′ to 14′, and the heights of men varied from 2′1″ to 14′3″, we might be more likely to assume that the 5-inch difference in group means could be attributed to chance fluctuation.

FIGURE A.7

The variability of the groups on the left is smaller than the variability of the groups on the right. Thus, it is more likely that the difference between the means of the groups on the left is statistically significant.

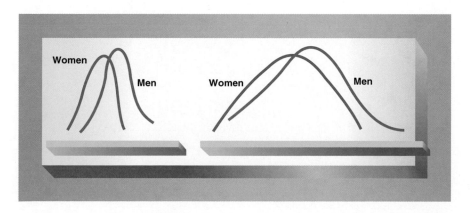

SAMPLES AND POPULATIONS.   Inferential statistics are mathematical tools that psychologists apply to samples of scores to determine whether they can generalize their findings to populations of scores. Thus, they must be quite certain that the samples involved actually represent the populations from which they were drawn.

As you learned in Chapter 2, psychologists often use the techniques of random sampling and stratified sampling of populations to draw representative samples. If the samples studied do not accurately represent their intended populations, it matters very little how sophisticated the statistical techniques of the psychologist may be. We could use a variety of statistical techniques on the heights of the New York Apples and California Quakes, but none would tell us much about the height of the general population.

GLOSSARY

A

A–B problem The issue of how well we can predict behavior on the basis of attitudes.

Abreaction In psychodynamic theory, the expression of previously repressed feelings and impulses to allow the psychic energy associated with them to spill forth.

Absolute refractory period A phase following a neuron's firing during which an action potential cannot be triggered.

Absolute threshold The minimal amount of energy that can produce a sensation.

Abstinence syndrome A characteristic cluster of symptoms that results from sudden decrease in the level of usage of a drug on which one is physiologically dependent.

Accommodation According to Piaget, the modification of existing concepts or schemas so that new information can be integrated or understood.

Acculturation The process of adaptation in which immigrants and native groups identify with a new, dominant culture by learning about the culture and making behavioral and attitudinal changes.

Acetylcholine A neurotransmitter that controls muscle contractions. Abbreviated *ACh.*

Achievement Accomplishment; that which is attained by one's efforts and presumed to be made possible by one's abilities.

Acoustic code Mental representation of information as a sequence of sounds.

Acquired drives Drives that are acquired through experience, or learned.

Acquired immunodeficiency syndrome A fatal, sexually transmitted disease caused by the human immunodeficiency virus (HIV) that destroys cells of the immune system, leaving the body vulnerable to opportunistic diseases. Abbreviated *AIDS.*

Acquisition trial In conditioning, a presentation of stimuli such that a new response is learned and strengthened.

Acronym A word that is composed of the first letters of the elements of a phrase.

Acrophobia Fear of high places.

Action potential The electrical impulse that provides the basis for the conduction of a neural impulse along an axon of a neuron.

Activating effects The arousal-producing effects of sex hormones that increase the likelihood of dominant sexual responses.

Activation-synthesis model The view that dreams reflect activation by the reticular activating system and synthesis of activated cognitions by the cerebral cortex.

Active coping A response to stress that manipulates the environment or changes the response patterns of the individual to permanently remove the stressor or to render it harmless.

Actor–observer effect In attribution theory, the tendency to attribute our own behavior to situational factors but to attribute the behavior of others to dispositional factors.

Acupuncture The practice, originated in ancient China, of piercing parts of the body with needles to deaden pain and treat illness.

Adaptation stage See *resistance stage.*

ADH Abbreviation of antidiuretic hormone.

Adipose tissue Tissue that contains fat.

Adjustment The process of responding to stress.

Adolescence The stage of development between childhood and adulthood that is bounded by the advent of puberty and the capacity to assume adult responsibilities.

Adrenal cortex The outer part of the adrenal gland, which produces steroids.

Adrenaline A hormone produced by the adrenal medulla that stimulates the sympathetic division of the autonomic nervous system. Also called *epinephrine.*

Adrenal medulla The inner part of the adrenal gland, which produces adrenaline.

Adrenocorticotrophic hormone A pituitary hormone that regulates the adrenal cortex. Abbreviated *ACTH.*

Adult In transactional analysis, a rational, adaptive ego state.

Aerobic exercise Exercise that requires sustained increase in oxygen consumption.

Affective disorders Disorders characterized primarily by prolonged disturbances of mood or emotional response. (Now referred to as *mood disorders.*)

Afferent neuron A neuron that transmits messages from sensory receptors to the spinal cord and brain. Also called *sensory neuron.*

Affiliation The social motive to be with others and to cooperate.

Afterimage The lingering impression made by a stimulus that has been removed.

Age regression In hypnosis, taking on the role of childhood, frequently accompanied by vivid recollections of the early years.

Agoraphobia Fear of open, crowded places.

AIDS Acronym for *Acquired Immunodeficiency Syndrome.* A disorder of the immune system caused by human immunodeficiency virus (HIV) and characterized by suppression of the immune response, leaving the body prey to opportunistic diseases.

Alarm reaction The first stage of the general adaptation syndrome, which is triggered by the impact of a stressor and characterized by heightened sympathetic activity.

Alcoholism Drinking that persistently impairs personal, social, or physical well being.

Algorithm A specific procedure such as a formula for solving a problem that will work invariably if it is applied correctly.

All-or-none principle The principle that a neuron fires an impulse of the same strength whenever its action potential has been triggered.

Alpha waves Rapid, low-amplitude brain waves that have been linked to feelings of relaxation.

Altered states of consciousness States other than the normal waking state, including sleep, meditation, the hypnotic trance, and the distorted perceptions that can be caused by use of certain drugs.

Alternate-form reliability The consistency of a test as determined by correlating scores attained on one form of the test with scores attained on another form. The Scholastic Assessment Tests and Graduate Record Exams, for example, have many forms.

Altruism Selflessness; unselfish concern for the welfare of others.

Alzheimer's disease A progressive disease that is associated with degeneration of hippocampal cells that produce acetylcholine. It is symptomized by the inability to form new memories and the loss of other cognitive functions.

Ambiguous Having two or more possible meanings.

Amenorrhea Absence of menstruation.

American Sign Language The communication of meaning through the use of symbols that are formed by moving the hands and arms and associated gestures. Abbreviated *ASL.*

Amino acid Protein involved in metabolism.

Amniocentesis A method for tapping amniotic fluid and examining fetal chromosomes that have been sloughed off, making it possible to determine the presence of genetic abnormalities and the sex of the fetus.

Amniotic fluid Fluid within the amniotic sac, formed largely from the fetus's urine, that protects the fetus from jarring or injury.

Amniotic sac A sac within the uterus that contains the embryo or fetus.

Amotivational syndrome Loss of ambition or motivation to achieve.

Amphetamines Stimulants such as Dexedrine and Benzedrine that are derived from *a*lpha-*m*ethyl-beta-*ph*enyl-*et*hyl-*amine.* Abuse can trigger symptoms that mimic schizophrenia.

Amplitude Height. The extreme range of a variable quantity.

Amygdala   A part of the limbic system that apparently facilitates stereotypical aggressive responses.

Anabolic steroids   Steroids, the chief of which is testosterone, that promote the growth of muscle tissue by creating protein and other substances. Anabolic steroids also foster feelings of invincibility. See also *corticosteroids*.

Anaerobic exercise   Exercise that does not require sustained increase in oxygen consumption, such as weight lifting.

Anal expulsive   A Freudian personality type characterized by unregulated self-expression such as messiness.

Anal fixation   In psychodynamic theory, attachment to objects and behaviors characteristic of the anal stage.

Analgesia   (1) A conscious state in which pain is reduced or terminated. (2) A method for inducing such a state.

Analogous hues   Colors that lie next to one another on the color wheel, forming families of harmonious colors such as yellow and orange, and green and blue.

Anal retentive   A Freudian personality type characterized by self-control such as excessive neatness and punctuality.

Anal stage   In psychodynamic theory, the second stage of psychosexual development, in which gratification is obtained through anal activities like eliminating wastes.

Analyst   A person who practices psychoanalysis, Freud's method of psychotherapy.

Analytical psychology   Jung's psychodynamic theory, which emphasizes archetypes, a collective unconscious, and a unifying force of personality called the Self.

Anchoring and adjustment heuristic   A decision-making heuristic in which a presumption or first estimate serves as a cognitive anchor. As we receive additional information, we make adjustments, but tend to remain in the proximity of the anchor.

Androgen   Male sex hormone.

Anger   (1) A negative emotion frequently characterized by a provocation, cognitions that one has been taken advantage of and should seek revenge, and aggressive behavioral tendencies. (2) The second stage in Kübler-Ross's theory of dying.

Angiotensin   A kidney hormone that signals the hypothalamus of depletion of body fluids.

Animism   The belief, characteristic of preoperational thought, that inanimate objects move because of will or spirit.

Anorexia nervosa   An eating disorder characterized by maintenance of an abnormally low body weight, intense fear of weight gain, a distorted body image, and, in females, amenorrhea.

Anosmia   Lack of sensitivity to a specific odor.

ANS   Abbreviation for *autonomic nervous system.*

Antecedent   An event or thing that occurs before another. (An *antecedent* of behavior is not necessarily a *cause* of behavior.)

Anterograde amnesia   Failure to remember events that occur after physical trauma because of the effects of the trauma.

Antibodies   Substances formed by white blood cells that recognize and destroy antigens.

Antidepressant drug   A drug that acts to relieve depression.

Antidiuretic hormone   A pituitary hormone that conserves body fluids by increasing the reabsorption of urine. Abbreviated *ADH.*

Antigen   A substance that stimulates the body to mount an immune-system response to it. (The contraction for *anti*body *gen*erator.)

Antisocial personality disorder   The diagnosis given a person who is in frequent conflict with society yet is undeterred by punishment and experiences little or no guilt and anxiety. Also referred to as *psychopathy* or *sociopathy.*

Anvil   A bone of the middle ear.

Anxiety   A psychological state characterized by tension and apprehension, foreboding and dread.

Aphagic   Characterized by undereating.

Aphasia   Impaired ability to comprehend or express oneself through speech.

Apnea   A life-threatening sleep disorder that is characterized by temporary discontinuation of breathing during sleep.

Applied psychology   The application of fundamental psychological methods and knowledge to the investigation and solution of human problems.

Applied research   Research conducted in an effort to find solutions to particular problems.

Approach–approach conflict   Conflict involving two positive but mutually exclusive goals.

Approach–avoidance conflict   Conflict involving a goal with positive and negative features.

Aptitude   A natural ability or talent.

Archetypes   In Jung's personality theory, primitive images or concepts that reside in the collective unconscious.

Arousal   (1) A general level of activity or preparedness for activity in an organism. (2) A general level of motivation in an organism.

Arteriosclerosis   A disease characterized by thickening and hardening of the arteries.

Artificialism   The belief, characteristic of preoperational thought, that natural objects have been created by human beings.

Assertiveness training   A form of social-skills training—including techniques such as coaching, modeling, feedback, and behavior rehearsal—that teaches clients to express their feelings and seek fair treatment.

Assimilation   According to Piaget, the inclusion of a new event into an existing concept or schema.

Association areas   Parts of the cerebral cortex involved in learning, thought, memory, and language.

Asthma   Recurrent attacks of difficult breathing and wheezing.

Astigmatism   A visual disorder in which vertical and horizontal contours cannot be focused on simultaneously.

Astrology   A pseudoscience that is based on the notion that the positions of the sun, the moon, and the stars affect human affairs and that one can foretell the future by studying the positions of these bodies.

Asylum   (1) An early institution for the care of the mentally ill. (2) A safe place, or refuge.

Attachment   The enduring affectional tie that binds one person to another.

Attachment-in-the-making phase   According to Ainsworth, the second phase in forming bonds of attachment, characterized by preference for familiar figures.

Attention-deficit/hyperactivity disorder   A disorder that begins in childhood and is characterized by a persistent pattern of lack of attention, with or without hyperactivity and impulsive behavior.

Attitude   An enduring mental representation of people, places, or things that evokes feelings and influences behavior.

Attitude-discrepant behavior   Behavior that is inconsistent with an attitude and may have the effect of modifying an attitude.

Attraction   A force that draws bodies or people together. In social psychology, an attitude of liking (positive attraction) or disliking (negative attraction).

Attribution   A belief about why people behave in a certain way.

Attributional style   One's tendency to attribute one's behavior to internal or external factors, stable or unstable factors, and so on.

Attribution process   The process by which people draw conclusions about the motives and traits of others.

Auditory   Having to do with hearing.

Auditory nerve   The axon bundle that transmits neural impulses from the organ of Corti to the brain.

Authoritarianism   Belief in the importance of unquestioning obedience to authority.

Autism   (1) Self-absorption. Absorption in daydreaming and fantasy. (2)

A childhood disorder marked by problems such as failure to relate to others, lack of speech, and intolerance of change.

Autogenic training   A method for reducing tension involving repeated suggestions that the limbs are becoming warmer and heavier and that one's breathing is becoming more regular.

Autokinetic effect   The tendency to perceive a stationary point of light in a dark room as moving.

Autonomic nervous system   The division of the peripheral nervous system that regulates glands and involuntary activities like heartbeat, respiration, digestion, and dilation of the pupils. Abbreviated *ANS*. Also see *sympathetic* and *parasympathetic* branches of the *ANS*.

Autonomy   Self-direction. The social motive to be free, unrestrained, and independent.

Autonomy versus shame and doubt   Erikson's second stage of psychosocial development, during which the child develops (or does not develop) the wish to make choices and the capacity to exercise self-control.

Availability heurisitc   A decision-making heuristic in which our estimates of frequency or probability of events are based on how easy it is to find examples.

Average   The central tendency of a group of measures, expressed as *mean, median,* or *mode.*

Aversive conditioning   A behavior-therapy technique in which a previously desirable or neutral stimulus is made obnoxious by being paired repeatedly with a repugnant or offensive stimulus.

Avoidance–avoidance conflict   Conflict involving two negative goals in which avoidance of one requires approaching the other.

Avoidance learning   An operant conditioning procedure in which an organism learns to exhibit an operant that permits it to avoid an aversive stimulus.

Axon   A long, thin part of a neuron that transmits impulses to other neurons from branching structures called *terminals.*

B

Babbling   The child's first verbalizations that have the sound of speech.

Babinski reflex   An infant's fanning of the toes in response to stimulation of the sole of the foot.

Backward conditioning   A classical conditioning procedure in which the unconditioned stimulus is presented prior to the conditioned stimulus.

Balance theory   The view that people have a need to organize their perceptions, opinions, and beliefs in a harmonious manner.

Barbiturate   An addictive depressant used to relieve anxiety or induce sleep.

Bargaining   The third stage in Kübler-Ross's theory of dying, in which the terminally ill try to bargain with God to postpone death, usually by offering to do good deeds in exchange for time.

Barnum effect   The tendency to believe in the accuracy of a generalized personality report or prediction about oneself.

Basal ganglia   Ganglia located in the brain between the thalamus and the cerebrum that are involved in motor coordination.

Basic anxiety   Horney's term for enduring feelings of insecurity that stem from harsh or indifferent parental treatment.

Basic hostility   Horney's term for enduring feelings of anger that accompany basic anxiety but that are directed toward nonfamily members in adulthood.

Basilar membrane   A membrane to which the organ of Corti is attached. The basilar membrane lies coiled within the cochlea.

Behavior   The observable or measurable actions of people and lower animals.

Behavioral competencies   Skills.

Behavior genetics   The study of the genetic transmission of structures and traits that give rise to behavior.

Behaviorism   The school of psychology that defines psychology as the study of observable behavior and investigates the relationships between stimuli and responses.

Behaviorist   A psychologist who believes that psychology should address observable behavior and the relationships between stimuli and responses.

Behavior modification   Use of principles of learning to change behavior in desired directions.

Behavior-outcome relations   A kind of expectancy in social-cognitive theory; predictions as to the outcomes (reinforcement contingencies) of one's behavior.

Behavior rating scale   A systematic means of recording the frequency with which target behaviors occur. (An alternative to self-report methods of personality testing.)

Behavior rehearsal   Practice.

Behavior therapy   Use of the principles of learning in the direct modification of problem behavior.

Benzodiazepines   A class of drugs that reduce anxiety. Minor tranquilizers.

Bimodal   Having two modes.

Binocular cues   Stimuli that suggest depth by means of simultaneous perception by both eyes. Examples: retinal disparity and convergence.

Biofeedback training   The systematic feeding back to an organism information about a body function so that the organism can gain control of that function. Abbreviated *BFT.*

Biological psychologist   A psychologist who studies the relationships between biological processes and behavior.

Bipolar cells   Neurons that conduct neural impulses from rods and cones to ganglion cells.

Bipolar disorder   A disorder in which the mood inappropriately alternates between extremes of elation and depression. Formerly called *manic-depression.*

Blind   In experimental terminology, unaware of whether one has obtained a treatment.

Blind spot   The area of the retina where axons from ganglion cells meet to form the optic nerve. It is insensitive to light.

Blocking   In conditioning, the phenomenon whereby a new stimulus fails to gain the capacity to signal an unconditioned stimulus (US) when the new stimulus is paired repeatedly with a stimulus that already effectively foretells the US.

B lymphocytes   The white blood cells of the immune system that produce antibodies.

Bottom-up processing   The organization of the parts of a pattern to recognize, or form an image of, the pattern they compose.

Brainstorming   A group process that encourages creativity by stimulating a large number of ideas and suspending judgment until the process is completed.

Breathalyzer   A device that measures the quantity of alcohol in the body by analyzing the breath.

Brief reactive psychosis   A psychotic episode of less than 2 weeks in duration that follows a known stressful event.

Brightness constancy   The tendency to perceive an object as being just as bright even though lighting conditions change the intensity with which it impacts on the eye.

Broca's aphasia   A speech disorder caused by damage to Broca's area of the brain. It is characterized by slow, laborious speech and by difficulty articulating words and forming grammatical sentences.

Bulimia nervosa   An eating disorder characterized by recurrent episodes of binge eating followed by purging and by persistent overconcern with body shape and weight.

Bureaucracy   An administrative system characterized by departments and subdivisions whose members frequently are given long tenure and inflexible work tasks.

C

Cannon–Bard theory   The theory of emotion that holds that events are processed by the brain and that the brain induces patterns of activity and autonomic arousal *and* cognitive activity — that is, the experiencing of the appropriate emotion.

Carcinogen   An agent that gives rise to cancerous changes.

Cardinal trait   Allport's term for pervasive traits that steer practically all of a person's behavior.

Cardiovascular disorders   Diseases of the cardiovascular system, including heart disease, hypertension, and arteriosclerosis.

Case study   A carefully drawn biography that may be obtained through interviews, questionnaires, psychological tests, and, sometimes, historical records.

Catastrophize   To exaggerate or magnify the noxious properties of negative events; to "blow out of proportion."

Catatonic schizophrenia   A subtype of schizophrenia characterized by striking impairment in motor activity.

Catch 30s   Sheehy's term for the fourth decade of life, which is frequently characterized by major reassessment of one's accomplishments and goals.

Catecholamines   A number of chemical substances produced from an amino acid that are important as neurotransmitters (dopamine and norepinephrine) and as hormones (adrenaline and norepinephrine).

Catharsis   In psychodynamic theory, the purging of strong emotions or the relieving of tensions. Also called *abreaction.*

CD4 cells   The white blood cells of the immune system that recognize invading pathogens and are attacked by the human immunodeficiency virus (HIV). Also called *T helper cells* or T_4 *cells.*

Cellular-aging theory   The view that aging occurs because body cells lose the capacity to reproduce and maintain themselves.

Center   According to Piaget, to focus one's attention.

Central fissure   The valley in the cerebral cortex that separates the frontal and parietal lobes.

Central nervous system   The brain and spinal cord.

Central traits   Characteristics that are outstanding and noticeable but not necessarily all-pervasive.

Cephalocaudal   Proceeding from top to bottom.

Cerebellum   A part of the hindbrain involved in muscle coordination and balance.

Cerebral cortex   The wrinkled surface area of the cerebrum, often called "gray matter" because of the appearance afforded by the many cell bodies.

Cerebrum   The large mass of the forebrain, which consists of two hemispheres.

Chain breaking   A behavior-therapy self-control technique in which one disrupts problematic behavior by complicating its execution.

Chemotherapy   The use of drugs to treat medical problems or abnormal behavior.

Child   In transactional analysis, an irresponsible, emotional ego state.

Childhood amnesia   Inability to recall events that occurred before the age of 3. Also termed *infantile amnesia.*

Chorionic villus sampling   The detection of genetic abnormalies by sampling the membrane that envelops the amniotic sac and the fetus within. Abbreviated *CVS.*

Chromosomes   Genetic structures consisting of genes that are found in the nuclei of the body's cells.

Chronological age   A person's actual age—as contrasted with *mental age.*

Chunk   A stimulus or group of stimuli that are perceived or encoded as a discrete piece of information.

Circadian rhythm   (sir-KADE-ee-an). Referring to cycles that are connected with the 24-hour period of the earth's rotation. (A scientific term coined from the Latin roots, *circa,* meaning "about," and *diem,* meaning "day.")

Circular explanation   An explanation that merely repeats its own concepts instead of offering additional information.

Cirrhosis of the liver   A disease caused by protein deficiency in which connective fibers replace active liver cells, impairing circulation of the blood. Alcohol does not contain protein; therefore, people who drink excessively may be prone to acquiring this disease.

Clairvoyance   The term means ability to perceive things in the absence of sensory stimulation. However, most psychologists do not believe that this ability exists. (A French word meaning "clear-sightedness.")

Classical conditioning   (1) According to cognitive theorists, the learning of relations among events so as to allow an organism to represent its environment. (2) According to behaviorists, a form of learning in which one stimulus comes to evoke the response usually evoked by a second stimulus by being paired repeatedly with the second stimulus. Also referred to as *respondent conditioning* or *Pavlovian conditioning.*

Classic organization theories   Theories that hold that organizations should be structured from the skeleton (governing body) outward.

Claustrophobia   Fear of tight, small places.

Clearcut-attachment phase   According to Ainsworth, the third phase in forming bonds of attachment, which is characterized by intensified dependence on the primary caregiver.

Client-centered therapy   See *person-centered therapy.*

Clinical scales   Groups of test items that measure the presence of various abnormal behavior patterns, as on the Minnesota Multiphasic Personality Inventory.

Closure   The tendency to perceive a broken figure as being complete or whole.

Cocaine   A powerful stimulant derived from coca leaves that is usually snorted, brewed, or injected.

Cochlea   The inner ear; the bony tube that contains the basilar membrane and the organ of Corti.

Cognitive   Having to do with mental processes such as sensation and perception, memory, intelligence, language, thought, and problem solving.

Cognitive-dissonance theory   The view that we are motivated to make our cognitions or beliefs consistent.

Cognitive map   A mental representation or picture of the elements in a learning situation, such as a maze.

Cognitive therapy   A form of psychotherapy that focuses on how people's cognitions (expectations, attitudes, beliefs, etc.) lead to distress and may be modified to relieve distress and promote adaptive behavior.

Collective unconscious   Jung's hypothesized store of vague racial memories and archetypes.

Collectivist   A person who defines herself or himself in terms of relationships to other people and groups and gives priority to group goals.

Color constancy   The tendency to perceive an object as being the same color even as lighting conditions change its appearance.

Common fate   The tendency to perceive elements that move together as belonging together.

Community psychology   A field of psychology, related to clinical psychology, that focuses on the prevention of psychological problems and the maintenance of distressed persons in the community.

Companionate love   A type of nonpassionate love characterized by intimacy, respect, trust, and commitment.

Competences   Within social-learning theory, knowledge and skills.

Competing response   In behavior therapy, a response that is incompatible with an unwanted response.

Complementary   (1) In sensation and perception, descriptive of colors of the spectrum that, when combined, produce white or nearly white light. (2) In transactional analysis, descriptive of a transaction in which the ego states of two people interact harmoniously.

Componential level   According to Sternberg, the level of intelligence that consists of metacomponents, performance components, and knowledge-acquisition components.

Compulsion   An apparently irresistible urge to repeat an act or engage in ritualistic behavior, such as handwashing.

Computerized axial tomography   Formation of a computer-generated image of the anatomical details of the brain by passing a narrow X-ray beam through the head and measuring from different angles the amount of radiation that passes through. Abbreviated *CAT scan.*

Concept   A mental category that is used to classify together objects, relations, events, abstractions, or qualities that have common properties.

Concordance Agreement.

Concrete operational stage Piaget's third stage of cognitive development, characterized by logical thought processes concerning tangible objects, conservation, reversibility, and subjective morality.

Conditional positive regard In Rogers's self theory, judgment of another person's basic value as a human being on the basis of the acceptability of that person's behaviors.

Conditional reasoning A form of reasoning about arguments that is used to reach conclusions about if–then relationships.

Conditioned reinforcer Another term for *secondary reinforcer*.

Conditioned response In classical conditioning, a learned response to a previously neutral stimulus. A response to a conditioned stimulus. Abbreviated *CR*.

Conditioned stimulus A previously neutral stimulus that elicits a conditioned response because it has been paired repeatedly with a stimulus that had already elicited that response. Abbreviated *CS*.

Conditioning A simple form of learning in which responses become associated with stimuli. See *classical conditioning and operant conditioning*.

Conditions of worth Standards by which the value of a person, or the self, is judged.

Conductive sensory deafness The forms of deafness in which there is loss of conduction of sound through the middle ear.

Cone A cone-shaped photoreceptor in the eye that transmits sensations of color.

Confederate In experimental terminology, a person who pretends to be a participant in a study but who is in league with the experimenter.

Confidential Secret, not to be disclosed.

Conflict (1) Being torn in different directions by opposing motives. (2) Feelings produced by being in conflict.

Conform To change one's attitudes or overt behavior to adhere to social norms.

Conformity Behavior that is in accordance with group norms and expectations.

Congruence In Rogers's self theory, a fit between one's self-concept and one's behaviors, thoughts, and feelings. A quality shown by the person-centered therapist.

Conscious Aware, in the normal waking state.

Consciousness A complex and controversial concept in psychology. Consciousness has several meanings in addition to the normal waking state; see *sensory awareness, direct inner awareness,* and *self*.

Consensus General agreement.

Conservation According to Piaget, recognition that certain properties of substances remain constant even though their appearance may change. For example, the weight and mass of a ball of clay remains constant (are conserved) even if the ball is flattened into a pancake.

Consolidation The fixing of information in long-term memory.

Consonant In harmony.

Construe Interpret.

Consultation The provision of professional advice or services.

Consumer psychology The field of psychology that studies the nature, causes, and modification of consumer behavior and mental processes.

Consummate love In Sternberg's triangular model, the kind of love characterized by passion, intimacy, and commitment.

Contact comfort (1) The pleasure attained from physical contact with another. (2) A hypothesized primary drive to seek physical comfort through physical contact with another.

Context-dependent memory Information that is better retrieved in the context in which it was encoded and stored, or learned.

Contextual level According to Sternberg, those aspects of intelligent behavior that permit people to adapt to their environment.

Contiguous Next to one another.

Contingency theory (1) In conditioning, the view that learning occurs when stimuli provide information about the likelihood of the occurrence of other stimuli. (2) In industrial/organizational psychology, a theory that holds that organizational structure should depend on factors such as goals, workers' characteristics, and the overall economic or political environment.

Continuity As a rule of perceptual organization, the tendency to perceive a series of stimuli as having unity.

Continuous reinforcement A schedule of reinforcement in which every correct response is reinforced. See *partial reinforcement*.

Control group A group of participants in an experiment who do not receive the experimental treatment but for whom all other conditions are comparable with those of individuals in the experimental group.

Conventional level According to Kohlberg, a period of moral development during which moral judgments largely reflect social conventions. A "law and order" approach to morality.

Convergence A binocular cue for depth based on the inward movement of the eyes as they attempt to focus on an object that is drawing nearer.

Convergent thinking A thought process that attempts to narrow in on the single best solution to a problem.

Conversion disorder A disorder in which anxiety or unconscious conflicts are "converted" into physical symptoms that often have the effect of helping the person cope with the anxiety or conflicts.

Cooing Prelinguistic, articulated, vowel-like sounds that appear to reflect feelings of positive excitement.

Cornea Transparent tissue that forms the outer surface of the eyeball.

Corpus callosum A thick bundle of fibers that connects the two hemispheres of the cerebrum.

Correlational research A method of scientific investigation that studies the relationships between variables. Correlational research can imply but cannot show cause and effect, because no experimental treatment is introduced.

Correlation coefficient A number ranging from +1.00 to −1.00 that expresses the strength and direction (positive or negative) of the relationship between two variables.

Corticosteroids Steroids produced by the adrenal cortex that regulate carbohydrate metabolism and increase resistance to stress by fighting inflammation and allergic reactions. Also called *cortical steroids*.

Cortisol A hormone (steroid) produced by the adrenal cortex that helps the body cope with stress by counteracting inflammation and allergic reactions.

Counterconditioning A behavior-therapy technique that involves the repeated pairing of a stimulus that elicits a problematic response (such as fear) with a stimulus that elicits an antagonistic response (such as relaxation instructions) so that the first stimulus loses the capacity to evoke the problematic response. See also *systematic desensitization* and *aversive conditioning*.

Countertransference In psychoanalysis, the generalization to the client of feelings toward another person in the analyst's life.

Covert reinforcement A behavior-therapy self-control technique in which one creates pleasant imagery to reward desired behavior.

Covert sensitization A behavior-therapy self-control technique in which one creates aversive imagery and associates it with undesired behavior.

CR Conditioned response.

Creative self According to Adler, the self-aware aspect of personality that strives to achieve its full potential.

Creativity The ability to generate novel solutions to problems. A trait characterized by originality, ingenuity, and flexibility.

Cretinism A condition caused by thyroid deficiency in childhood and characterized by mental retardation and stunted growth.

Criteria Plural of *criterion*.

Criterion A standard; a means for making a judgment.

Criterion-referenced testing A testing approach in which scores are based on whether or not one can perform up to a set standard.

Critical period A period in an organism's development during which it is capable of certain types of learning.

CS Conditioned stimulus.

Cultural bias A factor hypothesized to be present in intelligence tests that provides an advantage for test takers from certain cultural or ethnic backgrounds but that does not reflect actual intelligence.

Culture-fair Describing a test in which there are no cultural biases. On such a test, test takers from different cultural backgrounds would have an equal opportunity to earn scores that reflect their true abilities.

Cumulative incidence The occurrence of an event or act by a given time or age.

Cumulative recorder An instrument used in operant conditioning laboratory procedures to automatically record the frequency of targeted responses.

D

Daily hassles Notable daily conditions and experiences that are threatening or harmful to a person's well-being.

Dark adaptation The process of adjusting to conditions of lower lighting by increasing the sensitivity of rods and cones.

Debrief To receive information about a procedure that has been completed.

Decibel A unit expressing the loudness of a sound. Abbreviated *dB*.

Deductive reasoning A form of reasoning about arguments in which conclusions are deduced from premises. The conclusions are true if the premises are true.

Deep structure The underlying meaning of a sentence as determined by interpretation of the meanings of the words.

Defense mechanisms In psychodynamic theory, unconscious functions of the ego that protect it from anxiety-evoking material by preventing accurate recognition of this material.

Defensive coping A response to stress that reduces the stressor's immediate effect but frequently at some cost to the individual. Defensive coping may involve self-deception and does not change the environment or the person's response patterns to permanently remove or modify the effects of the stressor. Contrast with *active coping*.

Deindividuation The process by which group members may discontinue self-evaluation and adopt group norms and attitudes.

Delayed conditioning A classical-conditioning procedure in which the CS is presented several seconds before the US and remains in place until the response occurs.

Delirium tremens A condition characterized by sweating, restlessness, disorientation, and hallucinations that occurs in some chronic users of alcohol when there is a sudden decrease in the level of drinking. Abbreviated *DTs*.

Delta-9-tetrahydrocannabinol The major active ingredient in marijuana. Abbreviated *THC*.

Delta waves Strong, slow brain waves usually emitted during stage 4 sleep.

Delusions False, persistent beliefs that are unsubstantiated by sensory or objective evidence.

Delusions of grandeur Erroneous beliefs that one is a grand person, like Jesus or a secret agent on a special mission.

Delusions of persecution Erroneous beliefs that one is being threatened or persecuted.

Dendrites Rootlike structures attached to the soma of a neuron that receive impulses from other neurons.

Denial (1) A defense mechanism in which threatening events are misperceived to be harmless. (2) The first stage in Kübler-Ross's theory of dying.

Dependent variable A measure of an assumed effect of an independent variable. An outcome measure in a scientific study.

Depersonalization disorder A dissociative disorder characterized by persistent or recurrent feelings that one is not real or is detached from one's own experiences or body.

Depolarization The reduction of the resting potential of a cell membrane from about 70 millivolts toward zero.

Depressant A drug that lowers the nervous system's rate of activity.

Depression (1) A negative emotion frequently characterized by sadness, feelings of helplessness, and a sense of loss. (2) The fourth stage in Kübler-Ross's theory of dying.

Descriptive statistics The branch of statistics that is concerned with providing descriptive information about a distribution of scores.

Desensitization The type of sensory adaptation in which we become less sensitive to constant stimuli. Also called *negative adaptation*.

Determinant A factor that defines or sets limits.

Deviation IQ A score on an intelligence test that is derived by determining how far an individual's score deviates from the norm. On the Wechsler scales, the mean IQ score is defined as 100, and approximately two of three scores fall between 85 and 115.

Diabetes A disorder caused by inadequate secretion or utilization of insulin and characterized by excess sugar in the blood.

Diagnosis A decision or opinion about the nature of a diseased condition.

Dialogue A Gestalt therapy technique in which people verbalize confrontations between conflicting parts of their personality.

Dichromat A person who is sensitive to the intensity of light and to red and green or blue and yellow and who thus is partially color-blind.

Difference threshold The minimal difference in intensity that is required between two sources of energy so that they will be perceived as being different.

Differentiation The modification of tissues and organs in structure, function, or both during the course of development.

Diffusion of responsibility The spreading or sharing of responsibility for a decision or behavior among the members of a group.

Direct coping See *active coping*.

Direct inner awareness One of the definitions of consciousness: knowledge of one's own thoughts, feelings, and memories, without use of sensory organs.

Discovery learning Bruner's view that children should work on their own to discover basic principles.

Discrimination (1) In conditioning, the tendency for an organism to distinguish between a conditioned stimulus and similar stimuli that do not forecast an unconditioned stimulus. (2) In social psychology, the denial of privileges to a person or a group on the basis of prejudice.

Discrimination training Teaching an organism to show a conditioned response to only one of a series of similar stimuli by pairing that stimulus with the unconditioned stimulus and presenting similar stimuli in the absence of the unconditioned stimulus.

Discriminative stimulus In operant conditioning, a stimulus that indicates that reinforcement is available.

Disinhibit In social-cognitive theory, to trigger a response that is usually inhibited, generally as a consequence of observing a model engage in the behavior without negative consequences.

Disorganized schizophrenia A subtype of schizophrenia characterized by disorganized delusions and vivid hallucinations. Formerly *hebephrenic schizophrenia*.

Disorientation Gross confusion. Loss of awareness of time, place, and the identity of people.

Displacement (1) In information processing, the causing of chunks of information to be lost from short-term memory by adding too many new items. (2) In psychodynamic theory, a defense mechanism that involves the transference of feelings or impulses from threatening or unacceptable objects onto unthreatening or acceptable objects. (3) As a property of language, the ability to communicate information about events in other times and places.

Dispositional attribution An assumption that a person's behavior is determined by internal causes such as personal attitudes or goals. Contrast with *situation attribution*.

Dissociative amnesia A dissociative disorder marked by loss of episodic memory or self-identity. Skills and general knowledge are usually retained. Formerly termed *psychogenic amnesia*.

Dissociative disorder A disorder in which there is a sudden, temporary change in consciousness or self-identity, such as dissociative amnesia, dissociative fugue, dissociative identity disorder, or depersonalization disorder.

Dissociative fugue A dissociative disorder in which one experiences amnesia, then flees to a new location. Formerly termed *psychogenic fugue.*

Dissociative identity disorder A dissociative disorder in which a person has two or more distinct identities or personalities. Formerly termed *multiple personality disorder.*

Dissonant Incompatible, discordant.

Divergent thinking A thought process that attempts to generate multiple solutions to problems. Free and fluent associations to the elements of a problem.

Dizygotic twins Twins who develop from separate zygotes. Fraternal twins. Abbreviated *DZ twins.* Contrast with *monozygotic twins.*

DNA Deoxyribonucleic acid. The substance that carries the genetic codes and makes up genes and chromosomes.

Dominant trait In genetics, a trait that is expressed. See *recessive trait.*

Dopamine A neurotransmitter that is involved in Parkinson's disease and theorized to play a role in schizophrenia.

Double approach–avoidance conflict Conflict involving two goals, each of which has positive and negative aspects.

Double-blind study A study in which neither the participants nor the persons measuring results know who has obtained the treatment.

Down syndrome A chromosomal abnormality caused by an extra chromosome in the 21st pair ("trisomy 21") and characterized by slanted eyelids and mental retardation.

Dream A form of cognitive activity—usually a sequence of images or thoughts—that occurs during sleep. Dreams may be vague and loosely plotted or vivid and intricate.

Drive A condition of arousal within an organism that is associated with a need.

Drive for superiority Adler's term for the desire to compensate for feelings of inferiority.

Drive-reduction theory The view that organisms are motivated to learn to engage in behaviors that have the effect of reducing drives.

DSM The *Diagnostic and Statistical Manual of the Mental Disorders,* a publication of the American Psychiatric Association. A frequently used compendium of psychological disorders.

Duct Passageway.

Duplicity theory A combination of the place and frequency theories of pitch discrimination.

Dyslexia A severe reading disorder characterized by problems such as letter reversals, reading as if one were seeing words reflected in a mirror, slow reading, and reduced comprehension.

Dyspareunia Persistent or recurrent pain during or after sexual intercourse.

E

Eardrum A thin membrane that vibrates in response to sound waves, transmitting them from the outer ear to the middle and inner ears.

Eating disorders Psychological disorders that are characterized by distortion of the body image and gross disturbances in eating patterns. See *anorexia nervosa* and *bulimina nervosa.*

Echo A mental representation of an auditory stimulus that is held briefly in sensory memory.

Echoic memory The sensory register that briefly holds mental representations of auditory stimuli.

Eclectic Selecting from various systems or theories.

ECT Acronym for *electroconvulsive therapy.*

Educational psychology The field of psychology that studies the nature, causes, and enhancement of teaching and learning.

Efferent neuron A neuron that transmits messages from the brain or spinal cord to muscles or glands. Also called *motor neuron.*

Effort justification In cognitive-dissonance theory, the tendency to seek justification (acceptable reasons) for strenuous efforts.

Ego In psychodynamic theory, the second psychic structure to develop. The ego is governed by the reality principle and its functioning is characterized by self-awareness, planning, and capacity to tolerate frustration and delay gratification.

Ego analyst A psychodynamically oriented therapist who focuses on the conscious, coping behavior of the ego instead of the hypothesized unconscious functioning of the id.

Egocentric According to Piaget, assuming that others view the world as oneself does. Unable or unwilling to view the world as through the eyes of others.

Ego identity Erikson's term for the sense of who one is and what one stands for.

Ego identity versus role diffusion Erikson's fifth stage of psychosocial development, which challenges the adolescent to connect skills and social roles to career objectives.

Ego integrity Erikson's term for a firm sense of identity during the later years, characterized by the wisdom to accept the fact that life is limited and the ability to let go.

Ego integrity versus despair Erikson's eighth stage of psychosocial development, which challenges persons to accept the limits of their own life cycles during the later years.

Eidetic imagery The maintenance of detailed visual memories over several years.

Elaboration likelihood model The view that persuasive messages are evaluated (elaborated) on the basis of central and peripheral cues.

Elaborative rehearsal A method for increasing retention of new information by relating it to information that is well known.

Electra complex In psychodynamic theory, a conflict of the phallic stage in which the girl longs for her father and resents her mother.

Electroconvulsive therapy Treatment of disorders like major depression by passing an electric current through the head, causing a convulsion. Abbreviated *ECT.*

Electroencephalograph An instrument that measures electrical activity of the brain (brain waves). Abbreviated *EEG.*

Electromyograph An instrument that measures muscle tension. Abbreviated *EMG.*

Elicit To bring forth, evoke.

Embryo The developing organism from the third through the eighth weeks following conception, during which time the major organ systems undergo rapid differentiation.

Embryonic period The period of prenatal development between the period of the ovum and fetal development, approximately from the third through the eighth weeks following conception.

Embryo transfer Transfer of an embryo from the fallopian tube of its mother into the uterus of another woman, where it becomes implanted and develops.

Emetic Causing vomiting.

Emotion A state of feeling that has cognitive, physiological, and behavioral components.

Emotional appeal A type of persuasive communication that influences behavior on the basis of feelings that are aroused instead of rational analysis of the issues.

Empathic understanding Ability to perceive a client's feelings from the client's frame of reference. A quality of a good person-centered therapist.

Empathy Ability to understand and share another person's feelings.

Empirical Experimental. Emphasizing or based on observation and measurement, in contrast to theory and deduction.

Empty-nest syndrome A sense of depression and loss of purpose that is experienced by some parents when the youngest child leaves home.

Encoding Modifying information so that it can be placed in memory. The first stage of information processing.

Encounter group A structured group process that aims to foster self-awareness by focusing on how group members relate to each other in a setting that encourages frank expression of feelings.

Endocrine system The body's system of ductless glands that secrete hormones and release them directly into the bloodstream.

Endorphins Neurotransmitters that are composed of amino acids and are functionally similar to morphine.

Engram (1) An assumed electrical circuit in the brain that corresponds to a memory trace. (2) An assumed chemical change in the brain that accompanies learning.

Enkephalins Types of endorphins that are weaker and shorter-acting than beta-endorphin.

Enuresis Lack of bladder control at an age by which control is normally attained.

Environmental psychology The field of psychology that studies the ways in which people and the physical environment influence one another.

Epilepsy Temporary disturbances of brain functions that involve sudden neural discharges.

Epinephrine A hormone produced by the adrenal medulla that stimulates the sympathetic division of the *ANS*. Also called *adrenaline*.

Episodic memory Memories of specific events experienced by a person.

Equilibrium Another term for the *vestibular sense*.

Erogenous zone An area of the body that is sensitive to sexual sensations.

Eros In psychodynamic theory, the basic life instinct, which aims toward the preservation and perpetuation of life.

Estrogen A generic term for several female sex hormones that promote growth of female sexual characteristics and regulate the menstrual cycle.

Estrus The periodic sexual excitement of many female mammals, during which they are capable of conceiving and are receptive to sexual advances by males.

Ethical Moral; referring to one's system of deriving standards for determining what is moral.

Ethologist A scientist who studies behavior patterns that are characteristic of various species.

Euphoria Feelings of extreme well-being elation.

Eustress Stress that is healthful.

Evaluation apprehension Concern that others are evaluating our behavior.

Exceptional students The term applied to students whose educational needs are special because of physical and health problems, communication problems, behavior disorders, specific learning disabilities, mental retardation, or intellectual giftedness.

Excitatory synapse A synapse that influences receiving neurons in the direction of firing by increasing depolarization of their cell membranes.

Excitement phase The first phase of the sexual response cycle, characterized by erection in the man and by vaginal lubrication and clitoral swelling in the woman.

Exhaustion stage The third stage of the general adaptation syndrome, characterized by parasympathetic activity, weakened resistance, and possible deterioration.

Existentialism The view that people are completely free and responsible for their own behavior.

Expectancies A person variable in social-learning theory. Personal predictions about the outcomes of potential behaviors—"if–then" statements.

Experiential level According to Sternberg, those aspects of intelligence that permit people to cope with novel situations and process information automatically.

Experiment A scientific method that seeks to discover cause-and-effect relationships by introducing independent variables and observing their effects on dependent variables.

Experimental group A group of participants who obtain a treatment in an experiment.

Expository teaching Ausubel's method of presenting material in an organized form, moving from broad to specific concepts.

Expressive vocabulary The sum total of the words that one can use in the production of language.

External eater A person who eats predominantly in response to external stimuli, such as the time of day, the smell of food, or the presence of people who are eating. See *internal eater*.

"Externals" People who have an external locus of control—who perceive the ability to attain reinforcement as largely outside themselves.

Extinction An experimental procedure in which stimuli lose their ability to evoke learned responses because the events that had followed the stimuli no longer occur. (The learned responses are said to be *extinguished*.)

Extinction trial In conditioning, a performance of a learned response in the absence of its predicted consequences so that the learned response becomes inhibited.

Extrasensory perception Perception of external objects and events in the absence of sensation. Abbreviated *ESP*. A controversial area of investigation. (*Not* to be confused with hallucinations, which typify certain psychological disorders and are defined as confusion of fantasies with reality.)

Extroversion A source trait in which one's attention is directed to persons and things outside the self, often associated with a sociable, outgoing approach to others and the free expression of feelings and impulses. Opposite of *introversion*.

F

Facial-feedback hypothesis The view that stereotypical facial expressions can contribute to the experiencing of stereotypical emotions.

Factor A cluster of related items such as those found on an intelligence test.

Factor analysis A statistical technique that allows researchers to determine the relationships among a large number of items such as test items.

Fallopian tube A tube that conducts ova from an ovary to the uterus.

Family therapy A form of therapy in which the family unit is treated as the client.

Farsighted Capable of seeing distant objects with greater acuity than nearby objects.

Fat cells Cells that store fats. Also called *adipose tissue*.

Fear A negative emotion characterized by perception of a threat, sympathetic nervous system activity, and avoidance tendencies.

Feature detectors Neurons in the visual cortex that fire in response to specific features of visual information, such as lines or edges presented at particular angles.

Feedback Information about one's own behavior.

Feeling-of-knowing experience See *tip-of-the-tongue phenomenon*.

Female sexual arousal disorder A sexual dysfunction characterized by difficulty in becoming sexually aroused, as defined by vaginal lubrication, or sustaining arousal long enough to engage in satisfying sexual relations.

Feminists People (of both genders) who seek social change and legislation to reverse discrimination against women and to otherwise advance the concerns of women.

Fetus The developing organism from the third month following conception through childbirth, during which time there are maturation of organ systems and dramatic gains in length and weight.

Fight-or-flight reaction Cannon's term for a hypothesized innate adaptive response to the perception of danger.

File-drawer problem In research, the tendency to file away (and forget) negative results, such that positive results tend to achieve greater visibility or impact than they may deserve.

Final acceptance The fifth stage in Kübler-Ross's theory of dying, which is characterized by lack of feeling.

Fissure Valley—referring to the valleys in the wrinkled surface of the cerebral cortex.

Fixation In psychodynamic theory, arrested development. Attachment to objects of an earlier stage.

Fixation time The amount of time spent looking at a visual stimulus. A measure of interest in infants.

Fixed-action pattern   An instinct; abbreviated *FAP*.

Fixed-interval schedule   A partial reinforcement schedule in which a fixed amount of time must elapse between the previous and subsequent times the reinforcement is made available.

Fixed-ratio schedule   A partial reinforcement schedule in which reinforcement is made available after a fixed number of correct responses.

Flashbacks   Distorted perceptions or hallucinations that occur days or weeks after usage of a hallucinogenic drug (usually LSD) but that mimic the effects of the drug.

Flashbulb memories   Memories that are preserved in great detail because they reflect intense emotional experiences.

Flat affect   Monotonous, dull emotional response.

Flooding   A behavioral fear-reduction technique that is based on principles of classical conditioning. Fear-evoking stimuli (CSs) are presented continuously in the absence of actual harm so that fear responses (CRs) are extinguished.

Foot-in-the-door technique   A method of persuasion in which compliance with a large request is encouraged by first asking the recipient of the request to comply with a smaller request.

Forced-choice format   A method of presenting test questions that requires a respondent to select one of a number of possible answers.

Forensic psychology   The field that applies psychological knowledge within the criminal-justice system.

Formal-operational stage   Piaget's fourth stage of cognitive development, characterized by abstract logical and theoretical thought and deduction from principles.

Fovea   A rodless area near the center of the retina where vision is most acute.

Frame of reference   In self theory, one's unique patterning of perceptions and attitudes, according to which one evaluates events.

Framing effect   The influence of wording, or the context in which information is presented, on decision making.

Free association   In psychoanalysis, the uncensored uttering of all thoughts that come to mind.

Free-floating anxiety   Chronic, persistent anxiety. Anxiety that is not tied to particular events.

Frequency distribution   An ordered set of data that indicates how frequently scores appear.

Frequency theory   The theory that the pitch of a sound is reflected in the frequency of the neural impulses that are generated in response.

Frontal lobe   The lobe of the cerebral cortex that is involved with movement and that lies to the front of the central fissure.

Frustration   (1) The thwarting of a motive. (2) The emotion produced by the thwarting of a motive.

Functional analysis   A systematic study of behavior in which one identifies the stimuli that trigger it (antecedents) and the reinforcers that maintain it (consequences).

Functional fixedness   The tendency to view an object in terms of its name or familiar usage; an impediment to creative problem solving.

Functionalism   The school of psychology, founded by William James, that emphasizes the uses or functions of the mind.

Fundamental attribution error   A bias in social perception characterized by the tendency to assume that others act predominantly on the basis of their dispositions, even when there is evidence suggesting the importance of their situations.

G

g   Spearman's symbol for general intelligence, a general factor that the hypothesized underlay more specific abilities.

Galvanic skin response   A sign of sympathetic arousal detected by the amount of sweat in the hand. The greater the amount of sweat, the more electricity is conducted across the skin, suggesting greater sympathetic arousal. Abbreviated *GSR*.

Ganglia   Plural of *ganglion*. A group of neural cell bodies found elsewhere in the body other than the brain or spinal cord.

Ganglion   See *ganglia*.

Ganglion cells   Neurons whose axons form the optic fiber.

Ganzfeld procedure   In ESP research, a method for studying telepathy in which a "sender" tries to mentally transmit information to a "receiver" whose eyes and ears are covered. (*Ganzfeld* is German for "whole field.")

GAS   Abbreviation for general adaptation syndrome.

Gay male   A male who is sexually aroused by, and interested in forming romantic relationships with, other males.

Gender   The state of being female or male.

Gender constancy   The concept that one's gender remains the same, despite superficial changes in appearance or behavior.

Gender identity   One's sense of being female or male.

Gender polarization   The tendency in Western culture to view women and men as opposites in terms of personality and appropriate behavior patterns.

Gender role   A complex cluster of behaviors that characterizes traditional female or male behaviors.

Gender-schema theory   The view that gender identity plus knowledge of the distribution of behavior patterns into feminine and masculine roles motivates and guides the gender-typing of the child.

Gender stability   The concept that one's gender is a permanent feature.

Gender-typing   The process by which people acquire a sense of being female or male and acquire the traits considered typical of females or males.

Gene   The basic building block of heredity, which consists of deoxyribonucleic acid (DNA).

General adaptation syndrome   Selye's term for a theoretical three-stage response to stress. Abbreviated GAS.

General anesthetics   Methods that control pain by putting a person to sleep.

Generalization   (1) The process of going from the particular to the general. (2) In conditioning, the tendency for a conditioned response to be evoked by stimuli that are similar to the stimulus to which the response was conditioned.

Generalized anxiety disorder   Feelings of dread and foreboding and sympathetic arousal of at least 6 months' duration.

Generalized expectancies   In social-learning theory, broad expectations that reflect extensive learning and that are relatively resistant to change.

Generativity versus stagnation   Erikson's seventh stage of psychosocial development; the middle years during which persons find (or fail to find) fulfillment in expressing creativity and in guiding and encouraging the younger generation.

Genetic counseling   Advice or counseling that concerns the probability that a couple's offspring will have genetic abnormalities.

Genetics   The branch of biology that studies heredity.

Genital stage   In psychodynamic theory, the fifth and mature stage of psychosexual development, characterized by preferred expression of libido through intercourse with an adult of the opposite gender.

Genuineness   Recognition and open expression of one's feelings. A quality of the good person-centered therapist.

Germinal stage   The first stage of prenatal development during which the dividing mass of cells has not become implanted in the uterine wall.

Gestalt psychology   The school of psychology that emphasizes the tendency to organize perceptions into wholes, to integrate separate stimuli into meaningful patterns.

Gestalt therapy   Fritz Perls's form of psychotherapy which attempts to integrate conflicting parts of the personality through directive methods designed to help clients perceive their whole selves.

Glass ceiling   The unspoken limits that prevent many women from being promoted into the upper levels of management in organizations. The "ceiling" is the limit itself, and the concept of "glass" refers to women's ability to see through the limit they cannot penetrate.

Glaucoma   An eye disease characterized by increased fluid pressure within the eye. A cause of blindness.

Glial cells   Cells that nourish and insulate neurons, direct their growth, and remove waste products from the nervous system.

Grasp reflex   An infant reflex in which an object placed on the palms or soles is grasped. Also called *palmar* or *plantar reflex.*

Gray matter   In the spinal cord, the neurons and neural segments that are involved in spinal reflexes. They are gray in appearance. Also see *white matter.*

Groupthink   A process in which group members, as they make decisions, are influenced by cohesiveness and a dynamic leader to ignore external realities.

Growth hormone   A pituitary hormone that regulates growth.

Growth hormone releasing factor   A hormone produced by the hypothalamus that causes the pituitary to secrete growth hormone.

GSR   Abbreviation for *galvanic skin response.*

H

Habit   A response to a stimulus that becomes automatic with repetition.

Habituate   To become accustomed to a stimulus, as determined by no longer showing a response to the stimulus.

Hallucination   A sensory experience in the absence of sensory stimulation that is confused with reality.

Hallucinogenic   Giving rise to hallucinations.

Halo effect   The tendency for one's general impression of a person to influence one's perception of aspects of, or performances by, that person.

Hammer   A bone of the middle ear.

Hashish   A psychedelic drug derived from the resin of *Cannabis sativa.* Often called "hash."

Hassle   A source of annoyance or aggravation.

Health psychology   The field of psychology that studies the relationships between psychological factors (e.g., attitudes, beliefs, situational influences, and overt behavior patterns) and the prevention and treatment of physical illness.

Hebephrenic schizophrenia   See *disorganized schizophrenia.*

Hemoglobin   The substance in the blood that carries oxygen.

Heredity   The transmission of traits from one generation to another through genes.

Heroin   A powerful opioid that provides a euphoric "rush" and feelings of well-being.

Hertz   A unit expressing the frequency of sound waves. One Hertz, or *1 Hz,* equals one cycle per second.

Heterosexual   A person who is sexually aroused by, and interested in forming romantic relationships with, people of the opposite gender.

Heuristic device   A rule of thumb that helps us simplify and solve problems.

Higher-order conditioning   (1) According to cognitive psychologists, the learning of relations among events, none of which evokes an unlearned response. (2) According to behaviorists, a classical-conditioning procedure in which a previously neutral stimulus comes to elicit the response brought forth by a *conditioned* stimulus by being paired repeatedly with that conditioned stimulus.

Hippocampus   A part of the limbic system of the brain that plays an important role in the formation of new memories.

Histogram   A graphic representation of a frequency distribution that uses rectangular solids.

HIV   See *human immunodeficiency virus.*

Holocaust   The name given the Nazi murder of millions of Jews during World War II.

Holophrase   A single word used to express complex meanings.

Homeostasis   The tendency of the body to maintain a steady state, such as body temperature or level of sugar in the blood.

Homosexuality   See *sexual orientation, gay male, lesbian.*

Homunculus   Latin for "little man." A homunculus within the brain was once thought to govern human behavior.

Hormone   A substance secreted by an endocrine gland that promotes development of body structures or regulates bodily functions.

Horoscope   A forecast based on astrological (pseudoscientific) principles. (From Greek roots referring to observation *[skopos]* of the hour *[hora]* during which one was born.)

Hot reactors   People who respond to stress with accelerated heart rate and constriction of blood vessels in peripheral areas of the body.

Hue   The color of light, as determined by its wavelength.

Human factors   The field that studies the efficiency and safety of person–machine systems and work environments.

Human immunodeficiency virus   The virus that gives rise to acquired immune deficiency syndrome (AIDS) by destroying cells of the immune system and leaving the body prey to opportunistic diseases. Abbreviated *HIV.* Sometimes referred to as "the AIDS virus."

Humanism   The philosophy (and school of psychology) that asserts that people are conscious, self-aware, and capable of free choice, self-fulfillment, and ethical behavior.

Humanistic psychology   The school of psychology that assumes the existence of the self and emphasizes the importance of consciousness, self-awareness, and the freedom to make choices.

Human-relations theories   Theories that hold that efficient organizations are structured according to the characteristics and needs of the individual worker.

Hyperactivity   A disorder found most frequently in young boys, characterized by restlessness and short attention span. It is thought to reflect immaturity of the nervous system.

Hyperglycemia   A disorder caused by excess sugar in the blood that can lead to coma and death.

Hypermnesia   Greatly enhanced memory.

Hyperphagic   Characterized by excessive eating.

Hypertension   High blood pressure.

Hyperthyroidism   A condition caused by excess thyroxin and characterized by excitability, weight loss, and insomnia.

Hypnagogic state   The drowsy interval between waking and sleeping, characterized by brief, hallucinatory, dreamlike experiences.

Hypnosis   A condition in which people appear to be highly suggestible and behave as though they are in a trance.

Hypoactive sexual desire disorder   Persistent or recurrent lack of sexual fantasies and of interest in sexual activity.

Hypochondriasis   Persistent belief that one has a medical disorder despite the lack of medical findings.

Hypoglycemia   A metabolic disorder that is characterized by shakiness, dizziness, and lack of energy. It is caused by a low level of sugar in the blood.

Hypothalamus   A bundle of nuclei below the thalamus involved in the regulation of body temperature, motivation, and emotion.

Hypothesis   An assumption about behavior that is tested through research.

Hypothesis testing   In concept formation, an active process in which we try to ferret out the meanings of concepts by testing our assumptions.

Hypothyroidism   A condition caused by a deficiency of thyroxin and characterized by sluggish behavior and a low metabolic rate.

Hysterical disorder, conversion type   Former term for *conversion disorder.*

I

Icon   A mental representation of a visual stimulus that is held briefly in sensory memory.

Iconic memory   The sensory register that briefly holds mental representations of visual stimuli.

Id   In psychodynamic theory, the psychic structure that is present at birth and that is governed by the pleasure principle. The id represents physiological drives and is fully unconscious.

Idealize To think of as being perfect, without flaws.

Ideas of persecution Erroneous beliefs (delusions) that one is being victimized or persecuted.

Identification (1) In psychodynamic theory, unconscious incorporation of the personality of another person. (2) In social-learning theory, a broad, continuous process of imitation during which children strive to become like role models.

Identity crisis According to Erikson, a period of inner conflict during which one examines his or her values and makes decisions about life roles.

Identity diffusion See *role diffusion*.

Ill-defined problem A problem in which the original state, the goal, or the rules are less than clear.

Illusions Sensations that give rise to misperceptions.

Imbalance In balance theory, an uncomfortable condition in which persons whom we like disagree with us.

Immune system The system of the body that recognizes and destroys foreign agents (antigens) that invade the body.

Imprinting A process that occurs during a critical period in an organism's development, in which that organism forms an attachment that will afterward be difficult to modify.

Incentive An object, person, or situation perceived as being capable of satisfying a need.

Incest taboo The cultural prohibition against marrying or having sexual relations with a close blood relative.

Incidence The extent to which an event occurs.

Incubation In problem solving, a hypothetical process that sometimes occurs when we stand back from a frustrating problem for a while and the solution suddenly appears.

Incus A bone of the middle ear. Latin for "anvil."

Independent variable A condition in a scientific study that is manipulated so that its effects may be observed.

Indiscriminate attachment The showing of attachment behaviors toward any person.

Individualist A person who defines herself or himself in terms of personal traits and gives priority to her or his own goals.

Individual psychology Adler's psychodynamic theory, which emphasizes feelings of inferiority and the creative self.

Individuation The process by which one separates from others and gains control over one's own behavior.

Inductive reasoning A form of reasoning in which we reason from individual cases or particular facts to a general conclusion.

Industrial psychology The field of psychology that studies the relationships between people and work.

Industry versus inferiority Erikson's fourth stage of psychosocial development in which the child is challenged to master the fundamentals of technology during the primary school years.

Infant A very young organism, a baby.

Infantile autism A developmental disorder of childhood, characterized by extreme aloneness, communication problems, preservation of sameness, and ritualistic behavior.

Infer Draw a conclusion.

Inference Conclusion.

Inferential statistics The branch of statistics concerned with the confidence with which conclusions drawn about samples may be extended to the populations from which they were drawn.

Inferiority complex Feelings of inferiority hypothesized by Adler to serve as a central source of motivation.

Inflammation Increased blood flow to an injured area of the body, resulting in redness, warmth, and increased supply of white blood cells.

Inflections Grammatical markers that change the forms of words to indicate grammatical relationships such as number and tense.

Information processing The processes by which information is encoded, stored, and retrieved.

Informed consent Agreement to participate in research after receiving information about the purposes of the study and the nature of the treatments.

Inhibited orgasm Persistent or recurrent delay in, or absence of, orgasm in a sexually excited person who has been engaging in sexually stimulating activity.

Inhibited sexual desire Lack of interest in sexual activity, usually accompanied by absence of sexual fantasies.

Inhibited sexual excitement Persistent lack of sexual response during sexual activity.

Inhibitory synapse A synapse that influences receiving neurons in the direction of not firing by encouraging changes in their membrane permeability in the direction of the resting potential.

Initial-preattachment phase According to Ainsworth, the first phase in forming bonds of attachment, which is characterized by indiscriminate attachment.

Initiative versus guilt Erikson's third stage of psychosocial development, during which the child is challenged to add planning and "attacking" to the exercise of choice.

Innate Existing at birth. Unlearned, natural.

Innate fixed-action pattern An instinct.

Inner ear The cochlea.

Insanity A legal term descriptive of a person judged to be incapable of recognizing right from wrong or of conforming his or her behavior to the law.

Insecure attachment A negative type of attachment, in which children show indifference or ambivalence toward attachment figures.

Insight (1) In Gestalt psychology, the sudden perception of relationships among elements of the perceptual field, allowing the sudden solution of a problem. (2) In psychotherapy, awareness of one's genuine motives and feelings.

Insomnia A term for three types of sleeping problems: (1) difficulty falling asleep (sleep-onset insomnia); (2) difficulty remaining asleep; and (3) waking early.

Instinct An inherited disposition to activate specific behavior patterns that are designed to reach certain goals.

Instinctive Inborn, natural, unlearned.

Instructional objective A clear statement of what is to be learned.

Instrumental conditioning Another term for *operant conditioning*, reflecting the fact that in operant conditioning, the learned behavior is instrumental in achieving certain effects.

Instrumental learning See *instrumental conditioning*.

Insulin A pancreatic hormone that stimulates the metabolism of sugar.

Intellectualization A defense mechanism in which threatening events are viewed with emotional detachment.

Intelligence A complex and controversial concept: (1) Learning ability, as contrasted with achievement. (2) Defined by David Wechsler as the "capacity . . . to understand the world [and the] resourcefulness to cope with its challenges."

Intelligence quotient (1) Originally, a ratio obtained by dividing a child's mental age on an intelligence test by his or her chronological age. (2) Generally, a score on an intelligence test. Abbreviated *IQ*.

Interactionism An approach to understanding behavior that emphasizes specification of the relationships among the various determinants of behavior instead of seeking the first cause of behavior.

Interference theory The view that we may forget stored material because other learning interferes with it.

Internal eaters People who eat predominantly in response to internal stimuli, like hunger pangs. See *external eater*.

"Internals" People who have an internal locus of control—who perceive the ability to attain reinforcements as being largely within themselves.

Interneuron A neuron that transmits a neural impulse from a sensory neuron to a motor neuron.

Interpersonal attraction See *attraction*.

Interposition A monocular cue for depth based on the fact that closer objects obscure vision of objects behind them.

Interpretation In psychoanalysis, an analyst's explanation of a client's utterance according to psychodynamic theory.

Intimacy versus isolation Erikson's sixth stage of psychosocial development; the young adult years during which persons are challenged to commit themselves to intimate relationships with others.

Intonation The use of pitches of varying levels to help communicate meaning.

Intoxication Drunkenness.

Intrapsychic Referring to the psychodynamic movement of psychic energy among the psychic structures hypothesized by Sigmund Freud.

Introjection In psychodynamic theory, the bringing within oneself of the personality of another individual.

Introspection An objective approach to describing one's mental content.

Introversion A trait characterized by intense imagination and the tendency to inhibit impulses. Opposite of *extroversion*.

Intuitive The direct learning or knowing of something without conscious use of reason.

Involuntary Automatic, not consciously controlled—referring to functions like heartbeat and dilation of the pupils.

IQ Intelligence quotient. A score on an intelligence test.

Iris A muscular membrane whose dilation regulates the amount of light that enters the eye.

J

James–Lange theory The theory that certain external stimuli trigger stereotypical patterns of activity and autonomic arousal. Emotions are the cognitive representations of this behavior and arousal.

Just noticeable difference The minimal amount by which a source of energy must be increased or decreased so that a difference in intensity will be perceived. Abbreviated *jnd*.

K

Kinesthesis The sense that provides information about the position and motion of parts of the body.

Knobs Swellings at the ends of axon terminals. Also referred to as *bulbs* or *buttons*.

Knowledge-acquisition components According to Sternberg, components of intelligence that are used in gaining knowledge, such as encoding and relating new knowledge to existing knowledge.

Korsakoff's syndrome See Wernicke-Korsakoff syndrome.

L

La belle indifférence A French term descriptive of the lack of concern shown by some persons with conversion disorder.

LAD Acronym for *language acquisition device*.

Language The communication of information through symbols that are arranged according to rules of grammar.

Language acquisition device In psycholinguistic theory, neural "prewiring" that is theorized to facilitate the child's learning of grammar. Abbreviated *LAD*.

Larynx The structure in the throat that contains the vocal cords.

Latency stage In psychodynamic theory, the fourth stage of psychosexual development during which sexual impulses are repressed.

Latent content In psychodynamic theory, the symbolized or underlying content of dreams.

Latent learning Learning that is not exhibited at the time of learning but is shown when adequate reinforcement is introduced.

Lateral fissure The valley in the cerebral cortex that separates the temporal lobe from the frontal and parietal lobes.

Lateral hypothalamus An area at the side of the hypothalamus that appears to function as a start-eating center.

Law of effect Thorndike's principle that responses are "stamped in" by rewards and "stamped out" by punishments.

Learned helplessness A model for the acquisition of depressive behavior, based on findings that organisms in aversive situations learn to show inactivity when their operants are not reinforced.

Learning (1) According to cognitive theorists, the process by which organisms make relatively permanent changes in the way they represent the environment because of experience. These changes influence the organism's behavior. (2) According to behaviorists, a relatively permanent change in behavior that results from experience.

Least-restrictive placement Placement of exceptional students in settings that are as normal and as much in the maintstream of education as possible, in accord with the Education for All Handicapped Children Act.

Lens A transparent body between the iris and the vitreous humor of the eye that focuses an image onto the retina.

Lesbian A female who is sexually aroused by, and interested in forming romantic relationships with, other females.

Lesion An injury that results in impaired behavior or loss of a function.

Leukocytes The white blood cells of the immune system.

Libido (1) In psychodynamic theory, the energy of Eros, the sexual instinct. (2) Generally, sexual interest or drive.

Lie detector See *polygraph*.

Life-change units Numbers assigned to various life events that indicate the degree of stress they cause.

Light Electromagnetic energy of various wavelengths. The part of the spectrum of energy that stimulates the eye and produces visual sensations.

Limbic system A group of brain structures that form a fringe along the inner edge of the cerebrum. These structures are involved in memory and motivation.

Linguistic relativity hypothesis The view that language structures the way in which we perceive the world. As a consequence, our thoughts would be limited by the concepts available in our languages.

Linguists Scientists who study the structure, functions, and origins of language.

Locus of control The place (locus) to which an individual attributes control over the receiving of reinforcements—either inside or outside the self.

Long-term memory The type or stage of memory capable of relatively permanent storage.

Love A strong, positive emotion with many meanings. See, for example, *romantic love* and *attachment*.

Low-balling A sales method in which extremely attractive terms are offered to induce a person to make a commitment. Once the commitment is made, the terms are revised.

LSD Lysergic acid diethylamide. A hallucinogenic drug.

Lucid dream A dream in which we seem to be awake and aware that we are dreaming.

Lysergic acid diethylamide A hallucinogenic drug. Abbreviated *LSD*.

M

Magnetic resonance imaging Formation of a computer-generated image of the anatomical details of the brain by measuring the signals that these structures emit when the head is placed in a strong magnetic field. Abbreviated *MRI*.

Mainstreaming The practice of placing exceptional students in education environments that are as normal as possible.

Maintenance rehearsal Mental repetition of information in order to keep it in memory.

Major depression A severe mood disorder in which the person may show loss of appetite, psychomotor symptoms, and impaired reality testing.

Major tranquilizer   A drug that decreases severe anxiety or agitation in psychotic patients or in violent individuals.

Male erectile disorder   A sexual dysfunction characterized by difficulty in becoming sexually aroused, as defined by achieving erection, or in sustaining arousal long enough to engage in satisfying sexual relations.

Malingering   Pretending to be ill to escape duty or work.

Malleus   A bone of the middle ear. Latin for "hammer."

Mania   A state characterized by elation and restlessness. (A Greek word meaning "madness.")

Manic-depression   Former term for *bipolar disorder.*

Manifest content   In the psychodynamic theory of dreams, the reported or perceived content of dreams.

Mantra   A word or sound that is repeated in transcendental meditation as a means of narrowing consciousness and inducing relaxation.

Marijuana   The dried vegetable matter of the *Cannabis sativa* plant. A mild hallucinogenic drug that is most frequently taken in by smoking.

Masochism   The attainment of gratification, frequently sexual, through the receiving of pain or humiliation.

Masturbation   Self-stimulation of the sexual organs.

Matching hypothesis   The view that people tend to choose persons similar to themselves in attractiveness and attitudes in the formation of interpersonal relationships.

Maturation   Changes that result from heredity and minimal nutrition but that do not appear to require learning or exercise. A gradual, orderly unfolding or developing of new structures or behaviors as a result of heredity.

Mean   A type of average calculated by dividing the sum of scores by the number of scores.

Means–end analysis   A heuristic device in which we try to solve a problem by evaluating the difference between the current situation and the goal.

Median   A type of average defined as the score beneath which 50% of the cases fall.

Mediation   In information processing, a method of improving memory by linking two items with a third that ties them together.

Medical model   The view that abnormal behavior is symptomatic of underlying illness.

Meditation   A systematic narrowing of attention that slows the metabolism and helps produce feelings of relaxation.

Medulla   An oblong-shaped area of the hindbrain involved in heartbeat and respiration.

Meiosis   A process of reduction division in which sperm and ova are formed, each of which contains 23 chromosomes.

Memory   The processes by which information is encoded, stored, and retrieved.

Memory trace   An assumed change in the nervous system that reflects the impression made by a stimulus. Memory traces are said to be "held" in sensory registers.

Menarche   The onset of menstruation.

Menopause   The cessation of menstruation.

Menstrual synchrony   The convergence of the menstrual cycles of women who spend time in close quarters.

Menstruation   The monthly shedding of the uterine lining by nonpregnant women.

Mental age   The accumulated months of credit that a test taker earns on the Stanford–Binet Intelligence Scale.

Mental set   (1) Readiness to respond to a situation in a set manner. (2) In problem solving, a tendency to respond to a new problem with an approach that was successful with similar problems.

Mescaline   A hallucinogenic drug derived from the mescal (peyote) cactus. In religious ceremonies, Mexican Indians chew the buttonlike structures at the tops of the rounded stems of the plant.

Metabolism   In organisms, a continuous process that converts food into energy.

Metacognition   Awareness and control of one's cognitive abilities, as shown by the intentional use of cognitive strategies in solving problems.

Metacomponents   According to Sternberg, components of intelligence that are based on self-awareness of our intellectual processes.

Metamemory   Self-awareness of the ways in which memory functions, as shown by use of cognitive strategies to foster the effective encoding, storing, and retrieval of information.

Methadone   An artificial narcotic that is slower acting than, and does not provide the rush of, heroin. Methadone allows heroin addicts to abstain from heroin without experiencing an abstinence syndrome.

Methaqualone   An addictive depressant often referred to as "ludes."

Method of constant stimuli   A psychophysical method for determining thresholds in which the researcher presents stimuli of various magnitudes and asks the subject to report detection.

Method of loci   A method of retaining information in which chunks of new material are related to a series of well-established or well-known images.

Method of savings   A measure of retention in which the difference between the number of repetitions originally required to learn a list and the number of repetitions required to relearn the list after a certain amount of time has elapsed is calculated.

Microspectrophotometry   A method for analyzing the sensitivity of single cones to lights of different wavelengths.

Middle ear   The central part of the ear that contains three small bones, the "hammer," "anvil," and "stirrup."

Midlife crisis   According to theorists of adult development, a crisis experienced by many people at about age 40 when they realize that life may be halfway over and they feel trapped in meaningless life roles.

Migraine headache   A throbbing headache, usually occurring on one side of the head, that stems from change in the blood supply to the head. It is often accompanied by nausea and impaired vision.

Mind   That part of consciousness that is involved in perception and awareness.

Minor tranquilizer   A drug that relieves feelings of anxiety and tension.

Mitosis   The process of cell division by which the identical genetic code is carried into new cells in the body.

Mnemonics   A system for remembering in which items are related to easily recalled sets of symbols such as acronyms, phrases, or jingles.

Mode   A type of average defined as the most frequently occurring score in a distribution.

Model   In social-cognitive theory: (1) As a noun, an organism that engages in a response that is imitated by another organism. (2) As a verb, to engage in behavior patterns that are imitated by others.

Monoamine oxidase inhibitors   Antidepressant drugs that work by blocking the action of an enzyme that breaks down norepinephrine and serotonin. Abbreviated *MAO inhibitors.*

Monochromat   A person who is sensitive to the intensity of light only and thus colorblind.

Monocular cues   Stimuli that suggest depth and that can be perceived with only one eye, such as perspective and interposition.

Monozygotic twins   Twins who develop from the same zygote, thus carrying the same genetic instructions. Identical twins. Abbreviated *MZ twins.* See *dizygotic twins.*

Moral principle   In psychodynamic theory, the governing principle of the superego, which sets moral standards and enforces adherence to them.

Moro reflex   An infant reflex characterized by arching of the back and drawing up of the legs in response to a sudden, startling stimulus. Also called the *startle reflex.*

Morpheme   The smallest unit of meaning in a language.

Morphine   A narcotic derived from opium that reduces pain and produces feelings of well-being.

Morphology   The study of the units of meaning in a language.

Motion parallax   A monocular cue for depth based on the perception that nearby objects appear to move more rapidly in relation to our own motion.

Motive   A hypothetical state within an organism that propels the organism toward a goal.

Motor cortex   The section of cerebral cortex that lies in the frontal lobe, just across the central fissure from the sensory cortex. Neural impulses in the motor cortex are linked to muscular responses.

Multiple approach–avoidance conflict   A type of conflict in which a number of goals each produces approach and avoidance motives.

Multiple personality disorder   The earlier term for *dissociative identity disorder*. A dissociative disorder in which a person has two or more distinct identities or personalities.

Mutation   Sudden variations in the genetic code that usually occur as a result of environmental influences.

Mutism   Refusal to talk.

Myelination   The process by which the axons of neurons become coated with a fatty, insulating substance.

Myelin sheath   A fatty substance that encases and insulates axons, permitting more rapid transmission of neural impulses.

N

***n* Ach**   The need for achievement; the need to master, to accomplish difficult things.

***n* Aff**   The need for affiliation; the need to be associated with groups.

Narcolepsy   A sleep disorder characterized by uncontrollable seizures of sleep during the waking state.

Narcotics   Drugs used to relieve pain and induce sleep. The term is usually reserved for opioids.

Native-language approach   A method of teaching a second language in which children are at first taught in the language spoken in the home.

Naturalistic observation   A method of scientific investigation in which organisms are observed carefully and unobtrusively in their natural environments.

Nature   In behavior genetics, inherited influences on behavior, as contrasted with *nurture*.

Nearsightedness   Inability to see distant objects with the acuity with which a person with normal vision can see distant objects.

Need   A state of deprivation.

Need for achievement   The need to master, to accomplish difficult things.

Need for affiliation   The need for affiliation; the need to be associated with groups.

Negative correlation   A relationship between two variables in which one variable increases as the other variable decreases.

Negative feedback   Descriptive of a system in which information that a quantity (e.g., of a hormone) has reached a set point suspends action of the agency (e.g., a gland) that gives rise to that quantity.

Negative instance   In concept formation, events that are *not* examples of a concept.

Negative reinforcer   A reinforcer that increases the frequency of operant behavior when it is removed. Pain, anxiety, and disapproval usually, but not always, function as negative reinforcers. See *positive reinforcer*.

Neodissociation theory   A theory that explains hypnotic events in terms of an ability to divide our awareness so that we can focus on hypnotic instructions and, at the same time, perceive outside sources of stimulation.

Neo-Freudians   Theorists in the psychodynamic tradition who usually place less emphasis than Freud did on the importance of sexual impulses and unconscious determinants of behavior. Instead, they place more emphasis than Freud did on conscious motives and rational decision making.

Neonate   A newborn child.

Nerve   A bundle of axons from many neurons.

Neural impulse   The electrochemical discharge of a neuron, or nerve cell.

Neuron   A nerve cell.

Neuropeptide   A short chain of amino acids (peptide) that functions as a neurotransmitter.

Neurosis   One of a number of psychological disorders characterized chiefly by anxiety, feelings of dread and foreboding, and avoidance behavior. Neuroses are theorized to stem from unconscious conflict. (Contemporary systems of classifying psychological disorders focus more on observable behavior and therefore deemphasize this concept.)

Neuroticism   A trait in which a person is given to emotional instability, anxiety, feelings of foreboding, inhibition of impulses, and avoidance behavior.

Neurotransmitter   A chemical substance that is involved in the transmission of neural impulses from one neuron to another.

Nicotine   A stimulant found in tobacco smoke.

Nightmare   A frightening dream that usually occurs during rapid-eye-movement (REM) sleep.

Night terrors   See *sleep terrors*.

Node of Ranvier   A noninsulated segment of an otherwise myelinated axon.

Noise   (1) In signal-detection theory, any unwanted signal that interferes with perception of the desired signal. (2) More generally, a combination of dissonant sounds.

Nonbalance   In balance theory, a condition in which persons whom we dislike do not agree with us.

Nonconscious   Descriptive of bodily processes, such as the growing of hair, of which we cannot become conscious. We may know that our hair is growing, but we cannot directly experience the biological process.

Non-rapid-eye-movement sleep   Stages 1 through 4 of sleep, which are not characterized by rapid eye movements. Abbreviated *NREM sleep*.

Nonsense syllables   Meaningless sets of two consonants, with a vowel sandwiched in between, that are used to study memory.

Norepinephrine   A neurotransmitter whose action is similar to that of the hormone *epinephrine* and which may play a role in depression.

Normal curve   A graphic presentation of a normal distribution, showing a bell shape.

Normal distribution   A symmetrical distribution in which approximately two thirds of the cases lie within a standard deviation of the mean. A distribution that represents chance deviations of a variable.

Normative data   Information concerning the behavior of a population.

Norm-referenced testing   A testing approach in which scores are derived by comparing the number of items answered correctly with the average performance of others.

Novel stimulation   (1) New or different stimulation. (2) A hypothesized primary drive to experience new or different stimulation.

Noxious   Harmful, injurious.

Nuclear magnetic resonance   See *magnetic resonance imaging*.

Nuclei   Plural of *nucleus*. A group of neural cell bodies found in the brain or spinal cord.

Nurturance   The quality of nourishing, rearing, and fostering the development of children, animals, or plants.

Nurture   In behavior genetics, environmental influences on behavior, including factors such as nutrition, culture, socioeconomic status, and learning. Contrast with *nature*.

O

Objective   Of known or perceived objects rather than existing only in the mind; real.

Objective morality   According to Piaget, objective moral judgments assign guilt according to the amount of damage done rather than the motives of the actor.

Objective tests   Tests whose items must be answered in a specified, limited manner. Tests that have concrete answers that are considered to be correct.

Object permanence   Recognition that objects removed from sight still exist, as demonstrated in young children by continued pursuit.

Observational learning   In social-learning theory, the acquisition of expectations and skills by observing the behavior of others. As opposed to operant conditioning, skill acquisition by means of observational learning occurs without the emission and reinforcement of a response.

Obsession   A recurring thought or image that seems to be beyond control.

Occipital lobe   The lobe of the cerebral cortex that is involved in vision. It lies below and behind the parietal lobe and behind the temporal lobe.

Odor   The characteristic of a substance that makes it perceptible to the sense of smell. An odor is a sample of the molecules of the substance being sensed.

Oedipus complex   In psychodynamic theory, a conflict of the phallic stage in which the boy wishes to possess his mother sexually and perceives his father as a rival in love.

Olfactory   Having to do with the sense of smell.

Olfactory membrane   A membrane high in each nostril that contains receptor neurons for the sense of smell.

Olfactory nerve   The nerve that transmits information about odors from olfactory receptors to the brain.

Opaque   (1) Not permitting the passage of light. (2) In psychoanalysis, descriptive of the analyst, who is expected to hide her or his own feelings from the client.

Operant behavior   Voluntary responses that are reinforced.

Operant conditioning   A simple form of learning in which an organism learns to engage in behavior because it is reinforced.

Operational definition   A definition of a variable in terms of the methods used to create or measure the variable.

Opioid   An addictive drug derived from the opium poppy, or similar in chemical structure, that provides a euphoric rush and depresses the nervous system.

Opponent-process theory   (1) In sensation and perception, the theory that color vision is made possible by three types of cones, some of which respond to red or green light, some to blue or yellow light, and some to the intensity of light only. (2) In motivation and emotion, the view that our emotions trigger opposing emotions.

Optic nerve   The nerve that transmits sensory information from the eye to the brain.

Optimal arousal   A level of arousal at which an organism has the greatest feelings of well-being or functions most efficiently.

Oral fixation   In psychodynamic theory, attachment to objects and behaviors characteristic of the oral stage.

Oral stage   The first stage in Freud's theory of psychosexual development, during which gratification is obtained primarily through oral activities like sucking and biting.

Organizational analysis   Evaluation of the goals and resources of an organization.

Organizing psychology   The field of psychology that studies the structure and functions of organizations.

Organizational effects   The directional effects of sex hormones—for example, along stereotypical masculine or feminine lines.

Organ of Corti   The receptor for hearing, which lies on the basilar membrane in the cochlea. Called the command post of hearing, it contains the receptor cells that transmit auditory information to the auditory nerve.

Orgasm   The height or climax of sexual excitement, involving involuntary muscle contractions, release of sexual tensions, and, usually, intense subjective feelings of pleasure.

Orienting reflex   An unlearned response in which an organism attends to a stimulus.

Osmoreceptors   Receptors in the hypothalamus that are sensitive to depletion of fluid in the body.

Osteoporosis   A condition caused by calcium deficiency and characterized by brittleness of the bones.

Outer ear   The funnel-shaped outer part of the ear that transmits sound waves to the eardrum.

Oval window   A membrane that transmits vibrations from the stirrup of the middle ear to the inner ear.

Ovaries   The female reproductive organs located in the abdominal cavity. The ovaries produce egg cells (ova) and the hormones estrogen and progesterone.

Overextension   Overgeneralizing the use of words into situations in which they do not apply (characteristic of the speech of young children).

Overregularization   The formation of plurals and past tenses of irregular nouns and verbs according to rules of grammar that apply to regular nouns and verbs (characteristic of the speech of young children).

Overtones   Tones higher in frequency than those played on an instrument. Overtones result from vibrations throughout the instrument.

Ovulation   The releasing of an egg cell (ovum) from an ovary.

Oxytocin   A pituitary hormone that stimulates labor (childbirth).

P

Paired associates   Nonsense syllables presented in pairs in experiments that measure recall. After viewing pairs, participants are shown one member of each pair and asked to recall the other.

Palmar reflex   See *grasp reflex.*

Pancreas   A gland behind the stomach whose secretions, including insulin, influence the level of sugar in the blood.

Panic disorder   The recurrent experiencing of attacks of extreme anxiety in the absence of external stimuli that usually elicit anxiety.

Paradoxical intention   Achieving one's goals by undertaking an apparently opposing course of action.

Paradoxical sleep   Another term for the period of sleep during which rapid eye movements occur. The term *paradoxical* reflects the fact that brain waves found during REM sleep suggest a level of arousal similar to that shown during the waking state.

Paranoia   A rare psychotic disorder in which a person shows a persistent delusional system but not the confusion of the paranoid schizophrenic.

Paranoid personality disorder   A disorder characterized by persistent suspiciousness but not the disorganization of paranoid schizophrenia.

Paranoid schizophrenia   A subtype of schizophrenia characterized primarily by delusions—commonly of persecution—and by vivid hallucinations.

Paraphilia   A disorder in which the person shows sexual arousal in response to unusual or bizarre objects or situations.

Parasympathetic nervous system   The branch of the autonomic nervous system that is most active during processes such as digestion and relaxation that restore the body's reserves of energy. See *sympathetic division.*

Parent   In transactional analysis, a moralistic ego state.

Parietal lobe   The lobe of the cerebral cortex that lies behind the central fissure and that is involved in body senses.

Partial reinforcement   One of several types of reinforcement schedules in which correct responses receive intermittent reinforcement, as opposed to *continuous reinforcement.*

Participant modeling   A behavior-therapy technique in which a client observes and imitates a person who approaches and copes with feared objects or situations.

Passionate love   See *romantic love.*

Pathogen   An organism such as a bacterium or virus that can cause disease.

Pathological gambler   A person who gambles habitually despite consistent losses. A compulsive gambler.

PCP   Phencyclidine; a hallucinogenic drug.

Peak experience   In humanistic theory, a brief moment of rapture that stems from the realization that one is on the path toward self-actualization.

Pelvic inflammatory disease   Inflammation of the woman's abdominal region that is caused by pathogens such as the gonorrhea bacterium and characterized by fever, local pain, and, frequently, fertility problems. Abbreviated *PID.*

Penis envy   In psychodynamic theory, jealousy of the male sexual organ attributed to girls in the phallic stage.

Pepsinogen   A substance that helps the body digest proteins.

Perceived self-efficacy   In social-learning theory, a person's belief that she or he can achieve goals through her or his own efforts.

Perception   The process by which sensations are organized into an inner representation of the world — a psychological process through which we interpret sensory information.

Perceptual organization   The tendency to integrate perceptual elements into meaningful patterns.

Performance anxiety   Fear concerning whether or not one will be able to perform adequately.

Performance components   According to Sternberg, the mental operations used in processing information.

Period of the ovum   The period following conception before the developing ovum (now fertilized) has become securely implanted in the uterine wall. Another term for the *germinal stage.*

Peripheral nervous system   The part of the nervous system consisting of the somatic nervous system and the autonomic nervous system.

Permeability   The degree to which a membrane allows a substance to pass through it.

Personality   The distinct patterns of behaviors, including thoughts and feelings, that characterize a person's adaptation to the demands of life.

Personality disorder   An enduring pattern of maladaptive behavior that is a source of distress to the individual or to others.

Personality structure   One's total pattern of traits.

Personal space   A psychological boundary that surrounds a person and permits that person to maintain a protective distance from others.

Person-centered therapy   Carl Rogers's method of psychotherapy, which emphasizes the creation of a warm, therapeutic atmosphere that frees clients to engage in self-expression and self-exploration.

Person variables   In social-learning theory, determinants of behavior that lie within the person, including competencies, encoding strategies, expectancies, subjective values, and self-regulatory systems and plans.

Perspective   A monocular cue for depth based on the convergence (coming together) of parallel lines as they recede into the distance.

pH   A chemical symbol expressing the acidity of a solution.

Phallic stage   In psychodynamic theory, the third stage of psychosexual development, characterized by shifting of libido to the phallic region and by the Oedipus and Electra complexes.

Phallic symbol   In psychodynamic theory, an object that represents the penis.

Phencyclidine   A hallucinogenic drug whose name is an acronym for its chemical structure. Abbreviated *PCP.*

Phenomenological   Having to do with subjective, conscious experience.

Phenothiazines   Drugs that act as major tranquilizers and that are effective in treating many cases of schizophrenic disorders.

Phenylketonuria   A genetic abnormality transmitted by a recessive gene, in which one is unable to metabolize phenylpyruvic acid, leading to mental retardation. Abbreviated *PKU.*

Pheromones   Chemical secretions detected by the sense of smell that stimulate stereotypical behaviors in other members of the same species.

Phi phenomenon   The perception of movement as a result of sequential presentation of visual stimuli, as with lights going on and off in a row on a theater marquee.

Phobic disorder   Excessive, irrational fear. Fear that is out of proportion to the actual danger and that interferes with one's life. Formerly called *phobic neurosis.*

Phoneme   A basic sound in a language.

Phonology   The study of the basic sounds in a language.

Photographic memory   See *iconic memory.*

Photoreceptors   Cells that respond to light. See *rod* and *cone.*

Phrenology   An unscientific method of analyzing personality by measurement of the shapes and protuberances of the skull.

Physiological   Having to do with the biological functions and vital processes of organisms.

Physiological dependence   Addiction to a drug, which occurs when regular usage renders the presence of the drug within the body the normal state.

Physiological drives   Unlearned drives with a biological basis, such as hunger, thirst, and avoidance of pain. Also called *primary drives.*

Physiological psychologists   Same as biological psychologists.

Pitch   The highness or lowness of a sound, as determined by the frequency of the sound waves.

Pituitary gland   The body's master gland, located in the brain, that secretes growth hormone, prolactin, antidiuretic hormone, and other hormones.

Placebo   A bogus treatment that controls for the effects of expectations. A so-called sugar pill.

Placenta   A membrane that permits the exchange of nutrients and waste products between the mother and the fetus but that does not allow the maternal and fetal bloodstreams to mix.

Place theory   The theory that the pitch of a sound is determined by the section of the basilar membrane that vibrates in response to it.

Plantar reflex   See *grasp reflex.*

Plateau phase   An advanced state of sexual arousal that precedes orgasm.

Pleasure principle   In psychodynamic theory, the principle that governs the id; the demanding of immediate gratification of instinctive needs.

Polarization   (1) In physiological psychology, the readying of a neuron for firing by creating an internal negative charge in relation to the body fluid outside the cell membrane. (2) In social psychology, the taking of an extreme position or attitude on an issue.

Polygenic   Determined by more than one gene.

Polygraph   An instrument that is theorized to be sensitive to whether or not an individual is telling lies by assessing four measures of arousal: heart rate, blood pressure, respiration rate, and galvanic skin response (GSR). Also called a *lie detector.*

Pons   A structure of the hindbrain involved in respiration.

Population   A complete group of organisms or events.

Positive correlation   A relationship between variables in which one variable increases as the other variable also increases.

Positive instance   In concept formation, an example of a concept.

Positive reinforcer   A reinforcer that increases the frequency of operant behavior when it is presented. Food and approval are usually, but not always, positive reinforcers. See *negative reinforcer.*

Positron-emission tomography   Formation of a computer-generated image of the neural activity of parts of the brain by tracing the amount of glucose used by the various parts. Abbreviated *PET scan.*

Postconventional level   According to Kohlberg, a period of moral development during which moral judgments are derived from moral principles and people look to themselves to set moral standards.

Posthypnotic amnesia   Inability to recall material presented while hypnotized, following the suggestion of the hypnotist.

Post-traumatic stress disorder   A disorder that follows a distressing event outside the range of normal human experience. It is characterized by symptoms such as intense fear, avoidance of stimuli associated with the event, and reliving of the event.

Pragmatics   The practical aspects of communication. Adaptation of language to fit the social context.

Precognition   The term means ability to foresee the future; however, most psychologists do not believe that this ability exists. (From the Latin *prae-,* meaning "before," and *cognitio,* meaning "knowledge.")

Preconscious   In psychodynamic theory, descriptive of material of which one is not currently aware but which can be brought into awareness by focusing one's attention. Also see *unconscious.*

Preconventional level   According to Kohlberg, a period of moral development during which moral judgments are based largely on expectation of rewards and punishments.

Prefrontal lobotomy   A form of psychosurgery in which a section of the frontal lobe of the brain is severed or destroyed.

Pregenital   In psychodynamic theory, characteristic of stages less mature than the genital stage.

Prejudice   The unfounded belief that a person or group—on the basis of assumed racial, ethnic, sexual, or other features—will possess negative characteristics or perform inadequately.

Prelinguistic   Prior to the development of language.

Premature ejaculation   Ejaculation that occurs before the couple are satisfied with the duration of coitus.

Premenstrual syndrome   A cluster of symptoms—which may include tension, irritability, depression, and fatigue—that some women experience before menstruating.

Premise   A statement or assertion that serves as the basis for an argument.

Prenatal   Prior to birth.

Preoperational stage   The second of Piaget's stages of cognitive development, characterized by illogical use of words and symbols, egocentrism, animism, artificialism, and objective moral judgments.

Presbyopia   Brittleness of the lens, a condition that impairs visual acuity for nearby objects.

Primacy effect   (1) In information processing, the tendency to recall the initial items in a series of items. (2) In social psychology, the tendency to evaluate others in terms of first impressions.

Primary colors   Colors that we cannot produce by mixing other hues; colors from which other colors are derived.

Primary drives   Unlearned drives; physiological drives.

Primary mental abilities   According to Thurstone, the basic abilities that compose human intelligence.

Primary narcissism   In psychodynamic theory, the type of autism that describes the newborn child who has not learned that he or she is separate from the rest of the world.

Primary prevention   In community psychology, the deterrence of psychological problems before they start.

Primary reinforcer   A stimulus that has reinforcement value without learning. Examples: food, water, warmth, and pain. See *secondary reinforcer*

Primary sex characteristics   Physical traits that distinguish the sexes and that are directly involved in reproduction.

Primate   A member of an order of mammals including monkeys, apes, and human beings.

Prism   A transparent triangular solid that breaks down visible light into the colors of the spectrum.

Proactive interference   Interference from previously learned material in one's ability to retrieve or recall recently learned material. See *retroactive interference.*

Proband   The family member first studied or tested.

Procedural memory   Knowledge of ways of doing things; skill memory.

Productivity   A property of language; the ability to combine words into unlimited, novel sentences.

Progesterone   A sex hormone that promotes growth of the sexual organs and helps maintain pregnancy.

Prognosis   A prediction of the probable course of a disease.

Programmed learning   A method of learning, based on operant conditioning principles, in which complex tasks are broken down into simple steps. The proper performance of each step is reinforced. Incorrect responses go unreinforced but are not punished.

Progressive relaxation   Jacobson's method for reducing muscle tension, which involves alternate tensing and relaxing of muscle groups throughout the body.

Projection   In psychodynamic theory, a defense mechanism in which unacceptable ideas and impulses are cast out or attributed to others.

Projective test   A psychological test that presents questions for which there is no single correct response. A test that presents ambiguous stimuli into which the test taker projects his or her own personality in making a response.

Prolactin   A pituitary hormone that regulates production of milk and, in lower animals, maternal behavior.

Propinquity   Nearness.

Prosocial   Behavior that is characterized by helping others and making a contribution to society.

Prototype   A concept of a category of objects or events that serves as a good example of the category.

Proximity   Nearness. The perceptual tendency to group together objects that are near one another.

Proximodistal   Proceeding from near to far.

***Psi* communication**   (SIGH). The term means the transfer of information through an irregular or unusual process—not the usual senses. However, most psychologists do not believe that psi communication exists.

Psychedelic   Causing hallucinations or delusions or heightening perceptions.

Psychiatrist   A physician who specializes in the application of medical treatments to psychological disorders.

Psychic structure   In psychodynamic theory, a hypothesized mental structure that helps explain various aspects of behavior. See *id, ego,* and *superego.*

Psychoactive   Describing drugs that give rise to psychological effects.

Psychoanalysis   The school of psychology, founded by Sigmund Freud, that emphasizes the importance of unconscious motives and conflicts as determinants of human behavior. Also the name of Freud's methods of psychotherapy and clinical investigation.

Psychodynamic   Descriptive of Freud's view that various forces move within the personality, frequently clashing, and that the outcome of these clashes determines behavior.

Psychogenic amnesia   The earlier term for *dissociative amnesia.* A dissociative disorder marked by loss of episodic memory or self-identity. Skills and general knowledge are usually retained.

Psychogenic fugue   The earlier term for *dissociative fugue.* A dissociative disorder in which one experiences amnesia, then flees to a new location.

Psychokinesis   The term means ability to manipulate objects by thought processes. However, most psychologists do not believe that this ability exists.

Psycholinguist   A psychologist who studies how we perceive and acquire language.

Psycholinguistic theory   The view that language learning involves an interaction between environmental influences and an inborn tendency to acquire language. The emphasis is on the innate tendency.

Psychological androgyny   Possession of both instrumental and warmth–expressiveness traits.

Psychological dependence   Repeated use of a substance as a way of dealing with stress.

Psychological disorders   Patterns of behavior or mental processes that are connected with distress or disability and are not expectable responses to particular events.

Psychological hardiness   A cluster of traits that buffer stress and that are characterized by commitment, challenge, and control.

Psychology   The science that studies behavior and mental processes.

Psychomotor retardation   Slowness in motor activity and, apparently, in thought.

Psychoneuroimmunology   The field that studies the relationships between psychological factors (e.g., attitudes and overt behavior patterns) and the functioning of the immune system.

Psychopath   Another term for a person who shows an antisocial personality disorder.

Psychophysics   The study of the relationships between physical stimuli, such as light and sound, and their perception.

Psychophysiological   Having to do with physical illnesses that are believed to have psychological origins or to be stress related. Also termed *psychosomatic*.

Psychosexual development   In psychodynamic theory, the process by which libidinal energy is expressed through different erogenous zones during different stages of development.

Psychosexual trauma   A distressing sexual experience that may have lingering psychological effects.

Psychosis   A major psychological disorder in which a person shows impaired reality testing and has difficulty meeting the demands of everyday life.

Psychosocial development   Erikson's theory of personality and development, which emphasizes the importance of social relationships and conscious choice throughout eight stages of development, including three stages of adult development.

Psychosomatic   Having to do with physical illnesses that are believed to have psychological origins or to be stress-related. Also termed *psychophysiological*.

Psychosurgery   Biological treatments in which specific areas or structures of the brain are destroyed to promote psychological changes or to relieve disordered behavior.

Psychotherapy   A systematic interaction between a therapist and a client that brings psychological principles to bear on influencing the client's thoughts, feelings, or behaviors to help that client overcome psychological disorders or adjust to problems in living.

Puberty   The period of early adolescence during which hormones spur rapid physical development.

Punishment   An unpleasant stimulus that suppresses the frequency of the behavior it follows.

Pupil   The apparently black opening in the center of the iris, through which light enters the eye.

Pupillary reflex   The automatic adjusting of the irises to permit more or less light to enter the eye.

Pure research   Research conducted without concern for immediate applications.

Q

Quality circle   A regularly scheduled meeting in which a group of workers discusses problems and suggests solutions in order to enhance the quality of products.

R

Rage response   Stereotypical aggressive behavior that can be brought forth in lower animals by electrical stimulation of the brain.

Random sample   A sample drawn in such a manner that every member of a population has an equal chance of being selected.

Random trial and error   In operant conditioning, refers to behavior that occurs prior to learning what behavior is reinforced. The implication is that in a novel situation, the organism happens upon the first correct (reinforced) response by chance.

Range   A measure of variability; the distance between extreme measures or scores in a distribution.

Rapid-eye-movement sleep   A stage of sleep characterized by rapid eye movements that have been linked to dreaming. Abbreviated *REM sleep*. See also *paradoxical sleep*.

Rapid flight of ideas   Rapid speech and topic changes, characteristic of manic behavior.

Rapid smoking   A type of aversive conditioning in which cigarettes are inhaled every few seconds, making the smoke aversive.

Rational-emotive therapy   Albert Ellis's form of cognitive psychotherapy, which focuses on how irrational expectations create negative feelings and maladaptive behavior and which encourages clients to challenge and correct these expectations.

Rationalization   In psychodynamic theory, a defense mechanism in which an individual engages in self-deception, finding justifications for unacceptable ideas, impulses, or behaviors.

Reaction formation   In psychodynamic theory, a defense mechanism in which unacceptable impulses and ideas are kept unconscious through the exaggerated expression of opposing ideas and impulses.

Reaction time   The amount of time required to respond to a stimulus.

Readiness   In developmental psychology, referring to a stage in the maturation of an organism when it is capable of engaging in a certain response.

Reality principle   In psychodynamic theory, the principle that guides ego functioning; consideration of what is practical and possible in gratifying needs.

Reality testing   The capacity to form an accurate mental representation of the world, including socially appropriate behavior, reasonably accurate knowledge of the motives of others, undistorted sensory impressions, and self-insight.

Reasoning   The transforming of information to reach conclusions.

Rebound anxiety   Strong anxiety that can attend the suspension of usage of a tranquilizer.

Recall   Retrieval or reconstruction of learned material.

Recency effect   (1) In information processing, the tendency to recall the last items in a series of items. (2) In social psychology, the tendency to evaluate others in terms of the most recent impression.

Receptive vocabulary   The extent of one's knowledge of the meanings of words that are communicated to one by others.

Receptor site   A location on a receiving neuron that is tailored to receive a neurotransmitter.

Recessive trait   In genetics, a trait that is not expressed when the gene or genes involved have been paired with *dominant* genes. However, recessive traits are transmitted to future generations and expressed if paired with other recessive genes. See *dominant trait*.

Reciprocity   (1) Mutual action. Treating others as one is treated. (2) In interpersonal attraction, the tendency to return feelings and attitudes that are expressed about us.

Recitation   A teaching format in which teachers pose questions that are answered by students.

Recognition   In information processing, a relatively easy memory task in which one identifies objects or events as having been encountered previously.

Reconstructive memories   Memories that are based on the piecing together of memory fragments with general knowledge and expectations rather than a precise picture of the past.

Reflex   A simple, unlearned response to a stimulus.

Refractory period   (1) In discussion of the nervous system, a period following firing during which a neuron's action potential cannot be triggered. (2) In human sexuality, a period following orgasm when a male is insensitive to further sexual stimulation.

Regression   In psychodynamic theory, return to a form of behavior characteristic of an earlier stage of development. As a defense mechanism, regression to less mature behavior is a means of coping with stress.

Reinforcement   A stimulus that follows a response and increases the frequency of that response. See *positive* and *negative*, *primary* and *secondary* reinforcers.

Relative refractory period   A phase following the absolute refractory period during which a neuron will fire in response to stronger-than-usual messages from other neurons.

Relaxation response   Benson's term for a cluster of responses brought about by meditation that lower the activity of the sympathetic division of the autonomic nervous system.

Relearning   A measure of retention. Material is usually relearned more quickly than it is learned initially.

Releaser   In ethology, a stimulus that elicits an instinctive response.

Reliability   In psychological measurement, consistency. Also see *validity*.

Replication   The repetition or duplication of scientific studies in order to double-check their results.

Representativeness heuristic   A decision-making heuristic in which people make judgments about events (samples) according to the populations they appear to represent.

Repression   In psychodynamic theory, the ejection of anxiety-provoking ideas, impulses, or images from awareness, without the awareness that one is doing so. A defense mechanism.

Resistance   During psychoanalysis, a blocking of thoughts, the awareness of which could cause anxiety. The client may miss sessions or verbally abuse the analyst as threatening material is about to be unearthed.

Resistance stage   The second stage of the general adaptation syndrome, characterized by prolonged sympathetic activity in an effort to restore lost energy and repair damage. Also called the *adaptation stage*.

Response   A movement or other observable reaction to a stimulus.

Response cost   A behavior-therapy self-control technique in which one uses self-punishment for practicing a bad habit or failing to meet a goal.

Response prevention   A behavior-therapy self-control technique in which one makes unwanted behaviors difficult or impossible.

Response set   A tendency to answer test items according to a bias—for example, with the intention of making oneself appear perfect or bizarre.

Resting potential   The electrical potential across the neural membrane when it is not responding to other neurons.

Restriction of the stimulus field   A behavior-therapy self-control technique in which a problem behavior is gradually restricted from more environments.

Reticular activating system   A part of the brain involved in attention, sleep, and arousal. Abbreviated *RAS*.

Retina   The area of the inner surface of the eye that contains rods and cones.

Retinal disparity   A binocular cue for depth based on the difference of the image cast by an object on the retinas of the eyes as the object moves closer or farther away.

Retrieval   The location of stored information and its return to consciousness. The third stage of information processing.

Retroactive interference   The interference by new learning in one's ability to retrieve material learned previously. See *proactive interference*.

Retrograde amnesia   Failure to remember events that occur prior to physical trauma because of the effects of the trauma.

Reversibility   According to Piaget, recognition that processes can be undone, leaving things as they were before. Reversibility is a factor in conservation of the properties of substances. See *conservation* and *concrete operational stage*.

Reward   A pleasant stimulus that increases the frequency of the behavior it follows.

Risky shift   The tendency to make riskier decisions as a member of a group than as an individual acting independently.

Rod   A rod-shaped photoreceptor in the eye that is sensitive to the intensity of light. Rods permit "black and white" vision.

Role diffusion   According to Erikson, a state of confusion, insecurity, and susceptibility to the suggestions of others; the probable outcome if ego identity is not established during adolescence.

Role theory   A theory that explains hypnotic events in terms of the person's ability to act *as though* he or she were hypnotized. Role theory differs from faking in that people cooperate and focus on hypnotic suggestions instead of cynically pretending to be hypnotized.

Romantic love   An intense, positive emotion that involves arousal, a cultural setting that idealizes love, feelings of caring, and the belief that one is in love. Also called *passionate love*. Within Sternberg's triangular model, the kind of love that is characterized by passion and intimacy.

Rooting   (1) A reflex in which an infant turns its head toward a touch, such as by the mother's nipple. (2) In adult development, the process of establishing a home, which frequently occurs in the second half of the 30s.

Rorschach inkblot test   A projective personality test that presents test takers the task of interpreting inkblots.

Rote   Mechanical associative learning that is based on repetition.

"Roy G. Biv"   A mnemonic device for remembering the colors of the visible spectrum.

S

s   Spearman's symbol for specific or "s" factors, which he believed account for individual abilities.

Saccadic eye movement   The rapid jumps made by a reader's eyes as they fixate on different points in the text.

Sadism   The attainment of gratification, frequently sexual, from inflicting pain on, or humiliating, others.

"SAME"   The mnemonic device for remembering that *s*ensory neurons are called *a*fferent neurons and that *m*otor neurons are termed *e*fferent neurons.

Sample   Part of a population.

Satiety   The state of being satisfied; fullness.

Saturation   The degree of purity of a color, as measured by its freedom from mixture with white or black.

Savings   The difference between the number of repetitions originally required to learn a list and the number of repetitions required to relearn the list after a certain amount of time has elapsed.

Scapegoat   A person or group upon whom the blame for the mistakes or crimes of others is cast.

Scatter diagram   A graphic presentation formed by plotting the points defined by the intersections of two variables.

Schachter–Singer theory   The theory of emotion that holds that emotions have generally similar patterns of bodily arousal, and that the label we give to an emotion depends on our level of arousal and our cognitive appraisal of our situation.

Schema   A way of mentally representing the world, such as a belief or an expectation, that can influence perception of persons, objects, and situations.

Schizoid personality disorder   A disorder characterized by social withdrawal.

Schizophrenia   A psychotic disorder of at least 6 months' duration in which thought processes and reality testing are impaired and emotions are not appropriate to one's situation. Also see *schizophreniform disorder, brief reactive psychosis,* and *schizotypal personality disorder*.

Schizophreniform disorder   A disorder whose symptoms resemble schizophrenia but that is relatively brief (2 weeks to less than 6 months in duration).

Schizotypal personality disorder   A disorder characterized by oddities of thought and behavior but not involving bizarre psychotic symptoms. Formerly called *simple schizophrenia*.

Scientific method   A method for obtaining scientific evidence in which a hypothesis is formed and tested.

Secondary colors   Colors derived by mixing primary colors.

Secondary prevention   In community psychology, the early detection and treatment of psychological problems.

Secondary reinforcer   A stimulus that gains reinforcement value through association with other, established reinforcers. Money and social approval are secondary reinforcers. Also called *conditioned reinforcer*. See *primary reinforcer*.

Secondary sex characteristics   Physical traits that differentiate the genders, such as the depth of the voice, but that are not directly involved in reproduction.

Secondary traits   Allport's term for traits that appear in a limited number of situations and govern a limited number of responses.

Secure attachment   A type of attachment characterized by positive feelings toward attachment figures and feelings of security.

Sedative   A drug that soothes or quiets restlessness or agitation.

Selective attention   The focus of consciousness on a particular stimulus.

Selective avoidance   Diverting one's attention from information that is inconsistent with one's attitudes.

Selective exposure   The deliberate seeking of, and attending to, information that is consistent with one's attitudes.

Self   The totality of one's impressions, thoughts, and feelings. The center of consciousness that organizes sensory impressions and governs one's perceptions of the world.

Self-actualization   According to Maslow and other humanistic psychologists, self-initiated striving to become what one is capable of being. The motive for reaching one's full potential, for expressing one's unique capabilities.

Self-efficacy expectations   A kind of expectancy in social-cognitive theory. Beliefs that one can bring about desired changes through one's own efforts.

Self-esteem   One's evaluation of, and the placement of value on, oneself.

Self-fulfilling prophecy   An expectation that is confirmed because of the behavior of those who hold the expectation.

Self-ideal   A mental image of what we believe we ought to be.

Self-insight   In psychodynamic theory, accurate awareness of one's own motives and feelings.

Self-monitoring   A behavior-therapy technique in which one keeps a record of his or her behavior in order to identify problems and record successes.

Self-serving bias   The tendency to view one's successes as stemming from internal factors and one's failures as stemming from external factors.

Self theory   The name of Carl Rogers's theory of personality, which emphasizes the importance of self-awareness, choice, and self-actualization.

Semantic code   Mental representation of information according to its meaning.

Semanticity   Meaning. The property of language in which words are used as symbols for objects, events, or ideas.

Semantic memory   General knowledge, as opposed to episodic memory.

Semantics   The study of the relationships between language and objects or events. The study of the meaning of language.

Semicircular canals   Structures of the inner ear that monitor body movement and position.

Sensation   The stimulation of sensory receptors and the transmission of sensory information to the central nervous system.

Sensitive period   In linguistic theory, the period from about 18 months to puberty when the brain is thought to be particularly capable of learning language because of plasticity.

Sensitization   The type of sensory adaptation in which we become more sensitive to stimuli that are low in magnitude. Also called *positive adaptation.*

Sensorimotor stage   The first of Piaget's stages of cognitive development, characterized by coordination of sensory information and motor activity, early exploration of the environment, and lack of language.

Sensorineural deafness   The forms of deafness that result from damage to hair cells or the auditory nerve.

Sensory adaptation   The processes by which organisms become more sensitive to stimuli that are low in magnitude and less sensitive to stimuli that are constant or ongoing in magnitude.

Sensory awareness   One of the definitions of consciousness. Knowledge of the environment through perception of sensory stimulation.

Sensory cortex   The section of the cerebral cortex that lies in the parietal lobe, just behind the central fissure. Sensory stimulation is projected in this section of cortex.

Sensory deprivation   (1) In general, insufficient sensory stimulation. (2) A research method for systematically decreasing the stimuli that impinge on sensory receptors.

Sensory memory   The type or stage of memory first encountered by a stimulus. Sensory memory holds impressions briefly, but long enough so that series of perceptions are psychologically continuous.

Sensory register   A system of memory that holds information briefly, but long enough so that it can be processed further. There may be a sensory register for every sense.

Septum   A part of the limbic system that apparently restrains stereotypically aggressive responses.

Serial position effect   The tendency to recall more accurately the first and last items in a series.

Serotonin   A neurotransmitter, deficiencies of which have been linked to affective disorders, anxiety, and insomnia.

Serotonin reuptake inhibitor   An antidepressant medication that works by slowing the reuptake of serotonin in the synaptic cleft.

Serum cholesterol   A fatty substance (cholesterol) in the blood (serum) that has been linked to heart disease.

Set point   A value that the body attempts to maintain. For example, the body tries to maintain a certain weight by adjusting the metabolism.

Sex chromosomes   The 23rd pair of chromosomes, which determine whether a child will be male or female.

Sex flush   A reddish hue on body surfaces that is caused by vasocongestion during sexual excitement.

Sexism   The prejudgment that a person, on the basis of his or her gender, will possess negative traits or perform inadequately.

Sex norms   Social rules or conventions that govern the ways in which males and females interact.

Sex role   See *gender role.*

Sex therapy   A number of cognitive and behavioral methods that seek to reverse sexual dysfunctions by reducing performance anxiety, reversing defeatist expectations, and fostering sexual competencies.

Sex-typing   See *gender-typing.*

Sexual apathy   Lack of interest in sexual activity.

Sexual dysfunctions   Persistent or recurrent problems in achieving or maintaining sexual arousal or in reaching orgasm.

Sexual orientation   The directionality of one's erotic and romantic interests — that is, toward people of the opposite gender, people of the same gender, or in the case of bisexuality, people of both genders. See *heterosexual, gay male, lesbian.*

Sexual response cycle   A four-phase process that describes response to sexual stimulation in males and females.

Shadowing   A monocular cue for depth based on the fact that opaque objects block light and produce shadows.

Sham   False, pretended.

Shape constancy   The tendency to perceive an object as being the same shape even though its retinal image changes in shape as the object rotates.

Shaping   In operant conditioning, a procedure for teaching complex behaviors that at first reinforces approximations of these behaviors.

Short-term memory   The type or stage of memory that can hold information for up to a minute or so after the trace of the stimulus decays. Also called *working memory.*

Siblings   Brothers and sisters.

Signal-detection theory   In psychophysics, the view that the perception of sensory stimuli is influenced by the interaction of physical, biological, and psychological factors.

Significant others   Persons who have a major influence on one's psychosocial development, including parents, peers, lovers, and children.

Similarity   As a rule of perceptual organization, the tendency to group together objects that are similar in appearance.

Simple phobia   Persistent fear of a specific object or situation.

Simultaneous conditioning   A classical conditioning procedure in which the CS and US are presented at the same time, and the CS remains in place until the response occurs.

Situational attribution   An assumption that a person's behavior is determined by external circumstances, such as social pressure. Contrast with *dispositional attribution.*

Situational variables   In social-learning theory, external determinants of behavior, such as rewards and punishments.

Size constancy   The tendency to perceive an object as being the same size even as the size of its retinal image changes according to its distance.

Skewed distribution   A slanted distribution, drawn out toward the low or high scores.

Sleep-onset insomnia   Difficulty falling asleep.

Sleep spindles   Short bursts of rapid brain waves that occur during stage 2 sleep.

Sleep terrors   Frightening, dreamlike experiences that usually occur during deep stage 4 sleep.

Social-cognitive theory   A cognitively oriented learning theory in which observational learning and person variables such as values and expectancies play major roles in individual differences. Also termed *cognitive social-learning theory* or *social-learning theory*.

Social-comparison theory   The view that people look to others for cues about how to behave in confusing situations.

Social decision schemes   Rules for predicting the final outcome of group decision making on the basis of the initial positions of the members.

Social facilitation   The process by which a person's performance is increased when other members of a group engage in similar behavior.

Social influence   The area of social psychology that studies the ways in which people influence the thoughts, feelings, and behavior of others.

Socialization   Guidance of people—and children in particular—into socially desirable behavior by means of verbal messages, the systematic use of rewards and punishments, and other methods of teaching.

Social-learning theory   See *social-cognitive theory*.

Social loafing   The process by which a person's performance is decreased as a function of being a member of a group.

Social motives   Learned or acquired motives such as the needs for achievement and affiliation.

Social norms   Explicit and implicit rules that reflect social expectations and influence the ways people behave in social situations.

Social perception   A subfield of social psychology that studies the ways in which we form and modify impressions of others.

Social phobias   Irrational fears that involve themes of public scrutiny.

Social psychology   The field of psychology that studies the nature and causes of people's thoughts, feelings, and behavior in social situations.

Sociobiology   A biological theory of social behavior that assumes that the underlying purpose of behavior is to ensure the transmission of an organism's genes from generation to generation.

Sociocultural perspective   The perspective in psychology that focuses on the roles of ethnicity, gender, culture, and socioeconomic status in personality formation, behavior, and mental processes.

Sociopath   Another term for a person who shows an antisocial personality disorder.

Soma   A cell body.

Somatic nervous system   The division of the peripheral nervous system that connects the central nervous system (brain and spinal cord) with sensory receptors, muscles, and the surface of the body.

Somatoform disorders   Disorders in which people complain of physical (somatic) problems although no physical abnormality can be found. See *conversion disorder* and *hypochondriasis*.

Source traits   Cattell's term for underlying traits from which surface traits are derived.

Spectrograph   An instrument that converts sounds to graphs or pictures according to their acoustic qualities.

Sphincter   A ringlike muscle that circles a body opening such as the anus. An infant will exhibit the sphincter reflex (have a bowel movement) in response to intestinal pressure.

Spinal cord   A column of nerves within the spine that transmits messages from the sensory receptors to the brain and from the brain to muscles and glands throughout the body.

Spinal reflex   A simple, unlearned response to a stimulus that may involve only two neurons.

Split-brain operation   An operation in which the corpus callosum is severed, usually in an effort to control epileptic seizures.

Split-half reliability   A method for determining the internal consistency of a test (an index of reliability) by correlating scores attained on half the items with scores attained on the other half of the items.

Spontaneous recovery   Generally, the recurrence of an extinguished response as a function of the passage of time. In classical conditioning, the eliciting of a conditioned response by a conditioned stimulus after some time has elapsed following the extinction of the conditioned response. In operant conditioning, the performance of an operant in the presence of discriminative stimuli after some time has elapsed following the extinction of the operant.

Sports psychology   The field of psychology that studies the nature, causes, and modification of the behavior and mental processes of people involved in sports.

Stage   In developmental psychology, a distinct period of life that is qualitatively different from other stages. Stages follow one another in an orderly sequence.

Standard deviation   A measure of the variability of a distribution, obtained by taking the square root of the sum of difference scores squared divided by the number of scores.

Standardization   The process of setting standards for a psychological test, accomplished by determining how a population performs on it. Standardization permits psychologists to interpret individual scores as deviations from a norm.

Standardized tests   Tests for which norms are based on the performance of a range of individuals.

Stapes   A bone of the middle ear. Latin for "stirrup."

Startle reflex   See *moro reflex*.

State-dependent memory   Information that is better retrieved in the physiological or emotional state in which it was encoded (stored) or learned.

Statistically significant difference   As indicated by inferential statistics, a difference between two groups that is so large that it is not probable that it results from chance fluctuation.

Statistics   Numerical facts assembled in such a manner that they provide useful information about measures or scores.

Stereotype   A fixed, conventional idea about a group.

Steroids   A family of hormones that includes testosterone, estrogen, progesterone, and corticosteriods.

Stimulant   A drug that increases the activity of the nervous system.

Stimuli   Plural of *stimulus*.

Stimulus   (1) A feature in the environment that is detected by an organism or that leads to a change in behavior (a response). (2) A form of physical energy, such as light or sound, that impinges on the sensory receptors.

Stimulus control   A behavior-therapy self-control technique in which one places oneself in an environment in which desired responses are likely to occur.

Stimulus discrimination   The eliciting of a conditioned response by only one of a series of similar stimuli.

Stimulus generalization   The eliciting of a conditioned response by stimuli that are similar to the conditioned stimulus.

Stimulus motives   Motives to increase the stimulation impinging on an organism.

Stimulus-outcome relations   A kind of expectancy in social-cognitive theory. Predictions as to what events will follow certain stimuli or signs.

Stirrup   A bone of the middle ear.

Storage   The maintenance of information over time. The second stage of information processing.

Strabismus   A visual disorder in which the eyes point in different directions and thus do not focus simultaneously on the same point.

Stratified sample   A sample drawn in such a way that known subgroups within a population are represented in proportion to their numbers in the population.

Stress   The demand made on an organism to adjust or adapt.

Stressor   An event or stimulus that acts as a source of stress.

Stroboscopic motion   A visual illusion in which the perception of motion is generated by presentation of a series of stationary images in rapid succession.

Structuralism   The school of psychology, founded by Wilhelm Wundt that argues that the mind consists of three basic elements—sensations, feelings, and images—that combine to form experience.

Structure-of-intellect model   Guilford's three-dimensional model of intelligence, which focuses on the operations, contents, and products of intellectual functioning.

Stupor   A condition in which the senses and thought processes are dulled.

Subject   A participant in a scientific study. Many psychologists consider this term dehumanizing and no longer use it in reference to human participants.

Subjective   Of the mind; personal; determined by thoughts and feelings rather than by external objects.

Subjective morality   According to Piaget, subjective moral judgments assign guilt according to the motives of the actor. See *objective morality*.

Subjective value   The desirability of an object or event.

Sublimation   In psychodynamic theory, a defense mechanism in which primitive impulses—usually sexual or aggressive—are channeled into positive, constructive activities.

Subordinate   Descriptive of a lower (included) class or category in a hierarchy; contained by another class; opposite of *superordinate*.

Substance abuse   Persistent use of a substance despite the fact that it is disrupting one's life.

Substance dependence   A term whose definition is in flux: Substance dependence is characterized by loss of control over use of a substance, but some professionals consider *physiological* dependence, as typified by tolerance, withdrawal, or both, is essential to the definition.

Successive approximations   In operant conditioning, a series of behaviors that gradually become more similar to a target behavior.

Superego   In psychodynamic theory, the psychic structure that is governed by the moral principle, sets forth high standards for behavior, and floods the ego with feelings of guilt and shame when it falls short.

Superordinate   Descriptive of a higher (including) class or category in a hierarchy; containing another class; opposite of *subordinate*.

Suppression   The deliberate, or conscious, placing of certain ideas, impulses, or images out of awareness. Contrast with *repression*.

Surface structure   The superficial construction of a sentence as defined by the placement of words.

Surface traits   Cattell's term for characteristic, observable ways of behaving. See *source traits*.

Survey   A method of scientific investigation in which large samples of people answer questions.

Symbol   Something that stands for or represents another thing.

Sympathetic nervous system   The branch of the autonomic nervous system that is most active when the person is engaged in behavior or experiencing feeling states that spend the body's reserves of energy, such as fleeing or experiencing fear or anxiety.

Synapse   A junction between neurons, consisting of a terminal knob of a transmitting neuron, the space between the neurons (synaptic cleft), and a dendrite or soma of a receiving neuron.

Synaptic cleft   The space between neurons, across which messages are transmitted by means of neurotransmitters.

Syndrome   A cluster of symptoms characteristic of a disorder.

Syntax   The rules in a language for placing words in proper order to form meaningful sentences.

Systematic desensitization   A behavior-therapy fear-reduction technique in which a hierarchy of fear-evoking stimuli are presented while the person remains in a state of deep muscle relaxation.

Systematic random search   An algorithm for solving problems in which each possible solution is tested according to a particular set of rules.

T

TA   Abbreviation for *transactional analysis*.

Tactile   Of the sense of touch.

Target behavior   Goal.

Task analysis   The breaking down of a job or behavior pattern into its component parts.

Taste aversion   A kind of classical conditioning in which a previously desirable or neutral food comes to be perceived as repugnant because it is associated with aversive stimulation.

Taste buds   The sensory organs for taste. They contain taste cells and are located on the tongue.

Taste cells   Receptor cells that are sensitive to taste.

TAT   Thematic Apperception Test.

Taxonomy   Classification system.

Telegraphic speech   Speech in which only the essential words are used, as in a telegram.

Telepathy   The term refers to the direct transference of thought from one person to another. However, most psychologists do not believe that telepathy exists.

Temporal lobe   The lobe of the cerebral cortex that is involved in hearing. It lies below the lateral fissure, near the temples.

Terminal   A small branching structure found at the tip of an axon.

Territory   In sociobiology, the particular area acquired and defended by an animal, or pair of animals, for purposes of feeding and breeding.

Tertiary colors   Colors derived by mixing primary and adjoining secondary colors.

Tertiary prevention   In community psychology, the treatment of ripened psychological problems. See *primary* and *secondary prevention*.

Testes   The male reproductive organs that produce sperm and the hormone testosterone.

Testosterone   A male sex hormone (steroid) that is produced by the testes and promotes growth of male sexual characteristics and sperm.

Test–retest reliability   A method for determining the reliability of a test by comparing (correlating) test takers' scores on separate occasions.

Texture gradient   A monocular cue for depth based on the perception that nearby objects appear to have rougher or more detailed surfaces.

Thalamus   An area near the center of the brain that is involved in the relay of sensory information to the cortex and in the functions of sleep and attention.

THC   Delta-9-tetrahydrocannabinol. The major active ingredient in marijuana.

The Dream   Levinson's term for the overriding drive of youth to become someone important, to leave one's mark on history.

T-helper lymphocytes   The white blood cells of the immune system that recognize invading pathogens and are attacked by the human immunodeficiency virus (HIV). Also called *CD4 cells* and T_4 *cells*.

Thematic Apperception Test   A projective test devised by Henry Murray to measure needs through the production of fantasy.

Theory   A formulation of relationships underlying observed events. A theory involves assumptions and logically derived explanations and predictions.

Theory of social comparison   The view that people look to others for cues about how to behave when they are in confusing or unfamiliar situations.

Theory Y   McGregor's view that organizational goals should be congruent with workers' goals.

Theory Z   Ouchi's view that adapts positive features of the Japanese workplace to the U.S. workplace.

Theta waves   Slow brain waves produced during the hypnagogic state.

Thinking   Mental activity that is involved in understanding, manipulating, and communicating about information. Thinking entails paying attention to information, mentally representing it, reasoning about it, and making decisions about it.

Threshold   The point at which a stimulus is just strong enough to produce a response.

Thyroxin   The thyroid hormone that increases the metabolic rate.

Timbre   The quality or richness of a sound. The quality that distinguishes the sounds of one musical instrument from those of another.

Time out   In operant conditioning, a method for decreasing the frequency of undesired behaviors by removing an organism from a situation in which reinforcement is available as a consequence of showing the undesired behavior.

Tip-of-the-tongue phenomenon The feeling that information is stored in memory although it cannot be readily retrieved. Also called the *feeling-of-knowing experience*.

TM Transcendental meditation.

Token economy A controlled environment in which people are reinforced for desired behaviors with tokens (such as poker chips) that may be exchanged for privileges.

Tolerance Habituation to a drug, with the result that increasingly higher doses of the drug are required to achieve similar effects.

Tolerance for frustration Ability to delay gratification, to maintain self-control when a motive is thwarted.

Top-down processing The use of contextual information or knowledge of a pattern to organize parts of the pattern.

Total immersion A method of teaching a second language in which all instruction is carried out in the second language.

Trace conditioning A classical-conditioning procedure in which the CS is presented and then removed before the US is presented.

Trait A distinguishing quality or characteristic of personality that is inferred from behavior and assumed to account for consistency in behavior.

Tranquilizers Drugs used to reduce anxiety and tension. See *minor* and *major tranquilizer*.

Transaction In transactional analysis, an exchange between two people.

Transactional analysis A form of psychotherapy that deals with how people interact and how their interactions reinforce attitudes, expectations, and "life positions." Abbreviated *TA*.

Transcendental meditation The simplified form of meditation brought to the United States by the Maharishi Mahesh Yogi in which one focuses on a repeated mantra. Abbreviated *TM*.

Transference In psychoanalysis, the generalization to the analyst of feelings toward another person in the client's life.

Trauma An injury or wound.

Treatment In experiments, a condition obtained by participants and whose effects are observed by the researchers.

Trial In conditioning, a presentation of the stimuli.

Triangular model Sternberg's model of love, which refers to combinations of passion, intimacy, and decision/commitment.

Triarchic Governed by three. (Referring to Sternberg's triarchic theory of intelligence.)

Trichromat A person with normal color vision.

Trichromatic theory The theory that color vision is made possible by three types of cones, some of which respond to red light, some to green, and some to blue.

Tricyclic antidepressants Antidepressant drugs that work by preventing the reuptake of norepinephrine and serotonin by transmitting neurons.

Trust versus mistrust The first of Erikson's stages of psychosocial development, during which the child comes to (or not to) develop a basic sense of trust in others.

Trying 20s Sheehy's term for the third decade of life, which is frequently characterized by preoccupation with advancement in the career world.

Two-point threshold The least distance by which two rods touching the skin must be separated before an individual will report that there are two rods, not one, on 50% of occasions.

Type In personality theory, a group of traits that cluster in a meaningful way.

Type A behavior Behavior characterized by a sense of time urgency, competitiveness, and hostility.

U

Ulcer An open sore, as in the lining of the stomach.

Umbilical cord A tube between the mother and her fetus through which nutrients and waste products are conducted.

Unconditional positive regard In self theory, a consistent expression of esteem for the basic value of a person, but not necessarily an unqualified endorsement of all that person's behaviors. A quality shown by the person-centered therapist.

Unconditioned response An unlearned response. A response to an unconditioned stimulus. Abbreviated *UR*.

Unconditioned stimulus A stimulus that elicits a response from an organism without learning. Abbreviated *US*.

Unconscious In psychodynamic theory, descriptive of ideas and feelings that are not available to awareness, in many instances because of the *defense mechanism* of *repression*.

Unobtrusive Not interfering.

Uplifts Notable pleasant daily conditions and experiences.

UR Unconditioned response.

US Unconditioned stimulus.

Uterus The hollow organ within women in which the embryo and fetus develop.

V

Vaccination Purposeful infection with a small amount of an antigen, or weakened antigen, so that in the future the immune system will recognize and efficiently destroy the antigen.

Vaginismus Persistent or recurrent spasm of the muscles surrounding the outer part of the vaginal barrel, making entry difficult or impossible.

Validity The degree to which a test or instrument measures or predicts what it is supposed to measure or predict. Also see *reliability*.

Validity scale A group of test items that suggests whether or not the results of a test are valid—whether a person's test responses accurately reflect his or her traits.

Variable A condition that is measured or controlled in a scientific study. A variable can be altered in a measurable manner.

Variable-interval schedule A partial reinforcement schedule in which a variable amount of time must elapse between the previous and subsequent times that reinforcement is available.

Variable-ratio schedule A partial reinforcement schedule in which reinforcement is provided after a variable number of correct responses.

Vasopressin Another term for *antidiuretic hormone*.

Ventromedial nucleus A central area on the underside of the hypothalamus that appears to function as a stop-eating center. Abbreviated *VMN*.

Vestibular sense The sense that provides information about the position of the body relative to gravity. Also referred to as the sense of *equilibrium*.

Vicarious Taking the place of another person or thing. In vicarious learning, we learn from the experiences of others.

Visible light The band of electromagnetic energy that produces visual sensations.

Visual accommodation Automatic adjustment of the thickness of the lens in order to focus on objects.

Visual acuity Keenness or sharpness of vision.

Visual capture The tendency of vision to dominate the other senses.

Visual code Mental representation of information as a picture.

Volley principle A modification of the *frequency theory* of pitch perception. The hypothesis that groups of neurons may be able to achieve the effect of firing at very high frequencies by "taking turns" firing—that is, by firing in volleys.

Volt A unit of electrical potential.

W

Waxy flexibility A symptom of catatonic schizophrenia in which the person maintains a posture or position into which he or she is placed.

Weaning Accustoming the child not to suck the mother's breast or a baby bottle.

Weber's constant The fraction of the intensity by which a source of physical energy must be increased or decreased so that a difference in intensity will be perceived.

Well-defined problem   A problem in which the original state, the goal, and the rules for reaching the goal are clearly spelled out.

Wernicke-Korsakoff syndrome   An alcohol-related disorder that is characterized by loss of memory and that is thought to reflect nutritional deficiency.

Wernicke's aphasia   An aphasia caused by damage to Wernicke's area of the brain. It is characterized by difficulty comprehending the meaning of spoken language and by the production of language that is grammatically correct but confused or meaningless in content.

White matter   In the spinal cord, axon bundles that carry messages from and to the brain.

White noise   Discordant sounds of many frequencies, which often produce a lulling effect.

Wish fulfillment   In psychodynamic theory, a primitive method used by the id—such as in fantasy and dreams—to attempt to gratify basic impulses.

Working memory   See *short-term memory*.

Y

Yerkes-Dodson law   The principle that a high level of arousal increases performance on a relatively simple task, whereas a low level of arousal increases performance on a relatively complex task.

Z

Zygote   A fertilized egg cell or ovum.

REFERENCES

AAUW. (1992). *How schools shortchange women: The A.A.U.W. report.* Washington, DC: American Association of University Women Educational Foundation.

Abbey, A. (1987). Misperceptions of friendly behavior as sexual interest: A survey of naturally occurring incidents. *Psychology of Women Quarterly, 11,* 173–194.

Abraham, L. K. (1993). *Mama might be better off dead: The failure of health care in urban America.* Chicago: University of Chicago Press.

Abramowitz, A. J., & O'Leary, S. G. (1991). Behavioral interventions for the classroom: Implications with students for ADHD. *School Psychology Review, 20,* 220–234.

Adair, J. G., Dushenko, T. W., & Lindsay, R. C. L. (1985). Ethical regulations and their impact on research practice. *American Psychologist, 40,* 59–72.

Ader, D. N., & Johnson, S. B. (1994). Sample description, reporting, and analysis of sex in psychological research: A look at APA and APA division journals in 1990. *American Psychologist, 49,* 216–218.

Ader, R. (1993). Conditioned responses. In B. Moyers (Ed.), *Healing and the mind.* New York: Doubleday.

Adeyemo, S. A. (1990). Thinking imagery and problem-solving. *Psychological Studies, 35,* 179–190.

Adler, N. E., and others. (1994). Socioeconomic status and health: The challenge of the gradient. *American Psychologist, 49,* 15–24.

Adler, T. (1990). Distraction, relaxation can help "shut off" pain. *APA Monitor, 21*(9), 11.

Adler, T. (1993a). Shy, bold temperament? It's mostly in the genes. *APA Monitor, 24*(1), 7, 8.

Adler, T. (1993b). Sleep loss impairs attention—and more. *APA Monitor, 24*(9), 22–23.

Agras, W. S., & Kirkley, B. G. (1986). Bulimia: Theories of etiology. In K. D. Brownell & J. P. Foreyt (Eds.), *Handbook of eating disorders.* New York: Basic Books.

Agras, W. S., Southam, M. A., & Taylor, C. B. (1983). Long-term persistence of relaxation induced blood pressure lowering during the working day. *Journal of Consulting and Clinical Psychology, 51,* 792–794.

Aiken, L. S., West, S. G., Woodward, C. K., & Reno, R. R. (1994). Health beliefs and compliance with mammography-screening recommendations in asymptomatic women. *Health Psychology, 13,* 122–129.

Ainsworth, M. D. S. (1989). Attachments beyond infancy. *American Psychologist, 44,* 709–716.

Ainsworth, M. D. S., & Bowlby, J. (1991). An ethological approach to personality development. *American Psychologist, 46,* 333–341.

Akhtar, N., & Bradley, E. J. (1991). Social information processing deficits of aggressive children: Present findings and implications for social skills training. *Clinical Psychology Review, 11,* 621–644.

Albert, M. S. (1981). Geriatric neuropsychology. *Journal of Consulting and Clinical Psychology, 49,* 835–850.

Aldag, R. J., & Fuller, S. R. (1993). Beyond fiasco: A reappraisal of the groupthink phenomenon and a new model of group decision processes. *Psychological Bulletin, 113,* 533–552.

Alexander, R. A., & Barrett, G. U. (1982). Equitable salary increase judgments based upon merit and nonmerit considerations: A cross national comparison. *International Review of Applied Psychology, 31,* 443–454.

Allen, L. (1993, August). Integrating a sociocultural perspective into the psychology curriculum. G. Stanley Hall lecture presented to the American Psychological Association, Toronto, Canada.

Allison, K. W., Crawford, I., Echemendia, R., Robinson, L. V., & Knepp, D. (1994). Human diversity and professional competence. *American Psychologist, 49,* 792–796.

Alloy, L. B., Abramson, L. Y., & Dykman, B. M. (1990). Depressive realism and nondepressive optimistic illusions: The role of the self. In R. E. Ingram (Ed.), *Contemporary psychological approaches to depression.* New York: Plenum.

Alloy, L. B., & Ahrens, A. H. (1987). Depression and pessimism for the future: Biased use of statistically relevant information in predictions for self versus others. *Journal of Personality and Social Psychology, 52,* 366–378.

Alloy, L. B., & Clements, C. M. (1992). Illusion of control: Invulnerability to negative affect and depressive symptoms after laboratory and natural stressors. *Journal of Abnormal Psychology, 101,* 234–245.

Allport, G. W., & Odbert, H. S. (1936). Trait names: A psycholexical study. *Psychological Monographs, 47,* 2–11.

Altman, L. K. (1991, June 18). W.H.O. says 40 million will be infected with AIDS virus by 2000. *The New York Times,* p. C3.

Altman, L. K. (1993, May 4). Rise in asthma deaths is tied to ignorance of many physicians. *The New York Times,* p. C3.

Amabile, T. M. (1990). Within you, without you: The social psychology of creativity, and beyond. In M. A. Runco & R. S. Albert (Eds.), *Theories of creativity.* Newbury Park, CA: Sage.

Amaro, H. (1995). Love, sex, and power: Considering women's realities in HIV prevention. *American Psychologist, 50,* 437–447.

Amato, P. R. (1983). Helping behavior in urban and rural environments: Field studies based on taxonomic organization of helping episodes. *Journal of Personality and Social Psychology, 45,* 571–586.

American Cancer Society. (1995). Document ID: ACS061. [On-line]. America Online.

American Psychiatric Association. (1990). *The practice of electroconvulsive therapy.* Washington, DC: Author.

American Psychiatric Association (1994). *Diagnostic and statistical manual of the mental disorders* (4th ed.). Washington, DC: Author.

American Psychological Association, Committee on Gay and Lesbian Concerns. (1991). Avoiding heterosexual bias in language. *American Psychologist, 46,* 973–974.

American Psychological Association (1992a). *Big world, small screen: The role of television in American society.* Washington, DC: Author.

American Psychological Association. (1992b). Ethical principles of psychologists and code of conduct. *American Psychologist 47,* 1597–1611.

American Psychological Association. (1993). Guidelines for providers of psychological services to ethnic, linguistic, and culturally diverse populations. *American Psychologist, 48,* 45–48.

American Psychological Association. (1994). *Publication manual of the American Psychological Association* (4th ed.). Washington, DC: Author.

Anastasiow, N. J., & Hanes, M. L. (1976). *Language patterns of children in poverty.* Springfield, IL: Charles C Thomas.

Andersen, B. L. (1992). Psychological interventions for cancer patients to enhance the quality of life. *Journal of Consulting and Clinical Psychology, 60,* 552–568.

Anderson, B. L., Kiecolt-Glaser, J. K., & Glaser, R. (1994). A biobehavioral model of cancer stress and disease course. *American Psychologist, 49,* 389–404.

Anderson, C. A., & DeNeve, K. M. (1992). Temperature, aggression, and the negative affect escape model. *Psychological Bulletin, 111,* 347–351.

Anderson, J. R. (1991). Is human cognition adaptive? *Behavioral and Brain Sciences, 14,* 471–517.

Andreasen, N. C. (1990, August/September). Schizophrenia. In American Psychiatric Association, *DSM-IV Update.* Washington, DC: American Psychiatric Association.

Andrews, B., & Brown, G. W. (1993). Self-esteem and vulnerability to depression. *Journal of Abnormal Psychology, 102,* 565–572.

Aneshensel, C. S., & Huba, G. J. (1983). Depression, alcohol use, and smoking over one year: A four-wave longitudinal causal model. *Journal of Abnormal Psychology, 92,* 134–150.

Angell, M. (1993). Privilege and health—What is the connection? *New England Journal of Medicine, 329,* 126–127.

Angier, N. (1993, August 13). Scientists detect a genetic key to Alzheimer's. *The New York Times,* pp. A1, A12.

Angier, N. (1994a). Benefits of broccoli confirmed as chemical blocks tumors. *The New York Times,* p. C11.

Angier, N. (1994b). Factor in female sexuality. *The New York Times,* p. C13.

Angier, N. (1995, May 14). Why science loses women in the ranks. *The New York Times,* p. E5.

Annunziata, J., & Jacobson-Kram, P. (1995). *Solving your problems together: Family therapy for the whole family.* Washington, DC: American Psychological Association.

Antoni, M. H. (1987). Neuroendocrine influences in psychoimmunology and neoplasia: A review. *Psychology and Health, 1,* 3–24.

Antoni, M. H. (1992, July). *Behavioral intervention effects on coping strategies, emotional expression and immune measures among individuals dealing with traumatic events: Implications for psychooncology?* Paper presented at the Second International Congress of Behavioral Medicine, Hamburg, Germany.

Antoni, M. H., and others. (1990). Psychoneuroimmunology and HIV-1. *Journal of Consulting and Clinical Psychology, 58,* 38–49.

Antoni, M. H., and others. (1991). Cognitive-behavioral stress management intervention buffers distress responses and immunologic changes following notification of HIV-1 seropositivity. *Journal of Consulting and Clinical Psychology, 59,* 906–915.

Antonuccio, D. (1995). Psychotherapy for depression: No stronger medicine. *American Psychologist, 50,* 452–454.

Apter, T. (1995). *Secret paths: Women in the new midlife.* New York: W. W. Norton.

Archer, R. P., & Cash, T. F. (1985). Physical attractiveness and maladjustment among psychiatric patients. *Journal of Social and Clinical Psychology, 3,* 170–180.

Archer, S. L. (1991). Gender differences in identity development. In R. M. Lerner, A. C. Peterson, & J. Brooks-Gunn (Eds.), *Encyclopedia of Adolescence,* I. New York: Garland.

Archer, S. L. (1992). A feminist's approach to identity research. In G. R. Adams, T. P. Gullotta, & R. Montemayor (Eds.), *Adolescent identity formation.* Newbury Park, CA: Sage.

Argyris, C. (1972). *The applicability of organizational psychology.* Cambridge: Cambridge University Press.

Arnold, D. H., Lonigan, C. J., Whitehurst, G. J., & Epstein, J. N. (1994). Accelerating language development through picture book reading: Replication and extension to a videotape training format. *Journal of Educational Psychology, 86,* 235–243.

Aronson, E. (1990). Applying social psychology to desegregation and energy conservation. *Personality and Social Psychology Bulletin, 16,* 118–132.

Asarnow, J. R., Carlson, G. A., & Guthrie, D. (1987). Coping strategies, self-perceptions, hopelessness, and perceived family environments in depressed and suicidal children. *Journal of Consulting and Clinical Psychology, 55,* 361–366.

Asch, S. E. (1952). *Social psychology.* Englewood Cliffs, NJ: Prentice-Hall.

Ashe, A. (1992). Cited in A hug for Arthur Ashe. (1992, April 14). *The New York Times,* p. A24.

Aslin, R. N., Pisoni, D. B., & Jusczyk, P. W. (1983). Auditory development and speech perception in infancy. In P. H. Mussen (Ed.), *Handbook of child psychology* (4th ed.). New York: Wiley.

Atkins, C. J., Kaplan, R. M., Timms, R. M., Reinsch, S., & Lofback, K. (1984). Behavioral exercise programs in the management of chronic obstructive pulmonary disease. *Journal of Consulting and Clinical Psychology, 52,* 591–603.

Atkinson, R. C. (1975). Mnemotechnics in second-language learning. *American Psychologist, 30,* 821–828.

Atkinson, R. C., & Shiffrin, R. M. (1968). Human memory: A proposed system and its control processes. In K. Spence (Ed.), *The psychology of learning and motivation* (Vol. 2). New York: Academic Press.

Audrain, J. E., Klesges, R. C., & Klesges, L. M. (1995). Relationship between obesity status and the metabolic effects of smoking in women. *Health Psychology, 14,* 116–123.

Ayanian, J. Z. (1993). Heart disease in Black and White. *New England Journal of Medicine, 329,* 656–658.

Ayanian, J. Z., and others. (1993). The relation between health insurance coverage and clinical outcome among women with breast cancer. *New England Journal of Medicine, 329,* 326–331.

Ayllon, T., & Haughton, E. (1962). Control of the behavior of schizophrenic patients by food. *Journal of the Experimental Analysis of Behavior, 5,* 343–352.

Azar, B. (1994a). Women are barraged by media on "the change." *APA Monitor, 25*(5), 24–25.

Azar, B. (1994b). Outcomes measurement is debated by profession. *APA Monitor, 25*(5), 29.

Azar, B. (1995a). Several genetic traits linked to alcoholism. *APA Monitor, 26*(5), 21–22.

Azar, B. (1995b). Which traits predict job performance? *APA Monitor, 26*(7), 30–31.

Azar, B. (1995c). Breaking through barriers to creativity. *APA Monitor, 26*(8), 1, 20.

Babcock, J. C., Waltz, J., Jacobson, N. S., & Gottman, J. M. (1993). Power and violence: The relation between communication patterns, power discrepancies, and domestic violence. *Journal of Consulting and Clinical Psychology, 61,* 40–50.

Bachrach, L. L. (1992). What we know about homelessness among mentally ill persons: An analytical review and commentary. In H. R. Lamb, L. L. Bachrach, & F. I. Kass (Eds.), *Treating the homeless mentally ill.* Washington, DC: American Psychiatric Press.

Baddeley, A. (1994). Working memory: The interface between memory and cognition. In D. L. Schacter & E. Tulving (Eds.), *Memory systems 1994.* Cambridge, MA: The MIT Press, a Bradford Book.

Bahrick, H. P., Bahrick, P. O., & Wittlinger, R. P. (1975). Fifty years of memory for names and faces: A cross-sectional approach. *Journal of Experimental Psychology: General, 104,* 54–75.

Bailey, J. M., & Pillard, R. C. (1991). A genetic study of male sexual orientation. *Archives of General Psychiatry, 48,* 1089–1096.

Baker, L. A., DeFries, J. C., & Fulker, D. W. (1983). Longitudinal stability of cognitive ability in the Colorado adoption project. *Child Development, 54,* 290–297.

Bal, D. G. (1992). Cancer in African Americans. *Ca-A Cancer Journal for Clinicians, 42,* 5–6.

Bandura, A. (1973). *Aggression: A social learning analysis.* Englewood Cliffs, NJ: Prentice-Hall.

Bandura, A. (1986). *Social foundations of thought and action: A social-cognitive theory.* Englewood Cliffs, NJ: Prentice-Hall.

Bandura, A. (1989). Human agency in social cognitive theory. *American Psychologist, 44,* 1175–1184.

Bandura, A. (1990). Perceived self-efficacy in the exercise of control over AIDS infection. *Evaluation and Program Planning, 13,* 9–17.

Bandura, A. (1991). Human agency: The rhetoric and the reality. *The American Psychologist, 46,* 157–162.

Bandura, A., Blanchard, E. B., & Ritter, B. (1969). The relative efficacy of desensitization and modeling approaches for inducing behavioral, affective, and cognitive changes. *Journal of Personality and Social Psychology, 13,* 173–199.

Bandura, A., & McDonald, F. J. (1963). Influence of social reinforcement and the behavior of models in shaping children's moral judgments. *Journal of Abnormal and Social Psychology, 67,* 274–281.

Bandura, A., Reese, L., & Adams, N. E. (1982). Microanalysis of action and fear arousal as a function of differential levels of perceived self-efficacy. *Journal of Personality and Social Psychology, 43,* 5–21.

Bandura, A., & Rosenthal, T. L. (1966). Vicarious classical conditioning as a function of fear arousal. *Journal of Personality and Social Psychology, 3,* 54–62.

Bandura, A., Ross, D., & Ross, S. A. (1963a). A comparative test of the status envy, and the secondary reinforcement theories of identificatory learning. *Journal of Abnormal and Social Psychology, 67,* 527–534.

Bandura, A., Ross, S. A., & Ross, D. (1963b). Imitation of film-mediated aggressive models. *Journal of Abnormal and Social Psychology, 66,* 3–11.

Bandura, A., Taylor, C. B., Williams, S. L., Medford, I. N., & Barchas, J. D. (1985). Catecholamine secretion as a function of perceived coping self-efficacy. *Journal of Consulting and Clinical Psychology, 53,* 406–414.

Bangert, R., Kulik, J., & Kulik, C. (1983). Individualized systems of instruction in secondary schools. *Review of Educational Research, 53,* 143–158.

Banks, M. S., & Shannon, E. (1993). Spatial and chromatic visual efficiency in human neonates. In C. E. Granrud (Ed.), *Visual perception and cognition in infancy.* Hillsdale, NJ: Erlbaum.

Banks, S. M., and others. (1995). The effects of message framing on mammography utilization. *Health Psychology, 14,* 178–184.

Baquet, C. R., Horm, J. W., Gibbs, T., & Greenwald, P. (1991). Socioeconomic factors and cancer incidence among Blacks and Whites. *Journal of the National Cancer Institute, 83,* 551–557.

Barbaree, H. E., & Marshall, W. L. (1991). The role of male sexual arousal in rape: Six models. *Journal of Consulting and Clinical Psychology, 59,* 621–631.

Bard, P. (1934). The neurohumoral basis of emotional reactions. In C. A. Murchison (Ed.), *Handbook of general experimental psychology.* Worcester, MA: Clark University Press.

Barlow, D. H. (1986). Causes of sexual dysfunction: The role of anxiety and cognitive interference. *Journal of Consulting and Clinical Psychology, 54,* 140–148.

Barlow, D. H. (1991). Introduction to the special issue on diagnoses, definitions, and *DSM-IV:* The science of classification. *Journal of Abnormal Psychology, 100,* 243–244.

Barlow, D. H. (1994). Cited in Howard, K., Barlow, D., Christiensen, A., & Frank, E. *Evaluating outcomes of psychological interventions: Evaluating the effectiveness of psychotherapy.* Symposium conducted at the meeting of the American Psychological Association, Los Angeles.

Barlow, D. H. (1995). Cited in Goleman, D. (1995, June 21). "Virtual reality" conquers fear of heights. *The New York Times,* p. C11.

Barnett, W. S., & Escobar, C. M. (1990). Economic costs and benefits of early intervention. In S. J. Meisels & J. P. Shonkoff (Eds.), *Handbook of early childhood intervention.* New York: Cambridge University Press.

Baron, R. A. (1990). Countering the effects of destructive criticism: The relative efficacy of four interventions. *Journal of Applied Psychology, 75,* 235–245.

Baron, R. A., & Byrne, D. (1991). *Social psychology: Understanding human interaction* (6th ed.). Boston: Allyn and Bacon.

Barr, C. E., Mednick, S. A., & Munk-Jorgensen, P. (1990). Exposure to influenza epidemics during gestation and adult schizophrenia: A 40-year study. *Archives of General Psychiatry, 47,* 869–874.

Barr, H. M., Streissguth, A. P., Darby, B. L., & Sampson, P. D. (1990). Prenatal exposure to alcohol, caffeine, tobacco, and aspirin. *Developmental Psychology, 26,* 339–348.

Barringer, F. (1989, June 9). Divorce data stir doubt on trial marriage. *The New York Times,* pp. A1, A28.

Barringer, F. (1993a, April 15). Sex survey of American men finds 1% are gay. *The New York Times,* pp. A1, A18.

Barringer, F. (1993b, April 28). For 32 million Americans, English is a second language. *The New York Times,* p. A18.

Barsalou, L. W. (1992). *Cognitive psychology: An overview for cognitive scientists.* Hillsdale, NJ: Erlbaum.

Bartecchi, C. E., MacKenzie, T. D., & Schrier, R. W. (1994). The human cost of tobacco use. *New England Journal of Medicine, 330,* 907–912.

Bartek, S. E., Krebs, D. L., & Taylor, M. C. (1993). Coping, defending, and the relations between moral judgment and moral behavior in prostitutes and other female juvenile delinquents. *Journal of Abnormal Psychology, 102,* 66–73.

Bartoshuk, L. M., & Beauchamp, G. K. (1994). Chemical senses. *Annual Review of Psychology, 45,* 419–449.

Bashore, T. R., & Rapp, P. E. (1993). Are there alternatives to traditional polygraph procedures? *Psychological Bulletin, 113,* 3–22.

Bates, E., Thal, D., & Janowsky, J. S. (1992). Early language development and its neural correlates. In I. Rapin & S. Segalowitz (Eds.), *Handbook of neuropsychology: Vol. 6. Child neurology.* Amsterdam: Elsevier.

Batson, C. D., and others. (1989a). Negative state relief and the empathy-altruism hypothesis. *Journal of Personality and Social Psychology, 56,* 922–933.

Batson, C. D., and others. (1989b). Religious prosocial motivation: Is it altruistic or egoistic? *Journal of Personality and Social Psychology, 57,* 873–884.

Baum, A., & Fleming, I. (1993). Implications of psychological research on stress and technological accidents. *American Psychologist, 48,* 665–672.

Baum, W., & Heath, J. I. (1992). Behavioral explanations and intentional explanations in psychology. *American Psychologist, 47,* 1312–1317.

Baumeister, R. F., & Covington, M. V. (1985). Self-esteem, persuasion, and retrospective distortion of initial attitudes. *Electronic Social Psychology, 1,* 1–22.

Baumeister, R. F., Stillwell, A. M., & Heatherton, T. F. (1994). Guilt: An interpersonal approach. *Psychological Bulletin, 115,* 243–267.

Baumgardner, A. H., Heppner, P. P., & Arkin, R. M. (1986). Role of causal attribution in personal problem solving. *Journal of Personality and Social Psychology, 50,* 636–643.

Baumrind, D. (1985). Research using intentional deception: Ethical issues revisited. *American Psychologist, 40,* 165–174.

Baumrind, D. (1986). Sex differences in moral reasoning: Response to Walker's (1984) conclusion that there are none. *Child Development, 57,* 511–521.

Baumrind, D. (1991a). The influence of parenting style on adolescent competence and substance abuse. *Journal of Early Adolescence, 11,* 56–95.

Baumrind, D. (1991b). Parenting styles and adolescent development. In J. Brooks-Gunn, R. Lerner, & A. C. Petersen (Eds.), *Encyclopedia of Adolescence, II.* New York: Garland.

Baumrind, D. (1993). The average expectable environment is not good enough: A response to Scarr. *Child Development, 64,* 1299–1317.

Beauchamp, G. K. (1981). Paper presented to the Conference on the Determination of Behavior by Chemical Stimuli, Hebrew University, Jerusalem.

Beauchamp, G. K. (1993). Cited in Blakeslee, S. (1993, September 7). Human nose may hold an additional organ for a real sixth sense. *The New York Times,* p. C3.

Beck, A. T (1991). Cognitive therapy: A 30-year retrospective. *American Psychologist, 46,* 368–375.

Beck, A. T. (1993). Cognitive therapy: Past, present, and future. *Journal of Consulting and Clinical Psychology, 61,* 194–198.

Beck, A. T., Brown, G., Berchick, R. J., Stewart, B. L., & Steer, R. A. (1990). Relationship between hopelessness and ultimate suicide. *American Journal of Psychiatry, 147,* 190–195.

Beck, A. T., Epstein, N., Brown, G., & Steer, R. A. (1988). An inventory for measuring clinical anxiety: Psychometric properties. *Journal of Consulting and Clinical Psychology, 56,* 893–897.

Beck, A. T., & Freeman, A. (1990). *Cognitive therapy of personality disorders.* New York: Guilford.

Beck, A. T., & Haaga, D. A. F. (1992). The future of cognitive therapy. *Psychotherapy, 29,* 34–38.

Becker, L. B., and others. (1993). Racial differences in the incidence of cardiac arrest and subsequent survival. *New England Journal of Medicine, 329,* 600–606.

Bee, H. L., and others. (1982). Prediction of IQ and language skill from perinatal status, child performance, family characteristics, and mother–infant interaction. *Child Development, 53,* 1134–1156.

Beilin, H. (1992). Piaget's enduring contribution to developmental psychology. *Developmental Psychology, 28,* 191–204.

Belchetz, P. E. (1994). Hormonal treatment of postmenopausal women. *New England Journal of Medicine, 330,* 1062–1071.

Bell, A. P., Weinberg, M. S., & Hammersmith, S. K. (1981). *Sexual preference: Its development in men and women.* Bloomington: University of Indiana Press.

Bell, P. A. (1992). In defense of the negative affect escape model of heat and aggression. *Psychological Bulletin, 111,* 342–346.

Belle, D. (1990). Poverty and women's mental health. *American Psychologist, 45,* 385–389.

Belsky, J. (1990). Developmental risks associated with infant day care: Attachment insecurity, noncompliance and aggression? In I. S. Cherazi (Ed.), *Psychosocial issues in day care* (pp. 37–68). New York: American Psychiatric Press.

Belsky, J., Fish, M., & Isabella, R. (1991). Continuity and discontinuity in infant negative and positive emotionality: Family attachments and attachment consequences. *Developmental Psychology, 27,* 421–431.

Belsky, J., & Rovine, M. (1988). Nonmaternal care in the first year of life and infant–parent attachment security. *Child Development, 59,* 157–167.

Bem, S. L. (1993). *The lenses of gender.* New Haven: Yale University Press.

Benbow, C. P., & Stanley, J. C. (1980) Sex differences in mathematical ability: Fact or artifact? *Science, 210,* 1029–1031.

Benderly, B. L. (1993, June 20). The perps are almost always male. *The New York Times Book Review,* p. 10.

Bennett, D. (1985). Rogers: More intuition in therapy. *APA Monitor, 16*(10), 3.

Benson, H. (1975). *The relaxation response.* New York: Morrow.

Benson, H., Manzetta, B. R., & Rosner, B. (1973). Decreased systolic blood pressure in hypertensive subjects who practiced meditation. *Journal of Clinical Investigation, 52,* 8.

Benson, P. L., Karabenick, S. A., & Lerner, R. M. (1976). Pretty pleases: The effects of physical attractiveness, race, and sex on receiving help. *Journal of Experimental Social Psychology, 12,* 409–415.

Berenbaum, H., & Connelly, J. (1993). The effect of stress on hedonic capacity. *Journal of Abnormal Psychology, 102,* 474–481.

Berger, B. G. (1993). Exercise and the quality of life. In R. N. Singer, M. Murphey, & L. K. Tennant (Eds.), *Handbook of research on sport psychology* (pp. 729–760). New York: Macmillan.

Berkowitz, L. (1987). Mood, self-awareness, and willingness to help. *Journal of Personality and Social Psychology, 52,* 721–729.

Berkowitz, L. (1988). Frustrations, appraisals, and aversively stimulated aggression. *Aggressive Behavior, 14,* 3–11.

Berkowitz, L. (1994). Is something missing? Some observations prompted by the cognitive-neoassociationist view of anger and emotional aggression. In L. R. Huesmann (Ed.), *Aggressive behavior: Current perspectives.* New York: Plenum.

Berliner, D. (1993). Cited in Blakeslee, S. (1993, September 7). Human nose may hold an additional organ for a real sixth sense. *The New York Times,* p. C3.

Berman, J. S., Miller, R. C., & Massman, P. J. (1985). Cognitive therapy versus systematic desensitization: Is one therapy superior? *Psychological Bulletin, 97,* 451–461.

Bernal, M. E., & Castro, F. G. (1994). Are clinical psychologists prepared for service and research with ethnic minorities? *American Psychologist, 49,* 797–805.

Berne, E. (1976). *Beyond games and scripts.* New York: Grove Press.

Bernstein, W. M., Stephenson, B. O., Snyder, M. L., & Wicklund, R. A. (1983). Causal ambiguity and heterosexual affiliation. *Journal of Experimental Social Psychology, 19,* 78–92.

Berntzen, D., & Götestam, K. G. (1987). Effects of on-demand versus fixed-interval schedules in the treatment of chronic pain with analgesic compounds. *Journal of Consulting and Clinical Psychology, 55,* 213–217.

Berquier, A., & Ashton, R. (1992). Characteristics of the frequent nightmare sufferer. *Journal of Abnormal Psychology, 101,* 246–250.

Bersoff, D. (1994). Cited in DeAngelis, T. (1994). Experts see little impact from insanity plea ruling. *APA Monitor, 25*(6), 28.

Betancourt, H., & López, S. R. (1993). The study of culture, ethnicity, and race in American psychology. *American Psychologist, 48,* 629–637.

Beutler, L. E. (1991). Have all won and must all have prizes? *Journal of Consulting and Clinical Psychology, 59,* 226–232.

Beutler, L. E., & Kendall, P. C. (1991). Ethical dilemmas. *Journal of Consulting and Clinical Psychology, 59,* 245–255.

Bevan, W., & Kessel, F. (1994). Plain truths and home cooking: Thoughts on the making and remaking of psychology. *American Psychologist, 49,* 505–509.

Bexton, W. H., Heron, W., & Scott, T. H. (1954). Effects of decreased variation in the sensory environment. *Canadian Journal of Psychology, 8,* 70–76.

Birren, J. E. (1983). Aging in America: Roles for psychology. *American Psychologist, 38,* 298–299.

Bishop, J. E. (1993, March 17). When smokers quit is a key to cancer risk. *The Wall Street Journal,* pp. B1, B7.

Bjorklund, D. F., & de Marchena, M. R. (1984). Developmental shifts in the basis of organization in memory: The role of associative versus categorical relatedness in children's free recall. *Child Development, 55,* 952–962.

Blakeslee, S. (1992a, January 7). Scientists unraveling chemistry of dreams. *The New York Times,* pp. C1, C10.

Blakeslee, S. (1992b, January 22). An epidemic of genital warts raises concern but not alarm. *The New York Times,* p. C12.

Blakeslee, S. (1992c, October 27). Nerve cell rhythm may be key to consciousness. *The New York Times,* pp. C1, C10.

Blakeslee, S. (1993, September 7). Human nose may hold an additional organ for a real sixth sense. *The New York Times,* p. C3.

Blakeslee, S. (1994, April 13). Black smokers' higher risk of cancer may be genetic. *The New York Times,* p. C14.

Blakeslee, S. (1995a, March 21). How the brain might work: A new theory of consciousness. *The New York Times,* pp. C1, C10.

Blakeslee, S. (1995b, March 28). How do you stop agonizing pain in an arm that no longer exists? A scientist does it with mirrors. *The New York Times,* p. C3.

Blakeslee, S. (1995c, May 16). The mystery of music: How it works in the brain. *The New York Times,* pp. C1, C10.

Blanchard, E. B. (1992a). Introduction to the special issue on behavioral medicine: An update for the 1990s. *Journal of Consulting and Clinical Psychology, 60,* 491–492.

Blanchard, E. B. (1992b). Psychological treatment of benign headache disorders. *Journal of Consulting and Clinical Psychology, 60,* 537–551.

Blanchard, E. B., and others. (1990a). A controlled evaluation of thermal biofeedback and thermal feedback combined with cognitive therapy in the treatment of vascular headache. *Journal of Consulting and Clinical Psychology, 58,* 216–224.

Blanchard, E. B., and others. (1990b). Placebo-controlled evaluation of abbreviated progressive muscle relaxation and of relaxation combined with cognitive therapy in the treatment of tension headache. *Journal of Consulting and Clinical Psychology, 58,* 210–215.

Blanchard, E. B., and others. (1991). The role of regular home practice in the relaxation treatment of tension headache. *Journal of Consulting and Clinical Psychology, 59,* 467–470.

Blanck, P. D., Bellack, A. S., Rosnow, R. L., Rotheram-Borus, M. J., & Schooler, N. R. (1992). Scientific rewards and conflicts of ethical choices in human subjects research. *American Psychologist, 47,* 959–965.

Blass, E. M., & Smith, B. A. (1992). Differential effects of sucrose, fructose, glucose, and lactose on crying in 1- to 3-day-old human infants: Qualitative and quantitative considerations. *Developmental Psychology, 28,* 804–810.

Blass, T. (1991). Understanding behavior in the Milgram obedience experiment: The roles of personality, situations, and their interactions. *Journal of Personality and Social Psychology, 60,* 398–413.

Blatt, S. J., Quinlan, D. M., Pilkonis, P. A., & Shea, M. T. (1995). Impact of perfectionism and need for approval on the brief treatment of depression: The National Institute of Mental Health Treatment of Depression Collaborative Research Program revisited. *Journal of Consulting and Clinical Psychology, 63,* 125–132.

Block, J. (1995). A contrarian view of the five-factor approach to personality description. *Psychological Bulletin, 117,* 187–215.

Bloom, B. L. (1992). Computer assisted psychological intervention: A review and commentary. *Clinical Psychology Review, 12,* 169–197.

Bloom, J. D., & Williams, M. H. (1994). *Management and treatment of insanity acquittees: A model for the 1990s.* Washington, DC: American Psychiatric Press.

Bloom, L., Lahey, L., Hood, L., Lifter, K., & Fiess, K. (1980). Complex sentences: Acquisition of syntactic connectives and the semantic relations they encode. *Journal of Child Language, 7,* 235–261.

Bloom, L., Merkin, S., & Wootten, J. (1982). *Wh*-questions: Linguistic factors that contribute to the sequence of acquisition. *Child Development, 53,* 1084–1092.

Bloom, L., & Mudd, S. A. (1991). Depth of processing approach to face recognition: A test of two theories. *Journal of Experimental Psychology: Learning, Memory, and Cognition, 17,* 556–565.

Bly, R. (1990). *Iron John.* Reading, MA: Addison-Wesley.

Boden, M. A. (1994). What is creativity? In M. A. Boden (Ed.), *Dimensions of creativity.* Cambridge, MA: The MIT Press, a Bradford Book.

Bodenhausen, G. V. (1988). Stereotypic biases in social decision making and memory. *Journal of Personality and Social Psychology, 55,* 726–737.

Boneau, C. A. (1992). Observations on psychology's past and future. *American Psychologists, 47,* 1586–1596.

Bootzin, R. R., Epstein, D., & Wood, J. N. (1991). Stimulus control instructions. In P. Hauri (Ed.), *Case studies in insomnia.* New York: Plenum.

Bordo, S. (1993). *Unbearable weight: Feminism, Western culture, and the body.* Berkeley: University of California Press.

Borgida, E., & Campbell, B. (1982). Belief relevance and attitude-behavior consistency: The moderating role of personal experience. *Journal of Personality and Social Psychology, 42,* 239–247.

Borkovec, T. D., & Costello, E. (1993). Efficacy of applied relaxation and cognitive-behavioral therapy in the treatment of generalized anxiety disorder. *Journal of Consulting and Clinical Psychology, 61,* 611–619.

Borod, J. C. (1992). Interhemispheric and intrahemispheric control of emotion: A focus on unilateral brain damage. *Journal of Consulting and Clinical Psychology, 60,* 339–348.

Boskind-White, M., & White, W. C. (1983). *Bulimarexia: The binge/purge cycle.* New York: W. W. Norton.

Boston Women's Health Book Collective. (1992). *The new our bodies, ourselves.* New York: Simon & Schuster.

Bothwell, R. K., Deffenbacher, K. A., & Brigham, J. C. (1987). Correlation of eyewitness accuracy and confidence: Optimality hypothesis revisited. *Journal of Applied Psychology, 72,* 691–695.

Botvin, G. J., and others. (1990). Preventing adolescent drug abuse through a multimodal cognitive-behavioral approach: Results of a 3-year study. *Journal of Consulting and Clinical Psychology, 58,* 437–446.

Bouchard, C. (1991). Is weight fluctuation a risk factor? *New England Journal of Medicine, 324,* 1887–1889.

Bouchard, T. J., Jr., Lykken, D. T., McGue, M., Segal, N. L., & Tellegen, A. (1990). Sources of human psychological differences: The Minnesota study of twins reared apart. *Science, 250,* 223–228.

Bower, G. H. (1981). Mood and memory. *American Psychologist, 36,* 129–148.

Bowlby, J. (1988). *A secure base.* New York: Basic Books.

Bowman, M. L. (1989). Testing individual differences in ancient China. *American Psychologist, 44,* 576–578.

Boyatzis, R. E. (1974). The effect of alcohol consumption on the aggressive behavior of men. *Quarterly Journal for the Study of Alcohol, 35,* 959–972.

Boyd-Franklin, N. (1995, August). A multisystems model for treatment interventions with inner-city African American families. Master lecture delivered to the meeting of the American Psychological Association, New York.

Bracha, H. S., Torrey, E. F., Gottesman, I. I., Bigelow, L. B., & Cunniff, C. (1992). Second-trimester markers of fetal size in schizophrenia: A study of monozygotic twins. *American Journal of Psychiatry, 149,* 1355–1361.

Bradley, R. H., and others. (1989). Home environment and cognitive development in the first 3 years of life: A collaborative study involving six sites and three ethnic groups in North America. *Developmental Psychology, 25,* 217–235.

Bransford, J. D., Nitsch, K. E., & Franks, J. J. (1977). Schooling and the facilitation of knowing. In R. C. Anderson, R. J. Spiro, & W. E. Montague (Eds.), *Schooling and the acquisition of knowledge.* Hillsdale, NJ: Erlbaum.

Braun, B. G. (1988). *Treatment of multiple personality disorder.* Washington, DC: American Psychiatric Press.

Bray, N. W., Hersh, R. E., & Turner, L. A. (1985). Selective remembering during adolescence. *Developmental Psychology, 21,* 290–294.

Bray, R. M., & Sugarman, R. (1980). Social facilitation among interaction groups: Evidence for the evaluation-apprehension hypothesis. *Personality and Social Psychology Bulletin, 6,* 137–142.

Breckler, S. J., & Wiggins, E. C. (1989). Affect versus evaluation in the structure of attitudes. *Journal of Experimental Social Psychology, 25,* 253–271.

Brenner, J. (1992). Cited in Williams, L. (1992, February 6). Woman's image in a mirror: Who defines what she sees? *The New York Times,* pp. A1, B7.

Brent, E., & Granberg, D. (1982). Subjective agreement with the presidential candidates of 1976 and 1980. *Journal of Personality and Social Psychology, 42,* 393–403.

Brewin, C. R., Andrews, B., & Gotlib, I. H. (1993). Psychopathology and early experience: A reappraisal of retrospective reports. *Psychological Bulletin, 113,* 82–98.

Bridges, K. (1932). Emotional development in early infancy. *Child Development, 3,* 324–341.

Bridgwater, C. A. (1982). What candor can do. *Psychology Today, 16*(5), 16.

Brigham, J. C. (1980). Limiting conditions of the "physical attractiveness stereotype": Attributions about divorce. *Journal of Research in Personality, 14,* 365–375.

Brody, J. E. (1989, January 5). How women can begin to cope with premenstrual syndrome, a biological mystery. *The New York Times,* p. B12.

Brody, J. E. (1991, April 9). Not just music, bird song is a means of courtship and defense. *The New York Times,* pp. C1, C9.

Brody, J. E. (1992a, January 8). Migraines and the estrogen connection. *The New York Times,* p. C12.

Brody, J. E. (1992b, December 30). How weight loss changes risk. *The New York Times,* p. C6.

Brody, J. E. (1993, December 1). Liberated at last from the myths about menopause. *The New York Times,* p. C15.

Brody, J. E. (1994, March 16). Cancer pain is beatable, but too few know it. *The New York Times,* p. C12.

Bronstein, P., & Quina, K. (1988). (Eds.). *Teaching a psychology of people: Resources for gender and sociocultural awareness.* Washington, DC: American Psychological Association.

Broughton, R. S. (1991). *Parapsychology: The controversial science.* New York: Ballantine.

Brown, B. B., & Altman, J. (1981). Territoriality and residential crime. In P. A. Brantingham & P. L. Brantingham (Eds.), *Urban crime and environmental criminology.* Beverly Hills, CA: Sage.

Brown, D. E. (1991). *Human universals.* Philadelphia: Temple University Press.

Brown, L. S. (1992). A feminist critique of the personality disorders. In L. Brown & M. Balou (Eds.), *Personality and psychopathology: Feminist reappraisals.* New York: Guilford.

Brown, R., & Kulik, J. (1977). Flashbulb memories. *Cognition, 5,* 73–99.

Brown, R., & McNeill, D. (1966). The tip-of-the-tongue phenomenon. *Journal of Verbal Learning and Verbal Behavior, 5,* 325–337.

Brown, S. A. (1985). Expectancies versus background in the prediction of college drinking patterns. *Journal of Consulting and Clinical Psychology, 53,* 123–130.

Brown, S. A., Goldman, M. S., & Christiansen, B. A. (1985). Do alcohol expectancies mediate drinking patterns of adults? *Journal of Consulting and Clinical Psychology, 53,* 512–519.

Browne, A. (1993). Violence against women by male partners: Prevalence, outcomes, and policy implications. *American Psychologist, 48,* 1077–1087.

Browne, M. A., & Mahoney, M. J. (1984). Sport psychology. *Annual Review of Psychology, 35,* 605–625.

Browne, M. W. (1995, June 6). Scientists deplore flight from reason. *The New York Times,* pp. C1, C7.

Brownell, K. D. (1993). Whether obesity should be treated. *Health Psychology, 12,* 339–341.

Brownell, K. D., & Rodin, J. (1994). The dieting maelstrom: Is it possible and advisable to lose weight? *American Psychologist, 49,* 781–791.

Brownell, K. D., & Wadden, T. A. (1992). Obesity: Understanding a serious, prevalent, and refractory disorder. *Journal of Consulting and Clinical Psychology, 60,* 505–517.

Brownell, W. E. (1992). Cited in Browne, M. W. (1992, June 9). Ear's own sounds may underlie its precision. *The New York Times,* pp. C1, C8.

Bruner, J. S. (1983). *Child's talk: Learning to use language.* New York: W. W. Norton.

Bryant, P. (1982). Piaget's questions. *British Journal of Psychology, 73,* 157–163.

Buchanan, C. M., Eccles, J. S., & Becker, J. B. (1992). Are adolescents the victims of raging hormones? Evidence for activational effects of hormones on moods and behavior at adolescence. *Psychological Bulletin, 111,* 62–107.

Budd, L. S. (1993). *Living with the active alert child.* St. Paul, MN: Parenting Press.

Buffone, G. W. (1984). Running and depression. In M. L. Sachs & G. W. Buffone (Eds.), *Running as therapy: An integrated approach.* Lincoln: University of Nebraska Press.

Bullock, M. (1985). Animism in childhood thinking: A new look at an old question. *Developmental Psychology, 21,* 217–225.

Bulman, R. J., & Wortman, C. B. (1977). Attribution of blame and coping in the "real world": Severe accident victims react to their lot. *Journal of Personality and Social Psychology, 35,* 351–363.

Burish, T. G., Carey, M. P., Krozely, M. G., & Greco, F. A. (1987). Conditioned side effects induced by cancer chemotherapy: Prevention through behavioral treatment. *Journal of Consulting and Clinical Psychology, 55,* 42–48.

Burish, T. G., Snyder, S. L., & Jenkins, R. A. (1991). Preparing patients for cancer chemotherapy: Effect of coping preparation and relaxation interventions. *Journal of Consulting and Clinical Psychology, 59,* 518–525.

Burman, B., & Margolin, G. (1992). Analysis of the association between marital relationships and health problems: An interactional perspective. *Psychological Bulletin, 112,* 39–63.

Burns, D. D., & Nolen-Hoeksema, S. (1992). Therapeutic empathy and recovery from depression in cognitive-behavioral therapy: A structural equation model. *Journal of Consulting and Clinical Psychology, 60,* 441–449.

Burns, G. L., & Farina, A. (1987). Physical attractiveness and self-perception of mental disorder. *Journal of Abnormal Psychology, 96,* 161–163.

Burnstein, E. (1983). Persuasion as argument processing. In M. Brandstatter, J. H. Davis, & G. Stocker-Kreichgauer (Eds.), *Group decision processes.* London: Academic Press.

Burnstein, E., & Schul, Y. (1982). The informational basis of social judgments: Operations in forming an impression of another person. *Journal of Experimental Social Psychology, 18,* 217–234.

Burt, M. R. (1980). Cultural myths and supports for rape. *Journal of Personality and Social Psychology, 38,* 217–230.

Busch, M. P., and others. (1991). Evaluation of screened blood donations for HIV-1 infection by culture and DNA amplification of pooled cells. *New England Journal of Medicine, 325,* 1–5.

Bushman, B. J., & Cooper, H. M. (1990). Effects of alcohol on human aggression: An integrative research review. *Psychological Bulletin, 107,* 341–354.

Buss, A. H. (1983). Social rewards and personality. *Journal of Personality and Social Psychology, 44,* 553–563.

Buss, A. H.(1986). *Social behavior and personality.* Hillsdale, NJ: Erlbaum.

Buss, D. M. (1992). Is there a universal human nature? *Contemporary Psychology, 37,* 1262–1263.

Buss, D. M. (1994). *The evolution of desire: Strategies of human mating.* New York: Basic Books.

Buss, D. M. (1995). Psychological sex differences: Origins through sexual selection. *American Psychologist, 50,* 164–168.

Byrnes, J., & Takahira, S. (1993). Explaining gender differences on SAT-math items. *Developmental Psychology, 29,* 805–810.

Cacioppo, J. T., Martzke, J. S., Petty, R. E., & Tassinary, L. G. (1988). Specific forms of facial EMG response index emotions during an interview. *Journal of Personality and Social Psychology, 54,* 552–604.

Califano, J. A. (1995). The wrong way to stay slim. *New England Journal of Medicine, 333,* 1214–1216.

Campbell, A. (1993). *Men, women, and aggression.* New York: Basic Books.

Campbell, J. (1994). *Past, space, and self.* Cambridge, MA: The MIT Press, a Bradford Book.

Campos, J. J., Hiatt, S., Ramsey, D., Henderson, C., & Svejda, M. (1978). The emergence of fear on the visual cliff. In M. Lewis & L. Rosenblum (Eds.), *The origins of affect.* New York: Plenum.

Campos, J. J., Langer, A., & Krowitz, A. (1970). Cardiac responses on the visual cliff in prelocomotor infants. *Science, 170,* 196–197.

Cannon, W. B. (1927). The James–Lange theory of emotions: A critical examination and an alternative theory. *American Journal of Psychology, 39,* 106–124.

Cantor, N. (1990). From thought to behavior: "Having" and "doing" in the study of personality and behavior. *American Psychologist, 45,* 735–750.

Cantrell, R. P., Stenner, A. J., & Katzenmeyer, W. G. (1977). Teacher knowledge, attitudes, and classroom teaching correlates of student achievement. *Journal of Educational Psychology, 69,* 180–190.

Capaldi, E. D. (1993, August). The psychology of eating: Why we like the foods we like. G. Stanley Hall lecture presented to the American Psychological Association, Toronto, Canada.

Cappella, J. N., & Palmer, M. T. (1990). Attitude similarity, relational history, and attraction: The mediating effects of kinesic and vocal behaviors. *Communication Monographs, 5,* 161–183.

Carey, G. (1992). Twin imitation for antisocial behavior: Implications for genetic and family environment research. *Journal of Abnormal Psychology, 101,* 18–25.

Carey, G., & DiLalla, D. L. (1994). Personality and psychopathology: Genetic perspectives. *Journal of Abnormal Psychology, 103,* 32–43.

Carey, M. P., & Burish, T. G. (1987). Providing relaxation training to cancer chemotherapy patients: A comparison of three delivery techniques. *Journal of Consulting and Clinical Psychology, 55,* 732–737.

Carey, M. P., & Burish, T. G. (1988). Etiology and treatment of the psychological side effects associated with cancer chemotherapy: A critical review and discussion. *Psychological Bulletin, 104,* 307–325.

Carling, P. J. (1990). Major mental illness, housing, and supports: The promise of community integration. *American Psychologist, 45,* 969–975.

Carlson, J. G., & Hatfield, E. (1992). *Psychology of emotion.* Fort Worth, TX: Harcourt Brace Jovanovich.

Carmichael, L. L., Hogan, H. P., & Walter, A. A. (1932). An experimental study of the effect of language on the reproduction of visually perceived form. *Journal of Experimental Psychology, 15,* 73–86.

Carpenter, W. T., Jr., & Buchanan, R. W. (1994). Schizophrenia. *New England Journal of Medicine, 330,* 681–690.

Carroll, K. M., Rounsaville, B. J., & Nich, C. (1994). Blind man's bluff: Effectiveness and significance of psychotherapy and pharmacotherapy blinding procedures in a clinical trial. *Journal of Consulting and Clinical Psychology, 62,* 276–280.

Carver, C. S., & Gaines, J. G. (1987). Optimism, pessimism, and postpartum depression. *Cognitive Therapy and Research, 11,* 449–462.

Case, R. (1992). *The mind's staircase: Exploring the conceptual underpinnings of children's thought and knowledge.* Hillsdale, NJ: Erlbaum.

Castelli, W. (1994). Cited in Brody, J. E. (1994, February 8). Scientist at work—William Castelli: Preaching the gospel of healthy hearts. *The New York Times,* pp. C1, C10.

Cattell, R. B. (1949). *The culture-free intelligence test.* Champaign, IL: Institute for Personality and Ability Testing.

Cattell, R. B. (1965). *The scientific analysis of personality.* Baltimore: Penguin.

Caulfield, M., and others. (1994). Linkage of the angiotensinogen gene to essential hypertension. *New England Journal of Medicine, 330,* 1629–1633.

Ceci, S. J., & Bruck, M. (1993). Suggestibility of the child witness: A historical review and synthesis. *Psychological Bulletin, 113,* 403–439.

Celis, W. (1991, January 2). Students trying to draw line between sex and an assault. *The New York Times,* pp. A1, B8.

Celis, W. (1993, January 10). College curriculums shaken to the core. *Education Life (The New York Times),* Section 4A, pp. 16–18.

Center for Women in Government. (1992). Women in Public Service Survey. Rockefeller College of Public Affairs and Policy. Cited in Few women found in top public jobs. (1992, January 3). *The New York Times*, p. A12.

CDC (Centers for Disease Control). (1985). *Suicide surveillance: 1970–1980.* Washington, DC: U.S. Department of Health and Human Services.

CDC (Centers for Disease Control). (1991). Mortality attributable to HIV infection/AIDS—United States, 1981–1990. *Journal of the American Medical Association, 265,* 848.

CDC (Centers for Disease Control and Prevention). (1993, October). *HIV/AIDS surveillance: Third quarter edition. U.S. AIDS cases reported through September 1993.* Atlanta, GA: U.S. Department of Health and Human Services.

CDC (Centers for Disease Control and Prevention). (1995). Children aged 10 to 14 [on-line]. (1995, April 21). America Online.

Cepeda-Benito, A. (1993). Meta-analytical review of the efficacy of nicotine chewing gum in smoking treatment programs. *Journal of Consulting and Clinical Psychology, 61,* 822–830.

Chadwick, P. D. J., & Lowe, C. F. (1990). Measurement and modification of delusional beliefs. *Journal of Consulting and Clinical Psychology, 58,* 225–232.

Chaiken, S., & Eagly, A. H. (1983). Communication modality as a determinant of persuasion: The role of communicator salience. *Journal of Personality and Social Psychology, 45,* 241–256.

Chan, C. (1992). Cultural considerations in counseling Asian American lesbians and gay men. In S. Dworkin & F. Gutierrez (Eds.), *Counseling gay men and lesbians: Journey to the end of the rainbow.* Alexandria, VA: American Association for Counseling and Development.

Chartrand, S. (1993, July 18). A split in thinking among keepers of artificial intelligence. *The New York Times,* p. E6.

Chassin, L., Mann, L. M., & Sher, K. J. (1988). Self-awareness theory, family history of alcoholism, and adolescent alcohol involvement. *Journal of Abnormal Psychology, 97,* 206–217.

Chesney, M. A. (1993). Health psychology in the 21st century: Acquired immunodeficiency syndrome as a harbinger of things to come. *Health Psychology 12,* 259–268.

Chesney, M. A., & Coates, T. J. (1990). Health promotion and disease prevention: AIDS puts the models to the test. In S. Petro and others (Eds.), *Ending the HIV epidemic* (pp. 48–62). Santa Cruz, CA: ETR Associates.

Chesno, F. A., & Kilmann, P. R. (1975). Effects of stimulation intensity on sociopathic avoidance learning. *Journal of Abnormal Psychology, 84,* 144–151.

Cheung, F. K., & Snowden, L. R. (1990). Community mental health and ethnic minority populations. *Community Mental Health Journal, 26,* 277–291.

Childs, E. K. (1990). Therapy, feminist ethics, and the community of color with particular emphasis on the treatment of Black women. In H. Lerman & N. Porter (Eds.), *Feminist ethics in psychotherapy* (pp. 195–203). New York: Springer.

Chitayat, D. (1993, February). Presentation to the Fifth International Interdisciplinary Congress on Women, University of Costa Rica, San Jose, Costa Rica.

Chomsky, N. (1980). Rules and representations. *Behavioral and Brain Sciences, 3,* 1–16.

Chomsky, N. (1991). Linguistics and cognitive science: Problems and mysteries. In A. Kasher (Ed.), *The Chomskyan turn.* Cambridge, MA: Basil Blackwell.

Christiensen, A. (1994). Cited in Howard, K., Barlow, D., Christiensen, A., & Frank, E. *Evaluating outcomes of psychological interventions: Evaluating the effectiveness of psychotherapy.* Symposium conducted at the meeting of the American Psychological Association, Los Angeles.

Chronicle of Higher Education (1992, March 18), p. A35–A44.

Chwalisz, K., Diener, E., & Gallagher, D. (1988). Autonomic arousal feedback and emotional experience: Evidence from the spinal cord injured. *Journal of Personality and Social Psychology, 54,* 820–828.

Cialdini, R. B., & Fultz, J. (1990). Interpreting the negative mood-helping literature via "mega"-analysis: A contrary view. *Psychological Bulletin, 107,* 210–214.

Cinciripini, P. M., Lapitsky, L., Seay, S., Wallfisch, A., Kitchens, K., & Van Vunakis, H. (1995). The effects of smoking schedules on cessation outcome: Can we improve on common methods of gradual and abrupt nicotine withdrawal? *Journal of Consulting and Clinical Psychology, 63,* 388–399.

Clark, E. V. (1993). *The lexicon in acquisition.* New York: Cambridge University Press.

Clark, L. A., Watson, D., & Mineka, S. M. (1994). Temperament, personality, and the mood and anxiety disorders. *Journal of Abnormal Psychology, 103,* 103–116.

Clarke-Stewart, K. A. (1989). Infant day care: Maligned or malignant? *American Psychologist, 44,* 266–273.

Clarke-Stewart, K. A. (1990). The 'effects' of infant day care reconsidered: Risks for parents, children, and researchers. In N. Fox & G. G. Fein (Eds.), *Infant day care: The current debate* (pp. 61–86). Norwood, NJ: Ablex.

Clarke-Stewart, K. A. (1991). A home is not a school: The effects of child care on children's development. *Journal of Social Issues, 47,* 105–123.

Clement, J. (1991). Nonformal reasoning in experts and in science students: The use of analogies, extreme cases, and physical intuition. In J. Voss, D. Perkins, & J. Siegel (Eds.), *Informal reasoning and education.* Hillsdale, NJ: Erlbaum.

Clkurel, K., & Gruzelier, J. (1990). The effects of active alert hypnotic induction on lateral haptic processing. *British Journal of Experimental and Clinical Hypnosis, 11,* 17–25.

Coe, C. (1993). Cited in Adler, T. (1993). Men and women affected by stress, but differently. *APA Monitor, 24*(7), 8–9.

Coe, W. C., & Yaskinski, E. (1985). Volitional experiences associated with breaching posthypnotic amnesia. *Journal of Personality and Social Psychology, 48,* 716–722.

Cohen, L. A. (1987, November). Diet and cancer. *Scientific American,* 42–48, 53–54.

Cohen, S., Evans, G. W., Stokols, D., & Krantz, D. S. (1986). *Behavior, health, and environmental stress.* New York: Plenum.

Cohen, S., Tyrrell, D. A. J., & Smith, A. P. (1993). Negative life events, perceived stress, negative affect, and susceptibility to the common cold. *Journal of Personality and Social Psychology, 64,* 131–140.

Cohen, S., & Williamson, G. M. (1991). Stress and infectious disease in humans. *Psychological Bulletin, 109,* 5–24.

Cohen, E. G. (1990). Weather and violent crime. *Environment and Behavior, 22,* 280–294.

Cohn, L. D., Macfarlane, S., Yanez, C., & Imai, W. K. (1995). Risk-perception: Differences between adolescents and adults. *Health Psychology, 14,* 217–222.

Coie, J. D., and others. (1993). The science of prevention: A conceptual framework and some directions for a national research program. *American Psychologist, 48,* 1013–1022.

Colby, A., Kohlberg, L., Gibbs, J., & Lieberman, M. (1983). A longitudinal study of moral judgment. *Monographs of the Society for Research in Child Development, 48*(Serial No. 200).

Coleman, L. (1990). Cited in Goleman, G. (1990, August 2). The quiet comeback of electroshock therapy. *The New York Times,* p. B5.

Coleman, M., & Ganong, L. H. (1985). Love and sex role stereotypes: Do macho men and feminine women make better lovers? *Journal of Personality and Social Psychology, 49,* 170–176.

Collaer, M. L., & Hines, M. (1995). Human behavioral sex differences: A role for gonadal hormones during early development? *Psychological Bulletin, 118,* 55–107.

Collier, G. (1994). *Social origins of mental ability.* New York: Wiley.

Collins, P. H. (1990). *Black feminist thought: Knowledge, consciousness, and the politics of empowerment.* Boston: Unwin Hyman.

Collins, W. A. (1990). Parent–child relationships in the transition to adolescence: Continuity and change in interaction, affect, and cognition. In R. Montemayor, G. R. Adams, & T. P. Gullotta (Eds.), *From childhood to adolescence: A transitional period.* Newbury Park, CA: Sage.

Collins, W. A., & Russell, G. (1991). Mother–child and father–child relationships in middle childhood and adolescence: A developmental analysis. *Developmental Review, 11,* 99–136.

Comas-Diaz, L. (1994, February). Race and gender in psychotherapy with women of color. *Winter roundtable on cross-cultural counseling and psychotherapy: Race and gender.* New York: Teachers College, Columbia University.

Cools, J., Schotte, D. E., & McNally, R. J. (1992). Emotional arousal and overeating in restrained eaters. *Journal of Abnormal Psychology, 101,* 348–351.

Coon, H., Fulker, D. W., DeFries, J. C., & Plomin, R. (1990). Home environment and cognitive ability of 7-year-old children in the Colorado Adoption Project: Genetic and environmental etiologies. *Developmental Psychology, 26,* 459–468.

Cooney, J. L., & Zeichner, A. (1985). Selective attention to negative feedback in Type A and Type B individuals. *Journal of Abnormal Psychology, 94,* 110–112.

Cooper, J. R., Bloom, F. E., & Roth, R. H. (1991). *The biochemical basis of neuropharmacology.* New York: Oxford University Press.

Cooper, M. L., Peirce, R. S., & Huselid, R. F. (1994). Substance use and sexual risk taking among Black adolescents and White adolescents. *Health Psychology, 13,* 251–262.

Copeland, L. J., Jarrell, J. F., & McGregor, J. A. (Eds.). (1993). *Textbook of gynecology.* Philadelphia: W. B. Saunders.

Corkin, S., and others. (1985). Analyses of global memory impairments of different etiologies. In D. S. Olton, E. Gamzu, & S. Corkin (Eds.), *Memory dysfunction.* New York: New York Academy of Sciences.

Corter, J. E., & Gluck, M. A. (1992). Explaining basic categories: Feature predictability and information. *Psychological Bulletin, 111,* 291–303.

Coryell, W., Endicott, J., & Keller, M. (1992). Major depression in a nonclinical sample: Demographic and clinical risk factors for first onset. *Archives of General Psychiatry, 49,* 117–125.

Costa, E. (1985). Benzodiazepine/GABA interactions: A model to investigate the neurobiology of anxiety. In A. H. Tuma & J. D. Maser (Eds.), *Anxiety and the anxiety disorders.* Hillsdale, NJ: Erlbaum.

Costa, P. T., Jr., & McCrae, R. R. (1984). Personality as a lifelong determinant of wellbeing. In C. Z. Malatesta & C. E. Izard (Eds.), *Emotion in adult development.* Beverly Hills, CA: Sage.

Cousins, N. (1979). *Anatomy of an illness as perceived by the patient: Reflections on healing and regeneration.* New York: W. W. Norton.

Cox, M. J., Owen, M. T., Henderson, V. K., & Margand, N. A. (1992). Prediction of infant–father and infant–mother attachment. *Developmental Psychology, 28,* 474–483.

Coyne, J. C., & Downey, G. (1991). Social factors and psychopathology: Stress, social support, and coping processes. *Annual Review of Psychology, 42,* 401–425.

Crabtree, A. (1994). *From Mesmer to Freud: Magnetic sleep and the roots of psychological healing.* New Haven, CT: Yale University Press.

Craighead, L. W., & Agras, W. S. (1991). Mechanisms of action in cognitive-behavioral and pharmacological interventions for obesity and bulimia nervosa. *Journal of Consulting and Clinical Psychology, 59,* 115–125.

Craik, F. I. M., & Lockhart, R. S. (1972). Levels of processing: A framework for memory research. *Journal of Verbal Learning and Verbal Behavior, 11,* 671–684.

Craik, F. I. M., & Watkins, M. J. (1973). The role of rehearsal in short-term memory. *Journal of Verbal Learning and Verbal Behavior, 12,* 599–607.

Cramer, R. E., McMaster, M. R., Bartell, P. A., & Dragna, M. (1988). Subject competence and minimization of the bystander effect. *Journal of Applied Social Psychology, 18,* 1133–1148.

Crawford, C. (1979). George Washington, Abraham Lincoln, and Arthur Jensen: Are they compatible? *American Psychologist, 34,* 664–672.

Crawford, H. J., & Barabasz, A. (1993). Phobias and fears: Facilitating their treatment with hypnosis. In J. Rhue, S. Lynn, & I. Kirsch (Eds.), *Clinical handbook of hypnosis.* Washington, DC: American Psychological Association.

Crawford, H. J., Brown, A. M., & Moon, C. E. (1993). Sustained attentional and disattentional abilities: Differences between low and highly hypnotizable persons. *Journal of Abnormal Psychology, 102,* 534–543.

Creamer, M., Burgess, P., & Pattison, P. (1992). Reaction to trauma: A cognitive processing model. *Journal of Abnormal Psychology, 101,* 452–459.

Crews. D. (1994). Animal sexuality. *Scientific American, 270,* 108–114.

Crichton, M. (1992). *Rising sun.* New York: Knopf.

Crick, F., & Koch, C. (1992). The problem of consciousness. *Scientific American, 267,* 152–159.

Crick, N. R., & Dodge, K. A. (1994). A review and reformulation of social information-processing mechanisms in children's social adjustment. *Psychological Bulletin, 115,* 74–101.

Crits-Christoph, P., & Mintz, J. (1991). Implications of therapist effects for the design and analysis of comparative studies of psychotherapies. *Journal of Consulting and Clinical Psychology, 59,* 20–26.

Cross, W. (1991). *Shades of identity.* Philadelphia: Temple University Press.

Crusco, A. H., & Wetzel, C. G. (1984). The Midas touch: The effects of interpersonal touch on restaurant tipping. *Personality and Social Psychology Bulletin, 10,* 512–517.

Cummings, E. M., Iannotti, R. J., & Zahn-Waxler, C. (1985). Influence of conflict between adults on the emotions and aggression of young children. *Developmental Psychology, 21,* 495–507.

Cummings, N. A. (1979). Turning bread into stones: Our modern antimiracle. *American Psychologist, 34,* 1119–1129.

Cunningham, M. R., Shaffer, D. R., Barbee, A. P., Wolff, P. L., & Kelley, D. J. (1990). Separate processes in the relation of elation and depression to helping: Social versus personal concerns. *Journal of Experimental Social Psychology, 26,* 13–33.

Curb, J. D., & Marcus, E. B. (1991). Body fat and obesity in Japanese Americans. *American Journal of Clinical Nutrition, 53,* 1552S–1555S.

Curfman, G. D. (1993a). The health benefits of exercise: A critical reappraisal. *New England Journal of Medicine, 328,* 574–576.

Curfman, G. D. (1993b). Is exercise beneficial—or hazardous—to your heart? *New England Journal of Medicine, 329,* 1730–1731.

Curry, S. J., Wagner, E. H., & Grothaus, L. C. (1991). Evaluation of intrinsic and extrinsic motivation interventions with a self-help smoking cessation program. *Journal of Consulting and Clinical Psychology, 59,* 318–324.

Cutler, B. L., Penrod, S. D., & Martens, T. K. (1987). Improving the reliability of eyewitness identification: Putting content into context. *Journal of Applied Psychology, 72,* 629–637.

Damasio, A. R., & Damasio, H. (1992). Brain and language. *Scientific American, 267,* 88–95.

Danforth, J. S., and others. (1990). Exercise as a treatment for hypertension in low-socioeconomic-status Black children. *Journal of Consulting and Clinical Psychology, 58,* 237–239.

Darkes, J., & Goldman, M. S. (1993). Expectancy challenge and drinking reduction: Experimental evidence for a mediational process. *Journal of Consulting and Clinical Psychology, 61,* 344–353.

Darley, J. M., & Latané, B. (1968). Bystander intervention in emergencies: Diffusion of responsibility. *Journal of Personality and Social Psychology, 8,* 377–383.

Darwin, C. A. (1872). *The expression of the emotions in man and animals.* London: J. Murray.

Davey, L. F. (1993, March). *Developmental implications of shared and divergent perceptions in the parent–adolescent relationship.* Paper presented at the biennial meeting of the Society for Research in Child Development, New Orleans.

Davidson, J. R., & Foa, E. G. (1991). Diagnostic issues in posttraumatic stress disorder: Considerations for the DSM-IV. *Journal of Abnormal Psychology, 100,* 346–355.

Davidson, N. E. (1995). Hormone-replacement therapy—Breast versus heart versus bone. *New England Journal of Medicine, 332,* 1638–1639.

Davidson, T. M., & Bowers, K. S. (1991). Selective hypnotic amnesia: Is it a successful attempt to forget or an unsuccessful attempt to remember? *Journal of Abnormal Psychology, 100,* 133–143.

Davis, J. H. (1989). Psychology and law: The last 15 years. *Journal of Applied Social Psychology, 19,* 119–230.

Davis, J. H., Tindale, R. S., Nagao, D. H., Hinsz, V. B., & Robertson, B. (1984). Order effects in multiple decisions by groups: A demonstration with mock juries and trial procedures. *Journal of Personality and Social Psychology, 47,* 1003–1012.

Davis, K. L., Kahn, R. S., Ko, G., & Davidson, M. (1991). Dopamine in schizophrenia: A review and reconceptualization. *American Journal of Psychiatry, 148,* 1474–1486.

Dawes, R. M. (1989). Statistical criteria for establishing a truly false consensus effect. *Journal of Experimental Social Psychology, 25,* 1–17.

Dawkins, R. (1995). *River out of Eden.* New York: Basic Books.

DeAngelis, T. (1993a). Law helps American Indians enter field. *APA Monitor, 24*(3), 26–27.

DeAngelis, T. (1993b). It's baaack: TV violence, concern for kid viewers. *APA Monitor, 24*(8), 16.

DeAngelis, T. (1994a). Educators reveal keys to success in classroom. *APA Monitor, 25*(1), 39–40.

DeAngelis, T. (1994b). Poor kids are focus of asthma studies. *APA Monitor, 25*(3), 26–27.

DeAngelis, T. (1994c). Psychologists' expertise is often essential in court. *APA Monitor, 25*(6), 1, 29.

DeAngelis, T. (1995a). Firefighters' PTSD at dangerous levels. *APA Monitor, 26*(2), 36–37.

DeAngelis, T. (1995b). Mental health care is elusive for Hispanics. *APA Monitor, 26*(7), 49.

DeCasper, A. J., & Prescott, P. A. (1984). Human newborns' perception of male voices: Preference, discrimination, and reinforcing value. *Developmental Psychobiology, 17,* 481–491.

Decline in smoking levels off and officials urge a tax rise. (1993, April 2). *The New York Times,* p. A10.

deGroot, G. (1994a). The community teaches more than any textbook. *APA Monitor, 25*(5), 44.

deGroot, G. (1994b). Tutors help students boost self-esteem. *APA Monitor, 25*(5), 45.

deGroot, G. (1994c). Psychologists are keys to school reforms. *APA Monitor, 25*(6), 38–39.

deJong, P. F., & Das-Smaal, E. A. (1995). Attention and intelligence: The validity of the Star Counting Test. *Journal of Educational Psychology, 87,* 80–92.

De La Cancela, V., & Guzman, L. P. (1991). Latino mental health service needs: Implications for training psychologists. In H. F. Myers and others (Eds.), *Ethnic minority perspectives on clinical training and services in psychology* (pp. 59–64). Washington, DC: American Psychological Association.

Delanoy, R. L., Merrin, J. S., & Gold, P. E. (1982). Moderation of long-term potentiation (LTP) by adrenergic agonists. *Neuroscience Abstracts, 8,* 316.

Delgado, J. M. R. (1969). *Physical control of the mind.* New York: Harper & Row.

Delgado-Gaitan, C. (1993). Parenting in two generations of Mexican American families. *International Journal of Behavioral Development, 16,* 409–427.

Delprato, D. J., & Midgley, B. D. (1992). Some fundamentals of B. F. Skinner's behaviorism. *American Psychologist, 47,* 1507–1520.

Denmark, F. L. (1994). Engendering psychology. *American Psychologist, 49,* 329–334.

Dennett, D. C. (1995). *Darwin's dangerous idea.* New York: Simon & Schuster.

DePaulo, B. M. (1992). Nonverbal behavior and self-presentation. *Psychological Bulletin, 111,* 203–243.

Depue, R. A., and others. (1981). A behavioral paradigm for identifying persons at risk for bipolar depressive disorder. *Journal of Abnormal Psychology, 90,* 381–438.

Derryberry, D., & Tucker, D. M. (1992). Neural mechanisms of emotion. *Journal of Consulting and Clinical Psychology, 60,* 329–338.

Despite better diets, adults in their 20s are weighing more. (1994, March 18). *The New York Times,* p. A17.

DeValois, R. L., & Jacobs, G. H. (1984). Neural mechanisms of color vision. In I. Darian-Smith (Ed.), *Handbook of physiology* (Vol. 3). Bethesda, MD: American Physiological Society.

Devine, P. G. (1989). Stereotypes and prejudice: Their automatic and controlled components. *Journal of Personality and Social Psychology, 56,* 5–18.

Diaz, R. M. (1985). Bilingual cognitive development: Addressing three gaps in current research. *Child Development, 56,* 1376–1388.

DiClemente, C. C., and others. (1991). The process of smoking cessation. *Journal of Consulting and Clinical Psychology, 59,* 295–304.

Diener, E. (1980). Deindividuation: The absence of self-awareness and self-regulation in group members. In P. Paulus (Ed.), *The psychology of group influence.* Hillsdale, NJ: Erlbaum.

Digman, J. M. (1990). Personality structure: Emergence of the five-factor model. *Annual Review of Psychology, 41,* 417–440.

DiLalla, L. F., & Gottesman, I. I. (1991). Biological and genetic contributors to violence—Widom's untold tale. *Psychological Bulletin, 109,* 125–129.

Dinsmoor, J. A. (1992). Setting the record straight: The social views of B. F. Skinner. *American Psychologist, 47,* 1454–1463.

Dix, T. (1991). The affective organization of parenting: Adaptive and maladaptive processes. *Psychological Bulletin, 110,* 3–25.

Dockery, D. W., and others. (1993). An association between air pollution and mortality in six U.S. cities. *New England Journal of Medicine, 329,* 1753–1759.

Doctors tie male mentality to shorter life span. (1995, June 14). *The New York Times,* p. C14.

Dodge, K. A., Price, J. M., Bachorowski, J., & Newman, J. P. (1990). Hostile attributional biases in severely aggressive adolescents. *Journal of Abnormal Psychology, 99,* 385–392.

Dollard, J., Doob, L. W., Miller, N. E., Mowrer, O. H., & Sears, R. R. (1939). *Frustration and aggression.* New Haven, CT: Yale University Press.

Donnerstein, E. I., & Wilson, D. W. (1976). Effects of noise and perceived control on ongoing and subsequent aggressive behavior. *Journal of Personality and Social Psychology, 34,* 774–781.

Doob, A. N., & Wood, L. (1972). Catharsis and aggression: The effects of annoyance and retaliation on aggressive behavior. *Journal of Personality and Social Psychology, 22,* 236–245.

Dovidio, J. H., Evans, N., & Tyler, R. B. (1986). Racial stereotypes: The contents of their cognitive representations. *Journal of Experimental Social Psychology, 22,* 22–37.

Doyle, W. (1986). Classroom organization and management. In M. Wittrock (Ed.), *Handbook of research on teaching* (3rd ed). New York: Macmillan.

Draguns, J. G. (1988). Personality and culture: Are they relevant for the enhancement of quality of mental life? In P. R. Dasen, J. W. Berry, & N. Sartorius (Eds.), *Health and cross-cultural psychology: Toward applications.* Newbury Park, CA: Sage.

Dubbert, P. M. (1992). Exercise in behavioral medicine. *Journal of Consulting and Clinical Psychology, 60,* 613–618.

Duckitt, J. (1992). Psychology and prejudice: A historical analysis and integrative framework. *American Psychologist, 47,* 1182–1193.

Dugan, K. W. (1989). Ability and effort attributions: Do they affect how managers communicate performance feedback information? *Academy of Management Journal, 32,* 87–114.

Duke, M. P., & Norwicki, S. (1972). A new measure and social learning model for interpersonal distance. *Journal of Experimental Research in Personality, 6,* 119–132.

Dumas, J. E., & LaFreniere, P. J. (1993). Mother–child relationships as sources of support or stress: A comparison of competent, average, aggressive, and anxious dyads. *Child Development, 64.*

Dweck, C. S. (1990). Self-theories and goals: Their role in motivation, personality, and development. In R. A. Dienstbier (Ed.), *Nebraska Symposium on Motivation:* Vol. 38 (pp. 199–235). Lincoln: University of Nebraska Press.

Dywan, J., & Bowers, K. S. (1983). The use of hypnosis to enhance recall. *Science, 222,* 184–185.

Eagly, A. H. (1983). Gender and social influence: A social psychological analysis. *American Psychologist, 38,* 971–981.

Eagly, A. H. (1987). *Sex differences in social behavior: A social-role interpretation.* Hillsdale, NJ: Erlbaum.

Eagly, A. H. (1995). The science and politics of comparing women and men. *American Psychologist, 50,* 145–158.

Eagly, A. H., Ashmore, R. D., Makhijani, M. G., & Longo, L. C. (1991). What is beautiful is good, but . . . : A meta-analytic review of research on the physical attractiveness stereotype. *Psychological Bulletin, 110,* 109–128.

Eagly, A. H., & Chaiken, S. (1993). *The psychology of attitudes.* Fort Worth, TX: Harcourt Brace Jovanovich.

Eagly, A. H., & Steffen, V. J. (1984). Gender stereotypes stem from the distribution of men and women into social roles. *Journal of Personality and Social Psychology, 46,* 735–754.

Ebbinghaus, H. (1913). *Memory: A contribution to experimental psychology* (H. A. Roger & C. E. Bussenius, Trans.). New York: Columbia University Press. (Original work published 1885).

Eckholm, E. (1994, March 6). AIDS still immune to the onslaught of medical science. *The New York Times,* pp. E1, E4.

Edgerton, J. W. (1994). Working with key players for psychological and mental health services. *American Psychologist, 49,* 314–321.

Edgley, C. (1989). Commercial sex: Pornography, prostitution, and advertising. In K. McKinney & S. Sprecher (Eds.), *Human sexuality: The societal and interpersonal context.* Norwood, NJ: Ablex.

Edwards, D. J. A. (1972). Approaching the unfamiliar: A study of human interaction distances. *Journal of Behavioral Sciences, 1,* 249–250.

Edwards, D. L. (1991). A meta-analysis of the effects of meditation and hypnosis on measures of anxiety (Doctoral dissertation, Texas A&M University, 1990). *Dissertation Abstracts International, 52,* 1039B.

Edwards, R. (1995). American Indians rely on ancient healing techniques. *APA Monitor, 26*(8), 36.

Egeth, H. E. (1993). What do we not know about eyewitness identification? *American Psychologist, 48,* 577–580.

Ehlers, A., & Breuer, P. (1992). Increased cardiac awareness in panic disorder. *Journal of Abnormal Psychology, 101,* 371–382.

Eidelson, R. J., & Epstein, N. (1982). Cognition and relationship maladjustment: Development of a measure of dysfunctional relationship beliefs. *Journal of Consulting and Clinical Psychology, 50,* 715–720.

Eisenberg, N., Cialdini, R. B., McCreath, H., & Shell, R. (1987). Consistency-based compliance: When and why do children become vulnerable? *Journal of Personality and Social Psychology, 52,* 1174–1181.

Ekman, P. (1980). *The face of man.* New York: Garland.

Ekman, P. (1992). Are there basic emotions? *Psychological Review, 99,* 550–553.

Ekman, P. (1993a). Facial expression and emotion. *American Psychologist, 48,* 384–392.

Ekman, P. (1993b). Cited in D. Goleman (1993, October 26). One smile (only one) can lift a mood. *The New York Times,* p. C11.

Ekman, P. (1994). Strong evidence for universals in facial expression. *Psychological Bulletin, 115,* 268–287.

Ekman, P., Davidson, R. J., & Friesen, W. V. (1990). The Duchenne smile: Emotional expression and brain physiology II. *Journal of Personality and Social Psychology, 58,* 342–353.

Ekman, P., and others. (1987). Universals and cultural differences in the judgments of facial expressions of emotion. *Journal of Personality and Social Psychology, 53,* 712–717.

Ekman, P., Levenson, R. W., & Friesen, W. V. (1983). Autonomic nervous system activity distinguishes among emotions. *Science, 221,* 1208–1210.

Ekman, P., & Oster, H. (1979). Facial expressions of emotion. *Annual Review of Psychology* (Vol. 30). Palo Alto, CA: Annual Reviews.

Ekstrand, M. L. (1992). Safer sex maintenance among gay men: Are we making any progress? *AIDS, 6,* 875–877.

Elkins, R. L. (1980). Covert sensitization treatment of alcoholism. *Addictive Behaviors, 5,* 67–89.

Ellickson, P. L., Hays, R. D., & Bell, R. M. (1992). Stepping through the drug use sequence: Longitudinal scalogram analysis of initiation and regular use. *Journal of Abnormal Psychology, 101,* 441–451.

Ellis, A. (1977). The basic clinical theory of rational-emotive therapy. In A. Ellis & R. Grieger (Eds.), *Handbook of rational-emotive therapy.* New York: Springer.

Ellis, A. (1993). Reflections on rational-emotive therapy. *Journal of Consulting and Clinical Psychology, 61,* 199–201.

Ellis, L. (1990). Prenatal stress may effect sex-typical behaviors of a child. *Brown University Child Behavior and Development Letter, 6*(1), pp. 1–3.

Ellis, L. (1991). A synthesized (biosocial) theory of rape. *Journal of Consulting and Clinical Psychology, 59,* 631–642.

Ellis, L., & Ames, M. A. (1987). Neurohormonal functioning and sexual orientation: A theory of homosexuality–heterosexuality. *Psychological Bulletin, 101,* 233–258.

Ellsworth, P. C., Carlsmith, J. M., & Henson A. (1972). The stare as a stimulus to flight in human subjects. *Journal of Personality and Social Psychology, 21,* 302–311.

Emde, R. (1993). Cited in Adler, T. (1993). Shy, bold temperament? It's mostly in the genes. *APA Monitor, 24*(1), 7, 8.

Engels, G. I., Garnefski, N., & Diekstra, R. F. W. (1993). Efficacy of rational-emotive therapy: A quantitative analysis. *Journal of Consulting and Clinical Psychology, 61,* 1083–1090.

Engen, T. (1991). *Odor sensation and memory.* New York: Praeger.

Epstein, L. H., and others. (1995). Effects of decreasing sedentary behavior and increasing activity on weight change in obese children. *Health Psychology, 14,* 109–115.

Erikson, E. H. (1963). *Childhood and society.* New York: W. W. Norton.

Ernst, N. D., & Harlan, W. R. (1991). Obesity and cardiovascular disease in minority populations: Executive summary. *American Journal of Clinical Nutrition, 53,* 1507S–1511S.

Eron, L. D. (1982). Parent–child interaction, television violence, and aggression of children. *American Psychologist, 37,* 197–211.

Eron, L. D. (1993). Cited in DeAngelis, T. (1993b). It's baaack: TV violence, concern for kid viewers. *APA Monitor, 24*(8), 16.

Espenshade, T. (1993). Cited in Barringer, F. (1993, April 25). Polling on sexual issues has its drawbacks. *The New York Times,* p. A23.

Esterling, B. A., Antoni, M. H., Kumar, M., & Schneiderman, N. (1993). Defensiveness, trait anxiety, and Epstein–Barr viral capsid antigen antibody titers in healthy college students. *Health Psychology, 12,* 132–139.

Estes, W. K. (1972). An associative basis for coding and organization in memory. In A. W. Melton & E. Martin (Eds.), *Coding processes in human memory.* Washington, DC: Winston.

Etaugh, C., & Rathus, S. A. (1995). *The world of children.* Fort Worth, TX: Harcourt Brace.

Etcoff, N. L. (1994). Cited in Brody, J. E. (1994, March 21). Notions of beauty transcend culture, new study suggests. *The New York Times,* p. A14.

Evans, D. A., and others. (1989). Prevalence of Alzheimer's disease in a community population of older persons. *Journal of the American Medical Association, 262,* 2551–2556.

Evans, G. W., Jacobs, S. V., & Frager, N. B. (1982). Behavioral responses to air pollution. In A. Baum & J. E. Singer (Eds.), *Advances in environmental psychology* (Vol. 4) Hillsdale, NJ: Erlbaum.

Eysenck, H. J. (1991). *Smoking, personality, and stress: Psychosocial factors in the prevention of cancer and coronary heart disease.* New York: Springer-Verlag.

Eysenck, H. J. (1993). Comment on Goldberg. *American Psychologist, 48,* 1299–1300.

Eysenck, H. J., & Eysenck, M. W. (1985). *Personality and individual differences.* New York: Plenum.

Fabricius, W. V., & Wellman, H. M. (1983). Children's understanding of retrieval cue utilization. *Developmental Psychology, 19,* 15–21.

Fairstein, L. A. (1993). *Sexual violence: Our war against rape.* New York: William Morrow.

Fallon, A. E., & Rozin, P. (1985). Sex differences in perceptions of desirable body shape. *Journal of Abnormal Psychology, 94,* 102–105.

Farina, A., Burns, G. L., Austad, C., Bugglin, C. S., & Fischer, E. H. (1986). The role of physical attractiveness in the readjustment of discharged psychiatric patients. *Journal of Abnormal Psychology, 95,* 139–143.

Farley, F. (1993a). Wisconsin on the Potomac. *APA Monitor, 24*(4), 3.

Farley, F. (1993b). Cited in Michaelson, R. (1993). Farley calls for more money for health, behavior research. *APA Monitor, 24*(4), 7.

Farrell, A. D., Camplair, P. S., & McCullough, L. (1987). Identification of target complaints by computer interview: Evaluation of the Computerized Assessment System for Psychotherapy Evaluation and Research. *Journal of Consulting and Clinical Psychology, 55,* 691–700.

Fazio, R. H. (1990). Multiple processes by which attitudes guide behavior:

The MODE model as an integrative framework. In M. P. Zanna (Ed.), *Advances in experimental social psychology*. San Diego, CA: Academic Press.

Fehr, B., & Russell, J. A. (1991). The concept of love viewed from a prototype perspective. *Journal of Personality and Social Psychology, 60*, 425–438.

Feingold, A. (1992a). Gender differences in mate selection preferences: A test of the parental investment model. *Psychological Bulletin, 112*, 125–139.

Feingold, A. (1992b). Good-looking people are not what we think. *Psychological Bulletin, 111*, 304–341.

Ferin, M., Jewelewicz, R., & Warren, M. (1993). *The menstrual cycle: Physiology, reproductive disorders, and infertility*. New York: Oxford University Press.

Feshbach, S. (1994). Nationalism, patriotism, and aggression: A clarification of functional differences. In L. R. Huesmann (Ed.), *Aggressive behavior: Current perspectives*. New York: Plenum.

Festinger, L. (1957). *A theory of cognitive dissonance*. Evanston, IL: Row, Peterson.

Festinger, L., & Carlsmith, J. M. (1959). Cognitive consequences of forced compliance. *Journal of Abnormal and Social Psychology, 58*, 203–210.

Festinger, L., Riecken, H. W., Jr., & Schachter, S. (1956). *When prophecy fails*. Minneapolis: University of Minnesota Press.

Field, T. M. (1991). Young children's adaptations to repeated separations from their mothers. *Child Development, 62*, 539–547.

Findley, M. J., & Cooper, H. M. (1983). Locus of control and academic achievement: A literature review. *Journal of Personality and Social Psychology, 44*, 419–427.

Fischbach, G. D. (1992). Mind and brain. *Scientific American, 267*, 48–57.

Fischer, K. W., Shaver, P. R., & Carochan, P. (1990). How emotions develop and how they organize development. *Cognition and Emotion, 4*, 81–127.

Fisher, C. B., & Fyrberg, D. (1994). Participant partners: College students weigh the costs and benefits of deceptive research. *American Psychologist, 49*, 417–427.

Fisher, H. E. (1992). *Anatomy of love: The natural history of monogamy, adultery and divorce*. New York: W. W. Norton.

Fiske, S. T. (1993). Controlling other people: The impact of power on stereotyping. *American Psychologist, 48*, 621–628.

Fiske, S. T., & Taylor, S. E. (1984). *Social cognition*. Reading, MA: Addison-Wesley.

Fitzgerald, L. F. (1993). Sexual harassment: Violence against women in the workplace. *American Psychologist, 48*, 1070–1076.

Fitzgibbon, M. L., Stolley, M. R., & Kirschenbaum, D. S. (1993). Obese people who seek treatment have different characteristics than those who do not seek treatment. *Health Psychology, 12*, 342–345.

Flaherty, J. F., & Dusek, J. B. (1980). An investigation of the relationship between psychological androgyny and components of self-concept. *Journal of Personality and Social Psychology, 38*, 984–992.

Flavell, J. H., Miller, P. H., & Miller, S. A. (1993). *Cognitive development* (3rd ed). Englewood Cliffs, NJ: Prentice-Hall.

Flor, H., & Birbaumer, N. (1993). Comparison of the efficacy of electromyographic biofeedback, cognitive-behavioral therapy, and conservative medical intervention in the treatment of chronic musculoskeletal pain. *Journal of Consulting and Clinical Psychology, 61*, 653–658.

Flor, H., Fydrich, T., & Turk, D. C. (1992). Efficacy of multidisciplinary pain treatment centers: A meta-analytic review. *Pain, 49*, 221–230.

Foa, E. B. (1990, August/September). Obsessive-compulsive disorder. *DSM-IV Update*. Washington, DC: American Psychiatric Association.

Folkman, S., & Lazarus, R. S. (1985). If it changes it must be a process: Study of emotion and coping during three stages of a college examination. *Journal of Personality and Social Psychology, 48*, 150–170.

Ford, E. S., and others. (1991). Physical activity behaviors in lower and higher socioeconomic status populations. *American Journal of Epidemiology, 133*, 1246–1256.

Foreyt, J. P. (1986). Treating the diseases of the 1980s: Eating disorders. *Contemporary Psychology, 31*, 658–660.

Fowler, R. D. (1992). Solid support needed for animal research. *APA Monitor, 23*(6), 2.

Francis, D. (1984). *Will you still need me, will you still feed me, when I'm 84?* Bloomington: Indiana University Press.

Frankel, K. A., & Bates, J. E. (1990). Mother–toddler problem solving: Antecedents in attachment, home behavior, and temperament. *Child Development, 61*, 810–819.

Franzoi, S. L., & Herzog, M. E. (1987). Judging physical attractiveness: What body aspects do we use? *Personality and Social Psychology Bulletin, 13*, 19–33.

Freedman, D. (1994). *Brainmakers: How scientists are moving beyond computers to make a rival to the human brain*. New York: Simon & Schuster.

Freedman, D. X. (1993, August 8). On "Beyond wellness." *The New York Times Book Review*, p. 6.

Freedman, J. L., & Fraser, S. C. (1966). Compliance without pressure: The foot-in-the-door technique. *Journal of Personality and Social Psychology, 4*, 195–202.

Freedman, J. L., Wallington, S. A., & Bless, E. (1967). Compliance without pressure: The effect of guilt. *Journal of Personality and Social Psychology, 7*, 117–124.

Freeman, A. M. (1990, December 18). Deadly diet. *The Wall Street Journal*, pp. 1, B1.

Freeman, M. S., Spence, M. J., & Oliphant, C. M. (1993, June). *Newborns prefer their mothers' low-pass filtered voices over other female filtered voices*. Paper presented at the annual convention of the American Psychological Society, Chicago.

French, S. A., & Jeffery, R. W. (1994). Consequences of dieting to lose weight: Effects on physical and mental health. *Health Psychology, 13*, 195–212.

Freud, S. (1959). Analysis of a phobia in a 5-year-old boy. In *Collected papers* (Vol. 3) (A. & J. Strachey, Trans.). New York: Basic Books. (Original work published 1909).

Freud, S. (1961). *Civilization and its discontents* (J. Strachey, Trans.). New York: W. W. Norton. (Original work published 1930).

Freud, S. (1964a). New introductory lectures. In *Standard edition of the complete psychological works of Sigmund Freud* (Vol. 22). London: Hogarth. (Original work published 1933).

Freud, S. (1964b). A religious experience. In *Standard edition of the complete psychological works of Sigmund Freud* (Vol. 21). London: Hogarth. (Original work published 1927).

Friedman, H. S., & Booth-Kewley, S. (1987). Personality, Type A behavior, and coronary heart disease: The role of emotional expression. *Journal of Personality and Social Psychology, 53*, 783–792.

Friedman, M., & Ulmer, D. (1984). *Treating Type A behavior and your heart*. New York: Fawcett Crest.

Friedman, M. A., & Brownell, K. D. (1995). Psychological correlates of obesity: Moving to the next research generation. *Psychological Bulletin, 117*, 3–20.

Friedman, R. C., & Downey, J. I. (1994). Homosexuality. *New England Journal of Medicine, 331*, 923–930.

Friman, P. C., Allen, K. D., Kerwin, M. L. E., & Larzelere, R. (1993). Changes in modern psychology: A citation analysis of the Kuhnian displacement thesis. *American Psychologist, 48*, 658–664.

Frodi, A. M., Macauley, J., & Thome, P. R. (1977). Are women always less aggressive than men? A review of the experimental literature. *Psychological Bulletin, 84*, 634–660.

Fuchs, C. S., and others. (1995). Alcohol consumption and mortality among women. *New England Journal of Medicine, 332*, 1245–1250.

Furedy, J. J. (1990, July). *Experimental psychophysiology and pseudoscientific polygraphy: Conceptual concerns and practical problems*. Symposium at the 5th International Congress of Psychophysiology, Budapest, Hungary.

Furumoto, L. (1992). Joining separate spheres—Christine Ladd-Franklin, woman-scientist. *American Psychologist, 47*, 175–182.

Gable, D. (1993, July 26). Public wants TV crime reined in. *USA Today*, p. D3.

Galambos, N. L. (1992, October). Parent–adolescent relations. *Current Directions in Psychological Science*, 146–149.

Galambos, N. L., & Almeida, D. M. (1992). Does parent–adolescent conflict increase in early adolescence? *Journal of Marriage and the Family, 54*, 737–747.

Galassi, J. P. (1988). Four cognitive-behavioral approaches: Additional considerations. *The Counseling Psychologist, 16*(1), 102–105.

Gallucci, W. T., and others. (1993). Sex differences in sensitivity of the hypothalamic-pituitary-adrenal axis. *Health Psychology, 12*, 420–425.

Ganellen, R. J., & Blaney, P. H. (1984). Hardiness and social support as moderators of the effects of life stress. *Journal of Personality and Social Psychology, 47*, 156–163.

Garcia, J. (1981). The logic and limits of mental aptitude testing. *American Psychologist, 36*, 1172–1180.

Garcia, J. (1993). Misrepresentation of my criticism of Skinner. *American Psychologist, 48*, 1158.

Garcia, J., Brett, L. P., & Rusiniak, K. W. (1989). Limits of Darwinian conditioning. In S. B. Klein & R. R. Mowrer (Eds.), *Contemporary learning theories: Instrumental conditioning theory and the impact of biological constraints on learning*. Hillsdale, NJ: Erlbaum.

Garcia, J., & Koelling, R. A. (1966). Relation of cue to consequences in avoidance learning. *Psychonomic Science, 4*, 123–124.

Gardner, H. (1983). *Frames of mind: The theory of multiple intelligences*. New York: Basic Books.

Gardner, H., & Hatch, T. (1989). Multiple intelligences go to school: Educational implications of the theory of multiple intelligences. *Educational Researcher, 18*(8), 4–10.

Garland, A. F., & Zigler, E. (1993). Adolescent suicide prevention: Current research and social policy implications. *American Psychologist, 48*, 169–182.

Garnets, L., & Kimmel, D. (1991). In J. D. Goodchilds (Ed.), *Psychological perspectives on human diversity in America*. Washington, DC: American Psychological Association.

Gauthier, J., Côté, G., & French, D. (1994). The role of home practice in the thermal biofeedback treatment of migraine headache. *Journal of Consulting and Clinical Psychology, 62*, 180–184.

Gayle, H. D., and others. (1990). Prevalence of human immunodeficiency virus among university students. *New England Journal of Medicine, 323*, 1538–1541.

Gaziano, J. M., and others. (1993). Moderate alcohol intake, increased levels of high-density lipoprotein and its subfractions, and decreased risk of myocardial infarction. *New England Journal of Medicine, 329*, 1829–1834.

Gazzaniga, M. S. (1992). *Nature's mind*. New York: Basic Books.

Gebhardt, D. L., & Crump, C. E. (1990). Employee fitness and wellness programs in the workplace. *American Psychologist, 45*, 262–272.

Geen, R. G., Stonner, D., & Shope, G. L. (1975). The facilitation of aggression by aggression: Evidence against the catharsis hypothesis. *Journal of Personality and Social Psychology, 31*, 721–726.

Geisinger, K. (1992). *Psychological testing of Hispanics*. Washington, DC: American Psychological Association.

Gelernter, D. (1994). *The muse in the machine: Computerizing the poetry of human thought*. New York: Free Press.

Geller, E. S. (1990). Preventing injuries and deaths from vehicle crashes: Encouraging belts and discouraging booze. In J. Edwards and others (Eds.), *Social influence processes and prevention*. New York: Plenum.

Gelman, R., & Baillargeon, R. (1983). A review of some Piagetan concepts. In J. Flavell & E. Markman (Eds.), *Handbook of child psychology*. New York: Wiley.

Gentry, J., & Eron, L. D. (1993). American Psychological Association Commission on Violence and Youth. *American Psychologist, 48*, 89.

Gershon, E. S., & Rieder, R. O. (1992). Major disorders of mind and brain. *Scientific American, 267*, 126–133.

Gerstner, L. V., Jr. (1994, May 27). Our schools are failing. Do we care? *The New York Times*, p. A27.

Getzels, J. W., & Jackson, P. W. (1962). *Creativity and intelligence: Explorations with gifted students*. New York: Wiley.

Gfeller, J. D., Lynn, S. J., & Pribble, W. E. (1987). Enhancing hypnotic susceptibility: Interpersonal and rapport factors. *Journal of Personality and Social Psychology, 52*, 586–595.

Gibbs, J. T. (1992). Negotiating ethnic identity: Issues for Black–White biracial adolescents. In M. P. P. Root (Ed.), *Racially mixed people in America*. Newbury Park, CA: Sage.

Gibbs, N. (1991, June 3). When is it rape? *Time*, pp. 48–54.

Gibson, E. J., & Walk, R. D. (1960, April). The visual cliff. *Scientific American, 202*, 64–71.

Gibson, M., & Ogbu, J. (Eds.). (1991). *Minority status and schooling: A comparative study of immigrant and involuntary minorities*. New York: Garland.

Gigerenzer, G., Hoffrage, U., & Kleinbölting, H. (1991). Probabilistic mental models: A Brunswikian theory of confidence. *Psychological Review, 98*, 506–528.

Gilbert, S. (1993, April 25). Waiting game. *The New York Times Magazine*, pp. 70–72, 92.

Gilbert, S. J. (1981). Another look at the Milgram obedience studies: The role of the gradated series of shocks. *Personality and Social Psychology Bulletin, 7*, 690–695.

Gilligan, C. (1982). *In a different voice*. Cambridge, MA: Harvard University Press.

Gilligan, C., Lyons, P., & Hanmer, T. J. (Eds.). (1990). *Making connections*. Cambridge, MA: Harvard University Press.

Gilligan, C., Rogers, A. G., & Tolman, D. L. (Eds.). (1991). *Women, girls, and psychotherapy*. New York: Haworth.

Gilligan, C., Ward, J. V., & Taylor, J. M. (1989). *Mapping the moral domain: A contribution of women's thinking to psychological theory and education*. Cambridge, MA: Harvard University Press.

Gillin, J. C. (1991). The long and the short of sleeping pills. *New England Journal of Medicine, 324*, 1735–1736.

Gillis, A. R., Richard, M. A., & Hagan, J. (1986). Ethnic susceptibility to crowding. *Environment and Behavior, 18*, 683–706.

Gillis, J. S., & Avis, W. E. (1980). The male-taller norm in mate selection. *Personality and Social Psychology Bulletin, 6*, 396–401.

Gilman, A. G., and others. (1990). *Goodman and Gilman's the pharmacological basis of therapeutics* (8th ed.). New York: Pergamon.

Gilovich, T. (1983). Biased evaluation and persistence in gambling. *Journal of Personality and Social Psychology, 44*, 1110–1126.

Ginsburg, G., & Bronstein, P. (1993). Family factors related to children's intrinsic/extrinsic motivational orientation and academic performance. *Child Development, 64*, 1461–1474.

Glaser, R., and others. (1991). Stress-related activation of Epstein-Barr virus. *Brain, Behavior, and Immunity, 5*, 219–232.

Glaser, R., and others. (1993). Stress and the memory T-cell response to the Epstein-Barr virus. *Health Psychology, 12*, 435–442.

Glasner, P. D., & Kaslow, R. A. (1990). The epidemiology of human immunodeficiency virus infection. *Journal of Consulting and Clinical Psychology, 58*, 13–21.

Gleason, J. B., & Ratner, N. B. (1993). Language development in children. In J. B. Gleason & N. B. Ratner (Eds.), *Psycholinguistics*. Fort Worth, TX: Harcourt Brace Jovanovich.

Gleaves, D. H., Williamson, D. A., & Barker, S. E. (1993). Confirmatory factor analysis of a multidimensional model of bulimia nervosa. *Journal of Abnormal Psychology, 102*, 173–176.

Glenn, S. S., Ellis, J., & Greenspoon, J. (1992). On the revolutionary nature of the operant as a unit of behavioral selection. *American Psychologist, 47*, 1326–1329.

Glover, J. A., Ronning, R. R., & Bruning, R. H. (1990). *Cognitive psychology for teachers*. New York: Macmillan.

Godden, D. R., & Baddeley, A. D. (1975). Context-dependent memory in two natural environments: On land and underwater. *British Journal of Psychology, 66*, 325–331.

Goelet, P., and others. (1986). The long and short of long-term memory—A molecular framework. *Nature, 322*, 419–422.

Gold, M. S. (1993). *Cocaine: Drugs of abuse: A comprehensive series for clinicians* (Vol. 3). New York: Plenum.

Goldberg, L. R. (1993). The structure of phenotypic personality traits. *American Psychologist, 48*, 26–34.

Goldberg, L. W. (1978). Differential attribution of trait-descriptive terms to oneself as compared to well-liked, neutral, and disliked others. *Journal of Personality and Social Psychology, 36*, 1012–1028.

Goldfarb, L. A., Dykens, E. M., & Gerrard, M. (1985). The Goldfarb Fear of Fat Scale. *Journal of Personality Assessment, 49,* 329–332.

Goldman, J. A., & Harlow, L. L. (1993). Self-perception variables that mediate AIDS-preventive behavior in college students. *Health Psychology, 12,* 489–498.

Goldman, K. (1993, June 1). Jordan & Co. play ball on Madison Avenue. *The Wall Street Journal,* p. B9.

Goldman-Rakic, P. S. (1992). Working memory and the mind. *Scientific American, 267,* 110–117.

Goldman-Rakic, P. S. (1995). Cited in Goleman, D. (1995, May 2). Biologists find site of working memory. *The New York Times,* pp. C1, C9.

Goldsmith, H. H. (1993). Cited in Adler, T. (1993). Shy, bold temperament? It's mostly in the genes. *APA Monitor, 24*(1), 7, 8.

Goldstein, I. L., & Buxton, V. M. (1982). Training and human performance. In M. D. Dunnette & E. A. Fleishman (Eds.), *Human Performance and Productivity, 1,* 135–177.

Goldstein, T. (1988, February 12). Women in the law aren't yet equal partners. *The New York Times,* p. B7.

Goleman, D. J. (1992, January 8). Heart seizure or panic attack? Disorder is a terrifying mimic. *The New York Times,* p. C12.

Goleman, D. J. (1993, April 6). Studying the secrets of childhood memory. *The New York Times,* pp. C1, C11.

Goleman, D. J. (1995a, March 28). The brain manages happiness and sadness in different centers. *The New York Times,* pp. C1, C9.

Goleman, D. J. (1995b, May 2). Biologists find site of working memory. *The New York Times,* pp. C1, C9.

Gomez, J., & Smith, B. (1990). Taking the home out of homophobia: Black lesbian health. In E. C. White (Ed.), *The Black women's health book: Speaking for ourselves.* Seattle: Seal Press.

Goodchilds, J. D. (1991). (Ed.). *Psychological perspectives on human diversity in America.* Washington, DC: American Psychological Association.

Goodgame, R. W. (1990). AIDS in Uganda—Clinical and social features. *New England Journal of Medicine, 323,* 383–389.

Goodman, L. A., Koss, M. P., Fitzgerald, L. F., Russo, N. F., & Keita, G. W. (1993). Male violence against women: Current research and future directions. *American Psychologist, 48,* 1054–1058.

Goodwin, F. K., & Jamison, K. R. (1990). *Manic-depressive illness.* New York: Oxford University Press.

Gortmaker, S. L., and others. (1993). Social and economic consequences of over-weight in adolescence and young adulthood. *New England Journal of Medicine, 329,* 1008–1012.

Gotlib, I. H., Lewinsohn, P. M., Seeley, J. R., Rohde, P., & Redner, J. E. (1993). Negative cognitions and attributional style in depressed adolescents: An examination of stability and specificity. *Journal of Abnormal Psychology, 102,* 607–615.

Gottesman, I. I. (1991). *Schizophrenia genesis: The origins of madness.* New York: Freeman.

Gottfried, A. E., Fleming, J. S., & Gottfried, A. W. (1994). Role of parental motivational practices in children's academic intrinsic motivation and achievement. *Journal of Educational Psychology, 86,* 104–113.

Graesser, A. C., & Nakamura, G. V. (1982). The impact of a schema on comprehension and memory. In G. H.Bower (Ed.), *The psychology of learning and motivation* (Vol. 16). New York: Academic Press.

Granberg, D., & Brent, E. (1983). When prophecy bends: The preference expectation link in U.S. presidential elections. *Journal of Personality and Social Psychology, 45,* 477–491.

Grant, I., & Heaton, R. K. (1990). Human immunodeficiency virus-type 1 (HIV-1) and the brain. *Journal of Consulting and Clinical Psychology, 58,* 22–30.

Green, S. K., Buchanan, D. R., & Heuer, S. K. (1984). Winners, losers, and choosers: A field investigation of dating initiation. *Personality and Social Psychology Bulletin, 10,* 502–511.

Greenberg, J., & Kuczaj, S. A., II. (1982). Towards a theory of substantive word-meaning acquisition. In S. A. Kuczaj II (Ed.), *Language development: Vol. 1. Syntax and semantics.* Hillsdale, NJ: Erlbaum.

Greenberg, P. D. (1987). Tumor immunology. In D. P. Stites and others (Eds.), *Basic and clinical immunology* (6th ed). Norwalk, CT: Appleton & Lange.

Greenberg, R., Pearlman, C., Schwartz, W. R., & Grossman, H. Y. (1983). Memory, emotion, and REM sleep. *Journal of Abnormal Psychology, 92,* 378–381.

Greene, A. L., & Grimsley, L. D. (1990). Age and gender differences in adolescents' preferences for parental advice: Mum's the word. *Journal of Adolescent Research, 5,* 396–413.

Greene, A. S., & Saxe, L. (1990). *Tall tales told to teachers.* Unpublished manuscript. Brandeis University.

Greene, B. (1986). When the therapist is White and the patient is Black: Considerations for psychotherapy in the feminist heterosexual and lesbian communities. *Women & Therapy, 5,* 41–65.

Greene, B. (1990). Sturdy bridges: The role of African American mothers in the socialization of African American children. *Women & Therapy, 10,* 205–225.

Greene, B. (1991). Personal communication.

Greene, B. (1992). Still here: A perspective on psychotherapy with African American women. In J. Chrisler & D. Howard (Eds.), *New directions in feminist psychology.* New York: Springer.

Greene, B. (1993). African American women. In L. Comas-Diaz & B. A. Greene, (Eds.), *Women of color and mental health.* New York: Guilford.

Greene, B. (1994). Ethnic-minority lesbians and gay men: Mental health and treatment issues. *Journal of Consulting and Clinical Psychology, 62,* 243–251.

Greene, J. (1982, September). The gambling trap. *Psychology Today, 16,* 50–55.

Greenfield, S. A. (1995). *Journey to the center of the mind: Toward a science of consciousness.* New York: W. H. Freeman.

Greeno, C. G., & Wing, R. R. (1994). Stress-induced eating. *Psychological Bulletin, 115,* 444–464.

Greenwald, A. G. (1992). New Look 3: Unconscious cognition reclaimed. *American Psychologist, 47,* 766–779.

Greist, J. H. (1984). Exercise in the treatment of depression. *Coping with mental stress: The potential and limits of exercise intervention.* Washington, DC: National Institute of Mental Health.

Griffin, E., & Sparks, G. G. (1990). Friends forever: A longitudinal exploration of intimacy in same-sex friends and platonic pairs. *Journal of Social and Personal Relationships, 7,* 29–46.

Grinspoon, L., & Bakalar, J. B. (1994). The war on drugs—A peace proposal. *New England Journal of Medicine, 330,* 357–360.

Grob, G. (1994). *The mad among us: A history of America's care of the mentally ill.* New York: Free Press.

Gronlund, N. E. (1985). *Measurement and evaluation in teaching* (5th ed.). New York: Macmillan.

Grove, W. M., and others. (1991). Familial prevalence and coaggregation of schizotypy indicators: A multitrait family study. *Journal of Abnormal Psychology, 100,* 115–121.

Growdon, J. H. (1992). Treatment for Alzheimer's disease. *New England Journal of Medicine, 327,* 1306–1308.

Gruber, V. A., & Wildman, B. G. (1987). The impact of dysmenorrhea on daily activities. *Behavior Research and Therapy, 25,* 123–128.

Gruber-Baldini, A. L. (1991). *The impact of health and disease on cognitive ability in adulthood and old age in the Seattle Longitudinal Study.* Unpublished doctoral dissertation, Pennsylvania State University.

Gruder, C. L., and others. (1993). Effects of social support and relapse prevention training as adjuncts to a televised smoking-cessation intervention. *Journal of Consulting and Clinical Psychology, 61,* 113–120.

Grunberg, N. (1993a). Cited in Adler, T. Gum, patches aren't enough; to quit, counseling is advised. *APA Monitor, 24*(5), 16–17.

Grunberg, N. (1993b). Cited in Adler, T. Nicotine gives mixed results on learning and performance. *APA Monitor, 24*(5), 14–15.

Grush, J. E. (1980). The impact of candidate expenditures, regionality, and prior outcomes on the 1976 Democratic presidential primaries. *Journal of Personality and Social Psychology, 38,* 337–347.

Guilford, J. P. (1967). *The nature of human intelligence.* New York: McGraw Hill.

Guilford, J. P. (1988). Some changes in the structure-of-intellect model. *Educational and Psychological Measurement, 48,* 1–4.

Guisinger, S., & Blatt, S. J. (1994). Individuality and relatedness: Evolution of a fundamental dialectic. *American Psychologist, 49,* 104–111.

Gunther, V., Gritsch, S., & Meise, U. (1992). Smoking cessation—Gradual or sudden stopping? *Drug and Alcohol Dependence, 29,* 231–236.

Guralnik, J. M., Land, K. C., Blazer, D., Fillenbaum, G. G., & Branch, L. G. (1993). Educational status and active life expectancy among older Blacks and Whites. *New England Journal of Medicine, 329,* 110–116.

Guthrie, R. V. (1990). Cited in Korn, J. H., Davis, R., & Davis, S. F. (1991). Historians' and chairpersons' judgments of eminence among psychologists. *American Psychologist, 46,* 789–792.

Gutknecht, M. (1992). The "postmodern mind": Hybrid models of cognition. *Connection Science: Journal of Neural Computing, Artificial Intelligence and Cognitive Research, 4,* 339–364.

Haaf, R. A., Smith, P. H., & Smitley, S. (1983). Infant response to facelike patterns under fixed trial and infant-control procedures. *Child Development, 54,* 172–177.

Haaga, D. A. F., & Davison, G. C. (1993). An appraisal of rational-emotive therapy. *Journal of Consulting and Clinical Psychology, 61,* 215–220.

Haaland, K. Y. (1992). Introduction to the special section on the emotional concomitants of brain damage. *Journal of Consulting and Clinical Psychology, 60,* 327–328.

Haber, R. N. (1969). Eidetic images. *Scientific American, 220,* 36–55.

Haber, R. N. (1980, November). Eidetic images are not just imaginary. *Psychology Today, 14,* 72–82.

Hainline, L., & Abramov, I. (1992). Assessing visual development: Is infant vision good enough? In C. Rovee-Collier & L. P. Lipsitt (Eds.), *Advances in Infancy Research* (Vol. 7). Norwood, NJ: Ablex.

Haith, M. M. (1990). Progress in the understanding of sensory and perceptual processes early in infancy. *Merrill-Palmer Quarterly, 36,* 1–26.

Hall, J. (1989). *Learning and memory* (2nd ed.). Boston: Allyn & Bacon.

Hall, J. A., and others. (1990). Performance quality, gender, and professional role: A study of physicians and nonphysicians in 16 ambulatory-care practices. *Medical Care, 28,* 489–501.

Hall, S. M., Havassy, B. E., & Wasserman, D. A. (1990). Commitment to abstinence and acute stress in relapse to alcohol, opiates, and nicotine. *Journal of Consulting and Clinical Psychology, 58,* 175–181.

Hall, S. M., Muñoz, R. F., Reus, V. I., & Sees, K. L. (1993). Nicotine, negative affect, and depression. *Journal of Consulting and Clinical Psychology, 61,* 761–767.

Halldin, M. (1985). Alcohol consumption and alcoholism in an urban population in central Sweden. *Acta Psychiatrica Scadinavica, 71,* 128–140.

Halpern, D. F. (1986). *Sex differences in cognitive abilities.* Hillsdale, NJ: Erlbaum.

Halpern, D. F. (1989). *Thought and knowledge: An introduction to critical thinking* (2nd ed.). Hillsdale, NJ: Erlbaum.

Halpern, D. F., Hansen, C., & Riefer, D. (1990). Analogies as an aid to understanding and memory. *Journal of Educational Psychology, 82,* 298–305.

Hamer, D., and others. (1993). Cited in Henry, W. A. (1993, July 26). Born gay? *Time,* pp. 36–39.

Hamilton, L. C. (1985). Self-reported and actual savings in a water conservation campaign. *Environment and Behavior, 17,* 315–326.

Hamilton, M., and others. (1990). *The Duke University Medical Center book of diet and fitness.* New York: Fawcett Columbine.

Hamilton, R. J. (1985). A framework for the evaluation of the effectiveness of adjunct questions and objectives. *Review of Educational Research, 55,* 47–86.

Hamm, N. M., Baum, M. R., & Nikels, K. W. (1975). Effects of race and exposure on judgments of interpersonal favorability. *Journal of Experimental Social Psychology, 11,* 14–24.

Hammen, C., & Mayol, A. (1982). Depression and cognitive characteristics of stressful life-event types. *Journal of Abnormal Psychology, 91,* 165–174.

Haney, M., and others. (1994). Cocaine sensitivity in Roman high and low avoidance rats is modulated by sex and gonadal hormone status. *Brain Research, 645*(1–2), 179–185.

Hanson, K. A., & Gidycz, C. A. (1993). Evaluation of a sexual assault prevention program. *Journal of Consulting and Clinical Psychology, 61,* 1046–1052.

Harackiewicz, J. M., Sansone, C., Blair, L. W., Epstein, J. A., & Manderlink, G. (1987). Attributional processes in behavior change and maintenance: Smoking cessation and continued abstinence. *Journal of Consulting and Clinical Psychology, 55,* 372–378.

Hardy, J., and others. (1991, February 21). *Nature.*

Hare, R. D., Hart, S. D., & Harpur, T. J. (1991). Psychopathy and the *DSM-IV* criteria for antisocial personality disorder. *Journal of Abnormal Psychology, 100,* 391–398.

Hare-Mustin, R. (1983). An appraisal of the relationship between women and psychotherapy: 80 years after the case of Dora. *American Psychologist, 38,* 593–601.

Harkins, S. (1987). Social loafing and social facilitation. *Journal of Experimental Social Psychology, 23,* 1–18.

Harlow, H. F. (1959). Love in infant monkeys. *Scientific American, 200,* 68–86.

Harlow, H. F. (1965). Sexual behavior in the rhesus monkey. In F. A. Beach (Ed.), *Sex and behavior.* New York: Wiley.

Harlow, H. F., Harlow, M. K., & Meyer, D. R. (1950). Learning motivated by a manipulation drive. *Journal of Experimental Psychology, 40,* 228–234.

Harlow, H. F., & Zimmerman, R. R. (1959). Affectional responses in the infant monkey. *Science, 130,* 421–432.

Harlow, M. K., & Harlow, H. F. (1966). Affection in primates. *Discovery, 27,* 11–17.

Harnishfeger, K. K., & Bjorklund, D. F. (1990). Children's strategies: A brief history. In D. F. Bjorklund (Ed.), *Children's strategies: Contemporary views of cognitive development* (pp. 1–184). Hillsdale, NJ: Erlbaum.

Harris, G. T., Rice, M. E., & Quinsey, V. L. (1994). Psychopathy as a taxon: Evidence that psychopaths are a discrete class. *Journal of Consulting and Clinical Psychology, 62,* 387–397.

Harris, T. A. (1957). *I'm OK—You're OK.* New York: Harper & Row.

Hartmann, E. L. (1981, April). The strangest sleep disorder. *Psychology Today, 15,* 14–18.

Hartz, A. J., and others. (1984). The association of girth measurements with disease in 32,856 women. *American Journal of Epidemiology, 119,* 71–80.

Harwood, A. (1981). Mainland Puerto Ricans. In A. Harwood (Ed.), *Ethnicity and medical care.* Cambridge, MA: Harvard University Press.

Hashimoto, N. (1991). Memory development in early childhood: Encoding process in a special task. *Journal of Genetic Psychology, 152,* 101–117.

Hasselhorn, M. (1992). Task dependency and the role of typicality and metamemory in the development of an organizational strategy. *Child Development, 63,* 202–214.

Hatfield, M. O. (1990). Stress and the American worker. *American Psychologist, 45,* 1162–1164.

Hatsukami, D., LaBounty, L., Hughes, J., & Laine, D. (1993). Effects of tobacco abstinence on food intake among cigarette smokers. *Health Psychology, 12,* 499–502.

Hauser-Cram, P., Pierson, D. E., Walker, D. K., & Tivnan, T. (1991). *Early education in the public schools.* San Francisco: Jossey-Bass.

Hawkins, S. A., & Hastie, R. (1990). Hindsight: Biased judgments of past events after the outcomes are known. *Psychological Bulletin, 107,* 311–327.

Hayes, P. (1993). Cited in Chartrand, S. (1993, July 18). A split in thinking among keepers of artificial intelligence. *The New York Times,* p. E6.

Hayes, S. C. (Ed.). (1989). *Rule-governed behavior: Cognition, contingencies, and instructional control.* New York: Plenum.

Hayes, S. L. (1981). Single case design and empirical clinical practice. *Journal of Consulting and Clinical Psychology, 49,* 193–211.

Hays, K. F. (1995). Putting sport psychology into (your) practice. *Professional Psychology: Research and Practice, 26,* 33–40.

Hays, R. B., Turner, H., & Coates, T. J. (1992). Social support, AIDS-related symptoms, and depression among gay men. *Journal of Consulting and Clinical Psychology, 60,* 463–469.

Heaton, R. K., & Victor, R. G. (1976). Personality characteristics associated with psychedelic flashbacks in natural and experimental settings. *Journal of Abnormal Psychology, 85,* 83–90.

Hedge, J. W., & Kavanaugh, M. J. (1988). Improving the accuracy of performance evaluations: Comparison of three methods of performance appraiser training. *Journal of Applied Psychology, 73,* 68–73.

Hefferline, R. F., & Keenan, B. (1963). Amplitude-induction gradient of a small-scale (covert) operant. *Journal of the Experimental Analysis of Behavior, 6,* 307–315.

Hegarty, M., Mayer, R. E., & Monk, C. A. (1995). Comprehension of arithmetic word problems: A comparison of successful and unsuccessful problem solvers. *Journal of Educational Psychology, 87,* 18–32.

Heider, F. (1958). *The psychology of interpersonal relations.* New York: Wiley.

Heim, M. (1993). *The metaphysics of virtual reality.* New York: Oxford University Press.

Heingartner, A., & Hall, J. V. (1974). Affective consequences in adults and children of repeated exposure to auditory stimuli. *Journal of Personality and Social Psychology, 29,* 719–723.

Hellams, R. P. (1993). Personal communication.

Heller, D. A., de Faire, U., Pedersen, N. L., Dahlén, G., & McClearn, G. E. (1993). Genetic and environmental influences on serum lipid levels in twins. *New England Journal of Medicine, 328,* 1150–1156.

Hellige, J. B. (1990). Hemispheric assymetry. *Annual Review of Psychology, 41,* 55–80.

Helmes, E., & Reddon, J. R. (1993). A perspective on developments in assessing psychopathology: A critical review of the MMPI and MMPI-2. *Psychological Bulletin, 113,* 453–471.

Helms, J. E. (1992). Why is there no study of cultural equivalence of standardized cognitive ability testing? *American Psychologist, 47,* 1083–1101.

Helson, R., & Moane, G. (1987). Personality change in women from college to midlife. *Journal of Personality and Social Psychology, 53,* 176–186.

Helzer, J. E. (1987). Epidemiology of alcoholism. *Journal of Consulting and Clinical Psychology, 55,* 284–292.

Hendrick, C. D., Wells, K. S., & Faletti, M. V. (1982). Social and emotional effects of geographical relocation on elderly retirees. *Journal of Personality and Social Psychology, 42,* 951–962.

Hendrick, S. S., & Hendrick, C. (1977). *Aging in mass society: Myths and realities.* Cambridge, MA: Winthrop.

Hendrick, S. S., Hendrick, C., Slapion-Foote, M. J., & Foote, F. H. (1985). Gender differences in sexual attitudes. *Journal of Personality and Social Psychology, 48,* 1630–1642.

Henkin, W. A. (1985). Toward counseling the Japanese in America: A cross-cultural primer. *Journal of Counseling and Development, 63,* 500–503.

Hensley, W. E. (1981). The effects of attire, location, and sex on aiding behavior: A similarity explanation. *Journal of Nonverbal Behavior, 6,* 3–11.

Hepworth, J. T., & West, S. G. (1988). Lynchings and the economy: A time-series reanalysis of Hovland and Sears (1940). *Journal of Personality and Social Psychology, 55,* 239–247.

Herbert, T. B., & Cohen, S. (1993). Depression and immunity: A meta-analytic review. *Psychological Bulletin, 113,* 472–486.

Herek, G. M. (1993). Sexual orientation and military service: A social science perspective. *American Psychologist, 48,* 538–549.

Herrmann, D. J. (1991). *Super memory.* Emmaus, PA: Rodale.

Hershey, D. A., Walsh, D. A., Read, S. J., & Chulef, A. S. (1990). Relationships between metamemory, memory predictions, and memory task performance in adults. *Psychology and Aging, 5,* 215–227.

Herzog, D. B., Keller, M. B., & Lavori, P. W. (1988). Outcome in anorexia and bulimia nervosa: A review of the literature. *Journal of Nervous and Mental Disease, 176,* 131–143.

Hewitt, P. L., & Flett, G. L., (1993). Dimensions of perfectionism, daily stress, and depression: A test of the specific vulnerability hypothesis. *Journal of Abnormal Psychology, 102,* 58–65.

Higgins, E. T. (1990). Personality, social psychology, and person–situation relations: Standards and knowledge activation as a common language. In L. A. Pervin (Ed.), *Handbook of personality: Theory and research* (pp. 301–338). New York: Guilford.

Hilgard, E. R. (1977). *Divided consciousness: Multiple controls in human thought and action.* New York: Wiley.

Hilgard, E. R. (1978). Hypnosis and pain. In R. A. Sternbach (Ed.), *The psychology of pain.* New York: Raven Press.

Hill, C. (1978). Affiliation motivation: People who need people . . . but in different ways. *Journal of Personality and Social Psychology, 52,* 1008–1018.

Hilts, P. J. (1995, May 30). Brain's memory system comes into focus. *The New York Times,* pp. C1, C3.

Hiltz, S. R. (1993). Correlates of learning in a virtual classroom. *International Journal of Man-Machine Studies, 39,* 71–98.

Hineline, P. N. (1992). A self-interpretive behavior analysis. *American Psychologist, 47,* 1274–1286.

Hines, C. V., Cruickshank, D. R., & Kennedy, J. (1985). Teacher clarity and its relation to student achievement and satisfaction. *American Educational Research Journal, 22,* 87–99.

Hinton, G. E. (1992). How neural networks learn from experience. *Scientific American, 267,* 144–151.

Ho, D. Y. F. (1985). Cultural values and professional issues in clinical psychology: Implications from the Hong Kong experience. *American Psychologist, 40,* 1212–1218.

Hoberman, H. M., Lewinsohn, P. M., & Tilson, M. (1988). Group treatment of depression: Individual predictors of outcome. *Journal of Consulting and Clinical Psychology, 56,* 393–398.

Hobfoll, S. E., Jackson, A. P., Lavin, J., Britton, P. J., & Shepherd, J. B. (1993). Safer sex knowledge, behavior, and attitudes of inner-city women. *Health Psychology, 12,* 481–488.

Hobfoll, S. E., Ritter, C., Lavin, J., Hulsizer, M. R., & Cameron, R. P. (1995). Depression prevalence and incidence among inner-city pregnant and postpartum women. *Journal of Consulting and Clinical Psychology, 63,* 445–453.

Hobson, J. A. (1992). Cited in Blakeslee, S. (1992, January 7). Scientists unraveling chemistry of dreams. *The New York Times,* pp. C1, C10.

Hoffman, C., & Hurst, N. (1990). Gender stereotypes: Perception or rationalization? *Journal of Personality and Social Psychology, 58,* 197–208.

Hogan, R., Curphy, G. J., & Hogan, J. (1994). What we know about leadership: Effectiveness and personality. *American Psychologist, 49,* 493–504.

Holahan, C. J., & Moos, R. H. (1990). Life stressors, resistance factors, and psychological health: An extension of the stress-resistance paradigm. *Journal of Personality and Social Psychology, 58,* 909–917.

Holahan, C. J., & Moos, R. H. (1991). Life stressors, personal and social resources, and depression: A 4-year structural model. *Journal of Abnormal Psychology, 100,* 31–38.

Holahan, C. J., Moos, R. H., Holahan, C. K., & Brennan, P. L. (1995). Social support, coping, and depressive symptoms in a late-middle-aged sample of patients reporting cardiac illness. *Health Psychology, 14,* 152–163.

Holland, J. (1993). Cited in Rosenthal, E. (1993b, July 20). Listening to the emotional needs of cancer patients. *The New York Times,* pp. C1, C7.

Hollinger, L. M., & Buschmann, M. B. (1993). Factors influencing the perception of touch by elderly nursing home residents and their health caregivers. *International Journal of Nursing Studies, 30,* 445–461.

Hollingshead, A. B., & Redlich, F. C. (1958). *Social class and mental illness: A community study.* New York: Wiley.

Hollon, S. D., & Beck, A. T. (1986). Research on cognitive therapies. In S. L. Garfield & A. E. Bergin (Eds.), *Handbook of psychotherapy and behavior change* (3rd ed.). New York: Wiley.

Hollon, S. D., Shelton, R. C., & Loosen, P. T. (1991). Cognitive therapy and pharmacotherapy for depression. *Journal of Consulting and Clinical Psychology, 59,* 88–99.

Holmes, D. S. (1984). Meditation and somatic arousal reduction: A review of the experimental evidence. *American Psychologist, 39,* 1–10.

Holmes, T. H., & Rahe, R. H. (1967). The social readjustment rating scale. *Journal of Psychosomatic Research, 11,* 213–218.

Holyoak, K., Koh, K., & Nisbett, R. E. (1989). A theory of conditioning: Inductive learning within rule-based default hierarchies. *Psychological Review, 96,* 315–340.

Honts, C., Hodes, R., & Raskin, D. (1985). *Journal of Applied Psychology, 70*(1).

Hopper, J. L., & Seeman, E. (1994). The bone density of female twins discordant for tobacco use. *New England Journal of Medicine, 330,* 387–392.

Horm, J., & Anderson, K. (1993). Who in America is trying to lose weight? *Annals of Internal Medicine, 119*(7, Pt. 2, Suppl.), 672–676.

Horn, J. M. (1983). The Texas adoption project: Adopted children and their intellectual resemblance to biological and adoptive parents. *Child Development, 54,* 268–275.

Horney, K. (1967). *Feminine psychology.* New York: W. W. Norton.

Horvath, T. (1981). Physical attractiveness: The influence of selected torso parameters. *Archives of Sexual Behavior, 10,* 21–24.

House, J. S., Robbins, C., & Metzner, H. L. (1982). The association of social relationships and activities with mortality: Prospective evidence from the Tecumseh Community Health Study. *American Journal of Epidemiology, 116,* 123–140.

Howard, L., & Polich, J. (1985). P300 latency and memory span development. *Developmental Psychology, 21,* 283–289.

Howard-Pitney, B., LaFramboise, T. D., Basil, M., September, B., & Johnson, M. (1992). Psychological and social indicators of suicide ideation and suicide attempts in Zuni adolescents. *Journal of Consulting and Clinical Psychology, 60,* 473–476.

Hubel, D. H., & Wiesel, T. N. (1979). Brain mechanisms of vision. *Scientific American, 241,* 150–162.

Hudson, J. (1993). Cited in Goleman, D. J. (1993, April 6). Studying the secrets of childhood memory. *The New York Times,* pp. C1, C11.

Huesmann, L. R. (1993). Cited in DeAngelis, T. (1993a). It's baaack: TV violence, concern for kid viewers. *APA Monitor, 24*(8), 16.

Huesmann, L. R., Eron, L. D., Klein, R., Brice, P., & Fischer, P. (1983). Mitigating the imitation of aggressive behaviors by changing children's attitudes about media violence. *Journal of Personality and Social Psychology, 44,* 899–910.

Huesmann, L. R., & Miller, L. S. (1994). Long-term effects of repeated exposure to media violence in childhood. In L. R. Huesmann (Ed.), *Aggressive behavior: Current perspectives.* New York: Plenum.

Hugdahl, K., & Ohman, A. (1977). Effects of instruction on acquisition and extinction of electrodermal response to fear-relevant stimuli. *Journal of Experimental Psychology: Human Learning and Memory, 3,* 608–618.

Hughes, J. R. (1993). Pharmacotherapy for smoking cessation: Unvalidated assumptions, anomalies, and suggestions for future research. *Journal of Consulting and Clinical Psychology, 61,* 751–760.

Hughes, P. L., and others. (1986). Treating bulimia with desipramine. *Archives of General Psychiatry, 43,* 182–186.

Hull, J. G., Levenson, R. W., Young, R. D., & Sher, K. J. (1983). Self-awareness-reducing effects of alcohol consumption. *Journal of Personality and Social Psychology, 44,* 461–473.

Hultquist, C. M., and others. (1995). The effect of smoking and light activity on metabolism in men. *Health Psychology, 14,* 124–131.

Humphrey, L. L. (1986). Family dynamics in bulimia. In S. C. Feinstein and others (Eds.), *Adolescent psychiatry.* Chicago: University of Chicago Press.

Hunter, J. E., & Schmidt, F. L. (1983). Quantifying the effects of psychological interventions on employee job performance and work force productivity. *American Psychologist, 38,* 473–478.

Hurford, J. R. (1991). The evolution of the critical period for language acquisition. *Cognition, 40,* 159–210.

Hurvich, L. M. (1981). *Color vision.* Sunderland, MA: Sinaver Associates.

Huxley, A. (1939). *Brave new world.* New York: Harper & Row.

Hyde, J. S. (1993, August). Teaching the psychology of women and gender for undergraduate and graduate faculty. Workshop of the Psychology of Women Institute presented at the meeting of the American Psychological Association, Toronto, Canada.

Hyde, J. S., Fennema, E., & Lamon, S. J. (1990). Gender differences in mathematics performance: A meta-analysis. *Psychological Bulletin, 107,* 139–155.

Hyde, J. S., & Linn, M. C. (1988). Gender differences in verbal ability: A meta-analysis. *Psychological Bulletin, 104,* 53–69.

Hyde, J. S., & Plant, E. A. (1995). Magnitude of psychological gender differences: Another side to the story. *American Psychologist, 50,* 159–161.

Imber, S. D., and others. (1990). Mode-specific effects among three treatments for depression. *Journal of Consulting and Clinical Psychology, 58,* 352–359.

Insko, C. A. (1985). Balance theory, the Jordan paradigm, and the Wiest tetrahedron. In L. Berkowitz (Ed.), *Advances in experimental social psychology.* New York: Academic Press.

Insko, C. A., Smith, R. H., Alicke, M. D., Wade, J., & Taylor, S. (1985). Conformity and group size: The concern with being right and the concern with being liked. *Personality and Social Psychology Bulletin, 11,* 41–50.

Ironson, G. (1993). Cited in Adler, T. (1993). Men and women affected by stress, but differently. *APA Monitor, 24*(7), 8–9.

Ironson, G., Antoni, M. H., Schneiderman, N., LaPerriere, A., & Fletcher, M. A. (1992, July). *Stress management interventions and psychological predictors in HIV.* Paper presented at the Second International Congress of Behavioral Medicine, Hamburg, Germany.

Isabella, R. A. (1993). Origins of attachment: Maternal interactive behavior across the first year. *Child Development, 64,* 605–621.

Isay, R. A. (1990). Psychoanalytic theory and the therapy of gay men. In D. P. McWhirter, S. A. Sanders, & J. M. Reinisch (Eds.), *Homosexuality/heterosexuality: Concepts of sexual orientation* (pp. 283–303). New York: Oxford University Press.

Isen, A. M., & Baron, R. A. (1990). Positive affect and organizational behavior. In B. M. Staw & L. L. Cummings (Eds.), *Advances in experimental social psychology* (Vol. 12). Greenwich, CT: JAI Press.

Isomura, T., Fine, S., & Lin, T. (1987). Two Japanese families: A cultural perspective. *Canadian Journal of Psychiatry, 32,* 282–286.

Israel, E., and others. (1990). The effects of a 5-lipoxygenase inhibitor on asthma induced by cold, dry air. *New England Journal of Medicine, 323,* 1740–1744.

Ivancevich, J. M., Matteson, M. T., Freedman, S. M., & Phillips, J. S. (1990). Worksite stress management interventions. *American Psychologist, 45,* 252–261.

Iversen, I. H. (1992). Skinner's early research: From reflexology to operant conditioning. *American Psychologist, 47,* 1318–1328.

Izard, C. E. (1984). Emotion–cognition relationships and human development. In C. E. Izard, J. Kagan, & R. B. Zajonc (Eds.), *Emotions, cognition, and behavior.* New York: Cambridge University Press.

Izard, C. E. (1990). Facial expression and the regulation of emotions. *Journal of Personality and Social Psychology, 58,* 487–498.

Izard, C. E. (1992). Basic emotions, relations among emotions, and emotion–cognition relations. *Psychological Review, 99,* 561–565.

Izard, C. E. (1994). Basic emotions, relations among emotions, and emotion–cognition relations. *Psychological Bulletin, 115,* 561–565.

Jackson, J. (1993). Human behavioral genetics, Scarr's theory, and her views on interventions: A critical review and commentary on their implications for African American children. *Child Development, 64,* 1318–1332.

Jackson, J. (1995, August). The new immigrants in urban America: Implications for education, employment, and service delivery. Master lecture delivered to the meeting of the American Psychological Association, New York.

Jacob, T., Krahn, G. L., & Leonard, K. (1991). Parent–child interactions in families with alcoholic fathers. *Journal of Consulting and Clinical Psychology, 59,* 176–181.

Jacobs, T. J., & Charles, E. (1980). Life events and the occurrence of cancer in children. *Psychosomatic Medicine, 42,* 11–24.

Jacobson, N. S., & Addis, M. E. (1993). Research on couples and couples therapy: What do we know? Where are we going? *Journal of Consulting and Clinical Psychology, 61,* 85–93.

Jacox, A., Carr, D. B., & Payne, R. (1994). New clinical-practice guidelines for the management of pain in patients with cancer. *New England Journal of Medicine, 330,* 651–655.

James, W. (1890). *The principles of psychology.* New York: Henry Holt.

James, W. (1904). Does "consciousness" exist? *Journal of Philosophy, Psychology, and Scientific Methods, 1,* 477–491.

Janerich, D. T., and others. (1990). Lung cancer and exposure to tobacco smoke in the household. *New England Journal of Medicine, 323,* 632–636.

Janis, I. L. (1982). *Groupthink: Psychological studies of policy decisions and fiascoes* (2nd ed.). Boston: Houghton Mifflin.

Janowitz, H. D., & Grossman, M. I. (1949). Effects of variations in nutritive density on intake of food in dogs and cats. *American Journal of Physiology, 158,* 184–193.

Janus, S. S., & Janus, C. L. (1993). *The Janus report on sexual behavior.* New York: Wiley.

Jeffery, R. W. (1991). Population perspectives on the prevention and treatment of obesity in minority populations. *American Journal of Clinical Nutrition, 53,* 1621S–1624S.

Jemmott, J. B., and others. (1983). Academic stress, power motivation, and decrease in secretion rate of salivary secretory immunoglobin A. *Lancet, 1,* 1400–1402.

Jemmott, J. B., and others. (1990). Motivational syndromes associated with natural killer cell activity. *Journal of Behavioral Medicine, 13,* 53–73.

Jenkins, A. H. (1985). Attending to self-activity in the Afro-American client. *Psychotherapy, 22,* 335–341.

Jenkins, C. D. (1988). Epidemiology of cardiovascular diseases. *Journal of Consulting and Clinical Psychology, 56,* 324–332.

Jensen, M. P., & Karoly, P. (1991). Control beliefs, coping efforts, and adjustment to chronic pain. *Journal of Consulting and Clinical Psychology, 59,* 431–438.

Jensen, M. P., Turner, J. A., & Romano, J. M. (1994). Correlates of improvement in multidisciplinary treatment of chronic pain. *Journal of Consulting and Clinical Psychology, 62,* 172–179.

Jeste, D. V., and others. (1992). Cognitive deficits of patients with Alzheimer's disease with and without delusions. *American Journal of Psychiatry, 149,* 184–188.

Johnson, B. T., & Eagly, A. H. (1989). Effects of involvement on persuasion: A meta-analysis. *Psychological Bulletin, 106,* 290–314.

Johnson, C. A., and others. (1990). Relative effectiveness of comprehensive community programming for drug abuse prevention with high-risk and low-risk adolescents. *Journal of Consulting and Clinical Psychology, 58,* 447–457.

Johnson, D. (1990, March 8). AIDS clamor at colleges muffling older dangers. *The New York Times,* p. A18.

Johnson, D. J. (1992). Developmental pathways: Toward an ecological theoretical formulation of race identity in Black–White biracial children. In M. P. P. Root (Ed.), *Racially mixed people in America.* Newbury Park, CA: Sage.

Johnson, G. (1995, June 6). Chimp talk debate: Is it really language? *The New York Times,* pp. C1, C10.

Johnson, J. T., & Judd, C. M. (1983). Overlooking the incongruent: Categorization biases in the identification of political statements. *Journal of Personality and Social Psychology, 45,* 978–996.

Johnson, W., Emde, R. N., Pannabecker, B., Stenberg, C., & Davis, M. (1982). Maternal perception of infant emotion from birth to 18 months. *Infant Behavior and Development, 5,* 313–322.

Johnston, L. D., Bachman, J. G., & O'Malley, P. M. (1991, January 23). Monitoring the future: A continuing study of the lifestyles and values of youth. Ann Arbor: University of Michigan News and Information Services.

Johnston, L. D., O'Malley, P. M., & Bachman, J. G. (1993). National survey results on drug use from the Monitoring the Future Study, 1975–1992. The University of Michigan Institute for Social Research; National Institute on Drug Abuse, 5600 Fishers Lane, Rockville, MD 20957; USDHHS, Public Health Service, National Institutes of Health.

Johnston, W., & Dark, V. (1986). Selective attention. *Annual Review of Psychology, 37,* 43–75.

Jones, E. E. (1961). *The life and work of Sigmund Freud.* New York: Basic Books.

Jones, E. E. (1990). *Interpersonal perception.* New York: W. H. Freeman.

Jones, J. (1991). In J. D. Goodchilds (Ed.), *Psychological perspectives on human diversity in America.* Washington, DC: American Psychological Association.

Jones, J. L., & Leary, M. R. (1994). Effects of appearance-based admonitions against sun exposure on tanning intentions in young adults. *Health Psychology, 13,* 86–90.

Jones, M. C. (1924). Elimination of children's fears. *Journal of Experimental Psychology, 7,* 381–390.

Jordan, J. V., Kaplan, A. G., Miller, J. B., Stiver, L. P., & Stiver, J. L. (Eds.). (1991). *Women's growth in connection.* New York: Guilford.

Josephson, W. D. (1987). Television violence and children's aggression: Testing the priming, social script, and disinhibition prediction. *Journal of Personality and Social Psychology, 53,* 882–890.

Juarez, R. (1985). Core issues in psychotherapy with the Hispanic child. *Psychotherapy, 22,* 441–448.

Judd, C. M., & Park, B. (1988). Out-group homogeneity: Judgments of variability at the individual and group levels. *Journal of Personality and Social Psychology, 54,* 778–788.

Julien, R. M. (1988). *A primer of drug action* (2nd ed.). San Francisco: Freeman.

Kahle, L. R., & Beatty, S. E. (1987). Cognitive consequences of post-purchase behavior. *Journal of Applied Social Psychology, 17,* 828–843.

Kahn, M. W. (1982). Cultural clash and psychopathology in three aboriginal cultures. *Academic Psychology Bulletin, 4,* 553–561.

Kail, R. (1990). *The development of memory in children* (3rd ed.). New York: W. H. Freeman.

Kamin, L. J. (1982). Mental testing and immigration. *American Psychologist, 37,* 97–98.

Kandel, E. R., & Hawkins, R. D. (1992). The biological basis of learning and individuality. *Scientific American, 267,* 78–86.

Kanner, A. D., Coyne, J. C., Schaefer, C., & Lazarus R. S. (1981). Comparison of two modes of stress measurement: Daily hassles and uplifts versus major life events. *Journal of Behavioral Medicine, 4,* 1–39.

Karabenick, S. A., & Sharma, R. (1994). Perceived teacher support of student questioning in the college classroom: Its relation to student characteristics and role in the classroom questioning process. *Journal of Educational Psychology, 86,* 90–103.

Karasek, R. A., and others. (1982). Job, psychological factors and coronary heart disease. *Advances in Cardiology, 29,* 62–67.

Karasek, R. A., & Theorell, T. (1990). *Healthy work: Stress, productivity, and the reconstruction of working life.* New York: Basic Books.

Katzell, R. A., & Thompson, D. E. (1990). Work motivation: Theory and practice. *American Psychologist, 45,* 144–153.

Kazdin, A. E. (1993). Adolescent mental health: Prevention and treatment programs. *American Psychologist, 48,* 127–141.

Keating, C. F., and others. (1985). Psychosocial enhancement of immunocompetence in a geriatric population. *Health Psychology, 4,* 25–41.

Keefe, F. J., Dunsmore, J., & Burnett, R. (1992). Behavioral and cognitive-behavioral approaches to chronic pain. *Journal of Consulting and Clinical Psychology, 60,* 528–536.

Keen, S. (1991). *Fire in the belly.* New York: Harper & Row.

Keesey, R. E. (1986). A set-point theory of obesity. In K. D. Brownell & J. P. Foreyt (Eds.), *Handbook of eating disorders: Physiology, psychology, and treatment of obesity, anorexia, and bulimia.* New York: Basic Books.

Keil, J. E., and others. (1993). Mortality rates and risk factors for coronary disease in Black as compared with White men and women. *New England Journal of Medicine, 329,* 73–78.

Keinan, G. (1987). Decision making under stress: Scanning of alternatives under controllable and uncontrollable threats. *Journal of Personality and Social Psychology, 52,* 639–644.

Keita, G. P. (1993, February). Presentation to the Fifth International Interdisciplinary Congress on Women, University of Costa Rica, San Jose, Costa Rica.

Keita, G. P., & Jones, J. M. (1990). Reducing adverse reaction to stress in the workplace. *American Psychologist, 45,* 1137–1141.

Keller, M. B., First, M., & Koscis, J. H. (1990, August/September). Major depression and dysthymia. *DSM-IV Update.* Washington, DC: American Psychiatric Association.

Kellerman, J., Lewis, J., & Laird, J. D. (1989). Looking and loving: The effects of mutual gaze on feelings of romantic love. *Journal of Research in Personality, 23,* 145–161.

Kelley, H. H., & Michela, J. L. (1980). Attribution theory and research. *Annual Review of Psychology, 31,* 457–501.

Kellman, P. J., & von Hofsetn, C. (1992). The world of the moving infant: Perception of motion, stability, and space. In C. Rovee-Collier & L. P. Lipsitt (Eds.), *Advances in Infancy Research* (Vol. 7). Norwood, NJ: Ablex.

Kelly, G. A. (1955). *The psychology of personal constructs* (Vols. 1 & 2). New York: W. W. Norton.

Kelly, J. A., Murphy, D. A., Sikkema, K. J., & Kalichman, S. C. (1993). Psychological interventions to prevent HIV infection are urgently needed. *American Psychologist, 48,* 1023–1034.

Kemeny, M. E. (1993). Emotions and the immune system. In B. Moyers, *Healing and the mind.* New York: Doubleday.

Kemeny, M. E., Weiner, H., Taylor, S. E., Schneider, S., Visscher, B., & Fahey, J. L. (1994). Repeated bereavement, depressed mood, and immune parameters in HIV seropositive and seronegative gay men. *Health Psychology, 13,* 14–24.

Kemper, P., & Murtaugh, C. M. (1991). Lifetime use of nursing home care. *New England Journal of Medicine, 324,* 595–600.

Kendler, H. H. (1993). Psychology and the ethics of social policy. *American Psychologist, 48,* 1046–1053.

Kenrick, D. T., & MacFarlane, S. W. (1986). Ambient temperature and horn honking: A field study of the heat/aggression relationship. *Environment and Behavior, 18,* 179–191.

Kerr, N. L., & MacCoun, R. J. (1985). The effects of jury size and polling method on the process and product of jury deliberation. *Journal of Personality and Social Psychology, 48,* 349–363.

Kershner, J. R., & Ledger, G. (1985). Effect of sex, intelligence, and style of thinking on creativity: A comparison of gifted and average IQ children. *Journal of Personality and Social Psychology, 48,* 1033–1040.

Kessler, D. A. (1995). Nicotine addiction in young people. *New England Journal of Medicine, 333,* 186–189.

Kiecolt-Glaser, J. K. (1993). Cited in Adler, T. (1993). Men and women affected by stress, but differently. *APA Monitor, 24*(7), 8–9.

Kiecolt-Glaser, J. K., & Glaser, R. (1992). Psychoneuroimmunology: Can psychological interventions modulate immunity? *Journal of Consulting and Clinical Psychology, 60,* 569–575.

Kihlstrom, J. F. (1980). Posthypnotic amnesia for recently learned material: Interactions with "episodic" and "semantic" memory. *Cognitive Psychology, 12,* 227–251.

Kihlstrom, J. F., Brenneman, H. A., Pistole, D. D., & Shor, R. E. (1985). Hypnosis as a retrieval cue in posthypnotic amnesia. *Journal of Abnormal Psychology, 94,* 264–271.

Kihlstrom, J. F., Glisky, M. L., & Angiulo, M. J. (1994). Dissociative tendencies and dissociative disorders. *Journal of Abnormal Psychology, 103,* 117–124.

Kilborn, P. T. (1995, March 16). Women and minorities still face "glass ceilings." *The New York Times,* p. A22.

Killen, J. D., Fortmann, S. P., Newman, B., & Varady, A. (1990). Evaluation of a treatment approach combining nicotine gum with self-guided behavioral treatments for smoking relapse prevention. *Journal of Consulting and Clinical Psychology, 58,* 85–92.

Kimble, D. P. (1992). *Biological psychology* (2nd ed.). Fort Worth, TX: Harcourt Brace Jovanovich.

Kimble, G. A. (1994). A frame of reference for psychology. *American Psychologist, 49,* 510–519.

Kimerling, R., & Calhoun, K. S. (1994). Somatic symptoms, social support, and treatment seeking among sexual assault victims. *Journal of Consulting and Clinical Psychology, 62,* 333–340.

Kimmel, A. J. (1991). Predictable biases in the ethical decision making of American psychologists. *American Psychologist, 46,* 786–788.

Kimura, D. (1992). Sex differences in the brain. *Scientific American, 267,* 118–125.

Kinnunen, T., Zamansky, H. S., & Block, M. L. (1994). Is the hypnotized subject lying? *Journal of Abnormal Psychology, 103,* 184–191.

Kinsey, A. C., Pomeroy, W. B., & Martin, C. E. (1948). *Sexual behavior in the human male.* Philadelphia: W. B. Saunders.

Kinsey, A. C., Pomeroy, W. B., Martin, C. E., & Gebhard, P. H. (1953). *Sexual behavior in the human female.* Philadelphia: W. B. Saunders.

Kintsch, W. (1994). Text comprehension, memory, and learning. *American Psychologist, 49,* 294–303.

Kirsch, I., Montgomery, G., & Sapirstein, G. (1995). Hypnosis as an adjunct to cognitive-behavioral psychotherapy: A meta-analysis. *Journal of Consulting and Clinical Psychology, 63,* 214–220.

Klatzky, R. L. (1980). *Human memory: Structures and processes* (2nd ed.). San Francisco: W. H. Freeman.

Klatzky, R. L. (1983). The icon is dead: Long live the icon. *Behavioral and Brain Sciences, 6,* 27–28.

Klatzky, R. L. (1994). Cited in Goleman, D. (1994, September 6). Sonic device for blind may help in navigation. *The New York Times,* pp. C1, C9.

Klein, D. N., Depue, R. A., & Slater, J. F. (1985). Cyclothymia in the adolescent offspring of parents with bipolar affective disorder. *Journal of Abnormal Psychology, 94,* 115–127.

Kleinke, C. L. (1977). Compliance to requests made by gazing and touching experimenters in field settings. *Journal of Experimental Social Psychology, 13,* 218–223.

Kleinke, C. L. (1986). Gaze and eye contact: A research review. *Psychological Review, 100,* 78–100.

Kleinke, C. L., & Staneski, R. A. (1980). First impressions of female bust size. *Journal of Social Psychology, 110,* 123–134.

Kleinmuntz, B., & Szucko, J. J. (1984). Lie detection in ancient and modern times: A call for contemporary scientific study. *American Psychologist, 39,* 766–776.

Klesges, R. C., Klesges, L. M., & Meyers, A. W. (1991). Relationship of smoking status, energy balance, and body weight: Analysis of the Second National Health and Nutrition Examination Survey. *Journal of Consulting and Clinical Psychology, 59,* 899–905.

Klorman, R., Brumaghim, J. T., Fitzpatrick, P. A., Borgstedt, A. D., & Strauss, J. (1994). Clinical and cognitive effects of methylphenidate on children with attention deficit disorder as a function of aggression/oppositionality and age. *Journal of Abnormal Psychology, 103,* 206–221.

Klosko, J. S., Barlow, D. H., Tassinari, R., & Cerny, J. A. (1990). A comparison of alprazolam and behavior therapy in treatment of panic disorder. *Journal of Consulting and Clinical Psychology, 58,* 77–84.

Kneip, R. C., and others. (1993). Self- and spouse ratings of anger and hostility as predictors of coronary heart disease. *Health Psychology, 12,* 301–307.

Knight, M. (1994). Darwinian functionalism: A cognitive science paradigm. *The Psychological Record, 44,* 271–287.

Knowlton, W. A., Jr., & Mitchell, T. R. (1980). Effects of causal attributions on a supervisor's evaluation of subordinate performance. *Journal of Applied Psychology, 65,* 459–466.

Kobasa, S. C. (1979). Stressful life events, personality, and health: An inquiry into hardiness. *Journal of Personality and Social Psychology, 37,* 1–11.

Kobasa, S. C., Maddi, S. R., and Kahn, S. (1982). Hardiness and health: A prospective study. *Journal of Personality and Social Psychology, 42,* 168–177.

Kobasa, S. C., & Puccetti, M. C. (1983). Personality and social resources in stress resistance. *Journal of Personality and Social Psychology, 45,* 839–850.

Koch, C. (1992). Cited in Blakeslee, S. (1992c, October 27). Nerve cell rhythm may be key to consciousness. *The New York Times,* pp. C1, C10.

Koffka, K. (1925). *The growth of the mind.* New York: Harcourt Brace Jovanovich.

Kohlberg, L. (1969). *Stages in the development of moral thought and action.* New York: Holt, Rinehart and Winston.

Kohlberg, L. (1981). *The philosophy of moral development: Moral stages and the idea of justice.* San Francisco: Harper & Row.

Köhler, W. (1925). The mentality of apes. New York: Harcourt Brace World.

Kohn, P. M., Barnes, G. E., & Hoffman, F. M. (1979). Drug-use history and experience seeking among adult male correctional inmates. *Journal of Consulting and Clinical Psychology, 47,* 708–715.

Kolata, G. (1991a, February 26). Alzheimer's researchers close in on causes. *The New York Times,* pp. C1, C7.

Kolata, G. (1991b, November 8). Studies cite 10.5 years from infection to illness. *The New York Times,* p. B12.

Kolata, G. (1993a, February 7). AIDS group dismayed by report they see as discounting concern. *The New York Times,* p. 30.

Kolata, G. (1993b, May 6). Cancer-causing gene found with a clue to how it works. *The New York Times,* pp. A1, B15.

Kolata, G. (1993c, October 24). Scientist clones human embryos, and creates an ethical challenge. *The New York Times,* pp. 1, 22.

Kolata, G. (1993d, October 26). The hot debate about cloning human embryo. *The New York Times,* pp. A1, C3.

Kolata, G. (1994, February 16). Debate on using marijuana as medicine turns to question of whether it works. *The New York Times*, p. C12.

Kolata, G. (1995, May 2). New evidence on fetal cells. *The New York Times*, p. C3.

Kolko, D. J., & Rickard-Figueroa, J. L. (1985). Effects of video games on the adverse corollaries of chemotherapy in pediatric oncology patients: A single-case analysis. *Journal of Consulting and Clinical Psychology, 53,* 223–228.

Koocher, G. P. (1991). Questionable methods in alcoholism research. *Journal of Consulting and Clinical Psychology, 59,* 246–248.

Korn, J. H., Davis, R., & Davis, S. F. (1991). Historians' and chairpersons' judgments of eminence among psychologists. *American Psychologist, 46,* 789–792.

Kosonen, P., & Winne, P. H. (1995). Effects of teaching statistical laws on reasoning about everyday problems. *Journal of Educational Psychology, 87,* 33–46.

Koss, M. P. (1993). Rape: Scope, impact, interventions, and public policy responses. *American Psychologist, 48,* 1062–1069.

Koss, M. P., Butcher, J. L., & Strupp, H. H. (1986). Brief psychotherapy methods in clinical research. *Journal of Consulting and Clinical Psychology, 54,* 60–67.

Koss, M. P., Gidycz, C. A., & Wisniewski, N. (1987). The scope of rape: Incidence and prevalence of sexual aggression and victimization in a national sample of higher education students. *Journal of Consulting and Clinical Psychology, 55,* 162–170.

Kosslyn, S. M. (1994). *Image and brain: The resolution of the imagery debate.* Cambridge, MA: The MIT Press, a Bradford Book.

Kramer, P. D. (1993). *Listening to Prozac.* New York: Viking.

Krantz, D. S., Contrada, R. J., Hill, D. R., & Friedler, E. (1988). Environmental stress and biobehavioral antecedents of coronary heart disease. *Journal of Consulting and Clinical Psychology, 56,* 333–341.

Krantz, D. S., Grunberg, N. E., & Baum, A. (1985). Health psychology. *Annual Review of Psychology, 36,* 349–383.

Kring, A. M., Kerr, S. L., Smith, D. A., & Neale, J. M. (1993). Flat affect in schizophrenia does not reflect diminished subjective experience of emotion. *Journal of Abnormal Psychology, 102,* 507–517.

Krosnick, J. A. (1989). Attitude importance and attitude accessibility. *Personality and Social Psychology Bulletin, 15,* 297–308.

Kübler-Ross, E. (1969). *On death and dying.* New York: Macmillan.

Kübler-Ross, E., & Magno, J. B. (1983). *Hospice.* Santa Fe, NM: Bear.

Kuczaj, S. A., II. (1982). On the nature of syntactic development. In S. A. Kuczaj II (Ed.), *Language development: Vol. 1. Syntax and semantics.* Hillsdale, NJ: Erlbaum.

Kuczmarski, R. J. (1992). Prevalence of overweight and weight gain in the United States. *American Journal of Clinical Nutrition, 55*(Suppl.), 495S–502S.

Kushler, M. G. (1989). Use of evaluation to improve energy conservation programs. *Journal of Social Issues, 45,* 153–168.

Lacks, P., & Morin, C. M. (1992). Recent advances in the assessment and treatment of insomnia. *Journal of Consulting and Clinical Psychology, 60,* 586–594.

LaCroix, A. Z., and others. (1991). Smoking and mortality among older men and women in three communities. *New England Journal of Medicine, 324,* 1619–1625.

LaFramboise, T. (1994). Cited in DeAngelis, T. (1994). History, culture affect treatment for Indians. *APA Monitor, 27*(10), 36.

LaFramboise, T. D., Coleman, H. L. K., & Gerton, J. (1993). Psychological impact of biculturalism: Evidence and theory. *Psychological Bulletin, 114,* 395–412.

Laguerre, M. S. (1981). Haitian Americans. In A. Harwood (Ed.), *Ethnicity and medical care.* Cambridge, MA: Harvard University Press.

Lakka, T. A., and others. (1994). Relation of leisure-time physical activity and cardiorespiratory fitness to the risk of acute myocardial infarction in men. *New England Journal of Medicine, 330,* 1549–1554.

Lamb, M. E., Sternberg, K. J., & Prodromidis, M. (1992). Nonmaternal care and the security of infant–mother attachment: A reanalysis of the data. *Infant Behavior and Development, 15,* 71–83.

Lambert, W. E. (1990). Persistent issues in bilingualism. In B. Harley and others (Eds.), *The development of second language proficiency.* Cambridge, England: Cambridge University Press.

Lambert, W. E. (1992). Challenging established views on social issues. *American Psychologist, 47,* 533–542.

Lambert, W. E., Genesee, F., Holobow, N., & Chartrand, L. (1991). *Bilingual education for majority English-speaking children.* Montreal: McGill University.

Landy, F. J. (1992, August). The roots of organizational and industrial psychology. Master lecture presented to the annual meeting of the American Psychological Association, Washington, DC.

Lang, A. R., Goeckner, D. J., Adesso, V. J., & Marlatt, G. A. (1975). Effects of alcohol on aggression in male social drinkers. *Journal of Abnormal Psychology, 84,* 508–518.

Lang, P. J., & Melamed, B. B. (1969). Case report: Avoidance conditioning therapy of an infant with chronic ruminative vomiting. *Journal of Abnormal Psychology, 74,* 1–8.

Lang, S. S., & Patt, R. B. (1994). *You don't have to suffer.* New York: Oxford University Press.

Langer, E. J., Rodin, J., Beck, P., Weinan, C., & Spitzer, L. (1979). Environmental determinants of memory improvement in late adulthood. *Journal of Personality and Social Psychology, 37,* 2003–2013.

Langford, H. G., and others. (1985). Dietary therapy slows the return of hypertension after stopping prolonged medication. *Journal of the American Medical Association, 253,* 657–664.

Langlois, J. H. (1994). Cited in Brody, J. E. (1994, March 21). Notions of beauty transcend culture, new study suggests. *The New York Times,* p. A14.

LaPerriere, A. R., and others. (1990). Exercise intervention attenuates emotional distress and natural killer cell decrements following notification of positive serologic status for HIV-1. *Biofeedback and Self-Regulation, 15,* 229–242.

LaPerriere, A. R., and others. (1991). Aerobic exercise training in an AIDS risk group. *International Journal of Sports Medicine, 12,* S53–S57.

Laroche, S., & Bloch, V. (1982). Conditioning of hippocampal cells and long-term potentiation. An approach to mechanisms of posttrial memory facilitation. In C. Ajmone Marsan & H. Matthies (Eds.), *Neuronal plasticity and memory formation.* New York: Raven Press.

Larrick, R. P. (1993). Motivational factors in decision theories: The role of self-protection. *Psychological Bulletin, 113,* 440–450.

Larson, R., & Richards, M. H. (1991). Daily companionship in late childhood and early adolescence: Changing developmental contexts. *Child Development, 62,* 284–300.

Larson, R. K. (1990). Semantics. In D. N. Osherson, & H. Lasnik (Eds.), *An invitation to cognitive science: Language* (Vol. 1). Cambridge, MA: The MIT Press, a Bradford Book.

Lashley, K. S. (1950). In search of the engram. In *Symposium of the Society for Experimental Biology* (Vol. 4). New York: Cambridge University Press.

Lasnik, H. (1990). Syntax. In D. N. Osherson, & H. Lasnik (Eds.), *An invitation to cognitive science: Language* (Vol. 1). Cambridge, MA: The MIT Press, a Bradford Book.

Latané, B., & Dabbs, J. M. (1975). Sex, group size, and helping in three cities. *Sociometry, 38,* 180–194.

Latané, B., & Nida, S. (1981). Ten years of research on group size and helping. *Psychological Bulletin, 89,* 308–324.

Lau, M. A., Pihl, R. O., & Peterson, J. B. (1995). Provocation, acute alcohol intoxication, cognitive performance, and aggression. *Journal of Abnormal Psychology, 104,* 150–155.

Lau, R. R., & Russell, D. (1980). Attributions in the sports pages. *Journal of Personality and Social Psychology, 39,* 29–38.

Laube, D. (1985). Premenstrual syndrome. *The Female Patient, 6,* 50–61.

Laudenslager, M. L., and others. (1983). Coping and immunosuppression: Inescapable but not escapable shock suppresses lymphocyte proliferation. *Science, 221,* 568–570.

Laumann, E. O., Gagnon, J. H., Michael, R. T., & Michaels, S. (1994). *The social organization of sexuality.* Chicago: University of Chicago Press.

Lawler, E. E., III. (1985, January/February). Quality circles after the fad. *Harvard Business Review,* pp. 65–71.

Lazar, I., & Darlington, R. (1982). Lasting effects of early education: A report from the Consortium of Longitudinal Studies. *Monographs of the Society for Research in Child Development, 47*(2–3, Serial No. 195).

Lazarus, A. A. (1990). If this be research . . . *American Psychologist, 45,* 670–671.

Lazarus, R. S. (1991a). Cognition and motivation in emotion. *American Psychologist, 46,* 352–367.

Lazarus, R. S. (1991b). *Emotion and adaptation.* New York: Oxford University Press.

Lazarus, R. S., DeLongis, A., Folkman, S., & Gruen, R. (1985). Stress and adaptational outcomes: The problem of confounded measures. *American Psychologist, 40,* 770–779.

Lazarus, R. S., & Folkman, S. (1984). *Stress, appraisal, and coping.* New York: Springer.

Leary, W. E. (1991, October 22). Black hypertension may reflect other ills. *The New York Times,* p. C3.

Leary, W. E. (1995, May 2). Billions suffering needlessly, study says. *The New York Times,* p. C5.

LeBon, G. (1960). *The crowd.* New York: Viking. (Original work published 1895).

LeBow, M. D., Goldberg, P. S., & Collins, A. (1977). Eating behavior of overweight and nonoverweight persons in the natural environment. *Journal of Consulting and Clinical Psychology, 45,* 1204–1205.

Lederberg, A. R., & Mobley, C. E. (1990). The effect of hearing impairment on the quality of attachment and mother–toddler interaction. *Child Development, 61,* 1596–1604.

LeDoux, J. E. (1986). The neurobiology of emotion. In J. E. LeDoux & W. Hirst (Eds.), *Mind and brain: Dialogues in cognitive neuroscience.* Cambridge, England: Cambridge University Press.

Lee, C. C., & Richardson, B. L. (1991). *Multicultural issues in counseling: New approaches to diversity.* Alexandria, VA: AACD.

Lee, F. R. (1994, January 5). Grappling with how to teach young speakers of Black dialect. *The New York Times,* pp. A1, D22.

Lefcourt, H. M., & Martin, R. A. (1986). *Humor and life stress: Antidote to adversity.* New York: Springer-Verlag.

Lefcourt, H. M., Miller, R. S, Ware, E. E., & Sherk, D. (1981). Locus of control as a modifier of the relationship between stressors and moods. *Journal of Personality and Social Psychology, 41,* 357–369.

Lefley, H. P. (1990). Culture and chronic mental illness. *Hospital and Community Psychiatry, 41,* 277–286.

Lehrer, P. M., Sargunaraj, D., & Hochron, S. (1992). Psychological approaches to the treatment of asthma. *Journal of Consulting and Clinical Psychology, 60,* 639–643.

Leibel, R. L., Rosenbaum, M., & Hirsch, J. (1995). Changes in energy expenditure resulting from altered body weight. *New England Journal of Medicine, 332,* 621–628.

Leigh, B. C. (1993). Alcohol consumption and sexual activity as reported with a diary technique. *Journal of Abnormal Psychology, 102,* 490–493.

Leigh, B. C., & Stall, R. (1993). Substance use and risky sexual behavior for exposure to HIV. *American Psychologist, 48,* 1035–1045.

Leippe, M. R. (1985). The influence of eyewitness non-identifications on mock-jurors' judgments of a court case. *Journal of Applied Social Psychology, 15,* 656–672.

Lenneberg, E. H. (1967). *Biological foundations of language.* New York: Wiley.

Lerner, M. J., Miller, D. T., & Holmes, J. G. (1975). Deserving versus justice: A contemporary dilemma. In L. Berkowitz & E. Walster (Eds.), *Advances in experimental social psychology* (Vol. 12). New York: Academic Press.

Levi, L. (1990). Occupational stress: Spice of life or kiss of death? *American Psychologist, 45,* 1142–1145.

Levine, I. S., & Rog, D. J. (1990). Mental health services for homeless mentally ill: Federal initiatives and current service trends. *American Psychologist, 45,* 963–968.

Levine, S. R., and others. (1990). Cerebrovascular complications of the use of the "crack" form of alkaloidal cocaine. *New England Journal of Medicine, 323,* 699–704.

Levinson, D. J., Darrow, C. N., Klein, E. B., Levinson, M. H., & McKee, B. (1978). *The seasons of a man's life.* New York: Knopf.

Levinson, H. (1994). Why the behemoths fell: Psychological roots of corporate failure. *American Psychologist, 49,* 428–436.

Levy, S. M., Herberman, R. B., Maluish, A. M., Schlien, B., & Lippman, M. (1985). Prognostic risk assessment in the primary breast cancer by behavioral and immunological parameters. *Health Psychology, 4,* 99–113.

Lewinsohn, P. M., Rohde, P., & Seeley, J. R. (1994a). Psychosocial risk factors for future suicide attempts. *Journal of Consulting and Clinical Psychology, 62,* 297–305.

Lewinsohn, P. M., and others. (1994b). Adolescent psychopathology: II. Psychosocial risk factors for depression. *Journal of Abnormal Psychology, 103,* 302–315.

Lewis-Fernández, R., & Kleinman, A. (1994). Culture, personality, and psychopathology. *Journal of Abnormal Psychology, 103,* 67–71.

Lieber, C. S. (1990). Cited in Barroom biology: How alcohol goes to a woman's head (January 14). *The New York Times,* p. E24.

Liebert, R. M., Sprafkin, J. N., & Davidson, E. S. (1989). *The early window: Effects of television on children and youth* (3rd ed.). New York: Pergamon.

Linden, W., Chambers, L., Maurice, J., & Lenz, J. W. (1993). Sex differences in social support, self-deception, hostility, and ambulatory cardiovascular activity. *Health Psychology, 12,* 376–380.

Lindpaintner, K. (1995). Finding an obesity gene—a tale of mice and man. *New England Journal of Medicine, 332,* 679–680.

Lindsay, D. S., & Johnson, M. K. (1989). The reversed eyewitness suggestibility effect. *Bulletin of the Psychonomic Society, 27,* 111–113.

Lindsay, R. C. L., Lim, R., Marando, L., & Culley, D. (1986). Mock-juror evaluations of eyewitness testimony: A test of metamemory hypotheses. *Journal of Applied Social Psychology, 16,* 447–459.

Lindsey, K. P., & Paul, G. L. (1989). Involuntary commitments to public mental institutions: Issues involving the overrepresentation of Blacks and assessment of relevant functioning. *Psychological Bulletin, 106,* 171–183.

Linville, P. W., Fischer, G. W., & Salovey, P. (1989). Perceived distribution of the characteristics of in-group and out-group members. *Journal of Personality and Social Psychology, 57,* 165–188.

Lipsey, M. W., & Wilson, D. B. (1993). The efficacy of psychological, educational, and behavioral treatment: Confirmation from meta-analysis. *American Psychologist, 48,* 1181–1209.

Lipton, D. N., McDonel, E. C., & McFall, R. M. (1987). Heterosocial perception in rapists. *Journal of Consulting and Clinical Psychology, 55,* 17–21.

Llinás, R. (1995). Cited in Blakeslee, S. (1995, March 21). How the brain might work: A new theory of consciousness. *The New York Times,* pp. C1, C10.

Lochman, J. E. (1992). Cognitive-behavioral intervention with aggressive boys: Three-year follow-up and preventive effects. *Journal of Consulting and Clinical Psychology, 60,* 426–432.

Lochman, J. E., Coie, J. D., Underwood, M. K., & Terry, R. (1993). Effectiveness of social relations intervention program for aggressive and nonaggressive, rejected children. *Journal of Consulting and Clinical Psychology, 61,* 1053–1058.

Lochman, J. E., & Dodge, K. A. (1994). Social-cognitive processes of severely violent, moderately aggressive, and nonaggressive boys. *Journal of Consulting and Clinical Psychology, 62,* 366–374.

Locke, E. A., & Latham, G. P. (1990). Work motivation and satisfaction: Light at the end of the tunnel. *Psychological Science, 2,* 131–132.

Loftus, E. F. (1979). *Eyewitness testimony.* Cambridge, MA: Harvard University Press.

Loftus, E. F. (1983). Silence is not golden. *American Psychologist, 38,* 564–572.

Loftus, E. F. (1993a). Psychologists in the eyewitness world. *American Psychologist, 48,* 550–552.

Loftus, E. F. (1993b). The reality of repressed memories. *American Psychologist, 48,* 518–537.

Loftus, E. F. (1994). Conference on memory. Harvard Medical School. Cited in D. Goleman (1994, May 31). Miscoding is seen as the root of false memories. *The New York Times,* pp. C1, C8.

Loftus, E. F., & Burns, T. E. (1982). Mental shock can produce retrograde amnesia. *Memory and Cognition, 10,* 318–323.

Loftus, E. F., & Klinger, M. A. (1992). Is the unconscious smart or dumb? *American Psychologist, 47,* 761–765.

Loftus, E. F., & Loftus, G. R. (1980). On the permanence of stored information in the brain. *American Psychologist, 35,* 409–420.

Loftus, E. F., & Palmer J. C. (1974). Reconstruction of automobile destruction: An example of interaction between language and memory. *Journal of Verbal Learning and Verbal Behavior, 13,* 585–589.

Loftus, G. R. (1983). The continuing persistence of the icon. *Behavioral and Brain Sciences, 6,* 28.

Loftus, G. R., & Loftus, E. F. (1976). *Human memory: The processing of information.* Hillsdale, NJ: Erlbaum.

Lohr, J. M., & Staats, A. (1973). Attitude conditioning in Sino-Tibetan languages. *Journal of Personality and Social Psychology, 26,* 196–200.

Lonergan, E. T., & Krevans, J. R. (1991). A national agenda for research on aging. *New England Journal of Medicine, 324,* 1825–1828.

Long, G. M., & Beaton, R. J. (1982). The case for peripheral persistence: Effects of target and background luminance on a partial-report task. *Journal of Experimental Psychology: Human Perception and Performance, 8,* 383–391.

Lopez, S., & Hernandez, P. (1986). How culture is considered in evaluations of psychopathology. *Journal of Nervous and Mental Diseases, 176,* 598–606.

Lore, R. K., & Schultz, L. A. (1993). Control of human aggression: A comparative perspective. *American Psychologist, 48,* 16–25.

Lorenz, K. Z. (1981). *The foundations of ethology.* New York: Springer-Verlag.

Louie, V. (1993, August 8). For Asian-Americans, a way to fight a maddening stereotype. *The New York Times,* F9.

Luborsky, L., Barber, J. P., & Beutler, L. (1993). Introduction to special section: A briefing on curative factors in dynamic psychotherapy. *Journal of Consulting and Clinical Psychology, 61,* 539–541.

Lucariello, J., & Nelson, K. (1985). Slot-filler categories as memory organizers for young children. *Developmental Psychology, 21,* 272–281.

Luchins, A. S. (1957). Primary-recency in impression formation. In C. I. Hovland (Ed.), *The order of presentation in persuasion.* New Haven, CT: Yale University Press.

Ludwick-Rosenthal, R., & Neufeld, R. W. J. (1993). Preparation for undergoing an invasive medical procedure: Interacting effects of information and coping style. *Journal of Consulting and Clinical Psychology, 61,* 156–164.

Lundeberg, M. A., Fox, P. W., & Puncochar, J. (1994). Highly confident but wrong: Gender differences and similarities in confidence judgments. *Journal of Educational Psychology, 86,* 114–121.

Lurie, N., and others. (1993). Preventive care for women: Does the sex of the physician matter? *New England Journal of Medicine, 329,* 478–482.

Lykken, D. T. (1982, September). Fearlessness: Its carefree charm and deadly risks. *Psychology Today, 16,* 20–28.

Lykken, D. T., McGue, M., Tellegen, A., & Bouchard, T. J., Jr. (1992). Emergenesis: Genetic traits that may not run in families. *American Psychologist, 47,* 1565–1577.

Lynn, R. (1982). IQ in Japan and the United States shows a growing disparity. *Nature, 297,* 222–223.

Lynn, R. (1991). Educational achievements of Asian Americans. *American Psychologist, 46,* 875–876.

Lyons, J. S., Rosen, A. J., & Dysken, M. W. (1985). Behavioral effects of tricyclic drugs in depressed patients. *Journal of Consulting and Clinical Psychology, 53,* 17–24.

Lyons-Ruth, K., Alpern, L., & Repacholi, B. (1993). Disorganized infant attachment classification and maternal psychosocial problems are predictors of hostile-aggressive behavior in the preschool classroom. *Child Development, 64,* 572–585.

Maas, J. W., and others. (1993). Studies of catecholamine metabolism in schizophrenia/psychosis—I. *Neuropsychopharmacology, 8,* 97–109.

Maccoby, E. E. (1990). Gender and relationships: A developmental account. *American Psychologist, 45,* 513–520.

Maccoby, E. E., & Jacklin, C. N. (1974). *The psychology of sex differences.* Stanford, CA: Stanford University Press.

Maccoby, E. E., & Jacklin, C. N. (1989). Sex differences in aggression: A rejoinder and reprise. *Child Development, 51,* 964–980.

MacDonald, K. (1992). Warmth as a developmental construct: An evolutionary analysis. *Child Development, 63,* 753–773.

Mack, D., & Rainey, D. (1990). Female applicants' grooming and personnel selection. *Journal of Social Behavior and Personality, 5,* 399–407.

MacKenzie, T. D., Bartecchi, C. E., & Schrier, R. W. (1994). The human costs of tobacco use. *New England Journal of Medicine, 330,* 975–980.

Mackett-Stout, J., & Dewar, R. (1981). Evaluation of public information signs. *Human Factors, 23*(2), 139–151.

Mackie, D. M., & Worth, L. T. (1989). Processing deficits and the mediation of positive affect in persuasion. *Journal of Personality and Social Psychology, 57,* 27–40.

Mackie, D. M., Worth, L. T., & Asuncion, A. G. (1990). Processing of persuasive in-group messages. *Journal of Personality and Social Psychology, 58,* 812–822.

Macmillan, N. A., & Creelman, C. D. (1991). *Signal detection theory.* New York: Cambridge University Press.

Maddi, S. R., & Kobasa, S. C. (1984). *The hardy executive: Health under stress.* Homewood, IL: Dow Jones-Irwin.

Madigan, S., & O'Hara, R. (1992). Short-term memory at the turn of the century: Mary Whiton Calkin's memory research. *American Psychologist, 47,* 170–174.

Maher, B. A., & Maher, W. B. (1994). Personality and psychopathology: A historical perspective. *Journal of Abnormal Psychology, 103,* 72–77.

Maier, N. R. F., & Schneirla, T. C. (1935). *Principles of animal psychology.* New York: McGraw-Hill.

Maier, S. F., Watkins, L. R., & Fleshner, M. (1994). Psychoneuroimmunology: The interface between behavior, brain, and immunity. *American Psychologist, 49,* 1004–1017.

Malamuth, N. M., Sockloskie, R. J., Koss, M. P., & Tanaka, J. S. (1991). Characteristics of aggressors against women: Testing a model using a national sample of college students. *Journal of Consulting and Clinical Psychology, 59,* 670–681.

Malatesta, V. J., Sutker, P. B., & Treiber, F. A. (1981). Sensation seeking and chronic public drunkenness. *Journal of Consulting and Clinical Psychology, 49,* 282–294.

Malgady, R. G., Rogler, L. H., & Costantino, G. (1990). Hero/heroine modeling for Puerto Rican adolescents: A preventive mental health intervention. *Journal of Consulting and Clinical Psychology, 58,* 469–474.

Mann, J. M. (1992). AIDS—The second decade: A global perspective. *Journal of Infectious Diseases, 165,* 245–250.

Mann, L. (1981). The baiting crowd in episodes of threatened suicide. *Journal of Personality and Social Psychology, 41,* 703–709.

Mann, L., Newton, J. W., & Innes, J. M. (1982). A test between deindividuation and emergent norm theories of crowd aggression. *Journal of Personality and Social Psychology, 42,* 260–272.

Manson, J. E., and others. (1990). A prospective study of obesity and risk of coronary heart disease in women. *New England Journal of Medicine, 322,* 882–889.

Manucia, G. K., Baumann, D. J., & Cialdini, R. B. (1984). Mood influences on helping: Direct effects or side effects? *Journal of Personality and Social Psychology, 46,* 357–364.

Maratsos, M. (1983). Some current issues in the study of the acquisition of grammar. In J. H. Flavell & E. M. Markman (Eds.), *Handbook of child psychology: Vol. 3. Cognitive development.* New York: Wiley.

Marecek, J. (1995). Gender, politics, and psychology's ways of knowing. *American Psychologist, 50,* 162–163.

Marenberg, M. E., and others. (1994). Genetic susceptibility to death from coronary heart disease in a study of twins. *New England Journal of Medicine, 330,* 1041–1046.

Margolick, D. (1994, January 22). Lorena Bobbitt acquitted in mutilation of husband. *The New York Times,* pp. 1, 7.

Margraf, J., and others. (1991). How "blind" are double-blind studies? *Journal of Consulting and Clinical Psychology, 59,* 184–187.

Marin, P. (1983, July). A revolution's broken promises. *Psychology Today, 17,* 50–57.

Markman, H. J., Renick, M. J., Floyd, F. J., Stanley, S. M., & Clements, M. (1993). Preventing marital distress through communication and conflict management training: A 4- and 5-year follow-up. *Journal of Consulting and Clinical Psychology, 61,* 70–77.

Marks, G., Miller, N., & Maruyama, G. (1981). Effect of targets' physical attractiveness on assumption of similarity. *Journal of Personality and Social Psychology, 41,* 198–206.

Markstrom-Adams, C. (1992). A consideration of intervening factors in adolescent identity formation. In G. R. Adams, T. P. Gullotta, & R. Montemayor (Eds.), *Adolescent identity formation.* Newbury Park, CA: Sage.

Markus, H., & Kitayama, S. (1991). Culture and the self: Implications for cognition, emotion, and motivation. *Psychological Review, 98*(2), 224–253.

Marriott, M. (1991, June 5). Beyond "yuck" for girls in science. *The New York Times,* p. A26.

Marston, A. R., London, P., Cohen, N., & Cooper, L. M. (1977). In vivo observation of the eating behavior of obese and nonobese subjects. *Journal of Consulting and Clinical Psychology, 45,* 335–336.

Martin, R. A., & Lefcourt, H. M. (1983). Sense of humor as a moderator of the relation between stressors and moods. *Journal of Personality and Social Psychology, 45,* 1313–1324.

Martin, S. (1994). Music lessons enhance spatial reasoning skills. *APA Monitor, 27*(10), 5.

Martinez, C. (1986). Hispanics: Psychiatric issues. In C. B. Wilkinson (Ed.), *Ethnic psychiatry.* New York: Academic Press.

Martinez, F. D., Cline, M., & Burrows, B. (1992). Increased incidence of asthma in children of smoking mothers. *Pediatrics, 89,* 21–26.

Martinez, J. (1992). Personal communication.

Maruyama, G., Fraser, S. C., & Miller, N. (1982). Personal responsibility and altruism in children. *Journal of Personality and Social Psychology, 42,* 658–664.

Marx, E. M., Williams, J. M. G., & Claridge, G. C. (1992). Depression and social problem solving. *Journal of Abnormal Psychology, 101,* 78–86.

Maser, J. D., Kaelber, C., & Weise, R. E. (1991). International use and attitudes toward *DSM-III* and *DSM-III-R:* Growing consensus in psychiatric classification. *Journal of Abnormal Psychology, 100,* 271–279.

Maslow, A. H. (1963). The need to know and the fear of knowing. *Journal of General Psychology, 68,* 111–124.

Maslow, A. H. (1970). *Motivation and personality* (2nd ed.). New York: Harper & Row.

Maslow, A. H. (1971). *The farther reaches of human nature.* New York: Viking.

Masters, W. H., & Johnson, V. E. (1970). *Human sexual inadequacy.* Boston: Little, Brown.

Matarazzo, J. D. (1990). Psychological assessment versus psychological testing. *American Psychologist, 45,* 999–1017.

Matarazzo, J. D. (1993). Cited in Michaelson, R. (1993). Behavior gets big billing in medical schools today. *APA Monitor, 24*(8), 56.

Matefy, R. (1980). Role-playing theory of psychedelic flashbacks. *Journal of Consulting and Clinical Psychology, 48,* 551–553.

Matlin, M. (1993). *The psychology of women* (2nd ed.). Fort Worth, TX: Harcourt Brace Jovanovich.

Matlin, M. (1994). *Cognition* (3rd ed.). Fort Worth, TX: Harcourt Brace College Publishers.

Matteson, M. T., & Ivancevich, J. M. (1987). *Controlling work stress.* San Francisco: Jossey-Bass.

Matthews, K. (1994). Cited in Azar, B. (1994). Women are barraged by media on "the change." *APA Monitor, 25*(5), 24–25.

Maugh, T. H. (1982). Marijuana "justifies serious concern." *Science, 215,* 1488–1489.

Maxwell, K. (1994). *The sex imperative: An evolutionary tale of sexual survival.* New York: Plenum.

Mayer, R., and Goodchild, F. (1990). *The critical thinker.* Dubuque, Iowa: Wm. C. Brown.

Mazzella, R., & Feingold, A. (1994). The effects of physical attractiveness, race, socioeconomic status, and gender of defendants and victims on judgments of mock jurors: A meta-analysis. *Journal of Applied Social Psychology, 24*(15), 1315–1344.

McCann, I. L., & Holmes, D. S. (1984). Influence of aerobic exercise on depression. *Journal of Personality and Social Psychology, 46,* 1142–1147.

McCarley, R. W. (1992). Cited in Blakeslee, S. (1992, January 7). Scientists unraveling chemistry of dreams. *The New York Times,* pp. C1, C10.

McCarthy, K. (1993). Research on women's health doesn't show whole picture. *APA Monitor, 24*(7), 14–15.

McCarthy, M. J. (1990, February 26). Anti-smoking groups grow more sophisticated in tactics used to put heat on tobacco firms. *The Wall Street Journal,* pp. B1, B3.

McCaul, K. D., & Haugvedt, C. (1982). Attention, distraction, and cold-pressor pain. *Journal of Personality and Social Psychology, 43,* 154–162.

McCauley, C. (1989). The nature of social influence in groupthink: Compliance and internalization. *Journal of Personality and Social Psychology, 57,* 250–260.

McCauley, C., Woods, K., Coolidge, C., & Kulick, W. (1983). More aggressive cartoons are funnier. *Journal of Personality and Social Psychology, 44,* 817–823.

McClelland, D. C. (1958). Methods of measuring human motivation. In J. W. Atkinson (Ed.), *Motives in fantasy, action, and society.* Princeton, NJ: Van Nostrand.

McClelland, D. C. (1965). Achievement and entrepreneurship: A longitudinal study. *Journal of Personality and Social Psychology, 1,* 389–392.

McConnell, J. V., Shigehisa, T., & Salive, H. (1970). Attempts to transfer approach and avoidance responses by RNA injections in rats. In K. H. Pribram & D. E. Broadbent (Eds.), *Biology of memory.* New York: Academic Press.

McCrae, R. R. (1992). Editor's introduction to Tupes and Christal. *Journal of Personality, 60,* 217–219.

McDougall, W. (1904). The sensations excited by a single momentary stimulation of the eye. *British Journal of Psychology, 1,* 78–113.

McDougall, W. (1908). *An introduction to social psychology.* London: Methuen.

McFadden, E. R., Jr., & Gilbert, I. A. (1994). Exercise-induced asthma. *New England Journal of Medicine, 330,* 1362–1367.

McGaugh, J. L. (1983). Preserving the presence of the past: Hormonal influences on memory storage. *American Psychologist, 38,* 161–174.

McGaugh, J. L., Martinez, J. L., Jr., Jensen, R. A., Messing, R. B., & Vasquez, B. J. (1980). Central and peripheral catecholamine function in learning and memory processes. In *Neural mechanisms of goal-directed behavior and learning.* New York: Academic Press.

McGovern, T. V., Furumoto, L., Halpern, D. F., Kimble, G. A., & McKeachie, W. J. (1991). Liberal education, study in depth, and the arts and sciences major—Psychology. *American Psychologist, 46,* 598–605.

McGowan, R. J., & Johnson, D. L. (1984). The mother–child relationship and other antecedents of childhood intelligence: A causal analysis. *Child Development, 55,* 810–820.

McGrath, E., Keita, G. P., Strickland, B. R., & Russo, N. F. (1990). *Women and depression: Risk factors and treatment issues.* Washington, DC: American Psychological Association.

McGregor, D. (1960). *The human side of enterprise.* New York: McGraw-Hill.

McKeachie, W. (1994) Cited in DeAngelis, T. (1994). Educators reveal keys to success in classroom. *APA Monitor, 25*(1), 39–40.

McLeod, J. D., Kessler, R. C., & Landis, K. R. (1992). Speed of recovery from major depressive episodes in a community sample of married men and women. *Journal of Abnormal Psychology, 101,* 277–286.

McMinn, M. R., & Wade, N. G. (1995). Beliefs about the prevalence of dissociative identity disorder, sexual abuse, and ritual abuse among religious and nonreligious therapists. *Professional Psychology: Research and Practice, 26,* 257–261.

McNally, R. J. (1990). Psychological approaches to panic disorder: A review. *Psychological Bulletin, 108,* 403–419.

Mead, M. (1935). *Sex and temperament in three primitive societies.* New York: Dell.

Meade, V. (1994). Psychologists forecast future of the profession. *APA Monitor, 25*(5), 14–15.

Medin, D. L., & Ross, B. H. (1992). *Cognitive psychology.* Fort Worth, TX: Harcourt Brace Jovanovich.

Mednick, S. A. (1962). The associative basis of the creative process. *Psychological Review, 69,* 220–232.

Meichenbaum, D. (1993). Changing conceptions of cognitive behavior modification: Retrospect and prospect. *Journal of Consulting and Clinical Psychology, 61,* 202–204.

Meichenbaum, D., & Jaremko, M. E. (Eds.). (1983). *Stress reduction and prevention.* New York: Plenum.

Melzack, R. (1980). Psychological aspects of pain. In J. J. Bonica (Ed.), *Pain.* New York: Raven Press.

Melzack, R. (1990). Phantom limbs and the concept of a neuromatrix. *Trends in Neurosciences, 13,* 88–92.

Mendez, M., and others. (1992). Disturbances of person identification in Alzheimer's disease: A retrospective study. *Journal of Nervous & Mental Disease, 180,* 94–96.

Metalsky, G. I., Joiner, T. E., Jr., Hardin, T. S., & Abramson, L. Y. (1993). Depressive reactions to failure in a naturalistic setting: A test of the hopelessness and self-esteem theories of depression. *Journal of Abnormal Psychology, 102,* 101–109.

Metcalfe, J. (1986). Premonitions of insight predict impending error. *Journal of Experimental Psychology: Learning, Memory, and Cognition, 12,* 623–634.

Mevkens, F. L. (1990). Coming of age—The chemoprevention of cancer. *New England Journal of Medicine, 323,* 825–827.

Michael, R. T., Gagnon, J. H., Laumann, E. O., & Kolata, G. (1994). *Sex in America: A definitive survey.* Boston: Little, Brown.

Michaelson, R. (1993a). Behavior gets big billing in medical schools today. *APA Monitor, 24*(8), 56.

Michaelson, R. (1993b). Tug-of-war is developing over defining retardation. *APA Monitor, 24*(5), 34–35.

Michels, R., & Marzuk, P. M. (1993a). Progress in psychiatry. (Part 1). *New England Journal of Medicine, 329,* 552–560.

Michels, R., & Marzuk, P. M. (1993b). Progress in psychiatry. (Part 2). *New England Journal of Medicine, 329,* 628–638.

Mikesell, R. H., Lusterman, D., & McDaniel, S. (Eds.). (1995). *Family psychology and systems therapy.* Washington, DC: American Psychological Association.

Milgram, S. (1963). Behavioral study of obedience. *Journal of Abnormal and Social Psychology, 67,* 371–378.

Milgram, S. (1974). *Obedience to authority.* New York: Harper & Row.

Milgram, S. (1977). *The individual in a social world.* Reading, MA: Addison-Wesley.

Millar, J. D. (1990). Mental health and the workplace. *American Psychologist, 45,* 1165–1166.

Millar, M. G., & Millar, K. (1995). Negative affective consequences of thinking about disease detection behaviors. *Health Psychology, 14,* 141–146.

Miller, A. G. (1986). *The obedience experiments: A case study of controversy in social science.* New York: Praeger.

Miller, C. A. (1985). Infant mortality in the United States. *Scientific American, 235,* 31–37.

Miller, G. A. (1956). The magical number seven, plus or minus two: Some limits on our capacity for processing information. *Psychological Review, 63,* 81–97.

Miller, J. L. (1990). Speech perception. In D. N. Osherson, & H. Lasnik (Eds.), *An invitation to cognitive science: Language* (Vol. 1). Cambridge, MA: The MIT Press, a Bradford Book.

Miller, J. L. (1992). Trouble in mind. *Scientific American, 267,* 180.

Miller, M. E., & Bowers, K. S. (1993). Hypnotic analgesia: Dissociative experience or dissociated control. *Journal of Abnormal Psychology, 102,* 29–38.

Miller, M. F., Barabasz, A. F., & Barabasz, M. (1991). Effects of active alert and relaxation hypnotic inductions on cold pressor pain. *Journal of Abnormal Psychology, 100,* 223–226.

Miller, N. B., Cowan, P. A., Cowan, C. P., Hetherington, E. M., & Clingempeel, W. G. (1993). Externalizing in preschoolers and early adolescents: A cross-study replication of a family model. *Developmental Psychology, 29,* 3–18.

Miller, N. E. (1969). Learning of visceral and glandular responses. *Science, 163,* 434–445.

Miller, N. E., & Dollard, J. (1941). *Social learning and imitation.* New Haven, CT: Yale University Press.

Miller, P. H., Heldmeyer, K. H., & Miller, S. A. (1975). Facilitation of conservation of number in young children. *Developmental Psychology, 11,* 253.

Miller, R. L. (1992). The human ecology of multiracial identity. In M. P. P. Root (Ed.), *Racially mixed people in America.* Newbury Park, CA: Sage.

Miller, W. R. (1982). Treating problem drinkers: What works? *The Behavior Therapist, 5*(1), 15–18.

Millette, B., & Hawkins, J. (1983). *The passage through menopause.* Reston, VA: Reston Publishing.

Million Mrs. Bobbitts, A. (1994, January 28). *The New York Times,* p. A26.

Millon, T. (1991). Classification in psychopathology: Rationale, alternatives, and standards. *Journal of Abnormal Psychology, 100,* 245–261.

Mills, J., & Harvey, J. (1972). Opinion change as a function of when information about the communicator is received and whether he is attractive or expert. *Journal of Personality and Social Psychology, 21,* 52–55.

Milner, B. R. (1966). Amnesia following operation on temporal lobes. In C. W. M. Whitty & O. L. Zangwill (Eds.), *Amnesia.* London: Butterworth.

Mindell, J. A. (1993). Sleep disorders in children. *Health Psychology, 12,* 151–162.

Mineka, S. (1991, August). Paper presented to the annual meeting of the American Psychological Association, San Francisco. Cited in Turkington, C. (1991). Evolutionary memories may have phobia role. *APA Monitor, 22*(11), 14.

Mintz, L. B., Bartels, K. M., & Rideout, C. A. (1995). Training in counseling ethnic minorities and race-based availability of graduate school resources. *Professional Psychology: Research and Practice, 26,* 316–321.

Mischel, W. (1990). Personality dispositions revisited and revised: A view after three decades. In L. A. Pervin (Ed.), *Handbook of personality: Theory and research* (pp. 111–134). New York: Guilford.

Mischel, W. (1993). *Introduction to personality* (5th ed.). Fort Worth, TX: Harcourt Brace Jovanovich.

Mishkin, M., & Appenzeller, T. (1987). The anatomy of memory. *Scientific American, 256,* 80–89.

Mitchell, J. E., & Eckert, E. D. (1987). Scope and significance of eating disorders. *Journal of Consulting and Clinical Psychology, 55,* 628–634.

Mittelman, M. A., and others. (1993). Triggering of acute myocardial infarction by heavy physical exertion—Protection against triggering by regular exertion. *New England Journal of Medicine, 329,* 1677–1683.

Mohrman, A. M., Jr., Resnick-West, S. M., & Lawler, E. E., III. (1989). *Designing performance appraisal systems: Aligning appraisals and organizational realities.* San Francisco: Jossey-Bass.

Moliterno, D. J., and others. (1994). Coronary-artery vasoconstriction induced by cocaine, cigarette smoking, or both. *New England Journal of Medicine, 330,* 454–459.

Moncher, M. S., Holden, G. W., & Trimble, J. E. (1990). Substance abuse among Native-American youth. *Journal of Consulting and Clinical Psychology, 58,* 408–415.

Money, J. (1977). Human hermaphroditism. In F. A. Beach (Ed.), *Human sexuality in four perspectives.* Baltimore, MD: The Johns Hopkins University Press.

Money, J. (1987). Sin, sickness, or status? Homosexual gender identity and psychoneuroendocrinology. *American Psychologist, 42,* 384–399.

Montemayor, R., & Flannery, D. J. (1991). Parent–adolescent relations in middle and late adolescence. In R. M. Lerner, A. C. Petersen, & J. Brooks-Gunn (Eds.), *Encyclopedia of adolescence.* New York: Garland.

Monti, P. M., and others. (1993). Cue exposure with coping skills treatment for male alcoholics: A preliminary investigation. *Journal of Consulting and Clinical Psychology, 61,* 1011–1019.

Moon, J. R., & Eisler, R. M. (1983). Anger control: An experimental comparison of three behavioral treatments. *Behavior Therapy, 14,* 493–505.

Moore, R. Y. (1995). Vision without sight. *New England Journal of Medicine, 332,* 54–55.

Morales, E. (1992). Latino gays and Latina lesbians. In S. Dworkin & F. Gutierrez (Eds.), *Counseling gay men and lesbians: Journey to the end of the rainbow.* Alexandria, VA: American Association for Counseling and Development.

Moran, D. (1993). Cited in Blakeslee, S. (1993, September 7). Human nose may hold an additional organ for a real sixth sense. *The New York Times,* p. C3.

Moran, J., & Desimone, R. (1985). Selective attention gates visual processing in the extrastriate cortex. *Science, 229,* 782–784.

Moriarty, T. (1975). Crimes, commitment, and the responsive bystander: Two field experiments. *Journal of Personality and Social Psychology, 31,* 370–376.

Morin, C. M., Kowatch, R. A., Barry, T., & Walton, E. (1993). Cognitive-behavior therapy for late-life insomnia. *Journal of Consulting and Clinical Psychology, 61,* 137–146.

Morris, W. N., Miller, R. S., & Spangenberg, S. (1977). The effects of dissenter position and task difficulty on conformity and response conflict. *Journal of Personality, 45,* 251–256.

Morrison, A. M., & Von Glinow, M. A. (1990). Women and minorities in management. *American Psychologist, 45,* 200–209.

Moscovitch, M. (1994). Conference on memory. Harvard Medical School. Cited in Goleman, D. (1994, May 31). Miscoding is seen as the root of false memories. *The New York Times,* pp. C1, C8.

Moser, C. G., & Dyck, D. G. (1989). Type A behavior, uncontrollability, and the activation of hostile self-schema responding. *Journal of Research in Personality, 23,* 248–267.

Mowrer, O. H. (1947). On the dual nature of learning—A reinterpretation of "conditioning" and "problem-solving." *Harvard Educational Review, 17,* 102–148.

Moyers, B. (1993). *Healing and the mind.* New York: Doubleday.

Muelenhard, C. L., & Falcon, P. L. (1990). Men's heterosocial skill and attitudes toward women as predictors of verbal sexual coercion and forceful rape. *Sex Roles, 23,* 241–259.

Mullen, B., and others. (1987). Newscasters' facial expressions and voting behavior of viewers: Can a smile elect a president? *Journal of Personality and Social Psychology, 53.*

Muñoz, R. F., Hollon, S. D., McGrath, E., Rehm, L. P., & VandenBos, G. R. (1994). On the AHCPR *Depression in Primary Care* guidelines: Further considerations for practitioners. *American Psychologist, 49,* 42–61.

Murray, B. (1995). Black psychology relies on traditional ideology. *APA Monitor, 26*(6), 33–34.

Murray, E. A., & Mishkin, M. (1985). Amygdalectomy impairs cross-modal association in monkeys. *Science, 228,* 604–606.

Murray, H. A. (1938). *Explorations in personality.* New York: Oxford University Press.

Murstein, B. I., & Fontaine, P. A. (1993). The public's knowledge about psychologists and other mental health professionals. *American Psychologist, 48,* 839–845.

Murtagh, D. R. R., & Greenwood, K. M. (1995). Identifying effective psychological treatments for insomnia: A meta-analysis. *Journal of Consulting and Clinical Psychology, 63,* 79–89.

Muslim Women Bridging Culture Gap. (1993, November 8). *The New York Times,* p. B9.

Myers, D. G. (1983). Polarizing effects of social interaction. In H. Brandstatter, J. H. Davis, & G. Stocker-Kreichgauer (Eds.), *Group decision processes.* London: Academic Press.

Myers, L. B., & Brewin, C. R. (1994). Recall of early experience and the repressive coping style. *Journal of Abnormal Psychology, 103,* 288–292.

Nadol, J. B., Jr. (1993). Hearing loss. *New England Journal of Medicine, 329,* 1092–1102.

Nathan, P. (1991). Substance use disorders in the *DSM-IV. Journal of Abnormal Psychology, 100,* 356–361.

Nathans, J., Thomas, D., & Hogness, D. S. (1986). Molecular genetics of human color vision: The genes encoding blue, green, and red pigments. *Science, 232,* 193–202.

National Institute of Mental Health. (1982). *Television and behavior: Ten years of scientific progress and implications for the eighties.* Washington, DC: National Institute of Mental Health.

National Institute of Mental Health. (1985). *Electroconvulsive therapy: Consensus Development Conference statement.* Bethesda, MD: US Department of Health and Human Services.

National Institute of Occupational Safety and Health. (1990). *A proposal: National strategy for the prevention of psychological disorders.* Draft paper provided to the U.S. Senate Appropriations Subcommittee on Labor, Health, and Human Services, and Education and Related Agencies by NIOSH.

Neisser, U. (1993). Cited in Goleman, D. J. (1993, April 6). Studying the secrets of childhood memory. *The New York Times,* pp. C1, C11.

Nelson, J. (1990, May 28). Listen to your body for top performance. *The New York Times,* p. A39.

Nelson, K. (1973). Structure and strategy in learning to talk. *Monographs for the Society for Research in Child Development, 38* (Whole No. 149).

Nelson, K., Hampson, J., & Shaw, L. K. (1993). Nouns in early lexicons: Evidence, explanations, and implications. *Journal of Child Language, 20,* 228.

Nelson, M. B. (1994, June 22). Bad sports. *The New York Times,* p. A21.

Nevid, J. S. (1984). Sex differences in factors of romantic attraction. *Sex Roles, 11*(5/6), 401–411.

Nevid, J. S., Rathus, S. A., & Greene, B. A. (1997). *Abnormal psychology in a changing world* (3rd ed.). Englewood Cliffs, NJ: Prentice-Hall.

Newcombe, N., Bandura, M. M., & Taylor, D. G. (1983). Sex differences in spatial ability and spatial activity. *Sex Roles, 9,* 377–386.

Newlin, D. B., & Thomson, J. B. (1990). Alcohol challenge with sons of alcoholics: A critical review and analysis. *Psychological Bulletin, 108,* 383–402.

Newman, F. L., & Howard, K. I. (1991). Introduction to the special section on seeking new clinical research methods. *Journal of Consulting and Clinical Psychology, 59,* 8–11.

Newman, J., & McCauley, C. (1977). Eye contact with strangers in city, suburb, and small town. *Environment and Behavior, 9,* 547–558.

Newman, R. (1994). Prozac: Panacea? Psychological steroid? *APA Monitor, 25*(4), 34.

Newman, R. S. (1990). Children help seeking in the classroom: The role of motivational factors and attitudes. *Journal of Educational Psychology, 82,* 71–80.

Newport, E. L. (1994). Cited in Senior, J. (1994, January 3). Language of the deaf evolves to reflect new sensibilities. *The New York Times,* pp. A1, A12.

Newport, E. L., & Supalla, T. (1993). *Critical period effects in the acquisition of a primary language.* Unpublished manuscript, University of Rochester.

Nezu, A. M., & Ronan, G. F. (1985). Life stress, current problems, problem solving, and depressive symptoms: An integrative model. *Journal of Consulting and Clinical Psychology, 53,* 693–697.

Nickerson, R. A., & Adams, N. J. (1979). Long-term memory for a common object. *Cognitive Psychology, 11,* 287–307.

Nides, M. A., and others. (1995). Predictors of initial smoking cessation and relapse through the first 2 years of the lung health study. *Journal of Consulting and Clinical Psychology, 63,* 60–69.

Nigg, J. T., & Goldsmith, H. H. (1994). Genetics of personality disorders: Perspectives from personality and psychopathology research. *Psychological Bulletin, 115,* 346–380.

NIMH. See National Institute of Mental Health.

Nisan, M. (1984). Distributive justice and social norms. *Child Development, 55,* 1020–1029.

Nogrady, H., McConkey, K. M., & Perry, C. (1985). Enhancing visual memory: Trying hypnosis, trying imagination, and trying again. *Journal of Abnormal Psychology, 94,* 195–204.

Nolen-Hoeksema, S. (1991). Responses to depression and their effects on the duration of depressive episodes. *Journal of Abnormal Psychology, 100,* 569–582.

Nolen-Hoeksema, S., & Girgus, J. S. (1994). The emergence of gender differences in depression during adolescence. *Psychological Bulletin, 115,* 424–443.

Nolen-Hoeksema, S., Morrow, J., & Fredrickson, B. L. (1993). Response styles and the duration of depressed mood. *Journal of Abnormal Psychology, 102,* 20–28.

Noller, P., & Callan, V. J. (1991). Adolescents' perceptions of the nature of their communication with parents. *Journal of Youth and Adolescence, 19,* 349–362.

Norman, D. A. (1988). *The psychology of everyday things.* New York: Basic Books.

Norris, F. H., & Kaniasty, K. (1994). Psychological distress following criminal victimization in the general population: Cross-sectional, longitudinal, and prospective analyses. *Journal of Consulting and Clinical Psychology, 62,* 111–123.

Northwestern National Life Insurance Company. (1991, July 10). Job stress: Rating your workplace. *The New York Times,* p. C11.

Norvell, N., & Belles, D. (1993). Psychological and physical benefits of circuit weight training in law enforcement personnel. *Journal of Consulting and Clinical Psychology, 61,* 520–527.

Novick, L. R., & Coté, N. (1992). The nature of expertise in anagram solution. In *Proceedings of the Fourteenth Annual Conference of the Cognitive Science Society.* Hillsdale, NJ: Erlbaum.

Novick, L. R., & Holyoak, K. J. (1991). Mathematical problem solving by analogy. *Journal of Experimental Psychology: Learning, Memory, and Cognition, 17,* 398–415.

Novin, D., and others. (1983). Is there a role for the liver in the control of food intake? *American Journal of Clinical Nutrition, 9,* 233–246.

Nowlis, G. H., & Kessen, W. (1976). Human newborns differentiate differing concentrations of sucrose and glucose. *Science, 191,* 865–866.

Oberdorfer, M. (1994). Cited in Goleman, D. (1994, September 6). Sonic device for blind may help in navigation. *The New York Times,* pp. C1, C9.

ODEER (1994). See Office of Demographic, Employment, and Educational Research.

Oetting, E. R., & Beauvais, F. (1990). Adolescent drug use: Findings of national and local surveys. *Journal of Consulting and Clinical Psychology, 58,* 385–394.

Offerman, L. R., & Gowing, M. K. (1990). Organizations of the future: Changes and challenges. *American Psychologist, 45,* 95–108.

Office of Demographic, Employment, and Educational Research (1994). Summary report doctorate recipients from United States universities. Washington, DC: American Psychological Association.

Ogbu, J. U. (1993). Differences in cultural frame of reference. *International Journal of Behavioral Development, 16,* 483–506.

Ogden, J. (1994). Effects of smoking cessation, restrained eating, and motivational states on food intake in the laboratory. *Health Psychology, 13,* 114–121.

O'Grady, K. E. (1982). Sex, physical attractiveness, and perceived risk for mental illness. *Journal of Personality and Social Psychology, 43,* 1064–1071.

Ohman, A., Fredrikson, M., Hugdahl, K., & Rimmo, P. (1976). The premise of equipotentiality in human classical conditioning: Conditioned electrodermal responses to potentially phobic stimuli. *Journal of Experimental Psychology: General, 105,* 313–337.

Olds, J. (1969). The central nervous system and the reinforcement of behavior. *American Psychologist, 24,* 114–132.

Olds, J., & Milner, P. (1954). Positive reinforcement produced by electrical stimulation of the septal area and other regions of the rat brain. *Journal of Comparative and Physiological Psychology, 47,* 419–427.

O'Leary, A. (1990). Stress, emotion, and human immune function. *Psychological Bulletin, 108,* 363–382.

Olson, S. L., Bates, J. E., & Kaskie, B. (1992). Caregiver–infant interaction antecedents of children's school-age cognitive ability. *Merrill-Palmer Quarterly, 38,* 309–330.

O'Malley, S. S., and others. (1988). Therapist competence and patient outcome in interpersonal psychotherapy of depression. *Journal of Consulting and Clinical Psychology, 56,* 496–501.

Orr, S. P., Pitman, R. K., Lasko, N. B., & Herz, L. R. (1993). Psychophysiological assessment of posttraumatic stress disorder imagery in World War II and Korean combat veterans. *Journal of Abnormal Psychology, 102,* 152–159.

Ortega, D. F., & Pipal, J. E. (1984). Challenge seeking and the Type A coronary-prone behavior pattern. *Journal of Personality and Social Psychology, 46,* 1328–1334.

Ouchi, W. (1981). *Theory Z: How American business can meet the Japanese challenge.* Reading, MA: Addison-Wesley.

Outlook, The. (1993, January 6). Positive implications of new population projections. *Author,* pp. 10–11.

Paffenbarger, R. S., Jr., Hyde, R. T., Wing, A. L., & Hsieh, C. C. (1986). Physical activity, all-cause mortality, and longevity of college alumni. *New England Journal of Medicine, 314,* 605–613.

Paffenbarger, R. S., Jr., and others. (1993). The association of changes in physical-activity level and other lifestyle characteristics with mortality among men. *New England Journal of Medicine, 328,* 538–545.

Pagan, G., & Aiello, J. R. (1982). Development of personal space among Puerto Ricans. *Journal of Nonverbal Behavior, 7,* 59–68.

Page, R. A. (1977). Noise and helping behavior. *Environment and Behavior, 9,* 311–334.

Paige, K. E. (1971). Effects of oral contraceptives on affective fluctuations associated with the menstrual cycle. *Psychosomatic Medicine, 33,* 515–537.

Paige, K. E. (1973, July). Women learn to sing the menstrual blues. *Psychology Today, 41.*

Paikoff, R. L., & Brooks-Gunn, J. (1991). Do parent–child relationships change during puberty? *Psychological Bulletin, 110,* 47–66.

Paikoff, R. L., & Collins, A. C. (1991). Editor's notes: Shared views in the family during adolescence. In R. L. Paikoff & A. C. Collins (Eds.), *New Directions for Child Development* (Vol. 51). San Francisco: Jossey-Bass.

Pajares, F., & Miller, M. D. (1994). Role of self-efficacy and self-concept beliefs in mathematical problem solving: A path analysis. *Journal of Educational Psychology, 86,* 193–203.

Palac, L. (1994). Cited in Tierney, J. (1994, January 9). Porn, the low-slung engine of progress. *The New York Times,* pp. H1, H18.

Palladino, J. (1994). Cited in DeAngelis, T. (1994). Educators reveal keys to success in classroom. *APA Monitor, 25*(1), 39–40.

Pandurangi, A. K., and others. (1988). Schizophrenic symptoms and deterioration: Relation to computerized tomographic findings. *Journal of Nervous and Mental Disease, 176,* 200–206.

Pantin, H. M., & Carver, C. S. (1982). Induced competence and the bystander effect. *Journal of Applied Social Psychology, 12,* 100–111.

Papini, D. R., & Roggman, L. A. (1992). Adolescent perceived attachment to parents in relation to competence, depression, and anxiety: A longitudinal study. *Journal of Early Adolescence, 12,* 420–440.

Papousek, M., Papousek, H., & Symmes, D. (1991). The meanings of melodies in motherese in tone and stress languages. *Infant Behavior and Development, 14,* 415–440.

Pappas, G., Queen, S., Hadden, W., & Fisher, G. (1993). The increasing disparity of mortality between socioeconomic groups in the United States, 1960 and 1986. *New England Journal of Medicine, 329,* 103–109.

Pardes, H., and others. (1991). Physicians and the animal-rights movement. *New England Journal of Medicine, 324,* 1640–1643.

Parkes, C. M., & Weiss, R. S. (1983). *Recovery from bereavement.* New York: Basic Books.

Parron, D. L., Solomon, F., & Jenkins, C. D. (Eds.). (1982). *Behavior, health risks, and social disadvantage.* Washington, DC: National Academy Press.

Parrot, W. G., & Sabini, J. (1990). Mood and memory under natural conditions: Evidence for mood incongruent recall. *Journal of Personality and Social Psychology, 59,* 321–336.

Pascual-Leone, J. (1980). Constructive problems for constructive theories: The current relevance of Piaget's work and a critique of information-processing simulation psychology. In R. H. Kluwe & H. Spada (Eds.), *Developmental models of thinking.* New York: Academic Press.

Patrick, C. J., Bradley, M. M., & Lang, P. J. (1993). Emotion in the criminal psychopath: Startle reflex modulation. *Journal of Abnormal Psychology, 102,* 82–92.

Patterson, C. J., Kupersmidt, J. B., & Vader, N. A. (1990). Income level, gender, ethnicity, and household composition as predictors of children's school-based competence. *Child Development, 61,* 485–494.

Patterson, G. R. (1993). Orderly change in a stable world: The antisocial trait as a chimera. *Journal of Consulting and Clinical Psychology, 61,* 911–919.

Patterson, M. L. (1991). Functions of nonverbal behavior in interpersonal interaction. In R. S. Feldman & B. Rime (Eds.), *Fundamentals of nonverbal behavior.* Cambridge, England: Cambridge University Press.

Patterson, S. J., Sochting, I., & Marcia, J. E. (1992). The inner space and beyond: Women and identity. In G. R. Adams, T. P. Gullotta, & R. Montemayor (Eds.), *Adolescent identity formation.* Newbury Park, CA: Sage.

Pattison, E. M. (1977). *The experience of dying.* Englewood Cliffs, NJ: Prentice-Hall.

Pavlov, I. (1927). *Conditioned reflexes.* London: Oxford University Press.

Pearlman, K., Schmidt, F. L., & Hunter, J. E. (1980). Test of a new model of validity generalization: Results for job proficiency and training criteria in clerical occupations. *Journal of Applied Psychology, 65,* 373–406.

Pedersen, N. L., Plomin, R., McClearn, G. E., & Friberg, L. (1988). Neuroticism, extraversion, and related traits in adult twins reared apart and reared together. *Journal of Personality and Social Psychology, 55,* 950–957.

Pelham, W. E., Jr., and others. (1993). Separate and combined effects of methylphenidate and behavior modification on boys with attention deficit-hyperactivity disorder in the classroom. *Journal of Consulting and Clinical Psychology, 61,* 506–515.

Penfield, W. (1969). Consciousness, memory, and man's conditioned reflexes. In K. H. Pribram (Ed.), *On the biology of learning.* New York: Harcourt Brace Jovanovich.

Penner, L. A., Thompson, J. K., & Coovert, D. L. (1991). Size overestimation among anorexics: Much ado about very little? *Journal of Abnormal Psychology, 100,* 90–93.

Perkins, D. N. (1993). Teaching for understanding. *American Educator, 17*(3), 8, 28–35.

Perkins, K. (1993a). Cited in Adler, T. (1993). Nicotine gives mixed results on learning and performance. *APA Monitor, 24*(5), 14–15.

Perkins, K. (1993b). Weight gain following smoking cessation. *Journal of Consulting and Clinical Psychology, 61,* 768–777.

Perls, F. S. (1971). *Gestalt therapy verbatim.* New York: Bantam.

Perrett, D. I. (1994). Nature. Cited in Brody, J. E. (1994, March 21). Notions of beauty transcend culture, new study suggests. *The New York Times,* p. A14.

Persons, J. B., Burns, D. D., Perloff, J. M., & Miranda, J. (1993). Relationships between symptoms of depression and anxiety and dysfunctional beliefs about achievement and attachment. *Journal of Abnormal Psychology, 102,* 518–524.

A perverse choice. (1993). Cited in Kolata, G. (1993d, October 26).

The hot debate about cloning human embryo. *The New York Times,* pp. A1, C3.

Peterson, L. R., & Peterson, M. J. (1959). Short-term retention of individual verbal items. *Journal of Experimental Psychology, 58,* 193–198.

Petraitis, J., Flay, B. R., & Miller, T. Q. (1995). Reviewing theories of adolescent substance use: Organizing pieces in the puzzle. *Psychological Bulletin, 1995,* 67–86.

Petrie, T. A., & Diehl, N. S. (1995). Sports psychology in the profession of psychology. *Professional Psychology: Research and Practice, 26,* 288–291.

Pettingale, K. W., and others. (1985). Mental attitudes to cancer: An additional prognostic factor. *Lancet, 1,* 750.

Petty, R. E., & Cacioppo, J. T. (1986). The elaboration-likelihood model of persuasion. In L. Berkowitz (Ed.), *Advances in experimental social psychology* (Vol. 19). New York: Academic Press.

Petty, R. E., Gleicher, F., & Baker, S. M. (1991). Multiple roles for affect in persuasion. In J. Forgas (Ed.), *Emotion and social judgments.* London: Pergamon.

Phillipson, E. A. (1993). Sleep apnea—A major public health problem. *New England Journal of Medicine, 328,* 1271–1273.

Phinney, J. S., Chavira, V., & Williamson, L. (1992). Acculturation attitudes and self-esteem among high school and college students. *Youth and Society, 23*(3), 299–312.

Phinney, J. S., & Rosenthal, D. A. (1992). Ethnic identity in adolescence: Process, context, and outcome. In G. R. Adams, T. P. Gullotta, & R. Montemayor (Eds.), *Adolescent identity formation.* Newbury Park, CA: Sage.

Piaget, J. (1962). *The moral judgment of the child.* New York: Collier.

Piaget, J. (1963). *The origins of intelligence in children.* New York: W. W. Norton.

Pick, A. D. (1991). Perception. In R. M. Thomas (Ed.), *The encyclopedia of human development and education theory, research, and studies* (pp. 249–254). Oxford, England: Pergamon.

Pihl, R. O., Peterson, J., & Finn, P. (1990). Inherited predisposition to alcoholism: Characteristics of sons of male alcoholics. *Journal of Abnormal Psychology, 99,* 291–301.

Pike, K. M., & Rodin, J. (1991). Mothers, daughters, and disordered eating. *Journal of Abnormal Psychology, 100,* 198–204.

Pillard, R. C. (1990). The Kinsey Scale: Is it familial? In D. P. McWhirter, S. A. Sanders, & J. M. Reinisch (Eds.), *Homosexuality/Heterosexuality: Concepts of sexual orientation* (pp. 88–100). New York: Oxford University Press.

Pillard, R. C., & Weinrich, J. D. (1986). Evidence of familial nature of male homosexuality. *Archives of Sexual Behavior, 43,* 808–812.

Pinderhughes, E. (1989). *Understanding race, ethnicity and power: The key to efficacy in clinical practice.* New York: Free Press.

Pinker, S. (1990). Language acquisition. In D. N. Osherson, & H. Lasnik (Eds.), *An invitation to cognitive science: Language* (Vol. 1). Cambridge, MA: The MIT Press, a Bradford Book.

Pinker, S. (1994a, June 19). Building a better brain. *The New York Times Book Review,* pp. 13–14.

Pinker, S. (1994b). *The language instinct: How the mind creates language.* New York: William Morrow.

Pinpointing chess moves in the brain. (1994, May 24). *The New York Times,* p. C14.

Pitman, R. K., and others. (1990). Psychophysiologic responses to combat imagery of Vietnam veterans with posttraumatic stress disorder versus other anxiety disorders. *Journal of Abnormal Psychology, 99,* 49–54.

Plutchik, R. (1984). A general psychoevolutionary theory. In K. Scherer & P. Ekman (Eds.), *Approaches to emotion.* Hillsdale, NJ: Erlbaum.

Polivy, J., & Herman, C. P. (1987). Diagnosis and treatment of normal eating. *Journal of Consulting and Clinical Psychology, 55,* 635–644.

Polivy, J., Zeitlin, S. B., Herman, C. P., & Beal, A. L. (1994). Food restriction and binge eating: A study of former prisoners of war. *Journal of Abnormal Psychology, 103,* 409–411.

Pomazal, R. J., & Clore, G. L. (1973). Helping on the highway: The effects of dependency and sex. *Journal of Applied Social Psychology, 3,* 150–164.

Pomerleau, O. F., Collins, A. C., Shiffman, S., & Pomerleau, C. S. (1993). Why some people smoke and others do not: New perspectives. *Journal of Consulting and Clinical Psychology, 61,* 723–731.

Pool, R. (1994). *The dynamic brain.* Washington, DC: National Academy Press.

Pope-Davis, D. B., Reynolds, A. L., Dings, J. G., & Nielson, D. (1995). Examining multicultural counseling competencies of graduate students in psychology. *Professional Psychology: Research and Practice, 26,* 322–329.

Porter, R. H., Makin, J. W., Davis, L. B., & Christensen, K. M. (1992). Breast-fed infants respond to olfactory cues from their own mother and unfamiliar lactating females. *Infant Behavior and Development, 15,* 85–93.

Portes, A., & Stepick, A. (1993). *City on the edge: The transformation of Miami.* Berkeley: University of California Press.

Posner, M. I., Raichle, M. E. (1994). *Images of mind.* New York: W. H. Freeman.

Potter, W. Z., Rudorfer, M. V., & Manji, H. (1991). Drug therapy: The pharmacologic treatment of depression. *New England Journal of Medicine, 325,* 633–642.

Poussaint, A. (1990, September). An honest look at Black gays and lesbians. *Ebony,* pp. 124, 126, 130–131.

Powell, E. (1991). *Talking back to sexual pressure.* Minneapolis: CompCare Publishers.

Pratkanis, A. R., Breckler, S. J., & Greenwald, A. G. (1989). *Attitude structure and function.* Hillsdale, NJ: Erlbaum.

Premack, A. J., & Premack, D. (1975). Teaching language to an ape. In R. C. Atkinson (Ed.), *Psychology in Progress.* San Francisco: W. H. Freeman.

Prentky, R. A., & Knight, R. A. (1991). Identifying critical dimensions for discriminating among rapists. *Journal of Consulting and Clinical Psychology, 59,* 643–661.

Prewett, M. J., van Allen, P. K., & Milner, J. S. (1978). Multiple electroconvulsive shocks and feeding and drinking behavior in the rat. *Bulletin of the Psychonomic Society, 12,* 137–139.

Price, L. H., & Heninger, G. R. (1994). Lithium in the treatment of mood disorders. *New England Journal of Medicine, 331,* 591–598.

Prigatano, G. P. (1992). Personality disturbances associated with traumatic brain injury. *Journal of Consulting and Clinical Psychology, 60,* 360–368.

Proulx, E. A. (1994, May 26). Books on top. *The New York Times,* p. A23.

Putallaz, M., & Heflin, A. H. (1990). Parent–child interaction. In S. R. Asher & J. D. Coie (Eds.), *Peer rejection in childhood.* New York: Cambridge University Press.

Pyszczynski, T., Holt, K., & Greenberg, J. (1987). Depression, self-focused attention, and expectancies for positive and negative future life events for self and others. *Journal of Personality and Social Psychology, 52,* 994–1001.

Qualls, P. J., & Sheehan, P. W. (1981). Imagery encouragement, absorption capacity, and relaxation during electromyographic feedback. *Journal of Personality and Social Psychology, 41,* 370–379.

Quattrone, G. A. (1982). Overattribution and unit formation: When behavior engulfs the person. *Journal of Personality and Social Psychology, 42,* 593–607.

Quindlen, A. (1993, April 11). The good guys. *The New York Times,* p. E13.

Quinn, J. C., Murphy, L. R., & Hurrell, J. J. (1992). *Stress and well-being at work: Assessments and interventions for occupational mental health.* Washington, DC: American Psychological Association.

Raichle, M. E. (1994). Visualizing the mind. *Scientific American, 270,* 58–64.

Rajecki, D. J. (1989). *Attitudes.* Sunderland, MA: Sinaver Associates.

Rao, S. M., Huber, S. J., & Bornstein, R. B. (1992). Emotional changes with multiple sclerosis and Parkinson's disease. *Journal of Consulting and Clinical Psychology, 60,* 369–378.

Rapoport, K., & Burkhart, B. R. (1984). Personality and attitudinal characteristics of sexually coercive college males. *Journal of Abnormal Psychology, 93,* 216–221.

Rappaport, N. B., McAnulty, D. P., & Brantley, P. J. (1988). Exploration of the Type A behavior pattern in chronic headache sufferers. *Journal of Consulting and Clinical Psychology, 56,* 621–623.

Rathus, S. A. (1973). A 30-item schedule for assessing assertive behavior. *Behavior Therapy, 4,* 398–406.

Rathus, S. A., & Boughn, S. (1994). *AIDS—What every student needs to know.* Fort Worth, TX: Harcourt Brace College Publishers.

Rathus, S. A., & Fichner-Rathus, L. (1994). *Making the most of college* (2nd ed.). Englewood Cliffs, NJ: Prentice-Hall.

Rathus, S. A., & Nevid, J. S. (1995). *Adjustment and growth: The challenges of life* (6th ed.). Fort Worth, TX: Harcourt Brace.

Rathus, S. A., Nevid, J. S., & Fichner-Rathus, L. (1997). *Human sexuality in a world of diversity* (3rd ed.). Boston: Allyn & Bacon.

Ratner, N. B., & Gleason, J. B. (1993). An introduction to psycholinguistics: What do language users know? In J. B. Gleason & N. B. Ratner (Eds.), *Psycholinguistics.* Fort Worth, TX: Harcourt Brace Jovanovich.

Ravo, N., & Nash, E. (1993, August 8). The evolution of cyberpunk. *The New York Times,* p. V9.

Rebok, G. (1987). *Life-span cognitive development.* New York: Holt, Rinehart and Winston.

Redd, W. H., and others. (1987). Cognitive/attentional distraction in the control of conditioned nausea in pediatric cancer patients receiving chemotherapy. *Journal of Consulting and Clinical Psychology, 55,* 391–395.

Reeder, G. D., Henderson, D. J., & Sullivan, J. J. (1982). From dispositions to behaviors: The flip side of attribution. *Journal of Research in Personality, 16,* 355–375.

Reeder, G. D., & Spores, J. M. (1983). The attribution of morality. *Journal of Personality and Social Psychology, 44,* 736–745.

Rehm, L. P. (1978). Mood, pleasant events, and unpleasant events. *Journal of Consulting and Clinical Psychology, 46,* 854–859.

Reid, P. T. (1993, August). Teaching the psychology of women and gender for undergraduate and graduate faculty. Workshop of the Psychology of Women Institute presented at the meeting of the American Psychological Association, Toronto, Canada.

Reid, P. T. (1994). The real problem in the study of culture. *American Psychologist, 49,* 524–525.

Reid, T. R. (1990, December 24). Snug in their beds for Christmas Eve: In Japan, December 24th has become the hottest night of the year. *The Washington Post.*

Reinke, B. J., Holmes, D. S., & Harris, R. L. (1985). The timing of psychosocial changes in women's lives. *Journal of Personality and Social Psychology, 48,* 1353–1364.

Reis, H. T., and others. (1990). What is smiling is beautiful and good. *European Journal of Social Psychology, 20,* 259–267.

Reiser, M. (1992). *Memory and mind and brain: What dream imagery reveals.* New York: Basic Books.

Reiss, M., Rosenfeld, P., Melburg, V., & Tedeschi, J. T. (1981). Self-serving attributions: Biased private perceptions and distorted public descriptions. *Journal of Personality and Social Psychology, 41,* 224–231.

Remafedi, G. (1990). Study group report on the impact of television portrayals of gender roles on youth. *Journal of Adolescent Health Care, 11*(1), 59–61.

Rempel, J. K., Holmes, J. G., & Zanna, M. P. (1985). Trust in close relationships. *Journal of Personality and Social Psychology, 49,* 95–112.

Renninger, K. A., & Wozniak, R. H. (1985). Effect of interest on attentional shift, recognition, and recall in young children. *Developmental Psychology, 21,* 624–632.

Repetti, R. L. (1993). Short-term effects of occupational stressors on daily mood and health complaints. *Health Psychology, 12,* 125–131.

Rescorla, R. A. (1967). Pavlovian conditioning and its proper control procedures. *Psychological Review, 74,* 71–80.

Rescorla, R. A. (1988). Pavlovian conditioning: It's not what you think it is. *American Psychologist, 43,* 151–160.

Rescorla, R. A., & Holland, P. C. (1982). Behavioral studies of associative learning in animals. *Annual Review of Psychology, 33,* 265–308.

Rescorla, R. A., & Solomon, R. L. (1967). Two-process learning theory: Relationships between Pavlovian conditioning and instrumental learning. *Psychological Review, 74,* 151–182.

Resnick, H. S., Kilpatrick, D. G., Dansky, B. S., Saunders, B. E., & Best, C. L. (1993). Prevalence of civilian trauma and posttraumatic stress disorder in a representative national sample of women. *Journal of Consulting and Clinical Psychology, 61,* 984–991.

Resnick, M., and others. (1992, March 24). *Journal of the American Medical Association.* Cited in Young Indians prone to suicide, study finds. *The New York Times,* March 25, 1992, p. D24.

Rest, J. R. (1983). Morality. In P. H. Mussen, J. Flavell, & E. Markman (Eds.), *Handbook of child psychology: Vol. 3. Cognitive development.* New York: Wiley.

Reynolds, A. G. (1991). The cognitive consequences of bilingualism. In A. G. Reynolds, (Ed.), *Bilingualism, multiculturalism, and second language learning: The McGill Conference in Honour of Wallace E. Lambert.* Hillsdale, NJ: Erlbaum.

Rhodes, J. E., & Jason, L. A. (1990). A social stress model of substance abuse. *Journal of Consulting and Clinical Psychology, 58,* 395–401.

Rice, M. E., Quinsey, V. L., & Harris, G. T. (1991). Sexual recidivism among child molesters released from a maximum security psychiatric institution. *Journal of Consulting and Clinical Psychology, 59,* 381–386.

Rich, C. L., Ricketts, J. E., Thaler, R. C., & Young, D. (1988). Some differences between men and women who commit suicide. *American Journal of Psychiatry, 145,* 718–722.

Richman, J. (1993). *Preventing elderly suicide.* New York: Springer.

Ridon, J., & Langer, E. J. (1977). Long-term effects of control-relevant intervention with the institutionalized aged. *Journal of Personality and Social Psychology, 35,* 897–902.

Rieff, D. (1993). *Cuba in the heart of Miami.* New York: Simon & Schuster.

Rieser, J., Yonas, A., & Wilkner, K. (1976). Radial localization of odors by human newborns. *Child Development, 47,* 856–859.

Riggio, R. E., & Woll, S. B. (1984). The role of nonverbal cues and physical attractiveness in the selection of dating partners. *Journal of Social and Personal Relationships, 1,* 347–357.

Riley, V. (1981). Psychoneuroendocrine influences on immunocompetence and neoplasia. *Science, 212,* 1100–1109.

Rinn, W. E. (1991). Neuropsychology of facial expression. In R. S. Feldman & B. Rime (Eds.), *Fundamentals of nonverbal behavior.* Cambridge, England: Cambridge University Press.

Riordan, T. (1994, April 18). Patents: Mapping the shape of human emotions to give computers more realistic speaking skills. *The New York Times,* p. D2.

Robbins, C., & Ehri, L. C. (1994). Reading storybooks to kindergartners helps them learn new vocabulary words. *Journal of Educational Psychology, 86,* 54–64.

Robbins, S. P. (1989). *Organizational behavior* (4th ed.). Englewood Cliffs, NJ: Prentice-Hall.

Robertson, T. S., Zielinski, J., & Ward, S. (1984). *Consumer behavior.* Glenview, IL: Scott, Foresman.

Robins, C. J., & Hayes, A. M. (1993). An appraisal of cognitive therapy. *Journal of Consulting and Clinical Psychology, 61,* 205–214.

Robinson, L. A., Berman, J. S., & Neimeyer, R. A. (1990). Psychotherapy for the treatment of depression: A comprehensive review of controlled outcome research. *Psychological Bulletin, 108,* 30–49.

Robinson, P. (1993). *Freud and his critics.* Berkeley: University of California Press.

Rodin, J. (1986). Aging and health: Effects of the sense of control. *Science, 233,* 1271–1276.

Rogers, C. R. (1951). *Client-centered therapy.* Boston: Houghton Mifflin.

Rogers, C. R. (1959). A theory of therapy, personality and interpersonal relationships, as developed in the client-centered framework. In S. Koch (Ed.), *Psychology: A study of science* (Vol. 3). New York: McGraw-Hill.

Rogers, C. R. (1974). In retrospect: 46 years. *American Psychologist, 29,* 115–123.

Rogers, D. E., & Ginzberg, E. (1993). *Medical care and the health of the poor.* Boulder, CO: Westview Press.

Rohsenow, D. J. (1983). Drinking habits and expectancies about alcohol's effects for self versus others. *Journal of Consulting and Clinical Psychology, 51,* 752–756.

Rosch, E. H. (1978). Principles of categorization. In E. H. Rosch & B. L. Lloyd (Eds.), *Cognition and categorization.* Hillsdale, NJ: Erlbaum.

Rose, R. J. (1995). Genes and human behavior. *Annual Review of Psychology, 46,* 625–654.

Rose, S. A. (1983). Differential rates of visual information processing in full-term and preterm infants. *Child Development, 54,* 1189–1198.

Rosenberg, H. (1993). Prediction of controlled drinking by alcoholics and problem drinkers. *Psychological Bulletin, 113,* 129–139.

Rosenberg, J., Perlstadt, H., & Phillips, W. R. (1993). Now that we are here: Discrimination, disparagement, and harassment at work and the experience of women lawyers. *Gender & Society, 7,* 415–433.

Rosenblatt, R. (1994, March 20). How do tobacco executives live with themselves? *The New York Times Magazine,* pp. 34–41, 55, 73–76.

Rosenfeld, A. (1995). Cited in Collins, C. (1995, May 11). Spanking is becoming the new don't. *The New York Times,* p. C8.

Rosenstock, I. M., & Kirscht, J. P. (1979). Why people seek health care. In G. C. Stone, F. Cohen, & N. E. Adler (Eds.), *Health psychology: A handbook.* San Francisco: Jossey-Bass.

Rosenthal, A. M. (1994, March 15). The way she died. *The New York Times,* p. A23.

Rosenthal, D. M. (1980). The modularity and maturation of cognitive capacities. *Behavior and Brain Science, 3,* 32–34.

Rosenthal, E. (1991, December 3). Study of canine genes seeks hints on behavior. *The New York Times,* pp. C1, C12.

Rosenthal, E. (1993a, March 28). Patients in pain find relief, not addiction, in narcotics. *The New York Times,* pp. A1, A24.

Rosenthal, E. (1993b, July 20). Listening to the emotional needs of cancer patients. *The New York Times,* pp. C1, C7.

Roses, A. D. (1993). Cited in Angier, N. (1993, August 13). Scientists detect a genetic key to Alzheimer's. *The New York Times,* pp. A1, A12.

Roskies, E., and others. (1986). The Montreal Type A Intervention Project: Major findings. *Health Psychology, 5,* 45–69.

Ross, C. (1993). Cited in Adler, T. (1993). If parents are unhappy, are children the reason? *APA Monitor, 24*(4), 17.

Ross, L., & Nisbett, R. E. (1991). *The person and the situation.* New York: McGraw-Hill.

Rossouw, J. E., and others. (1990). The value of lowering cholesterol after myocardial infarction. *New England Journal of Medicine, 323,* 1112–1119.

Rothbart, M. K., & Ahadi, S. A. (1994). Temperament and the development of personality. *Journal of Abnormal Psychology, 103,* 55–66.

Rothbaum, B. O. (1995). *American Journal of Psychiatry.*

Rothbaum, B. O., Foa, E. B., Riggs, D. S., Murdock, T., & Walsh, W. (1992). A prospective examination of post-traumatic stress disorder in rape victims. *Journal of Traumatic Stress, 5,* 455–475.

Rotheram-Borus, M. J., Koopman, C., & Haignere, C. (1991). Reducing HIV sexual risk behaviors among runaway adolescents. *Journal of the American Medical Association, 266,* 1237–1241.

Rotheram-Borus, M. J., Trautman, P. D., Dopkins, S. C., & Shrout, P. E. (1990). Cognitive style and pleasant activities among female adolescent suicide attempters. *Journal of Consulting and Clinical Psychology, 58,* 554–561.

Rotter, J. B. (1972). Beliefs, social attitudes, and behavior: A social learning analysis. In J. B. Rotter, J. E. Chance, & E. J. Phares (Eds.), *Applications of a social learning theory of personality.* New York: Holt, Rinehart and Winston.

Rotter, J. B. (1975). Some problems and misconceptions related to the construct of internal versus external control of reinforcement. *Journal of Consulting and Clinical Psychology, 43,* 56–67.

Rotter, J. B. (1990). Internal versus external control of reinforcement. *American Psychologist, 45,* 489–493.

Rounsaville, B. J., and others. (1987). The relation between specific and general dimensions of the psychotherapy process in interpersonal psychotherapy of depression. *Journal of Consulting and Clinical Psychology, 55,* 379–384.

Rozin, P., & Fallon, A. (1988). Body image, attitudes to weight, and misperceptions of figure preferences of the opposite sex: A comparison of men and women in two generations. *Journal of Abnormal Psychology, 97,* 342–345.

Rudman, D., and others. (1990). Effects of human growth hormone in men over 60 years old. *New England Journal of Medicine, 323*(1), 1–6.

Ruiz, P., & Ruiz, P. P. (1983). Treatment compliance among Hispanics. *Journal of Operational Psychiatry, 14,* 112–114.

Ruiz, R. A. (1981). Cultural and historical perspectives in counseling Hispanics. In D. W. Sue (Ed.), *Counseling the culturally different: Theory and practice* (pp. 186–215). New York: Wiley.

Rule, B. G., Taylor, B. R., & Dobbs, A. R. (1987). Priming effects of heat on aggressive thoughts. *Social Cognition, 5,* 131–143.

Russo, N. F. (1990a). Cited in Korn, J. H., Davis, R., & Davis, S. F. (1991). Historians' and chairpersons' judgments of eminence among psychologists. *American Psychologist, 46,* 789–792.

Russo, N. F. (1990b). Overview: Forging research priorities for women's mental health. *American Psychologist, 45,* 368–373.

Rutkowski, G. K., Gruder, C. L., & Romer, D. (1983). Group cohesiveness, social norms, and bystander intervention. *Journal of Personality and Social Psychology, 44,* 545–552.

Rymer, R. (1993). *Genie: An abused child's flight from silence.* New York: HarperCollins.

Saarni, C. (1990). Emotional competence: How emotions and relationships become integrated. In R. Thompson (Ed.), *Nebraska Symposium on*

Motivation: Vol. 36. Socioemotional development. Lincoln: University of Nebraska Press.
Saccuzzo, D. (1994, August). Coping with complexities of contemporary psychological testing: Negotiating shifting sands. G. Stanley Hall lecture presented at the annual meeting of the American Psychological Association, Los Angeles.
Sachs, A. (1994, January 31). Now for the movie. *Time,* p. 99.
Sackheim, H. A. (1990). Cited in Goleman, G. (1990, August 2). The quiet comeback of electroshock therapy. *The New York Times,* p. B5.
Sadalla, E. K., Kenrick, D. T., & Vershure, B. (1987). Dominance and heterosexual attraction. *Journal of Personality and Social Psychology, 52,* 730–738.
Sadalla, E. K., Sheets, V., & McCreath, H. (1990). The cognition of urban tempo. *Environment and Behavior, 22,* 230–254.
Sadker, M., & Sadker, D. (1994). *How America's schools cheat girls.* New York: Scribner's.
Sadowski, C., & Kelley, M. L. (1993). Social problem solving in suicidal adolescents. *Journal of Consulting and Clinical Psychology, 61,* 121–127.
Saegert, S. C., & Jellison, J. M. (1970). Effects of initial level of response competition and frequency of exposure to liking and exploratory behavior. *Journal of Personality and Social Psychology, 16,* 553–558.
Salgado de Snyder, V. N., Cervantes, R. C., & Padilla, A. M. (1990). Gender and ethnic differences in psychosocial stress and generalized distress among Hispanics. *Sex Roles, 22,* 441–453.
Sanchez-Craig, M., Annis, H. M., Bornet, A. R., & MacDonald, K. R. (1984). Random assignment to abstinence or controlled drinking: Evaluation of a cognitive-behavioral program for problem drinkers. *Journal of Consulting and Clinical Psychology, 52,* 390–403.
Sanders, G. S. (1984). Effects of context cues on eyewitness identification responses. *Journal of Applied Social Psychology, 14,* 386–397.
Sanders, G. S., & Chiu, W. (1988). Eyewitness errors in the free recall of actions. *Journal of Applied Social Psychology, 18,* 1241–1259.
Sanna, L. J., & Shotland, R. L. (1990). Valence of anticipated evaluation and social facilitation. *Journal of Experimental Social Psychology, 26,* 82–92.
Santee, R. T., & Maslach, C. (1982). To agree or not to agree: Personal dissent amid social pressure to conform. *Journal of Personality and Social Psychology, 42,* 690–700.
Sarbin, T. R., & Coe, W. C. (1972). *Hypnosis.* New York: Holt, Rinehart and Winston.
Sattler, J. M. (1988). *Assessment of children.* San Diego, CA: Jerome M. Sattler.
Saunders, C. (1984). St. Christopher's hospice. In E. S. Shneidman (Ed.), *Death: Current perspectives* (3rd ed.). Palo Alto, CA: Mayfield.
Saxe, L. (1991a). Lying. *American Psychologist, 46,* 409–415.
Saxe, L. (1991b). Science and the CQT polygraph: A theoretical critique. *Integration of Physiological and Behavioral Sciences, 26,* 223–231.
Sayette, M. A. (1993). An appraisal-disruption model of alcohol's effects on stress responses in social drinkers. *Psychological Bulletin, 114,* 459–476.
Scarr, S. (1985). An author's frame of mind. [Review of the book *Frames of mind.*] *New Ideas in Psychology, 3,* 95–100.
Scarr, S., & Kidd, K. K. (1983). Developmental behavior genetics. In M. Haith & J. J. Campos (Eds.), *Handbook of child psychology.* New York: Wiley.
Scarr, S., & Weinberg, R. A. (1976). IQ test performance of Black children adopted by White families. *American Psychologist, 31,* 726–739.
Scarr, S., & Weinberg, R. A. (1977). Intellectual similarities within families of both adopted and biological children. *Intelligence, 1,* 170–191.
Scarr, S., & Weinberg, R. A. (1983). The Minnesota adoption studies: Genetic differences and malleability. *Child Development, 54,* 260–267.
Schachter, S. (1959). *The psychology of affiliation.* Stanford, CA: Stanford University Press.
Schachter, S., & Latané, B. (1964). Crime, cognition, and the autonomic nervous system. In D. Levine (Ed.), *Nebraska Symposium on Motivation.* Lincoln: University of Nebraska Press.
Schachter, S., & Singer, J. E. (1962). Cognitive, social, and physiological determinants of emotional state. *Psychological Review, 69,* 379–399.
Schafer, J., & Brown, S. A. (1991). Marijuana and cocaine effect expectancies and drug use patterns. *Journal of Consulting and Clinical Psychology, 5,* 558–565.
Schaie, K. W. (1993). The Seattle Longitudinal Studies of adult intelligence. *Current Directions, 2,* 171–175.
Schaie, K. W. (1994). The course of adult intellectual development. *American Psychologist, 49,* 304–313.
Schaie, K. W., & Willis, S. L. (1991). Adult personality and psychomotor performance: Cross-sectional and longitudinal analyses. *Journal of Gerontology: Psychological Sciences, 46,* P275–284.
Schaller, M., & Maas, A. (1989). Illusory correlation and social categorization: Toward an integration of motivational and cognitive factors in stereotype formation. *Journal of Personality and Social Psychology, 56,* 709–721.
Scheier, M. F., & Carver, C. S. (1985). Optimism, coping, and health: Assessment and implications of generalized outcome expectancies. *Health Psychology, 4,* 219–247.
Scheier, M. F., and others. (1989). Dispositional optimism and recovery from coronary artery bypass surgery: The beneficial effects on physical and psychological well-being. *Journal of Personality and Social Psychology, 57,* 1024–1040.
Schein, E. H. (1990). Organizational culture. *American Psychologist, 45,* 109–119.
Schenker, M. (1993). Air pollution and mortality. *New England Journal of Medicine, 329,* 1807–1808.
Schiffman, H. (1990). *Sensation and perception.* New York: Wiley.
Schmauk, F. J. (1970). Punishment, arousal, and avoidance learning in sociopaths. *Journal of Abnormal Psychology, 76,* 443–453.
Schmidt, F. L., Hunter, J. E., & Pearlman, K. (1981). Task differences as moderators of aptitude test validity in selection: A red herring. *Journal of Applied Psychology, 66,* 161–185.
Schneider, B. H., & Byrne, B. M. (1987). Individualizing social skills training for behavior-disordered children. *Journal of Consulting and Clinical Psychology, 55,* 444–445.
Schneider, W., & Bjorklund, D. (1992). Expertise, aptitude, and strategic remembering. *Child Development, 63,* 461–473.
Schotte, D. E., Cools, J., & Payvar, S. (1990). Problem-solving deficits in suicidal patients: Trait vulnerability or state phenomenon? *Journal of Consulting and Clinical Psychology, 58,* 562–564.
Schutte, N. S., Malouff, J. M., Post-Gorden, J. C., & Rodasts, A. L. (1988). Effect of playing videogames on childrens's aggressive and other behavior. *Journal of Applied Social Psychology, 18,* 454–460.
Schwartz, R. M., & Gottman, J. M. (1976). Toward a task analysis of assertive behavior. *Journal of Consulting and Clinical Psychology, 44,* 910–920.
Schwarz, N., Bless, H., & Bohner, G. (1991). Mood and persuasion: Affective states influence the processing of persuasive communications. In M. Zanna (Ed.), *Advances in experimental social psychology* (Vol. 24). New York: Academic Press.
Schweinhart, L. J., & Weikart, D. P. (Eds.). (1993). *Significant benefits: The High/Scope Perry Preschool Study through age 27.* Ypsilanti, MI: High/Scope Press.
Scott, J. (1994, May 9). Multiple-personality cases perplex legal system. *The New York Times,* pp. A1, B10, B11.
Scruggs, T. E., & Mastropieri, M. A. (1992). Remembering the forgotten art of memory. *American Educator, 16*(4), 31–37.
Segal, N. (1993). Twin, sibling, and adoption methods. *American Psychologist, 48,* 943–956.
Seligman, M. E. P., Abramson, L. Y., Semmel, A., & von Baeyer, C. (1979). Depressive attributional style. *Journal of Abnormal Psychology, 88,* 242–247.
Selkoe, D. J. (1992). Aging brain, aging mind. *Scientific American, 267,* 134–142.
Selye, H. (1976). *The stress of life* (Rev. ed.). New York: McGraw-Hill.
Seyle, H. (1980). The stress concept today. In I. L. Kutash and others (Eds.), *Handbook on stress and anxiety.* San Francisco: Jossey-Bass.
Senior, J. (1994, January 3). Language of the deaf evolves to reflect new sensibilities. *The New York Times,* pp. A1, A12.
Seta, J. J. (1982). The impact on comparison processes on coactors' task performance. *Journal of Personality and Social Psychology, 42,* 281–291.
Severn, J., Belch, G. E., & Belch, M. A. (1990). The effects of sexual and non-sexual advertising appeals and information level on cognitive processing and communication effectiveness. *Journal of Advertising, 19,* 14–22.
Shader, R. I., & Greenblatt, D. J. (1993). Drug therapy: Use of benzodiazepines in anxiety disorders. *New England Journal of Medicine, 328,* 1398–1405.
Shadish, W. R., Hickman, D., & Arrick, M. C. (1981). Psychological problems of spinal injury patients: Emotional distress as a function of time and locus of control. *Journal of Consulting and Clinical Psychology, 49,* 297.
Shah, M. & Jeffery, R. W. (1991). Is obesity due to overeating and inactivity or to a defective metabolic rate? A review. *Annals of Behavioral Medicine, 13,* 73–81.
Sham, P. C., and others. (1992). Schizophrenia following prenatal exposure to influenza epidemics between 1939 and 1960. *British Journal of Psychiatry, 160,* 461–466.
Shapley, R, & Enroth-Cugell, C. (1984). Visual adaptation and retinal gain controls. In N. Osborne & G. Chaders (Eds.), *Progress in retinal research* (Vol. 3). Oxford, England: Pergamon.
Shatz, C. J. (1992). The developing brain. *Scientific American, 267,* 60–67.
Shavitt, S. (1990). The role of attitude objects in attitude functions. *Journal of Experimental Social Psychology, 26,* 124–148.
Sheehy, G. (1976). *Passages: Predictable crises of adult life.* New York: Dutton.
Sheehy, G. (1995). *New passages: Mapping your life across time.* New York: Random House.
Sheingold, K., & Tenny, Y. J. (1982). Memory for a salient childhood event. In U. Niesser (Ed.), *Memory observed: Remembering in natural contexts.* San Francisco: Freeman.
Sheppard, J. A., & Strathman, A. J. (1989). Attractiveness and height: The role of stature in dating preference, frequency of dating, and perceptions of attractiveness. *Personality and Social Psychology Bulletin, 15,* 617–627.
Shepperd, J. A. (1993). Productivity loss in performance groups: A motivation analysis. *Psychological Bulletin, 113,* 67–81.
Sher, K. J., & Trull, T. J. (1994). Personality and disinhibitory psychopathology: Alcoholism and antisocial personality disorder. *Journal of Abnormal Psychology, 103,* 92–102.
Sher, K., J., Walitzer, K. S., Wood, P. K., & Brent, E. E. (1991). Characteristics of children of alcoholics: Putative risk factors, substance use and abuse, and psychopathology. *Journal of Abnormal Psychology, 100,* 427–448.
Shinn, M., Rosario, M., Morch, H., & Chestnut, D. E. (1984). Coping with job stress and burnout in the human services. *Journal of Personality and Social Psychology, 46,* 864–876.
Shneidman, E. S. (1985). *Definition of suicide.* New York: Wiley.
Shoham-Salomon, V. (1991). Introduction to special section on client-therapy interaction research. *Journal of Consulting and Clinical Psychology, 59,* 203–204.
Shotland, R. L., & Heinold, W. D. (1985). Bystander response to arterial bleeding: Helping skills, the decision-making process, and differentiating the helping response. *Journal of Personality and Social Psychology, 49,* 347–356.
Shumaker, S. A., & Hill, D. R. (1991). Gender differences in social support and physical health. *Health Psychology, 10,* 102–111.
Shusterman, G., & Saxe, L. (1990). *Deception in romantic relationships.* Unpublished manuscript. Cited in Saxe, L. (1991). *Lying. American Psychologist, 46,* 409–415.
Siegler, R. S., & Liebert, R. M. (1972). Effects of presenting relevant rules and complete feedback on the conservation of liquid quantity task. *Developmental Psychology, 7,* 133–138.
Signorielli, N. (1990). Children, television, and gender roles: Messages and impact. *Journal of Adolescent Health Care, 11*(1), 50–58.
Silver, E., Cirincione, C., & Steadman, H. J. (1994, February). *Law and human behavior.* Cited in DeAngelis, T. (1994). Public's view of insanity plea quite inaccurate, study finds. *APA Monitor, 25*(6), 28.
Silverstein, L. B. (1991). Transforming the debate about child care and maternal employment. *American Psychologist, 46,* 1025–1032.
Simoni, G., and others. (1990). Direct chromosome preparation and culture using chorionic villi: An evaluation of two techniques. *American Journal of Medical Genetics, 35,* 181–183.
Simons, A. D., and others. (1985). Exercise as a treatment for depression: An update. *Clinical Psychology Review, 5,* 553–568.
Simons, A. D., Angell, K. L., Monroe, S. M., & Thase, M. E. (1993). Cognition and life stress in depression: Cognitive factors and the definition, rating, and generation of negative life events. *Journal of Abnormal Psychology, 102,* 584–591.
Simons, A. D., Gordon, J. S., Monroe, S. M., & Thase, M. E. (1995). Toward an integration of psychologic, social, and biologic factors in depression: Effects on outcome and course of cognitive therapy. *Journal of Consulting and Clinical Psychology, 63,* 369–377.
Simpson, M., & Perry, J. D. (1990). Crime and climate: A reconsideration. *Environment and Behavior, 22,* 295–300.
Simpson, M. L., Olejnik, S., Tam, A. Y., & Supattathum, S. (1994). Elaborative verbal rehearsals and college students' cognitive performance. *Journal of Educational Psychology, 86,* 267–278.
Sims, C. (1993, December 19). The uncertain promises of interactivity. *The New York Times,* p. F6.
Skinner, B. F. (1938). *The behavior of organisms: An experimental analysis.* New York: Appleton.
Skinner, B. F. (1948). *Walden Two.* New York: Macmillan.
Skinner, B. F. (1957). *Verbal Behavior.* New York: Appleton.
Skinner, B. F. (1960). Pigeons in a pelican. *American Psychologist, 15,* 28–37.
Skinner, B. F. (1972). *Beyond freedom and dignity.* New York: Knopf.
Skinner, B. F. (1979). *The shaping of a behaviorist.* New York: Knopf.
Skinner, B. F. (1983). Intellectual self-management in old age. *American Psychologist, 38,* 239–244.
Skinner, B. F. (1987). Whatever happened to psychology as the science of behavior? *American Psychologist, 42,* 780–786.
Sleek, S. (1994). Bilingualism enhances student growth. *APA Monitor, 25*(4), 48.
Sleek, S. (1995). Group therapy: Tapping the power of teamwork. *APA Monitor, 26*(7), 1, 38–39.
Slobin, D. I. (1973). Cognitive prerequisites for the development of grammar. In C. A. Ferguson & D. I. Slobin (Eds.), *Studies of child development.* New York: Holt, Rinehart and Winston.
Slobin, D. I. (1983). *Crosslinguistic evidence for basic child grammar.* Paper presented to the biennial meeting of the Society for Research in Child Development. Detroit.
Small, M. Y. (1990). *Cognitive development.* San Diego, CA: Harcourt Brace Jovanovich.
Smetana, J. G. (1993, March). *Parenting styles during adolescence: Global or domain-specific?* Paper presented at the biennial meeting of the Society for Research in Child Development, New Orleans.
Smetana, J. G., Yau, J., Restrepo, A., & Braeges, J. L. (1991). Conflict and adaptation in adolescence: Adolescent–parent conflict. In M. E. Colten & S. Gore (Eds.), *Adolescent stress: Causes and consequences.* New York: Aldine deGruyter.
Smith, B., & Sechrest, L. (1991). Treatment of aptitude by treatment interactions. *Journal of Consulting and Clinical Psychology, 59,* 233–244.
Smith, D., King, M., & Hoebel, B. G. (1970). Lateral hypothalamic control of killing: Evidence for a cholinoceptive mechanism. *Science, 167,* 900–901.
Smith, G. F., & Dorfman, D. (1975). The effect of stimulus uncertainty on the relationship between frequency of exposure and liking. *Journal of Personality and Social Psychology, 31,* 150–155.
Smith, M. L., & Glass, G. V. (1977). Meta-analysis of psychotherapy outcome studies. *American Psychologist, 32,* 752–760.
Smith, M. L., Glass, G. V., & Miller, T. I. (1980). *The benefits of psychotherapy.* Baltimore, MD: The Johns Hopkins University Press.

Smith, R. E., Smoll, F. L., & Ptacek, J. T. (1990). Conjunctive moderator variables in vulnerability and resiliency research: Life stress, social support and coping skills, and adolescent sport injuries. *Journal of Personality and Social Psychology, 58,* 360–370.

Smith, S. M., Glenberg, A. M., & Bjork, R. A. (1978). Environmental context and human memory. *Memory and Cognition, 6,* 342–355.

Smith, S. S., & Richardson, D. (1983). Amelioration of deception and harm in psychological research: The important role of debriefing. *Journal of Personality and Social Psychology, 44,* 1075–1082.

Smith, T. W., & Pope, M. K. (1990). Cynical hostility as a health risk: Current status and future directions. *Journal of Social Behavior and Personality, 5,* 77–88.

Smith, T. W., Snyder, C. R., & Perkins, S. C. (1983). The self-serving function of hypochondriacal complaints: Physical symptoms as self-handicapping strategies. *Journal of Personality and Social Psychology, 44,* 787–797.

Smitherman, G. (1994). Cited in Lee, F. R. (1994, January 5). Grappling with how to teach young speakers of Black dialect. *The New York Times,* pp. A1, D22.

Smoke rises. (1993, December 27). *The New York Times,* p. A16.

Smolowe, J. (1993, July 26). Choose your poison. *Time,* pp. 56–57.

Snarey, J. R. (1987, June). A question of morality. *Psychology Today, 21,* 6–8.

Snarey, J. R., Reimer, J., & Kohlberg, L. (1985). Development of social-moral reasoning among kibbutz adolescents: A longitudinal cross-cultural study. *Developmental Psychology, 21,* 3–17.

Snow, C. E. (1993). Bilingualism and second language acquisition. In J. Berko-Gleason & N. B. Ratner (Eds.), *Psycholinguistics.* Fort Worth, TX: Harcourt Brace Jovanovich.

Snow, R. E. (1991). Aptitude-treatment interaction as a framework for research on individual differences in psychotherapy. *Journal of Consulting and Clinical Psychology, 59,* 205–216.

Snyder, M., & DeBono, G. (1989). Understanding the functions of attitudes. In A. R. Pratkanis and others (Eds.), *Attitude structure and function.* Hillsdale, NJ: Erlbaum.

Snyder, M., Grether, J., & Keller, K. (1974). Staring and compliance: A field experiment on hitchhiking. *Journal of Applied Social Psychology, 4,* 165–170.

Snyder, S. H. (1977). Opiate receptors and internal opiates. *Scientific American, 236,* 44–56.

Snyderman, M., & Rothman, S. (1987). Survey of expert opinion on intelligence and aptitude testing. *American Psychologist, 42,* 137–144.

Snyderman, M., & Rothman, S. (1990). *The I.Q. controversy.* New Brunswick, NJ: Transaction Publishers.

Solomon, E. P., Berg, L. R., Martin, D. W., & Villee, C. (1993). *Biology* (3rd ed.). Philadelphia: Saunders College Publishing.

Solomon, R. L. (1980). The opponent-process theory of acquired motivation: The costs of pleasure and the benefits of pain. *American Psychologist, 35,* 691–712.

Sommer, R. (1991). James V. McConnell (1925–1990). *American Psychologist, 46,* 650.

Sommers-Flanagan, J., & Sommers-Flanagan, R. (1995). Intake interviewing with suicidal patients: A systematic approach. *Professional Psychology: Research and Practice, 26,* 41–47.

Sonstroem, R. J. (1984). Exercise and self-esteem. *Exercise and Sport Sciences Reviews, 12,* 123–155.

Sorce, J. F., Emde, R. N., Campos, J. J., & Klinnert, M. D. (1985). Maternal emotional signaling: Its effect on the visual-cliff behavior of 1-year-olds. *Developmental Psychology, 21,* 195–200.

Sorenson, S. B., & Rutter, C. M. (1991). Transgenerational patterns of suicide attempt. *Journal of Consulting and Clinical Psychology, 59,* 861–866.

Spanos, N. P., Jones, B., & Malfara, A. (1982). Hypnotic deafness: Now you hear it—Now you still hear it. *Journal of Abnormal Psychology, 91,* 75–77.

Spanos, N. P., Radtke, H. L., & Dubreuil, D. L. (1982). Episodic and semantic memory in posthypnotic amnesia: A reevaluation. *Journal of Personality and Social Psychology, 43,* 565–573.

Spanos, N. P., & Radtke-Bodorik, H. L. (1980, April). Integrating hypnotic phenomena with cognitive psychology: An illustration using suggested amnesia. *Bulletin of the British Society for Experimental and Clinical Hypnosis,* pp. 4–7.

Spanos, N. P., Weekes, J. R., & Bertrand, L. D. (1985). Multiple personality: A social psychological perspective. *Journal of Abnormal Psychology, 94,* 362–376.

Sparrow, S. S., Ballo, D. A., & Cicchetti, D. V. (1984). *Vineland Adaptive Behavior Scales.* Circle Pines, MN: American Guidance Service.

Spector, I. P., & Carey, M. P. (1990). Incidence and prevalence of the sexual dysfunctions: A critical review of the empirical literature. *Archives of Sexual Behavior, 19,* 389–408.

Spence, J. T., Helmreich, R., & Stapp, J. (1975). Ratings of self and peers on sex-role attributes and their relation to self-esteem and concepts of masculinity and femininity. *Journal of Personality and Social Psychology, 32,* 29–39.

Spencer, M. B., & Markstrom-Adams, C. (1990). Identity processes among racial and ethnic minority children in America. *Child Development, 61,* 290–310.

Sperling, G. (1960). The information available in brief visual presentations. *Psychological Monographs,* 74, 1–29.

Sperry, R. W. (1993). The impact and promise of the cognitive revolution. *American Psychologist, 48,* 878–885.

Spiegel, D., & Cardeña, E. (1991). Disintegrated experience. The dissociative disorders revisited. *Journal of Abnormal Psychology, 100,* 366–378.

Spinhoven, P., and others. (1989). Pain coping strategies in a Dutch population of chronic low back pain patients. *Pain, 37,* 77–83.

Spinhoven, P., Labbe, M. R., & Rombouts, R. (1993). Feasibility of computerized psychological testing with psychiatric outpatients. *Journal of Clinical Psychology, 49,* 440–447.

Spitzer, R. L., Forman, J. B. W., & Nee, J. (1979). *DSM-III* field trials: Initial interrater diagnostic reliability. *American Journal of Psychiatry, 136,* 815–817.

Spitzer, R. L., Gibbon, M., Skodol, A. E., Williams, J. B. W., & First, M. B. (1989). *DSM-III-R casebook.* Washington, DC: American Psychiatric Press.

Sporer, S. L. (1991). Deep—deeper—deepest? Encoding strategies and the recognition of human faces. *Journal of Experimental Psychology: Learning, Memory, and Cognition, 17,* 323–333.

Spreat, S., & Behar, D. (1994). Trends in the residential (inpatient) treatment of individuals with a dual diagnosis. *Journal of Consulting and Clinical Psychology, 61,* 43–48.

Sprecher, S., Sullivan, Q., & Hatfield, E. (1994). Mate selection preferences: Gender differences examined in a national sample. *Journal of Personality and Social Psychology, 66*(6), 1074–1080.

Squire, L. R. (1994). Cited in Pool, R. *The dynamic brain.* Washington, DC: National Academy Press.

Stacy, A. W., Bentler, P. M., & Flay, B. R. (1994). Attitudes and health behavior in diverse populations: Drunk driving, alcohol use, binge eating, marijuana use, and cigarette use. *Health Psychology, 13,* 73–85.

Stacy, A. W., Newcomb, M. D., & Bentler, P. M. (1991). Cognitive motivation and drug use: A 9-year longitudinal study. *Journal of Abnormal Psychology, 100,* 502–515.

Stampfer, M. J., and others. (1991). A prospective study of cholesterol, apolipoproteins, and the risk of myocardial infarction. *New England Journal of Medicine, 325,* 373–381.

Stasser, G., Taylor, L. A., & Hanna, C. (1989). Information sampling in structured and unstructured discussion of three- and six-person groups. *Journal of Personality and Social Psychology, 57,* 67–78.

Steck, L., Levitan, D., McLane, D., & Kelley, H. H. (1982). Care, need, and conceptions of love. *Journal of Personality and Social Psychology, 43,* 481–491.

Steele, C. M., & Aronson, J. (1985). Cited in Watters, E. (1995, September 17). Claude Steele has scores to settle. *The New York Times Magazine,* pp. 44–47.

Steele, C. M., & Josephs, R. A. (1990). Alcohol myopia: Its prized and dangerous effects. *American Psychologist, 45,* 921–933.

Steinberg, L. (1991). Parent–adolescent relations. In R. M. Lerner, A. C. Petersen, & J. Brooks-Gunn (Eds.), *Encyclopedia of adolescence.* New York: Garland.

Steinberg, L., Dornbusch, S. M., & Brown, B. B. (1992a). Ethnic differences in adolescent achievement. *American Psychologist, 47,* 723–729.

Steinberg, L., Lamborn, S. D., Dornbusch, S. M., & Darling, N. (1992b). Impact of parenting practices on adolescent achievement: Authoritative parenting, school involvement, and encouragement to succeed. *Child Development, 63,* 1266–1281.

Steinbrook, R., (1992). The polygraph test—A flawed diagnostic method. *New England Journal of Medicine, 327,* 122–123.

Stephan, C. W., & Langlois, J. H. (1984). Baby beautiful: Adult attributions of infant competence as a function of infant attractiveness. *Child Development, 55,* 576–586.

Steriade, M. (1992). Cited in Blakeslee, S. (1992, January 7). Scientists unraveling chemistry of dreams. *The New York Times,* pp. C1, C10.

Stericker, A., & LeVesconte, S. (1982). Effect of brief training on sex-related differences in visual–spatial skill. *Journal of Personality and Social Psychology, 43,* 1018–1029.

Stermac, L. E., Segal, Z. V., & Gillis, R. (1990). Social and cultural factors in sexual assault. In W. L. Marshall and others (Eds.), *Handbook of sexual assault: Issues, theories, and treatment of the offender.* New York: Plenum.

Sternberg, R. J. (1985). *Beyond IQ: A triarchic theory of human intelligence.* New York: Cambridge University Press.

Sternberg, R. J. (1988). Triangulating love. In R. J. Sternberg & M. J. Barnes (Eds.), *The psychology of love.* New Haven, CT: Yale University Press.

Sternberg, R. J. (1990). Wisdom and its relations to intelligence and creativity. In R. J. Sternberg (Ed.), *Wisdom: Its nature, origins, and development.* New York: Cambridge University Press.

Sternberg, R. J. (1995). *In search of the human mind.* Fort Worth, TX: Harcourt Brace.

Sternberg, R.J., & Davidson, J. E. (1994). *The nature of insight.* Cambridge, MA: The MIT Press, a Bradford Book.

Stevenson, H. W., Lee, S. Y., & Stigler, J. W. (1986). Mathematics achievement of Chinese, Japanese, and American children. *Science, 231,* 693–699.

Stewart, J. E., II. (1980). Defendant's attractiveness as a factor in the outcome of criminal trials: An observational study. *Journal of Applied Social Psychology, 10,* 348–361.

Stewart, M. W., Knight, R. G., Palmer, D. G., & Highton, J. (1994). Differential relationships between stress and disease activity for immunologically distinct subgroups of people with rheumatoid arthritis. *Journal of Abnormal Psychology, 103,* 251–258.

Stier, D. S., & Hall, J. A. (1984). Gender differences in touch: An empirical and theoretical review. *Journal of Personality and Social Psychology, 47,* 440–459.

St. Lawrence, J. S., Brasfield, T. L., Jefferson, K. W., Alleyne, E., O'Bannon, R. E., & Shirley, A. (1995). Cognitive-behavioral intervention to reduce African American adolescents' risk for HIV infection. *Journal of Consulting and Clinical Psychology, 63,* 221–237.

Stokols, D. (1992). Establishing and maintaining healthy environments: Toward a social ecology of health promotion. *American Psychologist, 47,* 6–22.

Storfer, M. D. (1990). *Intelligence and giftedness: The contributions of heredity and early environment.* San Francisco: Jossey-Bass.

Straube, E. R., & Oades, R. D. (1992). *Schizophrenia: Empirical research and findings.* San Diego, CA: Academic Press.

Strauss, M. (1994). *Beating the devil out of them: Corporal punishment in American families.* Lexington, MA: Lexington Books.

Stricker, G. (1991). Ethical concerns in alcohol research. *Journal of Consulting and Clinical Psychology, 59,* 256–257.

Strickland, B. (1991). Cited in DeAngelis, T. (1991). Hearing pinpoints gaps in research on women. *APA Monitor, 22*(6), 8.

Strom, J. C., & Buck, R. W. (1979). Staring and participants' sex: Physiological and subjective reactions. *Personality and Social Psychology Bulletin, 5,* 114–117.

Strom, S. (1993, April 18). Human pheromones. *The New York Times,* p. V12.

Struckman-Johnson, C., Struckman-Johnson, D., Gilliland, R. C., & Ausman, A. (1994). Effect of persuasive appeals in AIDS PSAs and condom commercials on intentions to use condoms. *Journal of Applied Social Psychology, 24*(24), 2223–2244.

Strupp, H. H. (1990). Rejoinder to Arnold Lazarus. *American Psychologist, 45,* 671–672.

Strupp, H. H. (1992). The future of psychodynamic psychotherapy. *Psychotherapy, 29,* 21–27.

Stunkard, A. J. (1959). Obesity and the denial of hunger. *Psychosomatic Medicine, 1,* 281–289.

Stunkard, A. J., Harris, J. R., Pedersen, N. L., & McLearn, G. E. (1990). A separated twin study of the body mass index. *New England Journal of Medicine, 322,* 1483–1487.

Stunkard, A. J., & Sørensen, T. I. A. (1993). Obesity and socioeconomic status—A complex relation. *New England Journal of Medicine, 329,* 1036–1037.

Suarez, E. C., Harlan, E., Peoples, M. C., & Williams, R. B., Jr. (1993). Cardiovascular and emotional responses in women: The role of hostility and harassment. *Health Psychology, 12,* 459–468.

Sue, S. (1988). Psychotherapeutic services for ethnic minorities: Two decades of research findings. *American Psychologist, 43,* 301–308.

Sue, S. (1991). In J. D. Goodchilds (Ed.), *Psychological perspectives on human diversity in America.* Washington, DC: American Psychological Association.

Sue, S., & Okazaki, S. (1990). Asian-American educational achievements. *American Psychologist, 45,* 913–920.

Suinn, R. A. (1982). Intervention with Type A behaviors. *Journal of Consulting and Clinical Psychology, 50,* 933–949.

Suinn, R. A. (1995). Anxiety management training. In K. Craig (Ed.), *Anxiety and depression in children and adults* (pp. 159–179). New York: Sage.

Sundstrom, E., De Meuse, K. P., & Futrell, D. (1990). Work teams: Applications and effectiveness. *American Psychologist, 45,* 120–133.

Susser, E. S., & Linn, S. P. (1992). Schizophrenia after prenatal exposure to the Dutch Hunger Winter of 1944–1945. *Archives of General Psychiatry, 49,* 983–988.

Sweeney, P. D., & Gruber, K. L. (1984). Selective exposure: Voter information preferences and the Watergate affair. *Journal of Personality and Social Psychology, 46,* 1208–1221.

Szasz, T. S. (1984). *The therapeutic state: Psychiatry in the mirror of current events.* Buffalo, NY: Prometheus.

Tahka, S., Wood, M., & Loewenthal, K. (1981). Age changes in the ability to replicate foreign pronunciation and intonation. *Language and Speech, 24,* 363–372.

Takaki, R. (1993). *A different mirror: A history of multicultural America.* Boston: Little, Brown.

Talbott, E., and others. (1985). Occupational noise exposure, noise-induced hearing loss, and the epidemiology of high blood pressure. *American Journal of Epidemiology, 121,* 501–514.

Tan, L. (1985). Laterality and motor skills in four-year-olds. *Child Development, 56,* 119–124.

Tanford, S., & Penrod, S. (1984). Social influence model: A formal integration of research on majority and minority influence processes. *Psychological Bulletin, 95,* 189–225.

Tangney, J. P. (1990). Assessing individual differences in proneness to shame and guilt: Development of the Self-Conscious Affect and Attribution Inventory. *Journal of Personality and Social Psychology, 59,* 102–111.

Tanzi, R. E. (1995). A promising animal model of Alzheimer's disease. *New England Journal of Medicine, 332,* 1512–1513.

Taub, A. (1993, April 8). Narcotics have long been known safe and effective for pain. *The New York Times,* p. A20.

Taylor, H. (1993). Cited in Barringer, F. (1993, April 25). Polling on sexual issues has its drawbacks. *The New York Times,* p. A23.

Taylor, I., & Taylor, M. M. (1990). *Psycholinguistics: Learning and using language.* Englewood Cliffs, NJ: Prentice-Hall.

Taylor, R. C., & Richards, S. B. (1991). Patterns of intellectual differences of Black, Hispanic and White children. *Psychology in the Schools, 28,* 5–9.

Taylor, S. E. (1990). Health psychology: The science and the field. *American Psychologist, 45,* 40–50.

Taylor, W. N. (1985, May). Super athletes made to order. *Psychology Today, 19,* 62–66.

Telch, C. F., & Telch, M. J. (1986). Group coping skills instruction and supportive group therapy for cancer patients: A comparison of strategies. *Journal of Consulting and Clinical Psychology, 54,* 802–808.

Télégdy, G. (1977). Prenatal androgenization of primates and humans. In J. Money & H. Musaph (Eds.), *Handbook of sexology.* Amsterdam: Excerpta Medica.

Teller, D. Y., & Lindsey, D. T. (1993). Motion nulling techniques and infant color vision. In C. E. Granrud (Ed.), *Visual perception and cognition in infancy.* Hillsdale, NJ: Erlbaum.

Teri, L., & Wagner, A. (1992). Alzheimer's disease and depression. *Journal of Consulting and Clinical Psychology, 60,* 379–391.

Terrace, H. S. (1987). *Nim* (2nd ed.). New York: Knopf.

Tetlock, P. E. (1983). Accountability and complexity of thought. *Journal of Personality and Social Psychology, 45,* 74–83.

Tharp, R. G. (1991). Cultural diversity and treatment of children. *Journal of Consulting and Clinical Psychology, 59,* 799–812.

Thigpen, C. H., & Cleckley, H. M. (1984). On the incidence of multiple personality disorder. *International Journal of Clinical and Experimental Hypnosis, 32,* 63–66.

Thompson, C. P., & Cowan, T. (1986). The neurobiology of learning and memory. *Science, 233,* 941–947.

Thompson, L. A., Detterman, D. K., & Plomin, R. (1991). Associations between cognitive abilities and scholastic achievement: Genetic overlap but environmental differences. *Psychological Science, 2,* 158–165.

Thompson, R. A. (1991a). Attachment theory and research. In M. Lewis (Ed.), *Child and adolescent psychiatry: A comprehensive textbook.* Baltimore: Williams & Wilkins.

Thompson, R. A. (1991b). Infant daycare: Concerns, controversies, choices. In J. V. Lerner & N. L. Galambos (Eds.), *Employed mothers and their children* (pp. 9–36). New York: Garland.

Thompson, W. C., Cowan, C. L., & Rosenhan, D. L. (1980). Focus of attention mediates the impact of negative affect on altruism. *Journal of Personality and Social Psychology, 38,* 291–300.

Thoresen, C., & Powell, L. H. (1992). Type A behavior pattern: New perspectives on theory, assessment, and intervention. *Journal of Consulting and Clinical Psychology, 60,* 595–604.

Thurstone, L. L. (1938). Primary mental abilities. *Psychometric Monographs, 1.*

Thurstone, L. L., & Thurstone, T. G. (1963). *SRA primary abilities.* Chicago: SRA.

Tierney, J. (1994, January 9). Porn, the low-slung engine of progress. *The New York Times,* pp. H1, H18.

Tobias, S. (1982, January). Sexist equations. *Psychology Today, 16,* 14–17.

Tolchin, M. (1989, July 19). When long life is too much: Suicide rises among elderly. *The New York Times,* pp. A1, A15.

Tolman, E. C., & Honzik, C. H. (1930). Introduction and removal of reward, and maze performance in rats. *University of California Publications in Psychology, 4,* 257–275.

Tomes, H. (1993). It's in the nation's interest to break abuse cycle. *APA Monitor, 24*(3), 28.

Tomes, H. (1995). Minorities' access to care is top priority. *APA Monitor, 26*(7), 52.

Topf, M. (1989). Sensitivity to noise, personality hardiness, and noise-induced stress in critical care nurses. *Environment and Behavior, 21,* 717–733.

Torgersen, S. (1983). Genetic factors in anxiety disorders. *Archives of General Psychiatry, 40,* 1085–1089.

Torrey, E. F., Bowler, A. E., & Rawlings, R. (1992). Schizophrenia and the 1957 influenza epidemic. *Schizophrenia Research, 6,* 100.

Trehub, S. E., Schneider, B. A., Thorpe, L. A., & Judge, P. (1991). Observational measures of auditory sensitivity in early infancy. *Developmental Psychology, 27,* 40–49.

Trenton State College. (1991, Spring). Sexual Assault Victim Education and Support-Unit (SAVES-U) Newsletter.

Triandis, H. C. (1990). Cross-cultural studies of individualism and collectivism. In J. J. Berman (Ed.), *Nebraska Symposium on Motivation, 1989. Cross-cultural perspectives.* Lincoln: University of Nebraska Press.

Triandis, H. C. (1994). *Culture and social behavior.* New York: McGraw-Hill.

Trimble, J. E. (1991). The mental health service and training needs of American Indians. In H. F. Myers and others (Eds.), *Ethnic minority perspectives on clinical training and services in psychology* (pp. 43–48). Washington, DC: American Psychological Association.

Trujillo, C. (Ed.). (1991). *Chicana lesbians: The girls our mothers warned us about.* Berkeley, CA: Third Woman Press.

Trull, T. J. (1992). DSM-III-R personality disorders and the five-factor model of personality. *Journal of Abnormal Psychology, 101,* 553–560.

Tsui, A. S., & O'Reilly, C. A., III. (1989). Beyond simple demographic effects. *Academy of Management Journal, 32,* 402–423.

Tulving, E. (1985). How many memory systems are there? *American Psychologist, 40,* 385–398.

Tulving, E. (1991). Memory research is not a zero-sum game. *American Psychologist, 46,* 41–42.

Tupes, E. C., & Christal, R. E. (1992). Recurrent personality factors based on trait ratings. *Journal of Personality, 60,* 225–251.

Turnbull, C. M. (1961). Notes and discussion: Some observations regarding the experiences and behavior of the Bambute pygmies. *American Journal of Psychology, 7,* 304–308.

Turner, A. M., & Greenough, W. T. (1985). Differential rearing effects on rat visual cortex synapses: I. Synaptic and neuronal density and synapses per neuron. *Brain Research, 329,* 195–203.

Turner, J. S., & Helms, D. B. (1991). *Lifespan development* (4th ed.). Fort Worth, TX: Harcourt Brace Jovanovich.

Turner, S. M. (1987). Psychopathology in the offspring of anxiety disorders patients. *Journal of Consulting and Clinical Psychology, 55,* 229–235.

Turner, S. M., Beidel, D. C., & Jacob, R. G. (1994). Social phobia: A comparison of behavior therapy and atenolol. *Journal of Consulting and Clinical Psychology, 62,* 350–358.

Tversky, A., & Kahneman, D. (1982). Judgment under uncertainty: Heuristics and biases. In D. Kahneman, P. Slovic, & A. Tversky (Eds.), *Judgment under uncertainty: Heuristics and biases.* New York: Cambridge University Press.

Ugwuegbu, D. C. E. (1979). Racial and evidential factors in juror attribution of legal responsibility. *Journal of Experimental Social Psychology, 15,* 133–146.

Unger, R. K., Hilderbrand, M., & Madar, T. (1982). Physical attractiveness and assumptions about social deviance: Some sex-by-sex comparisons. *Personality and Social Psychology Bulletin, 8,* 293–301.

USBC (U.S. Bureau of the Census). (1985). *Statistical abstract of the United States* (105th ed.). Washington, DC: U.S. Government Printing Office.

USBC (U.S. Bureau of the Census). (1990). *Statistical abstract of the United States* (110th ed.). Washington, DC: U.S. Government Printing Office.

USBC (U.S. Bureau of Census). (1993). *Statistical abstract of the United States* (113th ed.). Washington, DC: U.S. Government Printing Office.

U.S. Congress (1983, November). *Scientific validity of polygraph testing: A research review and evaluation* (OTA-TM-H-15). Washington, DC: Office of Technology Assessment.

USDHHS (U.S. Department of Health and Human Services). (1991, March). *Health United States 1990.* (DHHS Publication No 91-1232). Hyattsville, MD: Centers for Disease Control, National Center for Health Statistics.

USDHHS (U.S. Department of Health and Human Services). (1992). *For a strong and healthy baby.* (DHHS Publication No. 92-1915). Washington, DC: U.S. Government Printing Office.

USDHHS (U.S. Department of Health and Human Services). (1993, Winter). *Mothers target of passive smoking intervention effort. Heart Memo.* Public Health Service, National Institutes of Health, National Heart, Lung and Blood Institute, Office of Prevention, Education, and Control.

Vachss, A. (1993). *Sex crimes.* New York: Random House.

Vaillant, G. E. (1994). Ego mechanisms of defense and personality psychopathology. *Journal of Abnormal Psychology, 103,* 44–50.

Vaillant, G. E., & Milofsky, E. S. (1982). The etiology of alcoholism. *American Psychologist, 37,* 494–503.

Valenstein, E. S. (1986). *Great and desperate cures: The rise and decline of psychosurgery and other radical treatments for mental illness.* New York: Basic Books.

Van Brunt, L. (1994, March 27). About men. Whites without money. *The New York Times Magazine,* p. 38.

Vandell, D. L., & Corasaniti, M. A. (1990). Child care and the family: Complex contributors to child development. In K. McCartney (Ed.), *New Directions for Child Development* (Vol. 49, pp. 23–37). San Francisco: Jossey-Bass.

Vandenbergh, J. G. (1993). Cited in Angier, N. (1993, August 24). Female gerbil born with males is found to be begetter of sons. *The New York Times,* p. C4.

Van der Pligt, J., & Eiser, J. R. (1983). Actors' and observers' attributions, self-serving bias, and positivity bias. *European Journal of Social Psychology, 13,* 95–104.

Van der Velde, F. W., van der Pligt, J., & Hooykaas, C. (1994). Perceiving AIDS-related risk: Accuracy as a function of differences in actual risk. *Health Psychology, 13,* 25–33.

Van Kammen, D. P., and others. (1990). Norepinephrine in acute exacerbations of chronic schizophrenia. *Archives of General Psychiatry, 47,* 161–168.

Verplanken, B. (1991). Persuasive communication of risk communication: A test of cue versus message processing effects in a field experiment. *Personality and Social Psychology Bulletin, 17,* 188–193.

Visintainer, M. A., Volpicelli, J. R., & Seligman, M. E. P. (1982). Tumor rejection in rats after inescapable or escapable shock. *Science, 216,* 437–439.

Vitousek, K., & Manke, F. (1994). Personality variables and disorders in anorexia nervosa and bulimia nervosa. *Journal of Abnormal Psychology, 103,* 137–147.

Volchko, J. (1991). Cited in Celis, W. (1991, January 2). Students trying to draw line between sex and an assault. *The New York Times,* pp. A1, B8.

Von Békésy, G. (1957, August). The ear. *Scientific American,* pp. 66–78.

Voyer, D., Voyer, S., & Bryden, M. P. (1995). Magnitude of sex differences in spatial abilities: A meta-analysis and consideration of critical variables. *Psychological Bulletin, 117,* 250–270.

Wachtel, P. L. (1994). Cyclical processes in personality and psychopathology. *Journal of Abnormal Psychology, 103,* 51–54.

Walker, L. E. A. (1993). Cited in Mednick, A. (1993). Domestic abuse is seen as worldwide "epidemic." *APA Monitor, 24*(5), 33.

Walsh, M. R. (1993, August). Teaching the psychology of women and gender for undergraduate and graduate faculty. Workshop of the Psychology of Women Institute presented at the meeting of the American Psychological Association, Toronto, Canada.

Wardlaw, G. M., & Insel, P. M. (1990). *Perspectives in nutrition.* St. Louis: Times Mirror/Mosby College Publishing.

Wardle, J., & Solomons, W. (1994). Naughty but nice: A laboratory study of health information and food preferences in a community sample. *Health Psychology, 13,* 180–183.

Watkins, C. E., Jr., Campbell, V. L., Nieberding, R., & Hallmark, R. (1995). Contemporary practice of psychological assessment by clinical psychologists. *Professional Psychology: Research and Practice, 26,* 54–60.

Watkins, M. J., Ho, E., & Tulving, E. (1976). Context effects on recognition memory for faces. *Journal of Verbal Learning and Verbal Behavior, 15,* 505–518.

Watson, J. B. (1913). Psychology as the behaviorist views it. *Psychological Review, 20,* 158–177.

Watson, J. B. (1924). *Behaviorism.* New York: W. W. Norton.

Watson, J. B., & Rayner, R. (1920). Conditioned emotional reactions. *Journal of Experimental Psychology, 3,* 1–4.

Watson, T. J., & Petre, P. (1990). *Father and son.* New York: Bantam.

Webb, W. (1993). Cited in Adler, T. (1993). Sleep loss impairs attention—and more. *APA Monitor, 24*(9), 22–23.

Weber, R., & Crocker, J. (1983). Cognitive processes in the revision of stereotypic beliefs. *Journal of Personality and Social Psychology, 45,* 961–977.

Wechsler, D. (1975). Intelligence defined and undefined: A relativistic appraisal. *American Psychologist, 30,* 135–139.

Weekes, J. R., Lynn, S. J., Green, J. P., & Brentar, J. T. (1992). Pseudomemory in hypnotized and task-motivated subjects. *Journal of Abnormal Psychology, 101,* 356–360.

Weidner, G., Istvan, J., McKnight, J. D. (1989). Clusters of behavioral coronary risk factors in employed women and men. *Journal of Applied Social Psychology, 19,* 468–480.

Weinberg, J., & Levine, S. (1980). Psychobiology of coping in animals: The effects of predictability. In S. Levine & H. Ursin (Eds.), *Coping and health.* New York: Plenum.

Weinberg, S. L., & Richardson, M. S. (1981). Dimensions of stress in early parenting. *Journal of Consulting and Clinical Psychology, 49,* 688–693.

Weiner, B. (1991). Metaphors in motivation and attribution. *American Psychologist, 46,* 921–930.

Weiner, K. (1992). Cited in Goleman, D. J. (1992, January 8). Heart seizure or panic attack? Disorder is a terrifying mimic. *The New York Times,* p. C12.

Weinraub, M., & Wolf, B. M. (1983). Effects of stress and social supports on mother–child interactions in single- and two-parent families. *Child Development, 54,* 1297–1311.

Weinstein, N. D. (1980). Unrealistic optimism about future life events. *Journal of Personality and Social Psychology, 39,* 806–820.

Weinstein, N. D. (1984). Why it won't happen to me: Perceptions of risk factors and susceptibility. *Health Psychology, 3,* 431–457.

Weinstein, N. D. (1993). Testing four competing theories of health-protective behavior. *Health Psychology, 12,* 324–333.

Weisinger, H. (1990). *The critical edge: How to criticize up and down your organization and make it pay off.* New York: Harper & Row.

Weiss, J. M. (1972). Psychological factors in stress and disease. *Scientific American, 226,* 104–113.

Weiss, J. M. (1982, August). *A model for the neurochemical study of depression.* Paper presented to the American Psychological Association, Washington, DC.

Weisse, C. S. (1992). Depression and immunocompetence: A review of the literature. *Psychological Bulletin, 11,* 475–489.

Weissman, M. M., and others. (1991). Affective disorders. In N. L. Robins & D. A. Regier (Eds.), *Psychiatric disorders in America: The Epidemiologic Catchment Area Study.* New York: Free Press.

Weisz, J. R., Sweeney, L., Proffitt, V., & Carr, T. (1993). Control-related beliefs and self-reported depressive symptoms in late childhood. *Journal of Abnormal Psychology, 102,* 411–418.

Welch, K. M. A. (1993). Drug therapy of migraine. *New England Journal of Medicine, 329,* 1476–1483.

Wells, G. L. (1993). What do we know about eyewitness identification? *American Psychologist, 48,* 553–571.

Wells, G. L., & Luus, C. A. E. (1990). Police lineups as experiments: Social methodology as a framework for properly conducted lineups. *Personality and Social Psychology Bulletin, 16,* 106–117.

Wentzel, K. R. (1994). Relations of social goal pursuit to social acceptance, classroom behavior, and perceived social support. *Journal of Educational Psychology, 86,* 173–182.

Werner, C. M., Brown, B. B., & Damron, G. (1981). Territorial marking in a game arcade. *Journal of Personality and Social Psychology, 41,* 1094–1104.

Westerman, M. A. (1990). Coordination of maternal directives with preschoolers' behavior in compliance-problem and healthy dyads. *Developmental Psychology, 26,* 621–630.

Wetzler, S. E., & Sweeney, J. A. (1986). *Childhood amnesia.* In D. C. Rubin (Ed.), *Autobiographical memory.* New York: Cambridge University Press.

Wexler, B. E., & Cicchetti, D. V. (1992). The outpatient treatment of depression: Implications of outcome research for clinical practice. *Journal of Nervous and Mental Disease, 180,* 277–286.

Whalen, C. K., & Henler, B. (1991). Therapies for hyperactive children: Comparisons, combinations, and compromises. *Journal of Consulting and Clinical Psychology, 59,* 126–137.

What is sexual harassment? (1993, June 19). *The New York Times,* p. L9.

Whisman, M. A., Miller, I. W., Norman, W. H., & Keitner, G. I. (1991). Cognitive therapy with depressed inpatients: Specific effects on dysfunctional cognitions. *Journal of Consulting and Clinical Psychology, 59,* 282–288.

White, J. L., & Nicassio, P. M. (1990, November). *The relationship between daily stress, pre-sleep arousal and sleep disturbance in good and poor sleepers.* Paper presented at the annual meeting of the Association for the Advancement of Behavior Therapy, San Francisco.

White, J. L., and others. (1994). Measuring impulsivity and examining its relationship to delinquency. *Journal of Abnormal Psychology, 103,* 192–205.

Whitehead, W. E. (1994). Assessing the effects of stress on physical symptoms. *Health Psychology, 13,* 99–102.

Whitten, L. A. (1993). Infusing Black psychology into the introductory psychology course. *Teaching of Psychology, 20*(1), 13–21.

Whittle, J., and others. (1993). Racial differences in the use of invasive cardiovascular procedures in the Department of Veteran Affairs medical system. *New England Journal of Medicine, 329,* 621–627.

Whorf, B. (1956). *Language, thought, and reality.* New York: Wiley.

Widiger, T. A. (1990, August/September). Antisocial personality disorder. *DSM-IV update.* Washington, DC: American Psychiatric Association.

Widiger, T. A., & Costa, P. T., Jr. (1994). Personality and personality disorders. *Journal of Abnormal Psychology, 103,* 78–91.

Widiger, T. A., and others. (1991). Toward an empirical classification for the *DSM-IV. Journal of Abnormal Psychology, 100,* 280–288.

Wiens, A. N., & Menustik, C. E. (1983). Treatment outcome and patient characteristics in an aversion therapy program for alcoholism. *American Psychologist, 38,* 1089–1096.

Wiggins, J. G., Jr. (1994). Would you want your child to be a psychologist? *American Psychologist, 49,* 485–492.

Wilcox, V. L., Kasl, S. V., & Berkman, L. F. (1994). Social support and physical disability in older people after hospitalization. *Health Psychology, 13,* 170–179.

Wilder, D. A. (1986). Social categorization: Implications for creation and reduction of intergroup bias. In L. Berkowitz (Ed.), *Advances in experimental and social psychology.* Orlando, FL: Academic Press.

Wilder, D. A. (1990). Some determinants of the persuasive power of in-groups and out-groups: Organization of information and attribution of independence. *Journal of Personality and Social Psychology, 59,* 1202–1213.

Wildman, B. G., & White, P. A. (1986). Assessment of dysmenorrhea using the Menstrual Symptom Questionnaire: Factor structure and validity. *Behavior Research and Therapy, 24,* 547–551.

Willett, W. C., and others. (1990). Relation of meat, fat, and fiber intake to the risk of colon cancer in a prospective study among women. *New England Journal of Medicine, 323,* 1664–1672.

Williams, L. (1992, February 6). Woman's image in a mirror: Who defines what she sees? *The New York Times,* pp. A1, B7.

Williams, R. L. (1974, May). Scientific racism and IQ: The silent mugging of the Black community. *Psychology Today, 8.*

Williamson, D. A., Cubic, B. A., & Gleaves, D. H. (1993). Equivalence of body image disturbances in anorexia and bulimia nervosa. *Journal of Abnormal Psychology, 102,* 177–180.

Willich, S. N., and others. (1993). Physical exertion as a trigger of acute myocardial infarction. *New England Journal of Medicine, 329,* 1684–1690.

Willis, S. L., Jay, G. M., Diehl, M., & Marsiske, M. (1992). Longitudinal change and prediction of everyday task competence in the elderly. *Research on Aging, 14,* 68–91.

Willoughby, T., Wood, E., & Khan, M. (1994). Isolating variables that impact on or detract from the effectiveness of elaboration strategies. *Journal of Educational Research, 86,* 279–289.

Wills, T. A. (1986). Stress and coping in adolescence: Relationships to substance use in urban school samples. *Health Psychology, 5,* 503–530.

Wilson, G. L. (1991). Comment: Transgenerational patterns of suicide attempt. *Journal of Consulting and Clinical Psychology, 59,* 869–873.

Wilson, G. T. (1993). Cited in O'Neill, M. (1993, September 29). Diet sabotage: The new battle of the sexes. *The New York Times,* pp. C1, C6.

Wilson, G. T., & Fairburn, C. G. (1993). Cognitive treatments for eating disorders. *Journal of Consulting and Clinical Psychology, 61,* 261–269.

Wilson, G. T., & Walsh, T. (1991). Eating disorders in the *DSM-IV. Journal of Abnormal Psychology, 100,* 362–365.

Wilson, K. G., and others. (1991). Effects of instructional set on self-reports of panic attacks. *Journal of Anxiety Disorders, 5,* 43–63.

Wilson, K. G., and others. (1992). Panic attacks in the nonclinical population: An empirical approach to case identification. *Journal of Abnormal Psychology, 101,* 460–468.

Wilson, R. S. (1983). The Louisville twin study: Developmental synchronies in behavior. *Child Development, 54,* 298–316.

Wink, P., & Helson, R. (1993). Personality change in women and their partners. *Journal of Personality and Social Psychology, 65,* 597–606.

Winkleby, M., Fortmann, S., & Barrett, D. (1991). Social class disparities in risk factors for disease: Eight-year prevalence patterns by level of education. *Preventive Medicine, 19,* 1–12.

Winson, J. (1992). Cited in Blakeslee, S. (1992, January 7). Scientists unraveling chemistry of dreams. *The New York Times,* pp. C1, C10.

Wirtz, P. W., & Harrell, A. V. (1987). Effects of postassault exposure to attack-similar stimuli on long-term recovery of victims. *Journal of Consulting and Clinical Psychology, 55,* 10–16.

Wlodkowski, R. J. (1982). Making sense out of motivation. *Educational Psychologist, 16,* 101–110.

Wolf, N. (1991). *The beauty myth: How images of beauty are used against women.* New York: Morrow.

Wolf, S., & Bugaj, A. M. (1990). The social impact of courtroom witnesses. *Social Behaviour, 5,* 1–13.

Wolinsky, J. (1982). Responsibility can delay aging. *APA Monitor, 13*(3), 14, 41.

Woloshyn, V. E., Paivio, A., & Pressley, M. (1994). Use of elaborative interrogation to help students acquire information consistent with prior knowledge and information inconsistent with prior knowledge. *Journal of Educational Psychology, 86,* 79–89.

Wolpe, J. (1990). *The practice of behavior therapy* (4th ed.). New York: Pergamon.

Wolraich, M. L., and others. (1990). Stimulant medication use by primary care physicians in the treatment of attention-deficit hyperactivity disorder. *Pediatrics, 86,* 95–101.

Women scientists lagging in industry jobs. (1994, January 18). *The New York Times,* p. C5.

Wood, J. M., & Bootzin, R. R. (1990). The prevalence of nightmares and their independence from anxiety. *Journal of Abnormal Psychology, 99,* 64–68.

Wood, J. M., Bootzin, R. R., Rosenhan, D., Nolen-Hoeksema, S., & Jourden, F. (1992). Effects of the 1989 San Francisco earthquake on frequency and content of nightmares. *Journal of Abnormal Psychology, 101,* 219–224.

Wood, P. D., and others. (1991). The effects on plasma lipoproteins of a prudent weight-reducing diet, with or without exercise, in overweight men and women. *New England Journal of Medicine, 325,* 461–466.

Woods, S. W., and others. (1987). Situational panic attacks: Behavioral, physiologic, and biochemical characterization. *Archives of General Psychiatry, 44,* 365–375.

Wood, W. (1982). Retrieval of attitude-relevant information from memory: Effects on susceptibility to persuasion and on intrinsic motivation. *Journal of Personality and Social Psychology, 42,* 798–810.

Woolfolk, A. E. (1995). *Educational psychology* (6th ed.). Boston: Allyn & Bacon.

Worchel, S., & Brown, E. H. (1984). The role of plausibility in influencing environmental attributions. *Journal of Experimental Social Psychology, 20,* 86–96.

Wu, C., & Shaffer, C. R. (1987). Susceptibility to persuasive appeals as a function of source credibility and prior experience with the attitude object. *Journal of Personality and Social Psychology, 52,* 677–688.

WuDunn, S. (1995, July 9). Many Japanese women are resisting servility. *The New York Times,* p. A10.

Wulfert, E., & Wan, C. K. (1993). Condom use: A self-efficacy model. *Health Psychology, 12,* 346–353.

Wyer, R. S., Jr. (1988). Social memory and social judgment. In P. R. Solomon and others (Eds.), *Perspectives on memory research.* New York: Springer-Verlag.

Yamamoto, J. (1986). Therapy for Asian Americans and Pacific Islanders. In C. B. Wilkinson (Ed.), *Ethnic psychiatry.* New York: Academic Press.

Yarmey, D. A. (1986). Verbal, visual, and voice identification of a rape suspect under different levels of illumination. *Journal of Applied Psychology, 71,* 363–370.

Yates, A., and others. (1983). Running—An analogue of anorexia? *New England Journal of Medicine, 308,* 251–255.

Yeates, K. O., MacPhee, D., Campbell, F. A., & Ramey, C. T. (1983). Maternal IQ and home environment as determinants of early childhood intellectual competence: A developmental analysis. *Developmental Psychology, 19,* 731–739.

Ying, Y. (1988). Depressive symptomatology among Chinese-Americans as measured by the CES-D. *Journal of Clinical Psychology, 44,* 739–746.

Yoder, J. D., & Kahn, A. S. (1993). Working toward an inclusive psychology of women. *American Psychologist, 48,* 846–850.

Yonas, A., Granrud, C. E., & Pettersen, L. (1985). Infants' sensitivity to relative size information for distance. *Developmental Psychology, 21,* 161–167.

Yoshikawa, H. (1994). Prevention as cumulative protection: Effects of early family support and education on chronic delinquency and its risks. *Psychological Bulletin, 115,* 28–54.

Young, T., and others. (1993). The occurrence of sleep-disordered breathing among middle-aged adults. *New England Journal of Medicine, 328,* 1230–1235.

Youngblade, L. M., & Belsky, J. (1992). Parent–child antecedents of 5-year-olds' close friendships: A longitudinal analysis. *Developmental Psychology, 28,* 700–713.

Yutrzenka, B. A. (1995). Making a case for training in ethnic and cultural diversity in increasing treatment efficacy. *Journal of Consulting and Clinical Psychology, 63,* 197–206.

Zahn-Waxler, C., & Kochanska, G. (1990). The origins of guilt. In R. A. Thompson (Ed.), *Nebraska Symposium on Motivation: Vol. 38. Socioemotional development.* Lincoln: University of Nebraska Press.

Zajonc, R. B. (1968). Attitudinal effects of mere exposure. *Journal of Personality and Social Psychology, Monograph Supplement 2*(9), 1–27.

Zajonc, R. B. (1980). Compresence. In P. Paulus (Ed.), *The psychology of group influence.* Hillsdale, NJ: Erlbaum.

Zajonc, R. B. (1984). On the primacy of affect. *American Psychologist, 39,* 117–123.

Zajonc, R. B. (1985). Cited in B. Bower (1985). The face of emotion. *Science News, 128,* 12–13.

Zamansky, H. S., & Bartis, S. P. (1985). The dissociation of an experience. *Journal of Abnormal Psychology, 94,* 243–248.

Zane, N., & Sue, S. (1991). Culturally responsive mental health services for Asian Americans: Treatment and training issues. In H. F. Myers and others (Eds.), *Ethnic minority perspectives on clinical training and services in psychology* (pp. 49–58). Washington, DC: American Psychological Association.

Zeki, S. (1992). The visual image in mind and brain. *Scientific American, 267,* 68–76.

Zigler, E. (1995, August). Modernizing early childhood intervention to better serve children and families in poverty. Master Lecture delivered to the meeting of the American Psychological Association, New York.

Zigler, E., Abelson, W. D., Trickett, P. K., & Seitz, V. (1982). Is an intervention program necessary to improve economically disadvantaged children's IQ scores? *Child Development, 53,* 340–348.

Zigler, E., Taussig, C., & Black, K. (1992). Early childhood intervention: A promising preventative for juvenile delinquency. *American Psychologist, 47,* 997–1006.

Zimbardo, P. G., LaBerge, S., & Butler, L. D. (1993). Psychophysiological consequences of unexplained arousal: A posthypnotic suggestion paradigm. *Journal of Abnormal Psychology, 102,* 466–473.

Ziv, T. A., & Lo, B. (1995). Denial of care to illegal immigrants—Proposition 187 in California. *New England Journal of Medicine, 332,* 1095–1098.

Zuckerman, M. (1980). Sensation seeking. In H. London & J. Exner (Eds.), *Dimensions of personality.* New York: Wiley.

Zuckerman, M. (1992). What is a basic factor and which factors are basic? Tumbles all the way down. *Personality and Individual Differences, 13,* 675–681.

Zuckerman, M., Klorman, R., Larrance, D. T., & Spiegel, N. H. (1981). Facial, autonomic, and subjective components of emotion. *Journal of Personality and Social Psychology, 41,* 929–944.

Zuroff, D. C., & Mongrain, M. (1987). Dependency and self-criticism: Vulnerability factors for depressive affective states. *Journal of Abnormal Psychology, 96,* 14–22.

Copyright Acknowledgments

Photo Credits

Name Index

A

Abbey, A., 712
Abraham, L. K., 669
Abramov, I., 459
Abramowitz, A. J., 244
Adair, J. G., 61
Addis, M. E., 622
Ader, D. N., 18, 44
Ader, R., 665
Adeyemo, S. A., 318
Adler, A., 515, 605, 609
Adler, N. E., 669
Adler, T., 179, 180, 387
Affleck, 658
Agras, W. S., 582, 633, 671
Ahadi, S. A., 568
Ahrens, A. H., 569
Aiken, L. S., 677
Ainsworth, M. D. S., 462, 463, 466
Akhtar, N., 428
Aldag, R. J., 730
Allen, L., 18
Allison, K. W., 627
Alloy, L. B., 567, 569, 657
Allport, G. W., 505
Almeida, D. M., 479
Alston, J. H., 21
Altman, L. K., 673, 677
Alzheimer, A., 299
Amabile, T. M., 328, 330
Amaro, H., 667
American Association of University Women, 707
American Cancer Society, 667
American Polygraph Association, 433
American Psychiatric Association, 185, 553, 553n, 634
American Psychological Association, 36n, 59, 60, 61, 416n, 428, 607, 627, 629, 630
Ames, M. A., 417
Anastasi, 53, 384
Andersen, B. L., 668, 675
Anderson, J. R., 320
Anderson, R., 648
Andreasen, N. C., 555, 575
Andrews, B., 568
Aneshensel, C. S., 188
Angell, M., 665, 667, 673
Angelou, M., 410
Angier, N., 19, 298, 299, 300, 415, 677
Annunziata, J., 623
Antoni, M. H., 673, 674
Antonuccio, D., 634
Apter, T., 485
Archer, R. P., 720
Archer, S. L., 481

Aristotle, 9, 10, 84
Arnold, D. H., 343
Aronson, J., 388
Asarnow, J. R., 568
Asch, S. F., 726–727
Ashe, A., 677
Ashton, R., 183
Atkinson, R. C., 267, 288
Audrain, J. E., 195
Avis, W. E., 717
Ayanian, J. Z., 667, 668
Ayllon, T., 617
Azar, B., 186, 325, 329, 385, 624

B

Babcock, J. C., 622
Bach, G. R., 696
Bachrach, L. L., 574
Baddeley, A., 271, 285, 292
Bahrick, H. P., 287
Bailey, J. M., 417
Bakalar, J. B., 199
Baker, T. A., 387
Bal, D. G., 668
Baldwin, J., 704
Ballo, D. A., 379
Baltes, M., 488
Baltes, P., 488
Bandura, A., 17, 46, 247, 409, 428, 429, 476, 519, 521, 522, 560, 561, 615, 655, 678
Banks, M. S., 459
Banks, S. M., 335, 700
Baquet, C. R., 668
Barabasz, A., 203
Bard, P., 439
Barlow, D. H., 553, 625
Barnes, 721
Barnett, W. S., 388
Barr, C. E., 577
Barringer, F., 349, 350
Barsalou, L. W., 316
Bartecchi, C. E., 194, 195, 671, 673
Bartek, S. E., 698
Bartis, S. P., 204
Bartoshuk, L. M., 155, 156
Bashore, T. R., 433, 435
Bates, J. E., 463
Batson, C. D., 733
Baum, A., 559
Baumeister, R. F., 579, 580, 703
Baumgardner, A. H., 711
Baumrind, D., 61, 391
Beauchamp, G. K., 155, 156
Beauvais, F., 187, 192
Beck, A. T., 556, 571, 611, 612, 625
Becker, 568
Becker, L. B., 667

Bee, H. L., 388
Behar, D., 626
Beilin, H., 466, 468, 469, 473
Belchetz, P. E., 486
Bell, 486
Bell, A. G., 147
Bell, A. P., 417
Belle, D., 568
Belsky, J., 463
Bem, S. L., 409, 538, 706, 708
Benbow, C. P., 97, 535
Benderly, B. L., 537
Bennett, D., 608
Benson, 487
Benson, H., 200, 201, 671
Benson, P. L., 734
Berenbaum, H., 649
Berkman, 659
Berkowitz, L., 428, 430, 733
Berman, J. S., 626
Bernal, M. E., 627
Berne, E., 609
Bernstein, 676
Bernstein, W. M., 720
Berquier, A., 183
Betancourt, H., 17, 18n, 667
Beutler, L. E., 59, 626
Bevan, W., 526
Bexton, W. H., 419
Binet, A., 14, 368, 374, 530
Bishop, J. E., 194
Bjorklund, D., 283
Blakeslee, S., 88, 123, 147, 158, 390, 667
Blanchard, E. B., 626, 649, 670
Blanck, P. D., 60, 61
Blane, P. H., 657
Blass, E. M., 462
Blass, T., 725
Blatt, S. J., 483, 536, 537, 569, 732
Block, J., 508
Bloom, B. L., 530
Bloom, L., 287, 345
Boden, M. A., 328
Bodenhausen, G. V., 704
Boneau, C. A., 19
Booth-Kewley, S., 657
Bootzin, R. R., 183
Bordo, S., 582, 681
Borkovec, T. D., 626
Bornstein, 352
Borod, J. C., 96
Boskind-White, M., 584
Botvin, G. J., 186
Bouchard, C., 680
Bouchard, T. J., Jr., 386, 387
Bower, G., 439
Bower, G. H., 285
Bowers, K. S., 204
Bowlby, J., 462, 463, 466

Bowman, M. L., 530
Boyatzis, R. E., 57, 58
Boyd-Franklin, N., 628, 629
Bracha, H. S., 577
Bradley, E. J., 428
Bradley, R. H., 388
Bransford, J. D., 286
Braun, B. G., 562, 563
Bray, R. M., 729
Breckler, S. J., 698
Brenner, J., 582
Brent, E., 423, 721
Breslow, 659
Breuer, P., 557
Brewer, C. L., 294
Brewin, C. R., 46, 511
Bridges, K., 435
Bridgwater, C. A., 700
Brigham, J. C., 720
Brody, J. E., 340, 486, 668, 670, 675, 676, 681
Brokaw, T., 701
Bronstein, P., 45
Brown, D. E., 435
Brown, G. W., 568
Brown, L. S., 607
Brown, R., 282, 284
Brown, S. A., 186, 188
Browne, A., 45
Brownell, K. D., 97, 671, 681, 682
Brownell, W. E., 151
Bruck, M., 278
Bryant, W. C., 490
Buchanan, C. M., 414, 479
Buchanan, R. W., 79, 574, 577, 578, 632
Budd, L. S., 238
Burish, T. G., 676
Burman, B., 659
Burns, D. D., 624–625, 634
Burns, G., 487
Burns, G. L., 720
Burns, R., 722
Burnstein, E., 708
Buschmann, M. B., 713
Bush, G., 699
Bushman, B. J., 58
Buss, D. M., 435, 719, 721
Byrne, B. M., 617
Byrnes, J., 535
Byron, L., 515

C

Cacioppo, J. T., 436, 698, 699
Cahill, 298, 661
Califano, J. A., 195
Calkins, M. W., 20–21
Callan, V. J., 480

Subject Index